SunOS 4.1 Command	SunOS 5.x (SVR4) Changes
df	Add the −k option to display output in a format similar to that of just the df command. The −t option now displays a full listing with totals, rather than reporting on the type of files.
diff	The −c takes no argument and assumes a default of 3. −C requires an argument giving the number of lines to display for each difference. The −S option requires that you add a space between the −S option and the name to specify (e.g., diff −S *name*).
dkinfo	Use the prtvtoc command to display similar results.
fastboot	Use the boot, reboot, or init 6 commands for similar results.
fasthalt	Use the init 0 command for similar results.
file	The -L option is no longer available. When you use the file *filename* command (if the file indicated by *filename* is a symbolic link), the file command tests the file referenced by the link, rather than the symbolic link itself.
find	The −ncpio *device* option, which wrote the current file on the device indicated by *device* in the cpio command's −c format, is no longer available.
fsck	Now specify most options after you specify the file system type.
grep	The -w option searches for the regular expression (as a word), if surrounded by \< and \>.
hostid	Use the sysdef -h command to display similar results.
hostname	Use the uname −n command to display similar results.
init	When you use the -a *n* option, the value of *n* can only be 1 or 2. You can no longer use the value 3. There is now no restriction to the argument −j, which previously could only be 1 or 2.
leave	The cron and at commands display similar results.
ln	The ln *target* command now removes the *target* if it already exists, provided you have the proper permissions. The −f option now forces files to be linked without displaying permissions, asking questions, or reporting errors.
lockscreen	Use the xlock command for similar results.
lpq	Use the lpstat command to display similar results.
lpr	Use the lp command for similar results.
lprm	Use the cancel command for similar results.

(Continued on inside back cover)

Computer users are not all alike.
Neither are SYBEX books.

We know our customers have a variety of needs. They've told us so. And because we've listened, we've developed several distinct types of books to meet the needs of each of our customers. What are you looking for in computer help?

If you're looking for the basics, try the **ABC's** series. You'll find short, unintimidating tutorials and helpful illustrations. For a more visual approach, select **Teach Yourself,** featuring screen-by-screen illustrations of how to use your latest software purchase.

Mastering and **Understanding** titles offer you a step-by-step introduction, plus an in-depth examination of intermediate-level features, to use as you progress.

Our **Up & Running** series is designed for computer-literate consumers who want a no-nonsense overview of new programs. Just 20 basic lessons, and you're on your way.

We also publish two types of reference books. Our **Instant References** provide quick access to each of a program's commands and functions. SYBEX **Encyclopedias** and **Desktop References** provide a *comprehensive reference* and explanation of all of the commands, features, and functions of the subject software.

Sometimes a subject requires a special treatment that our standard series don't provide. So you'll find we have titles like **Advanced Techniques, Handbooks, Tips & Tricks,** and others that are specifically tailored to satisfy a unique need.

We carefully select our authors for their in-depth understanding of the software they're writing about, as well as their ability to write clearly and communicate effectively. Each manuscript is thoroughly reviewed by our technical staff to ensure its complete accuracy. Our production department makes sure it's easy to use. All of this adds up to the highest quality books available, consistently appearing on best-seller charts worldwide.

You'll find SYBEX publishes a variety of books on every popular software package. Looking for computer help? Help Yourself to SYBEX.

For a complete catalog of our publications:

SYBEX Inc.
2021 Challenger Drive, Alameda, CA 94501
Tel: (510) 523-8233/(800) 227-2346 Telex: 336311
Fax: (510) 523-2373

Mastering
Solaris 2

Mastering
Solaris™ 2

BRENT D. HESLOP & DAVID F. ANGELL

San Francisco • Paris • Düsseldorf • Soest

SYBEX®

ACQUISITIONS EDITOR: Dianne King
DEVELOPMENTAL EDITOR: Gary Masters
EDITOR: Kimn Neilson
PROJECT EDITOR: Kathleen Lattinville
TECHNICAL EDITOR: Jeff Horan
BOOK DESIGNER/PRODUCTION ARTIST: Suzanne Albertson
SCREEN GRAPHICS: John Corrigan
TYPESETTER: Ann Dunn
PROOFREADERS/PRODUCTION COORDINATORS: Arno Harris and Catherine Mahoney
INDEXER: Ted Laux
COVER DESIGNER: Archer Design
COVER PHOTOGRAPHER: David Bishop
COVER PHOTO ART DIRECTION: Ingalls + Associates

SYBEX is a registered trademark of SYBEX Inc.

TRADEMARKS: SYBEX has attempted throughout this book to distinguish proprietary trademarks from descriptive terms by following the capitalization style used by the manufacturer.

SYBEX is not affiliated with any manufacturer.

Every effort has been made to supply complete and accurate information. However, SYBEX assumes no responsibility for its use, nor for any infringement of the intellectual property rights of third parties which would result from such use.

Library of Congress Card Number: 92-83942
ISBN: 0-7821-1072-X

Manufactured in the United States of America
10 9 8 7 6 5 4 3 2 1

To Kim for her love, patience, and understanding

B.D.H.

*To Frank Meritt Angell, who inspired me
before I even realized it*

D.F.A.

ACKNOWLEDGMENTS

MANY people at SunSoft were instrumental in the writing of this book. We owe a huge debt of gratitude to Bentley Radcliff, who helped supply us with the needed materials to make the transition from Solaris 1 to Solaris 2. Robert Saft was invaluable to this project. He graciously shared his time and advice to help us solve problems and improve this book. He deserves credit for many of the insights and tips in the chapter on customizing Solaris. We also would like to acknowledge Don Charles, who helped us get our Solaris 2 system up and running.

If we had to choose one person at SunSoft who really helped us make this book a reality, Doug Royer would be at the top of the list. Doug proved not only to be one of the most knowledgeable people about Solaris 2, he was, without a doubt, the most supportive. He put up with several late-night calls at his home and even made a special weekend trip to our office to help us. Doug also saved us hours of time by introducing us to XV (a shareware graphics program by John Bradley) that we used for all the figures in this book. Doug, thank you. Jeff Horan at SunSelect deserves a great deal of credit for his technical assistance and expertise. Jeff worked with us on our first book on SunOS, *Mastering SunOS,* and continues to be a lifesaver.

We also want to extend our appreciation to Ron Lee, who cheerfully explained many of the idiosyncrasies of Solaris 2 that had us scratching our heads. John Linton also deserves an honorable mention for his advice on how to improve this book. Stuart Marks deserves credit for helping us resolve problems related to capturing the screens used in the figures.

Thanks also to Karin Ellison and Kim Ingram for helping us with Solaris 2 for x86 information.

Outside of SunSoft we want to thank Larry Goodman for his help with the command reference and the use of his workstation. Kudos to Kimn Neilson for applying her superior copyediting skills to our text. Thanks also go to Kim Merry who helped us take and edit screenshots for several of the figures in this book. The new chapter on communications and networking would not have been possible without the support of Brian Fudge at Portal Communications Company. Brian helped us with questions about networking and communications and let us use a connection at Portal to test the accuracy of our text. Thanks go to Joe Ballard and Mike Cerni at Distributed Processing Technology (DPT) for making it possible to run Solaris 2 for x86 by providing us with a DPT Smartcache controller. This is the easiest controller card to install, and it has proven to be incredibly fast and dependable. A note of thanks to Sue Glassberg at UniPress Software Inc. for supplying us with XVision, the best product for working with the X Window System and Microsoft Windows we have seen. Thanks also go to David Newman at Island Graphics for supplying us with Island Write Draw and Paint.

At SYBEX, several people made writing this book an enjoyable experience. First off we want to acknowledge Dianne King, Acquisitions Editor, and Rudy Langer, Vice President and Editor in Chief, who gave us the opportunity to work on this exciting project. We are also grateful to Gary Masters, who besides giving us advice and encouragement, finagled the time we needed to finish this massive job. A warm thanks to Kathleen Lattinville, our project editor, who brought such a positive attitude to this project that we didn't mind working late into the night to make the deadlines. Thanks also to Barbara Gordon, Managing Editor. And many thanks to the entire production staff at SYBEX for their efforts in seeing this book through production.

Contents
AT A GLANCE

Introduction   xxxv

PART ONE   **WORKING WITH THE OPENWINDOWS DESKSET**

1   Getting Started with OpenWindows and the DeskSet   3

2   Using the File Manager   51

3   The Multimedia Mail Tool Makes Mail Easy   99

4   Using the Text Editor, Shell Tool, and Command Tool   163

5   Get Organized with the Calendar Manager   200

6   Using the Print Tool, Audio Tool, and Other DeskSet Applications   245

7   Customizing the Workspace and Icons   311

PART TWO   **WORKING FROM THE SUNOS COMMAND LINE**

8   Getting Started with the SunOS Command Line   361

9   Navigating Directories and Working with Files   379

10   Improving Your Command-Line Productivity   407

11   Electronic Mail and Messages   439

12   Using the vi Editor   467

13   Formatting and Printing   499

14   Multitasking with SunOS   533

PART THREE   **BEYOND THE FUNDAMENTALS**

15   Customizing Solaris   555

16   Networking and Communications   613

17   System Administration Basics   643

PART FOUR   **COMMAND REFERENCE**

Index   865

CONTENTS

Introduction   xxxv

PART ONE   **WORKING WITH THE OPENWINDOWS DESKSET**

1 **Getting Started with OpenWindows and the
       DeskSet**   3

About OpenWindows and the DeskSet   4
Logging into Solaris   6
   System Login Messages   7
   Changing Your Password   8
Starting OpenWindows and the DeskSet   8
Using the Mouse   10
   Pointer Indicators   12
   Pointer Jumping   12
Working with Menus   13
   Pinning a Menu to the Workspace   14
   Choosing the Default Menu Item   14
   The Workspace Menu   16
Starting a DeskSet Application   17
Working with Windows   18
   The Parts of an Application Window   19
   Using the Scrollbar   22
   The Scrollbar Menu   24
   Splitting a Window Pane   25
   The Clipboard   26
   Pop-up Windows   27
   Types of Window Controls   29
   The Active Window   30
   The Window Menu   31
   Closing and Reopening a Window   33
   Quitting a Window   33
   Moving a Window   33

Moving Multiple Windows   34
Moving Windows to the Background   34
Resizing a Window   36
Redisplaying a Window   36
Dragging and Dropping Files   37
Drag-and-Drop Targets   37
Getting Online Help   38
Using Magnify Help   38
Using the Help Handbooks   39
Using the Help Viewer Icons   39
Magnifying the Help Viewer Window   41
Navigating a Handbook   42
Closing or Exiting the Help Viewer Window   42
Workspace Utilities   42
Refresh   43
Reset Input   43
Function Keys   44
Window Controls   44
Save Workspace   45
Lock Screen   46
Console   46
Exiting OpenWindows and the DeskSet   47
Logging Out of Solaris   48

2   Using the File Manager   51
An Overview of the Solaris File System   52
Starting the File Manager   53
An Overview of the File Manager Window   54
Path Pane   54
Control Area   55
File Pane   57
File Manager Icons   57
Performing Basic Operations   59
Selecting Folders and Files Using the Mouse   60

Selecting Folders and Files Using the Keyboard
and Wildcards   60
Changing the File and Pane Displays   61
Changing How Icons Are Displayed in
the File Pane   62
Changing the Tree Display in the Path Pane   63
Navigating the File System   64
Opening Folders   64
Opening Folders as Windows on the Workspace   65
Using Goto to Navigate Directly to Files and
Folders   65
Searching for Folders and Files   67
Opening Files   70
Dragging and Dropping Files to Other
Applications   71
Creating Folders and Files   72
Changing Folder and File Names   73
Deleting Files and Folders   73
Deleting Files and Folders Using the Clipboard   75
Copying and Moving Files and Folders   76
Using the Clipboard to Copy and Move Files
and Folders   77
Using Accelerator Keys to Copy and Move Files
and Folders   78
Copying Files to Other Systems   78
Printing Files   80
File and Folder Permissions   81
Changing File and Folder Permissions   83
Changing Permissions for Groups of Files or
Folders   84
Linking Files   84
Creating a Link   84
Removing a Link   86
Customizing the File Manager   86
Customizing the File Pane View   87

Using the Tool Properties Window | 90
Adding Commands to a Menu | 92

3 The Multimedia Mail Tool Makes Mail Easy | **99**

Starting the Mail Tool | 100
An Overview of the Mail Tool Header Window | 101
Receiving and Viewing Messages | 102
Manually Checking Your Mail | 103
Mail Message Headers | 103
Selecting and Viewing Messages | 104
Opening and Viewing Mail Attachments | 106
Opening Multiple View Message Windows | 106
Viewing Messages with Full Headers | 108
Saving Mail Tool Header Window Changes | 111
Composing and Sending Messages | 112
An Overview of the Compose Message Window | 113
An Overview of Mail Addresses | 114
Creating and Sending Mail Messages | 115
Adding Attachments to Messages | 117
Including Other Messages in a Message | 118
Replying to a Message | 121
Using Drag-and-Drop with the Mail Tool | 122
Managing Your Messages in the Mail Tool Header
Window | 122
Sorting Message Headers | 123
Finding Messages | 124
Deleting Messages | 125
Undeleting Messages | 126
Printing Messages | 127
Working with Attachments | 128
Copying Mail Attachments | 128
Renaming Mail Attachments | 128
Deleting Mail Attachments | 129
Forwarding Mail | 129

Vacation Mail   130
Using Mail Tool Templates   131
Working with Mail Files   133
    Specifying a Default Mail File Directory 133
    The Mail Files Pop-up Window   134
    Creating a New Mail File and Saving Messages
    in Mail Files   136
    Creating an Empty Mail File or Mail Files
    Directory   137
    Saving Messages to an Existing Mail File 137
    Loading Mail Files in the Mail Tool Header
    Window   138
    Managing Your Mail Files   140
Customizing the Mail Tool   141
    Header Window Properties   143
    Message Window Properties   147
    Compose Window Properties   149
    Mail Filing Properties   154
    Template Properties   156
    Alias Properties   157
    Expert Properties   159

**4 Using the Text Editor, Shell Tool, and
Command Tool**   **163**
The Text Editor   164
    The Text Editor Window   164
    Starting the Text Editor and Loading Files 166
    Saving a New or Existing Text File   168
    Entering and Selecting Text   169
    Controlling the Position of the Insert Point 169
    Copying, Moving, and Deleting Text   171
    Splitting the Text Editor Pane   176
    Merging Files   177
    Changing the Line Wrap Mode   177

Finding and Replacing Text in the Text Editor	178
The Text Pane's Extras Pop-up Submenu	185
The Shell Tool	186
The Shell Tool's Term Pane Pop-up Menu	187
Viewing Text in the Shell Tool	188
Copying and Pasting Text in the Shell Tool	189
Turning the Shell Tool into a Command Tool	190
The Command Tool	190
Working with the History Log File	190
Saving the History Log to a File	192
Displaying a Text Editor Pane	193
Turning the Command Tool into a Shell Tool	194
The Console Window	194
The xterm Window	194
The xterm Window Menus	195
Scrolling the xterm Window	197
Selecting, Copying, and Pasting Text	197
Logging an xterm Session	198
Displaying the xterm Window in Reverse Video	198
Changing the Size of Fonts in the xterm Window	199
5 Get Organized with the Calendar Manager	**200**
Starting the Calendar Manager	202
The Calendar Manager Window	203
The Four Views of the Calendar Manager	205
The Appointment List and ToDo List Views	207
Navigating the Calendars and Lists	208
Entering Appointments and ToDo Items into the Calendar Manager	209
The CM Appointment Editor Pop-up Window Settings	210
Creating an Appointment or ToDo List Entry	213
Deleting Existing Appointments or ToDo List Items	215

Changing Existing Appointments or ToDo List Items   217

Finding a Calendar Appointment   217

Printing Calendar Views, Appointment Lists, and ToDo Lists   218

Working with the Multi-Browser Window   220

The Multi-Browser Window   222

Adding a User's Calendar to the Multi-Browser   224

Deleting a User's Calendar from the Multi-Browser   225

Determining an Appointment Time   225

Scheduling an Appointment for a Group of Users   227

Sending a Mail Appointment Notification   230

Browsing Another User's Calendar Using the Browse Menu   231

Setting the Calendar Manager Time Zone   233

Customizing Your Calendar Manager   233

Changing Appointment Alarm Defaults   236

Changing Display Settings   237

Specifying Who Can Browse and Change Your Appointments   238

Changing the Default Printer Settings   241

Changing Date Formats   242

6   Using the Print Tool, Audio Tool, and Other DeskSet Applications   245

The Print Tool   246

Printing a File   247

Choosing Another Printer   248

Checking the Print Queue Status   249

Stopping Printing Jobs   249

Adding a Custom Print Tool Filter   249

The Audio Tool   251

The Audio Tool Window   253

CONTENTS

Loading Sound Files	254
Recording a Sound	255
Playing Back a Recording	256
Saving Sound Files	256
The Edit Menu	258
Editing a Sound File	260
Inserting a Sound File into Another Sound File	260
Customizing the Audio Tool	261
The Play Volume Pop-up Window	263
The Record Volume Pop-up Window	264
The Snapshot Application	265
Taking a Snapshot of a Window	267
Taking a Snapshot of a Region	268
Taking a Snapshot of the Screen	269
Viewing a Snapshot	270
Printing a Snapshot	271
The Clock Application	273
Customizing the Clock	274
The Performance Meter	280
The Performance Meter Pop-up Menu	280
Customizing Performance Meters	282
The Calculator	285
Performing Simple Calculations	286
Modes of Operation	286
Number Bases	287
Changing the Display Type	288
Miscellaneous Functions	288
Memory Registers	289
User-Defined Functions	290
Number Manipulation Operators	291
The Financial Calculator	292
Logical Functions	295
The Scientific Calculator	297
Customizing the Calculator	299

The Tape Tool   301
    Viewing and Editing a List
    of Files on a Tape   302
    Writing Files to a Tape   303
    Reading Files from a Tape   304
    Customizing the Tape Tool   305

7   Customizing the Workspace and Icons   **311**
Using the Workspace Properties Window   312
    Setting Colors for the Workspace and Windows   314
    Setting Default Locations for Icons   317
    Changing Menu Settings   318
    Changing Miscellaneous Settings   319
    Customizing Mouse Settings   321
    Language Localization   322
Creating Your Own Icons   324
    Color Control   325
    Drawing Controls   326
    Fill Choices   328
    Move Buttons   329
    Adding Text to an Icon   330
    Editing Icons Using the Edit Menu   332
    Displaying a Grid in the Canvas   333
    Working with the Properties Menu   333
    Saving an Icon File   335
    Loading an Icon File   336
    Printing an Icon   336
    Using the Color Chooser Palette   339
Binding an Icon   340
    The Binder Window   340
    Binder Databases   342
    Viewing Binder Entries   342
    Binder Entry Properties   343
    Binding an Icon to a File   353

Deleting a Binder Entry   356
Changing a Binding   357

PART TWO   **WORKING FROM THE SUNOS COMMAND LINE**

8   **Getting Started with the SunOS Command Line**   361
Logging into SunOS   362
    System Login Messages   364
    Changing Your Password   364
    The SunOS Shells   365
Entering SunOS Commands   366
    Correcting Mistakes   367
Useful SunOS Programs   367
    Displaying the Date and Time   367
    Displaying a Calendar   368
    Performing Simple Calculations   368
    Who Is Using the System?   369
    Echoing Text   370
    Displaying and Repeating Commands   371
    Clearing the Screen   372
Sending and Receiving Electronic Mail   372
    Reading Your Mail   373
Sending Mail   374
Getting Help with SunOS Commands   374
Command Summary   375

9   **Navigating Directories and Working with Files**   379
An Overview of the SunOS File System   380
    Types of Directories   381
Navigating Directories   382
    Navigating with Path Names   383
    Moving to Your Home Directory   384
    Displaying the Working Directory   384

Moving to a Parent Directory   384
Working with Directories   385
    Listing a Directory's Contents   385
    Creating a Directory   387
    Copying a Directory   387
    Removing a Directory   388
Working with Files   389
    Listing Files   390
    Determining File Types   390
    File Name Conventions   390
    Creating a File   391
    Creating an Empty File   391
    Displaying the Contents of a File   392
    Copying Files   393
    Moving and Renaming Files   394
    Removing Files   394
Listing and Changing Permissions   395
    Listing File and Directory Permissions   395
    Ownership of Files   398
    Changing Permission Modes   399
Creating and Removing Links to Files   402
    Creating a Link   403
    Removing a Link   403
Command Summary   404

10   Improving Your Command-Line Productivity   407
Getting the Most from the Command Line   408
    Performing Multiple Commands   408
    Listing Command Line Entries   409
    Reexecuting and Changing Command-Line
    Entries   410
Matching Patterns   410
    File Name Wildcards   411
    Character Class   411

Korn Shell Pattern-Matching Features   411
Working with Filters   412
　　Filters for Displaying the Contents of a File   413
　　Finding Files by File Names   414
　　Finding Files by Text in a File   417
　　Spell-Checking a File   419
　　Counting Words in a File   420
　　Comparing Text Files   420
　　Sorting a File   421
Combining, Grouping, and Controlling Commands   426
　　Command Substitution   426
　　Combining Commands   427
　　Grouping Commands   428
　　Controlling Command Execution   428
Redirecting Output and Input   429
　　Redirecting Output to a File   429
　　Protecting Existing Files from Redirection Output   430
　　Adding Text to an Existing File   430
　　Using Files as Input to Commands   431
　　Redirecting the Standard Error   431
　　Redirecting Combined Commands   432
　　Directing Data to More Than One Place   433
Useful SunOS Filters   434
Command Summary   436

11 Electronic Mail and Messages   439
Overview of SunOS's Electronic Mail   440
Receiving Mail   441
　　Listing Your Mail   441
　　Reading Your Mail   442
　　Replying to Mail   443
　　Deleting Mail   444
　　Undoing a Mail Deletion   444
Getting Help in the mailx Program   445

Quitting the mailx Program   447
The Mail Storage File   448
    Managing the Mail Storage File   448
    Holding Mail   448
    Saving Letters as Files   449
    Saving and Copying Letters in Folders   449
An Overview of Sending Mail   451
    Who Is Using the System?   452
    Sending Mail   453
    Aborting a Letter   455
    Undeliverable Mail   455
Sending Files Using mailx   456
Adding Carbon Copies   457
Using Tilde Escape Commands   457
Using Electronic Messages   459
    Talking with Other Users   459
    Writing Messages   461
    Broadcasting Messages   462
    System Messages   462
Command Summary   463

12   Using the vi Editor   467
About vi   468
Starting vi   469
    The Status Line   470
Command and Insert Modes   470
    The Command Mode   470
    The Insert Mode   471
Exiting vi   472
    Exiting vi and Saving Changes   472
    Exiting vi and Abandoning Changes   473
    Recovering Text after a System Crash   473
Units of Text in vi   474
Cursor Movement   475

Moving by Characters and Words 477

Moving by Lines, Sentences, and Paragraphs 478

Moving within a Screen Display 478

Scrolling through a File 479

Line Numbering and Line Movement 479

Editing Commands 480

Cleaning Up the Screen 481

Inserting and Appending Text 481

Deleting Text 482

Changing and Replacing Text 485

Changing Case in Command Mode 487

Joining Two Lines 487

Cutting and Pasting Text 487

Inserting Text from Another File 490

Searching vi Files 491

Searching vi Files for Patterns 491

Global Replacement 492

Setting vi Parameters 493

Using SunOS Commands in vi 494

Save Time When Starting vi 494

Command Summary 495

13 Formatting and Printing 499

An Overview of Formatting 498

Adding Formatting Requests to a File 499

Using Macros to Format a File 499

Viewing and Printing Formatted Documents 499

Character Formatting 500

Italicizing Text 501

Underlining Text 501

Boldfacing Text 502

Changing the Size of a Font 502

Inserting Special Characters 503

Formatting Lines 504

Filling and Justifying Lines 504

Changing Line Spacing 505

Inserting Blank Lines 505

Indenting Lines 506

Setting Tabs 506

Centering Lines 507

Formatting Paragraphs 508

Standard Paragraphs 508

Left-Block Paragraphs 509

Block Quotes 509

Indented Paragraphs 510

Outline Paragraphs 511

Changing the Page Layout 512

Number Registers 512

Setting Left and Right Margins 515

Setting Top and Bottom Margins 515

Determining Page Breaks 516

Keeping Text Together 516

Headers and Footers 517

Creating Multiple Columns 518

Creating Tables 520

Running Print Jobs 522

Printing nroff and troff Files 523

Printing Multiple-Page Files 523

Printing Multiple Copies of a File 524

Sending Multiple Files to the Printer 524

Printing the Output of a Command 524

Getting Notified When a Print Job Is Done 525

Changing or Suppressing the Banner Page 525

Checking the Printer Status 526

Removing Printer Jobs 527

Command Summary 528

14   Multitasking with SunOS   **533**

    Running a Command in the Background   534

        Redirecting a Background Command's Output   535

        Keeping Error Messages from Displaying on
        Your Screen   535

    Controlling Your Jobs   536

        Checking the Status of a Job   536

        Job Names   537

        Suspending and Restarting Jobs   537

        Logging Out of SunOS with Stopped Jobs   538

        Switching Jobs between Foreground and
        Background   538

        Terminating Jobs   539

        Waiting for a Background Job to Finish
        Executing   540

        Running Commands in the Background after
        Exiting   541

    Displaying and Terminating Processes   541

        Checking the Status of a Process   542

        Terminating a Process   544

    Scheduling Processes   545

        Performing a Process at a Later Time   546

        Displaying the Processes to Be Performed   547

        Running a Batch of Commands
        in the Background   547

        Removing at and batch Commands   548

        Scheduling Repeated Tasks   548

        Changing the Priority of a Command   550

        Suspending the Execution of a Command   550

    Command Summary   551

PART THREE **BEYOND THE FUNDAMENTALS**

15 **Customizing Solaris** 555

Working with Variables 556

Storing Variables 557

Listing Variables 557

Changing Variables 558

Displaying and Referencing Variables 560

Saving Time with the PATH Variable 561

Simplifying Directory Navigation 562

Specifying How Long to Wait for Input 562

Customizing Your Command Prompt 563

Creating Your Own Variables 564

Unsetting a Variable 564

Storing Commands and Path Names
as a Variable 565

Output Substitution and Variables 566

Customizing Korn Shell Options 567

Running Background Jobs at a Reduced Priority 568

Displaying and Changing a Logout Message 568

Marking Directories 569

Disabling File Name Substitution 569

Protecting Files 570

Displaying an Error Message for Unset Variables 570

Changing Command Line Editing Modes 570

Changing the Default File Permissions 571

Working with Aliases 572

Creating an Alias 572

Undoing an Alias 573

Customizing Mail Program Variables 573

Indicating How Often to Check for Mail 577

Specifying Where to Send Your Mail 577

Changing Your Mail Notification Message 577

Adding an Alias for Sending Mail to a Group   578
Customizing Your Terminal Settings   578
   Changing the Backspace and Delete Key
   Assignment   579
   Changing Keyboard Preferences   579
Modifying Your OpenWindows Environment   581
   Changing Screensavers   581
   Customizing the Workspace   584
   Changing the Mouse Pointer   592
   Customizing Fonts   594
   Customizing OpenWindows Menus   604

16   Networking and Communications   613

About Networking Systems   614
Networking Solaris   615
   Logging In Remotely with rlogin   615
   Transferring Files Remotely with rcp   617
   Executing Commands Remotely with rsh   618
   Viewing User Information with rusers   619
   Viewing User Information with finger   620
   Checking Machine Status with ping   622
Checking Machine Status with rup   622
Modem Communications   623
   Communicating with tip   624
   Communicating with cu   632
Working with the Internet   635
   Internet Addresses   636
   Connecting with telnet   636
   Transferring Files with ftp   638

17   System Administration Basics   643

Working as a Superuser   644
   Communicating with Users on Your Network   645
Booting and Rebooting Your System   647

Booting Your System	647
Rebooting Your System	648
Emergency Rebooting	648
Shutting Down Your System	649
Shutting Down a System	650
Shutting Down Your Workstation	651
Emergency Shutdown for a Single System	651
Managing Hard Drives and CD ROM Drives on Your Network	652
Understanding File Systems	652
Identifying a Drive by Its Device Name	653
Mounting a File System	654
Displaying Disk Information	660
Working with Floppy Disks	662
Using a Floppy Disk	663
Formatting a Floppy Disk in the SunOS Format	663
Creating a File System on a Floppy Disk	664
Formatting Disks for Use with MS-DOS	665
Write-Protecting Diskettes	666
Working with Tapes	666
Preparing a Tape for Data	667
Backing Up Files and File Systems to Tape	667
Copying Files with the tar Command	668
Retrieving tar Files from a Tape	668
Copying Files with cpio	669
Write-Protecting Tapes	671
Working with the Administration Tool	671
About Network Naming Services	673
Working with the Database Manager	673
Working with the User Account Manager	675
Working with the Host Manager	682
Working with the Printer Manager	687

xxx   CONTENTS

PART FOUR	COMMAND REFERENCE	

Making the Transition to SunOS 5.X (SVR4)	696
Command Reference Conventions	697
alias	697
at	698
atq	700
atrm	701
banner	701
batch	702
bc	703
cal	704
calendar	706
cancel	706
cat	707
cd	709
chgrp	710
chmod	712
chown	715
clear	716
cmp	716
comm	717
compress	718
cp	719
cpio	720
crontab	724
cu	726
cut	729
date	730
deroff	732
df	732
diff	734
dircmp	735

domainname	736
dpost	736
du	738
echo	739
eject	741
env	742
exit	743
expand	744
fdformat	744
fgrep	746
file	748
find	748
finger	754
fold	755
ftp	756
grep	761
groups	763
head	764
history	765
id	765
kill	766
last	768
ln	768
login	770
logname	770
look	771
lp	772
lpstat	774
ls	776
mail	777
mailx	779
man	779
mesg	780

mkdir	781
more	782
mount	784
mv	787
newgrp	788
nice	788
nohup	789
openwin	790
pack	792
passwd	793
paste	794
pcat	796
pg	796
ping	798
pr	799
ps	801
pwd	804
rcp	804
rlogin	805
rm	806
rmdir	807
rsh	808
rup	809
ruptime	809
rusers	810
rwho	811
script	812
set	812
sleep	814
sort	815
spell	816
strings	816
su	817

tail   818
talk   819
tar   820
tee   824
telnet   825
time   826
tip   827
touch   829
tr   829
tty   831
umask   831
unalias   833
uname   833
uncompress   834
unexpand   835
uniq   836
units   837
unpack   838
vacation   838
vi   839
wall   840
wc   840
which   842
who   842
who am i   843
write   843
xfd   844
xfontsel   845
xhost   847
xlock   848
xlsfonts   852
xman   853
xrdb   854

xset   856

xsetroot   860

xterm   861

zcat   864

Index   865

INTRODUCTION

SUN stands for Stanford University Network, a name given to a printed circuit board developed in 1981 that was designed to run the popular UNIX operating system. This board was instrumental in bringing UNIX to the desktop from its minicomputer roots and catapulting Sun Microsystems to dominance in the workstation market. Sun continues its leadership in the computer industry with Solaris 2.x, its new UNIX-based operating system. Solaris is a distributed computing environment from SunSoft (a subsidiary of Sun Microsystems) that includes the SunOS 5.x operating system and ONC+ networking, plus the OpenWindows graphical user interface. OpenWindows represents a new, friendly face for UNIX that rivals the ease of Microsoft Windows and the Macintosh computer. Solaris 2.x brings this new computing power to not only Sun workstations and Sun workstation clones, but extends the reach of the powerful UNIX operating system to Intel-based PCs with Solaris 2 for x86.

What Is Solaris?

Solaris 2.x is a multilayered operating system (see Figure 1 below) that includes SunOS 5.x, Open Network Computing, OpenWindows, and the DeskSet. At the core of Solaris is SunOS, the collection of programs that actually manages the system, which includes the kernel, the file system, and the shells. The next level of Solaris is its built-in ONC+ networking features, which allow for distributed computing. The top layer of the Solaris operating system is OpenWindows, the graphical user interface, based on OPEN LOOK and Sun's implementation of the X Window System. The following sections provide an overview of the components that make up Solaris.

SunOS

SunOS is a collection of UNIX programs that control the Sun workstation and provide a link between the user, the workstation, and its resources. The core programs manage the computer system and remain hidden from the user. The remaining programs are utility programs that provide the user with tools for working with SunOS.

UNIX was created by Ken Thompson and Dennis Ritchie at AT&T's Bell Laboratories to provide an environment that promoted efficient program development. AT&T later licensed UNIX to universities, and at the

FIGURE 1

The layers of Solaris

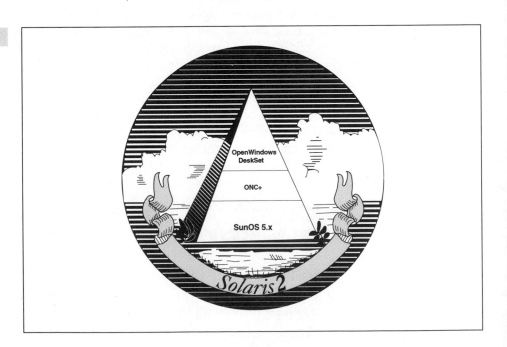

University of California at Berkeley it began a life of its own. Eventually the enhanced UNIX became known as Berkeley UNIX, or as it is more commonly called, BSD (Berkeley Software Distribution). Over time, UNIX matured into an easier to use, increasingly powerful operating system, incorporating such key features as portability, networking, security, and a friendly user interface.

SunOS has its roots firmly placed in the two most popular UNIX families: Berkeley UNIX (BSD) and AT&T's UNIX. Early versions of SunOS blended some of AT&T's UNIX with Berkeley UNIX and offered additional enhancements. AT&T and Sun Microsystems later worked together to create a new industry standard, AT&T UNIX System V Release 4, commonly known as SVR4. SunOS 5.x merges SunOS 4.1 and SVR4. Most of the new changes in SunOS come from SVR4. As a result, Solaris 2.x is based on SVR4 but contains a few additional BSD/SunOS features. To help in the transition from the old (largely BSD-based) SunOS to the new System V Release 4/SunOS 5.x, Solaris 2.x provides the BSD/SunOS Compatibility Package. This package is not covered in this book since these commands will eventually be removed from SunOS. The following sections briefly explain the major components of SunOS, including the kernel and file system, shell programs, and utility programs.

Kernel and File System

The *kernel* is the heart of SunOS; it resides in memory and manages the system's memory and hardware, such as terminals, printers, drives, and other devices. It schedules and terminates processes (programs being run) and keeps track of the file system and other important functions. The *file system* is integrated with the kernel and provides the organizing structure that stores your data. It enables you to organize files in a logical and structured manner, utilizing a hierarchical file system that allows related files to be grouped together in directories. These files are stored on a disk and organized into different levels with parent directories and subordinate directories called subdirectories, similar in structure to a family tree.

Shell Programs

A *shell* program (also called a *command interpreter*) manages the interaction of the user with the kernel. The shell first accepts, then interprets, and finally executes commands entered at the command-line prompt. There are three primary SunOS shells: the Bourne shell, the C shell, and the Korn shell. All three shells come with SunOS 5.x. The Bourne shell was developed by Steve Bourne for AT&T's UNIX. The C Shell was originally developed by Bill Joy as part of Berkeley UNIX. The Korn shell was developed by David Korn of AT&T Bell Laboratories as a response to the C shell. The Korn shell is noticeably more efficient than the C and Bourne shells because it has more built-in functions. However, many of the Korn shell commands are compatible with the C and Bourne shells. Because of the Korn shell's many benefits, and the fact that it is rapidly replacing the C and Bourne shells in popularity, this book focuses on the Korn shell.

Utility Programs

Beside the programs that transparently manage the computer system, SunOS 5.x includes over 300 UNIX utility programs. These utility programs allow you to perform a wide range of tasks from the command line, such as file management, text editing, sending and receiving electronic mail, performing calculations, and many other specialized functions. These utility programs share the same names as the commands used to execute them.

Distributed Computing

One of the key tenets of Sun Microsystems' computing philosophy is "The network is the computer." Solaris incorporates this philosophy by including built-in networking features clustered around the ONC+ (Open Network Computing) family of networking protocols and distributed services. ONC+ allows distributed computing so users can access everything on the network, including servers, printers, databases, and other resources, without having to know where it is, or what type of machine it resides on. To support distributed file systems, Solaris incorporates the Network File System (NFS) standard that was developed by Sun Microsystems to enable files and programs to be transparently accessed across a network.

Graphical User Interface

Solaris incorporates the OpenWindows graphical user interface to make working with SunOS substantially easier. OpenWindows includes on-screen objects that allow you to intuitively interact with UNIX without entering cryptic commands. In the OpenWindows environment, you use a mouse to work with icons, menus, and windows. OpenWindows is based on the OPEN LOOK graphical user interface, a set of standards for user interface design based on the X Window System. The X Window System is a network-independent, operating-system-independent graphical windowing system developed by MIT that has been adopted as an industry standard. The X Window System is sometimes referred to as X11. Solaris includes an impressive set of OpenWindows applications called the DeskSet that use the X Window System. These applications allow you to perform a wide variety of everyday tasks, such as managing files, editing text files, and sending email.

How This Book Is Organized

Mastering Solaris 2 explains how to work with Solaris using the graphical-based applications as well as using the traditional SunOS command-line prompt. This book provides a practical orientation supported by numerous step-by-step instructions that get you up and running quickly and efficiently.

Throughout this book you will find helpful tips, warnings, and notes that provide you with extra information. *Mastering Solaris 2* is organized into four parts. Part I, "Working with the OpenWindows DeskSet," explains working with all the applications in the OpenWindows DeskSet. In this part, you'll find detailed, hands-on instructions for performing everyday tasks using such DeskSet applications as the File Manager, the Multimedia Mail Tool, the Calendar Manager, the Audio Tool, and more. You'll also learn how to customize your OpenWindows environment to suit your needs.

INTRODUCTION

Part II, "Working from the SunOS Command Line," explains how to work with SunOS and Korn shell commands. In this part, you'll learn essential SunOS commands that are used to navigate the file system, manage files, send and receive mail, and create, edit, format, and print documents. Expanding your SunOS skills, you'll learn how to master advanced commands and techniques, such as learning how to locate files, search for text within files, perform sort operations, use redirection, pipes, and filters, and manage multiple tasks.

Part III, "Beyond the Fundamentals," explains how to harness the power of Solaris. It shows you how to customize Solaris to suit your own needs and how to communicate across your network or around the world from your workstation. You'll learn system administration basics for working with hard disk drives, tape drives, CD ROMs, and floppy disks. It also explains how to use the OpenWindows-based Administration Tool to add users, workstations, and printers to your network.

Part IV, "Command Reference," provides a comprehensive, practical reference guide to SunOS and Korn shell commands. This handy alphabetical command listing provides syntax, description, and real-world examples for using commands, showing not just how, but when and why to take advantage of a command.

PART ONE

Working with the OpenWindows DeskSet

CHAPTERS

1 Getting Started with OpenWindows and the DeskSet

2 Using the File Manager

3 The Multimedia Mail Tool Makes Mail Easy

4 Using the Text Editor, Shell Tool, and Command Tool

5 Get Organized with the Calendar Manager

6 Using the Print Tool, Audio Tool, and Other DeskSet Applications

7 Customizing the Workspace and Icons

Getting Started with OpenWindows and the DeskSet

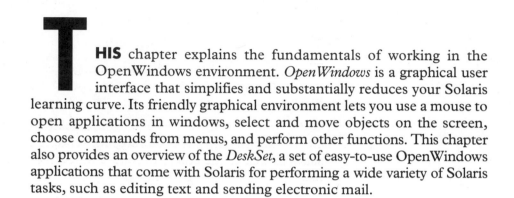

THIS chapter explains the fundamentals of working in the OpenWindows environment. *OpenWindows* is a graphical user interface that simplifies and substantially reduces your Solaris learning curve. Its friendly graphical environment lets you use a mouse to open applications in windows, select and move objects on the screen, choose commands from menus, and perform other functions. This chapter also provides an overview of the *DeskSet*, a set of easy-to-use OpenWindows applications that come with Solaris for performing a wide variety of Solaris tasks, such as editing text and sending electronic mail.

About OpenWindows and the DeskSet

The OpenWindows graphical interface rivals the ease of Microsoft Windows and the Macintosh computer, yet taps the power of UNIX. OpenWindows is based on the Open Look Graphical User Interface, a set of standards for user interface design. The background of the main OpenWindows screen is called the *Workspace*. The Workspace is the display area for objects such as windows, icons, and menus. It is analogous to a desktop that contains objects such as calculators, clocks, and file folders.

Solaris includes a set of default applications called the *DeskSet*. The DeskSet is a collection of basic applications for performing a wide range of tasks. These applications are also commonly referred to as *tools*. Each DeskSet application runs in its own window, and multiple applications can be run simultaneously. You interact with OpenWindows and DeskSet applications using the mouse, with the keyboard primarily used for entering text when needed. The following applications are included in the DeskSet:

- The Command Tool allows you easy access to the SunOS command line to enter SunOS commands.

- The Text Editor enables you to create and edit text files.

- The File Manager is a visual file management application for copying, moving, renaming, and deleting files and performing other file management tasks.

- The Mail Tool enables you to communicate with other users electronically. It includes features for sending and receiving messages as well as the ability to send and receive voice mail (when used in conjunction with the Audio Tool).

- The Calendar Manager allows you to create daily, weekly, monthly, and yearly calendars for upcoming appointments. It also lets you see the appointments of other users on the network for coordinating schedules.

- The Clock displays the current time, in either analog or digital form.

- The Calculator includes a financial and scientific calculator for performing both simple and complex calculations.

- The Print Tool allows you to easily manage your printing jobs.

- The Audio Tool lets you record and play audio files that contain recorded sounds.

- The Tape Tool provides a convenient way to back up or archive files onto a tape cartridge.

- The Binder allows you to connect a file to an application or icon so that you can start an application directly from the file.

- The Snapshot application lets you easily take snapshots of a part of the screen or the entire screen, print the image, and save the image to a file.

- The Icon Editor allows you to create your own icons which can be attached to files.

- The Performance Meter enables you to monitor many aspects of your system's performance, with either a graph or a dial meter.

- The Shell Tool lets you access the SunOS command line to enter commands.

- Demos includes a collection of special effects programs and utilities.

Logging into Solaris

NOTE If you have already logged in and want to work with OpenWindows, skip to the section "Starting OpenWindows and the DeskSet."

The process of getting into Solaris to start OpenWindows is called *logging in*. Before you can log into Solaris to get to OpenWindows and the Desk-Set, you need an *account* set up by the *system administrator*, the person responsible for managing the system. In setting up your account, the system administrator instructs Solaris to accept you as a user and establishes certain parameters for your use of the system. You are then assigned a *user name*. Your user name identifies you to the system and usually consists of the initial letter of your first name and your complete last name.

After you have been assigned an account and a user name, you need to choose a password that you can enter at the prompt Solaris displays after you have entered your user name. Your *password* prevents the use of your account by unauthorized users. Pick a password that is easy to remember, yet not easily deduced by others. You can change your password at any time, as explained later. The following are requirements for selecting a password for the first time.

- A password must have at least six characters. If you use a password of less than six characters in length, Solaris prompts you to use a longer password.

- A password must contain at least two alphabetic characters and at least one numeric or special character, such as an &, +, −, @, !, %. A password can contain uppercase or lowercase letters.

- Your user name, with its letters reversed or moved around *cannot* be used as a password.

To log in, at the `login` prompt, type in your user name in lowercase characters and press Return. If you typed a wrong character and have not yet pressed Return, use the Delete key to erase the incorrect character and type the correct character.

NOTE

If you enter a password more than three times that the system doesn't recognize, Solaris displays a message telling you there have been too many attempts and to try again later. This is a security feature to prevent unauthorized users from trying to guess a password.

After entering your user name, Solaris prompts you to enter your password. At the `password` prompt, type in your new password, then press Return. Your password will not be displayed as you type it. Solaris then logs you in and displays the system prompt, indicating that you are ready to start OpenWindows or enter SunOS commands.

System Login Messages

After you have logged in, you may see a *login message* displayed on your screen just before the system prompt. A login message usually displays information from the system administrator, such as a warning that the system will be shut down for maintenance. A message indicating that you have electronic mail from other system users may also appear. Some systems may prompt you to type **news** to display a news bulletin. For information on reading electronic mail messages, see Chapter 3, "The Multimedia Mail Tool Makes Mail Easy."

Changing Your Password

It is a good idea to change your password periodically in order to prevent unauthorized access to your files. Depending on how your system administrator set up your account, you may even be required to change your password at regular time intervals. The following are additional requirements for changing a password beyond those described earlier for entering your password for the first time.

- Uppercase and lowercase characters are not considered different by Solaris when changing a password.
- A new password must differ from the previous password by at least three characters.

The following steps explain how to change your password:

1. At the system prompt, type in the command **passwd** in lowercase characters and press Return. Solaris prompts you for your old password.

2. Type your old password and press Return. The system will not display the characters you type. The system will prompt you for your new password.

3. Type your new password and press Return. After you enter your new password, you will then be asked to retype your new password for verification.

4. Type your new password again and press Return.

Starting OpenWindows and the DeskSet

On some systems, OpenWindows comes up when you log in. If the system prompt (**$**) is displayed, you can start OpenWindows from the command line by typing

```
openwin
```

The Workspace appears with a default blue or gray background (depending on your screen type) and these DeskSet application windows appear on your screen (as shown in Figure 1.1):

- The `Console` window displays system messages. If a `Console` window does not appear on the Workspace, system messages will appear there instead, creating a cluttered screen. A new `Console` window can be opened and any system messages that appear on your screen can be removed by refreshing the Workspace, as explained in the "Workspace Utilities" section later in this chapter.

The default Open-Windows startup screen

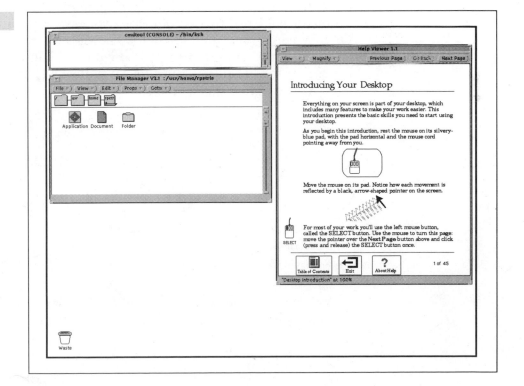

- The `File Manager` window is used to manage your files. The `Waste` (trash can) icon, which is part of the File Manager application, also appears on your screen.

- The `Help Viewer` window accesses information about Open-Windows and the DeskSet.

Using the Mouse

The mouse allows you to perform a variety of operations in OpenWindows by simply pressing a button. The arrow that appears on the screen pointing toward the upper left is the *pointer*. It changes location when you move the mouse. On most Sun workstations you must move the mouse on the metallic pad that accompanies your system. The key to mastering OpenWindows and the DeskSet is knowing where to move the pointer and which mouse button to push. Figure 1.2 shows the effects of each mouse button when used in OpenWindows. The following describes each mouse button and its related function.

FIGURE 1.2

Mouse button action

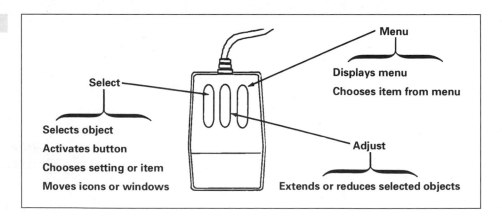

MOUSE BUTTON	FUNCTION
Left	Selects object, activates button, chooses setting or item, or move icons or windows. The left mouse button is also referred to as the *Select* button.
Middle	Extends or reduces selected objects. The middle mouse button is also referred to as the *Adjust* button.
Right	Displays menu or chooses item from menu. The right mouse button is also referred to as the *Menu* button.

N O T E

If you are using a two-button mouse with Solaris for x86, the middle mouse button's function is obtained by simultaneously pressing the left mouse button and the Shift key on the keyboard.

The following describes the seven basic mouse actions performed in OpenWindows.

ACTION	DESCRIPTION
Point	Move the mouse to change the location of the pointer.
Click	Quickly press and release a mouse button.
Double-click	Quickly press and release a mouse button twice (without moving the mouse).
Press	Hold down a mouse button without moving the mouse.
Drag	Hold a mouse button down while moving the mouse.

ACTION	DESCRIPTION
Drag and drop	Hold a mouse button down while moving the mouse. When the on-screen object is over an area that accepts the object as input, release the mouse button to drop it.
Control-drag	Press the Control key on the keyboard and drag the mouse.

Pointer Indicators

The pointer also acts as an indicator of different actions occurring in the system. For example, when an application is busy, the pointer changes to a stopwatch to indicate that the application is busy and cannot accept input. The standard pointer is an arrow pointing up to the left.

Pointer Jumping

In most cases, you move the pointer by moving the mouse. However, in some cases, the pointer moves directly to a specific place on the screen automatically. This is called *pointer jumping* and is used to indicate the default response. Figure 1.3 shows an example of a pointer jumping to a button in a Notice.

FIGURE 1.3

Pointer jumping to a button in a Notice

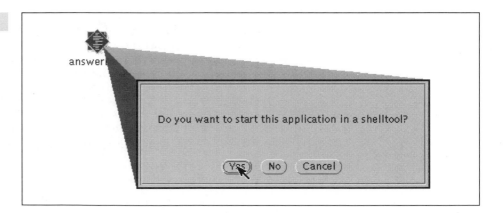

Do you want to start this application in a shelltool?

(Yes) (No) (Cancel)

Working with Menus

A menu lists the choices that can be made from the Workspace or a Desk-Set application window. You can display a menu without making a selection by clicking the right mouse button with the pointer on the Workspace, a menu button, a window border, or the work area of a window. For example, moving the pointer to the top border of the `Help Viewer` window and clicking the right mouse button displays the `Window` menu. You can then click the right mouse button on a menu option to execute the command. Otherwise, the menu will remain displayed until you click or press any mouse button again.

Pressing and holding the right mouse button on the Workspace, a menu button, a window border, or the work area of a window displays the menu and lets you drag the pointer to highlight a menu option. When you release the mouse button, the menu option is activated. For example, pressing and holding down the right mouse button with the pointer on the top border of `Help Viewer` window displays the `Window` menu. Dragging the pointer to highlight the `Quit` option and releasing the mouse button activates the `Quit` command, which removes the `Help Viewer` window from the Workspace. Moving the pointer off the menu and releasing the mouse button removes the menu from the screen. Menus that are accessed by moving the pointer to any area of the Workspace, a window border, or the work area of a window are referred to as *pop-up menus*.

Menus in OpenWindows incorporate standardized features. Each option in a menu is called an *item*. A dimmed menu item indicates the item is not available. The direction of the arrowhead indicates where a menu will appear. An arrowhead pointing downward, such as on a menu button, indicates the menu will appear below the arrowhead. An arrowhead appearing to the right of a menu item indicates that a submenu of options will appear to the right of that item. To display a submenu, press the right mouse button and move the pointer to the arrowhead. To choose an item in a submenu, continue to move the pointer to highlight the item you want, then release the mouse button.

Choosing a menu item followed by an ellipsis (...) displays an application or pop-up window. For example, choosing the `Properties...` item in the `Workspace` menu displays the `Workspace Properties` pop-up window. Pop-up windows are explained later in this chapter.

Pinning a Menu to the Workspace

Many menus include a pushpin in the upper-left corner of the menu. You can use the mouse to push the pin, pinning the menu to the Workspace. You can open and pin a menu by pressing the right button to display the menu, dragging the pointer on top of the pushpin, then releasing the button. You can also click the right mouse button to display the menu, then click the right or left mouse button on the pushpin. Figure 1.4 shows a menu before and after pinning it to the Workspace. The menu remains pinned until you unpin it or you close the application. A pinned menu can be moved anywhere on the Workspace by moving the pointer to the menu header, pressing the left mouse button, and dragging the menu to its new location.

To unpin a menu or pop-up window, click the left mouse button on the pushpin or choose `Dismiss` from the `Window` menu by clicking the right mouse button with the pointer on the menu's header, the area above the line at the top of the menu. The `Window` menu can also be accessed by moving the pointer on any part of the menu's border and pressing the right mouse button. The `Window` menu is explained in detail later in this chapter.

Choosing the Default Menu Item

The default menu item is usually the first item listed in a menu and is encircled with a small black border (Figure 1.5). Most menus have default menu items. The default item is activated by clicking the left mouse button on the menu button or choosing just the menu item that accesses the default item in the submenu. In both cases, you save the extra step of having to display the menu or submenu.

FIGURE 1.4

A menu before and
after pinning it to the
Workspace

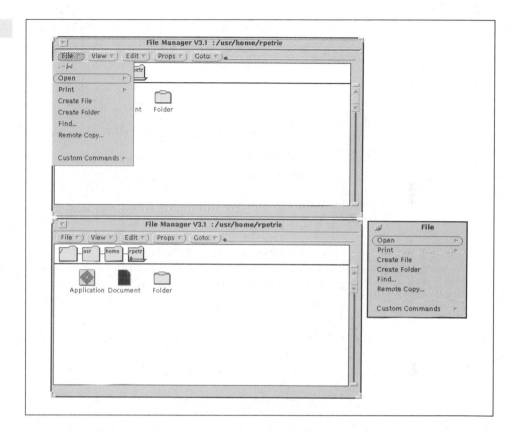

FIGURE 1.5

The default item in a
menu

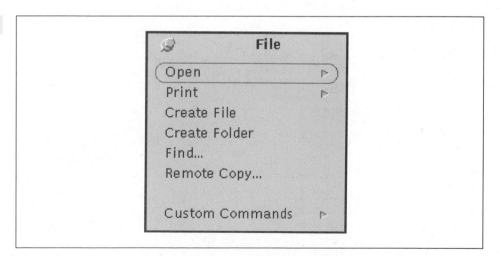

If you find that you frequently choose a menu item choice other than the default, you can define that item as the default item. To change the default choice, do the following:

1. Press the right mouse button to display the menu in which you want to change the default item.

2. Drag the pointer to highlight your new default menu item.

3. Press the Control key on your keyboard, release the right mouse button, then release the Control key.

The Workspace Menu

The Workspace menu is sometimes called the *root* menu because it is the primary menu you use to access applications and utilities. To display the Workspace menu, move the pointer anywhere on the Workspace background and press the right mouse button. The Workspace menu appears (Figure 1.6). To quit displaying the Workspace menu, move the pointer off the Workspace menu and release the right mouse button. The following describes the items displayed in the Workspace menu.

FIGURE 1.6

The Workspace menu

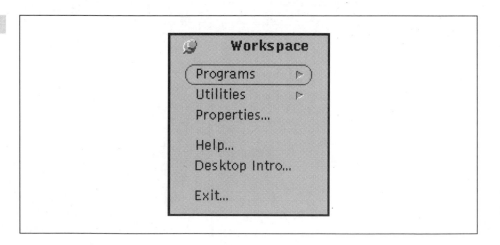

MENU ITEM	RESULT
Programs	Displays a submenu of DeskSet and other applications.
Utilities	Displays a submenu of services, including utilities for redisplaying (refreshing) the Workspace or windows, locking the screen, saving the Workspace layout, opening a new **Console** window, displaying a window's management menu, or displaying on-screen Function keys and their settings.
Properties	Displays a window containing settings for customizing your Workspace.
Help	Displays the help handbooks' Table of Contents in the **Help Viewer** window.
Desktop Intro	Displays the Desktop tutorial in the **Help Viewer** window.
Exit	Exits OpenWindows.

Starting a DeskSet Application

To start a DeskSet application, with the pointer on the **Workspace** menu and the highlight on the **Programs** item, drag the pointer to the right. The **Programs** submenu is displayed (Figure 1.7). You can pin the **Programs** submenu to the Workspace for easy access to your applications. Move the pointer to highlight the application item in the **Programs** submenu that you want to start and release the mouse button. The application appears on the Workspace as either an open window or as an icon.

FIGURE 1.7

The Workspace
Programs submenu

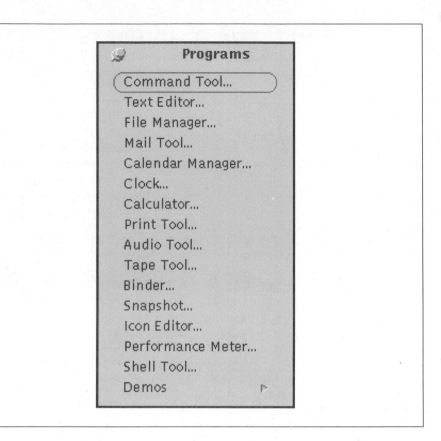

Working with Windows

All windows in the OpenWindows environment utilize a consistent interface. In other words, you perform the same tasks, such as opening or closing a window, using the same procedures, regardless of the application window. Some applications use more than one window. For example, the Mail Tool includes a *base window* that includes the main controls and also has a secondary window for composing mail messages. In addition to application windows, there are *pop-up windows*, which are usually connected to applications for changing settings. The following sections explain working with and managing windows on the Workspace.

The Parts of an Application Window

All application windows have similar features that make up the window. Figure 1.8 uses the DeskSet's `Text Editor` window to illustrate the parts of an application window. The following describes the main parts of the DeskSet's `Text Editor` window that are common to application windows.

WINDOW PART	DESCRIPTION
Window header	The wide stripe at the top of the window is called the window header. The contents of the header depend on the application you are using. The header typically tells you the name of the application associated with the window. If the application window contains a file, the path name for the file is usually included. You can access the `Window` menu by pressing the right mouse button with the pointer in the window header.
Control area	A region of a window where controls such as buttons, settings, and text fields are displayed.
Scrollbar elevator	The scrollbar elevator allows you to move (scroll) through the contents of a window using a mouse. You can also move the pointer to any part of the scrollbar and press the right mouse button to display the `Scrollbar` menu. The boxes at the ends of the scrollbar are cable anchors that allow you to move quickly to the beginning or end of a file by moving the pointer to a cable anchor and clicking the left mouse button.
Pane	The application window's work area.

FIGURE 1.8

The parts of the Text Editor window

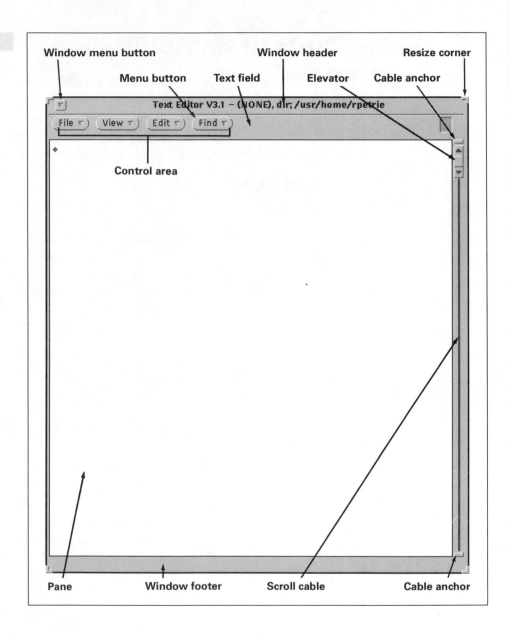

WINDOW PART	**DESCRIPTION**
Insert point	A symbol indicating where text or a command you type from the keyboard will appear in the window's pane. Some applications use a black triangle and others use a solid rectangle.
Menu button	Displays a menu when you click or press the right mouse button on the menu button. The button labels are command names. Menu buttons with an arrowhead beside the button label always have additional submenus layered underneath. An ellipsis (...) on a button indicates that a pop-up window will appear when you click on the button with the left mouse button.
Drag-and-drop target	The rectangle in the upper-right corner of the window's control area is a target (or source) for dragging and dropping files. The target's primary purpose is to act as a receptacle for loading files. Dragging an icon to the drag-and-drop target and dropping the icon (releasing the left mouse button) loads the selected file.
Resize corner	By moving the pointer onto any of the four resize corners and pressing the left mouse button, you can change the window to a new size, larger or smaller.

WINDOW PART	DESCRIPTION
Window menu button	This small triangle button in the upper-left corner of a window accesses the **Window** menu. When you click the right mouse button on the Window menu button, the **Window** menu appears with items for managing the window. Clicking the left mouse button on the Window menu button activates the default item from the **Window** menu, the **Close** item which allows you to easily close a window to an icon.
Window footer	This area at the bottom of the window displays messages and status information.

Using the Scrollbar

In most cases, the right side of a window displays a *scrollbar*. The scrollbar is made up of five major components: cable anchors, up arrow, drag box, down arrow, and the cable. Figure 1.9 identifies each of these parts of a scrollbar.

Pressing the left mouse button and dragging the drag box moves the contents up or down relative to the direction you drag the drag box. The following list explains how to use a scrollbar to move through a file.

MOVEMENT	ACTION
Beginning of a file	Place the pointer on the top cable anchor and click the left mouse button.
Bottom of a file	Place the pointer on the bottom cable anchor and click the left mouse button.

FIGURE 1.9

The parts of the
scrollbar

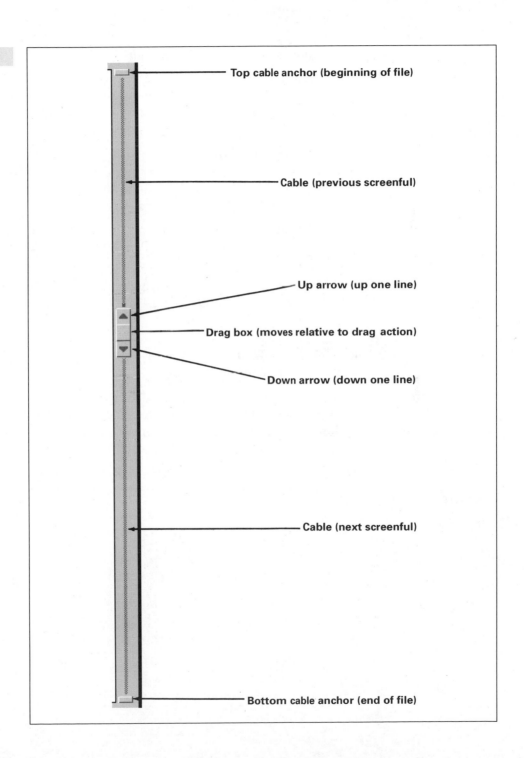

Top cable anchor (beginning of file)

Cable (previous screenful)

Up arrow (up one line)

Drag box (moves relative to drag action)

Down arrow (down one line)

Cable (next screenful)

Bottom cable anchor (end of file)

MOVEMENT	ACTION
Up a screen	Place the pointer on the cable between the top cable anchor and the Up arrow and click the left mouse button.
Down a screen	Place the pointer on the cable between the bottom cable anchor and the Down arrow and click the left mouse button.
Up one line	Place the pointer on the Up arrow and click the left mouse button.
Down one line	Place the pointer on the Down arrow and click the left mouse button.

The Scrollbar Menu

You can also use the **Scrollbar** menu to move to one of three locations in a window. To display the **Scrollbar** menu (Figure 1.10), move the pointer anywhere on the scrollbar and press the right mouse button. You choose the **Scrollbar** menu item by moving the pointer to highlight the item you want. The following explains the items in the **Scrollbar** menu.

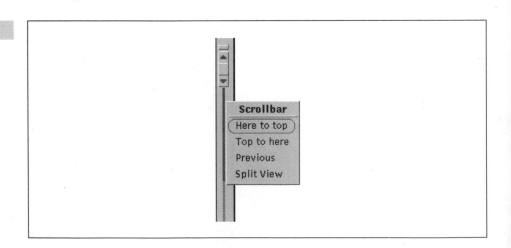

MENU ITEM	RESULT
`Here to top`	Moves the line where the pointer is located to the top of the text pane.
`Top to here`	Moves the text pane display towards the top of the file at a distance relative to the position of the pointer in the scrollbar.
`Previous`	Moves the text pane display to the position where you were located when you pressed a mouse button.
`Split View`	Creates another scrollable pane of the same document. A `Join View` item then appears in the `Scrollbar` menu, which is used to unsplit the last pane split.

Splitting a Window Pane

You can split a window pane into two or more parts, so you can work with different parts of a text file or file listing. Figure 1.11 shows a split `Text Editor` window pane. This allows you to have different vantage points for the same file or file listing from different panes. You can split a pane by dragging the top or bottom cable anchor, or by using the `Scrollbar` menu.

To split a pane using the cable anchor, move the pointer to the top or bottom cable anchor, press the left mouse button and drag the cable anchor to the position where you want to split the pane, then release the mouse button. To unsplit a pane, drag the cable anchor back to the top or bottom of the scroll bar.

To split a pane using the `Scrollbar` menu, move the pointer to the location on the scrollbar where you want to split the pane, press the right mouse button, then choose the `Split View` item.

FIGURE 1.11

A split Text Editor
window pane

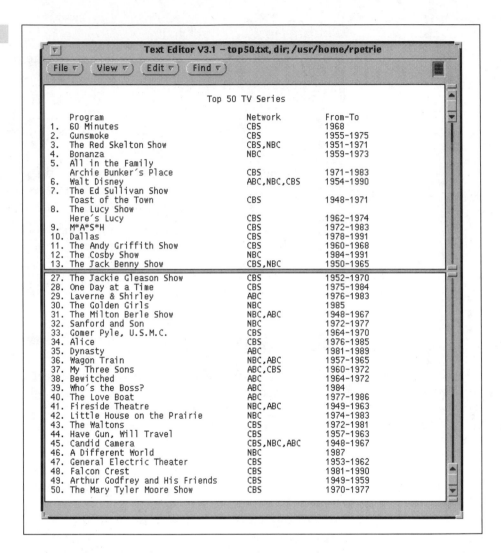

The Clipboard

The *clipboard* is a buffer, a storage place in memory that temporarily holds text or files during move or copy operations in or between application windows. Using an application's **Copy**, **Cut**, and **Paste** menu items automatically stores the selected information on the clipboard. Only one item or group of items is stored on the clipboard at a time.

WARNING If you choose a cut or copy operation while information is stored on the clipboard, or you quit OpenWindows, the information in the clipboard is lost.

Pop-up Windows

A pop-up window is a different type of window than an application window. Any button or menu item followed by an ellipsis (...) displays a pop-up window. Pop-up windows provide controls for conveniently changing specific attributes of an application. Most pop-up windows have pushpins in the upper-left corner so you can pin the window to the Workspace. Figure 1.12 shows a typical pop-up window. When you quit an application window, its related pop-up windows are also removed from the Workspace.

FIGURE 1.12

A pop-up window

| CM Appointment Editor: rpetrie@stv |

Date: 03/29/93
Month / Day / Year

Start: ▽ 09:00 AM PM

End: ▽ 5:00 AM PM

What: Developer's Conference

Appointments

9:00 Developer's Conference
2:00 Round Table
3:30 Staff Meeting

Appt ToDo My Eyes Only

Alarm:
Beep 5 ▽ mins
Flash 5 ▽ mins
PopUp 5 ▽ mins
Mail 2 ▽ hrs

Repeat: ▽ Daily

For: ▽ 3 days

Mail To: rpetrie@stv

(Insert) (Delete) (Change) (Clear) (Restore Size)

Pop-up windows have an associated Window menu (Figure 1.13) that is similar to an application window's Window menu. Because a pop-up window *cannot* be closed to an icon, there is no Close menu item. To display a pop-up window's Window menu, place the pointer in the window header and click the right mouse button. The following explains the pop-up window's Window menu items:

MENU ITEM	RESULT
Dismiss	Provides you with options for quitting the current pop-up window or dismissing all pop-up windows.
Move	Allows you to reposition the pop-up window using the arrow keys.
Resize	Allows you to resize the pop-up window using the arrow keys.
Back	Moves the current pop-up window to the back of the window stack.
Refresh	Redisplays the contents of the pop-up window.
Owner?	Flashes the window header of the window that the pop-up window was started from and moves the application window of the associated application to the foreground of the screen.

FIGURE 1.13

The pop-up window's Window menu

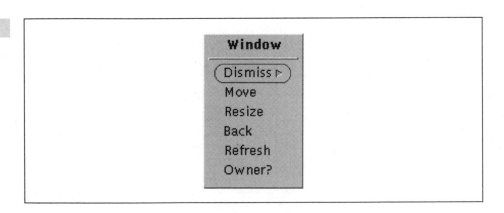

Types of Window Controls

In OpenWindows, there are standardized controls for working with settings in either application or pop-up windows. Figure 1.14 shows the different types of settings available in OpenWindows. You can navigate settings in a pop-up window by using the mouse, or you can press Return or the Tab key. The following list explains these window controls.

CONTROL	DESCRIPTION
Button	Displays menus or pop-up windows, or executes commands when you move the pointer onto them and click a mouse button.
Abbreviated menu button	Displays a menu of options.

FIGURE 1.14

Window controls

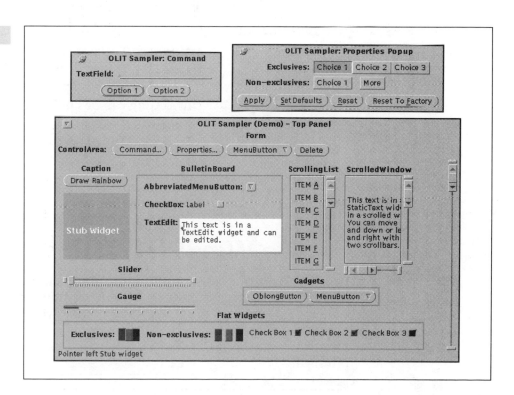

CONTROL	DESCRIPTION
Check boxes	Activates or deactivates settings by moving the pointer inside the check box and clicking the left mouse button.
Text field	Text input areas for entering text, such as specifying directories, files, or numeric settings. If a text field has more text than can appear in the field, a scrolling button automatically appears on the side of the text field where text is hidden. You can quickly delete all the text in any text field by triple-clicking the left mouse in the text field.
Numeric field	Text field with increment and decrement buttons for increasing and decreasing the value in the text field.
Scrolling list	List of options or settings that include a scrollbar. Scrolling lists include a `Scrolling List` pop-up menu that allows you to navigate and edit the list.
Exclusive setting	One setting can be chosen from a set of options.
Nonexclusive settings	Multiple settings can be chosen from a set of options.
Slider	Dragging the slider handle sets a value from a range of values.

The Active Window

Because there can be several windows open on the Workspace at once, OpenWindows must keep track of which window is currently active. To switch to a window and make it the active window, simply move the pointer to any location in the window you want active and click the left mouse button. An inactive window header lacks a 3-D effect or appears dimmed.

N O T E

You can change the default setting for activating a window from clicking the mouse button to simply moving the pointer to anywhere in the window, as explained in Chapter 7, "Customizing the Workspace and Icons."

When a text application window, such as the Text Editor, is active, the insert point appears as a black triangle, indicating it is ready for you to enter text or a command. In some applications windows, such as the Shell Tool, a solid rectangle appears, indicating the window is active. A dimmed diamond or a hollow rectangle indicates the window is inactive.

The Window Menu

Moving the pointer onto the Window menu button, an icon, a window header, or the border of a window and pressing the right mouse button displays the Window menu. The Window menu provides you with items to manage the application window, such as opening, closing, or resizing a window to take up the full screen. Figure 1.15 shows the Window menu.

FIGURE 1.15

The Window menu

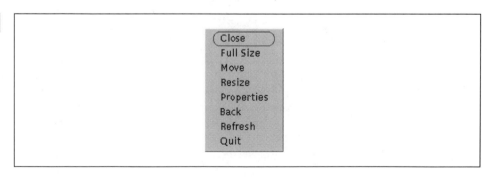

Closing and Reopening a Window

Closing an application window means reducing the window to an icon. The application is still active, but unavailable until you reopen it. Figure 1.16 shows the **Help Viewer** window closed to an icon. Every Open-Windows application window closes to an icon. The easiest way to close an application window is to move the pointer to the Window menu button (upper-left corner) and click the left mouse button to choose the default **Close** menu item. When you release the mouse button, the window shrinks to an icon.

FIGURE 1.16

The Help Viewer window closed to an icon

An application window can also be closed by moving the pointer to any part of the window header or the outside border of the window, pressing the right mouse button, then choosing the **Close** item from the **Window** menu.

To reopen a DeskSet application, place the pointer on top of the icon and double-click the left mouse button. The window is restored to the size it was when you closed it. You can also reopen the window by pressing the right mouse button on the icon to select it, then choosing **Open** from the **Window** menu.

NOTE

An alternative to using the mouse to open and close a window is to use the Open accelerator key on the left side of your Sun workstation keyboard. With the icon selected, press the Open accelerator key. This key acts as a toggle, so pressing it again with the pointer in an active window changes the window back into an icon.

Quitting a Window

The last menu item in the `Window` menu is `Quit`. Quitting is different from closing a window because the application is actually removed from the desktop. If you have unsaved changes, selecting `Quit` displays a confirmation Notice. The Notice usually contains two *buttons*, such as `Cancel, do NOT Quit` and `Discard edits, then Quit`. If the button outline is shown in boldface or a double outline surrounds the button, you can press Return to choose that choice; otherwise, you must move the pointer directly to the button you want to choose and click the left mouse button. If you want to quit the application and remove the icon or window from the Workspace, click the left mouse button or press Return, and the icon or window will disappear. Otherwise you can cancel the `Quit` operation by moving the pointer to the `Cancel, do NOT Quit` button and clicking the left mouse button.

Moving a Window

Windows and icons can be arranged anywhere on your screen, even on top of other windows or icons. When you move a window, an outline of it moves as you drag the pointer. This outline is known as a *bounding box*. To move a window, move the pointer to the window header of the window you want to move. Press the left mouse button and drag the bounding box to its new location. When you release the left mouse button, the window is moved to the location of the bounding box.

A less efficient way to move a window is choosing `Move` from the `Window` menu. To display the `Window` menu, press the right mouse button while the pointer is located in the window header, choose `Move`, then use the arrow keys to position the bounding box and press Return.

Moving Multiple Windows

Multiple windows can be selected as a group then moved together. For example, you might want to arrange several windows on the Workspace, then move the whole arrangement to a new location. Moving a group of windows involves selecting the group of windows you want, then moving them to the new location. You can select a group of windows by clicking the left mouse button on one window and the middle mouse button on each additional window or icon. You can also select a group of windows (and icons) by moving the pointer to any corner of the set of windows you want to group, pressing the left mouse button, then dragging the pointer diagonally to the opposite corner of the group and releasing the mouse button. After selecting a group of windows, place the pointer on the edge of one of the grouped windows, press the left mouse button, and drag the pointer to the new location. The group of windows moves to the new location. To ungroup the windows, click the left mouse button with the pointer anywhere in the Workspace.

Moving Windows to the Background

Windows (and icons) can be stacked up on your Workspace similar to the way you stack folders or papers on your desk. Anytime a window overlaps another window, the window in the background is inactive. You can switch between windows using the Window menu or by clicking the left mouse button on a window header or border.

To move a window that is in the background to the foreground, move the pointer to the window header or the border of the window you want and click the left mouse button. If the window is not available, move the foreground window to expose the window.

To move a window to the background behind another window, click the right mouse button on the window header or the border of the window you want. Choose the Back item from the Window menu. Figure 1.17 shows a Calendar window first in the foreground, then in the background.

FIGURE 1.17

The Calendar window
in the foreground and
background

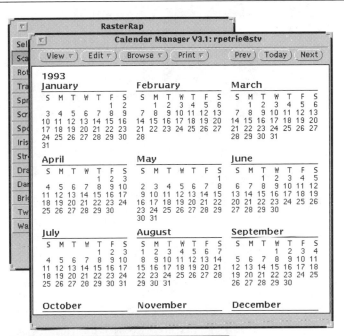

NOTE

You can also move a window to the background or foreground by moving the pointer to the window you want to move to the foreground, then pressing the Front accelerator key on Sun workstation keyboards. This key acts as a toggle, so pressing it again sends the window to the background.

Resizing a Window

Moving the pointer to any of the resize corners of a window causes the arrow pointer to change to a target pointer. Pressing the left mouse button and dragging the target pointer allows you to change a window's height and width. The bounding box changes size when you drag the pointer, and the window changes to the size of the bounding box when you release the mouse button.

A window can also be resized by using the `Resize` item from the `Window` menu. To display the `Window` menu, press the right mouse button with the pointer in the window header. Choose `Resize`, use the arrow keys to stretch the bounding box to the size you want, and press Return.

You can resize a window so that it takes up the full height of the screen by moving the pointer to the window header or border, pressing the right mouse button, and choosing `Full Size` from the `Window` menu. Once you release the left mouse button, the window is resized to the height of your screen, and the `Full Size` item in the `Window` menu changes to `Restore Size`. To return to the normal size of the window, choose `Restore Size` from the `Window` menu.

Redisplaying a Window

Sometimes fragments of previous work appear in a window, or a portion of the window appears to have a section missing. Choosing `Refresh` in the `Window` menu clears and redraws the window.

Dragging and Dropping Files

The OpenWindows drag-and-drop feature enables you to easily transfer text or files between applications, or open applications on the Workspace. For example, you can drag icons representing files from the File Manager and drop them into other windows or icons to enter them as input for the application. A file icon can also be dragged and dropped on the Workspace to open the file and the application associated with it. To delete files, you can easily drag and drop unwanted files onto the `Waste` icon.

To drag and drop a file into an application window, move the pointer onto the icon you want to drag and drop. Select a file using the left mouse button, drag the file inside the application window's pane, and release the left mouse button. Releasing this button is known as dropping a file. The file is inserted or a message appears in the window footer explaining why the action was unsuccessful.

NOTE — Chapter 2, "Using the File Manager" explains how to use the drag-and-drop feature to manage files.

Drag-and-Drop Targets

OpenWindows includes another feature for dragging and dropping files into applications called a *drag-and-drop target*. The Print Tool, Audio Tool, Tape Tool, and Snapshot DeskSet applications have drag-and-drop targets. The target is a rectangle located in the upper-right corner of a window's control area. If you drag a document icon or a piece of text and drop it into a text pane that already contains a file, the document will be inserted in the location the icon was dropped. If you drop the icon on the drag-and-drop target, the document replaces the existing text.

Some file icons can be dragged out of the drag-and-drop target. For example, you can drag a loaded text file icon out of the Text Editor's drag-and-drop target and drag and drop it onto the Print Tool icon to print the file.

Getting Online Help

OpenWindows comes with two kinds of online help, Magnify help and help handbooks. Magnify help is for immediate information on any specified object, such as a menu item, control, or window. Help handbooks supply information about how to use DeskSet applications. Help handbooks are available in the `Help Viewer` window. These help handbooks are organized by topic.

Using Magnify Help

Magnify help allows you to get specific information about a particular window or menu. To get online help about a window or menu item, move the pointer to the item (such as a window or menu) that you want to know about, then press the Help key on the keyboard. (The Help key is only available on the Sun workstation keyboard.) A help pop-up window appears with information about the item. If there is more text than appears in the pop-up window, a scroll bar appears for scrolling through the additional text. Figure 1.18 shows a sample Magnify help pop-up window. If there is more information available on the topic in a help handbook, a `More` button appears at the bottom of the window. Clicking the left mouse button on the `More` button opens the `Help Viewer` window, with the appropriate topic appearing in the window. If there is no Magnify help available for the item you specified, a small pop-up window appears that tells you there is no help for that item. The pointer jumps to the `OK` button. Click the left mouse button to continue.

A Magnify help pop-up window is closed when you close or quit an application. If you want to close the Magnify help window before you close or quit an application, click the left mouse button on the pushpin in the upper-left corner of the Magnify help window.

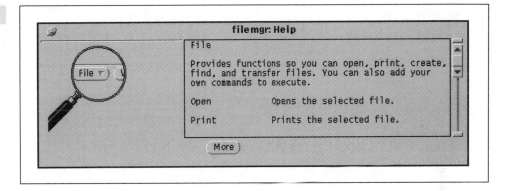

FIGURE 1.18

A sample Magnify help pop-up window

Using the Help Handbooks

The help handbooks include a tutorial and 15 additional help handbooks that provide information on working with the Workspace and DeskSet applications. Choosing `Desktop Intro` from the `Workspace` menu displays the first page of the tutorial in the `Help Viewer` window. This tutorial introduces and explains working with the Desktop. Choosing `Help` from the `Workspace` menu displays the Table of Contents for all the help handbooks in the `Help Viewer` window (Figure 1.19).

The help handbook can also be quickly accessed from any DeskSet application, icon, or menu by positioning the pointer over the area of interest, and pressing Shift, then Help on your keyboard. The `Help Viewer` window appears on the Workspace, displaying the appropriate handbook.

Using the Help Viewer Icons

The `Help Viewer` window uses standardized features to make navigating it easy. Handy icons located at the bottom of the `Help Viewer` window let you quickly return to the Table of Contents, display information about the Help Viewer itself, or exit the tutorial. Depending on your location in the Help Viewer window, one or more icons will appear at the bottom of the `Help Viewer` window. To choose an icon, you must double-click on it. The following describes each icon's function.

FIGURE 1.19

The help handbooks' Table of Contents in the Help Viewer window

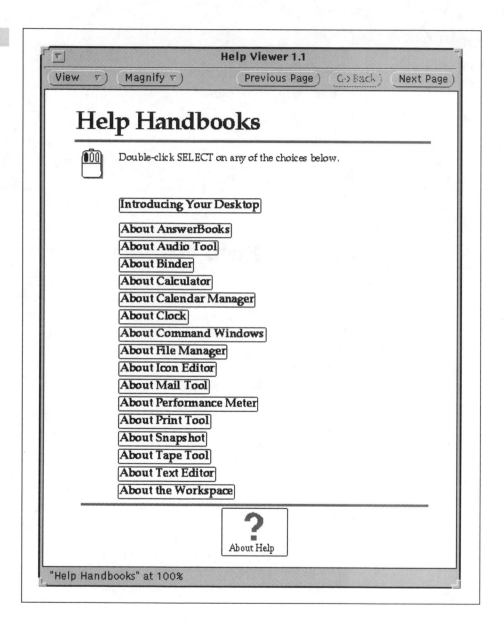

ICON	DESCRIPTION
About Help	Lets you view a description of how the help system works. Displays in all pages of the Help Viewer window.
Table of Contents	Displays the Table of Contents for the current help handbook. Appears after any first page of a help handbook.
Exit	Displays instructions on quitting the Desktop Introduction handbook. Appears only when the Desktop Introduction handbook is displayed.
More Handbooks	Displays the Table of Contents for all the help handbooks. Appears only on the first page of any help handbook.

Magnifying the Help Viewer Window

The Magnify menu contains items for changing the size of the Help Viewer window. By default, the Help Viewer window can be enlarged by 110% of its standard default size every time you click the left mouse button on the Magnify menu button, which chooses the default Larger item. Choosing Smaller shrinks the size of the Help Viewer window from any size larger than the standard size to no smaller than the standard window size. Choosing Standard returns the Help Viewer window to its default size.

NOTE   An easier way to magnify the Help Viewer window than using the Magnify menu button is to use the resize corners to stretch the window smaller or larger.

You can temporarily adjust the size of the Help Viewer window by choosing Custom Magnification to display the Custom Magnification pop-up window. Drag the slider control to specify the size you want, then click the left mouse button on the Apply button.

Navigating a Handbook

When you display a particular help handbook, you can page through the handbook using the buttons at the top of the Help Viewer window. Clicking the left mouse button on these buttons enables you to move backward (the Previous Page button) and forward (the Next Page button) one page at a time. The Go Back button redisplays the last page viewed. If you viewed pages in various parts of a handbook or in different handbooks, choosing the Go Back button allows you to retrace your steps, one by one. These navigation features are also available in the View menu.

The Help Viewer window also incorporates a handy navigation feature called *hypertext links*. Any text in a handbook that has a black outline indicates you can double-click the left mouse button on the text to move to related information.

Closing or Exiting the Help Viewer Window

The Help Viewer window can be closed to an icon by clicking the left mouse button on the Window menu button in the upper-left corner of any handbook. You can also close the Help Viewer window by clicking the left mouse button with the pointer on the window header and choosing Close from the Window menu. To exit the Help Viewer window, choose Quit from the Window menu.

Workspace Utilities

The Workspace menu includes the Utilities submenu (Figure 1.20). This menu includes several useful utilities for working with Open-Windows and the Workspace, such as options that save your Workspace configuration and lock your screen to keep unauthorized users out of your system when you are away from your workstation.

FIGURE 1.20

The Workspace
Utilities submenu

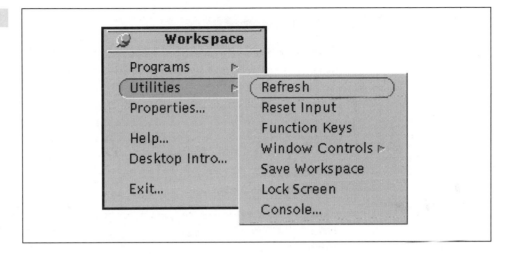

To open the `Utilities` submenu, press the right mouse button on the Workspace to display the `Workspace` menu. Drag the pointer to the `Utilities` item then to the right over the arrowhead to display the `Utilities` submenu. To choose an item, drag the pointer to the item you want and release the mouse button. The following sections explain these useful utility programs.

Refresh

Sometimes an application prints characters outside of a window, or leaves lines or other remnants from the window displayed after the window you quit is removed. For example, if you accidentally quit the `Console` window from the Workspace, there may be system messages printed on the Workspace. To redisplay the Workspace, choose `Refresh` from the `Utilities` submenu. The Workspace screen is redrawn.

Reset Input

If you're running several types of applications at once, you may occasionally find that characters you type in a window are garbled. This is because of an incompatibility between the way the different applications handle input data. The `Reset Input` item corrects the problem.

Function Keys

When you choose Function Keys, an on-screen display of the function keys on the keyboard (Figure 1.21) appears in a pop-up window at the bottom of the Workspace. Each function key on your keyboard appears as a button with a label of what the function key does. Placing the pointer on the function key and clicking the left mouse button is the same as pressing the key on your keyboard. The Function Key pop-up window can be pinned to the Workspace.

FIGURE 1.21

The Function Key
pop-up window

NOTE

You must have the Click Select option (the default setting) set in the Miscellaneous category of the Workspace Properties pop-up window for the Function Keys utility to work properly, as explained in Chapter 7, "Customizing the Workspace and Icons."

Currently, the Function Keys utility is not supported by DeskSet applications. If the application you are working with supports the Function Keys feature, the key labels display each key's function. The function key labels are automatically updated when the pointer is moved to another application that supports the Function Keys feature.

Window Controls

The Window Controls item displays a submenu of items for performing basic window operations for any selected window or group of windows on the Workspace. It is especially useful for performing operations on multiple windows simultaneously, instead of using each window's Window menu.

These basic operations include opening, closing, resizing, and moving windows behind other windows. Pinning this pop-up window to the Workspace allows you to quickly manage the windows on the Workspace.

To change a single window or icon, simply select the window or icon by clicking the left mouse button on it, then choose an item from the `Window Controls` submenu.

To select a group of windows or icons before using an item from the `Window Controls` submenu, either click the left mouse button on one window and the middle mouse button on each additional window or icon, or press the left mouse button and drag the pointer diagonally across the Workspace. Any windows or icons inside the rectangle formed by the dragging motion will be included in the group. The following explains each item in the `Window Controls` submenu.

MENU ITEM	DESCRIPTION
Open/Close	Opens selected icons or closes selected windows.
Full/Restore Size	Increases the size of selected application windows to the full height of the screen. Clicking the left mouse button on the `Full/Restore Size` item a second time (without deselecting the group of windows) decreases the size of selected windows to their former size.
Back	Moves selected application windows to the back of another window or group of windows.
Quit	Quits selected application windows or icons.

Save Workspace

Choosing the `Save Workspace` item saves an arrangement of windows and icons on the Workspace other than the default configuration that appears when you start OpenWindows. You can save your Workspace configuration as often as you like.

To save the Workspace, first arrange the application windows and icons in the locations you want them to remain, and close any windows that you want to be closed to icons whenever you start OpenWindows. After choosing Save Workspace, a Notice appears informing you that the Workspace layout has been saved. Click the left mouse button on the OK button to continue. The next time you start OpenWindows, the windows and icons appear on the Workspace exactly as you saved them.

Lock Screen

If you want to leave your terminal unattended, you can lock your screen to protect your work and prevent anyone else from using your system. The Lock Screen item also activates a feature called a *screen saver* that displays a series of changing images. This protects your screen from characters or images burning into the screen surface. For information on changing the default screen saver, see Chapter 15, "Customizing Solaris."

To unlock your screen, press any key (other than F1 or Lock Caps) or click a mouse button. Solaris displays a message instructing you to enter your password to unlock your screen, as shown in Figure 1.22. After you enter your password, the message validating login appears. If you entered your password correctly, you are returned to your original screen.

Console

The Console window, by default, normally appears in the upper left corner of the Workspace after you start up OpenWindows. Its primary function is to display messages from the network, and inform you of system errors. You should keep the Console window open at all times for important messages. If the Console window (or icon) is not on the Workspace, system messages appear on the Workspace. To open a new Console window, choose the Console item.

FIGURE 1.22

The locked screen
message

Exiting OpenWindows and the DeskSet

When you have finished using OpenWindows and the DeskSet, you can exit the OpenWindows environment by choosing `Exit` from the `Workspace` menu. Solaris displays a Notice that asks you to confirm if you want to exit, as shown in Figure 1.23. The pointer jumps to the `Cancel` button. Click the left mouse button with the pointer on the `Exit` button.

FIGURE 1.23

The Exit Notice

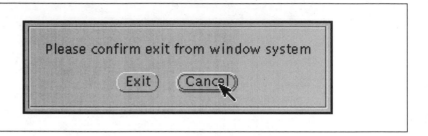

Logging Out of Solaris

After completing a Solaris session, it is important to *log out*. Otherwise, anyone who passes by your terminal can gain unauthorized access to your files. To log out of Solaris, first make sure the system prompt is displayed, then press Control-D or type

```
exit
```

and press Return. The system will display the login screen again. If the system prompts you with the message **there are stopped jobs**, type **exit** again. For more information on logging out with stopped jobs, see Chapter 14, "Multitasking with SunOS."

CHAPTER

2

Using the File Manager

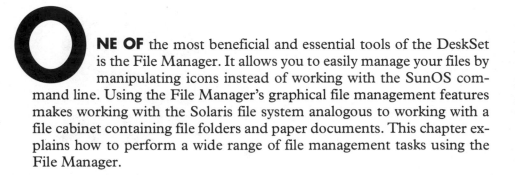

O **NE OF** the most beneficial and essential tools of the DeskSet is the File Manager. It allows you to easily manage your files by manipulating icons instead of working with the SunOS command line. Using the File Manager's graphical file management features makes working with the Solaris file system analogous to working with a file cabinet containing file folders and paper documents. This chapter explains how to perform a wide range of file management tasks using the File Manager.

An Overview of the Solaris File System

The File Manager is an easy-to-use tool for working with files and directories in Solaris. A *file* is a storage place for data or executable programs. Special files called *directories* contain indexes that are used to group and locate files. The File Manager uses a file folder icon to represent a directory and a single-page document icon to represent a text file. Other types of files, such as applications and picture files, have their own unique icons.

Solaris uses a hierarchical file structure, an inverted tree structure with the base of the tree at the top, similar to the structure of a family tree. The topmost directory of the tree is known as the *root* directory and is indicated by a slash (/). All other directories on your system branch out from the root directory. Although every directory, except the root directory, is a *subdirectory* of the root directory, a subdirectory is commonly referred to as a directory.

In keeping with the family tree analogy, directories in a hierarchical file structure are commonly referred to as *parent directories* and *child directories*. Any directory that has subdirectories is a parent directory and each subdirectory is a child directory of the parent directory that is above it.

Solaris relies on specific system directories to operate. In most cases, the system administrator organizes and restricts access to many of these directories. However, there are several important directories that you can work with using the File Manager. The following lists the main directories used by Solaris to store files and application programs.

DIRECTORY	DESCRIPTION
/export	Contains files you want to share with other users on the system.
/home	Contains home directories for all users on your system. The names of these home directories are usually based on user names, for example, /home/rpetrie.
/usr	A general purpose directory that contains several important subdirectories for users, including the openwin/bin directory, which contains OpenWindows application programs.
/bin	Contains SunOS program files or commands.
/tmp	Stores temporary files that can be deleted.

Starting the File Manager

By default, when you start OpenWindows, the File Manager window and its associated Waste icon, which is used for deleting files, appear on the Workspace (Figure 2.1). If the File Manager is not displayed on the Workspace, press the right mouse button anywhere on the Workspace to display the Workspace menu, then choose File Manager from the Programs submenu.

FIGURE 2.1

The File Manager and
Waste icons

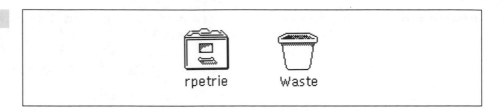

To close the `File Manager` window to an icon, click the left mouse button
on the Window menu button (the upside-down triangle in the upper-left
corner).When closed, the File Manager displays a filing cabinet drawer
icon with the name of the current directory appearing beneath the icon
(Figure 2.1). When you quit the File Manager, the `Waste` icon is also
removed from the Workspace.

An Overview of the File Manager Window

The `File Manager` base window consists of three main parts: the path
pane, the control area, and the file pane, as shown in Figure 2.2. Each part
of the `File Manager` window is described in the following sections.

Path Pane

The path pane displays your current location in the file system. A *path* is
the route through directories that Solaris must follow to access a file. By
default, the File Manager displays the path where you started Open-
Windows as a series of connected folders in a straight line. The path displayed in the path pane shows only the folders for the directory and subdirectory that lead to the current folder, which is the folder that is open.

The path pane display can be changed to a tree display, which displays a
hierarchical tree representation of directories in the file system (Figure 2.3).
To change the path pane to a tree display, click the left mouse button
on the `View` menu button. The `Show Tree` item in the `View` menu is the

FIGURE 2.2

The three main parts
of File Manager
window

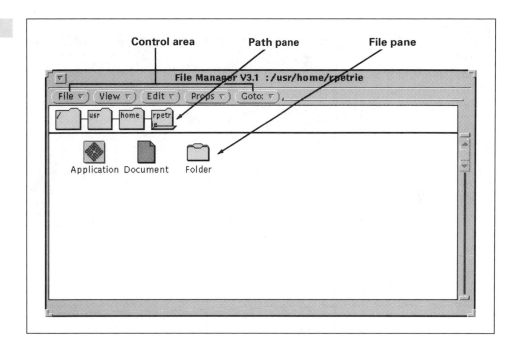

default item. Clicking the left mouse button on the **View** menu button
again switches you back to the path pane display.

Both the path and tree displays have associated pop-up menus. If you are
displaying the path, clicking the right mouse button in the path pane displays the **Path Pane** pop-up menu (Figure 2.4). If you are displaying the tree
display, clicking the right mouse button in the path pane displays the **Tree
Pane** pop-up menu (Figure 2.5). The default item in each pop-up menu
toggles to the other pane display.

Control Area

The control area of the **File Manager** window has five menu buttons:
File, **View**, **Edit**, **Props**, and **Goto**. To the right of the **Goto** button is a text
field for entering path names to find directories and files. Each of these
buttons displays menus that allow you to perform a variety of operations
on one or more selected files. Any of these menus can be displayed by
clicking or pressing the right mouse button on a menu button. The **File**,
View, and **Edit** menus have pushpins so you can pin them to the Workspace.

FIGURE 2.3

The File Manager
displaying directories
using the Show Tree
item

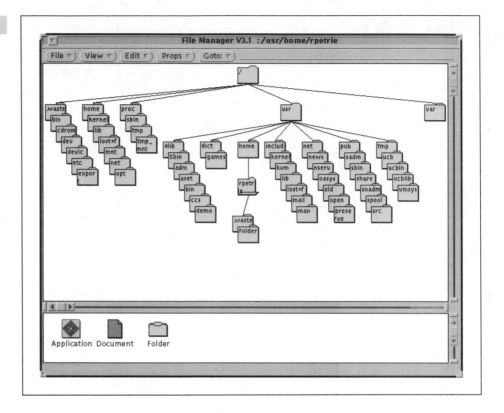

FIGURE 2.4

The Path Pane pop-up
menu

FIGURE 2.5

The Tree Pane pop-up
menu

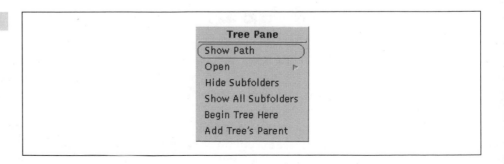

File Pane

The file pane is located directly below the path pane and displays the folders and files in the current directory. This area of the `File Manager` window allows you to navigate the file system and open folders and files. By default, folder and file icons are displayed in the standard size, but you can use smaller icons instead of the standard-size icons if you want to display more folder and file icons in the file pane. The file pane's elevator scrollbar lets you move up or down to display icons.

Folder and file icon names that cannot be completely displayed are followed by a "greater than" sign (>) to show that the full name is not displayed. If you want to see the complete file name, click the left mouse button on the icon name. The entire name is displayed in an editable text field.

The file pane can be split into two or more parts to allow you to view a file listing from more than one vantage point. To split the file pane, press the left mouse button on the top or bottom cable anchor, drag the cable anchor to where you want to split the pane, then release the mouse button. To unsplit a pane, return the cable anchor back to the top or bottom location you originally dragged it from. You can also split a pane by moving the pointer to where you want the pane split on the scrollbar, pressing the right mouse button, and choosing the `Split View` item from the `Scrollbar` menu. To unsplit the last pane split, choose the `Join Views` item from the `Scrollbar` menu.

The file pane provides a `File Pane` pop-up menu, which contains commands that are a subset of the commands you access from different menus in the File Manager's control area. To display the `File Pane` pop-up menu, press the right mouse button anywhere in the file pane. Figure 2.6 shows the `File Pane` pop-up menu.

File Manager Icons

Directories and files appear in the File Manager as icons. Different types of files are represented by different icons in the file pane. There are standard icons used by OpenWindows and DeskSet applications. If you are using a third-party application, its files may have unique file icons. The following are standard-size OpenWindows and DeskSet file icons.

FIGURE 2.6

The File Pane pop-up
menu

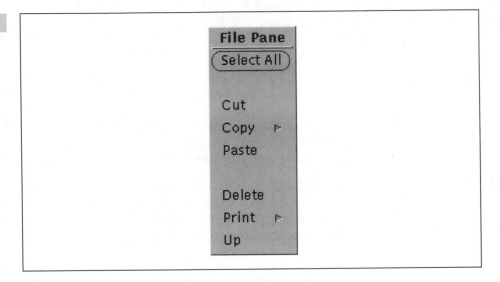

FILE TYPE	ICON
Directory file	Folder
Text file	Document
Raster file	Snapshot.rs
Audio file	Sound.au
PostScript file	Picture.ps
Mail file	Mail

FILE TYPE	ICON
Shell Script file	Script
DeskSet Application file	Application

Performing Basic Operations

The File Manager provides several ways to navigate the file system and perform file management operations such as copying, moving, deleting, and printing files. To open a single folder or file, double-click the left mouse button on the icon. The following methods can be used to perform file management operations on a single file or folder or on a group of files or folders.

- *Drag-and-drop icon(s)*. This is the easiest way to perform most file management operations. Dragging and dropping is performed by pressing the left mouse button on the file or folder icon you want, dragging the icon to any area that accepts the icon as input, and dropping it. You can drag icons onto the Workspace, application windows, window drag-and-drop targets, or other icons.

- *Select the icon(s) and choose a command from a menu.* For example, you can open selected files or folders by choosing `Open` from the `File` menu.

- *Select the icon(s) then press an accelerator key.* Accelerator keys are located on the left side of most Sun keyboards. For example, selecting a file and pressing the Cut accelerator key deletes the file.

Selecting Folders and Files Using the Mouse

When you drag and drop a single file or folder, it is automatically selected when you press the left mouse button on the icon. If you use a menu item or an accelerator key, or you want to drag and drop multiple folders or files, you must first select the file(s) or folder(s) you want before performing the operation.

To select a single file or folder, click the left mouse button on the file or folder you want. The icon turns black to indicate that the file or folder has been selected. You can then use the appropriate menu item or accelerator key to perform your file management task.

If you want to select multiple files or folders, click the left mouse button on the file or folder you want. Select additional files and folders by clicking the middle mouse button on the next file or folder you want. You can also select all the file and folder icons in the current folder by choosing **Select All** from the **File Pane** pop-up menu.

To unselect an icon, click the middle mouse button on a selected file or folder. Clicking the left mouse button in any blank area of the file pane unselects any selected files or folders in the file pane.

Another way to select multiple folders or files is by moving the pointer to any corner of a group of icons in the file pane you want to select, pressing the left mouse button, dragging the pointer diagonally to the opposite corner of the group, then releasing the mouse button.

Selecting Folders and Files Using the Keyboard and Wildcards

A file or folder, or a group of files or folders, can also be selected by moving the pointer to a blank area of the file pane and typing the name of the file you want to select. By naming files with the same character conventions, you can easily select a group of files.

The File Manager also supports the use of wildcards to select files and folders. *Wildcards* are special characters used to represent any single character or series of characters in a file or folder name. For example, to select a group of files ending with the letters .rs (a standard Raster file name extension), type *rs in the file pane. When you type the asterisk, the window footer displays the message `Building *`. After you type the letter r, the files containing the letter r are selected, and the message `Matching *r*` appears in the window footer. If a matching file is not found, the window footer displays a message telling you that it has not found any matching file names.

You can also use the question mark (?) wildcard character to represent any single character in a file or folder name. For example, you can type `hu?` to search for any file or folder that starts with hu followed by any character, such as hug, hub, and so on. You can use more than one question mark (?) in a file or folder name. For example, you can type `hu??` to search for any file or folder that starts with hu followed by any two characters, such as huge, hull, and so on.

Changing the File and Pane Displays

The File Manager allows you to change how icons are organized and displayed in the file pane and what folders appear in the path pane when you are using the tree display. The `View` menu button provides several items for specifying the organization and appearance of icons in the file pane. For example, file and folder icons can be sorted by their file size and displayed in a smaller size.

Because the tree display in the path pane can become extended as you navigate through the file system, the File Manager provides features for controlling which folders are displayed or not displayed. The following sections explain how to change the file and path pane displays.

Changing How Icons Are Displayed in the File Pane

The View menu (Figure 2.7) includes Icon items that let you display files and folders with standard-size icons. The List items in the View menu let you display the icons in a smaller size, so you can view more files and folders in the file pane and show more information about each file. The following describes the Icon and List items in the View menu.

The Customize item in the View menu lets you perform additional changes to the display of files and folders in the file pane. For information on working with the Customize item in the View menu, see "Customizing the File Manager" later in this chapter.

FIGURE 2.7

The View menu

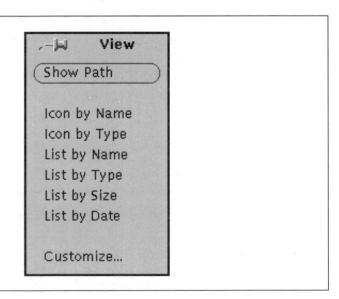

MENU ITEM	DESCRIPTION
Icon by Name	Displays standard-size folder and file icons sorted alphabetically.
Icon by Type	Displays standard-size icons grouped by file type. Folders are grouped first, followed by data files, then applications.
List by Name	Displays small folder and file icons sorted alphabetically by name in a multicolumn format.
List by Type	Displays small folder and file icons grouped by the file type in a multicolumn format. Folders are grouped first, followed by data files, then applications.
List by Size	Displays small file and folder icons in a multicolumn format sorted by file size in bytes, from largest to smallest.
List by Date	Displays small file icons in a multicolumn format sorted by date, from the newest file to the oldest.

Changing the Tree Display in the Path Pane

The Tree Pane pop-up menu displays items to selectively show all or part of the file system in the path pane when using the tree display. For example, using the Tree Pane pop-up menu, you can hide unwanted folders or display folders starting at a specific folder. Depending on which folder you have selected, one or more of the items in the Tree Pane pop-up menu are activated. The following explains the Tree Pane pop-up menu items that allow you to change the tree pane display.

MENU ITEM	DESCRIPTION
Hide Subfolders	Hides all subdirectory folders.
Show All Subfolders	Displays all subdirectory folders.
Begin Tree Here	Begins the tree display at the selected folder.
Add Tree's Parent	Displays the parent directory of the selected subdirectory.

Navigating the File System

The File Manager provides a collection of features for navigating the file system to find files. Navigating the file system using the File Manger involves opening folders and moving through the hierarchical structure of the file system to find files. In addition to navigating the Solaris file system folder by folder, you can also have the File Manager search the system to find files for you. The following sections explain working with the File Manager's navigation and file-searching features.

Opening Folders

To open a folder to view its contents, simply double-click on the folder icon either in the path pane or file pane. You navigate down the hierarchy of folders by double-clicking folders in the file pane. Double-click on the folder icon to the left of the open folder icon in the path pane to go back up to the parent directory. You can also move up to a parent directory by selecting a folder in the file pane then choosing **Up** from the **File Pane** pop-up menu. If you're using the tree display, the same folders remain displayed in the `Tree Pane`, even after you have moved up from the selected directory. The contents of the current opened folder appear in the file pane.

A folder can also be opened by selecting its icon in the file or path pane, clicking the left mouse button on it, and choosing `Open` from the `File` menu. The `Open` item is also available in the `Path Pane` or `Tree Pane` pop-up menus.

Opening Folders as Windows on the Workspace

The File Manager's file pane can display only the contents of the current folder. If you change to another folder, the contents of the previous folder are removed and the contents of the new folder appear. The File Manager allows you to open folders on the Workspace and keep the contents of multiple folders visible, regardless of which folder currently appears in the file pane. Opening folder windows on the Workspace makes it easier to perform file management tasks such as copying and moving files between folders.

To open a folder on the Workspace, drag and drop a folder or a selected group of folders onto the Workspace. A folder window contains the standard window features, including a scrollbar and `Window` menu for managing the window. You can resize the window by dragging the resize corners. Pressing the right mouse button in the file pane of the window displays the same `File Pane` pop-up menu that appears in the File Manager base window's file pane. Figure 2.8 shows several folder windows opened on the Workspace.

Using Goto to Navigate Directly to Files and Folders

When you know the path of the folder you want to open, or when you know the path and file name of a specific file you want to select, you can use the `Goto` text field to go directly to the folder or file. To use the `Goto`

FIGURE 2.8

Folders opened to
windows on the
Workspace

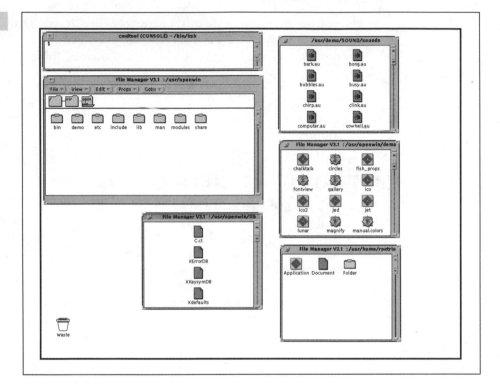

feature, click the left mouse button on the Goto text field then type the path and folder or file name you want to select in the Goto text field. After entering the path, press Return or click the left mouse button on the Goto button. For example, to select a folder named depositions in the /export/home/pmason directory, type

    /export/home/pmason/depositions

in the Goto text field and press Return. When you enter a path and a folder or file name, the folder or file appears selected in the file pane.

When you enter a path, the directory you specify becomes the current directory, and its contents are displayed in the file pane. If you have changed your location in the file system, click the left mouse button on the Goto button, and the current directory will change to the directory entered in the text field.

You can also use wildcard characters with the `Goto` text field to select groups of related files. For example, entering

    practice/*.c

finds and highlights all files in the practice directory ending in `.c`.

Clicking the right mouse button on the `Goto` menu button displays a menu listing the home directory and the last nine directory paths you navigated to, whether or not you used the `Goto` text field. Figure 2.9 shows an example of the `Goto` menu. You can move to any of the directories listed in the `Goto` menu by choosing the item from the menu. Your home directory is always the default item in the `Goto` menu. Clicking the left mouse button on the abbreviated `Goto` menu button quickly returns you to your home directory.

Searching for Folders and Files

If you do not remember the exact name of the file or folder you want to find, choose `Find` in the `File` menu to locate the file or folder. Choosing `Find` displays the `Find` pop-up window (Figure 2.10) with controls that allow you to perform file searches based on a variety of file attributes. To find a specific file or group of files, fill in some or all of the text fields according to the type of search you want to perform. The following explains each setting in the `Find` pop-up window.

FIGURE 2.9

A sample Goto menu

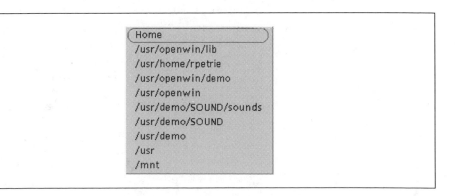

FIGURE 2.10

The Find pop-up window

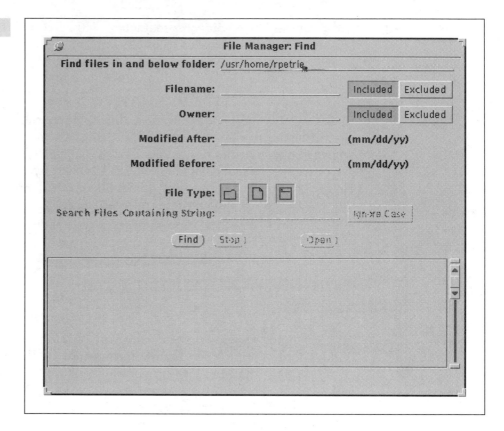

SETTING	DESCRIPTION
Find files in and below folder	Use this setting to specify where in the file system you want to start the search. The search begins in the folder you specify in this text field, and includes all subfolders.
Filename	Specifies a file name or pattern you want to match. Use the **Included** or **Excluded** setting to either include or exclude the file name or pattern you specified in the **Filename** text field.

SETTING	DESCRIPTION
Owner	Specifies searches for files by the owner of the file (file ownership is explained later in this chapter). Use the **Included** or **Excluded** setting to either include or exclude the owner specified in the **Owner** text field.
Modified After	Specifies searches for files with last modified dates after the date specified in this setting. Enter the date in the format indicated to the right, **mm/dd/yy** (month, day, year). **Modified After** and **Modified Before** entries can be combined to specify a range of file dates.
Modified Before	Specifies searches for files with last modified dates before the date specified in this setting. Enter the date in the format indicated to the right, **mm/dd/yy** (month, day, year). **Modified After** and **Modified Before** entries can be combined to specify a range of file dates.
File Type	Specifies whether you want to search all the files or only folders, document files, or application files. The mini-icons displayed in the **File Type** setting are the same icons that appear in the file pane when you choose a **List** item from the **View** menu.
Search Files Containing String	Specifies searches for files with a specific text content. This feature is active only if you restrict the search to document files in the **File Type** setting. Clicking on the **Ignore Case** setting removes any particular case specification from the search.

After filling in the fields to restrict the search, click the left mouse button on the **Find** button. If you want to cancel the search, click the left mouse button on the **Stop** button. When files that match the search criteria are found, their full path names are displayed in the scrolling list at the bottom of the **Find** window. Pressing the right mouse button in the scrolling list displays the **Scrolling List** pop-up menu, which contains items for managing entries in the scrolling list.

If more than one file is found, select the file you want from the scrolling list. When you select an item from the list, an outline appears around it and the **Open** button becomes active (changes to black). To open the file, click the left mouse button on the **Open** button. The file opens in the application window that the file is bound to. For example, if it is a text file, the file's contents appear in the **Text Editor** window.

Opening Files

Each DeskSet application's file in the File Manager is connected or bound to its related application so that when you open the file, you also open the application. In other words, opening a file means that the corresponding application is also automatically opened with the file you selected loaded in the application window. This OpenWindows feature is referred to as *binding* a file to an application. The *Binder* database, which is maintained using the DeskSet's Binder application, contains the information about each file and its corresponding application.

NOTE

Creating your own custom icons and working with the binder to connect them to an application using the DeskSet's Icon Editor and Binder applications is explained in Chapter 7, "Customizing the Workspace and Icons."

To quickly open a file, double-click the left mouse button on the file icon you want. You can also open an application without loading a file by double-clicking on the program icon. Another easy way to open a file is to drag and drop the file icon from the File Manager to the Workspace. Even though you can start an application by dragging it from the File Manager and dropping it onto the Workspace, you cannot quit the application by dragging and dropping it back onto the File Manager. You must use the application's `Window` menu's `Quit` item.

A file can also be opened by selecting the file icon you want, then clicking the left mouse button on the `File` menu button. This activates the default menu item in the `Open` submenu. You can select multiple files then open them using this method.

Dragging and Dropping Files to Other Applications

A file can be dragged and dropped onto another application outside the File Manager. The results of dragging and dropping a file onto another application depends on whether the file is dropped onto a window's drag-and-drop target, a window's work area, or an icon. Dragging and dropping a file onto a drag-and-drop target of an application window loads it into the application. Dragging and dropping a file onto a window pane inserts the file's contents into the application at the location of the pointer. When you drag and drop a file onto an icon, it loads the file into the application and opens the application window. If you drop an icon onto an application that has an inappropriate format, the move is not performed, and a message appears in the window footer informing you that the file is in an incorrect file format. For example, if you drag a file created with the Text Editor and drop it onto the Snapshot application window, the message `unrecognized file type` appears in the footer of the Snapshot window.

Creating Folders and Files

The `File` menu provides you with items to create folders or files. The file you create using the File Manager is a text file that when opened displays the file in the Text Editor. Working with text files in the Text Editor is explained in Chapter 4, "Using the Text Editor, Shell Tool, and Command Tool." When you create new files or folders, they are automatically added to the File Manager's path or file pane.

To create a folder, make sure you are located in the directory where you want to create a subdirectory. Press the right mouse button on the `File` menu button and choose `Create Folder`. An empty directory named `New-Folder` appears (Figure 2.11), highlighted and underlined with an active insert point at the end of the line. Subsequent new folders you create in the current session are numbered in sequence. To name the new folder, type the name you want (the new folder's text field is already selected), then press Return or click the left mouse button on the background of the file pane.

You create a file in the same way you create a folder, except that you choose `Create File` from the `File` menu. When you create a file, a file icon appears with the name `NewDocument` highlighted and underlined, and an active insert point at the end of the line. Figure 2.12 shows a new file icon. Subsequent new document files you create in the current session are numbered in sequence. To name the new file, type the name you want

FIGURE 2.11

A new folder icon

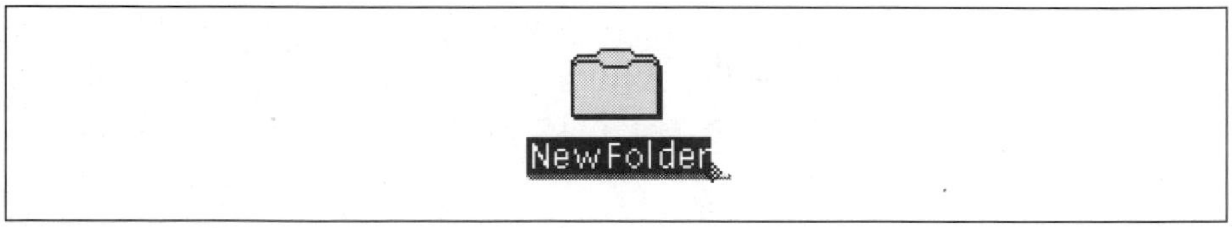

FIGURE 2.12

A new file icon

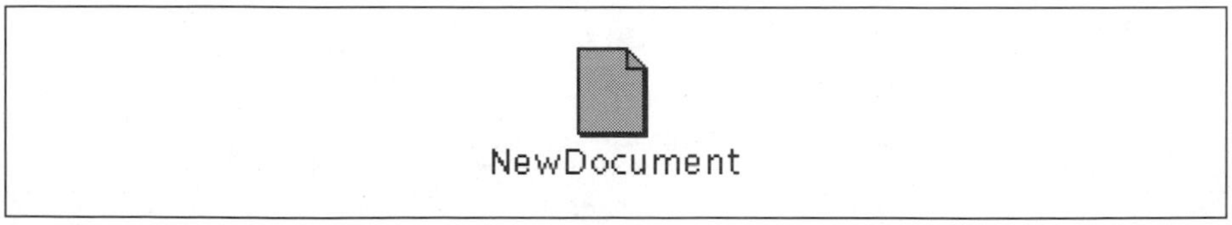

(the new folder's text field is already selected), then press Return or click the left mouse button on the background of the file pane.

N O T E Don't use spaces in your file or folder names. While the File Manager can handle spaces in file names, SunOS has trouble handling spaces when performing file management commands from the command line.

Changing Folder and File Names

To change the name of a new or existing folder or file, click the left mouse button on the folder or file icon. Then click the left mouse button on the file name. This selects the icon and displays the file or folder name highlighted and underlined with an insert point at the end. You can rename it by typing in a new name. When you are finished renaming the file or folder, press Return or click the left mouse button on the background of the file pane. The file or folder is sorted by the item specified in the `View` menu and displayed with its new name.

Deleting Files and Folders

The `Waste` icon is a holding tank for files you want to remove from the File Manager and permanently delete at a later time. Double-clicking on the `Waste` icon displays the `Wastebasket` window (Figure 2.13).

You can easily store files and folders you want to discard from the File Manager into the wastebasket by dragging and dropping them onto the `Waste` icon or the `Wastebasket` window. You can also select files and

FIGURE 2.13

The Wastebasket icon
and window

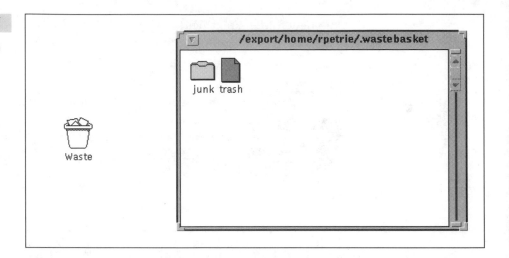

folders, then choose **Delete** from the File Manager's **File Pane** pop-up menu. If there are any files or folders in the wastebasket, overflowing papers appear in the **Waste** icon (Figure 2.13), or the file or folder icons appear in the **Wastebasket** window.

TIP

You can use **Undelete** in the **Wastebasket** pop-up menu to restore any selected files and folders in the **Wastebasket** window back to their original location.

Files remain in the wastebasket (even if you quit the File Manager) until you choose **Empty Wastebasket** for deleting all files and folders or **Delete** for selected files and folders from the **Wastebasket** pop-up menu (available in the **Wastebasket** window pane). Files you discard in the wastebasket are stored in a directory named **.wastebasket** in your home directory so that you can move them back to the File Manager if you change your mind. If the wastebasket file becomes full, a message warns you that you must empty the wastebasket before adding additional files.

To delete all the files and folders the **Waste** icon contains, do the following:

1. Double-click on the **Waste** icon to open the **Wastebasket** window.

2. Press the right button in the blank area of the file to bring up the `Wastebasket` pop-up menu.

3. Choose `Empty Wastebasket`. All the folders and files in the wastebasket are then permanently deleted.

To selectively delete individual files or folders stored in the `Waste` icon, do the following:

1. Double-click on the `Waste` icon to open the `Wastebasket` window.

2. Select the files you want to delete. Use the left mouse button to select the first file and the middle button for additional files. To unselect a file, click the middle mouse button on the selected file.

3. Press the right button in the blank area of the file pane to bring up the `Wastebasket` pop-up menu.

4. Choose `Delete` to permanently remove the files from the `Wastebasket` window.

If you quit the `Wastebasket` window, you can create a new one by selecting a file or folder in the file pane and choosing `Delete` from the `Edit` menu or the `File Pane` pop-up menu. A new wastebasket is created containing the file or folder you selected.

Deleting Files and Folders Using the Clipboard

The File Manager's `Edit` and `File Pane` menus also include a `Cut` item for removing selected icons. Using the `Cut` item removes the files or folders to the clipboard. The last item cut can be retrieved using `Paste` from either the `Edit` and `File Pane` menu. The `Wastebasket` pop-up menu also includes `Cut` and `Paste`, which remove and add selected files and folders.

Copying and Moving Files and Folders

Copying a file keeps the original file intact while making a copy of the file in the folder you specify. Moving a file copies the file to the new location then deletes the original file at the old location. The easiest way to copy or move files and folders is to drag and drop the file and folder icons.

TIP   Remember, you can open folders as windows on the Workspace to view the contents of each folder, which makes copying or moving files and folders easier.

To use the drag-and-drop method to move files and folders, simply drag the selected files and folders from the current folder in the File Manager to the folder where you want to move them, and release the left mouse button to finish the operation. You can display different folders by dragging and dropping them onto the Workspace. This makes copying and moving files between directories easier.

You can also copy files and folders by dragging and dropping them from the file pane onto folders displayed in the path pane. To copy one or more files, do the following:

1. Select the files you want to copy.

2. Hold down the Control key and press the left mouse button.

3. Drag and drop the files onto the target folder in the path pane, file pane, or folder window.

Whenever you perform a move or copy operation, a message appears in the window footer stating whether or not the copy or move action was successful.

Using the Clipboard to Copy and Move Files and Folders

The Copy, Cut, and Paste items are available in both the Edit menu and the pop-up File Pane menu. Using these items, you can *cut* or *copy* files and *paste* them into other folders or applications.

To copy a file using the clipboard, select the desired file then choose Copy from the Edit menu or the File Pane pop-up menu. To move a file using the clipboard, select the desired file then choose Cut from the Edit menu or the File Pane pop-up menu. Select the folder where you want to copy the file to then choose Paste from the File Pane pop-up menu in the File Manager's file pane or the file pane of a folder window on the Workspace.

WARNING

Only one item or group of items is stored on the clipboard at a time. If you choose Copy or Cut while information is already stored on the clipboard, the previous information is lost. If you quit the File Manager or exit OpenWindows, the contents of the clipboard are lost.

The following steps explain how to copy or move a group of files using the clipboard.

1. Click the left mouse button on the first file you want to select and click the middle button on each additional file you want. The selected files are highlighted in black.

2. Press the right mouse button on the Edit menu button or in the file pane, which displays the File Pane pop-up menu. Choose File from the Copy submenu. Choose Cut if you want to move the files.

3. Change to the folder where you want to copy or move the files.

4. Press the right mouse button on the Edit menu and choose Paste.

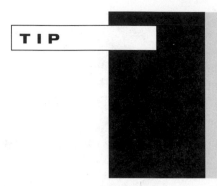

Using Accelerator Keys to Copy and Move Files and Folders

Another way to use the clipboard is to use the Copy, Cut, and Paste accelerator keys on the left side of the Sun workstation keyboard to copy or move file or folder icons. To use the accelerator keys, select the file(s) or folder(s) you want to copy or move, then press the Copy or Cut accelerator key. Move the pointer to where you want to copy or move the file(s) or folder(s) and press the Paste accelerator key.

Copying Files to Other Systems

The `Remote Copy` item in the `File` menu allows you to transfer copies of files between systems. You can copy between systems only if the permissions and ownership of directories and files allow you to perform the operation. For more information on permissions, see the "File and Folder Permissions" section later in this chapter.

NOTE

If your system is using the Automounter, you don't need to use the remote copy feature. With the Automounter running, directories located on different machines appear to be part of the same system. You can use the standard methods for copying and moving files. For more information about using the Automounter, see Chapter 17, "System Administration Basics."

When you choose `Remote Copy`, the `Remote Copy` pop-up window appears (Figure 2.14). To transfer files from your system to another system, follow these steps:

1. Choose `Remote Copy` from the `File` menu. If you have selected files, your host name will be displayed in the `Source Machine` text field, and the file names will be displayed in the `Source Path` text field of the `Remote Copy` pop-up window.

2. Type the destination machine name in the `Destination Machine` text field. For example, type `mayberry`.

3. Type the destination path in the `Destination Path` text field. For example, `/export/home/bfife`.

FIGURE 2.14

The Remote Copy
pop-up window

```
┌─────────────────────────────────────────────────────┐
│ ⊙              File Manager: Remote Copy             │
│       Source Machine: ◇_____      │
│                                                      │
│          Source Path: _____       │
│                                                      │
│   Destination Machine: _____      │
│                                                      │
│     Destination Path: _____       │
│                                                      │
│                     ( Copy )                         │
└─────────────────────────────────────────────────────┘
```

4. Click the left mouse button on the Copy button to initiate the copy process. While the transfer is in process, the Copy button displays the standard busy pattern.

Printing Files

There are sure to be times you want a printed copy of a document file. You can print files directly from the File Manager using Print File from the File submenu or the File Pane pop-up menu. Choosing Print File prints the selected file(s) using the default printer and print instructions from the application that is bound to the icon.

To print a file or group of files using Print from the File menu or the File Pane pop-up menu, do the following:

1. Select the file(s) in the file pane you want to print.

2. Press the right mouse button on the File menu button and choose Print File from the Print submenu.

NOTE Files can also be printed by dragging the file icons from the File Manager and dropping them onto the Print Tool. For more information on working with the Print Tool, see Chapter 6, "Using the Print Tool, Audio Tool, and Other DeskSet Applications."

The Custom Print item displays the Custom Print Properties pop-up window (Figure 2.15). Using this pop-up window allows you change the default printing settings for printing a file. The Print Method setting allows you to enter SunOS commands for formatting and printing a file. Initially, the default File Manager print script is displayed as cat $FILE | mp -lo | lp. If you are using a PostScript printer, you may need to change the default script to read as follows:

```
cat $FILE | mp -lo | lp -T postscript
```

You can change the default print script permanently by using the **File Manager** menu item in the **Props** menu, as explained later in this chapter. See Chapter 13, "Formatting and Printing," for more information on formatting and printing commands to enter in the **Print Method** setting. The **Copies** setting lets you specify the number of copies of a file you want to print.

FIGURE 2.15

The Custom Print
Properties pop-up
window

File and Folder Permissions

The Solaris security system is structured around permissions. Permissions determine which users can read, write, or execute files. Permissions can be changed for any file or folder you own (a file you created) or any file that the owner has given you permission to write to. Each folder and file in the file system has permissions assigned to it that can be changed to allow or restrict access.

You can change the permissions of files and folders using the **File Properties** pop-up window (Figure 2.16). To display the **File Properties**

FIGURE 2.16

The File Properties
pop-up window

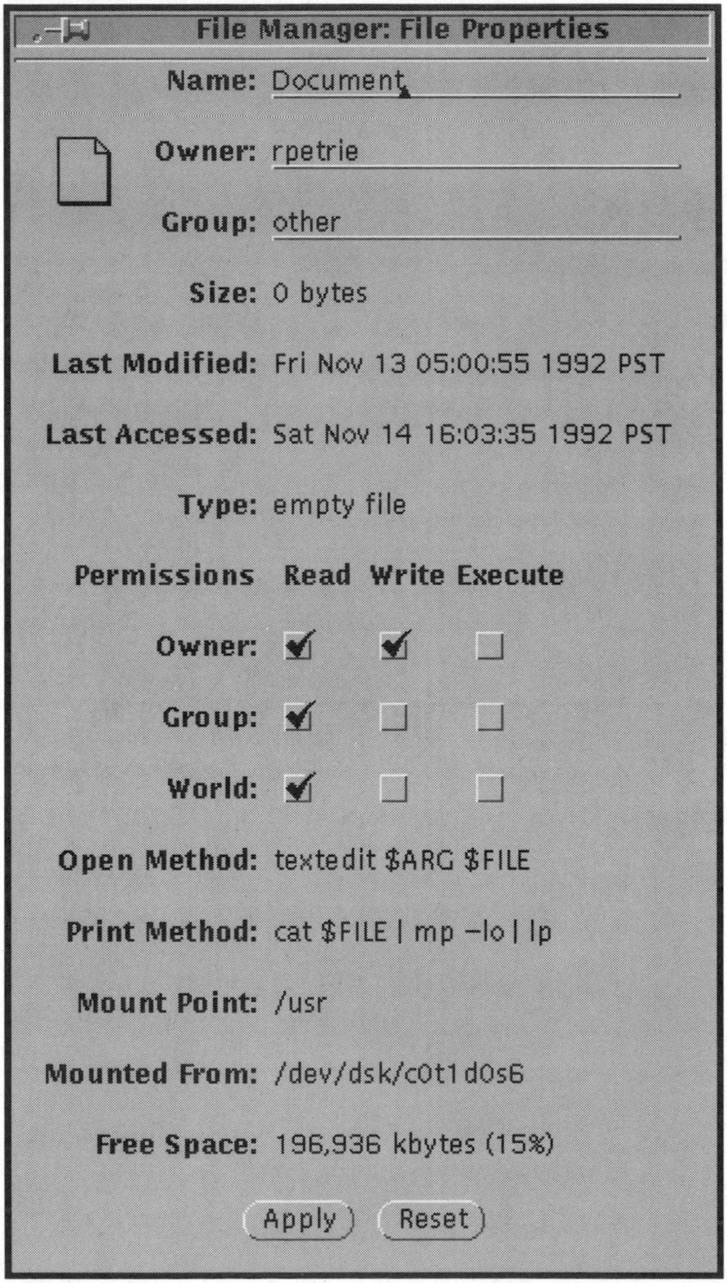

File Manager: File Properties

Name: Document

Owner: rpetrie

Group: other

Size: 0 bytes

Last Modified: Fri Nov 13 05:00:55 1992 PST

Last Accessed: Sat Nov 14 16:03:35 1992 PST

Type: empty file

Permissions	Read	Write	Execute
Owner:	☑	☑	☐
Group:	☑	☐	☐
World:	☑	☐	☐

Open Method: textedit $ARG $FILE

Print Method: cat $FILE | mp −lo | lp

Mount Point: /usr

Mounted From: /dev/dsk/c0t1d0s6

Free Space: 196,936 kbytes (15%)

(Apply)   (Reset)

pop-up window, first select the file or folder you want to change permissions for, then click the left mouse button on the **Props** button to choose the default **File** item. Remember, to make your permissions changes take effect, you must click the left mouse button on the **Apply** button.

Changing File and Folder Permissions

To change file or folder permissions, click the left mouse button on the boxes representing the permissions you want to change. The **Read**, **Write**, and **Execute** permission boxes are toggles that turn permissions on or off. If a box appears checked and you press the left mouse button on the check box, it then appears unchecked. The following explains the three types of permissions.

PERMISSION	DESCRIPTION
Read	Allows the authorized user to display the contents of the file or directory.
Write	Allows the authorized user to create or remove files and subdirectories from a folder or modify the file.
Execute	Allows the authorized user to change the directory, look at information about the files, or execute the file if the file is an executable program.

You can change read, write, and execute permissions for three types of users on the system.

USER TYPES	DESCRIPTION
Owner	The owner of the file or folder (usually the person who created the file or folder).
Group	The name of a specified group that can access the file.
World	All other users.

Changing Permissions for Groups of Files or Folders

The permissions of several files or folders can be changed at the same time. If you select more than one file, the file properties window shows those properties the selected files have in common. File or directory names and individual file or directory information are not displayed. You can change the permissions for the group of selected files the same way you change a single file, by clicking the left mouse button on the check boxes for the permissions you want to change to add or subtract.

Linking Files

Linking files allows several users to access a single file from different locations on the system, so there is one master file instead of many different copies or versions of the file. A *link* is a connection or pointer to a single file that allows access from more than one directory without having to move to the original directory where the file resides. When a file is linked, an icon appears in the directory where it is linked as though the file resides in that directory. Any editing changes you make to a file with links are reflected in all of the directories because there is really only one file.

Creating a Link

The Copy item in the File Manager's Edit menu or the File Pane pop-up menu allows you to create a link to a file using as a Link in the Copy submenu. To link a file, perform the following steps:

1. Select the file or files you want to link.

2. Press the right mouse button on the Edit menu and choose as a Link from the Copy submenu. The following message appears: Link these file(s) by opening the target folder and selecting 'Paste.'

3. Open the folder you want to add the link to.

4. Choose **Paste** from the **Edit** menu, the **File Pane** pop-up menu, or use the Paste accelerator key.

Once a link is established, the file's link information can be displayed using **File** from the **Props** menu. If you use a **List** item in the **View** menu, the linked file appears with an arrow pointing to the directory name that contains the file with which the file is linked. Figure 2.17 shows a linked file in **rpetrie**'s home directory.

T I P

If the display produced by your **List** item differs from Figure 2.17, activate the **Links** setting using the **Customize** item of the **View** menu.

FIGURE 2.17

A linked file displayed by using List by Type from the View menu

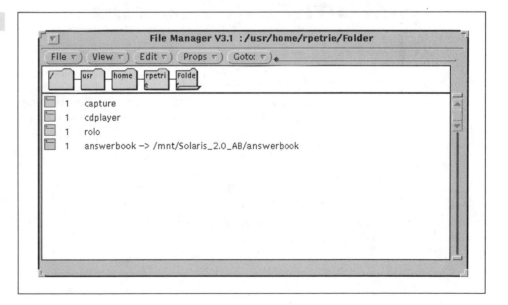

Removing a Link

To remove a link, select the file and choose **Delete** from the **Edit** sub-menu. Removing a link does not remove the original file. If you remove the original file without deleting the link, the icon for the link changes to display a broken chain, as shown in Figure 2.18.

FIGURE 2.18

A file icon representing a broken link

answerbook

Customizing the File Manager

The File Manager provides three different pop-up windows to customize various features. Using the **Customize View** pop-up window, you can customize the way the file system is displayed in the file pane. The **Tool Properties** pop-up window provides a collection of settings for changing default File Manager settings, such as specifying a different default printer or instructing the File Manager to automatically delete any files placed in the wastebasket. The **Create Command** pop-up window allows you to create and store commonly used SunOS commands as menu items. The following sections explain how to work with these customizing features.

N O T E There are additional customizing options that affect the File Manager that are executed from the command line. Working with these File Manager customization settings is explained in Chapter 15, "Customizing Solaris."

Customizing the File Pane View

The `Customize` item in the `View` menu displays the `Customize View` pop-up window, as shown in Figure 2.19. The settings in this pop-up menu allow you to change the default setting for how the File Manager displays and sorts your files. To change a setting, click the left mouse button on the setting you want to change. This will toggle the setting on or off. When a setting is on, it appears highlighted or with a bold border. After making your changes, click the left mouse button on the `Apply` button. The following explains each of the `Customize View` pop-up window options.

OPTION	DESCRIPTION
Display Mode	The `Icon` setting displays the current directory's files using standard-size icons. The `List` setting displays smaller icons so you can display more information about each file, as determined by options in the `List Options` settings. The `Content` setting displays the contents of an icon and raster files (files that contain images). The images are not displayed to scale. Using the `Content` setting slows scrolling through the file pane because the images must be drawn to the screen each time to change the display. The default is the icon setting.

FIGURE 2.19

The Customize View pop-up window

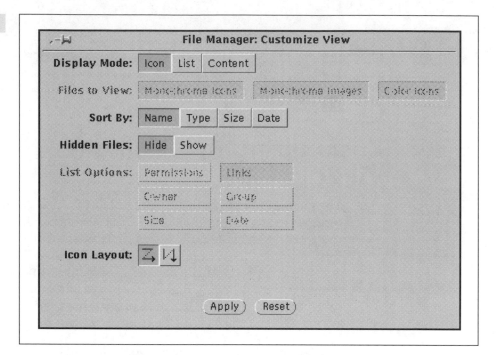

OPTION	DESCRIPTION
Files to View	Allows you to specify if icons appear in monochrome or color. This setting is only effective when the Display Mode is in the Content setting. You can choose from among three settings: Monochrome Icons, Monochrome Images, and Color. In most cases, the Files to View option is set with both monochrome settings on. The default monochrome settings speed up the display of icons and images.

OPTION	DESCRIPTION
Sort By	Allows you to arrange files in the file pane according to the option specified. The `Name` option sorts alphabetically by the file name. The `Type` option sorts files alphabetically by file type, with folders first, followed by document files, then by applications. The `Size` option sorts files by size, from largest to smallest. The `Date` option sorts the files in reverse chronological order, from the newest to the oldest file, based on the date the file was last modified. By default, the icons are sorted alphabetically by file names.
Hidden Files	Allows you to choose whether or not to display those files and folders ordinarily not displayed. Hidden file names begin with at least one period. Choosing the `Show` setting displays hidden files in the file pane. The default is `Hide`.
List Options	Allows you to choose how much information is displayed when you use the `List` option in the `View` menu. You can display one or more of the following options: `Permissions`, `Links`, `Owner`, `Group`, `Size`, and `Date`.
Icon Layout	Specifies whether icons wrap to the beginning of the next line or are displayed in a columnar format. The default is to wrap the icons to the beginning of the next row.

Using the Tool Properties Window

Choosing **File Manager** from the **Props** menu displays the **Tool Properties** pop-up window (Figure 2.20). This pop-up window provides you with options to customize how the File Manager displays and works with files and folders. Remember, after making changes in the **Tool Properties** pop-up window, you must click the left mouse button on the **Apply** button for the settings to take effect. These settings take effect immediately and are displayed in the **File Manager** window. The following list explains each of the options available in the pop-up window.

FIGURE 2.20

The Tool Properties pop-up window

File Manager: Tool Properties
Default Print Script: cat $FILE	mp −lo	lp
View Filter Pattern:
Longest Filename: 15
Delete: to wastebasket   really delete
Default Document Editor: texteditor   Other:
Apply   Reset

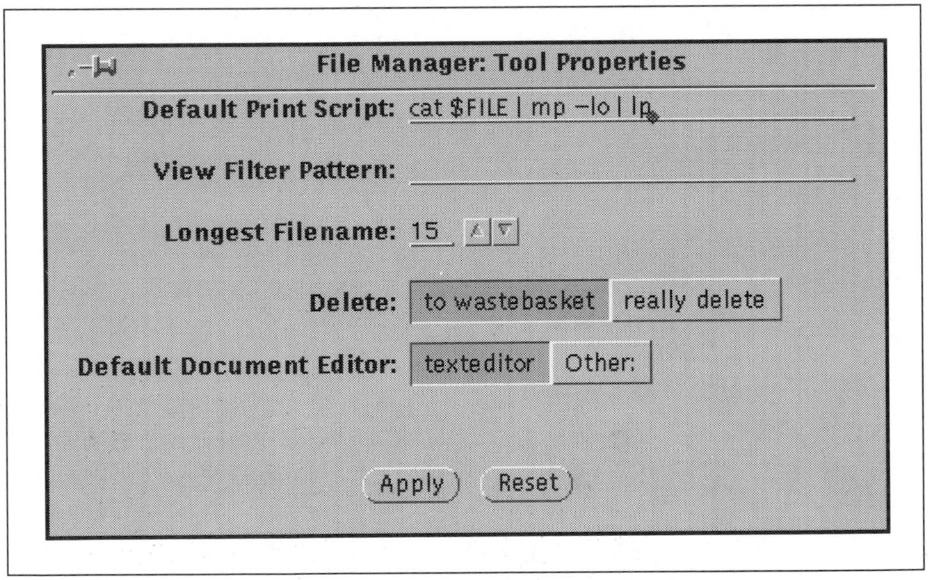

OPTION	DESCRIPTION
Default Print Script	Allows you to specify a print script for files that are printed using the `Print File` item in the File Manager's `File` menu that does not have a method defined by the DeskSet's Binder application. The print script shown in Figure 2.20 prints your files in landscape mode on your default printer, using the `mp` PostScript pretty-printer filter. The variable name `$FILE` acts as a placeholder for a file you select. If you are using a PostScript printer, you may need to change the print script to `cat $FILE	mp -lo	lp -T postscript`. The `-T postscript` argument specifies that you are using a PostScript printer. For more information on printing, see Chapter 13, "Formatting and Printing."
View Filter Pattern	Allows you to specify that only a certain type of file is displayed in the file pane of the File Manager. For example, entering `*.ps` lists all PostScript files that end with a `.ps`. The filter pattern used to filter files is always listed in the header of the window.
Longest Filename	Allows you to specify the number of characters that display for a file or folder name. You can type any number from 0 to 255 in this numeric field to choose how many characters of each file name are displayed in the file pane of the File Manager. The default is fifteen characters. The number of characters actually displayed for each file name may vary because the width of different fonts may vary.

OPTION	DESCRIPTION
Delete	Specifies whether or not a file is placed in the wastebasket or automatically deleted. The default `to wastebasket` option stores files you choose to delete in the wastebasket until you specify that they actually be deleted. The `really delete` setting instructs the File Manager to permanently delete a file. If you choose the `really delete` setting, the `Waste` icon will not appear the next time you log in because the File Manager will not hold files you want to delete.
Default Document Editor	Specifies the default editor the File Manager uses to display text data files not specifically bound to another application. The default setting is the DeskSet's Text Editor. Choosing the `Other` setting lets you specify a text editor; the default is the vi editor. If you want to specify an editor other than vi, you must type `shelltool`, followed by the name of the editor. Working with the vi editor is explained in Chapter 12, "Using the vi Editor."

Adding Commands to a Menu

NOTE

Working with the File Manager's custom commands feature requires that you have some working knowledge of working with SunOS commands. If you are not familiar with SunOS, see Part II, "Working from the SunOS Command Line."

The File Manager allows you to create and store commonly used commands. Once you have added the commands to the menu, you can use them at any time by choosing them from the **Custom Commands** menu. Figure 2.21 shows an example of the **Custom Commands** menu with custom commands created using the **Create Command** pop-up window.

To open the **Create Command** pop-up window, choose **Custom Commands** from the **File** menu, then from the submenu choose **Create Command**. The **Create Command** pop-up window appears (Figure 2.22). The scrolling list shows any custom commands that were created. You can use the items in the **Edit** menu (under the scroll list) to add, delete, and change the order of your custom commands.

The following steps explain how to add a new custom command in the **Create Command** pop-up window. This custom command allows you to move selected files to a directory you specify.

1. Click the left mouse button on the **New Command** button to activate and clear the settings below the scrolling list, if necessary. These settings are dimmed when you do not have a command selected in the scrolling list, or when you are not currently creating a new command.

FIGURE 2.21

Sample command items in the Custom Commands submenu

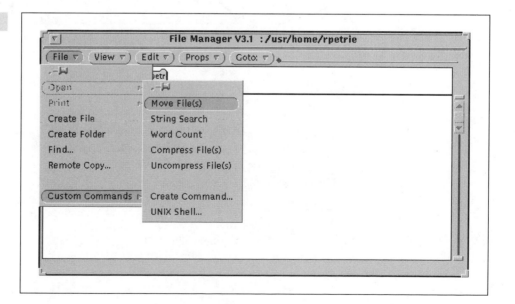

FIGURE 2.22

The Create Command
pop-up window

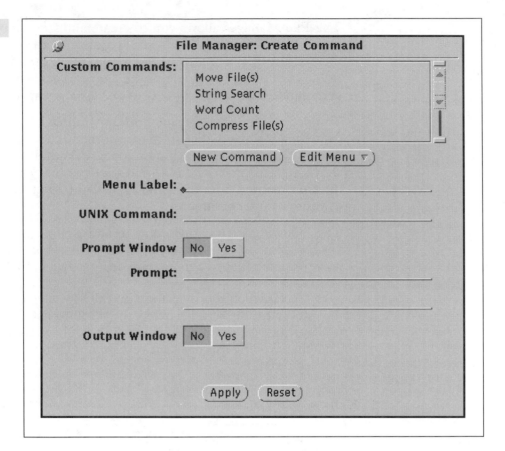

2. In the **Menu Label** text field, type the name for your custom command that you want to appear on the **Custom Commands** menu. The menu label should be descriptive enough to let you know what the custom command does. For this example, type

```
Move File(s)
```

NOTE

For information on working with the mv command, including setting arguments, see Chapter 9, "Navigating Directories and Working with Files."

3. Type the actual SunOS command in the UNIX Command text field. Adding $FILE or $ARG to the command creates a representation for the selected file(s) or special arguments (options) that you specify at the time you choose the command. For this example, type

```
mv $FILE $ARG
```

in the UNIX Command text field.

4. Change the Prompt Window setting to Yes. This causes the File Manager to display a prompt window for a command's arguments, if necessary, when executing the command. If you use a prompt window, when a custom command is chosen from the Custom Commands menu, a window is displayed with the prompt label. You use this pop-up window to type the command options.

5. In the Prompt field, enter the prompt that you want to display to instruct the user to enter argument and file variables. For example, in the previous example, you might use a prompt such as

```
Move Files to:
```

When you choose the custom command, a prompt window asks you to specify which directory to move the selected files to, as shown in Figure 2.23. If the command will produce output, such as a list of file names, change the Output Window setting to Yes. This causes an output window to be displayed when the custom command is chosen, where you can see the result of your command. In this case, there is no output.

6. Choose Apply to add the command to the Custom Commands submenu. Once you have added the command to the menu, you can use it at any time by choosing it from the Custom Commands submenu.

FIGURE 2.23

A sample prompt window

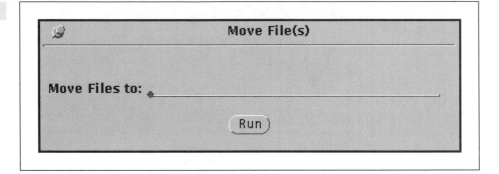

Editing a Custom Command

The `Edit Menu` button in the `Create Command` pop-up window displays a menu of options for copying, deleting, and moving commands in the `Custom Commands` submenu. To edit a command, first select the command in the list, press the right mouse button on the `Edit Menu` button, then choose the item you want to perform. For example, selecting a custom command and choosing `Cut` from the `Edit Menu` submenu removes the custom command from the `Custom Commands` submenu and stores it in the Clipboard. Selecting an item from the `Paste` submenu lets you move the custom command `Before` or `After` another custom command or to the `Top` or `Bottom` of the `Custom Commands` submenu.

The Multimedia Mail Tool Makes Mail Easy

THE DeskSet's multimedia Mail Tool, with its friendly graphical environment, is your gateway to communicating with other users, in the next office or around the world. It allows you to easily receive, write, send, and manage your electronic mail (commonly referred to as *email*), as well as attach files, such as audio and picture files, to your messages to make your point. This chapter explains Mail Tool fundamentals, as well as the rich collection of other features provided by the Mail Tool.

Starting the Mail Tool

To start the Mail Tool, choose `Mail Tool` from the `Workspace` menu's `Programs` submenu. The Mail Tool icon shows up on the Workspace. As shown in Figure 3.1, the icon for the Mail Tool appears differently depending on whether or not you have new mail, or if there is no old mail stored in your mail file. To open the Mail Tool from an icon to a window, double-click on the Mail Tool icon. The `Mail Tool Header` window appears (Figure 3.2).

FIGURE 3.1

The Mail Tool's icons

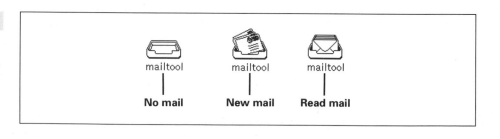

The Mail Tool Header window

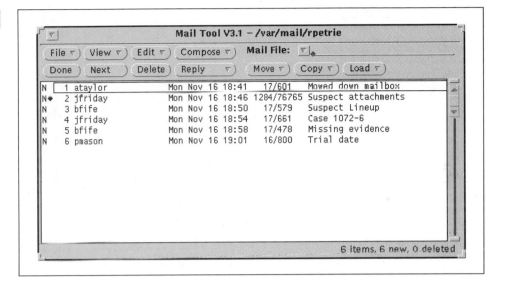

Mail Tool V3.1 – /var/mail/rpetrie

| File ▽ | View ▽ | Edit ▽ | Compose ▽ | **Mail File:** ▽ |

| Done | Next | Delete | Reply ▽ | Move ▽ | Copy ▽ | Load ▽ |

```
N   1 ataylor        Mon Nov 16 18:41    17/601    Mowed down mailbox
N♦  2 jfriday        Mon Nov 16 18:46 1284/76765 Suspect attachments
N   3 bfife          Mon Nov 16 18:50    17/579   Suspect Lineup
N   4 jfriday        Mon Nov 16 18:54    17/661   Case 1072-6
N   5 bfife          Mon Nov 16 18:58    17/478   Missing evidence
N   6 pmason         Mon Nov 16 19:01    16/800   Trial date
```

6 items, 6 new, 0 deleted

An Overview of the Mail Tool Header Window

The `Mail Tool Header` window is the base window that provides the main controls for the Mail Tool. Its headers pane displays the list of mail message headers and the status of your mail messages. Mail message headers provide information about the message such as the sender and subject. The headers pane contains a `Messages` pop-up menu (Figure 3.3) that includes some of the most frequently used Mail Tool menu items. To display the `Messages` pop-up menu, press the right mouse button anywhere in the headers pane. The `Messages` pop-up menu can be pinned to the Workspace.

The control area of the `Mail Tool Header` window has eleven menu buttons: `File`, `View`, `Edit`, `Compose`, `Done`, `Next`, `Delete`, `Reply`, `Move`, `Copy`, and `Load`. The first four buttons are the main buttons you use to store, view, edit, and send mail. The remaining buttons are custom buttons which can be used for quick execution of any item in the `File`, `View`, `Edit`, and

FIGURE 3.3

The Messages pop-up
menu

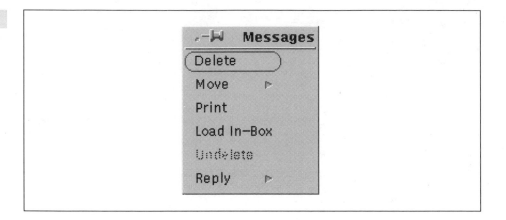

Compose menus. The mail file abbreviated menu button and the **Mail File** text field are used for storing mail messages. Changing the custom buttons and working with mail files is explained later in this chapter.

Receiving and Viewing Messages

Incoming messages are delivered to your electronic mailbox, a default mail file for all incoming messages, named **In-Box**. *Mail files* are special files that can contain multiple messages. As explained later in this chapter, you can create your own mail files. The Mail Tool periodically checks for new messages as specified from the **Mail Tool Properties** window. The default is every five minutes.

When messages are retrieved by the Mail Tool, their headers are displayed in the **Mail Tool Header** window. If the Mail Tool is closed to an icon, the icon changes to indicate new mail has arrived. In addition, any time you receive incoming mail, with the Mail Tool running on the Workspace, Solaris beeps.

Once mail message headers are in the **Mail Tool Header** window, you can select and open a mail message into a **View Message** pop-up window, which displays the contents of the message and shows file icons for any attachments to the message. A mail message *attachment* is a file of any type, such as a sound file generated from the Audio Tool or a Raster image file, that is sent along with the mail message. For example, a mail message might contain a picture and voice message attachment to provide the recipient with an illustration and voice mail. The following sections explain the fundamentals for reading your mail messages and any attachments.

NOTE If you have a problem receiving your mail, contact your system administrator or see Chapter 17, "System Administration Basics."

Manually Checking Your Mail

While the Mail Tool checks your `In-Box` mail file automatically at specified time intervals, you can also manually check for any new messages. To check your mail manually, click the left mouse button on the `File` button in the `Mail Tool Header` window. The default `Load In-Box` item is activated. If you have new mail, the new mail message headers appear in the `Mail Tool Header` window or the Mail Tool icon displays letters with canceled stamps.

Mail Message Headers

The mail message headers displayed in the `Mail Tool Header` window list information about the mail message. In addition, status messages, displayed at the right side of the window footer, tell you the total number of messages in your `In-Box`, the number of new messages, and how many messages you have deleted. Each header has nine columns of information. The following explains each column:

- The status of the mail message: an arrow points to the current message, an `N` indicates that the message is new, a `U` indicates that the message is unread, a blank indicates that you have viewed the message, and a diamond indicates that an attachment was sent with the message.

- A message number indicating the order in which your messages were received.

- The electronic mail address of the sender of the message.

- The day of the week the message was sent.

- The month the message was sent.

- The date the message was sent.

- The time the message was sent.

- The size of the message. The first number indicates the number of lines in the message, and the second number indicates the number of characters in the message.

- The subject of the message, if the person who sent the message provided a subject line.

Selecting and Viewing Messages

A single mail message can be quickly displayed by double-clicking the left mouse button on the mail message header you want. A selected mail message header can also be displayed by pressing the right mouse button on the **View** menu and choosing **Message**. The mail message appears in a **View Message** pop-up window (Figure 3.4) on the Workspace. Once you have displayed a mail message, its **New** status is removed from the message header listing in the **Mail Tool Header** window, whether or not you actually read the message.

Once you open a single mail message in the **View Message** window, you can select and open additional mail message headers by double-clicking on the header name. The previous mail message in the **View Message** window is replaced with the new selected message. The number of the mail message is displayed in the header of the **View Message** pop-up window.

Choosing the **Next** item or **Previous** item in the **Mail Tool Header** window's **View** menu allows you to view the previous or next mail message listed from the one currently displayed. You can also click the left mouse button on the **Next** button to display the next mail message.

FIGURE 3.4

The View Message
pop-up window

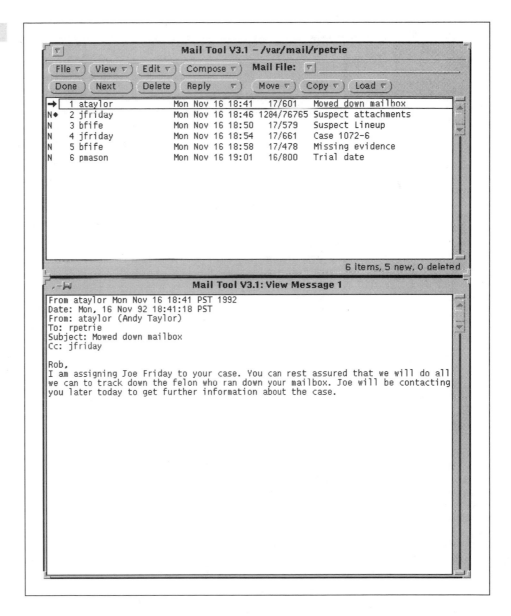

Opening and Viewing Mail Attachments

When you receive a mail message that contains one or more attachments, the `View Message` pop-up window displays a separate `Attachments` pane at the bottom, as shown in Figure 3.5. Attachments can be opened without moving them out of the Mail Tool. You can also open an attachment by moving it to the Workspace or any other application that accepts that type of file.

To open a mail message attachment, double-click the left mouse button on the attachment icon you want to open or drag and drop the attachment file icon onto the Workspace. The application bound to the attachment's file type is started, and the mail attachment is loaded into that application. For example, if you open a voice mail attachment created by the Audio Tool, the Audio Tool application window appears and the voice mail attachment is loaded. You can then work with the audio file using the Audio Tool.

A mail message attachment can also be opened by selecting the attachment and choosing `Open` from the `File` menu button at the top of the `Attachments` pane. Figure 3.6 shows a mail message with voice mail and picture attachments. For information on using the Audio Tool, see Chapter 6, "Using the Print Tool, Audio Tool, and Other DeskSet Applications."

Opening Multiple View Message Windows

Multiple mail messages can be opened, each appearing in a separate `View Message` window. To select multiple message headers in the `Mail Tool Header` window, click the left mouse button on the first message header then click the middle mouse button on each additional header you want to select. A mail message header can be unselected by clicking the middle mouse button on the mail message header. After selecting the messages, press the right mouse button on the `View` menu button and choose `Messages`. The `View Message` pop-up windows are displayed on top of one another in the numerical order of the messages listed (Figure 3.7).

FIGURE 3.5

The Attachments pane
in the View Message
window

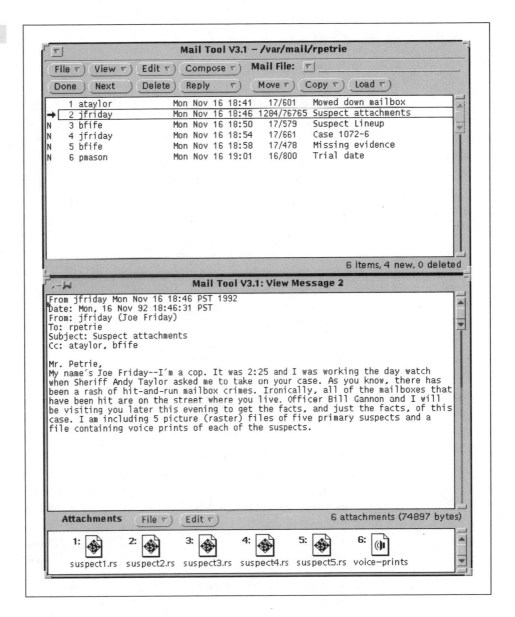

A mail message with voice and picture attachments

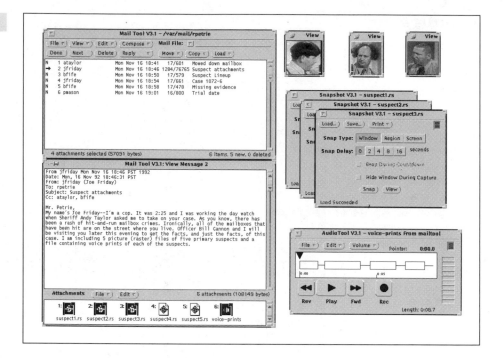

Viewing Messages with Full Headers

By default, the message header information appearing in the **View Message** window is in an abbreviated form. You can view messages with more information about the mail message appearing in the mail message header in the **View Message** window (Figure 3.8). For example, you can display information about the type of file and number of lines in the mail messages. The differences in the information that appears between the two displays are determined using the Mail Tool's **Properties** pop-up window.

To display a mail message with the full message header, first select the message in the **Mail Tool Header** window. Press the right mouse button on the **View** menu button, then choose **Full Header** from the **Messages** submenu.

FIGURE 3.7

Multiple messages
displayed

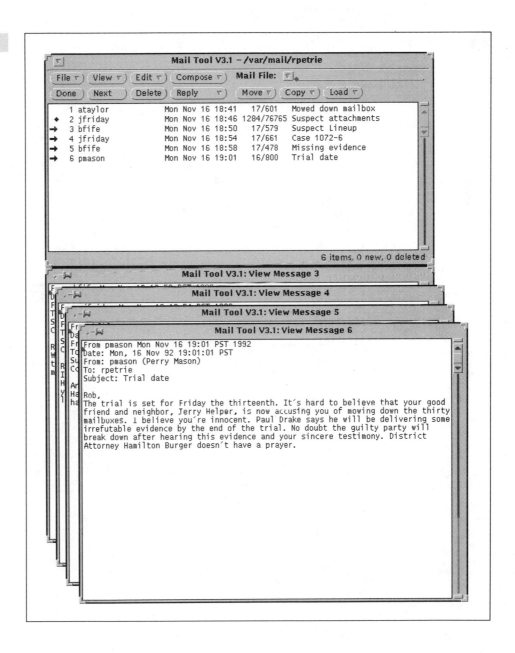

FIGURE 3.8

A full mail message header

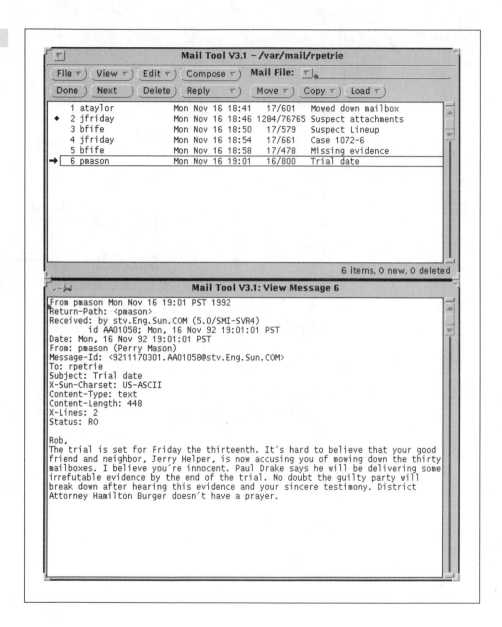

Saving Mail Tool Header Window Changes

If you attempt to quit the `Mail Tool Header` window after reading mail or after making any changes by using the `Quit` item in the `Window` menu, a Notice appears (Figure 3.9) informing you that changes have been made and prompting you for a confirmation. The following describes the options available in the Notice.

FIGURE 3.9

The Save Changes
Notice

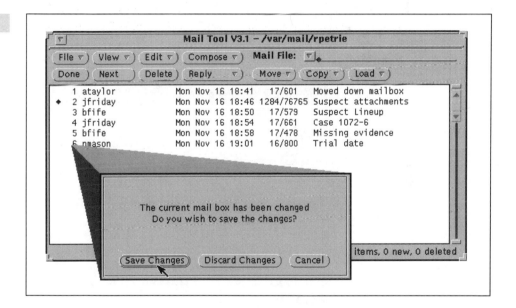

OPTION	DESCRIPTION
Save Changes	Saves any changes you have made and quits the Mail Tool, removing the icon from the workspace.
Discard Changes	Disregards changes you've made, restoring any deleted messages, and quits the Mail Tool, removing the icon from the Workspace.

OPTION	DESCRIPTION
Cancel	Aborts your request to quit the Mail Tool.

Changes can also be saved as you work by either using the **Save Changes** or **Done** item in the **Mail Tool Header** window's **File** menu or clicking the left mouse button on the **Done** button in the control area. The **Save Changes** item saves changes made in the Mail Tool without closing the **Mail Tool Header** window. The **Done** item or button closes the **Mail Tool Header** window and saves any changes.

Composing and Sending Messages

To create and send mail messages, use the Mail Tool's **Compose Message** window (Figure 3.10). The **Compose Message** window allows you to create mail messages using standard text editor functions. You can also add attachments to your mail messages, such as audio and image files.

The **Compose Message** window operates independently from the **Mail Tool Header** window. An opened **Compose Message** window can be closed to an icon for later use or you can keep the **Compose Message** window open while the **Mail Tool Header** window is closed to an icon. You can open several **Compose Message** windows at one time to reply to or compose several messages simultaneously. Once you have opened a **Compose Message** window, you can use it to write and send mail messages without having to reopen the **Mail Tool Header** window.

To display a **Compose Message** window, click the left mouse button on the **Compose** menu button in the **Mail Tool Header** window. The **Compose Message** window appears. When you close the **Compose Message** window without sending the message you are composing, its own icon (Figure 3.10) appears on the Workspace.

The Compose Message
icon and window

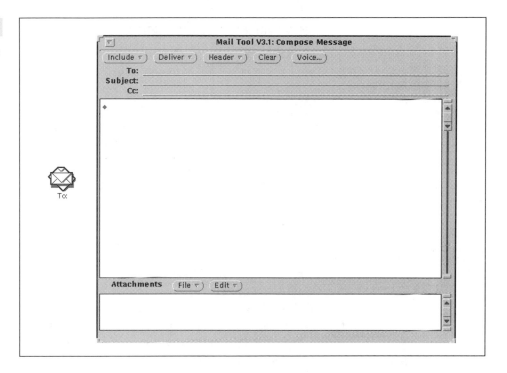

An Overview of the Compose Message Window

The `Compose Message` window has its own set of controls, which are displayed as five buttons in its control area: `Include`, `Deliver`, `Header`, `Clear`, and `Voice`. The following explains what each menu provides.

MENU BUTTON	DESCRIPTION
Include	Provides choices that allow you to include selected messages as part of the message you are composing and also provides you with a set of templates for creating different types of messages. This menu also includes an option that brings up the Attachments pane, which allows you to include attachments with your message (such as a voice file).

MENU BUTTON	DESCRIPTION
`Deliver`	Provides choices for how the Compose Message window behaves once the message is delivered.
`Header`	Provides choices for the number and type of text fields provided to create the message header.
`Clear`	Clears the contents of the Compose Message window and the `Attachments` pane.
`Voice`	Starts the Audio Tool, which lets you create audio files to attach to mail messages.

Just below the control area are three text fields: `To`, `Subject`, and `Cc`. These text fields allow you to include the addresses of the users you want to send your mail message to, the subject of the message, and the addresses of any users you want to send carbon copies of the mail message to. The text pane of the `Compose Message` window is where you type the contents of the message you want to send. The `Attachments` pane of the `Compose Message` window allows you to easily attach other files to your messages. It includes `File` and `Edit` menu buttons, which contain items for moving, copying, renaming, and deleting attachments.

An Overview of Mail Addresses

Before you send a mail message to a user, make sure you know the user address of the person you want to send your message to. The user address includes the user name and the name of the machine. The format for entering a user address is *username@machinename*. If the user is located on your system (sharing the same server), you don't need to add the machine name to the address.

Solaris includes a database system known as *alias mapping* that simplifies identifying users on the system. Alias mapping allows you send mail to users on other machines by just typing their user name without having to add the machine name. If you don't know the user name of the person you want to send a mail message to, see Chapter 11, "Electronic Mail and Messages," for information on using the `who`, `finger`, and `rusers` SunOS commands, which you can enter in the `Command Tool` or `Shell Tool` windows. Working with the `Command Tool` or `Shell Tool` windows is explained in Chapter 4, "Using the Text Editor, Shell Tool, and Command Tool."

Creating and Sending Mail Messages

Creating a mail message involves entering several standard items—including the user or users you are sending the message to, the subject of the message, and any user or users you want to send a carbon copy of the mail message—then entering the message text.

The `To` text field in the `Compose Message` window is where you enter the email address of the user or users you want to send the mail message to. To enter more than one email address, separate each address with a space. The `Subject` text field is an optional field, but entering information helps recipients identify what your message is about from the header listed in their `Mail Tool Header` window. The `Cc` (Carbon Copy) text field allows you to send a copy of the mail message to users other than those specified in the `To` text field. You can also send a blind carbon copy to another user so that the recipient does not know that the carbon copy was sent. To add the Blind Carbon Copy header for a message, choose the `Add Bcc` item from the Header menu in the `Compose Message` window.

You can create an *alias* that allows you to create your own distribution list containing a group of user email addresses. Then instead of typing a list of user email addresses that you frequently send mail to each time in either the `To` or `Cc` text fields, you can just enter the alias name. The Mail Tool automatically enters the group of user email addresses. Creating aliases is explained later in this chapter.

The area for entering your mail message text in the `Compose Message` window is a standard text pane that includes the `Text Pane` pop-up menu (Figure 3.11). This menu provides you with the standard text editing features that are available in the DeskSet's Text Editor, which is explained in Chapter 4 "Using the Text Editor, Shell Tool, and Command Tool." To

FIGURE 3.11

The Text Pane pop-up
menu

display the `Text Pane` pop-up menu, press the right mouse button anywhere in the text pane.

The following steps explain how to create and send a mail message.

1. If a `Compose Message` window is not displayed, click the left mouse
button on the `Compose` menu button. The `Compose Message` window is displayed.

2. Click the left mouse button on the `To` text field to set the insert
point. Type the address or series of addresses you want to send
your mail message to. If you type more than one address, separate
each with a space.

3. Move the insert point to the `Subject` field and type the subject of your message.

4. Move the insert point to the `Cc` field. Type the addresses of all those whom you want to receive a carbon copy of the message, if any.

5. Click the left mouse button in the `Compose Message` window's text pane to set the insert point in the text pane.

6. Type in your mail message. Pressing the right mouse button in the text pane displays the standard `Text Pane` pop-up menu. The `Edit` submenu lets you cut, copy, and paste text.

7. When you have finished composing the message, click the left mouse button on the `Deliver` button. The message is delivered and the `Compose Message` window is removed from the Workspace.

The `Deliver` menu button offers three additional items besides the default `Quit window` item, which removes the `Compose Message` window after sending a mail message. The `Close window` item closes the `Compose Message` window to an icon after sending a mail message. The `Clear message` item clears the `Compose Message` window after sending a mail message. The `Leave message intact` item leaves the message in the `Compose Message` window after sending the mail message.

Adding Attachments to Messages

Just as you can receive mail messages with attachments that can be files of any type, you can also add attachments to your outgoing mail messages. Attachments can be easily added to a mail message by dragging and dropping the file from the File Manager onto the `Attachments` pane of the `Compose Message` window. You can also drag and drop files or documents from the Text Editor or any other application that supports dragged and dropped files.

NOTE

By default the Attachments pane is displayed at the bottom of the Compose Message window; if it is not, choose the Show Attachments item from the Compose Message window's Include menu.

A mail attachment can also be added to a mail message using the **Add Attachment** window. Click the left mouse button on the **File** button at the top of the **Attachments** pane. The **Add Attachment** pop-up window is displayed, as shown in Figure 3.12. Type the directory name containing the file to be attached in the **Add Attachment Directory** text field, and type the name of the file in the **File Name** text field. Click the left mouse button on the **Add** button, and the file is added to the **Attachment** pane.

FIGURE 3.12

The Add Attachment pop-up window

> Mail Tool V3.1: Add Attachment
>
> Directory:
>
> File Name:
>
> (Add)

When you send a mail message with attachments, the receiver will see an **Attachments** pane at the bottom of the **View Message** window. The user can open the attachments by using the **Open** item in the **File** menu.

Including Other Messages in a Message

Other mail messages can be included in the mail message you are currently working on by using the **Include** menu button in the **Compose Message** window. The Include menu includes two items that allow you to specify how an included mail message is distinguished from the text you have entered in the mail message. The `Bracketed` item distinguishes a mail message by enclosing the message between dashed lines identifying the beginning and end of the included message, as shown in Figure 3.13. The `Indented` item displays a greater-than sign (>) preceding each line of an included text message, as shown in Figure 3.14. The greater-than sign is referred to as an *indent* character. A different indent character can be specified, as explained later in this chapter. The following steps explain how to include another mail message in the mail message currently displayed in a `Compose Message` window.

FIGURE 3.13

An included mail message using the Bracketed item

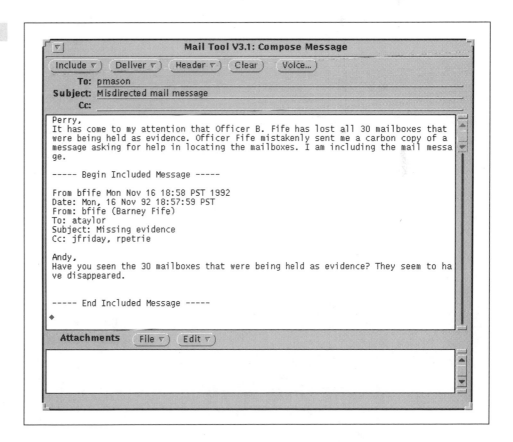

FIGURE 3.14

An included mail message using the Indented item

1. Open the mail message you want to include in the mail message currently opened in a **Compose Message** window.

2. Position the insert point at the location you want to insert the included mail message in the **Compose Message** window containing the mail message you want to add the mail message to.

3. Press the right mouse button on the **Include** menu button in the **Compose Message** window containing the mail message you want to insert the mail message into then choose **Indented** or **Bracketed**. The entire mail message is entered into the mail message at the location of the insert point.

Replying to a Message

Choosing `Reply` from the `Compose` menu automatically displays a `Compose Message` window, places the sender's address in the `To` text field, and places the subject of the mail message sent to you in the `Subject` text field of your reply message. The `Reply` submenu offers four choices for sending replies.

ITEM	RESULT
To Sender	Adds the name of the sender of the original message to the `To` field.
To All	Fills in the `To` and `Cc` fields with all the names in the selected message's text fields, including the originator of the message.
To Sender, Include	Fills in the `To` text field and puts a copy of the text of the original message into the `Compose Message` window pane.
To All, Include	Adds all the names from the original message to the `To` and `Cc` text fields, and puts a copy of the text of the message into the `Compose Message` window pane.

To reply to an individual message or to a group of messages, click the left mouse button on the `Reply` button or follow these steps:

1. Select the message header or headers that you want to answer by pressing the left mouse button on the first header and the middle mouse button on each additional header.

2. Press the right mouse button on the `Compose` menu and choose one of the four items from the `Reply` submenu. A `Compose Message` window is opened for each selected header.

Using Drag-and-Drop with the Mail Tool

You can drag mail messages from the `Mail Tool Header` window and drop them onto other applications. You can also drag and drop selected text or files from other applications onto the Mail Tool's `Compose Message` window to be included as text.

Single or multiple headers can be selected in the `Mail Tool Header` window and dragged to other DeskSet applications. When you drag a mail header, the entire mail message is moved along with it, including any mail attachments. The message headers can be dragged and dropped onto the File Manager, Text Editor, Print Tool, Calendar Manager, or any other application that accepts files via drag-and-drop. To drag and drop a copy of a mail message, select the message header, then drag it to the destination you want and drop it. A document object moves with the pointer to show that you are dragging a text file. When you select multiple headers, a group of three document objects is dragged with the pointer.

Managing Your Messages in the Mail Tool Header Window

The following sections explain Mail Tool features for managing and printing your mail messages in the `Mail Tool Header` window. To help you manage your messages, you can sort your messages, find specific messages by defining a search criteria, delete and undelete messages, and print messages directly from the `Mail Tool Header` window.

Sorting Message Headers

Mail messages in the `Mail Tool Header` window can be sorted by information contained in the mail message header. To sort mail message headers, choose an item in the `Sort By` submenu in the `View` menu (Figure 3.15). Immediately after you choose a sorting item, the message headers are redisplayed, sorted according to the item you selected. The following describes each sorting item available in the `Sort By` submenu.

FIGURE 3.15

The Sort By submenu

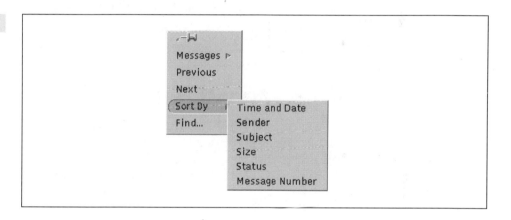

ITEM	DESCRIPTION
`Time and Date`	Sorts messages by receipt date and time with the most recently received messages at the bottom.
`Sender`	Sorts messages alphabetically by the name of the sender. This is useful for grouping together all messages from a particular person. Uppercase characters appear before lowercase characters in the alphabetical search.
`Subject`	Sorts messages alphabetically by mail message subjects. Uppercase characters appear before lowercase characters in the alphabetical search.

ITEM	DESCRIPTION
Size	Sorts messages by the size of the messages, from smallest to largest.
Status	Sorts messages by the read status of the messages. This puts the messages you have read first, the unread messages next, and the new messages last. This is useful to group together all unread mail after you read your messages in nonsequential order.
Message Number	Sorts messages by the message numbers assigned by the Mail Tool for each message.

Finding Messages

You can search through your messages using a number of different criteria to find a single message or group of messages. For example, you can find messages with a particular subject, or messages sent by a specific person. To find messages, choose Find from the View menu. The Find Messages

FIGURE 3.16

The Find Messages pop-up window

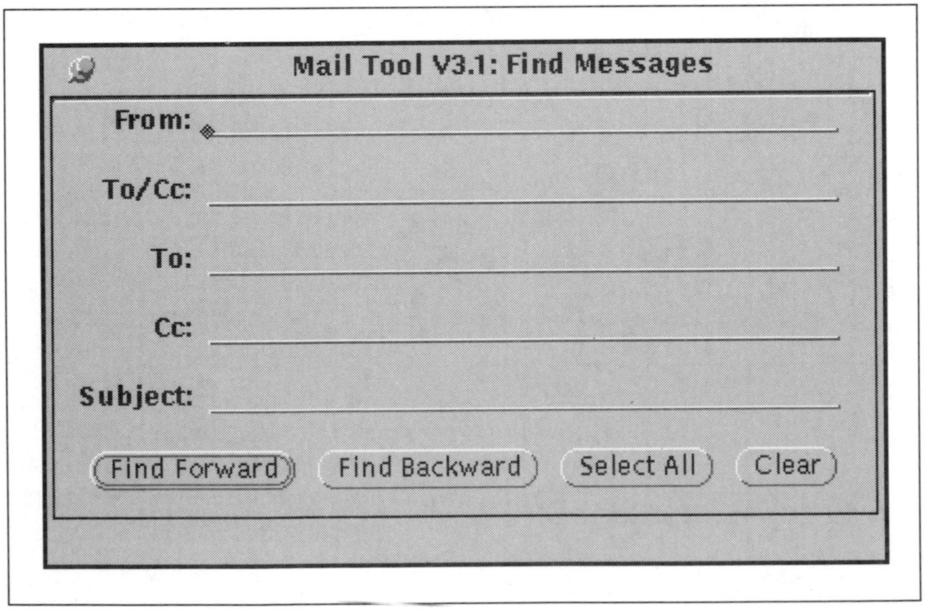

```
┌─────────────────────────────────────────────────┐
│         Mail Tool V3.1: Find Messages            │
│  From: ◆_____  │
│  To/Cc: _____  │
│    To: _____  │
│    Cc: _____  │
│ Subject: _____  │
│ (Find Forward)  (Find Backward)  (Select All)  (Clear) │
└─────────────────────────────────────────────────┘
```

pop-up window appears (Figure 3.16), which includes four text fields for entering search criteria. Searches can be based on information in a single field or combination of fields. The text fields do not distinguish between uppercase and lowercase characters and can match partial words and phrases. The following describes each setting in the `Find` pop-up window:

SETTING	DESCRIPTION
From	Searches the messages by the sender name. You don't need to type a complete sender name to find a match.
To/Cc	Searches for messages sent to an address or alias either directly or by Cc list.
To	Searches only for messages sent directly to an address; does not search for carbon copies.
Cc	Searches only for messages sent as carbon copies to an address or alias.
Subject	Searches for messages by subject.

After you fill out the search criteria text fields, click the left mouse button on one of the `Find` buttons located at the bottom of the `Find Messages` pop-up window. The `Find Forward` button selects the next message header that matches the specified information. The `Find Backward` button selects the previous message header with the specified information. The `Select All` button selects all message headers with the specified information. A status message displayed in the footer of the `Find Messages` window tells you how many messages are selected. The `Clear` button empties all text in the `Find Message` pop-up window's text fields.

Deleting Messages

Deleting messages that you no longer want from the `Mail Tool Header` window is easy. You can use the drag-and-drop method, the `Delete` button, or the `Delete` item from the `Edit` menu or `Messages` pop-up menu. To delete messages using the drag-and-drop method, select the mail message(s) you want, then drag and drop the mail message headers onto the

`Waste` icon or `Wastebasket` window. Remember, a file is not deleted from the `Wastebasket` window until you actually specify that the file be deleted.

To delete messages from the `Mail Tool Header` window using the `Delete` button or item, do the following:

1. Select the headers for messages you want to delete. Click the left button to select the first message, then click the middle button on each subsequent message to either add it to the group or remove it if it is already selected.

2. Click on the `Delete` button or choose the `Delete` item from either the `Edit` or `Messages` pop-up menu. The selected messages are deleted, and the status message in the footer reflects the current state of your `Mail Tool Header` window.

Undeleting Messages

If you deleted a message using the `Delete` item from either the `Edit` menu or `Messages` pop-up menu, and you have not chosen the `Save Changes` or `Done` items from the `File` menu, or the `Done` button, the deleted messages remain available for you to undelete. When no deleted messages are available, the `Undelete` item in the `Edit` or `Messages` menu appears dimmed.

NOTE Remember, if you deleted a message by dragging and dropping the header to the `Waste` icon or `Wastebasket` window, and you have not deleted the file, the file is still available in the `Wastebasket` window.

To undelete all the deleted messages, choose `Undelete` from the `Messages` pop-up menu or the `Edit` menu. You can also selectively undelete messages, as follows:

1. Choose `From List` in the `Edit` menu's `Undelete` submenu. The `Undelete` pop-up window appears, displaying a list of messages you have deleted since you last saved changes in the Mail Tool (Figure 3.17).

2. Select the headers you want to undelete. Click the left mouse button on the message header you want to undelete. Select additional message headers by clicking the middle mouse button on the message header. To unselect a message header, click the middle mouse button on the mail message header.

3. Click the left mouse button on the `Undelete` button in the bottom of the `Undelete` pop-up window.

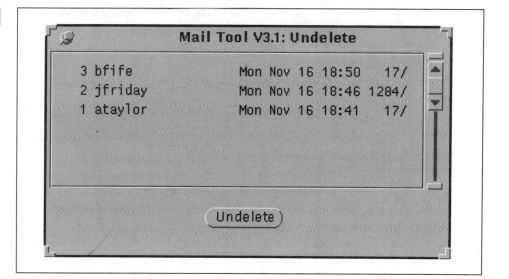

Printing Messages

Mail messages can be printed directly from the `Mail Tool Header` window using the `Print` item from the `File` menu or `Messages` pop-up menu. To print messages, first select the headers for the messages you want to print, then choose the `Print` item from the `File` menu or the `Messages` pop-up menu. The message is printed to the default printer for your system. The way to customize how your messages are printed is explained later in this chapter. Mail messages can also be printed by dragging and dropping messages from the `Mail Tool Header` window to the Print Tool's drag-and-drop target.

Working with Attachments

The Mail Tool allows you to manage mail message attachments from either the `Mail Tool Header` or `Compose Message` window. You can copy an attachment to store the file separately from the mail message, as well as rename or delete an attachment.

Copying Mail Attachments

The easiest way to copy an attachment is to simply drag and drop it into the File Manager or any other application that accepts files of the attachment's file type. You can also use the `Export Attachment` pop-up window to copy attachments to a specific directory. To copy an attachment to a specific directory, do the following:

1. Click the left mouse button on the attachment you want to copy. The attachment is then highlighted. To copy more than one attachment at a time, click the middle mouse button on each additional attachment that you want to copy.

2. Press the right mouse button on the `File` button at the top of the `Attachments` pane and choose `Copy Out`. The `Export Attachment` pop-up window is displayed.

3. In the `Export Attachment` pop-up window, type the name of the directory to which you want to copy the attachments in the `Directory` text field, and click the left mouse button on the `Export` button.

Renaming Mail Attachments

An attachment file can be renamed using the standard file name conventions used in the File Manager. You can only rename one attachment at a time. Follow these steps to rename a mail attachment in the `Attachments` pane:

1. Click the left mouse button on the attachment you want to rename. The attachment is highlighted.

2. Press the right mouse button on the `Edit` button at the top of the `Attachments` pane and choose `Rename`. The `Rename Attachment` pop-up window is displayed.

3. Type the new attachment name in the `Name` text field.

4. Click the left mouse button in the `Rename` button. The attachment file in the `Attachments` pane is renamed.

Deleting Mail Attachments

The easiest way to delete a mail attachment is to drag and drop the attachment icon from the `Attachments` pane to the `Waste` icon or `Waste-basket` window.

To delete a mail message attachment using the `Delete` item from the `Attachments` pane's `Edit` menu, click the left mouse button on the first attachment you want to delete. If you want to delete more than one attachment, click the middle mouse button on each additional attachment. Press the right mouse button on the `Edit` button at the top of the `Attachments` pane and choose `Delete`. The selected attachment or attachments are deleted from the mail message. You can use the `Undelete` item to restore the most recently deleted attachment.

Forwarding Mail

If you receive mail that you want to send to another user, you can forward it by selecting the mail message or messages and using the `Forward` item in the `Compose` menu of the `Mail Tool Header` window. When you forward a mail message, a `Compose Message` window opens, with the selected message appearing in the text pane and the subject field filled in. You can then forward the mail message by specifying the recipient of the forwarded message in the To text field. A carbon copy of the message can also be sent to another user by entering the person's name in the field labeled Cc.

Vacation Mail

When you are away from your terminal for an extended period of time, you can use the Mail Tool's Vacation feature to notify anyone sending you mail that you are not available to read it. When a user sends you a message, your Mail Tool automatically sends the user a reply indicating you are not available to read the message.

To display the Vacation Setup pop-up window, choose the Start/Change item from the Vacation submenu in the Mail Tool Header window's Compose menu. The default Start/Change item is chosen from the Vacation submenu and the Vacation Setup window appears (Figure 3.18).

You can edit the message template in the Vacation Setup pop-up window in the same way you edit messages in the Compose Messages window. The "$SUBJECT" string in the message text automatically extracts the subject from the message sent by the sender and includes it as part of the Vacation item's reply message.

To start the vacation reply message, click the left mouse button on the Start button. The word Vacation is displayed in the header of the Mail Tool Header window to remind you that Vacation mail is turned on. Incoming messages are stored in your In-Box and are readily available when you return to the office.

Once you've activated the Vacation mail feature, the Stop item on the Vacation submenu is available and becomes the new default setting. To stop Vacation mail, choose the Stop item from the Vacation submenu. If you decide you don't want to activate Vacation mail, choose Dismiss from the Window pop-up menu.

FIGURE 3.18

The Vacation Setup
pop-up window

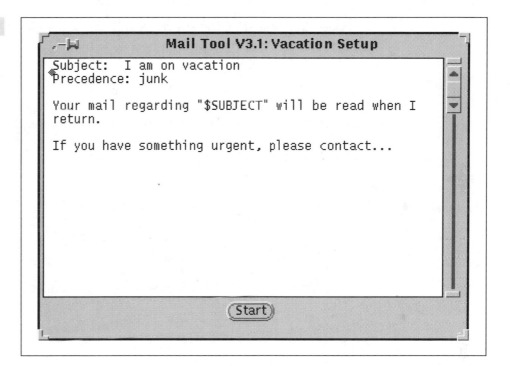

Using Mail Tool Templates

The Mail Tool allows you to use template files to create boilerplate messages of frequently used text such as a standard office memo. Each template is a text file that you can create using the DeskSet's Text Editor application, then add as an item on the **Templates** submenu of the **Compose Message** window's **Include** menu. Chapter 4, "Using the Text Editor, Shell Tool, and Command Tool," explains how to create a text file using the DeskSet's Text Editor. The Mail Tool includes a Calendar template, which inserts text information that can be added to the recipient's appointment calendar using the DeskSet's Calendar Manager application. To add a template to the Mail Tool, you use the Mail Tool's

`Template Properties` pop-up window, as explained in the "Template Properties" section later in this chapter.

To use a template as a basis for a mail message, press the right mouse button on the `Include` menu button in the `Compose Message` window and choose the template item you want from the `Templates` submenu. The template is inserted into the `Compose Message` window pane at the location of the insertion point. Figure 3.19 shows a sample template inserted in the `Compose Message` window text pane.

FIGURE 3.19

A sample template in the Compose Message window

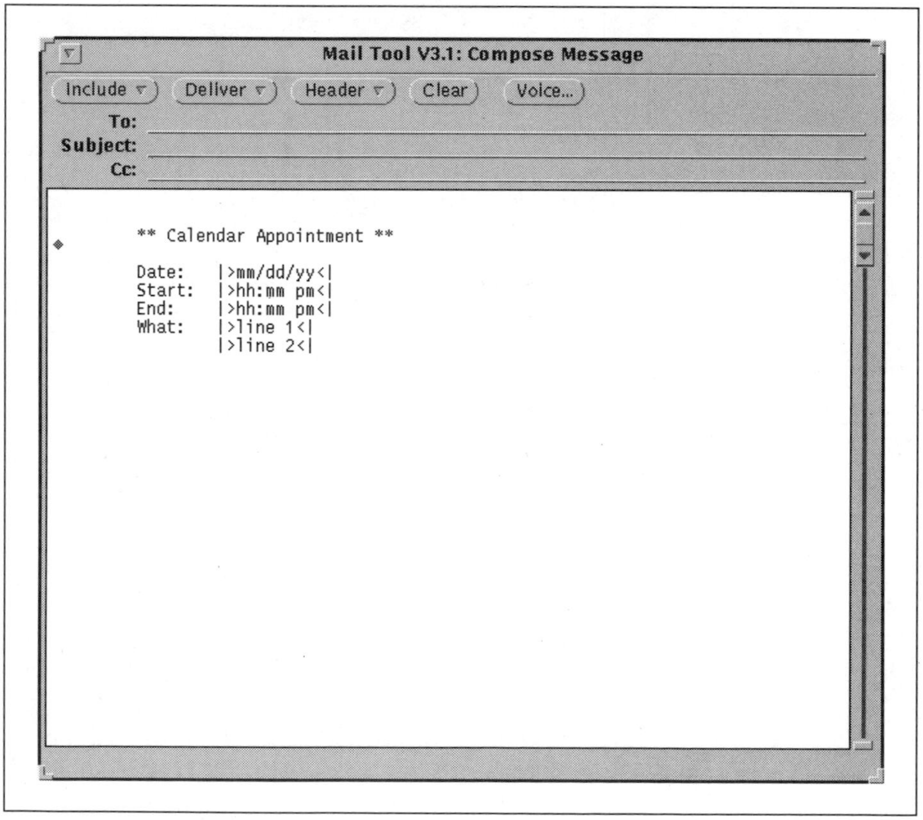

Working with Mail Files

As explained earlier, the In-Box is the default mail file (/var/mail/*user-name*) that receives and stores your incoming messages. Over time the In-Box becomes full of messages. While you can delete messages, it is better to save mail messages to another mail file. A mail file is a special file used by the Mail Tool for storing messages. Mail files allow you to store multiple messages in a single file. If you view a mail file outside of the Mail Tool, it looks like a single file with multiple messages appended to one another. When you view a mail file using the Mail Tool Header window, each separate message header is displayed in the header pane in the same way as messages from the In-Box. You can view, edit, delete, and respond to each message in any mail file in the same way you do for messages in the In-Box. The following sections explain how to manage your messages using the Mail Tool's mail file management features.

Specifying a Default Mail File Directory

By default, mail files are stored in your home directory. To keep your home directory organized, specify a new default mail file directory using the Mail Filing Properties window. To specify a new default directory for your mail files, do the following:

1. Choose Properties from the Edit menu in the Mail Tool Header window. The Mail Tool Properties pop-up window appears.

2. Choose Mail Filing from the Category menu (the abbreviated menu button in the upper-right corner of the window). The Mail Filing Properties window appears (Figure 3.20).

3. Enter the path for the directory where you want to store your mail files in the Mail File Directory text field. Unless a full path is specified, the directory you specify is considered a subdirectory of your home directory. In most cases, you want to create the directory in your home directory.

The Mail Filing
Properties pop-up
window

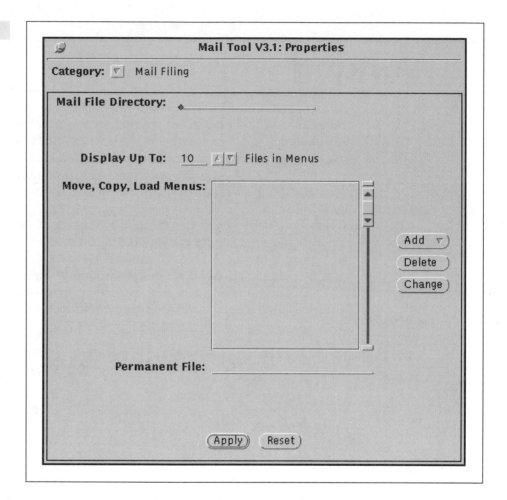

4. Click the left mouse button on the **Apply** button. If the directory name you specify does not exist, a Notice is displayed asking if you want to create the directory.

5. Click the left mouse button on the **Apply Changes** button.

The Mail Files Pop-up Window

The **Mail Files** pop-up window allows you to create, view, delete, and rename mail files, and add messages to a mail file. To open the **Mail Files** pop-up window (Figure 3.21), choose **Mail Files** from the **File** menu. The **Mail Files** pop-up window includes four menu buttons for working with mail files: **Save**, **Load**, **Create**, and **Edit**.

The scrolling list in the **Mail Files** pop-up window allows you to navigate directories and mail files in your default mail file directory. The scrolling list's first entry is your **In-Box** mail file. All files are indicated with a mailbox icon to the left of the name. If any folders are in the default mail file directory, they are listed after **In-Box** mail file with a folder icon appearing to the left of the folder name. Any additional files in the current directory are displayed after any subdirectories in the mail files scrolling list.

To navigate the **Mail Files** pop-up window's scrolling list, you can double-click on the folder icon to display any subdirectories and mail files in that directory. If you are in a subdirectory, the first entry in the list is

FIGURE 3.21

The Mail Files pop-up window

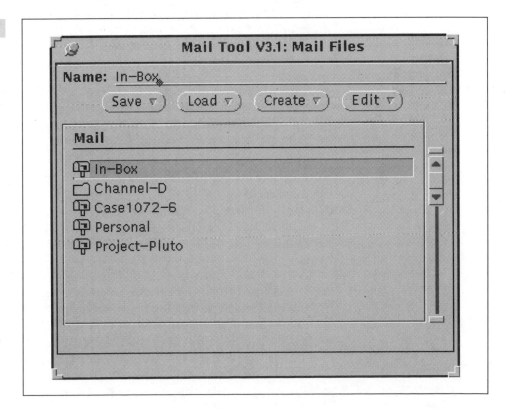

..(Go up 1 level). Press the right mouse button in the scrolling list to display the Scrolling List pop-up menu. If you are scrolling through a long list, choose the Locate Choice to return to the last selected file or folder.

Creating a New Mail File and Saving Messages in Mail Files

There are two ways to create a mail file and save messages to it. The easiest way is to use the Mail File text field in the Mail Tool Header window. In this procedure, you cannot create a new mail file without copying or moving messages. However, you can create a new mail file without having to copy or move mail messages by using the Mail Files pop-up window. To create a new mail file using the Mail File text field and copy or move multiple messages into it, do the following:

1. Type the name of the new mail file in the Mail File text field. For example, typing epistles will create a mail file named epistles.

2. Select the mail message headers from the Mail Tool Header window to move or copy to the new mail file.

3. Click the left mouse button on the Move or Copy button. The selected messages are moved or copied to the new mail file.

To create a new mail file using the Mail Files pop-up window, follow the steps below:

1. Choose Mail Files from the File menu in the Mail Tool Header window. The Mail Files pop-up window appears.

2. Type the name of the mail file in the Name text field.

3. If you want to copy or move any messages to the mail file, select the mail message headers from the Mail Tool Header window and choose Move Message into Mail File or Copy Message into Mail File from the Save menu in the Mail Files pop-up window. The selected messages are moved or copied to the new mail file.

Creating an Empty Mail File or Mail Files Directory

You can create subdirectories for storing mail files in the default mail directory or create a new, empty mail file using the `Mail Files` pop-up window, as follows:

1. Choose `Mail Files` from the `File` menu in the `Mail Tool Header` window.

2. Type the name of the new mail file or the new subdirectory in the `Name` text field. If you want to create a subdirectory to an existing directory listed in the `Mail Files` pop-up window's scrolling list, double-click on the folder name in the list to open the directory.

3. Choose either the `Mail File` or `Directory` item from the `Create` menu. The new mail file or directory is created and added to the scrolling list.

Saving Messages to an Existing Mail File

Additional mail messages can be added to a mail file at any time by using either the `Mail File` abbreviated menu button and the `Move` or `Copy` buttons in the `Mail Tool Header` window, or using the `Mail Files` pop-up window. To add messages to an existing mail file using the `Mail Tool Header` window, do the following:

1. Choose the name of the mail file to which you want to copy or move mail messages from the `Mail Files` menu by pressing the right mouse button on the abbreviated `Mail File` menu button. The mail file name appears in the `Mail File` text field.

2. Select the mail message headers in the `Mail Tool Header` window.

3. Click the left mouse button on the `Move` or `Copy` button. If there are messages already in the mail file, the newly added messages are appended to the existing messages.

To add messages to a mail file using the `Mail Files` pop-up window, do the following:

1. Choose the `Mail Files` item from the `File` menu in the `Mail Tool Header` window. The `Mail Files` pop-up window appears.

2. Click the left mouse button on the mail file name in the scrolling list.

3. Select the mail message headers to be moved or copied to the new mail file from the `Mail Tool Header` window.

4. Choose `Move Message into Mail File` or `Copy Message into Mail File` from the `Save` menu in the `Mail Files` pop-up window. The selected messages are moved or copied to the new mail file.

Loading Mail Files in the Mail Tool Header Window

Any mail file can be loaded into the `Mail Tool Header` window so you can work with its contents. By loading a mail file into the `Mail Tool Header` window you can perform all the tasks that you can with the `In-Box` messages, such as deleting, printing, and sorting messages. In addition, loading a mail file into the `Mail Tool Header` window allows you to move or copy messages from it to another mail file specified in the `Mail File` text field or using the `Mail Files` pop-up window.

You can load mail files using three different methods: using the `Mail File` text field and `Load` button in the `Mail Tool Header` window, using the `Mail Files` pop-up window, or dragging and dropping mail files from the File Manager to the `Mail Tool Header` window.

To load a mail file into the `Mail Tool Header` window using the `Mail Files` pop-up window, do the following:

1. Choose `Mail Files` from the `File` menu in the `Mail Tool Header` window. The `Mail Files` pop-up window appears.

2. Double-click on the mail file name that you want to load from the scrolling list. The mail message headers in that mail file will appear in the **Mail Tool Header** window. You can double-click on another mail file to display its mail headers in the **Mail Tool Header** window, replacing the previous mail file's contents.

To load a mail file into the **Mail Tool Header** window, do the following:

1. Press the right mouse button on the **Mail File** abbreviated menu button and choose the mail file you want to view. The mail file name appears in the **Mail File** text field.

2. Click the left mouse button on the **Load** button. All the messages saved to that mail file appear, as mail headers, in the **Mail Tool Header** window.

A mail file can be loaded from the **Mail Files** pop-up window or by dragging and dropping a mail file from the File Manager to the **Mail Tool Header** window. A mail file icon appears as a stack of envelopes in the File Manager's file pane, as shown in Figure 3.22. To load a mail file from the

FIGURE 3.22

Mail file incons in the File Manager's file pane

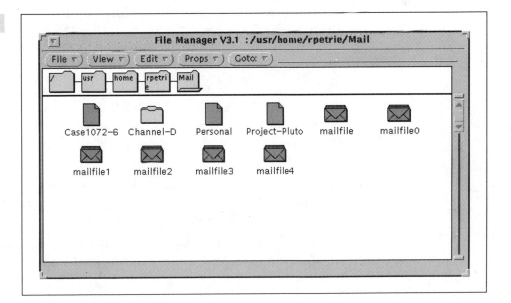

File Manager, do the following:

1. With the File Manager window open, navigate to the default mail file directory in your home directory.

2. Press the left mouse button on the mail file icon and drag it to the `Mail Tool Header` window's headers pane. The pointer changes to a target.

3. Drop the mail file icon onto the `Header` pane. The message headers in the mail file appear.

Managing Your Mail Files

You can empty a mail file, rename it, or delete it with the `Edit` menu of the `Mail Files` pop-up window. To empty, rename, or delete a mail file, you need to first select the mail file in the scrolling list in the `Mail Files` pop-up window. You can only work with one file at a time in the `Mail Files` pop-up window. If the mail file is in a subdirectory below the one displayed on the scrolling list, double-click the left mouse button on that subdirectory to display it. If the mail file is in a directory higher up from the one displayed in the scrolling list, double-click the left mouse button on the (`Go up 1 level`) folder item until the mail file you want is in the scrolling list. When the mail file is in the scrolling list, click the left mouse button on the mail file to select it.

To delete a mail file, select the mail file in the scrolling list. Then choose `Delete` from the `Edit` menu. The Mail Tool asks you to confirm that you want to delete the mail file. Click the left mouse button on the `Delete Mail File` button to delete the mail file.

To empty a mail file, select the mail file in the scrolling list. Then choose `Empty` from the `Edit` menu. The Mail Tool asks you to confirm that you want to empty the mail file. Click the left mouse button on the `Empty Mail File` button to empty the mail file.

To rename a mail file, select the mail file in the scrolling list, type the new name in the `Name` field, then choose `Rename` from the `Edit` menu.

Customizing the Mail Tool

The **Mail Tool Properties** pop-up window allows you to customize a wide variety of the Mail Tool's settings. To display the **Mail Tool Properties** window, choose **Properties** from the **Edit** menu. The **Mail Tool Properties** window appears (Figure 3.23).

FIGURE 3.23

The Mail Tool Properties pop-up window

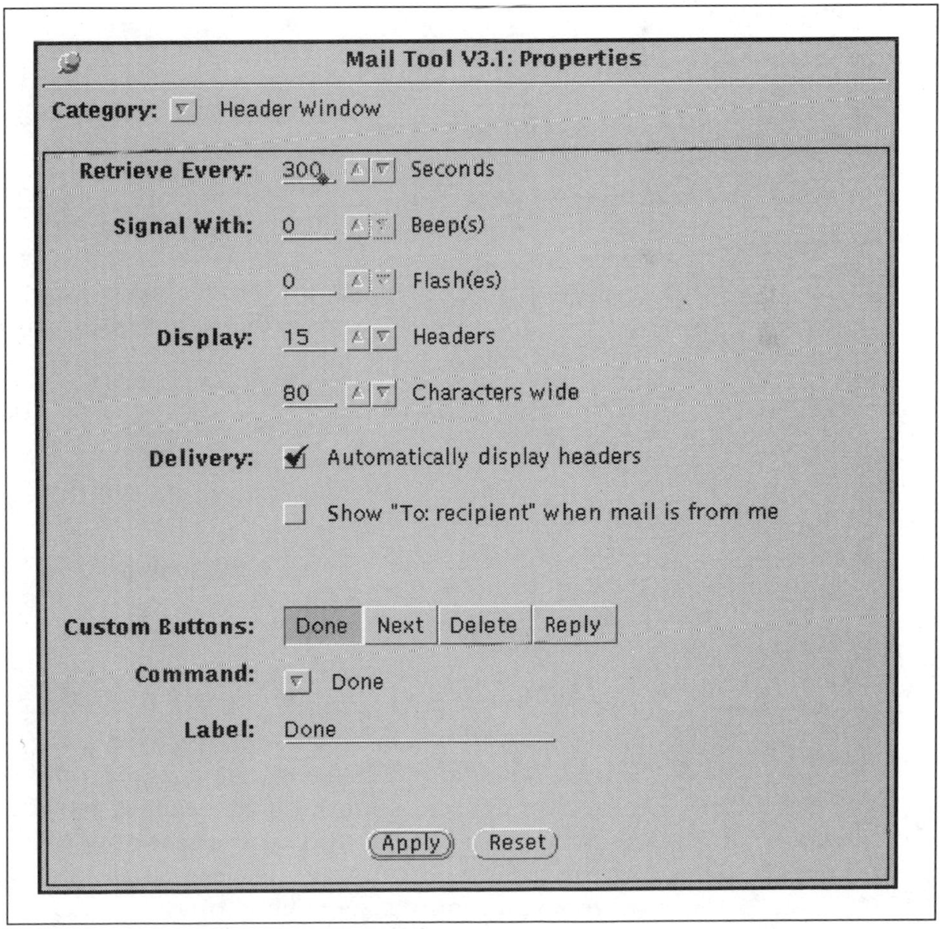

To display the menu that lists the categories of properties you can customize, click the right mouse button on the **Category** menu button. The **Category** menu (Figure 3.24) lists seven items: **Header Window**, **Message Window**, **Compose Window**, **Mail Filing**, **Template**, **Alias**, and **Expert**. Each of these menu items displays a pop-up window containing buttons and text fields for setting the category properties. To display the **Category** menu and choose a category item, press the right mouse button on the **Category** menu button and choose the category you want to change.

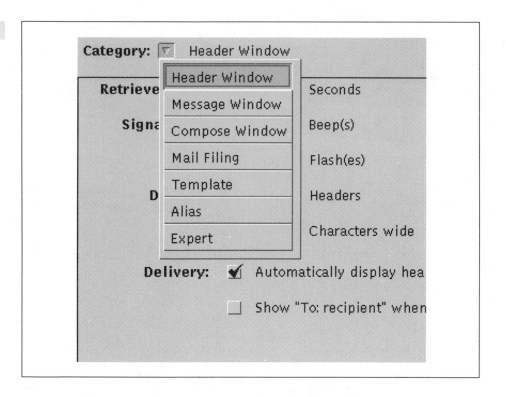

To save changes you make in any category window, click the left mouse button on the **Apply** button. If you want to cancel any changes you made, click the left mouse button on the **Reset** button. The properties window returns to their previous settings. But please note, if you click on the **Apply** button, you cannot reset your settings. If you make changes in any of the categories and attempt to leave the category without clicking the **Apply**

button, a Notice appears prompting you to save your changes. Click the left mouse button on the `Apply Changes` button to save your changes.

Header Window Properties

The `Header Window Properties` window is the default category that appears when the `Mail Tool Properties` window is opened (Figure 3.23). It allows you to change settings for the `Mail Tool Header` window. These settings include how often the Mail Tool checks for new mail, the way you are notified when new mail arrives, and whether headers are automatically displayed for new mail messages. You can also define the custom buttons that appear in the bottom row of the control area in the `Mail Tool Header` window, using the `Custom Buttons`, `Command`, and `Label` settings, as explained in the next section. The following explains the remaining settings in the `Mail Tool Properties` window.

SETTING	DESCRIPTION
`Retrieve Every`	Determines how often new mail is automatically retrieved. The default value is 300 seconds, or 5 minutes. To increase or decrease the number of seconds between mail checks, type a number in the numeric field or click the left mouse button on the appropriate scroll button to the left of the field.
`Signal With`	Determines how the Mail Tool signals that new mail has arrived. The `Beep(s)` setting causes the Mail Tool to beep the specified number of times when there is incoming mail. The `Flash(es)` setting causes the Mail Tool icon or the `Mail Tool Header` window to flash when there is incoming mail. To increase or decrease the number of beeps or flashes that signal the arrival of mail, type a number in the numeric field or click the left mouse button on the appropriate scroll button.

SETTING	DESCRIPTION
Display	The `Headers` setting determines how many headers are displayed in the `Mail Tool Header` window. The `Characters` setting determines the width of all Mail Tool panes and windows. To increase or decrease the number of headers to display or the number of characters wide, type a number in the numeric field or click the left mouse button on the appropriate scroll button.
Delivery	The `Automatically display headers` setting determines if the Mail Tool automatically displays or does not display the headers of incoming messages in the `Mail Tool Header` window. If you do not choose this option, the Mail Tool does not display headers for incoming messages unless you specifically request them by choosing `Load In-Box` or `Save Changes` from the `File` menu. If the `Show "To: recipient" when mail is from me` setting is checked, the header of the message sent to you will display who you sent the message to instead of your email address.

Customizing Mail Tool Buttons

The first four buttons on the second row of the `Mail Tool Header` window are custom buttons. These buttons can be changed to any of the items in the `File`, `View`, `Edit`, or `Compose` menus. If these menus contain items that you frequently use, you can change your custom buttons to easily access those items.

The **Custom Buttons** settings (**Done, Next, Delete,** and **Reply**) indicate the current four custom buttons that appear in the control area of the **Mail Tool Header** window, from left to right.

The **Command** abbreviated menu button provides a menu of all of the available commands from the **File, View, Edit,** and **Compose** menus (Figure 3.25). The first column in the **Command** menu displays all of the choices available from the **File** menu, the second column displays the choices from the **View** menu, the third displays the choices from the **Edit** menu, and the last column displays the choices from the **Compose** menu.

If space allows, the selected menu item name automatically becomes the custom button label. The **Label** text field allows you to change the label of a custom button.

FIGURE 3.25

The Command menu

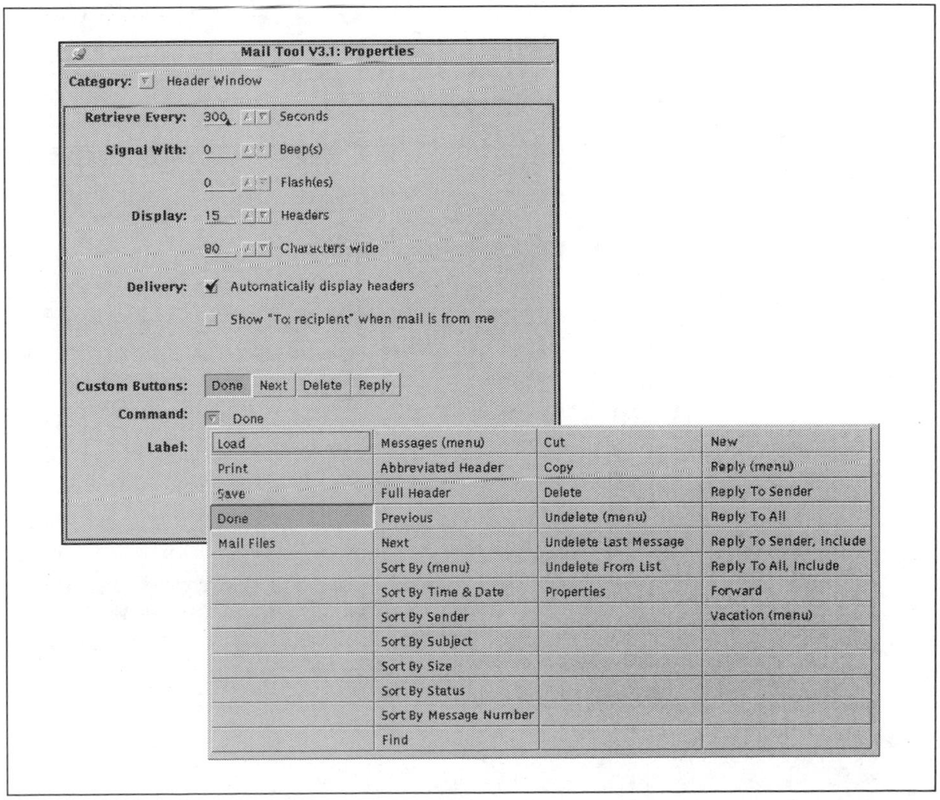

The following steps explain how to change a custom button.

1. Display the `Header Window Properties` window, if it's not already displayed.

2. Click the left mouse button on the `Custom Buttons` setting that you want to change.

3. Click the right mouse button on the `Command` menu button and click the left mouse button on the new command.

4. If you want, enter a new label for the selected command in the `Label` text field.

5. Click the left mouse button on the `Apply` button to change the custom button in the `Mail Tool Header` window. The changes are reflected in the current Mail Tool. Figure 3.26 shows new custom buttons appearing in the control area of the `Mail Tool Header` window.

FIGURE 3.26

New custom buttons added to the Mail Tool Header window

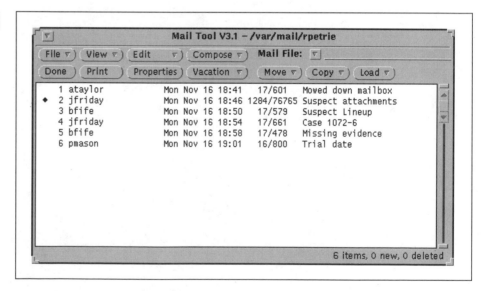

Mail Tool V3.1 – /var/mail/rpetrie		

File ▽ View ▽ Edit ▽ Compose ▽ **Mail File:** ▽
Done Print Properties Vacation ▽ Move ▽ Copy ▽ Load ▽

```
   1 ataylor      Mon Nov 16 18:41     17/601      Mowed down mailbox
 ◆ 2 jfriday      Mon Nov 16 18:46  1284/76765  Suspect attachments
   3 bfife        Mon Nov 16 18:50     17/579      Suspect Lineup
   4 jfriday      Mon Nov 16 18:54     17/661      Case 1072-6
   5 bfife        Mon Nov 16 18:58     17/478      Missing evidence
   6 pmason       Mon Nov 16 19:01     16/800      Trial date
```

6 items, 0 new, 0 deleted

Message Window Properties

The **Message Window Properties** window, shown in Figure 3.27, allows you to define the number of lines in the **View Message** pop-up window text pane, use a different print script for printing messages, and determine the information *not* displayed when viewing a message with abbreviated headers. The following explains the settings in the **Message Window Properties** window.

FIGURE 3.27

The Message Window Properties pop-up window

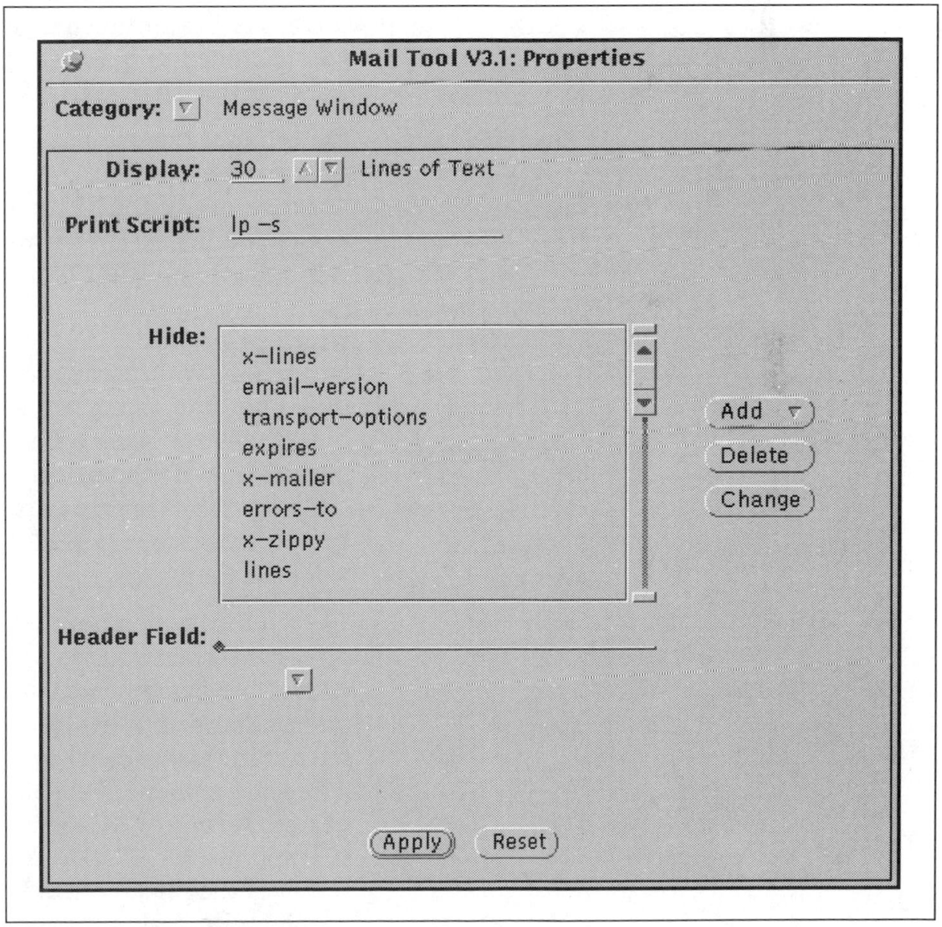

Mail Tool V3.1: Properties

Category: ▽ Message Window

Display: 30 △▽ Lines of Text

Print Script: lp −s

Hide:
- x−lines
- email−version
- transport−options
- expires
- x−mailer
- errors−to
- x−zippy
- lines

Add ▽
Delete
Change

Header Field: ◆

▽

Apply   Reset

SETTING	DESCRIPTION
Display	Determines the number of lines of text displayed in each View Message window text pane. The default setting is 30 lines of text. To increase or decrease the number of lines, type a number in the numeric field or click the left mouse button on the appropriate scroll button. After you click the left mouse button on the Apply button to change this field, you will need to quit and restart the Mail Tool for this change to take effect.
Print Script	Determines the print script used to print your messages when you choose the Print item from the File menu or the Header pane pop-up menu. For example, if you want to use the same print script used in the File Manager, which prints with a fancy border containing your name and the current time and date, enter cat $FILE	mp −lo	lp. If you are using a PostScript printer, specify the printer type by adding −T postscript argument to the lp command (cat $FILE | mp −lo | lp −T postscript).
Hide	Determines which headers are not displayed when you view your messages with abbreviated headers. You can add any header to this list by typing the header in the Header Field text field. The Add submenu lets you place the header Before or After the currently selected header. The Delete button removes the selected headers, and the Change button allows you to edit the selected header's text typed in the Header Field text field.

SETTING	DESCRIPTION
Header Field	Allows you to add any header to the Hide scrolling list.

Compose Window Properties

The **Compose Window Properties** window, shown in Figure 3.28, allows you to customize several settings for the **Compose Message** window. The **Included Text Marker** text field specifies the characters that precede each line of an included text message. These are referred to as indent characters.

The default is a greater-than sign (>). This puts the greater-than sign character at the start of the included message when you choose `Indented` from the `Include` menu of the `Compose Message` window. A different indent character can be specified by typing a new character in the `Included Text Marker` text field.

The `Logged Messages File` text field allows you to specify the name of a log file to log outgoing mail messages. If a log file is specified, the `Log` check box appears on the `Compose Message` window, as shown in Figure 3.29. When the `Log` check box is checked on your `Compose Message` window, the message is logged into the log file when it is sent. The log file lists who the message is from, the recipient of the message, the character set used to create the message, the number of characters and lines contained in the message, and the entire message. Use the `Log all messages`

FIGURE 3.29

The Log check box in the Compose Message window

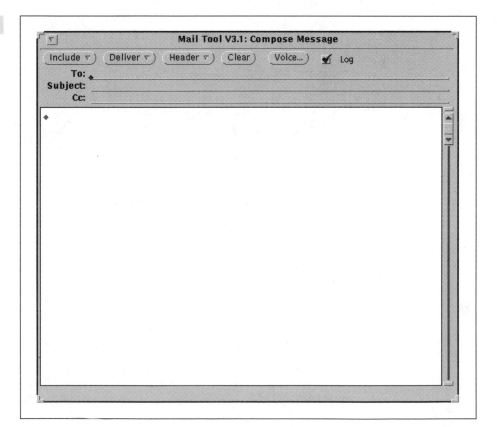

setting in the `Compose Window Properties` window to determine whether the `Log` check box in the `Compose Message` window is checked by default.

The `Defaults` setting's `Request confirmations` option determines if a Notice is displayed prompting you to confirm an operation or save any changes made in the following situations:

- When you have text or attachments in the `Compose Message` window and you choose the `Clear` button.

- When you have text or attachments in the `Compose Message` window and you quit the window.

- When you have made changes to a message in the `View Message` window, and you then display a new message, unpin the `View Message` window, or receive new incoming mail.

WARNING

If the Request Confirmations setting is not checked, any editing changes in the `View Message` window are automatically incorporated without notification. If you remove or change the `From` header of a message, your mail file will be corrupted and the message appended to the previous message in the mail file.

By default, a `Compose Message` window includes a pane at the bottom of the text area where you can add attachments to your message. If you rarely use attachments, you can use the `Show Attachment List` setting to specify whether the attachment pane is shown or not shown. If you turn off the default `Show Attachment List` setting, you can display the attachments pane on an as-needed basis by choosing `Show Attachments` from the `Include` menu.

Creating Custom Header Fields

The header of the `Compose Message` window always has `To`, `Subject`, and `Cc` header fields. A custom header field can be added to the `Header` menu in the `Compose Message` window by adding it to the `Custom Fields` scrolling list in the `Compose Window Properties` window. The following are some helpful predefined headers you can add to the headers menu.

HEADER FIELD	DEFAULT VALUE	DESCRIPTION
Precedence	junk	If the mail system cannot send a message with this header, no notices are sent to inform you that the message was not deliverable. This header can help keep mail notifications from cluttering up your mail file. However, it also keeps you from being informed that you entered an incorrect email address.
Reply-To	username @machinename	When you reply to a message containing this header, the reply is sent to the user specified instead of the sender of the message.
Return-Receipt-To	*yourusername @yourmachinename*	Similar to registered mail, adding this header informs the mail system to send you a transcript of the message after the message you sent is received. This header is useful for verifying that messages are received.

Any other custom headers you enter are added as text. The custom header is displayed in the header area of the **Compose Message** window. Figure 3.30 shows custom headers added to the **Header** menu in the **Compose Message** window. The following explains how to add the Return-Receipt-To header to the **Header** menu:

1. Type Return-Receipt-To in the **Header Field** text field in the **Compose Window Properties** window. A colon is automatically added to the end of the added text field.

2. Type your user name in the **Default Value** field.

FIGURE 3.30

The Header menu with custom header items

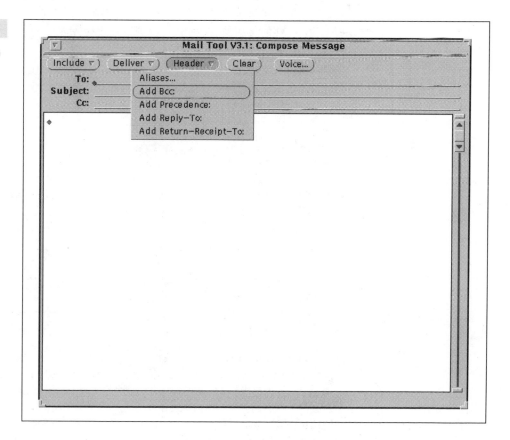

3. Click the left mouse button on the **Add** button. If you have other custom header fields displayed in the **Custom Fields** scrolling list, you can specify where you want to place the new custom header. Click the left mouse button on the custom header in the list you want your new entry before or after. Press the right mouse button on the **Add** button and choose either **Before** or **After**.

4. Click the left mouse button on the **Apply** button. The changes become effective immediately, adding the custom field to the **Header** menu of the **Compose Message** window.

To change a custom field, click the left mouse button on the item in the **Custom Fields** scrolling list, type the new values in the **Header Field** and **Default Value** text fields, click the left mouse button on the **Change** button, then click the left mouse button on the **Apply** button.

To delete a custom field, click the left mouse button on the item in the scrolling list, choose the **Delete** button, and click the left mouse button on **Apply**.

Mail Filing Properties

The **Mail Filing Properties** window (Figure 3.31) specifies where your mail files are stored and allows you to customize menus in the **Mail Tool Header** window. As explained earlier in this chapter, the **Mail File Directory** text field allows you to specify the directory where mail files you create are stored. Unless a full path name is specified, the directory will be located in your home directory. In most cases, it is recommended you store your mail files in your home directory or a subdirectory of your home directory to make backup of your files easier. If the directory name you specify does not exist, after you choose the **Apply** button, a Notice will be displayed asking you if you want to create the directory.

The **Move, Copy,** and **Load** menus in the **Mail Tool Header** window display up to ten of the most recently accessed mail files. You can change the maximum number of files in menus by changing the **Display Up To** setting of the **Mail Filing Properties** window. To increase or decrease the number of items displayed in these menus, type a number in the numeric fields or click the left mouse button on the appropriate arrow button to the left of the field.

FIGURE 3.31

Mail Filing Properties
pop-up window

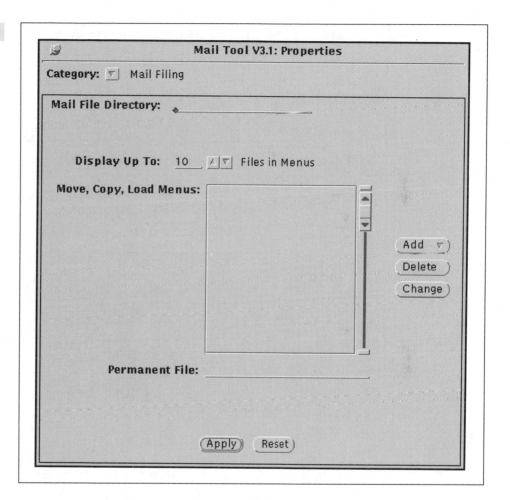

When you first start a new Mail Tool application, the `Move`, `Copy`, and `Load` menus are empty. Mail files are added to these menus as you access the mail files. You can specify mail files that you always want to appear at the top of these menus by adding them to the `Move, Copy, Load Menus` scrolling list setting.

To add any mail file to the list, type the name of the mail file in the `Permanent File` text field, then click the left mouse button on the `Add` button. If you already have mail files listed, select the mail file in the scrolling list that you want the new mail file to be listed before or after and choose `Before` or `After` from the `Add` submenu. The `Delete` button removes the currently selected mail file, and the `Change` button changes the currently selected mail file to the mail file typed in the `Permanent File` text field.

Template Properties

The Mail Tool allows you to use template files to create boilerplate messages of frequently used text such as a standard form letter. Each template is a text file that you create outside the Mail Tool. For example you can create a template using the DeskSet's `Text Editor`. Once you create a template, you use the `Template Properties` window (Figure 3.32) to add

FIGURE 3.32

The Template Properties pop-up window

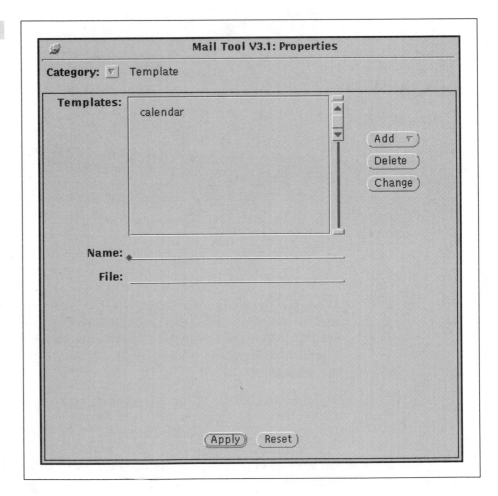

it as an item on the `Templates` submenu of the `Compose Message` window's `Include` menu. The following steps explain how to add a template to the `Templates` submenu in the `Compose Message` windows `Include` menu using the `Template Properties` window.

1. In the `Name` field in the `Template Properties` window, type the name of the template that you want displayed as an item in the `Include Templates` submenu of the `Compose Message` window.

2. Click the left mouse button in the `File` field and type the path and name of the file containing the template text. If the file is in your home directory, you can just enter the file name.

3. Press the right mouse button on the `Add` menu button and choose `Before` or `After`. If you select the `Before` item, the template name is inserted at the beginning of the templates list. If you select the `After` item, the template name is appended to the end of the list.

4. Click the left mouse button on the `Apply` button. The new template is placed in the scrolling list and added to the `Include Templates` submenu.

To delete a template name from the `Templates` submenu, first display the `Template Properties` window and click the left mouse button on the item in the scrolling list. Click the left mouse button on the `Delete` button.

Alias Properties

The `Alias Properties` window (Figure 3.33) allows you to create mail distribution lists of groups of users that you want to send a mail message to. Instead of repeatedly typing a list of names in the `To` or `Cc` text field, you only need to type the name you gave the alias in the `To` field in the `Compose Message` window. The alias name is replaced with the email addresses of all the users assigned to the alias.

The following explains how to create an alias that has more than one email address.

1. Type the alias name in the `Alias` text field in the `Alias Proper-ties` window.

2. Type the email address of each person in the **Address** text field. Separate each name with a comma or a space.

3. Click the left mouse button on the **Add** button. If you have other **Aliases** displayed in the **Custom Fields** scrolling list, you can specify where you want to place the new custom header. Click the left mouse button on the custom header in the list you want your new entry before or after. Press the right mouse button on the **Add** button and choose either **Before** or **After**.

4. Click the left mouse button on the **Apply** button.

To change an alias, click the left mouse button on the item in the **Aliases** scrolling list, type the new value in the **Aliases** and **Addresses** text fields, click the left mouse button on the **Change** button, then click the left mouse button on the **Apply** button.

FIGURE 3.33

The Alias Properties pop-up window

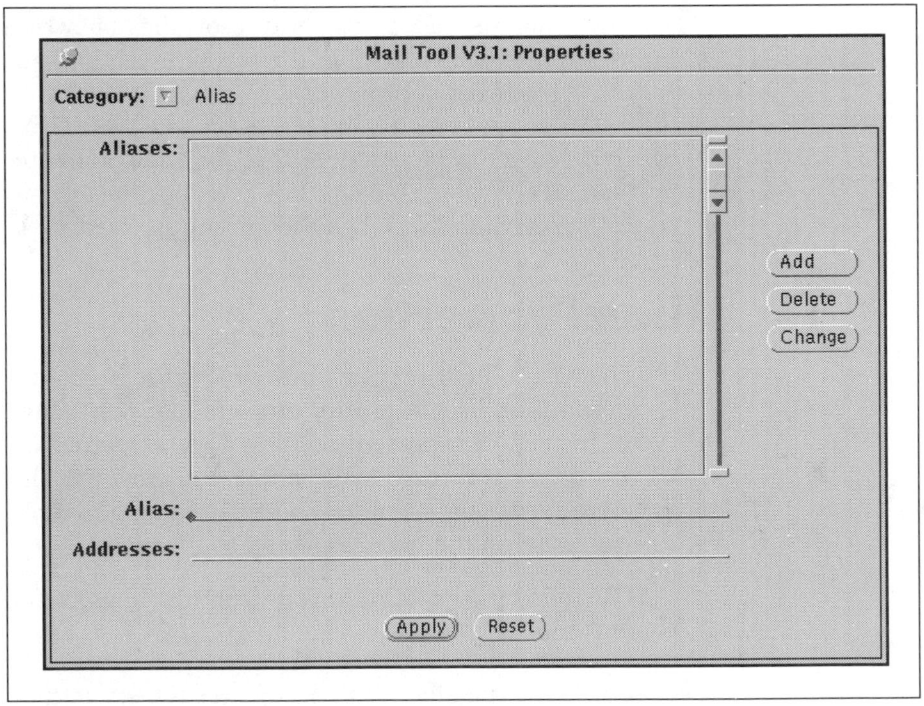

To delete an alias, click the left mouse button on the alias name in the `Aliases` scrolling list, choose the `Delete` button, and click the left mouse button on `Apply`.

Expert Properties

The `Expert Properties` window (Figure 3.34) includes settings that determine what happens when you choose the `To All` and `To All, Include` items from the `Compose` menu's `Reply` submenu in the `Compose`

FIGURE 3.34

The Expert Properties pop-up window

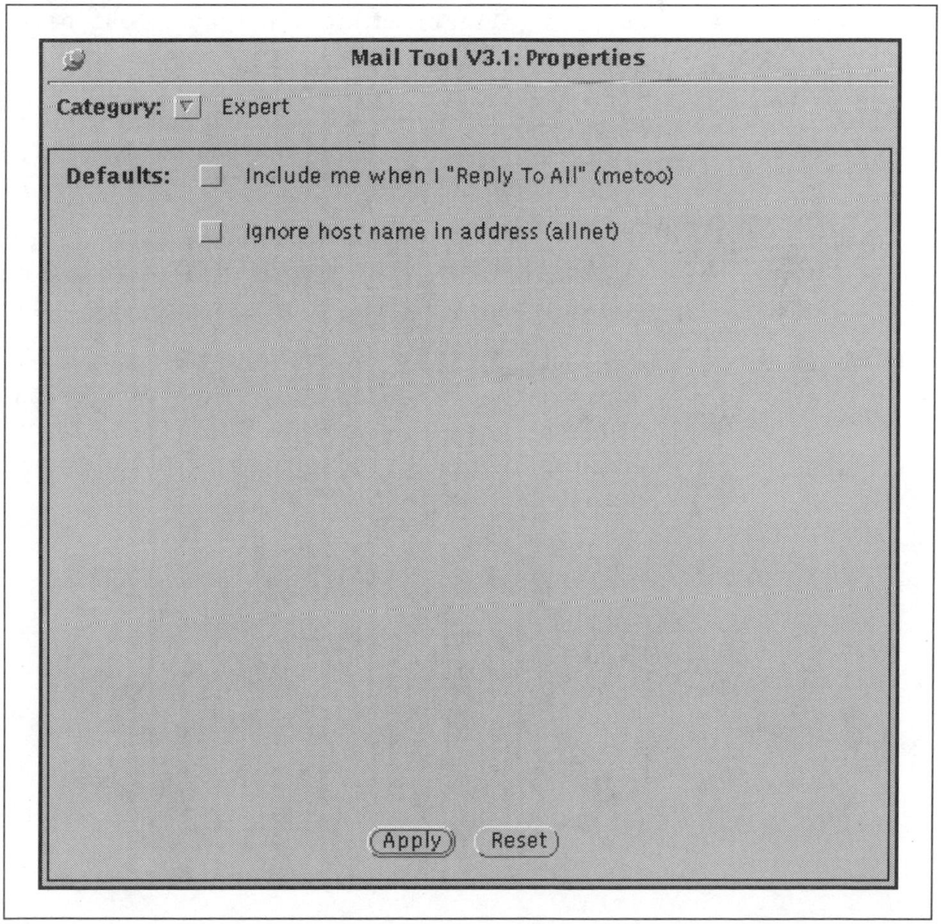

Mail Tool V3.1: Properties

Category: ▽ Expert

Defaults: ☐ Include me when I "Reply To All" (metoo)

☐ Ignore host name in address (allnet)

(Apply) (Reset)

`Message` window. These settings only apply when your email address appears in the `To` or `Cc` field's list of messages you are replying to.

If, when you do a Reply to All, the `Include me when I "Reply To All"` (`metoo`) setting is checked, and your email address appears in the `To` or `Cc` field, you will also receive the reply. Your email address is recognized in all forms that include your login address, such as *yourusername@machine* and *yourusername@host,* where "machine" is the name of your machine and "host" is the name of any host that is not your machine.

If the `Include me when I "Reply To All"` (`metoo`) setting is not checked, the message header of your reply depends on the `Ignore host name in address` (`allnet`) setting. The `Ignore host name in address` (`allnet`) setting determines whether your email address is recognized in all forms that include your login address, or only in the form of *yourusername@machine.* The `Ignore host name in address` (`allnet`) setting only has an effect when the `Include me when I "Reply To All"` (`metoo`) option is *not* checked.

If the `Ignore host name in address` (`allnet`) setting is checked and the `Include me when I "Reply To All"` (`metoo`) setting is not checked, and you do a `Reply to All`, your address is not included in any form in the `To` or `Cc` fields of your reply.

When neither the `Ignore host name in address` (`allnet`) nor the `Include me when I "Reply To All"` (`metoo`) settings are checked, your email address is only included in the `To` and `Cc` fields of the `Reply to All` item in the form *yourusername@host.*

CHAPTER

4

Using the Text Editor,
Shell Tool,
and Command Tool

THE DeskSet's Text Editor is an easy-to-use ASCII text editor that provides a friendly alternative to the SunOS vi editor. The Shell Tool and Command Tool let you easily access the SunOS command line without leaving the OpenWindows environment. Both tools are terminal emulators that allow you to work with the vast constellation of SunOS commands, which are explained in Part II, "Working from the SunOS Command Line." Because the DeskSet's Text Editor, Shell Tool, and Command Tool use similar commands, they are covered together in this chapter. In addition, this chapter also explains the DeskSet's `Console` window and the popular `xterm` window.

The Text Editor

The Text Editor simplifies creating and editing text files. It provides a friendly environment for working with text files. You can use the Text Editor to create text files as you would a word processor, or you can create programs to perform SunOS tasks. Once you create a text file using the Text Editor, you can easily cut and paste text directly between it and any other text pane in the DeskSet, such as the `Compose Message` window of the Mail Tool.

The Text Editor Window

The `Text Editor` window (Figure 4.1) has a control area that contains menu buttons and a text pane where you compose and edit text. The header of the `Text Editor` window always displays the path and the name of the file you are editing or the word `NONE` if you have not yet named your file. When you have made editing changes or have not yet saved a file, the word `edited` is displayed in parentheses following the file name. If you close the `Text Editor` window to an icon and you have created a new file but have not saved it, the icon displays the words `NO FILE`.

The rectangle located in the upper-right corner of the control area of the `Text Editor` window is the drag-and-drop target. You can drag text files directly from the File Manager to the drag-and-drop target to load them into the Text Editor or you can insert text or another text file into the

FIGURE 4.1

The Text Editor window and the Text Pane pop-up menu

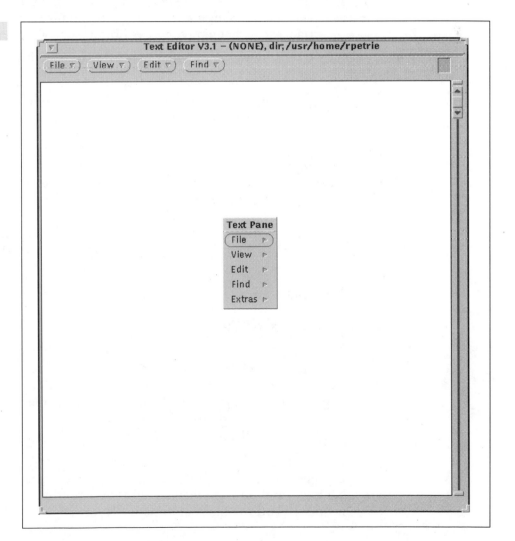

currently opened file by dragging and dropping a file in the Text Editor's text pane.

The control area of the `Text Editor` window has four menu buttons: `File`, `View`, `Edit`, and `Find`.

- The `File` menu includes items that allow you to load, save, merge, and clear text files.

- The `View` menu provides items for changing the position of the insert point, changing the portion of the file displayed in the text pane, and changing the Text Editor's line wrap feature.

- The `Edit` menu includes items for copying, moving, deleting, or undeleting text.

- The `Find` menu provides you with items to locate and replace any text selection in the text pane.

The text pane is the area in which you compose and edit your text. Placing the pointer inside the text pane and pressing the right mouse button displays the Text Editor's `Text Pane` pop-up menu. The `Text Pane` pop-up menu includes the same items as the menu buttons displayed in the Text Editor's control area, as well as an `Extras` submenu. The `Extras` submenu provides additional editing items, as explained later in this chapter. Figure 4.1 shows the `Text Editor` window and the `Text Pane` pop-up menu.

Starting the Text Editor and Loading Files

To start the Text Editor, press the right mouse button with the pointer anywhere in the Workspace to display the `Workspace` menu. Choose the `Text Editor` item from the `Programs` submenu. The `Text Editor` window appears on the Workspace. Move the pointer inside the text pane and click the left mouse button to activate the window. The insertion point appears as a black triangle, indicating the Text Editor is ready for you to enter text.

If you want to open the `Text Editor` window and load an existing file at the same time, move the pointer on the document file's icon in the File Manager and double-click the left mouse button. A `Text Editor` window is opened and the file is automatically loaded.

Loading Files Using the Drag-and-Drop Method

You can "drop" document file icons onto the `Text Editor` window's drag-and-drop target to *load* files into the Text Editor. Dragging and dropping a document file icon on the Workspace loads the document in the `Text Editor` window. You can also drop document file icons directly into the Text Editor pane to *insert* the file into an existing text file in the `Text Editor` window. Where you drop a document file determines how the `Text Editor` loads the file. If you want to open an existing file in the `Text Editor` window, drag the file icon to the drag-and-drop target (the rectangle located at the upper-right corner of the control area), and release the mouse button. If you want to insert the selected file into a file already loaded in the `Text Editor` window, drop the selected document file icon where you want the new text inserted.

Loading a File Using the File Menu

Another way to load a file into an open `Text Editor` window is to use the `Load File` item in the `File Menu` to display the `Load` pop-up window (Figure 4.2). To load a file using the `File` menu's `Load File` item, in the `Directory` text field, type the complete directory path and press Return. Type the name of the file you want to load in the `File` text field. Click the left mouse button on the `Load File` button. The file is loaded in the `Text Editor` window.

FIGURE 4.2

The Load pop-up window

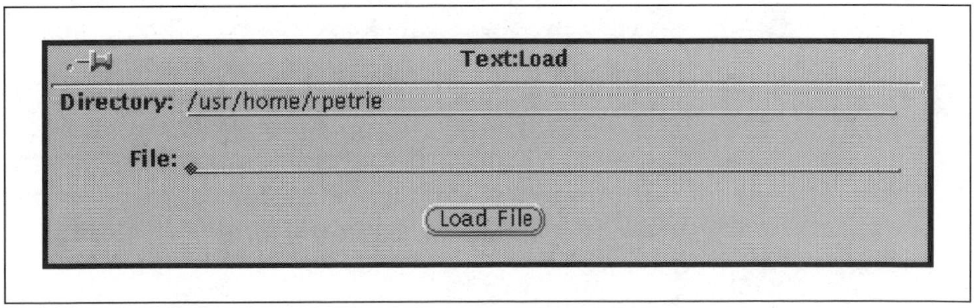

Text:Load
Directory: /usr/home/rpetrie
File:
(Load File)

Saving a New or Existing Text File

If NONE is shown as the file name, click the left mouse button on the File menu button. This is the same as choosing the File menu's Store as New File item to display a Store pop-up window (Figure 4.3), so you can store the new file. To save the file, in the Directory text field, type the directory path and press Return. If you do not specify a directory, the Text Editor uses the current directory. In the File text field, type the name that you want for the file. Click the left mouse button on the Store as New File button to save the contents of the Text Editor pane.

Once you have named your file, the Text Editor icon shows the first ten characters of the file name. When the file has been edited and you have not saved changes, the file name is preceded by a > symbol. Figure 4.4 shows an example of a named and edited file Text Editor icon.

The Save Current File item in the File menu saves changes to a named and edited file. Use the Save Current File item to save the contents of the Text Editor pane that has previously been saved. Remember that the name of the file is always displayed in the Text Editor's window header followed by the directory path name.

FIGURE 4.3

The Store pop-up window

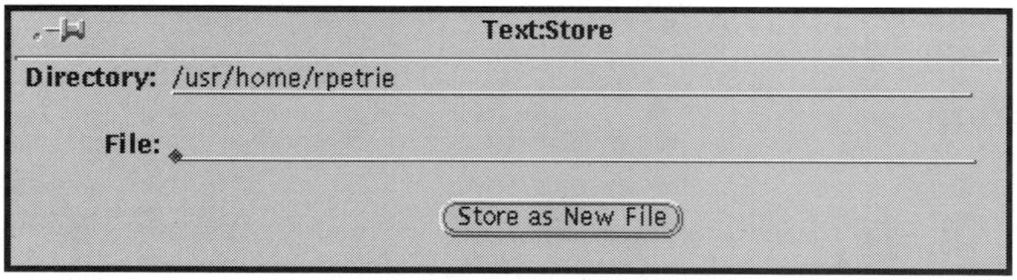

Text:Store
Directory: /usr/home/rpetrie
File:
(Store as New File)

FIGURE 4.4

Text Editor icon of an edited, named, but not saved, file

>sunspot

Entering and Selecting Text

Entering text is as easy as pointing to the location in the text pane where you want to add text, clicking the left mouse button then typing your text. By default, the Text Editor wraps at the word closest to window border.

You can easily select text in the Text Editor, so you can perform a variety of editing tasks such as copying or deleting. Selected text is highlighted in reverse video (white on black). If you type a character, the highlighted text is deleted and replaced with the typed character. The following list explains different methods of selecting text in a text pane.

SELECTION	OPERATION
Word	Double-click the left mouse button on the word you want to select.
Line	Click the left mouse button three times on the line you want to select.
Block of text	Click the left mouse button to set the insert point at the beginning of your text selection, move the pointer to the end of the selection, then click the middle mouse button.
Entire document	Click the left mouse button four times anywhere in the document.

You can also make a selection smaller by moving the pointer into the highlighted text where you want to end the selection and clicking the middle mouse button. Reducing a selection may not always work exactly as you expect because the adjustment depends on the method of the original selection and the starting position of the insert point.

Controlling the Position of the Insert Point

You can move the insert point anywhere in a text file by using the scrollbar to navigate to any location in the file then clicking the left mouse button.

You can also use the View menu, which provides three items for controlling the position of the insert point in a text file, or you can use the navigation keys on the numeric keypad on your keyboard.

The following describes the three items in the View menu used for controlling the position of the insert point.

ITEM	RESULT
Select Line at Number	Moves the cursor to the line number you specify. You can move the insertion point to any line in your text file by choosing the Select Line at Number item to display the Line Number pop-up window, as shown in Figure 4.5. Type the number of the line that you want selected, and click the left mouse button on the Select Line at Number button. The text on the specified line is selected, and the insertion point is moved to the beginning of the next line.
What Line Number?	Displays the line number of the selected text. The What Line Number? item allows you to locate the line number where the selected text begins. The line number is displayed in a Notice. When there is no current selection in the Text Editor window, the notice box displays an error message instead of a line number.
Show Caret at Top	Moves the insert pointer to the third line from the top of the *next* pane of text.

You can also use the keyboard to move the insert point to different positions in your text file. The following describes how to use keys to move
the insert point.

FIGURE 4.5

The Line Number
pop-up window

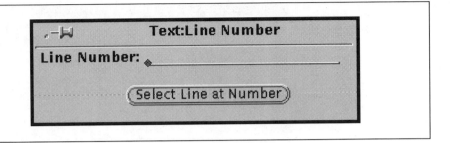

KEY	MOVES THE INSERT POINT
← or Control-B	One character to the left
→ or Control-F	One character to the right
Control-, (comma)	One word to the left
Control-. (period)	To the end of a word
Control-A	To the start of a line
Control-E	To the end of the line
↑ or Control-P	Up one line
↓ or Control-N	Down one line
Home or Shift-Control-Return	To beginning of text
End or Control-Return	To end of text

Copying, Moving, and Deleting Text

The **Edit** menu and the text pane's **Edit** submenu provide you with standard editing functions to copy, move, and delete text. Figure 4.6 shows the **Edit** menu and the text pane's **Edit** submenu. You can also perform any edit operations using the accelerator keys on the left side of most Sun keyboards. These keys are used in conjunction with the clipboard. The *clipboard* is a storage place in memory for selected text to be copied, moved, or deleted.

WARNING

Only one selection can be stored on the clipboard at a
time. If something is already on the clipboard and you
perform a copy or cut operation, the contents of the
clipboard are overwritten with the new information.

FIGURE 4.6

The Edit menu and the
Edit submenu of the
Text Pane pop-up
menu

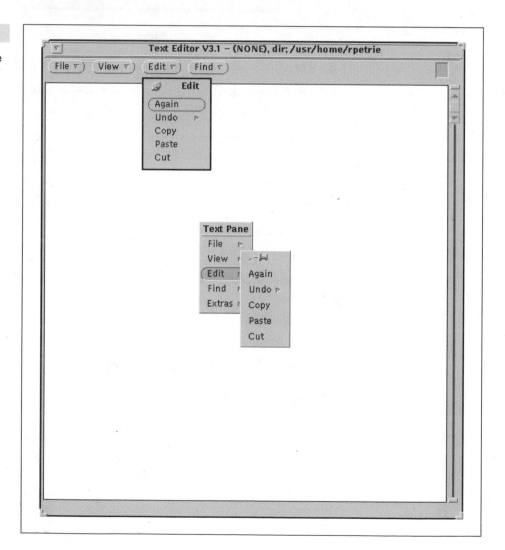

Copying a Text Selection

Select the text you want to copy. After you select the text, press the right mouse button on the **Edit** menu button and choose **Copy**. A copy of the selected text is stored on the clipboard. If you select the **Copy** item without first selecting text, a Notice will appear indicating that you must make a text selection. Once a text selection is copied, move the insertion point to where you want the copied text and choose **Paste** from the **Edit** menu.

The **Text Pane** pop-up menu and accelerator keys (on the left side of most Sun keyboards) allow you to perform the same copy operations. The **Text Pane**'s pop-up **Edit** submenu includes **Copy** and **Paste** items, which work in the same way as the **Edit** menu's **Copy** and **Paste** items. The Copy accelerator key on a Sun keyboard is identical to choosing the **Copy** item from an **Edit** menu. You can also copy text by pressing Diamond-c. If you are using another type of Sun keyboard, the Copy key is labeled L6 and the Paste key is labeled L8.

Copying Text Using the Drag-and-Drop Method

You can use the drag-and-drop method to copy selected text within the same file or to any location in the DeskSet environment that accepts ASCII text. The following explains the drag-and-drop method of copying text.

1. Select the text to be copied.

2. With the pointer on the selected text, press the Control key then press and hold down the left mouse button. Once you press the left mouse button, release the Control key. A Text Duplicate pointer appears, as shown in Figure 4.7. The first several characters of the selected text are displayed inside the rectangle.

3. Drag the pointer to the location where you want to copy the text (either within the Text Editor pane or anywhere on the DeskSet that accepts ASCII text), then release the left mouse button.

FIGURE 4.7

The Text Duplicate
Pointer

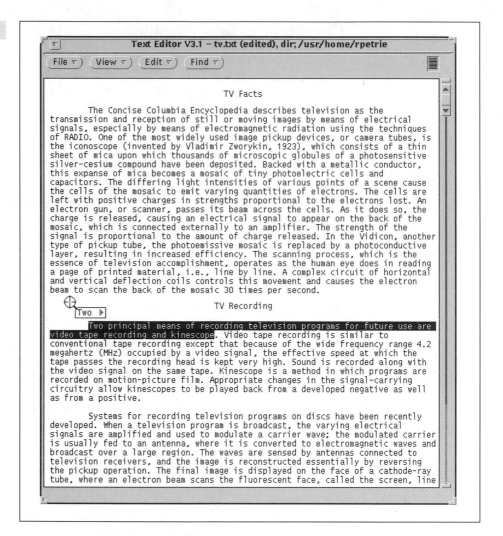

Deleting or Moving a Text Selection

There is no Delete item in the **Edit** menu or the text pane's **Edit** submenu; instead you use **Cut** to delete text. To delete text, simply select it then choose the **Cut** item from either the **Edit** menu or the text pane's **Edit** submenu. You can also use keys on your keyboard to perform a variety of text deletions. The following describes the keys and the text they delete.

KEY	DELETES
Backspace	Character to the left of the insert point.
Control-w	Word to the left of the insert point.
Shift-Control-w	Word to the right of the insert point.
Control-u	To the beginning of the line.
Shift-Control-u	To the end of the line.

The process of moving a selection is similar to the copying process, only instead of using the Copy item, you choose the Cut item from the Edit menu. The Cut item removes the selected text and stores it on the clipboard. Once text is stored on the clipboard, you can select the Paste item to move the text from the clipboard to its new location.

The Text Pane pop-up menu and the accelerator keys (on the left side of your keyboard) allow you to perform the same move operation. The Text Pane's pop-up Edit menu also provides Cut and Paste items, which work identically to the Cut and Paste items in the control area's Edit menu. The Cut and Paste accelerator keys on a Sun workstation keyboard are identical to choosing the Cut and Paste items from an Edit menu. You can also paste text by pressing Diamond-V. On some Sun keyboards, the Cut key is labeled L10 and the Paste key is labeled L8.

Repeating or Undoing Edits

You can repeat the last editing action that changed your text by selecting the Again item from either the Edit menu or the Text Pane pop-up menu. To choose the Again item from the Edit menu, click the left mouse button on the Edit menu button. You can also press the Again (L2) key to repeat the previous operation.

If you make a mistake and want to undo either the last editing action or all editing actions since you last saved your file, use either the Edit menu or the Text Pane pop-up menu by pressing the right mouse button and choosing the Undo item. You can undo the last editing action or all editing actions by choosing the Undo Last Edit or Undo All Edits items from the Undo submenu (Figure 4.8). If you are using a Sun keyboard, you can also press the Undo (L4) key to undo a previous operation.

FIGURE 4.8

The Undo submenu of
the Edit menu

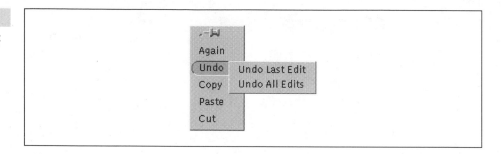

Clearing the Text Pane

If you want to clear the text pane of a window, use the `File` menu's `Empty Document` item. This clears the contents of the current text pane. If you have made editing changes and have not saved them, a Notice is displayed, asking you to confirm or cancel the operation. The Notice says `The text has been edited. Clear Log will discard these edits. Please confirm.` Click the left mouse button on the `Confirm, discard edits` button.

Splitting the Text Editor Pane

The Text Editor pane can be split into two or more panes so that you can view and edit different parts of a text file at the same time. The file itself is not split, so any editing changes you make in one view are reflected in the other views as well.

To split the Text Editor pane, drag the top or bottom cable anchor of the vertical scrollbar to the position where you want to split the Text Editor pane. To remove the split pane, return the cable anchor back to the top or bottom cable anchor where you originally dragged it from, and release the left mouse button. You can also split the Text Editor pane by dragging the vertical scrollbar's drag box down to where you want to split the pane, pressing the right mouse button on the drag box, and choosing the `Split View` item. To remove a split pane, choose the `Join Views` item from the `Scrollbar` pop-up menu.

Merging Files

The `File` menu's `Include File` item displays the `Include` pop-up window (Figure 4.9). The `Include` pop-up window allows you to merge two or more text files. To merge a file with the file in the text pane, type the directory in the `Directory` text field and the name of the file that you want to include in the `File` text field, then click the left mouse button on the `Include File` button. The file is inserted at the insert point in the text pane.

FIGURE 4.9

The Include pop-up window

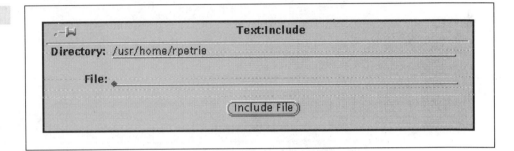

```
┌─╥                           Text:Include                              │
│  Directory: /usr/home/rpetrie                                         │
│                                                                       │
│       File: ◆                                                         │
│                      ( Include File )                                 │
```

You can also drag and drop a text file from anywhere on the Workspace to merge it with a file in the Text Editor. Drag the file icon to the spot in the text pane where you want the text inserted and release the mouse button.

Changing the Line Wrap Mode

The `View` menu's `Change Line Wrap` item provides you with a submenu listing three choices for line wrapping: `Wrap at Word`, `Wrap at Character`, and `Clip Lines`. The most commonly used wrapping method is to wrap at the end of words. If you choose `Clip lines`, the beginning of each line that ends with a Return is displayed. If you choose the `Wrap at Character` item, lines wrap at the closest character before the window's border.

Finding and Replacing Text in the Text Editor

The **Find** menu allows you to search for specific text strings, special characters, and delimiters. Using the **Find** menu's **Find and Replace** item, you can either search for text or search for *and* replace text. If the text string you want to search for is displayed in the Text Editor pane, you can select it before activating the **Find and Replace** item. The selected string is automatically displayed as the string you want to search for. To activate the **Find and Replace** item, click the left mouse button on the **Find** button. The Text Editor displays the **Find and Replace** pop-up window, as shown in Figure 4.10.

FIGURE 4.10

The Find and Replace pop-up window

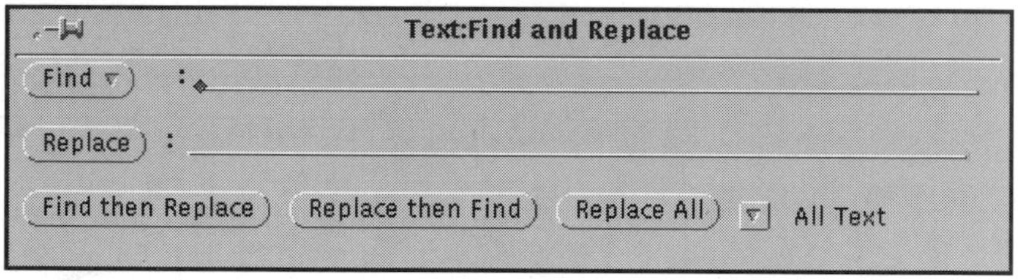

If you selected text before choosing the **Find and Replace** item, that text is displayed in the **Find** text field; otherwise, enter the text you want to search for.

If you only want to search ahead in the file for text, but not replace the text, leave the **Replace** field blank and click the left mouse button on the **Find** button. If you want to search backwards, press the right mouse button on the **Find** button and choose the **Backward** item.

To search and replace text, enter the text string you want to search for in the **Find** text field and the replacement string in the **Replace** text field. Click the left mouse button on the **Replace** button to search and replace the specified text. You can delete the text in the **Find** text field by leaving the **Replace** text field blank.

The buttons at the bottom of the `Find and Replace` pop-up window combine these find and replace operations: `Find then Replace`, `Replace then Find`, `Replace All`, and `All Text`. The following explains each of the `Find and Replace` pop-up window buttons:

ITEM	RESULT
Find then Replace	Searches for the next occurrence of the text string entered in the `Find` text field of the `Find and Replace` pop-up window, and replaces the matching text with the text entered in the `Replace` text field of the `Find and Replace` pop-up window.
Replace then Find	Replaces currently selected text (even if the text is different than the text in the `Find` text field) with the text in the `Replace` text field then searches for the next occurrence of the text in the `Find` text field.
Replace All	Replaces every occurrence of the text in the `Find` text field with the text in the `Replace` text field.
All Text	Specifies whether you want the find and replace operations to apply to the entire document or remain restricted to only the text between the insert point and the end of the document.

Searching for Selected Text

You can also search the file for another occurrence of a selected text string by using the `Find Selection` item in the `Find` menu in the Text Editor's control area. This item only *finds* selected text; it does not replace it. To find a text selection, select the text you want to search for, press the right mouse button on the `Find` button, then choose the `Find Selection` item. If you want to search forwards, release the mouse button. If you want to search backwards, choose the `Backward` item from the `Find Selection` submenu. The first match of the selected text in the file is then high-lighted. On Sun workstation keyboards you can use the keyboard to find selected text. Press Find (L9) to locate selected text to the right of the insert point. Press Shift-Find (L9) to locate selected text to the left of the insert point.

Searching for Delimiters

A *delimiter* is any character or combination of characters used to separate one item or set of data from another. For example, many databases use commas to delimit one field from another. You might think of a period as a type of delimiter used to separate sentences. The `Find Marked Text` item in the `Find` menu allows you to search for and highlight text between a matched set of delimiters. You can also insert or remove a matched set of delimiters. Eight types of delimiters are provided as items in the `Find Marked Text` pop-up window, as shown in Figure 4.11.

FIGURE 4.11

The Find Marked Text
pop-up window

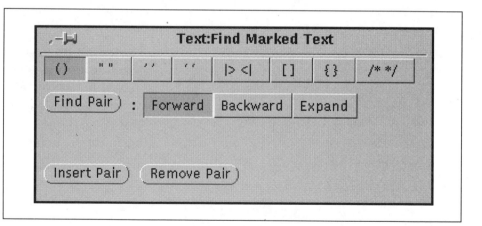

The `Forward`, `Backward`, and `Expand` buttons in the `Find Marked Text` pop-up window allow you to search for text between two or more sets of matched delimiters, such as two sets of matched parentheses (( )). When matched sets of delimiters are placed within another set of delimiters, they are referred to as *nested delimiters*. To select text within a set of nested delimiters, make sure the insert point precedes the delimiters you want to locate and do the following:

1. Choose `Find Marked Text` from the Text Editor's `Find` menu button. The `Find Marked Text` pop-up window is displayed.

2. Click the left mouse button on the type of nested delimiters that surround the text you want to locate.

3. Click the left mouse button on the `Forward` button.

4. Click the left mouse button on the `Find Pair` button.

Figure 4.12 shows the results of using the `Forward` setting and `Find Pair` button to select text and delimiters. Figure 4.13 shows the result of clicking the `Find Pair` button (using the `Forward` setting) three times to select text within two nested sets of matching delimiters. Figure 4.14 shows the result of changing to the `Expand` setting and clicking the left mouse button on the `Find Pair` button.

Inserting and Removing Delimiters

To surround selected text with delimiters, first select the text that you want to delimit then select a delimiter pair setting in the `Find Marked Text` pop-up window. Click the left mouse button on the `Insert Pair` button. The matching delimiters will surround your selection.

To remove the delimiters, click the left mouse button on the `Remove Pair` button. Be sure that your selection includes the delimiters specified in the delimiter settings. Otherwise, a notice box will appear telling you that the operation is aborted because the selection does not include the indicated pair.

Finding and Replacing Fields

The characters |> and <| act as text field delimiters, which indicate fields in a SunOS file. You can search forward through text from the insert point to find the text of each field and select the text using the `Replace |>field<|` item. Displaying the `Replace |>field<|` submenu provides you with three items explained below.

FIGURE 4.12

Using the Forward
setting and the Find
Pair button to select
text and delimiters

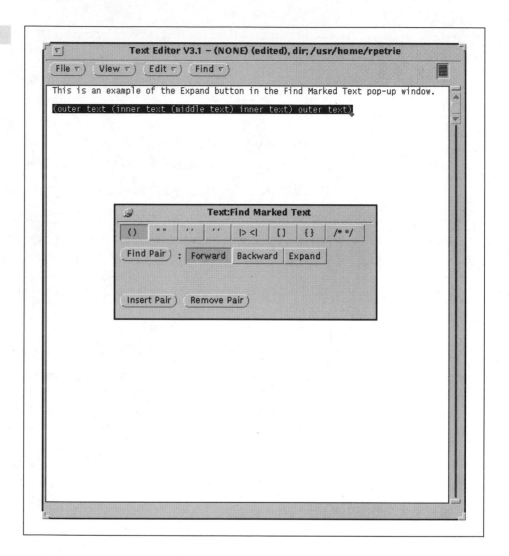

FIGURE 4.13

Using the Forward setting and clicking the Find Pair button three times to select text within two nested sets of matching delimiters

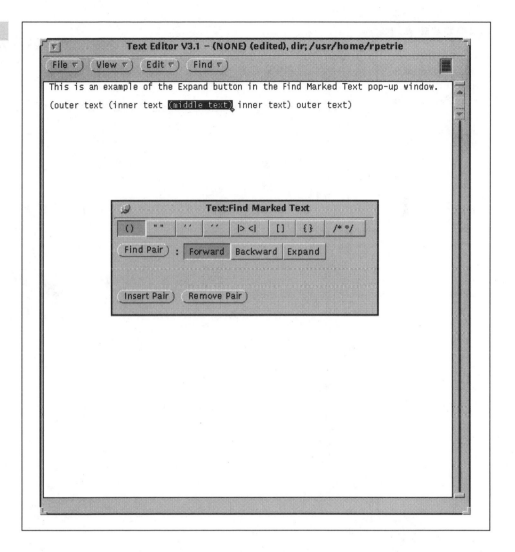

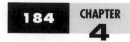
FIGURE 4.14

Using the Expand
setting and clicking
the left mouse button
on the Find Pair button

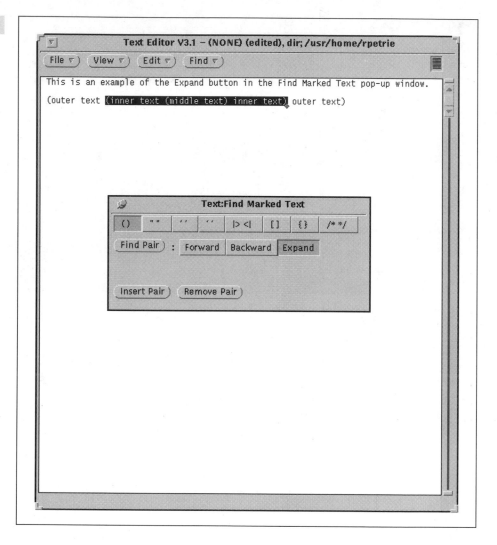

ITEM	RESULT
Expand	Searches in both directions and selects the entire field and its delimiters.
Next	Searches forward from the insert point and selects the next field.
Previous	Searches backward from the insert point and selects the previous field.

The Text Pane's Extras Pop-up Submenu

The text pane's `Extras` pop-up submenu (Figure 4.15) provides you with six items that allow you to format, indent, change the case of text, sort specified fields, insert brackets, or replace slashes. The following describes each of the items in the `Extras` submenu.

ITEMS	RESULTS
Format	Divides text into lines of not more than 72 characters. The **Format** item fills and joins lines, but it does not split words between lines.

FIGURE 4.15

The Text Pane pop-up menu's Extras submenu

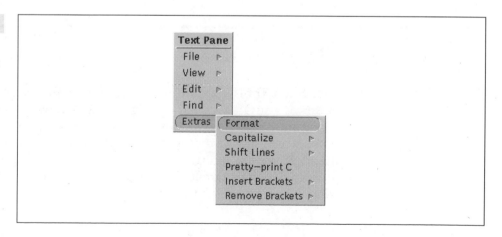

ITEMS	RESULTS
Capitalize	Changes the case of selected text from lowercase to uppercase (abcd ABCD), uppercase to lowercase (ABCD abcd), or capitalizes the first letter of every word in selected text (abcd -> Abcd).
Shift Lines	Inserts or removes a tab character at the beginning of each line in a selection. Choosing the Right item moves the selected lines to the right one tab stop. Selecting the Left item moves the selected lines one tab stop to the left.
Pretty-print C	Formats the selection to standard C program listing specifications.
Insert Brackets	Inserts matched parentheses, brackets, curly brackets, or quotation marks (( ), [ ], { }, or " ").
Remove Brackets	Removes matched parentheses, brackets, curly brackets, or quotation marks (( ), [ ], { }, or " ").

The Shell Tool

The Shell Tool is a command interpreter that accepts, interprets, and executes SunOS commands. Figure 4.16 shows the Shell Tool window. The pane of the Shell Tool window is referred to as a *terminal emulator* pane, which means that working in it is the same as working from a command prompt at a terminal. The text insertion point of the Shell Tool is indicated by a rectangle that appears as an outline when inactive and as a solid black block when active. To activate the insert point, move the pointer inside the `Shell Tool` window. If the insert point does not change to a solid block, click the left mouse button. After typing a SunOS command and pressing Return, the command is executed. For example, type the `ls` command and press Return while in the `Shell Tool` window to list the files in the current directory.

The Shell Tool's Term Pane Pop-up Menu

Pressing the right mouse button with the pointer in the text pane of the Shell Tool displays the Shell Tool's `Term Pane` pop-up menu (Figure 4.17).

FIGURE 4.16

The Shell Tool window

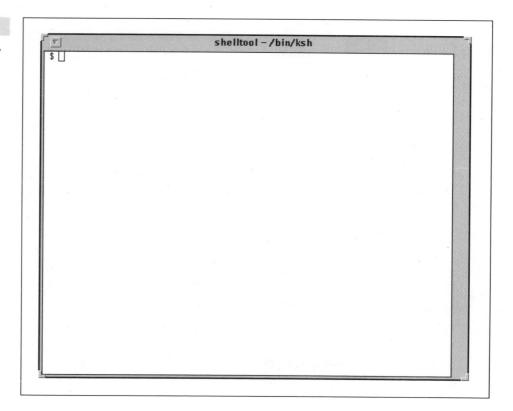

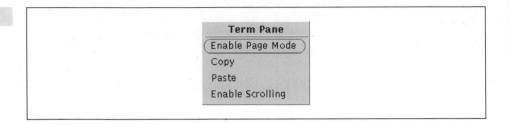

The four items in the `Term Pane` pop-up menu, include:

- `Enable Page Mode`, which displays text one pane of text at a time.
- `Copy`, which copies selected text from the Shell Tool window to the clipboard.
- `Paste`, which inserts the contents of the clipboard into a Shell Tool window.
- `Enable scrolling`, which turns the Shell Tool into a Command Tool.

Each of these items is described in the following sections.

Viewing Text in the Shell Tool

The `Enable Page Mode` item of the Shell Tool's `Term Pane` pop-up menu controls the scrolling of the screen so that you see only one paneful of text at a time. For example, if you have a directory listing that is longer than one pane, and you enter the `ls` command while `Enable Page Mode` is activated, the first paneful is displayed, and the pointer turns to a stop sign, as shown in Figure 4.18, indicating that the pane has stopped scrolling. To resume scrolling the contents of the Shell Tool, press the Space bar.

The `Enable Page Mode` item is replaced with the `Disable Page Mode` item when activated. If the `Disable Page Mode` item is activated, text scrolls without stopping until it reaches the end of the text to be displayed.

FIGURE 4.18

A partially scrolled
Shell Tool pane

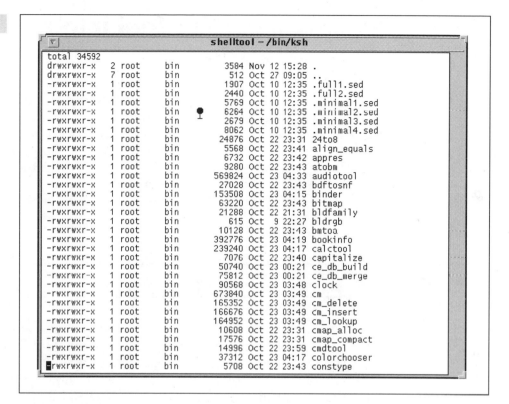

```
shelltool - /bin/ksh
total 34592
drwxrwxr-x   2 root      bin        3584 Nov 12 15:28 .
drwxrwxr-x   7 root      bin         512 Oct 27 09:05 ..
-rwxrwxr-x   1 root      bin        1907 Oct 10 12:35 .full1.sed
-rwxrwxr-x   1 root      bin        2440 Oct 10 12:35 .full2.sed
-rwxrwxr-x   1 root      bin        5769 Oct 10 12:35 .minimal1.sed
-rwxrwxr-x   1 root      bin        6264 Oct 10 12:35 .minimal2.sed
-rwxrwxr-x   1 root      bin        2679 Oct 10 12:35 .minimal3.sed
-rwxrwxr-x   1 root      bin        8062 Oct 10 12:35 .minimal4.sed
-rwxrwxr-x   1 root      bin       24876 Oct 22 23:31 24to8
-rwxrwxr-x   1 root      bin        5568 Oct 22 23:41 align_equals
-rwxrwxr-x   1 root      bin        6732 Oct 22 23:42 appres
-rwxrwxr-x   1 root      bin        9280 Oct 22 23:43 atobm
-rwxrwxr-x   1 root      bin      569824 Oct 23 04:33 audiotool
-rwxrwxr-x   1 root      bin       27028 Oct 22 23:43 bdftosnf
-rwxrwxr-x   1 root      bin      153508 Oct 23 04:15 binder
-rwxrwxr-x   1 root      bin       63220 Oct 22 23:43 bitmap
-rwxrwxr-x   1 root      bin       21288 Oct 22 21:31 bldfamily
-rwxrwxr-x   1 root      bin         615 Oct  9 22:27 bldrgb
-rwxrwxr-x   1 root      bin       10128 Oct 22 23:43 bmtoa
-rwxrwxr-x   1 root      bin      392776 Oct 23 04:19 bookinfo
-rwxrwxr-x   1 root      bin      239240 Oct 23 04:17 calctool
-rwxrwxr-x   1 root      bin        7076 Oct 22 23:40 capitalize
-rwxrwxr-x   1 root      bin       50740 Oct 23 00:21 ce_db_build
-rwxrwxr-x   1 root      bin       75812 Oct 23 00:21 ce_db_merge
-rwxrwxr-x   1 root      bin       90568 Oct 23 03:48 clock
-rwxrwxr-x   1 root      bin      673840 Oct 23 03:49 cm
-rwxrwxr-x   1 root      bin      165352 Oct 23 03:49 cm_delete
-rwxrwxr-x   1 root      bin      166676 Oct 23 03:49 cm_insert
-rwxrwxr-x   1 root      bin      164952 Oct 23 03:49 cm_lookup
-rwxrwxr-x   1 root      bin       10608 Oct 22 23:31 cmap_alloc
-rwxrwxr-x   1 root      bin       17576 Oct 22 23:31 cmap_compact
-rwxrwxr-x   1 root      bin       14996 Oct 22 23:59 cmdtool
-rwxrwxr-x   1 root      bin       37312 Oct 23 04:17 colorchooser
-rwxrwxr-x   1 root      bin        5708 Oct 22 23:43 constype
```

Copying and Pasting Text in the Shell Tool

Before you can copy and paste text, you must select the text you want to copy. You select text by moving the pointer to the beginning of the text you want to copy and clicking the left mouse button. Move to the end of the text and press the middle mouse button. Once you have selected the text, press the right mouse button to display the **Term Pane** pop-up menu then choose the **Copy** item. The selected text is copied onto the clipboard. If you don't select any text before selecting **Copy**, a notice box appears, indicating that you must first make a text selection. Move the insertion point to the location where you want to paste the text. Display the **Term Pane** pop-up menu and choose the **Paste** item.

Turning the Shell Tool into a Command Tool

The `Enable Scrolling` item in the `Term Pane` pop-up menu allows you to turn the Shell Tool into a Command Tool. The Command Tool provides more editing capabilities than the Shell Tool, as explained later in this chapter. When you choose the `Enable Scrolling` item, the tool name at the top of the Shell Tool window remains the same, but the Shell Tool now functions like a Command Tool. The Command Tool's `Term Pane` pop-up menu will appear instead of the Shell Tool's. To return to the Shell Tool, choose the `Disable Scrolling` item from the `Scrolling` submenu.

The Command Tool

The Command Tool is an enhanced Shell Tool with the added features of the standard Text Editor pane. The `Command Tool` icon looks the same as the `Shell Tool` icon. When opened, however, the `Command Tool` window (Figure 4.19) displays a scrollbar elevator and a different pop-up menu than the Shell Tool.

In addition to the same `Edit`, `Find`, and `Extras` items of the standard text editing pop-up menu, the Command Tool's `Term Pane` pop-up menu (Figure 4.20) has three additional items: the `History`, `File Editor`, and `Scrolling` submenus.

Working with the History Log File

The Command Tool automatically keeps track of commands you have typed in the Command Tool window for the current session in what is referred to as a *history log*. You can save this list of commands to a file, so you can choose a command from a list instead of entering it each time.

The Command Tool
window

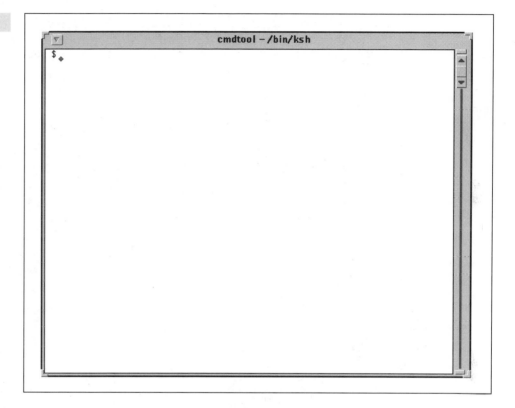

The Command Tool's
Term Pane pop-up
menu

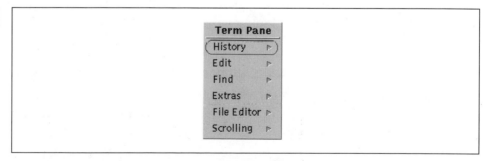

Repeating commands using the history log is explained in Chapter 10, "Improving Your Command Line Productivity." The **Term Pane** menu's **History** submenu provides items for saving and modifying the history log.

The `Mode` item determines whether the history log can be edited within the Command Tool. If you set the `Mode` item to `Read Only`, you cannot edit text in the Command Tool's terminal pane. However, you can still save the log to a file and edit that file using the `File Editor` item in the Command Tool's `Term Pane` pop-up menu. If the `Mode` item is set to `Editable`, you can edit text anywhere in the Command Tool's terminal pane, using the editing items on the `Term Pane` pop-up menu.

The `Store log as new file` item allows you to save the current history log to a file. The `Clear log` item clears the current history log. This resets the Command Tool history log as if you just started the Command Tool application. If the history log file has been edited, a Notice appears indicating that you've made changes and asks you to confirm the discard of your edits. Click the left mouse button on the `Confirm, discard edits` button to complete the discard operation or click on the `Cancel` button to return to the Command Tool without discarding the history log file's contents.

Saving the History Log to a File

The `Store log as new file` item allows you to save the current history log to a file. This history log file can be treated in the same way you would any other text file. You can edit it and save it again or drag and drop it from the File Manager onto a `Text Editor` window. The following steps explain how to save the current history log to a file.

1. In the Command Tool text pane, press the right mouse button to display the `Term Pane` pop-up menu.

2. Choose the `Store log as new file` item from the `History` submenu. The `Store` pop-up window is displayed.

3. In the `Directory` field, type your complete home directory path, then press Return.

4. In the `File` field, type the name under which you want to save the history log file.

5. Click the left mouse button on the `Store as New File` button.

Displaying a Text Editor Pane

The **File Editor** item in the **Term Pane** menu determines whether a Text Editor pane is displayed. To display the Text Editor pane in the **Command Tool** window, press the right mouse button to display the **Term Pane** pop-up menu and choose the **Enable** item from the **File Editor** submenu. The **Command Tool** window is then split into two panes: a Command Tool pane and a text editor pane, as shown in Figure 4.21. This Text Editor pane is the same as the pane that appears in the Text Editor window and includes the **Text Pane** pop-up menu. To remove the Text Editor pane, choose the **Disable** item in the **File Editor** submenu.

FIGURE 4.21

The Command Tool
with the Text Editor

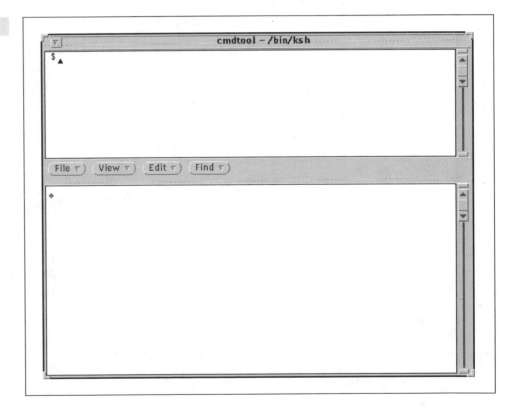

Turning the Command Tool into a Shell Tool

You can disable the editing capabilities of the Command Tool so that it appears and acts like a Shell Tool window by displaying the Command Tool's Term Pane pop-up menu and choosing Disable Scrolling from the Scrolling submenu. This item nearly doubles the performance of a Command Tool; when the scrolling feature is disabled, the window doesn't demand the overhead processing required to store commands. Choosing the Disable Scrolling item from the Scrolling submenu causes the Command Tool's Term Pane pop-up menu to appear the same as that of the Shell Tool window. To return to the original Command Tool Term Pane pop-up menu, choose the Enable Scrolling item.

The Console Window

A Console window is opened automatically whenever you start Open-Windows. The Console window is a special Command Tool that displays error and system messages for Solaris and some applications. If you accidentally quit a Console window, you can choose the Console item from the Workspace menu's Utilities submenu to open a new Console window.

It is not recommended that more than one Console window be open at a time since it is easy to miss important messages if you do not pay attention to which Console window is active. If no Console window is open, messages are displayed in large type at the bottom of the screen.

The xterm Window

One of the many layers of Solaris is the X Window System. The xterm window is not a part of the DeskSet, but a popular X window terminal emulator that comes with the X Window System and is included with Solaris. The `xterm` window is more versatile for copying and pasting text than the Shell Tool or Command Tool. It also lets you change font sizes, and display the window in reverse video using menus. The `xterm` program is usually stored in the `/usr/openwin/bin` directory.

To open an `xterm` window from the Shell Tool or Command Tool, enter

```
xterm -sb &
```

The `-sb` specifies opening the `xterm` window with a scrollbar. The `&` starts the program in the background, freeing up your Shell or Command Tool for additional commands. Figure 4.22 shows an example of an `xterm` window.

The xterm Window Menus

There are three menus available for working with the `xterm` window. All these menus are accessed by pressing the Control key on your keyboard

FIGURE 4.22

An xterm window

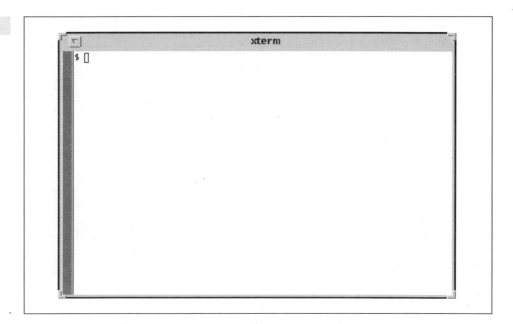

and pressing a mouse button. The following lists the key combinations used to display each of the three xterm menus:

KEY COMBINATION	DISPLAYS
Control and the left mouse button	Main Options menu.
Control and the middle mouse button	VT (video terminal) Options menu.
Control and the right mouse button	VT Fonts menu.

Figure 4.23 shows each of these menus. The following sections explain the most common operations and menu items for working in the xterm window.

FIGURE 4.23

The xterm Window menus

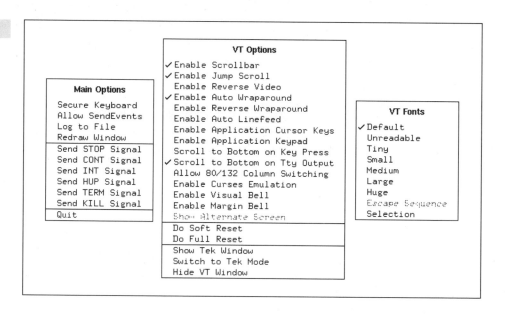

Scrolling the xterm Window

The highlighted area in the scrollbar is known as the *thumb*. The thumb reflects the amount of text stored in memory. By default, the last 64 lines are stored in memory. As more text is entered, the size of the thumb decreases. To scroll the text in an `xterm` window, move the pointer to the scrollbar. The pointer changes to a doubleheaded arrow. The extent of text scrolled depends on the position of the cursor in the scrollbar. The following explains how to use the mouse to scroll through text in an `xterm` window.

MOUSE BUTTON	ACTION
Middle	Scrolls text in direction of the cursor. To continue scrolling in a particular direction, keep the middle button pressed.
Left	Scrolls down the window.
Right	Scrolls up the window.

Selecting, Copying, and Pasting Text

The `xterm` window allows you to select and copy text within the same or other windows. The method of selecting text is similar to selecting text in a Shell or Command Tool. The last text selected replaces the previous text selection. The following lists ways to select text in the `xterm` window.

MOUSE ACTION	RESULT
Double-click	Selects the current word.
Triple-click	Selects the current line.
Drag the pointer to the end of the text	Selects a section of text.

To change the amount of text selected, move the pointer to the location where you want the text selection to end. Click the right mouse button. You can also press the right mouse button and drag the pointer to the

location where you want to end the text selection. To copy a selection of
text, simply select the text you want to copy, move the pointer to the xterm
window in which you want to paste the text, and press the middle mouse
button.

Logging an xterm Session

Just as you can log your commands in a history log using the Command
Tool, you can create a log file for xterm window commands. To send your
commands to a log file, press the Control key and the left mouse button
and highlight the Log to file item in the Main Options menu. A check
mark appears next to the Log to file item. All the xterm window output
is now sent to a file named XtermLog.*pid*. The *pid* indicates the xterm
program's Process ID number. The file is usually created in the directory
that the xterm program was started from. You can enable logging to the
default log file from the command line by adding -l to the xterm command.
To designate a file to store your terminal log, start the xterm program with
the -lf filename argument, where *filename* is the name of the log file. The
following example starts an xterm window with a scrollbar, enables logging, and writes to the file named xtermlog:

```
xterm -sb -l -lf xtermlog
```

Displaying the xterm
Window in Reverse Video

Displaying a window in reverse video (white on black) causes less eye strain.
The VT menu lets you display the xterm window in reverse video. To
change the current X window to display in reverse video, press Control and
the middle mouse button and drag the highlight to the Enable Reverse Video
item. To return to the previous display choose the Enable Reverse
Video item again.

Changing the Size of Fonts in the xterm Window

Pressing the Control key and the right mouse button displays a menu listing fonts that you can change for the current xterm window. You can choose from one of the following font sizes:

Default

Unreadable

Tiny (5x8)

Small (6x10)

Medium (8x13)

Large (9x15)

Huge (10x20)

N O T E

For more information on customizing the xterm window, such as changing to a specific font size and changing xterm window colors, see Chapter 15, "Customizing Solaris."

CHAPTER

5

Get Organized with the Calendar Manager

THE Calendar Manager is a handy appointment scheduler and reminder application that allows you to organize and plan your time on a daily, weekly, monthly, or yearly basis. It lets you easily schedule appointments then automatically reminds you of the upcoming appointments. The Calendar Manager also lets you enter and manage tasks using a ToDo list. Using the Calendar Manager, you can also enter appointments in a group of users' calendars and automatically notify the group of users via email. This chapter teaches you how to harness the powerful time-management features of the Calendar Manager.

Starting the Calendar Manager

To start the Calendar Manager, choose `Calendar Manager` from the `Workspace` menu's `Programs` submenu. The Calendar Manager icon appears on the Workspace, which displays the current month and date (Figure 5.1). To open the Calendar Manager icon to a window, double-click the left mouse button on the Calendar Manager icon. The `Calendar Manager` window appears, as shown in Figure 5.1.

The Calendar
Manager icon and the
Calendar Manager
window

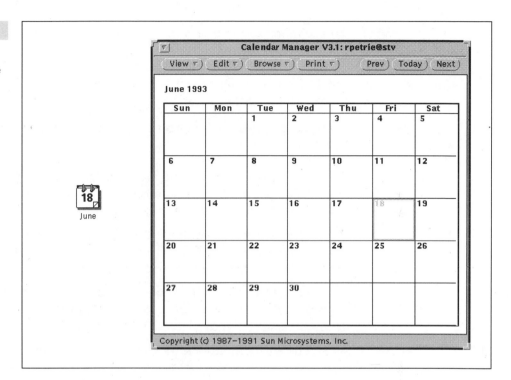

The Calendar Manager Window

The `Calendar Manager` window's default display shows the current month. The current day has a double border, or if you are using a color system, the border is the color of the window. The default display can be changed to show day, week, or year calendars. Any appointment entries for dates in the month view are displayed, although the information is usually clipped to accommodate the size of the date box. Each line in a date box is used for separate appointment text. The `Calendar Manager` window can be enlarged to view more text in a date box, or you can quickly display the day view to see your appointment information in more detail, as explained later in this chapter.

To see more appointment information in the month view, use one of the resize corners to stretch the window vertically or horizontally. You can also choose **Full Size** from the **Window** menu to expand the calendar view to the full size of your screen's height then use one of the resize corners to stretch the window horizontally.

The control area of the **Calendar Manager** window includes four menu buttons:

- The **View** menu lets you view a calendar, appointment list, or ToDo list by day, week, month, or year. It also provides a feature to search for specific appointments or ToDo list items.

- The **Edit** menu contains commands for entering and editing appointments or ToDo list items, specifying a different time zone, and customizing the Calendar Manager.

- The **Browse** menu contains commands to display single or multiple calendars, schedule group appointments, and add other users' calendars to your Calendar Manager.

- The **Print** menu allows you to print calendar views, appointment lists, and ToDo lists for any day, week, month, or year.

In the upper-right corner of the control area are three navigational buttons that allow you to quickly browse through the preceding or following time unit of the calendar view currently displayed. For example, with the **Month** view displayed, clicking the left mouse button on the **Prev** button displays the previous month's calendar. Clicking the left mouse button on the **Next** button displays the next month's calendar. Clicking the left mouse button on the **Today** button returns you to the current month with the current day selected.

The Four Views of the Calendar Manager

Four different calendar views, Day, Week, Month, and Year, are available in the Calendar Manager. The Day view (Figure 5.2) is useful for viewing in detail any appointment or ToDo list information scheduled for a particular day. The Week view (Figure 5.3) displays a weekly calendar based

FIGURE 5.2

The Day calendar view

on either the default current week or the week that includes the date you selected. The Week view displays an hourly box schedule with appointment times shaded. The Month view displays appointments from a monthly perspective. The Year view (Figure 5.4) displays a yearly calendar for any year from 1970 through 1999. The Year view does not display any appointment information.

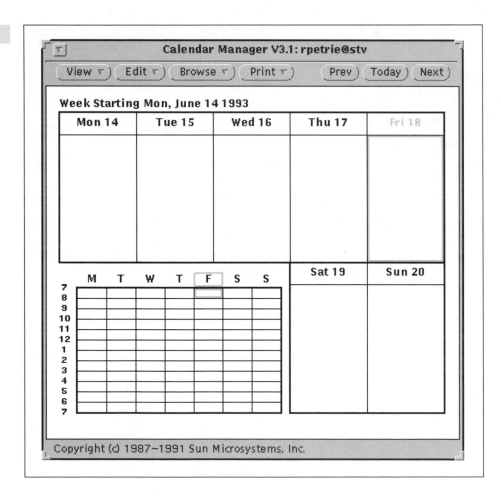

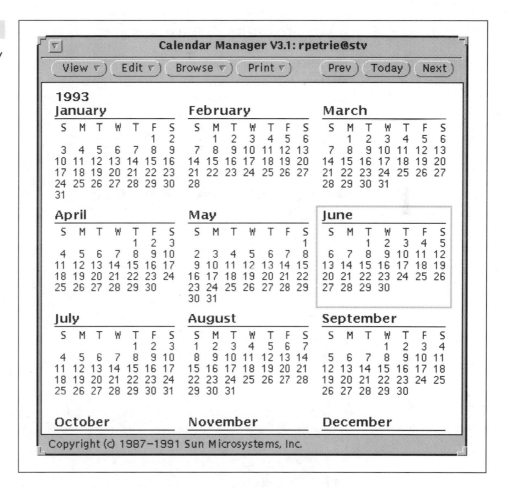

The Appointment List and ToDo List Views

In addition to displaying your schedule for a day, week, month, or year, you can also display pop-up windows of all your appointments and ToDo list items for a particular day, week, month, or year. Appointments are entered into any calendar view by using the CM Appointment Editor pop-up window. Appointments entered into any of the calendar views are also displayed in the other calendar views. Working with the CM Appointment Editor pop-up window is explained later in this chapter. Figure 5.5 shows a day calendar view displayed along with the appointment and ToDo lists for that day. An appointment list displays all the appointments for a particular time period, while a ToDo list displays all the ToDo items for a particular time period. To help you keep track of tasks that need to be accomplished, the ToDo list includes check boxes in which you can check off an item by clicking the left mouse button on the check box. To erase a check mark, click the left mouse button on the check box containing the check mark.

Navigating the Calendars and Lists

Several methods are available to navigate calendar views and their associated appointment or ToDo list views. To change calendar views with the **View** menu, press the right mouse button on the **View** menu button to display the **View** menu. If you want to display a calendar view, choose the calendar view item you want from the **View** menu. If you want to display a corresponding calendar view's appointment or ToDo list, choose **Appt List** or **ToDo List** from the appropriate calendar view's submenu.

FIGURE 5.5

A day calendar view with appointment and ToDo lists

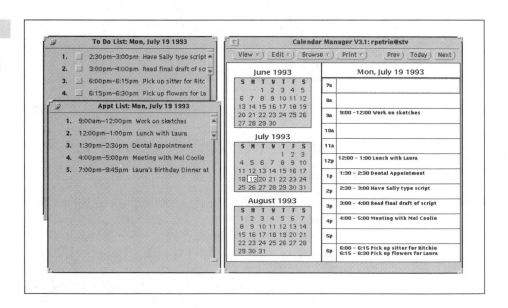

The Calendar Manager provides shortcuts to navigate between the Day, Week, Month, and Year calendar views. To display the Week view from the Month view, click the left mouse button directly on the number of the day within any date box. From the Week calendar view, you can display a Day view by clicking the left mouse button on the date for the day you want in any of the seven available date boxes.

You can also navigate to a specific day, week, or month by selecting it from the currently displayed calendar view, then using the appropriate calendar view item in the View menu. To access the Week view from the Month view, click the left mouse button on any day of the week you want, then choose the Week item from the View menu. The Week view is displayed with the day you selected outlined with a double line or a colored border. To access the Day view from the Month view, click the left mouse button on the date you want in the Month view, then click the left mouse button on the View menu button. Regardless of the view you're displaying, clicking the left mouse button on the View menu displays the selected Day view.

Entering Appointments and ToDo Items into the Calendar Manager

The CM Appointment Editor pop-up window (Figure 5.6) is used to enter appointments and ToDo list items into the Calendar Manager. It allows you to enter and set various parameters for your appointments. For example, you can choose the method the Calendar Manager uses to remind you of an appointment, such as beeping or sending an email message. Any appointment or ToDo list item entered using the Appointment Editor is available in all calendar views.

To display the CM Appointment Editor pop-up window, double-click the left mouse button on the day you want in either the Week or Month view. For the Day view, double-click the left mouse button on the starting hour of your

FIGURE 5.6

The CM Appointment
Editor pop-up window

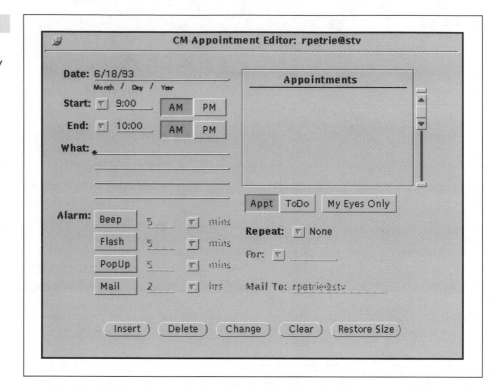

appointment. Clicking the left mouse button on the **Edit** menu button also
displays the **CM Appointment Editor** pop-up window for the day you selected
in either the **Week** or **Month** view or the hour for the **Day** view.

The CM Appointment Editor
Pop-up Window Settings

The initial display of the **CM Appointment Editor** pop-up window is full
size, meaning all the settings are displayed. Clicking the left mouse button
on the **Restore Size** button displays an abbreviated **CM Appointment
Editor** pop-up window, as shown in Figure 5.7. The abbreviated **CM
Appointment Editor** pop-up window does not display the settings that
allow you to set reminder alarm controls. To restore the **CM Appointment
Editor** pop-up window to the full size, click the left mouse button on the
Full Size button.

FIGURE 5.7

The abbreviated CM
Appointment Editor
pop-up window

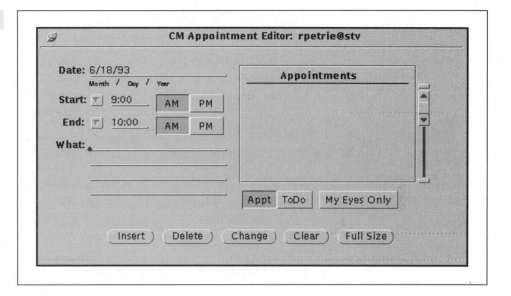

The following describes all the settings that appear in the full size CM Appointment Editor pop-up window.

- The Appointments scrolling list displays either the appointments or ToDo list items scheduled for the day that is currently displayed in the Date field.

- The Date text field displays the selected date. Changing the date entry in the Date text field changes the settings to display the information for the new date.

- The Start and End text fields allow you to set the time of the appointment. You can choose a time from the abbreviated menu buttons to the left of the text field. When you set the starting time, the Appointment Editor automatically inserts an ending time of one hour later. The AM and PM settings let you specify whether the hour is a.m. or p.m.

- The What text field provides a description of your appointment. Your description is not limited to the displayed space of this field; if your description is longer than the displayed space of the What text field, a scroll button appears on the side(s) of the text field where there is hidden text. Clicking the left mouse button on the scroll button scrolls through the hidden text.

- The `Appt` and `ToDo` settings under the `Appointments` scrolling list establish whether your entry is an appointment or a ToDo list item. The `My Eyes Only` setting allows you to hide your appointment or ToDo list item from other users that have permission to browse your calendar.

- The `Alarm` field includes four reminder settings: `Beep`, `Flash`, `PopUp`, and `Mail`. The `Beep` setting reminds you of an upcoming appointment with a beeping alarm sound. The `Flash` setting causes your calendar window or icon to flash to remind you of an upcoming appointment. The `PopUp` setting displays the `Reminder` pop-up window (Figure 5.8), to remind you of your upcoming appointment. The text field to the right of each reminder setting determines the advance time before being reminded for an upcoming appointment. The default is 5 minutes. The `Mail` reminder setting allows you to send the appointment reminder via email to yourself or any users on the system. The `Repeat` abbreviated menu button and `For` text field allow you to specify regularly repeated scheduled appointments. Reminder settings can be combined; for example you can use a pop-up window and send an email message.

- The `Insert`, `Delete`, and `Change` buttons enable you to enter, delete, or change an appointment or ToDo list entry. The `Clear` button clears any text in the `What` text field and resets the `Date`, `Start`, and `End` to their default settings.

FIGURE 5.8

The Calendar Reminder pop-up window

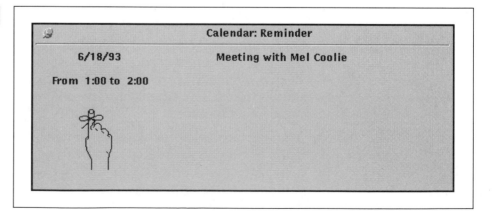

Calendar: Reminder

6/18/93   Meeting with Mel Coolie

From 1:00 to 2:00

- The `Full Size` button displayed in the abbreviated `CM Appointment Editor` pop-up window displays the full size `CM Appointment Editor` pop-up window. The `Restore Size` button, displayed in the full size `CM Appointment Editor` pop-up window, returns the window to its abbreviated size.

Creating an Appointment or ToDo List Entry

To create an appointment or ToDo list entry, first double-click on the day you want the appointment set for in the `Week` or `Month` view, or the hour in the `Day` view. A day can also be selected after displaying the `CM Appointment Editor` pop-up window by entering the exact date you want in the `Date` text field. With the `CM Appointment Editor` pop-up window displayed, follow these steps to enter a new appointment or ToDo list item:

1. If you want to change the date in the `Date` field, first delete the current date entry. Enter the date for the new appointment in any of these formats: mm/dd/yy (11/22/92), m/d/y (1/4/92), or month day, year (August 15, 1992).

2. If the entry is a ToDo item, click the left mouse button on the `ToDo` button under the `Appointments` scrolling list. Choosing the `My Eyes Only` button prevents other users from viewing your appointment or ToDo item.

3. Press the right mouse button on the `Start` abbreviated menu button to display an hour menu, as shown in Figure 5.9. You can choose an hour item or from one of three 15-minute intervals within each hour. Each hour has a submenu that lists these intervals as `00`, `15`, `30`, and `45` minutes. You also need to choose the correct a.m. or p.m. setting for your appointment. When you set a start time, the end time is automatically set to one hour later. If the appointment is shorter or longer than an hour, set a different end time, choosing the time item you want from the `End` abbreviated menu button. Times can also be entered in the `Start` and `End` text fields. Choosing the `All Day` item automatically sets `Start` to 12:00 a.m. and `End` to 11:59 p.m.

FIGURE 5.9

The hour items for the
Start submenu

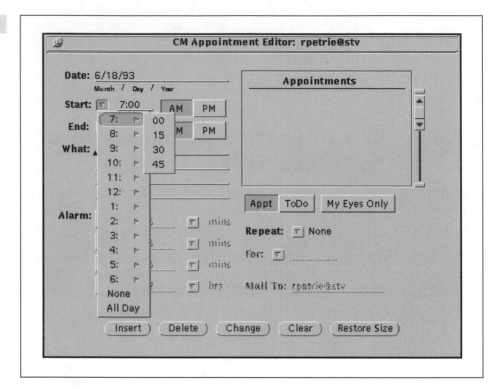

4. Click the left mouse button in the **What** text field to set the insert
   point. Type the appointment or ToDo list information; you can
   use up to four lines. Each line can be up to eighty characters in
   length. If the text is longer than the space in the **What** text field, a
   scroll button appears to the right or left of the text field to indicate
   that there is hidden text. Click the left mouse button on a scroll
   button to scroll through the hidden text.

NOTE

Be as descriptive as possible about the entry in the first
line of the What text field. The Calendar Manager
includes a feature that lets you search your appointment
and ToDo list entries based on text in the first line of the
What text field.

5. Choose an `Alarm` setting if you want to be reminded of your appointment. Click the left mouse button on the `Alarm` setting you want. The selected settings and the corresponding advance time fields are displayed in boldface. To change the default time for the specified `Alarm` setting, click the left mouse button on the setting's text field to set the insert point, and enter the time interval you want. You can specify minutes (the default), hours, or days by pressing the right mouse button on the corresponding advance-time abbreviated menu button to the right of the text field and choosing the time unit you want. If you choose the `Mail` setting, make sure you enter the email address in the `Mail To` text field.

6. If you want the appointment repeated regularly, press the right mouse button on the `Repeat` abbreviated menu button and choose the desired time interval: `None`, `Daily`, `Weekly`, `Biweekly`, `Monthly`, or `Yearly`. When you select a `Repeat` setting (other than the default `None`), the `For` menu button and text field are activated. The `For` setting allows you to specify the time frequency of the `Repeat` setting. For example, if you choose the `Daily` setting, you can set the number of days between recurring appointments. You can choose the time frequency using the `For` abbreviated menu button or you can enter your own number in the `For` text field.

7. After you have finished entering the information for the appointment or ToDo list item, click the left mouse button on the `Insert` button. The appointment is added to the scrolling list in the `CM Appointment Editor` pop-up window as well as to the current calendar view. The `CM Appointment Editor` pop-up window remains displayed, allowing you to enter another appointment or ToDo list item.

8. To quit the `CM Appointment Editor` pop-up window, click the left mouse button on the pushpin or choose `Dismiss` from the `Window` menu.

Deleting Existing Appointments or ToDo List Items

Appointments and ToDo items are constantly being changed or canceled, so the Calendar Manager makes it easy to remove a scheduled appointment or a ToDo list item from your calendar. To delete an existing appointment or ToDo list item from your Calendar Manager, follow these steps:

1. Double-click on the day containing the appointment or ToDo list item you want to delete in the `Week` or `Month` view, or the hour in the `Day` view. The `CM Appointment Editor` pop-up window is displayed.

2. Click the left mouse button on the appointment or ToDo item in the scrolling list you want to delete. The appointment or ToDo entry is highlighted and its information is displayed in the appropriate settings. The user name of the person who scheduled the appointment is displayed in the window footer.

3. Click the left mouse button on the `Delete` button. The appointment or ToDo list item is deleted from both the scrolling list and the calendar view and appointment or ToDo list view. If you select an appointment with a `Repeat` setting, when you click the left mouse button on the `Delete` button, a Notice is displayed (Figure 5.10) asking you if you want to delete the appointment for one or all dates or cancel the operation. Click the left mouse button on the `This One Only` button if you only want to delete the repeating appointment for the selected date. Click the left mouse button on the `All` button if you want to delete all repeating appointments regardless of the date.

FIGURE 5.10

The Delete
Appointment Notice

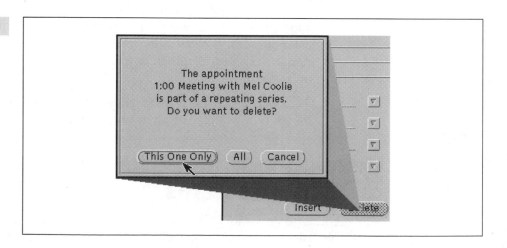

Changing Existing Appointments or ToDo List Items

Making changes to an existing appointment or ToDo item is performed in a similar way as creating a new appointment or ToDo item. The following steps explain how to make changes to existing appointments or ToDo items using the `CM Appointment Editor` pop-up window.

1. Double-click on the day that contains the appointment or ToDo list item you want to change in the `Week` or `Month` view, or the hour in the `Day` view. The `CM Appointment Editor` pop-up window is displayed.

2. Click the left mouse button on the appointment or ToDo item in the scrolling list you want to change. The appointment or ToDo entry is highlighted and its information is displayed in the appropriate settings. The user name of the person who scheduled the appointment is displayed in the window footer.

3. Edit any information for that appointment or ToDo list item.

4. Click the left mouse button on the `Change` button. If you made changes to an appointment with `Repeat` settings, a Notice appears asking if you want to change the appointment for the selected date only or for all dates that the appointment or ToDo item appears. Click the left mouse button on the `This One Only` button if you only want to delete the repeating appointment for the selected date. Click the left mouse button on the `All` button if you want to delete all repeating appointments regardless of the date.

Finding a Calendar Appointment

If you want to find an appointment, but you cannot remember the exact time it was scheduled, you can use the Calendar Manager's `CM Find` pop-up window (Figure 5.11). The `CM Find` pop-up window allows you to

FIGURE 5.11

The CM Find pop-up window

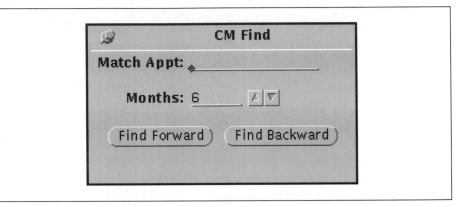

search for matching text in the appointment's **What** text field. To display the **CM Find** pop-up window, choose **Find** from the **View** menu.

The **Match Appt** text field is where you type text to match text entered in the first line of the appointment's **What** field. The text that you type can be either upper- or lowercase. Clicking the left mouse button on the **Find Forward** button searches forward for the number of months specified in the **Months** text field, starting with the currently displayed month. Clicking the left mouse button on the **Find Backward** button searches backward for the number of months specified in the **Months** text field, starting with the currently displayed month.

Printing Calendar Views, Appointment Lists, and ToDo Lists

The Calendar Manager allows you to print daily, weekly, monthly, and yearly calendars, appointment lists, and ToDo lists. The printed calendar views, appointment lists and ToDo lists match their screen counterparts. The `Print` menu provides settings for each calendar view along with a submenu for printing the respective calendar view's appointment and ToDo lists. The `CM Properties` window includes settings for changing the default printer settings, as explained later in this chapter.

The following explains how to print calendar views, appointment lists, and ToDo lists.

CALENDAR VIEW	PRINTING PROCEDURE
Day	To print the currently displayed day calendar view, click the left mouse button on the `Print` menu button. To print either the appointment list or ToDo list for the current day, press the right mouse button on the `Print` menu button, then choose `Appt List` or `ToDo List` from the `Day` submenu.
Week	To print the currently displayed week calendar view, press the right mouse button on the `Print` menu button and choose the `Week` item. To print the appointment or ToDo list for the currently displayed week, choose `Appt List` or `ToDo List` from the `Week` submenu.
Month	To print the currently displayed month calendar view, press the right mouse button on the `Print` menu button then choose the `Month` item. To print either the appointment or ToDo list for the currently displayed `Month`, choose `Appt List` or `ToDo List` from the `Month` submenu.

CALENDAR VIEW	PRINTING PROCEDURE
Year	To print the currently displayed year calendar view, press the right mouse button on the `Print` menu button and choose one of the two `Year` items. The `Year` item allows you to print two different calendars, the standard and alternate calendars. The standard year item, labeled (`Std`) is similar to the on-screen calendar, as shown in Figure 5.12. The alternate year item, labeled (`Alt`), prints the year calendar with each day denoted by a small box, as shown in Figure 5.13. To print either the Appointment or ToDo list for the currently displayed year, press the right mouse button on the `Print` menu button and choose `Appt List` or `ToDo List` from the `Year` submenu.

Working with the Multi-Browser Window

The Calendar Manager's `CM Multi-Browser` pop-up window lets you overlay the calendars of many users at one time to show the times when each user is busy, so you can coordinate appointment schedules. Once you find a convenient meeting time for the group, you can then use the `CM Multi-Browser` pop-up window to add an appointment to every user's calendar and send each user a mail message about the appointment.

The `CM Multi-Browser` pop-up window also allows you to add other users' calendars to your `Browse` menu. Adding users' calendars to your `Browse` menu allows you to view their calendars in the same way you view your own. In order to schedule appointments to another user's calendar or add another user's calendar to the `Browse` menu, you must have permission to use that user's calendar, as explained later in this chapter.

FIGURE 5.12

Printed standard year view

1993

06/25/93 02:38 AM   rpetrie@stv

January
S	M	T	W	T	F	S
					1	2
3	4	5	6	7	8	9
10	11	12	13	14	15	16
17	18	19	20	21	22	23
24	25	26	27	28	29	30
31						

February
S	M	T	W	T	F	S
	1	2	3	4	5	6
7	8	9	10	11	12	13
14	15	16	17	18	19	20
21	22	23	24	25	26	27
28						

March
S	M	T	W	T	F	S
	1	2	3	4	5	6
7	8	9	10	11	12	13
14	15	16	17	18	19	20
21	22	23	24	25	26	27
28	29	30	31			

April
S	M	T	W	T	F	S
				1	2	3
4	5	6	7	8	9	10
11	12	13	14	15	16	17
18	19	20	21	22	23	24
25	26	27	28	29	30	

May
S	M	T	W	T	F	S
						1
2	3	4	5	6	7	8
9	10	11	12	13	14	15
16	17	18	19	20	21	22
23	24	25	26	27	28	29
30	31					

June
S	M	T	W	T	F	S
		1	2	3	4	5
6	7	8	9	10	11	12
13	14	15	16	17	18	19
20	21	22	23	24	25	26
27	28	29	30			

July
S	M	T	W	T	F	S
				1	2	3
4	5	6	7	8	9	10
11	12	13	14	15	16	17
18	19	20	21	22	23	24
25	26	27	28	29	30	31

August
S	M	T	W	T	F	S
1	2	3	4	5	6	7
8	9	10	11	12	13	14
15	16	17	18	19	20	21
22	23	24	25	26	27	28
29	30	31				

September
S	M	T	W	T	F	S
			1	2	3	4
5	6	7	8	9	10	11
12	13	14	15	16	17	18
19	20	21	22	23	24	25
26	27	28	29	30		

October
S	M	T	W	T	F	S
					1	2
3	4	5	6	7	8	9
10	11	12	13	14	15	16
17	18	19	20	21	22	23
24	25	26	27	28	29	30
31						

November
S	M	T	W	T	F	S
	1	2	3	4	5	6
7	8	9	10	11	12	13
14	15	16	17	18	19	20
21	22	23	24	25	26	27
28	29	30				

December
S	M	T	W	T	F	S
			1	2	3	4
5	6	7	8	9	10	11
12	13	14	15	16	17	18
19	20	21	22	23	24	25
26	27	28	29	30	31	

Year view by Calendar Manager

FIGURE 5.13

Printed alternate year view

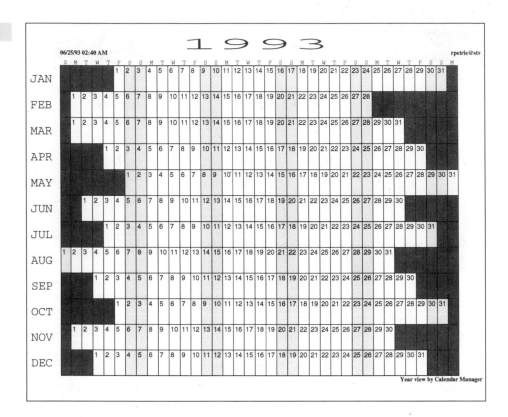

The Multi-Browser Window

To activate the CM Multi-Browser window, click the left mouse button on the Browse menu button. The CM Multi-Browser window appears, displaying the week time chart that includes the day you selected (Figure 5.14). The CM Multi-Browser window can be closed to an icon for added convenience (Figure 5.14). When you quit the Calendar Manager, the CM Multi-Browser window or icon is also removed. The CM Multi-Browser window includes the following controls:

- The Schedule button displays the CM Browser editor pop-up window, which is similar to the CM Appointment Editor pop-up window.

FIGURE 5.14

The CM Multi-Browser
window and icon

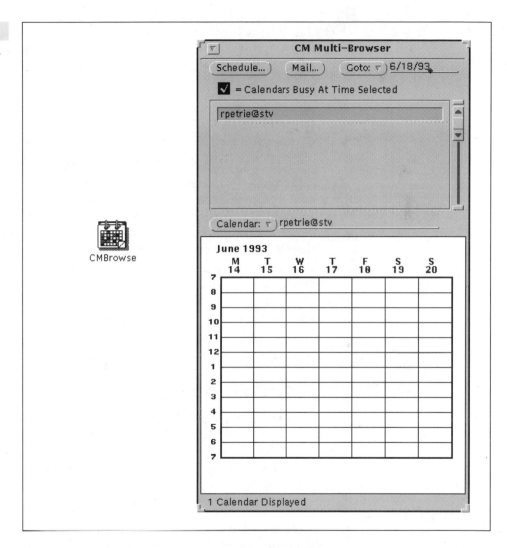

- The **Mail** button displays the Calendar Manager's **Compose Message** window for sending mail to notify users of your appointment scheduling.

- The **Goto** menu lists items to change in the Multi-Browser calendar display in order to show a different week or month.

- The Multi-Browser calendar list shows all the user names available in your `CM Multi-Browser` pop-up window. Each entry is the email address of the user.

- The `Calendar` menu button and text field allow you to add, delete, select, deselect, and sort the user names listed in the Multi-Browser calander list. Pressing the right mouse button in the Multi-Browser calendar list displays the `Calendar` pop-up menu, which is the same menu as the `Calendar` menu button.

- The Multi-Browser calendar display area displays any number of user calendars in an overlay manner to show a composite schedule. The number of calendars displayed in the calendar display area is noted in a message line in the bottom-left corner of the `CM Multi-Browser` window, directly below the calendar display area. The Multi-Browser only shows the times when each user is busy. To view the actual contents of a user's calendar, you need to choose the user name from the `Browse` menu, as explained later in the chapter.

Adding a User's Calendar to the Multi-Browser

In order to work with another user's calendar, you must first add it to the Multi-Browser calendar list. This scrolling list displays all of the calendars that are available to be browsed. These user names are also displayed as individual items in the Calendar Manager's `Browse` menu. New calendars are displayed on the `Browse` menu in the order in which you enter them in the Multi-Browser calendar list.

You must have browse permissions for each user's Calendar Manager, which are determined by the respective user, in order to work with the other users' calendars. The Calendar Manager does not confirm the validity of the user name nor the browse permissions for that calendar when you enter the user name in the calendar list. The Calendar Manager does check for such information when you select the calendar in the Multi-Browser calendar list, or when you choose the calendar from the `Browse` menu.

To add a user's calendar to the `Browse` menu:

1. Click the left mouse button on the `Browse` menu button. The `CM Multi-Browser` window appears.

2. Click the left mouse button on the `Calendar` text field to set the insert point and type in the user's login name, followed by `@`, then followed by the user's host machine name (for example, `ataylor@mayberry`).

3. Press the right mouse button on the `Calendar` menu button and choose `Add Calendar`. The calendar is added to the Multi-Browser calendar list and `Browse` menu.

You can sort the list of users in the Multi-Browser calendar list by choosing the `Sort List` item from the `Calendar` menu. The `Sort List` item sorts the user email addresses in alphabetical order.

Deleting a User's Calendar from the Multi-Browser

You can easily delete a user's calendar from the Multi-Browser calandar's list. If the `CM Multi-Browser` window is not open, click the left mouse button on the `Browse` menu button. Click the left mouse button on the user's name you want to delete as it appears in the calendar list. More than one user name can be selected by clicking the middle mouse button on each additional user's name. You can also type the user name of the user you want to delete in the `Calendar` text field. Choose the `Delete Selected` item from the `Calendar` menu. The selected user names are deleted from the Multi-Browser.

Determining an Appointment Time

When you open the `CM Multi-Browser` window, the week shown in the Multi-Browser calendar display is determined as follows:

- If the current view is the `Day` or `Month` view, the week containing the currently selected day is displayed.

- If the current view is the `Week` view, the current week is displayed.

- If the current view is the `Year` view, the first week of the currently selected month is displayed.

The Multi-Browser displays the days of the week and their corresponding dates at the top of the calendar display. On the left side of the calendar display are the one-hour blocks of appointment times. The 7 a.m. to 7 p.m. setting reflects the default `Day Boundaries` setting for the Calendar Manager, which can be changed using the `CM Properties` window.

The gray areas of the calendar indicate the times the selected users have scheduled appointments. If several calendars are being displayed, the gray blocks vary in shade. Darker blocks indicate that more users are busy during that time slot. There are up to three shades of gray, so a time slot when four people are busy does not appear any darker than a time slot when three people are busy. The white areas indicate times in which none of the selected users are busy.

The `Goto` menu provides several items for changing the Multi-Browser's Week display. Choose the `Prev Week` or `Next Week` item to display the previous or next week. Choose `This Week` to display the week of the day currently selected in the `Calendar Manager` window. Choose the `Prev Month` or `Next Month` to display a week one month before or after the current week. You can type any date in the `Goto` text field then click the left mouse button on the `Goto` button. The date can be entered in one of the following formats:

> `mm/dd/yy` or `m/d/yy` (for example, 1/15/92 or 10/5/92)
>
> `month day, year` (for example, June 30, 1992)

The following steps explain how to find free time slots for scheduling an appointment for a group of users.

1. Choose the `CM Multi-Browser` window by clicking the left mouse button on the `Browse` menu. Make sure that the calendars for all of the attendees are in the Multi-Browser calendar list.

2. Click the left mouse on each user name you want in the Multi-Browser calendar list. You can choose `Select All` from the `Calendar` menu to select every user name.

3. If the week you want is not currently displayed, use the `Goto` menu or enter the week you want in the `Goto` text field.

4. When all of the calendars are selected and overlaid, find an un-shaded block of time for the meeting. This represents a time when everyone is available.

5. If there is no time slot available on all the selected calendars, select a time slot that is lightly shaded and look at the selected user addresses in the Multi-Browser calendar list. If a user has an appointment scheduled for the selected time, a check mark appears to the left of the user's address, as shown in Figure 5.15. If you decide that a user does not have to be at the meeting, you can deselect that person's user name by clicking the left mouse button on it in the calendar list.

Scheduling an Appointment for a Group of Users

Once you have found a mutually convenient time, you can use the `CM Browser editor` pop-up window to mark the appointment in the calendars of all of the users. Remember, the user must give you permission (using the `Insert Setting` permission, which is explained later in this chapter) to add appointments to his or her calendar. Clicking the left mouse button on the `Schedule` button in the `CM Multi-Browser` pop-up window displays the `CM Browser editor` pop-up window (Figure 5.16). You can also double-click the left mouse button on the desired appointment time in the overlaid calendar area to display the `CM Browser editor` pop-up window.

The `CM Browser editor` pop-up window includes the same `Date`, `Start`, `End`, and `What` settings as the `CM Appointment Editor` pop-up window. The `Appointments` scrolling list displays appointments for all of the calendars selected in the `Calendars` scrolling list, at the time selected in the `CM Multi-Browser` window. When you select an appointment on the `Appointments` scrolling list, the appointment information is displayed in the `Date`, `Start`, `End`, and `What` text fields. The author of the selected appointment is displayed at the bottom-left corner of the `CM Browser editor` window.

FIGURE 5.15

The CM Multi-Browser
list showing busy users

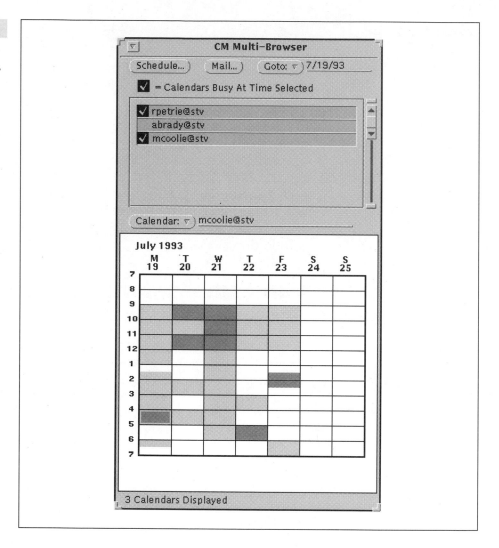

To schedule an appointment for a group of users, double-click the left mouse button on an available time slot for the new appointment, or select the time slot then click the left mouse button on the Schedule button. The CM Browser editor pop-up window is displayed. The Date, Start, and End text fields are automatically filled in and the selected calendars are listed in the Calendars Insert Access scrolling list.

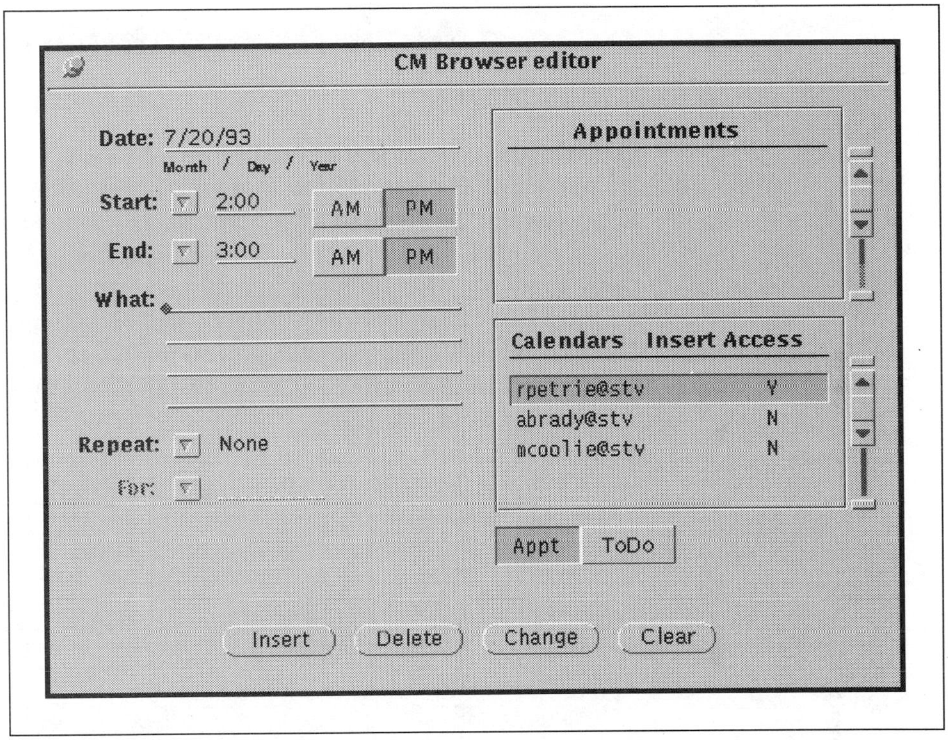

FIGURE 5.16

The CM Browser
editor pop-up window

If you have Insert Access permission (that is, permission to enter an appointment into that user's calendar), indicated by a Y in the **Calendars Insert Access** scrolling list, that calendar is automatically selected. If you do not have Insert permission, an N is displayed and the calendar is not selected. If any of the selected calendars has an appointment at the selected time, that appointment is displayed in the **Appointments** scrolling list, which is located just above the **Calendars Insert Access** list.

Fill out the new appointment information and click the left mouse button on the **Insert** button to add the appointment to the selected calendars. If the **Insert Access** column displays an N, you will need to send a mail message or contact that user to tell them to add the appointment to his or her calendar.

Sending a Mail Appointment Notification

The Multi-Browser's mail facility provides a convenient way to notify all the participants of a meeting that you have updated in their calendars and notify users who have not given you access to insert the appointment into their calendar. To display the Calendar Manager's **Compose Message** window (Figure 5.17), click the left mouse button on the **Mail** button in the **CM Multi-Browser** window. The **Compose Message** window is similar to the Mail Tool's **Compose Message** window, as explained in Chapter 3, "The Multimedia Mail Tool Makes Mail Easy." The information from the **CM Browser editor** pop-up window's **Date**, **Start**, **End**, and **What** text fields are automatically entered into the **Compose Message** window. The email addresses of all the users you have scheduled for the appointment

FIGURE 5.17

The Calendar Manager's Compose Message window

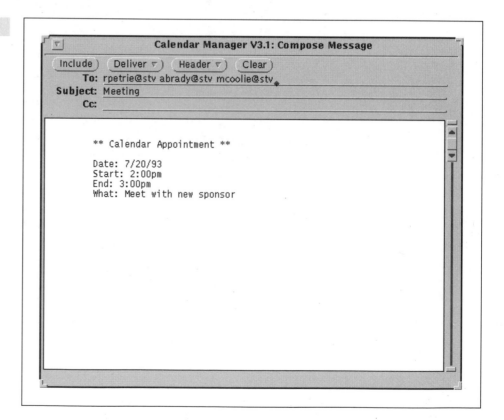

are displayed in the To text field, even if you were denied access to insert the appointment into a user's calendar. The default entry in the Subject text field is "Meeting," which you can change. The following steps explain how to send mail using the Calendar Manager's Compose Message window.

1. Before you send mail messages, make sure you have selected the recipient's user name in the CM Multi-Browser window. In the CM Browser editor pop-up window, make sure that you have filled in the Date, Start, End, and What fields for the appointment, and click the left mouse button on the Insert button.

2. Click the left mouse button on the Mail button in the CM Multi-Browser window to display the Compose Message window.

3. If you want to change the Subject field text or any text in the Compose Message window, click the left mouse button on any text area and edit the text.

4. Click the left mouse button on the Deliver button to send the mail message to the users listed in the To text field.

The mail message is sent in a format recognized by the Calendar Manager, so mail recipients can quickly add the appointment to their calendars, if it wasn't automatically added, by dragging the mail header to their Calendar Manager and dropping it anywhere on the window.

Browsing Another User's Calendar Using the Browse Menu

Once a calendar has been added to your Browse menu, you can display or edit the appointments for that user (depending on the access permissions that user has given you) by choosing the calendar from the Browse menu.

To choose a user's calendar from the **Browse** menu, press the right mouse button on the **Browse** menu button and choose the user's name you want. The user's calendar displays in your Calendar Manager in the same way as yours. If you do not have browse access for that user, you cannot see or edit that user's appointment information, but a scheduled appointment will appear as an **Appointment** entry for the specified time, as shown in Figure 5.18.

FIGURE 5.18

Browsing a user's calendar in the Week view without browsing permission

Calendar Manager V3.1: mcoolie@stv

View ▽   Edit ▽   Browse ▽   Print ▽   Prev   Today   Next

July 1993

Sun	Mon	Tue	Wed	Thu	Fri	Sat
				1 4:00p Appo 5:00p Appo	2 9:00a Appo 1:30p Appo	3
4	5 4:00p Appo	6 9:00a Appo	7	8 5:00p Appo	9 1:30p Appo	10
11	12	13 9:00a Appo	14	15 5:00p Appo	16 1:30p Appo	17
18	19 4:00p Appo	20 9:00a Appo	21	22 5:00p Appo	23 1:30p Appo	24
25	26	27 9:00a Appo	28	29 4:00p Appo	30	31 6:45p Appo

Setting the Calendar Manager Time Zone

When you browse another user's calendar, the Calendar Manager adjusts the times to your time zone. For example, if you are on the west coast of the United States, and you are browsing the calendar of someone on the east coast, a 9:00 a.m. appointment appears as 6:00 a.m. to you. This is an important feature when using the Multi-Browser, because it ensures that all users' calendars are in synch. If you are only browsing a single calendar, however, you might want to view the appointments in their native time zone. To change the time zone for the currently displayed calendar, press the right mouse button on the **Edit** menu and choose the **Time Zone** item you want from the **Time Zone** submenu (Figure 5.19). Notice there are several time zones with their own submenus, such as the **US** item. If you change your own time zone in order to browse another calendar, make sure to change it back to your native time zone when you are done.

Customizing Your Calendar Manager

The Calendar Manager's **CM Properties** pop-up window allows you to customize the Calendar Manager's settings. To display the **CM Properties** pop-up window, press the right mouse button on the **Edit** menu and choose the **Properties** item. The **Category** menu initially shows the **Editor Defaults** settings, which are currently displayed in the **CM Properties** pop-up window (Figure 5.20). The **CM Properties** pop-up window provides five groups of settings: **Editor Defaults, Display Settings, Access List and Permissions, Printer Settings**, and **Date Format**. To choose a group of settings in the **CM Properties** pop-up window, click the right mouse button on the **Category** button and choose the

FIGURE 5.19

The Time Zone submenu

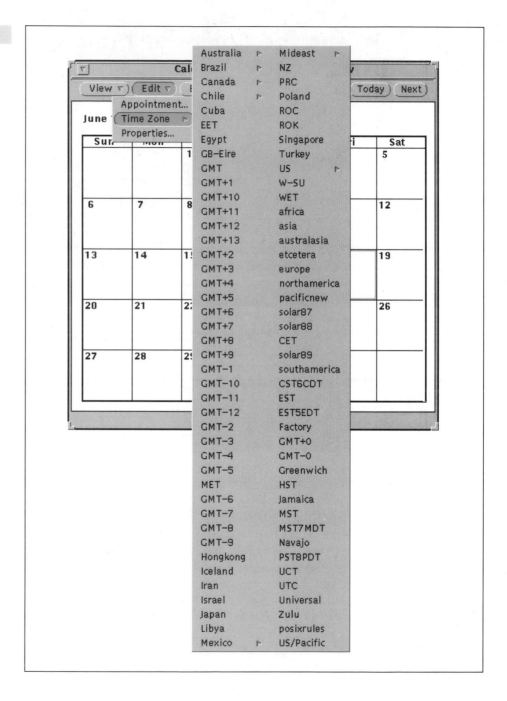

settings you want. There are three buttons at the bottom of the CM Properties pop-up window, regardless of which category is selected:

- The Apply button saves the changes made to the current CM Properties window. If you attempt to exit the CM Properties window after making changes without choosing the Apply button, a notice box appears requesting you either save or discard your changes, as shown in Figure 5.21.

- The Reset button restores the original properties settings to the current CM Properties window you had before you made changes in the current session.

FIGURE 5.20

The CM Properties
pop-up window

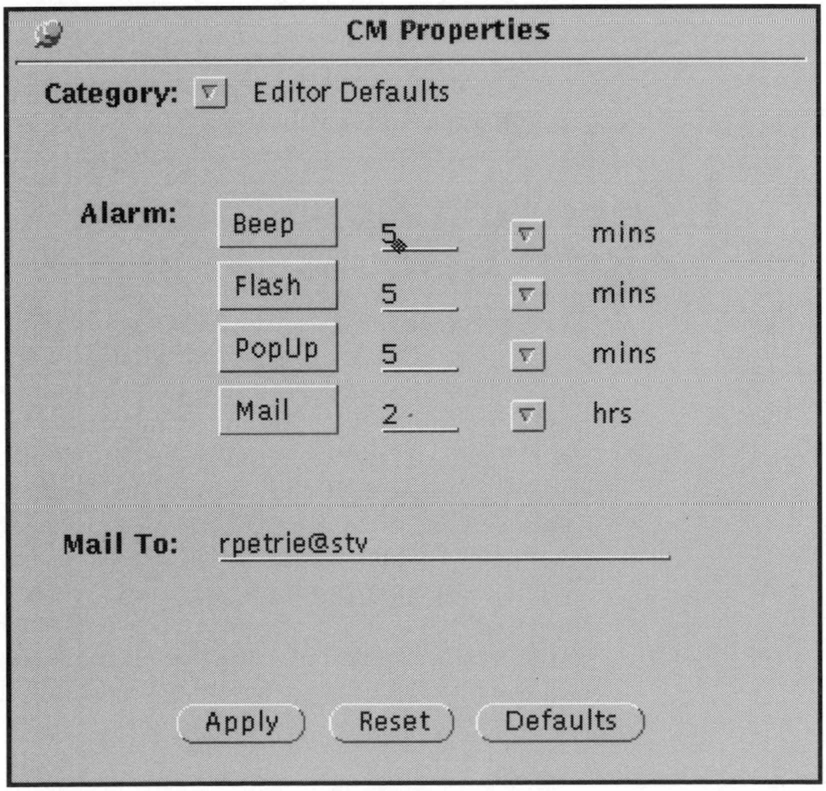

FIGURE 5.21

The CM Properties
notice box

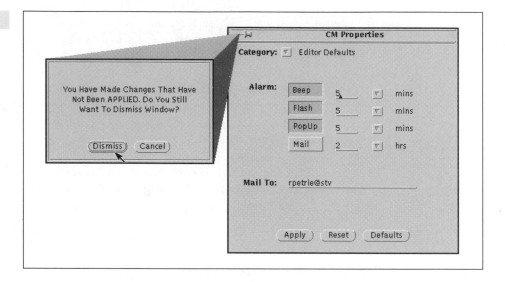

- The **Defaults** button restores the default settings for the current **CM Properties** window.

Changing Appointment Alarm Defaults

The **Editor Defaults** settings allow you to specify which of the four available **Alarm** settings are selected when you activate the **CM Appointment Editor** pop-up window. To select one or more **Alarm** settings, click the left mouse button on each **Alarm** setting you want. To enter a new time, click the left mouse button on the appropriate text field to set the insert point and type in a new number. To change the default time unit setting for an **Alarm** setting, press the right mouse button on the corresponding **Alarm** setting abbreviated menu button and choose the time unit item you want. You can also change the default **Mail To** text field entry, which specifies the email address for the **Mail** reminder setting. After making changes to the **Editor Defaults**, click the left mouse button on the **Apply** button, and the new defaults are saved and activated immediately.

Changing Display Settings

The `Display Settings` category lets you change the range of hours available for the `Start` and `End` fields in the `CM Appointment Editor` pop-up window, the `CM Multi-Browser` calendar display, and the `CM Browser editor` pop-up window. For example, if your normal working hours are 9 a.m. to 5 p.m., you would select 9 a.m. as your `Start` boundary and 5 p.m. as your `End` boundary.

The hour display for the Calendar Manager can be changed from the default `12 Hour` setting to a `24 Hour` setting using the `Hour Display` control. The `Default View` setting allows you to change the default calendar view when you activate the Calendar Manager application. The `Default Calendar` text field lets you specify the default user name you want to display in your Calendar Manager.

To change to the `Display Settings` settings (Figure 5.22), choose the `Display Settings` item from the `Category` menu. To change the Day Boundaries setting, follow these steps:

1. Press the left mouse button on the slider bar.

2. Drag the slider bar to the left or the right. Note that the time changes as you drag the slider. The pointer remains locked onto the slider as long as you keep the left mouse button pressed.

3. If you simply want to add or subtract an hour, click the left mouse button on the right (to increase the time) or on the left (to decrease the time) of the slider.

4. Once the Day Boundaries have been set, click the left mouse button on the `Apply` button to save your settings. The changes take effect immediately.

As explained earlier in this chapter, the `Month` view is displayed by default when you open the Calendar Manager. You can change this default view to `Day`, `Week`, or `Year`. To change the default view, click the left mouse button on the `Default View` setting you want, then click the left mouse button on the `Apply` button. The change takes effect the next time you activate the Calendar Manager.

FIGURE 5.22

The Display Settings
category

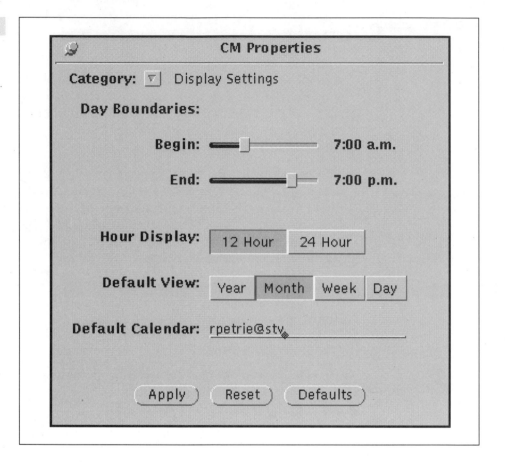

Specifying Who Can Browse and Change Your Appointments

The `Access List and Permissions` category in the `Category` menu lets you specify who may browse or change your appointments. Choosing the `Access List and Permissions` item displays the `Access List and Permissions` category window (Figure 5.23). The scrolling list displays a list of everyone who has access to your calendar. The default entry in the scrolling list, `world`, allows all users to browse your calendar and view your appointments, as indicated by the `B` (Browse) to the right of `world`.

FIGURE 5.23

The Access List and
Permissions CM
Properties pop-up
window

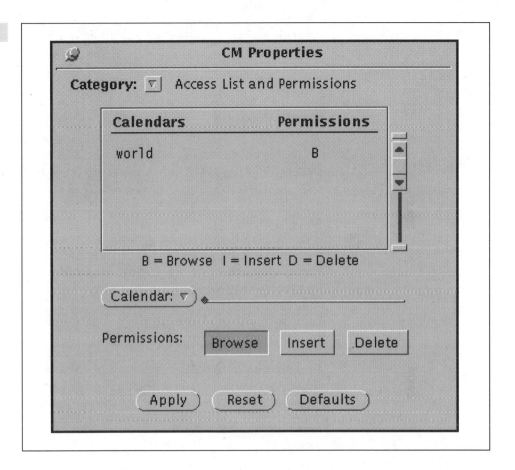

Three types of permissions can be establish for each user. The available permissions are:

Browse	Displayed as **B** in the scrolling list, the **Browse** permission allows the user to read your appointments.
Insert	Displayed as **I** in the scrolling list, the **Insert** permission allows the user to add new appointments into your calendar.

Delete   Displayed as `D` in the scrolling list, the
         `Delete` permission allows the user to
         delete appointments from your calendar.

You can combine any or all of the three permissions. If you give more permissions to the `world` entry than you give to an individual, that individual will still have the world permissions. If you delete the `world` entry from the access list, only the users you specifically add will be able to access your appointments. To give a user the ability to read, edit, and change appointments, you must give the user `Browse`, `Insert`, and `Delete` permissions. That user then has full permission to read appointments, insert new appointments, and delete or modify existing appointments. The following steps explain how to add a user to the access list:

1. In the `Calendar` text field, type the email address (such as, `ataylor@mayberry`) of the user you want to add.

2. Choose the permissions you want to give the user by clicking the left mouse button on the desired permissions.

3. Click the left mouse button on the `Calendar` menu button to add the user to the access list. You can also use the `Add Calendar` item from `Calendar` pop-up menu to add the user by pressing the right mouse button anywhere in the access scrolling list pane.

4. Click the left mouse button on the `Apply` button to save your changes.

To delete a user from the access list, select the user name in the scrolling list by clicking the left mouse button on the user name you want to delete, then choose the `Delete Calendar` item from the `Calendar` menu.

To change existing permissions for a user already on the access list, choose the user name from the scrolling list. Select the new permissions you want to give the user, then choose the `Add Calendar` item from the `Calendar` menu.

Changing the Default Printer Settings

You can change the default printer settings from the `Printer Settings` category window. To display the `Printer Settings` category window, choose the `Printer Settings` item from the `Category` menu. Figure 5.24 shows the `Printer Settings` category window with the default settings.

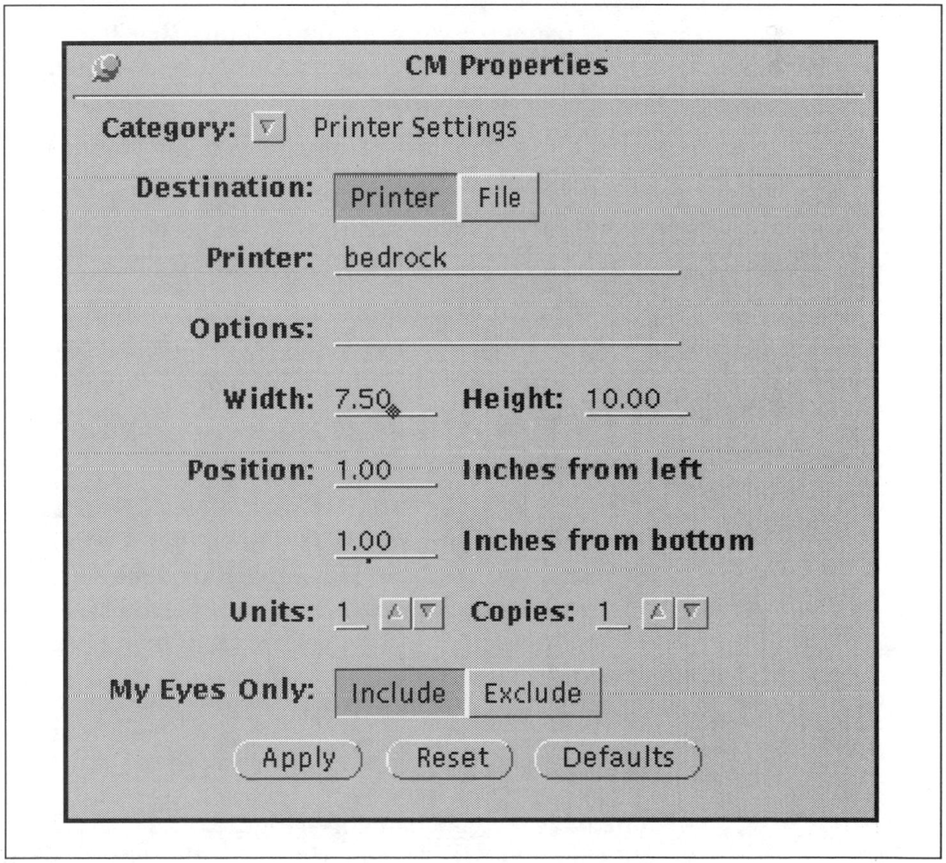

FIGURE 5.24

The Printer Settings CM Properties pop-up window

You can specify the following settings in the `Printer Settings` category window:

- The `Destination` setting specifies whether you want the Calendar Manager `Print` menu output sent to a printer or to a file. If the `Destination` setting is set to `Printer` (the default), the `Printer` and `Options` fields are displayed. If the `Destination` setting is set to `File`, the `Printer` and `Options` fields are replaced by `Directory` and `File` fields. The `Printer` field specifies the printer name and the `Options` field allows you to type in SunOS print commands to customize your printer defaults. The `Directory` and `File` fields allow you to type in the directory and file name of the file that you want to print to.

- The `Width` and `Height` fields allow you to specify the size of the printed output.

- The `Position` settings `Inches from left` and `Inches from bottom` specify the margins for printed output.

- The `Units` setting specifies the number of calendar view units from the selected day, week, month, or year calendar view to print. For example, when a day view is printed, the unit is `Days`.

- The `Copies` setting specifies the number of copies you want to print.

- The `My Eyes Only` settings allows to include or exclude printing any appointments or ToDo list items you have specified as for your eyes only. Choosing the `Include` setting allows them to be printed in an appointment or ToDo list. Choosing the `Exclude` setting blocks these entries from being printed in an appointment or ToDo list.

Changing Date Formats

The `Date Format` category (Figure 5.25) determines how the date in the `CM Appointment Editor` window is displayed. To display the date format set of controls, choose the `Date Format` item from the `CM Properties` window's `Category` menu. The `Date Ordering` settings determine the order in which the month, day, and year appear in the Appointment Editor's `Date` field. The `Date Separator` setting determines what separates each element of the date. To change the defaults, click the left mouse button on the settings you want, then click the left mouse button on the **Apply** button.

FIGURE 5.25

The Date Format CM
Properties window

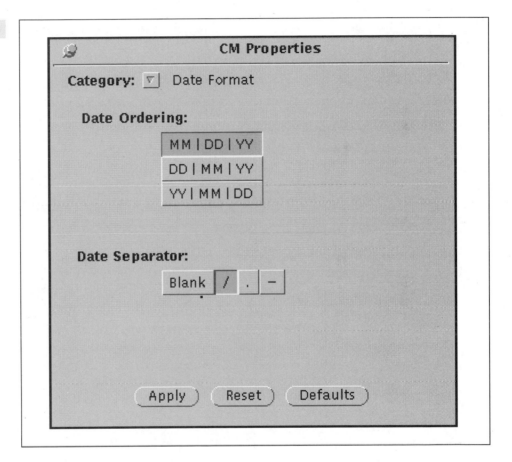

CHAPTER

6

Using the Print Tool, Audio Tool, and Other DeskSet Applications

TO **EXTEND** your mastery of the DeskSet, this chapter covers these DeskSet applications:

- The Print Tool, which prints your files.

- The Audio Tool, which allows you to create and edit sound files.

- The Snapshot application, which allows you to take pictures of part of or the entire screen.

- The Clock, which displays the current time and date.

- The Performance Meters, which allow you to monitor the performance of your system.

- The Calculator, which enables you to perform mathematical calculations.

- The Tape Tool, which allows you to read and write files to and from a tape cartridge or archive file.

All the applications in this chapter can be started in the same manner as other DeskSet applications—by displaying the **Workspace** menu then choosing the application item from the **Programs** submenu.

The Print Tool

The Print Tool makes printing easy by providing you with a friendly user interface that lets you send files to the printer. Figure 6.1 shows the **Print Tool** window and Print Tool icon. The name of the active printer is displayed at the bottom of the Print Tool icon. The Print Tool allows you to specify the printer you want to use, the number of copies you want to print, and the file format of the file you want to print.

FIGURE 6.1

The Print Tool window
and icon

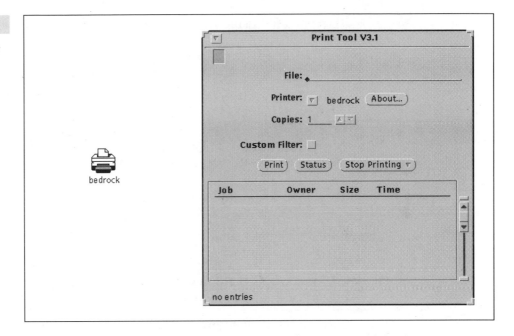

Printers are often in high demand in a networking environment because
multiple workstations are usually connected to a small number of printers.
To keep things running smoothly, Solaris normally feeds printing jobs to
printers on a first-come,first-served basis. A *print job* is a term for a file
sent to be printed as hard copy (on paper). Print jobs are sent to a *print
queue*, which stores the printing jobs in memory in the order they are
received. The status of your print jobs in the print queue can be quickly
displayed in the **Print Tool** window, and specific or all print jobs stopped.

Printing a File

The Print Tool allows you to print an ASCII file using the default printer
by either dragging and dropping files from the File Manager or typing the
file name of the file to be printed in the **File** text field. You can also drag
and drop a mail message header from the Mail Tool or the contents of a
Text Editor window into the Print Tool for printing.

To print a file using the drag-and-drop method, follow the steps below.

1. Select one or more files from the File Manager, or one or more mail message headers from the Mail Tool header pane.

2. Drag and drop the selected files or mail message headers onto the `Print Tool` window's drag-and-drop target. The file names are automatically entered in the `File` text field, the files are loaded into the print queue, and a message indicating the status of your print request is displayed in the footer of the window.

To print a file using the `Print Tool` window's `File` text field, type the complete path name of the file in the `File` text field. Click the left mouse button on the `Print` button to send your file to the print queue. In turn, one of the following printing status messages is displayed in the window footer: `Printing filename`, which indicates that your print request is printing, or `(n)Print Job(s) Submitted*`, which indicates your print request is waiting in a queue to be printed.

If you want to print more than one copy, enter the number of copies you want to print by typing a number in the `Copies` text field, or click the left mouse button on the arrow (increment/decrement) buttons.

Choosing Another Printer

The Print Tool automatically displays the default printer. Other printers available to you are listed in the `Printer` menu. You can display information that your system administrator has included about a printer by clicking the left mouse button on the `About` button.

To choose another printer, press the right mouse button on the `Printer` abbreviated menu button to display the Printer menu, then choose the name of the printer you want. The name of the printer you choose is displayed to the right of the `Printer` menu button.

Checking the Print Queue Status

Clicking the left mouse button on the `Status` button lets you view a list of print jobs in the print queue. When there are no entries, the message `no entries` is displayed at the bottom of the window. When there are entries in the print queue, the list of all the jobs for that printer (not just your jobs) is displayed in the scrolling list in the `Print Tool` window, as shown in Figure 6.2. Pressing the right mouse button in the scrolling list displays the `Scrolling List` pop-up menu.

Stopping Printing Jobs

The Print Tool allows you to stop printing all your jobs in the job queue by choosing the `All Print Jobs` item from the `Stop Printing` menu. To stop specific printing jobs, follow the steps below:

1. Click the left mouse button on the `Status` button to display jobs in the print queue.

2. Click the left mouse button on the name of the job in the scrolling list you want to stop. To stop more than one job at a time, click the middle mouse button on the additional jobs you want to stop.

3. When you have selected the jobs you want to stop, click the left mouse button on the `Stop Printing` button.

Adding a Custom Print Tool Filter

When the file you are printing has a print filter added, the filter format is automatically chosen when you drop a file on the Print Tool or type its file name in the `File` text field and click the left mouse button on the `Print` button. For example, when you print a raster image, such as a Snapshot file, a raster filter automatically filters the image file into instructions that the printer can understand. If you are printing a file that does not have a filter bound to it, such as an ASCII text file that includes `troff` formatting commands, you need to send the file through the `troff` filter so the file

FIGURE 6.2

The Print Tool window
with print jobs listed in
the scrolling list

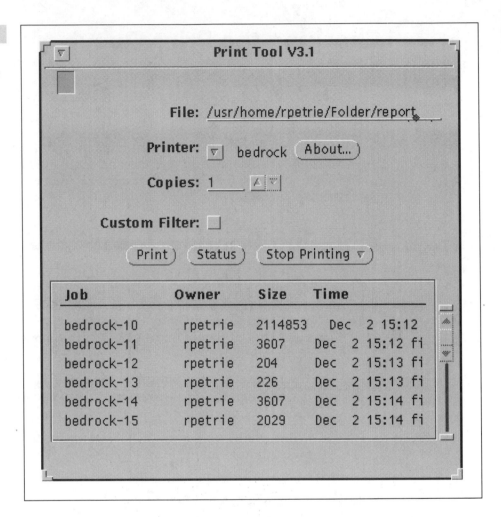

will print correctly. Chapter 13, "Formatting and Printing," explains
working with troff formatting commands.

To print a file using a filter, click on the Custom Filter check box. A check
appears in the Custom Filter check box along with a text field. In the text
field, type any command line print script. This text field accepts three variables. The $FILE variable substitutes the name of the specified file in the
print script. The $PRINTER variable substitutes the name of the printer cur-
rently selected in the Print Tool. The $COPIES variable substitutes the
number of copies currently specified in the Copies text field. For example,

to print a file containing `troff` commands to a PostScript printer, enter the following in the `Custom Filter` text field:

```
troff filename | dpost | lp -Tpostscript
```

This specifies that the file contains `troff` commands and sends the file to the `dpost` filter to convert the `troff` commands into PostScript instructions.

Using the mp PostScript Filter

Solaris includes a special PostScript printer filter to spruce up your standard output. The `mp` filter is included as the default custom filter for the File Manager and the Mail Tool. Both these tools use the following script:

```
cat $FILE | mp -lo | lp
```

The `-l` argument instructs the printer to print the file in landscape mode. The `o` argument identifies the format of the file as an ordinary ASCII file. If you are printing a PostScript file to a PostScript printer, you may need to add the `-Tpostscript` argument to the `lp` command as follows:

```
cat $FILE | mp -lo | lp -Tpostscript
```

The `-Tpostscript` argument specifies that the type of file you are printing is in a PostScript format.

Figure 6.3 shows a sample of the output using the `mp` filter. You can add arguments to the `mp` filter to print files in a format for use with personal organizers. For example, adding the `-f` argument to the `mp` command formats the output for use with a Filofax personal organizer, `-tm` formats the file for use with the Time Manager, and `-ts` formats the file for use with the Time/System International personal organizer.

The Audio Tool

The Audio Tool allows you to add a multimedia dimension to DeskSet environment. It provides features for recording, playing, editing sound files, and controlling your workstation's audio configuration parameters.

Listing for Robert Petrie   Sun Jun 20 02:34:41 1993   Page 1

```
* @(#)README   1.4    92/10/21 SMI

This directory hierarchy contains the sources and executables for demo
applications, a prototype audio programming library, and a set of
pre-recorded audio sound samples.  Manual Pages for the demo programs
are located in section 6: Games and Demos.

Note that the principal audio record/playback utility is AudioTool,
provided with the OpenWindows DeskSet applications (refer to the
DeskSet User's Guide and the audiotool(1) manual page).

Some of the XView demo programs contain spot help information.  To obtain
spot help, set the HELPPATH environment variable to include the directory
in which the files are located.  For example:

    % setenv HELPPATH "$HELPPATH:/usr/demo/SOUND/help"

The following is an overview of the contents of /usr/demo/SOUND:

/usr/demo/SOUND/bin        demo program executables
/usr/demo/SOUND/help       spot help files for the demos
/usr/demo/SOUND/include    header files for the prototype audio library
/usr/demo/SOUND/lib        libaudio.a, the prototype audio library
/usr/demo/SOUND/man        manual pages for libaudio functions
/usr/demo/SOUND/sounds     sample sound files
/usr/demo/SOUND/src        source code for the demo programs

Demo programs
-------------
soundtool(6)
    This is a prototype audio record/playback tool.  It demonstrates
    many of the features of the audio programming interface.  Since
    it is an XView application, it is written to obey the constraints
    of the XView Notifier and to issue only asynchronous i/o requests.
    Because Xt also attempts to keep an oscilloscope display synchronized
    during play and record, it is far more complex than most audio
    applications need to be.  However, it serves as a demonstration of
    the real-time audio capabilities of the SPARCstation.

gaintool(6)
    This is a prototype audio control panel.  It illustrates the ability
    to control various aspects of the workstation audio configuration
    outside of particular audio applications.  For instance, since play
    volume may be controlled from the panel, it is not necessary for all
    audio applications to provide an output volume control themselves.

    Gaintool also has a property sheet (activated from a menu over the
    main panel) that displays complete status information for the audio
    device.  This information can be useful for debugging audio programs.

Radio Free Ethernet
    Radio Free Ethernet is a suite of programs that allow broadcasting
    and receiving audio over the network.  The receiver and transmitter
    (radio_recv and radio_xmit) are command-line programs that are
    controlled by window programs (radio and xmit).  The command-line
    programs may also be invoked by shell scripts or through the cron(1n)
```

Listing for Robert Petrie   Sun Jun 20 02:34:41 1993   Page 2

```
    facility.  See the About Sound document for a general overview of
    this demo.

radio(6)
    Radio is the window-based tool for the radio receiver.  The interface
    is similar to that of a car radio.

xmit(6)
    Xmit is the window-based tool for the radio transmitter.  When running
    xmit for the first time, a radio station name must be entered in the
    Station configuration panel before transmission can be started.

radio_recv(6)
    Radio_recv is the command-line radio receiver program (normally invoked
    by the radio program).

radio_xmit(6)
    Radio_xmit is the command-line radio transmitter (normally invoked by
    the xmit program).

Prototype audio programming library
-----------------------------------
    A preliminary audio programming library, libaudio.a, is provided.
    Manual pages for the functions in libaudio.a are located in
    /usr/demo/SOUND/man/man3.  Header files for libaudio.a are in
    /usr/demo/SOUND/include/multimedia.

Sound files
-----------
    Some sample sound files are located in the /usr/demo/SOUND/sounds
    directory.  sample.au contains guidelines in setting the recording
    volume level.  The other files include sample sound effects and
    telephone control tones.

Building the demos from source code
-----------------------------------
    Source code is provided for all demo programs.  Before attempting to build
    the demo programs from source, ensure that the OpenWindows, SPARCcompilers,
    and Devguide (Version 3.0.1 or later) products are installed in your system.
    (Note that Devguide must be purchased separately.)  Refer to the system
    installation manual for instructions on installing these products.

    Be sure to set the GUIDEHOME environment variable to the directory where
    Devguide is installed.  Header files are included from $(GUIDEHOME)/include
    and libraries are linked from $(GUIDEHOME)/lib.

    To build the demo programs, do the following:

        % cd src
        % make

    To install them in /usr/demo/SOUND/bin, type:

        % make install
```

FIGURE 6.3

A sample of output using the mp filter

Before you can record anything, two additional pieces of hardware are needed: a microphone and an audio input/output adapter cable. The microphone can be any commercial variety that can be plugged into the audio I/O adapter cable. The adapter cable is part of the Sun workstation accessory package that comes with most Sun workstations. You can listen to audio output through a connected headphone or an externally powered speaker that is plugged into the headphone jack of the input/output adapter cable.

N O T E

If you are using Solaris 2 for x86, you need to have installed a supported sound board, such as the Sound Blaster Pro, to work with the Audio Tool.

The Audio Tool Window

The `Audio Tool` window uses a common tape recorder metaphor for working with sound files. Figure 6.4 shows both the Audio Tool window and icon. The `File` menu provides items for managing sound files. The `Edit` menu includes items for editing sound files, such as cutting and pasting sounds. The `Volume` menu provides items for adjusting the play and record volumes.

FIGURE 6.4

The Audio Tool window and icon

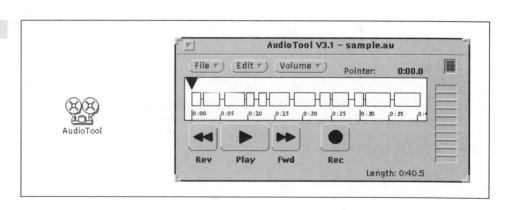

The display canvas area displays recorded sound graphically. Recorded information is represented with rectangle-shaped boxes that contain bands of sound, and silence is shown as a thin, flat horizontal line, as shown in Figure 6.4. Interval marks are displayed under the sound graph to measure recorded sound.

The four buttons located at the bottom of the window (`Rev`, `Play`, `Fwd`, and `Rec`) function like standard controls on a tape recorder. The drag-and-drop target allows you to drag sound files into the `Audio Tool` window. The `Level` meter, the boxes below the drag-and-drop target, graphically display the level of sound coming from the recording.

Loading Sound Files

There are several audio files included with Solaris, which are stored in the `/usr/demo/SOUND/sounds` and `/usr/openwin/lib/locale/C/help/hand-books/sounds` directories. Double-clicking the left mouse button on a sound file icon in the File Manager activates the Audio Tool and begins playing the recording.

A sound file can also be loaded into the Audio Tool using the drag-and-drop method. Dragging and dropping a sound file onto the drag-and-drop target loads the file into the Audio Tool, replacing any file currently in the Audio Tool. Dragging and dropping a sound file into the display canvas appends the sound file to any sound file already in the Audio Tool.

A sound file can also be loaded into the Audio Tool by clicking the left mouse button on the `File` menu to choose the default `Load` item. The `Load File` pop-up window appears (Figure 6.5). Select the file you want from the scrolling list and click on the Load button at the bottom of the window to load the file. Alternatively you can enter the directory path and file name of the sound file you want to load in the `Name` text field and click the left mouse button on the `Load` button.

FIGURE 6.5

The Load File pop-up
window

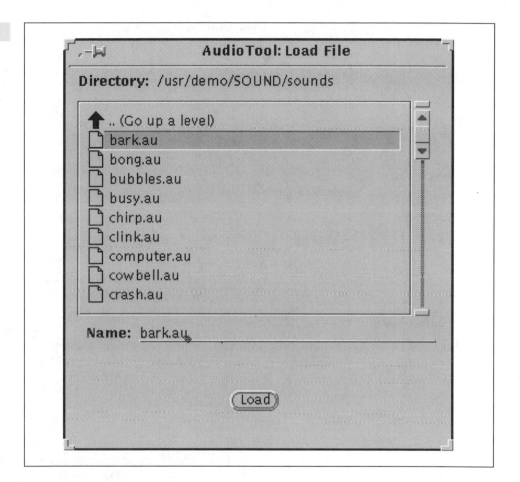

Recording a Sound

Recording a sound file in the `Audio Tool` window is similar to using a tape recorder. With the `Audio Tool` window displayed, make sure your microphone is turned on, and perform the following steps.

1. Click the left mouse button on the `Rec` button. The messages `Recording` and `Length` (elapsed time) are displayed in the status information area at the bottom of the Audio Tool window. The `Rec` button changes to a `Stop` button.

2. Record your sound or message.

3. To stop recording, click the left mouse button on the **Stop** button.
   The recording is stopped and your recorded sounds are displayed
   as boxes and lines in the **Display** canvas. You can append or record
   over a recording by repositioning the cursor in the display canvas
   and repeating steps 2 and 3.

The Audio Tool's status information is displayed below the recording
control buttons and the length of the sound file information is displayed
under the **Rec** button.

Playing Back a Recording

Playing back a recorded sound in the **Audio Tool** window is easy. With the
recorded sound displayed in the display canvas, do the following:

1. Click the left mouse button on the **Rev** (reverse) button or click
   the left mouse button with the pointer at the beginning of the
   recording in the display canvas. You can position the pointer at any
   location in the recording to start the playback at that location.

2. Click the left mouse button in the display canvas. The **Play** position pointer is displayed at that position.

3. Click the left mouse button on the **Play** button. The recording is
   played on your workstation's speaker, headphones, or external
   speaker. The **Play** button changes to a **Stop** button, on which you
   can click the left mouse button to stop the playback.

Saving Sound Files

To save a new sound file, choose the **Save** item from the **File** menu. The
Save File pop-up window appears (Figure 6.6). Enter the directory path
for the file and click on the **Save** button or press Return. In the **File Name**
text field, enter the file name for the sound file. Click the left mouse button on the **Save** button. An audio file icon (Figure 6.7) now appears in
the directory where you saved the audio file.

FIGURE 6.6

The Save File window

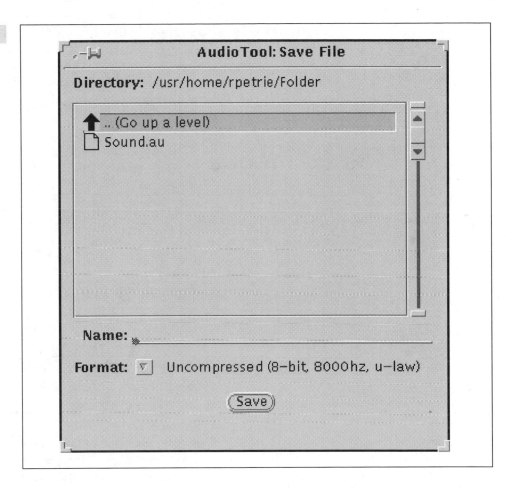

FIGURE 6.7

An Audio Tool file icon

Audio.au

If you're working on a sound file that has already been saved previously
by choosing **Save** from the **File** menu, you can save it with another file
name by choosing the **Save As** item from the **File** menu. This displays the
same **Save File** pop-up window as displayed when first saving a file. The
top center of the window displays the name of a sound file, along with its
status.

The Edit Menu

The **Edit** menu provides standard editing commands for working in the
Audio Tool window. If the editing command is dimmed, the use of that
command is not available for the operation being performed. The following explains the items in the **Edit** menu.

ITEM	DESCRIPTION
Again	Repeats the last **Edit** menu command.
Clear	Removes the displayed sound data from the display window. If the sound data has not been saved before choosing the **Clear** item, a Notice prompts you to confirm the discard of your unsaved edits.
Undo	Reverses the effect of the last editing command issued. A submenu provides the **Undo Last** and **Undo All** commands. The **Undo Last** command reverses the previous edit. The **Undo All** command restores all edited changes to their original status.
Redo	Reverses the effects of the **Undo** command. A submenu provides the **Redo Last** and **Redo All** commands. The **Redo Last** command restores the previous edit. The **Redo All** command restores all edited changes.
Cut	Removes the current selection from the sound file and places it in the clipboard. You can cut segments from the same file or other sound files.

ITEM	DESCRIPTION
Copy	Copies the current selection and places it in the clipboard without modifying the original sound file. You can copy segments from the same file or other sound files.
Paste	Pastes information currently stored in the clipboard (as a result of previous Copy or Cut commands) into any active sound file.
Delete	Displays a submenu of four deletion items. The first, Selection, removes the current selection from your sound file directory. The Unselected item removes all but the selected portion of the sound file. All Silence deletes all silent pauses from the sound file. The last item, Silent Ends, deletes any silence that occurs at the end of a sound file.
Select All	Selects the entire sound recording in the display canvas.

Pressing the right mouse button in the display canvas displays the Display pop-up menu (Figure 6.8). All the items in this menu, with the exception of the Reset pointer item, are also available in the Edit menu.

FIGURE 6.8

The Display pop-up menu

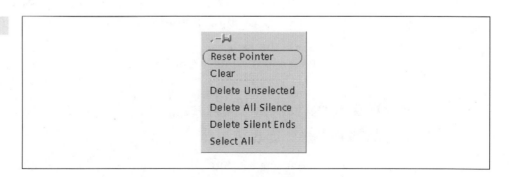

Editing a Sound File

Editing a sound file is similar to editing text in a text editor. You can copy, move, and delete sound data in the display canvas. Any time you move the pointer to the display canvas, the cursor becomes a thin vertical line. The position of the cursor is indicated by the cursor location status message in the upper-right corner. If you click the left mouse button while in the display canvas, the position pointer (an upside-down triangle located at the top of the display canvas) is displayed and its location is noted at the Pointer status message.

The following steps explain how to edit a sound file:

1. Load the sound file into the Audio Tool window.

2. Click the left mouse button at the beginning of the sound segment you want to edit in the display canvas. You can choose the Reset pointer item from the display canvas pop-up menu to move the pointer to the beginning of the display canvas.

3. Click the middle mouse button at the end of the sound segment you want to edit.

4. Press the right mouse button on the Edit menu button and choose either the Cut or Copy item. If you want to delete the selected sound data, choose the Delete item.

5. To copy or move the selected sound segment, move the cursor to the new position for the segment and click the left mouse button. The position pointer is displayed at the location.

6. Press the right mouse button on the Edit menu and choose the Paste item. The sound segment is pasted at the cursor's location.

Inserting a Sound File into Another Sound File

You can insert a sound file to an existing sound file in the Audio Tool window by using either the drag-and-drop method or the Include File item in the File menu. To insert a sound file using the drag-and-drop method, move the cursor in the display canvas to the location where you want to insert the sound file, and click the left mouse button. Drag and drop the sound file icon you want to insert on the display canvas.

To insert a sound file into an existing sound file in the `Audio Tool` window, first move the cursor in the display canvas to the location where you want to insert the sound file, and click the left mouse button. Choose the `Include File` itcm from the `File` menu to display the `Include File` pop-up window. In the scrolling list, select the file you want to insert in the `Audio Tool` pop-up window, and click the left mouse button on the `Include` button.

Customizing the Audio Tool

Choosing the `Properties` item menu in the `Edit` menu displays the Audio Tool's `Properties` window (Figure 6.9). The following list explains each control:

CONTROL	DESCRIPTION
Auto Play on Load	Instructs the Audio Tool to automatically play a file when it is loaded. The default setting is checked.
Auto Play on Selection	Automatically plays back any portion of a recorded sound selected in thc display canvas. The default setting is unchecked.
Confirm before clear	Determines whether a warning message is displayed when you choose the **Clear** item from the **Edit** menu.
Silence Detection	Silence in the Audio Tool is identified by a straight line, and sound is identified by boxes. Unless this setting is checked, the Audio tool does not differentiate between sound and silence, so silence and sound are indistinguishable in the display canvas.

FIGURE 6.9

The Audio Tool's
Properties window

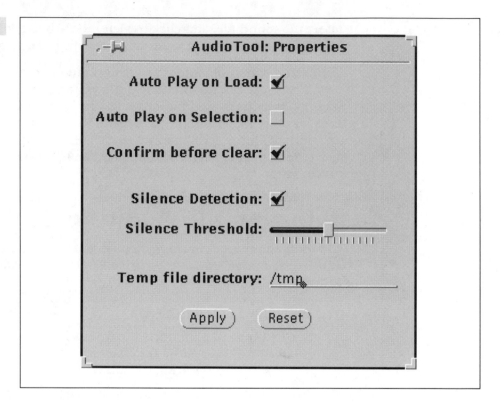

CONTROL	DESCRIPTION
Silence Threshold	Changes the degree with which silence is measured. It adjusts the sensitivity to pauses, determining when a pause should be interpreted as silence. Dragging the slider to the right decreases the sensitivity to short pauses, thus decreasing the number of sound-and-silence segments. Dragging the slider to the left increases the sensitivity to short pauses, thus increasing the number of sound-and-silence segments.

CONTROL	DESCRIPTION
Temp file directory	Lets you determine where temporary sound files are placed when working with the Audio Tool.

Clicking the left mouse button on the `Apply` button saves all the changes you make in the `Properties` pop-up window. Clicking the left mouse button on the `Reset` button before pressing the `Apply` button resets the most recent changes to their previous settings.

The Play Volume Pop-up Window

Choosing the `Play` item from the `Volume` menu displays the `Play Volume` pop-up window (Figure 6.10). The `Play Volume` pop-up window controls the volume of the audio input and output, and whether the audio output goes to the speaker or jack.

The `Play Volume` setting allows you to control the output volume to the internal workstation speaker. The `Monitor Volume` setting allows you to control the adjustment of the audio input signal. The `Spkr/Jack` control switches between your workstation's internal speaker and the external headphone jack. The default setting is `Spkr`, which sends the audio output to your workstation's speaker. The `Pause Play` button suspends and resumes all audio output from the Audio Tool.

FIGURE 6.10

The Play Volume pop-up window

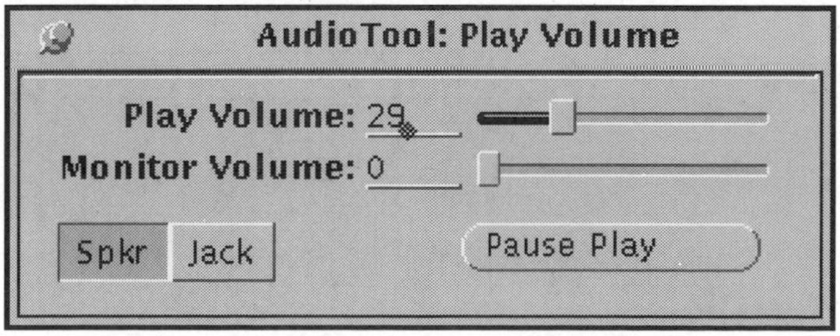

The Record Volume Pop-up Window

Choosing the `Record` item from the `Volume` menu displays the `Record Volume` pop-up window (Figure 6.11). The `Record Volume` pop-up window allows you to adjust the volume during recording using the `Record Volume` setting.

The `Auto-Adjust Record Volume` button sets the recording level to a programmed level adjustment, whereby the input sound data is scanned to determine its loudness. An input sensor meter is displayed on the window to show peaks and lows in the sound input. Once the volume is automatically adjusted, consistent loudness for each input device is set to an optimum signal level. If a microphone is connected to the audio input jack, adjustments can be made to voice input by selecting the `Auto-Adjust Record Volume` button. Speaking into the microphone in a normal tone until the process is complete automatically adjusts the voice input level.

FIGURE 6.11

The Record Volume
pop-up window

The Snapshot Application

The Snapshot application allows you to take color, gray-scale, and black-and-white snapshots of a region (a section of the screen), a window, or the entire screen. These snapshots are created and stored as raster files. *Raster files* store a picture as a matrix of dots. When you use the Snapshot application on a monochrome monitor, the images created are always black and white. When you take snapshots on a color monitor, the images are always in color, unless you are running OpenWindows in black-and-white mode. Some applications can handle black-and-white snapshots but cannot handle gray-scale or color snapshots. The **Snapshot** window and icon are shown in Figure 6.12. The following explains the controls in the **Snapshot** window.

FIGURE 6.12

The Snapshot window and icon

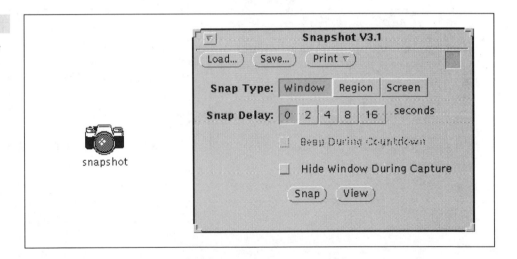

CONTROL	DESCRIPTION
Load button	Displays the **Load Options** pop-up window to allow you to load Snapshot files.

CONTROL	DESCRIPTION
`Save` button	Displays the `Save Options` pop-up window to allow you to save a snapshot to a file.
`Print` button	Lets you print your snapshots or displays the `Print Options` pop-up window to customize your printer settings.
`Snap Type`	Defines the area of the snapshot. The `Window` setting takes a snapshot of a single window. The `Region` setting takes a snapshot of part of the screen. The `Screen` setting takes a snapshot of the entire screen.
`Snap Delay`	Determines the time period between initiating the snapshot and taking it. The timer is especially useful if you are taking snapshots of menus that you must display after you start the snapshot. When the `Snap Delay` setting is set to 0 seconds, the snapshot is taken immediately. When the `Snap Delay` setting is set for more than 0 seconds, the `Beep During Countdown` setting becomes active and can be set.
`Beep During Countdown`	Activating the `Beep During Countdown` setting starts a bell beep each second between the time when you initiate the snapshot and when it is taken. Clicking the left mouse button on the `Beep During Countdown` setting acts as a toggle, setting it on or off.
`Hide Window During Capture`	Allows you to hide the `Snapshot` window when you're taking a snapshot of the screen.

CONTROL	DESCRIPTION
Snap	Activates the Snapshot application to take a snapshot.
View	Allows you to view the current snapshot in the View pop-up window.

Taking a Snapshot of a Window

To take a snapshot of a window, make sure the window or icon you want to capture is completely visible and not partly obscured by overlapping windows (unless you want to include them in the snapshot), and follow the steps below:

1. Make sure the Snap Type is set to Window in the Snapshot window. Set the Snap Delay and Beep During Countdown settings if you want to use them. When you have the Snap Delay set and are taking snapshots of windows or icons, Snapshot records the window position when the snap is initiated. However, if you move the window before the snapshot is completed, you may not get all the information you wanted in the window snapshot.

2. Click the left mouse button on the Snap button. A message appears in the window footer: SELECT–Select Window. ADJUST or MENU–Cancel. SELECT refers to the left mouse button. ADJUST refers to the middle button. MENU refers to the right mouse button. The Snap button appears shaded, indicating that it is waiting for you to select a window.

3. Click the left mouse button on the header of the window you want to snap to take the snapshot. To cancel the operation, click either the middle mouse button or the right mouse button. When the snapshot is complete, a message is displayed in the footer of the snapshot window indicating whether the snapshot succeeded or not. You can view the snapshot by clicking the left mouse button on the View button.

4. Click the left mouse button on the `Save` button. The `Save Op-tions` pop-up window is displayed, as shown in Figure 6.13. In the `Directory` text field, type the name of the directory to which you want to save the file. Type the file name for the snapshot in the `File` text field.

5. Click the left mouse button on the `Save` button in the `Save Op-tions` pop-up window.

Snapshot: Save Options

Directory: /usr/home/rpetrie

File: snapshot.rs

(Save)

Taking a Snapshot of a Region

Snapshots of any rectangular area of the screen you specify can be taken using the `Region` button. Before taking a snapshot of a region of the screen, make sure the screen is displaying the windows or icons you want to capture, and perform the following steps:

1. Click the left mouse button on the `Region` setting in the `Snapshot` window. Set the `Snap Delay` and `Beep During Countdown` settings if you want to use them.

2. Click the left mouse button on the `Hide Window During Capture` setting if you need to.

3. Click the left mouse button on the `Region` button. A message appears in the window footer: `SELECT—Position Rectangle, ADJUST—Snap Image, MENU—Cancel`. `SELECT` means to click the left mouse button. `ADJUST` means to click the middle mouse button. `MENU` means to click the right mouse button.

4. Move the pointer to the top left corner of the region you want to define and press the left mouse button. Drag the pointer to define the rectangular region to be included. A bounding box is displayed. Release the left mouse button. An outline of the snapshot region is displayed.

5. Click the middle mouse button. Snapshot takes the snapshot of the boxed region of the screen and displays a message in the Snapshot window footer indicating whether the snapshot was successful. If you want to cancel the snapshot, click the right mouse button. You can view the snapshot by clicking the left mouse button on the `View` button.

6. Click the left mouse button on the `Save` button. The `Save Options` pop-up window is displayed. Type the name of the directory in which you want to save the file in the `Directory` text field. Type the file name for the snapshot in the `File` text field.

7. Click the left mouse button on the `Save` button in the `Save Options` pop-up window..

Taking a Snapshot of the Screen

Taking a snapshot of the entire screen is the easiest type of snapshot to take; however, it takes longer and requires more disk space to store. Unless you need a snapshot of the entire screen, it is recommended you use `Window` or `Region`. To take a snapshot of the entire screen, make sure the screen is set up in the configuration you want and follow these steps:

1. Click the left mouse button on the `Screen` setting. Set the `Snap Delay` and `Beep During Countdown` settings if you want to use them.

2. Click the left mouse button on `Hide Window During Capture` unless you want the `Snapshot` window in the screen shot.

3. Click the left mouse button on the `Snap` button. After the snapshot is taken, a status message informing you whether the snapshot was successful or not is displayed in the window footer. You can view the snapshot by clicking the left mouse button on the `View` button.

4. Click the left mouse button on the `Save` button. The `Save Op-tions` pop-up window is displayed. Type the name of the directory in which you want to save the file in the `Directory` text field. Type the file name for the snapshot in the `File` text field.

5. Click the left mouse button on the `Save` button in the `Save Op-tions` pop-up window.

Viewing a Snapshot

The Snapshot application allows you to view a snapshot file at any time. You can use either the drag-and-drop method or use the `Load` button. To display a snapshot using the drag-and-drop method, drag a snapshot file from the File Manager and drop it onto the `Snapshot` window's drag-and-drop target. Click the left mouse button on the `View` button. The `View` pop-up window appears, displaying the selected file. Once the `View` pop-up window is displayed, you can view other snapshot files by dragging and dropping one file at a time onto the `Snapshot` window's drag-and-drop target.

To display a snapshot using the `Load` button, click the left mouse button on the `Load` button. The `Load Options` pop-up window is displayed. Type the name of the directory and the snapshot file you want to load in the `Directory` and `File` text fields. Click the left mouse button on the `Load` button. In the `Snapshot` window, click the left mouse button on the `View` menu. The `View` pop-up window is displayed (Figure 6.14), showing the contents of the snapshot file. To view a snapshot immediately after taking it, simply click the left mouse button on the `View` button. If you are using a black-and-white monitor, Snapshot automatically converts a copy of gray-scale or color images to black and white so that they can be displayed. The file itself is not changed.

Only one snapshot at a time can be viewed, unless you load and use multiple snapshot applications. When the `View` pop-up window is displayed, and you type a new snapshot file name in the `File` text field and click the left mouse button on the `View` button, the `View` window is cleared and automatically resized to match the size of the second snapshot file.

FIGURE 6.14

The View pop-up window displaying a snapshot

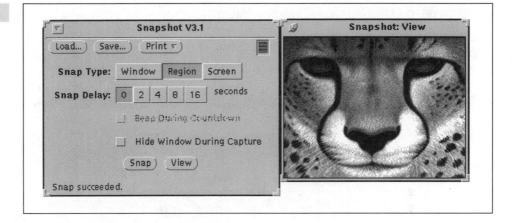

Printing a Snapshot

Snapshot files can be printed by clicking the left mouse button on the **Print** button. If you want to change the default printing settings, press the right mouse button on the **Print** button and choose the **Options** item. The **Print Options** pop-up window is displayed (Figure 6.15). This window allows you to change your printer settings for Snapshot. The following explains the controls in the **Print Options** window.

CONTROL	DESCRIPTION
Destination	Allows you to designate whether a snapshot is sent to a printer or to a file. When **Printer** is selected, use the text field to specify which printer you want to use. When **File** is selected, the **Directory** and **File** text fields are displayed.
Printer	Allows you to specify another printer.
Orientation	Determines the orientation of the printed image on the page. The **Upright** setting prints a portrait image. The **Sideways** setting prints a landscape image.

FIGURE 6.15

The Print Options
pop-up window

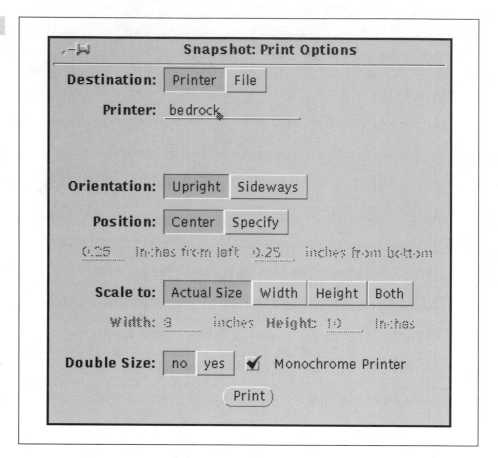

CONTROL	DESCRIPTION
Position	Controls the position of the snapshot on the printed page. The Center setting centers the printed snapshot. You can specify the left and bottom margins for the printed image by choosing the Specify setting. This activates the Inches from left and Inches from bottom text fields, which have default values of .25 inch.

CONTROL	DESCRIPTION
Scale to	The default `Actual Size` setting prints the snapshot in the actual size of the displayed snapshot. You can specify the width of the printed snapshot by choosing the `Width` setting and typing a value, either a whole number or decimal, in the `Width` text field. The snapshot is scaled to the width you select. You can also specify the height of the printed snapshot by choosing the `Height` setting, and typing a value in the `Height` text field. When you choose the `Both` setting, both the `Width` and `Height` text fields are activated, allowing you to specify the width and height dimensions for the snapshot.
Double Size	Choosing the `Yes` setting allows you to double the size of the snapshot.
Monochrome Printer	Unless you are using a color printer, keep the `Monochrome Printer` setting checked.
Print	Clicking the left mouse button on the `Print` button prints the specified file.

Once you change the settings in the `Print Options` pop-up window, they are recorded and used each time you click the left mouse button on the `Print` button until you exit or quit the `Snapshot` window.

The Clock Application

The Clock application displays an analog clock icon that shows the current time of day (Figure 6.16). When you open the Clock icon, the same clock is displayed in the pane of a window. The `Clock` window (Figure 6.16) has a header and resize corners to make the clock image larger or smaller.

FIGURE 6.16

The Clock icon and
window

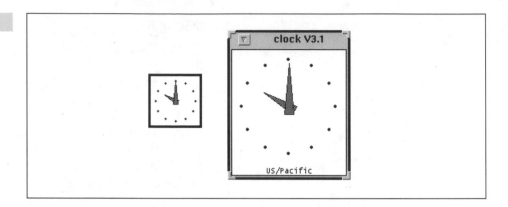

NOTE

Solaris also includes two X clock applications that
display analog clocks. To display the square X clock in a
Shell or Command Tool, enter xclock &. To display the
circular X clock in a Shell or Command Tool, enter
oclock &.

Customizing the Clock

The Clock can be customized using the settings in the Clock Properties
window. To display the Clock Properties window, press the right mouse
button in the Clock pane to display the Clock pop-up menu (Figure 6.17),
then choose the Properties item. The following explains the controls in
the Clock Properties pop-up window.

CONTROL	DESCRIPTION
Clock Face	The digital setting displays in the Clock window as a digital clock (Figure 6.18). The default analog setting displays a traditional clock face in the Clock window. The Clock icon always displays an analog clock, regardless of the Clock Face property setting.

FIGURE 6.17

The Clock Properties
pop-up window

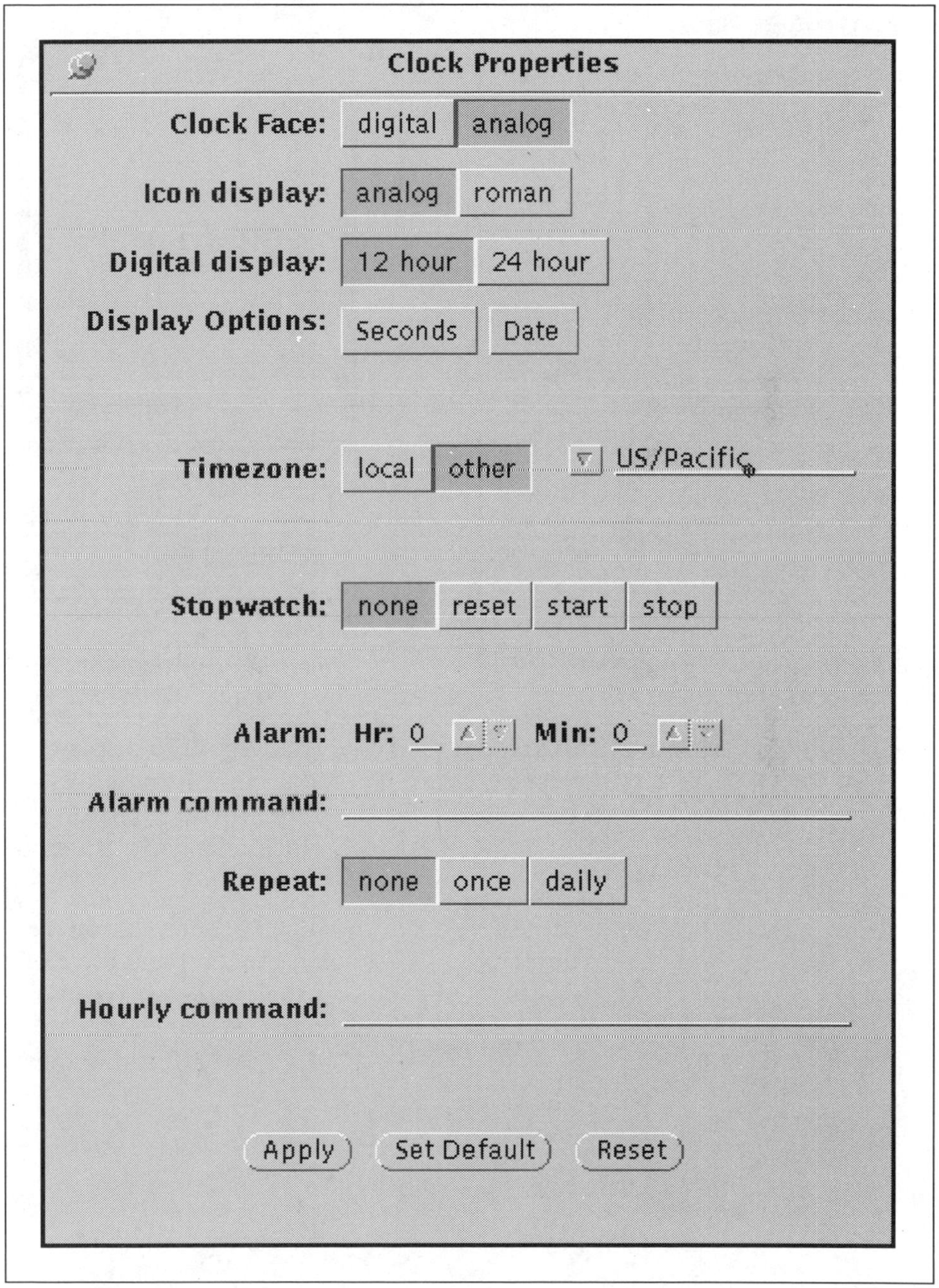

FIGURE 6.18

The digital clock

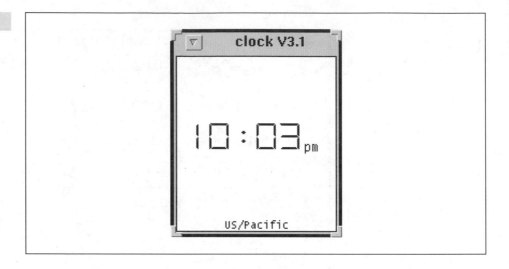

CONTROL	DESCRIPTION
Icon display	Allows you to choose whether the clock icon appears with dots representing numbers or with roman numerals.
Digital display	Allows you to display the digital clock in a 12-hour or 24-hour (military time) format. The digital 12-hour clock tells you if the time is a.m. or p.m.
Display Options	The Seconds setting displays seconds on the icon and the clock face in the Clock window. The Date setting displays the date in the Clock window but does not affect the icon display.

CONTROL	DESCRIPTION
Timezone	Allows you to display the time of a different time zone. By default, the time is displayed in your local time zone. You can set the clock to a different time zone by pressing the left mouse button on the `Other` setting to display the Timezone abbreviated menu button. Clicking the right mouse button on the Timezone abbreviated menu button displays a list of available time zones (Figure 6.19) so you can choose the time zone you want.
Stopwatch	The `reset` setting allows you to turn the clock display into a stopwatch. Using the `digital` setting in the `Clock Face` setting makes the stopwatch easier to read. To start the stopwatch, click the left mouse button on the `start` setting. To stop the stopwatch, click the left mouse button on the `stop` setting. The stopwatch settings take effect immediately, unlike the other settings, which take effect when you click the left mouse button on the `Apply` button.
Alarm	Allows you to specify the time for an alarm. You must specify the time, using a 24-hour format.

FIGURE 6.19

The Timezone submenu

CONTROL	DESCRIPTION
`Alarm command`	Enter the command that you want to take place at the alarm time in the `Alarm command` text field. If you don't specify a command, the Clock application will beep. If your workstation has audio capabilities, you can set the clock to crow like a rooster by entering `ksh -c "cat /usr/demo/ SOUND/sounds/ rooster.au > /dev/audio"`.
`Repeat`	Allows you to specify whether the alarm should be triggered just one time or daily at a given time. The alarm will not be triggered as long as the `Repeat` setting is `none`.
`Hourly command`	If you want a command to repeat hourly, type that command in the `Hourly` command text field. For example, you can enter `ksh -c "cat /usr/demo/SOUND/sounds/ rooster.au > /dev/audio"` to have the clock crow like a rooster on an hourly basis.

The `Set Default` button determines if the changes you make in the `Clock Properties` pop-up window will appear in each new clock you start. Unless you choose the `Set Default` button, the changes made in the `Clock Properties` pop-up window are not saved after the current Open-Windows session.

The Performance Meter

The DeskSet environment provides ten different Performance Meters that can be used to monitor various aspects of your system. One meter or a combination of meters can be run (displayed) at the same time. To display a Performance Meter, choose the `Performance Meter` item from the `Programs` submenu of the `Workspace` menu. The default `cpu Performance Meter` window is displayed in the size of a typical icon (Figure 6.20). Closing the performance meter window to an icon displays a graph icon, as shown in Figure 6.20.

FIGURE 6.20

An open and closed
Performance Meter

perfmeter

The Performance Meter Pop-up Menu

You can quickly change to another performance meter from any `Performance Meter` window using a `Performance Meter` pop-up menu (Figure 6.21). To display the `Performance Meter` pop-up menu, press the right mouse button in any `Performance Meter` window. The pop-up menu includes the ten Performance Meter items and a `Properties` item for customizing the Performance Meter. Choose the type of performance monitor you want to change to. The following is a brief description of what each of the items on this menu monitors.

The Performance
Meter pop-up menu

ITEM	MONITORS
Show cpu	Percent of CPU being used.
Show packets	Number of ethernet packets per second. (*Ethernet packets* are units for transmitting messages over a network.)
Show page	Paging activity in pages per second.
Show swap	Number of jobs swapped per second.
Show interrupts	Number of job interrupts per second.
Show disk	Disk traffic in transfers per second.
Show context	Number of context switches per second.
Show load	Average number of runnable processes over the last minute.
Show collisions	Number of collisions per second detected on the ethernet.
Show errors	Number of errors per second on receiving packets.

Customizing Performance Meters

The last item in the **Performance Meter** pop-up menu, **Properties**, allows you to customize the features of a Performance Meter. Choosing the **Properties** item displays the **Properties** pop-up window, as shown in Figure 6.22. The following explains the settings in the **Properties** pop-up window.

FIGURE 6.22

The Properties pop-up window

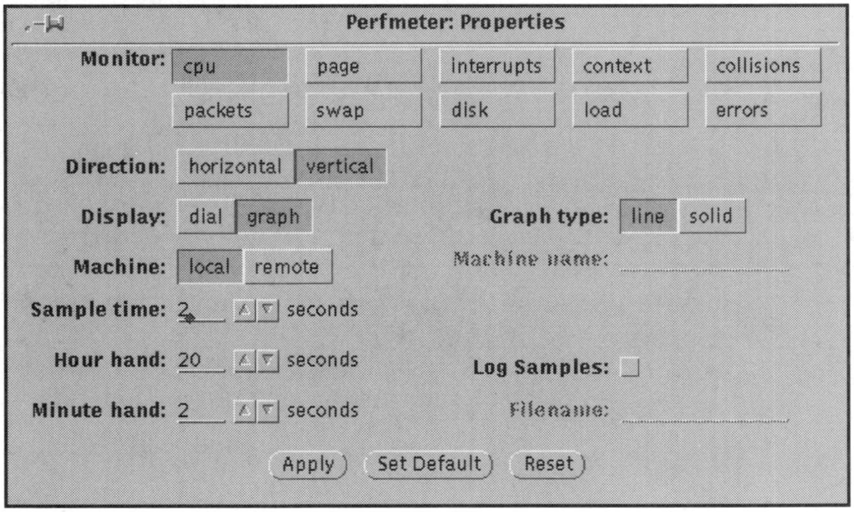

SETTING	DESCRIPTION
Monitor	Choosing one of the **Monitor** settings and clicking the left mouse button on the **Apply** button is the same as choosing one of the same items from the **Performance Meter** pop-up menu.

SETTING	DESCRIPTION
Direction	Determines if multiple Performance Meters are displayed side by side (horizontally) or stacked on top of one another (vertically).
Display	Determines if the Performance Meters are displayed as dials or as graphs. The **graph** setting is the default setting. Figure 6.23 shows a performance meter using a dial display.
Graph type	Choose the **line** setting to display a single line graph, and **solid** to display a solid graph.
Machine	Allows you to monitor the performance for your own machine (**local**, which is the default) or for another machine (**remote**) on the network. If you select the **remote** setting, the **Machine name** text field is activated to accept the name of the machine you want to monitor.

FIGURE 6.23

A performance meter using the dial display

SETTING	DESCRIPTION
Sample time	Allows you to change the frequency with which the meters are updated and units measured by the `Hour hand` and the `Minute hand` settings. The short needle, referred to as an *hour hand*, tracks average performance over a twenty-second interval, and the long one, referred to as the *minute hand*, tracks current performance over a two-second interval. The type of performance being measured is shown in the lower-left corner of the icon and its maximum value is shown in the lower-right corner.
Log Samples	Lets you save and examine individual samples. Samples are saved in the file typed in the `filename` text field. If no file is specified, then samples are saved in a file in your home directory called `perfmeter.logxxx`, where xxx is replaced by a unique identifier. If you use the `Log Samples`, do not leave the performance meter running for a long period of time. The `perfmeter.logxxx` file can increase in size and leave you with little or no disk space.

Clicking the left mouse button on `Set Default` saves your Performance Meter settings for use in each new Performance Meter you start. If you change the values of any of the performance meter properties, you need to click the left mouse button on the `Apply` button to record the changes. Pressing the left mouse button on the `Reset` button returns all settings to the system defaults.

The Calculator

The Calculator is designed to perform a wide variety of mathematical functions. It provides financial, logical, and scientific functions. It looks and works in much the same way as many hand-held calculators. The Calculator allows you to use decimal, binary, octal, or hexadecimal numbers, as well as scientific notation. It has ten different memory registers in which numbers can be easily stored, retrieved, and replaced. In addition, the Calculator allows you to store functions you create in a menu.

The `Calculator` window and icon are shown in Figure 6.24. The buttons of the calculator are the controls that activate its functions. It has six rows of eight buttons, some arranged as buttons within other buttons, to emulate a typical calculator. Buttons that have a menu mark (the upside-down triangle) display menus when you press the right mouse button on them.

FIGURE 6.24

The Calculator window and icon

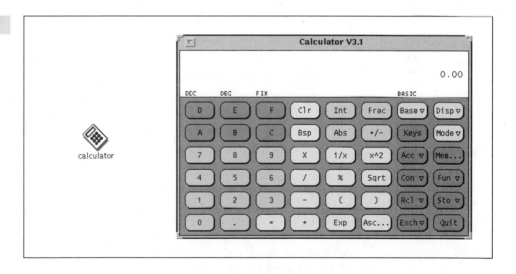

NOTE

Solaris also includes the X calculator. To start the X calculator program in a Shell Tool or Command Tool, enter `xcalc` &. For more information on using the X calculator, enter `xman` & in a Shell or Command Tool.

Performing Simple Calculations

While the DeskSet Calculator is a powerful financial, logical, and scientific calculator, it also allows you to perform simple arithmetic operations such as addition, subtraction, division, and multiplication. To perform a numerical operation, such as adding two numbers together, follow the steps below:

1. Click the left mouse button on the number you want to enter. Numbers can also be entered using the keyboard. The number is entered in the calculator's display in the upper-right corner.

2. Click the left mouse button on the operation button you want; for example, move the pointer to the plus sign (+) to add a number. Operators can also be entered using the keyboard.

3. Click the left mouse button on the next number in the equation.

4. Click the left mouse button on the equal sign (=). The result is displayed in the Calculator display area.

Modes of Operation

The Calculator has four modes of operation: `Basic`, `Financial`, `Logical`, and `Scientific`. The area above the Base key displays the current mode. To change modes, press the right mouse button on the `Mode` button and choose the mode you want.

Number Bases

Binary, octal, decimal, and hexadecimal number bases can be set using the **Base** button in the top row. Pressing the right mouse button on the **Base** button displays the menu of number bases. Drag the pointer to a number base item and release the right mouse button. The numeric keypad changes to display those numbers appropriate to the number base mode you chose. The following list gives a brief description of each of the calculator's number bases. Figure 6.25 identifies the binary, octal, decimal, and hexadecimal keypads.

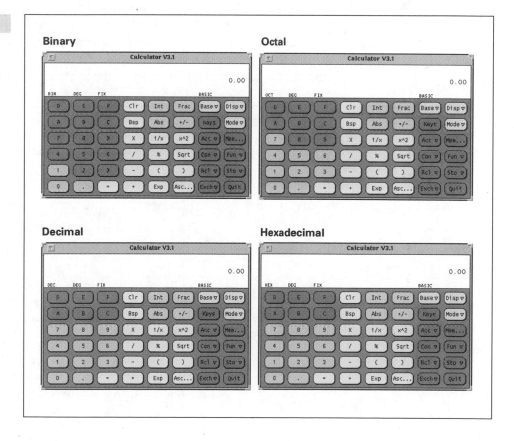

NUMBER BASE	DISPLAYS
Binary	Base 2, displays the digits 0 and 1.
Octal	Base 8, displays the digits 0 through 7.
Decimal	Base 10, displays the digits 0 through 9.
Hexadecimal	Base 16, displays the digits 0 through F.

Changing the Display Type

Normally the Calculator displays numbers in fixed-point notation. The Disp button lets you change the type of numeric display to engineering or scientific display. The Calculator display shows the notation type. Because the default is Fixed point notation, FIX is displayed in the Calculator display. To change to engineering or scientific display, press the right mouse button on the Disp button and choose the Engineering or Scientific item.

Miscellaneous Functions

The following list describes other helpful Calculator function keys:

KEY	DESCRIPTION
Clr (Clear)	Clears the value from the display.
Bsp (Backspace)	Removes the rightmost character from the current display and recalculates its value.
Acc (Accuracy)	Chooses the number of digits of precision used in the Calculator display and the memory registers.
Exp	Starts exponential input. Any numbers entered after you choose Exp are displayed exponentially. If no numerical input has occurred, a mantissa of 1.0 is assumed.

KEY	DESCRIPTION
Quit	Quits the Calculator.
Keys	Toggles the display of the keys to show the keyboard equivalents for mouseless operation of the Calculator.

Memory Registers

The Calculator has ten memory registers that can store and retrieve values for calculations. Registers are a handy way of storing calculation results for future computations. These memory registers can be accessed using the following keys:

MEMORY REGISTER	DESCRIPTION
Exch (Exchange registers)	Exchanges the value shown in the current display with a selected register number from the Exchange pop-up menu.
Mem (Memory)	Displays a pop-up window showing the values (in the current base and accuracy) of the ten memory registers.
Sto (Store)	Stores the current value in the memory register number you choose from the pop-up menu.
Rcl	Retrieves a value from the memory register number you choose from the pop-up menu.

The following steps explain how to store and retrieve register values.

1. Press the left mouse button on the number you want to store as a register value. The number appears in the Calculator's display area.

2. Press the right mouse button on the Sto (store) button at the far right, in the fifth row of keys, and choose the register you want to store the number in. The number is now in the register you selected.

3. Click the left mouse button on the `Mem` (memory) key, the second key in the top row, to view the stored register value.

4. To retrieve the register value you just stored, press the right mouse button on the `Rcl` button and choose the register value you want to retrieve. The value is displayed in the Calculator display.

User-Defined Functions

The Calculator allows you to enter your own set of constants and define your own functions using the `Con` (constant) and `Fun` (function) keys. Each of these keys contains a menu. Choosing the first item on the menu displays a pop-up window that lets you enter the name of a constant or a function and its value. Once you enter the number by clicking the left mouse button on the button at the bottom of the pop-up window, the number and its name are displayed as an item on the pop-up menu. To use the constant or the function, choose the appropriate item from the pop-up menu. The numbers you enter are stored in a file named `.calctoolrc` in your home directory. To edit or delete items from the `Constant` or `Functions` menus, you must edit the `.calctoolrc` file using the Text Editor or any other ASCII text editor. The following example describes how to create a function that determines the circumference of a circle.

1. Click the left mouse button on the `Fun` key (in the upper-right corner). The `Enter Function` pop-up window is displayed.

2. Enter a number to identify your function in the `Function no` text field and press Return. The insert point moves to the `Description` text field.

3. Enter a descriptive name (such as `circum`) for your function and press Return to move the insert point to the `Value` field.

4. Type a function in the `Value` field. For example, to create a function to determine the circumference of a circle, enter `3.14159 d *`.

5. Click the left mouse button on the `Enter Function` button to store the new function in your `.calctoolrc` file and add it to the `Functions` menu.

6. Press the right mouse button on the Fun (Function) key and choose the 3.14159 d * [circum] item, which displays 3.14. The next number you enter will be applied to the function.

7. Enter a number using the mouse or the keyboard to indicate the diameter of the circle you want to determine the circumference of, and either press Return or click the left mouse button on the = (equals) key.

Number Manipulation Operators

The Calculator provides the following number manipulation operators:

KEY	DESCRIPTION
Int	Returns the integer portion of the currently displayed value.
Frac	Returns the fractional portion of the currently displayed value.
Abs	Returns the absolute value of the currently displayed value.
+/-	Changes the arithmetic sign of the currently displayed value or the exponent being entered.
x	Returns the factorial of the currently displayed value.
1/x	Returns the current value of 1 divided by the currently displayed value.
x^2	Returns the square of the currently displayed value.
%	Calculates a percentage (determined from the next number entered) of the last number entered.
Sqrt	Returns the square root value of the currently displayed value.
Asc	Displays the ASCII value of a character.

The Financial Calculator

Choosing the Financial item from the Mode key pop-up menu, displays the Financial Mode pop-up window, as shown in Figure 6.26. The financial functions retrieve needed information from the memory registers. For example, in order to determine the amount of a loan payment, you must enter the amount of the loan, the interest rate, and the term of the loan. You store this information in the appropriate memory registers before you click the left mouse button on the financial function button.

The following describes each financial function and the memory register settings for each function.

FUNCTION	DESCRIPTION	EXCHANGE REGISTER SETTINGS
Ctrm	Computes the number of compounding periods it will take an investment of present value to grow to a future value, earning a fixed interest rate per compounding period.	*Reg. 0:* Periodic interest (*int*) rate. *Reg. 1:* Future value (*fv*) of the investment. *Reg. 2:* Present value (*pv*) of the investment.

FIGURE 6.26

The Financial Mode
pop-up window

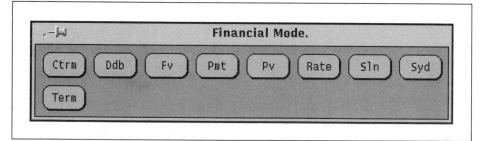

FUNCTION	DESCRIPTION	EXCHANGE REGISTER SETTINGS
Ddb	Using the double-declining balance method, Ddb commutes the depreciation allowance on an asset for a specified period of time.	*Reg. 0:* Amount paid for asset. *Reg. 1:* Salvage value of asset at end of life. *Reg. 2:* Useful life of an asset. *Reg. 3:* Time period for depreciation allowance.
Fv	The Fv function computes the future value of an investment based on a series of equal payments, earning a periodic interest rate over the number of payment periods in a term.	*Reg. 0:* Amount of each payment. *Reg. 1:* Interest rate. *Reg. 2:* Number of payments.
Pmt	Computes the periodic payment of a loan. Most installment loans are computed like ordinary annuities, in that payments are made at the end of each payment period.	*Reg. 0:* Amount of the loan. *Reg. 1:* Periodic interest rate of the loan. *Reg. 2:* Number of payments.

FUNCTION	DESCRIPTION	EXCHANGE REGISTER SETTINGS
Pv	The Pv function computes the present value based on a series of equal payments discounted at a periodic interest rate over the number of periods in the term.	*Reg. 0:* Amount of each payment. *Reg. 1:* Periodic interest rate. *Reg. 2:* Number of payments.
Rate	The periodic interest rate returns the periodic interest necessary for a present value to grow to a future value over the specified number of compounding periods in the term.	*Reg. 0:* Future value. *Reg. 1:* Present value. *Reg. 2:* Number of compounding periods.
Sln	The straight-line depreciation function divides the depreciable cost (actual cost less salvage value) evenly over the useful life of an asset. The useful life is the number of periods, typically years, over which an asset is depreciated.	*Reg. 0:* Cost of the asset. *Reg. 1:* Salvage value of the asset. *Reg. 2:* Useful life of the asset.

FUNCTION	DESCRIPTION	EXCHANGE REGISTER SETTINGS
Syd	The sum-of-the-years'-digits depreciation accelerates the rate of depreciation so that more depreciation expense occurs in earlier periods than in later ones. The depreciable cost is the actual cost less salvage value. The useful life is the number of periods, typically years, over which an asset is depreciated.	*Reg. 0:* Cost of the asset. *Reg. 1:* Salvage value of the asset. *Reg. 2:* Useful life of the asset. *Reg. 3:* Period for which depreciation is computed.
Term	The Term function computes the number of payment periods in the term of an ordinary annuity that are necessary to accumulate a future value earning a specified periodic interest rate.	*Reg. 0:* Amount of each periodic payment. *Reg. 1:* Future value. *Reg. 2:* Periodic interest rate.

Logical Functions

When you choose the Logical item from the Mode menu, the Logical Mode pop-up window is displayed, as shown in Figure 6.27. The Logical Mode Calculator provides the following logical functions.

FIGURE 6.27

The Logical Mode pop-up window

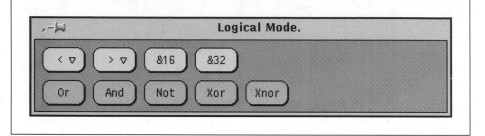

LOGICAL FUNCTION	DESCRIPTION
< (range 1 through 15)	Shifts the displayed binary value the designated number of places to the left.
> (range 1 through 15)	Shifts the displayed binary value the designated number of places to the right.
&16	Truncates the number displayed to return a 16-bit, unsigned integer.
&32	Truncates the number displayed to return a 32-bit, unsigned integer.
Or	Performs a logical OR operation on the last number and the next number entered, treating both numbers as unsigned long integers.
And	Performs a logical AND operation on the last number and the next number entered, treating both numbers as unsigned long integers.
Not	Performs a logical NOT operation on the current displayed value.
Xor	Performs a logical XOR operation on the last number and the next number entered, treating both numbers as unsigned long integers.

LOGICAL FUNCTION	DESCRIPTION
Xnor	Performs a logical XNOR operation on the last number and the next number entered, treating both numbers as unsigned long integers.

The Scientific Calculator

Choosing the `Scientific` item from the `Mode` menu displays the `Scientific Mode` pop-up window (Figure 6.28). The `Scientific Mode` pop-up window provides the following trigonometric functions.

KEY	DESCRIPTION
Trig	Displays a menu of trigonometric bases: `Degrees`, `Radians`, or `Gradients`. The current trigonometric base is indicated in the Calculator display.
Hyp	Sets or unsets the hyperbolic function flag. This flag affects the `Sin`, `Cos`, and `Tan` trigonometric functions.
Inv	Sets and unsets the inverse function flag. This flag affects the `Sin`, `Cos`, and `Tan` trigonometric functions.

FIGURE 6.28

The Scientific Mode pop-up window

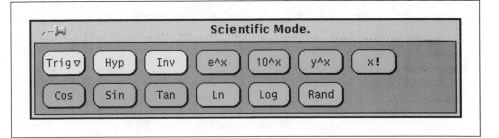

KEY	DESCRIPTION
e^x	Returns *e* raised to the power of the currently displayed value.
10^x	Returns 10 raised to the power of the currently displayed value.
y^x	Raises the last number entered to the power of the next number entered.
x!	Returns the factorial of the currently displayed value.
Cos	Returns the trigonometric cosine, arc cosine, hyperbolic cosine, or inverse hyperbolic cosine of the current value, depending on the settings of the Hyp and Inv flags. The result is displayed in the current units (degrees, radians, or gradients).
Sin	Returns the trigonometric sine, arc sine, hyperbolic sine, or inverse hyperbolic sine of the current value, depending on the setting of the Hyp and Inv flags. The result is displayed in the current units (degrees, radians, or gradients).
Tan	Returns the trigonometric tangent, arc tangent, hyperbolic tangent, or inverse hyperbolic tangent of the current value, depending on the settings of the Hyp and Inv flags. The result is displayed in the current units (degrees, radians, or gradients).
Ln	Returns the natural logarithm of the currently displayed value.
Log	Returns the base 10 logarithm of the currently displayed value.
Rand	Enters a random number (0 through 1) in the Calculator display.

Customizing the Calculator

You can change the appearance of the calculator. Pressing the right mouse button anywhere in the Calculator (other than on a button) displays the `Calculator` pop-up menu. Choosing the `Properties` item displays the `Calculator Properties` pop-up window, as shown in Figure 6.29. The following explains each of the Calculator settings.

FIGURE 6.29

The Calculator properties pop-up window

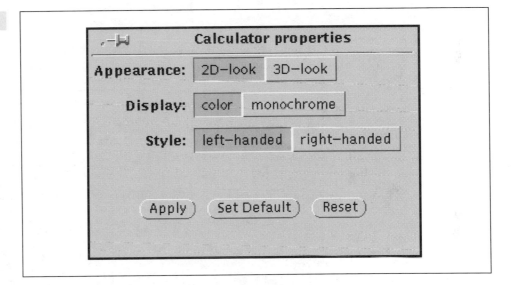

SETTING	DESCRIPTION
Appearance	Sets the calculator to display with two-dimensional or three-dimensional buttons.
Display	Sets the display to color or black and white.

SETTING	DESCRIPTION
Style	Changes the calculator keyboard layout. The `left-handed` setting is the default, with the numeric keys on the left side of the calculator. The `right-handed` setting moves the numeric keys to the right side of the Calculator keyboard. Figure 6.30 shows the calculator using the `right-handed` setting.

FIGURE 6.30

The Calculator using the right-handed setting

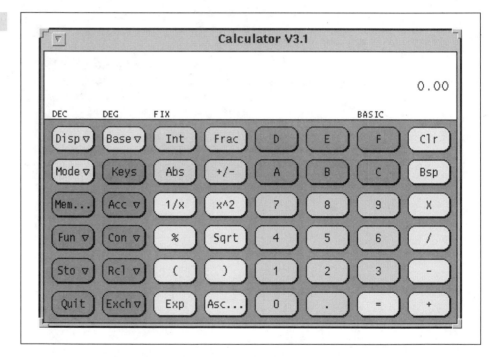

The `Set Default` setting saves your Calculator property settings, so the next time you start a calculator, the new **Appearance**, **Display**, and **Style** settings are applied. Be sure to click the left mouse button on the **Apply** button to apply your changes. If you make a mistake before pressing the **Apply** button, you can return to your original settings by clicking on the `Reset` button. If you want to return to the Calculator default settings, click on the `Set Default` button.

The Tape Tool

The Tape Tool lets you list files from a tape cartridge or an archive file that has been archived using the `tar` command. The Tape Tool cannot read tapes that have been written to using the `cpio` command. Working with `tar` and `cpio` commands are explained in Chapter 17, "System Administration Basics."

The `Tape Tool` window and icon is shown in Figure 6.31. You can drop files onto the `Tape Tool` window or onto the tape tool icon to select a file for archiving. The Tape Tool icon changes to display a unrewound tape, indicating the files have not been archived. Using the Tape Tool, you can read some or all of the files from a tape or archive file into the directory that you specify. You can write files or directories that you specify onto a tape cartridge or into an archive file.

FIGURE 6.31

The Tape Tool window and icon

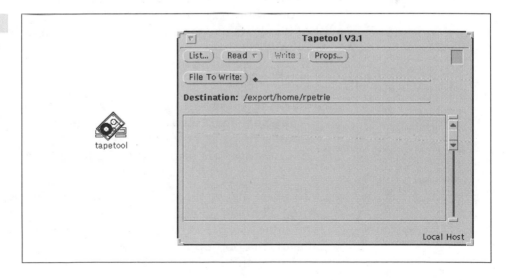

The `List`, `Read`, `Write`, and `Props` menu buttons provide controls for listing, reading from a tape, writing to a tape, and setting Tape Tool properties. The `File To Write` button and text field allow you to type in the
names of the files that you want to write to tape. After typing in the name
of a file to write, press Return or click the left mouse button on the `File
To Write` button. The scrolling list displays a list of the files you specify
by typing file names or by dragging and dropping icons from the File
Manager onto the drag-and-drop target.

The `Destination` field allows you to specify where in your file system files
are put when they are read from the tape. The default destination is your
current working directory. If the files on a tape have a complete path (absolute path), the files are always put in the directory specified on the tape,
regardless of what you type in the `Destination` field.

Viewing and Editing a List of Files on a Tape

By clicking the left mouse button on the `List` button, you can view a list
of files from a tape or archive file in the `Tape Contents/Files to Read`
pop-up window (Figure 6.32). Once the files are listed in the `Tape Con-
tents/Files to Read` pop-up window, you can edit the list to remove files
you do not want to retrieve. The following explains how to view and edit
a list of files from a tape or archive file in the Tape Tool window.

1. If you're viewing a list of files from a tape, insert the tape in the
    tape drive.

2. Click the left mouse button on the `List` button to display the
    `Tape Contents/Files to Read` pop-up window. This pop-up
    window displays a list of files on the tape in the scrolling list,
    and messages are displayed in the footer of the window telling
    you how many files have been found.

3. To select files to retrieve or remove from the list, click the left
    mouse button on each file you want. To select all the files in the
    scrolling list, press the right mouse button to display the `Read
    Functions` pop-up menu. Drag the mouse pointer to the `Select
    All` item and release the right mouse button.

FIGURE 6.32

The Tape
Contents/Files to Read
pop-up window

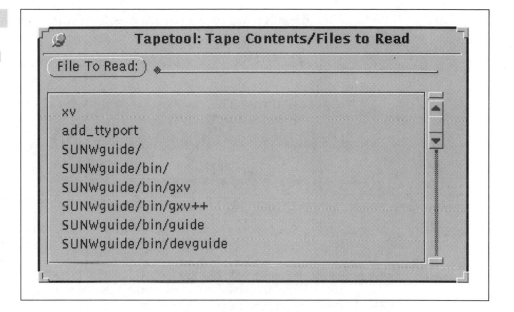

4. If you want to delete the selected files, press the right mouse button in the scrolling list and choose the **Delete Selected** item. If you inadvertently delete a file, you can place it back on the list by typing the file name in the **File To Read** text field, then pressing Return or clicking the left mouse button on the **File To Read** button. After editing your list, the Tape Tool will read only the selected files from the tape or archive file.

Writing Files to a Tape

Writing files to a tape copies the files you specify onto a tape cartridge. The following explains how to write files to a tape:

1. If you want to store files so they can be copied to a different directory than the one where they were originally stored, choose the **All** option in the **StripPath** setting in the Tape Tool's **Properties** window and choose Apply.

2. Select and drag files from the File Manager to the **Tape Tool** window's drag-and-drop target. You can also type the name of a directory or an individual file in the **File To Write** text field, and

press Return or click the left mouse button on the `File To Write` text field.

3. Check the tape cartridge to be sure that it is not write-protected, and insert it into the tape drive.

4. Click the left mouse button on the `Write` button. If you receive an error message, such as `/dev/rmt/0 I/0 error`, make sure that your tape drive is on.

Reading Files from a Tape

The `Read` menu provides three items— `Selected`, `Entire List`, and `Entire Tape` —for reading files from the tape or archive files to the directory specified in the `Tape Tool` window.

After listing and selecting the files you want to retrieve, choose the `Selected` item from the `Read` menu to copy the files to the destination directory specified in the `Destination` text field. When you have not listed the contents of a tape, choosing the `Selected` item displays the `Tape Contents/ Files to Read` pop-up window without a listing. If you know the names of specific files that you want to retrieve, you can type a name in the `File To Read` text field, then press Return or click the left mouse button on the `File To Read` button to add them to the list.

Choosing the `Entire List` item from the `Read` menu reads the entire list of files from the `Tape Contents/Files to Read` pop-up window. While the files are being read, messages are displayed in the footer of the `Tape Tool` window, indicating the percentage of the files that have been read. As the files are read, they are removed from the `Tape Contents/Files to Read` pop-up window. When the process is complete, a message is displayed in the footer of the `Tape Tool` window telling you how many files were read. If there are a large number of files, it may take several minutes for the files to be copied to your system.

Choosing the `Entire Tape` item from the `Read` menu copies all of the files on the tape to the destination directory without displaying the `Tape Contents/Files to Read` pop-up window.

WARNING   When you read files that have a path name in front of them, that path is always used as the destination.

Customizing the Tape Tool

You can customize the Tape Tool by using the `Properties` pop-up window (Figure 6.33). To display the `Properties` pop-up window, click the left mouse button on the `Props` menu button. After changing any setting, click the left mouse button on the `Apply` button (located at the bottom of the window) to save the changes. These changes remain in effect *only* until you quit the Tape Tool. Clicking the `Reset` button restores all your changes to the default settings.

The `Device` text field lets you identify the tape drive on your system. The most common device identifiers for a tape drive are `/dev/rmt/0` and `/dev/rmt/1`. You can also specify a file name in this field if you want to read or write files to and from one big archive file instead of to and from a tape cartridge.

The `Host Name` text field allows you to identify the name of the workstation where the reading or archiving of files is to take place. The default is your local host name.

The `Write` settings allow you to specify how you want to write files to a tape. You can choose none, some, or all of the settings listed. The following lists and describes each setting:

SETTING	RESULTS
No SCCS	Excludes all SCCS directories. SCCS stands for Source Code Control System. SCCS directories contain different revisions of source code for programs. Unless you are backing up directories containing source code for programs, leave this setting off.

FIGURE 6.33

The Properties pop-up window

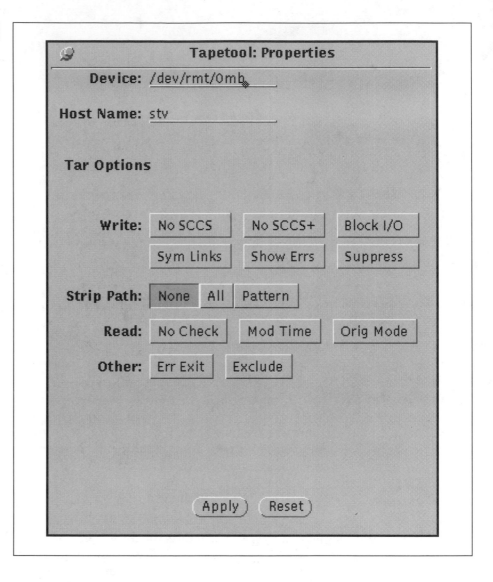

SETTING	RESULTS
No SCCS+	Excludes all SCCS directories, files with a suffix `.o`, and files named `errs`, `core`, and `a.out`. Unless you are backing up directories containing source code for programs, leave this setting off.
Block I/O	Specifies a blocking factor for better throughput. When you click the left mouse button on this setting, a text field is displayed in which you can type the blocking factor you want the Tape Tool to use. In most cases, you leave this setting alone and use the default.
Sym Links	Follows symbolic links to archive the linked files.
Show Errs	Displays error messages if all links to archived files cannot be resolved.
Suppress	Suppresses information showing owner and file modes for portability.

The `Strip Path` settings allow you to choose whether you want selected files to be stripped completely of their path names, to use complete path names, or to use a specific path name. Clicking the left mouse button on the `Pattern` setting displays a text field in which you can type the name of a path to use for all files.

The `Read` settings allow you to specify how you want to read files from a tape. The following explains each of the settings:

SETTING	RESULTS
No Check	Ignores directory checksum errors.
Mode Time	Keeps the Tape Tool from resetting the modification time of files that it reads from the tape.
Orig Mode	Restores the named files to their original mode, ignoring the default `umask` setting of `2`.

The `Other` setting `Err Exit` instructs the Tape Tool to exit the operation as soon as an error is encountered. The `Exclude` setting lets you specify a file name that contains a list of files and/or directories that you want to exclude from reading from the tape. This setting can be useful when the tape contains many files and you want to retrieve all but a few of them.

Customizing the Workspace and Icons

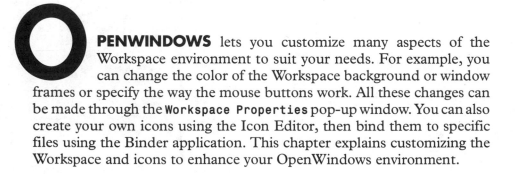

OPENWINDOWS lets you customize many aspects of the Workspace environment to suit your needs. For example, you can change the color of the Workspace background or window frames or specify the way the mouse buttons work. All these changes can be made through the **Workspace Properties** pop-up window. You can also create your own icons using the Icon Editor, then bind them to specific files using the Binder application. This chapter explains customizing the Workspace and icons to enhance your OpenWindows environment.

Using the Workspace Properties Window

The **Workspace Properties** pop-up window allows you to customize a number of Workspace settings. To open the **Workspace Properties** pop-up window, choose the **Properties** item from **Workspace** menu. The **Properties** pop-up window appears (Figure 7.1). The **Workspace Properties** pop-up window includes five property categories on a monochrome system and six categories on a color system. To view the property categories menu, click the right mouse button on the **Category** abbreviated menu button. Figure 7.2 shows the Category menu for a color system.

Changes you make using the **Workspace Properties** pop-up window are stored in the .**Xdefaults** file. This file contains all properties set for your Workspace. You can make additional modifications to the Workspace and DeskSet applications by manually editing the .**Xdefaults** file, as explained in Chapter 15, "Customizing Solaris."

FIGURE 7.1

The Workspace Properties pop-up window

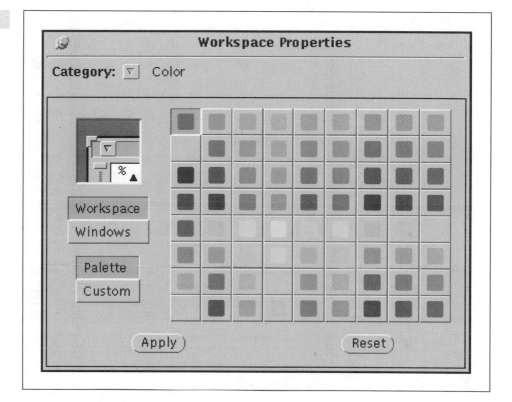

After making changes to the properties, you apply them by clicking the left mouse button on the **Apply** button. Although each category has its own **Apply** button, you only need to click the left mouse button on one **Apply** button after making changes to any Workspace properties category. For example, you can make changes in the **Color** category, then make changes in the **Mouse Settings** category and apply the changes for both categories by clicking the left mouse button on the **Apply** button in the **Mouse Settings** category. The following sections explain each category of property settings.

FIGURE 7.2

The Category menu

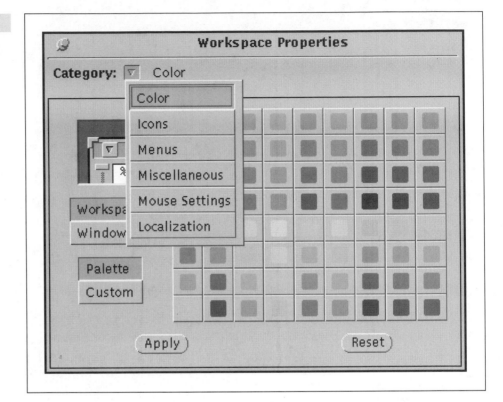

Setting Colors for the Workspace and Windows

If you have a color monitor, you have the option to modify the default colors for the Workspace and windows. When you open the Workspace Properties pop-up window, by default the Color category appears, as shown in Figure 7.2. You can modify the colors of the Workspace or windows by choosing from a palette of premixed colors or by mixing your own colors. The inset area located above the buttons displays a sample of the current color choice for either the Workspace or windows. The following steps explain how to change the Workspace and window colors using the palette in the Workspace Properties window.

1. Click on the **Windows** button to change the color of windows, or go to step two if you want to change the Workspace.

2. Click the left mouse button on the new color you want from the palette. The inset displays the current color choice.

3. Click the left mouse button on the **Apply** button to apply the new color. A Notice appears telling you that changes will be made to the **.Xdefaults** file (Figure 7.3).

4. Click the left mouse button on the **Yes** button. The Workspace or application windows change to the new color.

FIGURE 7.3

The .Xdefaults Notice

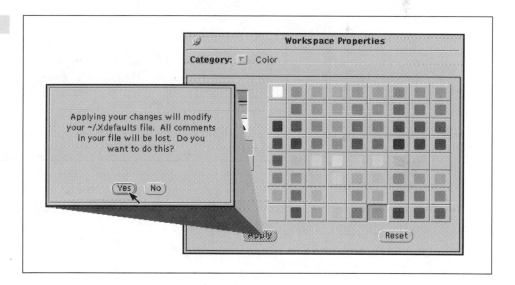

You can also create your own colors using the custom color palette. Click the left mouse button on the **Custom** button to replace the color palette with **Hue**, **Saturation**, and **Brightness** slider controls (Figure 7.4). To create a custom color, move the sliders as you watch the inset at the upper-left corner of the window. The following explains the three custom color settings.

- The **Hue** setting allows you to choose a gradation of color from the range of primary colors: red, green, and blue.

FIGURE 7.4

The Custom Color
Palette

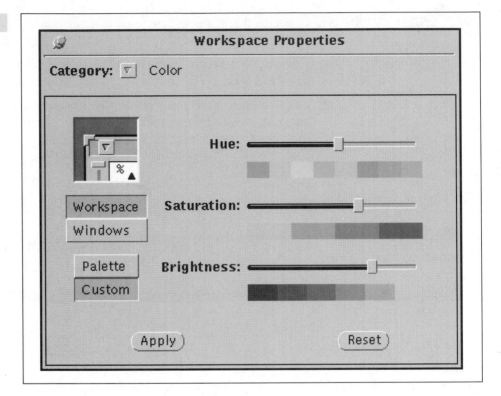

- The **Saturation** setting allows you to specify the deepness or richness of the color.

- The **Brightness** setting affects how much light is filtered into a color.

After creating your custom color, click the left mouse button on the **Apply** button, then click the left mouse on the **Yes** button in the Notice window. The changes you have made to the **Color** category will take place immediately.

Setting Default Locations for Icons

When you close a window to an icon on the Workspace, by default the icon appears at the bottom of the Workspace. You can change the default location where icons are placed on the Workspace by doing the following:

1. Press the right mouse button on the category abbreviated menu button and choose the **Icons** item. The **Icons** category appears (Figure 7.5).

2. Click the left mouse button on the appropriate **Location** setting: **Top**, **Bottom**, **Left**, or **Right**.

3. Click the left mouse button on the **Apply** button. The .Xdefaults Notice appears.

4. Click on the **Yes** button.

FIGURE 7.5

The Icons category

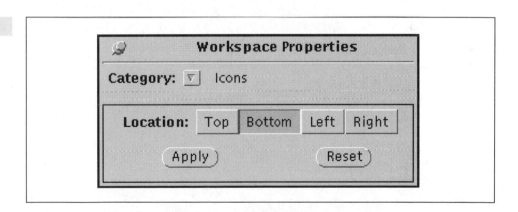

Changes to the **Icons** category take effect when you start a new application. Icons already displayed will not change location.

Changing Menu Settings

Choosing the Menus category enables you to change how you operate menus, including setting the distance you need to drag the mouse to the right to display a submenu, and determining whether the default menu item is chosen automatically when you click the left mouse button on a menu button.

The drag-right distance is the distance that you must move the pointer to the right before a submenu is displayed. This distance is measured on the screen in *pixels* (picture elements). The number of pixels available corresponds to the resolution of the monitor. Standard resolutions for most Sun monitors are 1152 by 900 and 1600 by 1280 pixels. The default pixel length for the drag-right distance is 100 pixels. Changes you specify in the Menus category take effect immediately.

NOTE

If you are using Solaris 2 for x86 the standard resolution is 1024 by 768.

To modify the drag-right distance, follow these steps:

1. Press the right mouse button on the Category abbreviated menu button and choose Menus. The Menus category appears (Figure 7.6).

FIGURE 7.6

The Menus category

> **Workspace Properties**
>
> Category: ▽   Menus
>
> Drag–Right distance (pixels): 100
>
> SELECT Mouse Press: Selects Default   Displays Menu
>
> (Apply)   (Reset)

2. Enter the drag-right distance in the `Drag-Right distance (pixels)` text field. The higher the value, the more distance you need to drag the pointer.

3. Click the left mouse button on the `Apply` button. The .Xdefaults Notice appears.

4. Click on the `Yes` button.

The `SELECT Mouse Press` setting determines whether the default menu item is chosen automatically when you click the left mouse button on a menu button or if the menu is presented for you to make a choice. The default setting, `Selects Default`, specifies that the default menu item is automatically chosen when you click the left mouse button on the menu button. The `Displays Menu` setting specifies that when you click the left mouse button on the menu button, the menu is displayed instead of the default menu item being executed. This means you need to click the left mouse button again to choose a menu item. Changes to the `SELECT Mouse Press` option do not take effect on any applications that are already opened, but they do take effect on any applications you open after changing the `SELECT Mouse Press` setting.

Changing Miscellaneous Settings

The `Miscellaneous` category allows you to change three settings: `Beep`, `Set Input Area`, and `Scrollbar Placement`. To change these settings, choose the `Miscellaneous` category from the `Workspace Properties` menu. The Miscellaneous category appears, as shown in Figure 7.7. The following explains each setting in the `Miscellaneous` category.

SETTING	DESCRIPTION
Beep	Always (the default setting) specifies whether your system beeps for all application-generated beep actions, such as errors in the Console window. Notices Only beeps only when a Notice is displayed. Never specifies no beeps.

FIGURE 7.7

The Miscellaneous
category

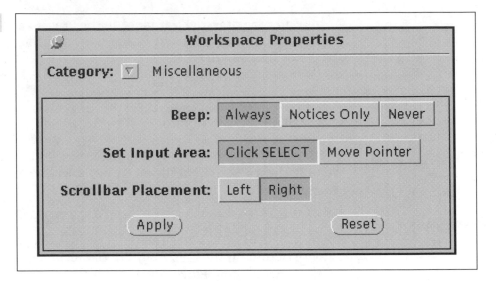

SETTING	DESCRIPTION
Set Input Area	Click SELECT (the default setting) specifies that you must click the left mouse button on the window to make it the active window. The Move Pointer setting lets you simply move the pointer into the window to make the window active.
Scrollbar Placement	Specifies whether scroll bars are displayed at the right and left of the pane. This setting applies to all scrollable application windows on the Workspace. The default is the Right setting.

TIP

Changing the Set Input Area to the Move Pointer setting makes working with multiple windows much easier than using the Click SELECT setting.

Changes made to the `Miscellaneous` category take place immediately after you apply them using the `Apply` button. However, the scroll bar changes do not affect application windows that are already on the Workspace.

Customizing Mouse Settings

The `Mouse Settings` category contains pointer jumping controls for scroll bars and pop-up windows, as well as a setting for changing the time interval between double-clicks of mouse buttons. To change these settings, choose the `Mouse Settings` category from the `Workspace Properties` menu. The `Mouse Settings` category appears, as shown in Figure 7.8. The following explains the settings in the `Mouse Settings` category window.

SETTING	DESCRIPTION
Scrollbar Pointer Jumping	Determines whether or not you want the pointer to move along the scroll bar elevator during scrolling actions. When the box is not checked, pointer jumping is disabled, so the pointer remains in a fixed position as the scroll bar elevator moves.

FIGURE 7.8

The Mouse Settings category

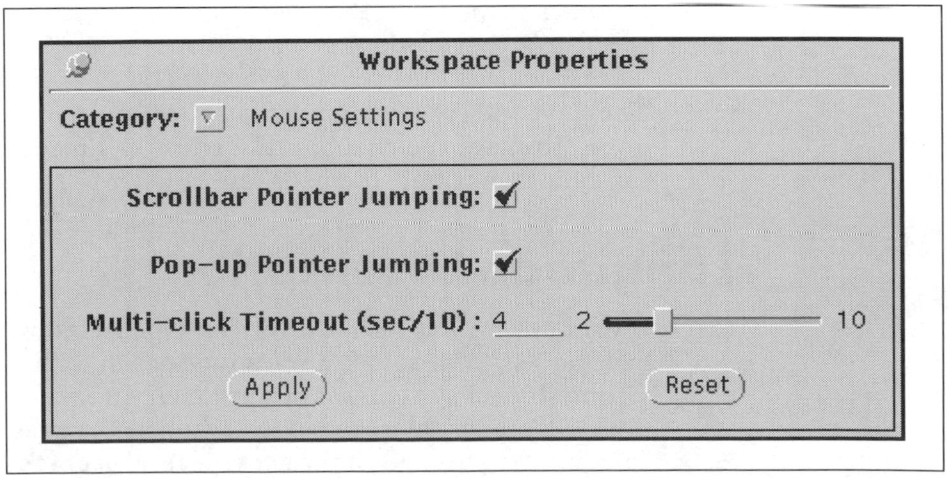

SETTING	DESCRIPTION
Pop-up Pointer Jumping	Determines whether or not you want the pointer to jump into a pop-up window automatically when it comes up. If this setting is chosen, the pointer jumps to the default choice whenever a pop-up window is displayed. When the box is not checked, the pointer does not jump to the default button in the pop-up window, but remains where it was when the pop-up window appeared.
Multi-click Timeout (sec/10)	Specifies how many tenths of a second can elapse between successive clicks on a mouse button before the first click is ignored. This affects how quickly you must double-click the left mouse button, for example, when you start an application from an icon. To set the multiclick time, you can either type in the number of tenths of a second in the numeric field, or you can drag the slider with the pointer.

Changes to the Scrollbar Pointer Jumping and Pop-up Pointer Jumping check boxes do not take place in applications already on the Workspace, but they do take effect when you open an application window. The Multi-Click Timeout option takes effect immediately in all applications. To make the changes take effect in already open applications you can quit then restart them, or restart OpenWindows.

Language Localization

If your system was installed with an OpenWindows localization CD, you have access to various European locales in addition to the basic U.S.A. setting. If your system was not installed with the OpenWindows localization CD, English is the only available language. The Localization category (Figure 7.9) of the Workspace Properties window provides you with controls for specifying an input and display language, as well as time,

FIGURE 7.9

The Localization
category

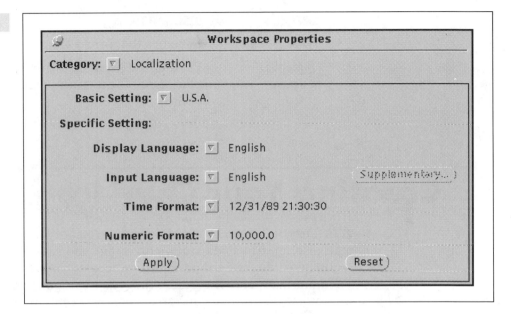

date, and numeric formats for different locales. If your system is not installed with an OpenWindows localization CD, these settings only reflect
your system's language, date, and time format. For those systems that allow
locale specifications, changes will apply when you start a new application.
It will not affect applications that already opened. The following describes
each setting in the `Localization` category.

SETTING	DESCRIPTION
Basic Setting	Specifies the name of the country or native language of the user interface. Specific setting choices listed below in the `Localization` category will vary depending on the basic locale setting.
Display Language	Specifies the language in which messages, menu labels, button labels, help files, etc., are displayed.
Input Language	Specifies the language to be used for input in application windows.

SETTING	DESCRIPTION
Time Format	Specifies the format for time and date.
Numeric Format	Defines the numeric format or placement of the comma and decimal point.

Creating Your Own Icons

The DeskSet's Icon Editor allows you to create your own icon images. You can also modify an existing icon image and save it with a new name in your home directory. The directory /usr/openwin/share/include/images contains many icon image files that you can modify and save in your home directory. Once you create a new icon, you can bind it an application and data file using the Binder application. Working with the Binder application is explained later in this chapter.

To start the Icon Editor, press the right mouse button on the Workspace to display the Workspace pop-up menu, then choose Icon Editor from the Programs submenu. The Icon Editor window appears on the Workspace. Figure 7.10 shows the Icon Editor window and icon.

The Icon Editor window's control area contains the File, View, Edit, Properties, and Palette menu buttons. The Preview area, located above the canvas to the right of the drawing controls, allows you to preview how the icon you are creating in the canvas pane of the Icon Editor window will look. The controls that you use to draw an image in the canvas appear to the left of the preview area. The drawing mode choices include tools for drawing and editing an image and adding text to an image. The Fill choices, below the Edit and Properties buttons, allow you to fill in a square or circle with a pattern. The Color choices allow you to choose between creating black-and-white or color images. The Move buttons allow you to adjust the position of the drawing on the canvas.

FIGURE 7.10

The Icon Editor icon
and window

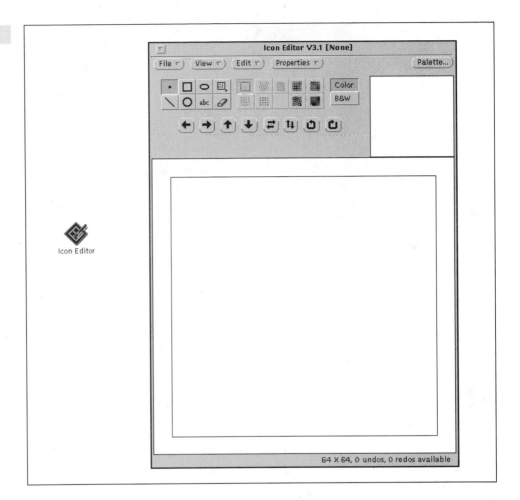

Color Control

You can create color or black-and-white icons by choosing the **Color** or
B&W setting. The **Color** setting is not available if you are working with a
black-and-white monitor. When the **Color** setting is selected, you can
draw using any of the colors provided on the **Color Chooser** pop-up window, which appears when you click the left mouse button on the **Palette**
button. Working with this pop-up window is similar to working with the
color setting window described in the section "Setting Colors for the Workspace and Windows," earlier in this chapter.

N O T E

If you change your icon from color to black and white, the colors will not be restored when you switch back to color. If you inadvertently switch from color to black and white, use the Undo item on the Edit menu to restore the color.

When the B&W setting is chosen, the Palette button on the Icon Editor header changes to display only Black and White settings. When Black is selected, your icon is drawn with a black pen. When White is selected, your icon is drawn with a white pen. If the icon you are creating is in color when you select B&W, the icon is converted to a black-and-white image.

Drawing Controls

The drawing controls (Figure 7.11), provide you with the tools for drawing an image. The following explains the available drawing mode choices.

FIGURE 7.11

Drawing controls

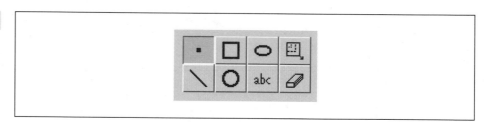

MODE	RESULT
Point	Click the left mouse button to insert one black pixel at the spot of the pointer on the canvas. Point to a black pixel and click the middle mouse button to turn the pixel from black to white.

MODE	RESULT
Line	Draws a line one pixel wide. To draw a line, position the pointer at one end of the line, press the left mouse button, drag the pointer to the other end of the line, and release the left mouse button. If you are in **B&W** mode, a white line can be drawn in the same way by selecting the `White` option in the upper right-hand corner of the `Icon Editor` window.
Square	Draws open or filled squares (or rectangles) using any of the fill patterns from the Fill area. Position the pointer at the top left corner, press the left mouse button, drag the pointer to the bottom opposite corner of the square or rectangle, and release the left mouse button.
Circle	Draws open or filled circles using any of the fill patterns from the Fill area. Position the pointer at the center of the circle and press the left mouse button, drag the pointer to the outside radius of the circle, and release the left mouse button.
Ellipse	Draws open or filled ellipses using any of the fill patterns from the Fill area. Position the pointer at the center of the ellipse and press the left mouse button, drag the pointer to the outside radius of the ellipse, and release the left mouse button. If you define a horizontal or vertical line, the ellipse is interpreted as a straight line.

MODE	RESULT
Text	Displays a pop-up window that allows you to type text to be displayed in your icon. Working with text is explained later in this chapter.
Region	Defines a rectangular region of the canvas that you can move, flip, or rotate by clicking the left mouse button on any of the Move buttons that are displayed directly above the canvas.
Eraser	Allows you to erase any pixels on the canvas by moving the pointer to the canvas, clicking the left mouse button, and dragging the eraser cursor over the areas you want to erase. Only the pixel under the front tip of the eraser is erased.

Fill Choices

The Fill choices (Figure 7.12) allow you to choose one of ten fill patterns to fill in squares, circles, ellipses, or irregular shapes with the specified pattern. To create and fill squares, circles, or ellipses, first choose a Fill option from the Fill choices area *before* using the draw mode. *You cannot fill previously drawn squares, circles, and ellipses.*

The first Fill choice, an open square, allows you to create an outline (unfilled) of the shape selected in the mode menu. Pressing the left mouse button and dragging the pointer defines the area of the square, circle, or ellipse. When you release the left button, the area you defined is filled with

FIGURE 7.12

Fill choices

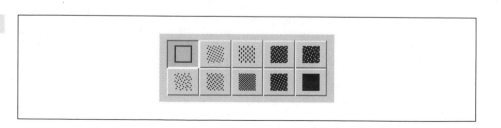

the pattern you specified. The other options represent patterns, from white to black, that create filled squares, circles, or ellipses.

Move Buttons

The series of eight move buttons in the Drawing Controls area (Figure 7.13) allow you to position the drawing on the canvas, or to move a region within the canvas. The first move buttons (left, right, up, and down arrows) in the Drawing Controls area adjust the position of the entire drawing or a region of the drawing in the canvas one pixel in the direction indicated.

FIGURE 7.13

The Move buttons

WARNING   If you move part of the image off the canvas, the pixels are cropped from the image and are not restored when you move the image in the opposite direction.

To move a defined region of your image, select the `Region` option from the mode menu, indicated by intersecting dimmed rectangles. To select a region, move the pointer to the left corner of the region you want to move, press the left mouse button, and drag the pointer to the bottom right of the region you want to affect. A bounding box indicates the selected region. Release the left mouse button and the region is selected.

To move the selected region or the entire drawing, click the left mouse button on one of the four arrow buttons. Each click will move the drawing one pixel in the designated direction. The fifth and sixth buttons in the row of the move buttons flip the image on the canvas or a defined region from left to right or top to bottom. The right two buttons rotate the image or a defined region 90 degrees in the direction of the arrow.

WARNING If you move part of the image over existing pixels, the pixels are removed from the image. Choose Undo from the Edit menu to restore the deleted pixels.

Adding Text to an Icon

Adding text to an icon is a simple operation. First choose Text (abc) from the Drawing Controls area and the Text pop-up window is displayed (Figure 7.14). To add text to the canvas, do the following:

1. Click the right mouse button on the Font abbreviated menu button and choose the font you want to use. Figure 7.15 shows the Font menu.

2. Click the right mouse button on the Weight abbreviated menu button and choose the weight (degree of bold) for the font you want to use.

3. Click the right mouse button on the Style abbreviated menu button and choose the font style you want to use.

FIGURE 7.14

The Text pop-up window

Icon Editor: Text
Text:
Font: ▼ avantgarde (itc)
Weight: ▼ book
Style: ▼ oblique
Size: ▼ default

FIGURE 7.15

The Font options of the
Text pop-up window

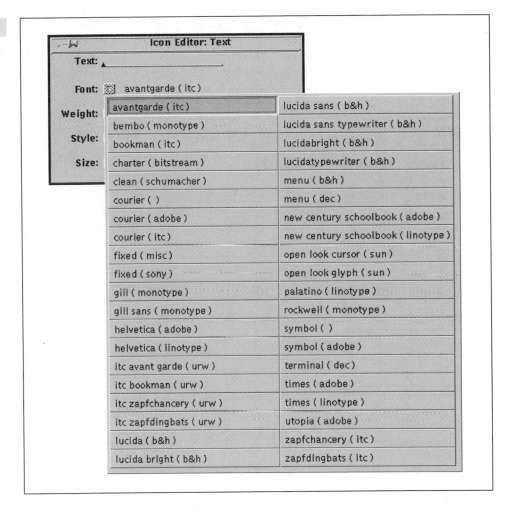

4. Click the right mouse button on the **Size** button and choose the font size you want.

5. Click the left mouse button on the **Text** text field and type the text you want to add to your icon.

6. Move the pointer onto the canvas and press the left mouse button to insert your text in the icon. A rectangle is displayed that shows the size of the text to be inserted. You can drag the rectangle anywhere within the canvas to position it.

7. When the rectangle is positioned correctly, release the left mouse button. The text is added to the canvas. White text can be typed on a dark background in the same way by selecting the `White` option. Once you have added text to the canvas, it can be edited as you would any other part of the image.

Editing Icons Using the Edit Menu

The `Edit` menu (Figure 7.16) provides you with seven editing items: `Undo`, `Redo`, `Clear`, `Cut`, `Copy`, `Paste`, and `Invert`. These editing items are also available in the `Edit` pop-up menu, which is displayed by clicking or pressing the right mouse button anywhere in the canvas.

You can undo up to seven of your last actions by choosing the `Undo` item. The status line at the bottom of the `Icon Editor` window informs you of the number of undos and redos available. After choosing `Undo`, you can then choose `Redo` to repeat the original action, which restores the canvas to its condition before you chose `Undo`. The `Clear` item allows you to erase the entire canvas. No warning Notice is displayed, since you can easily choose the `Undo` option to restore the contents of the canvas.

You can use the `Cut`, `Copy`, `Paste`, and `Invert` items in conjunction with the Region mode to move, copy, or invert selected regions of an icon. When you choose the `Cut` item, the current region is removed from the icon and placed on the clipboard. If you don't have a region currently

FIGURE 7.16

The Edit menu

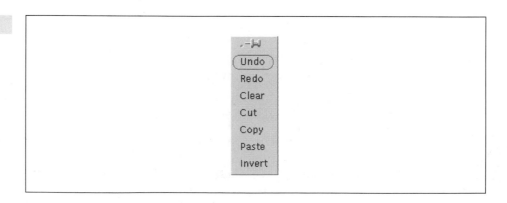

defined, the entire icon is deleted and placed on the clipboard. The `Copy` item copies the current region on the clipboard. Before choosing the `Paste` item, position the pointer so the upper-right corner of the copied or cut image matches the upper-right corner of the current region. If you use the Paste key from the keyboard, the contents of the clipboard are placed so that the upper-right corner is at the center of the icon. The `Invert` item simply inverts a black-and-white image. Black pixels become white and white pixels become black.

Displaying a Grid in the Canvas

Clicking the left mouse button on the `View` menu button activates the `Grid On` item, which allows you to display a grid background for your canvas. Figure 7.17 shows an example of the canvas with the grid turned on. The grid is useful for aligning and centering all or parts of the icon. You can toggle the grid on and off by clicking the left mouse button on the `View` menu button. When the grid is turned on, the `View` menu item changes to `Grid Off`.

Working with the Properties Menu

The `Properties` menu contains the `Format` and `Size` items. The `Format` item allows you to choose the format in which your icon file is saved. The `Format` submenu includes four format choices: `XView Icon`, `X Bitmap`, `Color X Pixmap`, and/or `Mono X Pixmap`.

In most cases you will save your icon images in the `XView Icon` format. A color image can also be saved as a color X Pixmap image. However, this type of icon can only be used for some XView applications. Save the icon as an XView icon if you want to display your icon in the File Manager by binding it to an application or data file using the Binder. If your icon is black and white, it can be saved as a regular XView icon, as an X Bitmap, or as a Monochrome X Pixmap image. You can save the icon as an X Bitmap if you want to include it in a C program.

FIGURE 7.17

The Icon Editor with the Grid item activated

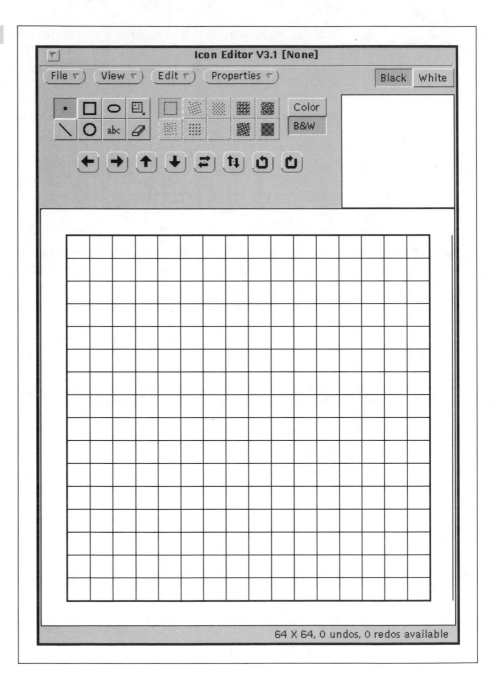

The **Properties** menu's **Size** submenu provides five icon-sizing options based on pixel measurements. The size for icons that appear in the File Manager window is 32 by 32 pixels. The **32** (**File manager Icon**) item is the default. If you need to create an icon for an application, choose the **64** (**Tool Icon**). This creates an icon that is 64 by 64 pixels, the standard size of an application icon on the Workspace. The other canvas sizes are 48 by 48 pixels, 16 by 16 pixels, and 128 by 128 pixels.

If you change the size of the canvas when an icon file is loaded, or load an icon into a different canvas size, the file is read from the upper-left corner. Larger images are cropped to fit the existing size of the canvas. The canvas can be changed to a larger size without losing data as long as you do not move the image. If you move the image, data outside the canvas is lost.

Saving an Icon File

To save an icon for the first time, click the left mouse button on the **File** button. A Notice appears informing you that no file was specified. Click the left mouse button on the **Continue** button. The **File** pop-up window appears, as shown in Figure 7.18. Type the name of the directory in which you want to store your icon in the **Directory** text field and the file name in the **File** text field. Press the right mouse button on the **Save** button and choose **XView** to save the icon. If you want to save an icon with a new or different file name, choose the **Save As** item from the **File** menu. The **File** pop-up window is displayed.

FIGURE 7.18

The File pop-up window

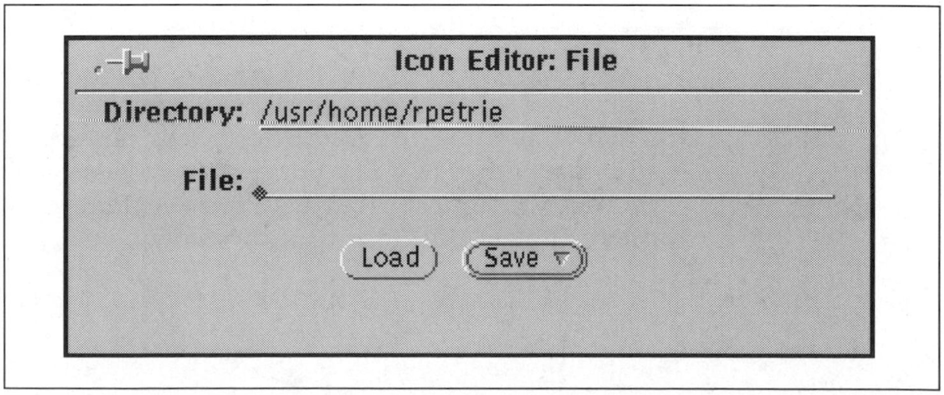

Icon Editor: File

Directory: /usr/home/rpetrie

File:

Load   Save ▼

In most cases, you will want to save your icon as an `XView Icon` so you can display your icon in the File Manager by binding it to an application or data file using the Binder, as explained later in this chapter. If your icon is in color, it can be saved as a `Color X Pixmap` image, which can be used for some XView applications. If your icon is black and white, you can also choose to save the icon as an `X Bitmap` or a `Mono X Pixmap` image.

Loading an Icon File

You can easily load an existing icon file by dragging it from the File Manager and dropping it onto the Icon Editor's canvas or onto the Icon Editor's preview window. The icon file appears in the `Icon Editor` window, as shown in Figure 7.19. An icon file can also be loaded by clicking the left mouse button on the `File` menu button, which displays the `File` pop-up window. Type the directory path in the `Directory` text field where you want to load the file from. Type the file name you want for your icon image file in the `File` text field. Click the left mouse button on the `Load` button to load the file into the canvas.

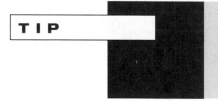

TIP

The DeskSet and supplementary icons are stored in /usr/openwin/share/include/images directory. These icons can used as a basis for creating your own custom icons.

Printing an Icon

Choosing the `Print` item from the `File` menu displays the `Print` pop-up window, as shown in Figure 7.20. You can print your icon image to a specified printer or a file. Printing an image to a file allows the file to be printed without using the Icon Editor application. The following explains the controls in the `Print` pop-up window.

FIGURE 7.19

An icon file icon in the
Icon Editor window

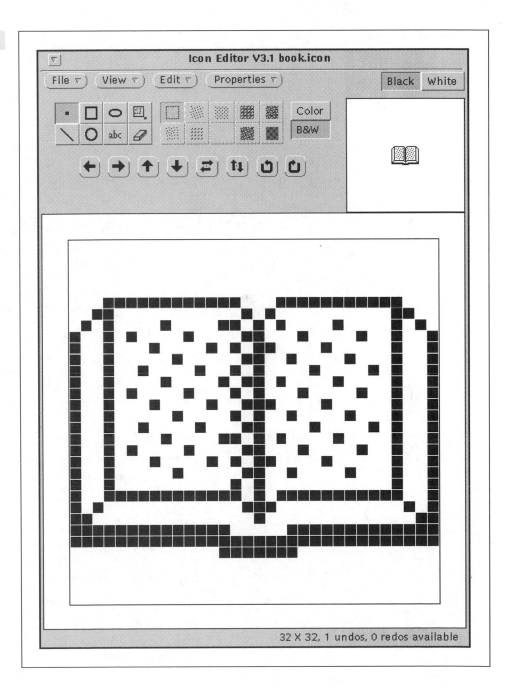

FIGURE 7.20

The Print pop-up
window

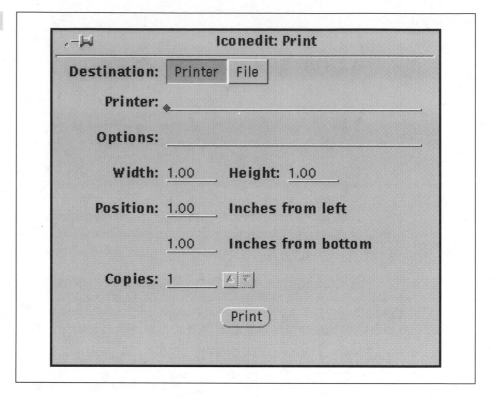

CONTROL	DESCRIPTION
Destination	Determines the destination of the printed output, which can be either a printer or a file. The default setting is **Printer**. If you choose the **File** setting, the **Printer** and **Options** settings change to **Directory** and **File** settings so that you can enter the path and file name of the file you want to print to.
Printer	Specifies the printer name.
Options	Allows you to type in SunOS commands that allow you to customize your printer option defaults.

CONTROL	DESCRIPTION
Width	Specifies the width of the printed image in inches.
Height	Specifies the height of the printed image in inches.
Position	The **Inches from left** specifies the left margin of the printed image. The **Inches from bottom** specifies the bottom margin of the printed image.
Copies	Specifies the number of copies. You can enter the number in the text field or click the left mouse button on the increment or decrement buttons to choose a number.
Print	Executes the printing of the current image in the canvas.

Using the Color Chooser Palette

If you're using the Icon Editor to create new icons for the File Manager, you should create black-and-white icons. You can use the Binder to specify foreground and background colors for your File Manager icons. However, you can create multicolor icons if you have a color workstation, and you can save them in a Color X Pixmap file format to be used with your own X applications.

If you want to create a color icon, select the **Color** choice button in the drawing controls area or click the left mouse button on the **Palette** button to display the **Color Chooser** pop-up window. The current color that the Icon Editor will use for drawing is displayed in the upper-left corner of the palette. The two colors at the top right of the palette are your Workspace and window colors, as defined in the **Workspace Properties Color** category window. The following explains how to use any of the colors displayed in the **Color Chooser** palette for the Icon Editor.

1. Click the left mouse button on the color you want in the **Color Chooser** palette. The selected color is highlighted and displayed in the **Color Chooser** preview area (the large square to the left of the palette).

2. Click the left mouse button on the **Apply** button to record the color change.

3. Move the pointer back to the Icon Editor to draw your icon with the chosen color. The pointer changes to the selected color as a reminder of the color you are drawing with.

Binding an Icon

The Binder application allows you to bind icons to files. It can also bind colors, applications, open methods, and print methods to files. A *binding* is a connection between file types and elements such as applications to be started when a file is opened, print scripts, or icons that the File Manager, Print Tool, Mail Tool, and other DeskSet applications use to display and operate on files. Because the DeskSet applications come with a default set of bindings, in most cases you will only need to use the Binder to bind customized icons to applications or files, or change the application used to open a file, or change the print script used to print a file. However, you may want to use the Binder to change the way particular files are displayed in the File Manager or other DeskSet applications, or to change the application used to open or print a file.

The Binder Window

To start the Binder application, press the right mouse button on the Workspace and choose the **Binder** item from the **Programs** submenu. Figure 7.21 shows the **Binder** window and icon. The **Binder** window has a control area, a scrolling list of Binder entries, and buttons at the bottom that you use to add a new binding or to modify or delete an existing binding. The Binder control area includes four menu buttons. The following explains each of these menus.

FIGURE 7.21

The Binder Window
and icon

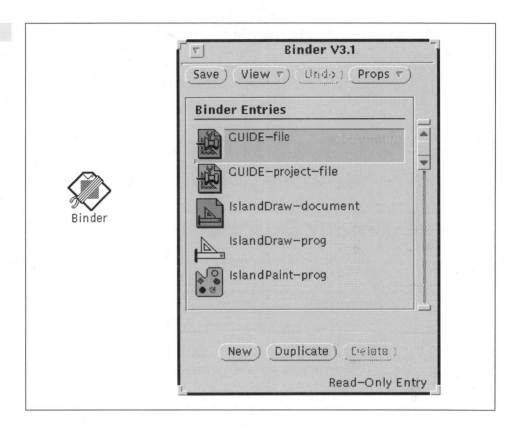

- The **Save** menu allows you to save your changes to the Binder database. The **Save** button replaces the standard **File** menu button because it is the only file operation used by the Binder.

- The **View** menu allows you to determine which Binder entries you want to display.

- The **Undo** menu allows you to undo the last operation. The operations that are undoable are the **New**, **Duplicate**, and **Delete** buttons at the bottom of the Binder window.

- The **Props** button allows you to display the properties of the selected Binder entry. There are two components for each Binder entry: Icon properties, which determine how a file is displayed and operated on by the DeskSet applications, and File Type properties, which determine which files are bound to the icon.

The scrolling list in the **Binder** window displays the bindings stored in three different databases: a network database, a system database, and a personal user database. The **New, Duplicate,** and **Delete** buttons at the bottom of the **Binder** window are used to work with Binder entries.

Binder Databases

The Binder databases are used by all applications in the DeskSet environment to determine how to display, print, and open any file. The network and system databases consist of the **Binder** entries shared by many workstations across the network. Your private database consists of the Binder entries that apply only to you.

In most cases, you cannot modify system or network (shared) database entries. If you select a shared network or system database entry, a message appears in the window footer of the **Binder** window telling you the selected entry is a read-only entry. The first time you run the Binder application, all your bindings will be system or network entries. If you want to customize a system or network entry, you can copy it to your personal database, then modify the user entry. When you add a new binding, it will be added as a personal Binder entry.

Viewing Binder Entries

The **View** menu allows you to determine the Binder entries displayed in the **Binder** window scrolling list. The **All Entries** item allows you to display a merged list of all private, system, and network entries. If you copy a system or network entry to your personal user database, only your personal version of the entry is displayed in the merged list. The **Shared Entries** item allows you to display all the system and network entries. The **Personal Entries** item displays only your entries.

Binder Entry Properties

Each Binder entry in the `Binder` window's `Binder Entries` scrolling list has associated properties, such as the application the entry is bound to or how the file is printed in the DeskSet environment. There are two types of properties associated with each Binder entry: Icon properties and File Type properties. The Icon properties include settings to determine how files of a particular type are displayed by DeskSet applications such as the File Manager, and what happens when files of that type are opened or printed. The Binder entry's File Type properties include defining the set of files that are bound to the icon. The `Props` menu button includes two items, `Icon` and `File Types`, for accessing pop-up windows that display the properties for the selected icon.

The Icon Properties Window

Selecting an entry in the `Binder Entries` scrolling list, then clicking the left mouse button on the `Props` menu button displays the Icon category `Properties` window (Figure 7.22) with the Icon properties for the selected icon. Clicking the left mouse button on the plus sign (+) button at the lower right of the `Properties` window, expands the window to display the full set of properties, as shown in Figure 7.23. You can shrink the window back down to the smaller size by clicking the left mouse button on the minus sign (−) button at the bottom of the expanded window. The following explains the controls in the expanded Icon category `Properties` window.

CONTROL	DESCRIPTION
Icon	Shows the current icon and Binder database entry name. You can use the text field to modify the entry name.

FIGURE 7.22

The Icon category
Properties window

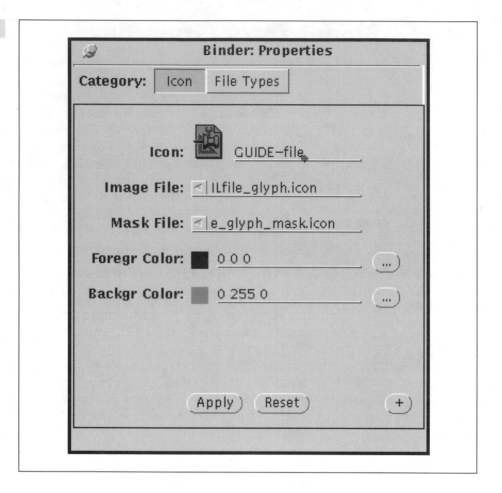

CONTROL	DESCRIPTION
Image File	Displays the path of the 32-by-32 pixel (XView format) icon that is bound to the current entry. This is the standard icon size displayed by the File Manager, Mail Tool, and other applications in the DeskSet Environment. The icon is displayed in the **Binder** window's **Binder Entries** scrolling list and the **Icon** field of the **Properties** window.

CONTROL	DESCRIPTION
Mask File	Displays the path of an icon color mask. A *color mask* defines the region of the icon to which the background color is applied. Think of a color mask as a background overlaid on top of your icon that indicates where the background color should be applied. If no icon mask file is specified, the entire icon is colored with the background color. For example, Figure 7.24 shows the icon and the icon mask for the **Audiotool-prog** Binder entry. The image in the Icon editor on the left is the icon image that determines the outline of the icon. The image in the Icon editor on the right is the icon mask that determines the icon area that will be colored with the background color.

N O T E

For a list of color settings, see the table in Chapter 15, or open the text file `rgb.txt` located in the `/usr/openwin/lib` directory.

FIGURE 7.23

The expanded Icon category Properties window

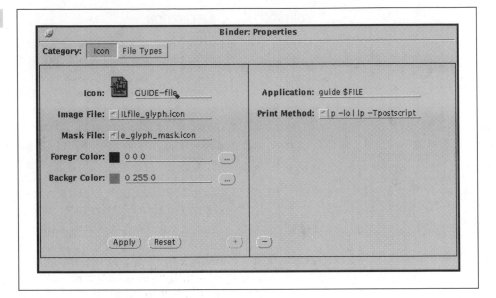

FIGURE 7.24

The Audiotool icon and Audiotool icon mask

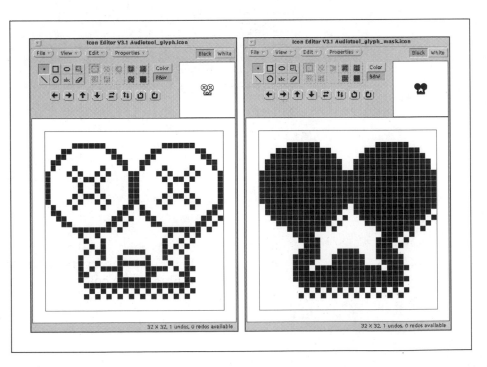

CONTROL	DESCRIPTION
Foregr Color	The foreground color is the color that the icon itself is drawn with in the File Manager and other DeskSet applications. If no value is given for this field, the foreground color is black. If you want to pick a new foreground color, click the left mouse button on the button to the right of the `Foregr Color` field to display the `Color Chooser` pop-up window. This is similar to the window that you used to change the Workspace and window colors. Alternatively, you can type three numbers in the `Foregr Color` field to indicate the amount each of red, green, and blue in the foreground color. Color saturation values range from 0 through 255; for example, 255 0 0 represents a solid red color. The zeros represent the amount of green and blue in the color.
Backgr Color	The background color is the color that the icon is colored with in the File Manager and other DeskSet applications. If no value is given for this field, the background color is white. If you want to pick a new background color, click the left mouse button on the button to the right of the `Backgr Color` field to invoke the `Color Chooser` pop-up window. Alternatively, you can type three numbers in the `Foregr Color` field to indicate the amount each of red, green, and blue in the background color. Color saturation values range from 0 through 255; for example, 0 255 0 represents a solid green color. The zeros represent the amount of red and blue in the color.

CONTROL	DESCRIPTION
Application	Defines the application that is invoked whenever any file, defined by the current binding, is opened in the File Manager, Mail Tool, or other applications.
Print Method	Defines how a file is printed. If no print method is specified, the default print method of the application the file is being printed from is used.

The File Types Properties Window

By default, the Properties pop-up window displays the Icon category settings for the selected Binder entry. Clicking the left mouse button on the File Types category button displays the File Types category settings in the Properties pop-up window for the selected Binder entry, as shown in Figure 7.25. You can display the File Types category Properties window from the Binder window by choosing the File Types item from the Props menu.

Clicking the left mouse button on the plus sign (+) button at the lower right of the Properties window, expands the window to display the full set of properties. Figure 7.26 shows the expanded File Types Properties window. You can shrink the window back down to the smaller size by clicking the left mouse button on the minus sign (−) button at the bottom of the expanded window. The following explains the controls in the File Types category Properties window.

FIGURE 7.25

The File Types
category Properties
window

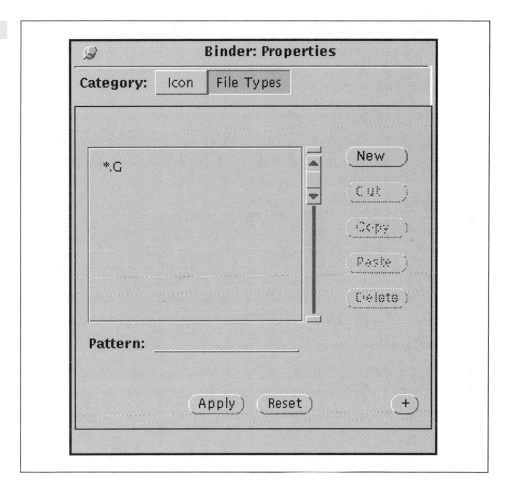

FIGURE 7.26

The expanded File Types category Properties window

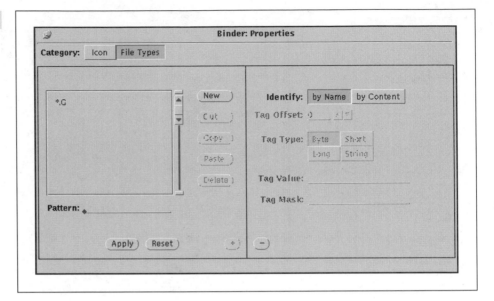

CONTROL	DESCRIPTION
File Types scrolling list	Each entry in the File Types scrolling list defines how a file, or group of files, is recognized by DeskSet applications. You can think of each entry in the File Types scrolling list as a class of files that consists of one or more files. Each class of files in this scrolling list (each File Type entry) is bound to the Icon properties of the current Binder entry. If you have two identical File Type entries in your Binder database, only the first one that the Binder reads is used. The first Binder entry to use the File Type entry is not necessarily the first Binder entry in the **Binder** window's scrolling list.

CONTROL	DESCRIPTION
Pattern	Modifies the name of a File Type entry. If the files are to be identified by a pattern, this pattern must be the name of the binding entry. If the currently selected File Type is identified by content, the `Pattern` text field is dimmed and unavailable. When there are no items selected in the scrolling list, you can type a pattern in the `Pattern` text field and press Return to create a new File Type entry.
File Types Properties buttons	The `New`, `Cut`, `Copy`, `Paste`, and `Delete` buttons to the right of the scrolling list allow you to create, delete, copy, and move entries in the File Types scrolling list. The `New` button creates a new File Type entry. Clicking the left mouse button on the `New` button creates a new entry in the scrolling list using the default name `unnamed_1`. If you create another new entry without renaming the first new entry, it is named `unnamed_2`. The `Cut` button allows you to remove the currently selected File Type entry and temporarily store it on the clipboard. The `Copy` button allows you to copy the currently selected File Type entry onto the clipboard. The `Paste` button allows you to add the File Type entry that is on the clipboard to the current Binder entry. The `Delete` button allows you to remove the File Type entry from the current Binder entry. The `Delete` button is inactive if the current Binder entry is a read-only entry. Deleting a Binder entry does *not* delete its File Type entry.

CONTROL	DESCRIPTION
`Identify`	Determines how the current class of files (the selected File Type entry) is recognized by DeskSet applications. A class of files is recognized either by name or by content. The default `by Name` setting recognizes files with names matching the text entered in the `Pattern` text field. For example, the File Type entry `*.ps` matches all the files that end with `.ps`. These are PostScript files, and they are displayed in the DeskSet environment with the postscript-file icon displayed in the Binder window's scrolling list. The asterisk (`*`) in the pattern means "match any file name here." The `by Content` setting recognizes files by matching file contents with the information entered in the `Pattern` field.
	If the `by Content` setting is activated, files are recognized by matching file contents instead of the file name. The four settings, `Tag Offset`, `Tag Type`, `Tag Value`, and `Tag Mask` define what the file contents should be in the current File Type. In most cases, you will only use the default `Tag Offset`, the `String Tag Type` setting, and `Tag Value` settings. The following briefly explains each of the `by Content` settings.
`Tag Offset` (numeric field)	Determines the starting position in the file (counting from 0) where the file contents should be matched. The default value is 0. The value 0 starts matching the contents at the first character of the file. A byte offset of 1 would start matching the contents at the second character of the file, 3 the fourth character, and so on.

CONTROL	DESCRIPTION
Tag Type	Determines the type of value that is to be matched in the file contents. The settings include `Byte`, `Short`, `Long`, or `String`. Most files are ASCII files consisting of the `String` data type (characters). A `Byte` type is a one-byte numerical value, a `Short` is a two-byte numerical value, and a `Long` is a four-byte numerical value. For example, to identify a file that begins with the word "project," choose the `String` setting.
Tag Value	Determines what to look for in the file contents. The `Tag Value` entry must be of the type defined in the `Tag Type` setting. In most cases, you will set the `Tag Type` setting to `String` and enter the text you want to match in the `Tag Value` text field. For example, enter "project" to match all files that begin with the text string "project."
Tag Mask	This optional field defines a mask value for `Byte`, `Short`, or `Long` data types. If a mask value is defined, a logical AND operation is performed on the `Tag Value` and the `Tag Mask` to determine the match value (the contents to be matched). The `Tag Mask` field is primarily intended for programmers developing applications to be integrated into the DeskSet Environment.

Binding an Icon to a File

Before you can bind an icon to a file, you first need to have created a 32-by-32 XView icon image. If you want to define the background area to apply a background color, you must also have created a mask file. Once you have created an icon, you can bind an icon image to a file by following the steps below.

1. Click the left mouse button on the **New** button at the bottom of the **Binder** window. The new entry **unnamed_1** appears in the Binder Entries scrolling list and in the Icon category **Properties** window, as shown in Figure 7.27.

2. Replace the name in the **Icon** text field with the name you want for the new Binder entry and press Return. This name will only appear in the binder; it is not a part of the icon. For example, you might enter "book-file" to identify that the icon indicates a text file associated with a book project.

3. Type the path and file name of your XView icon in the **Image File** text field and press Return.

4. If you want to specify a color mask (the area of the icon to be colored) you must have created another icon file that matches the size of your icon image to specify the area to apply the background color for the icon. Triple click in the **Mask file** text field to select the default entry, and enter the mask file name in the **Mask File** text field, then press Return. If you do not specify an icon mask file, the entire image appears in the background color.

FIGURE 7.27

The unnamed_1 entry appearing in the Icon category Properties window

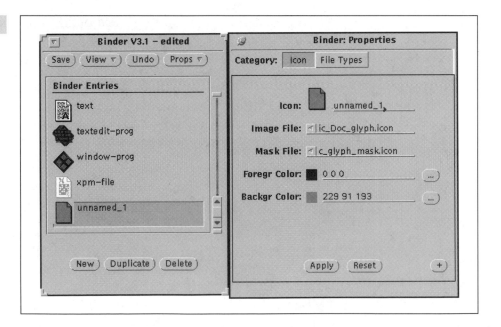

5. If you are using a color monitor, you can click on the buttons next to the `Foregr Color` text field and the `Backgr Color` text field to display the `Color Chooser` pop-up window. You can then select foreground and background colors for your icon. Be sure to click on `Apply` in the `Color Chooser` pop-up window to apply your selected colors.

6. Click the left mouse button on the + button in the lower left-hand corner. If you are defining the icon for an application other than the Text Editor, enter the application name in the `Application` text field. You can also define how a file prints by entering a print script (a series of print commands) in the `Print Method` text field. If you do not specify a print method, the print method of the application the file is being printed from is used.

7. Choose the `File Types` setting from the `Category` setting at the top of the `Properties` window. The `Properties` window now displays the File Types properties.

8. With the default `by Name` setting activated, type the file name pattern that you want to match in the `Pattern` text field. For example, to apply the icon to all files ending with the extension `.bk`, type `*.bk` in the `Pattern` text field and press Return.

9. Click the left mouse button on the `Apply` button to apply the icon file type and file type properties to your new binder entry.

10. Click the left mouse button on the `Save` button in the `Binder` window to save the new Binder entry in your personal database.

11. Choose `Close` from the Window menu to close the Binder to an icon.

12. Save a file using the file name pattern you indicated in step 8. Be sure that the file is not an empty file, or the new icon may not appear in the File Manager. In some cases, you must restart the File Manager or DeskSet application that your icon applies to. Figure 7.28 shows icons in the File Manager that match the file names ending with `.bk`.

FIGURE 7.28

A bound icon
displayed in the File
Manager window

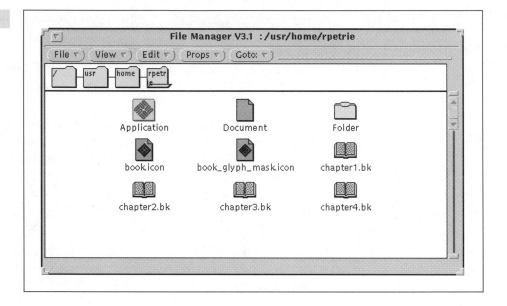

Deleting a Binder Entry

If you delete a Binder entry, the File Type entry associated with it is not deleted. If you want to delete the File Type entry, make sure to delete it from the File Type scrolling list before you delete the Binder entry. To delete the File Type entry, select the Binder entry in the base window scrolling list, display the File Type **Properties** window, select the entry or entries in the File Type scrolling list, and click the left mouse button on the **Properties** window's **Delete** button.

To delete a Binder entry, select the entry in the **Binder** window's scrolling list, and click the left mouse button on the **Delete** button. Then click the left mouse button on the **Save** button. Remember, the **Delete** button is dimmed and inactive if the currently selected entry is a system or network read-only entry.

Changing a Binding

To change a binding, select the entry in the **Binder** window's scrolling list, then modify the Icon and File Type properties fields that you want to change. If the binding that you want to change is a read-only entry, you can select the entry then click the left mouse button on the **Duplicate** button to make a private copy of the entry. You can then modify your private copy of the Binder entry. For example, suppose you want to change the color that the File Manager uses to display document files. Follow these steps:

1. Select the entry **default-doc** in the **Binder** window's scrolling list. A status message in the bottom-right corner of the Binder indicates that this is a read-only entry.

2. Click the left mouse button on the **Duplicate** button to copy the entry to your user database. A new Binder entry is created called **unnamed_1**, with all the same Icon properties as the original **default-doc** Binder entry. You can modify this new entry.

3. Rename the new Binder entry **default-doc**. This will put an entry called default-doc in your personal Binder database. This personal entry will take precedence over the system or network entry of the same name. If you later create a second user entry named **default-doc**, only the first entry you created will be recognized.

4. Change the background color to the new desired color. You can either type in the new RGB (red/green/blue) values in the **Backgr Color** text field, or click the left mouse button on the **Backgr Color** button to display the Color Chooser.

5. Click the left mouse button on the **Apply** button to update the icon name and color in the new Binder entry.

6. Click the left mouse button on the **Save** button in the **Binder** window. This updates your database to include the new Binder entry. Now when you view the merged Binder databases (the **All** item in the View menu), your personal entry will replace the shared entry

of the same name. If you want to use the shared entry again, simply delete the personal entry. The next time you start a new File Manager application, the color specified in your new personal entry will be used to display documents.

7. Choose Quit from the Window menu to quit the Binder.

NOTE   Changing the background of a default folder (default-dir) or document (default-doc) can change the background color of other icons.

PART TWO

Working from the SunOS Command Line

CHAPTERS

8 Getting Started with the SunOS Command Line

9 Navigating Directories and Working with Files

10 Improving Your Command-Line Productivity

11 Electronic Mail and Messages

12 Using the vi Editor

13 Formatting and Printing

14 Multitasking with SunOS

Getting Started with the SunOS Command Line

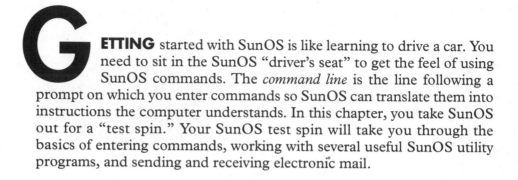

GETTING started with SunOS is like learning to drive a car. You need to sit in the SunOS "driver's seat" to get the feel of using SunOS commands. The *command line* is the line following a prompt on which you enter commands so SunOS can translate them into instructions the computer understands. In this chapter, you take SunOS out for a "test spin." Your SunOS test spin will take you through the basics of entering commands, working with several useful SunOS utility programs, and sending and receiving electronic mail.

Logging into SunOS

N O T E   If you have already logged in and want to work with SunOS commands in a Command Tool or Shell Tool window in the OpenWindows environment, skip to the section "Entering SunOS Commands."

The process of getting into SunOS is called *logging in*. Before logging into SunOS, you need an *account* set up by a *system administrator*, a person responsible for managing the system. In setting up your account, the system administrator instructs SunOS to accept you as a user and establishes certain parameters for your use of the system. When your account is established, you are assigned a user name. Your *user name* identifies you to the system. A common format for user names is the initial of your first name and your complete last name. Once you've been assigned an account and a user name, you are ready to log in.

After you have been assigned an account and a user name, you need to choose a password that you can enter when the system prompts you to after you have entered your user name. Your *password* prevents the use of your account by unauthorized users. Pick a password that is easy to remember, yet not easily deduced by others. You can change your password any time, as explained later. The following are requirements for selecting a password for the first time.

- A password must have at least six characters. If you use a password of less than six characters in length, the system prompts you to use a longer password.

- A password must contain at least two alphabetic characters and at least one numeric or special character, such as a &, +, −, @, !, or %. A password can contain uppercase or lowercase letters.

- Your user name, with its letters reversed or moved around, *cannot* be used as a password.

To log in, at the `login` prompt, type in your user name in lowercase characters then press Return. If you typed a wrong character and have not yet pressed Return, use the Delete key to erase the incorrect character, then type the correct character.

N O T E

If you enter a password more than three times that the system doesn't recognize, the system displays a message telling you there have been too many attempts and to try again later. This is a security feature to prevent unauthorized users from trying to guess a password.

After entering your user name, the system prompts you to enter your password. At the `password` prompt, type in your new password, then press Return. Your password will not be displayed as you type it. If your password is correct, the system logs you in and displays the system prompt, indicating that you are ready to start OpenWindows or enter SunOS commands.

System Login Messages

After you have logged in, you may see a *login message* displayed on your screen just before the system prompt. A login message usually displays information from the system administrator, such as when the system will be shut down for maintenance. A message indicating that you have electronic mail from other system users may also appear. Some systems may prompt you to type **news** to display a news bulletin. For information on reading electronic mail, see Chapter 11. For information on reading news messages, see Chapter 16.

Changing Your Password

It is a good idea to change your password periodically in order to prevent unauthorized access to your files. Depending on how your system administrator set up your account, you may even be required to change your password at regular time intervals. The following are additional requirements for changing a password beyond those described earlier for entering your password for the first time.

- Uppercase and lowercase characters are not considered different by Solaris when changing a password.

- A new password must differ from the previous password by at least three characters.

The following steps explain how to change your password.

1. At the system prompt, type in the command **passwd** in lowercase characters and press Return. Solaris prompts you for your old password.

2. Type your old password and press Return. The system will not display the characters you type. The system will prompt you for your new password.

3. Type your new password and press Return. After you enter your new password, you will then be asked to retype your new password for verification.

4. Type your new password again and press Return.

The SunOS Shells

A *shell* is the interface between you and SunOS; it translates commands you enter from the keyboard for the operating system. The system prompt is SunOS's way of saying it is ready and waiting for a command. How your SunOS prompt appears depends on which shell your system is using. The *Bourne shell* and *Korn shell* usually use the dollar sign ($) as the system prompt symbol. The Bourne shell is the standard shell for SunOS. However, your system may be using the *C shell*, which displays a percent sign (%) as its prompt. A system prompt may incorporate a system host name (also known as the name of the *file server*, the central computer on the network that enables you to access files throughout the system) followed by the system prompt. This is displayed as

```
bookware$
```

N O T E   Most of the examples in this book will not include the system prompt. Just be aware that this prompt will be displayed on your screen as you follow the exercises presented here.

The Korn shell, Bourne shell, and C shell all come with SunOS. Previously the Korn shell had to be purchased separately. The Korn shell uses a simpler syntax and performs commands faster than the C shell. In addition, the Korn shell provides many of the convenient features of the C shell. It is also compatible with the Bourne shell (the default), so any Bourne shell command will run using the Korn shell. New users will benefit from the Korn shell because it provides features for easily editing and repeating commands that are not available in the Bourne shell. Because of the Korn shell's many benefits and the fact that it is rapidly replacing the Bourne shell in popularity, this book focuses on using the Korn shell. If you're not already using the Korn shell, at the system prompt, enter

```
ksh
```

N O T E   Any Bourne shell command will run using the Korn shell.

Entering SunOS Commands

When you type in characters at the system prompt, you're entering characters into an area of memory called the *command-line buffer*. Pressing Return instructs SunOS to *execute* the command by accepting the contents of the command line in the buffer and processing it. The command line uses a simple standard *syntax* (rules governing the structure of a command line). Command lines can contain simple one-word commands or more complex commands that include *arguments*. Arguments modify commands and may be *options*, *expressions*, and *file names*. For example, adding a file name after a command identifies the file to be affected by the command. In SunOS you add an option to a command by typing a space then a hyphen before the first option letter. Options and expressions will be explained when commands that use them are introduced.

Keep in mind that the terms *commands* and *programs* are used interchangeably in SunOS because the names of the individual programs that make up the operating system are also the commands used to execute them. The general format for SunOS commands is as follows:

```
Command Option(s) Expression(s) Filename(s)
```

W A R N I N G   Keep in mind that SunOS is *case sensitive*, meaning that it treats lowercase and uppercase characters as two distinct character types.

Correcting Mistakes

There are several keyboard commands you can use to correct mistakes in the command line. The key combinations vary depending on how your system administrator has set up your system and account. Pressing the Delete key allows you to erase characters from the command line right to left. To erase an entire command line (as long as you haven't pressed Return), press Control-u. If you incorrectly type in a command and press Return, SunOS gives you an error message, such as `Command not found`. You can then retype the command. However, if you have typed in the wrong command, SunOS may execute a program you do not want to run. To terminate an executed program, press Control-c.

Useful SunOS Programs

SunOS contains over 300 utility programs that perform a wide variety of functions. To familiarize yourself with the SunOS environment, try running the utility programs described in this section. These programs enable you to display the date and time, display a calendar, perform simple mathematical calculations, establish who is using the system, echo text entered at the command line, and list and repeat commands you have entered previously. For more information on these and other SunOS commands, see Part IV, "Command Reference."

Displaying the Date and Time

To display the current date and time, type `date` at the system prompt, then press Return. SunOS uses a 24-hour clock and gives the time to the second. For example, SunOS might display the current date and time as

```
Tue Jan 30 10:52:35 PST 1999
```

Displaying a Calendar

The `cal` command displays a calendar on your screen for the month and year specified. Typing `cal` then pressing Return displays the calendar for the current month. You can enter arguments to the `cal` command to specify a particular month and year. There must be at least one space between the command and argument. The year can be in the range from 0 to 9999 A.D. The months are numbered 01 to 12, though you can use a one- or two-digit number for single-digit months, such as 5 or 05 for the month of May. To display the calendar for just one month of any year, enter

```
cal month_number year
```

To see the calendar for October 1999, enter

```
cal 10 1999
```

SunOS displays the calendar for October 1999 as follows:

```
      October 1999
  S   M  Tu  W Th   F   S
                    1   2
  3   4   5  6  7   8   9
 10  11  12 13 14  15  16
 17  18  19 20 21  22  23
 24  25  26 27 28  29  30
 31
```

Entering the command

```
cal 1999
```

displays the entire calendar for the year 1999.

Performing Simple Calculations

The `bc` program converts your computer into a handy desktop calculator. To start up the calculator program, type

```
bc
```

The `bc` command does not display a command prompt to let you know it has started. It simply waits for you to type your calculations. You can use standard operators to perform your calculations (plus +, minus -, multiplication *, and division /). To terminate the **bc** program, press Control-d. Type the calculation you want to perform. For example, the symbol recognized as the multiplication operator by **bc** is the asterisk (*), so entering

```
7*7
```

and pressing Return displays the result of the multiplication operation

```
49
```

In order to perform division operations with decimal places, you need to set the number of decimal places. The **scale** setting instructs **bc** how many decimal points to use in the division operation. To set the scale to two decimal places and divide 1 by 2, enter

```
scale=2
1/2
```

When you press Return, bc displays

```
.50
```

Press Control-d to return to system prompt.

Who Is Using the System?

SunOS is a multiuser system, which means more than one person can use the system at any one time. The **who** and **finger** commands are useful if you need to know a user's login name to send mail but only know their real name.

The **who** command lists the people logged into the system at that moment. The list contains user names, which terminals are being used, and the date and time each user logged in. To execute the **who** command, enter

```
who
```

SunOS displays a listing of current system users of your host machine. If your user name was **rpetrie**, the system might display

```
rpetrie    pts/06      Aug 30   11:35
bfife      pts/10      Aug 30   09:02
plane      pts/11      Aug 29   15:06
```

If you are working on a terminal other than your own, you may want to see the name that you are working under, or you may have access to more than one user name and want to remind yourself which name you used to logged in. To display information only about yourself simply enter

```
who am i
```

The `finger` command provides more detailed user information than the `who` command. Depending on what your system administrator has directed this command to display, it may list a user's full name, user name, terminal location, idle time, home directory, and more. To execute the `finger` command, enter

```
finger
```

SunOS then displays a `finger` command listing, such as

```
Login       Name  TTY Idle    When    Where
rpetrie     Rob Petrie        pts/06  12   Tue 10:30 NewRochelle
bfife       Barney Fife       pts/10  0    Wed 12:55 Mayberry
plane       Patty Lane        pts/11  20   Wed 15:06 Brooklyn
```

Echoing Text

The `echo` command is one of the simplest of SunOS commands. It displays on your screen whatever you type as its argument. The `echo` command can be very beneficial for displaying messages to yourself or other users. This command is frequently used when writing shell scripts, which are collections of commands stored in a file that can be run as a single program. To see just how the `echo` command displays text, enter

```
echo Is this the department of redundancy department?
```

when you press Return the `echo` command displays

```
echo Is this the department of redundancy department?
Is this the department of redundancy department?
```

The `echo` command prints on the line below the prompt, however you can move to the next line by adding the letter n followed by a backslash (\) and enclosing the text using single (') or double (") quotation marks. The backslash is used to identify the n as a special instruction for the `echo` command to perform, and the quotes or double quotes protect the back-slash from being mistaken for text. For example, entering

```
echo "line 1 \nline 2 \nline 3"
```

displays

```
echo "line 1 \nline 2 \nline 3"
line 1
line 2
line 3
```

The echo command includes additional options for controlling how the message is displayed. By adding "\c", you can force echo to display on the same line. By adding \07 you can sound a warning bell. You can also add more than one option to the echo command. For example, entering

```
echo To beep "\07"or not to beep "\c"
```

beeps and displays the following

```
To beep or not to beep $
```

Displaying and Repeating Commands

The Korn shell stores a list of previously issued commands that can be redisplayed on your screen using the history command then reexecuted from the list. This timesaving feature speeds up the task of reentering commands. By default, history remembers the last 128 commands and displays the last 16 commands. To see a list of the previous 16 commands that have been captured by the history command, type history at the system prompt, then press Return. You can display additional commands by entering the following:

```
history  -n
```

The letter n indicates the number of commands you would like to display. For example, entering

```
history  -20
```

instructs the Korn shell to display the last 20 executed commands. You can also list a range of previously executed commands by entering his-tory and separating the beginning and the ending number with a space.

Remember, you can check the numbering of the last 16 commands by entering `history`. To display commands 3 through 6, enter

```
history 3 6
```

For example, if you have entered each of the commands discussed in this chapter in the order in which they were introduced, entering `history 3 6` would produce this list:

```
3 cal 1999
4 bc
5 who
6 finger
```

The history list is dynamic, which means that it changes as you enter more commands at the system prompt. The commands issued first are the first to scroll off the list. You can reexecute any command in the `history` command list. To reexecute the last command in the list, type r at the system prompt and press Return. To execute any command in the list, type r n and press Return, where n is the number of the command in the list. For example, typing r 3 and pressing Return executes the third command in the `history` command list `cal 1999`.

Clearing the Screen

The more commands you enter, the more cluttered your screen becomes. The `clear` command lets you easily wipe your screen clean. To clear the screen so the cursor appears in the upper-left corner, simply enter

```
clear
```

Sending and Receiving Electronic Mail

SunOS's mail program allows you to send mail messages, called *electronic mail* or *email*, to other users on the network and receive electronic mail in return. Whenever you log in, SunOS checks the system mailbox. If any mail is addressed to your user name, you may see the message **you have mail** displayed on your screen. You can then display a listing of your mail messages and read your mail or ignore the mail message prompt and read your mail at any time later. You can send mail messages to other users whether they are online or not.

Reading Your Mail

If you get a message notifying you that you have mail, someone has sent you a mail message through the SunOS mail system. In order to read your mail, at the system prompt enter

```
mail
```

The system displays postmark message headers, followed by the **mail** program prompt, as shown below.

```
From buddy Thu Jul 23 14:17 PDT 1992
Date: Thu, 23 Jul 92 14:17:12 PDT
From: buddy (Buddy Sorrell)
Message-Id: <9207232117.AA00233@abradyshow>
Content-Length: 53

Rob,
Can we use Mel's bald head for the bowling ball sketch?
Buddy

?
```

The question mark (?), at the end of the message, prompts you for a filing disposition for the current mail message. Typing an asterisk * displays a complete list of disposition commands. The following describes the most common options for disposing and saving mail messages.

OPTION	DESCRIPTION
Press Return	Display the next mail message and save this mail message so it will still be there next time mail is read.
d	Delete the current mail message and display the next mail message.

OPTION	DESCRIPTION
s *filename*	Save the current mail message in *filename* (where *filename* is a file name you enter to store the message) and display the next mail message.
q	Quit reading mail; unread mail is available next time you execute the mail command.
x	Exit and abort the mail program; any mail messages that you deleted are restored.

Sending Mail

You send mail by specifying the user name of the person or persons you want to receive the mail after the `mail` command. You can use the `who` or `finger` command as explained earlier in this chapter to find a user's name if you don't know it. When you send mail to another user, it is stored in the recipient's electronic mailbox, and that person is notified that they have mail. To send mail to another user, at the system prompt, type `mail` `username`, then press Return. To send the same mail message to multiple users, separate each user name with a space. Type in the text of your mail message. If you want to create a new line, simply press Return at any point. If you decide you want to cancel your mail message, press Control-c. When you've finished entering your mail message text, press Return to move the cursor to a new line, then press Control-d. The mail program sends your mail message and the system prompt returns you to your screen.

Getting Help with SunOS Commands

SunOS includes the reference documentation for all SunOS commands, called *man pages* (short for manual pages). These man pages are not written for the beginning user. However, using man pages can come in quite handy when you have forgotten the syntax of a command or you want on-line help with a command from the command line. The man pages include a brief description, the command syntax, available options, system files that are referenced by the command, and lists related to commands. The man pages conclude with any known problems and limitations of a command. The `man` command uses the syntax

        man *command*

where *command* is the name of the command you want help with. For example, to get more information on the `mail` command, enter

        man mail

The `man` command displays only one screenful of text at a time and the percentage of the pages displayed. To continue displaying man pages, press the Spacebar or the Return key. To quit displaying the man pages, enter q.

Command Summary

The following lists the commands covered in this chapter and their functions.

COMMAND	RESULT
bc	Performs simple calculations.
cal	Displays calendar for month or year specified.
clear	Clears the screen.
date	Displays current time and date.
echo	Displays the text that follows the `echo` command.
finger	Lists detailed information about users currently on the system.
history	List commands previously executed.
mail	Allows user to read or send electronic mail.

COMMAND	RESULT
man	Displays manual pages for a command.
r	Reexecutes the last command (Korn shell only).
who	Lists users currently logged into system.
who am i	Lists information about the user currently logged into system.

CHAPTER

9

Navigating Directories and Working with Files

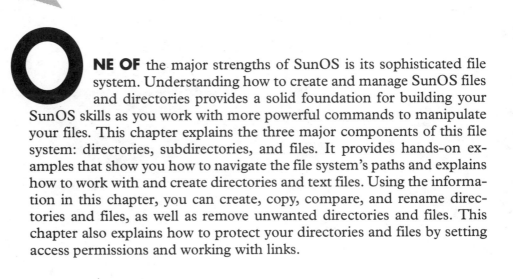

ONE OF the major strengths of SunOS is its sophisticated file system. Understanding how to create and manage SunOS files and directories provides a solid foundation for building your SunOS skills as you work with more powerful commands to manipulate your files. This chapter explains the three major components of this file system: directories, subdirectories, and files. It provides hands-on examples that show you how to navigate the file system's paths and explains how to work with and create directories and text files. Using the information in this chapter, you can create, copy, compare, and rename directories and files, as well as remove unwanted directories and files. This chapter also explains how to protect your directories and files by setting access permissions and working with links.

An Overview of the SunOS File System

SunOS uses a hierarchical file structure, an inverted tree structure similar to the structure of a family tree, with the base of the tree at the top. A *file* is a "container" that holds text or programs. *Directories* are files that contain indexes to aid SunOS in locating files. It's helpful if you think of directories as file cabinets and files as file folders containing the information that you want to access. That is, though directories really only contain indexes to files, you can think of them as actually containing the files themselves.

The topmost parent directory of the tree is known as the *root* directory and is indicated by a slash (/). The root directory contains files and *subdirectories*. Although every directory except the root directory is a subdirectory, subdirectories can be referred to as directories. In other words, the term subdirectory and directory are often used interchangeably. Your system may have a directory called **home** that contains home directories for all users. The names of these individual home directories are usually based on the names of the users.

Types of Directories

SunOS relies on specific system directories to operate. In most cases, the system administrator organizes and restricts access to these directories. The following list explains the primary types of directories that exist on a SunOS system.

DIRECTORY	DESCRIPTION
/ (root)	The first slash represents the top of the file system, or the root directory.
/bin	This is the binary files directory, which contains the SunOS program files or commands. For example, the commands you entered in Chapter 8 were executed from the **bin** directory.
/dev	This is the device directory, which contains files that support such devices as the screen, the mouse, and the disk drives.
/etc	This directory is used by the system administrator for machine-specific system maintenance. For example, the /etc/shadow file is used to keep user passwords in a file inaccessible to anyone except the system administrator and certain trusted programs.
/export	The /export directory contains files and file systems that a file server shares with other workstations on the network.

DIRECTORY	DESCRIPTION
/home	The /home directory contains user home directories. In some cases, user home directories are found in the /export directory so they can be accessed from other workstations on the network.
/kernel	The /kernel directory contains the program UNIX, which is also known as the *kernel*. The kernel is the heart of SunOS; it manages the system's hardware, and schedules and terminates processes.
/sbin	The /sbin directory contains programs for system administration.
/tmp	Temporary files are stored in this directory and are either periodically removed by your system administrator or deleted when you reboot your computer.
/usr	This is a general purpose directory that contains several important subdirectories for users. For example, /usr/bin contains many of the SunOS command programs, and /usr/share/man contains the online manual pages.
/var	This directory is maintained by the system administrator. It contains information that varies from machine to machine. For example, users' mail files are stored in the /var/mail directory.

Navigating Directories

When you want to move to another directory, enter the cd (change directory) command followed by the name of directory you want to move to.

The following sections describe more fully the **cd** command and explain additional techniques that you can use to move quickly through the file system. They also cover absolute and relative path names, on-screen displays of your current working directory, and shortcuts for returning to your home directory.

Navigating with Path Names

Every file has a path name. A *path name* tells SunOS which paths to take to find a specific directory or file, and so is similar to an address on a letter because both give specific directions for a final destination. You change from one directory to another by invoking the **cd** command with a path name. A path name consists of a directory name or series of directory names separated by slashes (/). For example, /usr indicates the directory usr, which is a subdirectory immediately below the root directory (indicated by the forward slash). There are two types of path names: absolute and relative.

Navigating with Absolute Path Names

You can construct the path name of a file by tracing a path from the root directory to the directory where the file resides. An *absolute path name* always begins with a slash (/) and lists the file name after the final slash. For example, /export/home/srogers/letter is the absolute path name for the file letter in the directory /export/home/srogers.

Navigating with Relative Path Names

Unless you specify an absolute path name by beginning the path name with a slash, SunOS assumes you are using a relative path name. A *relative path name* describes a path that starts from the directory in which you're currently working. In other words, relative path names trace the path from the working directory to the desired file or directory. Relative path names save you the time of typing in a complete, or absolute, path name to access a directory or file beneath the directory you are currently located in. For example, in the directory /export/home/srogers, the command

```
cd reports
```

moves you to the subdirectory /export/home/srogers/reports.

Moving to Your Home Directory

Your *home directory* is the directory that was created for you when you first logged into the system. Every user is assigned a home directory. Entering the **cd** command by itself moves you directly to your home directory. If you're using the Korn shell, the tilde character (~) can be used as a shortcut for typing in the entire path name for your home directory. For example, typing **cd ~/reports** moves you to the **reports** subdirectory of your home directory. You can also access another user's home directory by following the tilde character with the person's user name. For example, **cd ~mcooley** moves you to Melvin Cooley's home directory. Adding a plus sign to the tilde (~+) is the same as typing the absolute path name of the working directory. Adding a minus sign to the tilde (~+~−) is the same as typing the absolute path name of the directory you were previously in.

Displaying the Working Directory

The *working directory* is not a fixed directory but the directory in which you are currently located. A useful SunOS command is **pwd**, which prints (displays) on the screen the name of your working directory. When you use the **ls** command with the **-a** option to list the contents of a directory, SunOS may indicate the working directory path name as a single dot (.).

Moving to a Parent Directory

The *parent directory* is the directory located one level above your working directory. You can specify the path name of the parent directory of your working directory with two consecutive periods (. .). For example, entering **cd . .** moves you up one directory level. The following example prints the working directory before and after moving up a directory level using the double-dot shortcut. If entering the **pwd** command displays

```
/export/home/srogers
```

issuing the command **cd . .** then issuing the **pwd** command displays

```
/export/home
```

Working with Directories

Now that you know how to use absolute and relative path names, you can use several helpful commands to conveniently and strategically organize your files. Your ability to perform actions on a given file is governed by the type of access you have to that file. The type of access you have is controlled by *permissions* settings.

- *Read* permission allows you to view or copy the contents of a file.

- *Write* permission enables you to add or delete directories.

- *Execute* permission allows you to move into a directory and execute programs.

In most cases, if you try to move, copy, or remove a file for which you don't have these permissions, SunOS will respond with a `Permission denied` message. Permissions are covered in detail later in this chapter.

Listing a Directory's Contents

The `ls` command by itself lists the contents (directories and files) of the working directory. You can also specify a directory after the `ls` command to get a listing for that directory. For example, `ls /export/home/srogers` lists the files for the directory `srogers` no matter which directory you're using. There are a number of arguments the `ls` command can accept to display different information.

OPTION	RESULT
-1	Lists subdirectories and files with each entry on a separate line.
-a	Lists all subdirectories and hidden files (special system files that have a file name beginning with a dot or a period).
-c	Lists files by creation/modification time.

OPTION	RESULT
–F	Lists and flags directories with a slash (/), executable files with an asterisk (*), and symbolic links—used primarily by programmers—with an at sign (@). Text files appear without a flag.
–g	Shows the group ownership of a file in a long listing but omits the actual owner.
–l	Displays a long listing of the contents of the directory.
–m	Merges a listing of the contents of the directory into a series of names separated by commas.
–o	Shows the ownership of a file in a long listing but omits the group name.
–R	Recursively lists the contents of each subdirectory under a specified directory. Each subdirectory name is followed by its relative path name and a listing of the contents of that subdirectory until SunOS reaches the last level of the hierarchical structure.
–r	Reverses the order of listing to display a reverse alphabetical directory listing.
–t	Lists a directory sorted by time in order of newest to oldest files.
–u	Lists subdirectories and files according to file access time.

To help you quickly identify the different directories, files, and programs (executable files), enter the **ls** command with the –F option, **ls** –F. When you enter **ls** –F, a directory listing such as this one appears on your screen:

```
Desktop* examples/      info* memo
clients final     mail/ textfile
```

Below is a sample listing produced by ls -l.

```
-rw-r--r--  1  rpetrie staff  1094  Dec   1   17:08  clients
drwxr-sr-x  2  rpetrie staff   0    Nov   9   19:52  Temp
-rw-r--r--  1  rpetrie staff   0    Dec   1   17:08  info
drwxr-sr-x  2  rpetrie staff  512   Jan   30  19:52  mail
```

The different components of this listing are explained in the "Listing File and Directory Permissions" section later in this chapter.

Creating a Directory

The mkdir command creates directories. By creating a directory you are making the equivalent of a file drawer where you can keep related files. Before creating a directory, make sure you are in your home directory by typing cd and pressing Return. Enter mkdir followed by the name you want to give your new directory. For example, in the directory /export/home/srogers, entering

```
mkdir reports
```

creates the subdirectory /export/home/srogers/reports. If you attempt to make a new directory with a directory name that already exists, the message mkdir: failed to make directory "reports"; File exists appears. In order to create a directory outside your home directory, you must have write and execute permissions in the parent directory.

Copying a Directory

You can duplicate the contents of any directory using the cp (copy) command and the -r (recursive) option. This guarantees that all files and subdirectories of the source directory are duplicated. For example, in the directory /export/home/felix, issuing the command cp -r portfolio record copies all files and subdirectories from the portfolio directory to the directory named record, where record and portfolio are subdirectories of /export/home/felix. If the directory to which the copies are supposed to be sent doesn't exist, the cp command first creates it, then copies the files and directories to the new directory. If the directory to which the copies are supposed to be sent already exists, any files already there are overwritten. To allow you to avoid mistakenly overwriting existing files, use the -i (interactive) option. This option causes SunOS to ask if you really want to overwrite files in a directory that already exists. Pressing any key other than y causes the cp process to terminate.

As with many SunOS commands, you can use more than one option with the cp at a time. When you use multiple options you only need to precede the list of options with a single hyphen. For example, if you enter cp -ir portfolio record, the -i causes SunOS to ask if you really want to overwrite the existing files in record. Press y, and the -r (recursive) option then copies all the files and subdirectories of the portfolio directory to the record directory until SunOS reaches the last level of the hierarchical structure.

You can maintain the original modification times and permission modes of files and directories by using the -p (preserve) option. If you don't use the -p option, the files are assigned the current date and default permission modes. To interactively and recursively copy the contents of the directory bozo to the directory clone, while preserving the original modification times and permission modes, enter

```
cp -ipr /bozo /clone
```

WARNING Beware of a recursive copy that doesn't specify files to be copied, such as cp -r source source/backup. This copy command can ruin your day by recursively creating new backup subdirectories and copying files until it fills the entire file system.

Removing a Directory

You can delete a directory using the remove directory command, rmdir. The directory that you want to remove cannot be the working directory (the directory in which you're located). To remove a directory with rmdir, the directory needs to be empty; that is, it cannot contain any subdirectories or files. When removing subdirectories from your current directory, remember that you can refer to subdirectories using the shorthand convention of relative path names. For example, to remove the empty subdirectory `reports` from your current directory, simply enter `rmdir reports`. Adding the `-i` option causes SunOS to ask if you want the directory to be removed before SunOS deletes the directory. If you attempt to remove a directory that isn't empty, SunOS displays the message `rmdir: directoryname: Directory not empty`.

To remove directories that contain files or subdirectories, use `rm` with the `-r` (recursive) option, which deletes all existing files and subdirectories, then removes the directory. To interactively remove a directory and its contents, enter the command `rm -ir directory_name`. You can force files to be removed without SunOS displaying permissions, asking questions, and reporting errors by adding the `-f` (force) option; for example, `rm -rf directoryname`.

WARNING

Be careful when using the `-r` and `-f` options. All subdirectories are permanently deleted when you use these options. Before removing a directory, use the `ls` command with the `-a` (all) option to guarantee that the directory doesn't contain subdirectories or files that you'll later need. Then use the `rm` command with the `-ir` options to ensure you don't accidentally remove needed directories and files.

Working with Files

Manipulating files is the essence of SunOS. SunOS provides commands to perform just about any operation on a file you can imagine. The following section only scratches the surface in explaining the most essential commands and options you can use when working with files, such as displaying a file's type or contents, or copying, renaming, moving, or removing files. In many ways, working with files is similar to working with directories. Most of the commands you use with directories are the same as the commands you use with files.

Listing Files

The command for listing files is the same as that for listing the contents of a directory. You can list the files for any directory by following the `ls` command with the absolute or relative path name and any of the `ls` options. If the directory is empty and you use `ls -a` to list all your files, a single period (.) indicating the current directory and two consecutive periods (..) indicating the parent directory are displayed.

Determining File Types

If you enter `file` followed by a file name, SunOS lists that file's *type*, such as ASCII text, program files, or directory. For example, issuing the command

```
file clients
```

causes SunOS to display

```
clients: ascii text
```

indicating that clients is an ASCII text file. If the file is a program file, the command also lists the language it was written in and any pertinent information about the file.

File Name Conventions

A file name must be unique in the directory where it resides. File names can be up to 256 characters long, but it is recommended that you keep them under 14 characters to save time entering them. You can assign a file any name you want, provided you avoid using special characters such as `*?<>!/\`. Remember, SunOS is a case-sensitive operating system, so you need to enter the file name exactly as you created it in order to use it again. File names that begin with a period (.) indicate special hidden files that are used by the system and do not appear when you use `ls` by itself to list the files. But you can use a period anywhere else in a file name and it will not become a hidden file.

Be careful when naming files. To create file names that are easy to remember and don't conflict with SunOS's special characters, it is best to restrict file names to letters, digits, underscores, and periods (except as the first character). Don't create a file name that contains a nonprinting character, or a *control character*, by pressing a Control-key combination, such as Control-a. Although in most cases SunOS would substitute the control character with a question mark on screen, a file name with nonprintable characters can make that file inaccessible.

Creating a File

There are several ways you can create a file. You can use a text editor, such as vi, to create a file, use the `cat` command, or use the `touch` command to create an empty file. The `cat` command is an abbreviation of *concatenate*, which means to link or connect in a series. To create a file with the `cat` command, type `cat > `*`filename`*, where *`filename`* is the name you want your file to have. After typing the name for your file and pressing Return, you can begin entering the text you want your file to contain. When you are finished entering the text, press Control-d. For example, to create a file using the `cat` command, type in the following:

```
cat >myfile (press Return)
My first text file. (press Return)
(press Control-D)
```

The greater-than sign (>) is a *redirection operator* that channels your text into the file `myfile`. Control-d signals the end of the text that is to be put into the file. If you accidentally type `cat` without a redirection symbol or a file name, press Control-d to exit the `cat` command.

Creating an Empty File

The `touch` command is usually used to change the time and date of a file. It is also an easy way to create an empty file. When you first start working with files, you may want to create files with the `touch` command to practice copying, moving, and removing files. The `touch` command uses the following syntax:

```
touch filename
```

If *filename* is the name of an existing file, the date and time of the file is updated to the current time and date. If no existing files match the *filename* argument, the `touch` command creates an empty file with the name indicated by the *filename* argument.

Displaying the Contents of a File

Once you've created a file, you can look at its contents by entering the `cat` command followed by the file name. If you misspell the name of the file you want to view, SunOS displays the file name you typed followed by the message `cat: Cannot open file`. If the file contains more lines than the screen can display, the beginning text scrolls off the screen, leaving only the last screen of text visible. The following key combinations are useful in this situation:

Control-s	Temporarily halts scrolling
Control-q	Resumes scrolling
Control-c	Cancels scrolling

You can display more than one file in sequence on the screen by typing in the names of all the files you want to see after `cat`, making sure to separate the file names with a space. For example, `cat doc1 doc2` displays the contents of the file `doc1`, followed by the contents of the file `doc2`.

NOTE

Many SunOS files are binary files that contain instructions only the computer can understand. When you try to display these files, they appear as text resembling what you might find in a cartoon balloon to indicate cursing.

The following options are available when using the `cat` command:

OPTION	RESULT
-e	Displays a $ character at the end of each line. The -e option is ignored unless used with the -v option.
-s	Causes `cat` to suppress messages if the file does not exist.
-t	Displays tab characters as ^I and formfeed characters as ^L. The -t option is ignored unless it is used with the -v option.
-v	Lists control characters.

Copying Files

You copy files with the `cp` command. To copy one of your files, type `cp` and the name of the file to be copied, and the file name you want to copy this file to. For example, `cp rocky smooth` copies the file `rocky` to a file with the name `smooth`, leaving `rocky` intact. Unless you use the -p (preserve) option to record the original modification time and permission modes, the file is created with the current date and default permission modes. (Permission modes are explained later in this chapter.) When copying files, use the -i (interactive) option to ensure that the target name for the copy doesn't already exist. That way if the file does exist, SunOS inquires if you really want to overwrite the existing file. Pressing any key other than y causes the copying process to terminate. You can also copy more than one file. To copy two or more files at once, list all the files after the command `cp`, making sure you separate each file name with a space. For example, to interactively copy the files `onefile twofile` to their parent directory, enter

```
cp -i onefile twofile ..
```

If the file names exist in the parent directory, SunOS asks you, one file at a time, whether or not to overwrite the existing file. Pressing any key other than y aborts the copy process for that file, and SunOS then asks if you want to overwrite the next existing file.

Moving and Renaming Files

Moving a file and renaming a file both use the same command, mv (move). To move a file, type mv followed by the name of the file you want to move, then type the directory you want to move the file to. If you want to rename a file, type mv followed by the file name you want to rename, then type the new name. For example, the command mv sunrise sunset changes the file name sunrise to sunset. The mv (move) command deletes the original file after copying the file and moving it to its new location. Use the -i option to ensure that you don't move a file to another file that already exists and overwrite the text there. You can't rename more than one file at a time. You can, however, move several files at one time by listing all the files you want to move before the destination directory and separating each file name with a space. For example, if you are in Perry Mason's home directory, entering the command

```
mv letter1 letter2 memo letters
```

moves the files letter1, letter2, and memo to the letters subdirectory of pmason.

Removing Files

The rm command deletes one or more files. To remove a file you need to have write permission in the directory that contains the file as well as in the file itself. If you don't have write permission for the file, and you created the file, SunOS asks you whether or not to override the permissions feature and remove the file. To remove more than one file, list all the files you want to delete and separate each file name with a space. The command rm junk trash removes the files junk and trash from the working directory. The rm -i (interactive) option prompts you with the question rm: remove filename: (y/n)?. Type y to remove the file; any other response will cause SunOS to ask if you want to remove the next file in an argument list or, if you only have one file in the list, aborts the removal process. You can force files to be removed without displaying access permissions or having SunOS ask questions or report errors by using the -f (force) option. To remove all the files and subdirectories in the current directory, use the rm -r (recursive) option.

WARNING Be careful using the −r and −f options. Files and subdirectories are permanently deleted when you use these options. When removing files, use the −i option to ensure you don't accidentally remove the wrong files.

Listing and Changing Permissions

Because SunOS allows users to share the file system, it protects files and directories by defining types of users and access permission modes. Every file and directory has three types of users and four types of access permission modes. By changing permission modes, you can selectively share files and directories with some or all of the people on the system.

Listing File and Directory Permissions

By adding the −l (long) option to the ls (list) command, you can list permissions information about files. Entering ls −l displays a long format for your directory listing. This option can be used alone or in conjunction with the other options. This next example shows a listing of files using the −l (long) and −a (all) options with ls (ls −al), followed by an explanation of each of the file attributes from left to right.

```
drwxrwxrwx  7  rpetrie staff  2560  Dec  1  17:00  .
drwxrwxrwx  7  rpetrie staff  512   Dec  1  17:00  ..
-rw-r--r--  1  rpetrie staff  1094  Dec  1  17:08  clients
-rw-r--r--  1  rpetrie staff  0     Dec  1  17:18  info
drwxr-sr-x  2  rpetrie staff  512   Jan 30  19:52  mail
-rw-r--r--  1  rpetrie staff  1094  Dec  1  17:28  memo
drwxr-sr-x  2  rpetrie staff  512   Jul  4  12:26  temp
-rw-r--r--  1  rpetrie staff  179   Mar  1  10:35  test
-rw-r--r--  1  rpetrie staff  1327  Mar  1  15:00  textfile
```

COLUMN	DESCRIPTION
Permissions	Permissions are displayed in the *permissions list*, which is the first ten characters in the listing. The first character that appears in the leftmost column indicates the file type (regular, directory, or device). The remaining nine characters in the series specify the permission modes for the three types of users: yourself (owner), group, and others (three characters for each user type).
Links	The number that follows the first ten characters lists the number of files and directories linked to that file. Links are covered later in this chapter.
Owner	The user name of the person who created or owns the file.
Group	Users can be organized into groups. This enables members of a particular department to share access to files and directories. There can only be one group associated with a file or directory.
Bytes	The size of the file (a byte equals one character).
Date	The date and time the file was created or last modified.
File name	The name of the file or directory.

File and Directory Types

The first character in the permissions list indicates the file type. The most common types of files are referred to as *standard* files and are indicated by a hyphen (−). A directory is identified by the letter **d**. Outside your home directory you are likely to encounter other types of files. Here are some of the characters used to identify these types of files on the system.

CHARACTER	DESCRIPTION
−	Indicates that the file is a standard file.
b or c	Indicates that the device is a special device file.
d	Indicates that the file is actually a directory or subdirectory.
l	Indicates that the file is actually a symbolic link used to link one file with another. Symbolic links are discussed later in the chapter.
p	Indicates that the device is a special file.

Types of Permissions

There are seven types of permissions you can assign to your files or directories. By assigning different permissions, you can limit the access others have to that directory or file. Here is a list of the seven permission modes and the characters that represent them in a permissions list.

CHARACTER	DESCRIPTION
r	The read privilege allows a user to list the contents of the directory or file. The read permission is also necessary to copy a file from one location to another.
w	The write permission allows a user to change the contents of a file or directory. This permits a user to create, append, and remove existing files.
x	The execute permission allows a user to execute a file. The ability to search through directories is also a function of the execute permission. A directory can be read from or written to, but unlike a file, it can't be executed. When applied to a directory, the execute access permission allows you to search through and list the contents of the directory.

CHARACTER	DESCRIPTION
-	The no access permission is also referred to as the protection mode. It prevents a user from reading, writing to, or executing a file.

Ownership of Files

File access is defined for four types of users: owner, group, and all others. The following lists descriptions for each of these three types of ownership, and also includes examples of permissions modes.

TYPE OF USER	DESCRIPTION
Owner	This refers to the creator of the file or directory. The first three characters after the file type character list the types of permissions available to the owner. For example, a permissions list beginning with -rw- indicates the owner has read and write permissions but not execute permission.
Group	Each user is a member of a group defined by the system administrator. The fifth, sixth, and seventh characters in the list indicate the permissions available to users who are in the same group as the owner. For example, a file beginning with -rw-r-- indicates that group members have read, but not write or execute permissions. To find out which group or groups you belong to, enter the command groups.
Others	This means all other users. The third set of three characters after the file type lists the types of permissions available to users who are not members of the same group as the owner. For example, a file with -rw-r----- permissions indicates that users outside the owner's group have no access to the file.

TYPE OF USER	DESCRIPTION
All	Incorporates all three: owner, group, and others.

Changing Permission Modes

The owner of a file controls which users have permission to access and work with that file. You use the `chmod` command to change the permission modes of a file or directory. The permission modes of a file can only be changed by the person who created the file or by someone who has *super-user* privileges (additional access to files beyond those of a normal system user); usually this is your system administrator.

There are two forms of the `chmod` command you can use to change file and directory permission modes: the symbolic form and the numeric form.

Changing Permission Modes Using Symbolic Notation

The format for changing permission modes with symbolic notation is as follows:

```
chmod class(es) operation permission(s) filename(s)
```

Use the following abbreviations to identify the class for which you want to change permission modes:

u	User
g	Groups
o	Others
a	All

You then use operators to assign r for read, w for write, and x for execute permission modes. The following shows abbreviations for the possible arguments that can be added to the `chmod` command to assign, add, or remove permissions from a file using symbolic notation. If you omit class, the setting is applied to all three classes (user, group, and others).

CLASS	OPERATIONS	PERMISSIONS
u User (owner)	= assigns a permission	r read
g Group	+ adds a permission	w write
o Others	- removes a permission	x execute
a All		

The following example lists `chmod` commands to assign the file named **populace** read, write, and execute permissions for all classes of users and to remove all permissions for everyone but the user (owner) of the file named **restricted**.

```
chmod a=rwx populace
chmod go-rwx restricted
```

The command

```
chmod a=rx testfile
```

changes the mode of `testfile` so that it can be accessed and read but not written to by all users on the system. It's important to note that if you use = and do not specify all types of permissions (that is, if you omit r, w, or x), the permissions for the omitted types will be turned off. You can also change permissions for multiple files, provided you want them to have the same access permissions. You must separate the file names with a single space.

The following combines several aspects of `chmod`:

```
chmod u=rw, o=r redfish bluefish
```

This command

- allows the owner of the files `redfish` and `bluefish` to read and write to them.

- allows everyone else to read (but not write to) these files.

- prevents everyone, including the owner, from executing the files (because x was not specified).

Changing Permission Modes Using Numeric Notation

To assign permissions using numeric notation, you enter numbers to specify the permissions you want. If you enter only one number after `chmod`, that permission will apply to the other's class. If you enter two numbers, the first number will specify permissions for the group and the second will set the permissions for others. If you enter three numbers, the first number will set the owner's permissions, the second number will set group permissions, and the third number will apply to all others. The following lists the numeric values that can be used to change permissions.

VALUES	PERMISSIONS	DEFINITION
7	rwx	read, write, execute
6	rw–	read, write
5	r–x	read, execute
4	r––	read only
3	–wx	write and execute
2	–w–	write only
1	––x	execute only
0	–––	no access

To change modes using numeric notation, enter the `chmod` command followed by the numbers indicating the mode you want to assign to each class of user. For example, entering `chmod 750 fugu` indicates that the file named `fugu` can be read, written to, and executed by the owner, because the first number indicates the owner's permission mode is equal to 7. The next number, 5, indicates that the file can be read and executed by a member of the owner's group. The last number, 0, indicates there are no permissions for others on the system.

Here are two other examples of using the `chmod` command to change permissions mode:

```
chmod 64 project
```

assigns both read and write permissions to the group with access to the file **project** and assigns only the read permission to all other users. (Since only two numbers were entered after **chmod**, no permissions were assigned to the owner.)

```
chmod 544 document
```

assigns read and execute permissions for the owner of the file **document** and only read permission to both the group and all others.

Creating and Removing Links to Files

A *link* is a directory entry that acts as a pointer to locate files. In SunOS, you can create different names for a single file (that is, you can create additional links) by using the **ln** (link) command. For example, if you and another member of your group are both working on a file, you can have the file listed (under the same or different names) in both of your home directories. This ensures that two different versions of a file don't exist and also saves disk space. When you list files using the list command with the **-l** option, **ls -l**, the number displayed between the permissions modes and the file owner's name indicates the number of links to that file. In the following file listing, the file named **unite** has two links and **sole** has one.

```
-rw-r--r--  2  tcleaver  1024  Apr  1    19:05    unite
-rw-r--r--  1  tcleaver  256   Apr  1    19:35    sole
```

NOTE   If two users are working on a linked file simultaneously, only the user who first accessed the file will be able to write to it.

Creating a Link

When you create a file, SunOS places the file name in the appropriate directory and creates a link, or pointer, that points to the file so SunOS can locate it. Anytime you remove a file, the link is broken and the pointer is removed from the directory. Each file has at least one link, but other links can be created. To create a link to a file, you must have exccute permission for the directory in which you want to create a link. The syntax for the link command is as follows:

```
ln pathname\filename pathname\otherfilename
```

The `ln` command makes a file available from the directory in which you created the link. Once a file has been linked, it can be referenced without a path from that directory. If you wanted to link the file **chip** with the file **dale**, you would enter

```
ln chip dale
```

If the file originally named **chip** is the only file in the directory, entering `ls -l` would display

```
-rw-r--r--    2jfriday    lapd    23    May  5    12:35    chip
-rw-r--r--    2jfriday    lapd    23    May  5    12:35    dale
```

Removing a Link

Using the remove command, `rm`, to delete a file removes a single link. For instance, entering

```
rm dale
```

removes the link to the file **chip** created in the previous example. If a file has more than one link, you can remove one file name and still access the file from the other link. Oncc a file is down to a single link, however, the next time you use the `rm` command specifying that file, it is removed.

Command Summary

The following lists the commands covered in this chapter and their functions.

COMMAND	RESULT
..	Moves user to parent directory of working directory.
~	Changes working directory to user's home directory.
cat	Creates a file and displays a file's contents.
cd	Allows user to change directories.
chmod	Allows user to change permission modes of a file or directory.
cp	Copies contents of directories and files.
file	Lists file type of a given file.
ln	Creates links between files.
ls	Lists directories and files.
mkdir	Creates directories.
mv	Moves and renames files.
pwd	Prints the working directory on screen.
rm	Removes files and links to files.
rmdir	Removes directories.

Improving Your Command-Line Productivity

THIS chapter equips you with a variety of helpful commands, tips, and techniques to improve your command-line productivity. The commands in this chapter are the building blocks that enable you to control SunOS rather than having SunOS control you. A great deal of this chapter exploits the command-line features of the Korn shell. It includes additional information on repeating and editing commands, and explains pattern matching, stringing together commands using pipes, filtering information from files using a variety of filter commands, and redirecting output and input.

Getting the Most from the Command Line

Using the Korn shell, you can perform multiple commands in the same command line, and list and repeat commands from your command history list. The Korn shell also includes commands for modifying command-line entries to quickly fix commands incorrectly entered. These Korn shell features allow you to perform an assortment of operations with only a few keystrokes.

Performing Multiple Commands

To place more than one command on the command line, separate each command with a semicolon (;). When two or more commands are separated by a semicolon, they are treated as if they were sequentially entered on separate lines. For example, typing `cd; pwd; ls -la` and pressing Return brings you to your home directory, displays the directory name, and displays a long listing of all the files in that directory. You can continue a command line onto the next line by using the backslash (\\). For example, typing

```
cd; pwd; ls -la ; more file1\
```

and pressing Return displays

```
>
```

The greater than sign (>) indicates you can still continue to enter commands. When you press Return, the commands on both lines are executed.

Listing Command Line Entries

In Chapter 8 you learned how to use the `history` command to display a list of past commands. Adding `-l` to the `fc` command lists previously executed commands. For example, entering

```
fc -l -7
```

lists the last seven commands and their numbers, and entering

```
fc -l 10 15
```

lists commands 10 through 15 in the history command list. You can also list a previously executed command line by adding the name of the command after the `-l` option. To list the last `cat` command line and all subsequent commands up to the present command, enter

```
fc -l cat
```

Using the `fc` command with the `-ln` option, you can display the command list without the numbering that is displayed using the `-l` option. You can use an editor to edit a group of commands by using the `-e` option followed by vi and the beginning and ending lines of the history list that you want to edit. For example, entering `fc -e vi 10 15` displays the command lines 10 through 15 in the vi editor and also runs the commands when you exit vi. Working with the vi editor is explained in detail in Chapter 12, "Using the vi Editor."

Reexecuting and Changing Command-Line Entries

The r command allows you to edit and reexecute commands. You can reexecute a previously executed command line by adding the first letter of a command line after the r command. To reexecute the last `cat` command line, enter

```
r c
```

If you make a mistake in a command line, use the r command to replace the incorrect text and reexecute the command. This is also extremely beneficial for changing long command lines and replacing the entire command line. For example, if you entered

```
cp file1 fle2 file3 file4 /export/home/rpetrie/work; cd; ls -l f*
```

enter

```
r fle2=file2
```

to correct the spelling of the file `fle2` to `file2`. You can also replace text and reexecute a command in the command list. For example, entering

```
r report=letter m
```

reexecutes the last command that begins with the letter m and replaces the report to letter.

Matching Patterns

Several facilities are built into the shell to help you locate files using special characters called *metacharacters* or *wildcard* characters. Wildcard characters are analogous to the joker card in card games, where the joker can be any card. These characters can be used to indicate one character of a file name or parts of file names.

File Name Wildcards

The special characters used most often for pattern or wildcard searches are the question mark (**?**) and the asterisk (*****). The **?** represents any single character. Entering the command **ls letter?** lists all files beginning with the word **letter** and ending with one additional character, such as **letter1** and **letterA**.

The asterisk character (*****) matches any series of characters. Issuing the **ls** command followed by a single asterisk, **ls ***, lists every file in the working directory, except for hidden files. Entering the command **ls b*** lists every file beginning with the letter **b**, for example, **bard**, **beta**, **botany**, and **business**.

Character Class

Another way to search for files is to use the character-class option. A single character, or a *string* (a sequence of text characters) enclosed in brackets, is known as a *character class*. When you use brackets, you're instructing the Korn shell to match any character within the brackets. For example, **ls [Aabc]*** matches all file names beginning with an uppercase **A** or lowercase **a**, **b**, or **c**. You can also indicate a range of alphabetical characters by separating the beginning and ending range with a hyphen. For example, **ls [A-Z]*** matches all file names that begin with an uppercase alphabetical character, **ls [a-m]*** matches all file names that begin with lowercase alphabetical characters ranging from **a** through **m**, and **ls [1-9]** matches any numbers ranging from one to nine. You can match any character not enclosed in brackets by preceding the character with an exclamation point. For example **ls [!a-m]*** matches all file names that *do not* begin with lowercase alphabetical characters ranging from **a** through **m**.

Korn Shell Pattern-Matching Features

The Korn shell includes additional pattern-matching features. By using special metacharacters followed by patterns within parentheses, you can match a variety of different text and number patterns. The ***(*pattern*)** format matches any occurrences of the pattern within parentheses. Using the ***(*pattern*)** format you could find all files that begin with **s** by entering `ls *(s*)`. Multiple patterns can also be given, but they must be separated with a | character. For example entering

```
ls *(s*|t*)
```

displays all files beginning with the letter **s** and the letter **t**, such as `scratch`, `songs`, `temp`, and `totals`.

The `?(pattern)` format matches any occurrences of pattern. The following example matches and lists all file names that consist of only two or three letters:

```
ls ?(??|???)
```

The `+(pattern)` format matches one or more occurrences of the pattern within the parentheses. To list files containing `old` or `draft`, enter

```
ls *+(old|draft)*
```

The `!(pattern)` format matches anything except the pattern within the parentheses. To match any string that *does not* end with a `.c` or `.h` file name extension, enter

```
ls !(*.c|*.h)
```

Working with Filters

Filters are commands that accept text as input, transform it in some way, then produce text as output. For example, the `sort` command is a filter that sorts a file in alphanumeric order. Filters send their output to the screen by default, but the standard output can be redirected to files or system devices, as explained later in this chapter. Figure 10.1 shows a simple example of how a filter might process text.

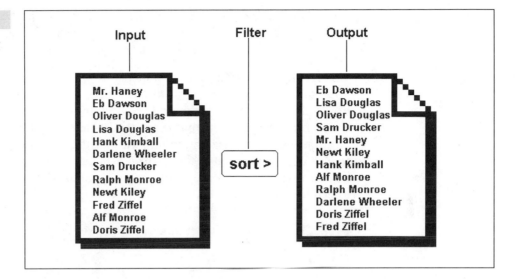

Filters for Displaying the Contents of a File

The `cat` command is an excellent vehicle for viewing the contents of a small file, but if the file is several pages long, it is easier to control how the text is displayed by using one of the many SunOS filter commands. Using a filter, you can display the contents of one or more files one screen of text at a time or display only the beginning or ending portion of a file. The following sections explain how to use filter commands to control the display of the contents of any text file.

Displaying a Long File One Screen at a Time

A convenient way to look at a long file is to use the `more` filter. The `more` filter simply transforms text into screen-sized blocks so the text of a file can be displayed one screen at a time. To use the `more` command, type `more filename(s)`, where `filename(s)` indicates the file or files you want to display. If you want to display multiple files, remember to separate each file name with a space. For example, `more doc1 doc2` displays the contents of `doc1`, followed by the contents of `doc2`, one screenful of text at a time.

To display the next screenful of text, press the spacebar. As you view a file using the `more` filter, the percentage of text that has been displayed is listed at the bottom of the screen in parentheses. To exit the `more` filter, type `q`.

Once you have started the `more` filter and the screen has stopped scrolling, you can display a specific number of lines at a time by typing in the number and pressing the spacebar or Return. For example, typing the number `5` and pressing the spacebar displays the next five lines of the file. You can change the display size by typing the number of lines you want the screen to show followed by `d` or Control-d. You can scroll back one page by pressing Control-b. If you are displaying a large file, backward scrolling can be excruciatingly slow.

Displaying the First or Last Lines of a File

If you want a quick look at the beginning or ending of a file, use the `head` or `tail` filters. The `head` filter displays the top 10 lines of a file by default. For example, `head jaeger` lists the first ten lines of the file named `jaeger`. Adding a minus sign followed by a number before the file name lists that number of lines from the top of the file. For example, `head -12 jaeger` lists the top twelve lines of the `jaeger` file.

The `tail` filter shows the tail end of a file. If you issue the `tail` filter without an option followed by the name of the file you want to view, `tail` lists the last ten lines of the file. You can change this display length by adding a hyphen and the number of lines you want displayed before the file name. For example, `tail -20 stocks` displays the last twenty lines of the file named `stocks`.

Finding Files by File Names

SunOS is a large file system. If you are working in several directories, it is easy to misplace a file, but you can discover where a file is located by using the `find` command. The `find` command searches for files that meet conditions you specify, starting at the top of the current or specified directory and automatically searching each subdirectory. A condition could be a file name matching a specific pattern, a file owned by a specific user or belonging to a specific group, or a file that has been modified within a specific time frame. The more specific your criteria, the narrower the field search becomes. The syntax for the `find` command is

    find *directory options*

The `find` options create a criterion for selecting a file. To see which files within your home directory and its subdirectories end in the letter **s**, type

    find ./ -name '*s' -print

The following explains each part of the preceding command-line entry.

`./`	Indicates that the search should begin at the top of the current directory. Remember the period is the symbol that specifies your working directory and the front slash begins the search at the highest directory.
`name *s`	Instructs `find` to find all file names ending with the letter **s**. If wildcards are used, as in this example, the file name character string and wildcard characters must be surrounded by single quotation marks.
`-print`	Indicates that you want the results to be displayed on your screen.

The following lists options that can be added to the `find` command to locate files.

OPTION	RESULT
`-exec` *command* `"{ } \;"`	Applies any command you specify to the files `find` calls up.
`-group` *groupname*	Finds files belonging to the specified group.
`-mtime` *n*	Selects files that have been modified in the last *n* days.

OPTION	RESULT
-name *filename*	Finds files that have names matching the character string you specify in single quotes.
-newer *filename*	Finds files that have been modified after the file specified.
-user *username* or *user ID number*	Selects files belonging to the user indicated.

You can reverse the meaning of an option by inserting a backslash (\) and an exclamation point before the option. The backslash is referred to as an *escape character*. It indicates that the special character or symbol following it has a different meaning than its normal meaning. In this instance, the exclamation point after the backslash indicates that SunOS should select files for which the option does *not* apply. For example, the command

```
find .\! -name 's*' -print
```

finds file names in the working directory and any subdirectories that *do not* begin with the letter **s**.

You can also use **find** to execute commands on the files it finds by adding the following option:

```
-exec command '{}' \;
```

For example, you can use **find** to locate and remove files that are named consistently. If the names of the files you want to remove begin with the string **junk** (such as **junk1**, **junk2**, and **junk3**), the following command line finds and removes them from the current directory:

```
find . -name 'junk*' -exec rm '{}' \;
```

Remember that a single period (.) refers to the working directory.

The quoted braces tell the command (`rm` in this case) to operate on the files the `find` selects.

Finding Files by Text in a File

The `grep` command is a powerful pattern-searching command that locates text in files. You can have `grep` search for an exact string of text, or you can use wildcards and brackets to broaden the search pattern. You must tell `grep` which files it should search. The most basic `grep` syntax is

```
grep string filename(s)
```

If `grep` only searches through one file, it will simply display any lines that contain the search string. If it searches more than one file, it will display the matching lines and also tell you the names of the files in which they occur.

Within a search string, a period (`.`) matches any single character in the same way the question mark (`?`) is used in file name substitution. For example, the command `grep .s namelists` preceded by a character (any character) in the file `namelist`. The equivalent of the asterisk wildcard is a period preceding an asterisk (`.*`). For example, the `grep 't.*' testfile` command locates every line in `testfile` containing the letter `t`. Note that the letter `t` and `*` wildcard character must be put in quotes.

A caret (`^`) instructs the pattern to match only the beginning of the line. The command `grep ^v` matches any line beginning with the letter `v`. A search string followed by a dollar sign (`$`) matches only those lines with that expression at the end of the line. For example, `grep s$ slist` displays all lines ending with the letter `s` in the file named `slist`. The command `grep ^v$` matches any line in which `v` is the only character.

Use double (`"`) or single (`'`) quotes to surround text that contains spaces. For example, if you use `grep` to search all files for the phrase **good work**, you would enter `grep 'good work'` and the name of the file to search. If you did not use the quotes, `grep` would only search for **good** and would consider **work** to be a file name.

Bracketed lists and ranges work just as they do for file name substitutions. For example, grep '[JE]' namelist, where the file namelist contains the names Jane, Judy, Elroy, and George, displays Jane, Judy, and Elroy but not George. Note that you must place quotation marks around the search string when you use brackets this way.

The characters &, !, $, ?, ., ;, and \ need to be preceded by a backslash when you want them to be treated as ordinary (literal) characters.

The following shows the characters that can be used to match or escape characters using the grep command.

CHARACTER	MATCHES
^	The beginning of a text line.
.	Any single character.
[ ]	Any character in the bracketed list or range.
[^]	Any character not in the list or range.
*	The preceding character or expression.
.*	Any characters.
\	Escapes special meaning of next character.
$	Any matching characters at the end of a line.

Using Options to Tailor grep's Output

There are several options that you can use to change the grep command's output to better fit your needs. The most useful of these are explained below. When you employ these options, use the following syntax:

```
grep option(s) string filename(s)
```

OPTION	RESULT
-v	Displays all lines that *do not* contain the search string.

OPTION	RESULT
-l	Causes `grep` to display only the names of any of the specified files that contain the search string. Does not display the lines that contain the search string.
-c	Causes `grep` to display the number of lines that contain the search string. If more than one file contains the string, displays the names of these files and the number of matching lines in each.

Spell-Checking a File

The `spell` command is a filter that checks an entire text file for words that do not match any of the words in the system dictionary. To check the spelling of a text file, type `spell`, followed by the name of the file you want to spell-check. If the spelling program hasn't been loaded into your system, SunOS displays the message `spell: command not found`. The `spell` command produces a list of words that don't match the entries in the SunOS online dictionary. For example, entering the command `spell brochure`, where `brochure` is a file than contains misspellings of the words `travel`, `oasis`, and `cruise`, displays the following results:

```
cruize
osais
travl
```

The `look` command lets you list words in SunOS's online dictionary that begin with the letters you enter. To use the `look` command, type `look` and the first few letters of a word for which you want to check the spelling.

Counting Words in a File

Another helpful filter for working with text files is the `wc` (word count) command. The `wc` command counts and displays the number of lines, words, and characters in a file. You can use these options with `wc`:

OPTION	RESULT
-l	Counts lines only.
-w	Counts words only.
-C	Counts characters only.
-c	Counts bytes only.

The following shows the results of using `wc` on a file named `jumbo`.

```
1625 2805 50545     jumbo
```

This indicates there are 1625 lines, 2805 words, and 50,545 characters in `jumbo`.

Comparing Text Files

Once you have copied a text file, you can use the `diff` command to ensure that the files are exactly the same. The `diff` command displays line-by-line differences between a pair of text files. You can check to make sure that a file has been copied using the `ls` command, but the `diff` command is helpful if you have two copies of a file and can't readily determine the differences between them. Entering the command

```
diff file1 file2
```

causes SunOS to display the differences between `file1` and `file2`. If no differences are found, the prompt is redisplayed without a message. Use the `diff3` command to display the differences between three files, such as `diff3 file1 file2 file3`. The following example shows the result of using `diff` on two files beginning with the same first line but with differences in the next three lines of text. The line containing numbers and an alphabetical character indicates the number of the lines and type of edits needed to make both files identical. If the letter **a** appears, it indicates that text needs to be appended. The letter **d** indicates text needs to be deleted. The letter **c** indicates text needs to be changed. In the following example, the first line indicates that lines 2 through 4 of **file1** need to be changed to match lines 2 through 4 of **file2**. The less-than signs (<) identify the differing lines in **file1**. The greater-than signs (>) identify the differing lines in **file2**.

```
diff file1 file2
2, 4c2,4
< line 2 in file1 contains the word incongruous
< line 3 in file1 contains the word disparate
< line 4 in file1 contains the word different
---
> line 2 in file2 contains the word analogous
> line 3 in file2 contains the word similar
> line 4 in file2 contains the word corresponding
```

Sorting a File

One of the most often used SunOS filters is the **sort** command. You can alphabetically sort the contents of a file in ascending order by issuing the **sort** command followed by the file name to be sorted. The **sort** command sorts lines in a file and displays the sorted list on your screen. To sort a file, you need to specify an output file using the –**o** (output) option. For example, to sort a list of customers in a file named **clients** and store the output in a file name **sclients**, enter

```
sort -o sclients clients
```

N O T E

Make sure the output file has a different name from the file you are processing. For example, if you are sorting a file called clients, do not send output to a file of the same name. This wipes out the original file before the information is sorted. Because the sorted clients information is directed into a file, it does not appear on the screen as it would if you simply typed sort clients. You can easily examine the clients file using the cat or more commands.

Selecting a Sort Field

The sort command begins numbering fields with the number zero. The second string of characters is considered field number one. The sort command allows you to sort by characters other than those at the beginning of a line. For example, say you have a file named clients in which you keep the following list of clients:

```
Buddy Sorrell
Melvin Cooley
Jerry Helper
Alan Brady
Sally Rogers
```

If you entered the command sort clients, the file would display on your screen sorted alphabetically by the first names of the clients. To sort the file by the last names, you have to specify which field to perform the sort on. *Fields* are character strings separated by spaces. The file clients contains two fields. The first field (field 0) comprises the first names and the second field (field 1) comprises the last names. The numbering scheme used with fields is illustrated in Figure 10.2.

NOTE Remember that the sort command begins numbering fields with the number zero. The second string of characters is considered field number one.

To specify where a sort begins, use this syntax:

```
sort +fieldnumber filename
```

The plus sign (+) followed by the field number indicates the field on which the sort begins. If you wanted to sort your list of clients by their last names, you would enter

```
sort +1 clients
```

where the number 1 specifies that the sort be performed on the field containing the last names. The output of this command, the sorted list, will then appear on the screen. Most likely you will want to save the sorted list

FIGURE 10.2

The numbering scheme of fields in sorts

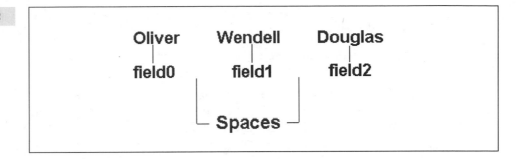

to another file, in which case you will have to enter a command such as this:

```
sort +1 -o clientsln clients
```

Here the output of sort, the sorted list of **clients**, is sent to a new file named **clientsln**.

In some instances, it is inconvenient to use spaces as field separators. For example, if your list of clients also included the name Dick Van Dyke and you tried to use the previous command to sort the list by last name, **sort** would only recognize Van and not include Dyke in the sort criteria. Of course, this would not affect the outcome of the sort on the current list, but if the file also contained the names Ella Vance, Jack Vance, and Jerry Van Heusen, it would cause problems. Fortunately, you can change the field separator to another character with the -t*c* option, where *c* is used to identify the new field separator. To add an option to the **sort** command, follow this general syntax:

```
sort option(s) +fieldnumber filename
```

If you inserted a symbol, say a colon, between the first and last names on your list and you specified the colon as the new field separator, you could sort by first or last names without worrying about spaces affecting the sort.

With the **sort** command you can sort on any range of characters you want as long as you specify where you want the sort to begin and end. This means you must indicate both the field number and character number to begin and end on. Use the following syntax to perform a sort on a specific range of characters:

```
sort option(s) +fieldnumber.characternumber
-fieldnumber.characternumber filename
```

Here the plus sign (+) indicates which field and character number to start the sort on and the minus sign (–) indicates which field and character number to end the sort on.

TIP   Remember, the first character in a field is numbered 0.

Let's say you added the amount of revenue of each client to the **clients** file. Your list might look like this:

```
Alan Brady:$1000.00
Buddy Sorrell:$4500.00
Jerry Helper:$250.00
Melvin Cooley:$500.00
Sally Rogers:$600.00
```

To produce a list of clients in order of lowest to highest revenue, enter

```
sort -o revenue -t: -n +1.1 -1.6 clients
```

Here the –t: indicates that the colon serves as the field separator, separating the list into two fields: names of clients and revenue. The –n (numeric) option allows you to sort in ascending numerical order. The +1.1 specifies that the sort begin with the second field (field 1) and second character of the field (character 1), or at the first number after the dollar sign. The –1.6 indicates that the sort ends with the sixth character (character 7) of the second field. The following output of the command is then sent to the file **revenues**:

```
Jerry Helper:$250.00
Melvin Cooley:$500.00
Sally Rogers:$600.00
Alan Brady:$1000.00
Buddy Sorrell:$4500.00
```

The following list reviews some of the options you can use with sort:

OPTION	RESULT
-f	Causes sort to ignore case when performing a sort. Otherwise the sort is performed according to ASCII number.
-n	Instructs sort to sort in numerical order.
-r	Produces a list sorted in reverse order (see next section).
-tc	Indicates the fields are separated by c. In the previous example the fields are separated by the colon (:) character.

Reverse Sorts

When you sort a file containing a field of numbers you may want to sort the file in descending numeric order to see the fields with the largest amounts first. Suppose you want to select the top three clients with the largest revenue from revenue. You can sort the file in reverse numeric order using the -r (reverse) and -n (numeric) options to produce a highest-to-lowest listing, then use the head command to select the top three entries. By using a pipe to combine the sort and head commands, you can get a list of the top three clients in the revenue file. Pipes are explained later in this chapter. Entering

```
sort -t: -r -n +1.1 -1.6 revenue|head -3
```

displays

```
Buddy Sorrell:$4500.00
Alan Brady:$1000.00
Sally Rogers:$600.00
```

Combining, Grouping, and Controlling Commands

The more you work with SunOS the more likely you will want to combine and control multiple commands. The Korn shell includes a variety of sequential control structures, so you can connect and control how commands are executed. For example, you may want to substitute part of a command line with the output of a command, feed the output of a command in directly as input to another command, or you may want to conditionally execute a group of commands. The following sections explain how to feed the output of one command into another, control the execution of a group of commands, and control whether or not a command is executed.

Command Substitution

The Korn shell lets you substitute the output from one command to form part of another command. This is known as *command substitution*. To substitute the output of one command, place the command within *back quotes*. The shell executes the command inside the back quotes and uses the output to form the input for the preceding command not included in back quotes. (Do not confuse the back quote with an apostrophe. A back quote (`) is usually on the same key as the tilde (~) next to the Return key. Also, do not confuse the back quote with the single quote mark found on the same key as the double quote mark.) Using command substitution, you can remove all files containing the word **paid** by entering

```
rm 'grep -l paid *'
```

The shell executes the **grep** command then performs the **rm** command using the list of file names generated by the **grep** command within the back quotes.

The Korn shell also lets you use a different format for command substitution: `$(command)`. Any commands can be used inside the parentheses, including pipes, redirection operators, and wildcards. Pipes are explained in the following section. To use the Korn shell's command substitution to inform you of the date, begin a new line, and inform you of the name of the working directory, enter

```
echo Today is $(date) '\n'Your working directory is $(pwd)
```

When you press Return, the screen appears similar to the following:

```
Today is Mon June 19 13:25:58 PDT 1992
Your working directory is /export/home/rpetrie
```

Combining Commands

One of the most useful features of the shell is the *pipe* (I). The pipe is used to feed the output from one command into another. The pipe (I) key is to the right of the F12 key on most Sun keyboards. A set of commands strung together is called a *pipeline*. Pipes have a wide variety of uses. You can string together multiple commands with pipes, as long as the command line does not exceed 256 characters.

Piping is a convenient alternative to a multiline command. Because a pipe passes output from one command to the input of another, instead of having to store data into temporary work files and perform several operations, you can join commands together so that output from one is used as input for another. For example, the command `ls -l |more` allows the user to view a long directory listing page by page. You can even connect groups of commands this way.

In addition to using pipes for file processing, you can pipe commands to simplify daily SunOS operations. For example, suppose you want a quick list of all the files you have changed today in your home directory. You can pipe the output of a long directory listing (`ls -l`) into **grep** and produce a list of files matching today's date. For example, if today is July 19, you can obtain a list of files using the following:

```
ls -l | grep 'Jul 19'
```

The listing produced might look something like this:

```
-rw-rw-rw-  1    rpetrie staff    1640 Jul   19   03:09   project
-rw-r-xr--  1    rpetrie staff    64   Jul   19   10:10   style
-rwxr-xrw-  1    rpetrie staff    256  Jul   19   12:07   clients
```

Grouping Commands

When you combine several commands on the same line, you can use parentheses to group them. Grouping commands starts up a new copy of the shell to execute the commands. Using parentheses to perform a group of commands, you can change directories and execute one or more commands, after which the shell returns to the original shell and directory. For example, to change to the directory named **docs**, make a subdirectory named **finished**, move and rename (**mv**) an existing file named **draft1** to a file named **report** in the **docs/finished** directory, enter

```
(cd docs; mkdir finished; mv draft1 finished/report)
```

The **cd** command applies only to the group of commands within the parentheses. If you enter the **pwd** command you will find that you are still in the same directory as you were before issuing the group of commands.

Controlling Command Execution

The Korn shell includes logical operators for controlling command execution. The double ampersand (**&&**) operator is sometimes called a logical AND operator. Separating two commands with the **&&** operator executes the command following the **&&** operator only if the previous command was successfully executed. For example, entering

```
grep 'Birth of Venus' artwork && echo The Birth of Venus was found
```

displays the message **The Birth of Venus was found** only if the **grep** command finds the text string **Birth of Venus** in the file named **artwork**.

Separating two commands with double vertical bars (**||**) is the opposite of using double ampersands; each command is executed only if the preceding command fails. The **||** operator is sometimes called a logical OR operator. For example, if you enter the command

```
grep 'Mona Lisa' artwork || grep 'Water Lilies' artwork
```

and `grep` fails to find `Mona Lisa` in the file named `artwork`, the Korn shell executes the second `grep` command, which looks for the text string `Water Lilies`.

NOTE Using the && and || to control command execution only works with two commands; you cannot add additional commands to the same command line using the semicolon (;).

Redirecting Output and Input

When you execute commands, the results are displayed on your screen. The screen is considered to be the *standard output*. A command normally gets information from the keyboard, which is referred to as *standard input*. You can control standard input and output and redefine where information is sent once a command has processed it. For example, you can store the output of commands into files for review or editing. You can send output from one command into another and further process the data, such as formatting text to be sent to a printer.

Redirecting Output to a File

The greater-than symbol (>), also known as "to," redirects output from commands into a specified file rather than to the screen. For example,

```
ls -a > myfiles
```

sends the output of the `ls -a` (list all) command to a file named **myfiles**. When you redirect output to a file, because the output is redirected to the target file, it isn't displayed on the screen. Specifying a target file automatically creates the target file with the name you specify (if a file with that name does not exist). Using the Korn shell, you can save a command line to a file. The following example saves the last five commands to a file named `viewme`:

```
fc -ln -5 > viewme
```

Anytime you want to view the saved command line, simply use the `cat` command to display the contents of `viewme`.

Protecting Existing Files from Redirection Output

If you use > to redirect output to a file that already exists, the contents of that file will be overwritten. For example, `cat file1 > newfile` redirects the contents of `file1` to `newfile`, overwriting the contents of `newfile` if that file already exists. You can prevent redirecting output to an existing file by setting the `noclobber` option as follows:

```
set -o noclobber
```

If you attempt to redirect output to an existing file, a message displays informing you that the file already exists. You can still overwrite an existing file even if noclobber is set by adding a pipe (|) after the >. For example, entering `ls -l >| fileout` overwrites `fileout` even if `noclobber` is set. To automatically protect files with the `noclobber` setting when you first log in, see Chapter 15, "Customizing Solaris."

WARNING When you use > to redirect output to a file that already exists, the contents of that file will be overwritten unless the `noclobber` option is set.

Adding Text to an Existing File

Two greater-than symbols in succession can be used to append text to the end of an existing file. This append feature is useful for keeping running logs or for accumulating information in a single file. The command

```
cat clients >> newclients
```

appends the file `clients` to a file named `newclients`.

Using Files as Input to Commands

Just as you can redirect the output of a command, you can also have a file or device provide input to a command. The less-than sign (<), referred to as "from," redirects the standard input of a command.

Input redirection is valuable for the few commands that don't use file name arguments. For example, the command

```
mail dobie < reply
```

mails the contents of the file `reply` to `dobie`. Another command that reads from a file instead of the terminal is the `tr` (translate) command. The following example sends the file `filei` to the `tr` command and translates all lowercase i's displayed on the screen to uppercase I's.

```
tr i I < filei
```

Redirecting the Standard Error

When a command performs without problems, it produces results as standard output to your screen. When a command encounters a problem, it uses a different channel to send error messages, or diagnostic output, to the screen. *File descriptors* identify open files to running commands. The Korn shell automatically assigns file descriptor 0 to standard input for reading, and file descriptor 1 to standard output for writing. File descriptor 2 identifies a standard error. By using file descriptor 2 before the redirection sign (2>), you can redirect the standard error output to a file for later review. For example,

```
cat testfile 2> errorfile
```

redirects the standard output and standard error to the file named `error-file`. If `testfile` doesn't exist, `errorfile` contains the error message:

```
cat: cannot open testfile
```

Command grouping lets you redirect the standard output to one file and the standard error output to another. For example, enter

```
(cat testfile > stdoutfile) 2> errorfile
```

The `cat` command output is redirected to the `stdoutfile` file and any error messages are sent to the file named `errorfile`.

You can also redirect error messages to the system wastebasket file. This file is located in the device directory and named `null` (`/dev/null`). Any output you redirect to this file disappears, so you can send output here when you don't want it displayed. The following lists and explains redirection commands with examples.

COMMAND	FUNCTION	EXAMPLE
>	Redirects the standard output.	`cat file1 > file2`
2>	Redirects the standard error.	`cat file1 2> errorfile`
>>	Appends the standard output to the file.	`cat file1 >> file2`
2>&1	Redirects the standard output to file1 and the standard error to file2.	`(cat file > file1) 2>file2`
<	Redirects the standard input.	`tr a A < filea`

Redirecting Combined Commands

When you want to redirect the output of a group of commands, enclose the group of commands in parentheses. An example of the output of grouped commands being sent to a file instead of the screen might appear as follows:

```
(ls -l | grep 'Jul 19') > todaysfile
```

You can combine any number of commands this way to consolidate output into a single file. Output from grouped commands can also be piped to other commands. For example, typing

```
(ls -l | grep 'Jul 19') | lp
```

prints the listing. Not all SunOS commands accept standard input, which means you can't pipe information into them. You can, however, pipe information into the `lp` (printing) command, because this command accepts standard input.

Directing Data to More Than One Place

Like pipes, the `tee` command is a term borrowed from the plumbing trade to describe a single pipe that splits into two directions. The `tee` command splits output into two or more separate destinations. As the `tee` stores data in a file, it also displays the output on the screen or channels it to another selected destination. This ability to split output is useful in many situations. For example, you can use it to send a sorted list to two files instead of one, or to view the list on the screen while simultaneously saving the data in a file. The command

```
sort clients|tee sclients
```

displays the sorted information on the screen as well as sending the sorted clients file to the file named sclients. Be aware that the `tee` command overwrites files. If you have a file named `userfile` and entered

```
who|tee userfile
```

the `tee` command displays a listing of who is using the system and overwrites the existing file named `userfile`. If the file does not exist, the `tee` command creates `userfile` and sends the output of the `who` command to the file.

WARNING   The `tee` command overwrites files without any warning.

If you use the `-a` option, `tee` appends the data into an existing file. For instance, the command

```
ls -l|tee -a userfile
```

displays a long directory listing and also adds this listing to the existing file `userfile`.

Useful SunOS Filters

The following lists useful SunOS filters, some of which were covered in earlier chapters. While they primarily use examples of filters processing files, keep in mind that filters can just as easily handle input from the keyboard or other commands.

COMMAND	PURPOSE OF FILTER	EXAMPLE
`cat`	Displays a file.	cat file1
	Creates a file from information typed at the keyboard.	`cat > newfile`
	Merges two or more files.	`cat file1 file2 > file3`
`echo`	Displays a message on the screen.	`echo 'Hi SunOS'`
`grep`	Searches a file or group of files for information you specify.	`grep 'Clients' file1`

COMMAND	PURPOSE OF FILTER	EXAMPLE
`head`	Displays the beginning lines of a file.	`head file1`
`more`	Displays one or more files, one screen at a time.	`more longfile`
`sort`	Sorts a file.	`sort clients`
	Sorts and merges multiple files.	`sort clients prospects > contacts`
`tail`	Displays the final lines of a file.	`tail prospects`
`tee`	Duplicates output to a file in addition to displaying output on the screen.	`sort comm |tee temp`
	Sends output to two files at once.	`cat file1 |tee register log`
`tr`	Translates one character or group into characters for another.	`tr a b < temp`
`wc`	Lists the number of lines, words, and characters in a file.	`wc temp`

Command Summary

The following lists the commands covered in this chapter and their functions.

COMMAND	RESULT
r	Repeats the last command.
r fle=file	Substitutes specified text and reexecutes last command.
r *n*	Repeats the command with the corresponding number in the history list.
r character(s)	Repeats the last command that matches the character string specified.
>	Redirects output.
>>	Appends text to the end of an existing file.
2>	Redirects standard error output.
<	Redirects input.
I	Takes command output and channels it into another command.
clear	Clears the screen.
diff	Compares and displays differences between files.
find	Locates files.
grep	Searches for specified patterns in text files.
head	Displays top lines of a file.
history	Lists commands previously used.

COMMAND	RESULT
`look`	Lists all the words from the system dictionary that begin with the characters the user specifies.
`more`	Displays text one screenful at a time.
`sort`	Sorts files.
`spell`	Checks a text file for words that do not match those in the system dictionary.
`tail`	Displays last lines of a file.
`tee`	Sends output to two destinations.
`tr`	Changes characters in a text file.
`wc`	Counts the number of lines, words, and characters in a file.

Electronic Mail and Messages

ONE OF SunOS's most useful features is its ability to send and receive electronic mail and messages. *Electronic mail* allows you to send and receive mail, including files, to and from other users, whether they're logged on or not. *Electronic messaging* allows you to interactively communicate with other users who are currently logged in. In this chapter, you'll learn how to receive, send, and manage your electronic mail using the `mailx` program. You'll also learn how to communicate with other users online using the `talk` and `write` commands, and how to view system news messages.

Overview of SunOS's Electronic Mail

Using SunOS's `mailx` program is similar to sending mail through the post office. When you send an electronic letter, the `mailx` program, like the post office, delivers your letter directly to the recipient's mailbox. The user login and machine name serve as the unique address of every user on the system. Each user on the system has a mailbox to receive electronic mail. This mailbox is usually a file with the same name as your login name, located in the `/var/mail` directory. Depending on how your system is set up, when someone on the system sends you mail, SunOS notifies you that you have mail in your mailbox. Once you've read your mail, the `mailx` program automatically stores these letters in a special storage file called `mbox`, which is located in your home directory. When you execute the `mailx` program, it displays its own unique prompt, the question mark symbol (**?**). After executing the `mailx` program, a working buffer is created in memory, where all tasks you perform within `mailx`, such as moving and deleting mail messages, are temporarily stored. These changes are stored to disk only when you quit the `mailx` program.

Receiving Mail

When you log in, your incoming mailbox, /var/mail/*username*, is checked for new mail. If there are any new letters, SunOS displays the message **you have mail** on your screen. If mail is sent to you while you're on the system, at the next SunOS prompt you are notified with the same message. SunOS checks your mailbox every few minutes to see if you have received mail. The time between these checks may vary, depending on how your system administrator has set up your account. You can choose to read your mail immediately after notification by SunOS or at a later time.

Listing Your Mail

To begin reading your mail, type `mailx` at the system prompt. If you don't have any mail, the `mailx` program displays the message, **No mail for** *username*. If you do have mail, the `mailx` program displays a list of mail headers from your /var/mail/*username* file followed by the `mailx` program prompt, as shown below.

```
mailx version 5.0 Mon Feb 15 00:20:20:58 PDT 1993  Type ? for
help.
"/var/mail/rpetrie": 3 messages 2 new 1 unread
 >N   1 plane   Mon Jan 25 16:51   20/619    Date tomorrow
  N   2 pmason  Wed Jan 20 15:55   19/610    Trial briefs
  U   3 bfife   Tue Dec 15 09:08   12/281    Lost my job
?
```

New letters are indicated by N, as shown in the first column above. The U (Unread) status indicates the letter was new but was not read before quitting the `mailx` program previously.

The > located to the far left of the first header in the list indicates the current letter. The current letter is either the first new letter in your mailbox or the last letter you read. The following list describes the information provided in each of the columns from left to right in the mail headers list:

COLUMN	DESCRIPTION
Mail letter status	Status of a letter in the mailbox.
Mail letter number	Number order in which the letter was received (you can use this number to specify a letter).
Sender	User name of the person who sent the letter.
Time sent	Date and time the letter was sent.
Size	Number of lines and number of characters in the letter (lines/characters).
Subject	Subject of the letter.

If you have numerous letters in your mailbox, the header list may not show all of your mail headers. Instead, it displays one screenful of mail headers at a time. You can display the next screenful of mail headers with the command

    z

To display the previous screenful of mail headers, enter

    h-

Anytime you want to redisplay the mail headers list, enter

    h

Reading Your Mail

After you've displayed the mail headers list, there are several ways to read the mail in your mailbox. The easiest way is simply to press Return. The current letter, indicated by the greater-than sign (>), is displayed. To continue reading your letters one by one, press Return again after each letter. When you've reached the end of the letters, `mailx` responds with the message `At EOF` (end of file), meaning `mailx` couldn't find any more mail letters in your mailbox.

NOTE Remember that if you enter q to quit mailx, the letters you have read are moved to your mbox file.

Another way to read your mail is to type the message number at the mailx prompt (?). Letter numbers are displayed in the second column of the mail headers list. For example, if you want to read mail letter number 2, type 2 at the mailx prompt. The mailx program then displays the mail letter number 2:

```
Message 2:
From pmason Wed Jan 13 15:55 1993
From pmason (Perry Mason)
Subject: Trial briefs

Just a reminder, we need those trial briefs this week.
```

TIP Another way to read a letter that is longer than a single screen is to save it as a file (explained later in this chapter), then use the more command.

If a letter is longer than the screen, it quickly scrolls down your screen. You can use Control-s to freeze the screen and Control-q to unfreeze it. You can check to see if a letter is longer than the screen by noting the number of lines in the size column of the mail headers list.

Replying to Mail

When you read your mail, mailx allows you to send a reply to the originator of any letter. Use the r (reply) command to quickly send a reply to the original sender of a letter. For example, to send a reply to the creator of mail message number 2, type r 2 at the mailx prompt. The mailx program responds with

```
To: pmason
Subject: Re: Trial briefs
```

The subject line of the reply will automatically hold the subject of the original letter, preceded by Re:. You can then type in your reply. When you complete your reply, press Return to place the cursor on a blank line, and press Control-d. Depending on how your system administrator has set up your mail account, the mailx program may then ask if you want to send any "carbon copies" by displaying a Cc: prompt. If you don't want to send duplicates of the reply to other users, simply press Return. The reply is sent to the author of the original letter. If you want to send a copy of the letter to another user, enter the user's name and address at the Cc: prompt, for example *username@machinename*.

Deleting Mail

After you've read or replied to mail letters, you may want to delete them rather than have them saved in your mbox file. You can delete the last letter you read by typing d at the mailx prompt. By typing h (header) you can verify that the letter was deleted. You can delete specific letters by typing d followed by the letter number. For example, typing d 3 deletes letter number 3. If you want to delete multiple letters, separate each letter number with a space; for example, if you wanted to delete letters 1 and 3, type d 1 3. You can also delete a range of letters. For example, to delete letters 2, 3, and 4, type d 2-4. Keep in mind that deleted mail files are permanently removed when you quit mailx with the q command. To cancel deletions, simply exit mailx using the x command.

Undoing a Mail Deletion

If you accidentally delete a message, you can restore the message using the u (undelete) command. To undo the last delete command, type u at the mailx program prompt immediately after the deletion. If you deleted multiple messages using the delete command, for instance, typing d4-7 to delete messages 4 through 7, you can undelete each message by typing u followed by the message number; for example, u6, u5, and so on.

Getting Help in the mailx Program

You can request help by entering a question mark (**?**) at the `mailx` prompt (**?**). Entering **?** displays a list of available mail program commands with descriptions, as shown below.

alias, group user	declare alias for user names
alternates user	declare alternate names for your login
cd, chdir [directory]	chdir to directory or home if none given
!command	shell escape
copy [msglist] file	save messages to file without marking as saved
delete [msglist]	delete messages
discard, ignore header	discard header field when printing message
dp, dt [msglist]	delete messages and type next message
echo string	print the string
edit [msglist]	edit messages
folder, file filename	change mailboxes to filename
folders	list files in directory of current folder
followup [message]	reply to message and save copy
Followup [msglist]	reply to messages and save copy
from [msglist]	give header lines of messages
header [message]	print page of active message headers

help,?	print this help message
hold, preserve [msglist]	hold messages in mailbox
inc	incorporate new messages into current session
list	list all commands (no explanations)
mail user	mail to specific user
Mail	mail to specific user, saving copy
mbox [msglist]	messages will go to mbox when quitting
next [message]	goto and type next message
pipe,| [msglist] shell-cmd	pipe the messages to the shell command
print, type [msglist]	print messages
Print, Type [msglist]	print messages with all headers
quit	quit, preserving unread messages
reply, respond [message]	reply to the author and recipients of the msg
Reply, Respond [msglist]	reply to authors of the messages
save [msglist] file	save (appending) messages to file
Save [msglist]	save messages to file named after author
set variable[=value]	set variable to value
size [msglist]	print size of messages
source file	read commands from file
top [msglist]	print top 5 lines of messages
touch [msglist]	force the messages to be saved when quitting

undelete [msglist]	restore deleted messages
undiscard, unignore header	add header field back to list printed
unread, new [msglist]	mark messages unread
version	print version
visual [msglist]	edit list with $VISUAL editor
write [msglist] file	write messages without headers
xit, exit	quit, preserving all messages
z [+/−]	display next [last] page of 10 headers

[msglist] is optional and specifies messages by number, author, subject, or type. The default is the current message.

Quitting the mailx Program

There are two commands for leaving the mailx program: the q (quit) command and the x (exit) command. The q command

- Moves the letters you have read from your mailbox (/var/mail/ *username*) and saves them in a file named mbox in your home directory.

- Saves any changes you've made to letters in your mailbox, such as deleting letters.

- Quits the mailx program, and returns you to the system prompt.

If you have any unread mail in your mailbox, mailx displays a message similar to the following

```
Saved 3 messages in /export/home/rpetrie/mbox
Held 2 messages in /var/mail/rpetrie
```

The x (exit) command leaves the mailx program but doesn't save any changes you made to mail in your mailbox, such as deleting a letter. It also doesn't move any letters you have already read into the mbox file.

The Mail Storage File

When you read a letter, it is marked to be moved to another file for storage. The default file name for this secondary mail file is mbox, and it is located in your home directory. Letters remain in the mbox file until you remove them. This mail storage file enables you to read your mail and store mail for reference at a later date, leaving your mailbox (/var/mail/ *username*) uncluttered.

Managing the Mail Storage File

When you want to access mail in your secondary mail storage file, mbox, use the mailx command with the -f option as follows:

```
mailx -f mbox
```

Your screen then displays a headers list similar to the headers list displayed when accessing your mailbox /var/mail/*username,* except the status of each message is replaced with the letter O. You can read, save, or delete letters using the same commands as you did when you used the mailx command without the -f option.

Holding Mail

To prevent letters from being automatically moved to your mbox file after reading them, you can use the hold command. The hold command instructs the mailx program to keep the letter(s) you have read in your /var/mail/*username* file after quitting mailx so that you can refer to the letter at a later time. Suppose you want to hold the last letter you've read; type hold at the mailx prompt. As with deleting letters, you can hold single or multiple letters, or a range of letters. For example, to hold letter number 3, type `hold 3` at the `mailx` prompt. If you wanted to hold multiple letters, such as letters 1 and 3, type `hold 1 3`. To hold a range of letters—for example, letters 2, 3, and 4—type `hold 2-4` at the `mailx` prompt. The hyphen (-) separates the beginning and end of the range of letters to be held.

Saving Letters as Files

You may want to save a letter as a file for editing or printing. To save the last letter you've read, including the header, into a file in your working directory, at the mail prompt (`?`) type

    s filename

Until you quit the `mailx` program, the letter `S` appears in the status column, indicating the message has been saved. In addition, you can save any letter by specifying its number from the mail headers list, as follows:

    s 4 filename

You can also save several letters in the same file at the same time. For example, to save letters 2, 4, 5, and 6 in a file, at the `mailx` prompt, type

    s 2 4-6 filename

You can also save a letter to a file using the `w` (write) command. This command is almost identical to the `s` (save) command, except it doesn't put the letter header into the file. Saved letters are marked in the mail headers list with the letter S. When you leave the `mailx` program using the `q` (quit) command, the marked letters are deleted from your mailbox (`/var/mail/username`) and saved in your `mbox` file.

Saving and Copying Letters in Folders

When you work with mail stored in files, you need to type the full path name in order to access the file. Saving and copying your mail to a mail folder, instead of separate files, saves time and keeps your mail files better organized. Folders are special files that are stored in a folder directory. Using a mail file automatically keeps your mail files together in the same directory, where they are easily accessible without typing long path names.

To use folders, you must first create a folder directory using the `mkdir` command. For example, if you wanted your folder directory to be called `messages`, you would create the directory messages as follows:

```
mkdir messages
```

You then need to use a text editor, such as vi, to edit the `.mailrc` file in your home directory (which contains `mailx` options) and set the folder directory path. Edit the "set folder" variable to include the full path name of your newly created folder directory. For example, you might enter

```
set folder=/export/home/rpetrie/messages
```

N O T E   For more information on setting `mailx` variables in the `.mailrc` file, see Chapter 15, "Customizing Solaris."

Saving Mail in Folders

You use the same commands to save or copy letters into folders as into files, except that the folder name is preceded by a plus sign (+) instead of a path name. The + tells `mailx` that the folder is to be kept in the folder directory. For example, to save message 3 to a folder called `memos`, at the `mailx` prompt type

```
s 3 +memos
```

`mailx` interprets this command as meaning save letter 3 into the `/messages/memos` directory. (If the folder doesn't already exist, `mailx` creates it.) To copy the letter into a folder, type

```
? c 3 +memos
```

If your mail account is set up to prompt you for carbon copies, you can send copies of your letters directly to a folder. To send a copy directly to a folder, simply type the folder name in either the `Cc:` or the `Bcc:` field. How to set up your mail account to prompt for carbon copies is explained later in this chapter.

Working with Mail in Folders

Working with mail in folders is similar to working with mail stored in files. To specify that the message is stored in a folder instead of a file, use the + sign. For example, if you want to read the letters stored in the **memos** folder, type

```
$ mailx -f +memos
```

This command starts **mailx** in the folder you specified. Only headers for the letters in the file or folder are displayed. Select a letter to read by typing its number at the **mailx** prompt and pressing Return. You can also work on mail folders within the **mailx** program. To display a list of your folders, at the **mailx** prompt, type

```
folders
```

To switch from your mailbox to a folder, or from one folder to another, type the command

```
folder +foldername
```

where *foldername* is the name of the folder you want to use. To return to the previous folder, type

```
#
```

An Overview of Sending Mail

You send mail with the **mailx** command by specifying the user name of the person or persons you want to receive a letter. You can use the **who**, **finger**, or **rusers** command to find a user's address if you don't know it. When you send mail to another user, it is stored in the recipient's electronic mailbox, and that person is notified that they have mail.

Who Is Using the System?

The who, finger, and rusers commands are useful if you need to know a user's login name but only know his or her real name. If the users you want to send mail to are logged into the same file server, you can address them using just their user names.

The who command lists the users logged into the system using the same file server at that moment. The list contains user names, identities of terminals being used, and the date and time each user logged in. Below is a listing produced by entering who.

```
wcleaver tty06  Jul 3 10:30
dreed    tty15  Jul 3 12:55
ataylor  tty19  Jul 3 12:56
```

The finger command provides more detailed user information than the who command. Depending on what your system administrator has directed this command to display, it may list a user's full name, user name, terminal number, idle time, home directory, and more. Idle time is the length of time in minutes since the last SunOS command was issued. When you enter the finger command, SunOS displays a listing of current system users, such as the following:

```
Login    Name           TTY   Idle  When
wcleaver Ward Cleaver    06    12    Fri 10:30
dstone   Donna Stone     15    0     Fri 12:55
ataylor  Andy Taylor     19    20    Fri 12:56
```

Listing Users on a Network

To find out who's logged in on other computers within your local network, use the rusers command. The rusers command by itself lists the machine name of each computer on the network, followed by the users currently on that computer. For example, entering rusers might display a listing similar to the one below. The left column lists the machine names.

```
mayfield      wcleaver
hilldale      dstone
mayberry      ataylor
```

N O T E If the person you want to send mail to is on a different computer on the same local network, you need to use both the user name and a machine name, separated by the at symbol (*username@machinename*).

If you know the relevant machine name but can't remember the specific user's name, enter `rusers` followed by the machine name to display user names for that specific computer. You can also add to `rusers` the `-1` (long) option, which lists the user name, machine name, terminal name, date and time the user logged on, idle time, and the name of the machine on which the user logged in. For example, entering `rusers -1 mayberry` might display

```
ataylor mayberry:console    Jul  3   11:00    12
bfife   mayberry:ttyp0      Jul  3   11:46    03 (sitcom)
```

Sending Mail

Once you've established the user name and the machine name (if needed) of the person you want to send mail to, you can use the following four simple steps to send them electronic mail.

N O T E SunOS has a special system database that includes a feature known as *alias mapping*. Alias mapping simplifies identifying users on a system. If your network supports this feature, you can send mail to users on other machines using just their user name.

1. If the person you want to send a letter to is using the same machine, at the system prompt type `mailx` *username*, then press

Return. If the person is on another machine, type `mailx` *username@machinename*. If you are already in the `mailx` program, you can simply type m followed by the user name of the person you want to send a letter to. To send the same letter to multiple users, separate each user name with a space. The `mailx` program then prompts you for the subject of the letter.

2. Type in the subject of your letter at the `Subject:` prompt, then press Return.

3. Type in the text of your letter. If at any point you want to create a new line, simply press Return. Remember, even though a sentence may wrap on your screen, it is not considered a line until you press Return. Each line of text can be up to 256 characters long. If you exceed 256 characters on your system, your screen may freeze up and you will have to abort the letter by pressing Control-c twice.

4. When you've finished entering your text, press Return to move the cursor to a new line, then press Control-d to end your letter. You can also type a period and press Return to end your letter. Either way, the message `EOT` (end of text) appears. Depending on how your system administrator has set up the `mailx` program, it may then display the `Cc:` (carbon copy) prompt. If this is the case, you can then enter the names of other users to whom you want to send copies of the letter. To specify more than one user, separate each user name with a space. When you are finished entering user names, or if you don't want to send any copies to other users, press Return to send your letter. As the `mailx` program delivers your mail, it displays several status lines similar to the following:

```
$ ataylor@mayberry...  Connecting to mayberry via ether...
Trying 129.144.65.110...  connected.
220 mayberry.Eng.Sun.COM Sendmail 5.0/SMI-SVR4 ready at Thu 26
Aug 93 17:02:31 PDT

>>> HELO bookware.Eng.Sun.COM
>>> MAIL From:<rpetrie@bookware>
250 mayberry.Eng.Sun.COM Hello bookware.Eng.Sun.COM, pleased to
meet you
250 <rpetrie@bookware>...Sender ok
RCPT To:<ataylor@mayberry>
>>>DATA
354 Enter mail, end with "." on a line by itself
>>> .
```

```
250 Mail accepted
>>> Quit
221 mayberry.Eng.Sun.COM delivering mail
ataylor@mayberry...  Sent
```

Aborting a Letter

If at any point you change your mind about sending a letter, press Control-c to abort the letter. The `mailx` program displays the message (`Interrupt -- one more time to kill letter`), asking you to press Control-c again to confirm aborting the letter. If you decide not to abort the letter, continue entering your text.

Undeliverable Mail

When you send a letter with an incorrect address through the postal service, it's either returned to you or ends up in a dead letter office. The SunOS mail system works much the same way. If you've created your letter and pressed Return, and have specified an incorrect user name, SunOS responds with the message *username*... `User unknown`, and the letter is returned to your mailbox (`/var/mail/username`). When you enter the `mailx` command again, the header states that you have returned mail, similar to the following example:

```
N 1 Mail Delivery Subs Wed Jul 3 12:55 19/61 Returned mail: User
unknown
```

When you view the returned letter, it will appear similar to the following returned mail message:

```
Message 1:
From dstone Fri Jul  3 12:53:21 PDT 1992
Date: Fri, 2 Jul 93 12:53:21 PST
From: Mailer-Daemon (Mail Delivery Subsystem)
Subject: Returned mail: User unknown
To: dstone

----- Transcript of session follows -----
550 wardcleaver... User unknown

----- Unsent message follows -----
Return-Path: <dstone>
Received: by hilldale (5.0/SMI-SVR4)
 id AA00305; Fri, 2 Jul 93 12:53:21 PDT
```

```
Date: Fri, 2 Jul 93 12:53:21 PDT
From: dstone (Donna Stone)
Message-Id: <9002060053.AA00305@hilldale.>
Errors-To: dstone
To: wardcleaver
Subject: hot water
Content-Length: 4

Meet me at the water fountain at 4:45.
```

The `mailx` program also sends this information without the letter's text to a person who is designated as the *postmaster* on your system. This person is usually the same as your system administrator. When a letter is interrupted by pressing Control-c or cannot be delivered as in the previous example, the file is also sent to a file named `dead.letter` in your home directory.

Sending Files Using mailx

If you have a file with information that you want to accompany a letter, such as a letter requesting payment and a file containing a list of outstanding invoices, you can mail the contents of a file as though it were a letter using the following command syntax:

```
mailx username < filename
```

The *username* is the name of the user you want to send the file to, and *filename* is the name of the file you want to send. For example, `mailx pmason < invoice` redirects the contents of the file named `invoice` to `pmason`'s mailbox.

When you send a file using the redirection symbol (<), `mailx` doesn't prompt you for a subject. If you want to add a subject line to the file, use the -s option followed by the text you want added as the subject. If the subject contains spaces, surround your subject text with quotation marks. The following is an example of adding a subject to a redirected file:

```
mailx -s "Outstanding 1993 invoices" pmason < invoice
```

Adding Carbon Copies

You can specify that a carbon copy of a letter is sent to other users. The `mailx` program even lets you send blind carbon copies so the recipient of your letter doesn't know that you sent a carbon copy to another user. In most cases, the system administrator sets up mail accounts by inserting the line

```
set askcc
```

in a hidden `mailx` configuration file named `.mailrc`. If this line doesn't exist, you can add it to the `.mailrc` file using any text editor. Once this line is added to your `.mailrc` file, the `mailx` program will prompt you with the carbon copy `Cc:` prompt to enter any users you want to send a carbon copy to after `mailx` displays the subject prompt. If you want to send multiple carbon copies, separate each address with a space. Another way to send carbon copies is to use the ~c and ~h tilde escape commands, which are explained in the following section.

Using Tilde Escape Commands

During the composition of a letter, that is, while you're entering the text of a letter, you can use tilde escape commands to perform a variety of functions. A *tilde escape* command usually consists of the tilde character (~) followed by a single character and possibly an argument. If you want to add a literal tilde to your letter, type two tildes in succession; only one tilde appears in your letter. The following lists some helpful tilde escape commands:

COMMAND	RESULT
~! *command*	Escapes to perform a SunOS command.

COMMAND	RESULT
~?	Displays a helpful list of tilde escape commands and brief explanations.
~.	Simulates Control-d or a period on a separate line to mark the end of the file (EOF).
~:*mailcommand*	In the mailx program, performs the indicated mail command.
~b *username(s)*	Adds user name(s) to a blind carbon copy (Bcc) list. This is similar to the carbon copy (Cc) list, but the names in the Bcc list aren't shown in the header of the letter.
~c *username(s)*	Adds user name(s) to the carbon copy (Cc) list.
~d	Reads the contents of dead.letter file in your home directory into the letter.
~f *messagenumber*	Inserts message indicated by *messagenumber*.
~h	Displays, one at a time, the header lines Subject, To, Cc, and Bcc. You can delete any header text by using the Back Space key; then enter any new text.
~m *messagenumber*	Inserts the text from the specified letters into the current letter.
~p	Prints the current letter to the screen.
~q	The equivalent of pressing Control-c twice. If the body of the letter is not empty, the partial letter is saved in the dead.letter file.

COMMAND	RESULT
~r *filename*	Reads text from *filename* into your letter.
~s *subject*	Changes the contents of the subject line to *subject*.
~t *name(s)*	Adds the specified **name(s)** to the To: list.
~v *filename*	Writes the letter text into *filename* without adding the header information.
~w *filename*	Writes the letter text into *filename* without adding the header information.
~x	Exits similar to ~q but doesn't save the letter in the **dead.letter** file.

Using Electronic Messages

There are three kinds of electronic messages: interactive, broadcast, and system. Interactive messages let you communicate with another person who is currently using a terminal on your machine or using another machine on your local network in a way that is similar to talking on a telephone. Broadcast messages are for important announcements for all current users of a system, such as an announcement that the system will be down for maintenance. System messages are the only messages that will be displayed for users who log on after the message was generated.

Talking with Other Users

The **talk** command is an interactive way of sending messages. You can use **talk** to communicate with other users who are currently on the system.

To find out who is currently on the system, issue the **who** command. To talk to another user, enter

    talk *username*

where *username* is the person on the system you want to talk to. If a user is on another computer in a network, enter the command **talk** *username* **@***machinename* where *machinename* is the name for the computer they're using. After entering this command, **talk**'s interactive screen appears and displays the message **No connection yet** until **talk** connects with the other user's machine. If you incorrectly enter the user name, or the other person isn't on the network, **talk** displays the message: **[Your party is not logged on]**.

If the person you want to talk to is logged on, **talk** connects your computer or terminal with the other user's computer or terminal, displays a line across the middle of your screen, and notifies you that it is still contacting the other user with the message **[Waiting for your party to respond]**. While this message is displayed on your screen, the other user's screen displays a message similar to the following:

    Message from Talk_Daemon@bradybunch at 01:11 ...
    talk: connection requested by wcleaver@mayfield
    talk respond with: talk wcleaver@mayfield

While the user is being notified that you want to talk, another message informs you that it is "ringing" the other user as follows:

    [Ringing your party again]
    [Ringing your party again]

The other person confirms that they want to be connected by typing in the user name and machine name, as displayed in the last line of the **talk** notification message.

    talk wcleaver@mayfield

If the other user is busy or simply doesn't respond, then you can type Control-c to exit **talk**. If the other user responds, you will see the message **[Connection established]**.

Now both users can type messages on the screen at the same time. The messages you send appear on the upper half of the screen. The other user's messages appear in the lower half of the split screen as shown below.

```
[Connection established]


Ward, how ya doin?
Eddie Haskell and Wally invited my kids to a party at your house
last week and they had a great time.
```

```
That's interesting, Mike, because June and I were in Mexico last
week.
```

The message you type appears on the other user's screen as you type it. You can correct any misspellings on a single line, but once you press Return, the line is sent. (Remember, even though a sentence may wrap on your screen, it is not considered a line until you press Return.) When either party wants to finish talking on the network, they can press Control-c to abort the `talk` program.

Writing Messages

The `write` command limits you to writing messages to only those users using terminals connected to the same computer as you. The `write` command doesn't use the entire screen like the `talk` command. To use the `write` command to send a message to another user, type `write` followed by the user name of the person you want to send the message to. The `write` command then displays the cursor on the next line without the prompt so that you can enter your message text. After typing the message text and pressing Return, the message is sent to the other user. The other person receives notification of the message directly below the command line, similar to the following:

```
Message from plane@brooklyn on ttyp3 at 11:58
When did you want that financial report?
```

If the other person wants to write you back, he or she can type `write`, followed by your (the receiver's) user name, press Return, and begin his or her reply message. The two users can then continue to send messages back and forth without reentering the `write` command. To stop conversing using the `write` command, type Control-d to end the session. When either user presses Control-d, the letters `EOT` (end of text) appear, indicating the end of the conversation. The other user must also press Control-d to get the system prompt back.

Broadcasting Messages

The `wall` (write to all) command allows you to broadcast messages to every user on your system. These messages should be reserved for important messages only, such as when the system is going to be down for maintenance. To broadcast a message to everyone, type `wall` then press Return. You can then enter the message you want to broadcast. Press Control-d and your message is sent immediately to everyone who is currently logged in.

WARNING Refrain from using `wall` unless your message is so important that everyone on the system should see it.

System Messages

Messages sent to you automatically (and possibly generated) by the SunOS system itself, such as error messages or a message informing you that you have mail, are known as *system messages*. If you are not logged on when such a message is sent, it will still appear when you do log on. The system administrator can also create system messages. The most common message of this type is the *message of the day*. This is an important or general interest message sent to all users of a system when they log in.

Another way that the system administrator can post announcements to you is by informing you that you should run the **news** command when you first log in. For example, after logging in, a message similar to the following may appear:

```
Type "news" TO READ news: framemaker
```

Enter the **news** command to display the title of the current news item and its time and date. Only the news items that you have not viewed before are displayed. To read a news message you have already viewed, add the `-a (all)` option. By using the `-n (name)` option, you can display the names of the current news items. For example, entering

```
news -n,
```

displays a line similar to the following:

```
news: framemaker party sunsoft downtime
```

To display news about when the system will be down for maintenance, enter

```
news downtime
```

If you just want to know how many current news messages exist, use the -s (sum) option. This displays any current news items that exist, without displaying their names or contents.

Command Summary

The following lists the commands covered in this chapter and their functions.

COMMAND	RESULT
?	Displays a list of available mail commands (at the mail prompt).
d	Deletes letters (at the mail prompt).
h	Displays mail headers list once in the mail program (at the mail prompt).
hold	Holds letters in the user's mail file (at the mail prompt).
mailx	Takes user into the mailx program and displays mail headers from the user's mail file.

COMMAND	RESULT
news	Displays news messages, such as announcing new programs available to the network and when the system will be down for maintenance.
q	Moves read letters to mbox, saves changes to letters, then exits the mailx program (at the mail prompt).
r	Mails a reply to sender of a letter (at the mail prompt).
rusers	Lists the machine name of each computer on the network.
s	Saves letters as files (at the mail prompt).
talk	Allows user to communicate interactively with another user.
u	Restores deleted letters (at the mail prompt).
wall	Allows user to broadcast messages to every user on your system.
write	Sends a message to another user without using the entire screen.
x	Exits the mailx program without saving changes (at the mail prompt).

CHAPTER

12

Using the vi Editor

THE vi editor (pronounced vee-eye) is a powerful, all-purpose file editor that edits everything from simple text files to complex program files. This editor provides an extensive collection of commands, many with overlapping functions, that can easily overwhelm new users. The purpose of this chapter is to provide you with a firm grasp of essential vi commands for editing and file management.

About vi

The vi (visual editor) program is a screen editor designed to display a text file one screen at a time. Early versions of UNIX forced users to work with line editors that only displayed one line at a time. While vi provides features for creating text documents, vi does not process text with the same ease associated with most commercial word processing software packages. For instance, vi cannot produce formatted printouts by itself. Instead, vi depends on the `nroff` and `troff` programs to format documents created or modified with vi before printing them. The `nroff` and `troff` programs are covered in Chapter 13. However, you can print files created or modified in vi using the SunOS `lp` command, which prints the text just as you see it on the screen.

Starting vi

To create or modify a file using vi, type vi *filename* at the system prompt, then press Return. For example, entering

```
vi evidence
```

executes vi and creates the new file, **evidence**. The following shows the last lines of the vi screen displayed with this file. The tilde (~) indicates empty lines.

```
    ~
    ~
    ~
    ~
    ~
    ~
    ~
    ~
    ~
    "evidence" [New file]
```

If you want to execute vi with an existing file, such as a file named **testimony**, enter

```
vi testimony
```

The resulting screen display might look something like the example below:

```
OK. I admit it.
I hid the gun.
I did not want my niece to go to the chair.
    ~
    ~
    ~
    ~
    ~
    ~
    ~
    "testimony" 3 lines, 67 characters
```

You can start vi without specifying a file name by simply entering vi. Later you can give your new file a name when you exit vi. A file name can be up to 256 characters in length and can include any characters except special characters (such as - * ? < > /).

The Status Line

The line at the bottom of the screen is called the *status line*. The status line shows the file name and the number of lines and characters in the file, as shown in the previous example. If you start vi to create a new file without a file name, no status line is displayed. Once you fill the screen with text, or move the cursor to the end of the file, the status line disappears. You can bring up the status line by pressing Control-g, which displays a new status line such as this:

```
"testimony" [Modified] line 2 of 3 --66%--
```

Command and Insert Modes

There are two modes of operation in vi, the command mode and the insert mode. The *command mode* allows you to enter commands for performing a wide range of vi functions, such as cursor movement and editing operations. The *insert mode* allows you to enter text into a file and is activated within vi by typing **i** while in the command mode. The vi program doesn't indicate which mode you're in, but pressing Esc always places you in the command mode.

The Command Mode

You start vi in the command mode. Most vi commands consist of one or two letters and an optional number, with uppercase and lowercase versions that usually perform related but different functions. For example, typing **x** deletes the character at the cursor, while typing **X** deletes the character preceding the cursor. You don't need to press Return after entering most vi commands. However, commands preceded by a colon do require you to press Return after the command. For example, to use the command :q! to quit vi and abandon changes, you must press Return after typing the exclamation point.

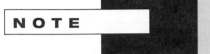

You don't need to press Return to enter a vi command unless it is preceded by a colon.

Undoing a Command

If you enter an incorrect vi command, you can undo it by typing u immediately after entering the command. (The insert mode command is an exception; if you mistakenly enter this command, press Esc to return to the command mode.) For example, if you've mistakenly deleted a line, immediately type u, and your deleted line is restored. You can also undo your last undo command. Typing U undoes all edits on a single line, as long as the cursor remains on that line. Once you move off a line, you can't use the U command for that line. The u command can be used to undo the U command.

Repeating the Previous Command

Any time you repeat the same editing command, you can save time duplicating the command by typing the repeat command (.) while in command mode. To repeat a command, position the cursor where you want to repeat the command and type a period (.). Keep in mind that you can only repeat the last command you executed, and that this command doesn't work with cursor movement or scrolling commands.

The Insert Mode

You leave the command mode and enter the insert mode by typing i (insert) while in the command mode. Typing i allows you to begin entering text at the cursor location. Characters you type subsequently appear to the left of the cursor and push any existing characters to the right. Remember, if you try to type a command while you're in the insert mode, the command characters are inserted as text. Press Esc any time you want to exit the insert mode and enter another command. The vi editor offers several other insert command options discussed later in this chapter.

Exiting vi

When you're creating or editing a file, you're actually working on a copy of the file that is stored in a *work buffer*, an area temporarily set aside in memory. Any changes you make to a file using vi only affect the file in the buffer until you instruct vi to save your file to disk. In other words, your edits don't affect your original file until you save your work. You can exit vi and abandon any changes you've made simply by not saving the contents of the work buffer. To quit vi, you must be in the command mode.

Exiting vi and Saving Changes

To save your changes to a file and quit vi, press Shift-ZZ while in command mode or type :x, then press Return to save your file and exit vi. Entering the command :w writes (saves) the buffer contents to the disk but doesn't exit vi.

WARNING   Use :w frequently during a work session to prevent losing your work in the event of a system crash or failure.

If you started vi without a file name, type :w, followed by a new file name to save your work to file. If you attempt to exit and save a new file you haven't named, vi responds with the message `No current filename`. You can also quit vi and save both an old version of a file and a new version of a file with your new edits. For example, if you made changes to a file originally named `evidence`, you can save your edits to a different file called `evidence.new` by typing the command

```
:w evidence.new
```

then pressing Return. Your old version of the file, `evidence`, remains unchanged, and the new file, `evidence.new`, contains your changes.

If you don't have a write permission for the file you've edited, when you use the Shift-ZZ command to exit vi and save the file, SunOS displays the message, `filename File is read only`. Enter `:w` with a different file name to save your file changes to disk. If you don't have write permission in the working directory, vi may still not be able to write your file to disk. Enter the `:w` command again, this time using a path name and a new file name in your home directory in place of the existing file name. For example, type

```
:w /usr/evidence/temp
```

Exiting vi and Abandoning Changes

You can quit vi without saving your changes by typing `:q!` then pressing Return. Entering `:q` and pressing Return quits vi if you haven't made any edits to the file; otherwise, vi prompts you with the message

```
No write since last change (:quit! overrides)
```

In this case, you can use the appropriate command to save your changes or abandon them. Type `:x` to exit vi and save changes or `:q!` to exit without saving your changes.

Recovering Text after a System Crash

If the system crashes while you're editing a file with vi, you can recover text that was not saved to disk before the crash. After the system is restored and you have a system prompt, type

```
vi -r filename
```

where *filename* is the name of the file you were working on when the system crashed. The displayed file reflects the changes you made, but did not save, before the system crash. Use the :w (write) command immediately to save the salvaged copy of the work buffer to disk. You can then continue to edit the file.

Units of Text in vi

As you will see, many vi commands affect specific units of text, such as characters, words, lines, sentences, and paragraphs. To improve your productivity using vi commands, it's helpful to understand how vi defines these units of text. The following explains vi's defined units of text.

UNIT	DESCRIPTION
Character	Whatever is stored in a single byte. The letter **a** is a character, a space is a character, and a tab is also considered a character.
Word	A string of one or more characters separated on each side by a punctuation mark, space, tab, digit, or newline character (Return). A word can also be defined to include adjacent punctuation marks. These punctuated words are separated by the space, tab, or newline (Return) characters only.
Line	A string of characters separated by a newline character (Return). A line can be more than the width of a line of text displayed across your screen.

UNIT	DESCRIPTION
Sentence	A string of characters that ends at a period, exclamation point, or question mark, followed by two spaces or a newline (Return) character. If only one space follows the period, exclamation point, or question mark, vi doesn't recognize it as the end of a sentence.
Paragraph	A group of one or more lines of characters preceded and followed by a blank line. Two newline (Return) characters in a row create a blank line in the text, which vi considers as the division between two paragraphs. A paragraph can be a single line or up to 45 lines.

Cursor Movement

There are vi commands to move the cursor up, down, left, or right; forward or backward by units of text, such as characters, words, sentences, or paragraphs; and through an entire file. However, you can't move the cursor below a tilde (~), which indicates a line without text or hidden control characters, such as for spaces, tabs, or returns. Keep in mind that all movement commands are executed in command mode.

With most cursor movement commands you can specify the number of times you want the cursor movement repeated. You can't use a repeat factor on any control commands, such as Control-d, which scrolls the screen down, or on any commands that position the cursor at a specific point on the screen. The following lists vi editor movement commands.

COMMAND KEY	CURSOR MOVEMENT
spacebar	Right (forward) one character position.
l	Right (forward) one character.
h	Left (backward) one character.
+	First character of next line.
–	First character of previous line.
↓	Same position in line below.
↑	Same position in line above.
j	Down to same position in line below; moves left to last position if line below is shorter.
k	Up to same position in line above; moves left to last position if line above is shorter.
w	Forward to first letter of next word or punctuation mark.
W	Forward to first letter of next word.
b	Backward to first letter of previous word or punctuation mark.
B	Backward to first letter of previous word.
$	End of current line.
0	Beginning of current line.
Return	Forward to beginning of next line.
(	Back to beginning of current sentence.
)	Ahead to beginning of next sentence.
{	Back to beginning of current paragraph.
}	Ahead to beginning of next paragraph.
H	Left end of top line on screen.
M	Left end of middle line on screen.
L	Left end of lowest line on screen.

COMMAND KEY	CURSOR MOVEMENT
G	Last line in work buffer.
*n*G	Move to line number *n*.
Control-d	Down half screen.
Control-u	Up half screen.
Control-f	Down almost a full screen.
Control-b	Up almost a full screen.
Control-e	Scroll down one line at a time.
Control-y	Scroll up one line at a time.
\<Return>	Scroll up or down a screen while leaving cursor on same line.

Moving by Characters and Words

The arrow keys provide the easiest method for moving the cursor through a file one character at a time. You can also use the keys h, j, k, and l as follows:

h	left
j	down
k	up
l	right

Adding a repeat factor multiplies the movement factor accordingly. For example, typing **7** before pressing the right arrow key moves the cursor seven characters to the right.

Typing the **w** command moves the cursor forward one word at a time, treating symbols and punctuation marks as words. Typing the **W** command moves the cursor forward one word at a time, ignoring symbols and punctuation. To move backward one word at a time, type the command **b**. This command also treats symbols and punctuation marks as words. Typing **B** moves the cursor backward one word at a time, ignoring symbols and punctuation marks. You can multiply the movement effects of the w, W, b, or B commands by entering a repeat factor before the command. For example, typing 3w moves the cursor forward three words; typing 6B moves the cursor back six words, ignoring punctuation marks.

Moving by Lines, Sentences, and Paragraphs

Typing + while in command mode moves the cursor to the next line's first character; typing − moves the cursor to the first character of the previous line. You can also use the up or down arrow keys to move through lines and add repeat factors to multiply their effect.

Typing $ moves the cursor to the end of the current line. To move the cursor to the beginning of the current line, type 0.

NOTE   Remember, in vi a line isn't necessarily the same length as the visible line (usually 80 characters) that appears on the screen.

You can move to the beginning of the current sentence by typing an open parenthesis ((). Typing a close parenthesis ()) moves the cursor to the beginning of the next sentence. You can move back to the beginning of the current paragraph by typing an open curly bracket ({), or ahead to the beginning of the next paragraph with a closed curly bracket (}). You can use repeat factors with any of these commands. If there is a sequence of blank lines, the cursor moves to the beginning of the first blank line.

Moving within a Screen Display

You can move the cursor to certain positions on the screen. Typing H moves the cursor to the home position in the upper-left corner of the screen. Typing M moves the cursor to the beginning of the middle line of the screen. Typing L moves the cursor to the beginning of the last line on the screen. You can't add a repeat factor to any of these commands.

Scrolling through a File

Several useful commands for scrolling through a file are provided by vi. Pressing Control-u scrolls up half a screen at a time. Pressing Control-d scrolls down half a screen at a time. To move up or down one screen at a time, press Control-f to see the next screen, and press Control-b to see the previous screen. To scroll down one line at a time, press Control-e. To scroll up one line at a time, press Control-y.

If you want to scroll the screen up or down, but you want the cursor to remain where it is on the current line, use the z command. Pressing z, then Return, moves the current line to the top of the screen. Typing z. moves the current line to the center of the screen. Typing z- moves the current line to the bottom of the screen.

Line Numbering and Line Movement

In vi, each line in a file is assigned a sequential line number. Line numbers, by default, are not displayed. They can be displayed on the screen by entering the command

```
:set nu
```

Line numbers are displayed in vi as shown in the example below:

```
1   OK. I admit it.
2   I hid the gun.
3   I did not want my niece to go to the chair.
~
~
~
~
~
~
~
"testimony" 3 lines, 67 characters
```

Only lines that include text are assigned numbers. Blank lines, those starting with the tilde character (~), are not numbered. These line numbers appear on the screen for convenience only and do not become part of your file. You can also display the current line number in the status line by pressing Control-g, which displays the current line number, the total number of lines in the file, and the percentage of the total lines of the file above the current line position.

Using the **G** (Goto) command, you can move directly to any line containing text. For example, typing **44G** moves the cursor to the beginning of line forty-four. Typing **G** without a line number moves the cursor to the last line of the file. Entering : *n*, where *n* is the specified line number, also moves the cursor to that line number in your file.

Editing Commands

There are four basic editing functions performed in vi.

- Inserting text in insert mode.
- Deleting text.
- Changing and replacing text.
- Cutting (or copying) and pasting text from one place to another in your file.

Most vi editing commands can also be combined with movement commands and repeat factors to further improve your productivity.

T I P

Remember, you can save time duplicating an edit command by using the repeat command. Simply position the cursor where you want to repeat the command and type a period.

Cleaning Up the Screen

Once you start making extensive changes to your file, the screen can get cluttered with leftover command symbols before vi redraws your screen. *Redrawing* a screen means updating the screen to reflect your changes and removing command symbols that have been executed. The vi editor doesn't automatically redraw your screen when you make changes, but instead redraws your screen periodically. You can redraw your vi screen at any time by pressing

```
Control-l
```

Inserting and Appending Text

In vi, there are several commands to insert text into your file. All of these commands are executed from insert mode. To enter the insert mode, first position the cursor at the location you want to insert text, then type **i** while in the command mode. You are now ready to begin entering text at the cursor location. The characters you type appear to the left or before the cursor position and push any following characters to the right. You can press Return to create a new line at any point while you are entering text.

Another way to enter the insert mode is by typing **a** for the append command. Characters you type after using the **a** (append) command are inserted to the right of the cursor. While in the command mode, you can insert a new line in your text by typing the **o** (open) command, which opens a new line below the cursor and automatically puts you in the insert mode. Typing **0** opens a new line above the cursor for text.

To leave the insert mode and return to the command mode, press Esc. The following lists vi insert mode commands.

COMMAND KEY	ACTION
i	Before cursor.
I	Before first nonblank character on line.
a	After cursor.
A	At end of line.
o	Opens a line next line down.
O	Opens a line next line up.
Esc	Quits insert mode.

Deleting Text

The vi editor provides a complete set of delete commands. Delete commands are performed in the command mode. After executing a delete command, vi remains in the command mode. Keep in mind that the u (undo) command, as explained earlier, is particularly useful in undoing deletion commands. The following lists and explains vi editor delete commands.

COMMAND KEY	DELETION
x	Character at cursor.
X	Character before cursor.
dw	To end of word.
dW	To end of word, including punctuation.
db	To beginning of word.
dB	To beginning of word, including punctuation.
d Return	Two lines, current and following.
dd	Entire line cursor is on.
d0	From cursor to the beginning of line.
d$	From cursor to the end of line.

COMMAND KEY	DELETION
d)	To end of sentence.
d (	To beginning of sentence.
d }	To end of paragraph.
d {	To beginning of paragraph.
dL	To last line on screen.
dH	To first line on screen.
dG	To end of the file.
d1G	To beginning of the file.

Deleting Characters and Words

Use the x command while in the command mode to delete a single character. Typing x deletes only the character the cursor is positioned on, unless you use a repeat factor. Typing X deletes the character before the cursor. You can delete multiple characters by typing the number of characters you want to delete before the command. For example, typing 10x deletes ten characters forward, starting with the character *at* the cursor; typing the command 8X deletes eight characters backward, starting with the first character *following* the cursor.

To delete units other than characters, type d, usually in combination with an argument that specifies the unit to be deleted. To delete a word, first position the cursor on the first or last character and type dw. If you want to delete a word, including any adjacent punctuation, type dW. You can include a repeat factor in these delete commands to delete a number of words. The number is placed following the d but preceding either the w or b, such as typing d4w to delete four words forward.

Deleting Lines and Sentences

Typing dd deletes the line where the cursor is currently located. If you type d, then press Return, vi deletes the entire line and the line following it. To delete more than two lines, precede the first d with the number of lines you want to delete. For example, typing 12dd deletes twelve lines down, starting with the current line.

You can also delete a part of a line. Typing d$ deletes from the cursor to the end of a line. Typing d0 deletes from the beginning of the line to the cursor. To delete a sentence from the cursor to the end of the sentence, type d). To delete a sentence from the cursor to the beginning of the sentence, type d(.

Placing the cursor at the very beginning or end of a sentence, then using the appropriate sentence deletion command, deletes an entire sentence. For example, typing d) with the cursor at the very beginning of the sentence deletes the entire sentence. As with other delete commands, you can add repeat factors to delete more than one sentence at a time. For example, typing d4) with the cursor located at the very beginning of a sentence deletes that entire sentence and the following three sentences.

Deleting Paragraphs and Other Sections of Your File

As with deleting sentences, placing the cursor at the very beginning or end of a paragraph and typing the appropriate delete command deletes the entire paragraph. To delete from the beginning of a paragraph to the cursor, type d{. To delete from the cursor to the end of the paragraph, type d}. You can also use the repeat factor to delete multiple paragraphs. For example, typing d3} with the cursor at the beginning of a paragraph deletes all of the current paragraph along with the two following paragraphs.

You can delete parts of your vi file displayed on your screen. Typing dH deletes text from the line the cursor is located on to the very top of the screen. Typing dL deletes text from the line the cursor is on down to the very last line on the screen. Typing dG deletes text from the line the cursor is on to the end of the file. Typing d1G deletes text from the line the cursor is located on to the very beginning of the file.

Changing and Replacing Text

The vi editor provides two commands to change text, the **c** (change) command and the **r** (replace) command.

- The change command combines the functions of deleting and inserting text in one command.
- The replace command allows you to overtype existing text.

Invoke both commands while in the command mode.

When you enter a change command, specify the text that will be replaced. The end of this text is then marked with a **$** (the cursor location marks the beginning of the text to be changed). You then overtype the marked text, then press Esc to complete the deletion and effect the change. Your changes can be shorter or longer than the marked text that will be deleted. You can use the change commands to change words, lines, sentences, and paragraphs. As with most vi editing commands, you can add repeat factors to change commands. The following lists vi editor change and replace commands.

COMMAND	CHANGE OR REPLACEMENT
cw	To end of word.
cW	To end of word, including punctuation.
cb	From beginning of word to cursor.
cB	From beginning of word, including punctuation, to cursor.
cc	Current line.
c$	From the cursor to the end of the line.
c0	From the cursor to the beginning of the line.
c)	From the cursor to the end of the sentence.
c(	From the cursor to the beginning of the sentence.

COMMAND	CHANGE OR REPLACEMENT
c}	From the cursor to the end of the paragraph.
c{	From the cursor to the beginning of the paragraph.
r	Replaces character at cursor.
R	Replaces characters until Esc is pressed.

Changing Words, Lines, Sentences, and Paragraphs

To change a word, type the command cw. The cw (change word) command instructs vi to delete the word at the cursor location and insert new text. You can change multiple words by adding a repeat factor for the number of words you want to change. For example, typing c3w allows you to change three words forward from the cursor.

To change an entire line, type the command cc, which marks the line and places you in the insert mode to begin entering replacement text. When you are finished entering text, press Esc. It doesn't matter where the cursor is located on the line; cc deletes the entire line of text and replaces it with the text you entered before pressing Esc. You can also use a repeat factor to change multiple lines. For example, typing 7cc marks the current line and the six following lines for deletion, then places you in the insert mode to begin replacing the lines.

You can remove part or all of a sentence or paragraph and enter the insert mode by using the commands c) (from the cursor to the end of the sentence), c((from the cursor to the beginning of the sentence), c} (from the cursor to the end of the paragraph), and c{ (from the cursor to the beginning of the paragraph). As with other change commands, you can also use repeat factors with sentence or paragraph change commands.

Replacing Text

The r (replace) command allows you to overtype a single character. You can multiply the effects of this command by typing the number of characters you want to affect before it. For example, typing 8r allows you to replace eight characters forward from the cursor. Typing R is particularly useful because it allows you to overtype characters until Esc is pressed.

Changing Case in Command Mode

To change the case of a character without leaving command mode, position the cursor on the letter whose case you want to change and type ~. The case of the letter changes, and the cursor moves to the next character. You *can't* add a repeat factor or an argument, such as w for a word, to the tilde command (~).

N O T E You can use the ~(tilde) command to change the case of any letter because it changes both lowercase letters to uppercase and uppercase letters to lowercase.

Joining Two Lines

You can merge shorter lines to form a longer line using the J (join) command. For example, to join two lines, first position the cursor anywhere on the first line, then type J to merge the line below it. You can also add a repeat factor to merge consecutive lines into one line and use the repeat command (.) to repeat the join command. To join these three lines

```
OK. I admit it.
I hid the gun.
I did not want my niece to go to the chair.
```

type **3J**, which results in the following:

```
OK. I admit it. I hid the gun. I did not want my niece to go to
the chair.
```

Cutting and Pasting Text

Cutting and pasting text means you mark pieces of text, *yank* (copy) them, then *put* (paste) them at another location. The vi editor performs cutting and pasting tasks by storing the yanked (or deleted) text in buffers, which are areas set aside in memory to store text. There are two types of buffers for cutting and pasting text, the general buffer and named buffers. The *general buffer* stores only the last text manipulation you performed in memory. Because so many commands use the general buffer, such as delete and change commands, vi provides a way to create your own buffers for storing and retrieving text. These are called *named buffers*. Don't confuse the general buffer with the work buffer, which holds your entire file in memory until you save it to disk.

NOTE   The u (undo) command always uses text placed in the general buffer as its source.

Using Named Buffers

You can establish up to 26 named buffers of your own, designated by lowercase letters ranging from **a** to **z**. These named buffers can store deleted, yanked, or changed text. You specify text stored in a named buffer by including a double quotation mark (**"**) and the name of the buffer before the delete, yank, or change command. For example, typing the command

```
"z3dd
```

with the cursor at the beginning of a sentence deletes five sentences and stores them in a buffer named **z**. To retrieve the text stored in the **z** buffer, you can use the **p** (put) command, which is explained after the following section.

Using a lowercase buffer name when instructing vi to save text to a named buffer *replaces* any text you have previously saved in that buffer. Using the uppercase version of a buffer name *appends* text you save to that buffer. For example, if you have text saved in a buffer named **z**, saving additional text by specifying **Z** in the command appends this text to the existing text in the buffer named **z**. You can use this technique to collect separate lines in your file and use the uppercase name to place them together in a named buffer. Named buffers work as temporary buffers that are only active during your vi work session for a particular file.

WARNING The contents of all named buffers will be erased if you quit vi or log out.

Copying Text Using Buffers

To copy text from one location to another in your file, you use the **y** (yank) command. Yank commands copy a specified unit of text into the general buffer or a named buffer, leaving the original text in place. To paste the yanked text, move the cursor to the location you want to copy the yanked text, then use the **p** (put) command. The put command is explained below. The following lists available yank commands. Each yank command puts the specified text into the general buffer unless you specify a named buffer.

COMMAND	TEXT YANKED
yw	From the cursor to end of word.
yW	From the cursor to end of word including punctuation.
yb	From the cursor to beginning of word.
yB	From the cursor to beginning of word including punctuation.
yy	Current line.
y Return	Two lines, current and following.
Y$	From the cursor to end of a line.
y0	From the cursor to beginning of a line.
y)	From cursor to end of sentence.
y(	From cursor to beginning of sentence.
y}	From cursor to end of paragraph.
y{	From cursor to beginning of paragraph.
yG	To end of file.

Retrieving Text from Buffers

The p (put) command by itself retrieves text from the general buffer into your file. If the contents of the general buffer are characters or words, typing p puts them *after* the character the cursor is located on. Typing P puts characters or words *before* the character the cursor is located on. If the general buffer contains lines, sentences, or paragraphs, typing p inserts the contents below the line, sentence, or paragraph the cursor is located on. Typing P inserts lines, sentences, or paragraphs from the general buffer into the line, sentence, or paragraph above the cursor. If your named buffer contains different units of text, such as a word and line, the put command places the buffer's text according to which unit of text was placed into the named buffer last. You can specify a named buffer to use with the put command. For example, typing the command "tz puts the contents of buffer tz after the cursor in the appropriate location, depending on what units of text the buffer contains.

Inserting Text from Another File

With vi you can read the contents of another file into the file you're currently working on using the :r (read) command.

    :r *filename*

The read command inserts the contents of *filename*, starting on the line after the cursor position in the current file. For example, suppose your user name is pmason and you are editing the file evidence and want to read in a file called testimony from another directory. To read the file testimony into the file evidence, first position the cursor one line above where you want the new data inserted in evidence. In the command mode, enter

    :r /home/pmason/testimony

The entire contents of the file testimony are read into your file evidence.

You can also combine the read command with a SunOS command to read the results of a SunOS command into your file. For example, entering

```
:r! date
```

will read the system's date information into your file.

Searching vi Files

Two powerful tools are provided by vi for searching through your files for specified strings of characters—the search command and the global replacement command. Search commands search your file for a specified pattern. When a match is found, you can make changes, then search for the next occurrence of the string. Global replacement commands search your file for a specified pattern and automatically replace it with another pattern you specify.

WARNING A forward search continues until the end of the file and a backward search continues until the beginning of the file. If you begin in the middle of a file, the entire file will not be searched.

Searching vi Files for Patterns

Search commands search your file for a pattern match, which means vi searches for a string of characters that matches your specified text. To search forward through a file, type the forward slash character (/) while in command mode, followed by the pattern you want to search for. For example, type

```
/SunOS
```

then press Return. This instructs vi to search forward through the file to find the first occurrence of the pattern SunOS. Typing a question mark before the search pattern, as in the following

`?SunOS`

then pressing Return searches backward through your file for the specified pattern. If no match is found after executing a search command, the message `Pattern not found` is displayed in the status line. When a search command locates the first occurrence of a pattern, you can then perform an editing task such as changing or deleting the pattern. Typing n continues the search to find the next occurrence of a pattern in the same direction. Typing N changes the direction of the search. The following lists vi search commands.

COMMAND	RESULT
/*pattern* \<Return\>	Searches forward in file.
?*pattern* \<Return\>	Searches backward in file.
n	Finds next pattern in same direction.
N	Find next pattern in opposite direction.

Global Replacement

The vi editor provides a powerful tool for searching and replacing incorrect text entries. With one command you can automatically replace a string of characters, such as a misspelled word, wherever it occurs in the file. The global replacement command syntax is

`:%s/oldpattern/newpattern/`

Once a global replacement command is entered, vi checks each line of a file for a given pattern. When the pattern is found, vi automatically replaces the old pattern with the new pattern you've specified. Suppose you wanted to search through your file and find each occurrence of the word Harry and change it to Larry. Type

`:%s/Harry/Larry`

then press Return. The vi editor searches through the entire file for each occurrence of Harry and replaces it with Larry. If vi doesn't find any matches, it responds with the message `Substitute pattern match failed`.

Setting vi Parameters

You can adapt vi to your preferences for a vi work session by setting vi parameters. The vi editor offers a number of parameter options. You can list these options on your screen by typing the command

> `:set all`

then pressing Return. The list shows the options available and their current status. You can set vi parameters to perform such functions as automatically inserting Returns, displaying line numbers, and displaying invisible characters such as tabs and end-of-line characters. To set a parameter while you're using vi, type `:set` followed by the option you want to change. For example, you can instruct vi to display line numbers by typing `:set nu` and pressing Return. To change back to the original set option, type `no` before the option. For example, typing the command

> `:set nonu`

then pressing Return now instructs vi *not* to display line numbers. The following lists several useful set command options.

OPTION	RESULT
`set all`	Displays the complete list of options, including options that you have set as well as vi's default settings.
`:set wrapmargin=`*n*	Specifies the size of the right margin used to wrap text as you type, and saves manually entering Return after each line. A typical value for *n* is 10 or 15.

OPTION	RESULT
`:set nu`	Displays line numbers of a file.
`:set ic`	Specifies that pattern searches should ignore case.
`:set window=`*x*	Sets the number of lines shown in the screen window, where *x* is the number of lines.
`:set list`	Displays invisible characters, with tabs displayed as `^I` and the end-of-line characters (Returns) displayed as `$`.

Using SunOS Commands in vi

You can temporarily exit vi to execute SunOS commands, such as checking your mail, then return to your vi work session without having to quit vi. Typing the command `:sh` while in vi returns you to the SunOS system prompt. You can then execute other SunOS commands. When you want to return to vi, at the system prompt enter

```
exit
```

Save Time When Starting vi

There are several options available when starting vi beyond the basic **vi** **filename** start-up command. You can start up vi, open an existing file, then have the cursor move to a particular line in the file by typing

    `vi +n filename`

where *n* is the number of the line on which you want the cursor to be placed. You can also start up vi, open an existing file, and move the cursor to the last line of the file by typing `vi + filename`. The start-up command

    `vi +/pattern filename`

opens a file and positions the cursor at the first occurrence of a particular text pattern. For example, typing `vi +/fired letter` opens up the file `letter` and places the cursor at the first character of the line containing the word `fired`.

Command Summary

The following lists the commands covered in this chapter that are not contained in the earlier tables.

COMMAND	RESULT
.	Repeats previous command.
Control-l	Redraws screen.
:q!	Quits vi and abandons changes.
Shift-ZZ	Quits vi and saves changes.
vi	Allows user to enter vi.
:w	Saves buffer contents without quitting vi.

CHAPTER
13

Formatting and Printing

IN THE last chapter, you worked with vi to create and edit text files. In this chapter, you learn how to use the nroff and troff formatting programs to enhance the appearance of your printed files. With the nroff and troff programs you can perform a wide range of formatting tasks from boldfacing a single word to changing your entire document's page layout. This chapter also teaches you how to use essential commands for performing basic formatting tasks. In addition, SunOS's printing commands and options are explained to provide you with a variety of ways to print your files.

An Overview of Formatting

SunOS provides several tools for formatting documents. The nroff and troff text formatting programs are two of these. One of the early text formatting commands in SunOS was named roff, which comes from the phrase to "run off" a document, used when a person wanted to format and print a document. The nroff command, which stands for "newer roff," is used primarily with line printers—printers that print one line of text at a time in a single style of typeface. The troff program is an adaptation of nroff for typesetters and laser printers. These printers can print a page at a time and change typeface size and styles, commonly referred to as *fonts*. Because of the prevalence of laser printers, this chapter focuses on using the troff text formatting program.

Adding Formatting Requests to a File

Before you can use `nroff` or `troff`, you must insert requests in the document you want to format. A *request* is simply a formatting instruction embedded in the text of the document to be formatted. You insert requests in a file with a text editor, such as vi, placing a request on a blank line above the text you want formatted.

Using Macros to Format a File

Certain types of documents may need extensive formatting, and could require you to insert many requests in the text. Instead of repeatedly typing the same commands, use macros to save time in formatting your documents. For our purposes, we will define a *macro* as a sequence of `nroff` or `troff` requests. Macros are distinguished from `nroff` and `troff` requests by case—macros use uppercase letters. In SunOS, these macros are grouped together in *macro packages*. This chapter explains how to use `troff` and some of the macros for formatting documents that are found in the `-ms` macro package. You format text with macros the same way as with `nroff` and `troff` requests. Use a text editor to insert the macro above the text you want to format.

Viewing and Printing Formatted Documents

Once you exit the text editor and return to the system prompt, you can view the document by entering

```
ntroff -ms filename | more
```

The `-ms` indicates that the macros embedded in your file belong to the `-ms` macro package. If you are not using `-ms` macros, you can exclude the `-ms` option.

To print a document containing -ms macro requests, use this general syntax:

```
troff -ms filename | lp -d destination
```

The nroff or troff program then formats your text according to the embedded requests. The lp command sends the formatted file to the printer specified by destination. If you are not using -ms macros, you can exclude the -ms option. The embedded requests will not appear on the printout.

When you filter a document that contains troff requests, it produces output in the ditroff format, which are instructions for the printer. If you are using a PostScript printer that doesn't recognize and convert the ditroff printing instructions into PostScript printing instructions, you may need to filter the document using the dpost filter. The dpost filter is stored in the /usr/lib/lp/postscript directory. To use the dpost filter you need to use the pipe to send the output from the troff command to the dpost filter, then use the pipe to send the filtered document to the lp command. Adding the -T postscript argument to the lp command indicates that the document you are printing is in a PostScript format. You must include the entire path name of the dpost filter or add the path to the PATH setting in your .profile file. For example, if you have not added the path to the dpost filter to your .profile file, enter

```
troff -ms filename | /usr/lib/lp/postscript/dpost | lp -T
postscript -d destination
```

If you add the /usr/lib/lp/postscript directory to your PATH setting, as explained in Chapter 15, "Customizing Solaris," you can simply enter the following:

```
troff -ms filename | dpost | lp -T postscript -d destination
```

Character Formatting

If you're using a laser printer or a typesetter, use troff requests and -ms macros to print characters in different fonts (both sizes and styles). The following explains the troff commands that allow you to use different fonts, such as italic and bold. You can use some of these requests, such as the underline request, with `nroff`, but `nroff` ignores requests for fonts it can't handle. In other words, `nroff` doesn't change the size or style of your font. This section also explains how to insert special characters, such as a bullet or a copyright symbol, using `nroff` and `troff`.

Italicizing Text

The `.I` macro is used to indicate italics. Italics are commonly used to set off a foreign word or expression or to indicate titles of books or magazines, as shown in the following example.

```
To inquire how the editors liked the manuscript for
.I
Les Miserables,
.R
Victor Hugo composed the following letter, quoted here in its en-
tirety: "?." The publisher responded: "!."
```

The text when printed then appears as follows:

> To inquire how the editors liked the manuscript for *Les Miserables*, Victor Hugo composed the following letter, quoted here in its entirety: "?." The publisher responded: "!."

If you use the `.I` macro with `nroff`, italicized characters are converted to underlined characters.

Underlining Text

To underline a word in a sentence, use the `.UL` macro; use the `.R` (roman) macro to stop underlining and return to a normal typeface. Unlike most formatting requests, the `.UL` request requires you to put the word to be underlined on the same line as the `.UL` request. You can also underline a certain number of words using the `nroff` request `.ul` *n*, where *n* is the number of words to underline. Unfortunately, neither `nroff` and `troff` provides a way to underline spaces between multiple words. The following is an example of underlining a single word in a text file.

```
The word "bug" in the slang expression "Don't bug me" comes from
the West African word
.UL bagu
.R
,meaning to annoy.
```

The text, when printed, appears as follows:

The word "bug" in the slang expression "Don't bug me" comes from the West African word <u>bagu</u>, meaning to annoy.

Boldfacing Text

Boldface is used to emphasize words or set headings apart from other text. To boldface text, use the .B macro; use the .R (roman) macro to return to normal roman typeface. The .B macro doesn't work with some line printers. For example

```
.B
Warning to all Personnel:
.R
Firings will continue until morale improves.
```

results in the printout

Warning to all Personnel: Firings will continue until morale improves.

Changing the Size of a Font

A laser printer or typesetter lets you print fonts in different sizes, measured in points. A *point* is $1/72$ of an inch. The default point size is 10 points. If you're using a laser printer or a typesetter, you can change the size of your font by using a few simple macros. The .LG macro makes the font two points larger. The .SM macro makes a font two points smaller, and the .NL macro returns your font to the normal size. To change the font size to a 12 points, enter

```
This text will print using a 10-point font.
.LG
This text will print using a 12-point font.
```

Inserting Special Characters

Not all the characters you can print are on your keyboard. The `nroff` and `troff` programs let you print a variety of characters not available on your keyboard by simply inserting a special code in your document. The following lists the most commonly used special characters that you can add using the standard fonts. Notice that the backslash escape character is used to identify the character code.

CHARACTER	CODE	DESCRIPTION
—	\(em	Em dash
–	\(hy	Hyphen
•	\(bu	Bullet
½	\(12	One-half
¼	\(14	One-quarter
→	\(->	Right arrow
←	\(<-	Left arrow
↑	\(ua	Up arrow
↓	\(da	Down arrow
		\br	Boxed rule
¢	\(ct	Cent sign
®	\(rg	Registered
©	\(co	Copyright
°	\(de	Degree
´	\(aa	Acute accent
`	\(ga	Grave accent

Formatting Lines

To the `nroff` and `troff` programs, a file is only a stream of words. Both programs ignore the line breaks you made when you pressed Return while creating or editing a file. Instead `nroff` and `troff` format text by filling the lines to fit in the margins. This process is called *line filling*. When they encounter a space at the beginning of a line, they interpret the space as a line break, stop filling the current line, and begin a new line.

Filling and Justifying Lines

The `-ms` macro package by default inserts spaces between words to make lines end with a flush right margin; this is commonly known as *justification*. To produce a nonjustified (ragged) margin, use the request `.na` (nonadjusted). To return to a right margin justification alignment, add the request `.ad`. Look at the following example to see the effects of using `.na` and `.ad`.

```
.na
Traditionally dinosaurs have been thought of as being cold-
blooded reptiles. However, contemporary evidence on posture,
skeleton, and eating habits indicates some dinosaurs may have
been warm-blooded. It is a mistake to think that dinosaurs and
cave dwellers lived at the same time.

.ad
Dinosaurs died out 65 million years ago, and the earliest human
dates back to no more than four million years.
It is also a myth that dinosaurs died during the Ice Age.
The last Ice Age, to which the myth presumably refers, ended
10,000 years ago.
```

Here is how this example would be printed:

Traditionally dinosaurs have been thought of as being cold-blooded reptiles. However, contemporary evidence on posture, skeleton, and eating habits indicates some dinosaurs may have been warm-blooded. It is a mistake to think that dinosaurs and cave dwellers lived at the same time.

Dinosaurs died out 65 million years ago, and the earliest human dates back to no more than four million years. It is also a myth that dinosaurs died during the Ice Age. The last Ice Age, to which the myth presumably refers, ended 10,000 years ago.

When you want to stop lines from being joined together, use the `.nf` request. For example, when you put an address in a letter, you don't want the city and state to be added to the end of the street address on the previous line. To prevent `nroff` from filling lines, use `.nf` (no fill). The `.nf` request doesn't justify your text, but stops the filling process and prints your text with line breaks as they appear in the file. To restart line filling, use the `.fi` (fill) request.

Changing Line Spacing

The `nroff` and `troff` programs both use single line spacing as the default. You can easily change the line spacing by adding the number of blank lines you want between each line using the request `.ls` *n*, where *n* is the number of the spaces you want between each line. The following request begins double spacing text then returns to single spacing.

```
.ls 2
A movie theater manager in Seoul, South Korea, decided that the
running time of the movie
I.
The Sound of Music
R.
was too long, so he shortened it by cutting out all the songs.
.ls
```

The double-spaced text when printed appears as follows:

A movie theater manager in Seoul, South Korea, decided

that the running time of the movie *The Sound of Music*

was too long, so he shortened it by cutting out all the songs.

Inserting Blank Lines

You can insert any number of blank lines using the `.sp` *n* request. The letter *n* indicates the number of line spaces you want to insert in the text. For example,

```
Rough draft
.sp 3
It was a dark and stormy night.
```

adds three lines between the first line of text and the text following the `.sp 3` request, printed as follows:

Rough draft

It was a dark and stormy night.

Indenting Lines

To indent text from the left margin, use the `.in` request followed by the number of spaces to indent. You can add spaces to an indent by preceding the number in the argument with a plus (+) sign or decrease spaces with a minus sign (–). For example, `.in +5` increases the current indent by five spaces.

Typically, the first line of a paragraph is indented. If you want to temporarily indent a single line of text, use the request `.ti` n, where n is the number of spaces you want to indent that one line.

Setting Tabs

Tabs are most frequently used to produce output in columns. The `troff` tab stops are set by default every half inch from the current indent. The `nroff` tab stops are set every .8 inch. You can set tabs using the `.ta` request followed by the tab position you want to set. For example,

```
.ta 1i 1.5i 2i 2.5i 3i 3.5i 4i 4.5i 5i 5.5i 6i
```

sets tabs every $1/2$ inch across a page. You can also set tabs relative to the previous tab stops by preceding the tab number with a plus (+) sign. For example,

```
.ta 1 +.5i +.5i +.5i +.5i +.5i +.5i +.5i +.5i +.5i
```

produces the same results as the previous `.ta` example. You can also create right-adjusted or centered tabs. To right-adjust a tab, add the letter `R` after the tab setting. When you right-adjust a tab, the text following the tab is lined up against the right margin. To center a tab entry, add the letter `C` after the tab setting.

The following shows how to create two columns of text using right-adjusted tabs. It is mandatory that you use the `.nf` (no fill) request at the beginning of this example to stop filling text. The `.fi` (fill) request at the end of this example is optional, depending on whether or not you want to resume filling text.

```
.nf
.ta 3.5iR
Date    Holiday
Jan 1   New Year's Day
Jan 15  Martin Luther King, Jr., Day
Feb 12  Lincoln's Birthday
Feb 14  Valentine's Day
Feb 22  Washington's Birthday
Mar 17  St. Patrick's Day
.fi
```

When printed this looks like this:

Date	Holiday
Jan 1	New Year's Day
Jan 15	Martin Luther King, Jr., Day
Feb 12	Lincoln's Birthday
Feb 14	Valentine's Day
Feb 22	Washington's Birthday
Mar 17	St. Patrick's Day

Centering Lines

The `.ce` request centers a single line of text. You can center multiple lines of text by following `.ce` with the number of lines of text you want centered. Blank lines are not counted when using the `.ce` request.

```
.ce 2
Men have become tools of their tools.
Thoreau
```

When printed, this appears as follows:

Men have become tools of their tools.

Thoreau

Formatting Paragraphs

You can produce several different kinds of paragraphs with the -ms macro package. For example, standard paragraphs begin with an indented first sentence, and left block paragraphs don't indent the first sentence. The following section shows examples of how text would appear using -ms macros for formatting standard, left-block, indented, and quoted paragraphs.

Standard Paragraphs

The standard paragraph is an indented, left-aligned paragraph. Insert the -ms macro .PP to format the following text as a standard paragraph:

```
.PP
Because of the radiant properties of the sun, people believe that
it consists of an entirely different material than earth. The sun
burns because of its size. It consists of the same cosmic matter
from which all of the planets are made.
```

When printed, the paragraph appears with an indent as follows:

Because of the radiant properties of the sun, people believe that it consists of an entirely different material than earth. The sun burns because of its size. It consists of the same cosmic matter from which all of the planets are made.

Left-Block Paragraphs

A left-block paragraph is the same as a standard paragraph, only without an indent. Left block paragraphs are indicated by the macro `.LP`, as shown here:

```
.LP
The sun contains 99.8 percent mass of the solar system and is a
million times larger than the earth. The effect of its size is to
produce pressure at the center so great that even atoms are
crushed, exploding their nuclei, and allowing them to smash into
each other. These collisions are actually nuclear reactions and
are felt and seen by us from 93 million miles away as heat and
light.
```

When printed the paragraph appears left-aligned, without an indent, as follows:

The sun contains 99.8 percent mass of the solar system and is a million times larger than the earth. The effect of its size is to produce pressure at the center so great that even atoms are crushed, exploding their nuclei, and allowing them to smash into each other. These collisions are actually nuclear reactions and are felt and seen by us from 93 million miles away as heat and light.

If you don't add an `.LP` or `.PP` request, all your paragraphs will be unindented with both the left and right margins aligned.

Block Quotes

The `.QP` (quoted paragraph) macro indents a paragraph on both sides, with blank lines above and below the paragraph.

```
.PP
The giant marlin has towed the old man's boat far off the coast
of Cuba. The old man is exhausted but has outlasted the fish. He
hoists a sail and begins heading for home. Hemingway writes,
.QP
They sailed well and the old man soaked his hands in the salt
water and tried to keep his head clear. There were high cumulus
clouds and enough cirrus above them so that the old man knew the
breeze would last all night. The old man looked at the fish con-
stantly to make sure it was true. It was an hour before the first
shark hit him.
.PP
```

The above example, when printed, appears as follows:

> The giant marlin has towed the old man's boat far off the coast of Cuba. The old man is exhausted but has outlasted the fish. He hoists a sail and begins heading for home. Hemingway writes,

> They sailed well and the old man soaked his hands in the salt water and tried to keep his head clear. There were high cumulus clouds and enough cirrus above them so that the old man knew the breeze would last all night. The old man looked at the fish constantly to make sure it was true. It was an hour before the first shark hit him.

Indented Paragraphs

Indented paragraphs are frequently used for creating bulleted or numbered lists. The syntax for creating an indented paragraph is as follows:

```
.IP label n
```

This command indents a paragraph n spaces after a "hanging" label. If a label is more than one word, the words must be enclosed in double quotation marks. If an indent isn't specified, an indent of five spaces is used. The following is an example of formatting indented paragraphs.

```
.IP (i) 5
Never use a metaphor, simile, or other figure of speech that you
are used to seeing in print.
.IP (ii) 5
Never use a long word where a short one will do.
.IP (iii) 5
If it is possible to cut a word out, always cut it out.
.IP (iv) 5
Never use the passive where you can use the active.
.IP (v) 5
Never use a foreign phrase, a scientific word, or a jargon word
if you can think of an everyday English equivalent.
.IP (vi) 5
Break any of these rules sooner than say anything outright
barbarous.
```

When printed, the above example appears as follows:

When printed, the above example appears as follows:

(i)   Never use a metaphor, simile, or other figure of speech that you are used to seeing in print.

(ii)   Never use a long word where a short one will do.

(iii) If it is possible to cut a word out, always cut it out.

(iv)   Never use the passive where you can use the active.

(v)   Never use a foreign phrase, a scientific word, or a jargon word if you can think of an everyday English equivalent.

(vi)   Break any of these rules sooner than say anything outright barbarous.

Outline Paragraphs

To create an outline, use the `.IP` (indented) macro with the `.RS` (right-shift) and `.RE` (right-shift end) macros. Each time you use the `.RS` request, the indention moves in another five spaces. The `.RE` request moves the indention back five spaces.

```
.IP I.
Making the Most of Priorities
.RS
.IP A.
The To Do list
.RS
.IP 1.
Setting priorities
.IP 2.
Grouping tasks
.RE
.RE
.IP II.
Tasks Better Left Undone
.RS
.IP A.
The 80/20 rule
.RS
.IP 1.
Skipping less important jobs
```

```
.IP 2.
Coping with information overload
.RE
.RE
```

The above example, when printed, appears as follows:

I. Making the Most of Priorities

  A. The To Do list

    1. Setting priorities

    2. Grouping tasks

II. Tasks Better Left Undone

  A. The 80/20 rule

    1. Skipping less important jobs

    2. Coping with information overload

Changing the Page Layout

You can change the layout of your document, such as margins or page sizing, if the default page-layout settings don't match your needs. Figure 13.1 shows the elements of page layout that you'll work with in this section.

Number Registers

In order to change the default page-layout settings, such as margins, you need to use number registers. *Number registers* are memory locations that store values of page-layout settings. You usually use one or two letters to specify a number register, that is, to say which part of the layout you want to change. Note however, that -ms number registers do not take effect immediately. If you need the effect immediately, use the `troff` command equivalent, which is a period and the lowercase equivalent of the register.

FIGURE 13.1

Elements of page layout

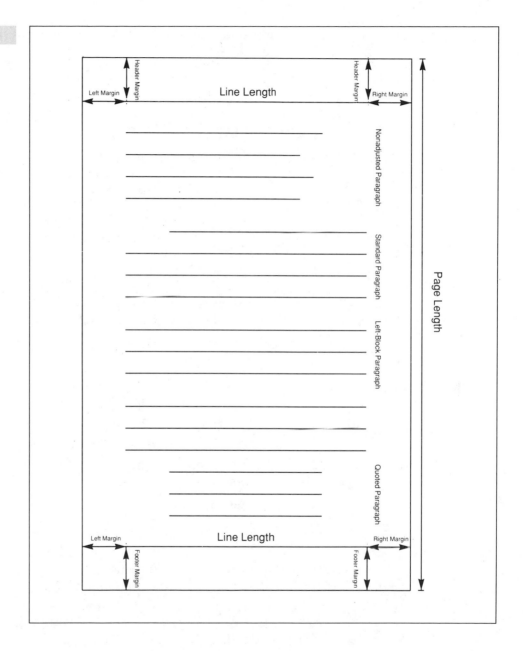

The following shows an example of using .nr to change the default point size to 9 points.

```
.nr PS 9
```

The following lists a summary of –ms number registers.

REGISTER	CONTROLS	TAKES EFFECT	DEFAULT
CW	Column width	The next occurrence of two-column text (next .2C)	$^7/_{15}$ of the set line length
FM	Footer margin	The next page	1 inch
GW	Gap width between columns	The next occurrence of two-column text (next .2C)	$^1/_{15}$ of the set line length
GM	Header margin	The next page	1 inch
LL	Line length	The next paragraph	6 inches
PD	Paragraph spacing	The next paragraph	0.3 of line spacing
PI	Paragraph indent	The next paragraph	5 spaces
PO	Page offset	The next page	$^{26}/_{27}$ inch
PS	Point size	The next paragraph	10 points
VS	Line spacing	The next paragraph	12 points

Setting Left and Right Margins

Margins are the white spaces at the top, bottom, left, and right of your printed document. By default, the `troff` program initially sets the margins to one inch (the `nroff` program sets the left margins to zero). To specify a one-and-a-half-inch-wide left margin, at the beginning of your text insert the command

```
.nr PO 1.5i
```

The `nr` in this command stands for number register. The `PO` stands for Page Offset; the number `1.5` followed by the letter `i` will offset the page 1.5 inches.

The right margin is determined by the left margin setting and the line length setting. To discover how wide your right margin is, subtract the length of your text line and the width of the left margin from the total width of the page, which is normally 8.5 inches. The result is the size of the right margin. The default line length is 6 inches. If you want one-and-a-half inch margins on both sides of the printout of your document, you need to offset the left margin by one-and-a-half inches and change the line-length setting to 5 inches. To do this, insert these commands above the first line of the file you want to format:

```
.br
.po 1.5i
.ll 5i
```

The `br` is a break that typically precedes the page offset and line length changes. The `.po` is the `troff` equivalent of `.nr Po`, which offsets the left margin. `ll` indicates the line length, which in this example is 5 inches.

Setting Top and Bottom Margins

The `.pl` (page length) request lets you change the number of lines on a page. This request actually specifies how many vertical inches of space the text should fill. At the top of the document, insert `.pl` *n*, where *n* indicates the number of inches the text should fill. The default page length is 11 inches.

For example, to change the page length to 10 inches, use the following command:

```
.pl 10i
```

Determining Page Breaks

Sometimes it is necessary to begin printing information on a new page. The `.bp` (break page) request ends the text at the bottom of a page and begins it at the top of the next page. Here is an example of using the `.bp` request to ensure that a list of paintings begins on a new page.

```
The following page lists the paintings that accompany this
document.
.bp
The List of Paintings

.nf
Old Woman
Old Guitarist
Les Demoiselles d'Avignon
The Three Musicians
Guernica
```

Keeping Text Together

The `nroff` and `troff` programs break pages when the text reaches the bottom margin. You can prevent a page break from occurring in the middle of a block of text by using the `.KS` and `.KE` macros. Suppose you have a paragraph that appears at the bottom of a page and you want it to appear with a paragraph on the next page. Precede the first paragraph with `.KS` and end it with `.KE`, as shown in the following example:

```
.KS
People look for a reflection of their own personalities or the
person they dream of being in the eyes of an animal companion.
That is the reason I sometimes look into the face of my dog Stan
(I have two) and see wistful sadness and existential angst, when
all he is actually doing is slowly scanning the ceiling for flies.
.KE
```

If you need to keep text together on the same page, try using the `.ne n` (need) request, where `n` is the number of lines to keep on the page. If there is room on the page, `.ne` places all the specified lines on that page.

Headers and Footers

Headers and footers are titles that appear at the top and bottom of a page. Titles that occur at the top of a page are called *headers*. Titles printed at the bottom of a page are called *footers*. If you want to use headers or footers, use `.pl` to change the page length and create space at the top and bottom of your printed pages. These spaces are called the *header margin* and the *footer margin*.

Headers and footers begin printing on the second page of your document. When you use `-ms` with `nroff`, date footers and page number headers are added automatically. Add the `.ND` macro request if you want to eliminate the date when using the `-ms` macro package with `nroff`. When `-ms` is used with `troff`, the date footers are not included. To create the header "Great Prime Time Shows," type the following request on the very first line of your file:

```
.ds CH Great Prime Time Shows
```

The `.ds CH` (define string Center Header) request clears the default setting of `CH`, which is the current page number surrounded by hyphens, and instructs `nroff` to instead center the text "Great Prime Time Shows" as the new header. Note that the quotes are not printed with your header. If you want to add a page number to your header, use the percent sign (`%`). The percent sign tells the automatic page counter to place page numbers in your header. To include page numbers in our previous example, insert

```
.ds CH Great Prime Time Shows %
```

at the top of the file.

You can create headers and footers and specify their location by using the requests listed below.

COMMAND	HEADER AND FOOTER TEXT PLACEMENT
`.ds LH`	Places header text at the left margin.
`.ds CH`	Centers header text.
`.ds RH`	Places header text at the right margin.

COMMAND	HEADER AND FOOTER TEXT PLACEMENT
`.ds LF`	Places footer text at the left margin.
`.ds CF`	Centers footer text.
`.ds RF`	Places footer text at the right margin.

Creating Multiple Columns

In order to get more information on a page, you may want to set your text in multiple columns. Use the following macros with the `col` command to create multiple columns.

MACRO	RESULT
`.2C`	Begins the first column of two-column text.
`.RC`	Begins the second column of two-column text.
`.1C`	Returns to single-column text. Switching from double- to single-column text causes an automatic page break.

The following excerpt from the *Virginia Pilot* shows how to create double columns with the `.2C` request.

```
.2C
.PP
A group calling itself the Partiers League for Christmas Cookie
Liberation kidnapped a Ronald McDonald statue from a Sacramento,
California, McDonald's. They sent a ransom note which read: "Mr.
McDonald is safe, unharmed, and, I assure you, entirely unable to
escape." The note demanded that McDonald's give a free box of
cookies to any child under eight who visited the restaurant on
Christmas Eve.
.PP
"This is not a hoax," said the note. "If any qualified child is
refused cookies, Ronald dies."
.RC
.PP
```

```
The note came with a photo of a blindfolded Ronald McDonald, a
stick of dynamite hanging from his neck. A note on the wall be-
hind the statue read: "Do as they say or I'm McHistory."
.PP
This is not the only case of a crime involving the theft of a res-
taurant statue. In Iron Mountain, Michigan, someone absconded
with a Big Boy restaurant statue and whisked it off to Niagara,
Wisconsin.
```

Entering the command

```
nroff -ms filename | col | lp
```

pipes the file name through the `col` filter to print this example as follows:

A group calling itself the Partiers League for Christmas Cookie Liberation kidnapped a Ronald McDonald statue from a Sacramento, California, McDonald's. They sent a ransom note which read: "Mr. McDonald is safe, unharmed, and, I assure you, entirely unable to escape." The note demanded that McDonald's give a free box of cookies to any child under eight who visited the restaurant on Christmas Eve.

"This is not a hoax," said the note. "If any qualified child is refused cookies, Ronald dies."

The note came with a photo of a blindfolded Ronald McDonald, a stick of dynamite hanging from his neck. A note on the wall behind the statue read: "Do as they say or I'm McHistory."

This is not the only case of a crime involving the theft of a restaurant statue. In Iron Mountain, Michigan, someone absconded with a Big Boy restaurant statue and whisked it off to Niagara, Wisconsin.

Creating Tables

It's easy to create simple tables in SunOS. Below is an example of a table that contains design elements you often use in tables.

	PHONE LIST	
Names	**Phone Numbers**	**Contact**
Sun Support	800-872-4786	Ann
Bookware	415-967-8283	Steve
SYBEX	510-523-8233	George

Here is the combination of formatting entries and text that was used to create this table.

```
.TS
tab(/);
c s s
l l l.
Phone List

Names/Phone Numbers/Contact

Sun Support/800-872-4786/Ann
Bookware/415-967-8283/Steve
SYBEX/510-523-8233/George
.TE
```

The following list explains the formatting entries used to create the table.

OPTION OR MACRO	RESULT
`.TS` (table start)	Begins the table.
`tab (/)`	Indicates that / will be used to delimit columns (the delimiting character will not be printed).

OPTION OR MACRO	RESULT
c s s	Specifies a table of three columns beginning with a centered header. (Only the `Phone List` line will be created because it is the only one without column delimiters.) You cannot use the letter **s** in the first column because the **s** indicates entries from a previous column span the following column.
l l l.	Indicates that each column is left aligned (include period).
.TE	Ends the table.

When you want to print a table, use the `tbl` command as follows:

```
tbl tablename | troff | lp
```

Below are some common formatting entries that were not used in the example table.

OPTION	RESULT
r	Right-adjusted column entry.
n	Numerical column entry.
s	Span previous column's text across this column.

The following list contains options you can use to affect the whole table.

OPTION	RESULT
allbox	Boxes each entry in the table in a box.
box	Frames the entire table with a box.
center	Centers the table on the page.
doublebox	Frames the table with a double line box.
linesize(n)	Sets the table text to n point size.
tab(x)	Uses x to separate table entries.

You can combine these options on one line. For example, an option line added after the `.TS` request might be

```
center allbox tab(/);
```

Be sure to end your option line with a semicolon, otherwise the system will display an error message.

Running Print Jobs

An essential capability of SunOS is to print files. The following section teaches you how to print files, check the status of print jobs, and cancel print jobs. Printers are often in high demand in a networking environment because multiple terminals are often connected to a small number of printers. To keep things running smoothly, SunOS usually feeds printing jobs to printers on a first-come, first-served basis. A *printing job* is a term for a file sent to be printed as hard copy (on paper). Printing jobs are sent to a print *queue*, which stores the printing jobs in memory in the order they're received.

Most networks have multiple printers available for you to choose from. Each printer in a network has a unique name. The `destination` acts as an address for sending your printing jobs to a specific printer. Usually, your system also has a *default printer*. If you don't specify a particular printer when sending a print job, the print job is automatically sent to the default printer. The command syntax for printing a file to the default printer is

```
lp filename
```

If you want to use a different printer than the default printer, you need to specify the printer after the `lp` command using the *-d destination* option. The command syntax for printing a file to a printer other than the default printer is

```
lp -d destination filename
```

The `lp` (line printer) command instructs SunOS to send to the print queue a copy of the file to be printed. The *-d destination* option requests the specific printer by its assigned name. For example, if you wanted to send a copy of the file `report` to the printer at a destination named `laserwriter`, you would type the following:

```
lp -d laserwriter report
```

Printing nroff and troff Files

If you want to print a document formatted using `nroff` and `-ms` macro requests to a line printer, enter

```
nroff -ms | lp
```

As explained earlier in this chapter, the `troff` formatting program is designed to format files for printing on typesetters or laser printers. If you're printing a file to a PostScript printer, you need to run the file through the `dpost` filter. To print a document formatted using `troff` and `-ms` macro requests to a PostScript printer, enter

```
troff -ms filename | dpost | lp -d destination
```

N O T E

The `dpost` filter file is stored in the `/usr/lib/lp/postscript` directory. In most cases, your system administrator will have set up your `.profile` file to include this path. If you cannot access the `dpost` filter, see Chapter 15, "Customizing Solaris," to add the path to your `.profile` file.

Printing Multiple-Page Files

SunOS provides a handy page formatting and printing utility called `pr`. The `pr` command separates text into pages and adds a left-aligned header to each page. The header starts printing at the second page and includes the current date, time, file name, and page number. The general command syntax for the `pr` command is

```
pr filename(s) | lp -d destination
```

You can print multiple files using the **pr** command by adding a space between each file name. For more information on the **pr** command, see Part IV, "Command Reference."

Printing Multiple Copies of a File

You can easily print multiple copies of the same file adding the **-n#** option to the **lp** command, where **#** is the number of copies you want. For example, suppose you want to use the default printer to print seven copies of the file **ratings**. Type the following:

```
lp -n7 ratings
```

Sending Multiple Files to the Printer

You can specify several files to be printed by separating file names with a space. For example, to print the files **report1** and **report2** on the default printer, type

```
lp report1 report2
```

Printing the Output of a Command

As with most SunOS utilities, you can connect the output of a command to the input of the print command using a pipe (|). For example, you can instruct SunOS to list the contents of a directory using the **ls** command, then send the output of the **ls** command to the printer as follows:

```
ls | lp
```

Getting Notified When a Print Job Is Done

You can instruct the print command to let you know when the printer has finished printing your job. When your print job is finished, at the next system prompt the message `You have mail` is displayed. To be notified that a print job is completed, type the command

```
lp -m filename
```

The `-m` option instructs the print command to send you a mail message at the next system prompt after your printed job has been completed. If you're entering commands in a Shell or Command Tool, you can instruct the print command to send a message to your console window by entering

```
lp -w filename
```

Changing or Suppressing the Banner Page

Each printing job is preceded by a single page called a banner page. The *banner page* contains information about the printer and the user issuing the print job. You can add a title line of up to eight characters to the banner page. Suppose you wanted to add the title "nocharge" to the banner page for the file `case101`. Enter the command

```
lp -t nocharge case101
```

If you want your title to include more than one word (that is, if there is a space between characters), such as "Perry Mason's Pro Bono Publico Case 101," you must place the title in quotes: `lp -t "Perry Mason's Pro Bono Publico Case 101" case101`.

In order to suppress the printing of the banner page, your system administrator must have set up the printer to allow the **-nobanner** option. If your printer is set up to print files without a banner page, enter

```
lp -o nobanner filename
```

to print the file without a banner page.

Checking the Printer Status

The `lpstat` command is used to display the status of the available printers, the status of print jobs, and the print request ID numbers of your print jobs in case you need to cancel a print job. To display a list of the printers that are configured on your system, type

```
lpstat -s
```

This displays a message similar to the following:

```
scheduler is running
system default destination: bedrock
system for dodge: longbranch
system for lapd: dragnet
```

If you want to check to see what printer is set up as the default printer, simply use the –d option. To see which printers are accepting requests, use `lpstat -a`. To list your printing jobs waiting in the default print queue, enter the command

```
lpstat -o
```

To determine how busy a printer is by viewing how many print jobs are waiting in a printer queue, add the *-p printername* option to the `lpstat` command, where *printername* is the name of the printer you want to check on. You can see all the characteristics for a printer by including the –l option after the *-p printername* option. For example, entering

```
lpstat -p bedrock -l
```

displays the following listing for the PostScript printer named bedrock:

```
printer bedrock is idle. enabled since Thu Jan 23 15:42:01 PDT
1993. available.
      Form mounted:
      Content types: PS
      Printer Types: PS
      Description: Epson EPL-7500 Bldg. #1
      Connection: direct
      Interface: /usr/lib/lp/model/standard
      After fault: continue
```

```
Users allowed:
   (none)
Forms allowed:
   (none)
Banner not required
Character sets
Default pitch:
Default page size: 80 wide 66 long
Default port settings:
```

Removing Printer Jobs

If you decide not to print a job after sending it to the default printer, you can remove it from the queue by typing the `cancel` command, followed by the job number, as shown below:

```
cancel jobnumber
```

You can find out the job number by first typing the command `lpstat` to list the print jobs and their assigned job numbers. If your printing job is already printing, the printing job isn't terminated. You can remove all your printing jobs from the default printer queue by typing the following:

```
cancel -u username
```

where *username* is your login ID.

T I P   If you have only one print job in a print queue to remove, it's easier to use cancel *-u username* than to find the job number, and use the command `cancel jobnumber`.

Command Summary

The following lists the commands and requests covered in this chapter and their functions.

COMMAND OR REQUEST	RESULT
`.ad`	Returns to justified right margin.
`.B`	Boldfaces text.
`.bp`	Ends text at the bottom of a page and begins it at the top of the next page.
`.ds`	Changes the default setting of headers and footers.
`.fi`	Restarts line filling.
`.I`	Changes type to italic.
`.in` *n*	Indents text *n* spaces.
`.IP` *n*	Indents a paragraph *n* spaces after a hanging indent.
`.KE`	Signifies end of text to keep on one page.
`.KS`	Keeps a specified block of text on one page.
`.LG`	Makes font two points larger.
`.LP`	Formats text into left-block paragraphs.
`lpstat`	Lists your print jobs waiting in the default print queue.
`lp`	Sends a copy of the file to be printed to the print queue.
`cancel`	Removes a print job from the print queue.

COMMAND OR REQUEST	RESULT
`.ls` *n*	Inserts *n* spaces between each line.
`.na`	Produces a nonjustified margin.
`.ND`	Eliminates date in headers when using the `-ms` macro package.
`.ne` *n*	Keeps *n* lines on one page.
`.nf`	Stops the line-filling process.
`.NL`	Returns font to normal size.
`.nr PO` *n*`i`	Offsets left margin *n* inches.
`nroff`	Text formatting command used with line printers.
`1C`	Returns from two-column to single-column text.
`pl` *n*	Changes the page length to n inches.
`.PP`	Formats text into standard paragraphs.
`pr`	Allows user to format and print multiple-page files.
`.ps` *n*	Changes the size of the font indicated by *n*.
`.QP`	Formats text into block quotes.
`.R`	Returns to normal typeface.
`RC`	Begins the second column of two-column text.
`.RE`	Moves the indent to the left five spaces.
`.RS`	Shifts indent five spaces to the right.
`.SM`	Makes font two points smaller.
`.sp` *n*	Inserts n line spaces in text.
`.ta`	Sets tabs.
`.TE`	Indicates the end of a table.

COMMAND OR REQUEST	RESULT
`ti n`	Temporarily indents a line n spaces.
`troff`	Text formatting command used with typesetters and laser printers.
`.TS`	Indicates the beginning of a table.
`.2C`	Begins the first column of two-column text.
`>UL word`	Underlines a word in a sentence.
`.ul n`	Underlines n words.

Multitasking with SunOS

SUNOS is a multitasking operating system, which means you can run several commands simultaneously. Up until now, all the commands in this book have been run one at a time in the *foreground*, so the results appear directly on your screen. Running jobs in the *background* allows you to run commands on your screen while other commands are being processed in the background. Both SunOS and the Korn shell provide you with a collection of commands for managing commands running in the background. This chapter helps you squeeze the maximum power out of Solaris by explaining how to run and manage commands running in the background.

Running a Command in the Background

Certain commands, such as formatting and printing a long text document with `troff`, take a long time to run. This type of time-consuming program is best run in the background so it doesn't tie up your screen and keep you from doing other work. To run a command as a background job, add the ampersand (`&`) at the end of the command line before you press Return. For example, typing

```
troff -ms schedules | lp &
```

instructs SunOS to format the file `schedules` using the `troff` program and run the job in the background. When you run a command in the background, the Korn shell executes the command and displays a job identification number similar to this:

```
[1]   183
```

Redirecting a Background Command's Output

A background job normally sends the result of its processing to the screen unless you redirect its output. Having the output of a background command appear on your screen while you are entering another command can be confusing. To redirect the output of a background command to a file, use the > redirection symbol. For example, entering

```
find . -name "chap*" -print > chapters &
```

redirects the standard output of the find command to a file named **chapters**. For more information on redirecting output, see Chapter 10, "Improving Your Command-Line Productivity."

Another way of preventing a background job from sending its output to your screen is to restrict writing to your terminal by entering

```
stty tostop
```

When the stty tostop command is activated, the stty tostop program suspends any background program that attempts to write to the screen. When the job has output, a message appears. For example, executing the command find . -name "chap*" -print & after issuing the stty tostop command, displays

```
[1] + Stopped (tty output) find . -name "chap*" -print &
```

To display the find command's output, you need to bring the job back into the foreground by typing

```
fg
```

To remove the screen output restriction, type

```
stty -tostop
```

Keeping Error Messages from Displaying on Your Screen

By default, standard error messages appear on your screen so you can find out immediately if there is a problem with the execution of the background command. For example, if you searched the entire system using the `find` command, error messages appear for directories that you do not have permission to read. To keep error messages from displaying on your screen, redirect the standard error as well as standard output either to the same file or to a different one, as shown in the following example.

```
find / -name "chap*" -print > chapters 2> errors &
```

This command line runs the `find` command in the background and saves standard output in the `chapters` file and any error messages in the file named `errors`.

To eliminate the error output, redirect it to `/dev/null`. The `/dev/null` is a device that acts like a trash can. Sending the information to this device causes the information to disappear. For example, enter

```
find / -name "chap*" > chapters 2> /dev/null &
```

to run the `find` command, send its output to `chapters`, and discard any error messages.

Controlling Your Jobs

The Korn shell provides job control commands for managing commands running in the background. Using the Korn shell you can list, suspend, resume, terminate, and switch jobs between the foreground and background. The Korn shell normally notifies you when background jobs change status, such as when a job terminates.

If you are using the Bourne shell, you will need to start a special shell, known as the job shell, to manage commands running in the background. To start the job shell, enter `jsh -i` at the system prompt.

Checking the Status of a Job

To check the status of jobs placed in the background, use the Korn shell's `jobs` command. The `jobs` command indicates if a job is done, running, or stopped. Typing `jobs` displays a list similar to the following:

```
[2]        Stopped    troff -ms yearend report93 &
```

```
[3]   -  Stopped    find / -name "a*" &
[4]   +  Stopped    vi program1.c &
[5]      Running    lp -t legal fees &
```

The first column identifies the job with a number in brackets. *Job numbers* are assigned by the Korn shell for jobs generated at your terminal. Job numbers are unique and relevant only to your work on the system. The current job is indicated by a plus sign (+), and the next job after that is indicated by a minus sign (−) to the right of the first column. If no jobs are running, entering **jobs** simply returns you to the shell prompt.

Job Names

In most cases, you refer to a job by its job number; however, the Korn shell gives you several alternatives to refer to a job. The Korn shell uses the percent sign to identify jobs. The following lists Korn shell job name equivalents.

% *n*	The letter *n* indicates the job number you want to refer to.
%+ or %%	The current job.
%−	The previous job.
%*string*	Job name that begins with *string*.
%?*string*	Job name matches part or all of *string*.

Suspending and Restarting Jobs

You can suspend a job you're currently working on in the foreground by typing Control-z. Using this command suspends the processing of the program, places the program in the background, and assigns the stopped program a job number. To resume the program in the background, enter **bg** *%n,* where *n* is the job number you want to resume. You can also stop a background job by typing **stop** *%n,* where *n* is the job number you want to stop. The **stop** command, like Control-z, suspends but doesn't terminate the command.

Logging Out of SunOS with Stopped Jobs

If you try to log out of SunOS while a job is stopped in the background, SunOS displays the warning message `There are stopped jobs`. Typing the `exit` command again logs you out and terminates any stopped jobs in the background. All other (unstopped) background jobs will be terminated when you log out. If you want to view which jobs are stopped before you log out, type `jobs`.

Switching Jobs between Foreground and Background

To move a running job from the background to the foreground, use the `fg` command followed by a percent sign and the job number. For example, typing `fg %2` moves job 2 into the foreground. Typing `fg` without a job number brings the current job (marked by the plus sign (+) in the `jobs` list) to the foreground.

Suppose you have a program running in the foreground and need to perform another task on your screen. You can quickly place the foreground command into the background. First, press Control-z, which automatically stops the program and places it in the background. Next, type `bg` to resume running the program in the background. To resume a stopped job in the background, type `bg %n`, where *n* is the job number. For example, typing `bg %4` instructs SunOS to resume running job number 4 in the background.

If a command running in the background needs a response from the user, the job is stopped. You need to use the `fg` command to bring the command to the foreground and respond to the command. For example, if you enter `rm -i backup* &`, the screen displays

```
[1]   375
rm: remove backup1: (y/n)?
```

Press Return to display the Korn shell prompt and enter `fg`. Press Return again and you can answer the `rm` command's prompts.

Remember, any time you need to know a job number, type jobs **for a listing of background jobs and their respective numbers.**

If you start a background job from a directory different from your working directory and bring that job to the foreground, SunOS changes your working directory to that directory. SunOS warns you when the system changes your working directory as a result of bringing a background job to the foreground.

Terminating Jobs

Any time you accidentally execute a wrong command or realize you don't want a particular program to run, you can terminate the job using the kill command. To terminate a program running in the background, type kill %*n*, where *n* is the number of the job you want to terminate. For example, typing kill %3 terminates job number three. Some programs need more than the kill command to be terminated. Strengthen the killing power of the kill command with this syntax:

```
kill -9 %n
```

To terminate a program running in the foreground, press Control-c. You can also terminate a foreground program by pressing Control-z to suspend it and move it to the background. Then use the kill command to terminate the program. The following lists essential job control commands.

COMMAND	DESCRIPTION
command &	Creates a background job.
Control-z	Stops the job you're working on.
jobs	Lists both stopped and background jobs, assigning them job numbers in brackets; for example, [1]. The current job is identified with a + and the next job with a -. With the -1 option, the listing includes the PID number. (PID numbers are explained in this chapter.)

COMMAND	DESCRIPTION
fg	Brings the current job (marked with a + in the jobs list) into the foreground, starting the job if it's stopped.
fg %*n*	Brings job *n* into the foreground, starting the job if it's stopped.
bg	Puts the current job (marked with a + in the jobs list) into the background, starting the job if it's stopped.
bg %*n*	Resumes job *n* in the background.
stop %	Stops the current job in the background.
stop %*n*	Stops background job *n*.
kill %*n*	Terminates background job %*n*.
stty tostop	Suspends background jobs that write to the screen.
stty - tostop	Allows background jobs to write to the screen.

Waiting for a Background Job to Finish Executing

If you need the results of a background command before you can continue working, use the **wait** command to wait for the background job to finish. The Korn shell keeps track of the commands it is performing. By entering

    wait $1

the Korn shell waits until the most recent background job is finished executing. You can specify another background job by entering the job ID after the **wait** command. For example, enter

    wait %243

to wait for the background job with the job ID of 243 to finish executing. If you omit a job number or the $1 argument, the Korn shell waits for all your background jobs to finish executing.

Running Commands in the Background after Exiting

By default, commands running in the background are terminated when you log out. You can ensure that a job is completed even after logging out. To continue running a command in the background even after logging out, use the `nohup` (no hang up) command. The `nohup` command causes standard output and standard error to be sent to `nohup.out`. For example, entering

    nohup spell folio

and issuing the `exit` command to log out ensures that the `spell` command continues checking the `folio` file and redirects any misspellings to the `nohup.out` file. The `nohup` command only works with a single command. If you entered the command line `nohup spell folio > mispelled | sort | lp` then logged out, only the output of the spell command is redirected to the file `mispelled`. In this instance, the `nohup` command does not apply to the `sort` and `lp` commands. However, you can enter multiple `nohup` commands, or you can place all the commands you want to execute in a file and enter

    nohup ksh *filename*

This executes all the commands in the file you specified and ensures that each command is not terminated when you log out.

Displaying and Terminating Processes

When you execute a command, the command and the data that it is working with are referred to as an active *process*. Just as the Korn shell includes job control commands, SunOS includes a collection of commands for managing processes.

Every command you run using SunOS, whether in the foreground or background, is assigned a unique *process ID* (PID) number. PID numbers are assigned by SunOS for all processes throughout the system. SunOS juggles its time and resources amongst the various processes currently running and uses the PID number to track the progress, current status, amount of time, and percentage of available memory each process uses.

Checking the Status of a Process

To see what processes you have running, type **ps** and press Return. SunOS takes a snapshot of the active processes and displays a list of processes generated from your account, similar to the one below:

```
PID   TTY     TIME   COMD
227   PTS/11  0:11   ksh
229   PTS/11  0:00   ps
```

In addition to showing the PID number for each process generated from your account, the **ps** command also lists the terminal where it originated, its current status, processing time used, and the command it's performing.

If you are using the Korn shell, you can list the PID numbers for running jobs by entering

```
jobs -l
```

Using the –l (long) option displays both job and PID numbers for all your background jobs, similar to the following:

```
[2]     194   Stopped    troff -ms yearend report93
[3]  -  207   Stopped    find / -name "a*"
[4]  +  211   Stopped    vi program1.c
[5]     243   Running    lp -t legal fees
```

Here the PID numbers are given in the third column. Alternatively, you can display the PID numbers of all jobs by entering **jobs -p**.

You can report on all processes that are being run on your system by typing

```
ps -e
```

This displays a listing similar to the following:

```
PID   TTY       TIME    COMD
0     ?         0:03    sched
1     ?         0:01    init
2     ?         0:00    pageout
3     ?         0:01    fsflush
173   ?         0:00    sac
150   ?         0:00    sendmail
174   console   0:01    ksh
110   ?         0:02    inetd
96    ?         0:00    rpcbind
88    ?         0:00    in.route
98    ?         0:00    keyserv
102   ?         0:00    kerbd
113   ?         0:00    statd
115   ?         0:011   ockd
126   ?         0:00    automoun
141   ?         0:011   psched
133   ?         0:00    cron
149   ?         0:001   Net
159   ?         0:00    syslogd
179   console   0:04    ps
176   ?         0:01    ttymon
```

For more information on finding the status of a process, you can add the –1 long option. Entering

```
ps -el
```

displays a listing similar to the following:

```
F   S UID PID PPID   C PRI  NI  ADDR       SZ    WCHAN   TTY TIME      COMD
39  T   0   0    0  80   0  SYf00b8eb0  0               ?  0:03     sched
28  S   0   1    0  80   1  20ff113800  50ff1139d0      ?  0:01      init
39  S   0        2  01   0  SYff113000  0f00b69a0       ?  0:00   pageout
39  S   0   3    0  80   0  SYff112800  0f00bbbac       ?  0:01   fsflush
28  S   0 173    1  32   1  20ff19f800  224ff28b24e     ?  0:00       sac
28  S   0 150    1  24   1  20ff27a800  300ff1d6d4e     ?  0:00sendmail
28  S5000 174   11  63   1  20ff1a0800  254ff1a0870console0:01       ksh
28  S   0 110    1  80   1  20ff214000  277f00b8c80     ?  0:02     inetd
28  S   0  96    1  47   1  20ff222800  299f00b8c80     ?  0:00   rpcbind
28  S   0  88    1  19   1  20ff213000  240f00b8c80     ?  0:00in.route
28  S   0  98    1   5   1  20ff222000  253f00b8c80     ?  0:00   keyserv
28  S   0 102    1  34   1  20ff21f800  289f00b8c80     ?  0:00     kerbd
28  S   0 113    1  45   1  20ff235000  280f00b8c80     ?  0:00     statd
28  S   0 115    1  80   1  20ff240800  375f00b8c80     ?  0:01     lockd
28  S   0 126    1   8   1  20ff23f000  247f00b8c80     ?  0:00automoun
28  S   0 141    1  80   1  20ff19f000  551f00b8c80     ?  0:01   lpsched
28  S   0 133    1  26   1  20ff26f800  139ff1a6f4e     ?  0:00      cron
```

```
28 S     0 149   141    29    1   20ff27c000 269f00b8c80    ? 0:00    lpNet
28 S     0 159     1    61    1   20ff288000 287f00b8c80    ? 0:00 syslogd
28 05000 180   174    20    1   20ff205000 133        console0:00      ps
28 S     0 176   173    54    1   20ff286000 251ff2861d0    ? 0:01 ttymon
```

The following lists a few key fields, you can check to find processes that may be hogging up your system resources. If necessary, use the kill command to terminate the processes. Killing a process is explained in the following section.

- Check the UID field for lots of processes owned by the same user. This may result from someone running a script that starts a lot of background jobs without waiting for any of the jobs to terminate.

- Check the S column for the letter Z. The letter Z, known as flag Z, stands for a zombie process. A *zombie* process is a process that has been killed but refuses to die. When you notice this, you should either become a superuser and kill the process or let your system administrator know. Be sure to double check this listing because some zombies do die when a device, such as a printer or tape drive, changes status.

- Check the TIME and C field for processes that have accumulated a large amount of CPU time. You can check the start time (STIME)of a process by entering ps -f. Processes with long time entries might be runaway processes that progressively use more and more CPU time. It is also possible that the process might be in an endless loop.

- Check the SZ field for processes that consume a large percentage of memory.

Terminating a Process

Any time you accidentally execute a wrong command or realize you don't want a particular program to run, you can terminate the command using the kill command with the PID number. First type the ps command to determine the PID number. Once you know the PID number, type kill, followed by the PID number. For example, type

```
kill 3193
```

terminates the command running in the background with the assigned PID number 3193. You can kill multiple processes by entering multiple PID numbers as arguments to the `kill` command. For example, type

```
kill 3193 3199 3200
```

to terminate processes 3193, 3199, and 3200.

In order to kill a process, SunOS sends the process a signal. A *signal* is a brief message that SunOS uses to communicate with a process. When you execute the `kill` command, SunOS sends signal 15 to the process you have specified. Depending on the process you are trying to kill, signal 15 may not terminate the process. If the process does not terminate using the `kill` command alone, use the command

```
kill -9 PIDnumber
```

to terminate a process. Signal 9 sends an unconditional kill signal to the process.

Scheduling Processes

Whether you're logged in at the terminal or not, you can execute commands at a time and date you specify, using one of SunOS's scheduling commands. The **at** command executes commands at a time and date you specify and sends the results of the process via electronic mail to whomever you indicate. The syntax of the **at** command is

```
at time date increment
```

NOTE   Your system administrator may restrict access to the at command. If you cannot use the at command on your system, check with your system administrator.

You specify the time for the **at** command as a one-, two-, or four-digit number. One- and two-digit numbers specify an hour, while four-digit numbers specify an hour and a minute. The **at** program assumes a 24-hour clock unless you place **am** or **pm** immediately after the number, in which case **at** uses a 12-hour clock. You can also use the word **now** in place of a time. If you do use **now**, you must also specify a date or an increment of time. An acceptable increment is a number followed by one of the following (plural or singular): minutes, hours, days, weeks, months, or years. For example, typing

```
at now + 30 minutes
```

means execute the command 30 minutes from the time the command is entered. You can also use the word **next** to specify when a command will be executed. For example

```
at now next week
```

means execute the command at the current time one week from now.

If you don't specify a date, **at** executes the job the same day if the hour you specify in time is greater than the current hour. If the hour is less than the current hour, **at** executes the process the next day. You can abbreviate the days of the week to the first three letters. To specify a date, use the name of the month followed by the number of the day in the month. You can also follow the month and day with a year.

Performing a Process at a Later Time

Suppose you want to send the text file **fired.ltr** to a user named **bfife**, but you want to hold its release until 8 a.m. the next morning. The following four steps demonstrate how to send the file at 8 a.m. the following day and let someone else know when the dirty deed has been done.

1. Type **at 8am** and press Return. If you are using the **at** command before 8 a.m. on the day before you're sending this file, you need to specify the day.

2. Enter **mail −s 'Greetings from Personnel' bfife < fired.let** then press Return. This command instructs SunOS to mail the file **fired.let** to the user **bfife**.

3. Enter `echo 'Message sent' | mail -s Message ihangman` then press Return. This command instructs SunOS to send a message to `ihangman`, confirming the file `fired.let` was sent to `bfife`.

4. Press Control-d to end the `at` command session. SunOS displays `<EOT>` and ends the `at` command session, displays a job confirmation message, then returns to the SunOS prompt, as shown in the following example:

```
$ at 8am
mail -s 'Greetings from Personnel' bfife < fired.let
echo 'Message sent' | mail -s Message ihangman
<EOT>
job 31629 at Thu Feb 22 08:00:00 1999
$
```

Displaying the Processes to Be Performed

Any **at** commands you enter are stored in a queue, a temporary storage file, until it comes time to execute the commands. The **atq** (at queue) command lists **at** command jobs that are queued for execution. The **atq** command lists the **at** jobs chronologically. You can list another user's **at** jobs by specifying the user's name after the **atq** command. By using the -c option you can display the jobs in the order they were created, rather than when the command is scheduled to be executed.

Running a Batch of Commands in the Background

The **batch** command is similar to the **at** command, except **batch** executes multiple commands one after another, waiting for the previous command to complete. Using the **batch** command ensures that you don't hog up the system's resources by running several background jobs simultaneously. The **batch** command can take input from a file name or you can specify commands. For example, entering

```
batch
```

```
find / -name "resume" -print
sort employees > colist
troff -ms manuscript
```

and pressing Control-d begins processing the commands. SunOS responds with a message similar to the following:

```
Warning: commands will be executed using /usr/bin/sh
job 715773735.a at Sun Sep 6 03:09:19 1993
```

The commands are then executed in the background and the results are sent to you via mail.

Removing at and batch Commands

The `atrm` (at remove) command removes jobs that were created with the `at` or `batch` command, but have not yet been executed. The `atrm` removes each job number you specify and/or all jobs, provided that you own the indicated jobs. Use the `-a` option to remove all unexecuted `at` jobs that you created. To have `atrm` prompt you before removing a job, use the `-i` (interactive) option. To suppress all information regarding the removal of the specified job, use the `-f` (force) option. The following example prompts for confirmation before removing jobs created using the `at` command for the user `rpetrie`:

```
atrm -i rpetrie
```

Scheduling Repeated Tasks

The `cron` command lets you run programs that you want to execute repeatedly at preset intervals you specify. This command is useful for doing timed backups, file transfers, mail forwarding, or file cleanup and maintenance. The commands that `cron` runs are listed in a file named `crontab`. You don't actually enter the `cron` command. Instead the system administrator activates the `cron` command, which executes the commands listed in the `crontab` file.

To enter the commands and scheduling information into the `crontab` file, use the following format for each command you want to run.

```
Min Hrs Day_of_Month Month Day_of_Week Command
```

The Time options are as follows:

FIELD	OPTIONS
Min	0–59
Hour	0–23 (0 is midnight)
Month	1–12
Day of Month	0–31
Day of Week	0–6 (0 is Sunday)

Each field entry is separated by a space or tab, and individual entries can be combined for repetition and separated by spaces. For example, if you want to remove core files from your home directory at 12:15 p.m. on the first day of every month, in your `crontab` file, type

```
0 12,15 1 * * find | / -name "core" -exec rm {} \;
```

The comma after the hour field specifies minute values past the hour. The asterisk (*) indicates that the schedule is valid for all possible values in the field. If you want to restrict a command to run only between a time interval, such as the hours of 9:00 a.m. and 5:00 p.m., separate the beginning and ending field entries with a hyphen. For example, the `crontab` entry

```
0 9-16  *  *  1-5 find | / -name "core" -exec rm {} \;
```

restricts the command to be run only on Monday through Friday between the hours 9:00 a.m. and 5:00 p.m. Using the 1-5 entry is the same as entering the values as 1,2,3,4,5.

To edit the `crontab` file or to create the entries, enter

```
crontab -e username
```

This starts the `ed` editor and loads or creates your personal `crontab` file for editing. For information on using the `ed` editor, open the Command or Shell Tool and at the prompt, enter `man ed`. Standard output from the timed commands, if it is not redirected to a file, is collected and mailed to you upon completion of the job.

Changing the Priority of a Command

The `nice` command is used to lower the scheduling priority of a command. This command is helpful, especially to other users, when you want to run a command that makes large demands of the system. If you don't need the output of a command right away, change the priority level using the following format:

```
nice -increment command
```

The default priority is set to 10. To lower the priority of a command, enter an increment higher than 10 but less than 20. For example, enter

```
nice -19 grep exam * &
```

to lower the priority of a `grep` command and run the command in the background. The priority of a command can only be increased by a super-user. A higher priority is indicated by a double minus sign. For example, the command

```
nice --10 grep exam * &
```

increases the priority of the `grep` command by 10 units.

Suspending the Execution of a Command

The `sleep` command suspends the execution of a command for a specified number of seconds. For example, entering

```
sleep 600;echo "\007 Call tech support again"
```

suspends the execution of the echo command for 10 minutes.

Command Summary

The following lists the commands covered in this chapter and their functions.

&	Executes commands in the background.
at	Executes commands at specified time and date.
atrm	Removes jobs created using the at and batch commands.
batch	Executes multiple commands in the background.
bg	Executes a job in the background (Korn shell).
exit	Logs you out and terminates any stopped jobs in the background.
fg	Executes a job in the foreground.
kill	Terminates the execution of a command.
nice	Changes the priority of a command.
nohup	Continues executing a command even after logging out.
ps	Lists processes currently running.
sleep	Suspends the execution of a command.
wait	Waits for background jobs to finish.

PART THREE

Personalizing Forms and Reports

CHAPTERS

15 Customizing Solaris

16 Networking and Communications

17 System Administration Basics

CHAPTER

15

Customizing Solaris

THERE is a treasure trove of options for customizing Solaris beyond the plain vanilla configuration that your system administrator has set up for you. Customizing Solaris can save you time and make working with Solaris a lot more comfortable. This chapter introduces you to a wide variety of options for enhancing your Solaris environment. It explores how to change the default settings for the Korn shell, the Mail Tool, and the `mailx` program, and how to customize your OpenWindows environment.

Working with Variables

A *variable* is a named memory location in which a value is stored. A number of variables provided by the Korn shell allow you to customize your working environment. Variables that affect your Solaris environment are commonly referred to as *environment variables*. For example, `HOME` is an environment variable that keeps track of your home directory. Some variables are automatically set by the Korn shell, some have a default value if not set, while others have no value unless specifically set.

After you log in, the Korn shell looks for the master profile file `/etc/profile`. The `/etc/profile` file contains *predefined variables* settings. Some of these variables are added by your system administrator. For example, a common predefined variable is `noclobber`. The `noclobber` variable ensures that you don't overwrite existing files when you use the `>` ("to") redirection symbol. All the customization options in this chapter can be changed on a temporary basis, so you can test out the option, or you can modify the related initialization file to permanently save your changes.

Storing Variables

If you enter a variable at the command line it is only effective for the current session. In most cases you will store variables in your `.profile` file. The `.profile` file is a hidden file stored in your home directory. After executing the master `/etc/profile` file, the Korn shell reads and executes the `.profile` file in your home directory. This `.profile` file contains your local environment settings, such as which directories are searched for commands and your default permissions settings. Modifying or adding a variable to your `.profile` file changes your Solaris environment for future sessions. You can also create your own variables to avoid repeatedly typing long strings of characters. The following sections explain how to list variable settings and how to change variable settings for a single session or permanently.

Listing Variables

To display your current environment variables, at the prompt, type

```
env
```

and press Return. A listing similar to the following appears:

```
HOME=/export/home/rpetrie
HISTORY=100
HZ=100
IFS=
LOGNAME=rpetrie
MAIL=/var/mail/rpetrie
MAILCHECK=600
MANPATH=/usr/openwin/share/man:/usr/man
MANSECTS=\1:1m:1c:1f:1s:1b:2:\3:3c:3i:3n:3m:3k:3g:3e:3x11:3xt:3w:
3b:9:4:5:7:8
OPTIND=1
OPENWINHOME=/usr/openwin
PATH=/usr/openwin/bin:/usr/bin:/bin:/etc:/usr/lib/lp/postscript
LD_LIBRARY_PATH=/usr/openwin/lib
PS1='$ '
PS2='> '
SHELL=/bin/ksh
TERM=sun
TZ=US/Pacific
XINTRC=/usr/openwin/lib/Xinitrc
```

The `env` command only lists the environment settings that have been set in the master `/etc/profile` file and the `.profile` file in your home directory. You can list all your Korn shell variables using the `set` command.

Changing Variables

A variable is set using a variable name, an equals sign (=), and what you want the variable set to. If you set a variable at the command line, it is only available during the current session. You must change your `.profile` file to make the variable setting effective the next time you log in. You can ignore variables in the `.profile` file by placing a pound (comment) sign (#) at the beginning of the line you want to ignore. You can also indicate multiple commands using the semicolon, just as you do when using the command line.

Before changing your `.profile` file, copy it to a file named `profile.bak` as a backup to ensure that you can return to your default settings. Once you have a backup of your original file, you can experiment with the settings and decide if you want to use the original. Because the `.profile` file is a hidden file, you may need to choose the `Customize` item from the File Manager's `View` menu to change the `Hidden Files` setting to `Show`. You cannot double-click on the `.profile` file to edit the file. Instead use the `Load` item from the Text Editor's `File` menu or drag and drop the `.profile` file into the Text Editor. Of course you can also edit the `.profile` file using the vi editor. Remember the global `profile` file with the file name `profile` is included in the `/etc` directory. The `/etc/profile` file can only be edited by your system administrator. The following lists some typical `.profile` file variable entries along with explanations.

VARIABLE	DESCRIPTION
`HOME=/home/`*`username`*	Sets the HOME variable to your default directory.
`HISTFILE=.`*`filename`*	Sets the file to store your last commands. If the HISTFILE variable is not set, the default `$HOME/` `.sh_history` file is used.

VARIABLE	DESCRIPTION
`HISTORY=25`	Sets the history mechanism to record the last 25 commands entered.
`IFS=`	Defines the internal field separator, normally the space or tab character, that is used to separate command words.
`LOGNAME=`*username*	Specifies your login name.
`MAIL=/var/mail/`*username*	Sets the path to your mailbox file for receiving mail.
`MAILCHECK=600`	Indicates in seconds how often your mailbox file is checked for mail.
`MANPATH=/usr/openwin/` `share/man:/usr/man`	Specifies which directories to check for online manual page files.

`MANSECTS=\1:1m:1c:1f:1s:1`
`b:2:\3:3c:3i:3n:3m:3k:3g:`
`3e:3x11:3xt:3w:`
`3b:9:4:5:7:8`
	Specifies the available sections of the online manual pages.

`OPENWINHOME=/usr/openwin`	Indicates the location of the OpenWindows directory.
`LD_LIBRARY_PATH=/usr/` `openwin/lib`	Specifies which directories to check for shared library files.
`SHELL=/bin/ksh`	Specifies the shell to use as the default.
`TERM=sun`	Sets your terminal type.

VARIABLE	DESCRIPTION
TZ=US/Pacific	Defines the time zone.
XINITRC=/usr/openwin/ lib/Xinitrc	Specifies which initialization script to run when starting OpenWindows.

NOTE

Any variables you don't add to the .profile file are lost when you log out of SunOS. In order to store your variables so that you don't have to recreate them each time you log in, add them to the .profile file, where SunOS stores your default variable settings.

Displaying and Referencing Variables

In order to display or reference a variable, you need to inform the Korn shell that you are referring to the contents of a variable. The dollar sign ($) indicates that a variable is being referenced. To display an existing variable's current value, enter the **echo** command followed by a $ and the variable name. For example, using the **echo** command on the variable **$OPENWINHOME** as follows,

```
echo $OPENWINHOME
```

displays

```
/usr/openwin
```

or the directory that the **$OPENWINHOME** variable is set to (where your OpenWindows program files reside).

Saving Time with the PATH Variable

The **PATH** variable is the most important variable in your `.profile` file. This variable identifies directories that the system should look in for commands you enter at the command line. Regardless of your current directory, SunOS will search through the directories, from left to right, in your **PATH** variable for the command you are executing. The path statement needs to exist to allow access to SunOS commands. If a command is not found, the following error message is displayed:

```
/bin/ksh: command:  not found
```

The default **PATH** is `/bin:/usr/bin`. A colon (:) by itself in the **PATH** statement specifies to check the current directory. Enter `$PATH` to display your **PATH** variable. The following is an example of a typical path statement:

```
PATH=:/bin:/usr/bin:/etc/:usr/lib/lp/postscript
```

This path setting instructs Solaris to check the current directory :, the `/bin` directory, then `/usr/bin`, `/etc/`, and lastly the `usr/lib/lp/postscript`. Note that each directory is separated by a space and each directory in the path statement is separated by a colon.

WARNING Adding several directories to your PATH can slow down system performance because each directory is checked each time you execute a command.

By default, the current directory is not checked. If you need to run a program that is in the current directory, use the period (.) to indicate the current directory. For example, if you changed to the `/usr/openwin/bin` directory to run the **openwin** command, you need to enter

```
./openwin
```

If you find that you are frequently changing to a directory to run a command, add the directory containing the command to your **PATH** variable. After adding the directory to your **PATH** variable, you can have your changes take effect without restarting OpenWindows. Make sure you are in your

HOME directory and at the shell prompt, enter

```
./.profile
```

Then you can execute the program without changing directories.

Simplifying Directory Navigation

The CDPATH variable contains a list of colon-separated directories to check when a full path name is not given to the cd command. Each directory in CDPATH is searched from left to right for a directory that matches the cd argument. A colon (:) alone in CDPATH stands for the current directory. For example, adding the line

```
CDPATH=:/home/ataylor:/usr/openwin
```

indicates to check the current directory first, /home/ataylor, then /usr/openwin, when cd is not given a full path name. Instead of typing cd /usr/openwin/lib, you can type cd lib; or to change directory to /home/ataylor/bin, you can type:

```
cd bin
```

By default the CDPATH variable is not set, so you will have to add it to your .profile file.

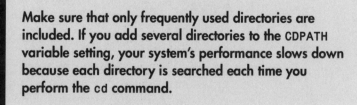

WARNING Make sure that only frequently used directories are included. If you add several directories to the CDPATH variable setting, your system's performance slows down because each directory is searched each time you perform the cd command.

Specifying How Long to Wait for Input

The TMOUT variable specifies the number of seconds that the Korn shell will wait for input before displaying a 60-second warning message and exiting. By default, the TMOUT variable is disabled (set to 0) meaning there is no time limit for the Korn shell to wait for input before displaying a 60-second warning message and exiting. This variable is usually set by the system administrator in the /etc/profile file. To set a 5-minute timer, add the following line to your .profile file.

```
TMOUT=300
```

Customizing Your Command Prompt

There are four prompt variables in the Korn shell. The prompt variable begins with PS and is followed by the number of the prompt. Typically you will only use PS1 and PS2; these contain the primary prompts displayed by the Korn shell when it is ready to read a command. If not specified, the default is $ for regular users, and # for superusers. PS2 specifies the secondary prompt string and is displayed whenever the Korn shell needs more input. For example, the PS2 variable is displayed when you press Return before a complete command has been given, or continue a command onto the next line with the \ character. If not specified, the default for PS2 is the > character, as shown in the following example.

```
$ print "This is the first line \
> This is the second"
```

You can change the prompt by assigning a new value to the PS1 variable. For example, entering

```
PS1="Your Wish, Master: "
```

displays a prompt message like this:

```
Your Wish, Master:
```

This is a cute prompt but not very helpful. To customize your prompt to display the current command number so you can easily reexecute commands and display the working directory, use the ! and the PWD variable.

```
PS1='!:${PWD} $ '
```

If you really want to display a ! in the prompt, type two exclamation points instead of one (!!). Using the single exclamation point changes the prompt to display the current history command number. The $PWD variable displays the current working directory. The following shows examples of changing directories using the prompt entry `PS1='!:${PWD} $ '`:

```
67:/home/ataylor $ cd /tmp
68:/tmp $ cd /usr/mail/ataylor
69:/usr/mail/ataylor $
```

Creating Your Own Variables

Besides the Korn shell's predefined variables in the `.profile` file, you can also create your own variables and add them to your `.profile` file. Remember, variables you create are lost when you log out, unless you add them to the `.profile` file. Be sure to make a backup copy of your `.profile` file to ensure that you can return to your default settings. Once you have a backup of your original file, you can experiment with the settings.

To assign the name and value of a variable, follow the variable name you want by an equal sign and the string of characters you want to assign to the variable. An example of setting a variable is to assign an abbreviation to a long path name. For example, the command

```
sounds=/usr/openwin/lib/locale/C/help/handbooks/sounds
```

allows you to type `$sounds` to indicate the `/usr/openwin/lib/locale/C/help/handbooks/sounds` directory.

WARNING
The Korn shell is sensitive to white space in variable settings. Don't add a space on either side of the equal sign. Only add a space in a variable setting that is within the double quotes.

Unsetting a Variable

The `unset` command lets you unset a variable. For example, if you have a variable named X and do not want the variable to be active, you can unset the variable as follows:

```
unset X
```

Storing Commands and Path Names as a Variable

Instead of typing out long, complicated commands or path names, you can store them as array variables. An array variable lets you specify one variable from a list of variables. You store a list of words as array variables by assigning each array variable a value using the following syntax:

```
variable[0]=value variable[1]=value variable[2]=value
variable[3]=value
```

For example, entering

```
opus[0]=frame/chaps opus[1]=frame/notes opus[2]=frame/docs
opus[3]=frame/tmp
```

specifies the directories `frame/chaps`, `frame/notes`, `frame/docs`, and `frame/tmp` as words in a variable list.

You specify a word in a variable list by entering a $ and inserting the word and word number in curly braces; for instance, using the **opus** variable example above and entering the command

```
echo ${opus[2]}
```

displays the second value in the list of variables, which in the previous example is

```
frame/docs
```

To display the first and last array variable in the previous example, enter

```
echo ${opus[0]} ${opus[3]}
```

This displays `frame/chaps` and `frame/tmp`.

Output Substitution and Variables

Output substitution allows you to use the output of a command as an argument for another command. Using output substitution with other commands, such as **echo**, can make displaying the output of a command a lot less cryptic. To substitute a variable with command output, use the following format:

```
variable=$(command)
```

You can also surround a command with back quote marks (`); the command within the back quote marks or parentheses is executed and substitutes the resulting output for the variable. For example, suppose you have a list of file names stored in a file called **printlist**; entering **lp `cat printlist`** prints each file listed in the file **printlist**. The following example uses output substitution to assign the current date to a variable named **day**.

```
day=$(date)
echo The date and time is $day
```

displays

```
The date and time is Sat Jan 22 12:00:00 PDT 1994
```

The **set** command can be used to set the words of the command line to variables **$0** through **$9**. This lets you extract selected pieces of data from the output of a command. For example, entering

```
set $(date)
```

sets the **$0** variable so that it refers to the command. The **$1** variable refers to Sat. Each following word is assigned the subsequent variable number. Therefore, by specifying the fifth word (**$4**) of the date command's output, you can extract the time. For example, entering

```
echo The time is $4 $5
```

displays

```
The time is 12:00:00 PDT
```

Customizing Korn Shell Options

The Korn shell has a number of options that specify your environment and control execution. There are options that cause background jobs to be run at a lower priority, prevent files from being overwritten with redirection operators, disable file name expansion, enable vi-style commands when editing the command line, and more.

Besides variables, the Korn shell lets you use a variety of options. Korn shell options are enabled with the **set -o** *option*, **set** *-option*, or **ksh -o** command. You can disable a command by entering the set +o *option* or set +*option* command. You can list settings to determine if they are on or off by entering

```
set -o
```

The first column lists the option name, and the second shows if the option is enabled or disabled, as shown in the following:

```
Current option settings
allexport       off
bgnice          on
emacs           off
errexit         off
gmacs           off
ignoreeof       off
interactive     on
keyword         off
markdirs        off
monitor         on
noexec          off
noclobber       off
noglob          off
nolog           off
nounset         off
privileged      off
restricted      off
trackall        off
verbose         off
```

```
vi              off
viraw           off
xtrace          off
```

As with variables, you can temporarily set an option from the command line. To permanently set an option, add it the `.profile` file in your home directory. Before changing your `.profile` file, be sure to copy it to a file named `.profile.bak` as a backup to ensure that you can return to your default settings. Once you have a backup of your original file, you can experiment with the settings and decide if you want to use the original. The following sections explain some common options you can use to customize the Korn shell.

Running Background Jobs at a Reduced Priority

The `bgnice` option runs in the background, saving you from having to run the `nice` command. When you enable the `bgnice` option, all background jobs are automatically run at a reduced priority, as if you had used the `nice` command to start them. To enable the `bgnice` option, enter

```
set -o bgnice
```

Any background jobs you start by adding an `&` at the end of the command line are run at a reduced priority.

Displaying and Changing a Logout Message

Typically, pressing Control-d at the system prompt logs you out or closes the active `Shell Tool` or `Command Tool` window. The `setignoreeof` option disables Control-d. To have the system prompt you to end a session by typing exit rather than using Control-d, enter

```
set -o ignoreeof
```

When you press Control-d, the message `Use 'exit' to logout` appears. If this variable is not set, pressing Control-d is the same as issuing the `exit` command. By default, this option is disabled.

Marking Directories

When enabled, the `markdirs` option appends directory names with a /
and list the contents of each subdirectory. The `markdirs` option is similar
to listing files using the `ls -F`, except that you only see the results when
using wildcard expansion. Enabling the `markdirs` option produces an organized listing of subdirectories and their contents, which makes listing
subdirectories and their contents a breeze. However, the `markdirs` option
is only effective for listing files using wildcard characters. By default, the
`markdirs` option is disabled. This means that entering `ls` displays a listing
similar to this:

```
Application    Document    bin    images    mail
```

enabling the `markdirs` option by entering

```
set -o markdirs
```

and entering `ls *` displays a listing similar to this:

```
Application              Document
bin/:
answerbook               cdplayer              killfish
images/:
book.icon                bricks                force.x
book_glyph_mask.icon     clouds                snapshot.rs
mail/:
letter                   proposal              report
```

Disabling File Name Substitution

The `noglob` option disables file name substitution and can be set using
either of these commands:

```
set -f
```

or

```
set -o noglob
```

Protecting Files

The `noclobber` option prevents redirection from overwriting (*clobbering*) existing files when using the > ("to") redirection symbol. By default, this option is disabled. To enable the `noclobber` option, enter:

```
set -o noclobber
```

If you enter a redirection command that will overwrite an existing file, the system responds with a message informing you that the file already exists. If `noclobber` is enabled, and you really want to overwrite a file, use the >| operator as follows:

```
ls>|out.txt
```

Displaying an Error Message for Unset Variables

The `unset` command lets you unset a variable. The `nounset` option causes the Korn shell to display an error message when it tries to expand a variable that is not set or has been unset. By default, the `nounset` option is disabled. The Korn shell interprets unset variables as if their values were null. To enable the `nounset` option, enter

```
set -o nounset
```

The Korn shell displays an error message when it encounters unset variables and causes the command to abort, as shown in the following example.

```
unset X
print $X
/bin/ksh: X: parameter not set
```

Changing Command Line Editing Modes

If you are familiar with the vi editor, you can make the same commands available for editing the command line. Using the vi editing commands, you can navigate and edit any part of the command line to make changes, just as you would to edit a line in vi. To enable vi command line editing, enter

    set -o vi

You can also substitute the vi argument with either **emacs** or **gmacs** to enable **emacs** or **gmacs** editing commands.

Changing the Default File Permissions

One of the first lines in the master `/etc/.profile` file contains the **umask** command. The **umask** command sets the default file and directory permissions assigned to the files and directories you create. The syntax for the **umask** command is

    umask *nnn*

where each *n* is a number that sets the permissions for files and directories for the owner, group, and public. The first number indicates the owner permissions; the second, group permissions; the last, public permissions. The **umask** command uses different values for permissions than the **chmod** command. The default setting for the **umask** command is usually **022**, which assigns *files* with read and write permissions for the owner and read only to other users (`-rw-r--r--`). The **022** setting assigns *directories* with read, write, and execute permissions for the owner, execute and read permissions for groups, and execute permissions to the public (`drwxr-xr-x`). The following lists the file and directory permissions used with **umask**.

NUMBER	FILE PERMISSION	DIRECTORY PERMISSION
0	rw-	rwx
1	rw-	rw-
2	r--	r-x
3	r--	r--
4	-w-	-wx

NUMBER	FILE PERMISSION	DIRECTORY PERMISSION
5	-w-	-w-
6	---	--x
7	---	---

Working with Aliases

Aliases give you the power to rename any command with a name you can more easily remember. For example, if you're new to Solaris but familiar with the MS-DOS operating system, you might frequently find yourself entering the DOS command dir instead of ls to list a directory's contents. Assigning an alias named dir to the command ls enables you to use the list command by typing either dir or ls. When Solaris processes your commands, the command line is scanned from left to right to see if it contains an alias. If a command line has an alias, the SunOS command that matches the alias is used. Aliases may already be available to you, depending on how your system administrator has set up your account. Typing the **alias** command by itself displays all defined aliases.

Some aliases may already be predefined by your system administrator. For example, the **cp** (copy) and **mv** (move) commands may have the interactive option (-i) added to prevent you from accidentally overwriting files by prompting you when existing files are going to be overwritten. If you want to save your alias for future sessions, simply add the alias to your .profile file.

Creating an Alias

To create an alias, type **alias** followed by the name you want to assign as the alias, then type the command you want to match the alias. For example, **alias dir=ls** enables you to type either dir or ls to obtain a directory listing. Using the **alias** command, you can abbreviate long command lines. To create an alias for multiword strings, enclose the multiword string in quotes. For example, typing **alias lc="ls -l chap*"** causes the system to display a long listing of all the files in the working directory beginning with `chap` whenever you enter `lc`. Note that the asterisk (*) wildcard character is enclosed *inside* the quotation marks. Both single and double quotation marks can be used to indicate multi-word text. If you frequently use the `history` command, try adding the following to your `.profile` file:

```
alias h=history
```

You can now get a `history` listing by simply typing the letter `h`.

Undoing an Alias

You remove an alias by entering the `unalias` command, followed by the alias name. For example, entering

```
unalias dir
```

removes the `dir` alias.

Customizing Mail Program Variables

The `.mailrc` file works similarly to the `.profile` file, except that it stores aliases and variables relating to the mail program for sending and receiving electronic mail. The `.mailrc` file is usually stored in your home directory. While the `.profile` file provides a few variables that allow you to specify how often to check for mail, where to send your mail, what your mail notification message is, and the search path for mailbox files, there are many additional mail variables that affect both the `mailx` program and the DeskSet.

The `.mailrc` file contains many predefined variables. You can turn default mail variable settings off by preceding the predefined variable with `no`. For example, to turn the variable `hold` off, add `no` to the `hold` variable as follows: `set nohold`. If a file is indicated by a variable, it's set with an equal sign; for example, `MBOX=mbox` sets the storage mailbox for your mail to the file named `mbox`. The following is a list of `.mailrc` variables and their default settings.

VARIABLE	PURPOSE	DEFAULT SETTING
append	Adds letters to the end of `mbox`.	off
askcc	Displays the carbon copy prompt `Cc:` when writing a letter.	on
asksub	Prompts for a subject when writing a letter.	on
autoprint	Displays the next letter in the mailbox when one is deleted.	off
DEAD	Stores partial letters in case of interruption, such as a power failure.	Sends the contents to a file called `dead.letter` in your home directory.
dot	Makes a single dot (period) act as the termination character to indicate the end of a letter.	off (set to on in the global start-up file)
EDITOR	Determines which editor to use when composing letters.	ed
folder	Determines which directory contains your mail folders.	`mail`

VARIABLE	PURPOSE	DEFAULT SETTING
header	Causes the header list to be displayed when you enter the `mail` command.	on
hold	Holds letters in your mailbox until you save or delete them.	off
ignoreof	Changes the end-of-file character to a period or the tilde character rather than Control-d.	off
keep	Retains your mailbox even if it's empty. When set to `nokeep`, the mailbox is removed until you receive mail.	off
keepsave	Prevents `mail` from deleting a letter from your mailbox when you save the letter in another file or folder.	off
MBOX	Specifies which file letters are stored in after they've been read.	The `mbox` file in your home directory.

VARIABLE	PURPOSE	DEFAULT SETTING
metoo	Sends letters to yourself when you send a letter to an alias group of which you're a member.	off
outfolder	Keeps a record of every letter you send in a folder named outfolder.	off
page	Ejects a page after each letter.	off
prompt	Sets the mail prompt.	&;
quiet	Suppresses the initial mail program display of its version number and a short sample letter.	off
save	Saves partial letters into the file specified in the DEAD variable setting.	on
SHELL	The name of the command interpreter.	Set from the environment setting.

VARIABLE	PURPOSE	DEFAULT SETTING
showto	Displays the letter's recipient rather than your name when sending copies of letters to yourself or letters to a group of which you're a member.	off

Indicating How Often to Check for Mail

The MAILCHECK variable specifies how often, in seconds, to check for new mail. If not set, or set to zero, new mail is checked before each new prompt is displayed. Otherwise, the default setting is **600** seconds (10 minutes).

Specifying Where to Send Your Mail

The MAIL variable contains the name of the mailbox file to check for new mail. It is not used if MAILPATH is set. The MAILPATH variable contains a colon-separated list of mailbox files to check for new mail and is used if you want to read multiple mailboxes. It overrides the MAIL variable if both are set. This MAILPATH setting specifies to check two mailbox files, /home/ataylor/mbox and /news/mbox.

    MAILPATH=/home/ataylor/mbox:/news/mbox

This only works if you have read permission on the mailbox file. If MAILPATH is not set, there is no default.

Changing Your Mail Notification Message

When you get new mail, the Korn shell displays this message on your terminal right before the prompt: you have mail in mailbox-file. You can also create your own mail notification message by appending a ? followed by your message to the mailbox files given in MAILPATH. If you wanted your message to be "Check your mail," then MAILPATH would be set like this:

```
MAILPATH=homeataylor/mbox?'Check your mail'
```

Adding an Alias for Sending Mail to a Group

You can add aliases to your .mailrc file to define a group of user names as a single name. For example, adding the following line to the .mailrc file

```
alias mailist lricardo@desilu sbertrille@santanco
janderson@springfield
```

allows you to send a letter to lricardo, sbertrille, and jandrson at their respective machines via the mail program, using the alias name mailist. The Mail Tool also lets you create and store aliases for sending mail to a group. This is explained in Chapter 3, "The Multimedia Mail Tool Makes Mail Easy."

Customizing Your Terminal Settings

The TERM variable is not used by the Korn shell, but several other programs, such as the vi editor, look for this variable. It specifies your terminal settings, and is usually set in the /etc/profile file by your system administrator. For example, if you start vi and open an existing file and get garbage on your screen, or the vi commands are not working correctly, try resetting the TERM variable. If you are using a Sun terminal, add the following line to your .profile file:

```
TERM=sun
```

If you are using Solaris 2 for x86, add the line

```
TERM=AT386
```

Changing the Backspace and Delete Key Assignment

In most cases, you will not need to change the default key assignment; however, if you find that the Delete or Backspace keys are not set correctly, you can easily change them. The `stty` command lets you set how the Backspace and Delete keys work. On some Sun workstation keyboards the default setting for the Backspace key is # and Delete is sometimes set to @. If your Backspace key doesn't work, try pressing Control-h to delete the previous character and pressing Control-u to delete an entire line. You can change the Backspace key so that you can erase the previous character when you press the Backspace key and erase an entire line by pressing Delete. The `stty` command is normally placed in your `.profile` file. To change the Backspace key setting, enter

```
stty erase <Back Space>
```

The notation `<Back Space>` indicates that you should press the Backspace key. You can also assign the Backspace key by specifying the ASCII code Control-h. Use the caret (^) to indicate the Control key as follows

```
stty erase \^H
```

To change the Delete key to delete the entire line, enter

```
stty kill <Delete>
```

The notation `<Delete>` indicates that you should press the Delete key. If you make an error before typing Return, you can press the Backspace to erase the error or press the Delete key to erase the entire line.

Changing Keyboard Preferences

The `xset` command lets you set how the keyboard bell sounds and the volume of the keyboard clicks, and lets you control the keyboard's auto-repeat feature. The `b` option lets you control the bell volume, pitch, and duration. The syntax for the `xset` option is

```
xset b volume pitch duration
```

The *volume* parameter can be any number from 1 to 100. The *pitch* is measured in hertz and can be set from 1 to 1000 hertz. The *duration* can be anywhere from 1 to 1000 milliseconds. If no parameters are given, the system defaults are used. You can turn off the keyboard bell by setting the volume parameter to 0. If only one parameter is given, the bell volume is set to that value. If two values are listed, the second parameter specifies the bell pitch. For example, the command:

```
xset b 50 500 50
```

sets the volume of the keyboard bell to 50 percent of its maximum loudness, the pitch to 500 hertz, and the duration to 50 milliseconds.

The `xset` command's `c` option sets the volume of the keyboard's key click. The syntax for the keyboard click is

```
xset c volume
```

The *volume* can be a value from 1 to 100, indicating a percentage of the maximum volume. For example,

```
xset c 100
```

sets each key to click at the highest volume. You can turn the key click off by using the value 0. Alternatively, you can also use the parameters on or off. If you specify the on parameter, the system default for volume is used.

If you hold a key down and the keystroke is repeated over and over again, the keyboard's auto-repeat feature is enabled. If the auto-repeat feature is not enabled, you can enable the keyboard's auto-repeat feature by entering

```
xset r on
```

Enter `xset -r off` to disable key repeat feature.

Modifying Your OpenWindows Environment

The `.Xdefaults` file contains the basic properties you set for the Workspace as well as any special settings you might add. To view and edit the `.Xdefaults` file, open the file from your home directory using any text editor. Figure 15.1 shows an example of an `.Xdefaults` file. The variables that you can edit appear after the colon on each line.

NOTE   The entries in the `.Xdefaults` file vary depending upon the type of monitor you have and the settings you choose from the Workspace Properties window. Additionally, the order of the settings varies.

Changing Screensavers

The `Lock Screen` item found in the `Utilities` submenu of the `Workspace` menu displays a screen of randomly appearing Sun logos and locks your screen so that a password needs to be entered to return to OpenWindows. This feature is especially helpful when you will be away from your terminal for an extend period of time. You don't have to use the standard screensaver; you can lock your screen and specify another screensaver feature by using the following syntax.

```
xlock -mode screensaver
```

Adding the `nolock` argument lets you enable a screensaver without locking your screen.

```
xlock -mode screensaver -nolock
```

FIGURE 15.1

A sample .Xdefaults file

```
Text Editor V3.1 - .Xdefaults, dir; /usr/home/rpetrie

File ▽    View ▽    Edit ▽    Find ▽

OpenWindows.WorkspaceColor:      #ffffff
OpenWindows.WindowColor:         #cccccc
OpenWindows.IconLocation:        bottom
OpenWindows.DragRightDistance:   100
OpenWindows.SelectDisplaysMenu:  False
OpenWindows.SetInput:    followmouse
OpenWindows.Beep:        always
OpenWindows.ScrollbarPlacement:  right
OpenWindows.PopupJumpCursor:     True
OpenWindows.MultiClickTimeout:   4
Scrollbar.JumpCursor:    True
*basicLocale:    C
*displayLang:    C
*inputLang:      C
*numeric:        C
*timeFormat:     C
```

Substitute the *screensaver* variable with one of the following screensavers.

SCREENSAVER	DESCRIPTION
hop	Shows the "real plane fractals" from the September 1986 issue of *Scientific American*.
life	Displays Conway's Game of Life.

SCREENSAVER	DESCRIPTION
`qix`	Displays spinning lines similar to those in the video game of the same name.
`image`	Shows several Sun logos randomly appearing on the screen.
`swarm`	Shows a swarm of bees following a wasp.
`roto`	Shows a swirling rotor.
`pyro`	Shows fireworks.
`flame`	Shows some interesting fractals.
`blank`	Shows a blank screen.
`random`	Picks a random mode of all the above except `blank` mode.

The **xset** command lets you enable a screensaver that makes the screen go blank after a period of no use. To use the **xset** command to enable the screensaver, enter

```
xset s on
```

You can specify how much time to wait before invoking the screensaver. For example, entering

```
xset s 300
```

sets the system to wait 5 minutes (300 seconds) before blanking the screen.

To restore your desktop, move the mouse in any direction. Although input from any keyboard key or mouse button will restore your screen, move the mouse instead. Pressing a key creates system input, so if the pointer is positioned in a text file, you may insert a character in the text. This option is turned off by default.

When you quit OpenWindows, the screensaver feature will be disabled again, and you must enter the **xset** command again to enable it. To disable the screensaver with the command line, enter

```
xset s off
```

Turning On the Screensaver Permanently

The `$OPENWIN/lib/Xinitrc/` file stores the initial OpenWindows startup script (a script is a file containing commands). If you want to turn the screensaver feature on automatically, you must copy and rename the Xinitrc file to .xinitrc in your home directory. To do this, enter

```
cp $OPENWINHOME/lib/Xinitrc $HOME/.xinitrc
```

Open the `.Xinitrc` file using any text editor and add the line

```
xset s on
```

to the end of the file. Save the changes and quit the editor. The next time you start OpenWindows, the screensaver will be active. If you want to disable the screensaver feature, simply add a # in front of the `xset` command line (comment out) or remove the `xset` command from the `.xinitrc` file and restart OpenWindows.

Customizing the Workspace

The `xsetroot` command allows you to tailor the appearance of the Workspace (background) window. The `xsetroot` command includes several options. You can display a solid color background, a pattern, or a tiled bitmap image as your background. The following explains how to change the Workspace using the `xsetroot` command.

To set the Workspace to a solid color, use the `-solid` option followed by the color you want to change the Workspace to. The next section includes a listing of some of the colors you can choose from when you want to change the color of the root window. For example, entering

```
xsetroot -solid lightsteelblue
```

changes the Workspace to a light steel blue color.

The `-bitmap` option followed by the name of the bitmap file lets you display a tiled image as your background. Entering the command line

```
xsetroot -bitmap $OPENWINHOME/share/include/X11/bitmaps/mensetmanus
```

displays the background shown in Figure 15.2.

FIGURE 15.2

A tiled bitmap image background

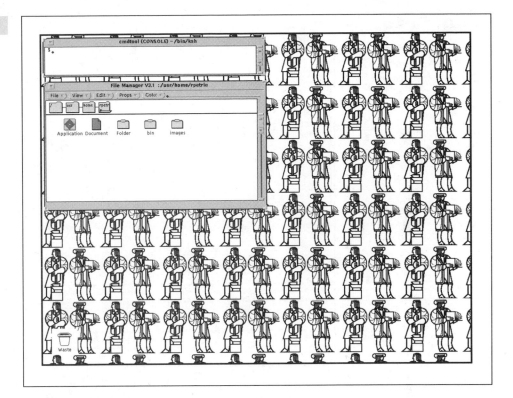

> **NOTE**
>
> Displaying a complex bitmap picture eats up more memory than a solid background. Each time a window is displayed, OpenWindows must repaint the screen. If you are running low on memory, use a solid background rather than a complex bitmap picture.

By default, the background color of a bitmap image is black and the foreground color is white. The `-fg color` option sets the foreground color of the Workspace. The `-bg color` option sets the background color of the Workspace. The following displays a bitmap image named `force.x` with a snow background and a gray foreground, as shown in Figure 15.3. Note

FIGURE 15.3

A bitmap image with
a snow background
and a gray foreground

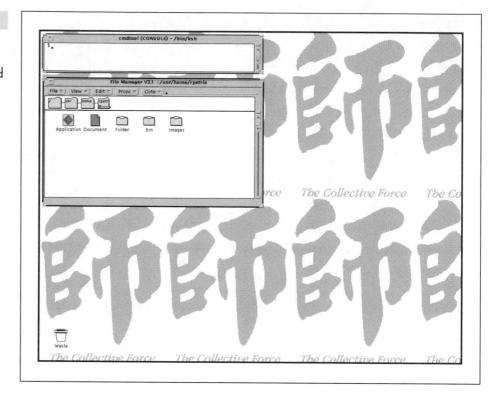

that the `force.x` file is used only as an example of foreground and background colors. It is not a file that comes with Solaris.

```
xsetroot -bitmap $HOME/images/force.x -bg snow -fg gray
```

You can reverse the foreground and background color by adding the `-rv` or `-reverse` option with another option. Using the `-rv` option without another specified option changes the Workspace to the default state. The following reverses the background color of the previous example.

```
xsetroot -bitmap $HOME/force.x -bg snow -fg gray -rv
```

The `-mod x y` option lets you display a grid pattern as your background. The x and y arguments can be any number from 0 to 16. For example, entering

```
xsetroot -mod 3 12
```

displays a plaid pattern as your Workspace background.

TIP

The OpenWindows demo program `realxfishdb` stored in the `$OPENWINHOME/demo` directory lets you create a background of a realistic aquarium with fish that swim behind your windows. You can change the types of fish in the aquarium by using the program `fish_props` in the same directory. A section on how to add a menu of options to display the aquarium background, change the fish, and remove the aquarium background is included at the end of this chapter.

Changing Windows to Display in Inverse Video

Some users find that it reduces eye strain to change windows to display white text on a black background instead of black text on a white background. To change your display, add the following two lines to the `.Xdefaults` file in your home directory using any text editor.

```
window.color.foreground: white
window.color.background: black
```

Save the changes and quit the editor.

In order for your changes to take effect, you need to run the **xrdb** command to read the contents of the `.Xdefaults` resource database. At the system prompt in a Command Tool or Shell Tool, enter

```
xrdb .Xdefaults
```

Any DeskSet applications you open after making this change are displayed in inverse video. To revert to black on white, just remove the **window.color** lines from the `.Xdefaults` file, save the changes, and again type the **xrdb** `.Xdefaults` command in a Command Tool or Shell Tool window.

Specifying a Window's Colors

One of the richest customization features of Solaris is the variety of colors that can be assigned to the Workspace, windows, and icons. There are over 900 colors that you can assign. The following is a list of some of the predefined colors. For a complete listing of the colors, enter the following command

```
showrgb | more
```

This displays the contents of the `rgb.txt` file that stores your color options. The `rgb.txt` file is located in the `/usr/openwin/lib` directory. Although some color names appear in the `rgb.txt` file as two or more words, you must eliminate any spaces when specifying a color. The following lists the primary RGB (Red Green Blue) color settings (0–255) that you can enter when using OpenWindows' Color Chooser (such as in the Icon Editor or the Binder), and the color names for setting colors from the command line.

COLOR CODE	COLOR
255 250 250	snow
248 248 255	ghostwhite
250 235 215	antiquewhite
255 228 196	bisque
255 218 185	peachpuff
255 222 173	navajowhite
255 248 220	cornsilk
255 255 240	ivory
255 250 205	lemonchiffon
255 245 238	seashell
240 255 240	honeydew
240 255 255	azure
230 230 250	lavender
255 240 245	lavenderblush
255 228 225	mistyrose
255 255 255	white
0 0 0	black
47 79 79	darkslategray
105 105 105	dimgray

COLOR CODE	COLOR
112 128 144	slategray
119 136 153	lightslategray
192 192 192	gray
211 211 211	lightgray
25 25 112	midnightblue
0 0 128	navy
100 149 237	cornflowerblue
72 61 139	darkslateblue
106 90 205	slateblue
123 104 238	mediumslateblue
132 112 255	lightslateblue
0 0 205	mediumblue
65 105 225	royalblue
0 0 255	blue
30 144 255	dodgerblue
0 191 255	deepskyblue
135 206 235	skyblue
135 206 250	lightskyblue
70 130 180	steelblue
176 196 222	lightsteelblue
173 216 230	lightblue
176 224 230	powderblue
175 238 238	paleturquoise
0 206 209	darkturquoise
72 209 204	mediumturquoise
64 224 208	turquoise
0 255 255	cyan

COLOR CODE	COLOR
224 255 255	lightcyan
95 158 160	cadetblue
102 205 170	mediumaquamarine
127 255 212	aquamarine
0 100 0	darkgreen
85 107 47	darkolivegreen
143 188 143	darkseagreen
46 139 87	seagreen
60 179 113	mediumseagreen
32 178 170	lightseagreen
152 251 152	palegreen
0 255 127	springgreen
124 252 0	lawngreen
0 255 0	green
127 255 0	chartreuse
0 250 154	mediumspringgreen
173 255 47	greenyellow
50 205 50	limegreen
154 205 50	yellowgreen
34 139 34	forestgreen
107 142 35	olivedrab
189 183 107	darkkhaki
240 230 140	khaki
238 232 170	palegoldenrod
250 250 210	lightgoldenrodyellow
255 255 224	lightyellow
255 255 0	yellow

COLOR CODE	COLOR
255 215 0	gold
238 221 130	lightgoldenrod
218 165 32	goldenrod
184 134 11	darkgoldenrod
188 143 143	rosybrown
205 92 92	indianred
139 69 19	saddlebrown
160 82 45	sienna
205 133 63	peru
222 184 135	burlywood
245 245 220	beige
245 222 179	wheat
210 180 140	tan
210 105 30	chocolate
178 34 34	firebrick
165 42 42	brown
250 128 114	salmon
255 160 122	lightsalmon
255 165 0	orange
255 140 0	darkorange
255 127 80	coral
240 128 128	lightcoral
255 99 71	tomato
255 69 0	orangered
255 0 0	red
255 105 180	hotpink
255 20 147	deeppink

COLOR CODE	COLOR
255 192 203	pink
255 182 193	lightpink
219 112 147	palevioletred
176 48 96	maroon
208 32 144	violetred
255 0 255	magenta
238 130 238	violet
221 160 221	plum
218 112 214	orchid
186 85 211	mediumorchid
138 43 226	blueviolet
160 32 240	purple
147 112 219	mediumpurple
216 191 216	thistle
3 3 3	gray1
127 127 127	gray50
255 255 255	gray100

Changing the Mouse Pointer

Besides customizing your background, the `xsetroot` command also lets you customize the mouse pointer. To change the mouse pointer, use the following syntax

```
xsetroot -cursor_name cursor-fontname
```

Figure 15.4 shows the available cursors and cursor names from which you can choose. To display the different types of cursor fonts and cursor font

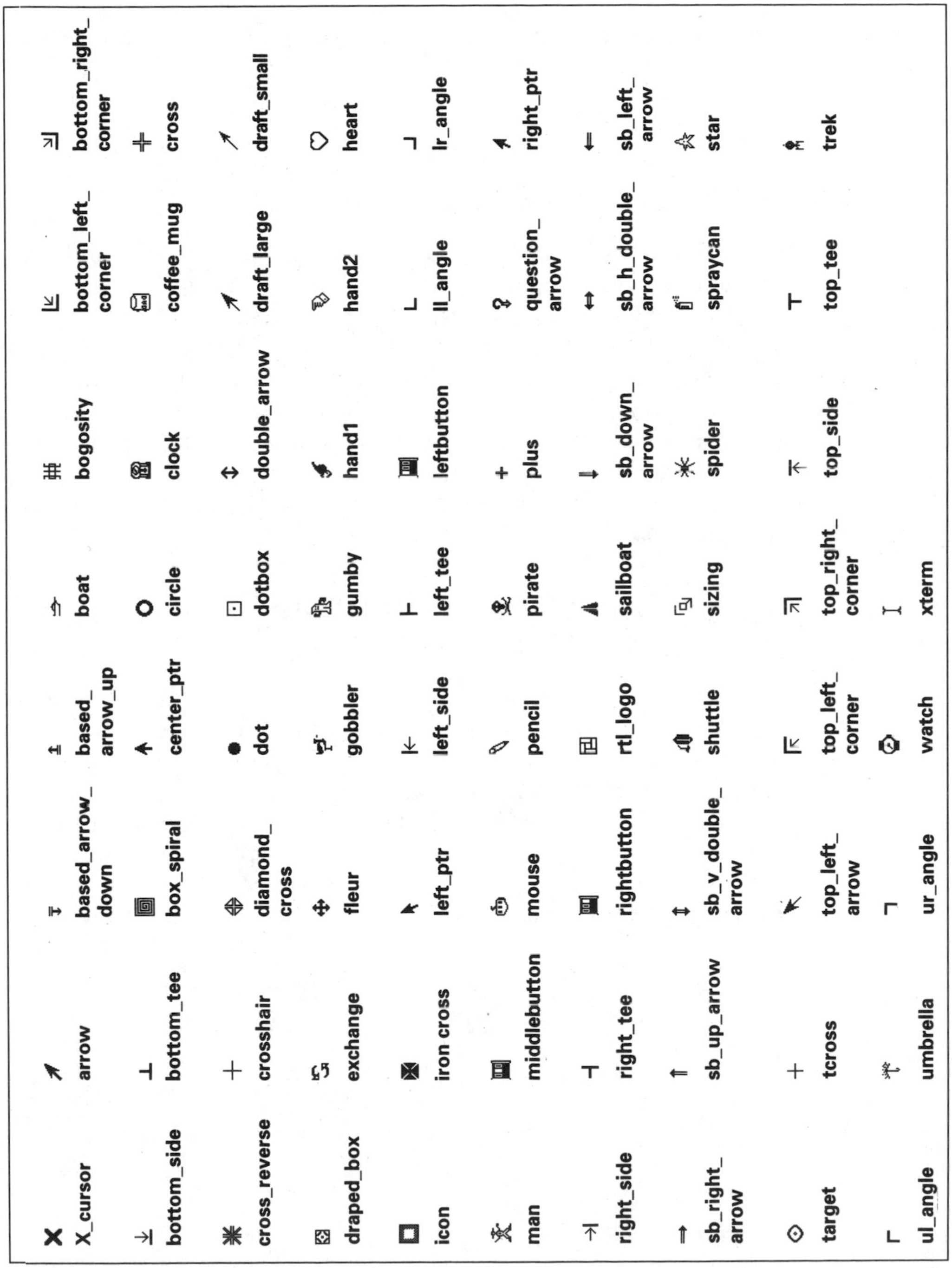

X_cursor	arrow	based_arrow_down	based_arrow_up	bogosity	bottom_left_corner	bottom_right_corner
bottom_side	bottom_tee	box_spiral	center_ptr	clock	coffee_mug	cross
cross_reverse	crosshair	diamond_cross	dot	double_arrow	draft_large	draft_small
draped_box	exchange	fleur	gobbler	gumby	hand1	hand2	heart
icon	iron_cross	left_ptr	left_side	leftbutton	left_tee	ll_angle	lr_angle
man	middlebutton	mouse	pencil	pirate	plus	question_arrow	right_ptr
right_side	right_tee	rightbutton	rtl_logo	sailboat	sb_down_arrow	sb_h_double_arrow	sb_left_arrow
sb_right_arrow	sb_up_arrow	sb_v_double_arrow	shuttle	sizing	spider	spraycan	star
target	tcross	top_left_arrow	top_left_corner	top_right_corner	top_side	top_tee	trek
ul_angle	umbrella	ur_angle	watch	xterm

FIGURE 15.4

The available cursors and cursor names

background masks on your screen, enter the following in a `Command Tool` or `Shell Tool` window

```
xfd -fn cursor
```

Customizing Fonts

OpenWindows DeskSet applications are set up with default fonts, that is characters available in a particular size, style, and weight, for icons, menus, and windows. However, you can change the default font style and size in windows and window headers. The following explain two methods of customizing fonts: changing the scale of the font (which also affects the window's size), and changing the font style and specifying a different point size. The first method simply increases or decreases the font size (to small, large, or extra large) and the corresponding size of the window, while the second provides greater flexibility in defining the style and specific size.

Specifying the Scale for One Application

You can open a single application with a modified font size from the Shell Tool or Command Tool. You must start a new application to display the new font. To open an application and change the font (and window) scale, type the application name followed by the scale command (-`scale`) and the desired size. The following example opens a Text Editor in the small size:

```
textedit -scale small &
```

Figure 15.5 shows a small and standard Text Editor window.

FIGURE 15.5

A small and standard
Text Editor window

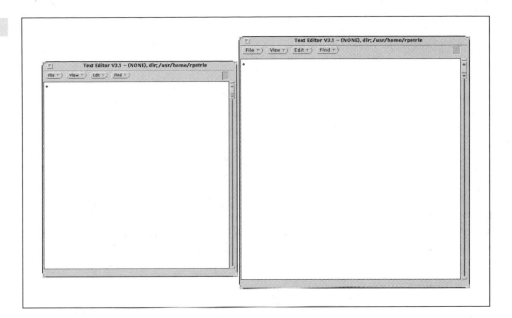

NOTE

The small Text Editor window appears open on
the Workspace. Adding the ampersand (&) returns the
window prompt and enables you to continue using the
Shell Tool or Command Tool window while the Text
Editor window is running. Otherwise, you would not
be able to use the Shell Tool or Command Tool
window until you quit the Text Editor.

The following lists the program names of the DeskSet Tools, which you
can use to execute the program from the Shell Tool or Command Tool.

```
audiotool
binder
calctool
clock
cm
cmdtool
filemgr
```

```
iconedit
mailtool
perfmeter
printtool
shelltool
snapshot
tapetool
textedit
```

Choosing a Font Scale

The scale utility enables you to choose from four font sizes for windows. You can make this change for one or more select windows, or you can change the default so that all applications subsequently open in the size you specify. When you scale the font, the window scales with it. Not all font styles and sizes appear on the screen satisfactorily. If the size is too large, some items, such as menu buttons, may be obscured. You can choose from these four sizes:

```
small
```

```
medium (the default)
```

```
large
```

```
extra_large
```

Specifying the Font Scale for All Default Applications

If you want to change the default scale of all DeskSet applications, you edit the `.Xdefaults` file as follows: Open the `.Xdefaults` file from your home directory using any text editor and add the following line, where size is `small`, `large`, or `extra_large`:

```
Window.Scale: size
```

Because medium is the default, using the medium size does not alter the scale. Save the changes and quit the editor. Type the following at the command line to update the `.Xdefaults` file's information on the window server:

```
xrdb .Xdefaults
```

Now any new DeskSet or other XView applications that you open from the command line or the Workspace menu appear in the specified scale. To make the changes take effect in existing applications, you can either quit them and restart them or restart the OpenWindows server.

Viewing and Listing Available Fonts

There are two demo programs included for viewing the available font styles and sizes. The `Text` demo program is available from the `Demos` submenu of the `Workspace` menu. It displays lines of text in a font you choose from a list. The `Text` demo window includes the `Text` pop-up window menu. Figure 15.6 shows the `Show Text` and `Show All` pop-up windows. Figure 15.7 shows a map of the `Text` demo items.

The `Fontview` demo is also available from the `Demos` submenu of the `Workspace` menu. It lets you see individual characters for any font as well as display a character grid to see the characters available for a font. The `Fontview` demo window includes the `Fontview` pop-up window menu. Figure 15.8 shows the `Fontview` pop-up window. Figure 15.9 shows a map of the `Fontview` demo items.

FIGURE 15.6

The Show Text and Show All pop-up windows

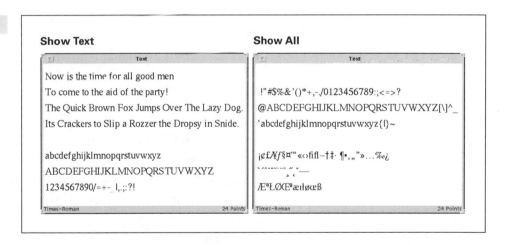

FIGURE 15.7

A menu map of the Text pop-up menu items and pop-up windows

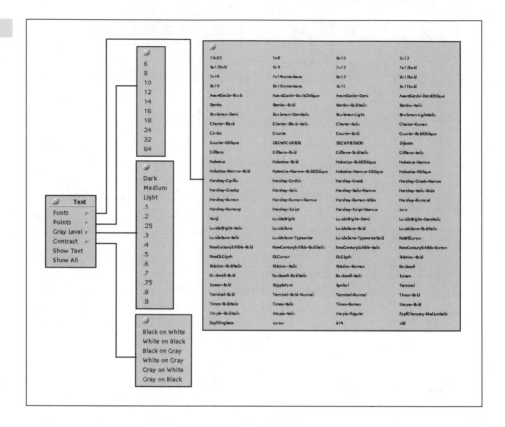

There are over 400 fonts available to OpenWindows applications. You can list the available font names by entering **xlsfonts** at the prompt in a Shell Tool or Command Tool window. To display the listing one screen at a time, enter **xlsfonts | more** or use the Command Tool window to scroll through the font list. Each font has a long name in addition to a shortened version. The full name for **-monotype-gill sans-medium**, is:

```
-monotype-gill sans-medium-i-normal--12-120-75-75-p-52-iso8859-1
```

FIGURE 15.8

Fontview pop-up
window

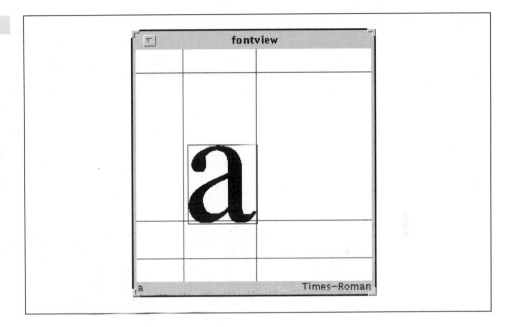

It is easier to reference a font by its short name. The following is a list of the short names of some popular fonts that you can use to customize windows.

avantgarde-book

avantgarde-bookoblique

avantgarde-demi

avantgarde-demioblique

bookman-demi

bookman-demiitalic

bookman-light

bookman-lightitalic

charter-black

charter-black-italic

charter-italic

charter-roman

FIGURE 15.9

A map of the Fontview demo items

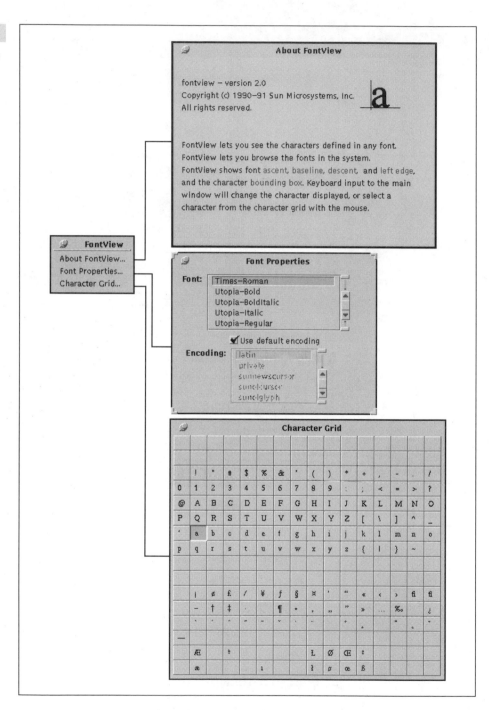

courier

courier-bold

courier-boldoblique

courier-oblique

gillsans

gillsans-bold

gillsans-bolditalic

gillsans-italic

helvetica

helvetica-bold

helvetica-boldoblique

helvetica-narrow

helvetica-narrow-bold

helvetica-narrow-boldoblique

helvetica-narrow−oblique

helvetica−oblique

lucida-bright

lucida-brightdemibold

lucida-brightdemibolditalic

lucida-brightitalic

lucidabright

lucidabright-demi

lucidabright-demiitalic

lucidabright-italic

lucidasans

lucidasans-bold

lucidasans-bolditalic

lucidasans-italic

lucidasans-typewriter

lucidasans-typewriterbold

newcenturyschlbk-bold

newcenturyschlbk-bolditalic

newcenturyschlbk-italic

newcenturyschlbk-roman

palatino-bold

palatino-bolditalic

palatino-italic

palatino-roman

terminal

terminal-bold

terminal-bold-normal

terminal-normal

times-bold

times-bolditalic

times-italic

times-roman

utopia-bold

utopia-bolditalic

utopia-italic

utopia-regular

zapfchancery-mediumitalic

zapfdingbats

Fixed-Width and Proportionally Spaced Fonts

There are two general categories of fonts, *fixed width* and *proportionally spaced*. Each character in a fixed-width font takes up the same amount of space as every other character. By contrast, the characters in a proportionally spaced font require varying amounts of space, depending upon their individual width. Proportionally spaced fonts are more pleasing to the eye.

The default font displayed in Command Tool and Shell Tool is a proportionally spaced font. Although this font is pleasing to the eye, problems occur in character alignment (when spacing and tabbing) with any proportionally spaced font in terminal windows. You may want to choose a fixed-width font for these windows.

Specifying a New Font Style and Size

The default font for windows is Lucida Sans in 12-point (medium); the default font for window headers is Lucida Sans Bold. The term point is a measurement used to indicate the height of a font. A point is approximately $\frac{1}{72}$ inch. You can specify another font style and size for windows and window headers. If the point size is not specified, the default (12-point) is used. You can make the change for a single window, you can make the change in several applications in your submenu, or you can make a permanent change for all your applications by editing your .Xdefaults file. Any changes you make do not apply to existing windows; you must start a new application to display the new font. To start a new application, type the application name on a command line followed by the -fn (font name) option, and the font style and size. The following changes the font style of the File Manager window.

```
filemgr -fn fontstyle-pointsize &
```

The following command starts a new Command Tool with the proportionally spaced font, Lucida Sans Typewriter Bold.

```
cmdtool -fn lucidasans-typewriter-bold &
```

To start a new Text Editor with the font Helvetica Bold in 14-point, enter:

```
textedit -fn helvetica-bold-14 &
```

Specifying the Font for Applications

If you want to make the font style and size permanent, edit your `.Xdefaults` file. Note that when you make any changes, the fonts in any applications that you have already started remain as before. Applications you start *after* making the change in your `.Xdefaults` file appear in the new font and size. Not all font styles and sizes appear the same. If the size is too large, some items, such as menu buttons, may be difficult to read.

To change the font style and size in all DeskSet applications, first, use any text editor to open the `.Xdefaults` file in your home directory. Insert the line

```
font.name:fontname-size
```

where `fontname` is the name of the font you want to specify and `-size` specifies the point size of the font. For example, the following line changes the text in your DeskSet applications to display in Lucida Sans Typewriter Bold font in 14-point. Be sure you press the Tab key when you encounter the <tab> reference in this example.

```
font.name:<tab>lucidasans-typewriter-bold-14
OpenWindows.TitleFont:<tab>lucidasans-typewriter-bold-14
```

Save the changes and quit the editor. Type the following command at the prompt in a Shell Tool or Command Tool to update the window from the `.Xdefaults` file.

```
xrdb .Xdefaults
```

Customizing OpenWindows Menus

You can customize your OpenWindows `Workspace` menu by copying and editing the `openwin-menu` file. The following sections explain how to modify the `openwin-menu` file to create a submenu in the `Workspace` menu and indicate the programs you want to start from the submenu. When you modify a menu, you can also customize how a window displays. For example you can change a window to display in inverse video (white type on a black background), or you can change the style and size of the fonts displayed in application windows.

Changing the Workspace Menu

The `openwin-menu` file specifies the submenus and applications included on the Workspace menu. The location of the system default Workspace menu is `$OPENWINHOME/lib`. `$OPENWINHOME` is a variable name for the location of the OpenWindows software (usually `/usr/openwin`), and `lib` is the directory that contains OpenWindows' system default files. Before customizing the `openwin-menu` file, copy the system default files in your home directory. The copy of the `openwin-menu` file is used to store your personal customizations. The changes you make to the menu file in your home directory override the system default `openwin-menu` file. To copy the file into your home directory, type the following at the system prompt in a Shell Tool or Command Tool:

```
cp $OPENWINHOME/lib/openwin-menu $HOME/.openwin-menu
```

This creates the file `.openwin-menu` in your home directory (specified with the variable $HOME). Placing the dot in front of the file name makes it a hidden file. When you open this file it appears as follows:

```
#
# @(#)openwin-menu    23.13 91/07/10 openwin-menu
#
#     OpenWindows default root menu file - top level menu
#

"Workspace" TITLE

"Programs" MENU          $OPENWINHOME/lib/openwin-menu-programs

"Utilities" MENU         $OPENWINHOME/lib/openwin-menu-utilities

"Properties..."          PROPERTIES

SEPARATOR

"Help..."      exec $OPENWINHOME/bin/helpopen
handbooks/top.toc.handbook

"Desktop Intro..."    exec $OPENWINHOME/bin/helpopen
handbooks/desktop.intro.handbook

SEPARATOR

"Exit..."         EXIT
```

Adding a Submenu to the Workspace Menu

Suppose you want to add a submenu of screensavers to the Workspace menu. Open the `.openwin-menu` file with any text editor and add the following line:

```
"Screensavers"        MENU        $HOME/screensavers-menu
```

This word in quotes (`"Screensavers"`) preceding `MENU` indicates the name of the menu that appears in the Workspace menu. You can change the order of any menu item by changing its placement in the `.openwin-menu` file. After adding this line save your changes and quit the editor. The new submenu, `Screensavers`, is not added to your `Workspace` menu until you create the `screensavers-menu`'s file that contains the `Screensavers` menu items.

Adding an Application to a Submenu

The following is an example of how to add a list of screensaver items to the `Screensavers` submenu. Using the text editor of your choice, create a file that contains the following lines:

```
#
# Screensaver Fun!
#

"Screensavers" TITLE PIN

     "Flame" exec xlock -password "Password, Please?" -invalid
"You've made an error, Please try again!" -validate "Validating
Password..." -mode flame -saturation 1
     "Fractals" exec xlock -password "Password, Please?" -invalid
"You've made an error, Please try again!" -validate "Validating
Password..." -mode hop -saturation 1
     "Life" exec xlock -password "Password, Please?" -invalid
"You've made an error, Please try again!" -validate "Validating
Password..." -mode life -saturation 1
     "Logo" exec xlock -password "Password, Please?" -invalid
"You've made an error, Please try again!" -validate "Validating
Password..." -mode image -saturation 1
     "Pyro" exec xlock -password "Password, Please?" -invalid
"You've made an error, Please try again!" -validate "Validating
Password..." -mode pyro -saturation 1
```

```
        "Qix" exec xlock -password "Password, Please?" -invalid
"You've made an error, Please try again!" -validate "Validating
Password..." -mode qix -saturation 1
        "Random" DEFAULT exec xlock -password "Password, Please?" -
invalid "You've made an error, Please try again!" -validate
"Validating Password..." -mode random -saturation 1
        "Rotor" exec xlock -password "Password, Please?" -invalid
"You've made an error, Please try again!" -validate "Validating
Password..." -mode rotor -saturation 1
        "Swarm" exec xlock -password "Password, Please?" -invalid
"You've made an error, Please try again!" -validate "Validating
Password..." -mode swarm -saturation 1
        "Unlocked (Random)" exec $OPENWINHOME/bin/xlock -mode random
-nolock -saturation 1

"Screensavers" END
```

Save the file with the file name **screensavers-menu** and quit the text
editor. The root workspace menu will now read this file whenever the
Screensaver item is chosen. Notice that the word **PIN** after the word
"TITLE" in the first line indicates that the menu can be pinned to the Workspace. The word **DEFAULT** after the title **"Random"** makes **"Random"** the
default item. You can add other screensavers to this menu. Just open a
blank line before or after entry, enclose the appropriate screensaver name
in quotes, and type in the screensaver's name and options. Figure 15.10
shows the result of adding the above screensavers example to the **Workspace** menu.

Creating Additional Submenus

You can also create additional submenus of items. The following example
lets you add a submenu that in turn lets you add an active aquarium as
your Workspace background or display a submenu of bitmaps to display
as your Workspace background. Use a text editor add the following line
to your openwin-menu.

```
"Backgrounds"        MENU        $HOME/backgrounds-menu
```

After adding this line, create a new file named **background-menu** that contains the following lines:

```
#
# Background screens
#
```

FIGURE 15.10

The newly added
Screensavers submenu

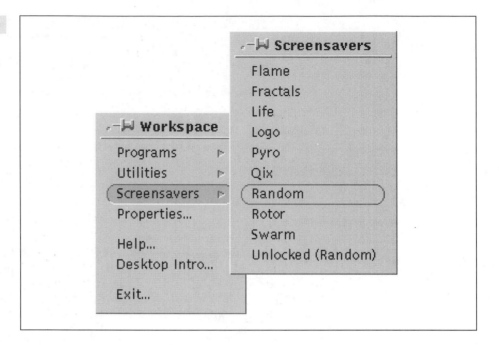

```
"Backgrounds"        TITLE PIN
"Aquarium"      MENU
     "Fish Background"       exec $OPENWINHOME/demo/realxfishdb
     "Fish Props..."             exec $OPENWINHOME/demo/fish_props
     "Kill Fish"          exec $HOME/killfish; REFRESH
"Aquarium"      END PIN
"X-Bitmaps"     MENU
     "Am I Blue"             $OPENWINHOME/bin/xsetroot -solid
lightblue
     "Collective Force" DEFAULT $OPENWINHOME/bin/xsetroot -bg
white -fg grey -bitmap $OPENWINHOME/share/include/X11/bit-
maps/wingdogs
     "Escherknot"            $OPENWINHOME/bin/xsetroot -bg cyan -fg
black -bitmap $OPENWINHOME/share/include/X11/bitmaps/escherknot
     "Hit the Bricks"        $OPENWINHOME/bin/xsetroot -bg firebrick
-fg black -bitmap $OPENWINHOME/share/include/X11/bitmaps/boxes
     "Mensetmanus"        $OPENWINHOME/bin/xsetroot -bg ghostwhite
-fg black -bitmap $OPENWINHOME/share/include/X11/bitmaps/menset-
manus
     "Night Sky"             $OPENWINHOME/bin/xsetroot -bg mid-
nightblue -fg ghostwhite -bitmap
$OPENWINHOME/share/include/X11/bitmaps/star
     "Weave"              $OPENWINHOME/bin/xsetroot -bg black -fg
ghostwhite -bitmap $OPENWINHOME/share/include/X11/bit-
```

```
maps/root_weave
"X-Bitmaps"        END PIN

"Backgrounds"       END
```

Figure 15.11 shows the newly added submenus displayed using the `Fish Background`. The `Aquarium` submenu items appear between the lines `"Aquarium Menu"` and `"Aquarium" End`. The `X-Bitmap` submenu items appear between the lines `"X-Bitmaps" Menu` and `"X-Bitmaps" End`. Notice the line beginning with the title "Kill fish" executes the `killfish` script file (a file containing commands). In order to change the aquarium background to another background, be sure you add and choose the `killfish` item. The `Kill Fish` item runs the Korn shell commands found in the `killfish` file. The following lists the contents of the `killfish` script file:

```
#!/bin/ksh
KILLFISH='ps -e | grep realxfis | cut -c1-6'
kill -9 $KILLFISH > /dev/null
xrefresh &
```

FIGURE 15.11

Newly added
submenus displayed
using the fish
background

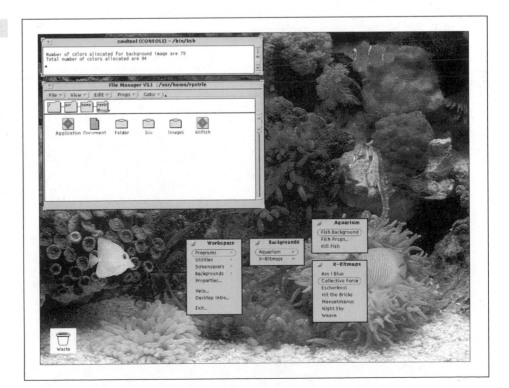

The `killfish` file runs a Korn shell script (a file containing commands) that sets the `KILLFISH` variable. This variable is set to execute a command line that finds the process number of the fish (`realxfis`) background screen, cuts the number of the process, kills the process, and redirects the standard output to a null device.

CHAPTER

16

Networking and Communications

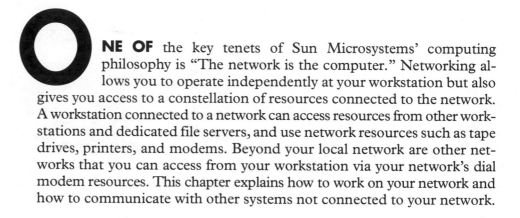

ONE OF the key tenets of Sun Microsystems' computing philosophy is "The network is the computer." Networking allows you to operate independently at your workstation but also gives you access to a constellation of resources connected to the network. A workstation connected to a network can access resources from other workstations and dedicated file servers, and use network resources such as tape drives, printers, and modems. Beyond your local network are other networks that you can access from your workstation via your network's dial modem resources. This chapter explains how to work on your network and how to communicate with other systems not connected to your network.

About Networking Systems

There are two networking systems that are widely used in the UNIX community: Networked File System (NFS) from Sun Microsystems, which runs on most Berkeley UNIX systems, as well as many System V-based UNIX systems, and the Remote File Sharing (RFS) from AT&T, which is part of System V, Release 4. Both of these networking systems are transparent, so the user does not have to know the network is there to use it. The files on the remote system are made available to the users on the local system in such a way that the files appear to be regular files on the local system.

Typically, networks center around a specialized computer, called a *file server*, which includes a powerful computer with large disk capacity that is connected to devices, such as laser printers, modems, and tape backups, that can be shared with other users. Software resources, such as application software that allows multiple users to work on the same file, are also shared on a network.

Different types of computers can communicate on the same network because they share a common language of communications, referred to as *protocols*. There are two primary types of networks: local-area networks (LANs) and wide-area networks (WANS). Local-area networks are networks connected via a coaxial cable or twisted-pair phone wiring. Wide-area networks connect LANs and other computers into a network connected by dial-up or dedicated phone lines, microwave links, or satellite communications.

Networking Solaris

There is a core of commands that allows you to access and use resources on the network. The commands `rlogin`, `rcp`, and `rsh` all allow you to work on other machines remotely from your workstation. To support working remotely on your network, there are several SunOS commands that let you find out information about other users and the network; these include `rusers`, `finger`, `ping`, and `ruptime`.

Logging In Remotely with rlogin

The `rlogin` command enables you to remotely log into other machines on your network. The system you start from is called the *local* system, and the system you want to log into is called the *remote* or *host* system. The `rlogin` command assumes that you have an account and home directory on the remote system. In most cases, you will be prompted for the correct user name and password before you can work on the remote machine. Once you make a connection using the `rlogin` command, you can enter commands on the remote system from your workstation as if you were sitting in front of that machine.

To log into a remote machine, use the following syntax:

```
rlogin hostname
```

where *hostname* is the name of the host (remote) machine. This syntax assumes you have the same login name on both systems. If you have a different login name on each system, you can use the −l option. For example, entering

```
rlogin -l bfife mayberry
```

logs you into the remote machine as the user bfife.

To end the rlogin session, you can press Control-d or enter

```
exit
```

which returns control back to your workstation.

NOTE   If you forget the name of the host machine, use the rusers or finger command, as explained later in this chapter.

You can set a system up so that you can avoid having to enter your login name and password when you log in remotely by creating a file called .rhosts in your home directory using a text editor. You then add a separate line to the .rhosts file that consists of the host machine name and your login name. For example, if you are bfife and want to log in on the mayberry machine on the primetime system, enter the following in the .rhosts file:

```
primetime bfife
```

When you log in from the primetime system, the mayberry machine checks bfife's .rhosts file. If the machine name and user name match the machine name and login name typed in from primetime, then mayberry lets you log in without prompting you for your login name and password.

Transferring Files Remotely with rcp

The `rcp` command enables files to be copied between machines connected to a network. This command works like the `cp` command, except that you need to identify the remote system. You do this by preceding the file path name with the name of the remote system and a colon (:). To copy one or more files from a remote machine to your machine, use the following syntax:

```
rcp hostname:source destination
```

where *hostname* is the name of the remote machine, *source* is the name of the file(s) you want to copy, and *destination* is the path name on your machine where you want the file(s) copied to.

To copy files from your local machine to a remote machine, the syntax is

```
rcp source hostname:destination
```

where *source* is the file(s) you want to copy, *hostname* is the name of the remote machine, and *destination* is the path name on the remote machine where you want the copied files to reside.

You can also copy a file from your machine to a remote machine while you are logged into a third machine. To do this, you must enter the host *name* identifier for both the *source* and *destination* using the following syntax:

```
rcp hostname source:hostname destination
```

For example, entering

```
rcp mayberry:/home/bfife/arrests newrochelle:/home/bfife/records
```

copies the file named `arrests` from bfife's home directory on the `mayberry` machine to the records directory on the `newrochelle` machine. If you omit the full path name for a remote destination, `rcp` assumes the path is relative to your home directory on that system.

If you have a different login name on the remote system than on the host system, you can prefix the remote system name with your login name on that system and an at symbol (@). For example, if your login name on the remote system is `pmason`, you can copy a file as follows:

```
rcp arrests pmason@mayberry:records
```

which copies the `arrests` file to the `records` directory of your home directory on the machine named `mayberry`.

You can copy directories and subdirectories by using the `-r` option. For example, typing

```
rcp -r testdir mayberry: /tmp
```

causes the subdirectory `testdir` and all of its subdirectories and files to be copied into the `/tmp` directory on `mayberry`. You can use normal shorthand commands for specifying directories, such as `$HOME` for your home directory or the period (`.`) for the current directory.

Executing Commands Remotely with rsh

The `rsh` (remote shell) command lets you connect to the specified host machine and execute the specified command. It can be a real timesaver when you only want to perform one task on the remote machine, because it automatically logs into the remote host. However, your user name must be in a list on the host machine in order to use this command. The commands available using the `rsh` command are specified by the system administrator. You cannot run an interactive command such as vi when using the `rsh` command.

To execute a command on a remote machine, type

```
rsh hostname command
```

If you use the `rsh` command without specifying a command, `rsh` logs you into the remote system using the `rlogin` command. Use the `-l username` option if your user name is different on the remote host machine.

As with the `rlogin` command, you can set up the remote system so that you do not have to enter your password when you remotely log in by creating a file called `.rhosts` (for remote hosts) in your home directory using a text editor, then entering the system name and your user name.

Viewing User Information with rusers

The `rusers` command produces a similar output to the **who** command, but for remote machines. The listing of users is in the order that responses are received after executing the `rusers` command. This default listing does not list a host machine if no users are logged into it. Typing

    rusers

displays the basic report that includes just the names of users logged into all the machines on the network. You can display the basic report for a specific remote host by typing

    rusers *hostname*

Adding the -1 option to the `rusers` command adds additional information about each user. For example, typing

    rusers -1

displays an output that includes the following information: user ID, host name, terminal, login date, login time, idle time, and login host.

You can use the following options with the `rusers` command.

OPTION	RESULT
-a	Displays idle machines as well as active machines. The `rusers` or `rusers` *hostname* commands by default do not display machines where no users are currently logged on.
-1	Provides more detailed information, including user names, machine and terminal names, the time each user logged in, how long each user's machine has been idle, and the name of the machine that each user logged in from.
-h	Sorts the listing of users alphabetically by the host name.

OPTION	RESULT
-i	Sorts the listing of users by idle time.
-u	Sorts the listing of users by the number of users logged onto a host.

Viewing User Information with finger

The `finger` command is useful for finding out if a user you want to reach is available on the system. It provides information about whether the user has been absent from their system by tracking the last time a keystroke was performed in a shell as well as when the last email message was read. The syntax for the `finger` command is

```
finger [options] username@hostname
```

For example, entering

```
finger bfife@mayberry
```

displays the information about the user `bfife` on the remote `mayberry` machine.

```
mayberry
Login name: bfife
Directory: /home/mayberry/bfife          Shell: /bin/ksh
on since Jan 5 10:10:52 on console
8 hours 40 minutes Idle Time
No unread mail
No plan
```

A `username` can be specified as either a first name, last name, or login name.

You can display information about all the users on a remote machine by using the following syntax:

```
finger [options] hostname
```

which displays the following information about the users on the remote machine:

Login name

Full user name

Terminal name

Idle time

Login time

Location

You can use the following options with the `finger` command.

OPTION	EFFECT
-b	Omits user's home directory and shell from display.
-f	Used with -s to omit the heading that is normally displayed in short format.
-i	Shows idle format, a terse format similar to -s.
-l	Forces long format (the default).
-m	Requires that the name indicated **username** match exactly, instead of also searching for a match of the first or last names.
-q	Displays a listing in a quick format. The quick format is similar to the short format except that only the login name, terminal, and idle time are printed. Requires an exact match of the user name.
-s	Displays listing in a short format. The short format displays the login name, name, terminal, idle time, when the user logged on, and where the user is located on the network.
-w	Used with -s to omit user's full name, which is normally displayed in short format.

Checking Machine Status with ping

The `ping` command informs you if another host machine on the network is up and running or not active. If a network is running, it is usually referred to as being up or alive. When you run the `ping` command, a network message is sent to the specified host machine asking for a response. If the remote machine is up, the message *hostname* `is alive` is displayed, indicating that the machine responded to the request. If the remote host machine is down or cannot receive the network message, the message `no answer from` *hostname* is displayed.

The syntax of the `ping` command is

    ping hostname

Adding the `-s` (statistics) option to the `ping` command reports the effectiveness of the data transfer between machines. This is useful if you want to see if the network is running slow. With the `-s` option, the `ping` command will continue to send packets until you press Control-c, then it will report the summary statistics. For example, entering

    ping -s mayberry

and then pressing Control-c might generate a report like this:

```
PING mayberry: 56 data bytes
64 bytes from 129.144.50.21: icmp_seq=0  time=80. ms
64 bytes from 129.144.50.21: icmp_seq=1  time=0. ms
64 bytes from 129.144.50.21: icmp_seq=2  time=0. ms
64 bytes from 129.144.50.21: icmp_seq=3  time=0. ms
.
.

.
----mayberry PING Statistics----
4 packets transmitted, 4 packets received, 0% packet loss
round-trip (ms) min/avg/max = 0/20/80
```

Checking Machine Status with rup

The `rup` command allows you to see the uptime and load average on a remote system. When you execute the `rup` command, it broadcasts a network message on the local network and displays the responses it receives. To display the uptime and load average for all the machines on your local network, enter

```
rup
```

which displays a table similar to this:

```
mayberry      up   2 days  4:14  load average: 0.00,  0.17,   0.27
newrochelle   up   5 day   2:03  load average: 1.43,  1.39,   1.46
primetime     up   3 days  1:00  load average: 0.00,  0.00,   0.00
```

This table contains the name of each host, whether the host is up or down, the amount of time each host has been up or down, the number of users on that host, and information on the average load on the past minute, 5 minutes, and 15 minutes.

Entering

```
rup hostname
```

displays the same table as the `rup` command for the specified host machine.

Normally the listing is in the order that responses are received, but this order can be changed by specifying one of the following options:

OPTIONS	EFFECT
-h	Sorts the display alphabctically by host machine name.
-l	Sorts the display by the load average values.
-t	Sorts the display by the uptime values.

Modem Communications

The `tip` and `cu` commands allow you to call up using a modem and connect to other UNIX and non-UNIX machines. You can also copy files between your machine and the remote machine with `tip`. The `tip` program, which stands for Telephone Interface Program, is newer and more versatile than cu. The **tip** and **cu** programs are not as powerful as many modern telecommunications packages. They do not support Xmodem protocols or transfer binary files. However, they are easy to use, and one or the other is available on most UNIX systems. Both your system and the remote system must have proper hardware installed to make a connection possible using the **tip** or **cu** commands, and you must have an account on the remote system.

N O T E   Many system administrators restrict the use of the tip and cu commands for security and to control telephone costs.

Communicating with tip

The **tip** command establishes a connection to a remote host machine. Once the connection is established, a remote session using **tip** behaves like an interactive session on a local terminal. The **tip** command checks the **remote** file in the /etc directory for information when making a connection. This file contains all the systems phone lines and modems that **tip** can work with.

To dial another system using **tip**, use the following syntax:

    tip -speed telephonenumber

where **-speed-entry** is the baud rate you want to set the modem to for communicating with the remote system. For example, **-9600** establishes the connection at the 9600 baud rate. The *telephonenumber* is the phone number of the other computer you want to access.

If your system administrator maintains an /etcremote file on your system, you can dial another system using the following syntax:

    tip -speed hostname

where the **hostname** entry makes the **tip** program find the appropriate telephone number in the /etcremote file and dial it.

The **tip** program displays the prompt **dialing...**, then places the call through your network's modem. When the call is answered by the remote system, `tip` indicates the connection is complete with the prompt `dial-ing...connected`. From this point on, you are connected with the other computer and can proceed to log into the system.

To disconnect from the remote system, enter

    ~.

The `tip` program responds with an `[EOT]`, meaning end of transmission, and returns you to your local prompt.

Transferring Files with tip

You can send a file from your system to the remote system or vice versa using the `tip` program. Entering

    ~p

tells `tip` that you want to send a file. Note that the tilde does not appear on the screen. The prompt changes to `[put]`, which notifies you that it is ready for you to specify the file you want to send. Entering

    filename

begins the sending of the specified file and displays the number of lines transferred. When the transfer is complete, `tip` will display the total number of lines transferred and an exclamation point (!) indicating the transfer is complete. Transferring a file from the remote machine to your machine is done in a similar manner to sending a file, except you use the ~t command.

The following are common `tip` commands that you can use to perform tasks while connected to the remote machine.

TILDE COMMAND	DESCRIPTION
~p	Puts (sends) a file to the remote machine.
~t	Takes (receives) a file from the remote machine.
~c	Changes directory on your local machine.

TILDE COMMAND	DESCRIPTION
~!	Escapes to a new shell, from which you can return to **tip** by typing exit. Lets you access your local machine while still being connected to the remote machine.
~Control-z	Suspends **tip** so you can perform commands on your (local) machine while still being connected to the remote machine. To return to **tip**, enter the **fg** command.
~Control-y	Suspends **tip** locally, but still displays the output of the remote machine.

Setting tip Variables

The **tip** program maintains a set of variables that can be used in normal operation or can be added to your .tiprc file. To set a variable during a **tip** session, enter

```
~s variable
```

To display a particular tip variable setting, enter the ~s, the variable name, and a question mark. For example, entering

```
~s record?
```

displays

```
record=tip.record
```

To display all the **tip** program variables, enter

```
~s all
```

When the **tip** program is run, it checks your home directory for a .tiprc file, which is an optional file where you can set **tip** environment variables. The **tip** program variables have Boolean, numeric, string, or character values. A **tip** variable assignment does not include any spaces. Numeric, string, and character values are set with the variable name, an equals sign (=), and a value; for example, entering

```
~s record=myfile
```

creates a log file named `myfile` for the current `tip` session. Boolean values are set by entering the variable name. To unset a variable, precede the variable name with an exclamation point (!). For example, to unset the verbose setting, enter

    ~s !verb

The following is a list of common `tip` environment variables.

VARIABLE	TYPE	DESCRIPTION
beautify or be, nb	Boolean	Discards unprintable characters so they are not placed into the captured file.
baudrate or ba	Numeric	Displays the baud rate at which the connection was initially established. The `baudrate` variable cannot be changed during a `tip` session.
dialtimeout or dial	Numeric	Displays the number of seconds to wait for a connection to be established. This defaults to 60 seconds. The `dialtimeout` variable cannot be changed during a `tip` session.
disconnect or di	String	Sets the string to send to the remote host when disconnecting. This defaults to the empty string " ". To log out when disconnecting, change the disconnect string to `disconnect=exit`.

VARIABLE	TYPE	DESCRIPTION
echocheck or ec	Boolean	Waits for the remote machine to echo the last character sent in order to synchronize with the remote machine during file transfers.
eofread or eofr	String	Specifies the string of characters that mark the end of transmission during a file transfer (~<). The default is the empty string " ".
eofwrite or eofw	String	Specifies the string that marks the end of transmission during a file transfer (~>). The default is the empty string " ".
eol or el	String	Specifies the string that tip uses to determine the end of a line. The escape character, ~, is recognized only if it is the first character following the end of a line. The default is the empty string " ". The Return key character is always an end-of-line character.
escape or es	Character	Specifies the escape character that informs tip you are entering tip commands rather than communicating with the remote machine. The default escape character is the tilde (~).

VARIABLE	TYPE	DESCRIPTION
`exceptions` or `ex`	String	Specifies the string of characters that should not be discarded when `beautify` is turned on. The default is `\t\n\f\b` for the tab, newline, formfeed, and backspace characters.
`framesize` or `fr`	Numeric	Sets the number of characters (bytes) for `tip` to store in a memory buffer when receiving files. When the internal buffer is full or when transfer is complete, `tip` writes the data to disk. The default is 1024 characters (bytes).
`halfduplex` or `hdx`	Boolean	Sets `tip` to run in half-duplex mode. In half-duplex mode, `tip` echoes the characters you type. If set off, `tip` will run in full-duplex mode, so the remote machine echoes the characters you type. The default is not set.
`localecho` or `le`	Boolean	Sets `tip` to run in half-duplex mode. `localecho` is exactly the same as the `halfduplex` variable.
`host` or `ho`	String	Displays the host name that you specified when running `tip`. If you ran `tip` with a phone number, then this will be the name of your local machine. The `host` variable cannot be changed during a `tip` session.

VARIABLE	TYPE	DESCRIPTION
parity or par	String	Specifies the parity setting. Parity is an error-checking procedure in which the number of 1's in transmitted data must match; that is, they must be either even or odd. Parity checking is used to check the accuracy of transmitted data. If the setting is **none**, parity is not checked. **zero** specifies that parity is not checked on input, and the parity bit is set to zero on output. **one** specifies that parity is not checked on input, and the parity bit is set to one on output. **even** specifies that parity of successfully transmitted data must be an even number. **odd** specifies the parity of transmitted data must be odd. The default is **none** (no parity).
phones	String	Specifies the name of the file containing phone numbers. By default, **phones** is set to **/etc/phones**. You can create your own file for system phone numbers by setting the environmental variable **PHONES** to the name of a file containing system names and phone numbers.

VARIABLE	TYPE	DESCRIPTION
prompt or pr	Char	Specifies the character that marks the end of line for the remote machine. The default is \n.
raise or ra	Boolean	Converts lowercase characters you type to uppercase. Characters you enter in response to the tip program's prompts will not be converted. The default is not set.
rawftp or raw	Boolean	Sends all characters during file transfers. This does not filter out nonprintable characters. Turns off all newline/carriage return pairs that are mapped to newlines. The default is on.
record or rec	String	Specifies the name of the file to record the current tip session when script is turned on. The default file is tip.record.
remote	String	Specifies the file name that tip refers to for descriptions of remote systems. The default is /etc/remote. You can change the default by setting the environment variable REMOTE to another file name. The remote variable cannot be changed during a tip session or in your .tiprc file.

VARIABLE	TYPE	DESCRIPTION
script or sc	Boolean	Records everything you type and everything the remote machine displays appended to the file whose name is defined by record. If **beautify** is turned on, only printable characters are saved. If **beautify** is turned off, everything is saved.
tabexpand or tab	Boolean	Converts tab characters to eight-space characters. The default is not set.
tandem or ta	Boolean	Controls data flow. If set to X, the ON/X OFF flow control is used. Control-s stops data flow and Control-q restarts data flow. The default is on.
etimeout or et	Numeric	Specifies the number of seconds that **tip** should wait for a character to echo when echo check is turned on. The default is 10 seconds.
verbose or verb	Boolean	Displays messages while dialing and during transfers. The default is on.

Communicating with cu

The cu program, like the tip program, enables you to connect to another machine using a modem. The cu program is not as powerful as the tip program. To connect onto another system using the cu command, enter

```
cu telephonenumber
```

The `cu` program's default baud rate is 300, which is excruciatingly slow. The -s option is used with the `cu` command to specify the baud rate you want. The most common baud rates are 1200, 2400, 9600, 19200, and 38400. For example, entering

```
cu -s9600 5551212
```

dials the number 555-1212 and connects using a 9600 baud rate.

The phone number can include an equal sign (=) as a wait-for-dial-tone code. For example, if you have to dial 9 to get an outside line, enter

```
cu 9=5551212
```

The following options allow you to change various `cu` default settings.

OPTION	DESCRIPTION
-s *speed*	Sets the baud rate to *speed*.
-e	Sets even parity on outgoing characters.
-o	Sets odd parity on outgoing characters.
-h	Sets half-duplex communications.
-t	Dials a terminal that has been set to autoanswer. The -t option also maps CR (Carriage Return) to CR/LF (Carriage Return/Line Feed) on incoming lines of text.

If the destination system has a name your system recognizes, you can use the system name instead of the phone number. For example, entering

```
cu mayberry
```

establishes a connection with the `mayberry` system.

To terminate a `cu` session, first log off the remote system by pressing Control-d, then type

```
~.
```

which terminates the `cu` connection.

After making the connection to the remote system, enter the commands for the remote machine as you would commands at your machine's command-line prompt. You can enter commands for your machine while still connected to the remote machine by preceding the command with a tilde (~). The following are tilde commands recognized by cu.

COMMAND	DESCRIPTION
~.	Terminates the connection.
~!	Escapes to the local system.
~!*command*	Runs the specified command on the local system.
~$*command*	Runs the specified command on the local system and sends its output to the remote system.
~%cd	Changes the directory on the local system.
~%take *filename1* *filename2*	Copies *filename1* from the remote system to the file *filename2* on the local system. If *filename2* is omitted, the name of *filename1* is used.
~%put *filename1* *filename2*	Copies *filename1* from the local system to the file *filename2* on the remote system. If *filename2* is omitted, the name of *filename1* is used.
~~*line*	Transmits ~*line* to the remote system. This is used when you call system B from system A, then call system C from system B. A single tilde (~) lets you execute commands on system A, and two tildes (~~) can be used to execute commands on system B.
~%break	Transmits a BREAK (Control-c) code to the remote system.

Transferring Files with cu

You can transfer a file from the remote system to your system using the cu program. Entering

```
~%take file
```

transfers *file* from the remote machine to your machine. If you want to copy the transferred file and name it with a different name, enter

```
~%take original copiedfile
```

where *original* is the name of the remote file to transfer and *copiedfile* indicates the name of the transferred file.

To send a file from your system to the remote system using the cu program, enter

```
~%put fromfile tofile
```

which tells cu that you want to send the file named *fromfile* to the file named *tofile* on the remote system. The cu program begins sending *fromfile* and displays the number of lines and characters transferred.

Working with the Internet

The Internet is a huge information superhighway that connects more than 5,000 networks and is used by 5 to 10 million users worldwide. The Internet has mushroomed from its early military-industrial-complex roots into a global system available to any computer user. The Internet uses the TCP/IP (Transport Control Protocol/Interface Program) protocol to allow communication among different operating systems. Three TCP/IP applications, mailx (electronic mail), telnet (remote login), and ftp (file transfer), are basic tools you need to work on the Internet. There are plenty of other applications available on the Internet, but these three programs are the workhorses and are available on nearly all networks connected to the Internet. Working with the mailx program was explained in Chapter 11, "Electronic Mail and Messages." The following sections provide an explanation of the Internet addressing system for sending email and connecting to machines on the Internet, as well as how to work with the telnet and ftp programs.

Internet Addresses

Each computer on the Internet has a name. An Internet computer name is usually several words separated by periods, such as `tyco.usno.navy.mil`. The naming system used by the Internet is known as the Domain Name System (DNS). The DNS is also the worldwide system of distributed databases of names and addresses. DNS names are constructed in a hierarchical fashion.

You can tell the type of network you are connecting to by checking the last part of the address name. For example, in the address `prep.ai.mit.edu`, the `edu` indicates an education domain. This address, by the way, is used for the Free Software foundation at MIT, which you can log into using the `ftp` program and the login name `anonymous`. The main domain-name categories on the Internet are EDU (educational), COM (commercial), GOV (government), MIL (military), ORG (organizations), and NET (networks). In addition, there are also two-letter country codes (like US for the United States and JP for Japan).

Connecting with telnet

The `telnet` program lets you log into host computers in a similar way to using the `rlogin` command, but it can operate with any computer that supports the Telnet protocol, including UNIX and non-UNIX systems. Once connected to a host system, you can usually access a database of on-line information available to any user. Depending on the host system you log into, the commands vary for navigating the host system.

The syntax for using the `telnet` command to connect to a remote system is

```
telnet remotehostname
```

After making the connection, you are prompted for a user name and password on the remote system. In most cases, you can log into a remote host system on the Internet using a public access login user name and password, or you'll know the user name and password before making the connection. For example, entering

```
telnet spacelink.msfc.nasa.gov
```

connects you to the NASA system. When prompted for a login user name and password, enter

```
newuser
```

You are then presented with a menu of options for reading entries about the history, current state, and future of NASA activities.

You can also make a `telnet` connection by typing `telnet` without a machine name, then at the `telnet` prompt entering

```
open remotehostname
```

Once the connection has been opened, the `telnet` program enters the terminal mode. In this mode, typed text is sent to the remote host system. You can switch from terminal mode to command mode by entering the `telnet` escape character `Control-]`. This returns you to the local machine and the `telnet` program.

The following `telnet` commands are used to start, suspend, and quit a `telnet` session.

COMMAND	DESCRIPTION
close	Terminates the connection but allows you to remain in the `telnet` program.
open remotehostname	Connects to the host machine specified by remotehostname.
bye or quit	Quits the current connection and exits the `telnet` program. You should log out of the remote host, using the `exit` command, before using the `quit` command.
z	Temporarily suspends the `telnet` session to allow other commands to be executed on the local system.
<Return>	Returns you to the shell at the remote host machine.

Transferring Files with ftp

A tremendous variety of public-domain software is available on the Internet. The most common way that these programs are distributed is via the `ftp` program. The `ftp` command implements the File Transfer Protocol (FTP) that allows files on different systems to be copied back and forth.

To make a connection using `ftp` to an Internet host system, enter

```
ftp remotehostname
```

You can also begin an `ftp` session with a remote host by entering

```
ftp
```

After the `ftp>` program prompt appears, enter

```
open hostname
```

For example, entering

```
open ftp.cs.widener.edu
```

accesses an archive of information about the Simpsons (stored in /pub/simpsons). At the login prompt, enter **anonymous**. Many resources that are accessible using the `ftp` program can be accessed by any user using a generic login name and password.

After the remote system has accepted your login name and password, you are ready to start transferring files. The `ftp` program can transfer files in two directions using the **get** and **put** commands. The **get** command copies files from the remote host machine to your system. The **put** command copies files from your system to the remote host machine. The **get** and **put** commands use the syntax

```
get source-file destination-file
put source-file destination-file
```

The *source-file* is the name of the file you want to copy. The *destination-file* is the name of the copied file. The *destination-file* name is optional; if it is omitted, the copied file is given the same name as the *source-file*.

Before copying a file, you need to make sure the correct transfer type is set. The default transfer type is ASCII. If you want to transfer an application or program file, you need to set the file transfer type to binary. To do this, at the `ftp>` prompt, enter

    binary

To set the file transfer type back to ASCII, use the `ascii` command. Once the file transfer type is set, you can use the `get` or `put` command. When you use either the `get` or `put` command, the `ftp` program reports that the transfer has begun, then reports when the file transfer has been completed and tells you how long the transfer took.

You can copy more than one file with the `mget` and `mput` commands, which use the same syntax as the `get` and `put` commands, except you can use metacharacters, such as (?) and (*) to specify multiple files.

To terminate an `ftp` session, at the `ftp>` prompt, enter

    quit

The following lists the most commonly used `ftp` commands.

COMMAND	ACTION
?	Lists available `ftp` commands.
append *localfile* *remotefile*	Appends the local file specified by *localfile* to the file on the remote host specified by *remotefile*.
ascii	Sets the file transfer type to ASCII (the default setting).
bell	Sounds a bell when a file transfer is completed.
binary	Sets the file transfer type to binary.
bye or quit	Terminates the `ftp` session.
cd *remote directoryname*	Changes the current directory on the remote machine to the directory specified.
close	Terminates the `ftp` session with the remote machine, but continues the `ftp` session on the local machine.

COMMAND	ACTION
delete *remotefilename*	Deletes the remote file name specified by *remotefilename*.
get *remotefilename* [*localfilename*]	Copies *remotefile* to the local host. If *localfilename* is not specified, the copy has the same name as the original file (*remotefilename*).
help	Lists available ftp commands.
help *command*	Describes the command specified by *command*.
lcd [*directoryname*]	Changes the current directory on the local machine to the directory specified by *directoryname*; if no directory is specified, lcd changes to the user's home directory.
mget *remotefilenames*	Copies the files specified by *remotefilenames* to the current directory on the local machine.
mkdir directory-name	Makes a directory with the name specified by *directoryname* on the remote host machine.
mput *localfilenames*	Copies the files specified by *localfilenames* to the current directory on the remote host.
open [*remotehostname*]	Sets up a connection with the host machine specified; if no host is specified, a prompt appears for entering the host machine name.
put *localfilename* [*remotefilename*]	Copies the file to the remote host with the file name specified.
pwd	Displays the name of the current directory on the remote host machine.

CHAPTER

17

System Administration Basics

THIS chapter explains essential system administration tasks. These tasks may need to be performed if your system administrator is unavailable or as routine tasks if your system administrator has issued you a superuser password. A *superuser* is a privileged user with unrestricted access to all files and commands. While there are some system administration tasks that a nonsuperuser can perform, in most cases you must be a superuser to perform system administration tasks that affect other users on your system or network. Basic system administration tasks include booting up and shutting down your system, accessing devices (such as disk drives), archiving files, and using the OpenWindows Administration Tool to perform the most elementary system administration tasks of adding or deleting a user, workstation, or printer to or from the network.

Working as a Superuser

The superuser is also referred to as a *root* user, and these terms are used interchangeably to describe the same privileged user status. When you have superuser privileges, the shell provides a special pound sign (#) prompt to remind you that you have privileged access to the system. The system keeps a log that records each time someone logs in as root or someone uses the superuser command.

To become a superuser if you are not already logged into the system, at the login prompt enter

    root

To become a superuser if you are already logged into the system as a user other than root, enter

```
su
```

To exit superuser status, type

```
exit
```

Communicating with Users on Your Network

An important part of performing system administrator tasks is to make sure you always let users know when you are about to perform a task that will affect them, such as rebooting a system or changing the environment. There are several ways you can communicate with users, such as using the `mailx` and `write` commands. The following sections explain how to create a login message to communicate with users as they log in, and how to use the `wall` and the `rwall` commands to communicate with all the users on your system or on the network.

Creating a Login Message

Each time a user logs into a system, any messages from the system administrator are displayed. These messages are not displayed to users already logged in. Login messages are stored in the file `/etc/motd` (message of the day), which is only accessible to the superuser.

To create a login message for the day, do the following:

1. Become a superuser.

2. Use an editor such as vi to open the `/etc/motd` file.

3. Delete any obsolete messages and type your new login message. Make sure your messages are short. If the message is longer than a screenful of text, users won't be able to read the beginning lines.

4. Save the changes. The message is changed and is displayed the next time a user logs into the system.

Sending a Message to All Users on a System or Network

You can send a message to every user on a system using the **wall** command, or send a message to every user on the network using the **rwall** command. You do not have to be a superuser to use either the **wall** or **rwall** command.

To send a message to all users on your system, do the following:

1. At the system prompt, type **wall** and press Return.

2. Type the message text you want to send.

3. When the message is complete, press Control-d. The message is displayed in the console window of each user or at the command line.

To send a message to all users on your network, do the following:

1. At the system prompt, type **rwall** −n *networkname* and press Return.

2. Type the message you want to send.

3. When the message is complete, press Control-d. The message is displayed in the console window of each user on the system or at the command line.

You can also use the **rwall** command to send a message to all users on a specific remote system by typing **rwall** *hostname*, where *hostname* is the name of the remote system you want to send the message.

NOTE Use the **rwall** command carefully, because it consumes extensive system and network resources.

Booting and Rebooting Your System

Booting is the process of powering up a system, testing to determine which attached hardware devices are running, and bringing up the operating system software. You normally don't have to boot your system because Sun workstations are designed to run continuously, preventing wear on system components. Each time you turn on the power, the machine reboots itself so that you can start using it again. In most cases, the system is set up to boot automatically from a local disk or over the network. In certain uncommon circumstances, such as when your system freezes up, you may have to manually boot or reboot your system to get it running again. The following sections explain how to manually boot and reboot your system.

N O T E   If your machine is set up to boot from a tape or diskette, you need to insert the appropriate disk or tape for the boot procedure to work.

Booting Your System

If your system is off, simply turning it on will usually cause the system to boot itself. If when you turn the system on, it displays a prompt similar to this:

```
console login type b (boot), c (continue), or n (new command mode)
>
```

at the boot prompt (>), enter

```
n
```

to enter the new command mode. The prompt changes to display

```
Type help for more information
ok
```

At the ok prompt, enter

`boot`

> **N O T E**
>
> Solaris 2 for x86 does not start the same way as Solaris for Sun Workstations. It boots off a hard disk or a floppy disk drive, so you cannot use these instructions.

Rebooting Your System

If the system is already running and you need to reboot the system from the command prompt, become a superuser by entering

`su`

and enter the superuser password. If you are not logged in, enter **root** at the login prompt to become a superuser. At the superuser prompt (#), enter

`reboot`

If you are adding new hardware to your system, you need to reboot with the –r option to reconfigure your system. To run a reconfiguration script for the new hardware, enter

`boot –r`

Emergency Rebooting

If you are using a Sun keyboard and the machine doesn't respond to keystrokes such as Control-c, then press Stop-a. (The Stop key is the accelerator key located in the upper-left corner of the keyboard.) On some Sun keyboards the Stop key is labeled L1. If a special prompt (> or ok) is not displayed, check the cables connecting the components of the system. If the system still doesn't respond, try turning off the power, waiting 60 seconds, and then turning the power back on.

WARNING Always allow 60 seconds between turning off the power and turning it back on again. This pause prevents possible damage to power supply components in your machine.

As a last resort if emergency rebooting does not solve the problem, contact Sun Customer Service (1-800-USA-4SUN). If the > boot prompt is displayed, type n and at the ok boot prompt, type **boot** and press Return to reboot the machine. A system login screen or prompt indicates that the system has booted properly and is awaiting a user to log in.

NOTE If you are using Solaris 2 for x86 and the machine doesn't respond to keystrokes, such as Control-c, you need to press the reset button on your computer to reboot.

Shutting Down Your System

The SunOS system software is designed to be left running continuously so that the network and email software can work correctly. However, there are situations that require the system be shut down, which means intentionally stopping execution of the system software. To shut down your workstation or a system, you must be a superuser. You should always shut down the machine before turning any of the power switches off. When you shut down your machine properly, you protect the machine from damage and prevent the loss of your data. You may need to shut down the system in the following circumstances.

- Turning off system power.
- Performing maintenance on a file system.
- Installing a new release of Solaris.
- Adding new hardware to the system.
- Moving the system to another location.

Shutting Down a System

Shutting down a system with multiple users using the **shutdown** command sends a warning message to all users who are logged in, waits for 60 seconds (the default), then shuts down the system to a single-user state (your workstation). You can choose a different default time to allow more time. You can check the activity before shutting down the network by typing **ps -ef** and pressing Return.

Follow these steps to shut down a multiuser system.

1. Become a superuser and change to the root (/) directory.

2. Enter **/usr/sbin/shutdown**. After a short wait, the system shuts down to a single-user state and you can perform any maintenance tasks. You can specify a longer period to wait before shutting down the system by adding the argument **-g** *time* to the **shutdown** command, where time is the amount of time to wait before shutting down the system.

3. Turn off the power to all units in the following order: monitor, external drive unit (if you have one), and system unit.

To quickly shut down and reboot a multiuser system, follow these steps:

1. Become a superuser and change to the root / directory.

2. Enter **/usr/sbin/shutdown -i6**. This command broadcasts a message to all users that the system is being shut down. After the system is shut down, it is restarted in its multiuser state.

3. Enter y when asked `Do you want to continue? (y or n):`. The system shuts down.

Shutting Down Your Workstation

Shutting down a single-user system is similar to shutting down a multi-user system except you use the `init 0` command instead of the `shutdown` command. The following steps explain how to shut down a single-user system.

1. Save any files you are presently editing with applications running on your machine, and quit any applications that will lose information when the machine shuts down.

2. Become a superuser by entering `su` at the system prompt, then entering the password assigned to a superuser.

3. Enter `init 0` and wait for either the `>` or `ok` prompt.

4. Turn off the power to all units in the following order: monitor, external drive unit (if you have one), and system unit.

To shut down and reboot a single-user system, follow these steps:

1. Change to the root directory by entering `cd /`.

2. Enter the `su` (superuser) command.

3. Enter `init 6`. No warning is displayed. After the system is shut down, it is restarted in its single-user state.

Emergency Shutdown for a Single System

If you need to shut down your system in a hurry, enter `uadmin 2 0`. Information is written to the disk and the system displays the boot prompt. To shut down a system that does not respond properly to the keyboard or to the mouse, follow these steps:

1. If you are using a Sun keyboard, press Stop-a (L1-A on some Sun keyboards). If you are using Solaris 2 for x86, there is no equivalent to Stop-a, so you must use the reset button on your PC.

2. Turn off the power to all units in the following order: monitor, external drive unit (if you have one), and system unit.

Managing Hard Drives and CD ROM Drives on Your Network

The system administrator is responsible for making sure that devices such as disk drives are available to users on the network. In order for a drive to be available, it must be formatted and contain a file system. Solaris allows users to work with different file systems, such as ufs (UNIX file system) and Sun's Network File System (NFS). The process of making a drive and its file system available to the system by attaching it into the directory tree at the specified mount point is called *mounting*. To mount and unmount drives, you must have superuser privileges. The following sections explain what file systems are, and how to identify a drive by its device name, list mounted drives, mount and unmount drives onto your network, and display information about a drive.

Understanding File Systems

A *file system* is a structure of directories used to locate and store files. The ufs (UNIX file system) is the default file system and Sun's network file system (NFS) is the network file system used by Solaris. NFS requests are translated from the UNIX file system to the network file system and sent across the network and translated back to the UNIX file system. *File systems are normally associated with a particular type of media.* File systems exist for floppy diskettes, hard disks, and CD ROMs. You can add the following types of file systems as a super user:

FILE SYSTEM	DESCRIPTION
ufs	UNIX file system. The ufs is the default file system for SunOS.
hsfs	High Sierra is the CD ROM file system. The hsfs is a read-only file system. The hsfs supports Rock Ridge extensions.
pcfs	PC file system, which allows you to read and write data on MS-DOS-formatted diskettes.

Identifying a Drive by Its Device Name

In some cases you will need to specify a disk drive by its device name, such as when you add a drive to your system and want to mount it. At first the device name of a disk may seem a little overwhelming, but if you break down the device name it is fairly easy to follow. The device name of a SCSI disk drive consists of four parts. The disk device name takes the following format:

```
/dev/rdsk/cwtxdysz
```

The following identifies the four parts of a disk device name.

- cw   Indicates the controller number. The controller is a device that can be a separate board in your workstation that your drive is connected to or it can be integrated into the SCSI disk drive. The controller is responsible for organizing data on the disk. If you only have one disk controller on your system, the controller identifier will always be 0.

- tx   Specifies the target address. To identify the target address, look at the switch that is set on the back of your disk drive.

d*y*   Displays the drive number. If the disk has an embedded controller, the drive number is always 0.

s*z*   Displays the slice (partition) number. The slice number can be a number 0 to 7. The most common assignments for disk slices are: slice 0, which is used by the operating system; slice 1, used for swapping data from memory to disk; slice 2, which indicates the entire disk; and slice 6, which typically contains the /usr directory and its subdirectories.

Mounting a File System

There are three ways that file systems can be mounted. The first method, called automounting, mounts and unmounts file systems shared through the network file system (NFS) automatically by simply changing directories. This method is totally transparent to the user. The second method is to manually mount a drive from the command line. You must be logged in as a superuser in order to manually mount a file system. The third method lets you add an entry into a special file (`/etc/vfstab`) so that a drive is automatically mounted when the system is booted. Adding an entry in this file also makes it so you can mount a file system by simply referring to its mount point (the directory the file system is mounted on). The following sections explain how to list mounted file systems, mount file systems using each of these three methods, and unmount file systems.

Listing Mounted File Systems

Any user can display which file systems are mounted by entering

```
mount
```

which displays a listing similar to this:

```
/ on /dev/dsk/c0t1d0s0 read/write on Mon Nov 28 15:23:09 1994
/usr on /dev/dsk/c0t1d0s6 read/write on Mon Nov 28 15:23:09 1994
/proc on /proc read/write on Mon Nov 28 15:23:09 1994
/dev/fd on fd read/write on Mon Nov 28 15:23:09 1994
/tmp on swap read/write on Mon Nov 28 15:30:13 1994
/opt on /dev/dsk/c0t1d0s5 setuid on Mon Nov 28 15:30:15 1994
/mnt on /dev/dsk/c0t0d0s6 setuid on Mon Nov 28 15:30:17 1994
```

Mounting Using the Automounter

You can mount file systems shared through the network file system (NFS) using a method called *automounting*. The `automount` program, commonly referred to as the *automounter*, runs in the background and mounts and unmounts remote directories as they are needed. The automounter mounts and unmounts file systems whenever a user changes into or out of a directory that is available through the automounter. The `automount` program mounts the file system on the user's system and remains mounted as long as the user remains in the directory or is using a file in a remote directory. If the remote file system is not accessed for a certain period of time, it is automatically unmounted.

Manually Mounting a File System

To manually mount a disk drive from the command line, you need to specify the disk drive's device name. The `mount` command adds a file system to the root file system to make it available to the network. The file system is attached to an existing directory, which is then considered the *mount point*. If the mount point directory has any files or subdirectories prior to the mount operation, they are hidden until the file system is unmounted. Manually mounting a file system adds an entry to the `/etc/mnttab` file. For example, to mount a disk set up as target disk 1 that is the first disk on the system (0), and mount its sixth slice (s6) and attach the disk drive at the `/disk1` directory, follow these steps:

1. Become a superuser.

2. At the superuser prompt, enter `mkdir /disk1`.

3. Enter `mount /dev/dsk/c0t1d0s6 /disk1` to attach the disk to the file system.

4. Type `exit` to return to exit the superuser privileges.

Adding the `-F` *filesystemtype* argument specifies the file system type on which to operate. The most common file systems are ufs (UNIX file system), hsfs (High Sierra file system), nfs (network file system), and pcfs (PC file system).

The following list describes generic options commonly supported by most file system types.

-m   Mounts the file system without making an entry in /etc/mnttab.

-r   Mounts the file system read-only.

-o   Specifies the file system type-specific options in a comma-separated (without spaces) list of suboptions. These are the standard ufs mount options:

     n   Mounts the file system without making an entry in the /etc/mnttab **file**.

     rw   Mounts the system as read and write.

     ro   Mounts the system so it is read-only.

To mount target disk 3 (t3) on the sixth partition (s6) on the /mnt directory, enter

```
mount /dev/dsk/c0t3d0s6 /mnt
```

Mounting a High Sierra File System

The hsfs (High Sierra file system) is the file system used with Sun CD ROMs. Sun's CD ROM drives are set to SCSI target 6 by default. The following example mounts a CD ROM using the High Sierra file system (hsfs) on the directory /cdrom.

```
mount -F hsfs -o ro /dev/dsk/c0t6d0s2 /cdrom
```

If the mount information for a drive is in your /etc/vfstab/ file, you can mount a drive by just adding the mount point. For example, enter

```
mount /cdrom
```

to mount the **cdrom** drive on the /cdrom directory. The **mount** command checks the /etc/vfstab for the information it needs to mount the drive.

Mounting a PCFS File System

In order to mount a PC file system (pcfs) to get access to files on a floppy diskette that came from a MS-DOS PC, you first need to create a directory to attach the pcfs file system to. To create the directory /`pcfiles` for mounting the MS-DOS floppy, enter

```
mkdir /pcfiles
```

You can now mount the floppy disk drive on the directory named /`pcfiles` by entering

```
mount -F pcfs /dev/diskette /pcfiles
```

The −`F` option specifies the type of file system to mount.

To unmount the floppy diskette mounted on the /`pcfiles` directory, first change to a directory in the file system other than the /`pcfiles` directory, and enter

```
umount /pcfiles
```

Mounting a Device Automatically

The /`etc`/`vfstab` (virtual file system table) file contains a list of devices that are automatically made available when booting the system. To see the list of disks that are in your /`etc`/`vfstab` file, enter

```
more /etc/vfstab
```

The following is a sample /`etc`/`vfstab` file listing.

```
#device             device            mount    FS     fsck mount  mount
#to mount           to fsck           point    type   pass atboot options
#
#/dev/dsk/c1d0s2    /dev/rdsk/c1d0s2  /usr     ufs    1    yes    -
/proc               -                 /proc    proc   -    no     -
fd                  -                 /dev/fd  fd     -    no     -
swap                -                 /tmp     tmpfs  -    yes    -
/dev/dsk/c0t1d0s0   /dev/rdsk/c0t1d0s0 /       ufs    1    no     -
/dev/dsk/c0t1d0s6   /dev/rdsk/c0t1d0s6 /usr    ufs    2    no     -
/dev/dsk/c0t1d0s5   /dev/rdsk/c0t1d0s5 /opt    ufs    3    yes    -
/dev/dsk/c0t1d0s1   -                 -        swap   -    no     -
/dev/dsk/c0t0d0s6   /dev/rdsk/c0t0d0s6 /int    ufs    2    yes    -
/dev/dsk/c0t6d0s2   /dev/rdsk/c0t6d0s2 /cdrom  hsfs   -    no     ro
```

When you boot up the system, the `mountall` command is performed to mount all the devices that are specified to be mounted in the `/etc/vstab` file. The `fsck` command is also run to check the file systems to be mounted when booting the system.

You can add a device to the `/etc/vfstab` file to have the device mounted automatically when you boot. Each entry in the `/etc/vfstab` file has seven fields that are separated by spaces or a tab. The following briefly explains each of the fields in the `/etc/vfstab` file.

FIELD	DESCRIPTION
device to mount	Identifies the device that you want to mount; for example, entering `dev/dsk/c0t1d0s6` indicates the drive set to target 1 on the sixth slice (partition).
device to fsck	Identifies the raw (character) device that corresponds to the file system you want to mount; for example, `/dev/rdsk/c0t1d0s6` is the raw device name for the `/dev/rdsk/c0t1d0s6` device. This determines that the device to check should be treated as a raw character device rather than a block device. Use a dash (−) when there is no applicable device, such as for a read-only file system or a network-based file system.
mount point	Specifies the directory to use for mounting the device; for example, the /usr directory might be the mount point for `/dev/dsk/c0t1d0s6`, or the /cdrom directory might be the mount point for `/dev/dsk/c0t6d0s2`.
FS type	Indicates the type of file system to be mounted. For example, enter ufs for a UNIX file system, hsfs for a CD ROM, or pcfs for a MS-DOS file system.

FIELD	DESCRIPTION
fsck pass	Specifies the pass number used by the fsck command to specify whether to check a file system. A dash (–) indicates that you do not want the file system to be checked. When the field contains a value of 1 or more, the file system is checked. A **ufs** file system with a zero (0) indicates that the file system should not be checked. When the field contains a value of 1, the file system is checked sequentially. Otherwise, the value of the pass number does not have any effect.
mount at boot	Specifies whether the file system should be automatically mounted by the **mountall** command when the system is booted. Enter **yes** to mount the file system or **no** *not* to mount the file system automatically. This field has nothing to do with the automounter program.
mount options	Specifies the options for mounting the file system. Options are separated by commas with no spaces. These are the same options commonly supported by the file system type (as explained earlier). For example, **ro** stands for read-only device (the default is **rw**). To specify no options, use a dash (–).

Unmounting a File System

To unmount a file system you must change to a directory that is in a file system other than the one to be unmounted, and enter the **umount** command followed by the file system's mount point. The **mount** command maintains a table of mounted file systems in **/etc/mnttab**. The **mount** command adds an entry to the mount table; the **umount** command removes an entry from the table.

Unmounting a file system removes it from the system's directory tree and removes the entry from the `/etc/mnttab` (mount table) file. Once a file is unmounted, any subdirectories and files that existed in the mount point's directory become available. File systems are automatically unmounted when shutting down the system. To unmount a specific disk drive, use the **umount** command followed by the name of the disk drive you want to remove. The following unmounts the file system mounted on the `/add` directory.

```
umount /add
```

You can also specify a drive to unmount by adding the device name to the **umount** command. The following example unmounts the file system for the target disk 3 (t3) mounted on the sixth partition (s6).

```
umount /dev/dsk/c0t3d0s6
```

You cannot unmount a disk that is being used. If the directory or files are being accessed, the message umount: `/add busy` is displayed.

Displaying Disk Information

To check the amount of space that you have available on a disk, use the **du** command. The du (disk usage) command reports the number of 512-byte disk blocks used per file or directory. If the directory contains subdirectories, the subdirectories and their files are included in the block count. Entering

```
du
```

displays a listing similar to this:

```
2     ./.wastebasket
16086    ./Folder/frame/chaps
26 ./Folder/frame/notes
226 ./Folder/frame/docs
314 ./Folder/frame/reports
16654    ./Folder/frame
19630    ./Folder
6    ./.cetables
162 ./.Mail
996 ./bin
3470./images
18    ./.menus
24484    .
```

You can display the total amount of allocated space in kilobytes, rather than 512-kilobyte blocks by entering

```
du -k
```

If you use the same disk as in the previous `du` example, the command `du -k` displays the following report:

```
1    ./.wastebasket
8043./Folder/frame/chaps
13   ./Folder/frame/notes
113 ./Folder/frame/docs
157 ./Folder/frame/reports
8327./Folder/frame
9815./Folder
3    ./.cetables
81   ./.Mail
498 ./bin
1735./images
9    ./.menus
12245  .
```

The `df` command reports the amount of occupied disk space, the amount of used and available space, and how much of the file system's storage space has been used. If you use the `df` command without any argument, the amount of space occupied and files for all mounted file systems are displayed. Entering

```
df -k
```

displays a listing of the amount in kilobytes of used and available space, similar to this:

```
Filesystem            kbytes     used   avail capacity   Mounted on
/dev/dsk/c0t0d0s0      24143    15954    5779      73%   /
/dev/dsk/c0t0d0s6     192151   171623    1318      99%   /usr
/proc                      0        0       0       0%   /proc
fd                         0        0       0       0%   /dev/fd
swap                   80180       16   80164       0%   /tmp
/dev/dsk/c0t0d0s5      95167    77279    8378      90%   /opt
/dev/dsk/c0t6d0s2     186723   180697       0     100%   /cdrom
```

To display a partition map of a disk, use the `prtvtoc` command. The `prtvtoc` command displays the volume table of contents for the disk you specify. You must be a superuser to use the `prtvtoc` command. Keep in mind this command only works when the slice (partition) you specify has space allocated to it. To display information about target disk 1 for the entire disk, become a superuser and enter

```
prtvtoc /dev/rdsk/c0t1d0s2
```

which displays output similar to this:

```
* /dev/rdsk/c0t1d0s2 partition map
*
* Dimensions:
*     512 bytes/sector
*      80 sectors/track
*       9 tracks/cylinder
*     720 sectors/cylinder
*    2500 cylinders
*    1151 accessible cylinders
*
* Flags:
*   1: unmountable
*  10: read-only
*
*                        First   Sector  Last
* Partition  Tag Flags  Sector   Count  Sector  Mount Directory
        0      2   00        0    51840  51839  /
        1      3   01    51840   164160 215999
        2      5   00        0   828720 828719
        5      6   00   216000   203040 419039  /opt
        6      4   00   419040   409680 828719  /usr
```

Working with Floppy Disks

If your workstation has a floppy disk drive, you can perform several tasks using Solaris to work with floppy disks. The following sections explain how to use a formatted disk, format a floppy disk for storing SunOS files, create a file system on a floppy disk, format a floppy disk for MS-DOS files, and write-protect floppy disks.

Using a Floppy Disk

To use a formatted disk, first insert the diskette into the drive, label side up. Push firmly to lock the diskette into place. To eject the diskette from the drive, type `eject` at the command prompt and press Return. If the diskette does not work correctly, it may need to be formatted.

Formatting a Floppy Disk in the SunOS Format

To format a diskette you must first know whether you are using a high-density (1.44Mb) diskette or a double-density (720K) diskette. By default, `fdformat` formats a high-density diskette (1.44 Mb) in the SunOS format. Before you format a diskette, make sure you can't see through the square hole in the upper-right corner of the diskette. If the notch is uncovered, push the plastic tab up to cover the notch. This makes it so you can format or write to the disk.

Remember, the format of your diskette must match the type of diskette you are using. You cannot format a high-density diskette with a double-density format. The `fdformat` command formats and verifies each track on the diskette, and terminates if it finds any bad sectors. All existing data on the diskette is destroyed by formatting.

To format a high-density diskette in the SunOS format, insert the diskette into the drive and at the command prompt enter

```
fdformat
```

The system displays the message

```
Press Return to start formatting floppy.
```

Pressing Return formats the diskette. If you want to abort the format command, type Control-c.

If you are using a double-density diskette, insert the diskette into the drive and enter

```
fdformat -l
```

To automatically eject the disk after formatting, add the −**e** (eject) option. You can only use the −**e** option on a Sun workstation. For example, to format a double-density 3.5" disk in a SunOS format and eject the disk after formatting it, enter

```
fdformat −l −e
```

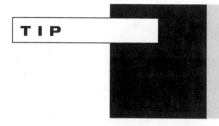

T I P

If you are using a Sun workstation and you cannot eject a diskette from a drive using the eject command, straighten a wire paper clip and insert it into the pinhole under the diskette slot. This manually ejects the floppy diskette.

Creating a File System on a Floppy Disk

As with a hard disk or a CD ROM, you can mount a floppy disk to your network. In order to mount a floppy disk, you must create a file system on it. After formatting the disk, become a superuser by typing **su** and your superuser password at the prompt, and enter

```
newfs /dev/rdiskette
```

This displays the following prompt:

```
newfs: construct a new file system /dev/rdiskette (y/n)?
```

Enter **y** to create the new UNIX file system on the floppy diskette or **n** to abort the **newfs** command. Typing **y** displays output similar to this:

```
/dev/rdiskette:       2880 sectors in 80 cylinders of 2 tracks, 18
sectors
     1.5MB in 5 cyl groups (16 c/g, 0.29MB/g, 128 i/g)
super−block backups (for fsck −F ufs −o b=#) at:
 32, 640, 1184, 1792, 2336,
```

To mount the new file system on the new diskette, make a directory to use as the mount point and enter

```
mount /dev/diskette /floppy
```

Replace /**floppy** with the directory you created as the mount point. If the floppy diskette is not in the drive, the following message appears:

```
fd0: drive not ready
mount: I/O error
mount: cannot /dev/diskette appears.
```

Formatting Disks for Use with MS-DOS

The **fdformat** command also lets you format a disk for use with MS-DOS. To format a high-density (1.44 Mb) diskette that installs an MS-DOS file system and boot sector on the disk after formatting, insert the diskette into the drive, label side up, and at the prompt, enter

```
fdformat  d
```

and press Return to format the floppy diskette. Any diskettes formatted using this option can be read by MS-DOS but are not bootable.

MS-DOS can include a label written to the diskette that identifies the disk when listing files. To add an MS-DOS label on the disk when formatting it, use the following syntax:

```
fdformat -d -b label
```

The text specified by label can be up to eleven characters, but cannot include spaces. For example, enter

```
fdformat -d -b DOS-DISK
```

at the prompt and press Return to format the floppy diskette and add the label **DOS-DISK** to the newly formatted disk.

To format a double-density disk (720K) for use with MS-DOS using a Sun workstation, insert the diskette into the drive, label side up, and enter

```
fdformat -d -l
```

If you're using Solaris 2 for x86, use the **-D** option instead of the **-d -l** options.

Both of these are the equivalent of entering **format a:/f:720** on an MS-DOS PC.

W A R N I N G Do not mix MS-DOS and SunOS files on the same diskette.

Write-Protecting Diskettes

Write-protecting a diskette prevents its contents from being erased or overwritten. To write-protect a diskette, follow the steps below:

1. Turn the diskette upside down and find the write-protect tab. The diskette is upside down when the metal circle at the center of the diskette is showing. If you hold the diskette at the label end, the write-protect notch is in the lower-right corner.

2. Using a ballpoint pen, pull the tab toward the edge until you can see through the notch.

Once you have write-protected a diskette, information cannot be saved on it. When you want to write information on the diskette, you need to change it back to its write-enabled status by pushing the tab back so that the hole is completely covered.

Working with Tapes

Tape drives are used primarily to store backup data on a network system. Solaris provides a number of features for archiving and managing your system backup files. The name for ¼-inch cartridge tape drives found on Sun workstations follows this format:

```
/dev/rmt/n
```

where *n* is the tape drive number for the ¼-inch cartridge tape drive.

Most SCSI drives automatically detect the density or format on the tape and read it accordingly. By default, the tape drive writes at the highest ("preferred") density it supports. If you need to specify the density for a tape drive, add the character that identifies the tape density after the tape drive number. For example, if you are using a tape drive that writes at a medium density, add the letter m after the tape device number (`/dev/rmt/0m`). The following is a list of characters used to specify different densities for SCSI tape drives.

`null`	Default, preferred (highest) density.
`l`	Low (800 bpi).
`m`	Medium (1600 bpi).
`h`	High (6250 bpi).
`u`	Ultra (reserved).

Preparing a Tape for Data

To insert a ¼-inch cartridge tape into an external tape drive unit, hold the cartridge with the label side up. The tape head faces the slide lock on the left side of the slot. Press the cartridge firmly into the slot and pull the slide lock to the right so that it holds the cartridge in place. When a cartridge is first loaded, it is a good idea to perform what is called a tensioning pass. This ensures an even distribution of tension throughout the tape. To run a tensioning pass on the ¼-inch cartridge tape in the first tape drive, insert the tape into the tape drive and enter the following:

```
mt -f /dev/rmt/0 retension
```

To release the cartridge, pull the slide lock to the left.

Backing Up Files and File Systems to Tape

The **tar** and **cpio** commands are the ones most commonly used to copy files and file systems to tape. Use the **tar** command to copy files and directory subdirectories to a single tape. Use the **cpio** command when you need to copy arbitrary sets of files, special files, or file systems that require multiple tape volumes. The **cpio** command packs data onto tape more efficiently than the **tar** command and skips over any bad spots in a tape when restoring data. The **cpio** command also provides options for writing files with different header formats (such as `tar`, `crc`, `odc`, `bar`), providing better portability between systems of different types.

After performing a backup or a retrieval, the system typically rewinds the tape. To prevent rewinding, the device name should be appended with the letter `n` at the end of the device name, such as `/dev/rmt/0n`.

Copying Files with the tar Command

The `tar` command includes several options for copying files. Adding the `c` option to the tar command instructs the `tar` command to copy files and overwrite any files existing on the tape. You can use wildcard characters to specify files that match a certain pattern. For example, to copy any files in your current directory that begin with the string `chap` to the default tape drive (`dev/rmt/0`), and overwrite any existing files on the tape, enter

```
tar cvf /dev/rmt/0 chap*
```

To display the files archived on a ¼-inch cartridge tape drive, enter

```
tar tvf /dev/rmt/0
```

WARNING The `tar` command stores the path name used when the archive was created. Use relative rather than absolute path names if you later extract files to a different directory. For more information on relative and absolute path names, see Chapter 9, "Navigating Directories and Working with Files."

Retrieving tar Files from a Tape

To extract (copy) all the files created using the `tar` command from a tape into the current directory, perform the following steps:

1. Insert the tape into the tape drive.

2. Change to the directory where you want to store the extracted files. For example, enter **cd** to change to your home directory.

3. Enter **tar xvf /dev/rmt/0**. Be sure to substitute the **0** with the appropriate drive number for your tape drive.

If you want to only extract some of the files on a tape, append the device name with a space and the file names you want to retrieve. You can use wild characters to extract a group of files matching a specified pattern. For example, entering

```
tar xvf /dev/rmt/0 chap*
```

extracts all files beginning with **chap** and copies them to the current directory. You can also list individual file names after the tape drive's name. For example, entering

```
tar xvf /dev/rmt/0 chap1 textfile report
```

extracts (copies) the three files **chap1**, **textfile**, and **report** into the current directory.

Copying Files with cpio

The **cpio** command can copy individual files, groups of files, or complete file systems in from or out to tape or disk. Unlike **tar**, the **cpio** command can create archives that require multiple tapes or diskettes. It also recognizes when the media is full and prompts you to insert another volume. The **cpio** command takes a list of files or path names and writes it to the standard output. Typically, the **cpio** command sends output to the standard output, so you need to redirect the output to a file or a device. You can also feed a command's output to the **cpio** command using the pipe (|). For example, to feed the output of the **ls** command to the **cpio** command to copy all files in the current directory and redirect the output to the first tape drive, enter

```
ls | cpio -oc > /dev/rmt/0
```

To verify a copy operation, list all the files archived on a tape by entering

```
cpio -civt < /dev/rmt/0
```

For information about the `cpio` command's options, see Part IV, "Command Reference."

Copying and Moving Directory Trees

To copy directory trees between file systems, make sure you are in the directory you want to copy and enter

```
find . -print -depth | cpio -pd /filesystem2
```

Replace `filesystem2` with the directory in the file system where you want the files copied to. The `find` command's `-print` option displays the names of the located files, and the `-depth` option instructs the `find` command to begin at the last subdirectory and search on up to the current directory. The output of the `find` command is sent via the pipe (|) to the `cpio` command. The `cpio` command's `-p` option creates the list of files, and the `-d` option creates the directories.

Moving a directory tree is similar to copying a directory tree, except you need to remove the original directory tree after verifying that the copy operation was successful. To verify a copy operation, change to the directory that you copied the files to and enter the `ls` command. The following explains how to copy and remove a directory tree.

```
find . -print -depth | cpio -pad /newdir
```

Be sure to replace `newdir` with the directory that you want the files moved to. To remove the old directory tree, change to a directory other than the directory you want to remove and enter

```
rm -rf /olddirectory
```

where `olddirectory` is the name of the directory you want to remove.

Retrieving Files

To retrieve all files from a tape and copy them into the current directory, enter

```
cpio -icv < /dev/rmt/0
```

To retrieve only some of the files from a tape, you must specify a pattern to match. The following example retrieves all files beginning with `report` and uses the `d` option to create subdirectories if needed.

```
cpio -icdv "report*" < /dev/rmt/0
```

In previous versions of SunOS, the bar format was frequently used to archive files to floppy disks. The bar format is no longer supported in SunOS 5.x. To restore files on a diskette created with the `bar` command, enter

```
cpio -ivH bar < /dev/diskette
```

Write-Protecting Tapes

To protect a ¼-inch cartridge tape so that it cannot be erased or written to, you will need a screwdriver or a coin. On the top of the tape is the word "SAFE," with an arrow and a notch for rotating the arrow. To write-protect the tape, insert the head of the screwdriver or coin in the notch and rotate the arrow to point to the word "SAFE." To enable writing to the tape, move the arrow so that it is pointing away from the word "SAFE."

Working with the Administration Tool

The Administration Tool is an OpenWindows application that greatly simplifies many common system administration tasks. The Administration Tool provides four separate applications for managing your system: the Database Manager, Printer Manager, Host Manager, and User Account Manager. Figure 17.1 shows the Administration Tool window. The following sections explain how to use the Administration Tool to view system

FIGURE 17.1

The Administration
Tool

database entries, and to add a user, a host, and a printer to your system. To start the Administration Tool, in a Command Tool or Shell Tool, enter

```
admintool &
```

Typically, you should not run the Administration Tool as a superuser or root unless you have root access to every system you need to administer. If you don't have root privileges, you can run the Administration Tool to affect your local machine, but you must be a member of the `sysadmin` group (GID 14). See your system administrator for more information on becoming a `sysadmin` group member.

About Network Naming Services

In order to work with the Database Manager, Printer Manager, Host Manager, and User Account Manager you need to know what type of naming service your network is using. NIS+ (Network Information Service+) is the new networking naming service for Solaris. NIS+ makes use of databases that store much more information than the older version of NIS. NIS is the network-naming service that is shipped with SunOS 4.1. NIS servers refer to NIS files that contain two-column maps that store information about the network, workstations, and users. You cannot add a workstation using the Host Manager if you select the NIS naming service. The Host Manager cannot directly update NIS database maps. If your network uses the NIS naming service, choose **None** rather than **NIS** when the **Select Naming Service** pop-up window appears. You will still need to update the NIS maps after adding the workstation, as explained later in this chapter. If you're not using a naming service, usually one workstation maintains network information files in the /etc directory.

Working with the Database Manager

The Database Manager is used to manage NIS+ tables and ufs files in the /etc directory. It allows you to view, search through, and edit different network databases, such as a database for hosts and groups.

To work with the Database Manager, follow these steps:

1. Click the left mouse button on the Database Manager icon to start the Database Manager. The **Load Database** pop-up window appears, as shown in Figure 17.2.

2. Click the left mouse button on the name of the database you want from the **Databases** scrolling list.

3. Click on the naming service your network is set up for. Check to make sure that the domain or host name is correct. The domain name defaults to the current workstation's domain. In most cases, you will want to use the default domain or host name.

FIGURE 17.2

The Load Database
pop-up window

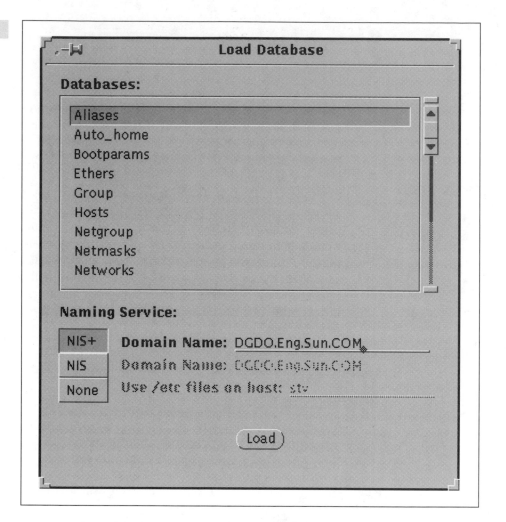

4. Click the left mouse button on the **Load** button. The window containing the database you selected is displayed. Figure 17.3 shows a sample Passwd (password) database displayed in the **Database Manager** window. Each database has a **File**, **View**, and **Edit** menu button at the top of the window for viewing and modifying system databases.

5. Click the right mouse button on the abbreviated window menu button and click on the **Quit** item to quit the Database Manager.

FIGURE 17.3

Sample Passwd
(password) database
listing in the Database
Manager

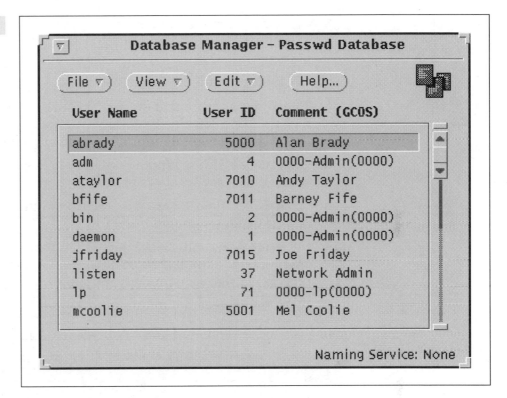

Working with the User Account Manager

The User Account Manager edits the database files that contain user information. It sets password security, creates the user's home directory, and specifies the user's default permission settings. Once you have added a user to the system, you can use the user's settings as a template for additional users.

Adding a User to the System

The following steps explain how to add a user using the User Account Manager.

1. Click the left mouse button on the User Account Manager button to start the User Account Manager. The `Select Naming Service` pop-up window is displayed, as shown in Figure 17.4.

2. Click on the naming service your network is set up for.

3. Check to make sure that the domain or host name is correct. The domain name defaults to the current workstation's domain. In most cases, you will want to use the default domain or host name.

4. Click the left mouse button on the `Apply` button. The `User Account Manager` window appears, as shown in Figure 17.5.

5. Click the left mouse button on the `Edit` button. The `Add User` pop-up window appears.

6. Fill in the fields and choose the settings for each entry in the `Add User` window. The table below describes each of the fields and settings in the `Add User` window, and supplies sample field and setting entries.

FIGURE 17.4

The Select Naming Service pop-up window

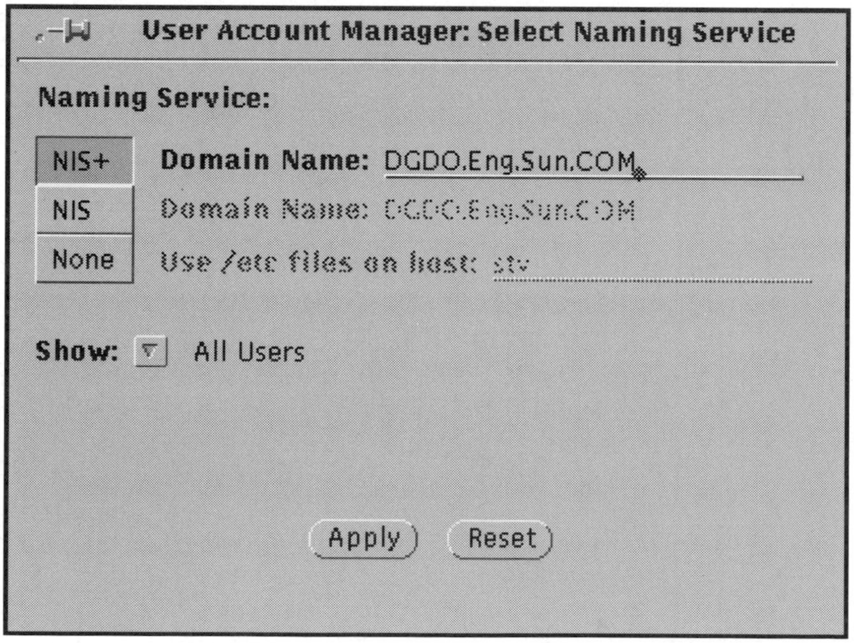

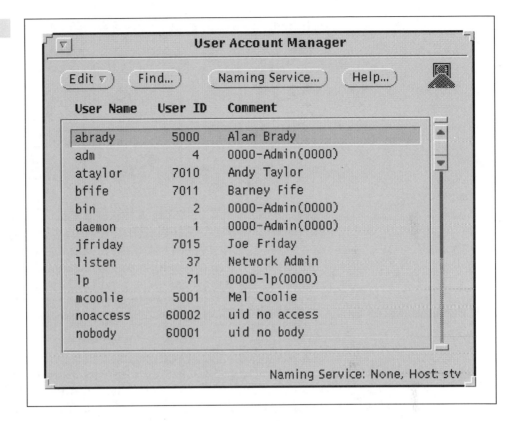

7. Click on the **Add** button to add the new user account to the system.

CONTROL	DESCRIPTION
User Name	Specifies a unique login name consisting of two to eight letters and numerals. The first character must be a letter, and the user name must contain at least one lowercase letter. Remember that the **login** command is case specific, so in order to log in, the user must enter his or her user name exactly as it is entered in this field.

CONTROL	DESCRIPTION
User ID	Specifies a unique number between 100 and 60000. The user ID number is stored in the `passwd` database file, and identifies the user account throughout the network.
Primary Group	Indicates the name of a preexisting group or a group ID number (GID). The group `other` is the default primary group.
Secondary Groups	Indicates additional names of preexisting groups or group ID numbers that you want the user to belong to. Each secondary group name is separated by a space. `Secondary Groups` is an optional field.
Comment	Identifies the user and includes any pertinent information about the user, such as his or her department and phone extension. `Comment` is an optional field, but typically is at least the user's name. For example, Robert Petrie is the `Comment` entry for the user `rpetrie`, who has been used as an example throughout this book.
Login Shell	Determines which default shell is started when the user logs in. The available shells are the Bourne shell (`/bin/sh`), the C shell (`/bin/csh`), the Korn shell (`/bin/ksh`), or Other (a shell you specify). For example, in this book all users use the Korn shell as the default shell.

CONTROL	DESCRIPTION
Password	Determines whether or not a password is required and how attempts to log in are handled. The `Cleared until first login` setting lets the user specify his or her password when he or she first logs in. The `Account is locked` setting disables the account with an invalid password. This allows a user to own files but not to log into the system. The `No password — setuid only` setting creates an account that cannot be logged into directly. This lets programs such as `lp` run under an account without allowing a user to log in under the account. In almost all cases, you will choose `Cleared until first login`.
Min Change	Specifies the minimum number of days required between password changes. The default is `0`, which lets you change your password any time.
Max Change	Specifies the maximum number of days before which, if the password is not changed, the account is locked. The `Max Change` is an optional field.
Max Inactive	Specifies the number of days the account may remain unaccessed before it is locked. This ensures that a user, such as a temporary employee, doesn't continue to have access to his or her account after termination. The `Max Inactive` is an optional field.
Expiration Date	Specifies the date on which the user account expires. The default is `None`.

CONTROL	DESCRIPTION
Warning	Specifies the number of days to begin warning the user before password expires. No warning is given if this field is left blank. The `Warning` setting is an optional field.
Create Home Dir	Determines whether to have the user's home directory automatically created. If you choose to have the home directory created, the `Yes if checked` box displays a check mark and the `Skeleton Path` field is activated. If this box is checked, you must fill in the `Path` and `Server` fields.
Path	Specifies the path of the user's home directory. For example, for a user named `rpetrie`, you might enter `/export/home/rpetrie`.
Server	Identifies the name of the host machine on which the user's home directory resides.
Skeleton Path	Specifies the path to the directory that stores initialization files. The files in this directory will be copied into the user's home directory. For example, the default home directory initialization files exist in the `/etc/skel` directory. The skeleton path must reside on the same host machine as the user's home directory. The `Skeleton Path` is an optional field.

CONTROL	DESCRIPTION
Auto Home Setup	Determines whether or not you want the user's home directory to be automatically mounted. This makes the user's home directory automatically accessible on any system on the network by entering /home/username, where *username* is the login name of the user.
Permissions	Determines who can read from, write to, and execute files in the user's home directory. Permissions enabled appear with a check mark. To disable a permission setting, click in the check box of the permission you want to change.

Copying a User's Settings

To copy a user's existing settings to create a new account from an already existing account, click on the user name of the account you want to copy and choose Copy User from the Edit menu. The Copy User window appears with most of the original user's settings displayed. The Name, User ID, and Password remain blank so you can change the fields for the new user. Note that the Comment and Path fields still contain the original user's information, which in most cases will need to be changed.

Deleting a User

To delete a user account from a network, in the User Account Manager window, click on the name of the user you want to delete. Next, click the right mouse button on the Edit menu and choose the Delete User item. The Delete User pop-up window is displayed, as shown in Figure 17.6. This pop-up window includes the user's name, ID, and any comments about the user. Two check boxes let you choose whether or not to delete the user's home directory and its contents and the user's mailbox and its

FIGURE 17.6

The Delete User
pop-up window

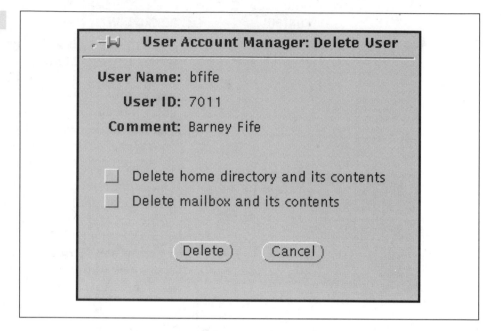

contents. Click on the check boxes to delete the user's home directory and mailbox files. Lastly, click the left mouse button on the **Delete** button to confirm the deletion.

Working with the Host Manager

The Host Manager lets you add or remove a workstation to or from the network. It lets you fill in blank fields to provide all the information that SunOS needs so users can log in. In order to add a host to a network, you need to know the type of naming information service (NIS) your network uses. As explained earlier, a network naming service is a method by which information about workstations is maintained. The three choices for specifying a network naming service are NIS+, NIS, and None.

Adding a Workstation to the Network

When Solaris is installed on a workstation, it prompts for several configuration settings. In order to add a workstation to an existing network, you need to include this information about your workstation in the **Host Manager** window. The following steps explain how to add a host workstation to a network.

1. Click the left mouse button on the **Host Manager** button to start the Host Manager.

2. Click on the naming service your network is set up for. If you are using NIS, be sure to choose **None**, and follow the instructions for updating the NIS maps in the next section.

3. Check to make sure that the domain or host name is correct. The domain name defaults to the current workstation's domain. In most cases, you will want to use the default domain or host name.

4. Click the left mouse button on the **Apply** button. The Host Manager window appears, as shown in Figure 17.7.

5. Click the left mouse button on the **Edit** button. The **Add Host** window appears.

6. Fill in the fields and choose the settings for each entry in the **Add Host** window. The following table describes each of the configuration fields and settings that the Host Manager requires to add a host workstation to the network and gives examples. Keep in mind that your entries will differ from the examples.

7. Click on the **Add** button to add the host account.

8. Click the right mouse button on the abbreviated window menu button and click on the **Quit** item to quit the Host Manager.

FIGURE 17.7

The Host Manager window

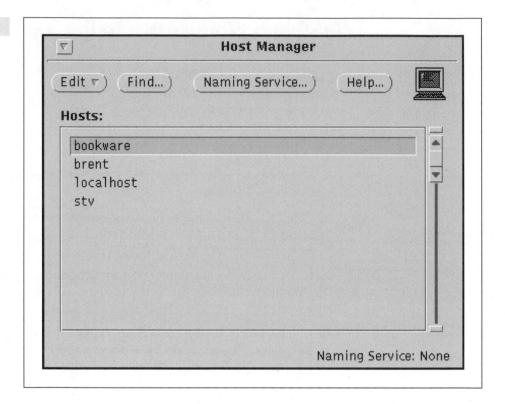

CONTROL	DESCRIPTION
Client Type	Specifies one of three types of client settings: **standalone**, **diskless**, and **dataless**. A **standalone** client is a computer that keeps all the file systems it needs on its own local disk. A **diskless** client gets all its file systems from another workstation, called a file server. A **dataless** client keeps the machine's root and swap file systems on a local disk, and stores the /usr and /home file systems on another workstation.

CONTROL	DESCRIPTION
Host Name	Specifies the unique name by which a workstation is known on the network. Type `uname -n` in a Command Tool or Shell Tool to display any installed system's host names. For instance, two host names used in examples in this book are `mayberry` and `primetime`.
IP Address	Identifies the unique Internet protocol address specified by four fields separated by periods. For example, a sample IP address might be `195.5.2.15`. Each field is a decimal number between 0 and 255. These addresses are required if your machines are connected to the Internet.
Ethernet Address	Indicates the workstation's ethernet address, specified by six fields separated by colons. Each field is a hexadecimal number between 0 and FF. The ethernet address can be obtained from a workstation during its boot sequence. For example, a sample ethernet address might be `02:60:8C:1B:7F:02`.
Timezone Region	Specifies the time zone for the region of the world you live in. SunOS recognizes world time zones and automatically adjusts the system clock for daylight saving time. You supply either the time zone for your area, or an offset from Greenwich mean time (GMT).
Timezone	The time zone for your area. For example, if you live in California choose `Pacific`.

Updating NIS Maps

Unless you are adding a host using the NIS network naming service with the Host Manager, you can skip this section. As previously mentioned, the

Host Manager does not directly support the NIS naming service. If you have added a host that is connected to a network using the NIS naming service by choosing `None` for the naming service, you need to manually add the new `/etc` entries into the NIS maps. When you use the Host Manager with an NIS network, you specify a workstation whose local `/etc` files are to be updated by the Host Manager. This workstation is known as a *database server*. The updated files include `/etc/hosts`, `/etc/ethers`, `/etc/timezone`, and `/etc/bootparams`. After you have finished using the Host Manager, do the following:

1. Write down the entries created in the four `/etc` files on the database server. For each new machine you added, there will be a new entry in the database server's `/etc/hosts`, `/etc/ethers`, `/etc/timezone`, and `/etc/bootparams` files.

2. On the NIS workstation that you added, copy each new entry that you noted previously into the corresponding files on the NIS master machine for your domain, so the new entries in the `/etc/hosts` file of the database server are also in the `/etc/hosts` file on the NIS master machine.

3. Do the same with each new entry in the `/etc/ethers`, `/etc/timezone`, and `/etc/bootparams` files.

4. At the shell prompt on the NIS master machine, enter the command line `cd /var/yp` to change to the `/var/yp` directory, then enter the `make` command. This remakes the NIS maps to allow the new workstations full access to the resources of the NIS network.

5. Once you have updated the NIS maps, remove the entries on the database server that were added by the Host Manager.

6. If you are adding a diskless client that is going to run SunOS 4.1.x, then change directories to the diskless client's root file system using the following command syntax: `cd /export/root/`*diskless-client*. Replace *disklessclient* with the diskless client's host name.

7. Enter `mv /var/yp- var/yp` to rename the `yp-` file to `yp` in the `var` directory.

8. Change the entry in the `/etc/defaultdomain` file to match your network's NIS domain name.

Deleting a Host from the Network

To delete a host from a network, in the `Host Manager` window, do the following:

1. Click on the name of the host you want to delete.

2. Click the right mouse button on the `Edit` menu and choose the `Delete Host` item.

3. Click the left mouse button on the `Delete` button to confirm the deletion.

Working with the Printer Manager

The Printer Manager lets you add printers to a host computer from any system in the network. Once a printer is added to a system, it is referred to as a *printer server*. You can also add access to remote printers (printers attached to a remote workstation), but the Printer Manager must be installed on each remote system you need to access. If you try to use the Printer Manager from your local machine to add or access printers across the network, it won't work.

WARNING

The Printer Manager will not help you install printers on workstations running SunOS 4.1 (BSD); however, it does allow you to access remote printers already attached to SunOS 4.1 printer servers.

Adding a Printer

The Printer Manager lets you add a printer either to the local system, the workstation on which you're running the Printer Manager, or to a remote printer server over the network. To add a printer do the following:

1. Click on the Printer Manager icon. The `Printer Manager` window appears, as shown in Figure 17.8.

The Printer Manager window

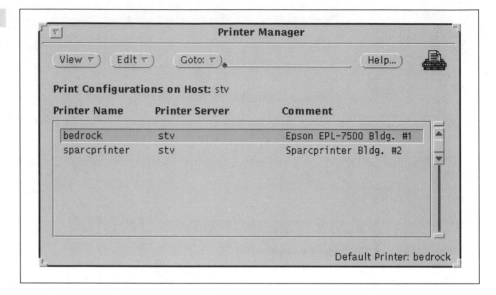

2. Click the right mouse button on the **Edit** button.

3. Choose the **Add Local Printer** item from the **Add Printer** submenu. The **Local Printer** window appears, as shown in Figure 17.9.

4. Fill in the fields in the **Local Printer** window. The following table describes each of the fields and settings, and supplies sample field entries and settings. Remember, your entries and settings may differ from these examples.

5. Click the left mouse button on the **Add** button to finish adding the printer.

6. Click the right mouse button on the abbreviated window menu button and click on the **Quit** item to quit the Printer Manager.

The following table describes each of the fields and settings, and supplies sample field entries and settings.

FIGURE 17.9

The Local Printer
window

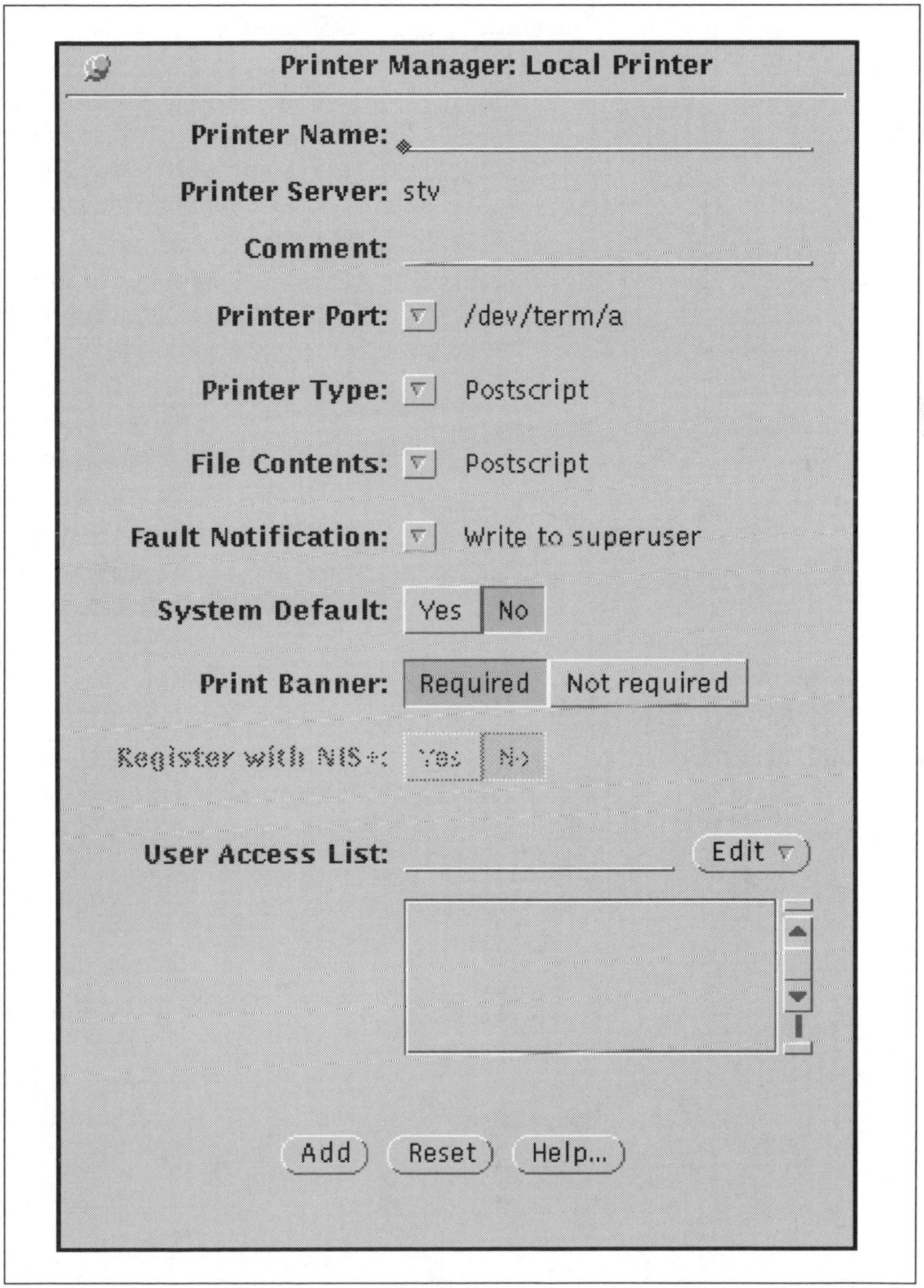

Printer Manager: Local Printer

Printer Name:

Printer Server: stv

Comment:

Printer Port: ▽ /dev/term/a

Printer Type: ▽ Postscript

File Contents: ▽ Postscript

Fault Notification: ▽ Write to superuser

System Default: Yes | No

Print Banner: Required | Not required

Register with NIS+: Yes | No

User Access List: (Edit ▽)

(Add) (Reset) (Help...)

CONTROL	DESCRIPTION
Printer Name	Specifies the unique name of the printer you are adding. A printer name can consist of up to 14 alphanumeric characters and underscores. For example, the printer name used in examples in this book is `bedrock`.
Printer Server	Identifies the name of the host workstation to which the printer is attached. For example, the printer server name shown in Figure 17.9 is `stv`.
Comment	Describes the printer or indicates its location. For example, you might enter the make of the printer and its location, `Epson EPL-7500 Bldg. #1`.
Printer Port	Specifies the device name of the port to which the printer is attached. The default is `/dev/term/a`.
Printer Type	Specifies the type of printer you are using. The default is `Postscript`.
File Contents	Determines what types of files can be printed. Common types include `Postscript` and `ASCII`.
Fault Notification	Indicates what action to take in case of printer error or problems. The three choices include writing a message to the root user, sending email, or no notification. The default is `Write to superuser`.
System Default	Determines whether or not the printer will be the default printer for users of the computer to which it is attached. The default is `No`.

CONTROL	DESCRIPTION
Print Banner	Specifies whether banner pages are required for each print job. Users still need to use the −o nobanner option with the lp command so that a banner page is not printed. The default is Required.
Register with NIS+	Creates a NIS+ table of all registered printers in the network. Unless you specified that you are using the NIS+ network-naming service, this setting is unavailable.
User Access List	Specifies, by user name, who will be able to access the printer. The Edit button next to the User Access List text field lets you insert user names into or delete user names from the scrolling list.

Adding a Remote Printer

The Printer Manager lets you add access to a remote printer. The remote workstation must be running the Printer Manager, or if the remote system is running SunOS 4.1, the printer must already be attached to the remote system. To add access to a remote printer, do the following:

1. Type the name of the remote system in the Goto text field.

2. Click the left mouse button on the Goto button. This is the same as choosing the Add Access to Remote Printer item from the Edit menu.

3. Click the left mouse button on the Edit item. The Access to Remote Printer pop-up window appears, as shown in Figure 17.10.

4. Fill in the fields in the Access to Remote Printer window. The following table describes each of the fields and settings and gives examples. Remember, your entries and settings may differ from these examples.

5. Click the left mouse button on the Add button.

FIGURE 17.10

The Access to Remote
Printer pop-up window

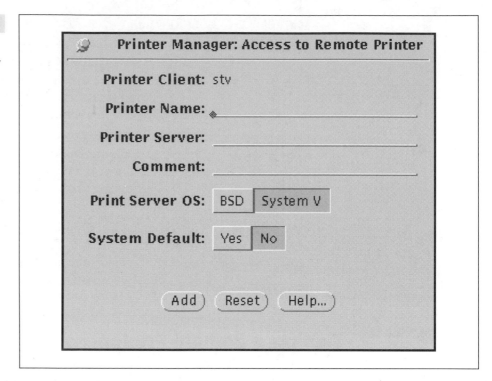

6. Click the right mouse button on the abbreviated window menu button and click on the `Quit` item to quit the Printer Manager.

CONTROL	DESCRIPTION
Printer Name	Specifies the unique name of the printer you are adding. A printer name can consist of up to 14 alphanumeric characters and underscores. For instance, the printer name used in examples in this book is `bedrock`.
Printer Server	Identifies the name of the host workstation to which the printer is attached. For example, the printer server name shown in Figure 17.10 is `stv`.

CONTROL	DESCRIPTION
Comment	Describes the printer or indicates its location. For example, you might enter the make of the printer and its location, `Postscript Bldg. #31`.
Printer Server OS	Specifies whether the workstation that is acting as a printer server is using SunOS 4.1 (`BSD`) or SunOS 5.x (`System V`).
System Default	Determines whether or not the system defaults to the remote printer. The default is `No`.

PART FOUR

Command Reference

THIS command reference covers the most common SunOS, Korn shell, and X Window System commands. Most of these commands were explained in this book. These commands can be entered from the DeskSet's Command Tool or Shell Tool, an `xterm` window, or from the SunOS command line. For clarity and quick referencing, obscure options have been omitted. If you want more information on a command's available options, use the `man` command followed by the command name.

Making the Transition to SunOS 5.X (SVR4)

If you are making the transition to SunOS 5.x (SVR4) from an earlier version of SunOS or from Berkeley Standard Distribution UNIX (BSD), keep in mind that many BSD commands are still available and are stored in the `/usr/ucb/` directory. Some of these commands have the same name as SunOS 5.x commands. If the PATH variable in your `.profile` file specifies `/usr/ucb` before the `/usr/bin` directory, you will end up running the BSD version of the command. If you are making the transition from System V Release 3 (SVR3), keep in mind that many additional commands are available with SVR4 that did not exist in SVR3. This command reference only explains how to use SunOS 5.x (SVR4) commands.

Command Reference Conventions

The conventions for this command reference are relatively simple. Text that appears in italicized brackets *[ ]* indicates an optional argument. Text that appears in italics indicates a place holder or text that varies; for example, *filename* would be replaced with an actual file name. Keystrokes that you press in the examples appear in angled brackets, for example, <Control-d>.

alias

Syntax

```
alias [name] [definition]
```

Description The `alias` command is a Korn shell command that lets you define shorthand ways to enter commands.

Options The `alias` command has no options.

Example If you want to always be prompted before copying over existing files, enter

```
alias cp="cp -i"
```

into your `.profile` file. This makes `cp` run `cp -i` instead, which prompts you before overwriting files.

Entering

```
alias cp
```

displays any definition in effect for `cp`.

Entering

```
alias
```

displays all `alias` definitions in effect.

See Also `unalias`, `set`

at

Syntax

```
at [options] time [date] [+ increment]
```

Description The `at` command runs a command or program from a file at some later time. By using `at`, it is possible to print long files after working hours or send reminders to yourself or others. It is also possible to set up a job to run and reschedule itself every day, week, month, and so on.

When scheduling a job to run at a later time, you have a great deal of latitude in specifying when it is to run. The time may be specified as either one, two, or four digits. One or two digits specifies hours, while four digits specifies hours and minutes. The time may also be specified with a colon separating hours and minutes (hour:minute). Either a 24-hour clock or an appended `am` or `pm` may be used. The special times `noon`, `midnight`, `now`, and `next` are also recognized. If no date is specified, the job runs at the next occurrence of *time*, the same day if *time* is after the current time, or the next day if *time* has already passed that day.

If *date* is included, it may take the form of either a month name followed by a day number or a day of the week. If a day of the week is used, it may be either fully spelled out or abbreviated with the first three letters. If the month given is before the current month, the next year is assumed.

An increment is a number followed by *minutes*, *hours*, *days*, *weeks*, *months*, or *years* (the singular form is used if appropriate). Thus, `at now + 15 minutes` means 15 minutes from the time the command is entered.

If no script file is specified (a script file is a file that contains SunOS commands, or programs, to be run together), `at` will take its input from the keyboard. If a script file is specified, it should contain the commands you would enter from the keyboard for `at` to run. If the script file named `run.at` contains

```
at -f run.me 15:00 today
```

```
at -f run.at 08:00 tomorrow
```

and the file `run.me` contains commands that print out memos that need to be routed every evening, then the system will automatically print out the memos every afternoon at 3:00 p.m. and reschedule the job the next morning.

Options

`-m`	Sends mail after the job has been run, even if the job is successful.
`-r` [*jobs*]	Removes jobs previously scheduled. The job number is determined by entering `at -l`.
`-l` [*jobs*]	Lists any jobs at has waiting to run.
`-f` [*scriptfile*]	Reads commands to be executed from `scriptfile`.

Example Entering

```
at -f atfile -m now + 15 minutes
```

runs commands from the file **atfile** in 15 minutes and displays

```
job 36983.a at Sat Oct 8 17:42:00 1994
```

where 36983 is the job queue entry number. Because the `-m` option was specified, this command sends mail when completed.

Entering

```
at -f atprint 1:00pm Friday
```

runs commands from the file **atprint** on the next Friday at 1:00 p.m. and displays

```
job 36984.a at Fri Oct 14 13:00:00 1994
```

Again, 36984 is the job queue entry number. To delete Friday's job, enter

```
at -r 36984.a
```

Had you not been sure of the queue entry number, you could have entered

```
at -l
```

which would have displayed

```
user = rpetrie 36983.a at Sat Oct 8 17:42:00 1994
user = rpetrie 36984.a at Fri Oct 14 13:00:00 1994
```

from which you could determine the job queue entry.

See Also atq, atrm, batch

atq

Syntax

```
atq [options] [usernames]
```

Description The atq command displays jobs created by the at command that are still in the job queue. Normally, jobs are sorted by the order in which they will execute. The superuser can display all jobs or specify the users whose jobs are in the queue he or she wants to display. Otherwise, only your jobs are displayed.

Options

-c	Displays the jobs in the queue sorted according to the time the at command was given.
-n	Displays the total number of jobs in the queue.

Example The following command displays the total number of jobs in the queue.

```
atq -n
```

See Also at, atrm, batch

atrm

Syntax

```
atrm [options] [users jobIDs]
```

Description The `atrm` command removes jobs that are in the queue by using the `at` command that matches the specified *jobIDs*. A superuser can also specify the users whose jobs are to be removed.

Options

`-a`	Removes all jobs belonging to the current user. This option lets a superuser remove all jobs.
`-f`	Removes jobs unconditionally and suppresses all removal information.
`-i`	Prompts to verify removal of a job. Press y to remove the job or n to leave the job.

Example To confirm that all jobs should be removed, enter

```
atrm -ai
```

See Also at, atq, batch

banner

Syntax

```
banner string
```

Description The `banner` command displays a string of characters as a poster on the standard output. The *string* can contain up to ten characters.

Options The `banner` command has no options.

Example

```
banner "Headline"
```

See Also echo

batch

Syntax

```
batch [options]
```

Description The `batch` command executes commands entered on standard input when the system load level permits. Input for the `batch` command ends when you press Control-d. Unlike `at`, which will execute commands at a specific time, `batch` executes commands one after another (waiting for each one to complete). Using the `batch` command avoids the high system load caused by running several background jobs at once. The output from commands are mailed to the person that started the `batch` command, unless it is redirected to a file.

Options The batch command has no options.

Example This is an example of how to run multiple commands from the command line using the `batch` command.

```
batch
find . -name "*.tmp" -exec rm {} \;
find . -name core -exec rm {} \;
troff -ms report I dpost I lp -Tpostscript
<Control-d>
```

The following example executes multiple commands stored in a file named `mycmds` and sends the output to another file named `mycmds.stats`.

```
batch
mycmds >mycmds.stats
<Control-d>
```

See Also at, atg, atrm, mail

bc

Syntax

```
bc [options] [files]
```

Description The **bc** command is an interactive arithmetic language processor and compiler that can also convert numbers from one base to another. Input can be taken from files or read from the standard input. You can use any of the following arithmetic symbols: + for addition, – for subtraction, * for multiplication, and / for division. To exit the **bc** command, type quit or Control-d.

Unless you specify otherwise, **bc** determines how many decimal places it should display. To specify a number of decimal places, after typing in the **bc** command, enter

```
scale=n
```

Where *n* is the number of decimal places you want.

The **bc** command can also convert between decimal, octal, hexadecimal, and any other bases. Special memory locations known as **ibase** and **obase** are used for converting and displaying values. To change how the base of numbers that are typed in are read, use the following format:

```
ibase=n
```

The **obase** location stores the base in which numbers are displayed. To change how the base of numbers are displayed, use the following format:

```
obase=n
```

Typically *n* will be the number 8 (octal), 10 (decimal), or 16 (hex). However, you can make any type of conversion by setting **ibase** to the base you have and **obase** to the base you want. Typing **ibase** or **obase** on a line by itself displays its current value.

Options

-c   Compile only.

-l   Makes available functions from the math library.

Example To use the bc command to multiply 3113*60, enter

```
bc
3113*60 <Return>
186780
<Control-d>
```

To set the number of decimals to 5 and divide 73 by 140, enter

```
bc <Return>
scale=5<Return>
73/140<Return>
0.52142
<Control-d>
```

To display the octal equivalent of the decimal number 10, type the following:

```
bc <Return>
ibase=8 <Return>
10<Return>
8
<Control-d>
```

To convert the decimal number 30 to its hexadecimal representation, enter

```
bc
obase=16
30
1E
<Control-d>
```

cal

Syntax

```
cal [month] year
```

Description The `cal` command by itself displays a calendar for the current month. The `cal` command followed by *month* and *year* gives a calendar for the month of the year specified. The `cal` command followed by *year* displays a calendar for the entire year. Note that entering `cal 11` displays the year 11 A.D., not November of the current year.

Options The `cal` command has no options.

Example If today's date is Saturday, October 5, 1999, then entering

```
cal
```

displays

```
    October 1999
 S   M   Tu  W   Th   F   S
                      1   2
 3   4   5   6   7    8   9
10  11  12  13  14   15  16
17  18  19  20  21   22  23
24  25  26  27  28   29  30
31
```

For the more historically minded, entering

```
cal 9 1752
```

displays

```
    September 1752
 S   M   Tu  W   Th   F   S
             1   2   14  15  16
17  18  19  20  21   22  23
24  25  26  27  28   29  30
```

This displays the month of September for the year the calendar changed from Gregorian to Julian.

See Also `calendar`, `date`

calendar

Syntax

```
calendar [option]
```

Description The `calendar` command is a reminder service. It looks for the file `calendar` in the current directory and displays lines that have today's or tomorrow's date. The `calendar` command recognizes `Aug. 31`, `august 31`, and `8/31` as valid dates, but not `31 August` or `31/8`. Designating the month as an asterisk (*) in the file `calendar` indicates all months.

Options

-	Allows a superuser to implement calendars for all users, searching each user's login directory for a file named `calendar`. Entries that match are sent to a user via mail.

Example Entering

```
*/15 PAYDAY!
```

in the file `calendar` causes the `calendar` command to display

```
*/15 PAYDAY!
```

if the command is run on the fifteenth (or the day before) of any month. On Fridays the `calendar` command considers tomorrow to be Monday.

See Also cal

cancel

Syntax

```
cancel [options] [printers]
```

Description The `cancel` command cancels requests for print jobs made with the `lp` command. A user can specify one or more *request-IDs* of print jobs to be canceled. The user can specify one or more printers to cancel current printing jobs. The `cancel` command also permits a user to cancel all of his or her own jobs on all printers. When used in this manner, the *printers* option identifies the printers on which the user's jobs will be canceled. When the printers option is used, all jobs queued for those printers will be canceled. Unless your system administrator has granted you special privileges, using the -u option will only allow you to cancel requests associated with your own login ID.

Options

request-ID	Cancels the print request for the print jobs *request-ID* specified.
-u *loginID*	Cancels the print request for the user identified by *loginID*.

Example

If there is only one request sent to a printer, entering

```
cancel sparcprinter
```

cancels the print request sent to the printer named **sparcprinter**. To cancel a specific print request, add the *request-ID*; for example, entering

```
cancel sparcprinter-119
```

cancels the print job with the *request-ID* **sparcprinter-119**. Entering

```
cancel -u bsimpson
```

cancels the print request sent by the user **bsimpson**.

See Also

lp, lpstat

cat

Syntax

```
cat [options] [filenames]
```

Description

The `cat` command creates, displays, and joins files.

Options

-e	Displays a $ character at the end of each line. The -e option is ignored unless used with the -v option.
-s	Causes cat to suppress error messages if the file does not exist.
-t	Displays tab characters as ^I and formfeed characters as ^L. The -t option is ignored unless it is used with the -v option.
-v	Makes control characters visible (for instance, Control-z appears on-screen as ^Z, Control-d as ^D, and so on). The Delete character prints as ^?. To display tabs and new lines as control characters, you must specify the -t option.

Example Entering

```
cat file1
```

displays the contents of file1 to the screen. Entering

```
cat file1 file2
```

displays the contents of file1 followed by the contents of file2. Entering

```
cat file1 file2 > file3
```

sends the contents of file1 followed by file2 to a new file called file3. Entering

```
cat > file1
```

takes input from the keyboard and sends the input to a new file called file1. Press Control-d to return to the prompt. Entering

```
cat file1 file2 >> file3
```

appends the contents of file1 and file2 to the already existing file3. Entering

```
cat
```

takes input from the keyboard (until a Control-d is entered) and sends its output to the screen.

See Also cp, echo, rm, more, pr, head, tail

cd

Syntax

    cd [directoryname]

Description The cd command changes the working directory to either your home directory (if no directory name is included) or to the directory indicated by *directoryname*. The main purpose of directories is to keep things organized. When working on multiple projects, you might make separate directories for each; thus, if two projects need a document called description, they will not conflict. By changing to the appropriate directory, you can avoid conflicting file names.

A directory is indicated by a relative or absolute path. A relative path references a subdirectory from the current directory when you type in the subdirectory's name, whereas an absolute directory always starts from the root directory. An absolute directory begins with a forward slash (/). A relative path can also use the dot (.) for the current directory or two dots (..) for the parent of the current directory.

Options The cd command has no options.

Example Entering

    cd

changes the current working directory to your home directory.

Entering

    cd /etc

changes the current working directory to the directory /etc. If your current directory is /games/scores, then entering

```
cd ..
```

changes the current working directory to the directory /games.

If you are a DOS user, you may be used to seeing your current path as part of your prompt. However, with Solaris you must reset the prompt string every time you change to another directory. The cd command only changes to the directory without the path. To reset the prompt every time you use the cd command, enter the following example. Note that the > prompt appears after you type the first line and press Return.

```
chdir() { <Return>
cd $* <Return>
PS1="${PWD}> "<Return>
}<Return>
```

After you press the last Return, the $ prompt returns. Now enter

```
alias cd="chdir"
```

To have the current path appear as part of your prompt, every time you use cd to change to another directory for future sessions, enter the previous examples into your .profile file. Adding these lines to your .profile file will cause the system's cd command to reset the prompt to display the current directory every time cd is used.

See Also pwd

chgrp

Syntax

```
chgrp [options] group filename(s)
```

Description The chgrp command changes the group association of a file (or files in the case of the -R option). Because Solaris is a multiuser system, built-in safeguards keep users from accidentally (or even deliberately) deleting one another's files. These safeguards protect against unauthorized reading, writing, copying, and deleting of files (as well as executing of executable files). See your system administrator about setting up groups.

Each file has a set of permissions associated with it: read, write, and execute. These three permissions may be applied to the owner of the file (usually the creator of the file), everyone else on the system, and specific groups of users. Entering the command **ls -lg** displays file names and information about their permission and group settings. The permissions are listed, then the number of links, the group ownership, the block size, the creation date, and finally, the file's name.

```
drwxrwxrwx     8     cntrct       4096    Feb     4    16:40           .
drwxr-xr-x    12     authrs       4122    Aug     7    17:00           ..
-rwxrwxrwx     1     cntrct     159360    Nov     5    11:40        file1
-rwx------     1     cntrct        658    Dec     1    15:30        file2
-r-xr-xr-x     1     cntrct      12555    Aug    13    08:30      archive
drwxrwxrwx    20     cntrct       1536    Oct    15    11:11       public
drwx------    11     cntrct        385    Jul     5    02:40      private
drwx-w--w-     2     cntrct         10    Oct     4    10:01     incoming
drwxr-xr-x     2     cntrct         10    Jul    21    17:32     outgoing
drwxrwx---    17     proj1        3072    Feb    17    09:48     project1
drwxrwx---    04     proj2        4096    May    21    08:45     project2
```

The **chgrp** command sets or changes the groups associated with a file's group permissions. To make the change, you must be the owner of the file as well as a member of the group to which you change the file.

Options

-h   Changes the group of a symbolic link.

-R   Causes **chgrp** to recursively descend through the directory (that is, into the subdirectories).

Example Entering

```
chgrp groupname filename
```

changes the group associated with *filename* to *groupname*.

See Also chown, ls, chmod

chmod

Syntax

```
chmod [-R] mode filename(s)
```

Description The `chmod` command changes the permissions (*mode*) associated with the file *filename* (or files in the case of the `-R` option). Built-in SunOS safeguards keep users from accidentally (or even deliberately) deleting one another's files. These safeguards prevent unauthorized reading, writing, copying, and deleting of files (as well as executing of executable files).

Each file has a set of permissions associated with it: read, write, and execute. These three permissions may be applied to the owner of the file (usually the creator of the file), everyone else on the system, and groups of people defined by entries in the file `/etc/passwd`. Entering the command `ls -l` displays file names and information about their permissions. The permissions are listed, then the number of links, the owner, the block size, the creation date, and finally, the file's name.

```
drwxrwxrwx   8  lgoodman   cntrct     4096  Feb   4  16:40       .
drwxr-xr-x  12  root       authrs     4122  Aug   7  17:00       ..
-rwxrwxrwx   1  lgoodman   cntrct   159360  Nov   5  11:40   file1
-rwx------   1  lgoodman   cntrct      658  Dec   1  15:30   file2
-r-xr-xr-x   1  lgoodman   cntrct    12555  Aug  13  08:30  archive
drwxrwxrwx  20  lgoodman   cntrct     1536  Oct  15  11:11   public
drwx------  11  lgoodman   cntrct      385  Jul   5  02:40  private
drwx-w--w-   2  lgoodman   cntrct       10  Oct   4  10:01incoming
drwxr-xr-x   2  lgoodman   cntrct       10  Jul  21  17:32outgoing
drwxrwx---  17  lgoodman   proj1      3072  Feb  17  09:48project1
drwxrwx---  04  lgoodman   proj2      4096  May  21  08:45project2
```

The first letter indicates the listing is for a directory (d) or a file (–). The next three letters are the permissions given the owner of the file: (`r` is read or copy permission, `w` is write or delete permission, `x` is execute or search permission). The next three letters are the permissions for the groups assigned. The last three letters are the permissions for everyone on the system. The listing shows that `file1` may be read, written, or executed by anyone on the system. `file2` may be read, written, or executed only by the owner, `lgoodman`. The file `archive` may be read by anyone, but no one (not even the owner) may overwrite the file. The directory `public` may have files read from, written to, or searched by anyone on the system. The directory `private` may only be written to, read from, or searched by the owner. The directory `incoming` may be written to by anyone, while no one but the owner may read or search it. The directory `outgoing` may be searched or copied from by anyone, but may only be written to by the owner. The directories `project1` and `project2` may be accessed only by the owner and the members of the respective groups `proj1` and `proj2`.

The modes are given in either of two formats for this command. An absolute mode is an octal number formed by summing up the following octal numbers representing the enabled permissions.

400	Read by owner allowed
200	Write by owner allowed
100	Execute (search in directory) by owner allowed
040	Read by associated group allowed
020	Write by associated group allowed
010	Execute (search in directory) by associated group allowed
004	Read by everyone allowed
002	Write by everyone allowed
001	Execute (search in directory) by everyone allowed

Thus a permission mode of **777** enables all to read, write, and execute. A permission of **744** enables the owner to read, write, and execute while allowing everyone else only read permission.

The other format uses letter symbols instead of numbers. The symbolic mode looks like this:

[who] operation permission

where *who* is

u	User's permissions
g	Group's permissions

o	Other's permissions
a	Permissions for everyone (equivalent to **ugo**)

The *operation* is

+	Adds the permission
-	Removes the permission
=	Explicitly assigns the permission and any permissions not listed will be disallowed

and the *permission* is a combination of

r	Read
w	Write
x	Execute

Options

-R	Sets the mode for all specified files in the current and any other appropriate subdirectories

Example Entering

```
chmod o-w file1
```

denies write permission to others not in your group on the file named **file1**. Entering

```
chmod a+r file1
```

gives everyone (the owner, members of your group, and everyone else) read permission on the file named **file1**. Entering

```
chmod 700 file1
```

gives the owner of `file1` read, write, and execute permission while deny-ing members of the owner's group and the rest of the users any permis-sions. Entering

```
chmod 222 file1
```

gives everyone write permission only.

See Also chgrp, chown, ls

chown

Syntax

```
chown [options] owner [group] filename
```

Description The chown command changes the owner of the file named *filename* to the user named *owner*. The user *owner* is specified by either the login name or the user identification number (UID). The *group* may likewise be specified as either a group name or group identification num-ber (GID).

Since Solaris is a multiuser system, built-in safeguards keep users from ac-cidentally (or even deliberately) deleting one another's files. These safeguards protect against unauthorized reading, writing, copying, and deleting of files (as well as executing of executable files). Another safeguard is that only someone logged in as a superuser (usually the sys-tem administrator) can execute chown.

Options

-h	Changes the owner of a symbolic link.
-R	Sets the mode for all specified files in the current and any other appropriate subdirectories.

Example Entering

```
chown ataylor chapter1
```

causes **ataylor** to become the owner of the file called **chapter1**.

See Also chgrp, chmod, ls

clear

Syntax

```
clear
```

Description The clear command clears the screen and returns the cursor to the upper-left corner. This is useful for clearing clutter from the screen.

Options The clear command has no options.

Example Entering

```
clear
```

clears the screen.

See Also set

cmp

Syntax

```
cmp [options] file1 file2
```

Description The cmp command compares *file1* with *file2* and displays the differing byte and line numbers.

Options

-l	For each difference, prints the byte number in decimal and the differing bytes in octal.
-s	Does not display file differences, but returns exit codes.
0	Exit code indicating files are identical.

1	Exit code indicating files are different.
2	Exit code indicating files are inaccessible.

Example This command prints a message if two files are the same (exit code is 0):

```
cmp -s old new && echo 'no changes'
```

See Also comm, diff

comm

Syntax

```
comm [options] file1 file2
```

Description The comm command reads *file1* and *file2* and displays three columns of output: lines unique to *file1*, lines unique to *file2*, and lines common to both files. The comm command is similar to diff in that both commands compare two files. But comm can also be used like uniq; that is, comm selects duplicate or unique lines between sorted files, whereas uniq selects duplicate or unique lines within the same sorted file. Before you run the comm command, sort the files to be compared using the sort command.

Options

–	Reads the standard input.
-1	Suppresses displaying lines unique from *file1* (column 1).
-2	Suppresses displaying lines unique from *file2* (column 2).
-3	Suppresses displaying lines in both *file1* and *file2* (column 3).
-12	Displays only lines common to *file1* and *file2* (displays only column 3).

-13	Displays only lines unique to *file2* (displays only column 2).
-23	Displays only lines unique to *file1* (displays only column 1).

Example To compare two lists of phone numbers, and display lines that appear in both lists, enter:

```
comm -12 blackbk phonelist
```

See Also diff, uniq

compress

Syntax

```
compress [options] [filename]
```

Description The compress command reduces the storage size of the file *filename* by use of a compression algorithm (Lempel-Ziv). The file *filename* is replaced by a file with a .Z extension. The .Z file is about half the size of the source file. The compression depends greatly upon the contents of the input file. To restore a compressed file, use the command uncompress. To view a file without changing the .Z file, use the command zcat.

Options

-c	Writes to the screen (or standard output); does not change any files. The zcat command is equivalent to the -c option.
-f	Forces compression regardless of whether the file actually shrinks (not all files shrink from compress) or the .Z file already exists.
-v	Displays the percentage of reduction attained by running compress.

Example Given a file, `report.text`, with a size of 4608 bytes, entering

```
compress report.text
```

results in a file `report.text.Z` with a size of 2696 bytes. To uncompress `report.text.Z`, enter

```
uncompress report.text
```

Note that with the `uncompress` command the `.Z` extension is optional.

See Also uncompress, zcat

cp

Syntax

```
cp [options] filename1 filename2
cp [options] directory1 directory2
cp [options] filenames directory
```

Description Entering `cp` *filename1 filename2* copies *filename1* to *filename2*. If *filename2* already exists, it is overwritten and the old file is lost. You might want to enter **alias cp cp −i** into your .profile file. The `cp −i` command asks for confirmation before overwriting a file.

Entering `cp −r` *directory1 directory2* copies all the files of *directory1* and any files in any subdirectories of *directory1* into *directory2*, creating *directory2*, if it does not already exist, and any subdirectories of *directory2*.

Entering `cp` *filenames directory* copies all of the files specified by *filenames* into *directory*. The destination directory must already exist.

For files that are linked (`ln`), `cp` copies the contents pointed to by a link, not the link itself; files that are linked will not have their copies linked.

Options

-i   Prompts for confirmation before overwriting an existing file. Pressing y confirms the copy should proceed; any other key aborts the **cp** operation.

-p   Copies the source file(s) and keeps the same modification time and permission modes.

-r   If any of the source files are directories, copies the directory, all its files, any subdirectories, and any files in the subdirectories.

Example Entering

```
cp file1 file2
```

copies the contents of **file1** to **file2**. If **file2** does not already exist, it is created; if it does exist, the old contents are replaced and lost.

Here is an example of using **cp** to copy directories:

```
cp -r rpetrie/part4 rpetrie/archive
```

This copies all of the directory **part4** into the directory **archive**, creating **archive** if necessary.

See Also mv, ln, rename, mkdir

cpio

Syntax

```
cpio -p [options]
cpio -o [options]
cpio -p [options]
```

Description The **cpio** command is an archiving program that can copy individual files, groups of files, or complete file systems in from or out to tape or disk. The `cpio` command can create archives that require multiple tapes or diskettes. It also recognizes when the tape or diskette is full and prompts you to insert another volume. The `cpio` command packs data onto tape more efficiently than the `tar` command.

Options

-i *[options]* *[patterns]*	Matches patterns from standard input to retrieve files. The command syntax cpio-i *[options]* *[patterns]* copies in files whose names match the patterns specified. Each pattern can include the ★ and ? wildcard characters. Patterns should be quoted or escaped so they are interpreted by `cpio`, not by the shell. If no pattern is used, all files are copied in. During extraction, existing files are not overwritten by older versions in the archive (unless –u is specified).
-o *[options]*	Reads and copies list of files whose names are specified to the standard output. The files are combined into an archive file.
-p *[options]* *directory*	Reads a list of files from the standard input and copies the files to another directory on the same system. Destination path names are interpreted relative to the named directory. This is useful for copying directories and their contents.
-a	Resets the access times of input files after performing the copy operation.
-A	Appends files to an archive (must use with *-o* option).
-b	Reverses the byte order in each word and half-word. Words are 4 bytes (only with –i).
-B	Blocks input or output using 5120 bytes per record (default is 512 bytes per record).

-c	Reads or writes header information as ASCII characters; you must use this option when the source and destination machines are of differing types.
-C *n*	Blocks input or output like -B, but block size can be any positive integer *n*.
-d	Creates directories as needed. This option is useful when some of the files you are copying are directories. (Do not use with the -o option).
-E *filename*	Extracts file names listed in file from the archives.
-f	Copies in all files that do *not* match the *pattern* specified with the -i option.
-H *header*	Reads or writes header information in *header* format. Values for *header* are bar (bar header and format), crc (ASCII header containing expanded device numbers), odc (ASCII header containing small device numbers), ustar (IEEE/PlOO3 Data interchange Standard header), or tar (tar header). This option is used only with the -i option.
-I *filename*	Reads input from *filename*.
-k	Skips corrupted file headers and I/0 errors.
-l	Links files rather than copies files. This option is used only with the -p option.
-L	Follows symbolic links.
-m	Retains previous file modification time. This option does not work for directories.

-M *string* Specifies a message (*string*) to use when switching media. To display the sequence number of the next tape or diskette, use the variable %d in the *string.* The -M string option modifier is valid only with -I or -O.

-O *filename* Sends the output to **filename**. Use only with the -o option.

-r Lets you interactively rename files as they are copied. When **cpio** copies each file, it waits for you to type a new name. If you press Return, the file is skipped. If you type a period (.), the original path and file name will be used.

-R *ID* Reassigns owner and group permissions for each file to the user's login ID. (This option is available to superusers only.)

-t Displays a table of contents of the input only; no files are created. When used with the -v option, the listing output resembles **ls** -l. This option cannot be used with -V.

-u Copies files unconditionally; old files can overwrite new files.

-v Displays a list of file names. When used with the -t option, the listing output resembles **ls** -l output.

-V Prints a dot for each file read or written. This shows that the **cpio** command is working without cluttering the screen.

Example To copy all files in a directory to a tape, enter

    ls | cpio -oc > /dev/rmt/0

To list all the files on tape, enter

    cpio -civt < /dev/rmt/0

To retrieve all files from a tape and copy them to the current directory, enter

```
cpio -icv < /dev/rmt/0
```

To retrieve only some of the files from a tape, you must specify a pattern to match. The following example retrieves all files beginning with report, and creates subdirectories if needed.

```
cpio -icdv "report*" < /dev/rmt/0
```

To copy directory trees between file systems, enter

```
cd /filesystem1
find . -print -depth | cpio -pdm /filesystem2
```

To restore files on a diskette created with the bar command, enter

```
cpio -ivH bar < /dev/diskette
```

See Also find, tar

crontab

Syntax

```
crontab [filename]
crontab [options]
crontab [options] [username]
```

Description The crontab command allows you to submit a list of commands that the system will run for you at times you specify. You can only work with the crontab program if your name is included in the /usr/sbin/cron.d/cron.allow file. The /usr/sbin/cron.d/cron.deny file contains the list of users not allowed to run crontab. If neither of these two files exist, only the superuser can start crontab. Your list of commands are stored in files that are referred to as crontab files. Numbers are supplied before each command to specify the execution time. The execution time and command to run in the crontab file must be on a new line. The system utility named cron reads your current crontab file and runs the commands in your crontab file. A superuser can run crontab for another user by adding the *username* argument. The format for each entry in the **crontab** file is:

```
minute hour day-of-the-month month day-of-the-week command
```

The range of acceptable numbers for each of these five fields is as follows:

minute	0–59
hour	0–23
day of the month	1–31
month	1–12
day of the week	0–6 (0 = Sunday)

You can use an asterisk (*) to indicate all possible values. Use a comma between multiple values and a hyphen (–) to indicate a range. Standard output and error output is mailed to the person who started the **crontab** command unless it is redirected to a file.

Options

-e	Edits the user's current **crontab** file (or creates one).
-l	Lists the user's file in the **crontab** directory.
-r	Deletes the user's file in the **crontab** directory.

Example The following shows a crontab entry that mails a reminder at noon on the 1st and 15th of each month to **rpetrie**.

```
0 12 1,15 * * echo "Time to submit biweekly report" | mail rpetrie
```

The following example installs a file named **cronfile** as the **crontab** file:

```
crontab cronfile
```

To list the **crontab** entries and send the output to a file named **cronlist**, enter

```
crontab -l >cronlist
```

To edit the `crontab` file using the default editor (`ed`), enter

```
crontab -e
```

For information on the `ed` editor, type `man ed`.

See Also at, atq, atrm, batch

CU

Syntax

```
cu [options] telephonenumber
```

Description   The `cu` command enables you to call another UNIX system, log in, and use that system while you are still logged into your own system. You can also use the `cu` command to connect to a non-UNIX system. In order for `cu` to operate correctly, your system administrator must have added it when installing Solaris and configured the files in the `/usr/lib/uucp` directory. If `cu` doesn't exist on your system, use the `tip` command. The `cu` command works by using your UNIX system's dial-out capability and connecting your terminal to an outgoing modem. You can use the equal symbol (=) to instruct `cu` to wait for a secondary dial tone before dialing the rest of the phone number. Adding the minus symbol (–) instructs `cu` to pause for four seconds before dialing the rest of the phone number. Once you are connected to another system, you follow normal procedures for logging in. Your terminal then becomes a remote terminal for the system you are connected to. You can also use the `cu` command to transfer files between your system and the remote system.

The `cu` command runs as two processes: transmit and receive. The transmit process reads lines from the standard input and transmits the standard input to the connected system. Lines beginning with a tilde (~) are treated as instructions to the calling system rather than lines to be transmitted. The receive process takes data from the remote system and echoes it on the standard output.

Options

−b*n*	Processes lines using *n*-bit characters; n can be either 7 or 8.
−c*name*	Searches UUCP's `Devices` file and selects the local area network that matches *name*.
−d	Displays diagnostic traces.
−e	Sends even-parity data to remote system.
−h	Sets communications mode to half-duplex. This emulates local `echo` and support calls to other systems expecting terminals to use half-duplex mode.
−l*line*	Specifies a device name to use as the communications line, such as (`/dev/term/a`).
−n	Prompts user for a telephone number.
−o	Uses odd parity.
−s*speed*	Sets transmission speed to *speed*. The standard transmission speeds are 1200, 2400, and 9600. The default is 1200.
−t	Dials an ASCII terminal that has auto-answer set.

The following are tilde commands for performing tasks on your local system while connected to the host system.

~.	Terminates the connection.
~!	Escapes to an interactive shell on the local system.
~!*command*	Runs *command* on local system.
~$*command*	Runs *command* locally and sends output to remote system as a command to be run on the remote system.
~o/%cd	Changes directory on the local system.

~%take file [target]	Copies *file* from remote system to *target* on the local system. If *target* is omitted, file is used in both places.
~%put file [target]	Copy *file* from the local system to *target* on the remote system. If *target* is omitted, file is used in both places.
~ ~.	Allows you to pass a line that begins with a tilde. This command lets you issue commands to more than one system in a cu chain.
~%b	Sends a BREAK sequence to remote system.
~%ifc	Turns the DC3/DC1 XON/XOFF control protocol (characters ^S, ^Q) on or off for the remainder of the session.
~ofc	Sets output flow control either on or off.

Example To connect to another system, enter

```
cu 5551234
```

where 5551234 is the modem phone number for the system you want to connect to. This command calls a computer using the first available device (modem).

Entering

```
cu -s9600 5551234
```

calls a computer that has a 9600 baud modem. The local computer will use the first available device supporting the speed.

To dial a 9 and wait for a secondary dial tone, enter

```
cu 9=5551234
```

To connect to a destination system that recognizes your system, you can use the system name instead of the phone number. For example, enter

```
cu mayberry
```

The `uuname` command lists the recognized systems. Systems that are recognized by your system are listed in the `/etc/uucp/Systems` file.

See Also `rcp`, `rlogin`

cut

Syntax

```
cut options [filename]
```

Description The `cut` command allows you to extract fields from lines of a file or columns from a table. It has two modes. The `-c` option selects columns from a file. Columns are one character wide and are identified by number. The `-f` option selects fields. Fields are recognized by a field delimiter (the default is tab) and identified by number. In both options, a hyphen is used to indicate a range of numbers and a comma is used to separate individual numbers or ranges. The list of identifying numbers follows the appropriate option without spaces.

Options

`-c`*list*	Cuts the column positions identified in list.
`-d`*c*	Used with `-f` to specify field delimiter as character *c* (default is tab); special characters such as spaces must be quoted.
`-f`*list*	Cuts the fields identified in list.
`-s`	Used with `-f` to suppress lines without delimiters.

Example Entering

```
cut -c3-6,9 report
```

displays columns three through six and column nine of the file `report`.

Entering

```
cut -f2,5 -d: sales
```

prints fields two and five of the file **sales**, with the fields separated by a colon.

To cut characters in the fourth column of a file named **file1**, and paste them back as the first column in the same file, enter

```
cut -c4 file1 | paste - file1
```

The **cut** command is often used with the pipe (|) to extract text when the characters appear in a fixed-width format, such as the output from the **ls -l** command. The following example cuts and displays the size and name of files from an **ls -l** file listing.

```
ls -l | cut -c33-40,54-
```

The notation **54-** indicates columns 54 through the end of the line.

See Also join, paste

date

Syntax

```
date [+format]
```

Description The **date** command displays this information: **day, month, date, hour:minute:second, time zone, year**, thus giving you access to current time and date information at your workstation. The **date** command is also used by the system administrator to set the system date and time.

Options

%n	Inserts newline character.
%t	Inserts tab character.
%m	Displays month as two digits (**01** to **12**).
%d	Displays day as two digits (**01** to **31**).
%y	Displays last two digits of the year (**00** to **99**).

`%D`	Displays date in `mm/dd/yy` format.
`%H`	Displays hour in 24-hour clock format.
`%M`	Displays minute as `00` to `59`.
`%S`	Displays seconds as `00` to `59`.
`%T`	Displays time as `hour:minute:second`.
`%j`	Displays day of the year as `000-365`.
`%w`	Displays the day of the week as `Sunday = 0`.
`%a`	Displays weekday abbreviated to three letters as `SUN, MON, TUE...`
`%h`	Displays the month abbreviated to three letters as `MAY, JUN, JUL...`
`%r`	Displays hour in 12-hour format as `AM/PM`

Example If today's date is Saturday, the 5th of October, 1999, and the time is 11:15 a.m., then entering

```
date
```

displays

```
Sat Oct 5 11:15:01 PDT 1999
```

For a gentle reminder every morning, you might add this into the `.login` file in your home directory:

```
date +'Good Morning! Today is %a %h %d %nThe time is: %r.'
```

which displays

```
Good Morning! Today is Fri Aug 13.
The time is 09:00:00 AM.
```

To change the date to December 25, 1999, 12:01 a.m., become a super-user and enter

```
date 1225001999
```

See Also `time`

deroff

Syntax

```
deroff [options] [filename(s)]
```

Description The `deroff` command removes all `nroff` and `troff` requests and macros, backslash escape sequences, and `tbl` and `eqn` constructs from the specified files and displays the remaining text on the screen. You can use the wildcard characters ? and * to indicate multiple files, or you can enter a list of file names by separating each name with a space.

Options

`-mm`	Suppresses text that appears on macro lines; paragraphs will print but headings might be stripped.
`-w`	Outputs the text as a list, one word per line.

Example To remove formatting instructions from two files named `status` and `text`, and display the text remaining in the two files, enter

```
deroff status text
```

To remove `troff` instructions from the file named `report1` and save the remaining text in a file named `report2`, enter

```
deroff report1 > report2
```

See Also `troff`

df

Syntax

```
df [options] [filesystem]
```

Description The `df` command reports the amount of occupied disk space, the amount of used and available space, and how much of the file system's storage space has been used. If you use the **df** command without any argument, the amount of space occupied and files for all mounted file systems is displayed.

Options

-b	Reports the amount of free disk space in kilobytcs.
-F *filesystemtype*	Reports on an unmounted file system specified by *filesystemtype*. Available file system types can be seen by displaying the **/etc/vfstab** file.
-g	Reports the amount of occupied and free disk space, the type of file system, the file system ID, file name length, block size, and fragment size.
-k	Reports the amount of occupied and free disk space in kilobytes, as well as the percent of capacity used.
-t	Reports the total allocated space as well as free space.

Example Entering

    df -k

displays a listing of the amount of used and available space similar to the following:

```
Filesystem            kbytes    used    avail  capacity  Mounted on
/dev/dsk/c0t0d0s0      24143    15954    5779    73%           /
/dev/dsk/c0t0d0s6     192151   171623    1318    99%        /usr
/proc                      0        0       0     0%       /proc
fd                         0        0       0     0%     /dev/fd
swap                   80180       16   80164     0%        /tmp
/dev/dsk/c0t0d0s5      95167    77279    8378    90%        /opt
/dev/dsk/c0t6d0s2     186723   180697       0   100%      /cdrom
```

See Also du

diff

Syntax

```
diff [options] filename1 filename2
```

Description The `diff` command compares *filename1* to *filename2* and identifies which lines to change to make the files identical. All differing lines are displayed, as are commands needed to convert *filename1* into *filename2*. The commands are **a**, **d**, and **c**. An **a** means that lines are added to *filename1* to match *filename2*; a **d** means that lines are deleted from *filename1* to match *filename2*; a **c** means that lines have changed from *filename1* to *filename2*.

Options

-b	Ignores trailing blanks (spaces and tabs) and treats all other strings of blanks as equals.
-i	Ignores the case of letters. Treats **A** as equivalent to **a**.
-w	Ignores all blanks (spaces and tabs). Treats **3 + 5 = 8** as equivalent to **3+5=8**.

Example Given two files, `file1`, which contains

```
Anne Addams      111 N 1st St      555-1111
Bill Browne      222 S 2nd St      555-2222
Cher Clarke      333 E 3rd Av      555-3333
Dave Durham      444 W 4th Av      555-4444
```

and `file2`, which contains

```
Anne Smythe      111 N 1st St      555-1111
Bill Browne      222 S 2nd St      555-2222
Carl Change      777 E 7th Av      555-7777
Dave Durham      444 W 4th Av      555-4444
Eddy Elliot      555 Park Pl       555-5555
```

entering

```
diff file1 file2
```

yields

```
1c1
< Anne Addams        111 N 1st St       555-1111
---
> Anne Smythe        111 N 1st St       555-1111
3c3
< Cher Clarke        333 E 3rd Av       555-3333
---
> Carl Change        777 E 7th Av       555-7777
4a5
> Eddy Elliot        555 Park Pl        555-5555
```

This shows that lines one and three have been changed and line five has been added.

dircmp

Syntax

dircmp [options] *directory1 directory2*

Description The dircmp command compares the contents of *directory1* and *directory2* and lists information on files that are unique to each directory. It then displays two-column output, listing the word same before all files that are the same in both directories. If you are comparing directories containing several files, it is easier to use the Command Tool window, because using a Shell Tool causes text to scroll past.

Options

-d	Compares the contents of files with the same name in both directories and outputs a list telling what must be changed in the two files to bring them into agreement.
-s	Suppresses all messages about identical files.
-w*n*	Changes the width of the output line length to *n* characters (the default is 72).

Example Entering

```
dircmp -S docs1 docs2
```

compares the directory *docs1* with *docs2* and returns to the prompt if the files are the same in both directories.

See Also cmp, diff

domainname

Syntax

```
domainname name
```

Description The domainname command sets or displays the name of the current Network Information Service (NIS) domain. Only the superuser can set the name of the domain. The domain name is usually set by your system administrator during the installation. Entering domainname displays the name of the current NIS domain name.

Options There are no options for the domainname command.

Example Entering

```
domainname
```

displays the current domain name.

If you have superuser privileges, entering

```
domainname mayberry
```

sets the domain name as mayberry.

dpost

Syntax

```
dpost [options] [files]
```

Description The `dpost` command translates files formatted by `troff` into PostScript for printing.

Options

`-c`*n*	Prints n copies of each page. The default is 1.
`-e`*n*	Sets the text encoding level to *n*. The recognized choices are 0, 1, and 2. The size of the output file and print time should decrease as *n* increases. Level 2 encoding will typically be about 20 percent faster than level 0, which is the default and produces output essentially identical to earlier versions of `dpost`.
`-m`*n*	Increases (multiplies) the size of logical pages by factor scale. The default is 1.0.
`-n`*n*	Prints *n* logical pages on each sheet of output. The default is 1.
`-o`*list*	Prints only pages contained in a comma-separated list.
`-p`*mode*	Specifies layout to be either portrait (long side is vertical; also the default) or landscape (long side is horizontal). Layout can be abbreviated to `p` or `l`.
`-w`*n*	Draws troff graphics (e.g., `pic`, `tbl`) using lines that are *n* points thick. The default is 0.3.
`-x`*n*	Offsets the x-coordinate of the origin *n* inches to the right (if *n* is positive).
`-y`*n*	Offsets the y-coordinate of the origin *n* inches down (if *n* is positive). Default origin is the upper-left corner of the page.
`-F` *directory*	Sets the font directory to *directory*. The default is `/usr/lib/font`.

-H *directory*	Sets the host-resident font directory to *directory*. Files there must describe PostScript fonts and have file names corresponding to a two-character **troff** font.
-L *filename*	Sets the PostScript prologue to file. The default is **/usr/lib/postscript/dpost.ps**.
-O	Omits PostScript pictures from output. Useful when running in a networked environment.

Example Entering

```
troff -ms myfile | dpost | lp -Tpostscript
```

formats the file named **myfile** with **troff**, translates the file to PostScript format, and sends the file to be printed on a PostScript printer.

Entering

```
troff file1 | dpost>file1.ps
```

formats the file containing **troff** requests named **file1**, sends the output to the **dpost** filter, and stores the translated output in a file named **file1.ps**.

See Also troff

du

Syntax

```
du [options] [directory]
```

Description The **du** command gives the number of 512K blocks used by a directory and all of its subdirectories. If no directory name is specified, it reports on the current directory and all subdirectories.

Options

-a   Reports on every directory and file instead of just each directory.

-k   Reports usage in kilobytes.

-r   By default, the **du** command ignores files and directories it cannot open. The -r option reports when **du** cannot open a file or directory.

-s   Reports the total disk usage for each specified directory, or the total for the current directory if a directory is not specified.

Example Entering

```
du -a
```

displays disk usage information on all subdirectories and files in the current directory. Entering

```
du /usr/
```

reports the number of 512k blocks contained in all files and all subdirectories under the directory /usr.

See Also df

echo

Syntax

```
echo [options] string
```

Description The echo command displays a string on the screen (or standard output). This command is often used within a script file to display the progress of the file or to request some user input. (A script file is a file that contains SunOS commands, or programs, to be run together.)

Options

-n   Does not output newline characters
              (carriage return characters).

The following are special options that can be used in the echo command's
argument.

\b   backspace

\c   display line without newline

\f   formfeed

\n   newline

\r   carriage return

\t   tab

\v   vertical tab

\n   Displays the ASCII value for the number
              indicated by *n*. The number *n* can be any 1-,
              2-, or 3-digit octal value; for example, \07
              rings a bell, because the ASCII value of the
              bell is octal 07.

\\   backslash

Examples Entering

```
echo "Hi Mom"
```

displays

```
Hi Mom
```

The echo command is useful for displaying the value of a variable, for example, entering

```
echo $OPENWINHOME
```

displays

```
/usr/openwin
```

or the name of the directory that is stored as your OPENWINHOME variable.

The echo command is often used with pipes. The following is an example of sending the output of the echo command so that it is sent to the mail program as a mail message to a user named lpartridge.

```
echo "Don't forget the battle of the bands today" | mail
lpartridge
```

eject

Syntax

```
eject [options] [device | nickname]
```

Description The eject command removes media from disk drives that do not have a manual eject button. The device can be specified by its name or by a nickname; if no device is specified, the default device is used. The default device is /dev/rdiskette. The eject command automatically searches for any mounted file systems that reside on the device and attempts to umount them prior to ejecting the media.

Options

-d	Displays the name of the default drive to be ejected.
-f	Forces the device to eject. The -f option can cause an ejection of a device that currently contains mounted partitions.
-n	Displays an assigned nickname for the device.
-q	Checks to see if the media is present.

Example The following ejects the floppy disk from the disk drive:

```
eject
```

If you have a CD ROM and a floppy diskette, entering

```
eject -n
```

displays a listing similar to this:

```
eject: nicknames are:
    fd -> /dev/rdiskette
    fd0 -> /dev/rdiskette
    floppy -> /dev/rdiskette
    /dev/rdiskette -> /dev/rdiskette
    /dev/fd0 -> /dev/rdiskette
    /dev/fd0a -> /dev/rdiskette
    /dev/fd0b -> /dev/rdiskette
    /dev/fd0c -> /dev/rdiskette
    diskette -> /dev/rdiskette
    /dev/diskette -> /dev/rdiskette
    sr -> /dev/rdsk/c0t6d0s0
    sr0 -> /dev/rdsk/c0t6d0s0
    cd -> /dev/rdsk/c0t6d0s0
    cdrom -> /dev/rdsk/c0t6d0s0
    /dev/sr0 -> /dev/rdsk/c0t6d0s0
    c0t6d0s0 -> /dev/rdsk/c0t6d0s0
```

See Also fdformat, mount

env

Syntax

```
env [option] [variable=value ...] [command]
```

Description The env command displays or alters environment variables. When issued without a command argument, the env command displays all global environment variables. When a command argument is specified, the variable's value is added to the environment.

Options

-    Ignores the current environment. Restricts the environment for command to that specified by the arguments.

name=value   Sets the environment variable file name to value and adds it to the environment before the given command is run.

Example To display your current environment, enter

```
env
```

To temporarily change your time zone setting from Pacific Standard Time to Eastern Standard Time and add it to the environment before running the `date` command, enter

```
env TZ=EST5EDT date
```

After issuing the `date` command, the `TZ` environment variable returns to its previous setting.

See Also `set`

exit

Syntax

```
exit
```

Description The `exit` command terminates a SunOS session. Entering `exit` is the same as pressing Control-d. The `exit` command is used to log out of the system. If you entered `su` to become a superuser, typing `exit` returns you to the previous shell. By requiring users to exit, the system is protected against unauthorized use and is able to reallocate resources no longer in use (such as memory and CPU time). If you type `exit` in a `Shell Tool` or `Command Tool` window, only the window is terminated.

Options The `exit` command has no options.

See Also `login`

expand

Syntax

```
expand [-n] [-tab1,tab2,...,tabn] [filename]
```

Description The expand command copies the file specified by *filename* to the standard output, converting tab characters to spaces. This is useful before sorting, looking at specific columns, or printing on some printers (those that have no tab capability, for instance). Specifying --*n* sets the tab width. The default is eight spaces. The -tab1,tab2...tab*n* arguments indicate numbers used to set tabs at columns.

Options The expand command has no options.

Example Enter

```
expand -2,10,18,30 report > report.notab
```

to make a copy of the file report with the tab stops set to the second, tenth, eighteenth, and thirtieth columns (just like setting tab stops on a typewriter).

Enter

```
expand -5 phonelist > phonelist.notab
```

to make a copy of phonelist (named phonelist.notab) with tabs converted to five spaces.

See Also unexpand

fdformat

Syntax

```
fdformat [options]
```

Description The fdformat command formats and verifies each track on the diskette, and terminates if it finds any bad sectors. All existing data on the diskette, if any, is destroyed by formatting. By default, `fdformat` formats high-density diskettes (1.44MB). Options exist to format medium-density diskettes (1.2MB) and double-density diskettes (720K). The `fdformat` command also lets you format a disk for use with MS-DOS.

Options

`-d`	Installs an MS-DOS file system and boot sector on the disk after formatting. This is equivalent to the MS-DOS FORMAT command. Any diskettes formatted using this option can be read by MS-DOS but are not bootable.
`-D`	Formats a double-density (720K) diskette on a machine running Solaris 2 for x86.
`-e`	Ejects the diskette when done. This option doesn't work with drives that require you to manually eject disks.
`-f`	Starts format without asking for confirmation.
`-1`	Formats a double-density (720K) diskette on a Sun workstation.
`-m`	Formats a medium-density (1.2MB) diskette.
`-v`	Verifies the floppy diskette after formatting.
`-b` *label*	Puts an MS-DOS *label* on the disk after formatting it. This option is only meaningful when the `-d` option is also set.

Example Entering

```
fdformat
```

formats a high-density diskette in a SunOS format.

Entering

```
fdformat -1
```

formats a 3.5" double-density disk in a SunOS format.

Entering

```
fdformat -d -b DOS-Disk
```

formats a high-density (1.44MB) diskette for use with MS-DOS and labels the disk DOS-Disk.

Entering

```
fdformat -d -l
```

formats a double-density disk (720K) on a Sun workstation for use with MS-DOS.

See Also cpio, tar

fgrep

Syntax

```
fgrep [options] ~'string~' [files]
```

Description The fgrep command searches one or more files for a character string and displays all lines that contain that string. The fgrep command searches for a string, instead of searching for a pattern that matches an expression like the grep command does. Because fgrep does not support regular expressions, it is faster than grep. (fgrep stands for fast grep.) Special characters like $, *, [, ^, (,), and \ are interpreted literally, but should be enclosed in quotes.

Options

-c	Displays only a count of matching lines.
-h	Displays matching lines but not file names (inverse of −l).
-i	Ignores case. Searches for both upper- and lowercase letters.

-l	Lists file names, but does not list matched lines.
-n	Displays lines and their line numbers.
-s	Works silently, that is, displays nothing except error messages. This is useful for checking error status.
-v	Displays all lines that don't match a pattern.
-x	Displays lines only if a *string* matches the entire line.
-e *string*	Searches for a string that begins with a hyphen (-).
-f *filename*	Gets a list of strings from *filename*.

Example To display the number of lines in a file named **phonefile** that contain (415), enter

```
fgrep -c '(415)' phonefile
```

To display lines in **file1** that don't contain any spaces, enter

```
fgrep -v ' ' file1
```

To display lines in a file named **textfile** that contain the words in the file named **searchme**, enter

```
fgrep -f searchme textfile
```

To display the number of lines in a file named **countfile** that do not contain 13, enter

```
fgrep -c -v '13' countfile
```

See Also find, grep

file

Syntax

```
file [-f namesfile] filename(s)
```

Description The `file` command determines what kind of information a file contains, and whether the file is executable, a text file, or a C program file, and so on. Be aware that the `file` command sometimes mistakenly identifies files.

Options

-f *namesfile*   *namesfile* is a file containing a list of files to identify. *namesfile* must contain only names of files.

Example Entering

```
file old.docs mygrep test.*
```

displays

```
old.docs:   directory
mygrep:     executable /bin/ksh script
test.c:     c program text
test:       ascii text
```

find

Syntax

```
find pathnamelist expression
```

Description The `find` command is an extremely powerful, useful, and adaptable tool. Although it is one of the more difficult commands to master, it is worth the effort. The `find` command searches all files and subdirectories of the directories in *pathnamelist* and checks for files that meet the criteria described by *expression*. *pathnamelist* is a list of directories to be searched. `find` searches all files and subdirectories in *pathnamelist*. *expression* is a list of selection criteria or actions to be taken. The selection criteria in *expression* are checked for each of the files in *pathnamelist*. The criteria are checked until one of them fails, at which point the next file is checked. It is possible to use `find` to perform such tasks as these:

- Check all files under a directory for the occurrence of a word, such as a group member's name.
- Check each file's creation date and list only those files created after or before a particular date.
- List only those files modified between two dates.

The *expression* list is traversed left to right. As long as the test in *expression* evaluates true, the next test is performed. In other words, the expression is evaluated as if the items are connected with logical ANDs. If a test is not met, the processing of the current file is ended, and the next file is checked. It is possible to cause a logical OR to be performed by using the –o argument; just because one check fails, this does not terminate further checking on the file. The criteria to be checked are separated by spaces.

Any action (as opposed to a test or check) in *expression* always counts as a test that is met; an action never causes an end to checking of the current file unless the action is the last item in the expression list.

Options

!	Negates the next argument. !`-name` *filename* checks true for files whose name is *not* *filename*.
`-atime` *n*	Indicates the expression is true if the file has been accessed in *n* days. The `find` command itself changes the access time of files in *pathnamelist*.

`-ctime` *n*	Indicates the expression is true if the file has been changed in *n* days. That is, either the file has been modified or the file's attributes (its owner, group, permissions, and so on) have changed.
`-depth`	Always yields true. This is an action to be performed, not a check to be made. The `depth` argument causes the `find` command to check the contents of subdirectories before any other files in the directory containing the subdirectories +.
`-exec` *command*	Indicates the expression is true if the executed *command* returns a zero value as an exit status. This usually means a requested command has occurred. (For instance, `grep` returns a zero if the requested string of characters was found, and returns a nonzero if the requested string of characters was not found.) The specified command must be followed by an escaped semicolon (\;). To specify the current file, use curly braces ({}).
`\(expression \)`	Indicates the expression is true if the parenthesized expression is true. Used for grouping expressions, usually with the `-o` operator. Parentheses must be preceded by backslashes, and the expression must be separated from the parentheses by spaces.
`-group` *groupname*	Indicates the expression is true if the file belongs to *groupname*.
`-links` *n*	Indicates the expression is true if the file has *n* links.

`-mtime` *n*	Indicates the expression is true if the file has been modified (that is, written to) in the last *n* days.
`-name` *filename*	Indicates the expression is true if `filename` matches the current file name. An `*`, `?`, or `[` and `]` can be used, but must be escaped (that is, put within quotes or preceded by a backslash).
`-newer` *filename*	Indicates the expression is true if the current file has been modified more recently than *filename*.
`-nogroup`	Indicates the expression is true if the file belongs to a group not in an assigned group in the `/etc/group` file.
`-nouser`	Indicates the expression is true if the file belongs to a user not in the `/etc/passwd` file.
`-o`	If two criteria are separated by spaces, this expression indicates they must both be true to continue checking; that is, both must be true to proceed, because as soon as a check fails, the next file is checked. Using `-o` between two arguments causes a logical OR to be performed. Thus `-name larry -o -name- brent` will evaluate to true if the current file has a name of either `larry` or `brent`.
`-ok` *command*	Like `-exec`, except `command` is written to the screen (`< command ... arguments>?`); input from the keyboard is then expected, and *command* is executed only if a `y` is input.

-perm *octalnumber*	Indicates the expression is true if the *octalnumber* matches the file permissions of the current file.
-print	This expression always yields true. This is an action to be performed, not a check to be made. It prints the current path name.
-prune	This expression always yields true. This is an action to be performed, not a check to be made. This is used to keep find from checking into directories—it prunes the search tree.
-size *n*	Indicates the expression is true if the file is n blocks long (there are typically 512 characters in a block). If *n* is followed by a c, the size is in characters instead of blocks.
-type *typechar*	Indicates the expression is true if the type of the current file is **typechar**, where **typechar** has the following values and associated meanings:
b	Block special files (that is, tape drives)
c	Character special files (that is, terminals)
d	Directories
f	Regular files
l	Symbolic links
s	Sockets
-user *username*	True if the file belongs to username

Example Entering

```
find . -print
```

displays the name of all files and all subdirectories under the current directory. Entering

```
find . -name test -print
```

displays the path name of all files or subdirectories under the current directory whose name is **test**. Entering

```
find . -name \*.doc -print
```

displays all files or subdirectories under the current directory whose name has a **.doc** extension. Entering

```
find . -perm 700 -print
```

lists all the files in your home directory with their permissions set to 700 (only the owner has read, write, and execute permissions). Entering

```
find /usr/home/rpetrie -type f -exec grep -l sunspots {} \;
```

displays the names of all files under the directory /usr/home/rpetrie (note the use of -**type f** to eliminate anything that is not a file) that contain the word **sunspots**. The **grep** command searches each file for **sunspots** and, since -**l** is specified, prints only the name of the file and not the line containing **sunspots**. Note the use of {} to mean the current file and the \;, which must follow any command to -**exec**. Entering

```
find . \( -user ataylor -o -user rpetrie \) -ok cp {} ~/temp \;
```

searches through the working directory and its subdirectories for files belonging to either **rpetrie** or **ataylor** and prompts for confirmation before copying them into the directory ~/temp. Entering

```
find . -type d -print
```

lists all the subdirectories of the working directory. Entering

```
find . \! -name '.' -type d -print -prune
```

lists all the main subdirectories of the working directory, but does not list the subsubdirectories as the previous example does. Entering

```
find . -type f -size +500c -atime +30 -ok rm {} \;
```

searches through your working directory for files larger than 500 characters that have not been accessed in the last 30 days, and asks whether you want to delete them.

See Also chgrp, chmod, ln, ls, passwd

finger

Syntax

```
finger [options] [username]
```

Description The finger command, with no user name specified, displays information about each user that is logged in. The information listed is as follows:

- Login name
- Full name
- Terminal name (preceded with an '*' if write permission is denied)
- Idle time
- Login time
- Location (which is taken from the comment field from the file /etc/ttytab)

If a user name is specified, the information is displayed about that user only. The user name can be specified as a first name, last name, or an account (login) name. When a user name is specified, the following information is also displayed:

- The user's home directory and login shell
- The time the user last logged in
- The terminal and terminal information from /etc/ttytab
- The last time the user received and read mail
- The contents of the file named .plan (if it exists) in their home directory
- The projects listed in the file named .project (if it exists) in their home directory

Options

`-m`	Matches only user name (not first or last name).
`-l`	Outputs long format.
`-s`	Outputs short format.

Example Entering

```
finger
```

displays information about all users currently logged in. Entering

```
finger -m lgoodman
```

displays information about user `lgoodman`. Entering

```
finger larry
```

displays information about any user whose first, last, or login name is `larry`.

See Also who, rusers

fold

Syntax

```
fold [-w width] filename
```

Description The `fold` command breaks lines at the maximum width as indicated by *width*. The default width is 80 characters. The *width* should be a multiple of eight if tabs are present; if it is not, you should use the **expand** command before using `fold`. (If you don't, when the tab character is printed, it will move the print head over eight spaces, which will throw off the row widths.) The `fold` command is useful for displaying files on screens with widths less than 80 characters wide, or for setting the width of a file. (For instance, a file's width might be made narrower to set it off from a file it is merged with.)

Options The `fold` command has no options.

Example Entering

```
fold -w 20 filename1 > filename2
```

copies *filename1* into *filename2*, but first adjusts the lines to a width of 20 characters.

ftp

Syntax

```
ftp [options] [hostname]
```

Description The ftp command is your gateway to the Internet's standard File Transfer Protocol (FTP). It allows you to log in and transfer files to and from a remote system. The ftp command is usually used to transfer binary or ASCII files during an Internet connection. If the client host with which ftp is to communicate is specified after the ftp command, ftp immediately attempts to establish connection to an FTP server on that host; otherwise ftp enters its command interpreter and awaits instructions from the user. When ftp is awaiting commands, it displays the prompt ftp>.

Options

-d	Enables debugging.
-g	Disables file name expansion so that file names are read literally.
-i	Disables interactive prompting during multiple file transfers.
-n	Does not attempt to automatically log in upon initial connection.
-v	Shows all responses from the remote host and transfer statistics.

The following are commands that can be entered at the `ftp` prompt after connecting with another system.

`!` *[command]*	Runs a shell command on the local system. If the command argument is not added, starts an interactive shell.
`account` *[passwd]*	Supplies a password required by the remote system. If the passwd argument is not added, the user is prompted to enter a password.
`append` *local-file [remotefile]*	Appends a local file to a file on the remote system. If the *remotefile* argument is not added, the local-file name is used.
`ascii`	Sets the file type to ASCII for file transfer.
`bell`	Sounds a bell after each command is complete.
`binary`	Sets the file type to binary for file transfer.
`bye`	Exits the `ftp` command.
`cd` *directory*	Changes the current directory on the remote system to directory.
`cdup`	Changes the remote directory to the parent directory, one level up.
`close`	Terminates the `ftp` session and returns to the command interpreter.
`cr`	Toggles return character stripping during ASCII file transfer.
`delete` *remotefile*	Deletes the specified *remotefile* from on the remote system.

`dir` `[remotedirec-tory] [localfile]`	The `dir` command without any arguments lists the directory contents of the remote system. If the `localfile` argument is added, `dir` puts the output in `localfile`.
`disconnect`	Terminates the `ftp` session and returns to the command interpreter. This is the same as entering the `close` command.
`get remotefile` `localfile`	Copies `remotefile` and stores it on the local system as `localfile`.
`help command`	Displays help messages for all `ftp` commands if no `command` argument is given. Otherwise, displays help for the specified `ftp` command.
`lcd [dir]`	Changes the working directory on the local system. The default is $HOME.
`ls` `[remotedirectory]` `[localfile]`	Without a `remotedirectory` or `localfile` argument, `ls` displays a list of the contents of a remote directory. Otherwise, it puts the listing of the remote directory into the contents of `localfile`. If no `remotedirectory` is given, `ls` uses the current remote directory.
`mdelete` `[remotefiles]`	Deletes `remotefiles` on a remote system.
`mdir` `remotefiles` `localfile`	Lists remote files, enabling you to specify multiple files. If the `localfile` argument is added, `mdir` puts the listing of remotefiles in `localfile`.
`mget remotefiles`	Executes the `get` command to transfer multiple files, specified by `remotefiles`, to local directory.

mkdir *directory*	Creates *directory* on the remote system.
mput *localfiles*	Expands the * wildcard in a list of local files and executes the **put** command to send the **localfiles** to a remote system.
open *host*	Establishes a connection to a specified *host*.
prompt	Toggles interactive prompting on or off. The default is on.
put *localfile* *[remotefile]*	Sends **localfile** to a remote system. You can specify a different file name by adding the **remotefile** argument. The **remotefile** argument specifies the name of the copied file.
pwd	Displays the remote host's current working directory.
quit	Exits the **ftp** command. This is the same as the **bye** command.
recv *remotefile* *[localfile]*	Retrieves a remote file and stores it on the local system. This is the same as the **get** command.
remotehelp *[command]*	Requests help from the remote **ftp** host. Displays help messages for all **ftp** commands if no *command* argument is given. Otherwise, displays help for the specified *command*.
rename *file1* *file2*	Renames *file1* on the remote host to *file2*.
rmdir *directory*	Deletes directory on the remote host.

send	Sends *localfile* to a remote system.
localfile	You can specify a different file name
[remotefile]	by adding the *remotefile* argument. The *remotefile* argument specifies the name of the copied file. This is the same as the **put** command.
status	Displays the current status of the **ftp** command.
type	Sets the representation type to ASCII, binary, image, or tenex (used to talk to TENEX machines).
user *username*	Identifies the user to the remote **ftp** host when autologin is disabled.
verbose	Toggles verbose mode on or off, which echoes the results of **ftp** commands to the screen.
?	Prints help message about **ftp** commands. This is the same as the **help** command.

Example Entering

```
ftp
```

activates the **ftp** program and displays the **ftp>** prompt. To connect to a host on the Internet that contains an archive of the Simpsons cartoon trivia, enter

```
open ftp.cs.widener.edu
```

The **ftp.cs.widener.edu** is the full domain name of the machine you are connecting to. After establishing the connection with the remote system, log in as **anonymous**.

At the **ftp>** prompt, enter the following to change to the directory **/pub/simpsons** and copy all the files beginning with the letter **s**,

```
cd pub/simpsons
mget s*
```

The `mget s*` command line will cause `ftp` to prompt you to confirm each copy operation. If you answer `y`, the file is copied to the current directory on your machine. Answering `n`, skips to the next file. To exit your connection, at the `ftp>` prompt, enter

        quit

See Also `rcp`, `rlogin`, `telnet`

grep

Syntax

        grep [options] [-e expression] filename

Description The `grep` command searches the file indicated by *filename* (or the standard input) for lines containing *expression*. If `grep` finds a line containing *expression*, it displays the line. If more than one file is specified by *filename*, the file name precedes the line.

The `grep` command can search a file for the string `word`, for instance. When searching for `word`, it also finds `wordy`, `wordless`, and `words`. If you want to locate `word` by itself, specify `word` in single close quotes, `' word '` (note the beginning and ending spaces inside the quote). To specify the beginning of a line use the caret (`^`), and use the dollar sign for the end of a line (`$`). To specify any of several characters, enclose the characters in square brackets. `[Bb]ill` matches `bill` or `Bill`, and `[A-Z]ill` matches any uppercase letter followed by `ill`. `[A-Za-z]ill` matches any letter (upper- or lowercase) followed by `ill`. A period (`.`) matches any single character (letters and special characters such as !, @, #...). Within a range delineated by square brackets, a caret (`^`) means any character except those in the brackets, so `[^0-9]` matches any nondigit. An asterisk (`*`) matches zero or more preceding characters. The string `ab*c` matches `a`, followed by zero or more `b`'s, followed by a `c`. For example, `abc`, `abbc`, and `ac` all match `ab*c` (note that the `ac` has zero occurrences of `b`). The string `ab.*c` matches `ab`, followed by zero or more of any other character, followed by `c`. For example, `abac`, `abdtzc`, and `abc` all match `ab.*c`.

To specify any special character ($, ^, [,], or \\), precede it with a backslash (\\). To use any of these special characters, you must enclose the string you are searching for in delimiters. A delimiter is a way to specify the beginning and ending of a string. The delimiter can be any character, such as ~, #, or /, so long as the delimiter does not appear in the string.

Options

-c	Displays a count of matching lines rather than displaying the matching lines.
-h	Inhibits the displaying of file names.
-i	Ignores the case of letters (for example, treats A as a).
-l	Lists only the file names of files with matching lines.
-n	Lists each matching line preceded by its line number from the beginning of the file.
-v	Lists lines that do not match the search string.

Example Entering

```
grep SunOS *
```

lists any files in the current directory that contain the word SunOS (note the capitals). To search for the string SunOS regardless of the case of the letters, enter

```
grep -i sunos *
```

To search for lines in files that contain numbers, enter

```
grep '[0-9]' *
```

Note the use of the single close quote to begin and end the search string; this enables the use of the square brackets ([ ]) to denote the range of zero to nine.

To search C program files for comments, enter

```
grep '/\*' *.c
```

The backslash is used to escape the wildcard usage of the asterisk. Also note the use of the single close quote (') as a delimiter, since this command looks for a slash (/), and needs the backslash (\) to precede the asterisk (*). To search for users on your system who do not have passwords, enter

```
grep '^[^:]*::' /etc/passwd
```

This example searches the /etc/passwd file for any number of characters besides colons followed by a double colon at the beginning of lines.

See Also fgrep, find

groups

Syntax

```
groups [username]
```

Description Shows the groups that the user belongs to. Groups are listed in /etc/passwd and /etc/group. Without arguments, the groups command displays the groups to which the current user belongs. With a user name specified as an argument, the **groups** command displays all the groups to which the user name belongs.

Options The groups command has no options.

Example Entering

```
groups bfife
```

displays the groups that **bfife** belongs to.

See Also newgrp

head

Syntax

```
head [-count] [filename]
```

Description
If you are not sure what is in a file, using **head** shows you; or if you cannot remember which file begins with some particular text, **head** can help you find out without loading many different files into a word processor or editor. The **head** command sends the beginning of a file (or the standard input) to the display (or the standard output). How many lines get sent is determined by count. If *count* is not specified, **head** sends 10 lines. Whether standard input or a file is used depends on whether a file name is added. If a file name is not specified, the standard input is used. If more than one file is specified, **head** begins each file's display with ==>filename<==.

Options
The **head** command has no options.

Example
Entering

```
head -2 file1 file2 file3
```

prints out the first two lines of each file indicated, such as:

```
==> file1 <==
  I. Introduction
For the image coding application, strictly speaking, all
==> file2 <==
The output of a discrete information source is a message
that consists of a sequence of symbols.  The actual message
==> file3 <==
Boolean logic is the logic we are all familiar with, the
logic we all think of when we think of mathematical logic.
```

See Also
cat, more, tail

history

Syntax

```
history [options] [n]
```

Description The `history` command displays a list of previously entered commands in the order of oldest to most recent. By default, the `history` command stores the last 128 commands in a file named **sh_history**. The shell stores a list of commands in the order you enter them. Erroneous commands, such as spelling errors, are stored in the `history` list as well as correct commands. You can repeat a command by entering r *n*, where *n* is the number of the command in the `history` list that you wish to repeat. Entering r reexecutes the last command.

Options

    -r   Reverses the order of commands listed to most recent first.

Example Entering

```
history -5
```

prints out the five most recent commands plus the `history` command you just entered. Such a list may look like this:

```
3 cd ./book/pt4
4 ls -al
5 cat log
6 cat log
7 rm log
8 history -5
```

id

Syntax

```
id
```

Description The `id` command displays your user name and ID, and your group name and ID.

Options The `id` command has no options.

Example Entering

     `id`

might display

     `uid=1230(lgoodman) gid=204(cntrcts)`

See Also `finger, who, who am i`

kill

Syntax

     `kill [-signal] processIDnumber`

Description A program is an executable file. When a program is loaded into memory and executed, it is called a process. If you and a coworker are both running a CAD package, there are two processes—one is yours, the other your coworker's.

A signal is a message sent to a process. For instance, if a program begins execution, and you want to stop it before it's done, you can send it a signal to stop. You may also want to stop a process for just a while, and later resume. Signals are also used when two or more processes are cooperating and need to send messages to each other.

Various system signals are defined within SunOS. Two defined signals are SIGKILL and SIGTERM. SIGKILL is the ninth defined signal (indicated by **-9**), which tells a program to abort itself. A process must shut itself down if it receives a SIGKILL message. SIGTERM is the fifteenth defined message (**-15**) and requests that a program shut itself down. A process may ignore a SIGTERM, but it can not ignore a SIGKILL.

The `kill` command terminates a process, as specified by its process ID number. Usually `kill` sends a signal -**15** to the process. Sometimes a process is harder to terminate; then a signal -**9** is needed. To determine the correct process ID number, use the `ps` command.

Options

-l   Prints a list of symbolic signal names.

Example If you were running a process in the background, such as the following:

```
find / -name "test*" -print &
```

entering

```
ps
```

would display a list similar to this one:

```
PID    TTY     TIME    COMD
15021 PS/08    0:00    ksh
15100 PS/08    0:02    find / -name "test*" -print&
15101 PS/08    0:00    ps
```

Notice the `find` command has a process ID number of 15100.

To terminate this process, enter

```
kill 15100
```

The screen should display this line:

```
[1]    Terminated              find / -name "test*" -print&
```

If the `kill` command did not terminate this process, you would then enter

```
kill -9 15100
```

See Also `ps`

last

Syntax

```
last [options] user
```

Description The `last` command reads the `/var/adm/wtmp` file and reports the last logins by a user or terminal. It is useful as a quick accounting log of who is accessing what systems.

Options

-n *number*	Limits the number of entries displayed to the `number` specified.
-f *filename*	Uses an alternative file name instead of `/var/adm/wtmp`.

Example Entering

```
last -n 10 rpetrie
```

displays the last ten times the user named `rpetire` logged in.

See Also `login`

ln

Syntax

```
ln [-fs] filename1 [filename2]
ln [-fs] filename(s) directory
ln [-fs] sourcefile1 newlink
```

Description When you create a file on disk, SunOS places the file name in the appropriate directory and creates a link (or pointer) that points to the physical file. The `ln` command creates a link (or pointer) between *filename1* and *filename2*. This makes it possible to refer to the same file by two different names. One person may prefer to name a file `phone.list`, while another prefers to call the file `numbers`. The `ln` command makes it possible for both names to point to the same file. The `ln` command can be used to point to the same file from different directories. If you are working on a project, and want to access a file from the `proj1` directory as if it were in your home directory, you could create a link from your home directory to the `project` directory.

There is an important difference between creating a link to a file and copying the file to another directory. With linked files, when one copy of the file is updated, all links to that file are simultaneously updated, whereas with a copy of the file, all copies must be updated individually. If you change the permissions of a file, any links to that file have their permissions changed also. Links are removed with the `rm` command. As long as a file has at least one link remaining, the file itself is not deleted.

The first form of the `ln` command creates a link called *filename2* to the existing file *filename1*. If *filename2* is not specified, the link is created in the current directory with the file name *filename1*. In the second form, `ln` creates a link in *directory* to *filename(s)*. In the last form, a symbolic link is made that may point to directories.

Options

−f	Forces a hard link to a directory. Only a superuser may use this option.
−s	Creates a symbolic link, which is useful for pointing to directories.
−n	Prevents the link file from overwriting the contents of an existing file with same file name.

Example If you are working on a file and want to call it `sanitation`, while a coworker wants to call the same file `garbage`, create a link to garbage called `sanitation`:

```
ln garbage sanitation
```

In your home directory you can link a subdirectory, `project`, to the already existing `proj1` directory by entering

```
ln proj1/* project
```

See Also rm, cp

login

Syntax

```
login [username]
```

Description The `login` command signs the user identified by *username* onto the system. By requiring users to log in, it is possible to protect the system from unauthorized use and to tailor the system to each user. This command may be used to change from one user to another in the middle of a session. If used without *username*, `login` will request a user name. In either case, `login` then prompts for a password.

Options

username   Establishes connection without first being prompted for entering *username*.

Example Enter

```
login pmason
```

to log in as **pmason**. The user indicated by **pmason** must be a valid user on the system in order to log in.

See Also exit, passwd

logname

Syntax

```
logname
```

Description The `logname` command displays your login name by displaying the contents of the LOGNAME environment variable. The LOGNAME environment variable setting is located in the /etc/profile file.

Options The `logname` command has no options.

Example If the current user logged in as `rpetrie`, entering

```
logname
```

displays

```
rpetrie
```

See Also `last`, `login`

look

Syntax

```
look string
look [options] string filename
```

Description The `look` command finds words in the system dictionary (`/usr/dict/words`) or lines in a sorted list that begin with a specified string.

Options

`-d`	Uses only letters, digits, tab, and space characters in the comparison.
`-f`	Ignores case.

Example Entering

```
look rece
```

displays

```
receipt
receive
recent
receptacle
reception
receptive
receptor
```

```
recess
recession
recessive
```

which are all the words in the dictionary file that begin with the characters "rece."

See Also grep, sort

lp

Syntax

```
lp [options] [files]
```

Description The **lp** command sends files to the print queue to be printed. This allows you to work on a file, print it out, then continue to work on the file while it is still printing out. The file prints in the same state as when you gave the print command. This command also allows you to print out several files at one time.

Options

-c	Makes copies of files before printing. If the -c option is not specified, any changes made to the named files after the request is made but before it is printed will be reflected in the printed output.
-d destination	Chooses the destination (printer) of the print job. By default, *destination* is taken from the environment variable **LPDEST**. Otherwise, the computer system's default destination is used.
-m	Sends a mail message informing you that the files have been printed. By default, no mail is sent upon completion of the print request.

-n *number*   Prints the specified number of copies of the output.

-o *option*   Specifies printer-dependent options. Several options may be specified by repeating the -o *option* (e.g., -o *option1* -o *option2*), or by specifying a list of options enclosed in double quotes (e.g., -o *"option1 option2"*). SunOS recognizes the following -o options: **nobanner** suppresses the printing of a banner page; **nofilebreak** suppresses the insertion of a formfeed between files; **length=[number][scale]** prints request with pages **number** lines long. The number can be followed by a scale character: **i** indicates inches and **c** indicates centimeters. A length setting without a scale indicator indicates lines. For example, **length=66** indicates a page length of 66 lines, **length=11i** indicates a page length of 11 inches, and **length=27.94c** indicates a page length of 27.94 centimeters. **width=[number][scale]** prints request with the page width set to **number** columns wide. A width setting without a scale indicator indicates columns. You can use the same scale indicators as with the length option. **lpi=[number][scale]** prints request with the line pitch set to **number** lines per inch. A line pitch setting without a scale indicator indicates lines per inch. You can use the same scale indicators as with the **length** option. **cpi=***number* prints request with the character pitch set to *number* characters per inch. For example, character pitch can be set to pica by entering 10 characters per inch, or elite by entering 12 characters per inch. There is no standard character-per-inch setting.

-P *pagelist*	Prints the pages specified in pagelist in ascending order. The pages specified in *pagelist* may consist of single page numbers, or a combination of both.
-q *priority-level*	Assigns this request a *priority-level* in the printing queue. The values that can be used to specify *priority-level* can range from 0, the highest priority, to 39, the lowest priority. The default priority is set by the system administrator. -t *title*, prints title on the banner page of the output. The default is no title. Enclose *title* in double quotes if it contains blanks.
-w	Writes a message on the user's terminal after the files have been printed. If the user is not logged in, then a mail message is sent instead.

Examples Entering

```
lp text.file
```

prints out the file text.file to the default printer. Entering

```
lp -d sparcprinter *.rpt
```

sends all files ending with .rpt to the printer named sparcprinter.

See Also cancel, lp, lpstat, pr

lpstat

Syntax

```
lpstat [options]
```

Description The lpstat command displays the status of a printer queue. SunOS takes files to be printed and places them into a queue (a storage place in memory). This allows you to print out a file or several files while you continue working on the same file.

For each of the jobs in the queue, the lpstat command reports the user requesting the print job, the job's current position in the queue, the name of the file to be printed, the print request number (needed to remove the job from the queue), and the size of the print job in bytes. If the print request number is specified, lpstat reports on that print job only. If -u *userID* is specified, lpstat reports on all print jobs requested by that user.

Options Several options allow you to enter a list of users and printers. The list can be the login ID of a user or the printer request ID number. The print request ID number is the printer's name followed by a hyphen and a number. A typical printer ID might be sparcprinter-12. When creating a list, separate each item in the list with a comma.

-d	Reports the system default destination for print requests.
-o *[list]*	Reports the status of all output requests. The list is optional and includes printer names and print request ID numbers.
-p *[list]*	Reports the status of printers identified in list.
-t	Reports all status information, including the print request ID numbers, the user who requested the print job, the file size in bytes, and the date and time the request was made.
-u *[userIDs]*	Displays the status of print requests for specific users. Replaces *userIDs* with the user's login IDs.

Example To list the status of all print requests waiting in the print queue, enter

```
lpstat -t
```

which displays output similar to this:

```
scheduler is running
system default destination: sparcprinter
device for sparcprinter: /dev/term/a
sparcprinter accepting requests since Jan 22 10:07
printer sparcprinter now printing sparcprinter-12. enabled since
Jan 22 10:07
sparcprinter-12 jrockford  512       Jul 1920:17 on sparcprinter
sparcprinter-13 jrockford  1024      Jul 1920:20
sparcprinter-14 jrockford  1152      Jul 1920:19
```

See Also cancel, lp, pr

ls

Syntax

```
ls [options] filename
```

Description   The ls command lists the files and subdirectories of a directory, as well as additional information about each file. The output is sorted alphabetically. When the *filename* argument is not added, the contents of the current directory are listed.

Options

-a	Lists all entries. Without this option, entries beginning with a dot (.) are not listed.
-c	Lists files sorted by the time of creation.
-d	If the ls argument *filename* is a directory, lists only its name.
-F	Marks directories with a trailing slash (/), executable files with a trailing asterisk (*), and links with a trailing at sign (@).
-g	Shows the group ownership of the file (used with the -1 option).

-l	Lists files in long format. This gives the permission modes, number of links to the file, owner of the file, and time of the file's creation or last modification.
-r	Reverses the order of the sort, listing files in reverse alphabetic order.
-R	Recursively lists any subdirectories encountered.
-t	Sorts by time of last modification instead of alphabetically, listing oldest files and directories first.
-u	Sorts by the time of the last access instead of the time of last modification when used with the -t option.

Example Entering

```
ls -altR
```

displays a list of all the files in the current directory and all subdirectories of the current directory, sorted by the time each was last modified.

mail

Syntax

```
mail
mail [options] [users]
```

Description The mail command reads or sends mail. If no user is listed, the mail program checks for and displays existing mail messages. Adding one or more user names after the mail command lets you compose and send mail to the specified user(s). Mail messages are read from standard input until the user presses Control-d or a line containing just a period is entered. For a quick summary of mail commands, after starting the mail command, type a question mark (?).

Options The following are options for reading mail.

-e	Tests to see if mail exists without printing it. Returns an Exit status code 0 if mail exists; otherwise returns an exit status code 1.
-f *mailboxfile*	Reads mail from alternate mailbox file indicated by mailboxfile.
-h	Displays a window of messages rather than the latest message.
-p	Displays all messages without pausing.
-P	Displays all messages with all header lines.
-q	Exits the mail program after an interrupt (Control-c).
-r	Displays mail messages with oldest messages displaying first.

The following are options for sending mail.

m *messagetype*	Adds a "Message-type:" line to the message header with the value of *messagetype*.
-t	Adds a "To:" line at the heading of the letter, listing the names of the recipients.
-w	Sends mail to remote users without waiting for remote transfer program to be completed.

The following are options for forwarding mail.

-F *recipients*	Forwards all incoming mail to recipients.
-F " "	Removes mail forwarding.

Example Entering

```
mail -h
```

displays mail headers for incoming mail messages and displays the **?** mail prompt. To read a message, enter the number at the right of list. To quit the mail program, at the **?** prompt, enter

```
q
```

Entering

```
mail sdrucker <Return>
Do you have Prince Albert in a can? <Return>
<Control-d>
```

sends the mail message "Do you have Prince Albert in a can?" to **sdrucker**.

Entering

```
mail -F fziffel
```

forwards the current user's incoming mail to the user named fziffel.

See Also `mailx, mesg, notify, talk, write`

mailx

Description The `mailx` command provides an interactive interface for reading or sending mail. The `mailx` command's options are covered in detail in Chapter 11, "Electronic Mail and Messages."

man

Syntax

```
man command
```

Description The `man` command displays information about commands from the online reference manuals usually located in the `/usr/share/man` directory. Not all systems have the manuals on line, but for those that do, this is a convenient command.

Options

-a	Displays all pages matching *command*.
-1	Like -**a**, but only lists the pages.
-f *files*	Displays a one-line summary of one or more reference *files*.
-t	Formats the manual pages with troff.
-k *keywords*	Displays any header line that contains one of the specified *keywords*.

Example Entering

```
man find
```

displays information on the find command.

mesg

Syntax

```
mesg [options]
```

Description The mesg command reports on the status of message posting to your screen.

Options

-n	Disables posting of messages to your screen through the write command.
-y	Enables posting of messages to your screen through the write command.

Example Entering

> `mesg`

displays

> `is y`

or

> `is n`

Entering

> `mesg-n`

displays just the prompt and disables posting messages to the screen.

See Also `write`, `talk`

mkdir

Syntax

> `mkdir` *`directoryname`*

Description The `mkdir` command makes directories.

Options *`-m mode`*

Specifies the access mode for new directories. For a listing of available modes, see the `chmod` command.

> `-p` Creates parent directories if they do not exist.

Example Entering

> `mkdir directory1`

creates a directory named **`directory1`** in the current directory. If `mkdir` cannot make a requested directory, it displays an error message. For instance, the command

```
mkdir .
```

causes the screen to display the message

```
mkdir:    Failed to make directory "."; File exists
```

The error is that `mkdir .` is telling the computer to make a directory with the name . (dot). Dot already refers to the directory in which you are currently working.

Entering

```
mkdir -m 444 directory2
```

creates a read-only directory named `directory2` in the current directory.

See Also chmod, rm, rmdir

more

Syntax

```
more [options]
```

Description The `more` command displays files one screenful at a time. This is useful when trying to view large files, which `cat` displays too fast to read. Using `more`, the display pauses after each screenful, until you enter either a Return or another command that `more` can interpret.

Options The `more` command interprets various keystrokes as commands. The numerical argument by default is one, but you can repeat any command by preceding it with *n*, the number of times you want that command repeated. The following list explains keystroke commands that can be used with `more`.

h	Displays help for `more` and a description of the `more` commands.
*n*b	Skips back *n* screenfuls, then displays a screenful. b alone skips back one screenful.

n/pattern	Searches for the *n*th occurrence of *pattern*. */pattern* alone moves to the first occurrence of *pattern*.
*n*s	Skips *n* lines, then displays a screenful. **s** alone skips one line.
q or Q	Exits the more command.
\<Return\>	Displays another line.
\<Spacebar\>	Displays the next screenful.
*n*z	If *n* precedes **z**, *n* sets the new default for the number of lines per screen. **z** alone is the same as a space.

The following are **more** command options.

-c	Clears the screen before displaying the file.
-d	Displays an error message rather than ringing the terminal bell if an unrecognized more command is used.
-1	Treats formfeeds as any other character, not as a page break. Without this, more treats formfeeds contained within the file as page breaks.
-linecount	Displays the number of lines indicated by *linecount* as a screenful instead of the default (typically 24 lines).
+linenumber	Starts display at the line indicated by **linenumber**, instead of the beginning of the file.
+/pattern	Starts display at the two lines before the line containing **pattern**. Note that there is no trailing slash (*/*). (If one is included, it becomes part of the search pattern.)
-s	Squeezes the output, replacing multiple, consecutive blank lines in the file with a single blank line.

Example Entering

```
more .profile
```

displays your `.profile` file, pausing at the end of each screenful. A good use for `more` is to use it with a pipe at the end of a command line; that way you can slow down the output to allow time to read. For instance, entering

```
ls -R | more
```

displays all directory and file names beginning at the root (/) directory. The `more` command allows you to read each screenful. If you enter the above command, type `q` to quit the `more` command.

See Also cat

mount

Syntax

```
mount [options]
umount mountpoint
```

Description The `mount` command adds a file system to the root file system to make it available to the network. The file system is attached to an existing directory, which is then considered the mount point. If the mount point directory has any files or subdirectories prior to the mount operation, they are hidden until the file system is unmounted. Only a superuser can mount file systems using the `mount` command. However, any user can change to the directory on which the file system is mounted. Any user can list mounted file systems by entering the `mount` command without an argument. If a superuser adds only a partial argument, `mount` will search `/etc/vfstab` for an entry to supply the missing arguments.

To unmount a file system, you must change to a directory that is in a file system other than the one to be unmounted, and enter the `umount` command followed by the file system's mount point. The `mount` command maintains a table of mounted file systems in `/etc/mnttab`. The `mount` command adds an entry to the mount table; the `umount` command removes an entry from the table.

Options

−F *filesystemtype*	Specifies the file system type on which to operate. The most common file systems are `ufs` (UNIX file system), `hsfs` (High Sierra file system), `nfs` (network file system), and pcfs (PC file system).
−V	Echoes the complete command line, but does not execute the command. The command line is generated by using the options and arguments provided by the user and adding to them information derived from `/etc/vfstab`. This option should be used to verify and validate the command line.
−p	Displays the list of mounted file systems in the `/etc/vfstab` format. Must be the only option specified.
−v	Displays the list of mounted file systems in verbose format. You cannot specify additional options when using the −v option.

Use −o to specify file system type-specific options. The following are generic options commonly supported by most file system types.

−m	Mounts the file system without making an entry in `/etc/mnttab`.
−ro	Mounts the file system so it is read-only.
rw	Mounts the system as read and write (the default).

Example Entering

```
mount
```

displays a list of the file systems currently mounted.

To mount target disk 3 (t3) on the sixth partition (s6) on the /mnt directory, enter

```
mount /dev/dsk/c0t3d0s6 /mnt
```

Sun's CD ROM drives are set to SCSI target 6 by default. The following example mounts a CD ROM using the High Sierra file system (hsfs) on the directory /cdrom.

```
mount -F hsfs -o ro /dev/dsk/c0t6d0s2 /cdrom
```

Keep in mind that not all CD ROM disks are in hsfs format. Some CD ROM disks use the standard ufs format. If the mount information for a drive is in your /etc/vfstab/ file, you can mount a drive by just adding the mount point. For example, enter

```
mount /cdrom
```

to mount the cdrom drive on the /cdrom directory. The **mount** command checks the /etc/vfstab for the information it needs to mount the drive.

To mount a PC file system (pcfs) on the directory /**pcfiles** to get access to files on a floppy diskette that came from an MS-DOS PC, enter

```
mount -F pcfs /dev/diskette /pcfiles
```

To unmount a file system mounted on the /mnt directory, first change to a directory in the file system other than the one attached at the /mnt directory, and enter

```
umount /mnt
```

You can also specify a drive to unmount by adding the device name to the **umount** command. The following unmounts the file system for the target disk 3 (t3) mounted on the 6th partition (s6).

```
umount /dev/dsk/c0t3d0s6
```

See Also umount

mv

Syntax

mv *[options] filename1 filename2*

or

mv *[options] directoryname1 directoryname2*

Description The mv command moves or renames *filename1* to *filename2* (that is, it makes a copy, then deletes the original file). If you are moving or renaming directories, mv moves all of *directoryname1* to *directoryname2;* if *directoryname2* does not exist, mv creates it. The mv command can be used to rename a file. It is also possible to use mv to copy a file over another file, thus deleting the old file. If you copy a .profile file from someone else's home directory into yours, their .profile file will replace yours.

The mv command returns to the system prompt if successful. It is a good idea for new users to use mv -i, as mv by itself does not give feedback to the user, which can lead to unknowingly deleting files. If you always want to use the -i option with mv, enter alias mv='mv -i' into your .profile file. This will cause ~ mv -i to be run whenever mv is entered.

Options

-f   Forces removal even if the file or directory permissions don't allow it.

-i   Asks for confirmation before replacing an existing file or directory.

Example Entering

mv /socrates/questions /delphi/answers

removes the file named questions in the directory socrates, places it into the delphi directory, and renames the file answers.

See Also rm, cp, alias

newgrp

Syntax

```
newgrp [group]
```

Description The `newgrp` command changes a user's group identification. Only the group ID is changed; the user remains a member of all groups previously assigned. The user remains logged in and the current directory is unchanged, but the group ID of newly created files is set to the new effective group ID. With no *group* specified, `newgrp` changes the group identification back to the group specified in the user's password file entry. Before you can use the `newgrp` command, your system administrator needs to have created the group.

Options The `newgrp` command has no options.

Example Entering

```
newgrp wildbunch
```

changes your group to the `wildbunch` group, which must already have been set up by a system administrator. If your group uses a password, you must enter the password to change the user's group identification.

See Also `chgrp`

nice

Syntax

```
nice [-n] command(s)
```

Description The `nice` command runs commands at low priority. Since Solaris is a multitasking system, it needs to know which jobs have priority. For instance, a user typing at the keyboard generally deserves priority over a file being printed to a printer. Various jobs are assigned various priorities. So if you decide to search the entire file system for a file you've misplaced, you can tell the operating system to give the command a low priority by using the `nice` command. The `nice` command is especially useful when running jobs in the background.

The *-n* argument tells `nice` how nice to be. The larger the number used for *-n*, the lower the priority the command gets and the slower it runs. *-n* should be in the range of zero to twenty; if no *-n* is present, `nice` defaults to `-10`.

Options The `nice` command has no options.

Example Entering

```
nice -19 grep jabberwocky *
```

executes the `grep` command, which looks for the word jabberwocky in all files indicated by the asterisk with a lower priority than usual.

nohup

Syntax

```
nohup command [arguments]
```

Description The `nohup` command runs a command immune to `hangup` signals and quits. The action of logging out sends a `hangup` signal that terminates all your processes. You can keep a job running after you log out by preceding the command with `nohup`. To execute a pipeline or list of commands, the list or pipeline must be in a script file. `nohup` recognizes only one command per line. Entering `nohup` *command1*; *command2* applies *nohup* only to *command1*. Note that entering `nohup` (*command1*; *command2*) is syntactically incorrect.

Example If you enter commands into a file named `script`, then enter

```
nohup sh script &
```

the commands are run in the background, and will continue to run even if you log out.

See Also `ps, jobs, kill`

openwin

Syntax

```
openwin [options]
```

Description The `openwin` command is the shell script that sets up Open-Windows, the windowing environment based on the OPEN LOOK graphical user interface. OpenWindows includes the DeskSet applications that let you perform a wide variety of Solaris tasks using a friendly graphical environment instead of the command line. To access Open-Windows, your environment variable `OPENWINHOME` must be set to the directory in which the OpenWindows software resides, usually `/usr/openwin`. The OpenWindows environment is usually set up automatically, so the `openwin` command's options are rarely used.

Once the OpenWindows environment is displayed, you can start any of the DeskSet applications using the `Workspace` menu's `Programs` submenu or by entering the command name for the application you want to start in the Shell or Command Tool. The following are the command names for the OpenWindows DeskSet.

APPLICATION	COMMAND NAME
Audio Tool	`audiotool`
Binder	`binder`
Calculator	`calctool`
Clock	`clock`
Calendar Manager	`cm`
Command Tool	`cmdtool`
File Manager	`filemgr`
Icon Editor	`iconedit`
Mail Tool	`mailtool`
Performance Meter	`perfmeter`
Print Tool	`printool`
Shell Tool	`shelltool`

Snapshot	`snapshot`
Tape Tool	`tapetool`
Text Editor	`textedit`

Options The following options are unique to the `openwin` command. The `openwin` command also accepts the same command-line options as the `xnews` command. For more information on `xnews` options, type `man xnews` at the prompt.

`-banner`	Displays the OpenWindows banner screen at startup. This option slightly increases the amount of time it takes to start up Open-Windows.
`-noauth`	By default, the OpenWindows' X11/NeWS server implements the "MIT-MAGIC-COOKIE" security mechanism. The `-noauth` option reverts to the security mode of previous X11/NeWS server versions. Running the server with this option enabled lowers your level of security.
`-includedemo`	Specifies that the path to the demo directory should be included in the user's search path.
`-nobanner`	Causes OpenWindows to start without displaying the banner screen at startup. This option slightly decreases the amount of time that it takes for OpenWindows to start.

Example Entering

```
openwin -nobanner
```

at the command prompt, starts the OpenWindows environment without displaying the banner screen that welcomes you to OpenWindows.

To start the OpenWindows' Text Editor after starting OpenWindows in a Shell Tool, enter

```
textedit &
```

Adding the ampersand (&) after the textedit command starts the Text Editor program in the background, making the Shell Tool window available for entering additional commands.

See Also xrdb

pack

Syntax

```
pack [options] filename(s)
```

Description The pack command compacts files and replaces them with compressed files with a .z appended to the file name. To restore the files to their original form, use the unpack command.

Options

-	Print number of times each byte is used, relative frequency, and byte code.
-f	Force the file to be compressed even when disk space isn't saved.

Example Entering

```
pack *.ps
```

compacts each file ending with .ps, replaces the file with a compressed file, and appends the file name with a .z. For example, compressing files butterfly.ps, porsche.ps, and tiger.ps replaces them with files named butterfly.ps.z, porsche.ps.z, and tiger.ps.z.

See Also compress, pcat, unpack, zcat

passwd

Syntax

```
passwd
```

Description The `passwd` command changes your login password. It prompts you for your old password, then for the new password, then for the new password again. Only a system administrator can change your password without knowing your current password.

When changing your password, the new password must be at least six characters and contain at least two alphabetical characters and at least one numeric or special character. The new password must differ by at least three characters from the old password. Remember, case counts, as do spaces and other control characters. You should avoid using names, dates, social security numbers, and so on as passwords, since they arc easy to guess.

Options

-s   Displays password information (**NP** indicates no password, **PS** indicates an active password, and **LK** indicates a locked password).

Example The following illustrates a sample password changing session. Enter

```
passwd
```

The system responds with

```
Old password:
```

When you enter your old password, it is not displayed on the screen. The screen then displays

```
New password:
```

Enter the new password. Note that it is not displayed. Then you reenter your new password at this prompt:

```
Re-enter new password:
```

and your old password is changed. If you enter a different password the second time, the system responds with this message:

```
Mismatch — They don't match; try again
```

and the prompt `New password` appears. Your password remains unchanged. If you fail to enter enough characters for the new password, the system responds with the message

```
Password is too short—must be at least 6 characters.
```

If you reenter the same password each time this prompt is displayed, on the third try, SunOS responds with `Too many failures — try later`.

paste

Syntax

```
paste [options] filename1 filename2
```

Description The `paste` command merges corresponding lines of several files. Each file is treated as a column, or series of columns, and the columns are concatenated horizontally. The `paste` command performs horizontal merging in a manner similar to the way the `cat` command performs vertical merging. The `paste` command replaces the newline character at the end of the first line in the first file with a tab (or another character with the -d option), then appends the first line in the second file, and so on.

Options

-d*list*   Without this option, the newline characters at the end of each line (in each file) except the last newline character, are replaced with a tab. This option allows the use of characters other than the tab character. The characters in list are substituted for the newlines. *list* is used circularly; when it is exhausted, it is restarted from the beginning. *list* may contain special escape sequences: \n (newline), \t (tab), \\ (backslash), and \0 (an empty string, not a null character).

Example If a file called men contains the following list:

```
Anthony
Othello
Romeo
Larry
```

and a file called women contains this list:

```
Cleopatra
Ophelia
Juliet
Rhonda
```

then entering

```
paste -d"+" men women
```

results in this display:

```
Anthony+Cleopatra
Othello+Ophelia
Romeo+Juliet
Larry+Rhonda
```

See Also cat, pr

pcat

Syntax

    pcat [options]

Description Displays the contents of one or more packed files.

Options The pcat command has no options.

Example Entering

    pcat file1.z file2.z

displays the contents of the packed files **file1.z** and **file2.z**.

See Also compress, pack, unpack, zcat

pg

Syntax

    pg [options] [files]

Description The **pg** command displays the specified files, one screenful at a time. When you enter the **pg** command, a : prompt appears for you to enter display commands. To display the next page, press the Return key. To get help with the **pg** command, press **h**. To quit displaying a file, press **q**.

Options

-c	Clears the screens before displaying each page.
-e	Does not pause between files.
-f	Does not split lines that are longer than the screen width.

-n	Issues a **pg** command without waiting for you to press Return.
-p *string*	Uses string for the command prompt. If *string* contains the special variable **%d,** the prompt is replaced with the current page number. The default prompt displays a colon (:).
-s	Displays messages in inverse video.
-n	Uses *n* lines for each window. The default is a full screen.
+n	Begins displaying at line number n.
+*/pattern/*	Begins displaying at first line containing *pattern.*

The following are display commands you can enter at the : prompt. To navigate by multiple pages or lines, most commands can be preceded by a number, as in: +1<Return> to move to the next page or -1 <Return> to return to the previous page.

h	Displays help.
q or Q	Quits the **pg** command.
<Return>	Displays the next page.
l	Displays next line.
d	Displays half a page more.
. or <Control-l>	Redisplays the current page.
f	Skips to the next page forward.
n	Moves to the next file.
p	Moves to the previous file.
$	Displays the last page.
*n*w	Sets window size to *n* and displays next page.
s *filename*	Saves the current file in *filename.*

/pattern/	Searches forward for *pattern*.
?pattern? or ^*pattern*^	Searches backward for *pattern*.
!command	Executes *command*.

Example Entering

```
pg -p 'Page %d : ' file1
```

displays `file1` and sets the prompt to display the page number.

Entering

```
pg -c file2
```

displays `file2`, clearing the screen after each page.

See Also cat, more, pr

ping

Syntax

```
ping [options] host [timeout]
ping [options] IPaddress [timeout]
```

Description The `ping` command is a network utility that tells you if another machine on the network is operational. It uses the ICMP protocol's ECHO_REQUEST datagram to check the specified host. The ICMP protocol is responsible for error handling on a TCP/IP network. If the datagram is sent and received successfully, the network is considered to be alive. Otherwise, `ping` informs you that there is no response from the host.

Options

-I*n*	Specifies the interval between successive transmissions. The number specified by *n* determines the number of seconds between transmissions. The default without the -I option is one second.
-n	Displays network addresses as numbers.
-s	Reports the effectiveness of the data transfer. This option sends packets to the host until you press Control-d or a timeout occurs.
-v	Lists any ICMP packets, other than ECHO_RESPONSE, that are received.

Example Entering

```
ping primetime
```

displays

```
primetime is alive
```

indicating that the host `primetime` responded to the ICMP data. You can also replace the host's name with the IP address. For example, if the host `primetime` has an Internet Protocol address of 192.9.200.1, you could enter the following:

```
ping 192.9.200.1
```

pr

Syntax

```
pr [options] [filename]
```

Description The `pr` command displays files according to options you specify. If no options are specified, the default format is 66 lines per page, with a five-line header and a five-line trailer. By default, each page includes a header containing the page number, file name, and the file's date and time. The pr command can also be used to prepare files for printing. The pr command reads standard input if *filename* is -, or no filename is specified.

Options

+*page*	Begins displaying at the page number indicated by **page**. The default is page one.
-*columns*	Produces output having *n* columns. The default is one column. The columns option does not work with the -m option.
-a	Displays the file in a multicolumn format. Lines that cannot fit in a column are truncated.
-d	Double-spaces the output.
-e*cn*	Expands tabs to positions to every nth position. The default is 8. The c specifies the input tab character. The default field delimeter is a tab.
-f	Separates pages using a single formfeed character instead of a series of blank lines.
-F	Folds input lines to fit in current column width (avoids truncation by -a or -m).
-h *string*	Replaces the default text line of the header with *string*. The -h is ignored when -t is specified or the -1 option is ten lines or less.
-i*cn*	Converts white space to the field delimiter indicated by c set at every *n*th position. The default field delimiter is a tab set at every 8th position.
-1*n*	Sets page length to *n*. The default is 66 lines per page.

-m	Merges up to eight files, displaying all files simultaneously, one per column. If a line is too long to fit in a column, the line is truncated (can't be used with -n and -a).
-n*cn*	Numbers lines with numbers n digits in length (default is 5), followed by the field separator indicated by *c*. The default field separator is tab.
-o*n*	Offsets each line *n* spaces. The default is 0 spaces.
-p	Pauses before displaying each page.
-r	Suppresses error messages for files that can't be found.
-s*c*	Separates columns with c. The default is a tab.
-t	Omits header and trailing blank lines.
-w*n*	Sets the line width to *n* characters. The default width is 72 characters.

Example To format a file named **report** with double spacing and add the header "Monthly Attendance Report" and send the formatted output to the default printer, enter

```
pr -dh "Monthly Attendance Report" report | lp
```

Entering

```
pr -m file1 file2
```

displays a side-by-side list of file1 and file2.

ps

Syntax

```
ps [options]
```

Description The ps command displays information about processes. Informally, processes can be thought of as jobs the system is running. Every job that runs on SunOS has a process ID number (PID) assigned to it. The column headings displayed in a ps listing depend on whether the f (full) or l (long) option is used. The following lists the headers, the option that displays the header, and a brief description of each header:

HEADER	DESCRIPTION
F	Indicates the status word. The status word is a special option associated with a process (represented by 00, 01, 02, 04, 08, and 10). For example, 00 indicates that the process has terminated; 10 indicates the process is currently in memory.
S	Indicates the state of the process. The state of a process is given as a single character. B and W mean that the process is waiting. I stands for idle. O means the process is running on a processor. R means that it is loaded as a runnable process in queue. S means sleeping. T means stopped and being traced. X indicates that the process is waiting for more primary memory. Z stands for Zombie, meaning the process has terminated.
UID (f,l)	User ID of the process owner.
PID (all)	Process ID number.
PPID (f,l)	Process number of the parent process.
C (f,l)	Processor utilization for scheduling.
STIME (f)	Starting time of the process.
PRI (l)	Priority of the process.
NI (l)	The nice value for priority.
ADDR (l)	Memory address or disk address of the process.
SZ (l)	Size of the swappable process in main memory.

WCHAN (l)	The event for which a process is sleeping.
TTY (all)	The controlling terminal ID.
TIME (all)	Cumulative execution time.
COM (all)	The command name.

Options

-e	Prints information about every process.
-f	Generates a full listing.
-l	Generates a long listing.
-p *processlist*	Lists only process data for the process ID numbers given in **processlist**.
-u *IDlist*	Lists only process data for the user ID number or login name given in IDlist. In the listing, the numerical user ID will be listed unless you specify the -f option.

Example Entering

```
ps
```

displays information about processes running on the system, similar to this:

```
PID   TTY    TIME   COMD
9084  p/10   0:00   ksh
9346  p/11   0:00   ps
```

Entering

```
ps -l
```

displays a listing similar to this:

```
F S  UID  PID PPID C PRI  NI   ADDR     SZ  WCHAN     TTY    TIME COMD
8 S 7001  386  384 80  1   20  ff227000 254 ff227070  pts/1  0:00 ksh
8 0 7001  391  386 22  1   20  ff229800 133           pts/1  0:00  ps
8 T 7001  389  386 20  1   24  ff3da800 228           pts/1  0:00  vi
```

See Also kill, nice

pwd

Syntax

```
pwd
```

Description The pwd command displays the path name of the current directory.

Options The pwd command has no options.

Example Remembering that cd changes the current directory to the directory specified, enter

```
cd /usr/lgoodman/book
```

then

```
pwd
```

This displays

```
/usr/lgoodman/book
```

See Also cd

rcp

Syntax

```
rcp [options] hostname:filename1 filename2
rcp [options] hostname:filename(s) directory
```

Description The rcp command copies files between systems on a network. The *hostname* can be omitted for a file on the local machine. If a path name is not included when specifying *filename2*, the files are placed in your home directory. If you have a different user name on the remote host, precede *hostname* with your user name and an at symbol (@) (*username@hostname:filename1*).

Options

-p	Preserves in copies the modification times, access times, and modes of the original files.
-r	If target and sources are both directories, -r copies each subtree rooted at *filename*.

Example Entering

```
rcp log.txt memo primetime:/tmp
```

copies the local files `log.txt` and memo to the `/tmp` directory on the system named `primetime`.

To copy the local `bin` directory and all subdirectories to the `/tmp` directory on the machine named primetime with times and modes unchanged, enter

```
rcp -rp /bin primetime:/tmp
```

See Also cp, ftp, rlogin, rsh

rlogin

Syntax

```
rlogin [options] system
```

Description The `rlogin` command logs users onto a remote system. The user is prompted for a password unless the `.rhosts` file in their home directory contains the host name and user name of the user.

Options

-8	Allows 8-bit data, instead of 7-bit data, to pass across the network.
-e*c*	Sets the escape character to c. The default is the tilde (~).

-l *username*	Logs into the remote system using *username* instead of the current user's name.

Example Entering

```
rlogin primetime
```

logs into the system with the host name `primetime`.

The `-l` option is especially useful when you are working on another person's machine and using their user name, and you need to log into your own machine as yourself. For example, entering

```
rlogin -l ataylor primetime
```

logs you onto the host machine named `primetime` as `ataylor`.

See Also `ftp`, `rsh`

rm

Syntax

```
rm [options] filename
```

Description The `rm` command deletes one or more files. You must have write permission in the directory that contains the file or files, but you need not have write permission for the file. If you do not have write permission, the permissions are displayed and you are prompted to confirm the deletion. If you have write permission, the `rm` command returns to the system prompt if successful unless the `-i` option is used. It is a good idea for new users to use this option, as `rm` runs without giving feedback to the user, which can lead to unknowingly deleting files. If you want to always use the `-i` option with the `rm` command, enter

```
alias rm 'rm -i'
```

into your `.profile` file. This will cause ~ `rm -i` to be run when `rm` is typed in.

Options

-f   Forces removal even if the file or directory permissions don't allow it. A file can have write permission disabled to keep the file from being overwritten or erased. If you try rm on a file that has its protection set to disable writing, then rm will not delete the file. If the -f option is used, the delete will occur regardless of what permissions are set.

-i   Asks whether to delete each file or to examine each directory if the -r option is used.

-r   Recursively deletes the files and subdirectories associated with a directory, as well as the directory itself.

Example Entering

```
rm lgoodman/temp
```

removes the file **temp** from the directory **lgoodman**. Entering

```
rm -r lgoodman/book
```

removes all the files from all the subdirectories of **book**, as well as the sub-directory **book**.

See Also mv, cp, alias

rmdir

Syntax

```
rmdir directoryname
```

Description The rmdir command removes directories. The directory must be empty (not containing any files or subdirectories) before using the rmdir command.

Options This command has no options.

Example Entering

```
rmdir tmp
```

removes the directory **tmp** from the current working directory.

See Also mkdir, ls, rm

rsh

Syntax

```
rsh [options] hostname command
```

Description The rsh command lets you execute a single command on a remote machine without having to formally log in using the rlogin command. Commands available using the rsh command are determined by the system administrator for the remote machine. If you omit the *command* argument, rsh logs you into the remote host using the rlogin command. A remote host may have a file named /etc/hosts.equiv that contains a list of trusted hostnames with which it shares usernames, or users can set up a .rhosts file in their home directories to use the rsh command. The .rhosts file contains the *hostname*, a space, and then the *username*. If the names of the local host and user name are not found in the /etc/hosts.equiv on the remote host machine, and the local user name and host name are not in the remote user's .rhosts file, access is denied.

Options

-l *username*	Uses a specific user name as the remote user name.
-n	Redirects the input of the rsh command to /dev/null.

Example Entering

```
rsh mayberry ls
```

executes the `ls` command on the remote machine, `mayberry`.

See Also `rlogin`, `rcp`

rup

Syntax

```
rup [options] hostname
```

Description The `rup` command shows the host status of local systems.

Options

-h	Sorts alphabetically by host.
-l	Sorts by load average.
-t	Sorts by up time.

Example Entering

```
rup mayberry
```

queries the host machine `mayberry` and displays its status.

See Also who

ruptime

Syntax

```
ruptime [options]
```

Description The ruptime command displays the status for all systems on the local network. If no options are added, ruptime displays the status sorted by host name.

Options

-a	Includes users even if they have been idle for more than an hour.
-l	Sorts the list of systems by load average.
-r	Reverses the sort order.
-t	Sorts the list of systems by the amount of time the system has been up and running.
-u	Sorts the list of systems by the number of users on the system.

Example Entering

```
ruptime -u
```

displays the system list, with the system being used by the most users listed first and the least number of users listed last.

See Also rwho

rusers

Syntax

```
rusers [options] hostname
```

Description The rusers command shows who is logged into local systems on the network.

Options

-a	Reports on a host machine even if no users are logged in.

-h	Sorts alphabetically by the host name.
-i	Sorts by idle time.
-l	Gives a long list, similar to that of the **who** command.
-u	Sorts by the number of users.

Example Entering

```
rusers
```

displays the users logged in on the local system.

Entering

```
rusers mayberry
```

displays the users logged in on the remote system **mayberry**.

See Also rup, who

rwho

Syntax

```
rwho [options]
```

Description The **rwho** command displays who is logged on for all machines on the local network.

Options

-a	Includes users even if they have been idle for more than an hour.

Example Entering

```
rwho -a
```

displays all users who are logged onto the local network.

See Also finger, rusers, who

script

Syntax

    script [option] [filename]

Description The script command keeps a record of your login session, storing in a file everything that displays on your screen. If a file name is not included after the script command, the record is stored in a file named typescript. The script command records nonprinting characters as control characters and includes prompts. The script ends when Control-d or exit is typed.

Option

  -a   Appends the script record to *filename,* rather than overwriting it.

Example Entering

    script mycmds

displays the message

    Script is started, file is mycmds

Any commands and output for the session are stored until you press Control-d or type exit. When you press Control-d or type exit, the message Script is done, file is mycmds displays before you are returned to the prompt.

set

Syntax

    set [variable=value]

Description The `set` command, without `variable` or `value`, displays the values of all shell variables. Shell variables are used from within the shell, as opposed to environment variables, which may be used within programs as well as within the shell. Shell variables are used to save typing in long commands often. For instance, a path variable tells the operating system where to look for executable files or scripts so that you don't have to type a path with each name of a program or script.

The `set` command followed by `variable` assigns a null value as the current value of `variable`. The `set` command with `variable` followed by `value` assigns the value indicated by `value` to the variable indicated by `variable`.

Options The `set` command has no options.

Example Entering

```
set
```

displays the current value of any defined shell variables, with a display similar to this:

```
DISPLAY=:0.0
ERRNO=10
FCEDIT=/bin/ed
FONTPATH=/usr/openwin/lib/fonts:/usr/openwin/lib/fonts/misc
HELPPATH=/usr/openwin/lib/locale:/usr/openwin/lib/help
HOME=/export/home/rpetrie
HZ=100
IFS=
LANG=C
LD_LIBRARY_PATH=/usr/openwin/lib
LINENO=1
LOGNAME=rpetrie
MAIL=/var/mail/rpetrie
MAILCHECK=600
MANPATH=/usr/openwin/share/man:/usr/man
MANSECTS=\1:1m:1c:1f:1s:1b:2:\3:3c:3i:3n:3m:3k:3g:3e:3x11:3xt:3w:
3b:9:4:5:7:8
NOSUNVIEW=0
OPENWINHOME=/usr/openwin
OPTIND=1
PATH=/usr/openwin/bin:/usr/sbin:/sbin:/usr/bin:/bin:/etc:/usr/lib
/lp/postscript:/usr/openwin/demo:
PPID=443
PS1=$
PS2=>
```

```
PS3=#?
PS4=+
PWD=/export/home/rpetrie
RANDOM=21942
SECONDS=89
SHELL=/bin/ksh
TERM=sun-cmd
TERMCAP=sun-cmd:te=\E[>4h:ti=\E[>4l:tc=sun:
TMOUT=0
TZ=US/Pacific
WINDOW_PARENT=/dev/win0
WINDOW_TERMIOS=
WINDOW_TTYPARMS=D,D,13107203,21509,13,13,127,21,1409614040,3,28,1
7,19,4,-1,26,25,18,15
WMGR_ENV_PLACEHOLDER=/dev/win3
XFILESEARCHPATH=/usr/openwin/lib/locale/%L/%T/%N%S:/usr/openwin/l
ib/%T/%N%S
XINITRC=/usr/openwin/lib/Xinitrc
_=/usr/openwin/bin/openwin
```

See Also env

sleep

Syntax

```
sleep time
```

Description The sleep command suspends execution of a process for a specified number of seconds.

Options The sleep command has no options.

Example Using sleep, you can execute a command at some later time, such as the following:

```
(sleep 600; echo try that phone call again ) &
```

which does nothing for 600 seconds (ten minutes), then displays

```
try that phone call again
```

See Also at

sort

Syntax

```
sort [options] [-o outfile] filename
```

Description The `sort` command sorts lines within the specified file and writes its output to either the screen or the file specified with the `-o outfile` option. Output lines are sorted character by character, left to right. If more than one file is specified as input, the files are sorted and collated.

Options

`-b`	Ignores leading blanks.
`-d`	Sorts by ascending dictionary order (uppercase letters first, then lowercase). Only letters, digits, and blanks are significant in comparison. The default is to sort using ASCII order, where all ASCII characters are significant.
`-f`	Ignores uppercase and lowercase differences.
`-i`	Ignores characters outside the ASCII range 040 to 0176 in nonnumeric comparisons.
`-n`	Sorts by numeric order.
`-r`	Reverses the collating sequence.

Example Entering

```
sort -o sorted namelist
```

sorts the file `namelist`, and writes the output to the sorted file `sorted`. Entering

```
sort dept[a-f] -o sorted.depts
```

sorts the six files, `depta` through `deptf`, and stores the output into the file `sorted.depts`.

See Also `tr, uniq`

spell

Syntax

```
spell [options] filename
```

Description The `spell` command checks a file for spelling errors. The output is an alphabetized list of all words that cannot be found in, or derived from, the system dictionary file.

Options

-b	Accepts British spellings, such as "centre," "colour," and "travelled."
-v	Displays all the words not literally in the system dictionary. Words that can be derived from the dictionary are displayed, showing the plausible derivation.
-x	Displays every possible stem for each word.

Example Entering

```
spell resume > corrections
```

reads in the file **resume**, checking for spelling errors, and writes any words not in the dictionary to the file **corrections**.

See Also `sort, uniq`

strings

Syntax

```
strings [options] files
```

Description The `string` command searches for ASCII characters in binary files.

Options

`-a`	Searches entire file, not just the initialized data portion of object files. You can also specify this option as `-`.
`-o`	Displays the string's offset position before the string.
`-n` *n*	Specifies the minimum string length as *n*. The default is to search for a string length of four ASCII characters.

Example Entering

```
strings program1
```

searches for and displays any string of four ASCII characters or more in the binary file program1.

SU

Syntax

```
su username
```

Description The `su` command temporarily switches your user ID to that of *username*. The `su` command prompts for a password, just as if you were logging in, and with a correct password changes your user ID and group ID to that of *username*. The `.profile` file is read. The current directory is not changed, but the HOME variable is changed. If no name is specified, `su` creates a shell for a privileged user.

Example To change to user `bjoy` enter

```
su bjoy
```

then enter the appropriate password for b'joy at the prompt

> password:

To become a privileged user, enter

> su

then enter the root password at the **password** prompt.

See Also login

tail

Syntax

```
tail [options] [filename]
```

Description The tail command sends the end of *filename* to the screen. The user can specify how many lines are sent. If the number of lines to be sent is not specified, tail sends ten lines. Whether standard input or a file is used depends upon whether or not the *filename* argument is used. If the *filename* argument is not specified, the keyboard (or standard input) is used. If you have a file that stores transactions, using tail you can quickly review the most recent activity.

Options

+*n* or -*n*	With no number specified, tail outputs the last ten lines of the input. If +*n* present, tail outputs the number of lines, characters, or blocks from the beginning of the input; if -*n* is present, tail counts back from the end of the file.
l	Refers to lines when added after +*n* or -*n*.
b	Refers to blocks when added after +*n* or -*n*.
c	Refers to characters when added after +n or -*n*.
r	Outputs the lines in reverse order.

Example Using the file named `phonelist` and entering

```
tail -31 phonelist
```

displays

```
Thomas, Ginger    (408) 555-2323
Williams, Greg    (408) 555-2916
Young, Charles    (415) 555-2380
```

Entering

```
tail -23c phonelist
```

displays

```
Charles (415) 555-2380
```

Note that if options **l**, **b**, or **c** are used, they must immediately follow any +n or -n with no intervening spaces.

See Also `cat`, `more`, `head`

talk

Syntax

```
talk username [tty]
```

Description The `talk` command establishes a two-way, terminal-to-terminal communication path. It allows users to send messages back and forth by typing them in.

Options The `talk` command has no options.

Example Entering

```
talk lgoodman
```

displays the following on `lgoodman`'s terminal:

```
Message from Talk_Daemon@primetime at 2:03…
talk:  connection requested by rpetrie@primetime
talk:  respond with:  talk rpetrie@primetime
```

where `primetime` is your computer's host name. `2:03` is the current time. `r.petrie` is your login name. The other user (in this case `lgoodman`) should then enter

```
talk yourname
```

This establishes the link between your terminals. To exit, just enter your system's interrupt character (on some systems press Control-o). Note that pressing Control-l redraws the screen while you are using the `talk` command.

See Also `mesg, who, write`

tar

Syntax

```
tar [key] [options] [tarfilename] [blocksize] [excludefile] [-I
includefile] [filename1] [filename2 ...] [-C directory filename3]
[filename4]
```

Description The `tar` command archives and recovers files. It can create, add to, list, and retrieve files from an archive. The first option following `tar` is the key. The key specifies these actions: create (creates a new tarfile); write (writes the designated files to the end of the tarfile); table of contents (lists the table of contents of the tarfile); update (adds the named files to the tarfile if they are not already present or current); extract (extracts files from an archive file). One of these must be entered. After the key comes any modifiers. An archive file may reside on a system disk, floppy disk, tape unit, or anywhere else SunOS can write or to read a file.

Common places to archive files are tape drives and floppy disks. The `/dev` directory has several files in it that are really devices such as a tape drive, terminal, system disk, or floppy disk drive. `/dev/rdiskette` is really a floppy drive, and `/dev/rmt/0` is really a tape drive.

The `tar` command knows about directory structures and can preserve absolute, relative, or no directory information. If the files specified to archive are given with a full path, that information is preserved, and when the file is recovered, it is placed back into the correct directory. If the files are specified with a relative path at the time of the archive, they are placed in the directory with the same relative path from the current working directory at the time of the recovery. If, at the time of the archive, the files are specified from the current directory with just a file name, they will be placed into whatever the current working directory is at the time of recovery.

The `tar` command keeps track of a great deal of information besides the file's contents. It keeps track of things like a *checksum*, which is a number used to help insure data integrity, the permissions associated with the files, their creation dates, and so on.

Examples of device names commonly found on Sun workstations include:

DEVICE NAME	DEVICE
`/dev/rmt/0`	¼-inch tape cartridge
`/dev/rdiskette`	3½-inch diskette

To specify the density for a tape drive, you need to add a character that identifies the tape density after the tape drive number. For example, if you are using a tape drive that writes at a medium density, add the letter `m` after the tape device number (`/dev/rmt/0m`). The following is a list of characters used to specify different densities for SCSI tape drives.

`null`	Default, preferred (highest) density
`l`	Low (800 bpi)
`m`	Medium (1600 bpi)
`h`	High (6250 bpi)
`u`	Ultra (reserved)

After performing a backup or a retrieval on some devices, the system typically rewinds the tape and resets the file pointers for diskettes. To prevent rewinding, the device name should be appended with an `n` at the end of the device name (`/dev/rmt/0mn`).

Keys

c   Creates a new archive file. This overwrites anything previously stored on the media (it overwrites files on floppies, for instance).

r   Appends the named files to an existing archive file. Any existing files in the archive are not changed. This does not work with ¼-inch tape.

t   Prints the names of any specified files as they appear in the archive file. If no files are specified, this key displays a directory of all files contained in the archive file.

u   Performs an update, appending files to the archive only if they are not already present or if they have been modified since they were last written to the tape. This option runs slowly due to the checking it must perform. This does not work with ¼-inch tape.

x   Extracts files from an archive file. Given a file list, this option only extracts the files specified. With no file list, this option extracts all the files in an archive.

Options

f   Uses the next argument as the name of the file to read or write as the archive file (instead of the default of /dev/rmt/0). If – is used, the standard input or standard output is used; thus tar can be used in a pipe.

FF   Excludes all SCCS directories, all files with .o as their suffix, and all files named errs, core, and a.out.

l   Displays error messages if links to archived files cannot be resolved. Without this option, error messages about unresolved links will not be displayed.

L   Follows symbolic links, which allows linked files to be treated as if they were normal files or directories. Without this option, `tar` does not support symbolic links.

m   Does not extract modification times with files. Sets the modification time to the time of the extraction.

o   Suppresses information specifying owner and permission modes normally placed into the archive. Such information makes previous versions of `tar` generate error messages like `filename: cannot create`.

v   Displays the name of each file archived or extracted. When used with the **t** key, displays a listing similar to `ls -l`.

w   Waits for user confirmation before taking any action. Displays the action to be taken followed by the file name and waits for a **y** entered from the keyboard. Anything other than a **y** causes no action to be taken for the named file.

-I   Uses `includefilename`, the next file name, as a list of files, one per line, entered on the command line for the `tar` command. Excluded files take precedence over included files. See the -x option.

Example To archive the current working directory to the default tape drive (`dev/rmt/0`), and overwrite anything else on the tape, enter

```
tar cv.
```

To list the files on a ¼-inch cartridge tape drive, enter

```
tar tvf /dev/rmt/0
```

To archive the files `memo` and `report` on a floppy disk, enter

```
tar cvf /dev/rdiskette memo report
```

To extract the files from a floppy diskette into the current directory, enter

```
tar xvf /dev/rdiskette
```

See Also `chdir`, `ls`, `cpio`

tee

Syntax

```
tee [options] [filename]
```

Description The `tee` command replicates the standard output. This command is usually used in a pipe. A pipe (I) is a way to connect the output of one command or program to the input of another command or program. The standard input is usually the keyboard, but by using pipes, you can get input from the output of a command or program instead. Sometimes when constructing long pipes, it is desirable to save intermediate results. If you form a `tee` in the pipe, you can siphon off some of the information and direct it to a file.

Options

`-a`	Appends the output to the specified file instead of overwriting the existing contents.
`-i`	Ignores interrupts.

Example Entering

```
pr final.draft | tee report.printed | lp
```

prepares the file `final.draft` for printing, saves a copy of the formatted file as `report.printed`, and sends a formatted copy to the printer.

See Also lp, ls, pr, wc

telnet

Syntax

```
telnet [hostname [port]]
```

Description The `telnet` command allows you to communicate with another machine using the TELNET protocol. If no host name is specified, `telnet` displays the prompt `telnet >`, indicating that it is in command mode. If a *hostname* or *port* is added, `telnet` opens the host indicated. After the connection is established, you are prompted for a user name and password on the remote system.

Commands The `telnet` command contains a command mode that offers many features and options. You can switch from terminal mode to command mode with the telnet escape character, which defaults to Control-]. After pressing Control-], a new prompt appears from the local telnet command mode. At this point you can enter any of several telnet commands. The following lists several `telnet` commands.

COMMAND	EFFECT
close	Terminates the connection but remains in the `telnet` program.
open *hostname*	Starts a connection to the named host machine.
quit	Quits the current connection and exits the telnet program. This command is the same as the `close` command.

COMMAND	EFFECT
z	Temporarily suspends the telnet session to allow other commands to be executed on the local system.
?	Prints help information on available telnet commands.
<Return>	Returns you to the shell at the remote host machine.

Example Entering

```
telnet spacelink.msfc.nasa.gov
```

connects you to the NASA system. When prompted for a login user name and password, enter

```
newuser
```

You are then presented with a menu of options for reading entries about the history, current state, and future of NASA activities.

See Also ftp, rlogin

time

Syntax

```
time [command]
```

Description The time command times how long a command takes to run, or with no command specified, tells how much time has been used for the current process.

Options The time command has no options.

Example Entering

```
time find / -name "*.ps" -print &
```

displays the results of the find command and something like

```
real  3m13.36s
user  0m10.29s
sys   1m35.74s
[1] +  Done                        find / -name "*.ps" -print &
```

The `real` time (`3m13.36s`) means that the process has been running for 3 minutes and 13.36 seconds. This is the total elapsed time from the execution of the `find` command to its completion. The `user` time (`0m10.29s`) is the amount of time the command takes to execute. The sys time (`1m35.74s`) indicates the amount of time used by the SunOS system to execute the command time. The total CPU time is the sum of the sys and user time measurements.

See Also date

tip

Syntax

```
tip telephonenumber
```

Description The `tip` program, which stands for Telephone Interface Program, allows you to dial up using a modem and log into other computers. You can also copy files between your machine and the remote machine. Once the connection is established, a remote session using `tip` behaves like an interactive session on a local terminal. The `tip` does not support Xmodem protocols or transfer binary files. Both your system and the remote system must have proper hardware installed to make a connection possible using the `tip` command, and you must have an account on the remote system.

Commands The following are common tilde commands that let you perform tasks on your local machine while connected to the remote machine using the `tip` program.

COMMAND	DESCRIPTION
~p	Puts (sends) a file to the remote machine.
~t	Takes (receives) a file from the remote machine.
~c	Changes the directory on your local machine.
~.	Disconnects from the remote system.
~!	Escapes to a new shell, from which you can return to **tip**. Lets you access your local machine while still connected to the remote machine.
~Control-z	Suspends, performs work locally, then returns **tip**. Lets you access your local machine while still connected to the remote machine.
~Control-y	Suspends **tip** locally, but still monitors the output of the remote machine. Lets you access your local machine while still connected to the remote machine.

Example To connect to a system at the phone number 555-1212, enter

```
tip 5551212
```

The **tip** program displays the prompt **dialing...** then places the call through your network's modem. When the call is answered by the remote system, **tip** indicates the connection is complete with the prompt **dialing...connected**. From this point on, you are connected with the other computer and can proceed to log into the system.

To send the file **humor** from your system to the remote system, enter

```
~p
```

then press Return and enter

```
humor
```

To transfer the file `macabre` from the remote machine to your machine, enter

`~t`

then press Return and enter

`macabre`

touch

Syntax

`touch [options] filename(s)`

Description The `touch` command sets the access and modification time of the file *filename* to the current time. The *filename* is created if it does not exist. The `touch` command is often used with the special programming command `make` to force a complete rebuild of a program.

Options

`-c`   Does not create `filename` if it does not
                             exist.

Example Enter

`touch *.c`

to change the access and modification of any files with the `.c` extension in the current directory.

tr

Syntax

`tr [options] [string1] [string2]`

Description The `tr` command copies the standard input to the standard output, translating occurrences from *string1* into corresponding characters in *string2*. A common use of `tr` is to convert a file to all uppercase or lowercase.

Options

-c Complements the set of characters in *string1* with respect to the set of ASCII codes 1-255 (so that `tr -cd 0-9` means to delete everything that's not a number).

-d Deletes all characters in `string1`. For example, `tr -d '^A-^Z' < in.ctrl > out.txt` can be used to strip all control characters from a file (for printing a file, for instance).

-s Squeezes strings of repeated characters from `string2` to single characters.

Example Entering

```
cat mixed.txt | tr "[A-Z]" "[a-z]" > lower.txt
```

translates the file `mixed.txt`, containing both upper- and lowercase, into the file `lower.txt`, containing only lowercase letters. Entering

```
cat infile.txt | tr " " "\012" > outfile.txt
```

translates the file `in.file` into a file, `out.file`, that converts spaces into newlines with one word per line. Note that this example has no effect on the case of the characters contained in any of the files.

Entering

```
tr -d "&" < textfile1 > textfile2
```

deletes the & character from *textfile1* and saves the output in *textfile2*.

See Also expand

tty

Syntax

    tty [option]

Description The `tty` command prints the path name of your terminal's device file.

Options

-l	Prints the synchronous line number.
-s	Returns only the codes: 0 (a terminal), 1 (not a terminal), 2 (invalid options used).

Example Entering

    tty

displays something similar to

    /dev/pts/1

umask

Syntax

    umask [mask]

Description The `umask` command displays or sets the file creation mode mask. Entering the `unmask` command alone displays the current file recreation mask. The numbers are like the numbers used for `chmod`, except that with `umask`, the numbers represent the permissions that are not granted, whereas with `chmod` the numbers represent the permissions that are granted. Because SunOS is a multiuser system, there are built-in safeguards to keep users from accidentally (or even deliberately) deleting another user's files. These safeguards protect against unauthorized reading, writing, copying, deleting, and executing of files.

The modes are given in either of two formats for this command. An absolute mode is an octal number formed by summing the following octal numbers representing the enabled permissions. There are three fields, one for the owner of the file, one for the group to which the file belongs, and one for everybody else.

0	Grants read and write permission for files, and read, write, and search permission for directories.
1	Grants read and write permission for files and directories.
2	Grants only read permission for files, and grants read and search permission for directories.
3	Grants only read permission for files and directories.
4	Grants only write permission for files, and write and search permission for directories.
5	Grants only write permission for files and directories.
6	Grants no permissions for files, and grants only search permission for directories.
7	Grants no permissions (denies all permissions) for files and directories.

By default, files are given the permissions mode 666 (rw-rw-rw-), which gives everyone read and write access. Directories are given the permissions mode 777 (rwxrwxrwx), which gives everyone read, write, and search permission.

Options The umask command has no options.

Example Entering

```
umask
```

displays the current setting of the file creation mask. Entering

```
umask 002
```

sets the file creation `mask` so the owner and group have all privileges, while the rest of the world has only read permission.

See Also `chgrp`, `chmod`, `chown`, `ls`

unalias

Syntax

```
unalias pattern
```

Description The `unalias` command is a Korn shell command that discards aliases. Any aliases that match *pattern* are discarded, so **unalias *** discards all previous aliases.

Options The `unalias` command has no options.

Example If you have previously aliased `ls` with

```
alias ls="ls -l"
```

which displays a long listing anytime `ls` is entered, you can undo the `alias` with

```
unalias ls
```

See Also `alias`

uname

Syntax

```
uname [options]
```

Description The `uname` command displays information about the operating system. If no options are specified, only the current operating system's name is displayed.

Options

−a	Displays all information about the current system.
−m	Displays the machine name.
−n	Displays the node name. The node name is the name by which the system is known to a network.
−p	Displays the current host's processor type.
−r	Displays the number of the operating system release.
−s	Displays the name of the operating system. This is the default.
−v	Displays the operating system version.

Example Entering

```
uname −a
```

is the same as entering **uname −mnprsv**, which displays a listing similar to this:

```
SunOS primetime 5.1 Generic sun4c sparc
```

uncompress

Syntax

```
uncompress [options] [filename]
```

Description The **uncompress** command recovers a compressed file.

Options

−c	Writes to the screen (or standard output). Does not change any files. (The **zcat** command is equivalent to the -c option.)
−v	Displays the percentage of reduction.

Example Given a file, `report.text`, with a size of 4608 bytes, entering

    compress report.text

results in a file, `report.text.Z`, with a size of 2696 bytes. To uncompress this file, enter

    uncompress report.text

Note that with the `uncompress` command, the `.Z` extension is optional.

See Also `compress`

unexpand

Syntax

    unexpand [option] filename

Description The `unexpand` command is the opposite of the `expand` command. It copies file names (or the standard input) to the standard output, putting tab characters back into the data. By default, only leading space and tab characters are converted to strings of tabs.

Options

`-a`	Inserts tab characters when replacing a run of two or more space characters would produce a smaller output file.

Example Entering

    unexpand myfile

reverses the effect of running the expand command on `myfile`.

See Also `expand`

uniq

Syntax

```
uniq [options] [inputfilename] [outputfilename]
```

Description   The `uniq` command is used to remove or report on adjacent duplicate lines within a file. Normally `uniq` removes the second and succeeding repeated lines, passing everything else through to the output. To be removed, duplicate lines must be adjacent.

Options

-c	Precedes each line by a count of the number of times it occurred in the input.
-d	Displays one occurrence of just the repeated lines from the input.
-u	Displays just those lines that were not repeated in the input.
+n	Ignores the first *n* characters when comparing lines.
-n	Ignores the first n fields, together with any blanks before each field. A field is a string of characters separated by space or tab characters.

Examples   Entering

```
cat singers musicians | sort | uniq > talent
```

combines the files **singers** and **musicians**, sorts the combined file, eliminates any duplicates, and stores the results in the file **talent**. Entering

```
cat singers musicians | sort | uniq -d > diverse
```

combines the files, sorts them, and saves only duplicate lines, thus showing entries common to two or more files.

See Also   sort

units

Syntax

```
units
```

Description

The `units` command converts between units of measure. (Be aware that the money conversions are not current.) For a complete list of known units, look in the file `/usr/share/lib/unittab`. Note that the `units` command only does multiplicative scale changes; thus it can convert Kelvin to Rankine, but not Celsius to Fahrenheit. The `units` command operates interactively.

Options

The `units` command has no options.

Example

Enter

```
units
```

and the `units` command displays

```
You have:
```

Enter

```
36 inch
```

and the `units` command displays

```
You want:
```

Enter

```
feet
```

and the `units` command displays

```
* 3.000000e+00
/ 3.333333e-01
```

To terminate the program, press Control-d.

unpack

Syntax

```
unpack filename(s)
```

Description Expands one or more files created with the `pack` command to their original form.

Options The `unpack` command has no options.

Example To unpack a previously packed file, `mucho.psz`, enter

```
unpack mucho.psz
```

See Also pack

vacation

Syntax

```
vacation [options]
```

Description Automatically return a mail message to sender announcing that you are on vacation. To disable the `vacation` command, type `mail -F " "`.

-I	Begins forwarding your mail and informing other users sending you mail that you are on vacation. If the -I option and the *username* argument are omitted, the `vacation` command lets you interactively turn `vacation` on or off. If the -I option is omitted but the `username` is included, `vacation` reads from the standard input for a line indicating who the vacation message is from (`From username`).

-a *alias* Indicates that *alias* is one of the valid aliases for the user running the `vacation` command, so that mail addressed to `alias` generates a reply.

-t *n*   Specifies the time interval between repeat replies to the same sender. You can specify seconds (-t*n*s), minutes (−t*n*m), hours (−t*n*h), days(−t*n*d), or weeks (−t*n*w). The default is one week.

Example The following is a sample listing of prompts displayed after entering the `vacation` command.

```
This program can be used to answer your mail automatically
when you go away on vacation.
You have a message file in /export/home/rpetrie/.vacation.msg.
Would you like to see it? y
Subject:  I am on vacation
Precedence: junk

Your mail regarding "$SUBJECT" will be read when I return.

If you have something urgent, please contact...
Would you like to edit it? n
To enable the vacation feature a ".forward" file is created.
Would you like to enable the vacation feature? y
Vacation feature ENABLED. Please remember to turn it off when
you get back from vacation. Bon voyage.
```

See Also `mail`, `mailx`

vi

Syntax

```
vi [options] [filename(s)]
```

Description The vi editor is a visual text editor. See Chapter 12, "Using the vi Editor" for detailed coverage on working with vi. Chapter 13, "Formatting and Printing" explains how to work with `nroff` and `troff` text-formatting commands.

wall

Syntax

```
wall [options] [filename]
```

Description The `wall` command writes to all logged-in users (as such it is usually used by the system administrator for important messages). The standard input is read until a Control-d is entered. It is then sent to all logged-in users preceded by the message "Broadcast Message." If `filename` is specified, the input is taken from the indicated file instead of from the standard input.

Options

    -a   Writes to all terminals.

Example Entering

```
wall fired
```

broadcasts the file `fired` to all users logged onto the network.

See Also `mesg`, `write`

wc

Syntax

```
wc [options] [filename]
```

Description The `wc` command counts the lines, words, and characters in `filename`. If `filename` is not specified, `wc` counts the standard input. Words are separated by spaces, tabs, or newlines (carriage returns). The `wc` command is very useful in piping. You can use the `who` command, which lists the users currently logged in (giving one user per line), and pipe its output to `wc`, which then counts the number of lines by entering `who | wc -l`. This counts and displays the number of currently logged-on users. Combining `ls`, a command to list the files in a directory, with `wc`, a command to count lines, as follows

```
ls | wc -l
```

counts the number of files in the current directory.

Options

-l   Counts the lines in the specified file.

-w   Counts the words in the specified file.

-C   Counts characters in the specified file.

-c   Counts bytes in the specified file.

Example
Entering the command

```
wc file1
```

displays

```
227  876  6220 file1
```

which means there are 227 lines, 876 words, and 6220 characters in the file **file1**.

Entering

```
wc -l file1
```

displays

```
227 file1
```

which means there are 227 lines in the file **file1**.

Entering

```
wc -C file1
```

displays

```
6220 file1
```

which means there are 6220 characters in the file **file1**.

which

Syntax

```
which filename
```

Description The `which` command locates a command and displays its path name The `which` command cannot find built-in shell commands such as `history` and `set`.

Options The `which` command has no options.

Example Entering

```
which vi
```

displays

```
/usr/bin/vi
```

Entering

```
which set
```

displays a path similar to this:

```
no set in /usr/openwin/bin /usr/sbin /sbin /usr/bin /bin /etc
/usr/lib/lp/postscript /usr/openwin/demo .
```

where everything after the `no set in` is a possible path setting, and the `which` command could not find a command named `set` in the path.

who

Syntax

```
who
```

Description The `who` command displays the login name, terminal name, and login time for each user currently logged in on the local host machine.

Options The `who` command has no options.

Example Entering

        who

displays something like

```
nbacon     tty6 Feb 29 09:18  (nbacon_tty)
rgoodman   tty3 Feb 29 13:12  (rgoodman_tty)
egoodman   tty9 Feb 29 08:10  (ecyr_tty)
```

See Also who am i, rwho

who am i

Syntax

        who am i

Description The who am i command displays your login name.

Options The who am i command has no options.

Example Entering

        who am i

displays something like

        lgoodman

See Also who

write

Syntax

        write *username*

Description The `write` command allows you to send a message to another user's terminal (if they have allowed it through the use of the `mesg` command). If the user is logged into more than one terminal, you must specify `tty`, which is a terminal number.

Options The `write` command has no options.

Example Entering

```
write bheslop
lunch in 10 minutes?
<Control-d>
```

displays on bheslop's terminal

```
Message from lgoodman on stv (pts/1) [Mon Dec 27 11:50:03 ...
lunch in 10 minutes?
```

See Also `mesg`, `talk`, `ps`

xfd

Syntax

```
xfd [options] -fn fontname
```

Description The `xfd` command is an X program that creates an X window for displaying all of the characters of the font indicated by the argument *fontname*. The window contains the name of the font being displayed, a grid containing one character per cell, and three buttons (`Prev Page`, `Next Page`, and `quit`). The text above the character grid displays the selected character's metrics. The characters are shown in increasing ASCII order from left to right, and top to bottom.

Options

-box	Displays a box filled with the background color (indicated by -**bc**) outlining the area of each character.

-bc *color*	Specifies the color used to make up the grid surrounding displayed characters.
-center	Centers each character in its grid for viewing characters at arbitrary locations in the font. The default is 0.
-columns *n*	Specifies the number of columns to use when creating the grid for displaying characters.
-rows *n*	Specifies the number of rows to use when creating the grid for displaying characters.
-start *n*	Displays as the first character the character that has position n.

Example Entering

```
xfd -fn rockwell &
```

displays all the characters in the Rockwell font.

Entering

```
xfd -columns 40 -rows 25 -start 1568 -fn kanji
```

displays, in a grid 40 columns by 25 rows, the kanji characters starting at character 1568 in the font named Kanji.

See Also xfontsel, xlsfonts

xfontsel

Syntax

```
xfontsel [options]
```

Description The xfontsel command is an X program that creates a window that allows you to show display font names by pointing and clicking. The window lets you display a font by choosing from a variety of menus, including the font foundry (**fndry**), font family (**fmly**), font weight (**wght**), font slant (**slant**), set width (**sWdth**), pixels points in tenths of a point (**ptSz**), horizontal resolution in dots per inch (resx), vertical resolution in dots per inch (resy), average width in tenths of a pixel (avgWdth).

Options

-pattern *fontname*   Specifies a subset of available fonts, with names that contain the pattern specified by *fontname*. The pattern can be a partial or full font name, but the pattern must occur somewhere in the full font name.

-print   Displays the selected font's name before returning to the command prompt after pressing the quit button.

-sample *text*   Displays the text to display the selected font. Be sure to put *text* containing spaces within quotation marks. The default *text* is lower-case and uppercase letters and the digits 0 through 9.

Example Entering

```
xfontsel
```

displays the xfontsel window with the alphabet and numbers 0 through 9 in the default display font.

To display the first font that contains "adobe-times" in its font name, enter

```
xfontsel -pattern *adobe-times*&
```

Entering

```
xfontsel -pattern *bitstream-charter*240* -sample "Bitstream
Charter (24 points)"&
```

displays the text "Bitstream Charter (24 points)" for the first font that contains "bitstream-charter" and "240" in its font name.

See Also xfd, xlsfonts

xhost

Syntax

xhost [*options*]

Description The xhost command is an X command that adds and deletes hosts from the list of machines that are allowed to make connections to the X host. The xhost command is often required to set up application programs on your machine. If no arguments are added to the xhost command, a message indicates whether or not access control is enabled, and a list of hosts you are allowed to connect to is displayed.

Options

[+]*hostname*	Adds *hostname* to the list of machines that are allowed to connect to the X server.
−*hostname*	Removes hostname from the list of machines that are allowed to connect to the X server. Existing connections are not broken, but new connection attempts will be denied.
+	Grants access to everyone, even if they aren't on the list of allowed hosts. In other words, access control is turned off.
−	Restricts access to only those machines on the list of allowed hosts. In other words, access control is turned on.

Example Entering

xhost +tvland +camelot

adds the hosts **tvland** and **camelot** to the X server access list.

Entering

```
xhost +
```

grants access to everyone on the network.

See Also openwin

xlock

Syntax

```
xlock [options]
```

Description The xlock command is an X command that locks the screen and starts a screen saver until you enter your password. While xlock is running, the screen displays a changing pattern of Sun logos. When you press a key or a mouse button, you are prompted for your password to return to OpenWindows. If the correct password is typed, the screen is unlocked. If you make a mistake when typing your password, press Control-h to backspace over the mistake, or press Control-u to start over. To return to the locked screen, click on the small icon version of the changing pattern.

Options

-mode *screensaver*	There are ten screensavers you can choose from. The following gives a brief description of each screensaver.
hop	Displays the "real plane fractals" from the September 1986 issue of Scientific American.
life	Displays Conway's game of life.

`qix`	Displays the spinning lines similar to the ones in the old video game by the same name.
`image`	Displays several Sun logos appearing randomly on the screen.
`swarm`	Displays a swarm of bees following a wasp.
`rotor`	Displays a swirling rotor.
`pyro`	Displays fireworks.
`flame`	Displays fractals.
`blank`	Displays nothing but a black screen.
`random`	Picks and displays a random screensaver from all of the above except the `blank` screensaver.
`-delay` *users*	Sets the speed at which a screensaver will operate. It sets the number of microseconds to delay between batches of animation. In the `blank` screensaver, it is important to set this to some small number of seconds, because the keyboard and mouse are only checked after each delay; so you cannot set the delay too high, but a delay of zero would needlessly consume CPU time by continuously checking for mouse and keyboard input, since `blank` screensaver has no work to do.

-batchcount *n*	Sets number of things to do for a screensaver to *n*. When you use the hop screensaver, *n* refers to the number of pixels rendered in the same color. When you use the life screensaver, *n* is the number of generations to let each species live. When you use the qix screensaver, *n* is the number of lines rendered in the same color. When you use the image screensaver, *n* is the number of Sun logos to display on the screen at once. When you use the swarm screensaver, *n* is the number of bees. When you use the rotor screensaver, *n* is the number of rotor things that whirr. When you use the pyro screensaver, *n* is the maximum number of flying rockets at one time. When you use the flame screensaver, *n* is the number of levels to recurse (larger numbers are more complex). When you use the blank screensaver, *n* means nothing.
-nice *n*	Sets the nice setting of the xlock process to *n*.
-timeout *seconds*	Sets the number of *seconds* before the password screen will time out.
-saturation *value*	Sets saturation of the color ramp used to *value*. 0 is gray-scale and 1 is very rich color. 0.4 is a nice pastel.
-font *fontname*	Sets the font to be used on the prompt screen.
-fg *color*	Sets the color of the text on the password screen to color.

-bg *color*	Sets the color of the background on the password screen to *color*.
-*username textstring*	The textstring is shown in front of user name, defaults to `Name:`
-password *textstring*	The *textstring* is the password prompt. The default is `Password:`
-info *textstring*	Informs the user what to do to unlock the screen. The default displays `Enter password to unlock; select icon to lock.`
-validate *textstring*	Specifies the message shown while validating the password. The default is `Validating login...`
-invalid textstring	Specifies the message shown when a password is invalid. The default is `Invalid login.`
-mono or +mono	Displays screensaver in monochrome (black and white), rather than the default color.
+nolock or -nolock	Causes `xlock` to only draw the patterns and not lock the display. Pressing a key or clicking a mouse button terminates the screensaver.
-echokeys or +echokeys	Causes `xlock` to echo the question mark (?) for each key typed at the password prompt. The default is to not echo keystrokes.
-usefirst or +usefirst	Causes `xlock` to use the keystroke that got you to the password screen as the first character in the password. The default is to ignore the first key pressed.
-v	Verbose mode; tells what options it is going to use.

Example Entering

```
xlock -mode rotor
```

displays a whirling rotor that saves the screen.

To display a screensaver that does not require you to enter a password, add the -nolock option. For example, to start the pyro screensaver without password protection, enter

```
xlock -mode pyro -nolock
```

To change the swarm of bees to include 100 bees in the swarm screensaver, enter

```
xlock -batchcount 100 -mode swarm
```

See Also xset

xlsfonts

Syntax

```
xlsfonts [options] -fn [pattern]
```

Description The xlsfonts command lists available fonts that match pattern. *The wildcard characters* * and ? can be used to match characters. If no pattern is given, * is assumed.

Options

-l[l[l]]	Generate medium (-l), long (-ll), and extremely long listings(-lll).
-c	Produces a list using multiple columns. This option is the same as using the argument -n 0.
-1	Produces a list using a single column. This option is the same as using the argument -n 1.

-w *width*	Specifies how many characters should appear in a column *width*. The default is a width of 79 characters.
-n *columns*	Uses number of columns in displaying the output. By default, the xlsfonts command attempts to fit as many columns of font names into the number of characters specified by -w *width*.
-u	Specifies not to sort the listing.

Example Entering

```
xlsfonts -fn \*linotype*
```

displays the available linotype fonts.

Entering

```
xlsfonts -l -fn \*monotype*
```

displays a long listing of available monotype fonts.

See Also xfd, xfontsel

xman

Syntax

```
xman [options]
```

Description The xman command displays a window for viewing the X manual pages for X commands. The initial Manual Browser window displays three buttons Help, Manual Page, and Quit. Clicking on the Manual Page or Help buttons displays the initial Manual Page window, containing instructions for displaying X manual pages. At the top of the Manual Page window are two menu buttons (Options and Sections) for displaying X manual pages. To scroll through the introductory text, press the right mouse button on the scrollbar at the left side of the Manual Page window.

Options

-helpfile *filename*	Uses an alternate file indicated by *filename* for help.
-bothshown	Displays both the manual page and manual directory in the same window.
-notopbox	Displays the Manual Page window without the displaying the initial Manual Browser window with the three buttons in it.

Example Entering

```
xman &
```

displays the initial Manual Browser window.

Entering

```
xman -notopbox -bothshown &
```

displays a split window with the directory of user commands at the top and the help manual page in the lower window.

See Also man

xrdb

Syntax

```
xrdb [options]
```

Description The xrdb command reads the .Xdefaults file and sets the basic properties for OpenWindows, such as the Workspace and window colors. The xrdb command also allows you to display or edit the contents of the .Xdefaults file. This program is run each time you start OpenWindows.

Options

`-help`	Displays a usage summary of command-line options. Using any unsupported option has the same effect.
`-query`	Displays the current contents of the `.Xdefaults` file.
`-quiet`	Does not warn about duplicate entries.
`-edit` *filename*	Copies the `.Xdefaults` file into *filename* replacing any values already listed. This allows you to put changes that you have made to your defaults back into your `.Xdefaults` file, preserving any comments.
`-backup` *string*	Generates a backup file appending an extension indicated by *string* to the file name used with the `-edit` option.

Example Entering

```
xrdb
```

reads and executes the `.Xdefaults` file.

To display the contents of your `.Xdefaults` file, enter

```
xrdb -query
```

See Also openwin, xset, xsetroot

xset

Syntax

```
xset [options]
```

Description The xset command lets you customize X environment settings for OpenWindows features, such as the bell, the key click, and the screensaver. Any X settings that you change are lost or reset to their default values when you log out unless you add them to the .xinitrc file in your home directory. If the .xinitrc file does not exist in your home directory, you need to copy and rename the $OPENWINHOME/lib/Xinitrc file to $HOME/.xinitrc.

Options

[-]b [volume [pitch [duration]]] [on | off]	Sets the volume, pitch, and duration of the bell. If no arguments are given, the bell is enabled and the system defaults are used. Unlike most options, preceding the b with a dash (-) turns the bell off. You can also turn the bell off by adding the off argument. If only one number is given, the bell volume will be set to that value, as a percentage of its maximum. The second number specifies the bell's pitch, in hertz, and the third number specifies the duration of the bell in milliseconds.

[−]c [value][on | off]	Sets the volume of the key click. The c option accepts an optional *value* from 0 to 100 that indicates the volume as a percentage of maximum. As with the b option, preceding the c with a dash (−) disables the key click. If no arguments are added, the system defaults are used. If the **off** argument is added, the keyclick is disabled.
fp=*path*	Sets the font path used by the server. The path must be a directory or a comma-separated list of directories.
fp default	Restores the default font path.
fp rehash	Rereads the font databases in the current font path. This is generally used only when adding new fonts to a font directory (after running *mkfontdir* to recreate the font database).
−fp *path* or fp− *path*	Removes elements from the current font path. *path* must be a directory or a comma-separated list of directories.
+fp *path* or fp+ *path*	Inserts or appends elements to the current font path, respectively. The path must be a directory or comma-separated list of directories.

led [*integer*] [*on* | off]

Turns LEDs (the lights on your keyboard) on or off. The *led* option without an argument turns all LEDs on. With a preceding dash or the *off* argument added, turns LEDs off. Adding an *integer* between 1 and 32 turns the respective LED on or off.

m [*acceleration* [*threshold*]] [default]

Sets how far the mouse pointer moves on the screen in relation to how far you move the mouse. The *acceleration* argument is a multiplier that is applied to the pointer motion. In other words, if the acceleration is set to 5, when you move the mouse, it will move 5 times as fast. To keep the mouse pointer from leaping around, you can also set a *threshold*. The *threshold* setting makes it so that the acceleration factor only takes effect if the pointer moves more than the number of pixels indicated by *threshold*. If no arguments are added, the system defaults are used.

`s [time [cycle]]`
`[blank | noblank]`
`[on | off] [default]`
	Sets up the screensaver. If no arguments are added, the system is set to its default screensaver characteristics. The off argument turns the screensaver off. The **blank** argument blanks the video instead of displaying a background pattern, while **noblank** sets the preference to display a pattern rather than blanking the video. The *time* and *cycle* arguments determine how many seconds the keyboard must be inactive for the screen blanker to start, and the period in which to change the background pattern to avoid damage to your screen, respectively.

`q`	Displays information on the current X settings.

Example Entering

    xset s 300

enables a screen blanker that starts after five minutes.

Entering

    xset c 75

sets a fairly loud key click sound.

Entering

    xset m 6 12

speeds up the acceleration of the mouse. This sets the mouse movement so that if you move more than 12 pixels, the mouse moves 6 times as many pixels on the screen as you moved the mouse.

```
xset b 100 1000 80
```

sets the volume of the bell to its maximum setting, the pitch to 1000 hertz, and the duration to 80 milliseconds.

See Also xsetroot

xsetroot

Syntax

```
xsetroot [options]
```

Description The `xsetroot` command sets the appearance of the Workspace's background. Without any options or if the `-def` option is added, the Workspace resets to its defaults. If you add the `-def` option with other options, only the nonspecified options are reset to their defaults.

Options

`-help`	Displays a summary of command-line options.
`-def`	Resets unspecified attributes to default values. The background defaults to a gray mesh pattern.
`-cursor cursorfile maskfile`	Sets cursor shape for the mouse pointer. The default mouse pointer is an arrow cursor.
`-cursor_name cursor name`	Changes the root window cursor to one of the standard cursors.

`-bitmap` *filename*	Uses the bitmap file specified by `filename` to set the Workspace background. The default is a gray mesh pattern.
`-mod` *x y*	Makes a plaid grid pattern on the screen. The *x* and *y* are integers ranging from 1 to 16. Zero and negative numbers are taken as 1.
`-gray` or `-grey`	Displays a gray background.
`-solid` *color*	Displays the Workspace background as a solid color.

Example Entering

```
xsetroot -solid turquoise3
```

displays a solid turquoise Workspace background.

To display a bitmap image as your background, enter

```
xsetroot -bitmap $OPENWINHOME/share/include/X11/bitmaps/xlogo64
```

which will display the background to a tiled series of X logos.

Entering

```
xsetroot -cursor_name gumby
```

changes the mouse pointer to a gumby figure.

See Also xset

xterm

Syntax

```
xterm [options]
```

Description The xterm command starts a terminal emulator for you to enter commands. It provides options for VT100- and Tektronics-compatible terminals. The xterm window provides four menus that allow you to manipulate the VT102 and Tektronics windows. To display the menus, press the Control key and one of the three mouse buttons. If you are using Solaris 2 for x86 with a two-button mouse, press both mouse buttons to simulate the middle mouse button. There are numerous options for the xterm command. The following section lists some of the most common options.

Options

-bg *color*   Sets the background color of the xterm window. The default is white.

-fg *color*   Sets the color of the foreground (text) of the xterm window. The default is black.

-fn *font*   Specifies a *font* to use instead of the default font.

-help   Displays a summary of available xterm options.

-j or +j   Specifies that the xterm window should do jump scrolling. Normally, text is scrolled one line at a time; this option allows the xterm window to move multiple lines at a time. Jump scrolling makes xterm much faster when you are scanning through large amounts of text. The +j option specifies that xterm window not do jump scrolling.

-1 *logname*	Sends `xterm` input and output into a file called `XtermLog.`*n*, where *n* represents the process ID number. Logging allows you to keep track of the sequence of commands and output data. The logging option can be turned on and off from the **Main Options** menu, which is displayed by pressing the Control key and the left mouse button.
-1f *filename*	Specifies the file in which the commands and output are written, rather than the default `XtermLog.`*n* where *n* represents the process ID number. The log file is created in the directory that `xterm` was started from.
-RV	Reverses the foreground and background colors. This option can also be turned on and off from the **VT Options** menu.
-sb or +sb	Displays a scroll bar for the `xterm` window and saves lines that are scrolled off the top of the window so they can be viewed.

Example Entering

```
xterm -sb &
```

displays an `xterm` window with a scroll bar.

To create an `xterm` window with a blue background and yellow text, enter

```
xterm -bg midnightblue -fg yellow &
```

If you want to store commands and output from the commands into a log file, named `mycmds`, enter

```
xterm -1 -1f mycmds &
```

See Also openwin

zcat

Syntax

```
zcat filename
```

Description The zcat command is like the cat command except it only displays uncompressed output for the contents of a compressed file (compressed files end with .Z). It leaves the compressed file unchanged.

Options The zcat command has no options.

Example Entering

```
zcat readme.Z
```

displays the compressed contents of the file readme.Z in an uncompressed format.

See Also compress, pack, pcat

INDEX

This index contains certain typographical conventions to assist you in finding information. **Boldface** page numbers are references to primary topics and explanations that are emphasized in the text. *Italics* indicate page numbers that reference figures.

A

abbreviated menu buttons, 29
About button for printer, 248
About Help icon, 41
Abs function, 291
absolute path names, **383**, 709
Acc function, 288
accelerator keys, 33, 59, 78
Access List and Permissions window, 238–240, *239*
access mode for directories, 781
Access to Remote Printer window, **691–693**, *692*
account command (ftp), 757
accounts, 6, 362, **675–682**
active processes, 541
active windows, **30–31**, 320
Actual Size setting for snapshots, 273
.ad request, 504
adapter cables, audio, 253
Add Attachment pop-up menu, 118, *118*
Add Bcc item for messages, 115
Add Calendar button and item, 225, 240
Add Local Printer item, 688
Add Tree's Parent item, 64
Add User window, 676
addresses
    on Internet, 636
    for messages, **114–116**, 158, **455–456**
    for workstations, 685
adjustments, mouse button for, 10–11, *10*
Administration Tool, **671–672**, *672*
    for Database Manager, **673–675**, *674–675*
    for Host Manager, **682–687**, *684*
    for Printer Manager, **687–693**, *688*

for User Account Manager, **675–682**, *677*
admintool command, 672
Again items
    for sound files, 258
    for Text Editor, 175
alarms
    for appointments, 212, 215, 236
    with Clock, 277, 279
    defaults for, 236
alias command, **572–573**, **697–698**
alias command (mailx), 445
Alias Properties window, 157–159, *158*
aliases
    for commands, **572–573**, **697–698**, **833**
    mapping, 114, 453
    for messages, **157–159**, 578
All buttons
    for changing appointments, 217
    for deleting appointments, 216
All Day item for appointments, 213
All ownership, 399
all parameter (vi), 493
All Print Jobs item for stopping printing, 249
All Text button for replacing text, 179
ampersands (&)
    for AND operators, 428–429
    for background commands, 534, 792
analog clocks, 273, *274*
AND operators, 296, 428–429, 749
Appearance setting for Calculator, 299
append command (ftp), 639, 757
append variable, 574
appending text
    with redirection, 430–432
    with vi editor, **481–482**, 488
Application control for Binder entries, 348

application windows, parts of, **19–22**, *20*
applications
  fonts for, **604**
  icons for, *59*. *See also* Binder application
  starting, 17, *18*
  submenus for, **606–610**
Apply buttons
  for calendars, 235
  for Mail Tool properties, 142–143
  for Workspace Properties, 313
appointments
  alarms for, 212, 215, 236
  with CM Multi-Browser window, **225–229**
  creating, **213–215**
  date formats for, **242–243**
  deleting, **215–216**, *216*
  editing, **217**
  entering, **209–217**
  finding, **217–218**
  for groups, **227–229**
  mail notification of, **230–231**
  permissions for, **238–240**
  printing, **218–220**
Appointments scrolling list, 211, 213, 227
Appt List item, 208
Appt setting, 212
aquarium background, 587
archives on tape
  with cpio, **669–671**, **720–724**
  with Tape Tool, **301–308**
  with tar, **667–669**, **820–824**
$ARG argument, 95
arguments for commands, 95, 366
arithmetic operations, 286
arrowheads on menus, 13
arrows for scrollbars, 22, *23*
as a Link item for copying files, 84
Asc function, 291
ascii command (ftp), 639, 757
askcc variable, 457, 574
asksub variable, 574
asterisks (*)
  with cron command, 549
  in grep searches, 417–418, 761–763
  in selecting files, 61, 411–412
at command, 545–546, **698–700**

at signs (@)
  in addresses, 617
  in custom commands, 92
  in Mail Tool messages, 114
atq command, **700**
atrm command, 548, **701**
Attachments pane, 106, *107*, 114, 117–118, 151
attachments to messages, 103, 114
  adding, **117–118**
  copying, **128**
  deleting, **129**
  displaying, 151
  dragging, 117, 122, 128
  opening and viewing, **106**, *108*
  renaming, **128–129**
audio files, icons for, *58*
Audio Tool, **251**
  customizing, **261–263**
  editing sound files with, **258–260**
  inserting sound files with, **260–261**
  loading sound files with, 254, *255*
  playing back sounds with, 256
  recording sounds with, **255–256**
  saving sound files with, 256, *257*, **258**
  volume settings for, **263–264**
  window for, **253–256**, *253*
Audio Tool window, **253–256**, *253*
Auto-Adjust Record Volume button, 264
Auto Home Setup control for users, 681
Auto Play on Load control for sound, 261
Auto Play on Selection control for sound, 261
Automatically display headers setting, 144
automount program, 79, 655
automounting file systems, **654–655**
autoprint variable, 574
autorepeat keyboard rate, **579–580**

B

.B macro, 502
Back item for windows, 28, 34, 45
back quotes (`) for command substitution, 426–427, 566
Backgr Color control for Binder entries, 347, 355, 357

background
    moving windows to, **34**, *35*, **36**
    of Workspace, **584–587**, *585–586*,
      860–861
background commands, **534–536**, 792
    batch command for, **547–548**, **702**
    after exiting, **541**, **789**
    priority of, 568
    waiting for, 540
backing up files to tape
    with cpio, **669–671**, **720–724**
    with Tape Tool, **301–308**
    with tar, **667–669**, **820–824**
backslashes (\)
    in grep searches, 418, 762–763
    for long commands, 409
    in messages, 370–371, 740
Backspace key, assignments for, 579
Backward item in Text Editor, 178–180
banner command, **701–702**
banner pages, printing, **525**, 691
bars (|)
    with metacharacters, 412
    for OR operators, 428–429
    for pipes, 427
Base button for Calculator, 287
base windows, 18
bases, number, **287–288**, **703**
Basic mode with Calculator, 286
Basic Setting for languages, 323
batch command, **547–548**, **702**
baud rate settings, 624, 633, 727
baudrate variable, 627
bc command, **368–369**, **703–704**
beautify variable, 627
beeping
    for appointments, 212
    for messages, 143
    settings for, 319
    for snapshots, 266–267
Begin Tree Here item for file display, 64
beginning of file
    displaying, 414, **764**
    scrolling to, 22
bell command (ftp), 639, 757
bell settings, 579–580, 856
bg command, 537–538, 540
bgnice command, 568
/bin directory, 53, 381

/bin:/usr/bin path, 561
binary command (ftp), 639, 757
binary files
    displaying, 392
    searching in, **816–817**
binary keypad, 287–288, *287*
Binder application, 324
    Binder database for, 70, 342
    binding icons with, **353–355**, *356*
    deleting entries in, 356
    editing entries in, **357–358**
    properties of entries in, **343–353**
    viewing entries in, 342
    window for, **340–342**, *341*
Binder database, 70, 342
Binder Entries scrolling list, 343
Binder window, **340–342**, *341*
binding icons to applications. *See* Binder
    application
bitmap files for backgrounds, **584–587**,
    585–586, 861
Biweekly setting for appointment alarms,
    215
black-and-white icons, 325–326
blank lines, **505–506**
blank screensaver, 583, 849
blind carbon copies, 115, 458
Block I/O setting for Tape Tool, 307
block quote paragraphs, **509–510**
blocks, selecting, in Text Editor, 169
boldfacing text, 502
boot command, 648
booting systems, **647–649**
bottom of file
    displaying, 414, **818–819**
    scrolling to, 22
bounding boxes, 33, 36, 329
Bourne shell, system prompt in, 365
.bp request, 516
.br request, 515
Bracketed item for including messages,
    119–120, *119*
brackets. *See* curly braces ({}); square
    brackets ([ ])
breaking lines, **755–756**
Brightness control, 315–316
broadcasting messages, 462, 840
Browse menu, 204, 231–233

Browse permission for appointments, 239–240
Bsp function, 288
buffers. *See also* clipboard
  command-line, 366
  with mailx, 440–441
  with vi editor, **488–490**
buttons, 29, 145–146, *146*
B&W setting for icons, 325–326
bye command (ftp), 639, 757
bye command (telnet), 637
bytes, counting, 420, **840–841**

C

C field in processes, 544
C shell, system prompt in, 365
cables and cable anchors for scrollbars, 19, *20*, 22, *23*, 25
cal command, **368**, **704–705**
.calctoolrc file, 290
calculations, bc program for, **368–369**, **703–704**
Calculator, 285
  customizing, **299–301**
  display type in, 288
  for financial functions, **292–295**
  for logical functions, **295–297**
  memory registers with, **289–290**
  miscellaneous functions with, 288–289
  modes of operation with, 286
  for number bases, **287–288**
  number manipulation operators with, **291**
  as scientific calculator, **297–298**
  user-defined functions with, **290–291**
Calculator Properties window, 299–301, *299*
Calculator window, 285, *285*
calendar command, **706**
Calendar Manager, 202
  browsing user calendars in, **220–233**
  customizing, **233–243**
  entering appointments in, **209–217**
  finding appointments in, **217–218**
  Multi-Browser window in, **220**, **222–231**

  navigating, **208–209**
  printing in, **218–220**
  starting, 202, *203*
  views in, **205–207**, *205–208*
Calendar Manager window, **202–204**, *203*
calendars
  browsing, **220–233**, *232*
  displaying, **368**, **704–705**
Calendars Insert Access scrolling list, 228–229
cancel command, 527, **706–707**
Cancel option for messages, 112
"Cannot open file" message, 392
Capitalize item for Text Editor, 186
carbon copies for messages, 114–115, 117, 125, 454, **457–458**
carets (^)
  for Control key, 579
  in grep searches, 417–418, 761
case changing with vi editor, 487
case-sensitivity
  of commands, 366
  of file names, 390
  in file searches, 69
  of passwords, 364, 793
  in sorts, 425, 815
cat command, **391–393**, **707–709**
Category menu, 142, *142*, 312, *314*
Cc settings on messages, 114–115, 117, 125, 444, 454
cd command, 382–384, **709–710**
cd command (ftp), 639, 757
cd command (mailx), 445
CD ROM file system, 653, 656, **785–786**
CDPATH variable, 562
/cdrom directory, 656
cdup command (ftp), 757
.ce request, 507–508
Center setting for snapshots, 272
centered tabs, 507
centering lines, 507–508
Change buttons
  for aliases, 158
  for appointments, 212
  for mail files, 156
Change Line Wrap item, 177
changing. *See* editing
character classes, 411

characters
    counting, 420, **840–841**
    formatting, **500–503**
    in message headers, 144
    in vi editor, 474, 477–478, 483
    wildcard, **410–412**
chdir command (mailx), 445
check boxes, 30
checksums, 821
chgrp command, **710–711**
child directories, 53
chmod command, **399–402**, **712–715**
chown command, **715–716**
Circle mode for icons, 327
classes
    character, 411
    of files, 352–353, 355
clear command, 372, **716**
clearing
    appointments, 212
    history logs, 192
    icons, 332
    messages, 114, 117, 125
    screen, 372, **716**
    sound files, 258
    text pane, 176
Click Select option, 44
clicking with mouse, 11
Client Type control for workstations, 684
Clip Lines item, 177
clipboard, 26–27
    for copying and moving files and
        folders, 77
    for custom commands, 96
    for deleting files and folders, 75
    for icons, 332–333
    with Shell Tool, 188–189
    for sounds, 258–260
    with Text Editor, **171–175**
Clock application, **273–279**
Clock Face control, 274
Clock Properties window, **274–279**, *275*
Clock window, 273, *274*
close command (ftp), 639, 757
close command (telnet), 637, 825
closing windows, **32–33**, 45
    Compose Message, 117
    File Manager, 54
    Help Viewer, 42

Clr function, 288
CM Appointment Editor window, 207,
    209–218, *210–211*
CM Find window, 217–218, *218*
CM Multi-Browser editor window, 222,
    227–230, *229*, 236–237
CM Multi-Browser window, **220**, **222–224**,
    223
    adding user calendars with, **224–225**
    appointment scheduling with, **225–229**
    deleting user calendars with, 225
    mail with, **230–231**
CM Properties window, 233–235, *235*
cmp command, **716–717**
collisions, monitoring, 281
color
    for Calendar Manager, 203
    for file views, 88
    for icons, 88, **324–326**, **339–340**, 345,
        347, 354–355, 357
    settings for, **314–316**
    for snapshots, 273
    for windows, **587–592**
Color category, 314
Color Chooser window and palette, 325,
    339–340, 347, 355
color masks, 345, *346*, 354
Color X Pixmap icon format, 333, 336, 339
columns, formatting, **518–519**
combining commands, **427–428**, **432–433**
comm command, **717–718**
!command command (mailx), 445
command interpreters. *See* Shell Tool
command line, 362
    buffer for, 366
    combining commands on, **427–428**
    controlling execution on, **428–429**
    editing commands on, **410**
    editing modes for, 570–571
    filters with. *See* filters
    grouping commands on, 428
    history of commands on, **409**
    multiple commands on, **408–409**
    pattern matching from, **410–412**
    redirecting I/O from, **429–434**
    substituting commands on, **426–427**
Command menu, 145–146, *145*
command mode in vi editor, **470–471**
"Command not found" message, 367

command prompts, variables for, **563–564**
Command setting for Mail Tool, 143
Command Tool
    history log file in, **190–192**
    from Shell Tool, 188, 190
    Shell Tool from, 194
    with Text Editor, 193, *193*
Command Tool window, 190, *191*
commands
    adding, to menus, **92–96**
    aliases for, **572–573, 697–698, 833**
    background. *See* background commands
    batch, **547–548, 702**
    with Clock alarms, 279
    combining, **427–428, 432–433**
    editing, 96, **410**
    entering, **366–367**
    execution of, 366, **428–429**
    grouping, 428
    help for, **374–375**
    history of, **190–192, 371–372, 409, 765**
    job control, **536–541**
    manuals for, 375, **779–780, 853–854**
    multiple, **408–409**
    path for, **842**
    priority of, **550, 788–789**
    remote execution of, **618, 808–809**
    substituting, **426–427, 566**
    suspending, 537, 550, **814**
    timing, **826–827**
    variables for, **565**
comments
    for printers, 690, 693
    in .profile file, 558
    for users, 678
comparing
    directories, **735–736**
    files, **420–421, 716–718, 734–735**
compatibility of input, 43
Compose Message window, 112–114, *113*,
    230, *230*
Compose Window Properties window,
    149–154, *149*
composing messages, **112–121, 149–154**
compress command, **718–719**
compressed files, displaying, **796, 864**
compressing files, **718–719, 792**
Con key for Calculator, 290
Confirm before clear control for sound, 261

confirmations
    for message editing, 151
    for quitting windows, 33
Console item, 194
Console window, 9, 46, 194
content settings
    for file classes, 352
    for file views, 87-88
context switches, monitoring, 281
control area, 19, **55**, *55*
    in Calendar Manager window, 204
    in Icon Editor window, 324
    in Mail Tool Header window, 101
    in Text Editor window, 164, 166
control characters in file names, 391
Control key
    with copying files, 76
    with mouse, 12
Control-c keys, 455–456, 539, 648
Control-d keys, 48, 454, 568, 702
Control-l keys, 481
Control-q keys, 443
Control-s keys, 443
Control-z keys, 537, 539
controller number for hard drives, 653
controls
    in icons, **326–328**, *326*
    in windows, **29–30**, *29*, **44–45**
converting
    measurement units, **837**
    number bases, **703**
    spaces to tabs, **835**
    tabs to spaces, **744**
copies, printing, 81, 242, 248, 339, 524,
    772–773
$COPIES variable, 250
copy command (mailx), 445
Copy items
    for links, 84
    for mail files, 137, 154–155
copying
    attachments, **128**
    to clipboard, 26
    directories, **387–388**
    file types, 351
    files, **76–80, 393, 719–720**
    folders, **76–78**
    icons, 332–333
    mail messages, 136–138

sounds, 259–260
text, 173, *174*, 188–189, 198, **489**
user settings, 681
counting words, **420**, **840–841**
cp command
for directories, 387–388
for files, **393**, **719–720**
cpio command, 667, **669–671**, **720–724**
cpu, monitoring, 280–281
cpu Performance Meter window, 280, *280*
cr command (ftp), 757
crashes with vi editor, 473–474
Create button for mail files, 135
Create Command window, 86, 93, *94*
Create File item, 72
Create Folder item, 72
Create Home Dir control, 680
cron command, 548, 724
crontab command, **724–726**
crontab file, 548–549
Ctrm function, 292
cu command, 623–624, **632–635**, **726–729**
curly braces ({})
in Text Editor, 186
with variables, 565
with vi editor, 478
current directory, 66
cursor movement in vi editor, **475–480**
cursors, 592, *593*
Custom button for Workspace Properties, 315
Custom Buttons setting for Mail Tool, 143, 145–146
Custom Color palette, 315–316, *316*
Custom Commands menu, 93, *93*
Custom Fields scrolling list, 152–154
Custom Filter check box, 250
Custom Magnification window, 41
Custom Print item, 80
Custom Print Properties window, 80–81, *81*
customer service, 649
Customize View window, 86–92, *88*
customizing
Audio Tool, **261–263**
buttons, 145–146, *146*
Calculator, **299–301**
Calendar Manager, **233–243**
Clock, **274–279**

file displays, 62, 85, 87
File Manager, **86–96**
fonts, **594–604**
header fields, **151–154**
Korn shell, **567–571**
Mail Tool, **141–160**
menus, **604–610**
mouse pointer, **592–594**
Tape Tool, 305–308, *306*
terminal settings, **578–580**
wastebasket, 92
Workspace, **584–592**, **860–861**
cut command, **729–730**
Cut items
and clipboard, 26
for file types, 351
for files, 75, 77
for icons, 332
for sound files, 258, 260
for Text Editor text, 174–175
cutting vi editor text, **487–489**
CW number register, 514

D

Daily setting for appointment alarms, 215
Database Manager, **673–675**, *674–675*
database servers, 686
Databases scrolling list, 673
date command, 367, **730–731**
Date Format window, 242–243, *243*
dates. *See also* Calendar Manager
for appointments, 211, 213, 227–228, 230, 242–243
with at command, 698
for clock, 276
displaying, 367, **730–731**
of file modification
changing, 391–392, **829**
displaying, 396
in searches, 69
sorting by, 63, 89
formats for, 233, 242–243, *243*, 324
listing files by, 385
on mailx mail, 442
sorting messages by, 123

Day Boundaries setting for calendars, 226
Day view in Calendar Manager, 205, *205*, 209, 219
Ddb function, 293
DEAD variable, 574
dead.letter file, 456, 458
decimal keypad, 287–288, *287*
decimal numbers, converting, 703
defaults
    for alarms, 236
    for appointment views, 237
    for document editors, 92
    for icon locations, **317**
    for Mail Tool directories, **133–134**
    for menu items, **14**, *15*, **16**
    for message change confirmations, 151
    for permissions, **571–572**
    for print scripts, 91
Degrees item for Calculator, 297
delays with Snapshot, 266–267
delete command (ftp), 640, 757
delete command (mailx), 445
Delete key, 367, 579
Delete permission for appointments, 240
Delete User window, 681–682, *682*
deleting
    access lists items, 240
    aliases, 159
    appointments, 212, **215–216**, *216*
    attachments, **129**
    Binder entries, 356
    custom header fields, 154
    delimiters, 181
    directories, **388–389**, **807–808**
    file types, 351
    files, 37, **73–75**, **394–395**, **806–807**
    folders, **73–75**
    hosts, 687, **847**
    links, 86, **403**, 769
    mail files, 101, 140, 155–156
    messages, **125–126**, 444
    printer jobs, 527
    queued jobs, **701**
    requests, 732
    sounds, 259–260
    tape files, 303
    template names, 157
    text, **174–175**, 178, **482–484**
    user calendars, 225

users, **681–682**, *682*
wastebasket option for, 92
delimiters
    for fields, 181, 185, 729
    in grep searches, 762
    searching for, **180–181**, *182*
Deliver button for messages, 114, 117
Delivery setting for messages, 144
density
    of floppy disks, 663, 665, 745
    of tape drives, 666–667, 821
depreciation functions, 293–295
deroff command, **732**
DeskSet and DeskSet applications, **4–6**
    Audio Tool, **251**, **253–264**
    Calculator, **285–301**
    Clock, **273–279**
    exiting, 47, *48*
    Performance Meter, **280–284**
    Print Tool, **246–252**
    Snapshot, **265–273**
    starting, **8–10**, 17, *18*
    Tape Tool, **301–308**
Desktop Intro menu, 17, 39
destinations
    for copying fields, 79
    for printing jobs, 242, 271, 338, 522, 772
    for Tape Tool, 304
/dev directory, 381, 820–821
device files, 397, **831**
device names for drives, **653–654**
Device text field for Tape Tool, 305
df command, 661, **732–733**
dials for Performance Meter, 283, *283*
dialtimeout variable, 627
dictionaries, 419, 771–772, **816**
diff command, **420–421**, **734–735**
diff3 command, 420
digital clocks, 274, *276*
dimmed menu items, 13
dir command (ftp), 758
dircmp command, **735–736**
Direction setting for Performance Meter, 283
directories, 52–53, 380
    comparing, **735–736**
    copying, **387–388**
    creating, 387, **781–782**

deleting, **388–389**, **807–808**
in File Manager, **57–59**
for icon files, 335
icons for, *58*
linked files in, 84
listing contents of, **385–387**, **396–397**, 712, **776–777**
for mail files, **133–134**, 137, 154
marking, **569**
navigating, **382–384**, **709–710**
for Text Editor, 167, 177
types of, **381–382**
"Directory not empty" message, 389
Disable item with Command Tool, 193
Disable Page Mode item, 188
Disable Scrolling item, 194
Discard Changes option for messages, 111
disconnect command (ftp), 758
disconnect variable, 627
disks. *See* floppy disks; hard disks
Dismiss items
for quitting windows, 28
for unpinning menus, 14
for Vacation mail, 130
Display canvas in Audio Tool, 256
Display Language setting, 323
Display pop-up menu, 259, *259*
Display settings
for Calculator, 299
for calendars, 233, 237, *238*
for Clock, 276
for files, 87
for Mail Tool, 144
for Message Window, 148
for Performance Meter, 283, *283*
Display Up To setting for mail files, 154
Displays Menu setting, 319
distribution lists for messages, 115, **157–159**, 578
dollar signs ($)
in file displays, 393
in grep searches, 417–418, 761
for system prompt, 8, 365
for variables, 560, 565–566
with vi editor, 485
Domain Name System (DNS), 636
domainname command, **736**
Done option for messages, 112
dot variable, 574

dots (.)
for directories, 384, 709
in grep searches, 417–418, 761
for hidden files, 390
with vi editor, 471
double-clicking, 11, 322
double-density floppy disks, 663, 665, 745
double quotation marks (")
in grep searches, 417
in messages, 370
with vi editor, 488
Double Size control for snapshots, 273
dp command (mailx), 445
dpost command, 251, **736–738**
dpost filters, 500, 523
drag-and-drop, **37–38**
with attachments, 117, 122, 128
for copying files, 76
for copying text, 173
with icons, 59
for loading files, 139, 167
with Mail Tool, **122**
for merging text, 177
with mouse, 12
for moving files, 71, 76
for printing, 80, 248
with sound files, 254, 260
drag-and-drop targets, 21, **37–38**, 71, 165
drag boxes for scrollbars, 22, *23*
Drag-Right distance text field for menus, 319
dragging with mouse, 11, 318–319
drawing in Icon Editor, 324, **326–328**, *326*
.ds request, 517–518
dt command (mailx), 445
du command, **660–661**, **738–739**
Duplicate button for Binder, 357
duplicate lines in files, **836**
duplicating. *See* copying
duration of bell, 580, 856

E

echo command, **370–371**, **739–741**
echo command (mailx), 445
ECHO_REQUEST datagram, 798–799
echocheck variable, 628

edit command (mailx), 445
Edit menu
    for attachments, 114
    for Audio Tool, **258–259**
    for calendars, 204
    for commands, 96
    for File Manager, 55
    for icons, 332–333, *332*
    for mail, 101, 135
    for sounds, 253
    for text, 166, **171–175**, *172*
    for time zones, 233
Editable item for history logs, 192
editing
    appointments, **217**
    audio files, **258–260**
    Binder entries, **357–358**
    commands, 96, **410**
    custom header fields, 154
    files. *See* vi editor
    history log files, 192
    icons, **332–333**, *332*
    sound files, **260**
    text, **169**, **171–176**
    vacation message templates, 130
editing commands in vi editor, **480–490**
editing modes for command line, 570–571
Editor Defaults settings for calendars, 236
EDITOR variable, 574
editors, default, 92
eject command, 663, **741–742**
ejecting floppy disks, 663–664, **741–742**,
    745
electronic mail. *See* messages
Ellipse mode for icons, 327
ellipses (...) on menus, 14, 27
emacs argument (vi), 571
email. *See* messages
emergency rebooting, **648–649**
emergency system shutdowns, 651–652
Empty Document item for Text Editor, 176
empty files, creating, 391–392
Empty Wastebasket item, 74–75
emptying mail files, 140
emulators, terminal, 186, 194–195,
    862–863
Enable item with Command Tool, 193
Enable Page Mode item, 188

Enable Reverse Video item, 198
Enable Scrolling item, 188, 190, 194
end of file
    displaying, 414, **818–819**
    scrolling to, 22
End text field for appointments, 211, 213,
    227–228, 230, 237
Engineering display with Calculator, 288
Enter Function window, 290
Entire List item for Tape Tool, 304
env command, 557–558, **742–743**
environment variables. *See* variables
eofread variable, 628
eofwrite variable, 628
eol variable, 628
equal signs (=) for variables, 564
Eraser mode for icons, 328
Err Exit setting for Tape Tool, 308
error messages
    Console window for, 194
    redirecting, **431–432**
    suppressing, **535–536**
    for unset variables, 570
escape characters, 416, **457–459**
escape variable, 628
/etc directory, 381, 686
/etc/group file, 763
/etc/mnttab file, 655, 659–660, 784–785
/etc/motd file, 645
/etc/passwd file, 763
/etc/profile file, 556–557
/etc/remote file, 624
/etc/vfstab file, 654, **657–659**, 784
Ethernet Address control, 685
etimeout variable, 632
exceptions variable, 629
Exch key for Calculator, 289
exclamation points (!)
    in finding files, 416
    with metacharacters, 412
Exclude setting for Tape Tool, 308
exclusive setting for controls, 30
execute permission settings, 81–83, 385,
    397, **712–714**
executing commands
    controlling, 366, **428–429**
    remote, **618**, **808–809**
exit command (mailx), 447–448

exiting
  handbooks, 41
  Help Viewer window, 42
  OpenWindows and DeskSet, 17, 47, *48*
  running background commands after,
    541, **789**
  sessions, 743
  and stopped jobs, 538
  superuser status, 645
  vi editor, 472–474
Exp function, 288
expand command, **744**
Expand item for delimiters, 180, *184*, 185
Expert item for Mail Tool, 142
Expert Properties window, 159–160, *159*
Expiration Date control for new users, 679
Export Attachment window, 128
/export directory, 53, 381
expressions with commands, 366
Extras menu, 166, **185–186**, *185*

F

factorial functions, 291, 298
Fault Notification control for printers, 690
fc command, **409**
fdformat command, **663–665**, **744–746**
fg command, 535, 538, 540
fgrep command, **746–747**
.fi request, 505, 507
fields
  for sorting files, **422–425**, *423*
  in tables, extracting, **729–730**
  in Text Editor, finding and replacing,
    181, 185
$FILE argument, 95
File buttons for messages, 103, 114
file command, 390, **748**
File Contents control for printers, 690
file descriptors, 431
File Editor item for history logs, 192–193
File field for templates, 157
File Manager and File Manager window,
    10, **52–53**, *54*, *56*
  adding menu commands to, **92–96**
  control area in, **55**, *55*
  for copying files and folders, **76–80**

for creating files and folders, **72–73**
customizing, **86–96**
for deleting files and folders, **73–75**
file pane in, *55*, 57, **61–63**, **87–89**
icons in, **57–59**, **61–63**
for linking files, **84–86**
for opening files, **70–71**
for opening folders, **64–65**
path pane in, **54–55**, *55*, **63–64**
for permissions, **81–84**
for printing files, **80–81**
for searching for files and folders, **67–70**
selecting files in, **59–61**
starting, 53–54
Tool Properties window for, **90–92**
File menus, 72
  in Audio Tool, 253–254
  in File Manager, 55
  for icons, 335, *335*
  in Mail Tool, 101
  in Text Editor, 166
File Name text field for attachments, 118
file pane, *55*, **57**
  customizing views in, **87–89**
  icons displayed in, **62–63**
  splitting, 57
File Pane pop-up menu, 57, *58*, 64–65
File Properties window, 81, *82*, 83–84
file servers, 365, 614
file systems, **380–381**, **652–653**. *See also*
    directories; files
  on floppy disks, **664–665**
  mounting, 652, **654–659**, **784–786**
  unmounting, **659–660**, 784
File text fields
  for Print Tool, 248
  for Tape Tool, 303–304
  for Text Editor, 167, 177
File Transfer Protocol (ftp), 635–636,
    638–640, **756–761**
File Type item for finding files, 69
File Types Properties window, **348–353**,
    349–350
File Types scrolling list, 350
$FILE variable, 91, 250
Filename item in searches, 68
files, 52, 380
  backing up. *See* tape backups
  comparing, **420–421**, **716–718**, **734–735**

compressing, **718–719**, **792**
copying, **76–80**, **393**, **719–720**
creating, **72–73**, **391–392**
date and time of. *See* dates
deleting, 37, **73–75**, **394–395**, **806–807**
displaying contents of, **392–393**, **707–709**
drag-and-drop feature for, **37–38**, 71
duplicate lines in, **836**
editing. *See* vi editor
filters for, **413–414**, **782–784**
finding, **67–70**, **414–419**, **748–754**, **761–763**
formatting requests in, 499
group associations for, **710–711**
hiding, 89
icons for, *58–59*, **61–64**
input from, 431
inserting, **260–261**, **490–491**
joining, 708
linking, **57–59**, **84–86**, 89, **396–397**, **402–403**, **768–769**
listing, 57, **301–303**, **385–387**, 390, **776–777**, **796–801**
loading. *See* loading
merging, **177**, **794–795**
for messages. *See* mail files
moving, **76–80**, **394**, **787**
names of. *See* names
navigating to, **65–67**
opening, **70–71**
owners of. *See* owners
permissions for. *See* permissions
printing, **80–81**, **247–248**, **523–524**
printing to, 242
protecting, 430, 570
redirecting output to, **429–431**
renaming, 73, 140, **394**, **787**
saving. *See* saving
saving mail as, **449**
searching through, **491–493**, **746–747**, **816–817**
selecting, **59–61**
sending, with mailx, 456
sorting, 63, 89, 386, **421–425**, **776–777**, **815**
substituting names of, 569
tabs in, **744**, **835**
on tape. *See* tape backups

transferring
    with cu, 635
    with ftp, **638–640**
    with rcp, **617–618**, **804–805**
    with tip, **625–626**
    types of, 89, 390, **396–397**, 748
    uncompressing, **834–835**, **838**
Files to View option, 88
Fill choices in Icon Editor, **328–329**, *328*
filling lines, **504–505**
filters, 412, **434–435**
    for controlling commands, **426–429**
    diff, **420–421**, **734–735**
    for file displays, 91
    find, **414–417**, **748–754**
    more, **413–414**
    with Print Tool, **249–251**, *252*
    for redirection, **429–434**
    sort, **421–425**, **815**
    spell, **419**, **816**
    wc, **420**, **840–841**
financial calculator, 286, **292–295**
Financial Mode window, 292, *292*
Find and Replace window, 178, *178*
find command, **414–417**, **748–754**
Find items and buttons
    for appointments, 218
    for files, **67–68**
    for messages, **124–125**
    for Text Editor, 178
Find Marked Text window, 180-181, *180*
Find Messages window, **124–125**, *124*
Find pop-up menu, **67–70**, *68*
finding
    appointment entries, 214, **217–218**
    files, **67–70**, **414–419**, **748–754**, **761–763**
    mail messages, **124–125**
    Text Editor text, **178–185**
finger command, 370, 452, 616, **620–621**, **754–755**
first lines of files, displaying, 414, **764**
fish_props program, 587
Fixed point notation for Calculator, 288
fixed-width fonts, 603
flame screensaver, 583, 849
flashing
    for appointment alarms, 212
    for messages, Tool, 143

floppy disks, **662**
ejecting, 663–664, **741–742**, 745
formatting, **663–666**, **744–746**
FM number register, 514
fold command, **755–756**
folder command (mailx), 445
folder variable, 574
folders
copying, **76–78**
creating, **72–73**
deleting, **73–75**
for directories, 52
hiding, 64
listing, 57
moving, **76–78**
names of, 72–73
navigating to, **65–67**
opening, **64–65**
permissions for, **81–84**
renaming, 73
saving mail in, **449–451**
searching for, **67–70**
selecting, **59–61**
as windows, 65, *66*
followup command (mailx), 445
fonts, 498
for applications, **604**
fixed-width and proportional, 603
for icon text, 330, *331*
listing and viewing, **597–602**, **844–846**, **852–853**
scales for, **594–597**
size of, 199, 331, 502, **594–597**, 603
style of, 603
xset command for, **857**
in xterm windows, 199
Fontview demo program, 597, *600*
Fontview window, 597, *599*
footers
in formatting, **517–518**
in windows, *20*, 22
For text field for appointments, 212
Foregr Color control for Binder entries, 347, 355
Format items for Text Editor, 185
formats
for dates, 233, 242–243, *243*, 324
for icons, 333, 335–336

formatting
documents, **498–499**
characters, **500–503**
columns, **518–519**
headers and footers, **517–518**
lines, **504–508**
pages, **512–516**, *513*
paragraphs, **508–512**
removing, **732**
tables, **520–522**
viewing and printing, **499–500**, 523
floppy disks, **663–666**, **744–746**
Forward button for Text Editor, 180–181, *182–183*
forwarding messages, **129–130**, 778
Frac function, 291
framesize variable, 629
Free Software foundation, 636
from command (mailx), 445
From List option for undeleting messages, 126
From setting for finding messages, 125
fsck command, 658
ftp program, 635–636, 638–640, **756–761**
full headers for messages, 108, *110*
Full/Restore Size item for windows, 45
Full Size items
for calendars, 204, 210, 213
for windows, 36
Fun key for Calculator, 290–291
Function Key window, 44, *44*
Function Keys item, 44
Fv function, 293
Fwd button in Audio Tool, 254

G

get command (ftp), 638, 640, 758
global replacement of text, **492–493**
GM number register, 514
gmacs argument (vi), 571
Go Back button for help, 42
Goto menu, 67, *67*
for calendars, 223, 226
in File Manager, 55
Goto text field, **65–67**
Gradients item for Calculator, 297

graphs for Performance Meter, 283
greater-than signs (>)
    with diff, 421
    in folder and file listings, 57
    for included mail messages, 119, 150
    as logical operators, 296
    with mailx mail, 441–442
    for redirection, 391, 429–432
    with Text Editor files, 168
grep command, **417–419**, **761–763**
grids for icons, 333, *334*
group associations for files, **710–711**
group identification numbers (GID), 715
group user command (mailx), 445
grouping
    commands, 428
    windows, 34
groups
    appointments for, **227–229**
    distribution lists for, 115, **157–159**, 578
    in file listings, 89, 386, 396
    finding files in, 415
    ownership by, 398
    permissions for, 83–84
    users in, changing, **788**
groups command, **763**
groups of files, copying and moving, 77
GW number register, 514

H

halfduplex variable, 629
handbooks for online help, **39**, *40*, **41–42**
hard disks
    information on, **660–662**, **732–733**,
        738–739
    managing, **652–662**
    monitoring traffic on, 281
    names and numbers for, **653–654**
head command, 414, 425, **764**
header command (mailx), 445
Header menu, 151–153, *153*
header variable, 575
Header Window item, 142
Header Window Properties window,
    143–146

headers
    for formatting, **517–518**
    for messages, **103–104**. *See also* Mail
      Tool Header window
    custom fields in, **151–154**
    for deleting messages, 126
    full, 108, *110*
    hiding, 148–149
    number of, 144
    sorting, **123–124**
    text fields for, 114
    for windows, 19, *20*
headphones, 253
Height settings in printing, 242, 273, 339
help
    for commands, **374–375**
    handbooks for, **39**, *40*, **41–42**
    with Magnify, 38, *39*, **41–42**
    in mailx program, **445–447**
help command (ftp), 640, 758
help command (mailx), 446
Help key, 38
Help menu, 17
Help Viewer window, 10, 13, 32, *32*, **39**, **41**
Here to Top item for scrollbar, 25
hexadecimal keypad, 287–288, *287*
hexadecimal numbers, converting, 703
hidden files, listing, 89, 385
hiding
    files, 89
    folders, 64
    message headers, 148–149
    Snapshot window, 266
hierarchical file structure, 52, 380
high-density floppy disks, 663, 745
HISTFILE variable, 558
history command, **371–372**, **765**
History menu, 191–192
history of commands, **190–192**, **371–372**,
    409, **765**
HISTORY variable, 559
hold command (mailx), 446, **448–449**
hold variable, 575
/home directory, 53, 381–382
    with Goto text field, 67
    for mail files, 133, 154
    moving to, **384**, 709
HOME variable, 556, 558
hop screensaver, 582, 848

Host Manager, **682–687**
Host Manager window, **683–687**, *684*
host variable, 629
hosts, 615
    adding and deleting, 687, **847–848**
    managing, **682–687**
    for Tape Tool, 305
Hour Display setting for appointments, 237
Hourly command control for clock alarms, 279
hsfs (High Sierra file system), 653, 656, 785
Hue control, 315
Hyp function, 297
hypertext links, 42

I

.I macro, 501
ibase location, 703
ic parameter (vi), 494
ICMP protocol, 798–799
Icon by Type item for file display, 63
Icon control for Binder entries, 343
Icon Editor, **324**, *325*
    for color of icons, **325–326**, **339–340**
    drawing controls in, **326–328**, *326*
    editing icons with, **332–333**, *332*
    Fill choices in, **328–329**, *328*
    loading icon files with, **336**, *337*
    Move buttons in, **329–330**, *329*
    printing icons with, **336**, **338–339**, *338*
    Properties menu for, **333**, **335**
    saving icon files with, **335–336**
    text with, 330–332, *330*
Icon Editor window, 324–325, *325*
Icon Layout item for file views, 89
Icon Properties window, **343–348**, *344*
Icon setting for file views, 87
icons
    arranging, 33
    for Audio Tool, *253*
    for Binder, *341*
    binding, **340–358**
    for broken links, *86*
    for Calculator, *285*
    for Calendar Manager, 202, *203*

    for Clock, *274*, 276
    for CM Multi-Browser, *223*
    color for, 88, **324–326**, **339–340**, 345, 347, 354–355, 357
    default locations for, **317**
    displaying, **61–64**
    drag-and-drop with, **37–38**, 59
    editing, **332–333**, *332*
    for files, **57–59**, *58–59*, **61–64**
    formats for, 333, 335–336
    grids for, 333, *334*
    for Icon Editor, *325*
    loading, **336**, *337*
    for Mail Tool, 100, *100*
    masks for, 345, *346*, 354
    for Print Tool, *247*
    printing, **336**, **338–339**, *338*
    saving, **335–336**
    size of, 57, 62, 87, 333, 335
    for Snapshot, *265*
    for sound files, 256, *257*
    for Tape Tool, *301*
    text for, 330–332, *330*
    wrapping, 89
Icons category, 317, *317*
id command, **765–766**
Identify control for file types, 352
IFS variable, 559
Ignore host name in address (allnet) setting for messages, 160
ignoreeof variable, 575
Image File control for Binder entries, 344
image screensaver, 583, 849
.in request, 506
In-Box file, 102–103, 133, 135
inc command (mailx), 446
Inches from settings in printing, 272, 339
Include me when I "Reply To All" (metoo) setting for messages, 160
Include Templates menu, 157
Include window, 177, *177*
including
    messages within messages, **118–121**, *119–120*, 149–150
    sound files, 260
    Text Editor files, 177
indent characters, 119, 149

indenting
    included messages, 119–120, *120*
    lines, 506
    paragraphs, **508–511**
init 0 command, 651
init 6 command, 651
input
    compatibility of, 43
    redirection of, 431, **829–830**
Input Language setting, 323
Insert Access permission, 229
insert mode in vi editor, **471–472**
Insert permission for appointments,
    239–240
insert point, 21
inserting
    appointments, 212, 215
    blank lines, **505–506**
    brackets, 186
    delimiters, 181
    sound files, **260–261**
    special characters, **503**
    text, 173, 175, 188–189, **481–482,**
        490–491
insertion point
    in Shell Tool, 186–187
    in Text Editor, **169–171**
Int function, 291
Internet, **635–640**
interrupts, monitoring, 281
Inv function, 297
inverse video, 587
Invert item for icons, 332–333
investment functions, **292–295**
IP Address control for workstations, 685
.IP macro, 510–511
italicizing text, 501
items, menu, 13

J

job control commands, **536–541**
jobs command, 536–539, 542
Join Views items
    for file panes, 57
    for scrollbar, 25
    for Text Editor panes, 176

joining
    files, 708
    lines, 487
jumping, pointer, 12, *12*, 321–322
justifying lines, **504–505**

K

.KE macro, 516
keep variable, 575
keepsave variable, 575
/kernel directory, 382
keyboard
    correcting mistakes on, 367
    preferences for, **579–580, 856–858**
    selecting files with, **60–61**
    for Text Editor insertion point, **170–171**
keyboard accelerator keys, 33, 59, 78
Keys function, 289
kill command, 539–540, 544–545, **766–767**
Korn shell
    Bourne shell commands with, 366
    customizing, **567–571**
    system prompt in, 365
.KS macro, 516
ksh command, 365

L

labels
    for floppy disks, 665
    for menus, 94, 145–146
landscape mode
    in printer filters, 251, 737
    for snapshots, 271
language localization, **322–324,** *323*
Larger item for Magnify help, 41
last command, **768**
last lines of files, displaying, 414, **818–819**
last logins, displaying, **768**
lcd command (ftp), 640, 758
LD_LIBRARY_PATH variable, 559
Leave message intact item, 117
left-block paragraphs, **509**
left-handed setting for Calculator, 300

Lempel-Ziv compression algorithm, 718
length of pages, 515–516
less-than signs (<)
    with diff, 421
    as logical operators, 296
    for redirection, 431–432
Level meter in Audio Tool, 254
.LG macro, 502
life screensaver, 582, 848
Line mode for icons, 327
Line Number window, 170, *171*
line numbering in vi editor, **479–480**
line setting for Performance Meter graphs,
    283
line wrap mode, 177
lines
    blank, **505–506**
    breaking, **755–756**
    centering, 507–508
    copying, 719
    counting, 420, **840–841**
    duplicate, **836**
    filling, **504–505**
    formatting, **504–508**
    indenting, 506
    scrolling by, 24
    selecting, 169
    spacing of, 505
    tabs in, **506–507**
    in vi editor, 474, 478, 483–484, 486,
    719
links for files, **84–86, 402**
    creating, 403, **768–769**
    deleting, 86, **403,** 769
    displaying, 89, 396–397
List by items for file display, 63
list command (mailx), 446
List item for linked files, 85, *85*
List menu for Tape Tool, 302
list parameter (vi), 494
List settings for file views, 87, 89
listing
    files, 57, **301–303, 385–387,** 390,
    776–777, 796–801
    folders, 57
    fonts, **597–602, 844–846, 852–853**
    jobs, **700**
    messages, **103–112,** 373–374, 441–443,
    778

mounted file systems, 654
    permissions, 89, 385, **395–398**
    users, **369–370, 452–453, 619–621,**
    754–755, 810–811, 842–843
    variables, **557–558, 742–743, 812–814**
LL number register, 514
ln command, **402–403, 768–770**
load averages on networks, **622–623, 809**
Load Database window, 673–674, *674*
Load File window, 254, *255*
Load Options window, 265, 270
Load window, 167, *167*
loading
    databases, 673–674, *674*
    icon files, **336,** *337*
    messages, 103, **138–140,** 154–155
    Snapshot files, 260, 265
    sound files, 254, *255*
    Text Editor files, **166–167**
local-area networks (LANs), 615
local network, status of, **809–810**
Local Printer window, 688, *689*
local setting for Performance Meter, 283
local systems, 615
localecho variable, 629
Localization category, **322–324,** *323*
Locate Choice item for mail files, 136
Location setting for icons, 317
Lock Screen item, 46, *47*, 581
Log check box for Mail Tool, 150–151, *150*
log files
    for commands, **190–192, 371–372, 409,**
    765
    for messages, 150–151
    for Performance Meter, 284
    for xterm commands, 198
logarithm functions, 298
logging in
    messages at, 7, 364, 645
    names for, 677
    prompt for, 7
    remote, **615–616, 805–806**
    to Solaris, **6–7**
    to SunOS, **362–366**
    to xterm sessions, **198**
logging out, **743**
    of Solaris, 48
    with stopped jobs, 538
logical functions, 286, **295–297**

logical operators, 428–429, 749
login command, **770**
login sessions, scripts of, **812**
Login Shell control, 678
logname command, **770–771**
LOGNAME variable, 559, **770–771**
logout messages, 568
Longest Filename item for file displays, 91
look command, 419, **771–772**
lp command, 433, 500, 522, **772–774**
.LP macro, 509
lpstat command, **526–527**, **774–776**
ls command, **385–387**, 390, **395–398**, **776–777**
ls command (ftp), 758
.ls request, 505

M

Machine setting for Performance Meter, 283
machine status in networking, **622–623**, **798–799**
macros for formatting files, 499–500
Magnify help, 38, *39*, **41–42**
Magnify menu, 41
mail. *See* messages
mail command, 373–374, **777–779**
Mail command (mailx), 446
mail files, 102. *See also* messages
    creating, 136–137
    deleting, 101, 104, 155–156
    icons for, *58*
    loading, **138–140**
    managing, **140**
    saving messages in, **136–138**
Mail Files window, **134–140**, *135*
Mail Filing Properties window, 133–134, *134*, 154–156, *155*
Mail Tool. *See also* Mail Tool Header window
    Alias Properties window for, 157–159, *158*
    attachments with. *See* attachments to messages
    Compose Window Properties window for, **149–154**, *149*

composing messages in, **112–121**
customizing, **141–160**
directories for, **133–134**
drag-and-drop with, **122**
Expert Properties window for, 159–160, *159*
for forwarding messages, **129–130**
Header Windows Properties window for, **143–146**
including messages in, **118–121**, 149–150
Mail Files window in, **134–140**
Mail Filing Properties window for, 154–156, *155*
Mail Tools Properties window for, 141–143, *141*
Message Window Properties window for, **147–149**, *147*
receiving messages in, 102–103
replying to messages in, **121**
sending messages in, **115–117**
starting, 100, *101*
Template Properties window for, 156–157, *156*
templates with, **131–132**, *132*
for vacation mail, 130, *131*
viewing messages in, **103–112**
Mail Tool Header window, **100–102**, *101*, 122
    deleting messages in, **125–126**
    finding messages in, **124–125**
    loading mail files into, **138–140**
    printing messages in, 127
    property settings for, **143–146**
    saving changes to, **111–112**
    sorting headers in, **123–124**
    undeleting messages in, **126–127**
Mail Tool Properties window, 141–143, *141*
mail user command (mailx), 446
MAIL variable, 559
MAILCHECK variable, 559, 577
MAILPATH variable, 577–578
.mailrc file, 457, **573–578**
mailx program, **440**
    electronic messages with, **459–463**
    help in, **445–447**
    quitting, **447–448**
    receiving messages in, **441–444**
    saving messages in, **448–451**

sending messages in, **451–459**, **843–844**
variables for, **573–578**
Main Options menu in xterm window,
196, *196*
make command, 829
man command, 375, **779–780**
man pages, **374–375**
MANPATH variable, 559
MANSECTS variable, 559
Manual Browser window, 853–854
manual mounting, **655–656**
manuals for commands, 375, **779–780**,
853–854
margins
justifying, **504–505**
setting, **515–516**
markdirs option, **569**
marking directories, **569**
masks
file creation mode, **831–833**
for icons, 345, *346*, 354
master files with linking, 84
Match Appt text field, 218
matching patterns, **410–412**
with grep, **417–419**, **761–763**
in vi files, 491–493
Max Change control for users, 679
Max Inactive control for users, 679
mbox command (mailx), 446
mbox file, 440, 443, **447–451**
MBOX variable, 573, 575
mdelete command (ftp), 758
mdir command (ftp), 758
measurement units, converting, **837**
Mem key for Calculator, 289–290
memory
for bitmap images, 585
for number registers, **512**, **514**
memory registers in Calculator, **289–290**
menu buttons, *20*, 21–22
menus, 13
adding commands to, **92–96**
customizing, **604–610**
default items on, 14, *15*, 16
mouse button for, 10–11, *10*
pinning, 14, *15*
Workspace, **16–17**
Workspace Properties window for,
318–319, *318*

Menus category, 318, *318*
merging files **177**, 794–795
mesg command, **780–781**
message of the day, 462, 645
Message Window Properties window,
147–149, *147*
messages, 372, 777, **819–820**
addresses for, **114–116**, 158, **455–456**
for alarms, 212, 215
for appointment notification, 223,
230–231
attachments to. *See* attachments to
messages
broadcasting, 462, 840
composing, **112–121**, **149–154**
Console window for, 194
copying, 136–138
deleting, **125–126**, 444
directories for, **133–134**
distribution lists for, 115, **157–159**, 578
drag-and-drop with, **122**
echo command for, **370–371**, **739–741**
forwarding, **129–130**, 778
headers for. *See* headers; Mail Tool
Header window
including messages within, **118–121**,
149–150
loading, 103, **138–140**, 154–155
login, 7, 364, 645
logout, 568
Mail Files window for, **134–140**
printing, 127, 148
receiving, 102–103
replying to, **121**, **443–444**
saving, **136–138**, 374, **448–451**
searching for, **124–125**
sending, **115–117**, **230–231**, 374,
453–459, 646, 778, 840, **843–844**
sorting, **123–124**
status of, 103–104, 124, 780–781
system, 7, 9, 194, 364, **462–463**
with talk, **459–461**, **819–820**
templates for, **131–132**, *132*, 142,
156–157, *156*
undeleting, **126–127**, 444
vacation, 130, *131*, **838–839**
viewing, **103–112**, **373–374**, **441–443**,
778
writing, **461–462**, **843–844**

Messages pop-up menu, 101, *102*
metacharacters, **410–412**
metoo variable, 576
mget command (ftp), 639–640, 758
Min Change control for users, 679
Miscellaneous category, **319–321**, *320*
miscellaneous settings for Workspace, **319–321**, *320*
mkdir command, 387, **781–782**
mkdir command (ftp), 640, 759
Mode item for history logs, 192
Mode Time setting for Tape Tool, 307
modem communications, **623**
    with cu, **632–635**, **726–729**
    with tip, **624–632**, **827–829**
modified files, finding, 69, 415–416, 750–751
Monitor setting for Performance Meter, 282
Monitor Volume setting for sound, 263
monitoring, Performance Meter for, **280–284**
Mono X Pixmap icon format, 333, 336
Monochrome Printer control for snapshots, 273
Monochrome settings for file views, 88
Month view in Calendar Manager, 206, 209, 219
Monthly setting for appointment alarms, 215
Months text field for finding appointments, 218
More button for help, 38
more command, **413–414**, **782–784**
More Handbooks icon, 41
mount command, 654–657, **784–786**
mount points, 655, 658, 784
mountall command, 658
mounting file systems, 652, **654–659**, **784–786**
mouse, **10–12**, *10*
    selecting files with, **60**
    settings for, **321–322**, *321*, **858**
mouse pointer, 10, 12, *12*, 321–322, **592–594**
Mouse Settings category, **321–322**, *321*
Move buttons in Icon Editor, 324, **329–330**, *329*

Move menu in Mail Tool, 101, 154–155
moving
    files, **76–80**, **394**, **787**
    folders, **76–80**
    to home directory, **384**, 709
    mail messages, 136–138
    text, **175**, 198, **487–490**
    in vi editor, **475–480**
    windows, 28, **33–36**
mp filters, 251, *252*
mput command (ftp), 639–640, 759
MS-DOS format, 653, 657, **665–666**, 785–786
~ms macro package, 499–500
Multi-Browser calendar list, 224
    adding user calendars to, **224–225**
    deleting user calendars from, 225
Multi-Click Timeout (sec/10) setting for mouse, 322
multiple commands, **408–409**
multiple files, selecting, 60
multiple-page files, printing, 523–524
multiple windows, moving, 34
multitasking, 534
mv command, **394**, **787**
My Eyes Only settings
    for appointments, 212
    for printing, 242

N

.na request, 504
Name option for file views, 89
named buffers, **488–489**
names
    of attachments, **128–129**
    of Binder entries, 354
    of commands, **572–573**, **697–698**
    of drives, **653–654**
    of file classes, 352, 355
    of files, 72–73, **390–391**, 396
    history log, 192
    mail, 136–137, 140
    renaming, **394**, **787**
    sorting by, 89
    sound, 256

substituting, 569
Text Editor, 168
vi, 469–470
of folders, 72–73
of functions, 290
of jobs, 537
login, 677
of NIS domain, 736
of printers, 690, 692
of snapshots, 268
sorting, 422
of templates, 157
of users, 369–370, **452–453, 619–621,
754–755, 810–811, 842–843**
window headers for, 19, *20*
of workstations, 685
naming services, 673, 676
navigating
Calendar Manager, **208–209**
directories, **382–384, 709–710**
to files and folders, **65–67**
handbooks, 42
.ND macro, 517
.ne request, 516
nested delimiters, 180–181, *183*
network naming services, 673, 676
Networked File System (NFS), 614, 652
networks and networking, **614–615**
with Internet, **635–640**
logging in with, **615–616, 805–806**
machine status in, **622–623, 798–799**
modem communications in, **623–635**
printers on, 247
remote commands in, **618, 808–809**
transferring files in, **617–618, 804–805**
user information in, **452–453, 619–621,
810–811**
New buttons
for Binder entries, 354
for file types, 351
new command (mailx), 447
New Command button, 93
newfs command, 664
newgrp command, **788**
news command, 462–463
next command (mailx), 446
next keyword with at command, 546
Next menus and items
for calendars, 204

for delimiters, 185
for messages, 101, 104
Next Month item for calendars, 226
Next Page button for help, 42
Next Week item for calendars, 226
.nf request, 505, 507
nice command, 550, **788–789**
NIS (Network Information Service), 682,
736
NIS+ (Network Information Service+),
673, 691
NIS maps, updating, **685–686**
.NL macro, 502
No Check setting for Tape Tool, 307
No SCCS settings for Tape Tool, 305
−nobanner option, 525
noclobber variable, 430, 556, 570
node names, 834
noglob option, 569
nohold variable, 573
nohup command, 541, **789**
nohup.out file, 541
nonexclusive setting for controls, 30
Not logical function, 296
nounset variable, 570
now keyword with at command, 546, 698
nroff command, 468, 498, 732. *See also* formatting
nroff files, printing, 523
nu parameter (vi), 493–494
nu variable, 479
null file, 432, 536
number bases, **287–288, 703**
number manipulation operators, **291**
number registers for formatting, **512, 514**
number signs (#)
in .profile file, 558
for superuser prompt, 644
numeric fields, 30
Numeric Format setting for languages, 324
numerical order in sorts, 425, 815

O

obase location, 703
octal keypad, 287–288, *287*
octal numbers, converting, 703

.1C macro, 518
online help, **39–42**, *39*
open command (ftp), 640, 759
open command (telnet), 637, 825
Open Look Graphical User Interface, 4
opening
    attachments, 106
    files, **70–71**
    folders, **64–65**
    windows, **32–33**, 45
openwin command, 9, **790–792**
.openwin-menu file, 604–606
OpenWindows, **4–6**
    exiting, 17, 47, *48*
    fonts in, **594–604**
    menus in, **604–610**
    mouse pointer in, **592–594**
    screensavers for, **581–584**
    script for, **790–792**
    starting, **8–10**
    Workspace in, **584–592**
OpenWindows localization CD, 322–323
OPENWINHOME variable, 559, 605, 790
operating system, information on, **833–834**
Options control for printing icons, 338
options for commands, 366
Or logical function, 296
OR operators, 428–429, 749, 751
order in dates, 242
Orientation control for snapshots, 271
Orig Mode setting for Tape Tool, 307
Other settings
    for default document editor, 92
    for Tape Tool, 308
Others ownership, 398
outfolder variable, 576
outline paragraphs, **511–512**
output, redirection of, **429–434**, **824–825**
Output Window setting for commands, 95
owners
    changing, **715**
    displaying, 89, 386, 396, 776
    in file searches, 69
    permissions for, 83
    types of, **398–399**
    of windows, 28

P

pack command, **792**
packed files, displaying, **796**
packets, monitoring, 281
page breaks, 516
page numbers in headers and footers, 517
page variable, 576
pages
    formatting, **512–516**, *513*
    monitoring, 281
Palette button for icons, 326
panes, 19, *20*, 25, *26*, 176
paragraphs
    block quote, **509–510**
    formatting, **508–512**
    left-block, **509**
    outline, **511–512**
    in vi editor, 475, 478, 486
parameters for vi editor, **493–494**
parent directories, 53, 384, 709
parentheses ()
    for command grouping, 428, 432
    for command substitution, 427
    for metacharacters, 411–412
    with vi editor, 478
parity variable, 630
partition maps, 661
partition numbers, 654
passwd command, 8, **793–794**
Passwd database listing, 674, *675*
Password control for users, 679
passwords, **6–7**
    changing, 8, **364**, **793–794**
    for screen savers, 46, 851
    selecting, **363**
    for superusers, 817–818
paste command, **794–795**
Paste items
    and clipboard, 26
    for files, 75, 77
    for icons, 332–333
    for links, 85
    for sound files, 259–260
Path control for users, 680
path pane, **54–55**, *55*, **63–64**
Path Pane pop-up menu, 55, *56*
PATH variable, **561–562**

paths, 54, **383**
   for commands, **842**
   for device files, **831**
   for mail file directories, 133
   variables for, **561–562**
"Pattern not found" message, 492
Pattern settings
   for file types, 351
   for Tape Tool, 307
patterns, **410–412**
   for file classes, 352, 355
   with grep, **417–419**, **761–763**
   in vi files, 491–493
Pause Play control for sound, 263
pcat command, **796**
/pcfiles directory, 657
pcfs (PC file system), 653, 657, 785–786
PD number register, 514
percent signs (%)
   for jobs, 537
   for system prompt, 365
perfmeter.log*xxx* directory, 284
Performance Meter, **280–284**
Performance Meter window, 280–281, *281*
periods (.). *See* dots (.)
Permanent File text field for messages, 155–156
"Permission denied" message, 385
permissions
   in adding users, 681
   for appointments, **238–240**
   changing, **81–84**, **399–402**, **712–715**
   default, **571–572**
   and file creation modes, **831–833**
   listing, 89, 385, **395–398**
   and ownership, **398–399**
   for user calendars, 224
personal Binder entries, 342
pg command, **796–798**
phones variable, 630
PI number register, 514
ping command, **622**, **798–799**
pinning menus to Workspace, **14**, *15*
pipe command (mailx), 446
pipes, **427–428**
   with echo command, 741
   with printing, 524
   with sorting, 425

   with tee command, 824
   with wc command, 840
pitch of bell, 580, 856
pixels, 318
.pl request, 515, 517
.plan file, 754
plans. *See appointments*
Play button in Audio Tool, 254, 256
Play Volume window, 263, *263*
playing back sounds, 256, 263
Pmt function, 293
PO number register, 514–515
.po request, 515
Point mode for icons, 326
pointers, mouse, 10, 12, *12*, 321–322, **592–594**
pointing with mouse, 11
points, 502, 603
Pop-up Pointer Jumping setting, 322
pop-up windows, 14, 18, 27–28, *27*
PopUp setting for appointment alarms, 212
portrait mode for snapshots, 271
Position controls in printing, 242, 272, 339
postmasters, 456
PostScript printers and files
   filters for, 251, 500, 523, **736–738**
   icons for, 58
   scripts for, 81, 91
pound signs (#)
   in .profile file, 558
   for superuser prompt, 644
.PP macro, 508
pr command, 523–524, **799–801**
Precedence header field, 152
preserve command (mailx), 446
pressing with mouse, 11
Pretty-print C item for Text Editor, 186
Prev items for calendars, 204, 226
preview area in Icon Editor window, 324
Previous items
   for delimiters, 185
   for messages, 104
   for scrollbar, 25
Previous Page button for help, 42
Primary Group control, 678
Print Banner control, 691
print command (mailx), 446
Print Options window for snapshots, 266, 271–273, *272*

Print Tool, **246–252**
Print Tool window, 246, *247*
Print window for icons, 336, 338–339, *338*
Printer Manager, **687–693**
Printer Manager window, **687–693**, *688*
printer servers, 687
Printer Settings window, 241–242, *241*
$PRINTER variable, 250
printers
    adding, **687–693**
    choosing, 248
    for icons, 338
    on networks, 247
    remote, **691–693**
    for snapshots, 271
    status of, **526–527**, **774–776**
printing
    appointments, **218–220**
    banner pages, **525**, 691
    Binder entries, 348
    files, **80–81**, **247–248**
    formatted documents, **499–500**, 523
    icons, **336**, **338–339**, *338*
    messages, 127, 148
    multiple-page files, 523–524
    scripts for, 91, 148
    snapshots, 266, **271–273**
printing jobs, 247
    canceling, 527, **706–707**
    running, **522–525**, **772–774**
    status of, 249, **526–527**, **774–776**
    stopping, 249
priority
    of background jobs, 568
    of commands, 550, **788–789**
    of printing jobs, 774
process IDs (PIDs), 198, 542–543, 802
processes
    displaying, **541–544**, 547
    monitoring, 281
    scheduling, **545–550**, **698–700**
    status of, **542–544**, **801–803**
    suspending, 550, **814**
    terminating, **539–540**, **544–545**, **766–767**
processor type, 834
.profile file, 557–558, 564, 568
    for aliases, 572
    for directories, 562
    for prompts, 710

.profile.bak file, 568
program files, directory for, 53
Programs menu, 17, *18*
.project file, 754
prompt command (ftp), 759
prompt variable, 576, 631
Prompt Window setting, 95, *96*
prompts, 8, 365
    for commands, 95
    directories displayed in, **710**
    for superusers, 644
    variables for, **563–564**
Properties menus and windows, 17, 108
    for Audio Tool, **261–263**, *262*
    for Icon Editor, **333**, **335**
    for Performance Meter, 282–284, *282*
    for Tape Tool, 305–308, *306*
properties of Binder entries, **342–353**
proportional fonts, 603
Props menus
    for Binder, 342
    for File Manager, 55
    for Tape Tool, 302
protecting files from redirection, 430, 570
protection mode, 398
protocols, 615
prtvtoc command, **661–662**
ps command, 542, 544, 650, **801–803**
PS number register, 514
PS variables, **563–564**
put command (cu), 635
put command (ftp), 638, 640, 759
putting text with vi editor, **487–490**
Pv function, 294
pwd command, 384, **804**
pwd command (ftp), 640, 759
PWD variable, **563–564**
pyro screensaver, 583, 849

Q

:q! command (vi), 473
qix screensaver, 583, 849
.QP macro, 509
question marks (?)
    with mail, 373, 440, 445
    as wildcard characters, 61, 411–412

queues, printer. *See* printing jobs
quiet variable, 576
quit command (ftp), 639, 759
quit command (mailx), 446, 449
quit command (telnet), 637, 825
Quit function for Calculator, 289
quitting
    messages, 117, **447–448**
    windows, 28, 33, 42, 45
quotation marks (`,")
    in grep searches, 417–418, 761, 763
    in messages, 370
    with vi editor, 488

R

r command, 372, **410**
.R macro, 501–502
Radians item for Calculator, 297
ragged margins, 504
raise variable, 631
random number functions, 298
random screensaver, 583, 849
ranges
    in grep searches, 418, 761
    sorting on, 423–424
raster files, 265
    contents of, 87
    icons for, *58*
Rate function, 294
rawftp variable, 631
.RC macro, 518
Rcl key for Calculator, 289–290
rcp command, **617–618, 804–805**
.RE macro, 511
Read Functions pop-up menu, 302
Read Only item for history logs, 192
read permission settings, 81–83, 385, 397,
    712–714, 832
reading
    files, on tape, 302, **304–305**, 307–308
    mail, **373–374, 442–443**, 778
really delete option, 92
realxfishdb program, 587
reboot command, 648
rebooting systems, **648–649**
Rec button in Audio Tool, 254–255

record variable, 631
Record Volume window, 264, *264*
recording sounds, **255–256**, 264
recursive file operations, 387–389
recv command (ftp), 759
redirection
    with background commands, 535
    of combined commands, **432–433**
    of errors, **431–432**
    of input, 431, **829–830**
    with messages, 456
    of output, **429–434, 824–825**
redirection operator, 391
redisplaying windows, 28, 36, 43
Redo items
    for icons, 332
    for sound files, 258
redrawing screens, 481
referencing variables, 560
refreshing windows, 28, 36, 43
Region mode for icons, 328
regions, snapshots of, 266, **268–269**
Register with NIS+ control for printers,
    691
relative path names, **383**, 709
Reminder window, 212, *212*
reminders, **706**. *See also* appointments
Remote Copy window, 79, *79*
Remote File Sharing (RFS), 614
remote operations
    command execution, **618, 808–809**
    copying files, **78–80**
    logging in, **615–616, 805–806**
    transferring files, **617–618, 804–805**
remote printers, **691–693**
remote setting for Performance Meter, 283
remote variable, 631
remotehelp command (ftp), 759
Remove Brackets item for Text Editor, 186
Remove Pair button for Text Editor, 181
removing. *See* deleting
Rename Attachment window, 129
rename command (ftp), 759
renaming
    attachments, **128–129**
    files, 73, 140, **394, 787**
    folders, 73
reopening windows, **32–33**

Repeat controls
    for appointment alarms, 212, 215
    for clock alarms, 279
repeated tasks, scheduling, **548–549**,
        724–726
repeating
    commands, **371–372**, **410**, 765
    Text Editor edits, 175
    vi editor commands, 471
replacing text
    with Text Editor, **178–185**
    with vi editor, **485–487**, **492–493**
reply command (mailx), 446
Reply-To header field, 152
replying to messages, **121**, **443–444**
Request Confirmation option for Mail
        Tool, 151
requests, formatting, 499, 732
reset button, 649
Reset buttons
    for calendars, 235
    for Mail Tool properties, 142
    for sound, 263
Reset Input item, 43
Reset pointer item for sound files, 259–260
resize corners, *20*, 21
resizing windows, 28, **36**, 45
resolution of monitors, 318
respond command (mailx), 446
restarting jobs, 537
Restore Size items and buttons
    for calendars, 210, 213
    for windows, 36
Retrieve Every setting for Mail Tool, 143
Return-Receipt-To header field, 152–153
Rev button in Audio Tool, 254, 256
reverse sorts, 425, 815
reverse video, 198
rgb.txt file, **588–592**
.rhosts file, 616, 618, 805, 808
right-handed setting for Calculator, 300,
        300
rlogin command, 615–616, **805–806**
rm command, **806–807**
    for directories, 389
    for files, **394–395**
    for links, 403, 769
rmdir command, 388–389, **807–808**
rmdir command (ftp), 759

roff command, 498–499
root command, 644
root directory, 52, 380–381
root menu, **16–17**, *16*
root users. *See* superusers
rotating icon images, 329
roto screensaver, 583, 849
.RS macro, 511
rsh command, 618, **808–809**
running print jobs, **522–525**, **772–774**
rup command, 622–623, **809**
ruptime command, **809–810**
rusers command, 452–453, 616, **619–620**,
        810–811
rwall command, 646
rwho command, **811–812**

S

Sample Time setting for Performance
        Meter, 284
Saturation control, 315–316
Save As items
    for icons, 335
    for sound files, 258
Save Changes Notice, 111, *111*
save command (mailx), 446, 449
Save File window, 256, *257*, 258
Save items, buttons, and menus, 138
    for Binder, 341
    for mail files, 135–136
    for snapshots, 266, 268
    for sound files, 256, 258
Save Options window for snapshots, 266,
        268–270, *268*
save variable, 576
saving
    Binder entries, 341
    history log files, **192**
    icon files, **335–336**
    Mail Tool Header window changes,
        111–112
    messages, **136–138**, 374, **448–451**
    snapshots, 266, 268–270
    sound files, 256, *257*, 258
    Text Editor files, **168**
    variables, 557

vi editor files, **472–474**
Workspace arrangement, 45–46
/sbin directory, 382
scale utility, 596
scales
    with calculator, 369
    for fonts, **594–597**
    for snapshots, 273
SCCS directories, 305, 822
Schedule buttons
    for appointments, 228
    for calendars, 222
scheduling. *See also* Calendar Manager
    processes, **545–550, 698–700**
    repeated tasks, **548–549,** 724–726
scientific calculator, 286, 288, **297–298**
Scientific Mode window, 297, *297*
screens
    clearing, 372, **716**
    redrawing, 481
    scrolling by, 24
    snapshots of, 266, **269–270**
screensavers, 46
    changing, **581–584, 848–852**
    xset command for, **859**
script command, **812**
script variable, 632
scripts
    with at command, 698
    with echo command, 739
    for File Manager, 81
    icons for, *59*
    of login sessions, **812**
    for OpenWindows, **790–792**
    for printing, 91, 148
scrollbar elevators, 19, *20*
Scrollbar menu, **24–25,** *24*
Scrollbar Pointer Jumping setting, 321
scrollbars
    for insertion point, 169
    placing, 320
    using, **22,** *23,* **24–25**
scrolling
    in Shell Tool, 188, *189*
    with vi editor, 479
    xterm window, 197
Scrolling List menu, 136, 249, *250*
scrolling lists, 30

SCSI tape drives, 666
Search Files Containing String item, 69
search permission settings, **832**
searching through files, **491–493, 746–747,**
    816–817. *See also* finding
Secondary Groups control for users, 678
Seconds setting for clock, 276
security. *See* passwords; permissions
Select All items and buttons
    for calendars, 226
    for files, 60
    for finding messages, 125
    for Tape Tool, 302
Select Line at Number item in Text Editor,
    170
SELECT Mouse Press setting, 319
Select Naming Service window, 673, 676,
    676
Selected item for Tape Tool, 304
selected text, searching for, 179–180
selecting
    files, **59–61**
    messages, **104–110**
    mouse button for, 10–11, *10*
    text, **169,** 197–198
Selects Default setting for menus, 319
semicolons (;)
    for multiple commands, 408–409
    in .profile file, 558
send command (ftp), 760
sender, sorting messages by, 123
sending messages, 374, **646,** 778, **840,**
    843–844
    for calendar, **230–231**
    Mail Tool, **115–117**
    Mailx, **453–459**
sentences in vi editor, 475, 478, 484, 486
separators
    for dates, 242–243
    for sort fields, 422–424
Server control for users, 680
sessions
    scripts of, **812**
    terminating, **743**
set command
    for variables, **558–560,** 566–567,
    812–814
    for vi editor parameters, **493–494**
set command (mailx), 446

Set Default buttons
    for Calculator, 300–301
    for clock, 279
    for Performance Meter, 284
Set Input Area setting, 320
setignoreeof option, 568
sh_history file, 765
shared Binder entries, 342
Shell Script files, icons for, *59*
Shell Tool, **186–187**
    from Command tool, 194
    Command tool from, 188, 190
    copying and pasting text in, 188–189
    Term Pane menu in, **187–188**, *188*
    viewing text in, 188, *189*
Shell Tool window, 186–187, *187*
SHELL variable, 559, 576
shells, SunOS, **365–366**
shelltool command, 92
Shift key with mouse, 11
Shift Lines item for Text Editor, 186
Show All Subfolders item, 64
Show All window, 597, *597*
Show Attachment List setting, 151
Show Attachments item, 118
Show Caret at Top item, 170
Show Errs setting for Tape Tool, 307
Show items for Performance Meter, 281
Show setting for file views, 89
Show Text window, 597, *597*
Show Tree item, 54, *56*
showto variable, 577
shutdown command, 650
shutting down systems, **649–652**
Sideways setting for snapshots, 271
SIGKILL signal, 766
Signal With setting for Mail Tool, 143
signals for processes, 545, 766
SIGTERM signal, 766
Silence Detection control for sound, 261
Silence Threshold control for sound, 262
Silent Ends item for sound files, 259
single quotation marks (')
    in grep searches, 417–418, 761, 763
    in messages, 370
size
    of files, 63, 89, 396
    of fonts, 199, 331, 502, **594–597**, 603
    of icons, 57, 62, 87, 333, 335

of printed output, 242
of processes, 544
of snapshots, 273
sorting messages by, 124
of windows, 28, **36**, 45
size command (mailx), 446
Skeleton Path control for users, 680
slashes (/)
    in path names, 383, 709
    for root directory, 52, 380–381
    in vi searches, 491–492
sleep command, 550, **814**
slice number for hard drives, 654
slider controls, 30
Sln function, 294
.SM macro, 502
Smaller item for Magnify help, 41
Snap controls for snapshots, 266–267
Snapshot application, **265–267**
    printing snapshots with, **271–273**
    for regions, **268–269**
    for screens, **269–270**
    viewing snapshots with, 270, *271*
    for windows, **267–268**
Snapshot window, 265, *265*
solid setting for Performance Meter graphs,
    283
sort command, 412, **421–425**, **815–816**
sorting
    files, 63, 89, 386, **421–425**, 776–777,
        815–816
    message headers, **123–124**
    user calendars, 225
sound boards, 253
sounds. *See* Audio Tool
Source Code Control System, 305, 822
source file command (mailx), 446
Source Machine text field in copying, 79
Source Path text field in copying, 79
.sp request, 505–506
spaces
    in folder and file names, 73
    in grep searches, 417, 761
    for sort fields, 422–423
    and tabs, **744**, **835**
    with variables, 564
spacing of lines, 505
special characters, inserting, **503**
special files, 397

spell command, **419, 816**
Spkr/Jack control, 263
split output, redirection for, **433–434, 824–825**
splitting
    file pane, 57
    Text Editor pane, 176
    windows, 25, *26*
Sqrt function, 291
square brackets ([ ])
    for character classes, 411
    in command references, 697
    in grep searches, 418, 761–762
    in Text Editor, 186
Square mode for icons, 327
stacked Performance Meters, 283
standard error, redirection of, **431–432**
standard files, 396–397
standard I/O, 429
Standard item for Magnify help, 41
standard paragraphs, 508
Start items for vacation messages, 130
Start menu, 213, *214*
Start text field for appointments, 211, 213, 227–228, 230, 237
starting
    Calendar Manager, 202, *203*
    Deskset applications, 17, *18*
    File Manager, 53–54
    Mail Tool, 100, *101*
    OpenWindows and DeskSet, **8–10**
    Text Editor, **166–167**
    vi editor, **469–470**
startup commands with vi editor, **494–495**
startup screen, *9*
status
    of local network, **809–810**
    of messages, 103–104, 124, 780–781
    of printer, **526–527, 774–776**
    of processes, 536–537, **542–544, 801–803**
status command (ftp), 760
status line for vi editor, 470
Sto key for Calculator, 289
Stop-a keys, 648, 652
Stop buttons
    in Audio Tool, 255–257
    for vacation messages, 130
stop command, 537, 540

Stop Printing menu, 249
stopped jobs, logging out with, 48, 538
stopping printing jobs, 249
Stopwatch control, 277
Store as New File item, 168
Store log as new file item, 192
Store pop-up menu, 168, *168*
storing. *See also* saving
strings
    in character classes, 411
    searching through files for, 69, **746–747, 816–817**
strings command, **816–817**
StripPath setting for Tape Tool, 303, 307
stty command, 579
stty tostop command, 535, 540
style
    of Calculator, 300
    of fonts, 603
    of icon text, 330
su command, 645, 648, **817–818**
subdirectories. *See* directories
subject, 442
    in composing messages, 114–115, 117, 454
    finding messages by, 125
    in replying to messages, 444
    sorting messages by, 123
$SUBJECT string, 130
submenus, 13
    adding, **606–610**
    settings for, 318–319
substituting
    commands, **426–427, 566**
    names of files, 569
    variables for, **566**
Sun Customer Service, 649
SunOS
    command line with. *See* command line
    entering commands in, **366–367**
    file system in, **380–403**
    help for, **374–375**
    logging into, **362–366**
    mail in, **372–374, 777–779.** *See also* mailx program
    transition to, 696
    utilities with, **367–372**
    and vi editor, 494

superusers, **644–646, 817–818**
    for mounting file systems, 652
    for permission modes, 399
    for shutting down systems, 649
Suppress setting for Tape Tool, 307
suspending commands, 537, 550, **814**
SVR4, transition to, 696
swapped jobs, monitoring, 281
swarm screensaver, 583, 849
switching jobs, **538–539**
Syd function, 295
Sym Links setting for Tape Tool, 307
syntax of commands, 366
sysadmin group, 672
system administration
    Administration Tool for. *See* Administration Tool
    booting and rebooting, **647–649**
    directory for, 382
    for floppy disks, **662–666**
    hard drive management, **652–662**
    shutting down systems, **649–652**
    superusers, **644–646**
    for tape drives, **666–671**
system administrators, 6, 362
system crashes with vi editor, 473–474
System Default control for printers, 690, 693
system dictionary, 419, 771–772, **816**
system directories, 53
system messages, 7, 9, 194, 364, **462–463**
system prompts, 8, 365
systems
    booting, **647–649**
    copying files between, **78–80**
    monitoring, **280–284**
    shutting down, **649–652**
SZ field in processes, 544

T

.ta request, 506–507
tabexpand variable, 632
Table of Contents for help handbooks, 39, *40*, 41
tables
    extracting fields from, **729–730**

formatting, **520–522**
tabs
    expanding, **744**
    in lines, **506–507**
    in Text Editor, 186
    unexpanding, **835**
tags for file classes, 352–353
tail command, 414, **818–819**
take command (cu), 635
talk command, 459–460, **819–820**
tandem variable, 632
tape backups
    with cpio, **669–671, 720–724**
    with Tape Tool, **301–308**
    with tar, **667–669, 820–824**
Tape Contents/Files to Read window, 302–303, *303*
Tape Tool, **301–308**
Tape Tool window, 301, *301*
tar command, 301, **667–669, 820–824**
target address for hard drives, 653
targets, drag-and-drop, 21, **37–38**, 71, 165
tbl command, 521
TCP/IP (Transport Control Protocol/Interface Program), 635, 798
.TE macro, 521
tee command, **433–434, 824–825**
Telephone Interface Program (tip), **623–632, 827–829**
telnet program, **635–637, 825–826**
Temp file directory control for sound, 263
Template Properties window, 132, 156–157, *156*
templates for messages, **131–132**, *132*, 142, 156–157, *156*
temporary files, directory for, 53, 382
Term function, 295
Term Pane pop-up menu, **187–188**, *188*
Term Pane window, 190, *191*
TERM variable, 559, 578
terminals
    customizing, **578–580**
    emulating, 186, 194–195, **862–863**
terminating
    processes, **539–540, 544–545, 766–767**
    sessions, **743**
text
    appending, 430–432, **481–482**, 488
    copying, 173, *174*, 188–189, 198, **489**

deleting, **174–175**, 178, **482–484**
echoing, **370–371**, **739–741**
editing, **171–176**
fonts for. *See* fonts
formatting. *See* formatting
for icons, 330–332, *330*
inserting, 173, 175, 188–189, **481–482**, **490–491**
moving, 175, 198, **487–490**
replacing, **178–185**, **485–487**, **492–493**
selecting, **169**, 197–198
with xterm window, **197–198**
Text demo program, 597, *598*
Text Duplicate pointer, 173, *174*
Text Editor
with Command Tool, 193, *193*
editing text in, **171–176**
finding and replacing text in, **178–185**
insertion point in, **169–171**
line wrap mode in, 177
loading files with, **166–167**
merging files in, **177**
saving files with, **168**
selecting text in, **169**
splitting pane for, 176
for templates, 156
window for, 164–166, *165*
Text Editor window, 19, *20*, 25, *26*, 164–166, *165*, 594, *595*
text fields, 30
text files
comparing, **420–421**
icons for, *58*
sorting, **421–425**
Text mode for icons, 328
text pane, 164, 166
clearing, 176
Extras menu in, **185–186**
Text Pane pop-up menu, 115, *116*, *165*, 166, *172*, 173, 175
Text pop-up menu, **330–332**, *330*, 597
text units in vi editor, **474–475**
"there are stopped jobs" message, 48, 538
This One Only buttons for appointments, 216–217
This Week item for calendars, 226
thumbs on scrollbar, 197
.ti request, 506

tildes (~) and tilde commands
with cu, 634, 726
for home directory, 384
with mailx, **457–459**
with tip, 625–626, 827
with vi editor, 469, 475, 480, 487
time
with at command, 698
clock for, **273–279**
with cron command, 549, **724–726**
displaying, 367, **730–731**
of files
changing, 391–392
displaying, 396
sorting by, 386, 776
formats for, 324
of messages, 123, 442
time command, **826–827**
TIME field in processes, 544
Time Format setting for languages, 324
Time Zone menu, 233, *234*
time zones
with Calendar Manager, 233, *234*
for clock, 277, *278*
for workstations, 685
timeouts, variables for, 562–563
Timezone menu, 277, *278*
timing commands, **826–827**
tip command, **623–625**, **827–829**
transferring files with, **625–626**
variables for, **626–632**
.tiprc file, 626
TMOUT variable, 562–563
/tmp directory, 53, 382
To text fields and items
for composing messages, 114–116, 121, 159–160
for finding messages, 125
Today menu for calendars, 204
ToDo lists, 202, 207–208, *208*
changing, **217**
creating, **213–215**
deleting items on, **215–216**, *216*
entering items on, **209–217**
printing, **218–220**
Tool Properties window, 86, 90–92, *90*
tools, 4
top command (mailx), 446
Top to Here item for scrollbar, 25

touch command, 391, **829**
touch command (mailx), 446
tr command, 431, **829–830**
transferring files
  with cu, 635
  with ftp, **638–640**
  with rcp, **617–618, 804–805**
  with tip, **625–626**
trash can icon, 10, 37, 53, *54*, 73–75, *74*
  for attachments, 129
  displaying, 92
  for mail messages, 126
tree display, 54, 61, **63–64**
Tree Pane pop-up menu, 55, *56*, 63–64
trigonometric functions, 297–298
troff command, 468, 498–499. *See also*
  formatting
troff files, printing, 523
troff filters, 249–250
troff requests, removing, 732
truncation on Calculator, 296
.TS macro, 520, 522
tty command, **831**, 844
tutorials, 17, 39
.2C macro, 518
type, sorting files by, 89
type command (ftp), 760
typescript file, 812
TZ variable, 560

U

uadmin 2 0 command, 651
ufs (UNIX file system), 652–653, 785
UID field in processes, 544, 802
.UL macro, 501
umask command, **571–572, 831–833**
umount command, 657, **659–660**, 784
unalias command, **833**
uname command, **833–834**
uncompress command, **834–835**
uncompressing files, **834–835, 838**
undelete command (mailx), 447
Undelete window, 126–127, *127*
undeleting
  attachments, 129
  files, 74

messages, **126–127**, 444
undeliverable mail, **455–456**
underlining text, 501–502
undiscard command (mailx), 447
undoing
  aliases, 573
  Binder operations, 341
  message deletions, 444
  sound file edits, 258
  Text Editor edits, 175, *176*
  vi editor edits, 471
unexpand command, **835**
ungrouping windows, 34
unignore command (mailx), 447
uniq command, **836**
units command, **837**
Units field for printing, 242
units of text in vi editor, **474–475**
UNIX Command text field for
  commands, 95
unmounting file systems, **659–660**, 784
unpack command, 792, **838**
unread command (mailx), 447
"unrecognized file type" message, 71
unset command, 564–565, 570
unset variables, error messages for, 570
updating
  NIS maps, **685–686**
  Performance Meter, 284
Upright setting for snapshots, 271
uptime on networks, **622–623, 809**
User Access List control for printers, 691
User Account Manager, **675–682**, *677*
user command (ftp), 760
user-defined functions, **290–291**
User ID control, 678
user identification numbers (UID), 544,
  678, 715, **765–766**, 802
User Name control, 677
user names, 6–7, 362, 677
users
  adding, **675–681**
  calendars for, **220, 222–233**, *232*
  communication with, **645–646**
  copying settings of, 681
  deleting, **681–682**, *682*
  group membership of, **763, 788**

listing, **369–370, 452–453, 619–621,
754–755, 810–811, 842–843**
logging in, **770**
/usr directory, 53, 382
/usr/bin directory, 696
/usr/demo/SOUND/sounds directory, 254
/usr/dict/words directory, 771
/usr/lib/lp/postscript directory, 500, 523
/usr/lib/uucp directory, 726
/usr/openwin/lib/locale/C/help/hand-
books/sounds directory, 254
/usr/openwin/share/include/images directory, 324, 336
/usr/sbin/cron.d directory, 724
/usr/share/lib/unittab file, 837
/usr/share/man directory, 779
/usr/ucb directory, 696
utilities
for SunOS, 367–372
for Workspace, **42–47,** *43*
Utilities menu, 17, **42–47,** *43*
uuname command, 729

V

vacation command, **838–839**
vacation mail, **130,** *131,* **838–839**
Vacation Setup window, 130, *131*
/var directory, 382
/var/adm/wtmp file, 768
/var/mail directory, 440 441
variables, **556**
changing, **558–560**
for command prompts, **563–564**
for commands, **565**
creating, **564**
displaying, 560, 740
listing, **557–558, 742–743, 812–814**
for mailx, **573–578**
for output substitution, **566**
for paths, **561–562**
referencing, 560
storing, 557
for timeouts, 562–563
for tip, **626–632**
unsetting, 564–565, 570
verbose command (ftp), 760

verbose variable, 632
version command (mailx), 447
vertical bars (|)
with metacharacters, 412
for OR operators, 428–429
for pipes, 427
vi editor, **468**
command mode in, **470–471**
cursor movement in, **475–480**
editing commands in, **480–490**
exiting, **472–474**
insert mode in, **471–472**
inserting files with, **490–491**
parameters for, **493–494**
searching files in, **491–493**
starting, **469–470**
startup commands with, **494–495**
SunOS commands with, 494
units of text in, **474–475**
View control for snapshots, 267, 270
View Filter Pattern item, 91
View menus, 61–62, *62*
for Binder, 341–342
for calendars, 204, 208
for File Manager, 55
for messages, 101, 104
for Snapshot, 267, 270, *271*
for Text Editor, 166
for Text Editor insertion point, **170**
View Message window, 102, 104, *105,* 106,
107
with full headers, 108, *110*
number of lines in, 147–148
viewing
Binder entries, 341–342
fonts, **597–602, 844–846, 852–853**
formatted documents, **499–500**
messages, **103–112, 373–374, 441–443,**
778
snapshots, 270, *271*
text, 188, *189*
views in Calendar Manager, **205–207,**
205–208, **218–220**
visual command (mailx), 447
Voice button for messages, 114
volume
in Audio Tool, **263–264**
of bell and keyboard clicks, 579–580,
856–857

Volume menu, 253, 263–264
VS number register, 514
VT Fonts menu, 196, *196*
VT Options menu, 196, *196*
VT terminal emulation, **862–863**

W

:w command (vi), 472–474
wait command, 540
waiting for background jobs, 540
wall command, 462, 646, **840**
Warning control for users, 680
Waste icon, 10, 37, 53, *54*, 73–75, *74*
    for attachments, 129
    displaying, 92
    for messages, 126
.wastebasket directory, 74
wastebasket option, 92
Wastebasket window, 73–75, *74*
    for attachments, 129
    customizing, 92
    for mail messages, 126
wc command, **420, 840–841**
Week view in Calendar Manager, 205–206, *206*, 209, 219
Weekly setting for appointment alarms, 215
weight of icon text, 330
What Line Number? item in Text Editor, 170
What text field for appointments, 211–212, 214, 218, 227, 230
which command, **842**
who command, **369–370**, 452, **842–843**
who am i command, 370, **843**
wide-area networks (WANs), 615
width
    of lines, **755–756**
    in printing, 242, 273, 339
wildcard characters, **410–412**
    with Goto text field, 67
    for selecting files, 61
Window Controls item, **44–45**
window footers, *20*, 22
window headers, 19, *20*
Window menu, 13, 31, *31*
    buttons for, *20*, 22

with pop-ups, **28**, *28*
window parameter (vi), 494
windows, 18
    active, **30–31**, 320
    closing, **32–33**, 45
    colors for, **314–316, 587–592**
    controls in, **29–30**, *29*, **44–45**
    folders as, 65, *66*
    moving, 28, **33–36**
    opening, **32–33**, 45
    parts of, **19–22**, *20*
    pop-up, 14, 18, 27–28, *27*
    quitting, 28, 33, 42, 45
    refreshing, 28, 36, 43
    resizing, 28, **36**, 45
    snapshots of, **266–268**
    splitting, 25, *26*
Windows button for Workspace Properties, 315
word processors. *See* Text Editor; vi editor
words
    counting, **420, 840–841**
    in Text Editor, 169
    in vi editor, 474, 477–478, 483, 486
working directory, 384, **804**
Workspace, 4, 9, *9*
    customizing, **584–592, 860–861**
    pinning menus to, **14**, *15*
    saving arrangement of, 45–46
    utilities for, **42–47**, *43*
Workspace menu, **16–17**, *16*, 605
Workspace Properties window, **312–313**, *313*
    for colors, **314–316**
    for icon locations, **317**
    for languages, **322–324**, *323*
    for menu settings, **318–319**, *318*
    for miscellaneous settings, **319–321**, *320*
    for mouse settings, **321–322**, *321*
workstations
    adding, **683–685**
    shutting down, 651
world permissions, 83, 240
wrapmargin parameter (vi), 493
wrapping
    icons, 89
    in Text Editor, 177
write command, **843–844**
write command (mailx), 447, 449, **461–462**

Write menu and settings for Tape Tool, 302, 305, 307
write permission settings, 81–83, 385, 397, **712–714, 832**
write-protecting
    floppy disks, 666
    tapes, 671
writing
    electronic messages, **461–462**
    files to tape, **303–304**

X Bitmap icon format, 333, 336
X calculator, 286
X clock applications, 274
X commands, manual for, **853–854**
X Window System, **194–199**
.Xdefaults file, 312, 315, 581, *582*, **854–855**
    for fonts, 603–604
    for inverse video, 587
    for scales, 596
xfd command, 594, **844–845**
xfontsel command, **845–847**
xhost command, **847–848**
.Xinitrc file, 584
XINITRC variable, 560
xit command (mailx), 447
xlock command, **848–852**
xlsfonts command, 598, **852–853**
xman command, **853–854**
Xnor logical function, 297

Xor logical function, 296
xrdb command, 587, 596, **854–855**
xset command, **860**
    for fonts, 857
    for keyboard preferences, **579–580, 856–858**
    for mouse, **858**
    for screensavers, **583–584, 859**
xsetroot command, 584, 592, **860–861**
xterm command, **861–863**
xterm window, **194–199**, *195*
XtermLog.*pid* files, 198
XView Icon format, 333, 335–336, 353

yanking text with vi editor, **487–489**
Year view in Calendar Manager, 206, *207*, 209, 220, *221–222*
Yearly setting for appointment alarms, 215
"you have mail" message, 441, 525

Z

z command (mailx), 447
z command (telnet), 637, 826
.Z extension, 718
.z extension, 792
zcat command, 718, **864**
zombie processes, 544

FREE BROCHURE!

Complete this form today, and we'll send you a full-color brochure of Sybex bestsellers.

Please supply the name of the Sybex book purchased.

_____

How would you rate it?

_____ Excellent   _____ Very Good   _____ Average   _____ Poor

Why did you select this particular book?

_____ Recommended to me by a friend

_____ Recommended to me by store personnel

_____ Saw an advertisement in _____

_____ Author's reputation

_____ Saw in Sybex catalog

_____ Required textbook

_____ Sybex reputation

_____ Read book review in _____

_____ In-store display

_____ Other _____

Where did you buy it?

_____ Bookstore

_____ Computer Store or Software Store

_____ Catalog (name: _____)

_____ Direct from Sybex

_____ Other: _____

Did you buy this book with your personal funds?

_____ Yes   _____ No

About how many computer books do you buy each year?

_____ 1-3   _____ 3-5   _____ 5-7   _____ 7-9   _____ 10+

About how many Sybex books do you own?

_____ 1-3   _____ 3-5   _____ 5-7   _____ 7-9   _____ 10+

Please indicate your level of experience with the software covered in this book:

_____ Beginner   _____ Intermediate   _____ Advanced

Which types of software packages do you use regularly?

_____ Accounting   _____ Databases   _____ Networks

_____ Amiga   _____ Desktop Publishing   _____ Operating Systems

_____ Apple/Mac   _____ File Utilities   _____ Spreadsheets

_____ CAD   _____ Money Management   _____ Word Processing

_____ Communications   _____ Languages   _____ Other _____
                                                          (please specify)

Which of the following best describes your job title?

_____ Administrative/Secretarial   _____ President/CEO

_____ Director   _____ Manager/Supervisor

_____ Engineer/Technician   _____ Other _____

                                                         (please specify)

Comments on the weaknesses/strengths of this book: _____

_____

_____

_____

_____

Name _____

Street _____

City/State/Zip _____

Phone _____

PLEASE FOLD, SEAL, AND MAIL TO SYBEX

SYBEX, INC.
Department M
2021 CHALLENGER DR.
ALAMEDA, CALIFORNIA USA
94501

SYBEX

SunOS 4.1 Command	SunOS 5.x (SVR4) Changes
ls	The −A option, which listed entries whose names began with a ., except the current directory (.) and the parent directory (. .), is no longer available. The ls command now defaults to a single column rather than multicolumn output when the output is a terminal.
mach	Use the uname −p command for similar results.
mail	The −i option, which ignored interrupts, is no longer available. Mail forwarding is now accomplished using the −F (forward) option. The n and dq commands, which were used to read mail, are no longer available.
mount	Most mount command options must now be specified after the file system type has been specified (mount −F *filesystem*), unless the file system is entered in the /etc/vfstab file.
mount_tfs	Use the mount -F *filesystem* command for similar results.
mountall	Use the mount −a command for similar results.
mv	The - option is no longer available. Instead use the −− option to explicitly mark the end of any command-line options so that mv can recognize file name arguments that begin with a −.
nice	This command now defaults to 10. The + option (nice +*n*) for the SunOS 5.x command increments the nice priority value by *n*; the C shell nice command sets the nice value to *n*. The C shell defaults to 4.
pack/unpack	The pack command's file name argument is no longer restricted to 12 characters; instead, the variable NAME_MAX −2 determines the length of the file name.
passwd	The -F *filename* (treat *filename* as the password file) and −y (change the password in the NIS database) options are no longer available. The −f option now forces the user to change the password at the next login. The −s option displays the password attributes for the user's login name, rather than changing the user's login shell.
pr	The −n option now displays balanced columns.
printenv	Use the env command for similar results.
ps	The −C, −k, −n, −r, −S, −U, −v, −w, and −x options are no longer available. The −c option displays six columns of process information, rather than just the associated command's name. The −e option displays information about all processes, instead of displaying the environment as well as the arguments to the command. The −g option is specified as −g idlist and restricts the listing to those processes whose process group IDs appear in *idlist*. The −u *uidlist* restricts the listing to processes whose user-ID numbers of login names appear in *uidlist*.

Lancashire Legacy

'A well-told, well-paced story'

Historical Novel Society on *Lancashire Lass*

'Spectacular saga'

Peterborough Evening Telegraph on *Lancashire Lass*

'Brilliant, no one can match her writing ability – *Lancashire Lass* is Anna Jacobs' new novel. I have just finished reading it, couldn't put it down, it held me absorbed on every page'

Amazon Reader Review on *Lancashire Lass*

'Catherine Cookson fans will cheer! A stirring saga of a Pennine village girl who marries to escape her drunken father'

Peterborough Evening Gazette on *Like No Other*

'A powerful and absorbing saga'

Hartlepool Mail on *Spinners Lake*

'A vivid saga'

Northern Lights on *Spinners Lake*

'Impressive grasp of human emotions'

The Sunday Times on *Spinners Lake*

'A well told, captivating story'

Dorset Evening Echo on *Jessie*

Lancashire Legacy

Anna Jacobs

CORONET BOOKS
Hodder & Stoughton

Copyright © 2001 by Anna Jacobs

First published in Great Britain in 2001
by Hodder & Stoughton
A division of Hodder Headline
This edition published in 2002

The right of Anna Jacobs to be identified as the
Author of the Work has been asserted by her in accordance
with the Copyright, Designs and Patents Act 1988.

A Coronet paperback

9

A CIP catalogue record for this title
is available from the British Library

ISBN 978 0 340 74829 9

Printed and bound by Clays Ltd, Elcograf S.p.A.

Hodder & Stoughton
A division of Hodder Headline
338 Euston Road
London NW1 3BH

I'd like to dedicate this book to the memory of my Uncle Jim, who died while it was in preparation.

James Norman Heyworth of Rochdale, Lancashire, was a lovely uncle, whom I shall miss very much. I'm proud that he served his country during World War II as a Commando in the Royal Marines and I feel the whole nation owes him and men like him a debt. I shall certainly not forget him.

I'd like to thank the following people
for sharing their expertise:

Lisa Chaplin, a writer friend who generously
used her Aboriginal background and studies
to help me with Dinny and her family.

Margaret Mendelawitz, who helped me
with some of the West Australian history
and local Aboriginal information.

PROLOGUE

January 1876: Western Australia

The man they called Fiery Dan took his time, slipping quietly through the West Australian bush, taking great care to avoid any cleared land or farms, always heading south. He was used to his own company and did not feel the need to hurry. This job must be done right because if he completed it successfully, he would have the thing he craved most, the only thing he craved now – enough money to return to England.

The damned Government had brought him out here when he was little more than a lad, had ill-treated him in almost every way known to man – yet he had survived, served his sentence, learning to live quietly beneath their yoke. Eventually they had set him free, certain he had been taught his lesson.

The shadow of a smile twitched at the corners of his mouth. Oh, yes, he'd been taught his lesson well and had not cared that some of his teachers had darker skins than his own, had only cared for what they could show him: the ways of this new land, especially the uses of fire. Fire had brought him out here, rick burning to be precise, and fire would get him home again to England. And in the meantime, fire had been his revenge — as two of his former tormentors had found out.

When he had been offered this job, he had sailed round the coast to Western Australia on the same ship as his employer. He had watched the family and seen the bitterness on Mrs Docherty's face. She had not wanted to come here to Perth, poor shrew. And though Mr Docherty spoke of revenge, Dan reckoned it was only habit, something to talk about. If he had really wanted to hurt his enemies, Docherty wouldn't have waited this long. Dan hadn't.

He turned off towards the small settlement they called Brookley, travelling openly and stopping at the inn there to order a glass of ale. Good ale, it was, too. He sipped it slowly, listening and watching, then ate appreciatively the hearty meal the inkeeper's wife brought him. She had been gentry once, he could tell. Wasn't gentry any more, though, for her hands were reddened and worn with work. It pleased him greatly to have a lady like her waiting on his needs. Serve the bitch right for coming to this god-forsaken land! But he spoke to her pleasantly, drank only moderately, then went on his way armed with the knowledge he needed.

He waited three days in the whispering shadows of the forest before he acted. The homestead was built of wood, dry old wood that had stood in the sun for years, slowly turning silver-grey. If sparks started flying, it'd catch fire easily and burn beautifully, with the bright colours and fierce crackling noises Dan loved so much.

How comfortably they all lived there! Why should these folk have so much and he so little? Well, that was going to change. He didn't know what they had done to offend

2

his employer, didn't really care. All Dan cared about was the money he was to be paid.

He woke before dawn, eager to finish his task. As the summer heat beat around him, teasing sweat from his scrawny body, he sipped sparingly from the lukewarm water left in his tin canteen, hoping the sea breeze would blow strongly enough today. Bloody breezes! Fickle as women, they were. All over you one minute and gone the next.

Mid-morning he sat up, nose raised to sniff like a questing hound. The air was stirring. Was that a hint of salt in it? Yes, yes! A feral grin stretched his features briefly then faded, leaving the sullen mask with which he habitually faced the world.

The breeze began to gust more strongly, bringing cooler air from the sea, making the gum leaves whisper and rustle. This breeze often blew on hot summer afternoons, bringing the relief of cooler air after the searing heat of the morning. It would be his tool today.

Purposefully he hurried towards the place he had chosen. There he set his first fire and lit it with one of his carefully protected safety matches. The wind whipped the smoke inland and sun-dried grass just beyond the tiny pile of dried grass and twigs caught fire, then a small gum tree which turned within minutes into a flaming torch. From there the fire spread quickly to other trees.

And still the wind blew, so strongly that there was no need for him to light other fires. As the blaze grew fiercer, clumps of burning leaves broke off here and there, floating through the air as the wind, the beautiful wind, bore them eastwards.

He laughed aloud, the sound hidden by the crackling of the flames which were roaring their pleasure as they fed from the eucalyptus oil in the leaves. He could not have stopped the fire now if he had wanted. No one could. Let it burn! Let the whole damned country burn as far as he was concerned!

CHAPTER ONE

January

———◆———

Cathie stood in the shadow of a big gum tree near the lake and stared across at her mother and stepfather, on the long veranda of Lizabrook homestead. She felt a sharp pang of jealousy at how close they always seemed to be, how much they still loved one another. At eighteen, she was of an age to want a man of her own, but since she and her family lived in the depths of the Australian bush, she wasn't likely to find one. She wanted other things, too, and if she'd been a man would have found a way to become a doctor. She'd been patching up her brothers, sisters and all the family pets since she had first developed an interest in the working of the human body at the age of nine.

But women weren't allowed to become doctors. It sometimes seemed to her women weren't allowed to do anything but marry and have babies and do endless housework and washing.

Feeling even more restless than usual she walked a few paces further on, taking care to keep out of sight. She stared down at the grave of her real father. Would things have been different if Josiah Ludlam had lived? She didn't really know because her mother rarely spoke of him, but Cathie doubted it.

Picking up some twigs and gum nuts, she began to vent her frustration by hurling them into the water. She had to find a way to escape from here or she would go mad with frustration. Even the lake wasn't a real lake, she thought scornfully, but only a band of shallow water lying beside a half-cleared swamp. It could look really pretty if her stepfather ever found the time to clear the rest of the swamp, but he was always too busy. All he cared about was that the partly finished lake gave them enough water to last through the long, hot summers. They weren't gentry to need fancy gardens for parading round in. Josiah Ludlam, her father, had been gentry, though, and her mother had once said the lake had been his idea.

'In another of your black moods?' a voice teased and she turned to smile at Brendan, her childhood playmate.

He smiled back, his teeth gleaming white against his dark skin. He was very like his mother's people, as if his body refused to acknowledge the part played in his creation by his Irish father, though his next brother's skin was much paler than his.

'Don't you ever get tired of living here at Lizabrook?' Cathie demanded.

Brendan's smile faded. 'You know I do. But at least I'm treated like a human being here. The minute I leave the homestead people treat me like an animal – and a worthless one at that – because of this.' He pointed to his skin.

She reached out to squeeze his arm. They were both misfits, but it was even harder for him. Maybe that was what drew them together. She was closer to him than to

6

her half-brothers. Glancing over her shoulder to make sure they were out of sight of the homestead, she took off her shoes and rolled down her stockings. 'Let's have a paddle. It's so hot today.'

'Aren't you supposed to be helping your mother?'

Cathie shrugged. 'The housework will still be there when I get back.' It always was. Boring, dreary work, the same day after day.

Liza Caine stood on the veranda and leaned against her husband, enjoying both the feel of his arm around her shoulders and the sea breeze which had just begun to blow, bringing some welcome cooler air. Smoke was drifting across the big external kitchen where Dinny was baking bread and roasting meat, for everyone at the homestead took the main meal of the day together. If you listened carefully you could hear her friend singing one of the little Aboriginal songs that went with the various daily tasks. Dinny seemed to have a song for everything.

Liza and Benedict often stood here together for a few moments before the midday meal, chatting quietly of this and that. She and her third husband had been happy together for thirteen years now, but with five young folk about the place it was sometimes difficult for them to find time alone. Their two younger children, Josie and Harry, were still in the schoolroom with Frau Hebel. Finding the money for a governess was a strain, but they weren't close enough to a school for a daily attendance. Both of them wanted their children to be decently educated, so when a friend had told them about Ilse Hebel and said she wanted to find a position in the country, they had appointed her simply on Agnes's recommendation, and had not regretted it.

From the far side of the house came the sound of Dinny's husband, Fergal, whistling happily as he worked in the small furniture manufactory in which he and Benedict were partners and which supplemented their farming income. Sadly, this had not done as well as they'd hoped because there simply weren't enough people with spare money in the colony of Western Australia to sell to, even though the pieces were beautifully crafted and embellished with Benedict's skilled carving. And some people were such snobs they were certain colonial goods must be inferior and only wanted furniture which had been brought out from the mother country. The same people continued to talk about England as 'home', but Liza didn't feel like that. Western Australia was her home now.

Across the beige, sun-burned grass of the paddock two figures came into view, arms waving as they paused to argue about something.

'That's where Cathie's got to, is it?' Liza muttered, frowning across at her elder daughter. 'I told her to give the parlour a good bottoming today. Just wait till she gets within reach of my tongue! And wasn't Brendan supposed to be working in the vegetable garden, Benedict?'

'He was indeed. He'll never make a farm worker, that one. But he's Fergal and Dinny's problem, not ours. I only pay him day rates now for the time he actually works.' Benedict glanced down at his wife's troubled face, thinking as he often did that she looked too young and pretty to have grown-up children. 'I'm getting worried about Cathie.

8

Be honest, love. She's been causing you a lot of trouble lately, hasn't she?'

Liza sighed. On good days her daughter was energetic and lively, making everyone around her feel happy – but the good days were getting fewer and she had taken to slipping away instead of helping about the house, spending hours tramping through the woods like a truant child. If these outings had made Cathie happy, Liza would have been more tolerant of them, but lately nothing seemed to please her daughter. 'I don't know what to do with her, that's for sure,' she admitted.

'It's about time I had a word with that young madam.' Benedict silenced his wife's protest with a kiss. 'She claims she's a woman grown, but she certainly doesn't act like it.'

Liza hesitated for a moment then said quietly, 'She needs to meet people, see new things. I don't think she'll settle down otherwise. And a lass of her age needs to meet young men, too.'

Benedict made a soft exasperated sound. 'She's too young to be thinking of marriage.'

'I was carrying a child by the time I was her age,' Liza pointed out.

'Not by your own choice!' he snapped.

Liza closed her eyes as his words brought back the memories of just why she had come to Australia. Her father had wanted her to marry their neighbour, a widower of thirty-five, and when she had refused, Teddy Marshall had raped her, to make sure she would have to marry him. Only she hadn't. She'd run away to Australia instead, sailing with her former employers, the Pringles, as their maid.

On board ship she'd discovered she was pregnant and

then Josiah Ludlam had married her, wanting the child more than he wanted her, for he'd never touched her as a wife. And that child had been Cathie. Was it any wonder that with a father like Teddy Marshall Cathie wasn't an easy girl to manage? And yet she was a warm, loving girl, the first to rush and help you in times of trouble.

Liza realized Benedict had asked her something. 'Sorry, my mind was wandering.'

'I was saying we can't afford to send Cathie back to England for a visit, let alone spare someone to go with her.'

'We could if we sold some of the jewellery.' She had inherited some pretty pieces from her first husband and they must be worth something.

'We can manage without touching that. I can't leave the farm and I don't want to lose my wife for a whole year, thank you very much, and the other children need you just as much as Cathie does, especially Josie.'

'We could send her back on her own.'

'And where would she stay when she got there? I've not heard from my brothers in England since my parents died.'

She knew that hurt him. Losing touch with your family was common out here, though. 'You've got a sister in Australia. You see her and her family sometimes.'

'Once a year, if I'm lucky.' Benedict stared blindly out across the lake.

After a moment's silence Liza resumed the discussion. 'Cathie keeps asking about the Ludlams lately. Do you think we should tell her the truth about who her real father is? She wants to know why Josiah's family never try to contact her and yesterday she threatened to write to them.

Well, she knows I keep in touch with Sophia Ludlam, his mother.'

Her husband made an angry growling sound in his throat. 'Eh, that wouldn't do! Mrs Ludlam's no true connection of Cathie's, for all the lass bears their name. I think we're going to have to tell her the truth — Josiah married you to give your baby a name but played no part in fathering her. We can't go on like this, love.'

'Perhaps we should make up some tale — say it was a stranger who attacked me and left me pregnant? If she ever met her real father, it'd break her heart.' Liza shuddered. You never forgot it when a man raped you. And the older Cathie grew, the more she resembled the Marshalls, for she was a tall, sturdy girl with a strong temper and a stubborn determination to get what she wanted from life — though she could be kind, too, and had a way with children and sick people that was nothing short of miraculous. Her younger brothers and sisters adored her, as did Dinny and Fergal's children.

Fortunately, in Cathie the strong Marshall features had been softened and she had her mother's thick dark hair, not dull light brown. Liza had told her many a time that she would be pretty if she would only stop frowning at the world, but Cathie considered herself too tall and solidly built, complaining that no man would ever love a great lump like her.

'It was a lot easier when they were younger,' Benedict murmured. 'Now there's Lucas too saying he wants to see a bit of the world before he settles down, though at least he wants to see the rest of Australia, not go back to England.'

'It's easier for a young man to travel, and anyway, he's

not so *angry* at the world as she is. Lucas is very sensible. His mother would have been very proud of him, I'm sure, if she'd lived.'

He looked down at Liza indulgently and could not resist planting a kiss on her rosy cheek. 'We have a confusion of children between us, don't we, my love? One of mine, by Grace, one of yours, by Marshall, and three of our own.'

'And another of mine whom I never see.' Her voice broke as she said that, for her eldest son Francis had been taken away from her by her second husband's family, the Rawleys, and had grown up in England. His loss was an abiding sadness to her.

Benedict gave her another hug and said bracingly, 'They're a fine healthy brood, thank God, except for Josie – and even she's better this year.'

Liza hesitated, wondering whether to tell him she might be expecting another child, but decided against it. It was too early yet to be sure and she'd had false alarms before. Besides, this had taken her by surprise, and she was not yet used to the idea of becoming a mother again.

Cathie and Brendan strolled by the edge of the lake for a while longer, both reluctant to return home and face a scolding.

Suddenly he sniffed the air. 'I can smell burning. The kitchen roof hasn't caught fire again, has it?'

They both swung round and saw blue-grey smoke rising behind the house.

'Hell, that's a bush fire – and the wind's blowing it in

this direction!' Brendan was starting to run towards the house even as he spoke.

Cathie raced after him, her skirts flapping about her legs and her boots pounding the ground, the untied laces whipping from side to side.

Bush fires were the thing everyone feared most in summer. They could destroy your life in an hour.

At almost the same moment, Benedict also stopped talking in mid-sentence to sniff the air, rush round the veranda and stare at the bush behind the house. 'Oh, my God! Liza, that's a big one! Let's hope our firebreaks will keep it back.'

Even as he spoke, the sea breeze seemed to grow stronger and they heard the dreaded roaring and crackling sounds of a fire burning out of control.

He ran to the emergency bell that would summon everyone on the farm. Even before he had let go of the rope he saw Brendan and Cathie running towards him and other people coming out of the various outbuildings. They all knew what to do because Benedict made them practise at the start of every summer. So far the cleared land had protected them, but this fire had a strong sea breeze behind it and was gaining ground fast.

Under the governess's supervision Josie and Harry rushed to gather some treasured possessions and clothes, stuffing them into the sacks kept in their bedrooms for that purpose. Liza did the same for herself and Benedict, then left Ilse to shepherd her charges down to the lake. Benedict had deliberately left a small spit of land jutting out into the water when he dug out the original swamp, because like all settlers he knew the dangers of bush fires.

Dinny's two youngest children were already rushing along the edge of the lake to join them, carrying some of their own family's possessions.

Liza dumped the box containing the family's main valuables on the ground by the water's edge and cast a quick glance at the sky behind the house, horrified to see how quickly the fire was spreading. A dark haze of smoke blurred the skyline now and below it flames were shooting high, racing along the ground and leaping from treetop to treetop as well. If only the breeze would drop! She decided to bring out a few more things, just in case. 'Josie, you stay here and keep an eye on the little ones. You two boys go back to the houses and grab whatever clothes and blankets you can. Anything useful. But keep an eye on the fire.'

Josie nodded, her thin face even paler than usual. With her tendency to wheeze, it was no use her trying to do things in a hurry. Harry was already rushing back towards the house. At seven he was almost as big as she was though nearly three years younger.

A chain of people formed to swing buckets of water up from the lake while Benedict dumped their contents on the wooden shingles of the roof, for the rainwater barrels were empty at this time of year. Liza was torn between saving possessions from the house and joining the others. Benedict shouted, 'Get what you can – just in case. Ilse, you help her! Brendan, get the animals out and shepherd them towards the water.'

By the time Liza made her second journey, clutching the bulging blanket, the flames had jumped the firebreaks and were racing across the tinder-dry grass towards the farm. She heard those passing buckets utter a groan of disappointment, but they kept on working.

Within minutes one of the outbuildings had caught fire. Liza paused to stare at it with tears in her eyes, then followed Ilse, the governess determinedly back into the house.

When Fergal moved towards the blazing building, Benedict yelled, 'Leave it to burn! Brendan, go with your father and see what you can rescue from the workshop. But be careful!' There was glue inside, which would fuel the fire, and piles of sawn wood were set out nearby to season. He didn't feel optimistic about their chances of saving much of that if this wind kept blowing so strongly, but perhaps some of the finished pieces of furniture and tools might be carried to safety. He went to pass buckets, standing in line next to his son Seth, the son who also thought Josiah was his father but who had none of Cathie's intensity and always said cheerfully that Benedict was his 'real' father as far as he was concerned, since he couldn't remember Josiah.

They held the fire at bay for over an hour, breaking line at Benedict's orders to beat out smaller blazes in the straw-like grass of summer. Fergal and his son managed to carry out the finished pieces of furniture and expensive tools from the workshop, stacking them on the little spit of land where the children were installed with a jumble of possessions. Even there they were keeping watch with buckets of water, standing ready to tip over anything which caught light from the sparks whirling everywhere.

By now smoke had turned the sunny day into a false

twilight and people were choking and coughing as they toiled frantically.

When the far end of the workshop suddenly burst into flames, Benedict groaned aloud and Liza sobbed. She knew how hard he had worked to develop the small furniture-making business so that they would not be totally at the mercy of the weather and the farm yield.

The whole workshop was soon burning fiercely, adding black and acrid smoke to the grey woodsmoke. Cathie ripped up a sheet, soaking the pieces in the lake and bringing them to people to tie across their mouths, for hot air burned harshly in the throat. Faces lost their identity as they became smoke-blackened. All they could think of were the buckets, heavy with water, tugging at their shoulders one after another.

As the fire approached the homestead itself, Liza went to join the line of those passing buckets. She found herself working side by side with her daughter and marvelled at Cathie's strength, for her own arms were aching and heavy. When she dropped a whole bucketful, she moved out of the line, panting, knowing she had to take a break for a moment or two.

Dinny and Fergal's house was closer to the fire. It seemed to catch light all of a sudden and be engulfed in flames within minutes. Liza saw Dinny stand still for a moment, rigid with pain, then move back into line with her lips pressed tightly together. Her heart ached for her friend, ached for them all.

Before Liza could move into the bucket line again, Benedict came and tugged her arm, saying hoarsely, 'It's no use, love. Our house has caught fire at the other side. We'll move out what furniture we can from this end, then we must retreat to the lake and leave it to burn.'

Liza stared at him blankly for a moment before the meaning of his words sank in. She saw the anguish in his eyes and knew it was mirrored in her own, then he turned to Cathie and said, 'Take your mother to safety, love. She's exhausted.' Even before he had finished speaking, he had turned to check that everyone else was all right, counting heads with a sooty finger, then leading the way towards the house.

Liza shook her head at her daughter, who was pulling her towards the water, and drove back the tears and momentary weakness with anger. 'I'm all right. I'm going to help carry things out.' She moved towards the house before anyone could try to stop her, following her son Seth inside.

People staggered past, carrying whatever came to hand from the smoke-filled interior, dumping their burdens near the water and then running back inside.

But after only a few journeys, the heat from the blazing end of the house was so intense, and the smoke inside so thick, that Benedict shouted to them to stop and take refuge near the water. He counted heads again and nodded in relief to find all accounted for. Neither he nor Liza would ever forget that her first husband, Josiah Ludlam, had been killed by a falling beam in another house fire — killed saving Cathie's life.

Liza wept openly as she stood there watching everything they had worked so hard for being devoured by the flames, which seemed to dance through the blackness of the smoke as if mocking the watchers with their searing power. As Cathie put an arm round her, Liza noticed paler stripes down her daughter's smoke-blackened face. It took her a moment to realise they were tear marks. She felt exhausted now, so leaned on the strong young arm, standing in the middle of a silent group of people.

Moving like an old man, Benedict came to join them. He nodded to Cathie. 'You've done well, lass.' Then he bent his head to kiss Liza's dirty cheek. 'I'll build you a new home, love. I promise.'

She forced back the tears. 'We'll build it together.'

Then they could only hold on to each other and watch their home burn to the ground. Ilse stood beside Josie, shocked to the core by what had happened, for she too had lost many of her possessions.

By sheer chance the fire only went round the southern part of the lake. To the north the cleared farmland inter-rupted its mad race until – too late to help the Caines – the sea breeze dropped. The swampy ground to the south had also slowed the flames' advance, but by then all the buildings that had made up Lizabrook homestead were reduced to ashes.

Lucas was the only member of the family missing and they were worried he might have got caught by the fire on his way home from Mandurah. There was no way to tell, no way to move through the burnt land till the layers of ash had cooled down.

'Lucas is a sensible chap. He'll be all right,' Benedict said, as much to reassure himself as Liza.

As night fell people slept on what they could, staying near the lake for safety. Benedict and Fergal took it in turns to keep watch, just in case a stray spark set the northern side of the lake afire.

The following morning Dinny and Brendan went to check the land which she and her son knew better than anyone. She might not have been born here, she might have Irish as well as Aboriginal blood, but she had put strong roots down and considered this her place now – and was equally sure it had accepted her, as had the Aboriginal tribe whose land it was.

They found that the main fire had burned out, though the ground was still hot in patches and the occasional tree trunk still smouldering. Everyone at Lizabrook homestead gathered to work out what to do and they were a solemn group, conscious of how very much they had lost. There was a grimness to Benedict's face that had not been there before.

Liza felt numb and disoriented. Once she looked at the governess and saw Ilse staring into the distance, tears welling in her eyes. 'It's a harsh land,' Liza said softly.

'I hadn't realised how quickly it could happen,' Ilse admitted.

'How much did you manage to save?'

'Most of my clothes and my books. Also the photographs of my family.'

'That's something, then.'

Benedict announced, 'We can start rebuilding almost immediately if we can get some sawn timber from Mandurah. We'll make mud bricks this time for the walls. They don't burn as easily. The new house will have to be smaller at first, I'm afraid.' He looked at the governess. 'I hope you'll still stay with us, Ilse?'

'Of course I will. And help in any way I can as we rebuild.'

Liza hugged her, then she and the governess set to work moving the pieces of furniture that had been saved to the shade of the few trees left standing in irregular groups near the water, covering the better pieces with what blankets and sacking remained.

'We'd just stocked up the provision shed with sacks of flour,' Liza mourned later as she worked with Dinny to take stock of the food that had been saved. 'Now it's all wasted.'

'Do you not have fire insurance?' Ilse asked.

Liza shook her head blindly. 'No. They don't insure places like this. You just look after yourselves.' Then she went back to work.

Benedict's oldest son, Lucas, appeared mid-morning from the direction of Mandurah, followed a short time later by some of their neighbours from Brookley. Liza burst into tears of sheer relief that he was still alive, for he was as dear to her as her own children.

Cathie, who had been watching her mother and worrying about how strained she looked, made her sit down on one of the chairs they'd saved.

'I'm sorry,' Liza gulped. 'It's just – I'm having another child and I always get t-tearful—'

Benedict overheard her and came striding across to kneel beside her and cradle her in his arms. 'What a way to tell us!' He turned to gaze at the blackened ruin of the home he had built with his own hands, adding quietly, 'And anyway, who does not want to weep today?'

Fifty miles away in Perth, Christina Docherty paced up and down the veranda of the house they had rented, waiting for her husband to return from a meeting in town. Her sons started shouting at one another nearby and she stood still for a moment to frown in their direction, then shrugged and left the governess to settle the fight.

When she saw Dermott striding back up the street, she jumped off the veranda and rushed to greet him, careless of her dignity. 'You've been gone for ages!' she complained, linking her arm in his. 'Did that man turn up?'

'Yes.' He grinned slyly. 'And I'm sorry to tell you my sister Liza's farm was burnt out by a bush fire.'

'Good. Now we can sort out our own lives. I'm fed up of living in this hovel.' She had never understood this stupid obsession of her husband's with getting revenge on his sister. To her mind, what had happened had been an accident and Niall Docherty a lout who deserved all he got. She had only met him once, when he came to her mother's inn, but that had been enough to take his measure. Dermott had always followed his brother's lead. The two of them had come to Australia, hoping to get money out of their sister's rich husband, and Niall had been about to rape Dinny when Liza shot him, as far as Christina could make out. Serve him right. She'd shoot someone who tried to rape her, too. But of course she didn't say that to her husband, who still idolised his brother's memory.

Dermott put his arm round her. 'Well, we'll be moving soon, though not back to England. I thought we'd spend some time at that farm I bought cheaply. It's closer than I'd realised to my dear sister's homestead.' He frowned. What if he'd burned his own property along with hers?

She looked at him in horror. 'Dermott Docherty, have you run mad? I thought you were just going to sell that place and make a nice little profit! You don't know the first thing about farming and I certainly don't want to live in the country, least of all here in Western Australia. I married you to *escape* all that!' She had been horrified when her father forced the Pringle family to emigrate to Australia. Her mother had made the best of it, but then Dorothy Pringle had always made the best of things throughout her unhappy marriage. Christina despised her for that. As for her father, he had lost all their money with his stupid schemes. No wonder she'd run away with Dermott.

'Well, I hadn't realised it was just down the road from Lizabrook. I swore when Niall died that I'd make my sister pay and—'

'She has paid! She's lost her home. Surely that's enough?' Even though Kitty had hated Liza, who had made all the eligible men fall for her, she didn't wish her any more ill.

He scowled at her. 'Might be enough. Might not. Anyway it won't hurt for me an' Matthieu to live fairly quietly for a year or two, and I fancy trying the life of a country gentleman. I can always sell the place later.'

She moved away from him, close to tears. When he set his mind on something he was bull-headed about it and she'd learned to fear his sudden whims. 'We're living quietly enough here in Perth, Dermott. I can't believe how small this place is and how backward compared to Melbourne. I don't call this a capital city! And the Australian countryside isn't like England, you know.'

'We'll do things my way, Christina!'

'I don't see why we have to stick with Matthieu Correntin, either. We don't need him any more. We've enough money now to live like gentry in England."

There was an edge of steel in his voice as Dermott answered, 'A bit more never hurts. I want to be really rich when we eventually go back to England and Matthieu's both clever and useful.' In fact, if Dermott had heeded his business partner's advice he'd never have had to leave Melbourne, something he regretted as much as his wife after spending a few weeks in a backwater like Perth – though he wasn't going to give her the satisfaction of telling her so.

Realising they were standing in the middle of the street arguing and that a neighbour was approaching, he muttered, 'Say hello to Mrs Fenton. She may be short of money, but she's still got some useful connections.'

Christina took a deep breath and turned to smile at their neighbour, who was taking the air dressed in her widow's black. 'And how are you today, Mrs Fenton?'

'I'm well, thank you.' Agnes started to move on.

Dermott said quickly, 'Perhaps you'd like to join us for a cup of tea to hear our news, Mrs F.? We've just bought ourselves a farm.'

'Another time, perhaps, Mr Docherty. It's a year since my husband died and I'm off to town to buy something a little lighter than unrelieved black. In fact,' Agnes looked down and grimaced, 'I don't think I'm even going into half-mourning. I've had enough of dark colours.' With a nod of her head, she walked briskly on.

As she passed a shop window, Agnes glanced at her own reflection with approval. She might be approaching fifty, but she had retained her figure and her health was still good.

Catching sight of a friend in the distance she hurried along the street, eager to chat. She was so bored with living alone! And with being a widow. What she needed was a man, both to support her and to share her bed. She had debated going back to England, but did not fancy living on her son-in-law's charity or even that of her son in Sydney. Besides, she'd have more chance of finding another husband here in Australia than in England because women were still in short supply – though this time she'd be a bit more careful. Her late husband had been a spendthrift and latterly a drunkard as well.

She needed to find someone else before what was left of her money ran out.

In Lancashire Magnus Hamilton went to see the doctor after tea on Friday evening to talk about his mother, whose behaviour was growing increasingly strange and who had recently taken to wandering the house at night, disturbing everyone's sleep.

Clifford Barnes, an earnest man in his late-forties with a reputation for caring about all his patients, rich or poor, showed Magnus into his consulting room, looked at the younger man sympathetically and gestured to him to sit down. He eased himself into his big comfortable chair behind the ornate mahogany desk, hesitated for a moment then said what he had to say bluntly because he knew of no way to soften this type of bad news. 'I'm afraid your mother is suffering from softening of the brain, which has led to a degeneration of the mental faculties. It – um – happens to some older folk.' He sighed and added, 'Regrettably, there is nothing medical science can do to help.'

Magnus stared down at the dark red carpet with its pattern of squares and lozenges, struggling to come to terms with this, his thoughts fragmenting and twisting away from the dreadful news. He had often wished he could afford a carpet as soft as this for his mother's swollen, aching feet to tread on. He had wished to do all sorts of things for her, because Janey Hamilton had been a good mother to them all, but although he earned an adequate living as foreman in the workshop of Ludlam's cotton mill, he had little put by. Since his father's death when he was eighteen years old, he had had to support his three brothers, sister and mother, so there had never been enough coming in for luxuries like fancy carpets.

He'd been foolish to indulge in such dreams! Should have grown out of that by now. He'd grown out of just about everything else – his own plans for finding a wife and having children, his desire to better himself, his love of learning. He had enough on his plate just surviving at the moment.

He looked down at his long legs, remembering the way he had grown out of his clothes so quickly in the years of his youth, until he reached his present height of six foot four inches. That had given them extra expense, for it cost more to find clothing that would cover his tall, spare frame decently. You couldn't buy suitable things from the second-hand clothes shop, but had to have them made specially. His mother had gone without new clothes for years in order that he be decently clad for work. He'd known that and been unable to do anything about it, for it was his wages that kept them all.

When Dr Barnes cleared his throat, Magnus realised

he'd been lost in his own thoughts and squared his shoulders to ask, 'What's going to happen to her, then? I mean – what can we expect?'

'I'm sorry to have to tell you that she'll grow more and more vague and will gradually lose the ability to care for herself. She'll have to be looked after like a helpless baby in the end. And that may happen quite quickly or slowly. One can never predict.'

'Oh, God!' For a few moments, Magnus buried his face in his hands and fought against his emotions.

'I can arrange for her to be taken into the Benevolent Home. They treat the poor creatures in their care pretty decently, I promise you, not like the old days. We're more enlightened about such things nowadays.' And the Ben was no longer dependent on the Ludlam family's grudging charity. The days of men, even millowners, acting as if they owned a town and its inhabitants, body and soul, were past.

'I'd never put her in there!' Magnus didn't even pause to consider it. His mother hated the Ben and had always tried to avoid even walking past it. The poor inmates who were not violent sat outside in the sun on fine days, their faces usually blank, and from inside there was always the sound of the ones who were really bad, moaning and screaming, especially when the moon was full. He would not confine his mother to a place like that for her final days, however sad her mental state. 'We'll continue to care for her at home, thank you, doctor. We'll manage somehow.'

Dr Barnes nodded. A decent fellow, Magnus Hamilton. Scottish originally, but the family had lived here in Pendleworth for many years. He'd always had a fancy that Magnus must have Viking blood in his ancestry, such a giant of a man he was with that bright red-gold hair. A woman would make the most of such hair, but Magnus cropped it as short as was decent and shaved his face too, as if he didn't want to be bothered with his appearance, though most men were wearing at least a moustache these days if not a full beard. The doctor let silence hang between them for a few seconds longer, then said simply, 'As you choose, Magnus. But the offer will always be open. People with your mother's affliction can be very difficult to care for towards the end.'

Magnus walked slowly home feeling sick to his soul. He hadn't needed a doctor to tell him something was dreadfully wrong. They'd been hiding his mother's vagaries for a year or two now and his sister Mairi had had to give up her job at the Emporium to care for her, though she had loved serving the customers and seeing half the town pass through the big haberdashery and fabrics shop. It was she who had insisted on calling in the doctor, saying she'd never forgive herself if they didn't try everything they could.

When he got home Magnus could hardly bear to look at his mother, who was sitting rocking quietly in front of the fire while his sister set the table, her expression grim.

'She's been bad again, today,' Mairi said abruptly. Her mother had pulled the tablecloth off, though luckily there had not been much on it, and then cast it aside to begin moving her hand backwards and forwards over the wood as if she were sandpapering it. When Mairi had tried to stop her, knowing that she would rub until her hand was raw, Janey had thrown a temper tantrum that had left them both exhausted. Sometimes Mairi felt she could not bear another day like this.

'Where's Hamish?' Magnus did not want to tell his news twice.

'Out at the Working Men's Institute.' Mairi hesitated, then added, 'Someone's giving a talk about Australia.'

The words burst out before Magnus could stop them. 'Not him as well!'

She shrugged. Not for her to fight her younger brother's battles. If Hamish was determined to emigrate, nothing she said would make any difference. It hadn't when their other brothers set their minds on Canada. 'What did the doctor say about Mum?'

Magnus glanced towards the rocking figure. 'I'll tell you later.'

'She doesn't understand what we're talking about now, you know.'

'She does sometimes so I'd rather wait. I don't want to upset her.'

'Then I'll tell you my news instead.' Mairi took a deep breath. 'Magnus, Elwyn Bebb at chapel has – well, he's asked me to walk out with him.'

'And you want to?'

She nodded vigorously. 'Aye, I do.'

'Then I'm glad for you.' But he could not prevent himself from feeling envious, though he tried not to show it. After all, Mairi was twenty-six, some might have said a confirmed spinster by now, and she was needed at home – desperately. If she married, how would he look after his mother? Well, time to worry about that when it happened. Mairi deserved some happiness. It had been hard for her these past two years. 'I *am* glad for you.' He went over and gave her a cracking great hug.

Afterwards she held him at arm's length and studied his face. 'Why don't you find yourself a lassie, Magnus?'

He shook his head, eyes going to his mother. 'What have I to offer anyone now but hard work? It's getting *you* down and she's your mother. How could we ask a stranger to live like this?'

Mairi leaned against him for a moment. 'You're a wonderful brother, Magnus, and a caring son. You'd make a good father.' She glanced up, seeing that grim expression return to his face. He seemed to have forgotten how to smile lately. She could remember him a few years ago, before their mother had started to grow vague and forgetful. How lively he had been then, in spite of the hard work! Always the one to lead a sing-song with his clear baritone voice. Going down to the Institute to hear a lecture on anything and everything, so eager was he for knowledge. And now? Now he spent his time mainly at home in the evenings. Oh, he still borrowed books from the library and still tramped across the moors occasionally on fine Sundays, something that he had always loved doing, but he was a quieter, sadder man.

First their brother Athol, always the adventurous one, had left the country and gone across the sea to Canada, then his twin, Dougal, had followed him, unable to live without his brother, though the two of them had parted in anger.

With each departure Magnus had grown a little quieter. Now, Hamish was talking of Australia and she — she had fallen in love with a plump little man with a heart of gold, whose kindness shone out of his face, and was hoping desperately that he loved her, too. Elwyn had asked her out walking, talked of going to the lantern show at church the following week, smiled at her warmly whenever they met and lingered to chat to her. Surely . . .

She shook away those thoughts. 'I'll make you a cup of tea, shall I?' Raising her voice, she added more loudly, 'Mum? Would you like a cup of tea as well?'

Once their mother would have jumped up and insisted on making it herself, now she just stared at them blankly as if she didn't understand the question. It was heartrending to see the changes in her.

Mairi looked at Magnus, her eyes brimming with tears, and saw that his eyes were over-bright, too.

CHAPTER TWO

January

———◆———

Fiery Dan returned to Brookley a week later with Mr Docherty, who insisted on covertly checking that the job had been done properly before he paid. Dan was delighted to see that the Caines' house had burnt to the ground, as had all the outbuildings. He glanced sideways at his employer, standing next to him behind the sturdy trunk of a huge gum tree. A man might expect a compliment or a thank you for a job well done, but he received no praise of any sort. Typical of rich folk. Never appreciated anything, they didn't.

'I burnt it down for you, then,' he prompted.

Dermott didn't even hear him. As he scowled at the busy scene before him, he was annoyed to see how many of their possessions his sister's family had managed to save and how quickly they were rebuilding the farm. Pieces of furniture stood under trees, covered in strips of bark or layers of branches to keep the sun off them. Beside the lake two men were busy making mud bricks, with many rows of them already standing in the sun to harden. 'Will nothing stop that damned Benedict Caine?' he muttered.

Dan sniggered. 'He thinks brick houses are safe, don't

he? Well, they burn too, because they've got wooden floors and roof timbers. Just need a bit more help to get started.'

As he had proved more than once.

Dermott ignored his remark. 'See that big pile of furniture over there, under the rough shelter?'

As he pointed one meaty finger, Dan nodded.

'Can you set it alight?'

'Easy.'

'Good. Do it then, as soon as it gets a bit darker. The big fire could have been an accident. I want this one to look deliberate so they'll start worrying about who's after them.' He poked Dan in the ribs. 'I'll go and look at that farm I bought hereabouts another time. Once that stuff's blazing we'll head back to Perth. You've earned your money. I've got a berth booked for you in five days' time under the name of John Roberts. I'll see you to the ship myself. And make sure you keep your mouth shut about all this. If I hear you've been talking to anyone . . .'

A week after the bush fire the biggest of the temporary shelters went up in flames just after nightfall. Benedict had been strolling by the water with his eldest son, Lucas, and quickly reached it, yelling for help. They both began dragging out the things stored there. Benedict let out a startled exclamation as a burning piece of the bark they'd used to make a temporary roof fell across his head but Lucas knocked it away quickly.

People came running with buckets of water and the flames were soon doused. Not much had been damaged.

'Now how the hell did that start?' Fergal wondered.

'There's only one way,' Benedict said grimly. 'It's nowhere near our cooking fire so someone must have set light to it deliberately.'

There was a gasp behind him and Liza came to clutch his arm, gripping him so tightly he could feel her fingernails digging in. 'Surely not?' Her voice had a pleading tone to it. 'Oh, Benedict, surely not?'

'I'm afraid so, love.' He raised his voice. 'We'll keep watch tonight. Everyone is to stay away from this shed. I want to examine the ground round it once it's daylight.'

Cathie was furious when her father refused to let any of the women help keep watch. After a short, sharp argument, she flung off to her makeshift bed in the rough shelter where all the family slept at night.

She lay down beside her little sister. It was always like that, she thought. She was bigger and stronger than many men but they wouldn't let her do anything interesting.

Josie reached over to cuddle her. 'Don't be mad, Cathie. You're always mad at something lately.'

She returned the cuddle. 'Not at you, chicken, never at you.'

'I know you want to go away.'

'Do you, indeed?'

'Yes, but I don't want you to.'

'Ah, Josie lovie, I'll go mad if I have to spend my whole life here in the bush. I want to meet people, see different things. I *need* to!'

She cuddled her little sister till Josie feel asleep and tried yet again to work out how to get away. It was England that called to her, the land her parents seemed happy to have left. She wanted to see the lively bustling Lancashire towns they had described, live close to other people, have something to see besides trees.

One day she'd find a way to get what she wanted. She was quite determined on that, whatever her mother said.

In the morning Dinny spent a long time checking the ground near the hut with her son Brendan. Like his mother and her people, he was at home with the ways of nature – unlike his younger brother, who was more concerned with furniture-making and seemed happy with a quiet life at the homestead.

'Someone with worn boots stood here.' Dinny pointed to marks in the dry sandy soil. She moved around the perimeter of the hut, pointing out this and that. Her mother had taught her enough about her people's ways to help her understand the messages the earth carried. 'Then he went off that way.' She pointed.

'Can you follow him?' Benedict asked.

'We can try, but it's probably too dry and if he's careful how he goes, we'll soon lose him. I'm not an experienced tracker.'

She was right. But before they lost the trail, they did find a place where horses had recently been tethered and where two people had stood, one of them a heavy man, one the man with worn boots who had set the first fire. They followed the horse tracks till they came to the main road to Perth, then lost them in the churned-up ground left by an ox wagon.

When they got back Benedict went to sit beside his wife on one of the rough benches he'd cobbled together after the fire, clasping her hand in his.

'Do you really think this fire was deliberately set?' she asked, sharing the thoughts that had kept her awake half the night.

'Undoubtedly.'

She shook her head in bewilderment. 'I can't imagine anyone who would hate us so much.' Then she remembered her brother Dermott's vow of revenge. No, surely even he would not do this to her?

'Neither can I. But I'm going to teach all the children to shoot from now on, even Josie. We've only got ourselves to rely on out here.' His lips twisted a little as he added, 'I hope that will cheer Cathie up a bit.'

But nothing seemed able to cheer her up now that the immediate crisis of the fire was over. As the weather was still quite warm they were living in rough bush shelters till the new house was built – and it would be a much smaller house than before. Cathie would have to share a bedroom with Josie, which meant she wouldn't be able to read in bed or even sit with the lamp on mending her clothes, enjoying her own company, because Josie wasn't strong and needed her sleep. And to add to Cathie's woes, most of their books had been burned. Though there had been nothing she hadn't read a dozen times before, still she missed them.

She confronted her stepfather about the situation as the new house took shape. 'Are we going to build a proper house again, or will this be it?' She waved a scornful hand towards the foundations of the new building.

'We can't do much else for a year or two. We lost quite a bit in the fire and it'll take us some time to recover from that.' He'd had to go up to Perth to sell one of Liza's pieces of jewellery even to do this, something he hated. They had considered letting Ilse go, but decided the children's education was more important than a bigger house — for the time being, anyway. But he intended to be careful with every penny and to see that his family were equally frugal.

Cathie scowled at the ground. 'I thought life here at Lizabrook couldn't get much worse, but it has.'

He looked at her sternly. 'You're behaving like a spoiled brat.'

'Maybe that's because you always treat me like a child,' she snapped back. 'Or a servant. I'm fit for nothing but housework, it seems. The boys have the furniture-making or the farm, while I have nothing to do but wash the same clothes week in, week out, or cook and clear up. I sometimes think I'll go mad stuck out here.' People did go mad from loneliness in the bush. Cabin fever, they called it. You read of it in the newspapers, which arrived at irregular intervals from Perth, passed round the small settlement by their old friend Dorothy Bennett at the inn, who had once been Dorothy Pringle, her mother's employer.

'We just have to make the best of things, Cathie,' he said quietly but with an edge to his voice.

'It's *your* best we're working for. This sort of life is not what I want for myself.'

'I'm your father and I'll decide what's best for you.'

'You're not even my real father. And you can't keep me prisoner here for ever! I won't *let* you. I'll find a way to escape — you'll see.'

He had promised Liza not to lose his temper again with their troublesome daughter, so he bit back the hasty words and strode away.

Cathie watched him go, already ashamed of her taunt for

he had always treated her just like his own children. But she was too upset to apologise now. Her life was being wasted, absolutely wasted. How would she ever find a husband stuck out here?

It wasn't that she didn't love her family. She did. But she'd seen spinsters who'd sacrificed themselves for their families, toiling until they died with nothing that was really their own. There was such a one living in Brookley, a pleasant, faded woman at the beck and call of her ageing parents, helping with her brother's children when they were ill, never seeming to do anything for herself, never looking happy and fulfilled as Cathie's mother had looked before the fire.

'I won't let that happen to me,' she vowed. 'I won't.'

A week later, in her desperation and loneliness, Cathie tried once more to persuade her mother to send her to England to visit her father's family. 'Don't you have any money left from selling that brooch? I'll go steerage. I won't mind the hardship. Anything would be better than this life. Surely Mrs Ludlam would let me stay with her for a little while? Next time you write you could ask her, just till I'd found a job in service or work in a shop — I'd do *anything*.'

'No! The Ludlams wouldn't even consider having you.'

Cathie stared, surprised at how sharp her mother's voice was. 'You always say that, but you never say why not. Yet when you read Mrs Ludlam's letters to us, she's always hoping you'll go and visit her one day.'

'She isn't the one with the power in that family. Josiah's brother is, and he's just like his father.' As her daughter stared at her in puzzlement, Liza added, 'When your father quarrelled with his family, they cast him off completely and made it plain they didn't want to see him again – ever. I took you back to England with me after I married Nicholas Rawley and Saul Ludlam behaved very badly towards us. You can never trust the Ludlam men and I don't want you going near them. They're still rich and powerful.'

Though she hoped things had improved since the time Josiah's father had found out that Cathie and Seth were not his son's children, and that Liza wanted to take them back to Australia. He had threatened to have her shut away in a mental asylum to prevent people from finding out. She had never forgotten that terrifying night when Saul had locked her in the stables and Benedict had rescued her. Even then they would not have got the children away if Sophia Ludlam hadn't stood up to her husband on their behalf. But since Liza had never told Cathie that Josiah wasn't her father, she could not tell her about all that now. She was sure it would upset her daughter to find out that her real father was a man called Teddy Marshall and that she was the result of a rape.

Cathie realised suddenly that her mother was avoiding her eyes and smoothing her apron over and over again. 'You're not telling me the truth,' she accused. 'There's something else. What is it? What's the real reason you're keeping me here? If you can't find the money, I'll sell my gold locket to pay for the fare.' She seized her mother's arm and shook it slightly, trying to make her understand. 'Please, I *have to* get away from here.'

Liza chose her words with care. 'I'm not telling you everything I will admit, love, but I'm telling you as much as I can. There are other people's feelings to consider as well as your own.' Cathie's arrival in Pendleworth might still trigger a scandal. Liza's first husband had not been like other men and had been her husband in name only, but he had given her and her bastard child respectability – and then died saving Cathie's life. Let him and his secrets rest in peace.

When her daughter continued to stare at her pleadingly, Liza said crisply, 'Please don't go on about it. You know we're going to be short of money for some time. Besides, you can't go halfway round the world on your own and I certainly couldn't go with you at the moment, even if I wanted to, which I don't.' She glanced down at her stomach which was beginning to show her condition.

'I could perfectly well go on my own,' Cathie pleaded. 'I'm eighteen not twelve, and I'm not exactly a helpless little flower.' She looked down at herself disparagingly, wishing yet again that she were not so strongly built. 'Besides, you've told me how carefully single women are supervised on the ships, so I'd be quite safe once I was on board. And after I'd arrived I could catch a train to Pendleworth.' She had never even seen a train but she had read of them. Everyone travelled round England on them, it seemed, so it couldn't be all that difficult to use them.

When her mother didn't answer Cathie let go of her arm and took a step backwards. 'You're just making excuses.' She laughed harshly. 'It's not only the convicts who got transported to Australia, you know. You've done it to me as well. But I'm *not* going to stay here for ever and I'm *not* marrying a farmer. I'll find a way to escape, you see if I don't.'

'When you love someone you don't mind where you live as long as you're with him,' Liza said softly. 'And I definitely don't want you to marry anyone you don't love. That's not,' she shuddered, 'at all comfortable.'

Cathie stared at her in shock. 'Didn't you love my father?'

'No!' It was out before Liza could stop herself.

'Why not?'

'I can't tell you.' Her voice softened. 'Please, Cathie darling, try to be satisfied with what you've got – you know we all love you.'

Why would they never tell her anything? Cathie's eyes strayed to her mother's swelling belly, to the hands that were cradling it unconsciously. 'You don't care where you live because you're besotted with your husband. Well, I think it's disgusting, a woman your age having more children. Haven't you got enough between you by now? If you had fewer children, you'd have more money to spare and—'

'*How dare you speak to your mother like that?*' a voice roared behind her.

Cathie turned round, stiffening, and fell silent.

'Apologise at once!' Benedict demanded.

'Sorry, Mother.' But she said it in an indifferent tone which left them in no doubt that she didn't mean it. Then she looked from one to the other, putting one hand to her mouth to hold back the sobs, and ran out of the tiny new house into the bush where no one would see her weeping.

Liza tried not to let her own tears show because she knew that would upset Benedict, but she cried easily when she was carrying a child and they spilled over anyway.

He came over to put his arms round her, making soothing sounds and kissing her forehead. 'I'm going to have a long talk with that young woman. And *you*, madam wife, are going to stop working so hard and rest more. You've been looking very drawn and weary lately.'

'I am a bit tired,' she admitted. 'I think we all are, Cathie as well. It's been a difficult few months. And she works very hard, for all her defiant talk. I don't know what I'd do without her.' Even Benedict had changed since the fire, grown grumpy and was always working too hard. Liza was worried about him as well as their daughter. When he drew her over to the shade of a tree and made her sit down on a stool there, she let him because it made him sit down, too.

'I blame myself.' He clasped her hand in his, patting it absent-mindedly. 'We'd not be in this position if I'd cleared bigger firebreaks. Before next summer I'm going to clear enough ground to make certain we're quite safe from fires.'

She leaned against him. 'Oh, Benedict, love, we've been over all that. You'd taken better precautions than anyone else in the district. It was just hard luck that there was a fire on such a windy day.'

'After the second fire we both know there's a good chance the first one was lit deliberately and one day I'll find out why. We won't be burnt out again. I'll make damned sure of that.'

She sighed. He had already cleared everything for a full two hundred yards beyond the new house and makeshift workshop, and was talking of clearing more. She missed having the bush nearby, for she loved to wander among the rustling, whispering gum trees when she had a few minutes free from her daily chores. But she hadn't told him that.

At bedtime Liza heard voices and paused outside the girls' tiny makeshift bedroom. Through the doorway, which had only a sacking curtain for a door, she could see Josie curled up against Cathie, with the older girl telling her little sister a story. She stayed watching her daughters for a moment, listening to the strong young voice spinning its story of magic and fairies, and the soft exclamations and questions with which Josie punctuated the story. With a smile Liza crept away again.

'I don't understand that girl,' she whispered to Benedict later as they lay in bed in the next room to the girls. 'If there's an emergency she's a tower of strength. Josie's not been feeling well lately – she always gets these breathless attacks when it's dusty like this – and suddenly Cathie's marvellous with her. And did you see her when Brendan cut his foot?' She burrowed against her husband for a moment, enjoying the feel of Benedict's hand stroking her hair, his big strong body against hers. 'Maybe we're wrong to keep Cathie here. Maybe we should help her get away for a while, even if it's only to Perth. Do you think Agnes would have her for a few days?'

'Does she deserve it? Even a short visit would cost money we can ill afford.'

'We can't afford to grow estranged from our daughter, either,' said Liza sadly. 'It's tearing me apart to see her so unhappy, Benedict love. Please, let's see if we can arrange something. It need not cost too much and there's a bit left from the brooch.'

Because he loved her and could deny her nothing he let her write to Agnes Fenton, who had travelled out to

Australia on the same ship and had remained their friend.

When Agnes wrote back saying she'd be delighted to have Cathie for a visit, Benedict agreed to take the girl and her luggage up to Perth in the cart.

Liza put the letter away and called Cathie over. 'Come for a walk by the lake, love. I've got some good news for you.'

Cathie shrugged and fell into step beside her, not at all convinced that her mother's idea of good news would be the same as hers.

'How would you like to spend a few weeks in Perth with Agnes while your father is finishing building the house?'

Cathie stopped dead, staring at her in disbelief, then swallowed hard. 'Oh, Mum! Do you really mean that?'

'Of course I do.'

Cathie threw her arms round her much smaller mother, weeping and laughing at the same time, then swept her round in a clumsy dance across the sandy ground near the lake.

'It was the right thing to do,' Liza told Benedict that night in bed.

'She was certainly sunny-tempered at dinner.'

'We've been wrong keeping her here. Farming is our life, not hers. If only . . .' She sighed.

'If only what?'

'If only there was someone in England she could go to.'

'I wouldn't let her.'

'Benedict, you can't mean that!'

'Oh, can't I? Look, love, she'd only stir up old trouble if she went to England. And do you really want to risk her meeting her real father?'

His voice had risen without his realising it and Cathie stiffened as the words echoed clearly in the stillness of the night. *Real father!* Did that mean Josiah Ludlam wasn't her father — and that her real father was still alive? How was that possible?

She lay straining her ears, for the thin walls of the temporary shelter were made only of hessian, and heard her mother say, 'No. Never that.'

Benedict's deep voice rumbled on, 'Then let's hope she'll be content with the trip to Perth, because it's all she's getting.'

Their voices fell to whispers again. Cathie lay awake for a long time, trying to take in what she had overheard. She felt like demanding to know who her real father was, but her step-father's voice had had that stubborn edge to it as he spoke that all his children recognised. That tone meant he would not be moved from what he had decided was best for her — and he took his fatherly duties very seriously.

So how, Cathie wondered, could she find out about her real father? Excitement hummed through her. Surely he would want to see her? And she certainly wanted to meet him. What harm could there be in that? Did he know about her or had her mother kept her existence a secret? She frowned as that thought brought another question. Why had Josiah Ludlam married her mother if she was already carrying someone else's child? Had he known Cathie wasn't his? Was that why they refused even to consider asking Sophia Ludlam to let her stay?

Who else could she ask about this? Mrs Bennett? Cathie considered their neighbour and sighed. No, Dorothy was her mother's friend, for all she was so much older, and would not go against Liza's wishes. She was another person who seemed content to live quietly, keeping the small inn and shop in nearby Brookley. Though she always looked sad when she spoke of her runaway daughter. She didn't even know whether Kitty was alive or dead, but clung to the hope that she'd see her again one day. Her second husband was a quiet man who was a cobbler and jack of many trades. He made and mended shoes, though some of the women got their fancier shoes from Perth. He grew vegetables for the inn, brewed the beer and helped his wife, seeming to have no ambitions beyond reading voraciously anything that came his way. He ran a small lending library, too, charging a penny to borrow a book for a month – or swapping book loans for other goods or services needed at the inn, because ready cash was always in short supply among the struggling settlers.

No, Cathie decided reluctantly as dawn brightened the sky, there was no one here to help her find out about her real father. But this meant she had even more of a reason to go to England. Surely he would want to meet her, even if she was – she faced the fact squarely – a bastard?

Mairi Hamilton waited till everyone had finished eating, then cleared her throat to gain her two brothers' attention. 'I would like to invite Elwyn to tea on Sunday. And – he wants to speak to you, Magnus.'

He smiled at her. 'Like that, is it?'

She flushed. 'Yes. Yes, it is.'

He was glad to find something happy to dwell on, for

their mother was growing stranger by the month. They had had to make the tiny bedroom over the stairs into a sort of — well, there was no word for it but 'prison cell' and the doctor had given them some medicine to make her drowsy at night. They needed their sleep even if their mother didn't.

He realised his brother was chuckling and looked up, banishing the sad thoughts.

'I don't know what you see in that little man, our Mairi,' Hamish teased. Unlike the other two, the youngest Hamilton's voice had no Scottish lilt in it at all, for he had been born here in Lancashire.

Mairi fired up at once. 'Elwyn's kind, that's what I see in him, and I love being with him, and—' She broke off, realising she was being teased. 'Oh, you two!' She flapped one hand at them. 'Just make sure you behave yourselves on Sunday, that's all.'

'Yes, Mairi.' Magnus hesitated, then looked sideways at their mother, who was making patterns in the crumbs on her plate with half the sandwich lying uneaten. 'What have you said to him about — our situation here?'

'Elwyn had an auntie who was the same. He understands and will be kind to Mum.' Well, he was kind to everyone, her Elwyn was.

On the Sunday, both Hamilton men put on their chapel clothes and Mairi set the table with the best china and tablecloth.

Their mother had been having one of her better days and had tried to help, carrying plates to and fro like a docile child, but setting them down wrongly and then drifting off in the middle of one journey to stand gazing into space, a plate cradled against her breast. She had even hugged Magnus, something she rarely did nowadays, which had made him remember with a pang how affectionate she used to be.

When the door knocker went, Magnus and Hamish ranged themselves in front of the fire and waited. They had met Elwyn Bebb, as they'd met most of the men at church, but they'd never had much to do with him. He was a little older than Hamish, a little younger than Magnus, and lived on his own in lodgings.

When he came in, Elwyn was carrying an oval box of Cadbury's chocolate dragees, with a picture of a little girl on the top. As he was introduced to Mrs Hamilton, he offered it to her.

She snatched it from him without a word of thanks and stared at it, running one finger across the top and muttering to herself, ignoring everyone. After staring at the picture for a moment she tried to open the box, but failed and began weeping in frustration.

Elwyn stepped forward and with gentle gestures showed her how it opened. Picking up a chocolate dragee, he offered it to her, but she only stared at his outstretched hand.

'Eat it, mum,' Mairi coaxed. 'It's nice.'

But Janey had turned stubborn and refused to open her mouth. When Magnus tried to take the box from her for safe keeping, she shouted, 'Mine! Mine!' and clutched it to her, so he slid the lid on quickly and left her to her rapt contemplation of the little girl's face.

'I'm sorry,' he said to Elwyn, hating to have his mother's weakness displayed like that to a stranger.

'She can't help it, poor thing,' said their visitor softly, his expression understanding. 'My auntie was just the same.'

'Let's have tea, shall we?' said Mairi, and they all took their places round the kitchen table, leaving their mother by the fire to continue crooning over the chocolate box, which seemed to have taken her fancy.

After the meal Elwyn turned to Magnus. 'May I have a word with you in private?'

'Aye. Come away into the front.'

Mairi closed her eyes in relief then began to clear the table. She had been terrified her mother's behaviour would put Elwyn off. There were younger and prettier women at chapel who didn't have her disadvantages.

'I like your Elwyn,' Hamish said, grinning at her and helping her carry the crockery into the scullery.

She paused for a moment. 'Do you really?'

'Yes. He may be shorter than you are but he'll do.' He glanced towards the closed door, hesitated, then said softly, 'I'm still thinking of going to Australia. It sounds so wonderful. Sunshine and parrots flying around. No snow. No chilblains.'

'Nothing's perfect,' she said flatly. 'And don't you think Magnus has lost enough of his brothers now?'

'I'm a man grown, Mairi. I have to make my own life — as you're doing.'

'I'll still be here to help with Mother. Will you?'

He didn't answer, just pushed past her with a closed

48

expression on his face. 'You don't need me now. I'm off to change and get a breath of fresh air.'

She stood motionless as she heard him leave the house, wondering what exactly he was planning. He was definitely up to something. She had always been able to tell.

CHAPTER THREE

January–February

In Melbourne, Matthieu Correntin strolled round to his current mistress's rooms. He intended to take his final leave of Alice tonight and give her a generous present, then he'd conclude his last remaining business deal and sail west to join Dermott in Perth. He preferred land travel, but there were as yet no roads from east to west of this huge country, let alone railways, so you had to travel round it by ship.

A grim expression sat briefly on his face at the thought of his partner. When he'd first started to work with Dermott he had not realised quite how reckless and unprincipled the man was. But they had made good money together, doing anything that came to hand – buying and selling, importing, running two or three eating houses, a pawnshop – even a brothel.

It was Dermott who had got them into this latter business without even asking Matthieu, who did not relish the thought of being a whoremaster. And it was this venture which had landed Dermott in trouble with Pat Blaney, who ran the district's other brothels and objected strongly to anyone encroaching on his territory. Blaney had made it clear that it would be dangerous for them to stay in Melbourne by burning down both their new brothel and one of their eating houses. Furious, but knowing when he was outclassed, Dermott had prudently left the state first and Matthieu had let it be known that he was winding up their business affairs before following his partner. He did not think Blaney would come after him with quite the same vengeful fury.

Christina had protested vigorously about the move, but she didn't know half the things her husband was up to; sometimes Matthieu suspected that *he* didn't know, either. The business they had conducted together was quasi-legal, a bit sharp at times, but Matthieu drew the line at some of the shadier deals which Dermott had suggested. He had no intention of landing himself in gaol, nor did he have his friend's confidence in the stupidity of the police. But he couldn't help enjoying Dermott's company. The man was a likeable rogue.

Although Matthieu wrote to his family from time to time, he doubted he would be able to go back and fit in again in France. Here the sky was wide and you were free to make money if you could without entrenched custom breathing down your neck — well, you were unless you tried to open a brothel in the wrong place and fell foul of a master criminal!

When Alice opened the door she looked flustered. A quick glance beyond her showed a man's trousers on a chair.

'It seems you are busy tonight, *chérie*,' Matthieu said mildly, but he was annoyed. He had been paying the rent on this room, more fool he! Then he saw who the other man was and gasped in shock.

Pat Blaney got out of bed and walked towards the open door, wrapped in a sheet, a nasty smile on his plump face. He put one hand on Alice's shoulder possessively. 'You should look after your property better, Correntin.'

Matthieu was so surprised he could not speak for a minute. Alice's eyes flew to something behind him and terror showed clearly on her face. He turned quickly, just in time to dodge the cudgel of the man who had crept up on him. Another fellow stood beside his assailant, grinning evilly and hefting a knife as if it were an extension of his hand.

Matthieu surprised them by rushing forward into the room, using his foot to shove the door shut in their faces and thanking providence for the quick reactions which had saved him from trouble before. He pushed Alice towards Pat, knocking him over easily enough because the over-confident fool was hampered by the sheet.

As Matthieu wrenched the french windows wider, he thanked God for hot nights. He leaped over the wooden rails of the veranda and made off swiftly through the back garden. From the crashing noises and curses behind him, he knew his way rather better than his pursuers.

He had no trouble losing them, but took a lot of care before re-entering his new, temporary lodgings. Did Blaney know where he lived? Probably. With a curse Matthieu sent his landlady's son out with an urgent message, then began to hurl the rest of his possessions into his half-packed trunk.

When the two men who had attacked him at Alice's

rooms arrived at his lodgings, they found their prey guarded by two men of similar ilk whom Matthieu had paid well for their services.

'You'd better get out of Melbourne if you know what's good for you, Correntin!' one of the Blaney men tossed across the few feet between them.

'I'm leaving, *mon ami.* Tell your master not to worry.'

'Don't mind if we tag along with you to the ship, do you? Just to be sure you get away safely. And don't try to come back to Melbourne again, either.'

'You can follow me if you want, but come any closer than that and you'll regret it.'

One of Matthieu's own bodyguards took a step forward at his words, fists bunched, and the two pursuers shrugged and stayed where they were.

Matthieu had to bribe the steward to let him board the ship early. He scribbled a hasty note to another friend, then handed it to the two bodyguards, who were waiting patiently on the docks and would do so until the ship sailed. More money exchanged hands for this extra favour, but Matthieu made sure of the note's safe delivery by promising them a further payment from Bob Sharpe once the letter was in his hands.

Then, having done all he could, Matthieu leaned on the rail and stared out across the moonlit water. He could only hope Bob was friend enough to tidy up his remaining business affairs – though he knew that favour would come at a price. He'd not been able to withdraw the rest of his funds from the bank before he left, either, something he had planned to do this morning before boarding, so he was not feeling at all happy about the situation. However, those funds would be safe enough and he could get them sent after him once he arrived in Perth.

But it would take weeks for his money to come through so he'd have to be a bit careful. Unlike Dermott, he did not have a huge fortune stashed away.

By the time the ship weighed anchor the following afternoon, Matthieu was able to laugh at himself – or at least to smile wryly. He had always found humour a saving grace because life had a way of tweaking your tail however hard you tried to arrange things to your liking.

A feeling of excitement followed the amusement. It was always like this when he set off for somewhere new. There was a sense of promise, a sense that this time he might find what he was looking for – or there again, he might not.

He tossed the stub of his cigar into the water and watched it swirl away. Why had he been cursed with this restless streak? Why could he never settle down as other men did?

Within the hour he had set his worries aside and was chatting to his fellow passengers. Western Australia, everyone told him gloomily, was the Cinderella Colony. If you didn't have a very good reason for going there you'd never bother to visit it. Two of the men on board were government officials and these Matthieu cultivated carefully, because even minor functionaries could be of use.

He made his way down to his tiny cabin that night somewhat the worse for wear since the ladies had retired early and the men had shared a bottle or two. He lay smiling into the darkness. He was alive, wasn't he? Still in possession of his faculties and looks – which made it easy to gain the ladies' attention. He twirled his moustache, then laughed at himself for doing so, and wondered whether to shave it off for a change.

He probably wouldn't stay in Western Australia for long, he decided, just until he got his money through from Melbourne and finalised his financial arrangements with Dermott. He did not want to make a habit of narrow escapes. Where should he go next? India, perhaps? Or America? There was a lot of the world still to see.

And why he couldn't think of a place he really wanted to visit this time he could not understand. Oh, he'd been too busy to think about it, that was all. It would come to him. It always did.

As the Caines' cart approached Perth, Cathie sighed in pleasure. 'Isn't it wonderful, Dad? So many people living here! So much to see and do! Heavens, how the city has changed since we were last here! Look at all those buildings.'

'I'd rather see fields and trees than city streets,' Benedict said flatly. 'I can't see why anyone would want to spend their whole life in towns.' He pointed into the distance at a clock tower. 'And what good does building fancy town halls do ordinary folk like us? Those who grow food do more good than those who build fancy monuments, and don't you forget it.'

She suppressed a sigh. Since the bush fire he had been so touchy. She knew he was working far too hard — but he had always worked hard and never been like this before. And her mother was clearly worried about him.

But even though Cathie felt sorry for them both in their

great loss, the thought that they had been lying to her about her father still galled her. She was not sure she could ever forgive them for that.

'Perth may be the capital of our colony,' Benedict went on, jabbing one finger towards the huddle of central buildings, 'and we who live here may call it a city, but it's still only a small town by English standards. I was reading somewhere that there are ten times as many people living in Manchester as in the whole of Western Australia. Just think of that.'

She sighed. He was always coming out with such information, culled from the newspapers he loved to read. What did she care?

'. . . and you'd be lost over there in the old country after growing up here, Cathie! Lost! Why, you'd never even seen a train till we crossed the timber line to Rockingham on this trip, yet over there even ordinary folk use them every day to get to and fro.'

They drew to a halt outside Agnes's house just then and Cathie sighed in relief. How she had kept her mouth shut on the slow, two-day journey up to Perth she didn't know.

When her things had been unloaded and carried inside to the small bedroom at the rear, her father drove off to find a livery stable for the horse and cart while the two women went back inside.

'I'm grateful to you for having me, Mrs Fenton!' Cathie felt shy all of a sudden, because she had never been on her own with her mother's friend before. Her hostess looked so elegant that the girl felt even bigger and clumsier next to her, with her limp, crumpled skirts hanging anyhow and not even the smallest of bustles at the back. She eyed Agnes Fenton's elegantly draped skirts surreptitiously, thinking how strange bustles looked – though no stranger than the crinolines her mother had once worn to please her first husband. Cathie had played at dressing up in them when she was a child, but the hoops, big spreading skirts and tightly fitted bodices had been lost along with many other possessions in the fire.

'It's my pleasure to have you. And do call me Agnes! "Mrs Fenton" makes me feel old. I was feeling a bit down, I must admit, till I got your mother's letter. It was such a bore being in mourning!' She spread her arms and twirled round. 'How do you like my new dress?'

'It's lovely.' Cathie looked down at herself ruefully. 'Mum's given me some money to buy material for a new dress or two, because all mine seem to be either torn or stained. And I've grown again, so these are a bit short for me, as well. Sometimes it seems as if I'll never stop growing till I hit the ceiling. I hate being so tall!'

'Goodness, and I'd sell my soul for some extra inches! How nice it would be to look gentlemen in the eye for a change, or even to look down my nose at one!'

They both laughed and Cathie began to relax. It had never occurred to her before that being short might have its problems as well, though she would still have preferred it. When her mother was dressed up for church, she might not be fashionably clad, but she looked so dainty and pretty that Cathie could not help feeling jealous sometimes.

*

'That must be her, because that's definitely Benedict Caine,' Christina Docherty said, peering out of the parlour window.

'She's a big strapping lass. How did my tiny sister have a child who looks like that? The daughter must take after Da's side of the family, like I do.' Dermott put the opera glasses to his eyes again. 'You know, this lass reminds me of someone else. Who the hell is it?'

'Let me have a look now.'

'In a minute. I want to . . .' His voice trailed away, then as Cathie scowled and made a vigorous gesture, he sucked in his breath suddenly. 'It can't be!'

'What? It can't be what?' His wife tried to snatch the opera glasses and he pushed her aside impatiently with any angry, *'Leave it!'*

While the three people across the road remained standing in the garden, he continued to study the girl. Could he be imagining things? Only as Caine drove away and the two women turned to go inside did he pass the opera glasses absent-mindedly to his wife.

'You might have let me see her face,' Christina grumbled when all she got was a brief glimpse of Cathie's back.

'Ach, you'll be meeting her in the next few days. We'll make sure of that. You can invite them both over to take tea and stare at her face for as long as you like then.'

Christina gave an exaggerated sigh. 'I'm sure I'll hate her as much as I hated Liza.'

'You'll do no such thing!' he corrected sharply. 'You're to become good friends and play the fond auntie. And you won't say anything, not a single word, to let her know how we really feel about her bloody mother. We'll be an aunt and uncle who're sad that we've never been welcome to keep in touch with my sister and her family, absolutely delighted to have a chance to get to know our niece. Don't let me down in this, now.'

Christina pulled a face. 'Oh, very well. But surely the fire has paid Liza back for what she did to your brother?'

'Mebbe. Mebbe not.' His sister had claimed it was an accident all those years ago, that she'd not meant to kill Niall only frighten him away. But she should have known better than to fire at him at point-blank range. As well as ruining Liza and her family, Dermott still wanted to find out where they'd buried Niall and see his brother's remains placed in a proper grave, with a headstone.

Christina, whose mother had always called her Kitty, frowned at him. Why did he go on about his stupid sister? When they were both young it had been Liza who'd attracted all the eligible men, leaving none for Christina. She had had to be satisfied with Liza's brother, who was not a gentleman and hadn't even married her till he'd got her with child. Even then, he'd forced her to convert to Catholicism first, a religion she still secretly despised. He'd been furious when she'd lost that first child and it had been years till she'd had the others. For a man who had been a thief and opportunist for most of his life, Dermott Docherty held singularly rigid views about his own family's respectability.

She remembered his other remark. 'Who is it the girl reminds you of?'

'One of our old neighbours in Pendleworth.'

His voice was abstracted and she could get no further information from him. He was the most frustrating man

59

on earth, but at least he provided for them all generously. Which was more than her own father had done, gentleman though he had been. All he'd done was waste the family's money on silly schemes, then drag them out to Australia almost penniless.

She stared round the little rented house. Oh, why had they left Melbourne? Life had been so much better there. But you couldn't talk sense into Dermott once he'd fixed his mind on something and she hated it when he did things impulsively, like buying this stupid farm. She could think of nothing worse than living in the country here in Australia, but would he listen to her? No, he rarely did these days. Tears welled in her eyes. She hated it in Western Australia, absolutely hated it.

The following day Cathie returned young James Docherty's ball when it sailed over the fence into the street near Agnes's house, then got talking to his governess.

'Go and join them!' hissed Dermott, poking his wife in the back. 'It's a heaven-sent opportunity to meet her.'

So Christina strolled out, smiling graciously and sending governess and children away with one sharp glance. 'I'm so pleased to meet you. I knew dear Mrs Fenton was expecting her young friend Cathie Ludlam to stay with her.' They had been astonished to hear that name and delighted that chance had given them an opportunity to meet Liza's daughter. She was amazed at how tall the girl was and how ill-dressed, looking more like a servant and a poor one at that, especially as Liza was a short woman who never had any style. Comparing that to her own affluence and modish clothes gave Christina deep satisfaction.

Cathie stood wondering why their neighbour had not introduced herself by name. 'It's very kind of Mrs Fenton to invite me to stay. She's taking me shopping later.' She looked down ruefully at her skirts, carefully ironed that morning but still limp and faded. 'I need some new clothes, something more stylish.' She gazed enviously at the other woman. 'Yours are beautiful.'

'Why, thank you.' Christina twirled to show off her elegant gown with its fashionable apron-front, the folds knotted up into a bustle at the back and the skirt flowing into a small train beneath it. 'That means you'll want something with a bustle and train, though to tell you the truth trains are very incovenient in winter.'

'I don't know how you manage them at all. Don't they get dirty?'

Christina caught up the hem to show the brush-like braid beneath it, speaking as one woman to another. 'See – this is to protect the underneath of the hem. And in wet weather one loops the train up, of course. We women are slaves to fashion, are we not?'

'I've never had the chance. But your dress is such a pretty colour. I love the deep rose with the paler pink. Is it real silk?'

'Yes. Mind you,' Christina leaned forward confidentially, as if treating the girl as an equal, inwardly amused at how the silly fool was drinking in her words as if she was the fount of all wisdom, 'one has to wear very tight lacing to get this straight appearance down the front.' With one hand she gestured to her own slender body. 'When we were living in Melbourne I used to get my clothes from England or France. We prided ourselves there on being only three months behind European fashions. But here in Perth,' she fluttered the hand scornfully, 'I don't know how I'm going to manage.'

'Perth seems wonderful to me. My family has a farm and I've not visited the city very often.'

'Then I mustn't spoil it for you. We can rest assured Perth will be more exciting than life in the country! May I hope that you and dear Mrs Fenton will come and take tea with me one day, perhaps tomorrow? I haven't had much chance to meet people here yet and, I must say, I'm missing my old friends.'

'Why did you leave Melbourne?' Cathie flushed then clapped one hand over her mouth. 'Oh, I'm sorry! That was rude of me.'

'No, just honest.' Stupid girl, thought Christina. She has no more style than a cart horse. 'We left for the usual reason – my husband's business interests. Ah, there is your kind hostess.' As Agnes came across the sandy unpaved street to join them, she cooed, 'My dear Mrs Fenton, I was just making the acquaintance of your young visitor and hoping the two of you would take tea with me tomorrow. Now do say you will!'

'We shall be delighted. But I must take Cathie away from you now. We have some shopping to do.'

As they re-entered the house Agnes murmured, 'She's a dreadful woman! What a pity you got talking to her. Now we shall have to pay a visit and listen to her going on forever about how wonderful Melbourne is and how behind the times we are in Perth.'

'She's very finely dressed,' Cathie said wistfully.

'For a woman at home in the morning, she's *over-dressed*,' corrected Agnes. 'And she wears too many bright colours for a woman of her age. It makes her skin look faded. You'd think she'd see that in her mirror. And did you see the amount of trimming on that dress? It was ridiculous!' She still privately wondered if these Dochertys were any connection of the girl's mother, who'd been plain Liza Docherty, lady's maid when they'd first met aboard ship – and who had horrified the cabin class passengers by contracting a shipboard marriage to Josiah Ludlam scandalously soon after his frail first wife Catherine died and was buried at sea. Dermott Docherty did not resemble Agnes's old friend in the slightest, but she would ask them about it the next day, though.

Cathie didn't know what to think about their neighbours. After the simple clothes she had worn all her life, the gorgeous colours of the neighbour's clothes had made her long for something more cheerful, and she'd have given anything for just a couple of those fringed frills on her own skirts. What were bustles made of? she wondered. Were they like little cushions, or where they small wire frames like crinolines? She would have to ask Mrs Fenton.

When Cathie and Agnes went round to take tea with their neighbour the following afternoon, they found Dermott sitting with his wife.

'I hope you don't mind if my husband joins us?' Christina asked, indicating seats on a plush-covered sofa.

Agnes inclined her head. 'Of course not, Mr Docherty.' She was a bit surprised to see him, however, since gentlemen did not usually participate in such tea parties.

Cathie stared at her host and hostess. 'Docherty? Why, that was my mother's maiden name!'

Dermott smiled at her. 'I know that, my dear. I hope you'll excuse this abrupt introduction but I'm your mother's brother.'

She could not think what to say, for her mother would not even speak the name of her eldest living brother and seemed to hate all mention of him. Cathie looked to Agnes for guidance.

'Does Liza know you're here?' her friend asked, startled.

'No. My sister and I – well, let's face it, Liza and I never got on. And I must confess it was mainly my fault. I was a rather, um, wild young man. Didn't treat my sister as well as I might have. I regret that now and am hoping for a reconciliation.'

Agnes was still frowning. 'Until you have seen Liza, I don't think Cathie should –'

Christina burst in, 'Oh, please don't deny us this chance to get to know our niece, Mrs Fenton! I have no close relatives and my husband doesn't know where the rest of his family is, so there's only Liza and her family left now.'

'This places me in a very difficult position,' Agnes protested, wondering why they hadn't said anything about the relationship when she'd told them about Cathie's proposed visit.

'Give us a few weeks, though, before you tell my sister. At least let us get to know our niece.' Dermott smiled across at Cathie. 'If you'd like that, of course, lass?'

Cathie studied her uncle, feeling unsure of herself. He had a commanding air to him that said he was used to having his own way, but at the same time his eyes twinkled with amusement and she had a strong desire to smile back at him.

It wasn't until she was lying in bed that night, thinking through this amazing day, that it suddenly occurred to her that her uncle might know who her real father was. That settled things. She would get to know him better and ask him.

After some thought, Agnes decided to write and tell Liza about the situation straight away. She didn't say anything to Cathie or the Dochertys. For all their show of friendliness to their niece, she still didn't quite trust her neighbours, though she couldn't say exactly why.

When she had put the letter in the post Agnes felt better. And until she got a reply, she would keep the girl busy, make sure Cathie didn't see too much of her relatives.

CHAPTER FOUR

February

Dinny saw Liza sigh as she contemplated the pile of washing. Her friend looked weary even before she started work. It was time to intervene. 'Let me do that today.'

'I can't ask you to—'

'You didn't ask. And you need more help now you haven't got Cathie,' Dinny went on, steering her away from the copper full of hot water.

As Liza leaned against her for a moment, the two women smiled at one another. They had been close friends ever since the day Liza had rescued Dinny from the two white men who had been keeping her prisoner and using her body.

Dinny had lived with Fergal O'Riordan, an ex-convict, for seventeen years now and been married to him for ten of those years, since his Irish wife's death, though the minister had been doubtful as to whether he should marry a native to a white man and would have refused to do it but for Benedict's intervention.

Life was good for the O'Riordans at Lizabrook, where no one cared about Dinny's colour, but if she went into Mandurah or Pinjarra she was at risk of being insulted in a variety of ways for being Aboriginal. And yet, ironically, her own mother had had to flee from New South Wales because she had met with equal hostility from her own people for going to live with a white man instead of the husband her father had chosen from their tribe. She had always been afraid of her people finding her, even though she had travelled right around Australia on a big ship to escape from them. Aboriginal fathers had the main say about marrying their daughters off, and about punishing any daughter who disobeyed them.

Unlike her son Brendan, whom she called by another name in her heart, Dinny was content with her small world. She might not have been born in this area, but she felt an affinity with the land and was sure it had accepted her. And the local tribe had accepted her as well, giving her a skin name and adopting her as one of them because she helped them when they were ill, especially the women. 'You're not carrying this baby as easily as you did the others,' Dinny observed to her friend, frowning.

'Well, I'm a lot older than I was when I had the last one,' Liza admitted, pulling away from her and rubbing her aching forehead.

'You shouldn't have any more children after this one. I'll give you something to stop them.'

'If you say so.' Liza trusted her friend's healing skills. 'Cathie said it was disgusting at my age to have another baby, but I've enjoyed all my children.'

'If you want to keep this child, from now on till it's born you must get help with the heavy work.'

'How can I? I can't ask Ilse to do the washing, except for her own. Governesses don't do things like that. And servants are scarce even in Perth, let alone here in the bush.'

Dinny hesitated. 'Would you try the girl I've taken on to live with me for a while? Willerin doesn't have many skills yet, but she's strong and learns quickly.'

Liza considered this for a minute, head on one side. 'I'd be happy to meet her and see if we like one another.'

Dinny smiled at her friend. 'Only you would say that.'

'Say what?'

'Only you would say, "see if we like one another". As if her feelings matter.'

'Well, of course they matter.'

'Not to most white people.'

So Willerin came to work, a shy young girl of fifteen, still somewhat overwhelmed by this close contact with white people.

A few days later as Liza took the mail from the man who brought it out to the homestead once a week the world seemed to waver around her then darkness swallowed her up.

Willerin saw her collapse and shouted for help.

Josie ran out from the schoolroom, sobbing, and tried to throw herself on her mother's still body. Ilse followed and pulled her away, before helping Willerin carry Liza into her bedroom. Noticing the letters blowing around she called to Josie to pick them up and the child did this hastily, still sobbing, not noticing one which had blown under a bush. From there it drifted towards the lake where it slowly sank.

Hearing the cries, Dinny came running across. When it came to child-bearing, with no doctors nearby even the white people of Brookley had learned to ignore the colour of her skin and trust her skills because the women she had attended did not fall ill as often after the birth and you could not fault her cleanliness.

'You'll have to stay in bed from now on if you want to keep this baby,' Dinny warned Liza, who was lying there looking boneless, her face chalky-white and the skin around her eyes shadowed.

With her head swimming and still feeling very distant, Liza said faintly, 'I don't think I *could* get up yet.'

Dinny went out to talk to Benedict, who was waiting anxiously nearby. She took the opportunity to warn him strictly not to have any more children after this one.

'It's Liza who matters, not the baby. Of course I'll be careful from now on. Is she going to be all right?'

'If she rests. She's a bit over-tired now.' Liza had carried her other children easily, but Dinny was worried that there might be something wrong this time.

Benedict ran one hand through his hair. 'How are we going to manage to slow her down?'

Ilse came up to join them and when he explained the problem, immediately said, 'If you don't mind my neglecting my teaching duties for a while, Mr Caine, I'd be happy to help out.'

He stared at her in surprise. She was usually so quiet and self-effacing. 'I can't ask you to do that!'

She smiled ruefully. 'You're not *asking* me, I'm volunteering.'

'I must admit I'd be grateful for any help you could give us. I think I'd better send for Cathie, though. We're going to need her.'

Dinny touched his arm. 'Don't do that yet, Benedict.

Your daughter's not been gone long and she needed to get away as much as you need to stay here.'

He hesitated, chewing the corner of his lip. 'Well – we'll try it for a few days, see how we go on, but I'm not having Cathie idling around in Perth if Liza needs her help.'

So Ilse found herself doing the household tasks she had once done for the husband she had come out to Australia to marry. How long ago that seemed now! Johannes had been far older than her, a widower in need of a young wife to care for him. He had been very set in his ways and had insisted on being absolute master in his own house. She had soon regretted letting her family persuade her to come to Adelaide to marry him, but by then it was too late. She was well and truly trapped in a loveless marriage.

Then Johannes had been killed in an accident and although she had been mildly sorry, she had also seen it as a way to find freedom at last – until she found he had left everything to his eldest son by his first marriage, with instructions for the heir to look after her. Andreas's charity was grudging and when he began to talk of finding her another husband, Ilse had refused point-blank to marry again. He had been very angry but she had stood her ground.

When he brought in the Minister and his wife to try to persuade her, and then locked her in her bedroom to 'think things over', she had realised that the only way to gain her freedom was to run away. She had pretended docility and made her plans carefully, guessing she would only get one chance. She had sailed to Western Australia because there was no ship due to leave for Sydney and had stayed in the west because she did not want to spend her precious savings on another sea voyage.

She had a facility for languages, speaking good French as well as her native German, and her English was by then almost perfect so she hoped to find a job as a governess but was prepared to do anything honest to earn a living. In the meantime she had found lodgings with another widow, Agnes Fenton, while she searched for employment. It had been harder to find a position than she had expected because of her nationality, so when Agnes had introduced her to the Caines, who were looking for a governess, she had been greatly relieved.

Her relief had not lasted. The Caines were very pleasant people, but like their daughter Cathie, Ilse found life in the country too quiet. In a year or so she intended to move back to Perth and try to find another husband, one more to her taste this time. Everyone said they were short of women out here and she knew she was not unpleasant to look at. Surely it should be possible?

With Liza spending her days on the sofa, Ilse took over running the house, enjoying the change from teaching. In the evenings after her work was done, she watched wistfully as the whole family cosseted Liza and conspired to keep her as happy and contented as possible. It must be wonderful to have such a family – children, a loving husband, your own home.

What worried Ilse was how, when she went back to live in Perth, she would meet suitable gentlemen and intimate to them that she was interested in marriage. She had not yet worked that out. But she would. She was very determined.

*

In Perth Dermott arranged to take Cathie out for a walk without Agnes keeping an eye on them. His niece was an energetic young woman and he liked to keep himself in good fighting fettle. He didn't invite Christina to go with them for she now considered it unladylike to go faster than a dawdle.

'So you're not ashamed to be seen out walking with your old uncle?' he teased as they strode off towards the city.

'Of course not.' As they walked along Cathie nerved herself to ask the question that had been hovering on the tip of her tongue ever since their first meeting. It came out in a rush. 'Uncle Dermott, I found out recently that Josiah Ludlam wasn't my real father.' She hesitated, not knowing how to continue.

'Now how did you discover that?' A sideways glance showed him an angry young face.

She avoided looking at him. 'I overheard Mum and Dad talking. Since the bush fire destroyed our home we've had to live in temporary accommodation while the new house is built and – and they don't realise how their voices carry at night.'

'What exactly did they say?'

'Just that they didn't want me going back to Lancashire, in case I met my *real father.*'

Dermott's voice was soft, coaxing more confidences from her. 'And did you ask them what that meant?'

She shook her head. 'I didn't even try, because I knew they wouldn't tell me. My mother once said it'd hurt other people if she told me everything about myself.' She stopped walking to plant herself squarely in front of him

72

and look him in the eyes. 'Do *you* know who my real father is, Uncle Dermott?'

'Yes. Well, at least, I'm pretty certain I do.'

She stood very still, hands clasped tightly at her breast. 'Will you tell me?'

He pursed his lips, pretending reluctance. 'Maybe I shouldn't, since your mother obviously doesn't want you to know.'

She grabbed his arm. 'Oh, please, Uncle! There's only you I can ask and I *have* to know.'

'Why?'

'Because one day I'm going to find a way to go back to England.' She stared into the distance, her expression determined. 'And if I have a father still living there, I want to meet him. What's he like?'

Dermott chose his words carefully. 'A strong man. He would have married your mother, you know, but she ran off to Australia. I suppose she didn't know then that she was carrying you.' To his relief Cathie didn't ask him how her mother had got pregnant in the first place to a man she didn't like enough to marry.

'What's my father's name?'

'Teddy Marshall. He's a clogger. Used to live across Underby Street from us. A bit rough, but earns an honest living and looks after his family. You have some half-brothers, too, you know.' But to his surprise, that information made her frown.

'Not more of them!' Her voice was bitter. 'I've got plenty of half-brothers already, thank you very much, including one in England whom I've never met.' She fell silent, frowning. 'What I don't understand is why a man like

Josiah Ludlam married my mother? She was his wife's maid, after all, and he was a gentleman. We have some of his furniture and it's lovely, though some got burned. I used to touch pieces and be glad they'd belonged to my father, that I still had something of his. Though I didn't, did I? It was all lies.'

A sob escaped her so she started walking again, sniffing away the tears that threatened. 'Now – well, I don't know who I *am*.'

And then Dermott realised what he could do with this situation that had been handed to him on a silver platter. It would be yet another way of getting back at Liza. 'If you want – well, I would be happy to pay your fare back to England. I've plenty of money, after all, and you're the only niece I've got.'

She went so white he took hold of her arm. 'Are you all right, lass?' And he found to his surprise that he didn't really want to hurt his niece.

Cathie's voice was a mere whisper. 'I can't believe you mean it.'

'Ah, it's nothing. I've done well for myself and if you can't use it to help your own kin, what's the point of having money?' He continued to watch her more carefully than she realised.

She had her head bent now and was walking along slowly, pretending to concentrate on where she was putting her feet. 'I don't think my parents would let you do that – even though *they* can't afford to send me back for a visit at the moment. There's some other reason they don't want me to go back, I think, apart from my real father. But I'm going one day, whatever they say. Surely I can find a way to earn a living over there? I'm no fine lady, afraid to dirty my hands. I know my father quarrelled with his older brother but I do have a half-brother there. His family took him away from my mother. Do you know *them*? They're called Rawley.'

'Of Rawley Hall? *Our Liza married a Rawley?*' This was news to Dermott. When Cathie nodded, he let out a long, low whistle. 'Imagine that, she only married into the two richest families in Pendleworth, my little sister did.' And must have done something to offend them both if she'd come back to Australia as a poor farmer's wife. How stupid could you get? They'd have kept her in luxury for the rest of her days if she'd buttered them up properly.

'I don't think she got on very well with the Rawleys. They took Francis away from her and won't let her contact him – though she won't say why. She pays for a report every year from a lawyer in Pendleworth about how my brother is and it always upsets her. So do Mrs Ludlam's letters sometimes. But that's nothing to do with me and whatever she and Dad say or do, I'm definitely going back there one day.' Cathie scowled into the distance.

'Then let me buy you the passage, lass.'

'I'll think about it.' And she did. In fact, she thought of little else during the next few days.

Once they'd finished their evening meal, Mairi looked at Magnus across the table. 'I need to talk to you so I'll get Mum to bed early.'

Not without some difficulty she persuaded her mother to go out and use the privy at the end of the back yard and then took her upstairs, getting her undressed, giving her the medicine that helped her sleep and putting her into bed in the small bedroom with the new lock on the door. When her mother sighed and lay back with a faint smile, she looked almost her old self, which made a lump come into Mairi's throat. But after a moment the blank expression returned and Mairi left the room quietly, bracing herself to talk to her eldest brother and break her news to him as gently as she could.

He was sitting staring into the fire, his expression so sad she almost changed her mind, then she summoned up her courage. Best get this over with. She'd been dreading telling him all day. Sitting down opposite him she said baldly, 'Magnus, there's a problem.'

He looked at her in surprise. 'What?'

'Elwyn and I want to get married.'

He smiled at her. 'Well, we know that. I don't see it as a problem.' His smile faded. 'Oh, you mean we'll need to get a bigger house once you're married. Yes, of course. I'm quite happy to move.'

Mairi swallowed hard. 'It's not that. I'd have done that and looked after Mother as we'd agreed only – well, things have changed. They want Elwyn to move to Bury, you see, as Assistant Manager of the shop there. When the present Manager retires, he's to take over. It's the chance he's been waiting for, his big chance. How can I ask him to give that up?' She saw Magnus swallow hard and bent her head to avoid his eyes as she answered her own question. 'I can't. I won't. And – and I won't give Elwyn up, either. I'm nearly twenty-seven and this may be my last chance of a normal family life.'

His words were so faint she could barely hear them.

'No. Why should you give up your life, lassie?'

'You shouldn't give yours up, either, Magnus. You've done enough, more than enough, for her. For all of us. We owe you so much. And the Benevolent Home isn't a bad place, you know. She'd be looked after there, kept clean and – made as comfortable as possible. You could visit her every week and—'

'No.' His voice was flat, determined. 'She'll not end her days in the Ben. I promised her that once.'

'But how will you look after her without me?'

'I don't know. I'll find a way, though.' Maybe he should look for a wife himself? No, who would take him on with a burden like his mother? 'How long can you give me to work things out – three months? Six would be better and—'

Mairi shook her head and interrupted before he could make any more plans, 'Barely four weeks, I'm afraid, love. Elwyn has to start in Bury next month. We hope to be married by then so that I can go with him.'

Magnus let a sigh sift out slowly. 'Aye. It makes sense for you.'

Her eyes filled with tears and she stretched out one hand to him, knowing how generous this was of him. His Scottish accent had grown stronger, which it only did when he was upset or particularly happy. She loved the soft musical sound of his voice normally, but today the thicker burr that slowed his words made her feel guilty. 'Oh, Magnus, I'm so sorry to do this to you.'

He leaned forward to take her hand between his big ones, patting it gently. 'It isna your fault.'

'It isn't yours, either, and yet you've had the burden of us for all these years since Father died. You're thirty now. Don't you think it's time you had a life of your own?'

'I've never regretted doing my duty. Family is the most important thing there is.'

Mairi closed her eyes and did not even try to answer that. If their mother could understand what was happening, it'd be different, but more and more Janey Hamilton was withdrawing from them to live in a world of her own – if you could call that blank stare living. Last year their mother had been anxious, restless, aggressive at times, and it had been a struggle to care for her. This year she was increasingly apathetic, forgetting how to do the most simple daily tasks, soiling herself sometimes, even.

Why had God let this happen to her?

Two weeks after she'd left home, Cathie received a letter from her stepfather. As usual with Benedict Caine's communications, it was curt and to the point:

> *You're needed at home again, Cathie. Your mother is not well, and Ilse is having to neglect the children's education to help out. I'll be coming up to Perth next Tuesday and will bring you home with me then.*

She stared at the piece of paper in horror. Go and live at home again! Already she could not bear the thought of it. To have no one new to talk to, nothing to see but trees and animals, day in, day out! No, never!

But her mother was ill! And Cathie loved her mother.

She frowned at the letter. How ill? And what was wrong? Her step-father didn't say. Was he just using it as an excuse to make her go back? It seemed likely. He hadn't wanted her to come to Perth in the first place, that was certain.

For an hour, her thoughts see-sawed to and fro. Her mother was never ill. She was probably just tired because of the baby. And that was *his* fault for getting a woman of her mother's age in the family way again. It was typical that he now expected his stepdaughter to give her own life up to deal with that. Men got the best of everything. They wouldn't have asked a son to do this.

Cathie shook her head, silently rejecting the demand. She was sorry for her mother, very sorry, but she wasn't going back.

She looked round the elegant little sitting room. Agnes was out taking tea with one of her friends but Cathie could guess what her hostess would say. *They must need you. You'll have to go, I'm afraid.* So she wasn't even going to tell Agnes about the letter.

With that thought she put down her sewing and marched across the street.

Her uncle was just going out, but one look at her face and he stopped. 'What's wrong?'

'I've had a letter from my stepfather *ordering* me to go home. My mother isn't well – she's expecting a baby – and they need another slave to work in the house. *And I'm not going to do it!*' She burst into tears.

He drew her into the house, winking at Christina behind her back. 'Come into the parlour, love, and let's talk about it.'

When they had her sitting down they offered soothing

words, then her uncle said, 'My offer of a passage to England still stands, you know.'

Cathie looked at him, swallowed hard and asked, 'But is there a ship sailing? If I have to wait a month or two he'll . . .' She didn't need to finish her sentence. Benedict could be a very determined man when he wanted something and she wasn't yet twenty-one.

'I believe there is a ship going shortly. I have to keep track of them because of my business dealings.' Which was a lie. Dermott had found out about sailings in case he could persuade her to go. 'I can easily get you a berth. Are you sure about this, though?'

'I am. But I insist on going steerage.'

He hadn't intended to offer her the luxury of cabin class, but made a token protest. 'No need for that, love.'

She wrapped her arms across her chest and stared at him. 'I mean it. I don't want to borrow more money from you than I have to – and one day I'll find a way to pay it all back, I promise.'

'Eh, lass, I don't need it back. It means nothing to me, that small sum.' But he was touched by her offer.

Cathie raised her chin. 'Well, it means a lot to me. I've not been raised to get into debt. It's only because you're my uncle and . . .'

He held up his hands in a gesture of surrender. 'All right, all right. I'll go and book you a passage right away – steerage.' He pretended to hesitate then said, 'You'd better not mention this to Mrs Fenton, though. She'll only try to stop you going.'

Cathie looked stricken. 'I don't like to deceive her. She's been so good to me.'

'Sometimes we have to think of ourselves. I haven't gone from poor to rich without some effort and, yes, some self-ishness too.'

'I suppose so.' Cathie took a deep breath. 'All right, then. I'll say nothing. Mrs Fenton doesn't know about the letter anyway.'

It was going to be hard to keep the secret, but as well as her desire to visit England, Cathie's longing to know who her father was ran deep and had been eating away at her ever since she had found out he was still alive. What if he died before she could meet him? How would she bear that? He couldn't be a young man if he was older than her mother.

No, there was no way out but to accept her uncle's offer. She was never going to work or live on a farm again as long as she lived.

Early the next morning a man turned up at the Dochertys' house, followed by a lad pushing a handcart with a pile of luggage on it. Cathie, who had been staring out of the front room window as she waited for Agnes to get up, saw the man arrive and lingered to watch, thinking how elegant and European he looked. He was not as old as her parents, but was older than she was, though still rather attractive in spite of being barely medium height. He was staring around him with a scornful twist to his lips, as if he didn't like what he saw.

When the two Docherty children saw him, they stopped playing in the garden to screech, '*Tonton* Matthieu! *Tonton* Matthieu!' and hurl themselves at him.

He swung them up in his arms, one after the other, laughing and teasing them about growing too big for this, then set them down and gave them a little push towards their governess who was smiling and blushing in a foolish way that made Cathie sniff in disgust. The front door of the house opened to show a beaming Christina and the stranger went to kiss her cheek before disappearing inside with his arm round her shoulders.

Cathie sighed. The newcomer must be her uncle's partner from Melbourne. They'd spoken of him a few times. But she was more concerned with how her uncle would go on today. Would he manage to book her passage? Did she really dare run away to England on her own?

She had nearly blurted out her news to Agnes several times and was feeling more weighed down by guilt with every hour that passed. Leaving like that would hurt her mother so much – and her stepfather, too.

Perhaps she shouldn't do it. No, she couldn't bear to go back to the farm and she absolutely *had to* meet her real father! She brushed away a tear impatiently. Her uncle was right. Sometimes you had to act selfishly and do what was right for yourself – but why did that have to hurt others?

'Well, you old devil,' Dermott greeted his business partner.

Matthieu Correntin grinned at him. 'What sort of greeting is that?'

'Would a glass of rum please you more?'

'I'd prefer a cognac.'

'You'll have rum and like it.' Dermott led the way into the parlour. 'I didn't expect you here yet.'

'No. I had to leave Melbourne rather suddenly. Our friends are still annoyed and wanted to take it out on me. Bob Sharpe is going to tie up the loose ends of the business for us.'

Dermott scowled as he passed Matthieu a glass. 'He'll take a percentage for that.'

'*Bien sûr.* But I didn't have much choice. It was get out or risk being killed. And Bob's more or less honest. I offered to work with him if he had any stuff to sell over here. We'll see what comes of that.' Matthieu rotated his shoulders, let out a soft relaxed sound and looked round. 'You seem quite cosy here. Is there a bedroom for me?'

'I'm afraid not. You can't get a decent house for love nor money here in Perth. You can sleep on the sofa tonight, but you'll not want to do that for long.' Dermott eyed the piece of furniture with disfavour. 'It's a damned uncomfortable thing, but this was the only furnished house available to rent — well, the only half-decent one.' He grinned. 'And even so, you should have heard Christina going on about how small it was when she first saw it!'

She sniffed. 'Well, after what we had in Melbourne, can you blame me?'

'The sofa will do me for a few days,' Matthieu said easily. 'Or even a mattress on the back veranda. It's warm enough still to sleep out. We have quite a few matters to discuss.'

'We do indeed.' Dermott drained his glass and stood up. 'But first I have a piece of business to deal with, so I'll have

83

to leave you to enjoy my wife's company. I've discovered a niece, would you believe, and she's staying right across the road. The poor lass is in trouble, so I'm sending her back to England.'

'Your sister's girl? Who's the baby's father?'

Dermott chuckled. 'Not that sort of trouble. No, Miss Cathie wants to run away from home and I'm helping by buying her a passage to England.'

'Which is more than you'll do for me!' Christina said in a voice grown suddenly hard and bitter.

He didn't even look in her direction. It was an old quarrel, though Christina had grown more pressing about it lately. He'd never seen her so upset about anything as she was about moving to the country and she was making all their lives uncomfortable.

Matthieu intervened. 'Why, Dermott? You're not usually a philanthropist.'

'Because it'll upset my dear sister, of course.'

His partner looked disapproving. 'Can you not let this matter of revenge drop, *mon ami*?'

'I'm getting there. We burned their farm down a few weeks ago.'

Matthieu whistled in amazement.

Christina gave a scornful sniff. 'It's gone to his head. Has he told you yet he's now planning to live on a farm he bought because it's near his sister's?'

'Is this true?'

'Aye.' Dermott nodded.

'Another of your wild impulses?'

'I have a fancy to become landed gentry. They tell me it's a good piece of land, with a decent house on it – though madam here will be sure to find fault with it. She's never satisfied, are you, my pet? Wants to go back to England, or Melbourne.'

'I doubt it'll ever be safe for us to return there,' Matthieu said thoughtfully. 'I'm not risking it, anyway. They tried to kill me after you'd left.'

'Ah, we'll see about that. There'll be plenty of room for you at the farm, if you want to stay for a while.'

Matthieu shrugged.

'It looks out on to a small lake, apparently.' Then Dermott glanced at the clock on the mantelpiece and clicked his tongue in annoyance. 'I haven't time to chat now. I've got to sort out my niece's passage.'

Christina put out a hand to prevent him from leaving. 'Why don't you let me travel to England with Cathie? My Aunt Nora keeps writing begging me to visit her. If we want her to leave me her money, I'd better go back before it's too late. We don't want her leaving it to some stray cousin.'

Dermott's expression was implacable. 'When you go back it'll be with me.' He didn't trust her to return to Australia if that aunt of hers really did have as much money as she said. Christina might not be the most comfortable wife in the world, but she was his and she was the mother of his sons. He wasn't letting her go anywhere without him.

CHAPTER FIVE

February

———————•———————

Late that afternoon Dermott came back from Fremantle looking smug, but as usual the horse he had hired looked jaded and weary. Matthieu watched him ride up the street and thought yet again that his partner must be one of the worst riders he'd ever seen. Dermott sat on his horse like a heavy sack of potatoes, wrenching at the reins whenever he wanted the poor creature to do anything. He took little care of the animals he rode, not even bothering to rest or water them properly on short journeys. When taxed with this, he said their health was the owner's concern.

Suddenly Matthieu could not stand to see it. He erupted out of the house and grabbed the horse's reins. 'What the hell have you been doing to this poor creature?'

Dermott shrugged. 'Riding it. That's what I hired it for.'

Matthieu saw James peering over the fence. 'Fetch me a clean bucket of fresh water – at once, lad!'

Dermott strolled into the house, leaving the horse's care to anyone stupid enough to wait on a dumb animal.

The boy returned with the bucket and watched as Matthieu tended the poor animal's needs, not allowing it to drink too much too quickly. 'Why *do* you bother doing all that? Da says it's for the livery stable to look after their horses and they're coming to pick it up later, so they can see to it then.'

Matthieu knew better than to tell Docherty's son that it was simply the right thing to do. 'I look after my mounts because you never know when you'll need to get the best out of an animal — same with a man. It makes more sense to treat them well.'

James traced a pattern in the loose sand of the street with one toe as he considered this. 'Da says it's everyone for himself in this world and only folk who let themselves get trodden on deserve it. He says animals don't count.'

'Your da grew up in a harder world than yours, lad. Times are changing. Besides, people notice if you ill-treat your animals and then they don't respect you. It's the same with dogs. That pup of yours would do anything for you if you were a bit kinder to it.'

'It's only a dog.'

'*Oui.* It is only a dog if you treat it like that. But it's a loyal watchdog and even a friend if you treat it well, the sort that'll die protecting you. You can't buy that sort of loyalty with money, only with kindness.'

He watched James slouch off and wondered why he bothered to offer these concealed lessons. But he knew really — because he hated to see children set such a poor example by a mother who alternately neglected or spoiled them and a father who hadn't the slightest idea how to bring out the best in them. The lads always hung about Matthieu when he was visiting, calling him '*Tonton*', the French word for 'uncle', and he felt he had softened their attitude to life a little. It made him smile sometimes to think of himself playing a father's role, for he had got on badly with his own father – though he had at least had a grandfather to care for him and teach him about life, and had not left France until old Hervé Correntin died.

That evening Dermott strolled across the road to thump heavily on Agnes's door. 'Could I have a word with my niece, please, Mrs Fenton?'

Agnes was beginning to wonder what was going on, because Cathie had been very edgy all day and had rushed towards the door the minute she heard her uncle's voice. She turned to look at the girl standing right behind her. 'Come in, Mr Docherty. Is something wrong?'

'No, nothing at all. Only it's such a lovely evening, I thought Cathie might like a stroll into town with her old uncle.'

So Agnes could do nothing but agree, even though it was obvious that this was merely a ploy for them to talk privately. Why hadn't she heard from Liza about the Dochertys? After fidgeting around for a while she wrote another letter to her friend, explaining the situation once again just in case the other note hadn't got through – though the post was pretty reliable these days. Then she went outside and paid a neighbour's lad to take it to the post office.

And why she should remain so uneasy about what Cathie and Mr Docherty were doing she could not think.

Once they were out of sight of Agnes, Cathie stopped walking and turned to face her uncle. 'Well?'

'There's a ship sailing next week from Albany.'

She looked at him in puzzlement. 'My mother's ship came to Fremantle.'

'They did sometimes in the early days and a lot of them got wrecked, too, they tell me — but Albany's the mail port and that's where most passenger ships sail from now.'

'Oh.'

'Don't look so upset. You've time to take the coaster and sail down to Albany in comfort. It leaves tomorrow. If you still want to go to England and meet your father, that is? I'll perfectly understand if you don't and—'

She didn't wait for him to finish. 'I *do* still want to go, of course I do!'

'How are we going to arrange it, then? I doubt Mrs Fenton will let you go openly.'

Cathie picked some leaves from a nearby bush and began to shred them. 'I'll have to find a way to leave without telling her.'

'Matthieu can drive us both to Fremantle tomorrow and I'll put you on the coaster myself. He's a dab hand with horses, that one.' Dermott chuckled but there was no real humour in the sound. 'We'll have to leave very early tomorrow morning, though. Can you slip out of the house at dawn, do you think? And what about your things?' He frowned, thinking it through. 'I've got a trunk I can let you have. Toss your things out of your bedroom window on to the back veranda and after Mrs Fenton's gone to bed, I'll nip round and get them, then your aunt can pack everything for you.'

'I haven't enough things with me to fill a trunk.'

'Oh, I dare say Christina can find you a few bits and pieces of clothing. She never wears anything out.'

'She's much smaller than I am.'

Dermott waved one hand dismissively. 'Well, you can alter them, can't you? It'll give you something to do on the ship.' He remembered his own journey to Australia and that was another reason why he'd delayed going back to England. He'd been seasick a lot of the time and had hated every minute of the voyage. Rotten food. No privacy at all in steerage. Half the time stinking hot, the rest freezing cold. He didn't envy his niece her coming experience.

Cathie considered her escape as they continued their walk and at one stage suggested they pop into a drapery so that she could buy a few things.

With an indulgent smile Dermott insisted on buying them for her.

As they walked on, Cathie said abruptly, 'Agnes never wakes till late because she stays up till midnight. She says only maidservants needed to rise at dawn. The woman who comes in daily to do the rough housework doesn't arrive till eight o'clock. She won't notice whether I'm in my room or not.' She swallowed hard. It all seemed to be happening too quickly.

Dermott saw her hesitation and said in a jollying tone, 'You're an adventurous lass – a bit like your old uncle, eh? It's natural to want to see something of the world.'

They walked on in silence for a while, then she asked, 'Will you give my mother a letter for me, Uncle Dermott?'

'Aye, of course I will. I'll be travelling down that way in a week or two on business and I'm going to see our Liza to try once more for a reconciliation.'

'I hope you manage to persuade her, but Mum is – well, she can be a bit stubborn and Dad's even worse. I'll give you the letter in the morning.' She would have to write to Agnes as well, Cathie decided. Another pang speared through her. This was not as easy to do as she'd expected.

Over the evening meal Dermott boasted to his partner about what he had arranged and Christina crowed with glee.

Matthieu scowled at him. 'You're a nasty devil, Dermott Docherty. What has that poor girl ever done to you?'

'Ah, she *wants* to go to England. She's just found out who her real father is and wants to meet him. I didn't put the idea of going into her head. I'm just – helping her do it.'

Matthieu knew his partner well enough to ask, 'What's the father really like? Is he worth meeting?'

Dermott shrugged. 'He's a bully. He raped my sister, which is how Cathie was born, no doubt. He was a nasty sod in those days and I don't suppose he's improved much with keeping. If he's still alive.' Actually, now he came to think of it, Niall had been paid to drag Liza across the street and hand her over to Teddy Marshall – who had wanted to make certain she'd be forced to marry him. She'd have been about as old then as Cathie was now. For the first time it occurred to Dermott that Niall hadn't been fair to their sister. If he himself had a daughter, he'd kill anyone who raped her. He blinked in surprise. Why was he thinking things like that? He'd never before questioned his brother's behaviour.

'Don't you even know whether this man is alive or not?' Matthieu demanded, horrified.

'How could I? I've never been back.'

'But you're sending that girl halfway round the world to meet him!'

Dermott shrugged. 'What I'm doing is sending her *away* from her mother and father. It doesn't matter a fart to me where she ends up. And Teddy Marshall probably is still alive. He was a tough old bugger. But I'd be grateful if you'd do the driving tomorrow. I don't want anything preventing us from getting her to Fremantle in time.' Those sodding horses sometimes turned stubborn on you.

Matthieu was tempted to go across the street and suggest very strongly to this Cathie that she think again about what she was doing. 'Everything will be very strange to her over there,' he said to Dermott. 'Are you sure—?'

'Oh, Teddy had several sons, so Cathie won't be without relatives even if someone has murdered the old sod.'

'She might not even tell this Marshall fellow who she is if she doesn't like the look of him,' Matthieu suggested.

'Mmm, you're right. I think I'd better send old Teddy a letter telling him about his little girl and suggesting he watch out for her in Pendleworth. It can go over on the same ship as she does!' Dermott laughed heartily.

The frown lines on Matthieu's forehead deepened.

When Dermott went into their bedroom, he found Christina weeping again and she turned her back on him in bed, something that rarely happened.

In the morning Cathie's departure went smoothly. There was no sound from Agnes's room as her guest crept out along the back veranda in the grey light of early dawn. Cathie paused a minute to mouth a silent and guilt-laden farewell then moved quietly round the side of the small house.

Her uncle had come for her things during the night. She'd heard him as she lay sleepless in bed. Now she found him and Mr Correntin waiting for her at their gate with a trunk on a handcart. 'Your aunt put in a few of her old things as well,' Dermott said as he took the bag holding the rest of her possessions from her and put it on top of the trunk. 'Look sharp now, lass!'

He set off at a brisk pace and she followed, casting one glance back over her shoulder then looking only ahead.

When they arrived in Fremantle, Cathie shivered. 'I hate that jail. It seems to loom over the town, doesn't it? I'd go mad if I was locked up in there.'

'Serve 'em right for getting caught,' Dermott said. 'They're the stupid ones.'

Cathie thought of Dinny's husband Fergal and decided she didn't agree with him, but it was not worth arguing.

Matthieu changed the subject firmly. 'We'll need to get you a ship's kit before you go on board, Cathie.'

'I don't want to cost my uncle any more.' She had no idea what a ship's kit would contain, but was determined not to be extravagant in any way.

'He's right. Come on, lass,' Dermott said, amazed that he hadn't thought of that himself. 'There's a ship's chandler's just down the street. They'll have what we need.'

'We'll get her one of the better kits,' Matthieu said firmly. 'And if you don't want to pay for it, I will.'

'I can bloody well afford it! She's my niece, so you keep your nose out of this.'

Cathie's face was scarlet with humiliation. 'Oh, please

don't quarrel over me. I'm sure I can manage without one.'

'*Chérie*, you need the right equipment for a long journey like this,' Matthieu said quietly. 'I've travelled a great deal and I know what a difference it makes.' He tied up the horse and signalled to a lad to come and watch it, then offered his right arm to her with such an imperative gesture that she could not refuse to take it, though she looked back apologetically at her uncle.

Sodding Frenchies always had to be gallant with women, Dermott thought grumpily as he followed them. If he treated Christina that way, she'd soon be ordering him around in the home he paid for.

However, when they got to the chandler's he made sure his niece got the best kit they had, containing bedding, toilet articles, a water bottle, wash basin, jug, plate and pint drinking mug, not to mention three pounds of marine soap.

Matthieu wandered off as Dermott was paying and came back with two smaller packs. One contained writing paper and ink, as well as a diary; the other contained some embroidery silks and a tablecloth. 'You will need something to pass the time during the journey.'

Cathie was overwhelmed by all this and pressed her hands against her hot cheeks. 'I never realised I'd be costing everyone so much! I'll pay you both back one day, I promise.' She had had so little money in her life that it seemed amazing how much these two men were spending on her.

Matthieu laughed. 'You can try, *chérie*, but I shall not let you.'

'Heavens, what a fuss!' growled Dermott. 'All for a few bits and pieces to keep you comfortable.'

They drove down to the quay and found the coaster. Cathie stood at the bottom of the gangway and hesitated as she looked at her uncle. England was so very far away. How would she ever find the money to return to Australia?

For the first time it occurred to her that she might not return, might never see her family again. And that was a truly shocking thought because, whatever their differences, she loved them all dearly. She tried desperately to hold the tears back, but they welled in her eyes and rolled down her cheeks.

'Don't go if you're at all doubtful, *chérie*.' Matthieu ignored the scowl his partner gave him and put one arm round her shoulders. 'You can always catch a later ship, after all.'

But the thought of returning to the farm in disgrace stiffened Cathie's spine and she shook her head emphatically. 'No, I must do this, Mr Correntin. It's just – it's a big thing to leave your family behind. I shall miss them so.'

Her uncle stared at her as if she'd said something stupid, but Matthieu said quietly, 'I know. I did the same thing myself.'

'And do you regret it?' she asked, feeling torn in a thousand different directions.

He shook his head, not even needing to think about it. 'No. I am not the sort to settle down quietly and follow in my father's footsteps.'

She looked at him for a moment, then nodded. 'I don't think I am, either.'

'*Bien*. What matters most is that this is the right thing

for you. It is not, after all, your family who are going to England.'

As she turned towards the ship again, Dermott surprised himself by thrusting a few sovereigns into her hand. 'Here. Take these, lass. You won't want to be without money when you arrive.'

A young woman who had stopped to watch them smiled at Cathie then walked past them.

Matthieu, who had already slipped some money secretly into the parcels he'd given Cathie, stared at his colleague in amazement. Dermott Docherty was normally the last man to perform acts of generosity.

Cathie had no such reservations. She flung her arms round her uncle and gave him a hug such as he had never experienced in his life before, pressing her smooth young cheek against his and saying huskily, 'Thank you, Uncle Dermott! For everything. You've been so kind to me. I'm sorry we haven't been able to spend more time together. Maybe if – when – I come back to Australia, we can get to know one another better.'

He gave her an awkward hug back. 'Ah, y're a good lass,' he muttered.

She walked a few steps, then turned and rushed back, fumbling in her handbag. 'I nearly forgot! This is the letter to my mother.' She thrust a crumpled, sealed envelope into his hand, tried to smile at the two men but failed signally, then hurried on to the ship, without looking back.

As she vanished from sight, Matthieu threw a dirty look at Dermott. 'You shouldn't have done this. It's cruel sending her so far away. *She* hasn't done you any harm.'

Already ashamed of his brief display of weakness,

Dermott made a rude noise. 'Ah, she'll be all right. She's got her head screwed on properly, that one has.'

'Sensible or not, she's a naïve young girl who's been brought up in the bush. She'll be prey for anyone and everyone.'

'She's a Docherty. She'll come through. Besides, I gave her some money, didn't I?'

Matthieu frowned. 'Yes, you did. What got into you?'

Dermott gave his rather hoarse chuckle. 'I'm wondering that myself. Must be getting soft in my old age. Come on, let's find ourselves a drink of ale. I've a hell of a thirst on me.'

Several drinks later, he said thoughtfully, 'You know, if I'd ever had a daughter I'd have wanted one like that — only I'd have taught her a few things, not left her so green and ready to be plucked.'

Matthieu had done his best for the girl and was now thinking about his own future. 'When do we go down to look at this land you've bought?'

Dermott grinned. 'When the ship's sailed from Albany. When a sailor I've got keeping an eye out for that lass sends me word she's definitely left with it.'

'I feel like a change. Shall I go down to the farm and look at it for you?'

'Why not? I'll sell it to you cheaply if you like it.' Dermott roared with laughter at his own joke, then looked at Matthieu in surprise. 'You're not joking, are you? I didn't have you figured for a country lover.'

'I enjoy a bit of peace from time to time.'

'Be my guest. There's plenty of peace in the bush.'

*

97

Cathie spent most of the daylight hours of the trip down to Albany on deck, not wanting to miss a thing. She could only vaguely remember the trip out from England to Australia when she was five and had heard her mother talk about shipboard life. Now she would experience it all herself. There were only two female passengers travelling alone, the other being the woman who had boarded just before her, so they were sharing a cabin. Bessie Downham was a rather coarse young woman three years older than Cathie and much battered by life.

'When my husband died I decided to go home to England,' she confided the first day. 'Can't stand it out here. Too quiet by half.'

'Do you have family there?'

'If they're still alive. A brother, Nat, in Liverpool. He'll help me settle in again. I'll get myself a job — I used to work in a pub. Nice lively work, that is. It'll seem like heaven after living in the stinking bush.'

That remark alone was enough to win her Cathie's friendship and sympathy.

Bessie didn't mention that working behind a bar had been only part of her duties. The rest had been to accommodate the sailors passing through the port — and steal their money if they were drunk enough. She'd been foolish enough to fall for one of them who was looking for a wife, and had believed his tales about a fine new life in the colonies. Well, that hadn't worked out and he'd been a lying sod about how easy it was to get rich in Australia! Once she'd decided to return to England, she'd written to her brother, who'd pimped for her before, to tell him she was coming back and which ship she'd be on.

She was sure Nat would come and meet her in Liverpool. She'd brought him in some good money before and he'd treated her better than her rat of a husband had. She smiled. They'd not find John's body, not in that god-forsaken spot. She hadn't really meant to kill him, had just swung out at him when he forbade her to go back, forgetting she was holding the carving knife and catching him in the throat. A good thing, really, because it had solved the problem of how to get away.

She eyed her companion shrewdly. She had seen the uncle press some money into Cathie's hand and hoped to get hold of some of it before they parted.

When they arrived at Albany Bessie took charge, telling the Matron on the ship that they were travelling together and arranging for them to get bunks in the same cabin. This was a modern ship and had small cabins opening off the main sitting area. Though they were more like cupboards than rooms, Bessie thought sourly, looking round theirs, and the rocking of the boat was already making her feel queasy.

She was so short-tempered that Cathie stared at her in surprise. 'Is something wrong, Bessie?'

'No. I'm just – not a good sailor.' She pressed one hand against her mouth.

By the time the Matron in charge of the single women came past to check that all was well, Bessie was vomiting into a bucket and her friend was helping her, looking very competent. Mrs Jebbings, who had made the journey several times since her husband had died and found acting as Matron an agreeable way of earning a living, made a mental note to keep an eye on Miss Caine. If the weather grew rough, they might need extra help from someone who was good at looking after people.

It turned out that all the single women of fourteen and over shared cramped quarters aft, which Cathie still thought of as the back of the ship. They were four to each tiny cabin, and already Matron had laid down rules about how they were to behave. In the middle of the ship were the married couples and their children, while the single men occupied the foremost compartment towards the bow, which was the name for the front end.

Cathie went up on deck, unperturbed by the way the ship was wallowing, to watch Albany disappear behind them. Bessie was still feeling poorly and had declined to leave the cabin.

Although Cathie was surrounded by other young women, some of whom smiled at her, it struck her all over again how far away she was going. As she stood by the rail she felt more alone than she ever had before in her life. They were mostly travelling with their families but she had no one, really, because you couldn't count Bessie. She had been with her mother and stepfather on her last voyage, with Seth as well, though he'd been only two. It was frightening to be on your own.

As she stared at the faint smudge that was all she could now see of Albany she could not hold back the tears. She wasn't the only one weeping, either.

At that moment, if she had been able to change her mind and go home, she would have done so.

Only she couldn't change things. She was on her way to England now and that was that. She would just have to make the best of it.

By the time she went below again she had calmed down. But she wept into her pillow that night and for several nights.

Benedict arrived in Perth several days after Cathie had left for Albany. Agnes watched him get down from the cart and stride down her garden path, looking grimly determined.

'Where's Cathie?' he demanded as he followed Agnes inside.

'I'm so sorry . . .' Her voice failed her for a moment or two, then she raised her head and forced herself to look him in the eye. 'I'm afraid she's run away – she's on her way to England.'

'What?'

'Benedict, please sit down and let me make you something to eat and drink, then I'll explain.'

He remained standing. 'Explain first.'

So she did, growing increasingly anxious as she saw the grim look on his face. 'I'm sorry,' she finished. 'I've failed you.'

'You have that! I thought we could trust you to look after her. Where's this damned uncle of hers?'

'I saw Mr Docherty go out earlier. I don't think he's back yet.'

'How am I to tell Liza?' he muttered. 'She'll be sick with worry. And how am I to find help for her now? Ilse is having to neglect the children to run the house.'

'Is Liza really ill?'

'Aye. She's gone so thin, except for the baby, that I fear

for her life.' He buried his face in his hands and groaned. 'What the hell am I going to do?'

Agnes was weeping openly now but after a while she pulled herself together and went over to take his arm. She had to shake it quite hard to make him pay attention to her. 'I'll come and look after the house and Liza, Benedict.'

'You?'

She nodded. 'I'm not completely helpless, you know. Living in Australia has taught me to look after myself. You'd be surprised what a good housewife I've become.' Though like many other ladies in her position she pretended that the housework got itself done.

'Nay, I can't expect you to do that. You have your own life here.'

She sighed. 'Not much of a life for a widow – and not much money, either, to tell you the truth. Gerard was always a poor manager and he got worse as he grew older. All I own now is this house, and I've been wondering whether to take in lodgers again.' She brightened. 'Look, why don't I come and stay with you till after the baby is born? I can rent this place out for six months and that'll help me financially.'

'Do you really mean that?'

'Of course I do.'

'Then I accept and gladly.'

Agnes looked at him. 'Cathie will be all right, I'm sure.'

He tried to smile and failed. 'She's so young – inexperienced. And we love her very much.'

He agreed to stay the night and allowed Agnes to feed him, but picked at his food and every time someone came along the street he went to the window and asked, 'Is that him?'

When a man of medium height, very neatly dressed, appeared from the direction of the town centre, Agnes hurried out to the gate. 'Good afternoon, Monsieur Correntin.'

He swept off his hat and inclined his head. 'Madame.'

She gestured to Benedict. 'This is Mr Caine, Cathie's father. He wants to speak to Mr Docherty.'

Matthieu studied Benedict, whose expression was grim. 'Dermott is away on business. He may not be back for days.'

'I don't believe you,' Benedict snapped.

Anger crackled between the two men then Matthieu gave a very French shrug, murmured, 'If you will excuse me?' and turned to leave. Inside the house he found Christina peering out of the window at the two people standing talking on Agnes's veranda.

'Benedict Caine's going grey now,' she said in some satisfaction. 'He's really showing his age.'

'You know him?'

'Oh, yes. I came out on the same ship as them. He had eyes only for Liza, even though he was married to someone else at the time, it turned out. And she fancied him, too – but since he wasn't free, she married Josiah Ludlam to give her baby a name – and of course that baby was Cathie. You'd better go and warn Dermott that Caine is here and he should stay away.'

Matthieu sighed. 'I suppose so. I'll slip out the back way.'

The following morning Benedict went across the street and banged on the door of the Dochertys' house. Christina fled to her bedroom with a muffled shriek, so Matthieu opened it.

'Is Docherty back?'

'Non.'

Benedict breathed deeply. 'He'll not avoid me for ever.'

'He'll be back in a day or two.'

'I've got to return to Lizabrook. My wife's ill. Tell him he's not heard the last of this, though.' He swung round and went back to help Agnes pack.

They worked until past midnight so that she could leave the place in her lawyer's hands to rent furnished for six months. Luckily, they would be able to carry all her more personal things back with them in the cart.

Even when he did get to bed Benedict lay fretting because it'd taken them two days to get home. He hated the thought of Liza being on her own – even though Dinny was there to help. Never again, he decided. My Liza's definitely not having any more children. She matters more to me than anything else. Or anyone. He could not imagine life without her now.

And he had failed her, failed to look after her daughter properly.

CHAPTER SIX

March–April

In Pendleworth Mairi Hamilton stood near the window of the front room, not bothering to light the gas, just gazing out at the moonlit street and enjoying the peace. Her mother was now dozing in front of the kitchen fire, but had had a bad day. There was no doubt in Mairi's mind that she was rapidly getting worse.

Magnus was sitting with her now, ostensibly reading but doing more gazing into the flames. Mairi knew he was worrying about what would happen after she got married the following Saturday. It was so hard to find someone to care for their mother as they would have wished. A few slatternly women who didn't even look clean themselves had applied for the job, but neither Mairi nor Magnus had taken to them, so with great reluctance she had postponed her wedding once.

But she wasn't postponing it again. The Benevolent Home was not all that bad and Magnus would simply have to put their mother in. If Mum had been able to recognise where she was it would be different, but she couldn't even recognise her own children now. All she did was wander round the house, pacing to and fro, often getting very agitated for no reason that anyone could understand.

Mairi knew that even if she were not getting married she could not go on like this. Some women made martyrs of themselves, caring for relatives for years. Much as she loved her mother, she wasn't one of them. She had had several very difficult years and had come to the end of her patience now. She had a life of her own to lead, a man she loved waiting to marry her.

Since Elwyn had moved to Bury they had written to one another almost daily and she missed him dreadfully, but he was coming across to Pendleworth on Friday, ready for their simple wedding ceremony on Saturday. Her heart sang at the thought of moving away from here, of being with him, and of leaving this dreadful, tedious life behind — even though at the same time she was riven with guilt for deserting Magnus. But at least her brother would have Hamish's company and help in the evenings, and they had now found a woman who seemed suitable and was prepared to come in six days a week.

She looked up, smiling as she heard a faint whistling from the far end of the street. That would be Hamish. He always whistled when he was in a particularly good mood. Going back into the kitchen, she smiled at Magnus and moved the kettle over to the hottest part of the range top ready to make their evening cup of cocoa.

The front door banged open and Hamish called out a greeting from the hall.

'Can he not do anything quietly?' Magnus muttered, putting his newspaper down.

'You know he can't. He's young and full of life. I like to see it.'

Hamish breezed in beaming at them both, then grabbed Mairi and waltzed her round the room, humming 'The Blue Danube' in his tuneful baritone.

'Let me go, you daft loon!'

He did, but with another of his great roaring laughs.

'What's got into you the night?' As he flung himself down by the table, she went to brew the cocoa.

Hamish beamed at her. 'The talk at the Institute has got into me, that's what. It sounds wonderful, Australia does.'

Magnus stiffened visibly. 'Aye, well, I'm happy with my own country, thank you very much.' He remembered how sad leaving Scotland had made him and could not imagine wanting to leave Lancashire and everything he had grown to love here.

Hamish stared down at the steaming cup Mairi had just placed in front of him, then blurted out, 'Well, I'm not happy here.'

There was dead silence until Magnus asked with a harsh edge to his voice, 'What does that mean?'

'It means there's no future for a man like me in Pendleworth. It's all right for you. You're foreman in Ludlam's workshop and the apple of Mr Reuben's eye, so you're set for life.' Hamish began to stir his cocoa round and round, slopping it into his saucer. 'I hate working in the mill, but in Australia — why, there's no limit to what a fellow can do out there.'

'Oh, aye? Paradise, is it?' Magnus snapped. 'Canada was the same, but don't you think that Dougal or Athol would have written by now if they'd done well for themselves? Or perhaps they just don't want to share the fortunes they've made with us.' His brothers had borrowed the fare money from him and promised faithfully to repay it, and the fact that they hadn't even written to say they couldn't manage that upset him greatly. Unless they were dead – and the idea of that was even worse.

'Oh, you always look on the black side.' Hamish set his spoon down in the saucer, avoiding Magnus's eyes and adjusting its position carefully, as if it mattered very much that he get it just so.

'Tell us what you've heard the night,' Mairi prompted quietly.

He started to tell them not only about what he had heard, but the sights he had seen on the lantern show. 'The sky's so blue out there. It never snows, you know – well, not in most places. And they're crying out for men on the land.'

'What the hell do you know about farming?' Magnus snapped.

'Nothing. But it's bred in me, isn't it?'

Magnus thumped the table. 'Bred in you! What are you talking about, man? You were born here in Pendleworth. All that's bred in you is a mill town.'

Hamish ignored that comment. 'And while we're at it, there's another thing we need to talk about. Our mother. Once Mairi's left—'

'We'll have Mrs Midner.'

'And if *she* leaves?'

'Then we'll find someone else.'

Hamish groaned. 'Magnus lad, are you out of your mind? We *can't* manage without Mairi. What do we know about looking after a house? And what happens after Mrs

Midner goes home at night? I'd die of shame if I had to tend my mother's naked body. I tell you flat I won't do it — and she wouldn't want me to. Besides—'

Her sister closed her eyes and prayed for him to stop but he didn't. He went right ahead and said the things she'd been afraid to hear, for she too had studied the posters outside the Institute and knew what they were offering.

'— I won't be here to help you.' Hamish stared at them both challengingly, his jaw jutting out and his head jerking as he looked from one to the other, then back again.

Mairi spoke before Magnus could. 'You can wait a year to go, surely? Australia will still be there next year. You can give Magnus that much after all he's done for you.'

Hamish gave a quick, tight shake of the head. 'There are people offering to pay your fare out if you'll work for them for two years after you arrive — *and* they'll pay you wages during those two years, as well as your keep. It's a great chance for a man like me to save a bit of money.' He paused then blurted out, 'So I signed the papers tonight. I leave for Australia in about two months.'

With an inarticulate mutter Magnus got up and strode out of the house, leaving the front door swinging open behind him and cold damp air swirling in.

'Did you have to tell us now?' Mairi demanded, getting up to close the door, then coming back to stand next to Hamish, hands on hips. 'Just as I'm about to get married! Couldn't you even let me have a happy wedding day?' Her voice broke and she bent her head, fighting the tears.

Hamish's voice was truculent. 'I've waited long enough. *You're* escaping. Why shouldn't I?' He stared across the room at their mother who was sitting gazing blankly into the fire, humming under her breath. 'She doesn't know what's going on. She's not our mother any more!'

'Magnus won't put her in the Ben. He never breaks a promise.'

'He'll have to now.'

It was two hours before Magnus came home again. They were all in bed, but Mairi was still awake, lying worrying. She heard her brother climb the stairs slowly, as if he were old and weary, and go into the big front bedroom he and Hamish shared, but she didn't call out to him. She knew she was being a coward but she could not face his distress again that night because she did not want to risk giving in to her guilty conscience and saying she'd wait to join her husband in Bury.

In the morning Hamish looked at his oldest brother across the breakfast table. 'Mother would be well looked after at the Ben, you know.'

So Magnus said it all over again, flatly and emphatically, for he had thought it through as he walked the dark streets. 'She's *not* going in there and it's no use telling me she wouldn't know, because it's not true. She still gets distressed if we so much as walk past it. And if none of you will help me to look after her at home, then I will just have to – to manage somehow.' He looked at his sister, eyes softening for a moment, then back at his brother with a stern expression. 'Our Mairi's done her share, more than. Surely you could wait a wee while and do yours now, Hamish?' It was as near as he could come to pleading.

'I'll not. It's not a job for a man. I'd die of embarrassment if I had to wash her and . . . other things.'

'Then you're no brother of mine!' Magnus thumped his fist down on the table.

'Magnus!' Mairi said sharply. 'Don't say something you'll regret for the rest of your life.'

'But he—'

'— has made his mind up to leave. As have I.' Her voice softened. 'And, laddie, you're wrong about the Ben.'

'I shallna break my word: not for you, nor for anyone!'

But he did not attack his brother again and when Hamish would have spoken, Mairi put a finger to her lips and shook her head at him. Least said soonest mended — if there was any mending possible.

Dermott laughed when Matthieu sent word that Benedict Caine had gone home to his farm and taken Agnes Fenton with him. 'Good riddance to them. I'll see them when I'm ready and not before.'

'I'm going to visit the farm in a day or two,' Matthieu said mildly. 'I may call on the Caines and tell them Cathie was all right, and well equipped for the voyage. They must be worried about her. Have you posted the letter to her mother?'

'I lost it.'

Matthieu stared at him in disgust. 'There was no need for that.'

'I'll judge the need where my sister is concerned. And you might want to stay here for a bit longer, because I've found a bit of business as'll bring us both in a few extra pence.'

The business was profitable, but Matthieu's conscience

kept pricking him, so in the end he sat down and wrote a brief letter to the Caines, saying that when Cathie had sailed to England she had been in good health and very excited about her trip. After some hesitation, he signed his name to it. He found out from the tenants who Mrs Fenton's lawyer was and visited his office to find out her present address.

Then there were not only the things Dermott had purchased to dispose of, but the first load of goods from Bob Sharpe in Melbourne, so Matthieu was soon too busy making sure they got the best returns on their investment to visit the farm.

'Bob's done well by us,' he said, once they'd found a suitable warehouse and inventoried the load.

Dermott looked round at the neat stacks of household goods. 'And we've done well by him, too. He's a fool. Could have forced us to give him a higher percentage. He won't even be able to check the prices we get.'

'He wants reliable contacts over here – and besides, he knows I shall not cheat him.' Matthieu gave his partner a very straight look.

'But we could—'

'We'll deal honestly with him – and with everyone else here in Perth. You keep saying you want to be known as a respectable member of the community once you've made your fortune. Well, here's your chance to make a new start.'

Dermott chewed the corner of his lip thoughtfully.

'And don't think you can cheat me, either,' Matthieu added. 'I'll find out if you do, one way or the other, and that'll be the end of our partnership.'

There was a pregnant pause, then Dermott chuckled. 'I

expect you're right, lad! I'll get Christina to come and help us. She's better than either of us at dealing with women's stuff.' She'd been in low spirits since Cathie's departure, weeping quite often, which was not like her. Having something to do would take her out of herself.

Matthieu nodded and let the matter drop, but promised himself to keep a very careful eye on what Dermott was doing. And since the Dochertys were not the most comfortable of companions, he found himself some lodgings a few streets away. A man needed a bit of peace sometimes. He was looking forward to getting away for a while to the quiet of the countryside.

Matthieu's letter arrived at the Caines' farm on a warm day in early April just as autumn was beginning to cool the land. Benedict read it through, then passed it on to his wife, saying in a voice choked with emotion, 'Cathie's definitely gone to England.'

Liza read the letter, tears rolling down her cheeks. 'It was kind of Mr Correntin to write.'

'It'd have been kinder still to stop her leaving.'

'How could he if both she and Dermott were set on it?'

With a snort of anger Benedict went out to tend the horses, while she went to tell the rest of the family what the letter had said.

Agnes watched her friend trying to maintain a cheerful front, for the sake of her younger children. *She* did not feel at all cheerful and was regretting that she'd volunteered to come and help here until after the baby was born. There was a sameness to days in this place that was beginning to wear her down. No wonder Cathie had been so desperate to escape.

After some thought, Agnes wrote to tell her lawyer not to allow the tenants to renew the lease on her house as she would be returning to Perth then. When she had finished her letter she went out to sit on the veranda, her favourite place.

Ilse joined her. 'When you go back to Perth' – she hesitated, looked over her shoulder and lowered her voice – 'I wonder if you'd consider taking a lodger again?'

'You?'

'Yes. Benedict and Liza have been good to me, but one does not meet many people living here. I'm not getting any younger and there's a shortage of respectable women there, they say, so—' She broke off, not daring to put her modest dreams into words and dreading the other woman's scorn.

Agnes finished for her '– you'd like to find yourself another husband before it's too late. And this time, one whom you can respect and like, perhaps?'

'Ja. Do you think I'm being foolish? Only I'm not ugly or malformed, so I thought . . .'

'I'd be happy to take you as a lodger again and I'm sure you'll have no difficulty whatsoever in finding yourself a husband in Perth.' Agnes smiled encouragingly. 'I even have hopes in that direction for myself. We'll go hunting together.'

That night Liza was wakened by cramping pains in her stomach and a stickiness between her legs. Her groans disturbed Benedict and he lit the lamp. By that time she was doubled up, rolling around in agony. 'Fetch Dinny!' she gasped.

When he had gone, the new bedroom seemed full of shadows and pain. Though she tried to muffle her cries in the pillow, the cramping was growing stronger. She didn't need anyone to tell her she was losing the child and when Dinny came hurrying through the door, started weeping helplessly.

By that time the rest of the household was awake. Agnes lit their lamp and looked at Ilse with whom she was sharing a room. 'Will you go and light a fire while I see if I can help? We'll need plenty of hot water.'

Ilse dragged on some clothes and went out to the small separate laundry at the rear to light a fire under the copper. She had been dreaming of a husband, children, a home. This was the reality for women: both pleasure and pain from marriage. She had failed to find happiness once. Did she dare risk trying again? A memory of the loving glances Benedict and Liza often shared made her nod. Yes, she would risk it.

In the bedroom Liza was alternately sobbing and groaning. Dinny tried to send Benedict away, but he would not leave and, after Liza had lost the baby, he held her in his arms and wept with her.

Relieved that this was taking place in the new house Benedict and Fergal had recently finished and which had proper doors to keep the noise down, Ilse went to sit with Josie. The child was terrified by the thought of her mother being ill, and within a few minutes an equally frightened Harry had crept in to join them. Ilse talked softly to them, telling them one of the fairy stories she had heard in her own childhood, pausing sometimes to fumble for the right English word. It seemed a very long time until Benedict came to see them.

The children threw themselves at their father and he hugged them close as he said gently, 'Your mother's lost the baby.'

Josie burst into tears and he spent a few minutes patting her shoulder and assuring her that although this was an unhappy thing, her mother would get better. Harry sat huddled in a heap, so Ilse pulled him into her arms and began to murmur meaningless endearments. As she looked down at the sturdy little body, she knew she wanted children of her own.

When Benedict left them he went to tell Lucas and Seth, then returned to his own bedroom. He found Dinny holding Liza in her arms, rocking her and letting her cry. She looked up at the sight of him, then said quietly, 'I have something to tell you both. Liza, listen to me.' When she had their attention, she said, 'The baby wasn't growing properly. It couldn't have lived, even if you'd managed to carry it for the whole nine months.'

There was silence then Liza pressed back against the pillows, her arm shielding her eyes. Dinny got up and gestured to Benedict to take her place before leaving the room quietly.

When Liza eventually fell asleep, he left Agnes sitting with her and went to find Dinny. 'Show me the baby!'

So she took him to see the poor deformed infant, with its twisted limbs and over-large head.

He stood there in silence looking down upon what would have been his son. 'Shall I bury him?'

'Not yet. Liza will need to see him, too.'

Two hours later, just as dawn was breaking, Liza awoke and demanded to see her child before they buried it. Dinny brought the baby in to her, washed and dressed in a little gown, its skin almost translucent in its whiteness. But nothing could hide its deformities.

'I want to give him a name!' Liza said suddenly. 'Ambrose.'

Dinny said nothing. Her people had different views on what happened after death but she usually kept these to herself.

Liza lay back and closed her eyes, beyond tears now, so deeply sad she could not think about anything but getting through each minute.

Benedict accepted Fergal's offer to dig the grave because he felt a great weariness as well as a sense of loss, but he made the baby's coffin himself in the new workshop, which had a roof of sorts, but no walls yet.

When evening came he carried his wife outside. Liza sat on a chair in the small cemetery by the lake and watched as he put the tiny coffin in the ground. Around them their other children stood silently and it was a comfort to see them, to know that they had not lost several to the various childhood ailments as so many of the settlers did. Afterwards they all prayed for Ambrose's soul.

When the short ceremony ended Ilse and Agnes shepherded the two younger children back to the house, relieved when they fell asleep, exhausted by their broken night and traumatic day.

Benedict and Liza stayed by the little grave and after a moment or two he sat on the ground at her feet, leaning against her knees, taking comfort from the hand that stroked his hair from time to time. He didn't say anything, nor did she. What could they say at a time like this? They were together and that was the important thing.

When Ilse went into the living room she found Agnes sitting with a glass of port in front of her and accepted a glass herself.

'I don't usually indulge but Benedict offered and it seems appropriate today,' Agnes said quietly.

The two women sat sipping the rich, sweet wine, not saying much but warmed by each other's company. Benedict joined them once Liza had gone to bed and he was sure she was asleep. Agnes poured him a glass too. He shook his head but she insisted. 'Drink it!'

Not until he had taken a few sips and had slumped back in the chair did she ask, 'Is Liza all right?'

He nodded. 'I think so. The funeral ceremony helped a little, I think, but we're both upset.' He stayed for a while then put his empty glass down, almost missing the edge of the table. When he got to bed, he expected to lie awake but fell deeply asleep from utter exhaustion.

Beside him Liza intermittently dozed and stared at the darkness outside the window. She wanted to weep but could not. She wanted to scream out a protest against the fate that had taken her child away from her so abruptly, but everyone else was asleep and this pain was hers more than theirs anyway. Her body felt strange and she missed the comfort of the baby moving gently in her stomach. But he was lost to her now. What would he have been like if he had lived?

As the slow hours passed, her thoughts turned inevitably to her other lost child. Where was Cathie? Was she all right? Then it occurred to her that she had two lost children. There was her son Francis as well, who had been taken from her when he was a baby. Anguish hit her again in a great black wave. Her second husband had left the guardianship of their son to his uncle, and when Nicholas had been killed that uncle, Alexander Stephenson, had sent her to live with the Ludlams. At first they had let her see her son every day or two — which was no substitute for seeing him every day, caring for him, being able to cuddle him.

When had she tried to take her children and go back to Australia, Saul Ludlam had refused to allow it, so had she told him they were not Josiah's children. He had been so furious about her deception that he had threatened to put her in an asylum so that the secret would never be revealed. When Benedict had rescued her, Cathie and Seth from the Ludlams they had had to leave Pendleworth quickly or face a rich man's wrath. She had not even been able to say goodbye to Francis.

She then she had paid a lawyer in Pendleworth, a kind man called Bernard Lorrimer, to send her a report on Francis every year, so that she at least knew he was all right. She had saved the reports from the fire among her other treasured possessions. But she had not seen her son for nearly fourteen years, and that was an abiding sadness for her. She tried not to let it show, but she knew Benedict understood when she had one of her sad days.

By the time light streaked the sky and birds began crooning in the bush, she had taken a resolve and in it she found her greatest comfort for the loss of the baby. She was going to find her other two lost children. She had to, could not rest until she had done it.

As soon as she found out where Cathie was, she would travel to England and make sure her daughter was all right, even if she could not persuade her to come home. Then she was going to find Francis. He was nearly fifteen now. Both Mr Lorrimer, her Pendleworth lawyer, and Sophia Ludlam, Josiah's mother, said he was a fine-looking youngster, tall for his age and very like his father. But Mr Lorrimer also said that his great-uncle allowed him to associate with no one but the Ludlams and the lads from his boarding school, so Francis didn't have any real friends in the neighbourhood.

She could imagine that only too well. Alexander Stephenson, Francis's guardian and great-uncle, was an arrogant man. The boy must be lonely. Well, Liza had been without him for all these years, had wept for him in the darkness of many a night, and now she knew that she would not be healed from this fresh loss until she had seen Francis and made sure he was all right.

Perhaps he needed to see her, too? What had they told him about her? Not the truth, she was sure, which was that Alexander Stephenson and Saul Ludlam had forced her to leave him behind and forbidden her ever to contact him.

During the voyage to England Cathie had a lot of time to think and all too often found her thoughts turning to her mother and family. She didn't really like having no direction to her life. Oh, there were activities organised on board ship, reading and sewing circles, choirs and concerts, and she joined in many of them, but they weren't enough to use up her abundant physical energy. And although she tried to write a diary, as many passengers did, she kept forgetting and putting it off, so that she had only a few entries.

At the sewing circle she managed to finish her second dress, with the help of a motherly passenger. Cathie intended to save it to wear after her arrival, however, contenting herself with her old worn clothes on board ship.

She had only vaguely remembered the journey from England to Australia when she was five. Her stepfather had travelled to England when his first wife died to ask Liza to marry him and had brought them all back. Now, memories of that voyage began to return. The way you could stand at the ship's rail and gaze out across the water which seemed to stretch for ever. Of standing there on one rough day with her stepfather holding her, the two of them laughing as the ship rose and fell. The way storms howled around the ship. The movements and sounds, because even if the passengers slept, the ship never did. It creaked and groaned and whispered around you.

Bessie hated it and said only desperation had driven her to come on a ship again, but Cathie enjoyed everything about it, relishing every new experience, thoroughly enjoying talking to anyone and everyone, playing with the children, helping Matron when a lot of people were seasick.

Inevitably she spent a lot of time with Bessie, who wasn't a very nice person but who made her laugh, at least. Having a friend of her own age to talk to was another new thing for Cathie, though some of the things Bessie said shocked her to the core. She had an uneasy feeling that her parents would not approve of her new friend but pushed that thought to the back of her mind and told herself it was because Bessie had been married that she spoke so freely.

The ship stopped to refuel and take on fresh food in Cape Town but the steerage passengers were not allowed ashore, although the Captain arranged for letters to be posted. Cathie sent one to her parents. When she tried to write it she wept so copiously that in the end she could only manage one page. But she was sure they'd be relieved to know she was still all right, and after all her uncle would have passed on her other, longer letter.

Crossing the Equator provided a little light relief, with mock ceremonies in which the First Mate took a leading role.

By now it felt as if Cathie had been travelling for ever and she could not help thinking how terrible it must have been on the longer journey in a sailing ship without auxiliary engines which her mother had experienced when going out to Australia the first time.

As they sailed further north the weather became much cooler, even though it was late spring in England now. Bessie lent Cathie a shawl because she hadn't taken her winter clothes to Perth and the shawls her Aunt Christina had packed for her were light things. She would have to buy herself some warmer clothing once they arrived, and if this was a sample of spring weather, how would she ever cope with an English winter? She had never seen snow, because it simply didn't get cold enough for that at home. Bessie told her snow gave you chilblains and had nothing good to say of it, but in the pictures Cathie had seen in books snow looked beautiful.

'What are you going to do when you get off the ship?' Bessie asked one day.

'I don't know. Get a train to Pendleworth, I suppose, and see if I can find my father.'

'You can stay with me and my brother for a day or two first, if you like,' Bessie offered.

Cathie could not help giving her a hug. 'Oh, how kind you are to me!' She was surprised to see tears in her friend's eyes. 'What's wrong?'

'You an' your soppy words,' Bessie sniffed.

'But you *are* being kind to me.'

Bessie began to sob in earnest and ran off to their cabin.

Cathie gave up trying to understand her friend, whose mood could change three times in as many minutes, and went back to gazing out across the grey-brown northern waters. The closer the ship got to England the more apprehensive she became. Not only were there the problems of where she would live and if she could find employment, but how did you approach a stranger and tell him he was your father? What if her uncle had not been right about this Teddy Marshall anyway? How could anyone be really sure who her father was except her mother?

And, oh, she did wish she had not left Australia this way! What had got into her to make her do it?

When the letter arrived from Cape Town Benedict recognised Cathie's handwriting and wondered whether this would make things better or worse. He went into the living room where Liza was dusting the furniture, working list-lessly without any of her old vigour. They were all worried about her. Pulling her down beside him on the sofa, he took her hand, trying in vain to find a gentle way to break the news. In the end he said simply, 'There's a letter from Cathie.'

Liza sat bolt upright, one hand flying up to cover her mouth. It was a moment before she could speak. 'What does she say?'

He held it out to her. 'I thought you'd like to open it yourself.'

She took it from him with a hand that trembled, staring at the handwriting they both knew so well. As the words of the address suddenly blurred and ran together, Liza held it out to him. 'You open it and read it to me. Quickly, please.'

He tore open the envelope and unfolded the single sheet of paper.

Dear Mum and Dad
By now you'll have received my other letter and you'll know
that I'm on my way to England. I explained all my reasons
in that letter, so I won't go into them again. I just hope you've
forgiven me.

He stopped reading to stare in puzzlement at Liza. 'What does she mean? We haven't received any other letter from her – only the one from Correntin.'

Liza could only shake her head and beg, 'Go on! Please.'

The voyage seems very long. I'm not used to being shut up like
this and I'll be glad when it's over.

I've made a friend called Bessie. She's a bit older than me and widowed, going back to her family in England. She's invited me to stay with them but I'd rather go straight to Pendleworth. I'll call and see your lawyer and Mrs Ludlam once I'm settled.

I'll write to you again after I arrive. And don't worry about me. I'm fine, truly I am — but so ashamed and sorry that I ran away like that, because I know it must have hurt you. I do love you.

Cathie

Liza stared at her husband and picked up the envelope as if expecting to find another sheet of paper inside it. 'Is that all?'

'She says she sent us another letter. I can't understand — oh, my darling, don't!' For Liza was weeping, great sobs racking her too-thin body. He took her in his arms and when Agnes came to the door and looked at him with an unspoken question in her eyes, said simply, 'We got a letter from Cathie.'

'At last! Is she all right?'

Liza tried to pull herself together, brushing ineffectually at the tears. 'She's on a ship — going to England. Only she says she sent us a letter when she left.'

'Maybe it's time I went and hunted out your brother,' Benedict said grimly. 'She probably gave it to him to post.'

'No!' Liza clutched his arm. 'You promised not to. I don't want you going after him. I don't want to see Dermott again as long as I live.' She had been having night-mares about him — something which hadn't happened for years — reliving that dreadful day when she had inadvertently killed Niall.

'I didn't like him all that much myself,' Agnes said, 'though he has a certain rough charm. His wife is an absolute shrew. You should hear her shriek at the children and she treats that governess of theirs like a slave.'

'I sometimes think we treat *you* like a slave,' Liza said ruefully. 'You've worked so hard since you came here.'

'I've quite enjoyed myself, though I wouldn't like to live here all the time,' Agnes said diplomatically.

'We're so grateful to you,' Liza said. 'I've never in my life felt like this. Always tired.'

'Well, make the most of it!' Benedict teased. 'We're going to have you slaving away for us again as soon as you've recovered fully.' Though he was beginning to wonder if she ever would. It had been weeks now since she'd lost the child and she still didn't look herself, still wept at night when she thought he was asleep.

'That girl's gone off again today, though,' Agnes said. 'She's not very reliable, is she?'

Benedict frowned. 'Brendan's gone off as well. I hope he and Willerin . . .' He broke off, not voicing his concerns. Liza had enough to worry about. But he'd ask Dinny to have a word with Brendan – again.

Later, when they were alone, Liza told Benedict of her determination to return to England and find her daughter.

He stared at her in consternation. 'But we can't leave the farm!'

She avoided his eyes. 'I know *you* can't, but if we ask Agnes and Ilse to help – maybe I can.'

'No! I'm not having you going so far on your own.'

She looked up then. 'I think I need to be on my own for a while, love, need a change of scenery, too. I can't seem to pull out of this – this Slough of Despond.'

He took her in his arms. 'You're the light of my life, Liza. I can't bear to think of you going away.'

'I love you, too, but I need to see Cathie – and Francis. Something tells me he needs me, don't ask me why. I'm not usually fanciful like that. But I shan't be on my own. I thought I'd take Josie with me. I think it'd do her good. I wondered about taking Harry as well, but I decided he'd be better off staying here with you and the other lads. You know how he follows Seth and Lucas around.'

Benedict stared at her in shock. 'You've decided to go, whatever I say, haven't you?'

She looked at him sadly. 'Yes. I must, love. We'll sell another piece of jewellery to pay the fares.'

He struggled to find arguments which would change her mind. 'But we don't know Cathie's address. How will you find her? Hadn't you better wait a while, think it over more carefully?'

'Cathie said she was going to Pendleworth and would contact Mr Lorrimer and Sophia. They'll help me find her, I'm sure. It's only a small town.'

'But the danger? No, I can't let you risk it!'

'Saul Ludlam is dead and I'm sure Alexander Stephenson won't try to put me into a lunatic asylum – especially with Mr Lorrimer to look after my interests.' Liza laid one hand over his. 'Benedict, darling Benedict – I *have* to go. I can't get better, won't feel right, until I've seen them – both of them.'

He pulled her against him, burying his face in her hair,

and they sat there together for a long time, not saying anything, just offering unspoken comfort and love. She knew he would let her go. Just as she knew how much they would miss one another.

But that didn't change her mind.

Benedict didn't need to ask Dinny to speak to her son. She was waiting for Brendan and Willerin when they came home from wandering through the woods.

'Go and help Mrs Fenton, Willerin. You should have been with her today.'

The girl shot a worried look sideways at Brendan but left quietly, as always.

'Don't do that again, Brendan!' Dinny said with an edge to her voice that all her children recognised and usually obeyed.

But today he was in no mood to do as he was told. 'Why not? You should be glad I'm spending time with your people.'

'Your people, too.'

'Well, it doesn't feel like it!' He glared down at his arm. 'Whatever colour my skin is.'

She sighed. 'Brendan, Willerin's father left her in my care so that I could teach her about bringing children into the world, as my mother taught me and as Willerin's mother would have taught her if she'd lived. He trusts me to look after her as if she were my own daughter – and you know she's already promised in marriage.'

'To a man she's afraid of, a much older man!'

'That's the custom. You can't change it.'

'If you ask me, customs like marrying young girls off to older men are meant to be broken.'

Dinny kept herself calm only with an effort. 'If you do anything, touch her in any way, they'll kill her as well as you.'

He stopped short and stared at her. 'They wouldn't.'

'They would feel it necessary, believe me.'

He avoided her eyes as he muttered, 'Not if I take her away first.'

'How will you do that? You never manage to save any money. You can't live on dust and air.'

'I'll find a way. If those convicts can manage to escape from Western Australia, surely I can, too?' Only the previous day his father had told him with great relish about the escape from the American whaling barge *Catalpa* of six transported Fenians, political prisoners like Fergal himself had once been, men whose sole crime was to want freedom for their country. He and Brendan had laughed together to think of Irishmen confounding the British authorities like that.

'Those Fenians were white men,' Dinny said firmly, 'and they had help from people in America. You're not white and if you try to leave with Willerin, her family will follow you, hunt you down and kill you both. And they'll be angry with me, too, perhaps punish me as well. When you throw a stone into a pond, son, it makes many ripples.' After a pause, she said firmly, 'I want your word that you'll not touch her, Beedit.'

He stiffened. When she used that special name she had for him, it lent more force to her words somehow. 'Mum, please—'

'And if you don't give me your word not to touch her, and not to go wandering through the woods with her again, then I'll send her back to her father tomorrow. To save her life. And yours. That I swear.'

'Can't she and I even be friends?' he pleaded.

'No. I've seen the way you look at her. She's younger than you, not sure of herself yet, easy to persuade. It's up to you to prevent things going further. Your word, Beedit!'

Fergal had come up behind her but said nothing, leaving this to her. Where their two cultures clashed, as they sometimes did, he left it to Dinny to mark the boundaries.

'All right, I promise!' Brendan flung at them, then turned and strode off into the bush.

Fergal and Dinny exchanged glances and sighed. Their son would not be back for a day or two, they knew. He did this sometimes, simply walked away when he needed time on his own.

'If only I had someone to send him to back home,' Fergal murmured, taking Dinny into his arms, leaning against her soft warmth. 'A change of scene would be the best thing for him.'

'He'll go away from here one day,' she said sadly, 'and not return. That's why I've perhaps been a bit more lenient with Brendan than he deserves sometimes.'

Fergal held her at arm's length. 'One of your presentiments?'

She nodded, too full of emotion to speak for a moment or two.

'Oh, no!' he exclaimed, for Dinny's visions of the future usually did come true. He hugged her close. They both loved their children dearly, whether they were troublesome or not.

She pulled herself together and went to help Agnes serve the evening meal, which everyone on the homestead took together as long as the weather was fine, sitting at benches along a huge table made from wood felled on the property, under the rough shelter they had built after the bush fire. It would soon be winter, too cold and rainy to do so, and most of them would miss this sociable evening hour. They were like one big family, really, on the homestead, though Dinny knew Ilse and Agnes did not accept her as wholeheartedly as Liza did.

She noticed that her friend was looking in low spirits and didn't need to ask why, having heard about the letter and Liza's decision to go to England. They were both suffering from the rebelliousness of their children.

The two of them went for a stroll afterwards and as they wandered beneath the trees, Dinny sang one of her mother's songs to give them both a little comfort.

> *Trees, trees, your voices are soft*
> *I can hear the song you sing*
> *When you sing of the moon and stars.*
> *Trees, trees, your voices are soft.*

CHAPTER SEVEN

May

As Cathie's ship docked in Liverpool, she stared in delight at the buildings. Such huge places some of them, and the city itself seemed to go on for ever to a young woman brought up in the isolation of the Australian bush.

'Ugly old place, ain't it?' Bessie pushed her way through the people at the rail to stand next to her friend.

'Not to me. I think it's beautiful! So many people.' Cathie sighed in delight. 'I can't wait to see more of it.'

'I thought you were going straight to this Pendleworth place?'

'I am. I'll definitely go there first and try to find my father, but I want to see other parts of England as well.' She spread her arms wide. 'London, Bath . . . they all sound so interesting.'

'Well, Liverpool will do me from now on. I was a fool ever to leave it.' As the ship moved gently into its berth beside the dock Bessie squealed loudly. 'There he is! Look, there's our Nat!'

Cathie smiled as Bessie jigged up and down in excitement, shrieking and waving, making as much noise as a whole flock of black cockatoos. The man her friend had pointed out was tall and plump, with rather a cruel face. If you didn't know he was Bessie's brother, you might pass such a man as quickly as you could on the other side of the street. Strange, that.

'Now remember,' Bessie said, linking her arm through Cathie's, 'me an' Nat will see you to the train. We don't want you getting lost on your first day in England, do we?'

Cathie suppressed a sigh. She wasn't a child to need looking after. 'I've got a tongue, haven't I? I can always ask directions.'

'Yes, but there are folk watching out for newcomers to rob them. You stick with us when we get off the ship.'

It was hours before they were allowed to disembark, then they had to wait for their luggage to be unloaded and find a porter to carry it for them.

The minute they stepped out of the big echoing customs shed, Nat appeared beside them, pushing a small handcart. His eyes flickered over Cathie then back to his sister. 'How are you, Bessie love? Had enough of travellin', then?'

'More than bloody enough. I'm never leavin' Liverpool again as long as I live.'

He turned to eye Cathie once more. 'This a friend of yours? Ain't you going to introduce me?'

To Cathie's surprise Bessie seemed nervous. In fact, she'd never seen her friend look so subdued.

'This is Cathie.'

He nodded and this time his gaze raked Cathie's body in a way that made her feel very uncomfortable. 'Pleased to meet you.'

She shook his hand reluctantly and let go of it as quickly as she could.

Bessie clung to her brother's arm for a minute. 'I said we'd see her to the railway station, Nat. She hasn't been on a train before. They don't have them in Perth yet. Talk about backward, that Australia! You've never seen such a nasty place.'

Cathie bit back the urge to defend her home. Everything about Australia wasn't bad, just living in the bush.

'Tell us about it later,' Nat said. 'Let's get your things loaded on my cart. We need to get a move on. I've got a busy evening ahead of me.' He made short work of piling up their trunks and bags.

'I don't like taking you from your work,' Cathie protested, seeking an excuse not to go with them because Nat made her feel uneasy. Even if he was Bessie's brother she couldn't like him, not at all. 'I can manage perfectly well by myself.'

'No, you come with us.' Bessie moved to link her arm in Cathie's and tug her until she started walking.

The girl suppressed a sigh. 'Well, if you're sure . . .'

Nat set off at a cracking pace. 'Keep up, you two. We'll go the back way. It's quicker.'

Bessie flung him a glance full of appeal but when he scowled at her began walking more quickly, still holding tight to her friend's arm.

Cathie was puzzled by this exchange but went along with them. It seemed strange that everyone else was going in a different direction and she began to feel uneasy. As they came to a deserted alley between two buildings she stopped. 'This can't be the right way, Bessie.'

'Oh, it is. It's a short cut. Most folk wouldn't know it,

but Nat's worked around the docks quite a lot, haven't you, love?'

'Aye. You two go ahead of me.' He bumped the back of Cathie's skirt with his handcart, so she moved on.

At the end of the alley, Bessie turned right into another one, just as narrow. Here they were completely out of sight of other people. Feeling even more uneasy, Cathie stopped. 'I don't want to go this way.'

Before she could do or say anything else, Nat dropped the handles of the cart and stepped round it towards her.

She backed away, suddenly afraid. 'Bessie?' She could hear how uncertain and wobbly her own voice was.

Bessie began to cry and beg, 'Don't hurt her, Nat.'

He didn't reply, just shoved his sister aside and grabbed Cathie. When she pulled away and began to struggle, he gave her a backhander across the face and she cried out in both shock and pain. After that she began to struggle in earnest, screaming at the top of her voice and calling on Bessie to help her.

But her friend did not move.

Nat cursed as Cathie's fist connected with his face and was followed by a kick which if it had landed on the intended spot would have seriously incapacitated him. As she struggled with him, Cathie continued to scream at the top of her voice.

'Shut her up, Bessie, if you don't want to get caught,' Nat roared, 'then go through her trunk.'

She hung back. 'Please, Nat.'

'Do as you're – ouch! – bloody well told.'

As Cathie screamed again something hit the back of her head and everything seemed to explode around her.

*

In Pendleworth Hamish looked round the room where he'd slept for so many years, then picked up his last bag and walked downstairs. Magnus and Mairi were waiting for him, both looking sad. 'Well, that's it, I think,' he said, trying to sound calm but not feeling it.

Mairi burst into tears and flung herself into his arms, hugging him convulsively. 'You will write, won't you? Promise me you'll write.'

'Of course I will.' Hamish was struggling to hold back his own tears. He hadn't expected it to hurt quite so much to leave them.

She sobbed against his chest. 'Athol promised to write. So did Dougal. But they didn't keep their promise.'

'Well, I definitely will.' He put his hands on her shoulders and moved gently back from her embrace. Drawing in a deep, ragged breath, he turned to the brother who had been more like a father to him. The two of them exchanged long glances which said more than either could have put into words, then Hamish squared his shoulders and said gruffly. 'I'm ready now.'

Magnus nodded. 'Aye, then. So am I. You'll want to kiss our mother goodbye, will ye not?'

With a sigh Hamish moved across to the figure rocking gently near the fire. 'Goodbye, Mother.'

She didn't turn, didn't even show she'd heard him. More to appease Magnus than anything else, Hamish gave her a quick hug. But his touch made her whimper and pull away, so he moved quickly backwards again. As far as he was concerned he'd said goodbye to his mother several months previously when she'd stopped recognising him. The warm, loving person who had once inhabited this body was no longer alive, and even being in the same room as her made him feel uncomfortable now. It would have been kinder if God had taken her cleanly rather than letting her linger like this, a mindless doll-thing. He was glad he'd not have to watch her any more and glad, too, that Mairi had got away. Surely it wouldn't take Magnus long to discover that he could not manage on his own?

As he left the kitchen and walked down the narrow hallway, Hamish resolved that he would remember only the old mother, who had been lively and full of fun.

Magnus turned at the kitchen door to ask, 'You're sure you'll be all right today, Mairi? I can still stay behind if you . . .'

'Of course I'll be all right. I don't have to leave till this evening and if you're late Mrs Midner has promised to come in. You should have plenty of time to get there and back, even with the Sunday train services. And you know full well you want to go with Hamish to Liverpool and see him safely on the ship.' Elwyn understood that she was glad to look after their mother occasionally, that it assuaged her guilt about leaving Magnus with the burden of daily care.

Such a wonderful man, her big brother – though he grew embarrassed if you tried to tell him so. She wished he could meet a woman, get married and have the normal family life he deserved. Why was he so determined to waste his life caring for a woman who no longer even recognised her own children? However, since nothing would change his mind about that, Mairi intended to continue coming over to Pendleworth now and then to give him some respite, even if only for a few hours. She knew better than anyone how wearing their mother could be, day in, day out.

Blinking her eyes in a vain attempt to rid them of tears she looked round and decided to give the place a good clean-through while she was here. That would mean tying her mother to the rocking chair, because you couldn't take your eyes off her for a minute nowadays or she did things which harmed herself as well as others.

This time tying her up meant a struggle for Mairi, who ended up sobbing in the other chair with a bruise and scratches on her face, while her mother moaned and tugged against the soft bonds that held her.

After a while, Mairi dried her tears and got started on the cleaning. But she felt sad all day. Her mother seemed to be worse each time she visited Pendleworth.

The two brothers were silent as they walked to the station carrying the big tin trunk between them, with canvas travelling bags in their other hands.

'Are you sure you should be coming with me?' Hamish asked yet again. 'You'll be exhausted tomorrow.'

'I want to come. Don't you want me with you?'

'Of course I do. I just – was worried about you.'

'Aye, well, and I'm going to be worried about you for a while now.'

There was silence, then, as the train pulled out of the station and passed the big mass of Ludlam's mill, Hamish laughed. 'I shan't miss that place.'

'I enjoy working there now that Mr Reuben is in charge of the workshop. He's much more reasonable than his father,' Magnus said mildly. Things had changed greatly since old Mr Ludlam's sudden death from a seizure ten years previously, and mostly for the better. Saul Ludlam's widow was still alive, though, living in a small house of her own out at Ashleigh and appearing happier than she'd ever done while her husband was alive. Everybody said so. Magnus passed her house sometimes when he went out walking and always received a nod and a greeting if he met her. She knew a lot of the men who worked at Ludlam's by sight and still helped their families if they were in trouble.

In Liverpool they made their way to the docks. Magnus had been here before to see off his other brothers and it brought back sad memories that made him close his eyes briefly. Like Hamish, they had been full of hope and suppressed excitement, looking round them as if they were children out for a treat.

And they hadn't written once! Would Hamish?

At the customs shed the two brothers hugged, then Magnus stepped back and let Hamish follow the porter inside. When his brother turned at the door to wave to him, Magnus called 'Good luck!' but wasn't sure his words had been loud enough to be heard above the noise and bustle. He raised his own hand, trying to force a smile on to his face, but couldn't manage it, so waved a couple of times, then swung round and strode away.

His eyes blinded by a sudden rush of tears, he looked for some private corner where he could get his emotions under control once more. A man did not weep in public.

When he found a narrow alley, he turned into it with relief, feeling almost overwhelmed by the pain of losing his third brother and the thought of going back to live alone with his poor demented mother.

Gulping back the unmanly sobs he moved a little way down the alley, so lost in his own grief that it took him a minute or two to realise that somewhere nearby a woman was screaming for help. He glanced quickly round. At one end of the alley people were hurrying past, not seeming to hear the screams.

He ran quickly to the blank wall at the other end and saw a young woman fighting off a man who seemed to be attacking her. Another young woman was hovering nearby. Even as Magnus watched she picked up a half brick and used it to clout the struggling female on the back of the head. As the woman collapsed, the one who had hit her tugged a big trunk off the cart, stepping hastily backwards as it thumped down near her feet, then pounding at its padlock with the brick. She didn't even turn to look at her victim, whose skirts the man was now lifting.

'Hey!' Magnus roared, realising the thief was intending to rape as well as rob her. He began to run towards them. Fury filled him, for he loathed violence and thievery – but there was also a savage delight at the prospect of venting his emotions. He had not fought very often because other men were afraid of his size, but just occasionally it had been necessary and he had always given a good account of himself.

The man and woman looked up in shock then the man picked up the handles of the cart and shoved it past the unconscious victim, while his accomplice tried to pull a handbag off the victim's arm. But as Magnus continued to run towards them she pulled something out of it instead and fled after her accomplice.

Magnus ran a little way after them.

The young woman looked over her shoulder and shrieked that they were being followed. The man stopped, snatched a piece of luggage from the top of the cart and threw it at Magnus with such force that it sent him stumbling backwards, flailing to keep his balance. The two attackers took off running again, disappearing round a corner with the handcart rattling and squeaking.

Deciding it would be wiser to remain with the unconscious woman to protect her from further attacks, he picked up the piece of hand luggage and went back to where she was lying, worried that she had not moved at all.

He knelt by her side. Had they killed her? Her face was badly bruised and there was blood matting the hair at the back of her head. He bent closer to check if she was still breathing and heaved a sigh of relief when he saw her chest rising and falling. Her cheeks were bone white and the bruises shockingly blue against the soft, fair skin. She would be quite pretty normally, he guessed, and was neatly dressed in the sort of clothes his sister wore. Respectable, the sort who had to earn her bread. For some reason, that touched him more than if she had been a fashionably dressed lady. Why had they been attacking her? Surely they did not think she was worth robbing?

'Miss! Miss!' Still kneeling beside her, he shook her shoulder slightly.

She didn't stir.

He looked around but there was no one in sight. Indeed, if the attackers came back with any companions, he could still be in trouble. He dragged the trunk across, positioned it carefully, then picked the young woman up and sat her on it with the smaller bag on her lap. He let her limp upper body fall back against him and then, grunting with the effort, began to drag the trunk and its burden slowly along the ground. It was hard work and a lesser man might not have managed it but he was grimly determined. All the time he kept glancing along the alley, afraid her attackers might return with reinforcements.

It was a relief to turn the corner and see people passing by. As he got to the street end of the alley he glanced back over his shoulder and saw the man who had robbed the girl step out from the corner and stand there, hands on his hips and a furious expression on his face. There were two other men behind him. When they saw Magnus staring at them, the newcomers dodged back out of sight and the attacker shook his fist before following them.

Magnus looked down, wondering what to do next. People were hurrying past them. Some glanced at the unconscious woman but none stopped to offer help. He propped the stranger against the wall and when he saw some ship's officers approaching moved to intercept them.

'Excuse me, gentlemen, but this young woman has been attacked and robbed and I need to find a policeman. Can you help me?'

One grimaced and said resignedly, 'I'll go and report it to the dock police. You stay here with her till they come.'

When Magnus turned back the girl was stirring.

A woman passing by said to her companions, 'Disgusting, I call it, to be drunk like that.'

'Madam! She's not drunk – she's been attacked,' Magnus protested.

The woman gasped and scurried away as if she might be assaulted herself.

'You'd think someone would stop and help!' he muttered. As he knelt beside the young woman, her eyelids fluttered open but she could not focus properly.

'Bide still, lassie,' he said gently. 'You've been hit on the head. Let yourself recover slowly.'

She let out a long trailing sigh and asked, 'Who – are you?'

Her voice was low and to his ear pleasing. He did not like shrill women. 'My name is Magnus Hamilton. I was passing and saw you being attacked, so came to your aid. I'm afraid they got some of your luggage.'

She made a mewing sound in her throat then tried again to focus on him. 'I can't see properly. Are there – two of you?'

'No, there's only me. You've had a thump on the head and it'll take a while for you to recover. What's your name?'

She blinked at him. 'It's—' Panic suddenly filled her face. 'I – can't remember!'

He patted her hand. She was a sturdy young woman with strong, capable hands. He liked her looks – well, he would have liked them normally, when she was not pale and dishevelled. 'That's all right, lassie. Just give yourself time to recover.'

She closed her eyes for a moment, then opened them to ask, 'Magnus, did you say you were called?'

'Aye.'

'You're Scottish.'

'Aye. And you?'

But again she shook her head and looked at him with haunted eyes. 'I can't remember *anything*.'

'It'll come back to you bit by bit. I was hit on the head once and it took a few days for me to remember why I'd been fighting.' He smiled reminiscently. 'When I did remember I went after the one who'd hit me from behind and made him very sorry.' He hesitated. 'There were a man and a young woman attacking you and she hit you on the head with a brick.'

She put one hand to the back of her head and winced. 'It hurts.'

He took the hand and clasped it in his own, finding it cold and clammy. 'We should be getting you warm. Where is that damned policeman?'

She seemed to lapse into semi-consciousness again and he could only crouch there and worry about her. It seemed a long time until a policeman came into sight, scanning the crowd until he saw them then hurrying forward.

As Magnus was explaining what had happened, she regained consciousness again and muttered, 'My head hurts.'

'We'd better get her back to the station,' the policeman decided.

'We're going to need help, then,' Magnus muttered. 'If we leave her luggage here, it'll be taken.'

A ragged fellow who had been watching agreed to help the policeman with the trunk and the bag, while Magnus pulled the young woman to her feet, drew one of her arms round his neck and helped her to stagger along. If he hadn't been there, she'd have fallen. As it was, he was more than half-carrying her.

At the police station they were taken into a small room, where they tried to question her. Even though she had not lapsed into unconsciousness again and had even regained a little colour in her cheeks, she still could not remember anything at all about the attack – or even her own name.

After gesturing to Magnus to join him outside, the policeman asked in a low voice, 'Do you know the young woman, sir?'

'No, I just happened to come along in time to save her.' He explained how the man who'd attacked her had returned with two other fellows.

'She's very lucky you intervened, and I congratulate you on doing your civic duty, sir. I'll write a report on the incident, but I don't know what we're going to do with her till she recovers. There's nothing in her handbag to say who she is. I think we'll have to put her into the poor house till she regains her senses – if she ever does. You can never tell with blows to the head. She might be damaged for life.'

Magnus had a sudden image of the Ben and this lassie stuck in a similar place among the drooling idiots. It was none of his business and he could never afterwards explain what made him do it but he found himself saying, 'Not that!'

The policeman shrugged. 'If there's no one to take care of her, what choice do we have, sir? She can't be turned loose on her own, and let alone she doesn't know who she is, they've taken all her money. We'll break the padlock on that trunk tomorrow and see if there are any more clues, but there's only me here on a Sunday and I have other things to see to.'

Magnus thought of the young woman with her poor battered face. She was younger than his sister, and at the moment, alone and defenceless. He smiled in relief as the solution came to him. 'I'll take her home to my sister. Mairi will know what to do.'

It was not quite as easy as that. First he had to give details of himself and prove who he was. Then he had to sign some papers. Finally the constable said that all the information would be passed on to Pendleworth Police Station and as soon as the young woman remembered what had happened, she was to report to them.

It was only then that Magnus looked at the clock and realised how late it was. He hated the extra expense but there was no way to avoid it. 'Is there anywhere I can find a cab? I've a train to catch. I'm going to be late home as it is and my sister is expecting me.'

'The ladies do worry if we're late, don't they, sir?' the Sergeant said sympathetically. 'But I'm sure your sister will forgive you when she sees this poor young woman and hears what happened.'

But the cab was slowed by a tangle of vehicles and didn't arrive at the station until some minutes after Magnus's train had left. The driver helped him find a porter and unload the young woman's trunk, then they had to wake her and persuade her to get out of the cab.

It being Sunday, it was an hour and a half until the next train. They sat on an iron bench and the young woman fell asleep with her head on Magnus's shoulder. He sat beside her, his annoyance at the delay subsiding and a wry smile taking its place as he listened to her breathing as softly as a baby. Her lashes were very long and as dark as her hair, which was in a sad tangle. Two ladies walking past frowned at them in disapproval. Already he was regretting his impetuousness, but it was too late now to do anything but take the lass home with him. Well, he still couldn't bear the thought of them putting her in the poor house. Once you were inside those places you had trouble getting out again.

After sleeping uneasily for half an hour she woke with a start, staring at him fearfully and then looked round in bewilderment.

'It's all right, lassie,' he said gently, not attempting to stop her from drawing away from him. 'You've been attacked and you're not feeling well, but I'm taking you home to my sister. Mairi will help you better than I can.'

She gazed at him doubtfully then her face cleared and she managed a small, uncertain smile. 'You're very kind – Magnus. You did say you were called Magnus?'

'Well, you've remembered my name at least,' he said softly. 'I dare say after a good night's sleep you'll remember your own, too.'

'It all feels strange, as if nothing is real.' She sighed and snuggled against him so that he had to put his arm round her again. 'Perhaps this is just a dream,' she murmured. 'But you're nice.'

He smiled down at her. What must it be like to regain consciousness and remember nothing? Perhaps they could find out who she was from her trunk? He realised suddenly what that probably meant. A trunk and her down at the docks . . . she was either just leaving the country or just arriving. Which one was it? He found himself hoping she was arriving, which was a silly thing to hope for when it was no business of his, but if so, why had no one met her?

Once she had remembered who she was, she'd go on to wherever she had been heading and he would probably never see her again. And if she didn't remember? a faint voice asked inside his head. What would happen to her if she didn't remember who she was? Well, he'd deal with that when it happened. For the moment he needed to get home as quickly as he could because he couldn't remember what time the last train went for Bury.

He had to wake the lassie to get her on the train and tip a porter for helping him get her trunk into the luggage van.

When they arrived at Pendleworth it was getting dark but at least she had recovered enough to stand up on her own while another porter helped him unload the trunk and find a cab to take them home. Another expense. If he went on at this rate, he'd have no money left.

There was a light on in his house and he sighed in relief at the thought of turning his charge over to his sister. After paying off the cab he dragged the trunk to the front door, surprised that Mairi hadn't come out to help him. She was usually watching out for him. As he reached for the handle the door opened. 'Mairi, I—' He looked up and saw Mrs Midner.

She stared at the stranger standing beside him, then looked back at him with disapproval writ large on her face. 'Your sister had to go home, Mr Hamilton. She thought you might have missed the train and paid me to come in to mind your mother. It's not what I like, working on the Lord's Day, and your mother's been in one of her funny moods. Did you meet a friend?' Her eyes went back to the stranger.

'This lassie has been hit on the head and doesn't remember who she is. I was going to ask Mairi to help her. Could you perhaps—'

A sour expression came over Mrs Midner's face and she folded her arms. '*I* can't do anything more today. I have to be getting home. My husband doesn't like me working on a Sunday and I only did it as a special favour because your Mairi was going to miss her last train if I hadn't come in. And I don't know what *you* think you're doing bringing strange young women home, Magnus Hamilton, I really don't. You must have taken leave of your senses as well as your brother today.'

'But she's—'

The woman pushed past him and hurried away, leaving him standing there with the stranger. He looked up and down the street, wondering about getting some other woman to help him. But there was no one outside at this time of day and most of the houses were dark. In the end he helped the lassie inside, installed her in his own armchair opposite his mother and went back to bring her things in. Well, he assumed they were hers. She didn't even know that.

When he returned to the kitchen the lassie had drifted off to sleep again and his mother was stirring the fire mindlessly, letting coals fall on to the rag rug which was smouldering and smelling of scorched wool. He rushed to snatch the poker from his mother's hand and she screamed at him, a mindless sound, then began to beat at him.

The stranger woke with a start and jerked upright, gaping at them in shock.

'What's wrong with her?' she asked once he'd got his mother a bit calmer again.

'Old age. Softening of the brain, the doctor calls it. She doesn't mean to do foolish things. She can't help it.'

The young woman came to stand beside them. 'There, there. It's all right,' she said soothingly.

Janey blinked at her and stretched out one hand to paw at the stranger's face and touch the dark hair, which seemed to please her. She then allowed herself to be seated in the chair and began to rock to and fro, crooning to herself.

'I'm sorry,' the stranger said with a blush, 'but I need to use the – the necessary.'

'It's down the back of the yard. Take a candle with you.' He gestured to the end of the mantelpiece. 'I'd come and show you the way, but I daren't leave my mother.' He sat down for a moment, feeling weary beyond measure and worrying about what to do with his unexpected guest.

After a few minutes the back door banged shut and she came in, rubbing her forehead as if it hurt. 'I'm sorry. My head aches so badly I can't think properly.'

'You need to rest. You can stay in my sister's old room, if you like. I have to lock my mother in the small bedroom or else she wanders the house. She doesn't seem able to tell night from day now. And she may call out, but just ignore it if she does.' He was going to ask the doctor if there was a stronger medicine to give her at night.

The young woman was staring at him owl-eyed. 'I don't feel I know you.'

'You don't. But you had nowhere else to go and I thought my sister would be here to help you. Only she'd already left. The trouble is, it's too late to find you somewhere else to go and I really can't leave my mother alone. Are you hungry?'

She was swaying on her feet. 'No. I'd like a drink of water, but what I really need is sleep.'

He glanced at his mother who was leaning back staring at the ceiling, then led the way upstairs. 'This is my sister's old bedroom. My mother sleeps in this one and the other is mine. I'll bring your trunk up once I've got Mum off to sleep.'

When he got downstairs he found that his mother had picked up the poker again and was staring at the fire as if it fascinated her. He took the poker out of her hand and drew her into the hall, murmuring soothingly as he left her standing there. Keeping an eye on her, he began to heave the trunk up the stairs. After shoving it into the stranger's bedroom, he nodded and ran back down to his mother.

She was pacing up and down the hall now, in a strange mood, beating one hand against her thigh as she walked. She no longer talked any sense at all, just uttered disjointed phrases. This upset him, remembering how she had loved to chat in the evenings.

He was feeling ravenous, so he made some porridge, then fed his mother and himself alternate spoonfuls from the pan. He had to put the food into her mouth, for she just sat and looked at the spoon in her hand as if she didn't know what to do with it. His own food tasted like bitter ashes in his mouth and he'd have pushed it aside but he needed to keep up his strength.

Then, just as they were finishing, his mother looked at him, really looked at him, and for a few moments her face was her own again. She raised one hand and stroked his cheek, a gesture she had often made when she was herself. Though the light faded from her eyes soon after, the incident heartened him. It was such moments which kept him going, made him sure he was doing the right thing in not locking her away.

After he'd cleared away the dishes he got his mother ready for bed. He hated having to deal with her so intimately and always felt embarrassed, but it was no use getting upset. It simply had to be done.

By the time he had given her the sleeping medicine and got her to bed, he was bone weary. He paused outside the visitor's room, listening, but there was no sound coming from it. He hoped she was all right, but did not like to go inside to check in case he frightened her.

What had he got himself into? he wondered as he got undressed. Wasn't his life difficult enough without taking on a stranger's problems? The tears he had been fighting all day welled in his eyes again and he brushed them away impatiently with the back of one hand. But a sudden memory of Hamish as a little lad – such an eager, energetic little fellow – brought a lump to his throat and he had to brush away another tear. He was going to miss Hamish; well, he missed all his brothers. And what he would do with himself after his mother died, he didn't know.

Would he try to find a woman then and marry? Maybe. But he was shy with women and had never been able to joke with them and tease them as other young men did. He knew he was too serious for most folk's liking. And being so tall was a problem, too. You grew tired of looking down at people.

The stranger was quite tall for a woman.

He clicked his tongue in exasperation at himself. What was he doing thinking about her again? She'd probably remember who she was within a day or two and be off to join her family. Or someone would report her missing and the police would direct them to Pendleworth.

A great yawn overtook him and he got into bed. Time enough to worry about this bizarre situation in the morning. For once he was too exhausted to lie there and worry, but fell instantly into a heavy sleep.

CHAPTER EIGHT

May

———◆———

In the end, several weeks passed and Matthieu's longing for some peace and quiet grew even stronger. 'I've nothing pressing to do here,' he declared one day, 'so I'll go down to the farm on my own, if you don't mind?'

Dermott shrugged. 'Whatever I decide to do with the place it needs keeping an eye on, so that suits me. We don't want squatters walking in and thinking they can just settle there.'

'*Bien*. I shall set off as soon as I find myself a spare horse.' The idea of living quietly in the countryside for a while was surprisingly appealing.

Matthieu rode south one chilly winter morning in June, riding a neat bay mare with a comfortable gait and leading a sturdy pack horse. He intended to take his time about the trip. The plants of the bush fascinated him, they were so different from those in France, and here they were different even from those in the east of Australia.

He camped out on the first night, humming as he cooked a piece of steak, glad of the crackling warmth of the fire and enjoying his own company.

Lying warmly wrapped in blankets looking up at the

154

brilliant stars overhead, different from those he had seen in the northern hemisphere, he let out a long breath and wondered why he still could not decide where to go next. Wondered, too, how he had got himself so closely involved with Dermott Docherty, who had plenty of easy charm when he chose to use it, but who was undoubtedly a rascal.

Morning dawned crisp but fine and as he set off Matthieu found himself singing a song of his youth, *'Auprès de Ma Blonde'*. He had always been attracted to blonde women for some reason.

He turned left at a signpost to Brookley, surprised when he got there to find it consisted of half a dozen houses only, widely spaced, each surrounded by gardens and work areas of various types. Why had Dermott not checked more carefully before buying a house in a place like this? He stared up and down the sandy street before going inside a neat little inn where he was served a tasty stew with large chunks of beef in it that reminded him of the *boeuf en daube* his grandmother had sometimes made in his youth.

The inn had a tiny shop at one side of the main room, hardly more than a large cupboard with shelves of basic provisions: barrels of flour, sugar, currants, salt and a cask of rum. Staple provisions for settlers, these. He smiled as he studied the contents of the shelves. No one, it seemed, earned their money in only one way in this country.

After the meal he bought some fresh foodstuffs to supplement his flour and the kangaroo meat he would kill for himself, and asked directions to the house.

'Oh, the old Bailey place.' The rather genteel landlady came outside with him and pointed along a narrow track opposite the inn. She looked hopeful. 'You and your family are coming to live here?'

He shrugged. 'Who knows? It was my partner who bought it, but he and his wife are too busy to move down here yet, so I've come to check that everything is all right.'

She smiled faintly. 'It should be. We don't get many people passing through Brookley.'

He rode off along the track, looking up at the sky, which was clouding over now, and wondering what the hell he was doing in such a lonely place after the pleasures of Melbourne. The horse stumbled suddenly, throwing him, and next thing he knew he was sprawled on the ground feeling shaken, which served him right for not paying attention.

From the distance a voice called, 'Are you all right?' and when he looked up he saw a woman and girl running along the track towards him.

He tried to pull himself together, but did not feel like sitting up yet. *Merde!* his head hurt. He must have bumped it on something.

'Don't try to move.' The woman knelt beside him, holding his shoulder with a slim, elegant hand and staring earnestly into his eyes. 'Does your head hurt?'

He stared back at her, enjoying her touch. It had been some time since he'd been near a lady. Unlike women of pleasure, this one radiated an air of cleanliness and smelled of soap and lavender, a strangely heady combination in the middle of the Australian bush. And she had the softest blonde hair he'd ever seen, so light in colour it was almost silver. She wore it simply in a chignon, without the frizzed fringes so popular with many women, which he detested.

'I will be all right in a minute or two.' He closed his eyes for a minute trying to gather his senses.

The child hovered nearby, jigging about from one foot to the other. 'Who is he, Frau Hebel?' she whispered. 'Why does he speak like that?'

'He's French, I think.'

So this woman wasn't the child's mother, Matthieu thought, and she was German which explained her slight accent. Not wanting to appear helpless, he managed to sit up and smile at the child. She was a scrawny little thing, pale and freckled with reddish-brown hair, but her eyes were very pretty and she had an alert, intelligent look to her. 'I'm Matthieu Correntin. And I am indeed French.' He inclined his head then winced as it throbbed.

'I think you should sit still, Monsieur Correntin,' Ilse said, worried by how pale he was. 'Josie, go and catch the gentleman's horses before they wander off.'

'One of them's limping, poor thing.' The child went and caught hold of the reins of Matthieu's mount, whispering to it and rubbing its nose, then leading the two animals slowly back.

He decided he could not appear at his best sitting on the ground and tried to stand up, but his head spun and he would have fallen had she not knelt to support him. He summoned up his small store of German to apologise. *Entschuldigen Sie, bitte, gnädige Frau.* I shall have to rest a moment longer before I move.'

'*Ça ne fait rien,*' she said, speaking his language far more easily than he had spoken hers. 'Perhaps I should send Josie home to fetch help?'

How long had it been since a woman had looked at him

with such concern, not simply assessing the state of his wallet but caring about him as a human being? Matthieu leaned against her shamelessly, breathing in that crisp linen-and-lavender smell with deep appreciation. '*Mais non!* I shall be all right soon, I'm sure.'

Her face was very close to his as she reached out and with firm, slim fingers turned his head slightly better to study his face. '*Il faut se reposer un peu, Monsieur.*'

Her accent was flawless. '*Vous parlez bien français, Madame.*'

'*Un peu seulement.* There isn't much chance to use it here.'

He smiled. What luck! He had been hungry for the sound of his own language lately. 'Your accent is good.'

She smiled back at him. 'I have some facility with languages, monsieur. It helps me gain employment as a governess.' Not that she used them much. Liza said frankly she preferred Josie and Harry to concentrate on getting their own language right before they learned any others, though Josie had insisted on learning a few French and German words for the fun of it.

'You are a governess? I thought you were – married.' He couldn't keep the surprise from his voice. She didn't look like a governess. They were, in his experience, dowdy women while this one was elegant in dress and graceful in even the slightest movement.

'Widowed,' she said curtly, hating even to think of Johannes now. 'I work for the Caines and—' She broke off. 'What's the matter?'

'I – um – moved my head suddenly.' Damnation! Why did she have to work for that family of all others? He gave a sniff of wry amusement. Fate was like that, giving with one hand, taking away with the other.

'Dad's coming!' Josie called and ran back along the track to grab her father's hand. 'This gentleman's had an accident and he's hurt his head.'

Matthieu got to his feet, helped unobtrusively by Frau Hebel and wondering what her first name was. He liked the fact that she was almost the same height as him, liked the clean lines of her face with its straight nose and pale skin, and relished the air of respectability that was stamped all over her. He had had enough of whores. Quickly, before Caine got close enough to hear, he whispered, 'Frau Hebel, this is not the way I would have wished to make your acquaintance. But be sure that we'll meet again under happier circumstances, I shall make certain of that.' He noted with satisfaction the delicate colour that tinged her cheeks then he turned. 'Monsieur Caine, we meet again.'

'Mr Correntin.' Benedict stared at him, wondering what the hell the fellow was doing here. Noticing the bruise on his forehead and the slightly glazed look in his eyes, he felt obliged to ask, 'Are you all right?'

'A little battered and rather embarrassed, monsieur. I was not paying attention and when my horse stumbled, I was thrown.'

Automatically Benedict offered, 'You're welcome to come back and spend the night with us.' In the bush you did not turn people away. However, he was somewhat suspicious at finding a man who was involved with Liza's brother so close to their farm. Perhaps she was right. Perhaps Dermott Docherty did still intend to do her harm?

Matthieu made a negative movement with his hand, not daring to shake his head again. '*Merci*, but no. I've come from Brookley and am looking for the farm which used to belong to the Baileys.'

'There's no one living there now.'

'Yes, I know.' He didn't volunteer the information that Dermott owned it because he hoped the Caines would assume he was just looking the place over with a view to buying it. He did not want them to prevent him from furthering his acquaintance with their governess.

Benedict's voice was crisp, businesslike. 'You took the wrong turn. Go back round the bend and turn right. The track is a bit overgrown at the moment but it's clearly marked.' He ran his hand down the riding horse's fore-leg. 'Your mare will be all right, I think. It's not far to the Baileys' place. Could you walk her for a bit? Let her recover as well?'

'I shall have to, shall I not?'

'Are you sure you'll be all right on your own, Monsieur Correntin?' the governess asked.

Matthieu turned to smile at her. '*Oui*. But I thank you for your concern, Frau Hebel.'

Ilse inclined her head and turned to Josie. 'Come along, dear. I promised to help Mrs Fenton with tea. *Au 'voir, Monsieur.*'

Matthieu managed to engage her eyes for a moment and smiled – pleased to receive a smile in return.

Benedict took a step backward. 'If you're sure you'll be all right, then, Mr Correntin . . . ?'

'I shall be fine, but I shall take more care how I ride in future.' Matthieu watched the three of them walk away, the child skipping and talking in her rather breathless voice. As they turned a bend in the track, the governess glanced back at him briefly, then bent her head again to listen to her charge.

Under other circumstances Matthieu might have liked Benedict Caine, who had a very direct manner. Under other circumstances he could have accepted the offer of hospitality and got to know Frau Hebel ... *Bon dieu*, why had he not asked her first name? But as things were it seemed better not to get too close to the family.

As he walked away, however, Matthieu cast prudence aside with one wave of his hand. Prudence be damned! He wanted very much to get to know the governess. She was not pretty exactly, but she had style which had always appealed to him much more than mere looks. And she spoke good French, too. How rare that was in Australia!

He remained thoughtful as he strolled back along the track, letting his mare pick her own pace. After the bend he turned right and found himself on an overgrown track just wide enough for a wagon. It might be almost winter but most of the trees were in full leaf. You never got the bare brown branches of his own country's winter. Something about these rustling woodlands appealed to him, he decided, as he continued to stroll along with the horses' hooves sounding muffled behind him on the sandy soil. There were pretty vistas with occasional huge trees and at this time of the year the dry, sunburned land of summer was turning green again with the occasional rain. It was not the same green as his home and this part of the country was very flat, too, but still it had its own beauty.

One twist in the path revealed a view of a small lake which reminded him abruptly of a certain part of the woods near his home and sent an unexpected pang of homesickness through him. He had spent many hours wandering those woods as a lad, and getting into trouble when he returned home for neglecting his studies and escaping from his tutor. His father, ambitious for his children to rise in the world, had wanted his third son to become a lawyer. Matthieu had hated the dusty books and convoluted phraseology, the hours of sitting on a high stool poring over precedents. He had been born for action and loved being outdoors. And so, when Grand-père died and his father proved intractable, he had left. At eighteen one did foolish things — and lived to regret them.

Baileys' Farm, when he came to it, turned out to be a neat building, a simple oblong in shape with a veranda along the back and front. When he went inside it smelled musty, so he left the front door open. There was furniture, plain but adequate, and a good stone fireplace. He turned slowly round, liking what he saw.

He went out on to the back veranda and found a tumble-down cooking area a few paces away, with a pile of sawn firewood nearby under a rough bark shelter. To his surprise he felt instantly at home. I had better be careful, he told himself with a wry smile. I do not want to turn into a settler.

He frowned and paused to stare around him. What did he want to do with the rest of his life, though? He was sure of nothing except that he was reluctant to change countries again. He must be getting old, though at thirty-five he did not feel it.

He banished his worries with one snap of his fingers and concentrated on unsaddling the two horses and turning them out into a small enclosure whose fence was still strong enough to keep them in. After that he lit a fire, cooked some food and made up his bed.

But his last thoughts as he drifted towards sleep in the quietness of a still night were of the governess. He must definitely see her again. That would cure him of this – this foolishness. She was bound to have faults which would lessen her attraction. All women did.

At Lizabrook the talk was all of Mr Correntin for the first part of the meal. There was much speculation as to whether he would buy the old Bailey place and why a Frenchman would even think of settling in the Brookley district.

Liza was more worried that he was her brother's partner. If he bought the farm, Dermott might come to visit him. She was leaving shortly for England, but she had never forgotten her brother's threat of vengeance. If Dermott found her gone, would he take out his anger on her family? As if she did not bitterly regret killing Niall! She saw Benedict's eyes on her, the worry in them, and tried to smile at him but failed miserably.

On the other side of the table Ilse was asked for her opinion of the stranger, but what she really wanted to do was go away and think about the encounter. 'This is not the way I would have wished to make your acquaintance,' Monsieur Correntin had murmured just before Benedict joined them. What had he meant by that?

The Frenchman was very handsome – no, not handsome exactly, but certainly attractive. 'Be sure we'll meet again,' he had whispered. Would they? What did he mean by that? Men did not usually show an interest in her. Well, not men like him. And did she even want him to? She had already decided that she wanted both kindness and solid worth in a husband, not mere physical attraction.

'Well, I thought Mr Correntin had a nice smile,' Josie said for the third time. 'Didn't he, Frau Hebel?'

'Er — yes. And he seemed very polite.' Ilse saw Agnes Fenton watching her from across the room. Her friend was rather too perceptive sometimes. 'I'll go and — um — clean my shoes.'

She fled to the back veranda and stood there with her hands pressed to her hot cheeks. She was being foolish. Very foolish. She would probably never see him again. Or if she did, he'd have forgotten her name.

When Cathie woke the morning after the attack, she was astonished to find herself in a strange room. It was just starting to get light so she slipped out of bed and went to stare through the window. The sound of her door opening made her whirl round to see a giant of a man with tousled red-blond hair standing in the doorway. She tensed, ready to defend herself. Who was he? How had she got here? His face seemed vaguely familiar so she searched through the muddles of her throbbing head for his name. Magnus, that was it.

He spoke in a deep rumbling bass voice. 'So you're awake, lassie. How are you feeling now?'

As he gave her a tentative smile she lost her fear of him. There was a gentleness to his gaze and he had made no attempt to come into the room. Looking down, she realised in surprise and relief that she had been sleeping in her clothes.

'Do you remember your name?' he asked.

'Cathie . . .' She frowned, then fear fluttered in her chest. 'I – can't remember the rest of it.'

'Last night you couldn't remember even your first name, so you must be starting to get better. I thought you would. You look like a strong lass to me.'

She looked up in puzzlement at the sound of someone yelling incoherently from the next room.

'That's my mother. She canna think or speak properly now. Do you remember how yesterday she nearly set the place on fire? I have to lock her in her room at night now, or she wanders.'

Cathie blinked as a vague memory of burning coals falling on to a rug came back to her.

He took a step backwards on to the landing. 'I have to go to work soon, so I'll just away and finish dressing. When you come downstairs I'll show you where everything is.'

Cathie tried to straighten her crumpled clothes. There was a trunk standing at the foot of the narrow little bed and it seemed familiar. In a tentative exploration of the back of her head she found a painful lump. How had that happened? And why had a complete stranger brought her back to his home?

Downstairs a fire was smouldering in the kitchen range so she found the damper and opened it up, watching the glowing centre of the ashes grow brighter. There were pieces of coal in a box by the side of the fire, so she picked one up and put it on. She'd never seen coal before, only heard of it, but she treated it like wood, using small pieces first, and by the time she heard his footsteps on the stairs, flames were beginning to show.

Her host came in, looking more tidy now. He frowned at the clock ticking away comfortably on the mantelpiece. 'The neighbour who looks after my mother is usually here by now. I'd better go and see what's keeping her. She only lives in the next street. Will you be all right for a moment or two?'

'Yes, of course.'

He was back within minutes, his face flushed and his movements tight with suppressed anger. 'She's not coming. Says she's not condoning our immorality.'

'Immorality?' Cathie gaped at him. 'But we haven't . . .' Surely she'd have remembered if he'd tried to – to— But she did remember a man's hands, only when she looked at Magnus's she knew they weren't the ones. The others had been dirty, with black-rimmed fingernails, while his were well-scrubbed. She spoke her thoughts out loud. 'I remember a man attacking me – a burly man, not very clean.' She could summon up a memory of a brutal face, too, though she could not put a name to it.

'Aye. And there was a young woman helping him steal your things. If I hadna come along, he'd have . . .' Magnus broke off and finished lamely, '. . . attacked your virtue. She hit you on the head with a brick and when they saw me they made off. They had your trunk which they were trying to open and a bag that he threw at me, so maybe you haven't lost everything. I think they got your purse, though. It wasn't in your handbag. I'm sorry for looking in it, but the policeman and I were trying to find out who you were.'

Cathie stood stock-still, trying to fit her own fragments of memory to this tale. She did vaguely remember a young woman, but the face was still misty and she could not put a name to it.

Magnus glanced at the clock. 'Look, do you think you could possibly look after my mother for me today? I have to go to work, you see.' He broke off to yawn loudly. 'I'm tired already. It was a long day yesterday, seeing my brother off on the ship to Australia and—'

'*Australia!*' She stared at him. 'I think – it sounds like – home.'

He nodded, not seeming surprised. 'I thought you might be newly arrived in Liverpool.'

He pronounced it 'thocht'. She liked the soft Scottish accent. 'Yes, I did come from Australia.' She was suddenly quite certain of that and relieved to have another piece of the puzzle revealed. Only why had she come to England? And why had no one met her at the docks? 'I can remember – a house burning down!' She clutched her head. 'Oh, why can't I remember things properly?'

His voice was gentle. 'Because you've been hurt. But at least you're starting to remember. And Cathie's a pretty name, though I prefer our Scottish version – Caitlin.' He stepped forward to lay one hand on her shoulder, a comforting, not a threatening gesture. 'It'll all come back to you, lassie, if you give it time.' Another glance at the clock brought the harried expression back to his face. He asked again, 'Could you – I know you're not well – but could you possibly look after my mother for me today? I'm the foreman at a local mill and I like to get there early to show a good example to the men.' He tried very hard not to let his mother's needs interfere with his work.

'Yes, of course. What do I need to do for her?'

'Whatever you can. Treat her like a baby, and a naughty baby at that, for it's what she is now, poor thing. And whatever you do, don't leave her alone with the fire.' He fumbled in his pocket and tossed some coins on to the table. 'There's a baker's shop at the end of the street. If you buy a loaf and mebbe some cheese from the grocer's shop next door, you'll have something to eat. You'll have to cut hers up for her in small pieces and put it in her mouth. She can't seem to remember how to feed herself.' His face was ravaged with sorrow as he added, 'She was a good mother to us. It's hard to see her like this.'

Cathie's heart went out to him. 'I'll do my best with her. Won't she be frightened of a stranger?'

'We're all strangers to her now. She likely won't notice you half the time. Tie her to the rocking chair if she gets troublesome. I have to do that sometimes or I'd get no work done about the house.' He flicked some strips of material hanging from the bars of the chairback and added sadly, 'I hate doing it, though.' At the door he paused to say, 'Her name's Janey and our surname's Hamilton, in case you don't remember. She doesn't answer to her name any more but it seems only fair to use it.'

And then he was gone.

Cathie stood there in the cramped little room, hearing other footsteps passing by outside. They made a lot of noise. What sort of shoes were the people wearing? No, they must be clogs. She remembered someone telling her once how practical they were for bad weather if they were made properly. Who had done that? The harder she tried to remember, the fuzzier her brain felt. With a sigh she abandoned the attempt and tiptoed into the front room to peer through the window. People were still clattering past, so many people. But within a minute or two the rush stopped. She jumped in shock as there was a loud noise like a ship's siren from somewhere close by. A man hurrying along the street set off running the minute he heard it.

And then it was silent, with not a soul to be seen on the street.

Standing in the middle of the room she turned slowly in a circle as she studied it. The furniture shone as if someone had polished it recently. Would that be the sister? Where did she live? Why could she not look after the mother?

There was a noise upstairs and she went up to unlock the other bedroom. The old woman was sitting up in bed with a blank expression on her face. There was a strong smell of urine and, when Cathie moved forward, the woman cowered back as if expecting to be hit.

Trying to sound soothing, Cathie coaxed her from the bed and stood her against the wall, then stripped the wet sheets, hoping the wetness had not spread to the feather mattress below. It had, and there were other similar stains that said it wasn't the first time this had happened.

It took her a while to coax the poor woman into coming downstairs. She picked up a bundle of clothing and took it with her, deciding to dress her charge in front of the fire so that she could wash her first. Pouring some hot water into a bowl from the big black kettle that stood at the side of the hob, she mixed it carefully with cold water and sponged Magnus Hamilton's mother down like a small child, continuing to make soothing noises as she did it because when she stopped speaking the poor creature started making sounds of distress.

Afterwards Janey Hamilton stood patiently as she was dressed. She spoke occasionally, but only disjointed phrases that had no relevance to what was being done to her.

Feeling hungry now, Cathie investigated the kitchen for food. There was oatmeal in a bin and not much else, so she made watery porridge, struggling to heat it on the small range. It was a messy business feeding the old lady and she decided she would not wash her until after breakfast the following day. That made her freeze for a moment. The following day? Was she intending to stay here with these strangers? Then she shrugged. What else could she do if her money had been stolen?

On that thought she raced up the stairs. Magnus had said something about a handbag and her purse being stolen.

She brought the bag back down to investigate its contents. A crumpled handkerchief, a small sewing kit, an unfinished letter. A sound made her turn round and she saw Mrs Hamilton approaching the fire with one hand outstretched. With a sigh Cathie tied the poor woman to the rocking chair, hating to do that because the whimpering started again, but desperate to see what she could learn about herself.

Sitting down at the table she picked up the letter again.

Dear Mother and Father
The voyage has continued well and now we're nearly there. I haven't been seasick once, not even in the stormy weather, but others have, so I've been helping Matron look after them. For

that she gave me half a crown. It's not a large sum, but it's the first money I've ever earned. I didn't want to put it with the rest of my coins, so it's in my trunk with the money Mr Correntin slipped into my bag when he kindly bought me the embroidery materials I told you about.

Cathie paused. Who was Mr Correntin? She could conjure up no face to go with that name.

We'll be arriving in Liverpool tomorrow and Bessie Downham, the girl I've made friends with, is going to see me to the train. She seems to think I can't manage on my own, but I have a tongue in my head and I'm not stupid. Still, an offer of friendship is not to be spurned, is it?

With a cry, Cathie clutched her head, which seemed to be full of booming sound. Pain throbbed through her as images came tumbling in: Bessie's brother, the narrow alley, being attacked. She could not remember, though, how Magnus Hamilton had saved her, but if he said he had, well, she believed him. He had a sternly honest face – nice, though. And his hair was a lovely colour. She remembered with a wry smile how he had towered over her, something few other men had ever done. Goodness, what a giant he was! But he was also gaunt, with an unhappy look on his face.

She leaned her head on one hand and as the tide of pain ebbed her thoughts strayed back to Magnus. If she was in trouble so was he, trying to look after a mother in this state, with his sister obviously living elsewhere. Yet he had still found time to help a stranger. That said a lot about the kind of man he was. What would have happened to her if he hadn't brought her home?

She tried to remember her own family but could not bring their faces to mind clearly, only that they lived in Australia. What was she doing here in England, then? Oh, it was so frustrating not to remember!

She realised that Mrs Hamilton was wriggling about uncomfortably, so removed the bonds and led her out to the privy, relieved when that worked. Afterwards she cleared up their breakfast things, talking to the woman as she did so. Though she received no answers the sound of her voice seemed to keep the poor thing quiet. She could see no sign that Magnus had had any breakfast and wondered if he'd simply dashed out to work.

It seemed obvious that the next thing to do was to go through her trunk and see what she had been left with. She took Mrs Hamilton upstairs with her and the old lady began to walk up and down the room, crooning tunelessly to herself. When Cathie investigated, she found the trunk filled mostly with dirty clothes but there was a small embroidered purse at the bottom containing several sovereigns and other coins. She bowed her head at the sight of that, feeling quite shaky with relief at not being penniless and muttering, 'Oh, thank goodness! Thank goodness!'

Before going downstairs again she looked into Magnus's bedroom, though she felt guilty about prying. She found it a spartan chamber, with a double bed which seemed longer than usual and of rather rough workmanship. Perhaps he'd made it himself to accommodate his long limbs. There was a chest of drawers and a small pile of dirty linen on the bare wooden floor in the corner. Like the rest of the house, the room was clean and the furniture free of dust.

Leading her charge downstairs again she kept hold of Janey's hand while she studied the front room in more detail. It was by far the grandest in the house, but had a totally unused feel to it. There was a table at one side covered by a plush cloth in a rich red colour with a Bible standing squarely in the middle, a sofa and a few chairs, a highly polished sideboard and a few ornaments on the mantelpiece. There was also a shelf of books. She examined the titles. No novels. Serious subjects like *The History of Scotland, Birds of the Lancashire Moors, Domestic Economy of Great Britain* – which said something about the owner of the house, she supposed.

She went back into the kitchen. She would do some washing today, she decided, starting with herself. So she heated water then tied Mrs Hamilton to the chair again. The clothes she donned afterwards seemed to be the only clean ones she possessed, but there were plenty of dirty ones so perhaps, as Magnus said, he had prevented Bessie and her brother from taking her things. Which meant that all they'd taken had been the money in her purse. She couldn't even remember how much that had been.

It felt wonderful to be clean again. She rinsed out some underclothes and Mrs Hamilton's soiled nightdress in the bowl of water she had washed in and hung them to dry on a line in the back yard, then put the soiled sheets to soak and found others for the bed. She'd ask Magnus if she could do a big wash the following day – and would offer to wash his clothes as well.

When the clock on the mantelpiece chimed she realised

it was midday. She found a shawl and bonnet hanging in the hall, and dressed Mrs Hamilton in them, then set out for the corner shops Magnus had mentioned. Feeling ravenously hungry she bought not only a loaf, but some cheese, jam, potatoes, onions and a cabbage, spending some of her own money as well as his. She'd find a butcher's shop later and get some meat to make a stew for tea. She asked the shopkeeper what time the mill workers finished and, although the woman seemed very disapproving, received a curt answer.

'Is something wrong?' Cathie asked in exasperation. 'You don't know me, yet you seem angry at me. What have I done?'

The woman gaped at her in shock at this blunt question, then pursed her lips and said with a sniff, 'You'll be the young woman who spent the night with Magnus Hamilton, I take it?'

Cathie suddenly realised where this was leading. 'I spent the night in his sister's old bedroom, actually, and I'm looking after his mother today because Mrs Midner didn't come to work this morning.'

'Martha Midner is a member of our chapel Ladies' Circle. She'd not share a house with an unmarried young woman like yourself – *given the circumstances.*'

Cathie leaned forward and said very clearly, 'Then you'd better tell her that I'm not sharing Magnus Hamilton's bed, nor shall I be doing that. I, too, was brought up to be respectable – but also taught not to judge others without first seeking the truth.' She paused and added bitterly, 'Which is that I was attacked at the docks when I arrived in England, though luckily for me, my' – inspiration suddenly struck and she changed what she had been intending to say to — 'Cousin Magnus arrived in time to drive off the attackers. I was still very dizzy last night and couldn't think properly. I slept,' she slapped her hand down on the counter for emphasis, '*in his sister's bed*. And so you can tell Mrs Midner and anyone else who asks.'

Two women who were waiting to be served gasped aloud at her frankness.

The shopkeeper looked at her suspiciously. 'He's your cousin? He never said anything about a cousin, only about taking his brother to the ship.'

'I'm his second cousin, actually, but he promised my parents he and Mairi would help me when I arrived in England. And so he'd have told Mrs Midner if she'd given him time to explain. Which she didn't.' Cathie had no compunction about lying to these women. Why should they sit in judgement on her and blindly approve of this Mrs Midner who had left poor Magnus in the lurch today? She only hoped he had not told Mrs Midner last night that she was a stranger. She managed to summon up a vague memory of an older woman looking at her disapprovingly.

'You're very blunt,' the shopkeeper said.

'We speak our minds in Australia.' Cathie picked up her purchases, stuffed them anyhow into the string shopping bag she had found in the kitchen and took hold of Mrs Hamilton's hand. 'Come on, Auntie Janey. Let's get you home again.'

She heard someone say, 'Well!' as she left the shop, but didn't turn her head.

Janey smiled as they walked back, holding her face up to the sun. The smile faded as Cathie opened the front door of their house and the old woman pulled back, whimpering in her throat.

Cathie studied her. 'Do you like going for walks? Well, so do I. We'll go out again after we've eaten, shall we?' They'd find a butcher's shop and when they came back she'd cook a hearty stew for the man who had saved her — before confessing to him that she'd claimed him as a cousin.

She smiled briefly. Would he mind? Would he agree to keep up the pretence? Well, if he didn't she'd just leave him to deal with the gossip however he thought best and find somewhere else to live.

But somehow she didn't think he would mind because he needed her to look after his mother for a while. She had noticed bruises on Mrs Hamilton's body which could have been caused by blows and indignation filled her at the mere thought, both on her own and Magnus Hamilton's behalf. How could anyone hurt a poor helpless creature like Janey Hamilton? If this was how Mrs Midner had looked after her, she should be ashamed of herself.

'I can certainly do better than that,' muttered Cathie.

CHAPTER NINE

May

When a letter arrived at the clogger's shop in Underby Street, Teddy Marshall stared at it in distrust. Who the hell was writing letters to him? He nearly tossed it in the fire then changed his mind and set it on the back of his work bench to wait till his eldest son came back. Those squiggly little lines meant nowt to him, but Bob could read and would tell him what was in the damned thing.

When his son returned, face ruddy, carrying a load of clog irons in a sack, Teddy scowled at him. He hated to see how strong his sons were, for they all took after him and were big men while he was fast losing what was left of his strength and his eyes weren't too good lately, either. Sodding old age! You worked hard all your life and this was your reward, a body that let you down. He couldn't even drink as much ale nowadays because it made him feel sick. Well, at least he had fathered five fine sons, and raised them to stand up for themselves, too. No one could take that away from him.

He picked up the letter and thrust it at his son. 'This arrived.'

Bob took it out of his hand and stared at the envelope. 'It's addressed to you.'

'Fat lot of good that is. I can't read the bloody thing, nor I don't want to. Throw it in the fire if you aren't going to read it to me.'

'It's come all the way from Australia.'

Teddy gaped. 'Australia? I don't know anyone in Australia. Who sent it? What do they want?'

'Only one way to find out.' Bob ripped open the envelope and pulled out a single sheet of paper, reading it carefully, then hissing in shock and reading it all over again.

'What does it say? Read it out to me.'

Dear Mr Marshall

I'm writing to tell you that you have a daughter and that she's coming to England on the same ship as this letter. Her name is Cathie Ludlam, or she may be calling herself Cathie Caine now because her mother married again. Remember her mother? Liza Docherty, my sister, who used to live opposite you in Underby Street?

Liza ran off to Australia and did pretty well for herself. Married Josiah Ludlam no less, then Nicholas Rawley, but is now married to a farmer, Benedict Caine, who also comes from Pendleworth.

If you keep an eye open, you might meet your daughter around the town and introduce yourself. The girl certainly looks like a Marshall, tall and sturdy. A daughter to be proud of.

Dermott Docherty

Bob grinned at his father. 'You lusty old bugger! How come you didn't know about this?'

Teddy didn't smile back at him. 'It ain't true. Someone's playing a trick on us.'

'Didn't you know this Liza Docherty, then?'

There was silence, then Teddy glanced over his shoulder to check that his wife wasn't within earshot and muttered, 'Might have.'

'Well, this Liza's brother says the daughter looks like us. Wonder why he bothered to write, though?' Bob waited as his father turned away from him, shoulders hunched, kicking absent-mindedly at the end of the wooden work bench with one clogged foot. Thud. Thud.

'Dad?' When he got no answer, Bob grinned and decided it must be true. The old devil! 'Are you all right? Not going to faint from shock, are you?'

Teddy didn't answer. He was remembering the time he'd forced himself on Liza. Pretty little thing she'd been. He'd felt a bit guilty afterwards because he'd hurt her. Suddenly he remembered her face the next morning, chalk white, her eyes dark-rimmed and her slender body bruised. He'd wanted to marry her right and proper, though. She'd been refusing to wed him, so he'd thought it best to make sure of her. Only it hadn't solved anything because she'd run off, the jade, and never been heard of again till she turned up in Pendleworth years later married to Squire Rawley's only son. Had she really been married to a Ludlam as well? Teddy scowled. Buggered if he could figure it all out. Buggered if he wanted to try.

'You don't want to go getting mixed up with that lot,' he muttered as his son kept staring at him.

'What lot?'

'Them Ludlams. Or the Rawleys.' Teddy explained

what had happened, enjoying the feeling of superiority that came from knowing more than his son for once. 'I saw her a few years ago when she come back to England with her husband – Mr Nicholas Rawley, no less. Well, she were a pretty piece, you have to give her that. I kept well away from her an' you should do the same with the daughter now. That old sod Stephenson is still alive and he's the meanest devil as ever rode in a carriage, that one is. You don't offend them nobs if you know what's good for you.'

A further minute or two of rumination and he added, 'That young Rawley is Liza's son, you know – what's his name again?'

'The heir?' Bob asked sharply.

'Aye, the son and heir.' Teddy spat a gob of phlegm triumphantly on to the floor as he remembered. 'Francis he's called.' He flicked the letter with one grimy finger-tip. 'He must be the half-brother of this lass in the letter.' He didn't really want owt to do with it, just wanted to live what was left of his life quietly without any trouble. Anyway, by the time he'd seen Liza again he'd married Sal Pocklington, more fool him. He sighed, mentally comparing Sal to Liza. Not a looker, Sal, though she'd enjoyed a bit of bed play when she was younger an' given him two sons, though what use were they to a man when they'd gone off on the tramp and never been heard of again? But what a mistake his second marriage had been! Sal might be scrawny, but she had ways of making you pay if you upset her. A man couldn't call his life his own with her around. 'Don't tell Sal about this,' he said automatically.

'Don't tell Sal what?' asked a sharp voice from behind him. 'What've you done now, Teddy Marshall?'

He cursed under his breath.

'Well?' she demanded, hands on scrawny hips and *that* look on her face. 'What don't you want Bob to tell me?'

'I just didn't want to upset you, love,' he offered placatingly.

Bob laughed and tossed the letter across to his stepmother. 'Read that. It seems I've got a half-sister I didn't know about.' Out of pity for his father he added, 'Before your time, Ma.'

Sal scanned the letter, mouthing the words as she slowly spelled her way through it. 'You old sod!' she said affectionately, clouting Teddy round the ears. Then she frowned. 'Why would this Dermott fellow bother to write to you? Was he a friend of yours?'

'That's what worries me. He weren't a friend of anyone, that one weren't. Used to hang out with his brother. Thick as thieves because they *was* thieves, them two. One of the nastiest sods I've ever met, Niall Docherty was. Born to be hung. Dermott weren't as bad, but bad enough.'

Bob chewed one side of his lip then said thoughtfully, 'He says the lass's family has a bit of money. Wonder if there's any chance of us getting our hands on some?' For he had a wife and three children at home and his wife was always asking for money for new clothes for them. Good thing he'd taken over his father's shop two years ago. The old fool had let it run down and had refused to change things till Bob had threatened to set up for himself as a clogger on the opposite side of the street.

He looked at his father sourly and picked up a piece of

181

wood from the bench, inspecting the shaping. Poor quality of work, as usual nowadays. 'Where are those spectacles I got you, Dad? You haven't gone and lost this pair as well, have you?'

'I keep 'em safe for him,' Sal said. 'I'll go an' fetch 'em.'

'Well, go on keeping 'em safe, because I'm not forking out for another pair.' He turned to his father and raised his voice. 'Why aren't you wearing them? You know bloody well you can't see for close work without.'

Teddy muttered something and scowled at him.

Bob picked the letter up. 'I'll keep this, Ma. It wants thinking about.'

'Well, this lass, whoever she may be, isn't getting anything out of us,' Sal cautioned. 'I don't scrub my hands raw to help *his* bastards.'

'No, you do it to pay for your gin.'

As Bob had hoped this jibe distracted her and she forgot about the letter in cursing him and arguing about a woman's right to a sip or two of comfort of an evening to ease the ache in her bones.

He called in on his next brother on the way home. Jim had just come in after a day at the mill and was grumbling about Magnus bloody Hamilton, the foreman, who'd been driving them all mad today fussing about nowt. What did it matter if they missed oiling a machine part once in a while? It'd get done the next time round, wouldn't it? Fussy buggers like Hamilton should be taken out and shot, and Jim would volunteer to do that any day, by hell he would.

When he had calmed down a bit, Bob explained about the girl who was supposed to have arrived in England on the same boat as this letter, and the two of them speculated as to whether they really did have a half-sister.

'If we have, it'll be you an' me as'll have to deal with it,' Jim said angrily. 'Pat's too soft.'

Later they called in at their youngest brother's, after a stop at the Railway Arms. Much mellowed by a couple of pints of beer, they showed Pat the letter.

'You mean, we've got a sister?' He beamed at them. 'I wonder what she's like. Cathie's a nice name. I allus wanted a sister.'

'She's only a half-sister and don't talk so bloody soft. Who cares what she's like? It's whether her family's got any money as is more to the point.' Bob didn't reckon much to sisters. His wife had three of 'em, always turning up and expecting a cup of tea and who knew what else?

But he couldn't get it through the daft bugger's head that this might be an opportunity for them and Pat's wife, Tess, was just as stupid. The pair of them deserved one another, they did that! Soft ha'porths! Allus helping other folk instead of helping themselves.

Well, Pat would fall into line eventually. You only had to say things like 'Family first' and 'Family need to stick together', and the silly sod would do anything for you.

When Magnus got home, he stood in the hall sniffing the aroma drifting out of the kitchen. Someone was cooking and it smelled wonderful. 'I'm back!' he called before he moved into the house, not wanting to frighten the lass.

He stopped again at the door of the kitchen, his breath catching in his throat at the sight of her, wrapped in one of his mother's pinafores, stirring something on the cooking range and humming to herself. She looked clean today – and so did his mother. He'd forgotten how rosy newly washed skin could look and that made him realise how sloppily Mrs Midner had cared for his mother, even if she hadn't been cruel to her.

Cathie smiled at him. 'I hope you like stew?'

'I love it. Especially when it smells like that.' He frowned. 'Did I leave you enough money to buy meat?'

'I found some of my own in my trunk. There's no reason you should be paying for my meals.'

They stared at one another across the room and the thought suddenly came to him that this was what it must be like to return home to a wife. Longing speared through him followed swiftly by scorn at his own weakness. 'I'll wash, then.' He clumped past her into the scullery, closing the door on the surprised expression on her face. He wanted to sit with her and tell her about his day, as he used to tell his mother. Jim Marshall had been causing trouble again. Give that fellow an inch and he slid out of any work he could. Lazy devil he was and infected others with that same laziness. Though he could do good work when pushed and was definitely not stupid.

When he went back into the kitchen, Magnus found Cathie trying to persuade his mother to move to the table for her meal. Forgetting his earlier embarrassment, he hurried across to help her.

Cathie took a step back and watched, surprised at how much more easily he did this than she had. It was as if his mother recognised his touch, even in her clouded state. 'I'll serve the food, then, shall I?'

'Please.' He watched her bustling to and from the kitchen range, getting dishes out and ladling the stew into them, then cutting big hunks of bread to go with it. 'How did you know what time to have it ready? I forgot to tell you when I finished.'

'I asked the woman in the corner shop.'

He saw a frown wrinkle her forehead as she said that. Well, he didn't like Mrs Naylor, either. The corner shop was convenient for a man with too few hours in the day and that was the best you could say of it. 'That old besom?'

She laughed. 'Besom! What a lovely word.'

'It's Scottish. Mum used to use it.' He looked sadly at his mother then smiled across the table. 'You've washed her. Thank you for that. She'd be grateful. She always liked to keep clean.'

Cathie hesitated. 'Didn't Mrs Midner do that – wash her, I mean?'

'Not very well. My mother looks different today – rosy and well cared for. I'm grateful to you for that.' He took a deep breath. 'I – um – asked around at work, but no one knows of a woman who can come and look after her, even temporarily.'

'I can do it for a while, if you like? In return for somewhere to live.'

He had been hoping she would say this – and yet afraid of hearing it, too. What would it do to her reputation if they lived together? But how could he refuse her offer when his mother so badly needed help? 'Do you really mean that? You don't mind?'

She nodded, putting another spoonful of stew into Janey's mouth, then one into her own.

He followed their example for a moment or two, chewing slowly and with relish. 'This is a fine meal. You must tell me how much I owe you for the meat, though.'

'Nothing.'

'But I canna let you—'

She changed the subject. 'I have something to confess.'

His heart lurched. What? What had she remembered?

'I told the woman in the shop that you were my cousin — well, second cousin.'

'Why?' He watched her wriggle uncomfortably and when she didn't speak, prompted, 'Why did you do that, lassie?'

'Well, she was suggesting — things. About us. You and me.'

He saw her face flame and felt anger surge through him. Not only because the things were untrue, but because he wished they could be true. 'Did she believe you?'

Cathie looked up and a smile twisted her mouth briefly. 'I don't know, but when I told her straight out that we were not sharing a bed, she got angry and' — she hesitated then continued in a rush of words — 'I don't think she believes I'm your cousin, but if I'm to stay and look after your mother, it'll sound better to say I am.'

He stared at her. 'Have you remembered much more about yourself? Won't someone be waiting for you, expecting you?'

Her smile faded. 'I haven't remembered much more. It's all very patchy. I remember scenes, faces . . . There's a child, a little girl called Josie — and I remember being attacked. But I can't fit things together properly. It's very frustrating.'

He was sorry he'd caused her smile to fade. It was such

a lovely smile, fresh and open. She was a sonsy lass, looking strong and healthy, a woman very much to his taste. 'It'll all come back to you eventually.'

She shook her head, her hands twisting together in her lap. 'Will it?'

He stretched out to take one of them and hold it still in his. 'Aye, lassie. I'm sure it will.'

For a moment their hands lay together on the table, both large and capable, hers reddened from the washing and his rough from his daily work. He didn't want to let go but he did, slowly, his eyes meeting hers and—

His mother began to choke and they had to pound her back and settle her down again. By then the moment had passed – and probably a good thing too, Magnus decided. He picked up his spoon and continued his meal, murmuring, 'You're a good cook, Caitlin.'

She didn't correct him. She liked his version of her name better than Cathie – well, when he said it with that soft Scottish lilt, anyway.

'All right,' he said as the meal ended. 'We'll say you're a second cousin from Australia – on my mother's side. They're Rutherfords, come from near Roxburgh. I don't usually approve of telling lies, but if it'll make things easier for you to stay, cause you less embarrassment . . .' He let the words trail away.

'Caitlin Rutherford,' she said slowly. 'All right.' But she could not help wondering what her real surname was.

It was only later when he was sitting reading in front of the fire that he remembered Mairi. 'I'd better write and let my sister know we've got a new cousin.' And then he had to explain about his sister, which somehow led on to his brothers and how they'd all gone away over the sea.

'And left you with the burden of your mother?' Cathie said softly, her feet tucked up on the rung of the chair, her arms clasped around her knees. 'That must be hard.'

'I'm the eldest. Head of the family. She's my responsibility.'

'You're a good man, Magnus Hamilton.'

He could feel himself flushing. He wasn't used to compliments. He got out the writing paper. It all sounded very far-fetched when he set it down and he was tempted to tear the letter up, but Mairi and Elwyn might come across on Sunday so they must be warned. Abandoning any thought of trying to make it sound better he scrawled across the bottom, 'I'll explain properly next time I see you, but Caitlin looks after Mum as well as you would, and far better than Mrs Midner did, so I think it's all happened for the best.'

He wasn't really sure of that, for seeing Caitlin like this with the firelight reflecting on her face and shining hair made him realise that his heart was already touched by her. The more fool he.

As they got his mother ready for bed, working together to persuade Janey to change into a nightgown, he smiled at Caitlin — he simply could not think of her as Cathie — and said softly, 'So you'll be staying for a while, eh, lass?'

'I'll be staying, but not for too long,' she warned. 'Just for a few weeks, maybe, till I get a bit more used to this England of yours. So it might be as well for you to keep your eyes open for someone else. I won't go until you've found other help, though.'

'I thank you for your help, Caitlin — Cathie, I mean.'

'Caitlin sounds more Scottish, so it's better to call me that if I'm to pretend I'm your cousin.'

Somehow he forgot his book as they settled downstairs, chatting like old friends in front of the fire.

He went to bed feeling better about life than he had for a long time. And dreamed of Caitlin. When he woke he didn't know whether to be upset about that or not.

In Australia Matthieu lingered at Baileys' Farm, considering his future. He took long walks, trying to work out where this property ended. The Caines' homestead marked one boundary very clearly, not only because there was a rough pole fence but also because the land beyond it had that indefinable air of being cared for. Fields had crops standing in them, because in this strange country, winter and spring were the main growing seasons. Even the patches of bushland on Caine land had well-used little paths curling around them without signs of new growth as if someone walked the perimeters regularly.

Had Caine's wife really killed her eldest brother, as Dermott claimed? Matthieu wondered. What was she like, then? He had met females who were whores and thieves but never, to his knowledge, one who was a murderess.

On one of his trips he met a young man and stopped to exchange greetings, surprised to be met by a scowl.

'Are you the new owner of Baileys'?' the young man demanded.

'No, I'm just keeping an eye on things for him.'

'Then I'll not trespass again.'

As he turned to leave Matthieu held out his hand. 'I'm

Matthieu Correntin.' When his companion stared at the hand as if he had not expected that, Matthieu looked down at it in puzzlement. 'Is there something wrong with my hand?'

'No, with mine. I'm part-native,' the lad said, scowling and eyeing him challengingly. 'You won't want to shake hands with such as me.'

Matthieu grinned. 'I'm French. Are *you* sure you want to touch me? After all, my people used to be enemies of Britain.' He did not drop his hand and when the young fellow took it hesitantly, gave his a hearty shake. 'We French are not so worried about the colour of a man's skin,' he said. 'We care more about what's inside his mind. Look, there are some things I'd like to ask you about this place. Would you share a pot of coffee with me? It's not good coffee, but it's all I have to offer.'

Still Brendan hesitated. He was not used to being treated like this and could not help doubting the man's sincerity. Did the French really not care as much about the colour of a man's skin? If so, what was their country like?

'I'm trying to find out where this farm ends and other people's land begins but it's not very clear, except along Caine's boundaries.'

Bemused, Brendan began to walk with him, intrigued by his companion's accent and his trim appearance, so different somehow from the other men round Brookley. When they got to the house Brendan was even more bemused by the ritual for making coffee, which meant grinding some black seeds and making a dark brown brew out of them.

'I've never seen people do that before,' he said abruptly.

Matthieu shrugged. 'It is my weakness, coffee. The English drink tea, but we French prefer coffee, so I bring the beans with me and make a small pleasure of preparing a drink. Though I would have preferred a good china cup to these clumsy things. The last owners have left most of their household goods. What happened to them? Did they die?'

'Mrs Bailey died. Mr Bailey was getting old. One day he loaded some things on his cart and drove away. We didn't see him again, but we heard that he'd gone over to Melbourne to join his son.'

'Do you live near here?'

Brendan shrugged. 'If you call it living, stuck in the middle of nowhere. My father is Irish. My mother is half-Irish, half-Aboriginal. They work for the Caines. I don't like it here – but I don't fit in anywhere else, either. People look at your skin and treat you as if you're stupid. And I'm *not* stupid.' And why he'd confided in a stranger like this he could not work out, for he usually avoided the company of white men. He raised the clumsy cup and sipped, frowning down at the dark liquid and rolling it round his mouth.

'You don't like it?' Matthieu asked.

'I'm not used to it. It seems very strong.'

'I shall add more hot water, then perhaps you will find it more palatable.' Matthieu did so and watched his young companion's valiant efforts to pretend he was enjoying it. He chuckled suddenly. 'I shall not be offended if you don't wish to finish it.'

And Brendan found himself smiling back. 'I'll finish it.

After all, it's a new experience for me and I don't enjoy many of those. We only drink tea at home.' After a pause he said gruffly, 'I can show you the boundaries of the farm, if you want.'

'I would be grateful. Do you not have work to do, *mon ami*?'

Again that defensive shrug. 'I'm supposed to work for Mr Caine, but sometimes I get fed up and just walk away for a time. I'm on day rates. He only keeps me on because of my parents and because there are few others to hire round here.'

'You don't like working on a farm?'

'No. But if I leave, I'll be treated as an ignorant native and that would be no better. When Cathie was here, it wasn't so bad, but since she's gone . . .' He shrugged and let the words trail away.

'She too hated living here in the country,' Matthieu agreed tranquilly.

Brendan looked at him in surprise. 'You've met her?'

'Yes. Her uncle is my partner.' He explained what had happened to her and saw the distress on the young man's face. 'She will be all right, *j'en suis sûr.*'

'She was my only friend and now I may never see her again.'

'It is hard indeed to lose a friend,' Matthieu agreed. 'But she'll be back one day, with tales to tell, no doubt. And I have no friends here, either, so perhaps you and I can find time for one another.'

The only response was a cynical stare.

'I mean that.' Matthieu waited for a comment. When none came, he looked at the sky. 'It's too late to survey the boundaries today and I'm sure your mother will be expecting you back, but if you would come again tomorrow, I too will pay you a suitable daily rate.'

'I'm not going home tonight.'

'You have quarrelled with your family?'

Brendan shook his head. 'No. But sometimes I need to be away from everyone, so I camp out in the bush.'

'If you wish to stay here tonight, there are other bedrooms and I shall be happy to share a meal. I shot a kangaroo this morning.'

And so began an unlikely friendship. Which was, Matthieu thought, going to cause complications once Dermott arrived, for his partner despised natives. He grinned into the darkness of his bedroom, then thought of the governess and made a soft sound of exasperation. He kept thinking of her, wanting to see her again. She intrigued him. He was sure there was fire behind that cool exterior.

But at least he had found out her given name from Brendan: Ilse. A beautiful name. It suited her.

Matthieu spent two days walking the boundaries with Brendan, learning a great deal about the local wildlife and also about the way Brendan's mother and her people thought of the land. In return he spoke of France, suddenly sure he would never return there again. Which might or might not be a step towards finding out where he did want to go next.

He found the young man intelligent and interested in the world, and sincerely pitied him. To his mind, the English placed too much importance on the whiteness of a person's skin.

A mile away Liza was equally wakeful. How could she leave when her brother's business partner had come to Brookley? Was there some plan to harm her family again?

And then there was Benedict. He was working too hard, looking grim and determined, and he had become very short-tempered, even with the children. Poor Josie and Harry could not understand why their father had changed so much. He, Seth and Lucas were working every minute of the day. And during the evenings he would not stop, but sit on the veranda with an oil lamp, carving pieces of wood to embellish the furniture he hoped to make again one day.

She knew he was still deeply upset about Cathie's departure. What with the bush fire and their daughter running away, he felt he had failed his family, and to Benedict family was the most important thing in his life. He was a good husband and Liza loved him dearly, but she wished she could persuade him to take life more easily. She did not need riches or luxuries to make her happy, just him and her children, but he seemed determined to wrest a fortune out of this harsh land. It was as if he still felt he had to prove to everyone that he had made a success of his life here.

He had not tried to prevent her from going to England, and she and Josie would be leaving very soon, but she knew he would worry about them and miss her desperately — as she would miss him. Before she went she was going to insist he sold some more pieces of jewellery so that he'd have money to finish the new house and build a proper furniture manufactory.

But whatever pain she caused him, she was still going.

She would not feel right until she'd done this. It wasn't just for her own sake now. She had a presentiment that both Francis and Cathie were going to need her.

Her own mother had sometimes talked about 'the sight' but Liza had not really believed in it until now.

CHAPTER TEN

May

As Matthieu was riding back to the farm he saw Ilse Hebel and the little girl strolling along in the distance and urged his horse to a faster trot, catching up with them well before they turned off towards Lizabrook. He reined the horse in and slid off it because he wanted to stand close to her.

'*Bonjour*, Frau Hebel, Mademoiselle Caine.' He bowed to the little girl as if she were a grown-up and as he'd expected she giggled. In other circumstances he would have enjoyed teasing her, because little girls of that age could be charming. The governess was very calm today, but a pulse was beating rapidly in her throat and he had seen for himself how her colour had risen slightly when she saw him.

'Monsieur Correntin.' She inclined her head. 'How are you feeling? Have you recovered from your fall?'

'*Mais oui*. I've been into Brookley to buy fresh vegetables from the inn.' He gestured around them. 'A pleasant day to take the air. I enjoy the Australian winters.'

'I enjoy the summers as well.'

There was a short silence. The child hopped up and down playing some complicated skipping game as she waited for the adults to finish their chat, mouthing rhymes under her breath to match her steps.

'It is unexpected to find a lady like yourself here in the middle of the bush, and one who speaks French moreover. I must confess, I've greatly missed the sound of my native tongue.'

Ilse opened her mouth as if to speak, then closed it again and looked at him warily.

'I wonder – would you and the child have time to come and visit the farm? I would really welcome a woman's opinion of the house.'

She swallowed hard, then glanced down at a little fob watch pinned to her bodice.

Before she could say anything Josie skipped forward to urge, 'Do say yes, Frau Hebel. I haven't been out there for ages. They used to have some apple trees at the back.' She stared at Matthieu calculatingly. 'Our trees got burned in a bush fire, but it missed the Baileys' farm. I used to enjoy picking apples and eating them straight away. They taste best of all that way.'

Ilse clicked her tongue at this blatant hint. 'Josie!'

Matthieu smiled warmly at the child. 'You must come and show me the orchard, if you please, Mademoiselle Josie. I have not seen it yet. If there are any ripe apples, you can try one straight from the tree and see if they still taste as good.' He offered his hand and she took it without hesitation, so he set off walking before the governess could say anything, leading the horse. After a moment's hesitation Ilse turned and followed them. He slowed down to let her catch up, giving her a warm smile that was not feigned.

As they walked they spoke of music and books. He

found her French excellent. 'How did you learn my language so well?' he asked.

'I was well educated and our home was so close to France we all spoke both French and German. And I've always had a particular gift for languages.'

He kept her engaged in unthreatening conversation until she grew more comfortable with him. He could tell the moment that happened because the constrained expression vanished. He was surprised to see how warm her smile could be. It transformed her so much that he guessed her emotions were normally kept under very firm control.

When they arrived at the farm he unsaddled the horse and turned it loose, then let the child show them the orchard. Some of the trees were early producers and were loaded with fruit, so he begged Josie to try one and pick as much as she wanted for her family, finding an old sack for her to put them in. Then he took the governess to inspect the house, ignoring her wary look when he offered her his arm.

'What a waste!' Ilse mourned as they walked back through the windfalls lying on the ground. 'You could make apple pies or dried fruit from those.'

'I shall gather some of them and leave them at your gates — in return for a pie or two, perhaps?'

'That seems fair.'

He led the way into the house. 'Would a woman like this place, do you think?' he asked as they stopped just inside the front door. Instead of the usual central breezeway with rooms to either side there was a huge room, which was entrance hall, kitchen and dining area all in one. At the moment it was filled with golden light from the sun shining through the dusty windows.

He strolled to the other side of the room, watching her covertly from there, seeing the way her hand fluttered up to her throat then down again as she struggled to maintain her composure. She was, he thought, quite unversed in flirtation and although she was widowed, there was something almost virginal about her, as if she had never been truly roused. He found that thought piquant. He would like to be the one to show her what love could be like. Then he looked at her again and knew it would not be fair to seduce her, for he was not a marrying man and she was most definitely a respectable woman.

She took a few paces forward, filling the silence with a rush of words. 'I've always liked this room and I know Mrs Bailey loved the place. Poor Mr Bailey never got over her death.' She walked slowly up and down, running a hand along the dresser as she passed then stopping to ask quietly, 'Have you bought the farm, monsieur?'

'*Non. Pas encore.* But I am considering it now that I've seen the other attractions the neighbourhood has to offer.' He looked at her in a way which emphasised his hidden meaning. He might not wish to hurt her, but a gentle flirtation could be fun.

Instead of replying in kind she walked away from him, going back up the room with her hands clasped so tightly together in front of her that the knuckles were white. At the far end she turned to ask, 'And your partner? Will Mr Docherty be coming down here to visit?'

'I believe so. Mrs Caine is his sister, is she not?'

'Yes. But they don't get on.'

'She is upset at the thought of him coming?'

'Yes, very. They've had enough trouble lately with the fire and then her losing the baby she was carrying. She's not worried for herself — she and Josie are leaving for England in a couple of days — but she's afraid Mr Docherty will cause trouble for her family. Couldn't you tell him she's gone, suggest it's a waste of time his coming here?'

As she looked at him with her clear, blue eyes, something twisted inside Matthieu but he pushed it aside. 'I doubt Dermott ever lets anyone tell him what to do. He is not that sort of a man. And I'm afraid since he owns this place, I cannot forbid him to come here.' After an awkward silence, he changed the subject. 'How are you all managing at Lizabrook since the fire?'

'Mr Caine has worked very hard to rebuild the place, though we're still living in rather restricted conditions.'

'That must be difficult for you. Could you not find yourself another employer? In Perth perhaps? You're a long way from civilisation here.'

'I get on well with the Caines. They've been good to me. Though I have been thinking . . .' She broke off abruptly, as if regretting this confidence, and said hastily, 'But I shouldn't like to leave them at present. Nor should I like to see anything else hurt them.'

Here was another person who thought well of the Caines. It did not match with what Dermott had said about his sister. 'I have suggested to him that it is time to forget the past.'

'And did he agree?'

'He is considering the matter. I can do no more.'

After consulting the pretty gold watch pinned to her

bodice Ilse moved towards the door. 'We must leave now. We have Josie's packing still to finish. It's a lovely house, though. I'm sure any woman would be happy to live here.' She didn't wait for him but hurried outside.

Josie had filled the sack with apples and was munching one with relish.

Matthieu went over to tie the top corners of the sack together. 'You've worked quickly, young lady. Let's saddle the pack horse. Ginger can carry that sack for us and another filled with windfalls, if you like. If we work quickly we can soon fill one.'

At the farm he lifted the sacks down and propped them by the back door, then turned to hold out his hand to the governess. *'Auf wiedersehen, Ilse.'*

She did not refuse to take his hand nor did she chide him for using her first name, so he clasped her hand for a moment longer than he should have done and murmured, 'It's a beautiful name. It suits you.' Only then did he let go and hold out his hand to the child. *'Au 'voir* to you as well, Joséphine. And *bon voyage!'*

'Merci beaucoup, Monsieur.' She giggled at her own temerity in using the French words Frau Hebel had practised with her the previous day.

He smiled as he watched them enter the house. The woman did not look back, but the child stopped at the door and waved vigorously.

He led the pack horse slowly back, thinking about her, this cool German woman with her silvery blonde hair and pale blue eyes. Did he really wish to pursue her? He shouldn't. The wisest thing to do would be to leave Brookley now.

Only he had never been wise where women were concerned. And Ilse was very different from others he had known, intriguingly different.

The following morning Cathie got up as soon as she heard the knocker-up coming along the street in the pre-dawn hush. He was rapping on bedroom windows with his long pole and calling out the time. Determined to earn her keep, she flung her clothes on anyhow and hurried downstairs to get the fire going and water boiling for Magnus's shave and cup of tea.

When he came downstairs he stared at her as if he didn't believe what he saw, then muttered a greeting before going out to the privy. By the time he returned she had toasted some pieces of bread on the fire, buttered them and put them on the edge of the hob to keep warm. She busied herself making some cheese sandwiches for his mid-day meal.

'I don't expect you to wait on me,' he said as he took his place at the table. 'You could have stayed in bed a little longer.'

'I always wake early, and anyway I wanted to talk to you – to ask if I could take your mother for a walk? She seemed to enjoy being outside yesterday and kept turning up her face to the sun. When we came back, she didn't want to come inside.'

'She used to love going for walks. You could try it, see how she goes. Mrs Midner rarely took her out.' He gave directions for a pleasant walk towards the outskirts of the town.

'And the other thing is, what do you want for tea tonight?'

'Eh, lassie, anything is fine. Lately I've not been used to . . .' his voice came out choked, '. . . being cared for like this.'

'All right.' She tended to the fire, thinking what a bleak time he must have been having.

His voice made her jump. 'I usually get my mother up before I go.'

'I can do that. You take your time today.'

A long silence, then, 'Thank you. It's a rare treat not to be rushing around.'

She turned and looked him in the eyes. 'I could be dead if you hadn't helped me. I owe you a great deal, Magnus Hamilton, and I shan't forget that.' And even if the work was more of the domestic drudgery she'd hated, she was surrounded by people, not trees, which made life much more interesting.

He loved the sound of his name on her lips. 'I'm very glad you're not dead, Caitlin,' he said before he could help himself, then picked up another piece of toast and concentrated on his food.

She said teasingly, 'Will you be coming home at the same time today, *Cousin* Magnus?'

That made him look up and smile. 'Aye. I will, *Cousin* Caitlin.'

When the front door closed behind him, she ran into the front parlour to watch him stride down the street, arms swinging, head held high, one of the first to leave for work. His bright hair caught the sunlight and his height and proud bearing made the other people seem like drab and dwarfish creatures. He was, she decided, the most attractive man she had ever met and she could not help wondering what he thought of her.

Then a noise from upstairs recalled her to her duties.

Later that morning Cathie took her 'Auntie Janey' out for a walk, noting again how willingly the older woman went outside. They took the route Magnus had recommended, heading west and avoiding the town centre. Since Janey did not seem to be tiring, Cathie followed the road as far as some large houses which stood quite a distance apart from one another, surrounded by luxuriant gardens. She had never seen anything like them and slowed down to gaze at the massed flower displays, entranced by their vivid colour and beauty, not to mention the soft green of the neatly trimmed lawns.

A vision of a sun-baked field of beige grass surrounded by dull green foliage flashed before her eyes. Australia. That was followed by another image, even more vivid: a small woman with dark hair, hands on hips, scolding, but in a fond voice. 'Mother,' Cathie whispered. A dark-haired man walked into the scene in her head. Her father – no, her stepfather. Then his name: Benedict Caine. Was her surname Caine, then? It didn't seem right. Had he not given her his name? She felt – no, she *knew* – she loved him, but she was equally sure that Caine wasn't her real surname.

Tears trickled down her cheeks. From the half-finished letter in her handbag she guessed that she had run away and that must have hurt them. As soon as she remembered their address she'd write to them again and assure them she was all right.

But why had she run away from people she loved?

Then Janey whimpered and tugged her onwards. So Cathie banished her memories and simply enjoyed the walk, getting to know the English countryside as she had once known the Australian bush.

Meanwhile in Rawley Manor – the largest of the houses Cathie had walked past – Alexander Stephenson was berating his great-nephew in a low, furious voice, for Francis had been sent home from school due to a lingering illness. A Rawley should be well educated, able to hold his own in any company, as Alexander prided himself on doing. But the latest report from the expensive boarding school for the sons of gentlemen was worse than the previous one and said bluntly that Francis was more interested in painting than in study, showing no aptitude for sport, either.

The boy was such a disappointment! For all the careful upbringing Alexander had bestowed on him, he had not been able to mould his nephew into a satisfactory future owner of a great estate. The lad was a poor rider and the county gentry regarded him scornfully because of this. To make matters worse he also refused point blank to join the hunt or go out shooting, and no threats or bribes would change his mind about that. When he could, he slid away from confrontations of any sort; when he could not avoid trouble, he accepted punishment sullenly, but it seemed to make little difference to his behaviour.

It must be his mother's Irish blood which had done this and it sickened Alexander that *her* son would inherit this great estate. Why his nephew had married such a common creature he had never understood. Liza might have been pretty, but so were dozens of other young women.

Well, Nicholas had come to regret his hasty match and at least he'd left his son to the guardianship of people of breeding, not to *her*. Alexander had swiftly made sure she left the country so that she could not interfere.

But would his efforts make a difference? They said what was bred in the bone would come out in the flesh. If Francis grew up feckless and let the estate run to rack and ruin, Alexander would not be there to prevent it. He was over eighty now, and felt his age sometimes. The previous year he had had a small seizure, though he had hidden that from everyone except his valet. It had left one leg a bit numb and made him forgetful for a time, but that had passed. But it was a warning that he must do something about the boy. If he died before Francis was twenty-one, there were only lawyers to act as guardians because there were no other close family members left – well, none that he would trust. This idle great-nephew of his was the last descendant of a once-proud name, the only one left to continue the line!

Alexander realised that he had been muttering to himself, a habit that had crept up on him since his sister's death, and that Francis was staring at him. He forced back the anger. Anger was dangerous for a man of his age. He *had* to live long enough to find Francis a suitable wife, one from a good family, who would put some backbone into the next generation.

'Go to your room!' he snapped, suddenly weary of scolding someone who wasn't really listening. 'And you're not to leave it until dinner time.'

He waited until the library door had closed then sank

into a chair, wiping his forehead with his handkerchief and willing his thudding heart to slow down. This happened occasionally. It meant nothing. Neither did the occasional forgetfulness. Just signs of old age.

Francis was glad to leave the library for his uncle's rages had become worse lately. He climbed slowly up the stairs to his bedroom, sighing in frustration as he looked through the landing window. He would have loved to stroll through the sun-dappled woods. Instead he had to sit in his stuffy room, treated like a child – again. He flung open the window and leaned out.

Life hadn't been so bad until his grandmother died because she'd always been there to cheer him up and intercede for him with her brother. He'd missed her greatly in the two years since her death. His uncle did nothing but scold. What did it matter whether a fellow did well at his studies or not? Francis wouldn't have to earn a living because the estate would take care of all that. He looked round him frowning. He had always loved his home, but lately it had begun to seem more like a prison. Dull, beige wallpaper with a small pattern in brown, dark furniture, faded green brocade curtains and a square of brown carpet. Dreary, faded colours to match a dreary place. How many unhappy hours had he spent here?

As soon as he reached his majority he would send his great-uncle packing. He wanted life at Rawley Manor to be happy and that wasn't possible with the old man in charge. He'd hated his uncle for as long as he could remember, just as he hated the mother who had abandoned him and never tried to visit him or even find out how he was doing. The thought that she was probably still alive somewhere in Australia with her other children always hurt. She hadn't abandoned *them*, just Francis.

But there were more than six years to get through until he reached his majority. He gave a low groan and beat out his frustration with one clenched fist against the wooden frame of the great bay window that overlooked the front gardens.

Once this had all been countryside dominated by the manor house, but in the past decade the town had reached out to swallow up the farmland and, to his uncle's annoyance, his father had sold some of their land, believing the days of great estates were past and money in the bank was what counted now. There were several large new houses close by, modern places with immaculate gardens, inhabited by people his uncle referred to scathingly as 'nouveaux riches'.

The new neighbours were not invited to visit the Manor, nor did Alexander Stephenson call on them. Some of them had youngsters whom Francis watched occasionally from the shelter of the woods. He'd have loved to join in their croquet matches or ride a bicycle along the lanes with the other young fellows, but not only was he not allowed to associate with them, he was not even allowed to possess a bicycle, which his uncle considered only suitable for mechanics and other common persons.

Francis slouched across the room to stare at himself in the mirror over the mantelpiece. He was still a bit pale after the influenza. All he really wanted was a peaceful, happy life and a few friends of his own age. Was it so much to ask? Apparently so. He had a couple of good friends at school, but dared not ask to invite them back because his uncle would sneer about their families, then write to the headmaster asking that the lads be kept apart. He had done that once when Francis was younger and had made an 'unsuitable' friend.

The lad leaned forward to examine his own features, something he had done many times before. Did he look like *her*, the mother who had abandoned him in return for money? His uncle denied any likeness, pointing out that not only did he have blond hair, like many of the Rawleys, but greatly resembled his father also. Francis's grandmother had more than once said that he had his mother's eyes, though.

He went back to sprawl on the window seat again, wishing he could go sketching in the woods. But his uncle had taken away his sketching equipment after reading the report from school and told him he'd only get his things back when he showed signs of buckling down to scholastic work. Crossing his arms behind his head Francis stared up at the ceiling, losing himself in dreams of better times.

When the bell rang for dinner it took him by surprise and he jumped up with a yelp of dismay. He hadn't changed his clothes and was so late that he rushed downstairs as he was, for his uncle detested unpunctuality.

Alexander took one look at him and breathed in deeply. 'You have not changed.'

'I forgot about the time. I thought you'd prefer me not to be late.'

'I'd prefer you to be both punctual *and* properly clad. You may return to your room and we'll see if hunger will teach you to behave like a gentleman in future.'

Francis walked out without another word. At nearly

fifteen he bitterly resented being treated like this, though at least the punishment got him out of another boring formal dinner with the two of them sitting opposite one another at the long, gleaming table. Anyway, Cook would find a way to slip him something to eat. She always did. He was very fond of Mrs Denham, who had arrived here when he was four and whose pet he had always been. Fortunately, her cooking exactly suited his uncle's troublesome digestion, so that the old man did not treat her as harshly as he did the other servants.

Ten minutes later Francis was working his way through a plate of sandwiches and an apple, knowing his uncle would not come upstairs until he had slowly picked his way through the four-course meal. The maid who had brought the food up to his room had begged him in a whisper to hide the plate under his bed afterwards or she'd be for it. While he ate, Francis bent his mind to how he was going to pass the time during the coming summer holidays and – most important of all – how to avoid his uncle as much as possible. It would be best to find some excuse for getting out of the house.

After a few minutes it came to him. Walking. He'd take up walking, claim it had been recommended to get him fitter for his return to school in the autumn. Would his uncle allow that? Well, he might if Francis pretended reluctance to take extra exercise.

The following morning his uncle asked curtly, 'Have you been set any tasks by your schoolmasters? I do not wish you to waste your time while you're recovering?'

'I'm supposed to read and do a lot of walking to get

myself fitter.' Enjoying this venture into deceit, Francis put on a sulky expression.

'I think exercise an excellent idea. You will go out for long walks on fine days and we'll find you some suitable indoor occupations for the wet ones. And I myself will select your reading material.'

Francis heaved a loud, aggrieved sigh.

His uncle breathed deeply and slowly.

When Francis got to the woods, he could hold back his amusement no longer. He threw back his head and roared with laughter, stamping to and fro gleefully and wishing he had someone to share the joke with.

When Janey Hamilton heard the laughter she suddenly broke away from Cathie to run towards the sound. It took a minute or two for Cathie, who had been lost in thought, to realise what had happened and chase after her.

She found her charge in a clearing, standing very close to a young man with her face thrust out, rocking from one foot to the other.

He was gazing at her in pop-eyed astonishment and looked up in patent relief as Cathie came to a halt and put one arm around Janey.

'I'm so sorry. She got away from me.' As he smiled, something about his appearance seemed familiar and Cathie frowned at him as she tried to work out what it was. If only she had all her memories back. 'Have I met you before?'

'No. Never.'

Janey began to walk round them, so Cathie let her.

'I say, is she——?' He tapped his forehead.

'Yes. It's very sad, but she's not dangerous. She's my auntie and I'm looking after her.'

He was staring at Janey as if fascinated. 'That can't be much fun for you.'

'I needed a job, so it suits me for a time.' Cathie tried to take hold of Janey's hand, intending to leave him, but Janey had her own ideas and let out a scream of defiance, reaching out towards the young man instead.

He patted the older woman's shoulder as he would have done a pet, and when she resumed her walking round them, he thrust out one hand to Cathie. 'I'm Francis Rawley.'

The name seemed faintly familiar and she still felt as if she knew his face. There was something about the eyes. 'I'm Caitlin Rutherford.'

Janey stopped beside him again.

'I'm sorry,' Cathie said, tugging in vain at her arm. 'She seems to have taken a fancy to you.'

'Look, I'll walk with you to the road, if that makes her move on. *I* don't mind you being here, but my uncle hates people trespassing in the woods.'

'He should put up stronger fences, then.' They began walking, but as they reached a gap in the trees the house came into view, a huge stone place, and Cathie stopped to gaze at it. 'Is that your uncle's?'

'Um – no. Actually it's mine.' He shrugged his shoulders, trying to act as if it didn't matter. 'Or it will be when I'm twenty-one. My uncle's in charge till then.' His face grew bitter.

'What happened to your parents?' she asked, then

realised how tactless this question was. 'Sorry, none of my business.'

He thrust his hands into his pockets and began to kick at some loose earth where a small animal had been digging. 'My father's dead and my mother left me to my uncle's tender mercies when I was quite little.'

She could hear the bitterness in his voice and laid one hand on his shoulder without thinking, squeezing it slightly as she would have done with one of her brothers. 'Have you never seen her again?'

'I've never seen her at all! I don't,' his voice broke on the words, 'even remember her face, though my grandmother used to say I had her eyes.'

'She must have been pretty, then.'

He glared at her. 'Are you saying I'm pretty? Like a girl? Thank you very much!'

He was so like her brother Seth, hiding his emotions behind a truculent attitude that she said without thinking, 'Oh, for heaven's sake, don't be so touchy.'

He jerked away from her, still scowling. 'The woods end there. You'd better get back on the road.' Then he walked off, shoulders hunched.

Janey tried to follow him, pulling at Cathie's arm, and did not calm down until he was out of sight.

That boy was very unhappy, Cathie decided as she turned her charge towards the town again. And very bitter towards his mother. Rightly so. How could any mother leave a child for others to bring up? Her own wouldn't have done such a thing – she paused on that thought. Strange how sure she felt of that. Again she saw the woman's face, dark-haired and laughing this time, and knew she'd been loved. Her mother's name was Liza! Liza Caine. Suddenly Cathie's own surname popped into her mind: Ludlam. Now how could that be? Ludlam's was the name of the mill where Magnus worked. She couldn't be related to them, could she? Her head began to throb and she realised Janey was growing restless, doing that mindless rocking movement again.

Taking a firmer hold of the older woman's hand, Cathie started walking briskly towards the town. Time to go back. And on the way she'd buy some food for the evening meal. But for some reason she couldn't stop thinking about poor Francis Rawley, who might be rich but wasn't happy and who was so bitter about his mother.

When they got back Janey fell asleep in the rocking chair and Cathie sat opposite her for a while, having no success in willing the phantom memories to return. Cathie Ludlam. Could she be related to the owners of the mill or was it a common name in Pendleworth?

Oh, it was so frustrating not to know things! But at least she was starting to get her memory back. And in the meantime she had somewhere to live and was earning her keep, even if the job was not very interesting. That would have to do for the time being.

CHAPTER ELEVEN

May–June

Josie burst into the house full of the tale of their visit to Baileys' Farm. Benedict listened with a scowl, but agreed that the apples would be most welcome. There was no sense in wasting good food, wherever it came from.

Liza asked, 'Is my brother intending to come and visit his friend?'

After a moment's hesitation, Ilse said, 'It's worse than that, I'm afraid.'

'What do you mean?'

'Your brother owns the farm.'

There was silence, then Liza covered her face with one shaking hand, making a faint, distressed sound.

'Is he so bad, your brother?' Ilse asked.

'He used to be dreadful, probably still is. I must warn Dinny. She might be in danger from him as well. Maybe I shouldn't go to England.' Liza saw the puzzlement in Ilse's eyes and realised that Agnes had stopped sewing to watch her. 'Dermott swore once to get his revenge on me.'

'What for?' Agnes asked quietly. 'May we know? It's better to be forewarned.'

Liza hesitated, then decided to tell them. Better they

heard it from her than from Dermott. She glanced round, but Josie had gone off to her room to continue sorting out her toys for the journey and Harry was helping Dinny sort through the apples. 'My oldest brother, Niall – he attacked Dinny. This was years ago, before I married Nicholas. So I got the shotgun and threatened Niall with it, told him to leave us alone. Only he kept coming towards me, laughing. There was no one to call to for help, just me and Dinny, so I fired.' She drew in a ragged breath and went on shakily, 'He was very close to me by then and it – killed him.'

Horror flooded through her in a black wave as it still did every time she remembered that dreadful night, but she was determined to tell them the rest of the story so that they would understand. 'I told Dermott to leave. I still had the gun with the other barrel loaded, so he did. But he said,' she gulped, 'he'd come back one day and make me sorry. I knew he would, I've always known that.'

'Oh, Liza!' Agnes got up and went to hug her. 'How brave you were!'

'I wasn't brave, just desperate, but I didn't mean to kill Niall. *I didn't!* Benedict helped me bury him next to my first husband, down by the lake. I go there sometimes to pray for his soul.' And for her own.

Agnes said thoughtfully, 'I don't like Mr Docherty myself, but surely he wouldn't attack you after all these years? You are still his sister, after all, and this is 1876, not the Dark Ages.'

'My being his sister doesn't mean anything to him. He was only ever close to Niall – and to Mum. Benedict believes the bush fires were set deliberately – and who else but Dermott would have done that? What if he does something else while I'm away, something worse?' Liza bowed her head for a moment. Thoughts like these were the demons that came to torment her in the night. 'What's his wife like?'

Agnes cocked her head on one side, thinking what to say. 'Bred a lady, I'd guess, but a shrew. Her name's Christina. She dresses in the height of fashion whether the occasion warrants it or not. I can't see her living down here in the bush for long. They have two sons, who are alternately spoilt and scolded from what I can see – which doesn't form very pleasing characters. Though Mr Correntin is very good with them, I will say.'

'He was good with Josie, too,' Ilse admitted. 'Treated her like a grown lady and she loved it. But if he's Mr Docherty's partner . . .' She let the words trail away. He was probably just using her to get information. His flirting didn't mean a thing.

She found it hard to settle to sleep that night because she kept going back over their conversation. They had not said anything personal, but she could not help being aware of him as a man – and a very attractive one. And she had felt that he was equally aware of her as a woman, until Liza told her about Mr Docherty.

A tear traced its way down Ilse's cheek. She should have known better than to believe a man like that could be interested in her. She should definitely have known better by now. Only old men seemed to like her.

Liza decided in the end that Dermott was less likely to attack her family if she was away, so she asked the governess to tell Mr Correntin as soon as she had left. Ilse could think of no reason for refusing, though she would have infinitely preferred not to see him alone.

Benedict was to drive his wife and daughter up to Fremantle where they would take the coaster down to Albany. Josie was wild with excitement and hardly slept a wink the night before. Harry was surly because he was not going with them.

With tears streaming down her face, Liza kissed each of her sons, for she considered Lucas just as much hers as the others. 'Be good and look after your father,' she said in a choked voice.

'Give Cathie our best love,' said Lucas, always the spokesman for the others. 'And don't worry, Mum. Seth and I are not children now.' He lowered his voice. 'We won't let anyone hurt him. And we'll look after Harry.'

So she had to give him another hug and wonder yet again what was driving her to go so far away. Was this worry about Cathie and Francis just a foolish fancy, or was it as real as Dinny believed?

Seth grinned at her, holding back his emotions with banter, as usual. 'I'm tempted to hide in your trunks,' he teased. 'Are you sure you don't want me to come and look after you on the journey?'

'I want you here, looking after your father.' And when she got back she intended to tell Seth that Benedict was his real father, even if that reflected badly on her. Cathie had run away to find her real father. It was important that Seth know the truth.

She turned to Harry, who was scowling at her, bottom lip pushed out. Not allowing him time to protest, she folded him in her arms. 'I'm relying on you to keep your father from getting sad,' she whispered. 'No one can make him laugh like you can. That's why I'm leaving you here.' And also because an energetic child would find the long voyage very frustrating.

He was only partly appeased. That bottom lip still stuck out.

'Oh, darling, I do love you!' Liza gave him a quick kiss and turned to the two women, standing together behind the children. 'Agnes, this wouldn't be possible without you. How can I ever thank you for postponing your return to Perth?'

'You don't need to thank me,' Agnes said. 'If I'd looked after your daughter properly, you wouldn't need to go.'

But Liza knew differently. There would still have been Francis. It was more than time she met him.

And then they were in the cart rumbling down the track. She turned for a last look at her home, then blinked away her tears and looked straight ahead.

The following day Ilse turned up at Baileys' Farm accompanied by Harry. Matthieu invited her in, but she declined. 'I need to speak to you – privately. Harry, will you wait for me here?' She began walking towards the orchard.

Matthieu thought she seemed embarrassed, so let her take her own time to speak.

When the child was out of earshot, she stopped and said, 'I came at Mrs Caine's request to tell you that she's left for England and to ask that you pass this information on to her brother.'

He whistled softly. 'She's left already?'

'Do you think – will he still try to harm her family now that she's not here?'

He looked at her and shrugged. 'I think not, but if I see anything happening, I shall try to prevent it.'

She stared at him in surprise. 'You will?'

'Of course. What sort of man do you take me for?'

'I don't know.' She turned to leave.

He caught hold of her arm and swung her round to face him, but resisted the temptation to kiss her smooth skin because that might frighten her off. 'When I come back from Perth, may I visit you?' She flushed and did not seem to know what to say, so he smiled and amended it to, 'I *shall* be coming back and I *shall* definitely call on you, Ilse.' He saw a pulse beating in the white skin of her elegant throat. He would kiss it one day and make it beat even faster.

This time he let her return to the child and stood watching as they walked away. He was not surprised when she did not look back.

He found a perverse and slightly malicious satisfaction in contemplating his partner's rage when Dermott found out that his sister had left for England. Well, serve him right! It was stupid to cling to a desire for revenge. He had spoken about it several times. And this Niall, whom his partner had clearly idolised, must have been a very unsavoury character. A woman was entitled to defend herself against rape.

He ought to go back to Perth and tell Dermott that his sister had gone to England but he wanted to stay here, and for the stupidest of reasons – a woman.

Matthieu stared round the large room. It was a good

house and an attractive piece of land, though his partner probably hadn't even noticed how pretty the bush was round here or how beautiful the lake could be made with a little effort. But the place had no prospect of growth in value as far as Matthieu could see, not unless someone put a lot of hard work in. It was not a good investment unless you liked the countryside and wanted to live there.

The thought came to him suddenly: he could farm it, plant some vines. They made wine over in New South Wales, so why not here?

Was Ilse the sort to live quietly in the country and raise a family? Did he want to find out? *Bon dieu*, he was a fool for even thinking of buying the place! How Dermott would laugh at him!

In Pendleworth Jim and Bob Marshall were enjoying a glass of beer together. 'Have you heard?' Jim asked.

'Heard what?' Bob stared at the froth on the top of his glass, wondering how long he could spin this one out. He did not allow himself to spend lavishly on beer, not with a family to feed, but he enjoyed the company at the pub, the warmth and the bright flaring gas lights.

'About Mr High and Mighty Hamilton. He's only got a lass living in his house now.' Jim sniggered. 'Says she's his cousin, but Ma Midner won't work for him any more so folk don't believe him.'

'He should stick that mother of his in the Ben. That's what it's for. I wish we could stick our Dad there, by heck I do. He's broken them spectacles again, the old devil. I shall take the cost of the new ones out of his wages, though.

He'll be sorry when he can't buy himself a glass of beer.'

'Never mind our dad, what do you think of Hamilton taking a girl in? She's from Australia, they say, and—'

'*What did you say?*' They stared at one another, then Bob said slowly, 'There can't be two lasses from Australia come to Pendleworth in one month, Jim lad. Maybe she's the one we're keeping an eye open for?'

'Nay, I thought of that, but this one's called Caitlin, not Cathie. She's looking after the loony, callin' her Auntie Janey, but folk are laughing behind their hands, thinking it's just a tale to make it look more respectable like, her warming Hamilton's bed.'

'Caitlin's not that much different from Cathie as a name. What's her surname?'

'They didn't say.'

'Then bloody well find out! We need to know.'

Cathie had now settled into a simple routine and her memory was gradually returning, though still not complete. She had, after some consideration, told Magnus what she thought her surname was and asked him about the Ludlams.

He frowned at her revelation. 'I heard Mr Matthew had a brother who was sent out to Australia in disgrace. Josiah Ludlam died out there, apparently.' He didn't intend to tell her what else they'd said about Josiah or how one or two of the older men still sniggered about him in unguarded moments. 'Do you think he could have been your father?'

'Josiah? Yes, that was the name of my mother's first husband. I grew up thinking he was my father, but one night I overheard my parents talking about my "real father" so now I'm not sure of anything.'

'That must be hard for you, lassie.'

She could only shrug. Everything had been hard since her arrival in England. And perhaps, if what she had remembered was correct, she deserved that, deserved even the penance of looking after an old lady who could offer her no companionship.

Magnus studied Caitlin's features as they ate their meal. He could not see any resemblance to the Ludlams in her face. Yes, she was dark-haired, but her hair was thick and bouncy while theirs was very straight. He thought of Mr Reuben and shook his head. No, they couldn't be related. She had broad features with an open, sunny expression most of the time, not a long, narrow Ludlam head like those on the medieval tombs in the parish church. The older Ludlams always had dour expressions, too, as if life had not been pleasant for them. Only Mr Reuben had an open look to him, and Magnus was glad he worked with *him*, not his father, Mr Matthew.

He was teased by some obscure resemblance in her face, however, something that did remind him of someone . . . but he could not pin it down so he said nothing. Maybe it would come to him.

Mairi had written to say she and her husband would be coming the following Sunday to meet the woman who was looking after their mother. It was a brief note, without the usual anecdotes of her daily life, and he realised how suspicious she was about their new 'cousin'. Well, he was sure once she'd met Caitlin, Mairi would feel better about the situation and realise he had not brought a mistress into his home but a decent, hard-working lass.

That conjured up a vision of Caitlin in his bed that brought a flush to his cheeks. He was a man, with a man's needs long unsatisfied, and could not help reacting to her, but he could not do anything about it. The way his mother was he had nothing to offer any woman but drudgery.

Though Caitlin seemed not to mind: singing about her work, chatting cheerfully in the evenings about what she had seen on her walks. Life had seemed so much brighter since her arrival. How would he ever manage without her now?

Before his sister arrived he suggested Caitlin take advantage of the fine day to go out for a brisk walk on her own. 'Please don't be offended, but my sister will not be satisfied until she has all the details of why you're living here and it'll be best if she and I have a talk in private first.'

'Will she pretend I'm her cousin, do you think?'

'Aye, I think so. Once she's met you and seen how well you're caring for Mum.'

'I hate people thinking I'm – you know—' Cathie broke off, her cheeks scarlet.

He nodded. 'Aye. So do I. I didn't mean that to happen.'

'It wasn't your fault. Who knows whether I'd even be alive if you hadn't intervened that day?'

He blurted out, 'Och, that doesna' bear thinking of!' which embarrassed them both greatly. So he went off to fill the coal scuttle while she dusted the front room, determined to have everything perfect for Mairi.

Cathie left soon afterwards. It felt strange to be out on her own and when her feet automatically took her in the direction of Rawley Manor she didn't question the wisdom of this. She wanted to see Francis Rawley again because she felt she knew the name. She sighed. It was another of the missing pieces of her memory. How long was it going to take to recover fully, to be certain of who she was and exactly why she was here in England? Surely she hadn't just come here on a whim?

She walked briskly, intending to go further out into the countryside than had been possible with Auntie Janey shuffling along beside her, but when she got to the Rawley estate, she slowed down and studied the distant house thoughtfully. Again it was almost as if she could recognise it, but she couldn't think why. Today being a Sunday there was no one to be seen working in the grounds and even the horses were standing quietly in the shade at one corner of a meadow to the right, tails flicking occasionally to dislodge a fly.

As she continued along the narrow road the hedges gave way to a wall, and then to a neat gatehouse. This time she didn't walk past, but stopped to study the view down the gravelled drive through the big wrought-iron gates.

A man came out. 'Are you lost, miss?'

'No. I was just admiring the house.'

'Begging your pardon, but Mr Stephenson doesn't like folk loitering round here.'

She was puzzled. 'Is this not a public road?'

'Well, it is, but if you'll take my advice, miss, and no offence intended, you'd best be on your way. Mr Stephenson has a way of making people sorry if they don't do as he wishes.' And had been even more unreasonable of late, so that everyone on the estate was afraid of angering him.

Cathie folded her arms and gave the man back stare for

stare. 'If this were private land, I would move away at once, but as it's a public road I'll decide for myself. I'm told England is still a free country.'

He stepped back, shaking his head. 'I'll have to report you, then.' Mr Stephenson always wanted to know if anyone had been 'hanging around'.

From behind some trees, Francis heard the exchange and grinned. She was a lively one. Then his smile faded. If she was living in a Rawley or Ludlam house in Pendleworth, she'd soon find out how easy it was for his uncle to get her evicted. Perhaps he'd better warn her?

When she moved on, he hurried along the inside of the wall until it gave way to hedges again. Only last year his uncle had suggested building a stone wall all the way round the park. For once, Francis had dredged up the courage to say he didn't want a wall round his home and if his uncle erected one, he would pull it down again the minute he attained his majority. That had cost him a few furious scoldings about ingratitude and young people thinking they knew better than their elders, but the question of the wall had not been raised again. If his uncle had really wanted to build one, however, they both knew he would have done so.

Francis was waiting for the young woman as she strolled around a bend in the road. 'Hello again! I heard you talking to our gatekeeper.'

She scowled at him. 'And are you also going to warn me not to walk along this road?'

'No. Well, not exactly. It's just that my uncle can make things pretty unpleasant for people who annoy him so you should take care.'

She set her hands on her hips, angry at having her lovely walk spoiled. 'Well! Who does your uncle think he is? Lord of all creation?'

Francis grinned. 'Pretty much. He seems to think we're still in medieval times and the rest of the world is divided into serfs and gentry.' Then the grin faded and he sighed. 'When I come into my inheritance I shan't behave like that, I promise you.'

'My stepfather always said the gentry in England had too much power, but I didn't realise what he meant until now.'

He could see her studying him as if he were a curiosity, and didn't like it. 'I'm not real gentry, you know. My father married a woman from the lower classes and my uncle has never forgiven him for it. He hates even to hear her name mentioned.'

Cathie's head started to thump. *Rawley.* She had been wondering where she had heard that name before. Suddenly another set of memories tumbled into place, each one triggering the next. She groaned and put one hand to her temple as pain stabbed through it.

'I say, are you all right?'

He stepped forward to put an arm round her and she leaned against him, unable to answer until the roaring inside her head stopped. Then she moved away, shaking her head to clear it. He was still standing close to her, looking anxious, and was the same height as she was for all he seemed younger. She stared at him and knew in a blinding flash who he resembled. Her mother! He had exactly her mother's eyes and that same way of holding his head.

'Was your father's name Nicholas?' she asked, her voice coming out haltingly as she struggled to take in all the new information that was echoing round her skull.

'Yes, it was.'

She could think of no way to soften the shock. 'Then you're my half-brother. My real name's Cathie. Cathie Ludlam.'

There was dead silence for several moments. If birds were still singing, Cathie didn't hear them, and even though a bee paused to study her dress before deciding it was not a flower and flying on, she heard no sound from it, because she was watching Francis, hoping desperately that he would not reject her.

'Are you sure of that?' he asked hoarsely.

'Very sure. And — and now I can remember you as a baby, too. When my mother married your father, we all lived there.' She gestured in the direction of the house. 'That's why I kept wanting to look at it, why it seemed so familiar.' She sighed. 'Other things in Pendleworth have seemed familiar, too, but I was only a small child when we left so they don't look the same now. I remember a big wall and now that I've grown so tall, I look at it again and it seems quite a small one. So I'm never quite sure if I'm really remembering something or not. And when memories do come back, as they did just now, they're all vague and jumbled at first. I feel so impatient to understand everything properly. My mother always says I—'

'I don't want to hear anything about *her*, thank you very much. She abandoned me when I was a baby. They paid her to leave me with them and *she took the money. Sold me!*'

He turned as if to leave and Cathie grabbed his arm.

'That's not true. Really it isn't!'

He let out a snort of disbelief. 'She didn't tell you the truth because she knew it wouldn't reflect well on her to have abandoned her own son.'

Cathie was about to inform him that her mother didn't lie to her, but suddenly remembered that both Liza and Benedict had lied about her real father, so instead she seized on another piece of information which had fallen into place in her mind. 'It'd be very easy to prove it one way or the other.'

'You think so?' He tried to tug his arm away.

She grasped it with both her hands and shook him to make him pay attention. 'I *know* so! Please don't run away, Francis. Can't you see – if we are brother and sister, we should get to know one another.'

He stopped pulling, but his expression was sullen. 'I won't believe anything unless it's proven beyond doubt.'

'You can do that. Mum and Dad have been paying a lawyer from Pendleworth to report on you once a year. His letter usually arrives a month or two after your birthday.'

'Oh? And when is my birthday?'

'You were born in 1861, on the eleventh of August. At the Manor.' She gestured towards the house.

He swallowed, looking suddenly younger and less certain of himself. 'How did you find that out?'

Another memory slotted into place. 'We children could never forget we had another brother, because every year on your birthday Mother used to get sad and go off for walks by herself. And – is there someone called Sophia Ludlam living nearby? She writes to Mother, too, and tells her how you are.'

He shook his head helplessly. Who to believe? His uncle or this girl with her fresh, open face who didn't look like a liar to him. The idea that he was not an only child pleased him, but he tried to conceal that as he asked, 'How many half-brothers and sisters do I have — if you're telling the truth?'

'Four, including me. Seth is sixteen this year, Josie ten, and Harry seven.' She could hear how uncertain his voice was and laid her hand on his arm, offering comfort by her touch.

'What's the lawyer's name?' he managed at last.

'Lorrimer.'

He stared at her. 'There *is* a lawyer called that in Pendleworth. He doesn't handle our affairs, Patenby does, but Bernard Lorrimer is well thought of in the town.' He backed away from her. 'I'm — I'm not discussing it any further until I've seen him, found out if . . .' He let the words trail away, then turned before he could ask her to tell him about the others, for questions were teeming in his brain. Two half-sisters and two half-brothers. What were they like? Were they all as tall and fresh-faced as she was?

No! He mustn't accept what she had told him. Not yet! It would be too hard if his hopes were dashed.

She didn't try to hold him back, but stood with her arms wrapped round herself, watching him stride towards the hedge. As he reached it he stopped and turned round.

'Can you come here next week at the same time?' There was a long pause, then he said her name, 'Cathie? Will you?'

She nodded.

He pushed his way through the hedge then broke into a run. When he was quite sure he was out of sight he stopped to wipe the tears from his eyes, only to find more welling in their place. Not until he had full control of his emotions did he return to the house. This was something he intended to inquire into for himself. If his uncle got one whisper of it, he'd send Cathie away – as he might have sent Francis's mother.

Once her half-brother had disappeared from sight, Cathie walked on for a while, her thoughts in turmoil, then realised that she was hungry and the sun was high in the sky, so began to tramp back. Not knowing another route, she had to go past the front gates of the Manor, but she marched past without pausing. This was no time to be causing trouble or getting herself noticed.

Mairi and Elwyn arrived at noon bringing a basket loaded with home-cooked food. It warmed Magnus's heart to see how happy they both looked and how fond of one another they were, exchanging glances and smiles without even realising what they were doing.

Magnus showed them round, proud of how well the house was looking, then they sat with their mother, who was also looking well cared for.

'She knows how to keep house, at least,' Mairi admitted. 'But I still can't see why you brought in a stranger. You might have known it'd cause talk. And now you want me to lie about her, say she's our cousin—'

'Second cousin.'

'It's the same thing.'

Elwyn patted her arm. 'We should meet her before we decide anything, love.'

She scowled at him. 'I still don't like telling lies.'

When Cathie returned, she found the table set for a meal and Mairi rather stiff for a few minutes. She studied his sister with great interest. Mairi was tall, about the same height as Cathie, but she was not particularly good-looking, being very thin with hair closer to ginger than Magnus's red-blond, and a skin covered in freckles. Her husband Elwyn was plump and genial, with thinning hair and the kindest expression in his eyes that Cathie had ever seen. Magnus had said several times how glad he was to see Mairi married to a man like this and Cathie could see why.

As the two of them discussed Janey's progress, Magnus's sister became rather more friendly, and in the end they found themselves in complete agreement on how best to look after her.

Mairi was equally relieved to find Cathie a decent young woman. She looked up once, catching Magnus staring at the lass with a fond smile. He called her Caitlin and there was a warmth in his voice as he said the name. If that had been any other man, she'd have said he was taken with the girl. She glanced quickly towards Elwyn and he grinned in a conspiratorial way. After that she could not feel as suspicious of the girl's motives. If Caitlin had managed to break through Magnus's reserve, bring that happier look to his face, then she could not be bad. More than anything else Mairi longed for her eldest brother to find the happiness and love she had discovered in her dearest Elwyn.

'So?' her husband said softly as they strolled through the town towards the station.

'What do you mean by that?' Mairi demanded.

'Eh, my love, don't pretend you didn't notice how Magnus looked at her.'

She was silent until they turned the next corner, then said slowly, 'If she makes him happy, I don't care what her past is. He deserves something for himself.' And had to stop to wipe her eyes and let Elwyn give her a quick hug. 'Though he'll never be as happy as I am,' she said quickly, still feeling tearful.

When the visitors had gone, Cathie poured out the story of her encounter with Francis to Magnus.

He sat frowning in thought for so long that she asked impatiently, 'Well? What do you think of that?'

'I find it hard to believe – that you can be related to the Rawleys,' he said at last.

She chuckled. 'So does my brother.' Then her smile faded. 'But what upsets me is that they've poisoned his mind against my mother, told him she took money from them to leave him behind. And she didn't. She wouldn't! They forced her to leave. I can remember now how she always grew sad when she mentioned him. It didn't really matter much to the rest of us. We knew we had a brother, but we never thought we'd meet him. Only now I have done and I like him. Isn't that wonderful?'

Magnus loved to see her excitement, and was beginning to think that this was her real personality, bubbling with enthusiasm for life. It was so contagious he was feeling happier by the day, in spite of his worries about his mother.

'Did you mebbe come to England to see him?' he wondered aloud.

She shook her head. 'No. Definitely not. I think – though I'm not perfectly sure of it yet – that I came to get away. And to find my real father. Only I still haven't remembered his name.'

'It'll come to you. Give it time, Caitlin lassie.'

She giggled, looking younger tonight. 'I like it when you call me "lassie". I love the way you talk.'

'Do ye now?'

'Aye, laddie,' she teased, trying and failing to imitate his Scottish lilt.

He watched her covertly as she got his mother ready for bed. At one stage she suddenly stopped and smiled at Caitlin, hugging her. Then the smile faded and she lapsed into the blank apathy that hurt him so much to see.

When Caitlin came down to join him for a quiet half hour in front of the fire, she said, 'Did you see how your mother smiled and hugged me?'

'Aye. I think in her own way she's grown fond of you. You look after her well. I'm grateful. So is Mairi.'

'I like to look after people. I just wish I could make your mother better, but I can't, can I?'

He sighed and shook his head.

Gradually the silence soothed him again. And Caitlin's company. Just to be with her in a room, not to be on his own . . . He cut those thoughts off short. He had no right to indulge in them. He leaned forward and lifted the coals to get the fire glowing more brightly. They didn't really need it, because it had been quite a warm day, but without it they'd not be able to heat the water for a last cup of cocoa, a ritual he looked forward to every night.

But once his mother died, what then?

Maybe — he hardly dared allow himself to hope — maybe then he could think of his own future.

CHAPTER TWELVE

June

———◆———

The following day Francis saw his uncle staring at him in a jaundiced manner from across the breakfast table and tensed, waiting for criticism.

'You should go out walking again today,' Alexander said at last, after letting the silence drag on. 'It's giving you a better colour, making you look fitter. Your teachers were right.'

Relief filtered through Francis, but he shrugged and tried to look sulky. He glanced surreptitiously towards the head of the table. Was there something different about the old man today? Yes. His uncle's mouth looked pulled down at the left and his colour was bad, skin papery and dry. But no one would ever dare ask Alexander Stephenson how he was feeling because he seemed to deny the needs of his own body. There were days when he looked really ill but still he held himself upright, never giving in for a moment to bodily weakness.

Francis finished the meal quickly, then had to sit hiding his eagerness to escape until his uncle finally laid down his knife and fork, wiped his mouth with the table napkin and nodded dismissal. The lad left the room as quickly as he could in case his uncle changed his mind.

He had decided to investigate his mother's actions today, though he felt afraid of what he might find. What if his uncle and his grandmother had lied to him? What if they really had sent his mother away from him? And – he hardly dared contemplate this – what if Cathie was right and their mother did care for him? Somehow he had no doubt that the young woman had been telling the truth when she had declared herself to be his half-sister.

If his uncle had really sent his mother away, he would never forgive him for it. Never.

There was a knock on the bedroom door. Hilda said, 'If you please, Master Francis, the master says you're to go out for your walk now.'

He scowled. There was no need to send the maids to chivvy him. 'Hilda, do you think there's something wrong with my uncle? His face looks different today.'

She glanced quickly over her shoulder. The servants had all noticed the same thing, but Mr Gower, the butler, had said they were to ignore it and Clifford, Mr Stephenson's manservant, said his master had refused to discuss it this morning and had acted as if everything was normal – though he'd moved more slowly, favouring his right side. 'When my granda had a seizure he looked like that, only he was much worse,' she told Francis in a low voice. 'There's nothing you can do about it. It made Granda right bad-tempered, though.'

She hoped it wouldn't make Mr Stephenson's temper worse because he had been really chancy lately, shouting at you for nothing then turning and walking off in the middle of saying something. Cook said it was old age.

Hilda reckoned her master had been born bad-tempered. She was wondering about giving notice come quarter day. She didn't enjoy working here any more, even if they did pay well. Horace, the head groom, was trying to take liberties and getting above himself because the master favoured him. But where else could you get such work in Pendleworth? There were only the Ludlams and they were known to be stingy with their staff. Nor did she want to work in another town because her parents were getting on a bit and she liked to keep an eye on them. With a sigh she went back to her duties.

Francis left the house by the rear door. A brisk walk brought him to the edge of Rawley land. He pushed through one of the hedges on to a narrow lane that was not much used, then as he reached the town itself, kept to the back streets with their rows of smoke-blackened houses. He walked quickly, eager to reach his destination and a bit nervous of being seen. He could be sure his uncle would never drive along these streets, but could only pray that no one else would see him and mention it.

The worst moment was when he had to cross Market Square to get to Lorrimer & Sons, whose offices were in one of the tall, grey-stone houses on the north side of the square. He slipped inside the front door quickly, panting from his haste and half-expecting to hear that thin dry voice behind him demanding what he was doing here and ordering him to come out at once.

'I'd like to see Mr Lorrimer,' he told the clerk. 'It's extremely urgent.'

'And your name, young sir?'

Francis hesitated then gave it, asking the clerk not to

mention his visit to anyone else. He saw the surprise on the man's face because everyone knew that Patenby was the Rawleys' lawyer.

Within minutes Francis was shown into a large office which had an excellent view of the square, nearly empty now, but always crowded with people and animals on Thursday when it was market day.

Bernard Lorrimer shook hands then gestured to a chair. 'How can I help you, Mr Rawley?'

Francis looked into the kindly face and all his carefully prepared speeches vanished from his head. 'Is it true that you report to my mother every year on how I am?'

'Yes. We've been doing it ever since she left Pendleworth.'

'Did she – leave of her own accord?'

Bernard studied the anguished young face and decided the lad was old enough now to be told the truth. 'No. She ran foul of both Mr Stephenson and Mr Saul Ludlam, and they forced her to leave. They wouldn't even let her say goodbye to you, from what my father told me. Your great-uncle's generation had a lot more power than yours will have. That sort of attitude is changing now.' And a good thing, too, he thought as he looked sympathetically at the young man who was clearly very distressed.

Francis found himself fighting a great wave of emotion that threatened to break and overwhelm him, so moved hastily to stand looking out of the window with his back to the lawyer. 'Did she take money from them for leaving?'

'No. Definitely not.' Bernard hesitated, then said gently, 'Mr Ludlam threatened to put her into an asylum for the mentally deranged, a dreadful place – the Ben hadn't been built then — and also threatened to accuse Mr Caine of theft. Your uncle prevented that injustice, at least, but he still sent your mother and Benedict Caine away to Australia without you.'

She had not wanted to leave him! The wave of anguish broke over Francis and nothing would hold it back.

Bernard got up and moved quickly to put an arm round the shoulders of the young man sobbing helplessly against his velvet curtains. He held the lad against him, patting his back and making soothing noises. Since he had sons of his own, he knew that lads of this age were not nearly as tough as they pretended.

It was some time before the storm of weeping abated. Bernard proffered a handkerchief and gave Francis time to pull himself together. 'I think a cup of tea might help, don't you?' he asked gently when the damp handkerchief was offered back to him.

Francis nodded and watched Mr Lorrimer go to the door and speak to his clerk in a quiet voice. He was wondering what to do next, but was feeling so emotionally drained he could not think straight. The lawyer said nothing until the clerk brought in a tea-tray, which allowed Francis time to pull himself together.

'How did you find out about this?' Bernard asked as he filled a cup and passed it over.

'I met my half-sister. She told me. I didn't believe her at first, so she sent me to see you, said you could prove everything.'

'Your half-sister?'

'Cathie. She says her surname is Ludlam.'

Bernard frowned. The sister's arrival could really upset

people and revive old scandals. 'I'd have thought your mother would have informed me of your sister's visit. Where is she staying? There might be difficulties with your uncle if he finds out she's here.'

Francis stared at him open-mouthed. 'Surely not?'

'He is still an influential man in this town and would be very averse to your meeting any of your mother's family. Since he'll be managing your affairs until you're of age, he has considerable power over your life. You'll need to take great care if you intend to go on meeting your sister, for her sake as well as your own.'

'Surely my uncle won't – he wouldn't *hurt* Cathie?'

Bernard shrugged. Who could tell? It was well known in Pendleworth that Alexander Stephenson still had a feudal attitude to life and to the estate he managed for his nephew. People employed there had to do what they were told or risk being thrown out. It was also known that he was getting grumpier and more unreasonable as he grew older. As he watched young Rawley sit up straighter, he had a sudden fancy that the lad had just grown up a little and this time when he spoke, Francis's tone was firmer.

'If my uncle tries to do anything to Cathie, he'll have me to answer to.' He frowned at Mr Lorrimer as something else occurred to him. 'Will *you* be in trouble if he finds out about the reports you've been sending?'

'None of my business is with the Rawley estate and I think I can look after myself legally.' Bernard hesitated, then said quietly, 'I shall deny saying this, but you might wish to check matters out very carefully once you take over as owner.'

Francis stared at him in shock. 'Is my uncle dishonest?'

This was the last thing he had expected to hear.

'No, definitely not. But he's very harsh in his dealings with people of the lower classes. He doesn't hesitate to throw those he considers troublemakers out of their jobs and houses. I hope someone of your generation will be more generous to those less fortunate than himself. And you may perhaps wish to remedy past injustices.'

Francis gave him a very direct look. 'My uncle won't allow me to play any part in business matters at the moment, but I'll remember what you've said when I come of age, I promise you.'

Bernard glanced at the clock. 'I'm afraid I have a client coming to see me shortly, but will you ask your sister to come and see me? And Francis — if you need anyone to talk to, not as a lawyer but as an older friend — please don't hesitate to turn to me. I have sons of your age and I know you've never had a father to guide you.' Had he gone too far? No, the lad didn't seem to resent this offer.

'Thank you. I'll remember that. I've seen your sons and I wish I could meet them. You live quite near to us, don't you?' Bitterness rang in Francis's voice. 'I'm not allowed to make friends with anyone who isn't my "social equal" — as my uncle judges it.'

'That's a great pity. You must be very lonely.'

Francis looked at him, head on one side, and asked hesitantly, 'If I called at your house, would you introduce me to your sons? Would they want to meet me?'

'How will you get permission to do that?'

The young face was grim. 'My uncle is about to find out that he will either have to lock me in my room until I'm twenty-one or give me more leeway.'

'Be a little careful how you confront him,' Bernard warned. 'He can be a dangerous enemy.'

'He's pushed me too far. It's not just my sister's arrival. Things have been getting on top of me lately for other reasons.' The constant nagging to go hunting, to 'act the man' — as if he'd want to kill little animals. He couldn't even bear the thought of it.

Bernard wondered what one boy could do against a man accustomed to wielding power. He had in the past helped more than one person Alexander Stephenson had decided to destroy and was not himself well thought of by the man, he knew. But since the Lorrimers had a few useful family connections, Stephenson had not dared to try to hurt them — so far. Would offering friendship to this lonely lad change that? Bernard couldn't even begin to guess but he intended to risk it, for his conscience would not allow him to draw back now from such an acute need for help.

'Come round to the house any Sunday afternoon and I'll introduce you to my lads. We often have young folk visiting us then.' He would explain the situation to his eldest son, who was about the same age as this young man but did not have that grim, unhappy look to his face, thank goodness.

Francis gave him a singularly sweet smile, then it was replaced by a determined expression as he stood up. 'Thank you for everything, sir. I won't forget what you've said.'

He walked home very slowly, lost in thought.

As she waited near the little wood the following Sunday afternoon, Cathie began to think that Francis was not coming. Just as she was thinking she ought to start back, she heard a sound and turned to see him running through the woods. She beamed at him as he came to a breathless halt beside her, gulping in air and trying to speak.

'I thought – I'd missed you. My uncle wanted me – to stay at home. I had to escape.' He glanced over his shoulder. 'We'd better get out of sight in case he sends the grooms out to look for me.' He led her further into the woods to a clearing where there was a fallen tree and flourished a bow, hiding the emotion he was feeling at seeing her again under a jesting tone. 'Your throne awaits you, my lady sister!'

She chuckled, dropped him a curtsy and sat down on it.

He took a place beside her and studied his clasped hands. 'I went to see Mr Lorrimer and you're right – about our mother, I mean. She does pay him to report on how I'm going every year and he told me why she left. She didn't take money to leave, she was driven away by threats.'

'They never told us children the details.'

He explained then said bleakly, 'I'm nearly fifteen, Cathie. I've missed *years* of knowing my mother. Can you imagine how that feels?' He'd lain awake every night of that long week filled with bitterness. He'd almost burst out with the accusation several times, but had held back because in spite of his brave words to Mr Lorrimer he didn't really know how to deal with his uncle – just that from now on he would no longer allow himself to be browbeaten without fighting back.

Cathie laid one hand on his and glanced at him compassionately. 'That's terrible. And you've missed knowing your brothers and sisters, too.'

He met her eyes, which were filled with tears like his own. 'At least I've met *you* now, Cathie. And will you please tell me where you live before we go any further? I was thinking as I ran through the woods that if I didn't get here on time, I'd not know how to contact you.'

She told him her address, then he passed on Mr Lorrimer's message, which seemed to surprise her.

'Shall you go and see him?'

'No. Not yet.'

He decided that he would write to tell Mr Lorrimer her address, just in case anything went wrong or his uncle tried to harm her.

They were silent for a few moments, sitting companionably together, then she grimaced and confessed, 'I've, um, got some more of my memory back.'

'And?'

She looked at him, her face full of sorrow, and the words burst out in a torrent. 'I'm so ashamed of myself. I ran away from home, let my uncle pay my fare to England – didn't even say goodbye to Mum and Dad. How could I have been so *stupid*? So cruel? And – and I knew Mum didn't get on with her brother, so it was even worse to let *him* persuade me to run away. I don't think he should have done it, so perhaps he isn't as kind as he seemed.'

It was the last thing Francis had expected to hear. 'Why did you run away? You said you loved your family. Did they ill-treat you?'

'No, of course not! Never think that! It's just – I do love them only, well, I hated living in the bush. It's very lonely and you hardly ever meet new people. I felt I was going mad, wasting my life doing the same thing every day. And also I ran away because,' she hesitated then told him the rest, 'I overheard them talking one night. I'd always thought Josiah Ludlam was my father, but it seems he wasn't and I wanted to find the real one. My uncle told me who he thinks my father is because I look like the man, but it's not absolutely certain he's the right one, even then. Only I can't remember the man's name. Why can't I remember something so important?'

Tentatively, because he wasn't used to touching anyone, let alone a girl, Francis put one arm round her and gave her a hug. 'You will remember it one day, I'm sure.'

'I hope so. I don't mind helping Magnus look after his mother – he's a lovely man, you must come and meet him – but the life I'm leading here is almost as limited as my life back home was.' She gave a wry smile as she looked down at her reddened hands and added, 'And there's just as much washing, which is harder to dry here. I don't call this summer!' She glanced up at the sky which was alternately clouding over and giving them brief glimpses of a cool sun.

When she explained more fully about her situation and Francis realised she was living with a man she had not previously known, he could not hide his shock. 'Look, you don't have to do that sort of thing! I'll give you some money and—'

'I don't need any money. I'm earning my own way.'

'Well, I'll *lend* you some money, then, and your – our – mother can pay me back.'

'My parents don't have much spare money because they lost so much in the bush fire.' Her lips set in an obstinate line. 'I'm not going to ask them for anything. I got myself into this and I'm going to prove that I can look after myself.'

'But you're living with a man. It looks so bad.'

She pulled away from him. 'I'm not doing anything wrong.'

There was silence while Francis thought about what she had said, then he muttered, 'I've never met anyone like you.'

'You've probably only met spoiled rich brats.'

'Yes.' Suddenly he understood why his father must have fallen for his mother, if she was at all like Cathie. 'I think you're marvellous.'

She chuckled. 'I'm not, you know. I'm very ordinary.'

He couldn't agree with her. After a few moments had passed, he said thoughtfully, 'But you'd still better go and see Mr Lorrimer in case my uncle finds out about you and tries to hurt you or the Hamiltons. I don't think you're living in one of our houses, but if the place belongs to the Ludlams, well, they'll throw you out without hesitation if my uncle asks them to.'

She stared at him in dismay. 'I didn't think of that! Oh, I'd never forgive myself if anything happened to Magnus.'

He hesitated, then blurted out, 'Perhaps you could move out and just go in daily to look after his mother. It's not at all respectable – your living with him, I mean.' He hated the idea of people thinking ill of her.

She realised suddenly that she didn't want to move out, that the main reason for staying was to be with Magnus and have those golden evenings chatting quietly together in front of the fire. 'It's very respectable, I promise you,' she said lightly. 'I have my own bedroom and we've told everyone I'm his second cousin Caitlin. Now don't forget that — I'm called Caitlin Rutherford here. His sister comes to visit us, so that helps stop the gossip. Mairi is very well thought of and is a regular churchgoer. People know she wouldn't associate with me if there was — well, any wrongdoing between me and Magnus.'

'I still don't like it.'

She changed the subject. 'Let me tell you more about our family . . .'

When she left him, he stood beneath some trees watching her stride out along the road, admiring her upright posture and air of sturdy health.

He looked down at himself and grimaced. She must think him a mere boy. He'd grown so much in the past year he was all spindly. He was glad he was six foot tall and Cook had once told him he'd fill out in a year or two and be a fine-looking man, but he wished he looked more manly now. Why, he hadn't even started shaving yet. And the cough and lassitude from his influenza were still lingering. Some days it was an effort to do anything.

It felt important not to go home again without making some sort of stand, so Francis strolled past his own driveway, conscious of Roskin the gatekeeper staring after him. When he got to the gate of the Lorrimers' house, he hesitated for a moment then went to knock on the front door.

The maid who opened it said placidly, 'The young folk are all out in the back garden, sir, if you'd like to go round.' She pointed to the left.

'Um — is Mr Lorrimer there?'

'No, of course not. The master's inside with the mistress.'

'Well, I think it best if I see him first. He's the one who asked me to call, really.'

She looked surprised but held the front door open. 'Come in then, sir, and I'll let him know you're here.' She moved away, then giggled and turned back. 'Oops, I nearly forgot to ask your name.'

When he told her she goggled at him, gulped audibly and rushed away at top speed.

He liked the idea of a maid not being afraid to giggle. The ones at the Manor were terrified of doing anything to offend his uncle, and when Hilda slipped food to him she only did so because she was also terrified of upsetting Cook. His nursemaid had been dismissed the day he was put into short coats. His uncle had simply told him one day that Jenny had left and that he was to act like a big boy from then on for a tutor who would be teaching him to read and write. He'd cried himself to sleep for many nights after that and been smacked by the tutor for it. His grandmother had, he was sure, loved him in her own way, but that had never included embraces which might disturb her clothes or hair.

In this house Bernard Lorrimer came out into the hall in person to greet him, clasped his hand and looked at his anxious face. 'First act of defiance?' he asked, understanding immediately what was happening.

Francis nodded.

'You're welcome here, lad, always, but don't try to push all the barriers down at once with your uncle. No one can do that.'

Francis nodded again, feeling a lump in his throat at the genuine caring shown for him by this man. He was taken round to the back to be introduced to 'the young people', which made him feel like a new boy at school again — terrified, alone against the world, as he had been when he was sent away at the age of eight.

Outside there were about a dozen youngsters. Four of them were playing croquet, two were sitting over a chess board, three were enjoying a lively discussion and three others were gathered around one of the new Ordinary bicycles, which a young fellow of about Francis's age was pushing to and fro with a proprietary air.

It was a moment before they noticed Mr Lorrimer's companion, then one by one they fell silent, staring.

When he had their attention, Bernard put an arm round his protégé's shoulders and said, 'Francis Rawley has come to visit us at my invitation. I doubt his uncle's going to approve, so I'd prefer you not to tell people yet about his coming here, but I'm truly delighted to see him.' He then drew Francis forward to the group round the bicycle. 'I don't know whether you're interested in cycling, but my son Johnny is a devotee — and I must confess he doesn't fall off the contraption all the time.'

Johnny grinned at his father and smiled tentatively at Francis. 'I've only had it for two weeks, but it's a wonderful improvement on my old boneshaker. Do you cycle?'

'I've never tried, but I wouldn't mind having a go — though I'm hopeless on horses, so I would probably fall off this as well.'

The three of them immediately assured him that the bicycle was really easy to ride, then began to explain the finer points of the Ordinary, with its huge front and small rear wheels, the sprung seat, the front and rear brakes, the superior bearings which made for a smooth ride, and above all its capacity to cope even with muddy conditions.

An hour later Francis reluctantly decided to return home and face the scolding he would no doubt receive for absenting himself without permission.

Johnny accompanied him to the gate. 'I'm glad you could come.' His tone was as friendly as his father's. 'We've seen you walking around the grounds of your house alone and felt a bit sorry for you.'

'My uncle is very old-fashioned and snobbish.'

'It must be hard for you not being allowed to make friends.'

Francis nodded, relieved when the other boy didn't press the point. Today had begun to show him what he'd been missing. These young people had all known one another for years and were comfortable together, and yet they'd welcomed him and tried to make him feel at ease. The lads at school were not nearly so kind.

'Come again any Sunday,' Johnny said as he opened the gate. 'We nearly always gather here because my parents don't mind the noise. If it's raining we go into the shed or conservatory.'

As Francis walked slowly home he felt deeply envious. If he couldn't have his family, he ought at least to have been allowed his friends. But his uncle had permitted him neither. He intended to change that, but it would mean making a stand and a lot of unpleasantness, too, he had no doubt.

Well, so be it.

*

As soon as he set foot indoors Francis was informed that his uncle was waiting for him in the library, the sort of message that usually sent a shiver of apprehension through him. Today he was glad the first confrontation had come at once so that he didn't have to sit and worry about it. Taking a deep breath, he made his way to the room which had been the scene of many scoldings.

As he hesitated outside the door, it suddenly occurred to him that this room, like the whole house, really belonged to him. It's mine, not my uncle's, he thought, looking round. That idea gave him a little more courage. He lifted his hand and knocked – loudly.

'Come.'

He went inside, looking round as if he had never seen it before. *His* room. *His* estate.

'Where have you been?' demanded Alexander in that carping snappish tone that meant his digestion was playing up again. 'I will not have you wandering off when you've been told to stay at home. I informed you that we were expecting guests. I was obliged to offer the Ludlams your apologies and say you were unwell.' The scolding continued for a long time, ending with, 'You will go to your room and . . .'

Somehow Francis could not stomach that after his golden afternoon. 'No.'

His uncle stared at him, open-mouthed. *'What did you say?'*

'I said no and I meant it. I'm not five years old, and I resent being treated as a child. I will not be sent to my room in that way again.'

'Oh, will you not?'

Francis stared at him. His uncle's lips had narrowed to a thin line and his face had gone white and chill. The old man's head was like a skull, set on top of its stringy neck. How yellow and unhealthy the whites of his eyes were and how frail he looked, yet how vicious! Francis forced himself to speak calmly because shouting never got you anywhere with his uncle. Only *he* was allowed to shout, and he had been doing a lot of that lately. 'I have no wish to be impolite or to quarrel with you, but I'm nearly a man now and expect to be treated accordingly.'

'A man? You'll never be half the man your father was! You can't even sit a horse like a gentleman, let alone behave like one.'

'My father was killed by his horse, for all his skill. I think I prefer my way.'

Alexander Stephenson's eyes bulged and he moved across to the bell pull and gave it a sharp tug.

Francis turned on his heel before any servant could answer. At the door he paused to say, 'If you're thinking of sending the head groom to use force on me,' something which had happened once or twice when he was younger, though not recently, 'you might like to consider how that will look to the world, for I promise you I will fight every inch of the way to my bedroom and I shall not keep quiet about being treated so brutally.'

He walked out of the room and made his way to the conservatory his grandmother had loved, which he was the only person to visit nowadays. In its soothing warmth he paced slowly up and down until the shuddering feeling in his belly had settled, listening to see whether his uncle would send Horace and some of the outdoor menservants to manhandle him to his room. The head groom seemed to do a lot of nasty business for his grandfather these days, terrorising the tenants for one thing. Francis intended to dismiss him the minute he turned twenty-one.

But although he stayed in the conservatory for over an hour no one came searching for him. In the end he heard the hall clock chime the quarter and went up to change for dinner, taking particular care with his clothes. He was downstairs again even before the clock chimed the hour.

His uncle entered the dining room by the other door and walked past him as if he didn't exist. When the first course had been removed, Francis addressed the roast beef and potatoes that followed, doggedly but without any real appetite, determined not to betray his nervousness. It was another of his uncle's tricks to use silence to punish him, but in some ways that was easier to handle than conversation. It was always a strain trying to think of something to say or working out an answer that would not provoke a sarcastic comment.

After the meal was over, Francis looked questioningly towards the head of the table. *His* table, really, he reminded himself.

His uncle stared at him coldly. 'I shall decline to converse with you until I have received an apology for your insolence and a promise to obey me in future.'

'I did not intend to be insolent and am sorry if that's how you regard what I said. I merely wished to tell you that I am no longer a child and that it is inappropriate to treat me as one. And I cannot promise to obey unfair commands.'

'You dare speak to me like that!' his uncle began to

shout, getting into such a passion that dribble trickled from the slack side of his lips.

It was a while before the tirade ceased, then Francis took a deep breath and said quietly, 'You're my uncle and I would not wish to be on bad terms, but I'm not a child any longer.' Before his uncle could start shouting at him again he pushed his chair back and walked out of the room. The anger that followed him seemed almost tangible, but he didn't turn round. If he had done, he might have said more than he had planned, might have accused his uncle of sending his mother away. Francis would never forgive him for that, but as Mr Lorrimer had said, it would not be wise to try to change or challenge everything at once.

He knew exactly what was to come now because it had happened once or twice before – chill silences, servants forbidden to do things for him. But something had changed inside him today and that something was fuelled by both anger and anguish. He had a mother who cared about him and yet had been kept from him. He had brothers and sisters who were complete strangers to him, except for Cathie. He had had to endure long, empty years living with a man who had no warmth in his character, not a single iota. And he still had nearly six years to go until he would be free from his uncle. How was he to endure that?

He went to the billiards room and hit a few balls up and down the table with his usual indifferent success. He had never been good at sports, didn't seem to have an eye for a ball or much interest in the stupid things, either, though he might have a go at riding one of the new bicycles. What had Johnny called it? An Ordinary. It didn't seem at all ordinary to Francis. It seemed very modern and dashing.

And unlike a horse, a bicycle could not bite or kick you.

When his usual bedtime of ten o'clock came, he debated staying up longer, but was tired and wished to mull over the events of the week. So he put the cues away and made his solitary way up the stairs.

He left the curtains open and as he lay staring at the patterns of moonlight on the bedroom floor, he acknowledged that life was going to be very unpleasant from now on. But then, it had never really been pleasant, so it was only a matter of degree.

What did his mother look like? He didn't even know. That thought brought tears to his eyes.

As soon as she got back Cathie poured out the tale of her encounter with her half-brother to Magnus and his sister, who had come on her own this week.

Afterwards Mairi asked hesitantly, 'What about old Mr Stephenson? He's going to be furious about this.'

Cathie shrugged. 'If he's angry, that's not my fault. He's kept my brother and mother apart all these years, and I won't let him keep *me* away from Francis. That poor boy looks like he's never had a good cuddle in his whole life. What can the old man do to me, after all? He's not my guardian.'

'He can have my brother thrown out of this house, though, and perhaps make him lose his job, too.' It had happened before and you couldn't hide things like that in a small town.

'But this has nothing to do with your brother!'

Magnus leaned forward, smiling reassuringly.

'Stephenson's a mean old devil, but I doubt it'll come to that, Mairi. It's the Ludlams who own this house and are my employers, and I think they value me as a worker.' Well, he knew they did.

She was not convinced. 'The gentry always help one another. Oh, Caitlin, please keep your meetings with your brother secret!'

'I'll do my best, for all our sakes.'

After Magnus had walked his sister to the railway station, he came back and helped Cathie put his mother to bed, then sat down at the kitchen table looking thoughtful.

She came to sit opposite him, clasping her hands together on the table and trying to read his expression. 'If he does try to throw you out because of me, then I promise you I'll leave at once.'

'I doubt he will. Mr Reuben is always very fair with us workers. He wouldn't allow it.' He looked at her and risked saying, 'I should be sorry to see you go, Caitlin lassie.'

'Should you?' She felt suddenly breathless.

'Aye.' He wondered whether to tell her that Jim Marshall had started asking questions about her, but decided against it.

Marshall was a good worker if you kept an eye on him, but he was a married man and not a womaniser so it couldn't be because she was such a pretty lass. Why then did he want to know?

CHAPTER THIRTEEN

June

One day Dermott turned up without warning in Brookley, riding a horse with his usual lack of care while his wife and sons rode behind in a cart driven by a man he'd hired to help about the place. They'd also brought along their young Irish maid to help Christina with the housework, but the governess had given notice when required to move to the bush.

By the end of a second long day of travelling with a wife alternating between a foul temper and floods of tears, Dermott was beginning to wonder why the hell he'd even considered living in the country. What would have been an easy day's journey in England or even in Victoria, and hadn't been too bad when he and Fiery Dan had ridden down here, had turned into an endurance feat with a cart and a wife who never stopped complaining about the insects, and the rain, and the lack of inns.

Matthieu had written to say that the farm was very close to the Caines' place. Dermott found that thought piquant. Thinking of Liza reminded him of his niece and he realised suddenly how much meeting Cathie had changed his attitude towards his sister. He wondered how the lass was doing in England. To his surprise he found himself hoping she was all right.

Which brought to mind the fact that his sister had several other children. For the first time he wondered if they were as pleasant to be with as Cathie. That thought was followed by a scowl. He was getting soft again and that wouldn't do at all. How Niall would have mocked him for that! Yet Matthieu, who was as mean a fighter as you'd hope to meet, didn't seem to mind acting soft sometimes. The man was a puzzle to Dermott. Oh, hell, life itself was a puzzle.

As they pulled up outside the inn in Brookley he edged his mount closer to where his wife was sitting in the cart, amused by the expression of disgust on her face. 'We're here, then,' he announced unnecessarily.

Christina stared at the inn in which she had lived as a young woman, then glared at the small settlement which now surrounded it. 'It hasn't changed much,' she declared, adding in a voice shaking with anger, 'How could you do this to me, Dermott Docherty? There's no *need* for us to come and live in a place like this!'

'Ah, shut your trap, woman! I'm sick and tired of your moaning.' He jerked his head towards the inn. 'Aren't you going in to say hello to your mother?'

She didn't move. 'I've told you and told you: I didn't want to meet *anyone* from my past.'

He leaned across to grasp her shoulder. 'Well, I do want to meet my ma-in-law. Either you get off that cart of your own accord or I'll drag you off it.'

Their eyes met for a moment, then she sniffed, gathered up her skirts and began to clamber down.

Dermott sat admiring her shapely legs till she was down, dismounted himself and went across to where she was standing. 'Come on, then.'

But as she straightened her skirts, he saw the apprehension in her face. 'You're nervous!' he said in surprise.

'Well, of course I am. My mother might refuse to speak to me.'

He took her arm and threaded it in his, patting her hand. 'Then we'll do this together.' As Christina threw him a grateful smile, he wished suddenly that she would smile like that more often. She almost looked pretty when she did. His steps faltered for a moment and he gave his head a little shake. Another moment of softness. It didn't do to be too kind to Christina or she took advantage and tried to rule the roost. Only — her eyes were red with weeping, she was desperately unhappy about coming to live here, and he didn't like to see that. She'd been a good wife to him in her own way.

When they walked into the inn Dorothy looked up, then gasped and turned bone white, clutching the counter as if about to faint.

With a muttered oath Dermott let go of his wife and hurried across the room to support the older woman. 'Are you all right, missus?' His ma-in-law was light enough in weight, but was sagging against him as if she had lost the power of her limbs and had not uttered a single word.

As she moved across to join them Christina decided her mother had aged better than she had expected, but now looked like a working woman not a lady, which did not please her at all. 'I'm sorry to give you such a shock, Mother. Come and sit down for a minute.'

There was a shout and a small man came rushing to Dorothy's aid, standing with one arm round her shoulders and demanding furiously, 'What have you done to her?'

Dorothy raised her head. 'It's all right, Jack. I'm just — being silly.' She stared at her daughter. 'Is it you, Kitty? Is it really you?'

'Well, of course it's me.' She leaned over to plant a kiss in the air just above her mother's cheek. 'Though I'm called Christina now. I much prefer it. I don't know why you ever wanted to shorten my name in the first place.' She gestured to the burly man standing beside her. 'This is my husband, Dermott Docherty. He's Liza's brother.'

He nodded and held out a huge hand.

Dorothy stared at him in open-mouthed shock but pulled herself together enough to shake the hand quickly then let it drop.

'And I have two sons, so you're a grandmother. James and Charlie are waiting outside.' Christina forced a smile. 'I wasn't sure if you'd forgiven me, you see.'

'Oh, Kitty darling!' Dorothy held out her arms and after a moment's hesitation Christina allowed herself to be embraced, but pulled away as soon as she could.

Dorothy remembered of old that her daughter didn't like to be cuddled. 'Perhaps we could bring the boys in? I'd love to meet them.'

Dermott ambled over to the door. 'I'll fetch 'em.'

His face expressionless, Jack watched him go then turned to his wife, who was looking flushed and tearful. 'You sit down, love, and I'll make us all a nice cup of tea.'

'Thank you.' But Dorothy's eyes were on the door and when the two boys came in, she clapped one hand across her mouth and blinked her eyes furiously, not wanting to embarrass them by weeping. 'They look so like your father,' she whispered to her daughter. 'They have his hair and mouth.'

Christina turned to stare at them. 'I suppose they do. James, Charlie, this is your grandmother. I said we'd meet her, didn't I?'

The two boys came across the room, taking care to keep out of reach of their grandmother's outstretched arms.

'We're a bit big for kisses and stuff now,' James explained.

Dorothy let her arms drop and, as Jack cleared his throat, turned and smiled at him. 'Sorry, dear. Kit— Christina, this is my husband, Jack Bennett. We – um – run the inn together. Brookley is quite a thriving little community now.'

Christine gave Jack, who was clearly of plebeian origin, a cool nod and made no attempt to take his outstretched hand. 'What happened to my father?'

'He died. The day you left, actually.'

'Oh! Oh, no!' Christina clapped both hands to her mouth. 'And I didn't know.'

Dermott put his arm round his wife and gave her a bracing hug. 'If only we'd known, we could have stayed to help you, but we were so taken with one another, we weren't thinking straight.' He dug his elbow into his wife's well-corseted side. 'Weren't we, love?'

'No.' She suddenly remembered that night: how he'd forced himself on her, then persuaded her to ride off with him through the moonlight, and how she'd been desperate enough to escape to do just that. Looking round, she wondered what would have happened if she hadn't met Dermott. Heavens, she might still be here! On a sudden impulse she put her arm through his and gave it a squeeze.

Dorothy was looking very tearful. 'Oh, Kitty, why *did* you run away? Why could you not have told me you'd met someone?'

'*Please* call me Christina. After all, you gave me the name in the first place.' She shrugged. 'I ran away because I was afraid Father would try to stop me marrying Dermott since he wasn't a gentleman. You know how rigid he could be about some things.'

'Yes, I do.' Dorothy smiled at her through a mist of tears. 'I never gave up hoping you'd come back, though, and now you have. Oh, I'm so glad, my darling, so very glad. You must tell me everything and then—'

'We've plenty of time for that, Ma,' Dermott interrupted. 'We'll be staying round here for a while because we've bought Baileys' Farm. Thought it'd be good for the boys – a healthy life in the country, getting to know their grandmother.' He looked through the kitchen door at the puny man busying himself making tea and wondered why his mother-in-law had not found someone better than this little snirp, who barely reached Dermott's shoulder.

Both his in-laws stared at them. '*You've* bought the Bailey place?' Jack exclaimed. 'Then what's Mr Correntin doing there?'

'Matthieu and I are business partners. He's keeping an eye on it for me.'

'Are you interested in farming?' Jack asked.

'No, I'm bloody not! I've brought a man to do the outdoor work, though I can turn my hand to most things if I have to. I'm not short of a bob or two, but I've been a bit busy over the past few years and I feel like taking things more easily for a while.'

'You're Matthieu Correntin's partner?' Dorothy said, still trying to understand what Dermott was doing here. 'Why did he not say anything to me?'

'He didn't know Christina was your daughter. Seen much of him, have you?'

'He's eaten here a few times. He's always very pleasant.'

Dermott chuckled. 'That's a Frenchie for you, charming all the ladies. 'Fraid you'll find me a bit blunt after him, Ma.'

She was frowning now. 'And you're Liza's brother?'

'Aye. I know she doesn't think much of me – well, I was a bit of a rough lad – but I'm hoping to mend things between us now.'

His smile was like that of a wolf about to pounce on a particularly choice morsel.

Dorothy, who knew the full story of how Liza had killed her brother by accident, and why, was still wondering what had persuaded her finicky daughter to marry a man like this. She decided to send a messenger to Lizabrook as soon as they had left for their farm. She needed to warn Benedict, who had just got back from putting his wife and daughter on the coaster in Fremantle – just in case Dermott meant to cause more trouble. Heavens, he was a large man and she'd guess he'd been in a few fights from the battered look to his face and fists!

And she definitely didn't want to be the one to tell Dermott that his sister had left for England, so she threw a quick warning glance at her husband, shaking her head.

As usual, he nodded agreement. He could read her thoughts in a way Andrew had never been able to or wanted to. Some might say her Jack was beneath her, but she was happy with him and had never regretted marrying him.

She looked back at her daughter, who had a sulky expression on her face and looked as if she'd been crying. That hadn't changed. Poor Kitty — Christina rather — didn't seem to have it in her to be happy. Dorothy bustled about getting them a meal, proud of the table she set and pleased when her grandsons and son-in-law expressed their appreciation of the food. Her daughter hardly ate a thing and when she wasn't talking, simply sat staring round glumly. Dermott ate plenty and made up for his wife's silence, talking easily of this and that, mostly of how he had made his fortune. He seemed a pushy sort of fellow and reminded Dorothy very much of his father, Con, whom she still remembered clearly from the days he'd come to collect Liza's wages, when she was working as a maid for her and her first husband in Lancashire.

When they left, Dorothy stood waving goodbye until the cart had trundled out of sight then turned to Jack and said abruptly, 'We'd better warn Benedict that he's here. Would you go and ask young Pete from next door if he'll take a message to Lizabrook for me?' While Jack was undertaking this errand, she got out her inkpot and scratched a hasty note explaining what had happened.

For all his affability towards her she had not taken to Dermott Docherty. How could her pretty, finicky Kitty have fallen in love with a man like that? And at first sight, too? It didn't make sense. No, her daughter could only have married him for money — and to escape from Brookley.

But even that hadn't made her happy.

Then Dorothy thought of her two grandsons and smiled. Well, some good had come out of it all, anyway. She hoped the boys would come and visit often. She had always longed for grandchildren. Perhaps it wasn't too late for her to play a part in their lives.

When the lad turned up at Lizabrook and proffered the note, panting from hurrying along the rough track, saying Mrs Bennett had told him to bring it over as fast as he could and to wait for an answer, Benedict took it listlessly. Already the place seemed empty without Liza's cheerful voice and presence. She and Josie would be out on the ocean now, getting further away from him by the day. He had hoped she'd change her mind, right until the last minute, but although she'd wept as she said goodbye, she'd still boarded the ship.

He stiffened as he read what their friend had written. So Dermott Docherty was here in Brookley! If the fellow had had enough money to buy Baileys' Farm, then he must have done well for himself financially. Which was all the more galling because Benedict and Liza had been struggling since the fire and he'd had to sell another piece of Josiah's first wife's jewellery to pay for this trip to England.

If Dermott really had set the bush fire – and who else could it be? – well, Benedict was forewarned this time. The farm and furniture workshops were now protected by huge fire breaks and Dinny had asked her people to keep watch on the comings and goings nearby, promising them food in return for this service. And although Brendan was very friendly with Correntin, Benedict was sure Dinny's son would not allow any harm to come to his mother or the other folk on the homestead.

After a few minutes' thought he sent a message back to Dorothy and went to warn Dinny and Fergal to be even more on their guard. The three of them went to sit on the Riordans' new veranda, which looked out over the small stretch of water they had cleared so painfully from the swamp. Maybe while Liza was away he'd make a real effort and dig out some more.

'I never thought I'd be glad that Liza was away,' Benedict said grimly, 'but I am.'

'I am, too,' Dinny said quietly. She had never forgotten the day Niall Docherty had tried to rape her and the other one had just smiled. It was Liza who had saved Dinny, killing her own brother accidentally as she did so. Then Liza had driven the other brother away. 'Why has that man come back here? This land means nothing to him. Surely he doesn't intend to get his revenge on me after all this time?'

Fergal put his arm round her shoulders. 'You're not alone now, though, darlin'. I'll not let him touch you.' He looked at them, his brow wrinkled in puzzlement. 'There's no proof *he* set the fires. Isn't it possible that he has indeed come for a reconciliation as he told Dorothy?'

Benedict gave Fergal a fond glance. His friend had a very tender heart and an idealistic nature, always believing the best of everyone — which had led to a betrayal back in Ireland that had landed him in trouble with the English law for his political activities, and had brought him out here as a convict. Since he'd received his freedom Fergal had hardly left the homestead and now lived only for his family.

'I'd better go and tell Ilse and Agnes of our fears,' Benedict decided. 'They need to be on their guard as well. Ilse has met that Correntin fellow a few times now and Agnes thinks she's rather taken with him.' He nodded to them both and left.

Ilse looked hard at her employer as he spoke to them. He sounded crisper, more like the old Benedict Caine, the man she had met when she first came to work here. He had been so energetic and decisive then – and cheerful, too. But since the fires he had become short-tempered, snapping at people, often looking grim as well as weary. When he had returned from taking Liza to Fremantle he had looked so sad she had felt sorry for him. Now, suddenly, she watched the energy within him flicker into a blaze and could see what he must have been like as a young man who had sailed across the world to carve himself out a piece of land in the colonies.

Later that evening Benedict went to stand on his own by the water, filled with determination not to let Dermott Docherty take away what they had gained from all their years of hard work. In the darkness he heard someone approaching and turned to see his older sons walking towards him. They came to stand beside him, one on either side, nearly as tall as him now.

'Lucas, Seth,' he acknowledged.

'We're old enough to help, Dad,' Lucas said. 'If

Mother's brother has come to cause trouble, you're not facing him alone.'

Benedict put an arm round each lad's shoulders, standing between them feeling proud of his sturdy sons. They stayed there together in silence for a while and the slight pain in his chest eased. With sons like this a man could do anything. And Liza would be back within the year. He'd use that time to make things better for her here.

When Matthieu heard the sound of wheels and horses' hooves and saw who it was, he cursed softly under his breath. Dermott was going to be furious when he found out that his sister had already left for England, and Matthieu still had not come to a decision about what he wanted to do with himself.

He had been fighting the urge to go and see Ilse for the past day or two, because with a respectable woman regular meetings could only lead to one thing and he did not want to get married. Well, he thought he didn't. He wasn't sure of anything lately.

Taking a deep breath, he went forward to greet the Docherty family. 'So you've decided to inspect your property at last, have you?'

Christina didn't even look at him after an initial glance. She glanced round her in disgust then turned to her husband. 'This is even worse than Brookley, Dermott Docherty. I'll never forgive you for bringing me here!' Clambering down without his help, she stormed into the house, totally ignoring Matthieu.

Dermott grinned at him and rolled his eyes heavenwards. 'Women!'

The two boys slipped down from the cart and began exploring outside the house, calling to one another. The maid had stayed in the vehicle, staring round her with an expression almost as dismayed as that of her mistress.

'I was not expecting you to come down so soon, *mon ami.*' Matthieu folded his arms and leaned against a veranda post.

Dermott swung off the horse. 'Well, I had nowt better to do.'

As they unloaded the cart, Christina bombarded her husband with a series of demands: for wood and rope to build more bed frames, for benches inside and out, for another table. 'There must be someone round here who can cobble furniture together, for I know you've no skill at carpentry.'

'Benedict Caine makes fine furniture,' Matthieu said softly.

Dermott grinned. 'There you are, then. And we'll invite your mother to tea soon.'

'Not till I have things straight here, we won't. The boys will have to sleep on the floor for a day or two.'

'Before you decide anything,' Matthieu said quietly, 'there's something you need to know, *mon ami.* Your sister left for England a few days ago.'

Dermott froze. 'Are you sure of that?'

'Very sure.'

'Why didn't Christina's mother tell us?'

'She was probably more concerned with seeing her daughter again.'

Without a word, Dermott turned and stormed into the house. He fumbled through the baskets of provisions piled here and there on the floor and pulled out a bottle of rum, opening it and taking a swig. Then he turned to Matthieu. 'Show me around, will you?'

Christina opened her mouth to protest that she needed his help, then shut it again, looking at him thoughtfully. Might this news make him change his mind about living here?

Dermott was gone for over an hour, by which time Christina was nearly at screaming point and had retreated to the bedroom to lie on the bed weeping.

When he came to join her, her husband looked thoughtful. 'What am I going to do with you, woman?'

Her reply was muffled by the pillows.

He touched her shoulder and when she tried to shrug his hand off, turned her over by force and studied her swollen eyes. 'That bad, is it?'

She nodded. 'It's brought back to me how unhappy I was here.'

'Eh, you daft bitch. We were never going to stay for long, were we?'

'I don't want to stay at all.'

So he took another of his impulsive decisions. 'Then we won't. We'll go back to Perth tomorrow.'

She gulped and stared at him. 'Do you really mean that?'

He nodded. 'After which we'll go to England.'

She stared at him as if she didn't believe what she'd heard, then flung her arms round him and burst into tears again. 'Oh, Dermott, thank you, thank you!'

'What the hell are you crying for now?'

'Because I'm so happy.'

So he rocked her for a bit and patted her shoulder, thinking over his decision. She had been unhappy for a while now, and although he liked to be the master in his own home, which was not always easy with Christina, it didn't please him to see her so deeply upset. He looked round at the so-called farm, which looked more like a bloody cabin in the wilderness to him. The house was roughly built. Gum trees had set seedlings in the pastures which would need clearing again; the gardens were a tangle of dead plants except for a new patch Matthieu had cleared. It was all a big disappointment to him, nothing like he'd imagined, though of course he'd got it dirt cheap and would probably not lose when he sold it. He'd seen proper farms over in Victoria, country estates you could be proud of, but here in the west, they'd hardly begun to tame the countryside.

And finally, his sister wasn't around to torment. That took all the savour out of coming here.

He patted Christina's heaving shoulders. Yes, this was the right thing to do. It wouldn't hurt to see the old country again before he worked out what he was going to do with the rest of his life. He had spent nearly twenty years concentrating on making his fortune and since he'd achieved it, his heart wasn't really in trading any more. He'd have to find some other way to occupy his time, and Perth wasn't at all the sort of place he wanted to settle in. Too small by far. Call it a capital city? He called it a town, and a small one at that.

He looked down, enjoying the glow of happiness on Christina's face as she nestled against him. 'You'd better sort out what you want to take and what you want to leave here. I'm not hanging about. We'll set off at dawn, so you'll need to get things ready tonight. And while we're in England, we'll go and visit that bloody aunt of yours you're always going on about.' He put her firmly away from him. 'Now, I need to discuss a few things with Matthieu. You get started on packing up again.'

His partner was standing by a ramshackle fence that any fool could have knocked down just by leaning on it. Dermott scowled round. Of all his impulsive acts, this was the worst. 'I want you to sell this place for me while I'm away. It's no use to me. We're following my bitch of a sister to England.'

Matthew gave him a long, level look. 'I might be interested in buying the farm myself. I'll give you ten per cent on what you paid, no more. If I don't buy it – and I haven't made up my mind yet – I'll sell it for you for ten per cent commission.' To his surprise it had upset him to see Dermott stalking around the place with such a proprietorial air.

'Done!' his partner said promptly.

Matthieu didn't allow his thoughts to take him any further than that for the moment. One step at a time. First he would get to know Ilse better, and persuade her employer that he wanted to be friends.

Only as he sank towards sleep that night did he acknowledge to himself what a decision to stay would really mean – marrying Ilse, if she would have him.

He dreamed of warming up her cool skin, of running his fingers through her soft blonde hair and smiling into her blue eyes.

And woke at dawn to the bustle of the Dochertys' departure, glad to see them go.

Christina was so full of joy at the thought of returning to England that she spent what was left of the day happily sorting out the things on the wagon. But as she studied the boys' clothes and possessions she grew thoughtful. She was not looking forward to looking after them on a long voyage because they were a lively pair and always into mischief. Dermott usually treated this as a great joke but other people did not find their antics so amusing.

As the sun sank low in the sky, she stood watching the boys pushing one another and shrieking, running round, getting in everyone's way. When Matthieu came into the big living area, however, she saw him deal easily with James and Charlie, getting them to sit down quietly to eat some bread and cold kangaroo meat.

Hearing Dermott's voice outside, Christina went to join him. 'I've got an idea I want to discuss with you.'

'I'm hungry.'

'This is important and it won't take long. Come on!' She tugged at his arm, only stopping when they were out of earshot of the house. 'I've been thinking about the boys. They'll drive us mad on the voyage to England. Why don't we ask my mother to look after them for a year or so? She'd love it and you can see how short of money she is. Those dreadful clothes she wears!' Christina shuddered. 'And there's Matthieu down here as well. He'll keep an eye on them for us. He's very fond of them and they of him. It would save us a lot of trouble.'

When Dermott didn't say anything, she waited a minute before continuing persuasively, 'If we want to win over my aunt and make sure she leaves her money to me, we'll do better without the boys banging around. She's a real fusspot about her house and garden and you know what a mess and noise they always make.'

Dermott chewed the inside of his cheek thoughtfully as he considered this, not even aware that he had stopped walking or that Christina was waiting with unwonted patience for his response. 'We'd have to go and see your ma before we said anything to them.' It didn't occur to him to ask the boys if they wanted to stay here, any more than it had to his wife.

Christina hugged him. 'That's wonderful! Oh, Dermott, I can't believe this is happening at last.' She twirled him round, laughing up at him.

He grinned down at her. 'Eh, you daft lump! Life in England won't be perfect.'

'It'll be better than this.' The boys could join them later, when they were a little older. Matthieu would find someone to escort them to England. It was done all the time.

She felt deep satisfaction well in her. Now was not the time to tell Dermott that she was utterly determined to stay in England and was sure her Aunt Nora would help her do so, since she was now a wealthy widow with no children of her own. The two of them wrote to one another regularly and there had been several offers to pay for them to visit England.

If it hadn't been for Christina's stupid, bull-headed father, she could have gone to live with her aunt all those years ago instead of going to Australia and married a gentleman of education not Dermott Docherty – though he did have his good points and she'd grown fond of him. But no, her father had insisted all the Pringles go out to the colonies together. And look where it had led? Her mother was now running an inn and was married to a common fellow.

Brendan was worried. If these newcomers were staying on at Baileys' Farm, would Matthieu have time for him? He decided to go and see him, forgetting to tell Benedict that he wasn't working that day. Because he had slept badly he rose before dawn, knowing Matthieu often rose early, too.

He heard the unaccustomed noise before he got to the farm, so slipped into the woods and stayed hidden, watching in fascination.

The newcomers were loading the cart as if they were leaving. And they'd only arrived yesterday! The wife was shouting and shrieking, there were bags and boxes everywhere, but the two boys were nowhere to be seen. Where had they gone? After a few minutes it became clear that Matthieu was getting all the work done and that the big fellow, Liza's brother, was deliberately leaving it to him. Was Matthieu leaving as well? Worried, Brendan found a place from which to watch.

When they had reloaded the cart, the maid climbed up on it, sitting in the back with the boxes, and the man who'd come down with the Dochertys to work on the farm got up into the driver's seat.

From what they shouted to one another, it was plain that

the man was driving them up to Perth, but Matthieu was staying! Brendan breathed a sigh of relief as the cart drove away.

When the dust had settled and quietness returned to the woods he walked out of the bush towards the farm, catching his friend making a cup of coffee in the kitchen.

'Come and join me!' Matthieu said, gesturing to a chair. Then he saw Brendan's expression. 'Is something wrong?'

'I want to know if you and that man intend to harm my family and friends?' Brendan stood very straight, feeling more like Beedit today, for some reason.

'I mean no harm to anyone at Brookley.'

'But your friend does. Only – why did he leave so quickly?'

'Because he found his sister wasn't here and took a dislike to this place. He's going back to England to see his wife's aunt, so you don't need to worry about him any more. His sons are staying here, though, with their grandmother at the inn.'

Brendan sighed in relief and went to join his friend at the table.

Matthieu smiled at him. 'Will you come and work with me for a while, help me set this place to rights? I'll pay you.'

'I'm supposed to work for Mr Caine.'

'But if you work with me I can teach you to speak French. You won't find what you're looking for here or in England, but you may just find it in France.'

'What is it I'm looking for?' Brendan asked, not sure that he knew himself.

'Acceptance. A chance to prove yourself as a man. I'll send you to my family, if you like. They'll find you a job.'

Brendan could make no sense of this. 'Why would you do that? You owe me nothing.'

Matthieu stared down at his steaming cup. 'Because I was once a restless lad like you and would have got myself into trouble if it hadn't been for a stranger helping me. It sounds stupid, but all the payment he wanted was for me to help someone in the same way one day. And that's the payment I'd ask from you.'

Brendan considered this, studying his companion's face, then nodded. There were no lies written there. In fact, his friend looked happier than he had for a while. 'You'll need to talk to my family if you want me to work here and I'll tell them what I'm thinking of doing. Cathie ran away without telling anyone. It hurt her family greatly. It'll hurt mine when I leave, but I'm going to do things openly at least and say goodbye properly.' Because if he found a place where people accepted him, he would probably not come back. He suspected his mother already knew he would leave one day.

Matthieu nodded. 'All right. Now, help yourself to coffee and sit down. I'm enjoying the peace.'

Brendan smiled wryly. 'I must learn to drink coffee now, must I not?'

The dark liquid was as bitter as the thought of leaving his family. But he drank it all.

CHAPTER FOURTEEN

June–July

At Fremantle Dermott found a small ship which was taking a miscellaneous range of goods and a few passengers to Cape Town. This was a scruffy vessel which plied whatever routes would earn its owners the best money, and its passenger accommodation was not very comfortable. It was sailing the next afternoon, however, so after booking passages for himself and Christina, he retrieved the horse and rode back to Perth as fast as he could persuade the stupid creature to move. She was right not to bring the boys and they'd seemed happy to stay with their grandmother.

He'd half expected his wife to fall into hysterics at the thought of leaving the next day, and on such a small ship, but she stood still for a moment then started ordering him around. Fetch this, find that! For once he didn't complain. This was Christina at her best, as he'd seen her when they were first making their fortune – efficient and capable, not fussing, just getting on with things.

An hour later the maid was sent into town with a big shopping list and Dermott followed her a short time later to buy some more luggage and crates for their household goods, as well as hay for packing their best crockery which they'd send down to the farm.

At six o'clock they ate a scratch meal then the work continued, with the maid promised a bonus and a good reference for working through the night if necessary.

At eleven, blinking tiredly, Dermott began a letter to Matthieu giving him instructions about closing down the Perth house and taking the rest of their possessions to the farm. He did not write easily and it took a few swigs of rum to get the information down.

Not feeling in the least bit tired because at last she was going back to the country she had never stopped considering her home, Christina sat down at midnight to write a more elegant note, describing to Matthieu exactly what she wished stored and what was to be sold.

It was past one o'clock by the time they got to bed and as they had to be up again by four in the morning they did not bother to undress. Dermott grinned as he pulled up the blankets and closed his eyes. He was looking forward to seeing the shock on his sister's face when she saw him in England.

On the first day out the weather blew up a storm and both Dermott and Christina retired to their bunks, feeling unwell. It was three days before they came on deck again, by which time he was in a foul mood. Stinking seasickness! He'd forgotten how bad it made a man feel.

The weather continued brisk, but they made good time and gradually the worst of the seasickness passed. The captain, it seemed, had a bonus promised from the owners if he made a quick trip. Food was plentiful but not fancy, and the worst problem was boredom. Dermott had forgotten what it was like on a long voyage. If he never made another one in his life it'd be too soon, he decided gloomily, and began to wonder if he should stay in England after all. It would have been better on a proper passenger ship, with more folk to keep you company and things arranged to amuse you, especially now he could afford to go cabin class. But there would still be the seasickness when the weather grew rough.

At Cape Town they had to disembark and wait for another ship going to England, but were lucky to find one about to sail to France and took that instead. Full of bloody foreigners, but beggars could not be choosers.

Christina remained in excellent spirits. He had never seen her so happy or enjoyed her company like this. The fact that most of the other passengers did not speak the same language threw them together.

'Did you hate Australia so much?' he asked one day, as they were strolling round the deck.

She considered this, head on one side. 'It was all right, I suppose, especially Melbourne, but I'm English, and I'll never stop being English.' She turned to give him a very level look. 'You'll have to drag me screaming on to a ship to get me back to Australia again, Dermott Docherty. I mean it.'

'Ah, we'll think about that when we see what England's like these days.'

'You mean — you'll consider staying there?'

'Aye. Eh, stop crying, you dafthead.' He pulled her into his arms and let her weep on his shoulder. She said she was crying because she was happy. Who could fathom women? But when she continued cheerful and unlike herself, he began to think very seriously about where their future lay.

'We need to get a better look at this lass as is living with Hamilton,' Bob Marshall told his brother. 'Have you seen her at all? Do you think she could be our sister?'

'When would I get a chance to gawp at her? I'm working too bloody hard and when I get home there's allus something needs doing. I never get time to feel the sun and wind on my face, shut up all day in that workshop. I'm fed up of it, I am that!'

'You still find time to come out for a sup of ale!'

'Ah, well, a man's throat gets dry after a day's hard work, doesn't it?'

Bob frowned. 'I suppose I'll have to go and take a look at the lass myself, then. As if I don't have enough on my plate with Dad.'

'You do that.' Jim counted up the change in his pocket and went to get another half-pint.

Bob went along Whalley Street the very next day, pushing his handcart and staring at the houses as if searching for a certain street number. He fell lucky. Just as he got near number twenty-two the door opened and out came a lass leading an old lady by the hand as if she were a small child. Pretending to shake a bit of grit out of his boot, he got a good look at her and what he saw made him whistle through his teeth. This had to be his half-sister! She had a look of the Marshalls to her, no doubt about that.

She was tall, sturdy, and though her hair was much darker than his, she had that twisty bit at the right of the forehead that would never lie smooth, as they all did.

'Bloody hell!' he muttered under his breath. 'Who'd ha' thought it?'

She most resembled his younger brother Pat, though, with that same soft expression on her face. Just asking for folk to take advantage of you, it was, that expression. And they did take advantage of Pat, who was forever being asked to help some lazy sod for nothing.

Bob frowned as he wondered yet again why Docherty had written to tell them about this Cathie, who was, after all, Docherty's own niece. Did the bugger want her hurt? Bob wasn't having that, not if she really was a Marshall. He frowned as he took another long, slow look while she calmed the old lady down. She looked respectable, not much different from his own wife, really. But why was she dressed so plainly and living in Whalley Street working for Hamilton if her family was well-to-do? It didn't make sense.

He let her and the old lady walk past him, then strolled slowly home, marvelling at this unexpected outcome to his dad's randiness. The old sod! Good thing his father was past that sort of thing now – at least according to Sal – or they'd have a whole house full of bastards to look after. Bob didn't intend to tell his father anything yet about the lass because this needed thinking through properly. If there was any advantage to be gained from her presence, he intended to be the one to benefit because unlike his father he had a bit of sense in his noddle.

On his way to the pub that night he met Pat, who asked

him if he'd had any luck in his search. He must have hesitated a bit too long because his younger brother beamed at him and exclaimed loudly, 'You did find our sister, then?'

Bob grabbed his arm and shook him. 'Shut up, you fool! Do you want everyone to know?'

'But what does it matter? Aren't we going to go and see her?'

'No, we're bleedin' well not. We're not going to do anything until I see my way straight.'

'What does Dad say?'

Bob scowled. 'Nothing, because I haven't told him.'

'He has a right to know you've found her.'

'Not in my book, he doesn't. Any road, he hasn't mentioned it again. It's us who'll have to think what to do — see if there's any money to be had from her family, mebbe.'

Pat gaped at him. 'Why should they give us money?'

'Have you forgot that our dear half-sister, bastard though she may be, is also half-sister to Master Francis Rawley? Because I haven't.' Bob snickered. 'Fancy *us* being related to them nobs. They'll hate that and they definitely won't want other folk to know about the connection, so if we play it right, they might give us a bit of money to keep our mouths shut.'

Pat stepped backwards, a disgusted expression on his face. 'I should have known you lot would mess things up. I were looking forward to having a sister an' I'm not threatening her with owt like that. Where is she?'

'Wouldn't you like to know?'

'I'll find out.' Pat turned on his heel and strode off.

Bob let out a scornful bray of laughter and called after

him, 'By the time you've found out, me an' Jim will have getten oursen some money. Only we'll not share it with you, nor with the old man neither.' He marched off in the other direction, muttering 'Stupid sod!' under his breath two or three times, his mind already busy with schemes to get money out of the Rawleys. Only he'd have to do it carefully, because he didn't want to anger old Stephenson.

On the following Friday Magnus came home with a frown on his face.

'Is something wrong?' Cathie asked at once.

He hesitated, then said slowly, 'Young Mr Reuben was asking me about you today, what you were doing in Pendleworth.'

'Oh.'

'I told him you were my cousin and had come to look after my mother.' Another hesitation then he added, 'I'm not sure he believed me, though. He gave me a lecture about fornication.' Magnus had had great difficulty in restraining himself while he stood and listened. He'd thought Mr Reuben knew better than to believe him slack in morals, and suspected that Mr Matthew had insisted on the lecture, because Mr Reuben had seemed embarrassed by it and had finished abruptly.

Cathie's face turned scarlet and she said, 'Oh!' in a small voice. 'I thought if we said we were cousins people wouldn't think . . .'

'Eh, lassie, they're bound to talk. I've definitely harmed your reputation and I'm sorry for that.'

'You've never laid a finger on me, never been anything but respectful towards me,' she said hotly.

'What does that matter? Folk hereabouts enjoy a bit of gossip. Don't they in Australia?'

She stared down at her feet, still too embarrassed to look him in the eyes. 'There were very few other people living nearby. From what I remember of our homestead, the nearest neighbour was about half a mile away. We often didn't see anyone outside the family from one week to the next. I'm not sorry I left, but I still can't remember my real father's name, however hard I try.' She looked at him in despair. 'What if I've wasted my time, hurt everyone – for nothing?'

'Eh, lassie, don't take on.'

Somehow his arms were round her and she was leaning against him, enjoying the rare sensation of feeling small and cherished against a man's hard body. When she looked up, Magnus was gazing down at her and she was sure that was fondness in his gaze. She smiled at him tentatively.

He brushed the back of his index finger up her cheek and said huskily, 'Och, we musna do this, lassie, not while you're living under my roof. Not even after you leave. With my mother how she is I have nothing to offer any woman but thankless hard work.' He glanced across the room towards the silently rocking figure as he said that, his expression sad.

'You have yourself to offer and most people work hard in one way or another,' Cathie corrected softly.

'It's not enough. I'm thirty with nothing saved.' He laid his hands on her shoulders and pushed her away from him, though a sigh escaped him as he did so. When his mother made a noise and stood up suddenly, he went across to make sure she didn't try to play with the fire again, but she did not respond to him, nor did she want to sit down, and in the end he had to push her gently into a sitting position.

Cathie didn't know what to say to him after that comment. Did it mean he was thinking seriously of her? She didn't know. But Magnus was wonderful, so patient and intelligent, and fun when he relaxed. Good-looking too in his own way, especially with that fierce expression on his face and that haughty way of holding himself as he strode about the town. A man of pride and integrity.

In fact, she admitted to herself, she liked him too much for her own good, thought about him during the day and dreamed of him sometimes at night.

She looked across the room to where he was trying to elicit some response from his mother. He loved his family very much and it was clear how upset he was about his brothers leaving. Oh, why was life never straightforward? Why were there always problems standing between you and happiness?

At Rawley Manor icy silence prevailed for several weeks. If Francis hadn't had the pleasure of his Sunday outings to look forward to, hadn't known he had a half-sister and was no longer alone in the world except for the great-uncle he'd grown to hate, he didn't know how he'd have borne it. Going over to visit the Lorrimers helped too, though he tried not to let his uncle know about that. It was reassuring to see a happy family who loved one another and welcomed visitors. Francis wanted a family and home like that himself some day, when he grew up.

Then one day he noticed his uncle looking at him differently, in a speculative way which made him suspect the old man was planning something. Silent scorn hadn't worked, but Francis was sure Alexander Stephenson would not let himself be easily beaten.

Worry about what the old man might do next, together with the thought that it was August and the date was fast approaching for him to go back to school, gave Francis some bleak moments. There was a perfectly good grammar school in Pendleworth, to which the Lorrimers' sons went, but he could see no prospect of persuading his uncle to allow him to go there.

'Can you not simply put up with the school for another two years?' Mr Lorrimer had asked the previous Sunday.

Francis didn't see why he should have to put up with it. He didn't fit in there and hated the rough discipline and poor food, not to mention the brutal teasing. Only he hated life at home too, so much that he was even wondering about running away to Australia to try to find his mother. Cathie was sure he'd be welcome at Lizabrook, but she insisted that running away caused more problems than it solved. And anyway, Francis was quite sure his uncle would send someone after him if he did try to escape — and would have the law on his side for years yet.

When Sunday morning came it was wet and very chilly, and although there were a couple of breaks the sky remained overcast and it rained heavily.

There was a knock on the bedroom door and Francis opened it to see Hilda standing there.

'If you please, Master Francis, your uncle says you're not to go out for a walk today. He doesn't want you catching your death of cold and the Ludlams are calling this afternoon.'

'He can't stop me,' Francis muttered.

She glanced over her shoulder. 'Oh, please, Master Francis, don't be setting his back up again. He's been that bad-tempered lately we're all afraid to open our mouths.'

'Thank you for delivering the message.'

He endured another silent luncheon, then returned to his room to change into his outdoor clothes. He thought he heard a sound outside and when he tried to open the bedroom door found it locked. Francis kicked it in fury. He could guess what had happened. He bent to stare under the door and thought he could make out a shadow. Was someone standing there?

Anger flared inside him and he pounded on the door. 'Let me out!'

'I have decided that your insolence must be checked. You will stay in your room today until our guests arrive, then you will join us,' Alexander said, the first time he had spoken to Francis in more than monosyllables for weeks. 'And from now on I shall take steps to ensure your complete obedience.'

Francis did not reply. After a few moments he saw the shadow move and heard footsteps moving away. Ever since the seizure, his uncle walked with a sort of shuffle, as if one leg wasn't as strong as the other.

Francis waited five agonisingly slow minutes by the clock on his mantelpiece, then got out the spare key to his bedroom that he'd filched from the board in the butler's pantry, just in case he ever needed it. Slipping it into the lock, he turned it gently. The click sounded very loud and he held his breath for a moment, but nothing happened, so he risked opening the door.

He breathed a sigh of relief as he saw that the corridor was empty. Turning quickly, he locked the door again, then crept along to the servants' stairs.

At the bottom he met Cook, who gasped and clapped one hand to her bosom, then shot a quick glance around before she whispered, 'It's not wise, Master Francis. The master's in a foul mood today.'

'I've had enough of being treated like a child. I told him that a while ago and I meant it.'

She shook her head and gestured to him to pass. 'I didn't see you,' she muttered.

Daringly he kissed her plump cheek.

'Get on with you!' she said under her breath, but he had already gone.

Tears welled in her eyes. Master Francis was heading for bigger trouble than he had ever met in his whole life. She had seen how ruthless the old master could be with tenants if he was crossed, and was surprised he'd held off so long from retaliating to his nephew's disobedience. She went back into the kitchen feeling really worried. There was only so much she could do to help Francis or she'd lose her place. And if she left, who would care for that poor lad?

Outside it was raining again and Francis realised that in his haste to escape he had forgotten his outdoor coat. He hesitated but did not dare go back for it. Detouring to visit the stables, he picked up a horse blanket, which he wrapped round himself, keeping a careful watch for Horace.

He did not allow himself to think what things would be like when he returned. Today he wanted desperately to see his sister, needing the comfort of an hour or two with her.

Cathie was waiting for him on the edge of the woods, her face hidden under a large black umbrella with one spoke broken. When she heard him coming, she raised the umbrella and beamed at him.

They hugged one another, then he led the way into the woods.

Neither of them saw the stable lad watching them from behind some bushes. They had been spotted here the previous week. All the outdoor staff knew Master Francis was for it, but no one knew who the girl was and even today her face was hidden by the umbrella.

The woods were dripping with rain and Cathie was shivering. 'I'm not used to this cold,' she admitted when she saw Francis looking at her in concern.

'It gets a lot colder in winter, but dampness always makes it feel worse.'

'Is wearing a blanket the latest fashion for young gentlemen?' she teased.

He chuckled. 'I forgot my coat and didn't want to go back.' He didn't like admitting it but she had to know. 'My uncle locked me in my room. I escaped.'

Her smile faded. 'Francis, are you sure that was wise?'

'I'm not sure of anything lately. I just know that I've had enough of his bullying ways. I'm still thinking of running away to Australia to meet our mother. No one here really cares about me.'

'Oh, Francis, surely there's *someone*?'

He shook his head, gazing blindly across the clearing. 'The only one who'd really care if I ran away is Cook. I'm certain my uncle has no love for anyone these days. I'm not surprised he never got married, he's such a cold fish. My grandmother is probably the only person he's ever cared about in his life. Since she died, he's grown harsher with everyone, especially me. I hate him, Cathie, really hate him.'

'Oh, Francis, that's dreadful!' She gave him a quick hug. 'Well, there is another person who cares about you now – me.'

His eyes filled with tears so she held him close as she would have one of her other brothers, not saying anything, letting him recover in his own time. How dreadful it must be not to have any family who loved you!

And how badly she'd treated her own family, who definitely loved her!

When the Ludlam carriage drew up in front of Rawley Manor only Matthew Ludlam got out, his son Reuben having pleaded a prior engagement. As head of the household, he considered it his duty to keep on good terms with the other big landowners in the district, so visited Stephenson regularly. This time, however, Matthew had been asked to call.

Inside the house he joined his host in the library and there, in a dry voice that rasped with restrained anger, the old man confided his problems with his nephew.

Matthew frowned as the tale unfolded, shocked at the

way the boy had behaved. 'Have you decided what to do about it?'

'Yes. That school hasn't toughened him up as I expected, so I've arranged to hire a private tutor. However, I also need a strong man to help the tutor keep Francis in order, by force if necessary, and to share the duties of supervising him every hour of the day. I've engaged the tutor myself and he'll be arriving shortly, but I wanted to ask if you knew anyone suitable to help — maybe someone from your mill?'

'Who is the tutor?' Matthew asked.

'A military man fallen on hard times.'

'Do you intend to keep the boy a prisoner, then?' he queried in some surprise.

'If necessary.'

'Don't you think that's a bit — extreme?'

'No, I do not!' Surreptitiously Alexander wiped a trickle of moisture from the sagging corner of his mouth and tried to control his anger. 'I cannot subscribe to this modern idea of pampering the young. My sister treated Francis far too leniently and look where it's led. I intend to pull him into line over the next few years. I must do, for the sake of our family's heritage.' If he had a few years left. The matter was growing urgent because this numbness was not getting any better, and in fact he was not feeling at all well lately.

Matthew did not like the way the old man's body trembled with anger. Stephenson's colour had gone from an angry flush to a bone-white bleached look, as if he hadn't got enough blood in his body, and there was a viciousness in his tone that Matthew did not approve of. 'I suppose I could find you a strong man,' he said slowly, knitting his brow in thought. 'There are any number of those at the mill. I'll ask Reuben what he thinks. He's in charge of the workshop and knows our operatives better than I do.'

'Good. And now I wonder if you'd accompany me upstairs to Francis's room? It's time he found out what I have planned. I would be most obliged if you would have a word with him, too, to show him that I am not being unreasonable.'

Matthew hesitated, but the look of fragility beneath the anger, and that slightly twisted lip, convinced him it was better to humour the old man.

But Francis was not in his room and as Matthew definitely did not approve of such blatant disobedience, he promised again to find a strong man to work with the tutor.

When Stephenson broached another matter, which he had found out about from his head groom, Matthew was surprised at the scope of the old man's virulence. He agreed to investigate Magnus Hamilton's home arrangements, however, because he did not condone immorality among his employees any more than Stephenson did among his tenants. It was a Christian employer's responsibility to keep an eye on his dependants' morals.

Within days the voyage to England had started to restore Liza's health and spirits. Things had improved greatly since her first voyage to Australia in a sailing ship without even an auxiliary steam engine. Best of all for her this time was watching Josie's pleasure and the improvement in her health.

Her younger daughter had always been frail, prone to wheezing and a little pale. On the ship the wheezing vanished entirely and Josie became a gleeful and sometimes naughty child, making friends for the first time in her life and confiding in her mother that she wished the voyage would go on for ever.

'It's so much more fun on the ship than it was at home,' she said sleepily one night from the top bunk. 'I can understand now why Cathie ran away, but I still miss her, don't you? I do hope we find her in England.'

'I'm sure we shall,' Liza promised.

What her younger daughter had said gave her much food for thought when she went to bed later after a pleasant evening spent talking to the other cabin passengers. You could not immure your children in the bush for ever, and though it hurt to let them go, she would do it in future with better grace and make sure Benedict did, too.

And why Josie should feel so well now that she was away from the farm needed further consideration too. Liza had talked to the ship's doctor about that and he had said that such wheeziness could be affected by the climate and where the sufferer lived.

She fell asleep, feeling a little guilty that she too was enjoying the change of routine. When she got back she would make sure Benedict left the farm more often. They could leave their sons in charge and travel to Melbourne or Sydney once they were on their feet financially again. Why not? And she'd definitely sell the rest of the Ludlam jewellery when she got back, except for the cameo ring for which she had a particular fondness. It was silly to keep something she never wore just because of Benedict's pride.

The ship made good time and soon there were only a couple of weeks left before their arrival in England. Much as she missed her husband and sons, Liza remained sure that she was doing the right thing coming to look for her lost children.

It made the young Lorrimers and their friends laugh to see Francis turn up wrapped in a horse blanket. He joined in because their merriment was not malicious. It was not unpleasant to be teased, he found, by people like this.

Mr Lorrimer walked outside with him when he left and gestured to the blanket. 'What happened?'

'They locked me in my room. I had a spare key so I escaped. But I forgot my overcoat.'

'Be careful not to push them too far.'

Francis blinked furiously. He hated to leave this happy house. 'They've pushed *me* too far, sir.'

Mr Lorrimer's only response was to pat him on the back.

Back at the Manor Francis returned the horse blanket then stood outside the stables for several minutes, his stomach churning with nervousness about facing his uncle.

He went into the house via the kitchen. Cook deliberately avoided his questioning glance, so he knew something had happened while he was away. He didn't ask, just nodded to her and the kitchen maid and walked up the back stairs, hoping to postpone the confrontation for a while longer.

His bedroom door was now unlocked, which showed someone had been in. He hid the key with even greater care than before, hanging it outside the window on a thread attached to the ivy so that it lay beneath the lush green leaves. Spit and dirt disguised the thread, so that even if anyone did look, they'd have trouble finding the key.

No one came to summon him to the library so he waited until dinner time, getting dressed with care. He had never felt less hungry in his life, but was not going to lurk in his room like a coward.

His uncle was already seated and looked up as he entered the dining room to ask in that rasping voice he had developed recently, 'How did you get out?'

'Through the door.'

'Kindly return the key.'

'I've already put it back in the butler's pantry.'

Francis noted that his uncle was eating with more appetite than usual, in fact cramming food into his mouth, which puzzled him from a normally fastidious eater. The triumphant expression on the old man's face made his heart sink even further.

But nothing else was said over the meal — nothing at all.

Francis went up to his room afterwards with apprehension churning in his belly and vomited up what he had eaten. He didn't sleep well, either.

CHAPTER FIFTEEN

July

'Is Hamilton living in sin?' Matthew Ludlam asked his son over breakfast the following day.

'Not to my knowledge.'

'He's renting one of our houses, isn't he? Stephenson told me about it, hinted we should turn him out.'

Reuben looked at his father in amazement. 'What's it got to do with him?'

'He was just being neighbourly, passing on a piece of information.'

'A piece of gossip! Anyway, I've already questioned Hamilton about the situation and he says the girl is his cousin, there to look after his mother who has softening of the brain and is getting worse by the month, poor soul. I've seen the woman myself — a very sad decline. And since Hamilton's sister has married and gone to live in Bury, he needs help.'

'Well, if you're sure . . .'

'I am sure they're not in an immoral relationship, Father.' Magnus Hamilton would have scorned to lie. Reuben wasn't sure whether the girl really was a cousin, however, but had not pressed that point. 'And either I'm in charge of the workshop and those who work there or Mr Stephenson is — in which case I'll leave today.'

'Don't be stupid. I just don't want to have a foreman setting a bad example.'

Reuben gave his father a very level look. 'I mean what I say. Grandfather kept you without power right until his death. I'll not put up with the same treatment. I can earn my living in other places and I'm not greedy for Ludlam wealth.'

'Oh, don't be so touchy. You know you're in charge of the workshop. Anyway, Stephenson has another problem and I promised we'd help him . . .' He began to explain.

By the time he got to the mill, Reuben had walked his anger off. As he moved round the workshop, he studied the men, deeply resenting the fact that his father had given his word to find someone suitable to discipline Francis Rawley. Men of Stephenson's generation thought they could ride roughshod over anyone in their power, and for all his father's protestations, he was still too influenced by the way his own father had done things. Reuben would not carry on those traditions when his time came. He could still remember being afraid of his grandfather; had seen his grandmother weep several times after Saul Ludlam had treated her scornfully. She was well rid of him, they all were, and now they lived a happier life at the Hall, or would do if his father would stop trying to copy Saul by acting the tyrant.

Reuben knew, because she often confided in him, that his grandmother had supported some of his grandfather's many bastards during their childhood, those born to the maidservants upon whom his grandfather had forced himself. He often visited her because her cosy little house with its cheerful atmosphere was a relief after the formality of the big house. He wished he could have such a place for himself, only his father had made such a fuss when he'd suggested moving out of the Hall that he'd let the matter drop. For the time being.

Nor was he going to marry one of the suitable girls his mother and father were pressing him to consider. He'd choose his own wife — and did not want to marry anyone yet.

He beckoned his capable foreman to join him.

A few minutes later Magnus went over to Jim Marshall and said, 'Mr Reuben wants to see you in his office.'

Jim cast him a resentful glance as he put his hammer down. 'What for? I've done nowt wrong.'

'You're not in trouble.' Magnus watched him leave, frowning. Mr Reuben had not looked in the best of humours this morning. Which usually meant his father had been interfering in workshop matters again.

In the office Reuben waved Jim to a seat and he sat down uneasily, never having been asked to sit in here before.

'I don't want this to go any further, Jim. In fact, I want your solemn promise on that before I start. What's more, if I find you *have* been talking, you'll be out on your ear.'

'Nay, sir, you can trust me. What you say will go no further.'

'Mr Stephenson at Rawley Manor is having trouble controlling his nephew Francis —'

Jim sat up a bit straighter, all attention now.

'— and wants a strong fellow to help the new tutor keep the lad in order.' Reuben made an exasperated sound in his throat. 'I may as well tell you that I don't like us getting involved in this. I feel sorry for that lad. He's not had a happy life and it looks as if things are about to get worse for him. However, my father has promised to find someone to help Mr Stephenson and I thought you might fancy a bit of a change. You don't always seem best pleased with what you're doing here and the job at the Manor will pay a bit more.'

'What exactly do they want me to do there?'

Reuben spread his hands wide in a gesture of puzzlement. 'Who can tell? If it involves beating the lad then' – he hesitated before adding – 'I'd like you to let me know about it.' He would rather have sent Hamilton to do a job like this, if he had to send anyone, but he needed his foreman's skills here and Magnus had his mother to care for. 'Well, what do you think?'

'How much extra money if I do it, sir? It's a long walk out to the Manor.'

'They want someone to stay there – though you'll get a day a week off to visit your family.'

'Stay there?' Jim goggled at him for a minute then grinned. 'Fancy me living at the Manor! That's a queer one, isn't it?'

'You'll be staying in the servants' quarters. You'll get the same money as now, part of it paid to your wife, plus your keep and an extra guinea a month.'

Jim didn't hesitate. 'I'll do it, sir.'

'Right then. You're to report there at eight o'clock tomorrow morning. Clear your things here. You can have the rest of the day off. Oh, and send Hamilton in to see me, if you please.'

Jim closed the office door behind him then grinned round the noisy workshop. Fate was being kind to him and Bob. They'd wanted to meet the lad and now here was Master Francis being handed over to them like a gift.

When he left he headed towards Underby Street to tell his brother about it.

Reuben summoned Magnus to his office, gesturing to the chair. 'Marshall accepted.'

'I thought he would.'

'I've asked Jim to let me know if they're ill-treating the lad. I don't like this at all. If *you* hear anything . . .'

'I'll let you know at once, sir.' Magnus knew Caitlin would be upset when he told her about this. She was getting very fond of her half-brother.

Reuben then turned the discussion to some modifications Magnus had suggested for some of the machinery. If things turned out as well as he expected, he would insist on the foreman being given a bonus for this and later a more important position in the mill. Almost as an afterthought he added, 'How's your mother, Magnus?'

'Worse, I'm afraid, sir. Caitlin couldn't even persuade her out for a walk yesterday. She just lay abed all day. I've asked the doctor to call in on his rounds tonight.'

'It's a hard time for you.'

'Aye, sir. I don't know what I'd do without Caitlin. She's marvellous with my mother. A born nurse, the doctor says.'

*

Later the same morning one of the Rawley carriages was sent to the station to fetch the new tutor who had been Sergeant Baxter until an injury left him with a pronounced limp and forced him to leave his regiment. The limp didn't stop him being a strong man still and he was well read for someone of his station, but his brief as 'tutor' was to make a man of Francis, not to mollycoddle him or worry too much about book learning.

Francis happened to be strolling in the gardens when the carriage returned from the station, for the weather had cleared today. He watched a stranger get out, surprised by what he saw. No gentleman, this, so what was he doing calling on Alexander Stephenson via the front door? Then the driver unloaded several items of luggage and it was clear that the man had come to stay. Apprehension shivered through Francis. What was his uncle planning now? He did not normally invite people to stay.

On a sudden impulse the lad hurried round the side of the house and concealed himself in some bushes near the library. One of the French windows was open because his uncle was a firm believer in the benefits of fresh air and since the old man was becoming increasingly deaf, the conversation was clearly audible from outside.

'Eli Baxter reporting for duty, sir!'

'Sit down, man.' There was a short silence, then, 'They explained to you what was required?'

'Yessir. But I'd like to hear it explained by you, if you don't mind. Can't beat first-hand information.'

'Yes, I suppose you're right.' Alexander took a deep breath and said the words aloud, distasteful though they might be. 'I want you to knock my great-nephew into shape. Literally if need be. He's a namby-pamby creature. Refuses to join the hunt or go shooting, wants to waste his time sketching, fools around at school. Lately he's been openly defiant of my orders and has been seen in the woods with a young woman of plebeian origin.'

Silence, then, 'What do you mean by "knock into shape"?'

'I mean that if necessary you will beat him until he learns to obey – not in a way that will mark him or injure him badly, of course. But I am not a young man and do not wish this estate to fall into the hands of a weakling, so the matter is urgent. You will spare no effort, do anything that is necessary to bring Francis up to scratch and as quickly as possible – as if he were a new recruit in your regiment.'

'If I treated him like that, it could be painful for him, sir.'

'It will be painful for the estate if the last of the Rawleys fails in his duty to care for it.'

Eli didn't comment on that. This was a rum situation if ever he'd seen one, but the old man was going to pay him handsomely and the extra money would help him buy himself a little inn he'd got his eye on. He'd give himself a year here, no more, and deal with this spoiled rich lad exactly as he'd dealt with unsuitable recruits in the regiment, not one of whom had ever got the better of him when he'd set his mind to it. Eli prided himself on that.

'My neighbour, Matthew Ludlam, is finding a man to help since you cannot be on duty twenty-four hours a day. The lad is cunning so will bear watching. We don't want him running off again.'

Francis closed his eyes and a sick feeling of dismay and

fear shuddered through him. If he had ever needed confirmation of how much his uncle despised him, here it was. Only he hadn't needed it, for he had already known. He had not, however, expected Uncle Alexander to be prepared to have him beaten into submission. Anger flooded through him. Well, he would not do what they wanted! He hated horses and always would. He hated blood sports, too, and refused to kill animals for pleasure. But most of all he hated his uncle and would not cave in to his bullying.

He swallowed hard. At least, he hoped he wouldn't. Could he manage to stand firm against them all? He'd have to find the courage somehow. He thought suddenly of the mother he had not been allowed to know. Yes, he would cling to that painful thought as he faced them.

How best should he do this? He would have to think about that. And quickly.

His uncle was speaking again. 'You will be given a room in the west wing next to my nephew, Mr Baxter, so that you can keep an eye on Francis at all times. The other man will be here tomorrow and will act as general servant to you both, but his main purpose is to act as guard and see the boy doesn't escape.'

'Yes, sir.'

There was the sound of a bell ringing and the library door opening. Francis stumbled to his feet and made for the woods. Perhaps he should run away now, while he could? But once under the trees he slowed down and acknowledged that it was impossible. He had no money with him and did not dare go back for any. And he had no one close enough to run to – only his half-sister, and he did not intend to bring trouble to Cathie who would be powerless if his uncle turned the full force of his anger on her.

After some thought Francis made his way across the fields to the Lorrimers' house, knocked on the door and asked to speak to Mrs Lorrimer. The maid recognised him and ushered him straight into the hall, then her mistress came out and took him into her sitting room.

'Is something wrong, Francis?'

His voice cracking with pain, he told her what he had overheard and asked her to pass the information on to her husband. 'I don't think there's anything he can do to help me, but I feel someone should at least know what's happening.'

'You poor boy.' Her voice was soft and warm and made him want to weep in her arms, so he stood up hastily and said, 'I'd better get back now. They'll be looking for me.'

'What exactly are you going to do?'

'Resist them. Any way I can.' He looked at her, his eyes very blue and over-bright, his soft blond hair gleaming in the sun. 'They may knock me about, but I doubt they'll kill me. And whatever they do, I won't let them turn me into a person like my uncle.'

As they walked towards the front door he stopped at a sudden thought. 'I wonder if I could write a note to my half-sister and ask you to send it to her? I've been meeting her on Sundays in the woods and she'll wonder what's happening if I don't turn up next week. I don't want her going to the house and asking for me, and I don't want them knowing who she is, though they do know I've been meeting a young woman.'

When Francis got back to the Manor he went in by the kitchen door. Cook looked at him pityingly, but said only, 'Your uncle wants to see you at once. He's sent the grooms out to look for you.'

'Where is he?'

'In the library.'

How he hated that room, Francis thought as he knocked on the door. When his uncle's reedy voice told him to enter, he found them waiting for him, his uncle and the new tutor, a burly man with a somewhat battered face.

'So they found you!' Uncle Alexander snapped.

'No one found me. I came home from a walk in the woods and received a message you wanted to see me, so I came at once.'

'You're not to go out on your own again.' With a triumphant, sneering smile, his uncle explained what had been arranged.

'So I'm not to go back to school in the autumn then?' Francis asked, trying to act as if this was all news to him, as if he didn't know what to expect from this 'tutor'.

'Did I not say so?'

'Well, I'm glad of that at least.'

Alexander was suddenly unable to bear the sight of his nephew. That the Rawleys, a fine old county family, had degenerated to the point where this milksop was the heir galled him more each day. 'Take him away, Baxter, and find out what he can and cannot do. You're in charge, now.' Anger beat so strongly within him that he felt dizzy, but a few deep breaths and he started to calm down. He had to conserve his strength. The second seizure had frightened him and now he was concentrating all his energy on the main thing he needed to do before he went to meet his Maker. He had to live long enough to make a man of his nephew.

He began to walk up and down the room, gesticulating and muttering, so that when Ethel peeped in, she backed out again hastily. The master was in one of his moods again. Gave her the shivers, it did, seeing him like that.

Upstairs Francis showed the tutor to the west wing, trying to keep his manner calm and polite even though his stomach was churning with nerves.

'Your uncle says we're to use the old schoolroom,' Eli prompted after he had nodded approval of the comfortable bedroom he'd been assigned next to the lad's.

'Did he? Very well.' Francis led the way up another flight of stairs, staring round yet another room where he had been unhappy.

Eli studied him assessingly. Weak physically, still a boy not a man, for all his height. He'd seen new recruits who looked like this before and had found out the hard way that you couldn't force muscles on to young bodies until they'd grown into their adult strength, whatever you did.

'I've a lot of experience with lads your age,' he warned. 'Your uncle wants me to teach you to ride properly, use a gun, hunt – all the usual gentlemanly pursuits.'

As quietly and politely as before Francis told him, 'I won't hunt. I'm a bad enough rider without risking myself over fences and hedges. And I won't shoot birds and animals, either, when I don't need them for food.'

'It's your duty to do as your uncle wishes.' He was

surprised at how steadily the lad gazed back at him, even though Eli had stared down generals in his time. Had the old man underestimated this boy?

'Only if it does not go against what I believe to be right, Mr Baxter.'

A firm believer in starting as you meant to go on, Eli lashed out and caught Francis on the side of the head, sending him staggering across the room. 'I have your uncle's permission to use force to persuade you into better behaviour and shall not hesitate to do so. It's not for you to make conditions, only to obey orders.'

'I can't stop you beating me, Mr Baxter,' Francis said. 'You're much bigger than I am. But I must tell you that you won't change my mind.'

Eli watched the lad steady himself against the table, realised his tone was that of one reasonable adult speaking to another, and again wondered what was going on here. The old man downstairs had not been reasonable, not at all, but sadly he held the purse strings. 'You'll have no chance of holding out against the three of us. If you think about it, you'll see that your wisest course is to do as you're told,' he warned.

Francis braced himself for another blow, but it didn't come.

'How about we start with target shooting? Your uncle says you've refused even to handle a gun.'

'Yes, I hate the things. So I'm sorry but I won't learn to shoot.' Another hefty thump was his answer and it hurt. His head ringing with pain, it took Francis a moment to stand up straight again. He moved to the other side of the table. No use making it easy for this brute to thump him.

'Who's the lass you've been meeting?' Eli watched the lad become very still and pale.

'Just a friend.'

'You young men will sow your wild oats!' his tutor jeered. 'Well, that's going to stop, too.'

Anger brought hot colour rushing into Francis's face. 'I've not been sowing any wild oats and I'm not lying! She's a friend and that's all! Who's been maligning her?'

'Your uncle simply informed me that you'd been meeting a lass in the woods and that it was to stop. Who is she?'

'None of your business.'

'You'll tell me. And you'll learn to answer smartly when I ask a question.'

'I'll not tell you.'

Eli thought he'd rarely seen a lad look so despairing and yet so steadfast. He wondered what had driven the old man to treat a youngster with such a steady, honest face in this cruel way. Well, that was enough violence for now. Give the lad something to think about then give him time to do that thinking, that was the trick of it.

'We'll go out for a walk, then, and you can show me these woods of yours. Walking is surely not against your principles?' As Francis moved reluctantly towards the door, Eli added sharply, 'And hold yourself upright as you walk. Slouching is bad for the spine and a sign of slovenliness.'

The lad stood and thought about the order — that was going to change very soon, Eli decided — then shrugged and squared his shoulders as if it didn't matter.

As they went outside the sunlight revealed a handsome young fellow with a clear, innocent face, not at all like the brutal youths Eli had mostly dealt with up to now. This was the sort of lad any father would be proud of. Eli had had a son once, but he'd died of cholera in India and so had Eli's wife.

He suddenly wished he had not taken this job. But having done so, he wasn't going to admit failure. And besides, a few beatings never hurt anyone. He was living proof of that and so were the many men he'd turned into good soldiers.

When Bernard Lorrimer came home that night, he listened in silence to his wife's tale. 'Unfortunately we have no right to interfere.'

'But surely we can do *something*?' she begged, still upset. No lad should have to face such callous treatment. No lad should ever have such a bleak look in his eyes.

'There's nothing we can do, not even if we can prove they've been beating him. The law gives them that right.'

'You mean we can't do anything officially,' she corrected, knowing him better than to think he'd turn his back on poor Francis.

They stared at one another then he said carefully, 'The situation would have to be very desperate indeed for me to intervene unofficially.'

'I know, dear. But Francis does have a mother in Australia who cares about him. Could we not send him to her?'

'If it becomes desperate I may consider that,' Bernard promised. He would also go and see Cathie Ludlam the very next day and deliver Francis's note in person. He was relieved to have found exactly where she was living and meant to discover whether she was in need of help of any sort.

As he walked slowly up the stairs to bed he thought yet again how glad he was that he had an independent income and useful connections so did not have to kow-tow to arrogant bullies like Alexander Stephenson. He was, however, surprised at the Ludlams' involvement in something like this.

That reminded him that Cathie still carried the Ludlam name and made him wonder whether to inform Sophia Ludlam that her son Josiah's adopted daughter was in Pendleworth. The old lady had apparently been very fond of her granddaughter as a child and might be glad to see her again and help, if necessary. No. Not yet. Best to wait and see what happened. You did not take action on mere suppositions.

But he would definitely go and see Cathie the following day.

His wife was equally wakeful and making her own plans. Her cook knew the cook at the Manor. She would ask Mrs Sark, who was the soul of discretion, to find out from her friend Barbara how things were going over there.

That evening Dr Barnes called at Magnus's house on his evening rounds, examined Janey, commented on how well cared for she was nowadays and shook his head over her lack of response to his questions. 'She is entering the final stage of the illness, I'm afraid, Mr Hamilton. They decline very rapidly when they get like this and often simply starve to death. Are you managing to feed her still?'

Magnus had to force the words through a throat suddenly constricted with tears. 'Not always. Caitlin is very good with her.'

'I can see that.' The doctor turned to the young woman and noted how clean she was in her own person. 'And how have you found your charge lately?'

'She wouldn't eat at all yesterday,' Cathie told him. 'Though she's been a bit better today.'

'You can only do your best with her. Afterwards, if you ever want a job as a home nurse, Miss Rutherford, I can find you work.'

She looked at him in surprise, then beamed at him. 'I never thought of that.' Her smile faded as she added, 'I shall have to earn my own living if anything happens to Aunt Janey. It wouldn't be proper for me to stay here on my own with Magnus.'

Clifford Barnes, who had also heard the gossip about her and Magnus Hamilton, decided yet again that gossip was usually a liar and he would continue to trust his own judgement about such matters. These were obviously two decent people doing their duty by an ageing relative, and so he'd tell the next person who hinted at anything else.

In the middle of the morning there was a knock on the front door and when Cathie went to answer it she found a stranger standing there, a gentleman by his appearance.

'Miss Ludlam?'

She wondered how he knew that when they'd told everyone she was called Rutherford. 'Yes.'

'My name is Bernard Lorrimer. May I have a word with you?'

She gaped at him. 'You're my mother's lawyer!'

'Yes.'

She held the door open. 'Come in.'

In the back room Janey Hamilton was slumped in a chair, not needing any bonds to restrain her because today she would only move when someone made her. 'I'm looking after Mrs Hamilton for Magnus and his sister,' Cathie said softly. 'She doesn't know what she's doing.'

'Poor thing. It can't be easy for you.'

'She wasn't too bad until the last few days. Now she lies or sits wherever I leave her. It's upsetting my cousin Magnus greatly.'

Bernard held up one hand. 'We both know he isn't your cousin.'

She looked at him nervously. 'Sorry. I've got into the habit of calling him that. You won't tell anyone, will you? Oh, please don't! We only say it to stop people saying such terrible things about us.' She stared him straight in the eye as she added, 'Things that are quite untrue.'

'I believe you, Cathie. Do you want to tell me what happened to bring you here?'

So yet again she had to explain what she had remembered about her flight and voyage to England. When she had finished, he sat looking thoughtful and she ventured to ask, 'Do you know who my real father is, sir?'

He shook his head. 'Your mother never told me anything except that you were not Josiah Ludlam's child. I gather someone forced himself upon her when she was quite young.'

Cathie gasped in shock: 'No!'

Her voice rang with such anguish that Bernard immediately regretted his tactless remark. 'You didn't know that?'

'No. At least, I don't think I did.' She shook her head, trying in vain to penetrate the veils which she suspected still concealed some of her memories. 'I can't believe I'd have come here looking for him if I'd known that. But now that I am here, I intend to find him and learn something about that side of my family – however he became my father.'

'Well, let's see. Your mother lived in Underby Street for many years, that I do know, and some of her old neighbours may still be there. You could ask them what they remember.' Bernard walked along that street sometimes as a short cut to vary his path home on fine days when he spurned using the carriage. 'I think the clogger's shop has been there for a good many years and in the same family, so the people there are most likely to have known your mother.'

Her expression brightened. 'I'll go and ask them.'

Bernard cleared his throat, seeking a tactful way to ask but not finding one, so just saying bluntly, 'Are you all right for money, my dear? If not, I could let you have some.'

She raised her head proudly. 'I'm earning my keep here, thank you.'

He frowned. 'Not very suitable employment for a girl like you.'

'Magnus needs me, and since he saved my life at Liverpool docks I'm happy to repay him by looking after his mother.' She looked sadly at the old woman. 'The doctor says Aunt Janey is probably nearing the end now and will soon refuse to eat at all. He's known patients like her choke if you try to force food on them, so has advised me not to do that. But I intend to look after her 'til she – 'til Magnus doesn't need me any more, then I'll decide what to do next.' With a hint of a smile, she added, 'The doctor has already offered me other nursing work.'

Lorrimer was surprised at that. 'Dr Barnes has?'

'Yes.'

'That's a great compliment coming from him. He and his nurses are well respected in Pendleworth.'

'I've always enjoyed that sort of thing. If I'd been a man, I'd have become a doctor.' She spread her hands wide in a helpless gesture. 'I read somewhere that a woman did become a doctor in America some years ago – Elizabeth Blackwell she was called. I've never forgotten her name.'

'There's a woman doctor in England, too. Another Elizabeth – Elizabeth Garrett Anderson. I remember reading about it – oh, it must be ten years ago now. She had a lot of trouble getting permission to study and take the exams, though. I don't think there's been another one brave enough since.'

Cathie sighed. 'I envy her. But I have no money and no family here, so I can't hope to follow in her footsteps.' She looked at him with determination in every line of her body. 'But I can earn a living nursing. That's something, at least. And it'll mean I can stay in England. I'm not going back to living in the bush.'

He wasn't sure what he thought of women becoming doctors and would definitely have forbidden his own daughters to try. Changing the subject, he produced the letter Francis had written. 'I'm afraid I have some bad news for you about your half-brother. He's written you this note. Perhaps you had better read it, then if you have anything to ask me about, you can.'

She read it quickly, murmuring in dismay, then exploding into angry words as she finished it. 'How can they treat him like this? Is there nothing *you* can do to help him? I'm sure my mother would pay whatever it cost.'

'Unfortunately the law is on Mr Stephenson's side. He is your half-brother's legal guardian and has a right to chastise him.'

Cathie closed her eyes and when she opened them again they filled with tears. 'Francis is such a lonely, unhappy boy! He doesn't deserve this. My other brothers and my sister and I have been so very lucky in our parents' love. I never realised how lucky till I met Francis. Oh, I do wish I had not hurt my parents so!' Then she began sobbing and Bernard was so upset by her distress he took her in his arms as he would have his own daughters.

Cathie didn't weep for long, but pulled away and wiped her eyes. 'I'm sorry.'

'My dear, you have good reason to be upset.'

She gave him a determined look. 'If I hear they're hurting Francis, I shall have to try to rescue him.'

Bernard did not try to hide his shock. 'My dear girl, you must do no such thing!'

'I can't leave him to endure such cruel treatment. He's my brother and I've grown very fond of him.'

Bernard produced one of his business cards. 'Please don't do anything rash. If you ever have reason to believe that Francis needs rescuing, come and see me at my chambers or at home — any time of day or night. Promise!'

317

He took out his little silver propelling pencil and scribbled his home address on the back of the card, explaining where his house was.

She took the card from him. 'Thank you, sir. I promise to let you know. But you'll not stop me if I see a need to act.'

He saw her looking at the pencil, which was a novelty to most people, and showed her how it worked, glad to introduce a lighter note into their conversation. He had been the first person in Pendleworth to have a propelling pencil, the first to ride on the underground railway in London a few years previously, the first to send his wife one of the new picture postcards purchased on one of his trips to London.

Talk of such novelties distracted her for a while, then he took his leave with the warning, 'Please don't try to do anything to help Francis without consulting me.'

'I'm not going to let them hurt him.'

Bernard was so worried by her stubborn expression that when he went home he discussed it with his wife. 'I had to admire her spirit,' he admitted. 'She's a fine young woman.'

'Is she – decent?'

'I believe so. It's not right, her living with a strange man, but I'm convinced there's nothing untoward going on between her and Magnus Hamilton.'

'Perhaps you should tell the Ludlams who she is?'

He pursed his lips. 'Perhaps. But Matthew Ludlam is a friend of Stephenson's and might tell him, which could only cause more trouble for Francis. Matthew is a weak reed under that pompous exterior, so terrified of jeopardising his damned dignity he never does anything out of the ordinary. His father destroyed his spirit when he was young — as Stephenson is trying to do to young Francis now. I pray he won't succeed.'

But if the need ever arose, he would go and see Matthew's mother Sophia, who was both kind and wise, he decided. He handled all her legal affairs now, because when her husband Saul died she had immediately moved out of the Hall and insisted on being independent from her sons. She not only enjoyed helping those worse off than herself, but had known and loved Cathie as a child. And best of all, she was not afraid of Alexander Stephenson, for whom she did not attempt to hide her dislike.

CHAPTER SIXTEEN

July

When Magnus got home from the workshop that evening, he found Cathie looking very downcast and his mother slumped in her chair, not even rocking to and fro. He tried in vain to coax a glance or a touch from Janey, then gave up.

'You must have had a bad day with her, Caitlin?'

'She hasn't misbehaved, but she hasn't eaten a thing.' Cathie hesitated then said, 'And I had some bad news of my own today as well.'

He could see she was holding back tears only with difficulty so said at once, 'Tell me. You can serve the meal afterwards. You need to talk to someone after a hard day with my mother.' Only – Janey did not seem like his mother any more. There had been no glimpses of her old self for several days and he longed for her to be released from her failing body – longed for it and yet felt guilty about those feelings.

'Oh, Magnus . . .'

He jerked out of his sombre thoughts to see Cathie's lips quivering and tears on her cheeks. In spite of his resolution not to touch her, he took her in his arms and drew her against him. 'Tell me, lassie,' he murmured against the soft dark hair.

So she poured out the news of Mr Lorrimer's visit and how Francis was to be imprisoned and ill-treated. Magnus found himself stroking her hair and making soothing noises as the tale faltered to a close.

She didn't tell him about the suggestion that she call and see the clogger because by the time she had told him that she was probably the result of a man forcing himself on her mother she was sobbing uncontrollably.

He let her weep, his heart twisting with anguish for her.

'I'm sorry,' she gulped as she began to calm down. She tried to pull away from him. 'You have enough troubles of your own — and bad ones, too. You don't need mine as well.'

'You're sharing my troubles. Why can I not share yours?' he said simply.

'Oh, Magnus.' She lifted her face and stared at him as she held back the words 'Magnus, my love', which she would have liked to add. The feeling had crept up on her as she watched him care so tenderly for his mother, saw his joy at his sister's visits and experienced his kindness towards a stranger like herself. And she loved his tall, strong body, too. The mere touch of his hand was enough to set her tingling with longing. Why had it taken her so long to realise what all this meant?

'Caitlin, lass, this is not . . . we mustn't . . .' He let the words trail away and stepped backwards.

She could only assume that he did not care about her as she cared for him, so took a deep breath and said with false brightness, 'Well, now that I've wept all over you, I suppose I'd better get you your tea.'

He told himself it was better to keep his distance for the moment because he was a man, with all a man's desires, and she was a very bonny lass. So he sat down by the table and watched her bustle about the kitchen, neat and careful in her work as always. He could at least enjoy watching her.

'I'm afraid they're sending another man to help guard your brother,' he said as she finished cooking his food. 'Mr Ludlam is helping his friend, Mr Stephenson, so they've sent Jim from the workshop. He's a rough fellow though not cruel, I think. But Mr Reuben was in a bad mood all day about it and your poor brother will be so carefully watched I don't see how you *can* do anything to help him.'

'Well, I'm not going to leave Francis to be ill-treated!'

'We'll keep an eye on the situation and if we find out that things are bad, the best thing is for us to go and see your Mr Lorrimer.'

She gave him a glowing look. 'You'll help — come with me, if necessary?'

'Aye, of course I will, Caitlin. But we'll keep our eyes and ears open first. A lad doesn't die of a strict upbringing.'

She thought of Francis, so soft-hearted he wouldn't even go shooting, of the way his eyes lit up when he saw her, the way he held on to her hand as if he needed the human contact. 'Perhaps his body won't die, but something inside him will wither, I'm sure, if he doesn't have anyone to care for him and only meets with ill-treatment.' She set a plate of fried ham and potatoes in front of Magnus and cut a thick slice of bread for him as well. He had a hearty appetite, which was not surprising in such a big man, and she loved to watch him enjoying his food.

She found her own appetite returning as they shared the meal.

As Cathie was lying in bed later she suddenly remembered her own mother saying once that it didn't matter where you lived as long as you were with the man you loved. She knew she could be happy with Magnus, was happy with him, even in the present difficult circumstances.

Oh, if only he loved her as she loved him. But how could he? He was older, far more sensible, must think her stupid — but he *had* held her in his arms today . . . and it had felt wonderful . . . and . . . on that thought she fell asleep.

The following day Janey was a little better, allowing herself to be dressed and moving willingly enough down the stairs and around the house. Cathie decided to take her out for a short walk, but was a bit worried when they started off at the way Janey's eyes did not focus on anything at all. She decided only to go to Underby Street, to ask about her mother at the clogger's shop, because it wasn't far.

The narrow street had small shops in it as well as terraced dwellings. She stopped for a minute to stare around. Had her mother really been born here? It could not have been more different from Lizabrook homestead. The clogger's shop was on the right, halfway along the street, with CLOGS painted in big red letters above the window. That same window was grimy and had a few clogs scattered about in a kind of display, with a panel of wood behind them so that she couldn't see inside.

She remembered suddenly looking at a picture in a book of Dutch people wearing clogs and wondering aloud how people could wear such stupid footwear. Her mother had laughed and told her that clogs were very comfortable and weatherproof, then had fallen silent and stared into the distance. Cathie could now guess that this was because she had once lived near a clogger's shop. She wished she knew which house had been her mother's.

She decided to go inside the clogger's, but had to pull Janey quite hard to make her move forward again and noticed with dismay that the older woman was standing limply, as if she might fall down at any moment. A bell rang as she opened the door and Cathie looked up to see it bouncing about on a spring above her, giving off a tinny tinkle. The interior was very dim because the panel at the back of the window blocked out the light. The shop was empty, but from the back room came the sound of hammering.

No one came out, so after a few moments Cathie picked up the handbell from the counter and rang it.

'I'll get it!' a man's voice called and a fresh-faced young fellow came out of the rear door. He greeted her with a friendly smile, saying, 'My brother will be with you in a minute. He's just finishing summat.'

'Oh. Right.' She stared at him, deciding he had a kind face and wondering if he'd know anything. Time seemed to pass very slowly and when no one came out from the back she risked saying, 'I didn't come for clogs, but to ask if anyone used to know my mother. She lived round here once. Her father had a second-hand clothing shop. Liza Docherty she was then.'

He gaped at her as if he couldn't believe what he was hearing, then beamed and came round the counter. 'You're Liza Docherty's daughter?'

'Yes.'

'Eh, lass, I'm that glad to see you!' he said, seizing her hand and shaking it vigorously.

'You are?'

'Aye. You see, I think you might be our half-sister.'

In the rear doorway Bob opened his mouth to tell Pat to shut up, but it was too late. The stupid sod had to let it all out, didn't he? Bob closed his eyes and breathed deeply. Bloody pity Pat hadn't been working that day. His brother worked in a variety of casual labouring jobs, which came and went in a chancy way that Bob would have hated. He liked to be sure that money would be coming in every single week, but the clogger's could only support one of them as well as their father, so his four brothers had had to find other ways of earning their living.

He studied the lass again before he spoke, liking what he saw. She didn't seem to have noticed him and was still staring at Pat in shock. Well, he didn't blame her. Fancy blurting it out like that! *I think you might be our half-sister.*

'You know about me?' she asked.

'Aye. Dad got a letter from Australia, saying you were coming to England,' Pat volunteered.

Bob closed his eyes in anguish. It was getting worse! Pat'd be telling her how short of money they were next.

'But no one knew . . .' Her voice trailed away. Two men had known: her Uncle Dermott and – she groped in her mind for a name and found Matthieu Correntin, which brought up an image of a small, neat man seeing her off on the ship. But only her uncle had known the people in Pendleworth, so he must have made it his business to warn them that she was coming, though why he should do that she could not think.

There was the sound of someone clearing his throat and she turned to see a man wearing a leather apron step forward from the back of the room, wearing clogs that made a thumping noise on the bare wooden floor.

He came across and held out his hand. 'I'm Bob Marshall and this is my brother Pat. You must be Cathie?'

She was beyond words as she took the hand, shook it briefly and studied the two men. She was suddenly quite sure they were her half-brothers. It was like looking in a warped mirror – faces, bodies, everything spoke of a connection between them and her. They were very alike, big men with broad shoulders and dusty brown hair. But Bob had a more closed sort of expression as if he never gave anything away without good reason, while Pat's expression was warm and friendly. Indeed, he was still beaming at her and she could not help returning his smile.

He reached out to touch her hairline. 'You've even got the twisty bit that won't lie flat. Aye, you're a Marshall all right.'

Bob decided they were both a right pair of soft ha'porths, so took charge. 'Dad's nipped out but he'll be back soon. Why don't you come through to the back, Cathie?' He looked at Janey as if not sure what to do about her.

'This is Mrs Hamilton,' Cathie said. 'She's not well. I'm being paid to look after her.'

'Eh, she's changed so much I hardly recognised her.

Used to see her around the town. Our other brother works with Magnus Hamilton so we knew his mother was poorly, but not how bad.' He indicated the rear door.

Cathie moved towards it, tugging Janey, but it was a minute before the older woman started moving, as if she'd forgotten how. 'I'll have to bring her with me,' Cathie said apologetically. 'She wanders off sometimes if I don't keep an eye on her.'

He shrugged. 'I don't suppose she'll do much harm.'

The small kitchen clearly doubled as a workshop and would have been better for having its stone-flagged floor swept and scrubbed. Janey would not sit down on the chair Bob pulled out from the table and made faint distressed sounds when Cathie tried to make her.

'Poor owd thing,' said Pat.

'Ah, leave her standing where she is,' said Bob, who didn't care two hoots about the old loony, but wanted to make a good impression on his half-sister.

'What's my father's name?' Cathie asked hesitantly. 'I was attacked and hit over the head in Liverpool and I still can't remember some things clearly, though they're coming back to me bit by bit.'

'Teddy Marshall. Edward, really, but no one ever calls him that.'

Cathie closed her eyes as the name fell into place and other things with it. She remembered her parents discussing her 'real father' one night in bed and worrying that meeting him might upset her. The main thing she wanted to know was out before she could prevent it. 'Why did he not marry my mother?'

'He offered, but she didn't want to marry him from what

he's let drop,' Bob told her, for he was old enough to remember all the fuss when Liza Docherty ran off. 'You can ask him yoursen when he gets back, if you don't believe me.'

Pat pulled a chair towards her. 'I allus wanted a sister,' he said with another of his warm smiles.

Before she could sit down there was a noise outside the back door and an old man came in. He must have been big once but he was stooped now and looked as if he was wearing a larger man's skin. He had a shiny pate, with a tangle of grey hairs scattered to either side of a rather square-shaped head. And he was distinctly dirty, smelling sour even from across the room.

Cathie looked at him in shocked dismay. This couldn't be her father, surely? She turned to see Bob watching her.

'He isn't very lovely, is he?' he said with a sneer. 'But he's the only father we've got.' He pronounced it 'feyther'.

Teddy scowled at them all impartially. 'What are you lot doing lazing around while I have to go out an' deliver the bloody clogs?' He cast an unfriendly glance in Cathie's direction as he added, 'And Sal won't want you bringing your women friends in here. She'll go hairless when she finds out and then you'll be for it.'

'Did you get the money?' Bob demanded, cutting him short and holding out one hand.

'A' course I did.'

'Give it here, then.'

Teddy wriggled his shoulders uncomfortably and held out a few coins.

Bob counted them. 'Where's the rest?'

Teddy's voice took on a whining tone. 'I had a real thirst

on me and me back was aching. It was just the one drink. You can't grudge your old father one little drink.'

Cathie shuddered and wondered how quickly she could get away.

'It'll come out of your wages,' Bob said implacably, then recalled that his half-sister was watching and turned to see the horror on her face. He gave a bitter laugh. 'Not much cop, is he? But he used to be a good clogger once – and at least he had enough about him to get us lot. I don't think us lads are owt to be ashamed of, and you look healthy enough.'

Teddy turned to stare at her. 'What're you talking about, our Bob? I'm used to daft talk from Pat here – soft as butter *he* is – but you usually talk sense. Not but what she's not a pretty lass. Reminds me of someone.' He frowned at Cathie and took a step in her direction, head on one side as he studied her.

She recoiled and bumped into Pat.

'Dad won't hurt you,' he said easily, steadying her. 'And he's not a bad father, really. He used to belt us when we were young, but he allus provided well for us and we never went hungry.'

She looked up at Pat. A bit taller than she was and his father was right – he did have a soft expression on his face. Turning, she looked across at Bob who was chewing one corner of his lip as if puzzled over what to do next. Well, she was puzzled, too.

Janey solved the problem by collapsing to the ground like a rag doll.

'Isn't she Magnus Hamilton's mother, the one as has gone crazy?' Teddy demanded. 'What's *she* doing here? She should be locked away in the Ben, that one should.'

Cathie ignored him and knelt by her charge. 'Come on, Aunt Janey,' she urged, tugging at the older woman's shoulders. 'Stand up and I'll take you home.'

But there was no light of comprehension in those dull eyes and Janey made no attempt whatsoever to move, just curled into a ball.

Pat knelt beside her. 'What can I do to help?'

Cathie sat back on her heels. 'I don't think there's anything much we can do. I shouldn't have brought her out today. I just wanted to see if you were . . .' Her voice faded and she blinked away tears of guilt at doing this to the poor creature on the floor next to her. After Janey's behaviour of the past few days, she definitely should have kept her at home.

Pat laid one hand on hers. 'Well, I'm right glad you've come, but you'll need help getting her back. I'll carry her for you, if you like.'

'Better we put her in the handcart,' Bob said abruptly from right behind them. 'And I think we need to talk before we say owt else, don't you?' His eyes slid for a moment towards their father.

Cathie nodded in relief. She did not want to tell the old man who she was and shuddered at the mere thought of him touching her.

'What's going on here?' demanded Teddy from across the room. 'Who is that lass?'

'She's the one as looks after the old lady, isn't she?'

'Well, what's she doing in our kitchen?'

'Come to look at some clogs.' Bob turned back to his brother. 'You carry the old lady out to the front, Pat lad, and I'll bring the handcart round.' He frowned at his father. 'And you can get on with shaping the next batch, Dad. Where are your glasses?'

His expression surly, Teddy went over to get them from a shelf and perch them on his nose.

'If you do some good work today, I'll maybe forget about the drink money,' Bob said.

'Ah, y're a good lad.' Teddy went to open a door, revealing a small room with a workbench along one wall. It was even untidier than the kitchen. He seemed to have completely forgotten Cathie's presence.

Bob went out of the back door without another word and Pat bent to pick up Janey, settling her carefully in his arms. 'Eh, she's light as a child. It's sad when they get like this, isn't it? But I'm right glad we've found you, Cathie lass.' At the door he hesitated, then added in a low voice, 'Our Bob can be a bit sharp sometimes and cares too much about money, but he's had a lot to put up with from Dad. We thought you'd be rich.'

'I don't have much money, just what I earn.'

Pat smiled again, still blocking the doorway. 'So you're living at Magnus Hamilton's house, are you?'

She nodded. 'Yes, and we're telling folk I'm his cousin, so they won't think we're . . . we're . . .' She flushed hotly.

Pat nodded and tactfully didn't pursue that point. 'I know where he lives. I'd like to bring my wife round to meet you, if that's all right? And we've got two little children, lasses they are – Gilly and Nan. You'll be their auntie. Eh, they'll like that.'

He was so blessedly normal it brought tears to Cathie's eyes as she followed him out. At the door she paused to glance over her shoulder at the old man. He threw her a suspicious look, then bent over his work again.

With a shudder she hurried after Pat, wishing desperately that she'd never started looking for her father. He was horrible! Absolutely horrible! No wonder her mother hadn't wanted to tell her about him.

What had she got herself into now?

Francis woke up to sunlight dancing on the walls of his room and a figure looming by the window. He jerked upright and felt sick at the sight of his so-called tutor standing there.

'Time to get up, lad!'

Francis blinked. 'What time is it?'

'Six o'clock.'

'But breakfast isn't till eight.'

'There will be no breakfast, no food at all, until you've fired a gun.'

'Do you intend to starve me, then?' Francis asked in amazement.

'It's your choice. There's plenty of food if you do as expected.' The old man had come up with this suggestion the evening before, though Eli wasn't sure he liked the idea.

'I'm not firing any guns.'

'You wait till you've hungered for a while and see how you feel about it then. Now up and get yourself washed. I've told them to bring cold water. We're not having you namby-pambying yourself.'

Francis got up, trying to keep his face expressionless.

332

When they got back another man was waiting in the passageway next to the kitchen, wanting to see Baxter.

'Jim Marshall?' Eli asked. 'Good. You'd better come upstairs. Bring your bag.' When they got to Francis's room, he explained, 'Jim's come here to help me, and will be keeping an eye on you when I'm not around. He'll be sleeping in here with you from now on, and you'll both be locked in at night. We don't want you going wandering through the woods again, do we? Or running off anywhere, either?'

And so began one of the longest days Francis could ever remember. He found the hunger difficult, but less difficult than being beaten. When his stomach growled, his new tutor smiled. The other man said nothing, doing as he was told and staring at Francis from time to time with a look of faint puzzlement on his face.

The hardest thing was that they required Francis to attend meals with his uncle when he had to watch them serving all his favourite foods to the old man, who ate with loud appreciation. All they allowed Francis was water. Marshall ate in the kitchen.

The maids avoided Francis's eyes as they served the others. Eli Baxter answered the occasional question from Alexander Stephenson about his experiences in India and attended to his own meal when not required to speak.

When they came out of the dining room, Jim was waiting for them in the hall.

'Master Francis has had his dinner now,' Alexander jeered. 'Take him up to his room. I want a private word with Baxter.'

As he slowly climbed the stairs, followed by his new keeper, Francis wondered what had made his uncle suddenly begin to treat him like this.

When Baxter came up to join them later, he said curtly, 'You two might as well go to bed now.' He closed the door on them and there was the sound of a key turning in the lock.

There was an awkward silence, then Jim said, 'I suppose he's right, lad.' He did not know how to address a young man like this, who would be rich one day, especially when he was here to guard and help bully him. He scowled at that thought. He hadn't realised what they were going to be doing. It seemed a bloody funny business to him, starving a rich lad, it did that! Weren't there enough folk in the world going short without this?

Francis walked slowly across to the bed, sitting down on it for a minute, eyes closed, feeling slightly disoriented.

'You all right?'

Francis looked up to find the man standing beside him. 'No, not really. I feel dizzy.'

'You might as well do as they ask. Never seen folk so determined t'get their own way.'

Another silence, then Francis said, 'Well, I'm not going to. And if they want to starve me to death, it seems I can't stop them.' He began to undress, ignoring the other man as he had ignored his schoolmates in the big dormitories.

He put his nightshirt on and got into bed, but found it hard to sleep. Had Cathie got his note? Was she thinking of him? A tear trickled down his cheek, but now that the lamp was out, the man lying down across the room would never know he was weeping.

On his own narrow bed Jim lay awake for a while, puzzling over what he should do. If they were going to kill the lad, he'd leave before it happened and tell Mr Reuben, he decided in the end. He wasn't going to get involved in something like that. That damned Baxter fellow might even try to blame him. As for the old sod, he was barmy. You only had to look at his eyes to see that. It happened like that sometimes when folk had a seizure as the old fellow clearly had. It affected their brains as well as their bodies. He should be locked up in the Ben.

Which led to another thought. If they killed this lad, how would he and Bob get any money out of Cathie's family? He wished he could ask his brother's advice. They'd said he could have Saturdays off, but that was three days away. And he had to keep an eye on the lad on Mondays on his own while Baxter took a break. They were going to send a groom to help him on those days. That damned sergeant had threatened to pound him senseless if he let the lad escape.

It was daft, all this was! And he'd been stupid to accept the job without finding out exactly what he'd have to do. He kept thinking how angry Bob would be if anything happened to Cathie's other half-brother.

Just as he was falling asleep, he suddenly realised what he could do — till he could ask Bob's advice. He could smuggle in some bread to the lad to keep him going, like. It'd be easy enough to filch a piece or two from the kitchen. And from what he'd overheard, that fat old woman they all called Cook wouldn't mind, even if she knew what he was doing. She was fond of Master Francis, one of the maids had said. Which no one else in this damned place seemed to be.

With a relieved sigh Jim let himself slide into sleep.

With Janey in this new and distressing phase, Cathie waited a day or two to tell Magnus about her family. Then one evening she could hold her news back no longer.

He stared at her in surprise. 'You're Jim Marshall's sister!'

'Half-sister. And I've not met Jim yet, only Bob and Pat.'

'I can't believe it!'

'Don't you like Jim?' she asked.

He shrugged. 'It's not so much a question of disliking him as of – well, understanding what he's like.'

'Tell me. And be honest, please.'

'Well, he's a bit of a rogue. A good worker when he sets his mind to it, but he'd rather find ways of avoiding too much work. The other men like him, though. And he's always pleasant enough. But you have to keep him up to the mark.'

'And the other brothers – have you had much to do with them?'

'No. I've seen Bob around the town, of course, and I've employed Pat a few times for labouring jobs. He's a good worker, but has no feel for the machinery or I'd have given him a steady job. And your father? What about him?' He couldn't remember what the clogger was like, because his mother had always insisted on them wearing proper shoes, however worn and scuffed.

'Horrible. I don't want to tell him who I am, though I

suppose it'll come out one day.' She hesitated, then said, 'I'm not sorry I came to England, and I think I could get very fond of Pat, but I wish I'd never met my father. Mr Lorrimer says he forced himself on my mother and Bob says he did it so she'd have to marry him, but—'

She could not hold back the tears and Magnus could not prevent himself from again taking her in his arms and comforting her. But he didn't kiss her. It was hard not to, but if they were to live together decently he did not dare start kissing that soft, generous mouth, or he might not be able to stop.

When she pulled away, she gave a half-ashamed laugh. 'I feel better for telling you, but I'm sorry to weep all over you again. Um – would you mind if my brothers visited me here? Pat said he'd bring my nieces round to meet me.'

'Of course not, lassie. They're your family.'

She smiled at him and the words were out before she could prevent them. 'You feel like family, too, Magnus. I've been calling you cousin for so long you seem like one.'

He could not say the same to her. She did not affect him as a cousin would, not at all. And she affected him so strongly it was getting harder by the day to hide his true feelings.

CHAPTER SEVENTEEN

August

———◆———

'Mummy?' Josie said one night as they were lying in their bunks.

'Yes, love.'

'I'm glad we're going to England. Is that wicked of me?'

'Why should it be wicked, darling?' Liza asked, puzzled.

'Because we wouldn't have come if Cathie hadn't run away and then the poor little baby died.

In the darkness Liza smiled, though her reaction was bittersweet. 'No, it's not at all wicked of you, Josie. And I'll tell you a secret: I'm glad we're going too. I'm missing Daddy and the others dreadfully, but I'm really looking forward to seeing England again. And most of all to seeing Cathie.' She hadn't told Josie about Francis, not wanting to have her purpose inadvertently revealed by the child.

'Won't she be surprised to see us?' Josie giggled at the thought. Soon she was asleep, her breathing soft and even with none of the gasping that had sometimes worried them all during the dry, dusty summers in Australia.

Liza lay awake for a long time, however, her thoughts turning as they often did to her two missing children. She prayed every night that she would find Cathie safe and happy in England. Only – if the poor girl had found her father, it must have upset her dreadfully. A man like Teddy Marshall could not possibly have grown pleasanter over the years and those boys of his had been bullies, full of suppressed energy and violence. What would they have said to a half-sister who suddenly turned up in Pendleworth?

And then there was Francis. Liza was not sure how she was going to manage to see him, but she would do it even if she had to camp on the doorstep of the big house where she had been so unhappy with her second husband.

Matthieu read Dermott's scrawled note, whistling softly in amazement.

Brendan, who had been working with him on clearing the vegetable garden, looked up and asked, 'Not bad news?'

'No, but Dermott and Christina have left for England already and want me to close up their house, so I'll have to go up to Perth. I wasn't really sure they'd go, you know.' He hesitated, then asked, 'Do you want to come with me?'

Brendan looked down, avoiding his eyes and shaking his head. 'People treat me like an animal up there.'

'Only if you let them. We'll dress you so smartly they won't dare do that. I think my clothes will fit you pretty well. And we might take the boys with us as well, to see if they want to keep anything from the house.' Trust Christina not to think of her sons' needs and wishes.

He smiled. Even though it had only been a few days, James and Charlie had already settled in happily with their grandmother, who was talking of building an extra bedroom on the back for them and who didn't seem to mind the little dog's presence in her inn yard at all, but who did insist on good manners and discouraged cruel practical jokes.

After some persuasion Brendan had a chat with his parents about Matthieu's suggestion. Dinny didn't know what to say, for she too avoided leaving the homestead, but Fergal encouraged him to go and face the demons that were keeping him imprisoned at Brookley, saying sadly, 'You haven't committed a crime as I did, son. There's no need for you to hide away from the world.'

The small cavalcade set off early one morning, taking their time about travelling to Perth. The boys were well behaved most of the time, and when they weren't Matthieu corrected them swiftly and firmly. He corrected Brendan, too, who grew nervous whenever they encountered other travellers, trying to teach the young man to behave with pride in everything he did, as Matthieu's old grandfather had taught him during his own years of youthful uncertainty and rebelliousness.

The house in Perth showed signs of a hasty departure, but three days' hard work soon sorted out its remaining contents. Matthieu then decided to buy a small all-purpose vehicle and found Brendan surprisingly knowledgeable about this, and even more so when it came to choosing some horses. 'You are good with animals, *mon ami*,' he commented.

'I like them.'

'It's a useful skill. I have a cousin who breeds horses in France. Maybe I should send you to him once your French is good enough.' They were talking regularly in that language now, and Matthieu made the two boys join in the lessons. They were very ignorant for a rich man's children, but touchingly responsive to praise and encouragement.

Matthieu had not realised how much he would enjoy guiding these young people and decided ruefully that he had a gift for it. The desire to have children of his own had taken him firmly by the throat now, as well as the desire to see more of Ilse.

When they'd taken the boys back to Brookley, they went on towards the farm. It felt like coming home and the shock of that made Matthieu fall silent.

'Is something wrong?' Brendan asked.

'*Je ne sais pas. J'ai . . .*' Matthieu hesitated, then admitted, 'It feels like coming home. It's a long time since anywhere gave me that feeling.'

'My mother would say the land is welcoming you.'

Matthieu shrugged, then brightened as they saw Ilse and Harry on the track ahead of them. The sight of her made him realise suddenly how he could arrange matters so that he would see more of her. He shoved the reins into his companion's capable hands. 'I'll see you at the farm.'

Brendan watched him stride towards Ilse and drew his own conclusions.

'Frau Hebel.' Matthieu raised his hat and the two of them stood looking at one another.

Ilse tried in vain to stay cold and correct with him, but things had been quiet since Josie and Liza had left, and Harry was more interested in tagging after his father than in his schoolbooks. Even Agnes seemed abstracted lately.

'You look well,' Matthieu said softly. 'How do you manage to remain so elegant in such surroundings?' He offered her his arm. 'I wonder, may I walk with you for a while? I need to ask you something privately.'

She did not answer directly, but looked down at Harry and said, 'Why don't you run home and help your father in the workshop?' He was off almost before she had finished speaking. Then she looked at Matthieu, flushed slightly and took the arm he was offering.

He used his free hand to clasp her hand as it lay on his arm, smiling when that brought a little extra colour into her cheeks. 'As you know, I'm now partly responsible for Mr Docherty's two sons, who are staying with their grandmother and are cousins of Harry's. I wondered – if Mr Caine approves, of course – whether you would consent to give them lessons as well? It would be good for Harry to have company of his own age, and of course Mr Docherty would be happy to pay you extra.'

She had hoped for something more personal because, heaven help her, she'd been thinking of him and wondering if he was thinking of her. But still, this would surely bring her into more contact with him? Was he doing it on purpose? 'I would be happy to do that, but only if Mr Caine agrees.'

'Then perhaps I could come back to Lizabrook with you now and ask him?'

They strolled along, with Matthieu telling her of his trip to Perth. He had been feeling tired, but now felt full of energy and made a humorous tale of it, pleased to make her chuckle.

She thought she had never walked with a man whose steps matched hers so well, or who took so much trouble to entertain her.

Forewarned by Harry of a visitor approaching, Benedict had stopped work and had a quick wash. He was not sure of how to greet Docherty's partner, but was glad of any company at the moment because the evenings dragged without Liza's company, pleasant as Agnes and Ilse were.

When Matthieu had explained his request, Benedict readily gave permission and after much discussion it was decided that Charlie and James should come across to Lizabrook in the mornings, since there was a schoolroom of sorts and equipment there already.

After all the arrangements had been settled Benedict hesitated, then asked Matthieu if he would like to share their evening meal.

'I'd love to, but Brendan will be waiting for me at the farm.'

'Oh, we'll send his brother to let him know there's a meal here.'

The two men sat down on the veranda and began to chat over a pot of tea. Matthieu feigned enjoyment, though at this time of day he would have preferred a glass of wine. He'd brought a few dozen bottles back with him from Perth and was seriously considering starting a vineyard here, since the rear part of his land lay on a gentle slope. He asked Benedict's opinion and that led to an enthusiastic discussion of viticulture, a topic in which Benedict had no experience but about which he was happy to learn.

'We have some grape vines planted,' he said, 'but the fruit is for eating, not wine making, and we dry some to make raisins. The fire missed them, fortunately, though it ruined our orchard. I can let you have some cuttings if you want.'

'Thank you. And we still have more apples than we can possibly use. Neighbours should help one another, do you not think?'

'I didn't realise you intended to settle here permanently, Mr Correntin,' Benedict was saying just as Ilse came to summon them to the big communal table.

She looked at Matthieu in surprise when she heard Benedict's words and saw him nod, then look across at her and smile.

When the meal was over, Matthieu asked Ilse to walk with him to the gate.

As they reached it, he stopped and took both her hands in his. 'My dear Ilse, I would very much like to court you. I wonder – would you give me a chance to show that I can make you happy?'

She stared at him in shock. 'You are very direct.'

He shrugged. 'I see no need to procrastinate. We are both free to make our own decisions.'

She bent her head, not moving, her thoughts in turmoil. At last she looked up at him and said painfully, 'I was not happy in my first marriage. I could not rush into anything, even though I am – not averse to the idea.'

'So we shall take the time to know one another better.' He watched one hand go up to her throat, saw the fear in her eyes and could not help asking, 'Was it very bad, your marriage?'

She nodded, her eyes suddenly bleak.

'I am not a hard man to live with, nor am I violent. And I am prepared to court you properly, give you as much time as you need.' He took her hand and raised it to his lips. 'Give me a chance, *chérie*.'

She nodded, then said softly, '*Ja. Warum nicht?*'

He smiled wryly. 'You do not sound — *enthousiaste.*'

'I'm sorry. It's just you've taken me by surprise. I had thought you were using me to gain information about the Caines.'

'*Chérie*, I would never do that.' He smiled gently at her, finding to his surprise that he too liked the idea of a gentle courtship. 'I shall come and take you for a stroll tomorrow evening. We shall talk and start getting to know one another.'

She could only nod, then stand and watch as he sauntered away. When he turned at the bend in the road to wave, she raised her own hand in response and made her way slowly back to the house. She would tell Agnes, ask her advice.

But she rather thought that Matthieu Correntin would make a charming husband.

At Rawley Manor Jim Marshall sat eating his tea, amazed at the plentiful feasts served to the servants, but also sickened that the poor lad who owned this house was now into his third day without food. And Eli had let slip that the old sod was happy about that. Eli wasn't, Jim could tell that. For all his shouting and blustering, he did not seem at all comfortable with what he was doing.

When no one was looking Jim slipped a piece of bread into his pocket, cursing himself for putting this easy job at risk by this act, but driven by a feeling that it was just not right to starve someone on purpose.

When the meal was over he got up with the rest, reluctant to return to his charge, wondering if Baxter and the old sod had again forced the lad to watch them eat in the big dining room in the main part of the house.

'A moment, if you please, Mr Marshall,' Cook said, leading the way into the small office to one side of the kitchen where she made up her menus and did her accounts.

Jim followed her and waited. What now?

'You put a piece of bread into your pocket, Mr Marshall.'

He stared at her, feeling resentful. What did it matter to her whether he took a piece of bread or not? There was more than enough for everyone. 'I get hungry sometimes between meals,' he muttered by way of an excuse.

She hesitated then said slowly, 'Or maybe you feel sorry for Master Francis?'

Oh, hell, she'd guessed! 'What if I do? I suppose you're going to tell the old man and get me into trouble? Lose me my job?' He pulled the bread out and flung it on the table, turning to leave. 'Well, go ahead then. Don't worry about my poor family and . . .'

She rushed to catch hold of his arm and bang the door shut again. 'I wouldn't say anything if I thought that bread was for Master Francis.' For a long moment they stared at one another then she asked quietly, 'Was it?'

Jim nodded, watching her warily, trying to read her expression. To his surprise he saw tears in her eyes.

'Oh, thank goodness!' She plonked a kiss on his cheek. 'Thank you!' The kiss was followed by a rib-cracking hug, for she was a buxom woman. 'Now you wait here, Mr

Marshall, and I'll find you something better than a piece of dry bread for that poor lad.'

'Well, make sure it isn't big enough to be noticed. That sod Baxter can see a fly thinking!' Jim rubbed at his cheek. What did she want to go a-kissing him for? She must have a soft spot for Master Francis. Bit of luck, that. He listened at the door and heard her outside sending the two maids on errands, then moving quickly to and fro in the kitchen.

After a short time she came back with something flat wrapped in a cloth and held it out to him. 'I don't want any of the maids involved in this. If I lose my place for it, I don't care. I'd have gone long since if it hadn't been for Francis. Here!' When Jim was slow to take it, she slapped it into his hand. 'It's bread and a slice of roast beef. I've squashed it flat so it won't show under your clothes, though if they find it, you can always say it's for you. And don't leave the cloth lying around. Bring it back to me tomorrow.'

Jim tucked the little parcel into his jacket pocket and nodded to her. 'All right, missus. Cook, I mean.'

She gave him a tearful smile. 'I don't know how to thank you, Mr Marshall. I've helped bring that lad up and I can't bear to see him tortured like this. He's a gentle soul, is my Francis, and what's wrong with that?' She blinked her eyes furiously. 'I'll have something else waiting for you tomorrow.'

When he had left, Cook wrote a note to her friend Hatty, who was the cook at Mr Lorrimer's house and who had said her employers wanted to be informed of what was going on with Francis Rawley.

The following day she sent the kitchen maid across to

deliver the note, something she did occasionally when things were quiet. Lasses that age worked better for the occasional brisk walk or other treat, to her mind.

Oh, she did hope the Lorrimers would be able to help poor Master Francis! She couldn't sleep for worrying about her lad. She stood frowning for a moment as she wondered again why Jim Marshall was helping him? He seemed the most unlikely person to have a soft heart.

Jim hid the sandwich under his pillow and waited until he and the boy were locked in the bedroom for the night. Francis lay down on his bed, not undressed yet, looking limp and totally exhausted.

Jim took the parcel across to the bed. 'I've got something for you,' he muttered, holding it out.

Francis didn't even open his eyes.

Jim laid a hand on the boy's shoulder and was upset when he flinched away, upset too at how wan he was looking. That Baxter was a master at hitting folk so it didn't show and strong with it, too, though Jim thought *he* might be able to hold his own if Baxter ever turned on him. The Marshall boys knew how to defend themselves, by hell they did! Lowering his voice he whispered, 'It's food.'

Francis jerked upright and stared at him. When he opened his mouth to speak, Jim clamped his hand across it and hissed, 'Howd your clack, you fool! Do you want *him* to hear us?' He pulled his hand away and was relieved when the boy swallowed and sat staring at him.

'Is this more torture?' he asked at last, his voice low enough not to be heard.

Jim breathed a sigh of relief before growling in an equally low voice, 'No, it bloody isn't! I don't go around starving folk or torturing them. If I'd known what I was getting into I'd not have taken this job. Here!' Again he held out the parcel.

When Francis unwrapped it and saw the food inside, tears began to pour down his cheeks.

Jim stayed where he was, ready to quieten the lad if necessary, but after a few moments the tears dried up and Francis picked up the flattened sandwich. 'Better eat it slowly, lad,' Jim advised. 'Or you'll just bring it straight back up. Best of all if you just ate half of it tonight and kept half for the morning.'

Francis nodded and took a small bite, chewing it carefully and closing his eyes in sheer bliss. When the sandwich was half-finished he stared down at it, reluctant to put it away.

Realising what he was thinking, Jim took the bread out of his hand, wrapping it in the cloth again and taking it over to his own bed. 'I'll keep it till morning for you. Baxter won't search my things, but he might search yours.'

Francis nodded and went across to get a drink of water. They allowed him a full carafe morning and evening, but yesterday Jim had filled the carafe a third time without Baxter realising it. 'How did you get the food?'

Jim shrugged, a bit embarrassed about his own soft-heartedness. 'That cook of yours saw me putting a piece of bread in my pocket and guessed what I was up to, so she give me a proper sandwich for you.'

'Why should you help me? You've been hired to watch me.'

'I can't abide to see folk go without food. Not when they don't need to. Never could.' Jim had made sure his own kids never clemmed, had always brought in a regular wage and slipped the odd jam buttie to Pat's kids when his younger brother was short of work. Not that he wanted folk knowing that, or they'd think him a soft touch.

Francis looked at him, the gaze of someone much older than a mere fifteen years. 'I'm grateful to you. I can't do anything to show my gratitude now, but when I come into my inheritance in six years' time, I'll see you're rewarded, I promise you.' In a tone of surprise, he added, 'It's my birthday soon. I'd forgotten that.'

Jim perked up. 'Well, I'd appreciate any help you can give. I do have a family to look after.'

Francis was trying to think, trying to ignore the hunger that the half-sandwich had done little to assuage. 'Can you get me some more food?'

'Cook says she'll have something ready for me tomorrow. But we'll have to be careful.'

'They didn't tell me your other name. Only Jim.'

Jim looked at him uneasily. 'They said I shouldn't tell you, that it'd be better for me if you didn't know.'

'I can't find you again to reward you if I don't know your full name, can I?'

Jim shrugged. 'Well, it's Marshall, Jim Marshall. And I work at Ludlam's normally, so I'm easy enough to find.'

Francis stared at him in the flickering light from the candle. 'What did you say?' he whispered.

'Marshall. And—'

'Do you know a girl called Cathie?' Francis asked in a low, urgent voice.

Jim stiffened. Now what? 'Might do,' he admitted, glancing instinctively over his shoulder towards the door. 'Why?'

'She's my half-sister.'

Jim grinned. 'Oh, that. I know. She's our half-sister, too.' Silence, then, 'She found her real father?'

'Aye. Just walked into the shop one day, Bob said, to ask if anyone in the street had known her mother.'

'My uncle doesn't know she's here in Pendleworth and he mustn't,' Francis said urgently. 'If he did, he might try to harm her.'

'He'd have us lot to deal with if he tried to hurt her,' Jim said, his hands bunching into fists at the mere thought. 'We look after our own, us Marshalls do.' Even that daft Pat could be relied on to stand by you in times of trouble.

Francis gave him a beaming smile. 'Look after her carefully, then. She's a wonderful person.' His gaze grew thoughtful. 'That makes us sort of step-brothers, doesn't it?'

'Eh, I dunno about that. What I do know is, if we go on talking they might hear us. An' any road, I'm tired if you aren't.' It was exhausting working for that sod Baxter, who kept you on the hop all day long. Magnus bloody Hamilton was nothing compared to the ex-sergeant and it'd be a relief to go back to Ludlam's, though Jim would miss the fresh air. He went across to his bed, embarrassed by all this show of emotion.

Francis nodded and began to get undressed, feeling better than he had for days – though he was still ravenous and light-headed. One sandwich a day wasn't nearly enough.

When his companion started snoring, gentle bubbles of sound that covered any other noises, Francis allowed himself to weep again. But these were tears of hope because he'd found a friend just when he'd given up hope. He smiled through the tears at that thought. No, not a friend. He had spent enough time with Jim Marshall to know that he would do nothing without hope of reward. An ally. That was a better word for it.

Francis frowned in the dark and wriggled into a better position to ease the strain on his bruised arm, which Baxter had twisted behind his back this morning till he'd thought it was going to break. Strange how the pain only made him feel more determined about resisting them. He had never thought of himself as a particularly brave person, still didn't, really. Maybe Jim would carry messages for him? Not written ones, though, which could fall into other people's hands, only verbal messages. He was sure Mr Lorrimer would reward Jim for that.

He slept badly and woke with a start at dawn as Baxter erupted into the room and shook him awake to get dressed. He didn't say anything in response to the petty bullying and slapping around. His uncle was not the only one to use silence as a weapon. And when he had washed and changed, he went down and watched them eat breakfast, sorry he had not been able to eat the half-sandwich. It was not until he was washing his hands before luncheon that he managed to eat it and later Jim slipped him some bread and cheese. Your courage held up even better when you had food in your belly. And an ally living beside you.

*

The following morning Hatty passed the note to her mistress, Edith Lorrimer, saying indignantly, 'I've heard from my friend Barbara at the Manor, ma'am. It seems they're trying to starve that nice young lad into obeying them.'

Edith read it through quickly, her heart sinking. 'Oh, heavens! May I keep this to show to Mr Lorrimer?'

'Certainly, ma'am.'

'Hatty, you're a treasure.'

Bernard read the note twice then closed his eyes for a moment, shaking his head in disbelief.

'Can't we do something to help him now?' Edith asked.

'I'm afraid not. It's only been a few days, and anyway, how can we prove anything?' After some thought he said slowly, 'I'd like to speak to this Jim Marshall in person, though. Who is he? Why is he helping Francis?'

They called Hatty in to ask what she knew about Jim Marshall.

'I'm afraid I don't know anything, sir.'

'Can you try to find out, Hatty?'

'I'll be seeing Barbara on Sunday, sir. We usually go to church together. I can't do anything till then. They don't like me visiting her at the Manor.' She went back to her kitchen, feeling disgusted by the cruel ways of some folk who ought to know better, 'deed they ought.

'I'll ask around, see if anyone knows who Marshall is,' Bernard said.

Edith looked at her husband, her eyes filled with tears. 'That old man is *wicked*.'

'I agree absolutely. But he is still Francis's lawfully appointed guardian.'

*

Jim found his brother Bob waiting for him at his home when he had his first Saturday off. He was a bit annoyed about that because he had wanted to spend time with his wife and kids. He was surprised at how much he'd missed them. But Bob insisted they go for a walk so that they could talk privately and wouldn't take no for an answer.

'Well?' he demanded as soon as they were clear of the house.

Jim scowled at him. 'Well, what?'

'Tell me about it.'

Feeling superior for once, Jim described his first few days at the Manor.

By the time he had finished, Bob was frowning. 'I think you're a fool to risk helping him.'

'Easy for you to say. You don't have to sit and watch a poor lad starving, do you?'

'Are they trying to kill him, do you think?'

Jim shrugged. 'I don't reckon so, just force him to do what they want. I don't know why he won't go hunting or shooting. Seems daft to me to argue about that sort of thing.'

'What's the lad like?'

'Soft, but all right. A bit like our Pat, really.'

Bob rolled his eyes. 'Just what we need. Another daft ha'porth to keep an eye on. But Francis did promise you a reward one day?'

'I told you he did.'

'Right then. You'd better keep feeding him. But you watch your step. Don't let them catch you.'

'He wants me to get word to his sister about what's going on.' Jim grinned. '*Our* sister. Funny to be related to the nobs, isn't it?'

'I'll go and see her for you and let her know what's happening.'

'Right then. I'm going home now.' His wife, not usually demonstrative and often sharp-tongued, had flung her arms round him and burst into tears when he returned this morning. It was a funny sodding world, it was that.

Francis realised one day that his fifteenth birthday had passed. He hadn't even noticed it himself, because the days seemed to run together, each one as unhappy as the last. He felt distant most of the time and very weak physically. In his bleakest moments he wondered how long it would be before he died.

His meetings with Cathie seemed like a distant dream now, a wonderful taste of what it meant to have a family. If it hadn't been for Jim, he did not know what he would have done. Killed himself, perhaps. The thought that there was someone who cared enough to help him, when the outside world seemed to be ignoring him, made a big difference. As did the food Jim smuggled in to him.

But Francis did not for one moment consider giving in to his uncle. He would not, could not, be like him. And if that meant betraying his class, well, so be it. He would not betray himself.

CHAPTER EIGHTEEN

August–September

———◆———

It took Janey Hamilton several weeks to die. Her body clung tenaciously to life, though it grew so frail and thin she hardly caused a bump under the covers. Her mind seemed completely dead now, and she never walked again or ate of her own accord after they returned from the clogger's shop.

The house was so quiet now that Cathie sometimes sang to keep herself cheerful, but the songs faded of their own accord and she spent a lot of time lost in her own thoughts – and regrets. She found time hanging very heavily on her hands and joined a penny library, devouring books as she sat with the old lady. It was ironic that she had come to England to avoid an isolated life, and found herself in a similar situation. But Magnus needed her and she would not let him down. Besides – she smiled – she had the evenings with him. That compensated a lot for the quiet days.

Bob Marshall had called one afternoon to tell her about the situation at the Manor, but with Janey dying inch by inch Cathie had to set aside her worries about Francis and concentrate on her charge. At least Jim was slipping her brother some food; looking after Janey was all she could do for Magnus now. His deep sadness had dimmed the bright energy he had always radiated before and he, too, often seemed lost in thought.

Knowing they would soon lose their mother, Mairi came over from Bury every single Sunday, sometimes with her husband, sometimes on her own. On one visit she thanked Cathie for what she was doing. 'I don't know what Magnus would have done without you, and it's relieved my mind knowing you're here. I felt guilty about leaving him with her, but Elwyn needed me, too, and I thought Magnus would have to put Mum in the Ben when I'd gone.' She sighed and changed the subject. 'You've remembered everything about your past now?'

'I think so.' Cathie reached out to poke the fire, avoiding her companion's eyes. 'It's a sorry tale of a wilful girl, I'm afraid. I ran away from home to find my real father – and to escape from life in the bush, which is very lonely. I'm not sorry I left and I'm never going back, but I'm very ashamed of the way I did things.'

'You've written to your family, though?'

'Several times. But it's not the same as saying goodbye properly, is it? At least your brothers said goodbye. And I haven't heard from home yet, because there hasn't been time for a reply to get here from Australia.'

Mairi let the silence lengthen for a few moments then asked hesitantly, 'What will you do after Mother dies?'

Cathie shrugged. That thought was worrying her as well. 'I don't know. Dr Barnes said once that he could find me a job nursing. I do have to earn a living and obviously I won't be able to stay here.'

'If you're stuck for somewhere to live, you could come and stay with Elwyn and me for a time. That'll help allay the rumours, make people think you really are our cousin.'

'Thanks, but I want to be near my brothers, especially Francis.'

'Well, if you're ever in need, the offer is still open.'

When Mairi left to catch her train, several neighbours were standing on their doorsteps gossiping. She gave Cathie a hug, winked at her and whispered, 'That'll make them think twice.'

She watched Mairi and Magnus walk along the street, then went inside again to wash up the tea things.

It was funny, she thought, how many half-brothers she had here now. Francis and Three Marshalls. She really liked Pat, though she deplored his lack of ambition and easy-going ways. There were times when his family went hungry, she guessed, but he was making little attempt to find himself a more permanent job. She was sure Bob's family didn't go hungry and had already discovered how hard he worked and how determined he was to better himself. But he wasn't nearly as nice as Pat. Too determined. Too sharp with everyone. And then there was Jim, who seemed to care for no one but himself, but who was sneaking food to Francis. He was a puzzle to her still.

Best not to think of her other half-brother, she told herself, plunging her hands into the hot water. Best just to get on with her work here till she was needed no more. Then she'd see if she could help Francis, whatever Mr Lorrimer said.

*

The day after Mairi's visit, Dr Barnes came to visit Janey just as Cathie was trying yet again to give her charge a drink of milk. He suggested gently that she was only prolonging the painful decline by doing this.

'But I can't just let her starve to death!' Cathie protested, horrified.

'My dear,' he put his big hand over hers and looked at her very solemnly, 'it'll be a merciful release. Let her go.'

'It's hard to do that to anyone.'

'Yes. But you're a good nurse and will have nothing to blame yourself for.'

She plucked up her courage. 'Afterwards, you did say you'd find me other nursing jobs?'

'I'll be happy to do that. There's always a call for good nurses. Have you ever assisted with childbirth?'

'No. It's mostly been accidents I've had to deal with, or nursing my younger brothers and sister when they were sick.' She pulled a wry face. 'I've done a lot of that. I'd like to learn more about childbearing, though. In fact, if I were a man I'd like to be a doctor.'

He laughed indulgently. 'Each to his own sphere, my dear. Or *her* own sphere, I should say. I find women better at nursing the sick than men, and we men are better at learning the complexities of doctoring. Don't let these foolish, strident "new women" turn your head. Elizabeth Garrett Anderson may *call* herself a doctor, but no one of sense is going to take her seriously. No wonder she treats mainly women and children. No man would let himself be examined by her or have faith in her capabilities. Women like her are going against nature by becoming doctors. It is a fad which will soon fade away.'

Cathie could see he felt strongly on this point so bit back a sharp response. She had better not contradict him if she wanted his help. Later that evening she complained about his attitude to Magnus.

'I'd not like to see you trying to become a doctor either, lassie,' he said. 'It's not that you couldn't learn what to do, never that – I know how intelligent you are – but I wouldn't want you to have to see the dreadful sights doctors face.'

'I think about *helping* people, not about whether they look nice or not when they're in pain,' she said quietly.

'Well, you're helping me more than I can say with what you're doing for my mother. She hasn't been easy to look after. I don't know how to thank you.' He hesitated, then added, 'You must get very bored here on your own now, so I brought you this.' He went across to where his jacket was hanging on the door and pulled a little parcel wrapped in brown paper out of it.

She opened it in delight, finding it a volume of poetry. 'Oh, I shall love this!' When she turned to the flyleaf she asked, 'Would you inscribe it for me?'

'Aye.' He went into the front room to fetch the ink and fitted a new nib into the holder with its mother-of-pearl handle. He held it out to show her. 'This was the last present Mam ever bought me and I shall always treasure it.' Then he dipped the nib carefully into the ink pot and wrote in her book in his fine copperplate script.

When he handed it to her, she read: *To Cathie, to whom I owe a great deal for her help with my mother. Fondest regards, Magnus.* 'I shall always treasure this.' She ran her fingers over the fine leather binding, wondering if the word 'fondest' meant anything special, then telling herself not to be so foolish.

'It's getting late now, but maybe we can read some of the poems together in the evenings. I can show you my favourites.'

'I shall look forward to that.' She clasped the book to her bosom.

He looked at her glowing expression and love surged up in him, so that he nearly spoke his feelings aloud. But he had vowed to do nothing about it while she was still under his roof. It would not feel right, somehow, as if he were taking advantage of her.

Bob had come to the house several times now with messages from Francis. They had stopped starving the lad, it seemed, but only because he'd grown very thin and weak. They didn't want to kill him, Jim reckoned. Well, Baxter had said as much one day, when frustration had made him confide that he'd never expected this one to be so hard to crack.

'Oh, I wish I could do something to help him!' Cathie exclaimed. 'But at least they're feeding him again.'

'Only bread and water.'

She clicked her tongue in distress. 'That's not fit food for a growing lad. Why, you should have seen what my brothers Seth and Lucas ate! Mother always said they had hollow legs.'

'Our Jim's took a real liking to your Francis,' Bob told her another day as he ate a piece of the cake Cathie had baked. He waved it at her. 'Good, this! I wish my wife could make 'em, but she says bread and jam come to the same thing.' After another appreciative bite, he returned to his topic. 'Never seen owt like it, our Jim getting upset. That sod don't usually care for anyone but hissen and his family.'

'I'm glad of it.' She sighed and confided, 'When Mrs Hamilton dies, I'm going to try to rescue Francis. Will you help me? Will Jim, do you think?'

Bob goggled at her. 'You can't be serious, lass!' He did not intend to risk prison by breaking into the Manor, or being thrown out of his home and shop, which would be almost as bad.

Her lips set in a mutinous line. 'I am serious. Very serious. What they're doing isn't right. Francis could go to our mother in Australia. I know she'd be delighted to have him.'

'Nay, they'd guess and have the ships searched for runaways.'

'Maybe. But if we rescued him just before a ship was leaving, they might not have time to do that. Magnus is going to find out about sailing dates for me.'

'Sweet on him, aren't you?'

She flushed. 'There's nothing going on between us.'

'The more fool him, then. If I had a bonny lass under my roof, I'd not let her sleep alone.' In contradiction of that he added, 'Mind you, I'm not having anyone messing around with my sister, so you let me know if he tries owt on.'

She smiled at him. She was getting to know the Marshalls now. Truculent, but loyal. Doing whatever it took to make a living for themselves and their families in a hard world.

Changing the subject, Bob asked suddenly, 'Do you still

want to keep who you are secret from my father? Only he's asking why I keep coming to see you. How the old sod knows about it, I don't know, because I haven't said a word. It's a good thing my Min knows the real reason because he went and told her about it. He'll not go running off with tales to her again, though, not if he wants the money for his ale.'

She spoke slowly, choosing her words with care. 'I don't see how any good can come from telling him, given the sort of man he is. At present the fewer people who know who I am the better. As far as everyone is concerned, I'm Caitlin Rutherford, Magnus's cousin.'

'Ah, but do they believe you?' There was still gossip about her and Magnus.

'They pretend they do because his sister is very respectable and she tells them I'm her cousin, too. The important thing is that no one should find out who I really am.'

'Aye, you're right. That old sod at the Manor might try to harm you, an' maybe us as well.'

That week the Lorrimers invited Reuben Ludlam to dine with them. When he arrived he found he was to be the only guest and could not hide his puzzlement because he did not know them nearly well enough for an intimate family evening like this, since they did not visit at the Hall and he'd only met them at his grandmother's.

'I need to talk to you privately about something,' Bernard said. 'This seemed the best way to do it. Come into my study for a few minutes, would you?'

Edith was already walking away, so Reuben followed him into the cosy, book-lined room just off the hall. 'What do we need to talk about?' he asked in puzzlement.

'Jim Marshall.'

Reuben stared at him. '*Jim Marshall!* What has he to do with anything?'

'He's guarding Francis Rawley.'

'Yes. Though not by my wish.' His father was still very vague about when Marshall would be returning to the workshop and what exactly he was doing at the Manor, which was annoying because for all his grumbling ways, Jim was a skilled and experienced workman who was sorely missed.

Bernard took the plunge and asked, 'Do you know that they're trying to starve young Francis into submission?'

'*Starve him!*'

'Yes. He's apparently grown very thin. At first they gave him only water, but now they've got him on bread and water.'

'That sounds a bit drastic, but my father says the lad's been seriously misbehaving.'

'Only to the extent of refusing to hunt or shoot. You must judge for yourself whether those are heinous crimes.'

Reuben frowned. 'I heard he'd been sent down from school for misbehaving as well.'

'No. He was sent home because he'd been ill. Stephenson has hired a private tutor to toughen him up.'

'But my father said —'

'— what Stephenson told him. I've written to a chap I know and he's been to see the headmaster. It appears Francis is a gentle lad who can't stand to kill things. He used to be teased by the other lads for that and he didn't work particularly hard, but that's all. No question of him misbehaving. Rather the reverse, in fact.'

There was a silence while Reuben took this in. 'I feel sorry for him, then,' he said eventually. 'Stephenson can be vicious when his pride is injured. In the past my father has kicked one or two families out of our houses to oblige him, though I've put a stop to that now. How do you know all this?'

'Their cook's been sending me messages and I arranged to meet Jim on his day off last weekend to question him in detail. He isn't happy about the situation, so with Cook's help he's been slipping extra food to Francis, but he has to be careful and can only smuggle so much in. The so-called tutor is an old military man and keeps a very firm hand on things. I'd — um — appreciate it if you didn't tell anyone else about that, though, or Jim too will be in trouble.'

'No, of course not. But I don't see what we can do about it. Stephenson *is* his guardian, after all.'

'Jim thinks Stephenson is behaving irrationally. He's apparently had a seizure of some sort and his behaviour has changed. All the women servants are terrified of upsetting him these days.' Jim's actual words were, 'The old sod's crazy. There are more sensible folk locked up in the Ben, there are that!'

Reuben let out a long, low whistle.

'This treatment could permanently damage Francis's health if it goes on. Growing lads need good food and he wasn't in the best of health anyway. So what I wondered was whether you could get your father to talk to the old man and see whether *he* thinks Stephenson is — well, completely rational.'

Reuben pursed his lips. 'I'll *ask* Father, though I'm not sure whether he'll agree to it. He believes people of our class should support one another. But I'll definitely ask him.'

'I'd be grateful.' Bernard could see that he'd given Reuben a lot to think of so said in a lighter tone, 'And now that is decided, let's go in to dinner.'

But although the food was excellent, none of them ate heartily or were very good company. It was hard to do justice to a plate full of good food when you knew a lad was being half-starved only a few hundred yards away.

As he took his leave, Reuben said, 'If you think of any other way for me to help, don't hesitate to ask. I take it you're prepared to do something yourself if things go on for too long?'

Bernard nodded his hand. 'Yes, I am. After all, he has a mother in Australia who'd give him a home and be thrilled to do so.'

'Bit drastic, sending him to Australia.'

'Very. And definitely against the law. I shall only do that in an emergency, to save his life.'

Janey Hamilton died during a stormy night in early September. She had been gasping for breath all day, faint pitiful sounds. Cathie had never kept watch over a deathbed before but she did that night, sitting quietly beside Magnus while the space between his mother's breaths seemed to grow longer and longer. Then suddenly the breathing stopped with a faint rattling sound.

Silence enfolded them and for a moment or two neither of them moved. Then Magnus murmured, 'Lord keep her safe!' and reached out to close his mother's eyes.

When Cathie laid her hand on his shoulder, he turned to her and raised his hand to cover hers. 'I'm glad she's gone. Is that wrong? She would have hated to be like this.'

Thunder shook the house and lightning slashed across the sky.

'I don't think it's wrong.' Cathie had once helped Dinny lay out an old man who had been brought to her when he fell ill and died while passing through Brookley, so she knew what to do. And the human body was not something she feared. 'I can lay her out if you'll bring me some warm water.'

'Is there no end to your kindness, lassie?' he said in a wondering tone.

She did not dare say it, but she thought: Not where you're concerned, Magnus, as she waved him away.

When she had finished her task, she realised with surprise that it had grown light and that the storm had passed, leaving a freshness and sparkle to the air, with droplets of water on the window panes catching the early rays of the sun. She opened the window wide and stayed for a moment beside it, breathing in the fresh scents.

When she went downstairs she found Magnus sitting at the kitchen table with his head propped on his hands. He looked up as she came in and she saw that his cheeks were wet.

Going across to push the kettle on to the hot centre of the range top she said quietly, 'I must move out of here now.' She had already found a place which offered lodgings to 'young women of decent character' and could only hope they would not heed the gossip about her.

'I suppose so. What shall you do? Do you need any money?' Not the time to speak of their future with his mother still unburied.

'I have a little money saved and Dr Barnes said he could find me a nursing job.'

'You're not leaving Pendleworth?' Magnus hesitated then added, 'I don't want you to go away, Caitlin. This isn't the time, but – well, there are things I want to say to you, lassie.'

She stared at him. Did this mean what it sounded like?

He looked back at her gravely. 'We'll talk about it later.'

Her heart lifted at the warmth in his eyes, but she remembered her brother and knew she must help him before she thought of herself and Magnus. 'I can't go away while they're ill-treating Francis – but I wouldn't want to anyway. My mother sometimes teased me, said I was her little legacy from Lancashire. And the strange thing is I feel at home here as I never felt at home on the farm, though my parents love it in Australia and so do my brothers.'

She liked the lively people of Pendleworth who faced hard lives with determination and good humour; even liked the sound of their rather raucous voices as they called to one another across the streets. She stopped sometimes to watch children play. If she ever had any children, she would not shut them away on a bush homestead. Her walks had shown her a different Lancashire as well, with its green rolling moors beckoning her to go striding across them. She would do one day.

Magnus's voice came out harsher than he had intended. 'Caitlin, ye canna go against a man in Alexander Stephenson's position.' He knew before she spoke that he was wasting his breath, for her face took on that determined expression he had come to know so well. She was unlike other young women of his acquaintance, more self-reliant and outgoing, and he didn't know whether this was because she had grown up in Australia or whether it was just her own nature.

'I can go against him if I have to,' she insisted. 'I've waited until your mother didn't need me any more, but I can't wait any longer. I'm going to ask Bob and Pat to help me, and if necessary we'll break in one night and rescue Francis.'

'Look – wait until we've buried my mother and I'll . . .' Magnus broke off to say, 'We can't discuss it now.' He'd have to think good and hard about this. He wasn't having her getting in trouble with the law. 'I need to tell my sister that Mother's dead and arrange a funeral. Caitlin, would you go over to Bury for me today and tell Mairi? There are plenty of trains and I'm sure she'll want to come back with you.'

'Of course.' That would also solve her problem about staying in the house without the nominal chaperonage of Janey.

Mairi might be able to talk sense to Caitlin about rescuing Francis, Magnus decided as he wrote a quick note to his sister, telling her of their mother's death and explaining Caitlin's situation. If they couldn't dissuade his lassie, well, he'd have to find a way to help her rescue her brother. He had never broken the law in his life before –

never had the time to get into trouble, for he had been busy helping raise his brothers and sister ever since he could remember – but for Caitlin he would do even that, he suddenly realised. 'And since Mairi will be here, you can stay another night or two, eh? Maybe she can help find you somewhere to stay among her old friends at church.'

And there they left it. Cathie went to get ready and he sat down to make a list of all he had to do. Once the funeral was over he would also have a quiet word with Bob Marshall and beg him to refuse if Caitlin asked him to do anything stupid. Stephenson employed gamekeepers and outdoor staff. They might even shoot at her. Magnus couldn't bear to think of her being hurt.

CHAPTER NINETEEN

September

———◆———

At Rawley Manor Jim woke up just before dawn and heard a sound he couldn't place for a minute or two. He lay there frowning as he tried to work out what it was, then suddenly realised it was coming from the other bed, so got up and padded across to see what was wrong. He found Francis tossing and turning, his breath rasping in his throat, his face flushed.

'You all right, lad?' Jim asked.

Francis rolled his head to stare at him, then muttered, 'Feel awful. Bit sniffly yesterday, dreadful s'morning.' He raised his head but let it drop almost immediately. 'Dizzy. Chest hurts.'

Jim got dressed rapidly and began to pound on the wall that adjoined Baxter's room. Trust the sod not to come early today. He heard signs of someone stirring next door, but Baxter didn't open the door for what seemed a very long time. Jim hadn't minded being locked in before because it meant they got a warning if someone was coming, but he minded it now. Very much. What if the lad went and died on him?

Suddenly that locked door seemed a stupid thing to

accept, but when he'd come here he'd thought these nobs knew everything. Only they didn't. And the old man was definitely barmy. Being rich didn't save you from that. Jim sighed in relief at the sound of boots clumping towards the door.

A key turned in the lock and Baxter erupted into the room with his usual noise and scowls. 'Why were you banging? And why is he still lying there?'

Before he could go across and yank Francis out of the bed, as he had done once or twice before, Jim grabbed his arm. 'The lad's ill.'

'He's pretending.'

'See for yourself.'

Baxter went over to the bed. Francis was muttering and tossing, seeming unaware of them now, his face flushed, his breathing stertorous. 'Stupid sod. Can't even stay healthy.' Baxter stared sourly down at the lad whose spirit he hadn't been able to break and whom he had grown to dislike intensely.

'It was getting wet two days ago what done it, I reckon,' Jim told him with relish. 'You should've let him change his clothes after that walk, like *you* did. He's caught his death o' cold an' it's all your fault.' He went to stand on the other side of Francis, looking down at him. 'I reckon he needs a doctor. Unless Mr Stephenson *wants* him to die.'

'Of course he doesn't.' Baxter breathed in deeply, still studying Francis and listening to his laboured breathing. 'You wait here. Don't let him get out.'

'Does he look like he can go anywhere?' Jim folded his arms and stayed where he was as Baxter went tramping off down the corridor again. Why did the stupid twit allus make so much noise when he walked?

It was a full half hour later before anyone came to see them, by which time Jim had bathed Francis's forehead and tried in vain to get him to drink some water. When he risked a peep out of the door, puzzled by the slowness of the approaching footsteps, he saw old Stephenson shuffling towards him. Darting back inside, he took up his position on the far side of the bed again, arms folded. If the old man didn't send for the doctor, he was leaving here and telling that Mr Lorrimer what was going on. And even if they did send for the doctor, once Francis was better Jim was still going to leave. He'd had enough of this, more than enough. Give him a good honest job in the mill any day, even with Magnus bloody Hamilton breathing down your neck.

Without saying a word Alexander Stephenson stood by the side of the bed and observed his great-nephew: thin and flushed with fever, definitely not faking. 'Damnation! Can the lad do nothing right?' he demanded.

Francis opened his eyes and stared at him. As he recognised who it was, hatred blazed in those eyes along with the fever. But he didn't say anything and nor did the old man. After a minute Francis sighed and closed his eyes again.

'Send for the doctor, then!' Stephenson ordered. 'And send a message to Cook to prepare some beef tea.' He went away feeling furious with his stupid great-nephew, muttering to himself in a way that made Hilda stare at him in astonishment as she passed him in the corridor. And when he insisted on going down to breakfast in his night-shirt, his manservant stared too.

Jim stayed by the bed, sponging the lad's body as the fever rose because he had seen his wife do this when one of his own kids was ill. He was more relieved than he'd have admitted when the doctor finally arrived towards the middle of the morning. Since Baxter was suffering from the belly gripes – and serve the bastard right for eating so much! – and had had to rush out a minute ago, Jim was on his own.

Dr Barnes looked down at the boy and frowned. 'Has he always been so thin?'

After a quick glance over his shoulder, Jim whispered, 'They've been starving him to force him to do what they want. No food at all for the first few days I were here, then only bread and water since, an' that's four or five weeks now. It's no wonder he's took ill.'

Footsteps came hurrying back.

'Don't say I told you or they'll turn me off an' then he'll have no one to look out for him.' Jim took a hasty step backwards.

Clifford Barnes closed his eyes for a moment in sheer horror. He could not believe that a lad who was the owner of all this should have been brought so low by deliberate ill-treatment.

'Why is the boy so thin?' he asked the tutor.

Baxter glanced sideways at Jim, but found him gazing at the floor. 'Outgrown his strength,' he offered.

Clifford bit back a sharp response. 'Well, whatever the cause, he needs feeding up. Beef tea, for a start. Some lightly poached fish. Stewed fruit. Custard. And get a fire lit in here. We don't want it too hot, mind you, just steady warmth and a little fresh air from the window.'

'The master doesn't believe in pampering young men,' Baxter said, as if a request for a fire on a chilly autumn day were unreasonable.

'It's a case of either pamper him or lose him!' the doctor snapped. 'I'll speak to Mr Stephenson myself before I go.'

When Clifford Barnes went downstairs, no one came into the hall so he went into the library which he knew to be Stephenson's usual refuge. Here there was a blazing fire in contrast to the icy temperature in the bedroom and the rest of the house. The old man was sitting in front of it with a tray full of food on a small table before him. Clifford Barnes's gorge rose at the contrast.

Alexander turned round. 'Who asked you to come in here?'

'I'm the doctor. You sent for me.'

'I don't need a doctor. Go away!' He flapped one hand irritably.

Clifford Barnes stared at him, seeing the signs of recent degeneration and a seizure of some sort, and wondering why he had not been called in when this happened. 'I need to speak to you. Your nephew is in a bad way.'

The old man stuffed another forkful of ham into his mouth and said indistinctly as he chewed it, 'He deserves it. Don't be misled by that angelic face of his. Francis is wicked and disobedient, should have been beaten into shape years ago. *Would* have been if it hadn't been for my sister's foolish fondness for him.' He cackled with sudden laughter. 'But he's learning to toe the line now. Oh, yes, he's learning what is expected of him.'

Clifford stared in shock as the old man started a rambling monologue about his nephew being the son of an ill-bred and coarse woman, and how shameful it was to see a good family brought down to this. From that the old man went on to decry modern manners then fell on his food again, muttering to himself as he picked among the plates with greasy fingers.

When he looked up a moment later to see the doctor still standing there, he rang a little handbell and laughed again, a high-pitched sound which sent a chill running down Clifford Barnes's spine. He knew seizures could cause changes in personality, but he had never seen a more marked case of it.

'Are you well?' he asked. 'Pardon me, but you seem to have—'

'I'm perfectly sound. Don't need your help.'

A maid came hurrying into the room and bobbed a curtsy.

'Show the doctor out!' Stephenson snapped.

'But what about your nephew?' Clifford demanded.

'Do what it takes to get him better, but don't spoil him. Deal with Baxter. And don't come near *me* again. Just send the bill. Doctors always send bills, don't they? Damned leeches.'

Clifford turned and left the room, pausing in the hall to say, 'I need to speak to your cook.'

The maid nodded and led the way to the rear of the hall.

'Wait!' He caught hold of her arm before she could push open a baize-covered door. 'Has Mr Stephenson been acting strangely lately?'

Fear settled on her face for a moment and she glanced round to check no one was near before nodding. Then, as if afraid of even that small action, she pushed the door open, hurrying ahead of him to prevent further speech.

'I'd like a word with you in private,' he told Cook.

'I'll join you if I may?' Baxter, who had been standing warming himself near the fire, moved forward.

'I have nothing further to say to you, sir,' said Clifford crisply.

'But I'm the boy's tutor.'

'Then I say shame on you for treating him like that.'

Baxter glared at him. 'What do you mean? Who's been saying things?'

'No one needs to say anything. If you think I'm blind to the bruises on his arms and legs, or to the way he has grown over-thin, then you're taking me for a fool — which I'm not. I have no confidence that you will heed my instructions, so prefer to give them to Cook.' He spoke loudly enough that the two maids in the kitchen could hear every word and by their expressions they were relishing what they were hearing.

Before Baxter could reply, Cook led the doctor into her own room and closed the door firmly on the tutor.

'I'm that glad to see you, sir,' she said, pulling out a large white handkerchief and mopping her eyes. Then, after a glance towards the door, she beckoned him across to the window and whispered, 'How is he, really?'

'Francis is very ill indeed,' Clifford admitted. 'He's got a raging fever.'

'That's because they wouldn't let him change his wet clothes the other day.'

'I have orders from Mr Stephenson to do what is necessary to ensure that the lad recovers, though I'm afraid I can't promise anything. His constitution has been weakened by this ill-treatment.' Clifford saw her shocked expression and said slowly, 'I think it will be best if I send a nurse to look after Francis. Your part will be to provide light, nourishing food. And you are to let me know personally if anyone tries to prevent that.'

'Mr Lorrimer is taking an interest in Mr Francis, too,' she whispered, with another glance towards the door. 'Me and his cook are friends and I let them know how things are.'

'Is he now?'

'Yes. Mr Francis got friendly with his sons, you see, though he was forbidden to talk to any of the young folk round here. Eh, they've treated that lad shamefully, they have that, even before Mr Baxter came to be his tutor – though he's like no tutor I've ever seen, 'deed he isn't, the brute.'

Clifford patted her shoulder. 'Pull yourself together, my good woman. And be sure you let your friend know how things stand.'

She blew her nose loudly and muttered, 'No use weeping. There's cooking to be done. Egg custard. Easily swallowed. Compôte of stewed fruit. Goes down without them noticing it.'

When Dr Barnes went back into the kitchen he approached the tutor who was still standing by the fire and didn't look too well himself. 'I'm sending a nurse to look after Francis.'

'I don't think that's necessary, sir. Jim can do what's needed.' Baxter gave a huge sneeze.

'I'll judge what is and isn't necessary. Mr Stephenson has given me express orders to ensure the lad's recovery –

though that I cannot guarantee. Moreover, if you have a cold, you should stay away from him.'

Baxter stared at him in amazement. 'He *can't* be that ill!'

'He is. And his poor physical condition makes me seriously worried about his ability to recover – some blame for which lies at your door, sir!'

'I've done nothing I wasn't ordered to,' he protested.

'Then shame on you for accepting such unreasonable orders from a man who is clearly in his dotage!' snapped the doctor.

As soon as he got home, Clifford sent a message round to Magnus Hamilton's house, for with Janey Hamilton dead he hoped the young cousin would be willing to take on another nursing job. Most of his regular nurses were out on jobs, there being a spate of babies among the town's more affluent families, but he had great confidence in Miss Rutherford. Some women had an instinct for caring for others and she was one of them.

The messenger was lucky enough to find Cathie packing her bags after Mairi's departure. The funeral had taken place the previous day and now she had to move out. One of Mairi's friends from chapel had agreed to take her as a lodger, but Cathie wished she did not have to leave Magnus on his own.

Within minutes of receiving the message she was round at the doctor's house.

'Miss Rutherford, are you free to nurse Francis Rawley?' he asked, tapping his pencil on the desk and scowling out of the window. 'The lad has been ill-treated at his uncle's orders. He's thin and covered in bruises, and sadly he has contracted a severe inflammation of the lungs.' Her face turned so white he stared at her in shock. 'Is something wrong?'

Cathie pulled herself together. If she betrayed her connection to Francis she was sure she would not be allowed to look after him. 'I've just been rushing around rather a lot and I haven't eaten yet today, but I'm well, really I am.'

'How soon can you be ready to go to the Manor?'

'Within the hour.'

'I'll arrange for a cab to pick you up, then. You will live in there till the patient recovers.' He paused, as if waiting for something, then prompted, 'You haven't asked about payment?'

How stupid of her! 'I – um – trust you to see that I receive a suitable wage. And I am relieved to get any job. I feel it proper to move out of my cousin's house now that my aunt has passed away.'

'Very well, then. You'd better go and get ready. I shall be calling to see Francis morning and evening, but these are my instructions . . .'

On the way back to the house, Cathie called to inform Mairi's friend that she would not now need the lodgings, then hurried home. She packed her bags at lightning speed and scribbled a note to Magnus, explaining what had happened and assuring him that she would find a way to send him a message once she was settled in.

She was delighted at this unexpected opportunity to see Francis, but her delight faded to terror when she saw how ill he was. He was stick-thin and looked dreadful, wheezing and struggling for breath. She could not bear to lose him now, not when she had just found him!

Standing opposite her by the sickbed Jim said quietly, 'Just tell me what to do, lass. I'm not used to nursing folk, but who else is there to help him save you and me? I don't trust that Baxter an inch! That sod would do owt for money.' He lowered his voice still further as he added, 'And old Stephenson is as barmy as they come, though he pulls hisself together when posh folk come to the house. You should see him the rest of the time, though. Eh, he should be locked away, he should that.'

As the ship neared France the weather calmed down again and Dermott staggered up on deck desperate for some fresh air. Christina had been an absolute shrew for the past two days, acting as if she was the only one feeling unwell.

Some children were playing near the rail and he stood watching them, wondering suddenly what his own sons were doing. He wished he hadn't left them in Australia. He was proud of his sturdy lads and their high spirits. Still, Matthieu wasn't a fool and he'd keep an eye on them.

Things had, Dermott decided gloomily, gone downhill rapidly since he'd left Melbourne. He was losing his grip and it was more than time he pulled himself together. He must have been mad to buy that sodding farm, even at such a low price.

His sister and her husband were fools. Who else but fools would settle in the middle of bloody nowhere and work themselves into an early grave clearing and farming a patch of sandy scrub? Let her rot there from now on, for all he cared! He hoped she found Cathie quickly and went right back to Australia and he never saw her again. Except he still needed to find out where she had buried their brother Niall. He couldn't feel easy till he knew that.

When he went back to the cabin, he pulled out his last bottle of rum and took a good big swig.

'Do you have to drink it like that?' Christina demanded. 'We do have glasses.'

'You should try a bit yourself. It helps in rough weather.'

'Nothing helps. I feel awful!' She moaned and pressed a hand to her forehead.

'Ah, pull yourself together, woman!' he told her. 'We need to plan what we're going to do when we get there.'

She raised her head. 'Go to see my aunt, of course. What else?'

Just to show he was still master and not getting soft, he said, 'Not till we've been to Pendleworth and visited my mother's grave, we aren't.'

That made her screech at him like a fishwife. But having made the decision, he wasn't backing off. He was still master in his own household and intended to remain so. Besides, he knew what Christina would be like when she got together with that aunt of hers. They'd both be looking down their nose at him. He was going to have a very serious talk with her before he let her anywhere near the old lady.

And, he realised, he did have a fancy to visit some of his childhood haunts again. He wanted to show the folk from Underby Street how well he'd done for himself. He wondered if Teddy Marshall was still alive, which reminded him again of his niece. Not a bad lass, Cathie.

He didn't wish *her* any harm. Maybe he'd see her again, too.

Only desperation would make him undertake such a long journey again. England it was going to be from now on. And respectability. Dermott grinned at the thought.

Liza watched the buildings of Liverpool grow more distinct as the ship approached the docks. The sky was grey and the wind icy, but although she was warmly wrapped she kept shivering and her head was aching. She turned to Josie, standing beside her wide-eyed. 'Are you cold, love? Would you like to go below?'

'No. I want to see everything. Isn't it big?'

So Liza stayed on deck with her daughter until her teeth were chattering, then had to go and rest in her cabin until they were allowed to disembark. What a time to feel poorly! She told herself not to give in to it and tried to remain cheerful.

When they disembarked, Josie laughed at how awkward it was to walk steadily on land, and remained bright-eyed and interested in everything she saw.

Feeling distinctly wobbly, Liza signalled to a porter, who took their luggage and found them a cab. Since the afternoon was drawing on, she asked him to recommend somewhere respectable to stay and he drove them to a small but comfortable lodging house.

While Josie was investigating every detail of their bedroom, Liza consulted the landlady about train timetables for the following day, determined to go straight to Pendleworth. Surely Cathie would be there?

'Never fear, we'll get you to the station on time,' the

landlady said genially. 'Excuse me for asking, but you don't look well.'

'I think I must be starting a cold. I feel very shivery.'

'I'll bring you up some tea and we'll give you a fine supper tonight too. That'll make you feel better. You'll be sick of ship food. It's got no nourishment in it by the time you've been at sea for a few weeks. My late husband was a sailor and you wouldn't believe the tales he had to tell.'

But in spite of the landlady's cosseting, Liza could not eat much of the evening meal and decided to go to bed early. It was wonderful to have so much space and not to be surrounded by the noises of other people, but if only her head would stop aching.

'Are you sure we'll be able to find Cathie?' Josie asked as they got ready for bed. She had asked the same question a dozen times already.

'We'll ask Mr Lorrimer to help us,' Liza said, not giving her a goodnight kiss because she didn't want to pass the cold on.

The following morning Liza felt so bad she could hardly lift her head. Josie flung on some clothes and went to fetch the landlady, who tutted and sent for the doctor.

He diagnosed influenza and insisted Mrs Caine spend the week in bed. She felt too ill to argue.

Josie proved as devoted a nurse as her big sister and the landlady was a cheerful soul who took everything in her stride, keeping an eye on Josie, taking her to market and sending her out on a sightseeing trip with a young neighbour on the Saturday, because Mrs Caine was looking a bit brighter.

But Liza could not help fretting. To come so far, then

to be held up like this! And although she was recovering she was still so weak and wobbly she could not think of travelling yet.

Cathie began to sponge Francis down again as his fever rose. Jim helped her turn him and it didn't occur to either of them to worry that he was naked. This was no time for false modesty. For the past two days, they'd taken it in turns to sleep and had hardly left his side. He was holding his own, but barely.

Baxter did little to help them, coming to stand in the doorway occasionally and watching them. He was now suffering from a streaming cold and the doctor insisted he was not to go near the sick lad.

They thought nothing of it when they heard footsteps in the corridor, then a rasping voice asked, 'Who's the young woman?'

Cathie turned to look at the man she guessed was Alexander Stephenson, shocked when she saw the wild look in his eyes. 'I'm Caitlin Rutherford, the nurse Dr Barnes sent to look after your nephew.'

'He didn't say you were young and pretty.' Alexander came to stand on the other side of the bed from her. She had a vague memory of an old gentleman who had come to the station and made her mother leave Pendleworth, but would not have recognised him in this wild-eyed person whose clothing was liberally stained with food.

She said nothing, just continued to sponge down her half-brother.

'Like it, do you?' he asked. 'Like tending men's bodies?'

'My job is to look after sick people, sir. It doesn't matter to me whether they're men or women. My last patient was an old woman.'

'Make sure nursing him is all you do. He doesn't deserve any of the extra comforts you women can offer a man.'

She became suddenly aware that Francis had come out of his delirium and was staring up at his uncle. 'Lie still,' she said quietly. 'Let us cool you down.'

He turned to stare at her and his mouth opened in shock as he recognised her.

Fortunately, Alexander Stephenson was already turning away. 'Get him better,' he threw over his shoulder, 'then we'll make a gentleman of him.'

When he had gone Francis said, 'Are you real?'

Cathie leaned closer to whisper, 'Yes. Very real. I've come to nurse you. But I'm called Caitlin now. Can you remember that?'

But he had fallen into another doze.

'It's to be hoped he don't give you away,' Jim said gloomily. 'The fat would be in the fire, then.'

His hopes were not realised. The very next morning, Francis said wonderingly, 'Cathie. You *are* real. I'll be all right now you're here.'

From the doorway Baxter said sharply, 'Why is he calling you Cathie?'

She shrugged. 'I don't know. Perhaps he's confusing me with someone. His mind is still wandering.'

He stared at her thoughtfully, but did not press the point. There was something going on here. She and Marshall were altogether too comfortable together. It was as if they were both working against him, and a good general didn't allow the troops to band together against him.

That evening he found Marshall talking to the cook in a corner of the kitchen and lingered behind the door, listening to them. What he saw made him swell with fury. The sod had been slipping the lad food all along. He went storming along to see the old man.

Alexander looked up in annoyance as Baxter came into the library. 'What do you want?'

'I want to fire Marshall. I'm not satisfied with him.'

The old man shrugged. 'Up to you. You can bring in one of the stable lads instead to help that nurse.'

Baxter hesitated. 'There's something else. Francis called that nurse Cathie. Does he know anyone called Cathie?'

'What did you say?'

'He called her Cathie.'

'I thought she was called Caitlin!'

'So did I.'

Stephenson scowled at him. 'Well, you just get rid of Marshall. I'll deal with the nurse if I have to.' He didn't like having a woman tending the lad. They were too soft, women were.

CHAPTER TWENTY

September

———◆———

Dermott handed Christina out of the train at Pendleworth station and paused to look around the platform. 'This place hasn't changed much, any road.'

She was more concerned with their baggage counting the trunks and cases off the train then tugging at her husband's arm because he was still staring round. 'Where are we going to stay?'

'Where's the best hotel?' he asked the porter, tossing him a coin.

'The new one, sir. Just opposite the station. I could wheel your luggage across easy.'

'You do that, lad.' He swept Christina a mocking bow and offered her his arm, ignoring the sour look she cast at Market Square.

When they were installed in the hotel's only suite, Dermott went to gaze out of the window. 'It's not raining for once. Come on, let's go and have a proper look around.'

'You go. Visit your mother's grave, or whatever it is you want to do, then we can leave this horrid town tomorrow.' She went to huddle by the fire which was just starting to blaze up in the grate of the large draughty sitting room.

'I'll go and see Mam's grave tomorrow. Today I want to go back to the street I was born. Don't you want to see your old house? We could get a cab out to Ashleigh.'

'I don't want to go anywhere, let alone our old house. I'm tired of travelling.' She flung herself down on a sofa. 'When you go down, ask them where that tea is. I ordered it ages ago.'

He grinned and left her to her misery. She'd been sulking ever since he refused to take her to Paris or let her go shopping in London. Tomorrow he'd drag her out for a stroll whether she wanted it or not. Today he was quite pleased at the thought of some time to himself.

It felt strange to be back. As he strolled along, he noted the civic improvements in the town centre with a snort of amusement. Library, floral gardens, new Town Hall. You might doll up the main street, but behind it on one side was the ugly mass of the gasworks and on the other the big chimney of Ludlam's mill. That damned thing stood where it always had, belching out black smoke as if to set its mark on the huddle of terraced streets that clustered around it.

Only, he thought in deep satisfaction, nowadays he'd not need to kow-tow to a Ludlam – or to a Rawley, either.

Underby Street looked different. What had been his da's secondhand clothing shop was now a haberdasher's, with a window crammed full of the bits and pieces women seemed to need. But opposite it, the clogger's shop was still there. New sign, same pile of clogs in the window. He sauntered across just as a fellow came barrelling along the street, bumping into him with a muttered apology and slamming open the door of the clogger's without looking behind him. Intrigued, Dermott followed and listened to the conversation.

The man started talking as soon as the back door of the shop was open. 'That sod Baxter's just sacked me. Didn't even give me time to pack. Said they'd send my luggage home before the end of the day.'

The other man put down his chisel. 'What have you been getting up to now, our Jim?'

'That's the whole point. I've done nowt but look after that lad.'

Jim took three steps one way, met the wall and retraced his steps till he hit the sagging sofa. 'Stephenson's up to summat. An' our sister's out there still. I don't like this, Bob, I don't like it at all. What if they're intending to hurt her?'

'Ah, you're imagining things. An' if they've sacked you, you'd better get over to the workshop, hadn't you? Make sure Ludlam's still have a job there for you.'

Dermott left the shop quietly. What had happened to old Teddy? Was he still alive? He grinned. The Marshall lads were still getting themselves into trouble and Cathie had obviously found her family. The sons seemed to accept her well enough and Dermott discovered with mild surprise that he was glad the lass was all right. Then he frowned and stopped walking for a moment. But was Stephenson really intending to harm her? Why should he do that? She was related to the old man through marriage.

A few paces later he stopped again, even more surprised to discover that he'd feel responsible if anything happened to Cathie. He'd sent her over here – but not for anyone to harm. He definitely wasn't having that.

As he moved on he decided to look into things. And when he met one of his old cronies walking along the street, the sort of fellow who was good at finding things out, it seemed meant to be.

Not till he was re-entering the hotel did Dermott realise this meant staying on a bit longer in Pendleworth. Christina would go mad about that. He grinned. Well, let her.

They would only go and see that aunt of hers when he was good and ready.

Grumbling all the way, Jim headed towards the mill, standing in the small gateway the workers used and gazing across the yard with a jaundiced eye. He hated being shut up inside this damned place. Ah, to hell with it! He'd give himself an hour or two at home first, then come back later. No one would know what time he'd been fired, would they?

But as luck would have it – this was definitely not his day – his foreman came into the yard just as Jim was turning to leave.

Magnus greeted him with, 'I thought you were working at the Manor.'

'I were. Only they don't want me no more.'

'Oh? Lost your place, did you? What have you been doing?'

Jim hunched one shoulder. 'Not helping 'em kill that young lad. I'm better out of that business. But our Cathie's still there, an' how they'll treat her without me to keep an eye on things, I don't know. Anyone as treats their own kin like that old sod's been treating his nephew wouldn't think twice about harming the lad's nurse.'

Magnus pulled him quickly round a corner. 'What do you mean? Who's trying to kill Francis Rawley? Is Caitlin all right?'

'If you ask me, nothing's right up there. That old fellow's lost his wits and gone nasty with it. He's got 'em starving and beating that poor lad.'

Magnus stared at him in horror. 'You're not making this up?'

Jim stuck his chin out. 'Cathie's my sister. Us Marshalls look after one another. An' young Francis is *her* half-brother, so he's a connection, too. He seems a nice lad to me, but that tutor is a nasty bit of work, does just what the old lunatic says. An' who's to stop 'em now I'm gone? Tell me that, eh!'

'I've got to go and bring her home again.'

Jim cocked one eye at him. 'Got an interest in our Cathie, haven't you? I thought as much. I hope your intentions are honest, then. We won't stand for you messing her around.' He loved saying that to Magnus Bloody Hamilton.

Realising he'd betrayed himself, Magnus shrugged. 'Yes, they are honest. And if I'd been at home when she got that offer, she'd never have gone to work for Stephenson in the first place. She doesn't realise the power rich folk have.' There had been tales of strange happenings out at the Manor for a while. Everyone in town knew it wasn't a good place to work.

'Ah, you're right there. They've got too much bloody power.' Jim kicked idly at a stone and watched it bounce off the mill wall. 'Talking of rescuing the lad, she was. Not afraid of anyone, that lass isn't. Only we couldn't rescue him till he got better because he was like to die.'

Reuben Ludlam walked past just then, then realised whom he had seen and turned back. 'What are you doing here, Marshall? I thought you were working up at the Manor.'

Jim shrugged. 'They don't want me no more.'

Reuben hesitated, then realised it wouldn't be wise to talk openly out here so said abruptly, 'Come into my office.'

Magnus began to follow them.

'I'll send him back to the workshop when I'm done, Hamilton.'

But Magnus could not bear to be left out, not when Caitlin might be in danger. 'Begging your pardon, sir, but my cousin's involved and I'm worried about her.'

'Cousin?'

'She's the one nursing Francis Rawley.'

'You'd better join us, then.' Reuben led the way into his office.

Jim was offered a chair and if he hadn't been so worried about what was happening at the Manor, would have enjoyed himself, sitting there like a bloody nob.

'Tell us what's going on!' Reuben ordered. When Jim had finished his tale, he began tapping his right index finger against his left in a way he had when thinking hard about something. 'Mr Lorrimer is worried about the lad, too. I think it's time for us to intervene. I'll send someone to – no, will *you* go to his rooms for me, Hamilton? Insist on seeing Mr Lorrimer straight away and tell him what's been going on. Ask him to come round here. I'm not helping harm someone.'

But before anyone could decide what to do, Cathie found herself in serious trouble. Alexander Stephenson had been puzzling over where he'd heard the name 'Cathie' and suddenly realised that it was the name of Francis's half-sister, the one who had borne Ludlam's name. Only she wasn't a Ludlam, it had turned out, but a bastard brat foisted on to Josiah by *that woman*.

Fury sizzled through him. *Her* daughter had wormed her way into the Manor and that could not be allowed.

When a maid knocked on the door and would have come in with a tray, he shouted to her to go away. 'Tell the servants to get their own food. I don't want mine yet.'

Once she had left, he began to pace up and down again, laughing as he suddenly thought of a solution.

He walked across to the door. Seeing no servants lurking in the hall he crept up the stairs, grinning at what he was going to do. Luck was with him. Even his own bedroom was unoccupied.

Taking a worn leather purse from his drawer, Alexander filled it with sovereigns and slipped it into his pocket. Then he tiptoed up the next flight of stairs to the nurse's bedroom and looked for somewhere to hide the purse. He found an empty travelling bag under the bed, hid the purse in it and pushed the bag back into place. There'd be no reason for her to look inside it – not till it was too late.

He went downstairs again and rang for his own food, eating it with a hearty appetite.

Afterwards he went up to his room to change his clothes, but no sooner had he got there than he rang for his manservant and made a big fuss about his missing purse, insisting it had been stolen. 'Send for the police!'

'But, sir—'

Stephenson raised his voice. 'Do as I say or you'll lose your job. What do I pay you for? I give the orders here and don't you forget it.'

Cathie heard the noise of the old man shouting in the distance, but ignored it. She was finding it hard to manage without Jim's help and was tired after several disturbed nights. But she had her reward when Francis woke up and looked at her, really looked at her for the first time with his eyes clear of fever brightness.

His eyes lit up. 'Cathie?' Then he looked round in terror. 'What are you doing here? You're in danger.'

'I'm nursing you. And it's all right, they don't know who I am. I go by the name of Caitlin Rutherford. Can you remember that? Caitlin. Besides, there's nothing your uncle can do but dismiss me.' She smoothed the sweaty tangle of fair hair from his forehead. 'How are you feeling, love?'

He closed his eyes. 'Dreadful.'

'Can you drink a little beef tea, do you think? I have some keeping warm by the fire.' She'd been spooning tiny amounts into his mouth as well as lukewarm water and milk. Every spoonful seemed a step forward in the battle to save his life.

'Not hungry.'

'Just have a sip or two.'

But although he struggled to do as she asked, after a few mouthfuls he pushed the spoon away. 'So tired.' Closing his eyes, he fell asleep again almost immediately.

Two hours later Baxter opened the door. 'You're wanted downstairs, Miss Rutherford.'

'Is something wrong?'

'Not my place to say.'

Her thoughts were more on her patient than herself. 'If Francis wakes, will you give him something to drink? Even a spoonful helps, I'm sure.'

'Yes.' Eli watched her go. Stephenson was up to something. There were two policemen downstairs with him and he had a triumphant look on his face. What was the old sod plotting now? Eli looked down at Francis, who was sleeping uneasily. He hoped the lad would not wake up. What did he know about sickrooms and invalids?

The head groom was waiting for Cathie at the top of the stairs. 'I'm to take you down, miss.'

She looked at Horace in puzzlement. She knew her own way down.

In the library were two policemen and Mr Stephenson, the latter sitting by the fire with a blanket over his knees. Cathie hesitated by the door.

'She's the one!' Alexander declared at once, pointing one bony finger. 'She's the only one who could have taken it. All the other servants were having their dinner. Besides, she's a stranger and they're not. I should have known better than to employ someone like her. The sort of women who go nursing are no better than they ought to be.'

The policemen, who had heard all this before as they waited, shifted uneasily. The young woman at the door not

only looked fresh-faced and respectable but bewildered –
though you couldn't always tell, of course. They exchanged
glances that told each they were not sure of this situation.

Cathie stepped forward, her heart thudding. She was
determined not to be cowed by anyone, so she addressed
Mr Stephenson directly. 'What are you accusing me of? I
haven't taken anything.'

'Then you won't object to us searching your room,
miss?'

Cathie stilled as Mr Stephenson smiled. She had taken
nothing, but she hadn't been near her room for hours. 'I
haven't taken anything,' she repeated. 'I haven't even been
near my bedroom since early this morning. I've been
looking after Francis who is still very ill.'

Alexander Stephenson leaned forward and nearly spat
the words at her, 'Don't you dare call him Francis in that
familiar way! A slut like you . . . I shouldn't have taken you
into my house.'

'I'm not a slut!' she exclaimed indignantly.

He ignored her and began to rant on again, going over
the same ground as he had already covered several times.
The droop to his mouth was even more marked this
morning and as he wiped moisture from it impatiently with
a crumpled handkerchief, his hand shook.

The two policemen exchanged another glance. The
sergeant had told them to obey Mr Stephenson, who was
rich and influential, but the old man was talking so
strangely that if he hadn't been who he was, they'd have
dismissed everything he said as rubbish.

When the flood of words eased, one of them said
quietly, 'Could you show us your room, miss?'

'What am I accused of taking?' Cathie asked on the way up, but they didn't answer.

They searched her bed, lifting the feather mattress, then the more solid mattress beneath it, while she stood there with her arms folded, getting angrier and angrier. They then began to investigate her drawers, pulling all her underwear out, to her great embarrassment, and leaving it scattered on the untidy bed. Finally, one of them looked beneath her bed and pulled out her travelling bag.

He opened it and said, 'Aaaah!' then looked sternly across at her. 'Is this yours, miss?' He held up a shabby leather purse.

'No. Definitely not. I've never seen it before.'

'Then how did it get here?'

'I should think,' she said bitterly, 'someone put it there to incriminate me while I was looking after Francis.'

They gave her disbelieving glances.

'We'll have to take you down to the police station,' one of them said. 'If you'd just put your coat and hat on, miss?'

'To the police station?' She could not believe this was happening to her.

'If you please, miss.' They were waiting for her in the doorway.

She looked from one to the other. 'But let alone I didn't take that purse, what's going to happen to Francis? He's ill and Mr Stephenson dismissed Jim Marshall this morning. There'll be no one to look after him. He could *die!*'

But they would not listen to her and she found herself being escorted outside and helped into a shabby cab, which then drove them into town.

Dermott's informant Bert came to find him at the hotel, but he was still out. The proprietor suggested the visitor see Mrs Docherty if the matter was so important. After some hesitation he agreed.

Christina swept down the stairs dressed in all her finery, took one look at the scruffy creature waiting in a small room at the rear of the entrance hall and nearly went back to her suite. Then she decided to find out what her husband was up to and controlled her annoyance. 'Well? What do you want?'

'I need to see Dermott. Urgent, it is.'

'*Mr Docherty* to you.'

He grinned. 'It weren't *Mr Docherty* this morning when him an' me had a chat an' he asked me to keep me eyes open.'

Ignoring his impudence, she said loftily, 'I'm his wife. Tell me and I'll see he's informed.'

Bert shook his head. Dermott had mentioned money and women never paid you as much. Mean buggers, women. 'It's for his ears only.'

'How much?' She had a little purse hanging under her skirt and pulled it through the side slit.

Bert pursed his lips, then breathed a sigh of relief as Dermott walked in.

'You're soon back, lad.'

'Ah. Heard summat, didn't I, *Dermott*?' The last was spoken with a mocking glance towards Christina.

'Tell me.'

'That nurse you was interested in has been arrested.

Down at the police station, she is. Stole a purse, they say.'

'Who's she supposed to have stolen it from?'

'Stephenson.' Bert scowled as he said the name. His brother had worked in the gardens up at the Manor till Stephenson took a dislike to him, and the head groom had beaten Tom up before they sacked him, saying he'd better keep his mouth shut about what was going on up there. Here was a chance to get even with the sods.

Dermott stood chewing his lip, thinking. 'Is she down at the police station now?'

'Yes. I come over here straight off soon as I heard.'

'Good lad.' He handed over a coin, the value of which made Christina suck in her breath angrily. 'And if you find out anything else, either about the young lady or the folk at the Manor, let me know at once.' He glanced sideways at his wife. 'No one else. Me.'

'Ye're a good lad, Dermott,' Bert said with a grin.

'Aye, but I'll be an angry lad if you go boozing before I've sorted this lot out.'

Bert's smile faded. 'Aw, just the one.'

'Up to you. But if you come to me with ale on your breath, I'm paying nowt more.'

Bert fingered the coin and decided he could wait to celebrate. He'd go and find his brother, who still knew folk up at the Manor.

When the man had gone, Christina turned to her husband. 'You're not going to get involved in this, surely?'

Dermott had been wondering why he was bothering, but this annoyed him. 'I'm going to find out what's happening before I do owt. She *is* my niece, after all.'

'The daughter of a woman you hate.'

'I don't hate Cathie, though.'

Cathie was feeling terrified. They'd questioned her again on arrival at the police station, then locked her in a cell while the sergeant 'considered the situation'. She didn't know what to do. Her first thought was to ask for Magnus, then her cheeks burned at the thought of him seeing her in this situation. She'd written to him from the Manor a few days ago, but had not received a reply.

After a few moments she remembered Mr Lorrimer with a sob of relief. She knocked on the door of the cell and called, 'Excuse me!' But no one came.

She went back to sit on the narrow bench, feeling quite sick with worry now. What was going to happen to her? She could be tried and put in prison. She shivered at the thought. Even being locked in this chilly cell was horrible. It made you feel as if you were suffocating. And it was so cold that in the end she wrapped the folded blanket round her shoulders, glad of its rough warmth.

When she heard the sound of a key in the door, she stood up, relieved. Surely they'd come to tell her it was a mistake?

But it was a woman with a tray on which was a piece of bread and butter and a thick cup of strong tea. A policeman stood just outside the door.

'Constable, could you ask the sergeant if I can speak to him, *please*?' Cathie pleaded.

He shook his head. 'Sergeant's having his dinner. He'll see you later.'

'But this is urgent. I need to—' He shut the door in her face and all she heard were footsteps tramping down the passage, then silence.

She couldn't hold back the tears as she picked up the cup of tea in fingers that trembled. What was she going to do? What if no one believed her?

CHAPTER TWENTY-ONE

September

Thinking about matters carefully over his midday meal Sergeant Horly decided he needed more information about this alleged theft at Rawley Manor. He had had considerable experience of criminals and prided himself on his ability to spot a liar at ten paces. He did not think Miss Caitlin Rutherford was either a criminal or a liar, unless she was the best actress he had ever met — which was just vaguely possible, but not probable. He chewed his lamb and mashed potatoes slowly as he turned things over in his mind, for he did his best thinking while eating. When he had pushed that plate away, he went on to eat his apple pie and custard with equal deliberation and enjoyment.

Mr Stephenson's message had referred to the young woman as a 'slut of a nurse'. Having met her, Sergeant Horly could not agree with this description and wondered at its use. What's more, his men said Mr Stephenson had spoken wildly and if he hadn't been a rich man they would not have believed a word he'd said. Only — Alexander Stephenson *was* a very rich man and therefore Sergeant Horly intended to treat this case with particular caution and care. He did not want to lose his job.

The first thing to do, he decided as he licked the last traces of the custard thoughtfully from his spoon, was to find out more about the situation. He swallowed a final mouthful of tea and heaved himself up from the table to send one of his men out to the Manor again to question the servants.

Constable Dimmott went to the back door of Rawley Manor, having no desire whatsoever to meet Mr Stephenson again. When a young maid opened it, she squeaked in shock, did not invite him in and called for Cook to, 'Come quick! There's a policeman at the door.'

Cook came to stand before him with arms folded and asked brusquely, 'Can I help you, constable?'

Cecil Dimmott seized the moment by giving her a winning smile. 'The sergeant needs a little more information about Miss Rutherford and I'm sure what *you* say is bound to be reliable.'

She glanced over her shoulder and lowered her voice. 'We've orders to let no one into the house, I'm afraid, but I'm happy to talk to you here if you're quick. More than happy, because you'll never persuade me that Caitlin Rutherford is a thief.' She swelled with indignation at the mere idea and repeated firmly, 'Never!'

'You wouldn't know anything about the nurse's whereabouts during the earlier part of the morning when the theft occurred, would you?'

'Indeed I would. I've asked the maids who were cleaning upstairs within hearing of the master's room and neither of them saw or heard a sign of her round there. Not a sign! And every time they passed Mr Francis's door, she was right there, looking after him. Though one of them did see the master go upstairs just after she'd taken his lunch tray away.'

'It was very sensible of you to make inquiries, ma'am, if you don't mind my saying so, because who can understand what's going on inside the house better than those who work here?' He waited and sure enough further information was forthcoming.

'Caitlin Rutherford is a devoted nurse and she's saved Master Francis's life, whatever *a certain person* says. You wouldn't find anyone more caring than her, not if you searched all of Lancashire, you wouldn't.' Cook hesitated, then added, 'And to tell you the truth, Mr Stephenson has been behaving very strangely of late. If it weren't for Master Francis I'd have left months ago.'

In her indignation her voice had risen on the last words and suddenly the man the constable thought of as 'that mad old bugger' erupted from behind an inner door, looking furiously angry.

Cecil Dimmott nearly dropped his helmet in shock and Cook let out a loud screech before clasping one hand to her bosom and muttering, 'Giving a body palpitations like that!'

'I'll give you palpitations,' Stephenson shouted in a piercing voice that could have been heard a hundred yards away. 'You're dismissed, you fat, stupid female! And make sure you get out of my house within the hour! You're as much a slut as *she* was. That's why you're defending her.'

Cook drew herself up with great dignity. 'I shall be glad to leave.'

'No references. And I'll make sure you don't find another job in Pendleworth.'

She did not answer, but turned and marched away with stately tread. When Stephenson darted forward and gave her a shove which sent her staggering into a wall, she righted herself quickly and glared at him. 'That is *not* the behaviour of a gentleman.'

He laughed wildly, then turned back to the constable. 'As for you . . .'

Cecil Dimmott, who had been observing this behaviour in utter amazement, took a step backwards, but the old man followed him, jabbing one finger into the constable's chest to emphasise his words.

'I shall be complaining to the Chief Constable. Daring to come here and question my servants without my permission.' Spittle dribbled unheeded out of one corner of his mouth and his words were slightly slurred. 'There was no need for it. *No need at all!* I've told the police what they need to know. It's their duty now to lock that slut up. Are they daring to challenge my word? Are you, fellow?'

Cecil retreated another step, but the old man followed, bony finger still jabbing.

'She's as bad as her mother before her, that one is. She stole my nephew out there in Australia, destroyed our good name. Women like her should be locked away. Blood and breeding will out. But I'll not let any more women near that boy till he grows up. Not one! He's to be made into a man, do you hear me, not a namby-pamby fool!'

Prudently Constable Dimmott continued to back away, unable to make head or tail of all this. After a few paces, the old bugger stopped following him, but the shrill voice followed him all the way to the edge of the kitchen gardens and when he looked back he could see Stephenson glaring at him.

As he hurried down the drive, Cecil shook his head and settled his helmet more firmly in place. There was something very strange happening here, no doubt about it, and he wouldn't be in his sergeant's boots for anything.

When the constable got to the end of the drive, he slowed down as the gatekeeper came out of his cottage, clearly wanting to speak. After a quick look behind him to make sure he couldn't be spotted from the house, Cecil stopped. 'Did you want to speak to me, sir?'

'Is summat else wrong at the big house, then?' Roskin the gatekeeper asked.

'Just pursuing inquiries.'

'There was a right old fussation up there this morning. They sacked Jim Marshall, then that tutor left as well. Baxter, he's called. Treated poor Master Francis something shocking, my wife tells me. She helps with the washing up there.' Roskin drew breath and rushed on, 'Just packed his bags, that Baxter did, and brought 'em down here hissen in a wheelbarrow. When I asked what were up, he telled me he knew when to beat the retreat. Said he'd had enough of working for a madman. Then he left his bags near my back door and walked into town. Came back in a cab to collect 'em half an hour later and off he went. What do you think of that, eh?'

'Very strange. Do you know where this Baxter has gone?'

'No. But I envy him, I do that. I wish I could leave here, too, only I'm tied to this house, aren't I? Wife came home proper upset today.' Roskin shook his head and sucked in air loudly through a gap in his teeth before continuing,

'Says she's never seen the likes of it. They've accused the nurse of stealing — as nice a lass as you'd ever hope to meet, my wife says — and that poor lad still at death's door, hardly able to draw breath. And who'll be next, tell me that, eh? At this rate we'll none of us have jobs here no more. We'll be turned out to starve in the streets — or he'll accuse *us* of theft next.'

A pause, then he added in a low voice, though there was no chance of anyone overhearing him, 'None of the maids don't think she did it, you know. They think the master must have put the purse in her room hissen.'

Which gave Cecil Dimmott a great deal to mull over on his way back into town, and set deep frown lines in his sergeant's brow when the constable passed the information on.

In Liverpool Liza's influenza lingered and it was lucky she had both a caring landlady and a daughter who, like her older sister, seemed to delight in looking after sick people. Josie bustled to and fro, full of importance, bringing drinks and helping her mother wash or change her nightgown. In the afternoons, when children got home from the new elementary school just down the road, Josie sometimes went out and played with the landlady's nieces if her mother didn't need her. The improvement in her health which had begun on the voyage had continued on land, and she was as loud and full of energy as any of them, without any of that dreadful wheezing.

After two long weeks, during which Liza fretted at her incarceration first in her bedroom, then in the landlady's front parlour, she declared herself fit to travel again. Josie and the landlady both protested that it was too soon, but she overrode them, even though she still did not feel her usual self.

By the time she got to the station, she was regretting her rashness but decided she could rest again when she got to Pendleworth. While a porter helped them on to the train and dealt with their large pile of luggage, she got into the carriage on legs that trembled and sank gratefully down on the seat, leaning her head back against the upholstery, infuriated that she was still so weak.

By the time they arrived Josie had told her mother several times that she was very pale, and indeed Liza was feeling so dizzy and weak that she found it difficult to think clearly.

A fatherly porter retrieved their luggage with Josie's help while Liza sat on a bench, then he escorted them across the square to a hotel which was new since she had lived here. They went into a very modern-looking reception hall, where small square tables and wooden settles were arranged along the walls with great precision and where the wall-paper pattern was so strong that it hurt Liza's eyes, especially when taken in conjunction with the equally strong pattern on the carpet that ran down the centre of the floor. The walls were also embellished by several pictures of Scotland grouped tastefully around a picture of Her Majesty, looking heavy and elderly and sombre.

As they were waiting for a fussy old lady in a virulently purple and green outfit to be attended to, Liza put a hand up to her aching forehead and rubbed it. She felt very wobbly and distant and was longing to lie down. Then she heard a loud voice she recognised and gasped in shock. Stiffening her spine, she turned to face the owner of that voice, hoping she had been mistaken.

But she had not.

At the other end of the hall Dermott broke off in mid-sentence and stopped moving so abruptly that his wife bumped into him. He continued to stand there, looking equally shocked.

Before either of them could say a word, everything began to whirl round Liza and the last thing she heard was her daughter's scream.

When she awoke she was lying on a sofa with Josie kneeling beside her sobbing and Dermott standing by a fireplace scowling. For a moment she could not speak, only meet his gaze and hope her fear of him did not show. She was amazed at how like Da he looked now, only he had a much healthier colour in his cheeks than Da had ever had and was far better dressed. She had not expected that resemblance and it threw her into confusion. Dermott was the one to break the silence and his deep voice also reminded her of Da's, even though it did not have the same lilting Irish accent.

'You look older,' he said abruptly. 'Nor I didn't expect you to faint at the sight of me.'

Josie bounced to her feet, hands on hips, to declare, 'She's been really ill with the influenza, that's why she fainted. And you're a very rude man, whoever you are. Go away and let me look after my mother.'

He stared at the diminutive defender in surprise, then chuckled. 'Eh, you're as feisty as your sister Cathie, you are. You'll be Josie, I suppose.'

'How do you know my name?'

Liza tugged at her daughter's skirt to pull her closer. She forgot her differences with her brother, for her main worry would not be held back. 'How long have you been in England, Dermott? Have you seen Cathie? Is she all right?'

'My wife and I only arrived in Pendleworth this morning, and no, I haven't seen her.' He gestured towards the woman standing beside him. 'I believe you two already know one another.'

As he hesitated, wondering whether to tell her that her daughter was in trouble, Christina stepped forward with a toss of her head and a shrill scrape of laughter. 'Your Cathie's in jail, actually.'

'I don't believe you!' Liza recognised Kitty Pringle with a further feeling of shock. How could *she* be Dermott's wife? She tried to sit up, but her head was still spinning and with a low groan she let it fall back on the cushions, raising her arm to shield herself from the light streaming through a window opposite.

Dermott could not stop staring at his sister. She hadn't looked like Mam when he'd seen her in Australia, because he didn't remember his mother as a young woman, let alone a vibrantly beautiful one like his sister had been then. But now Liza looked pale and drawn, as their mother often had, and there was a touch of grey in the hair at her temples. The resemblance shook him to the core and he regretted, as he had many times, not having written to his mother. It would have been grand to have seen Mam just once before she died, even better to tell her that her 'bad lad', as she had often called him, had done well for himself. The thought made a lump come into his throat.

'Cathie *is* in jail,' he said quietly, taking hold of his wife's arm and giving it a little shake as he muttered, 'Shut up, you!' Raising his voice again, he told his sister, 'I was just going out to see what it was all about when you turned up.'

Liza was so chalky white he let go of Christina and moved across the room to crouch beside her and say abruptly, '*You* aren't in any state to do owt about it, that's for sure. Let them show you to a room and leave me to see if I can help your lass.'

'*You?* After what you did to us?'

He ignored her accusation. 'Who else is there? You're in no fit state to do anything. And as it happens, I like my niece, in spite of her being *your* daughter. I wouldn't want owt bad to happen to Cathie.' He turned to his wife. 'An' while I'm gone, you mind that sharp tongue of yours, Christina Docherty, and help our Liza settle in. I'll be back when I can.'

Christina shrugged. 'Oh, very well. But why you want to help her after swearing you'd get your revenge all these years, I can't think.'

Still standing protectively beside her mother Josie looked at her uncle and said loudly, 'I won't let anyone hurt my mother.'

Dermott smiled, a genuine smile this time. 'Eh, lass, I'm frit at the mere thought of upsetting you.'

Josie stamped her foot. 'I mean it!'

Eh, he thought, what a nice little lass! He looked at his sister and said in a gentler voice, 'I'll see that Cathie's all right. I got quite fond of her in Perth.' Then he scowled at Liza again in a way that said he still had not completely forgotten what lay between them.

412

She could not hold back a sob at that look. 'It was an accident, Dermott, one I've rued every day since then.'

'What did you do with his body?'

'Buried it next to Josiah's. His grave's been carefully tended, believe me.'

The silence was so charged with anger and emotion that Josie looked from one to the other in apprehension and even Christina held her tongue.

Then Dermott turned away, saying with a harsh edge to his voice, 'I'm getting soft in my old age. I find I like my nieces so I'm not going to hurt their mother. I'll go and see what's up with Cathie.'

Christina watched him go, then turned to stare at Liza. 'Well, you *do* look a mess!' She patted her own elaborate hair-do, cast a complacent glance at herself in the mirror over the mantelpiece, then went to ring the bell. 'I suppose we'd better get you to a room now before you faint again.'

Some people never change, Liza thought as a sturdy maid helped her to another bedchamber and Christina followed, issuing sharp instructions but doing little to help.

Liza had a sudden desperate longing for Benedict. Dermott sounded as if he meant it about liking Cathie, but she still found it hard to trust her brother and would never forgive him for setting that fire and destroying all Benedict had worked so hard for. But the most important thing at the moment was to help Cathie.

Magnus pounded along the streets from the mill to Market Square and burst into the offices of Lorrimer & Sons. 'I need to see – Mr Bernard Lorrimer – right away,' he told the clerk, panting from his mad rush.

The clerk eyed his height uneasily and said in a nervous voice, 'I'm afraid he's with a client at the moment, but—'

'Then you'll have to disturb him, won't you?'

'I can't do that.'

Magnus came right up to the counter and gripped the edge of it. 'Look, I've got an urgent message from Mr Reuben Ludlam. Very urgent. If you tell Mr Lorrimer I'm here and why, he'll definitely see me.'

'If you give the message to me, I'll—'

Frustrated and desperately worried about Caitlin, Magnus pounded on the desk and roared, 'Show me where Mr Bernard Lorrimer is this minute or I'll open every door in the place till I find him myself!'

A door opened at the side and a gentleman Magnus recognised by sight came out. 'Is something wrong?'

'Very wrong,' Magnus said before the clerk could do more than open his mouth. 'Are you Mr Lorrimer?'

'Yes.'

'Mr Reuben sent me. It's urgent, about' – he didn't want to name Francis in public, so amended what he had been going to say to '– the lad who's ill.'

Bernard gave him a quick, assessing glance then said, 'Wait a moment, please.' He stuck his head round the door of the room he had just left and said, 'My deepest apologies, Mrs Grey. I'm called away urgently. But I will attend to that matter, I promise you.' He then led the way to another room. 'I presume you're talking about Francis Rawley?'

'Aye. Jim Marshall's just been dismissed – for no real

reason – so Caitlin's up there on her own with young Francis. Mr Reuben and I are worried that Stephenson is planning something nasty. He's been acting very strangely of late, by all accounts. So not only may that poor lad's life be in danger, but Caitlin's too if she gets in the way. Mr Reuben suggests you come over to the mill and speak to Jim yourself, then mebbe we can plan what to do.'

Bernard looked at him in surprise. 'Who are you? And what is your connection with this, if I may ask?'

'I'm Magnus Hamilton and Caitlin's my cousin.'

'I beg to differ – I have discussed this already with Miss Ludlam.'

'Sorry. I've got used to calling her that in public.' Magnus flushed as he added, 'I want to marry her. Only she took this job at the Manor before I could stop her. I was at work so I couldna even say goodbye, and although I've written to her I've not had a reply, which isna like her. So I'm more than a bit worried. I was going to walk out there on Sunday and see if I could catch sight of her, mebbe even speak to her – or at least ask one of the other maids how she is.'

Bernard was touched by the love glowing in the other man's eyes as he spoke of Cathie and warmed to him immediately. 'We'd better go and see Reuben at once, then. He and I have been worried about Francis for some time.'

The two men strode through the streets, coats flapping, with Bernard clutching his top hat to stop it blowing away while Magnus carried his cap in his hand, for he hated to wear anything on his head.

As they walked Bernard said, 'It was dangerous, her going to nurse her brother. If they find out who she is, she could be in real trouble and Stephenson is still a powerful man in these parts.'

'If he touches her, I'll make him sorry for it, powerful or not,' Magnus said curtly.

Again Bernard gave him a close scrutiny. 'Yes, I believe you would. But that might land you both in more trouble if the law is on Stephenson's side. We must take great care how we approach this.'

Magnus didn't bother to argue. What did laws matter if Caitlin was in danger? He should have spoken sooner of his feelings and to hell with convention. He *would* speak as soon as he found her. He couldn't believe how bleak life was without her.

At the mill Jim was watching Mr Reuben pace up and down his office while he enjoyed a cup of tea and some shortbread biscuits that a lad had brought in all fancied up on a tray with a lace-trimmed cloth on it. What it was to be one of the nobs and get waited on like this! When Mr Lorrimer and Magnus came in, however, he set the cup down and jumped to his feet, knowing it was not his place to sit in the company of his betters.

After Jim had told his story again and filled in more details about what had been happening at the Manor, it was decided that Bernard would go there and ask to speak to Cathie, pretending a legal reason to do with her family, while Reuben urged his father to call on Mr Stephenson and ask to see Francis.

Magnus and Jim could do nothing but go back to the workshop, though neither of them could settle to anything.

Matthew Ludlam flatly declined to intervene in the affairs at the Manor, and he and his son had a short, sharp argument after which Reuben returned to his own office near the workshop, waiting for his friend to return.

Bernard was back within the hour, jumping out of the cab before it had drawn up properly outside the mill and yelling at the driver to wait.

Magnus, who had been keeping an eye on the yard through the window of the workshop, shouted to his assistant to, 'Take over, Sam!' and raced along to the office, closely followed by Jim, who was determined not to be left out. They arrived in time to hear Bernard say, 'Cathie was arrested for theft this morning and is in custody at the police station.'

'That lassie would never steal anything!' Magnus said indignantly.

'What's she supposed to have took?' Jim asked, frowning.

'I don't know. Stephenson refused to speak to me except to say that I could find the slut in jail, where she belonged. And the gatekeeper told me that not only has the tutor packed his bags and left, but the cook also has been dismissed. The whole house is in an uproar, it seems.'

'Who's looking after Francis, then?' Jim asked. 'Eh, I were counting on Cook to do that. She's right fond of the lad.'

'I don't know who's caring for him.' Bernard moved towards the door. 'I'm going to the police station to see what I can do for Cathie before I worry about Francis.'

'I'm coming with you,' said Magnus at once.

'Shall I go and see what I can sniff out at the Manor?' Jim offered. 'Though I'd better take my brother with me. They've got a rough fellow running the stables and outdoor staff there.' And if that Horace wasn't benefiting from his master's strange behaviour, Jim would eat his hat.

'Good idea. Take a cab and tell it to wait for you while you're there. I'll pay.' Reuben tossed a coin towards him.

Jim raced through the streets and burst into the cobbler's shop. 'Hey up, lad. I need you to come out to the Manor with me. Mr Reuben's paying for a cab. I reckon if we can get hold of one of them maids, she'll tell us what's going on.'

'What the hell are you talking about?'

'They've arrested our Cathie for theft an' Mr Reuben wants to know what's happening to Francis. The poor sod's not out of danger yet an' if there's no one to nurse him anything could happen to him.'

Bob put down his tools and the unfinished clog and began untying his apron. 'Sod this Francis, I want to know how our sister is. That lass'd not steal a farthing.'

Jim glared at him. 'Cathie's got a fancy lawyer going to look after her, but there's no one to look after Francis.' He didn't know why he felt so responsible for the poor lad, but he did. 'Let alone I reckon he's our ticket to better things when he turns twenty-one, I like him an' he's our step-brother or summat like that. But them chaps in the stables would beat up anyone who looked sideways at 'em, and I don't want to go out there on my own.'

Bob shrugged. 'All right. But best be prepared, eh? No bugger's going to attack me without regretting it.' He went to a corner of the room and tossed Jim a walking stick his father used sometimes which had a hard knobbly handle, taking an old axe handle for himself and slotting it through his belt.

They hailed a cab at the station and set off for the Manor, burly men fairly radiating determination and a willingness to settle the hash of anyone who got in their way.

Dermott arrived at the police station just behind two men who seemed to be together. One was well-dressed, clearly a gentleman, the other a working man in oil-stained clothing. Dermott eyed the latter sideways, not used to meeting anyone so much taller than himself and wondering idly what this one would be like in a fight. He stood impatiently, waiting for the gentleman to finish his business first because he'd get nowhere by causing an upset.

'I believe you have a Miss Rutherford here,' Bernard said. 'She was working as a nurse out at the Manor.'

Dermott took a step closer. Was this fellow talking about Cathie? Why had she changed her name?

The policeman nodded and said 'Yes, sir' in an obsequious voice.

'I'm Miss Rutherford's lawyer. I'd like to see Sergeant Horly, if you please.'

The policeman looked surprised, but said politely, 'I'll go and fetch him, sir.'

While he was away, Dermott cleared his throat to attract attention. 'Excuse me, sir, but I think I'd better introduce myself. Dermott Docherty. If you were talking about a young lady whose real name is Cathie, I'm her uncle.'

'I wasn't aware she had an uncle still resident in Pendleworth.'

'I'm not resident here. I've just arrived from Australia – and so has her mother.'

'Mrs Caine is here?'

'Aye, but she's been ill, so she sent me to find out what's going on.'

The sergeant came in at that moment, annoyed at being disturbed while he was taking his afternoon tea. When he recognised one of the three men waiting at the counter, he straightened up. This one, at least, was well known to him and was respected in the town. 'Can I help you, Mr Lorrimer?'

'I'm representing Miss Rutherford. Has she been arrested?'

Sergeant Horly felt even more puzzled. 'Well, not exactly arrested, sir. More like – um – detained for questioning. We're still investigating the case.'

Dermott edged forward. 'I'm the lass's uncle. I don't believe she'd take anything.'

'The purse in question was found in her travelling bag, under her bed.' After some hesitation, the sergeant added, 'Sir.'

Magnus stepped forward, for he had no intention of being left out of this. 'Caitlin is innocent.'

Sergeant Horly drew himself up. 'And you are, sir?'

Magnus hesitated, then said rashly, 'The man who's going to marry her.'

This caused another dead silence as everyone stared at him.

Dermott grinned and gave him a quick nudge with one elbow. 'Well, if that's so, you'd better come and see her mother. Ask permission, like.'

'Aye, I will. Once we've got her out of here.'

Sergeant Horly decided that no harm could come from releasing the young woman into a lawyer's charge. In fact, it was a good way out, given his present doubts. 'If you'll come this way, Mr Lorrimer, I'll take you in to see Miss Rutherford. You other gentlemen will have to wait here, I'm afraid.'

Dermott considered this for a moment, then shrugged and took a step backwards, waving Bernard through the gate in the counter, which the constable was lifting to let him through. 'Give her my love and tell her her mother's here.'

He turned to study Magnus. 'What's this about marrying my niece, then? Isn't this a bit quick? She can't have been in England more than four months.'

Cathie looked up as heavy footsteps came along the stone-flagged corridor. She felt as if she had been here for an eternity, but it could only have been a few hours. What would happen next? What did they do with people they'd arrested? She wished she could send a message to Magnus, but they hadn't even brought the sergeant to see her when she asked, just left her sitting here.

'I didn't do it,' she declared as soon as the door opened. She'd decided to say that loudly at every opportunity.

'There's someone to see you.' Sergeant Horly's expression betrayed nothing.

'Who?'

'This way, if you please, miss.'

He gestured to her to follow him, so she did, wondering

who would know she was here. What if it were Magnus? She felt hot with embarrassment at the thought of him seeing her in this shameful dilemma, but pride stiffened her bearing. She knew she hadn't taken anything, whatever they said or did to her. She must hold on to that.

When the sergeant opened a door and waved her inside, she found herself in a small room which contained a table and two chairs only. Mr Lorrimer was waiting there for her and she blushed with shame that he should find her in this predicament.

'When I heard what had happened, I assumed you'd want me to represent you, Miss Ludlam.'

'I didn't do it.'

'I'm quite sure you didn't.' He pulled out one of the chairs and when she had taken it, he sat down opposite her, smiling reassuringly.

'Begging your pardon,' the sergeant asked, taking up position against the wall to one side, arms folded, 'but is the young lady's name not Rutherford?'

'No, it's Ludlam. She's a relative by marriage of the local family.'

The sergeant swallowed hard. This changed the situation considerably.

Bernard's tone was confident and easy. 'Miss Ludlam thought it wiser to use another name while in Pendleworth, Sergeant, because of Mr Stephenson's hostility towards her mother and family – though she kept me aware of what was happening, of course.'

'His hostility?'

'Yes, Sergeant. Miss Ludlam is Francis Rawley's half-sister and Mr Stephenson has been refusing to let her mother see or communicate with Francis since he was a baby.'

'I see.' Now here was a motive for harming the young woman. Sergeant Horly frowned as he considered it.

'Was the purse found on Miss Ludlam's person?' Bernard asked.

'Well, no, it wasn't, sir. It was found in her travelling bag, under her bed.'

'And when did the purse go missing?'

'Early this morning.'

'I was with Francis,' Cathie interrupted. 'I hadn't been near my room since the early hours of the morning, when Jim called me to take my turn with Francis.'

'Jim?' queried the Sergeant.

'Jim Marshall. He's been employed to help look after Francis.'

'Sent to the Manor by Mr Reuben Ludlam,' Bernard intervened. 'Jim is a trusted employee at the mill.'

The sergeant thought it over. 'Why was *he* not there this morning, then?'

'Mr Stephenson dismissed him, which is why Mr Reuben Ludlam and I are particularly worried about Francis. The lad could die if he's not properly cared for at this delicate stage in his recovery. And Mr Baxter left suddenly today as well.'

Sergeant Horly decided it was more than a bit suspicious for Marshall to be dismissed at the same time as the girl was accused of theft. And the tutor had slipped away without waiting for his wages from the sound of it. It took a lot to make a man do that.

Cathie turned to the stern, grey-haired policeman. 'Can't

you insist that someone go and look after Francis? He's been so ill.'

'I'm afraid we can't go into the house unless invited, Miss, any more than Mr Lorrimer can, and we certainly can't question what Mr Stephenson is doing in his own home.'

She looked back at the lawyer, tears welling in her eyes. 'I'm so afraid for Francis.'

'Let's deal with your problems first,' Bernard said quietly. 'Your Uncle Dermott is waiting for you outside, and there's also a tall, fierce young man with a Scottish accent.'

Her face softened at once. 'Magnus.'

'He says he's your intended.'

Rosy colour stained her face and for a moment her eyes glowed with happiness, then she slumped in dejection. 'I didn't want him to see me like this.'

Bernard turned to the sergeant. 'Could you release Miss Ludlam on my security? I'll see she doesn't leave Pendleworth, though I don't think she'll even want to, with a mother and fiancé here.'

Sergeant Horly nodded. 'That would be a useful solution' – his eyes met Bernard's as he added – 'for the time being.'

'Mother's here!' Cathie exclaimed. *My mother's here in England?*'

Bernard smiled at her. 'So I'm told. I haven't seen her myself. She's been ill and is waiting for us at the hotel.'

With that the two men went off to attend to the formalities, leaving Cathie locked in the little room which was only marginally better than being shut in a cell. If her mother had come all this way, it could only be to see her. What had happened about the baby? Had her mother brought it with her? Guilt flooded through Cathie once again for all the trouble she had caused, then her thoughts turned back to Magnus. Had he really said he was her intended? Did he mean it? She was lost for a few moments in a happy dream of being his wife, but then reality pressed down on her again and she got up to pace the room.

It seemed a long time before those heavy footsteps came clumping towards her again and the sergeant led her outside into the public room of the police station.

She stopped in the doorway with eyes for no one but Magnus.

He could wait no longer but pushed past the constable and went behind the counter to gather his beloved into his arms. 'Ah, lassie, my bonny lassie! Why did you leave me?' And heedless of the audience, he kissed her soundly.

When he drew away, they both became suddenly aware of where they were and flushed scarlet, but she still clung to him.

'Why did you no' answer my letter, Caitlin?' he asked softly as they moved back to the other side of the counter. 'I've been frettin' to hear from you. We didn't even manage to say goodbye properly.'

She looked up at his dear face. 'What letter? I've received none.'

Bernard exchanged amused glances with Dermott, then intervened. 'Shall we leave? I don't think any of us wants to linger here.'

'And have you no word of greeting for your uncle, lass?' Dermott asked as Magnus and Cathie turned towards the door, both still with dreamy expressions on their faces.

She gave him a very direct look. 'I don't think you deserve a kind word. You must have known sending me here would hurt my mother and that was cruel.'

'Ah, well, you wouldn't have accepted my offer if you hadn't wanted to come. And anyway, if she and I can let bygones be bygones, surely we can do that, too?'

She gave him a suspicious look. 'I need to see her first and say I'm sorry. And you should apologise, too.'

He chuckled. For the second time that day a niece had put him in his place.

'Are you all right, Miss Ludlam?' Bernard asked.

She stared round her as if she'd never seen Pendleworth before. 'I will be all right once I've seen my mother. And then we have to decide what to do about Francis.'

He blinked in surprise at the determined tone of her voice, but she was already striding ahead with Magnus, her arm threaded through his, his head bent over her and the two of them talking in low voices.

Liza was lying on a chaise longue in the bedroom, with Josie beside her begging her to eat a piece of fruit cake and drink some more tea, when there was a knock on the bedroom door.

'Come in!'

The door opened to show Cathie standing there uncertainly. Liza burst into tears and held out her arms. Josie shrieked with delight and the small table with the tray on it went flying as she rushed across to her sister.

As the three of them hugged one another, Magnus

smiled and closed the door. This was not the time for him to introduce himself to the mother.

He went to join Cathie's uncle and the lawyer in the Dochertys' sitting room. 'What are we going to do for the lad?' he asked. 'Caitlin's right. We canna leave him in that man's hands.'

CHAPTER TWENTY-TWO

September

When Francis awoke his head felt much clearer, but to his surprise no one was sitting with him and his room had not been tidied. The clock on the mantelpiece said four and he realised he had slept away the day. He stretched and decided he was hungry. Where was Cathie? And Jim?

With a huge effort because he still felt weak he managed to reach the bell pull and tug it. It seemed a very long time before steps came up the stairs and to his disappointment they didn't sound like Cathie's. Hilda peeped into his room but didn't come any closer.

'Where's C— Miss Rutherford?' he asked.

'She's left.'

Francis stared at her in horror. No! He needed his sister. 'Jim, then. I need help.'

'He's left as well, and so has Mr Baxter.'

'But why?' How would he manage without them? What was his uncle planning now?

'I'll send someone to help you, sir. Do you want something to eat or drink?'

Suddenly a cup of tea seemed the most desirable thing

on earth. 'Tea. And one of Cook's scones. Thank you, Hilda.'

Tears filled her eyes and she whispered quickly, 'Your uncle dismissed Cook this morning as well.'

At the sound of footsteps coming up the stairs, she put one finger to her lips and hurried away.

What on earth had happened? Before Francis could even begin to work it out, his uncle peered into the bedroom.

'So you're awake at last!'

'Yes.'

'She's gone, that slut has. Anyway, you're better now, I can see that. You don't need a nurse mollycoddling you.'

Francis felt too weak to do more than lie there. He made no attempt to contradict his uncle because this man seemed like a caricature of the upright and impeccably dressed man who had dominated his childhood, and a frightening caricature at that to someone who could barely lift his arm. His uncle's hair had not been brushed and his eyes were wild. Even his speech sounded different, slurred and rambling.

'No more women for you, boy! I'm going to take charge of you myself, make a man of you.' As he heard footsteps Alexander turned and left the room, but his voice echoed down the corridor as he began to berate the maid and order her to take the tray back and send it up with one of the male servants. 'None of you women is to go anywhere near him.' His voice faded away.

A few minutes later Mr Stephenson's valet came up with a tray and helped Francis to relieve himself then drink a cup of tea. He didn't feel hungry but forced down most of a piece of bread and butter because he knew he needed to build up his strength. Something was wrong here and he felt terrifyingly helpless at the moment.

After the valet had gone it seemed very quiet and Francis lay there worrying, before slipping gradually into another long, healing sleep.

Jim and Bob took a cab out to the Manor, but left it in a nearby lane. Reuben Ludlam's name had worked wonders with the driver and he didn't even ask for payment in advance, just nodded and went to put a nosebag on his horse.

'Nice out here, isn't it?' Jim said as they walked through the woods. 'No neighbours to pester you. That Lorrimer fellow lives just over there in that big house. Eh, these nobs have a nice time of it – well, all except poor Francis. Can't understand why his father left him in the care of that old fellow. Stephenson's as nasty a piece of work as I've ever met.'

'Shut up, you fool. Someone will hear us.' Bob did not share his brother's liking for the countryside. It gave him the creeps to have no one around.

When they got near the house Jim led the way through the gardens. A maid was taking in some washing from the long clothes lines hanging in a place like a barn without walls. It had amazed Jim that they'd build a place especially to dry clothes.

'Hey, Ethel!' he called in a low voice.

She jumped visibly then grabbed a clothes prop, holding it in front of herself in self-defence.

Jim showed himself. 'It's only me. I came to find out how the lad is.'

She cast a terrified glance around. 'Keep back near the wall, then. If they see you here, they'll dismiss me and come after you. Horace is in a nasty mood today and the master don't want no strangers near the house.'

'Where's Cook gone?' He trusted her more than anyone else.

'To Mr Lorrimer's.'

'Do *you* know how the lad is?'

'Hilda saw him last time she went upstairs. She said Master Francis looked a bit better. Only the men are allowed near him, though, and if they start ill-treating him again, me and her are leaving. Near drove him to his death last time, they did.' She clutched a pillow case to herself, looking near to tears, then shook her head and continued to unpeg the clothes and fold them.

'I was hoping to get a message to him,' Jim said.

'Well, you've no hope of that.'

'Is he still in his old bedroom?'

'Yes.' She didn't look at him but continued to work and speak in a low voice. 'What do you want to know all this for?'

'It's not me as wants to know, it's the lawyer, Mr Lorrimer.' Jim had a sudden idea. 'And if you have to leave here sudden-like, I think you should go to his house first. He'd probably pay you for information and help you if there were any problems.'

A man came out of the rear of the house and stood watching her, so Jim kept back in the lengthening shadows near the wall. Taking down the last few items, she picked up the heavy basket and returned to the house. The man continued to scan the grounds for another minute or two, then followed her inside.

'I don't reckon we'll discover owt else,' Jim said to his brother. 'Let's go back.'

In town Bob went home and Jim went to tell Mr Reuben what the maid had said and what he'd suggested to her.

Reuben smiled approvingly. 'Good thinking, Marshall. I'll send a note to Lorrimer about it. Now you'd better go and tell Magnus Hamilton what you've told me. He's not long been back and he's fretting for fear his lass will do something rash to help her brother.'

Jim nodded. As he got to the workshop the siren went so he waited till the other men had left, then told Magnus what he'd found out.

'We'd better leave things for the moment,' Magnus said.

'I don't agree,' Jim said thoughtfully. 'I think tonight would be a good time to get the lad out.'

Magnus stared at him in surprise. 'I didn't think you cared about anyone else but yourself.'

Jim wriggled uncomfortably. 'Aw, well, I never could abide cruelty. An' starving that lad were cruel. It brought him near to death. That old sod is planning summat else now, or why would he get rid of everyone?'

'I think we should give Mr Lorrimer and Mr Reuben a chance to rescue Francis first.'

'But—'

Magnus's tone was exasperated. 'We can't just break into the house, can we? You said yourself they've got men on guard out there.'

Since Bob had also refused point-blank to help him

break into Rawley Manor that night, Jim let matters drop. But he still thought they were missing a good opportunity.

The following morning Cathie woke up and lay for a few moments listening to Josie breathing softly and sweetly beside her. It was wonderful to see her mother and sister and to know herself forgiven, sad though she was that her mother had lost the baby. She had vowed never to let anyone down again as long as she lived, which meant she had to do something to help Francis escape.

She was relieved when Josie began to stir because she could not bear to stay still another minute. With much giggling and teasing, they both washed and dressed, then Cathie opened the door into her mother's room very gently.

'I'm awake, my darlings.'

'How are you feeling, Mum?'

'All right as long as I don't do anything. Oh, Cathie, I've been lying here worrying about Francis. I can't bear it if I lose him now, when I'm so close.' Her expression grew determined. 'I won't let them hurt him — or keep us apart — any longer.'

'We'll leave you to get dressed, then we'll have a council of war.'

By eight o'clock all three had had breakfast and had decided to seek help.

'Mr Lorrimer first,' said Cathie, 'then if he won't do anything, Uncle Dermott.' She hesitated and looked across at her mother. 'And there's Magnus, too.'

'Who is he?'

433

By the time Cathie had lost herself in a tangle of explanations, Liza had a very fair idea of what her daughter's feelings were about this young man. 'I'm looking forward to meeting him.'

'I think he — well, he said he'd be coming to see you to ask . . .' she blushed furiously, '. . . to ask if we can get married.'

Josie squealed and grabbed her sister's arm. 'You didn't tell me you had a sweetheart!'

'I had to tell Mum first.'

Liza smiled warmly. 'I'm so glad for you, darling, and I can't wait to meet your Magnus.' Trust Cathie to fall in love in the middle of a crisis. Nothing but love could have brought that glowing look to her daughter's face. Cathie looked older, more mature, and not once had she worn that sulky expression Liza had always hated to see marring her face.

Just before nine o'clock Cathie went round to Mr Lorrimer's office, determined to get things moving. She met him just as he was arriving for the day. 'We need to rescue Francis,' she said bluntly as soon as he had taken her inside.

'My dear, we can't just walk into someone else's house, however strong our suspicions that something is wrong. If we did that we'd be acting against the law.'

'If we don't do it, Francis may die, and law or no law, I won't let that happen.'

'I'm going out to the Manor again today and I shall insist on seeing Mr Stephenson. If he will not co-operate, then we'll work something out.'

So Cathie had to trail back to the hotel and wait around, fidgeting so much that Liza suggested the two girls go out for a walk.

In fact Bernard and Reuben only got as far as the front door of the Manor where they were greeted by the butler, looking embarrassed and unhappy as he told them he regretted that Mr Stephenson was not receiving guests today. Immediately he had finished speaking he attempted to close the door.

When Bernard put his hand out to prevent this, a large man with a ruddy complexion materialised from one side. 'My master doesn't want no visitors. And if you try to get in, I've only to shout for help and it'll come running.'

The two men were left looking at the closed door.

'What now?' Reuben asked.

'We go and see your father. He's a magistrate and can issue a warrant for us to see Francis and check that he's all right. I'll be acting as the lad's mother's lawyer. Will you come with me?'

'Yes, of course. Father should be in his office by this time.'

But once again Matthew Ludlam refused point-blank to help them.

'If that lad dies, how will you live with yourself, Father?' Reuben pleaded.

'You're grossly exaggerating the situation, all on the word of a young woman who is, by all accounts, no better than she ought to be. If she really is Francis's half-sister, then she was telling lies about her relationship with

Magnus Hamilton when she was living with him. Alexander was quite right about her lack of morals. I'd have dismissed her myself. And I'm not at all pleased with Hamilton's part in this, either. We need to be able to trust the men we place in positions of authority to set a good example to those beneath them.'

'Father, whether that's true or not, Mr Stephenson has still been behaving very irrationally and—'

'If people came to my house and tried to tell me how to manage my affairs, I'd be extremely angry, too. I don't blame him in the slightest for showing you the door. I don't know what the world is coming to when a gentleman cannot have his privacy and home respected. Your generation is altogether too hasty and reckless, Reuben, as I've told you many times before. And as a lawyer, Mr Lorrimer, you should know better than to get involved in what are essentially private matters. I'm only thankful I have no business dealings with you myself.'

'But Father—'

No more! Get about your business.' He glared at his son, who glared right back but said nothing, then he turned to the other man and said frostily, 'Now, Mr Lorrimer, I'm busy and so is my son. We have a mill to run. Reuben, I believe you have an appointment at the foundry this morning.' He waved one hand in dismissal, picked up a pen, dipped it carefully into the silver and glass inkwell and began to write in a precise copperplate script.

Outside the office Reuben ran one hand through his hair and looked unhappily at Bernard. 'I'd better go to the foundry. Once I've seen to that little matter, I've nothing else pressing so I'll come round to your office. And if my father complains about anything else, I'll give notice.'

'I didn't mean to put your livelihood at risk when I asked for your help.'

'I've been thinking of leaving for a while. He still treats me as a child, just as his father treated him. It's all right. I've had several other offers of employment and this episode has ended any sense of loyalty I might have felt towards my father and Ludlam's. I'll come and see you later. A few hours won't make much difference, surely?'

'All right. I'd better go and tell Mrs Caine about the impasse.' Bernard walked away feeling shaken by the depths of animosity Ludlam had shown, and deeply worried about Francis, as well as guilty about involving Reuben.

When his son had left the mill Matthew decided to act. He would be master in his own mill! He rang the little brass handbell that stood ready on his desk and told his senior clerk to send for Magnus Hamilton.

Magnus was shown into the owner's room but was not offered a seat.

'I hear that the young lady who was caring for your mother was not related to you in any way.'

How had he found that out? 'No.'

'I will not tolerate such moral lapses in my employees, especially those in positions of authority and trust. You're dismissed. Get your things and be out of this mill within the half-hour.'

Magnus gaped at him for a minute, then as it sank in what was happening and why, he went right up to the desk. 'I'll go nowhere until I've said my piece.'

'How dare you?' Matthew reached for the handbell.

Magnus took it out of his hand and sent it hurtling into the corner of the room. 'I merely wish to inform you, *sir*, that the young lady in question and I have never shared a bed, nor committed an immoral act. And if you say one word to harm her reputation, then I shall sue you for slander.'

Turning on his heel, head held high but colour flaring in his cheeks, he walked out past the clerk who had come running at the sound of the bell.

Matthew Ludlam gaped after him, then pulled himself together as he saw his clerk waiting for orders. 'I have just dismissed Hamilton. See that he leaves the premises within the half-hour. If necessary seek help and *throw* him out.'

Magnus stalked along the short corridor, slammed the door to the office back so that it crashed into the wall and left it swinging wide behind him. Hands clenched into fists, he strode across the yard and into the workshop without a word to anyone.

'Is something wrong?' his assistant asked, following him to the desk set in a corner.

'Aye, there is. I've just been dismissed.'

Sam's mouth dropped open. The men nearby, who had been shamelessly eavesdropping, stopped work to exchange glances of astonishment.

'But why?'

'Because Mr Ludlam chooses to believe a pack of lies about the young lady who was caring for my mother.' He scowled round and raised his voice. 'There has been nothing immoral between myself and my betrothed, Miss Rutherford, and if I hear of anyone saying there was, I'll take whatever action is necessary to shut that person's mouth. Whether it's a mill owner or a labourer.'

The clerk who'd entered the workshop behind him stood near the door with the air of one in fear for his life and everyone went reluctantly back to work.

Magnus slammed drawers open and shut, taking out his personal possessions.

Jim watched what was happening from the side of the workshop. Them bloody nobs allus stuck together. Stephenson must have put Matthew Ludlam up to this. Anyone who sacked a fellow as hard-working as Magnus Hamilton was a fool. He wondered if Mr Reuben knew about this. No, he couldn't. He wouldn't have let this happen. He thought the world of Magnus, Mr Reuben did. Jim forgot all his former animosity towards his foreman. To his mind, they were all in trouble. If old Ludlam got a taste for dismissing folk for nowt, who would it be next?

When Magnus had his possessions sorted out, he hesitated, then called Sam across again. He had to make sure they could not accuse him of something else that was untrue. 'I'd like you to check what I'm taking, Sam. Jim, you come over here for a minute as well and bear witness.'

In silence the two men looked over the small pile of personal possessions and nodded.

Magnus took off his working apron and piled his things into it. Then, without a word, his features stony, he put on his overcoat and cap, picked up his bundle and walked towards the door.

With a squeak of fright, the clerk moved out of the way then followed a few paces behind.

Magnus did not so much as glance at his companion but marched back across the yard, heedless of the rain, to fling open the door to the office and go into the senior clerk's room. 'I've come for my wages,' he declared.

The senior clerk goggled at him.

'I've worked this whole week except for today and I expect to be paid for that.'

'B-but you were dismissed.'

Magnus raised his voice. 'I wasna dismissed for anything to do with my work here, only because our employer chose to believe slander and calumny, so I canna see why I should forgo my rightful wages. And if I'm *not* paid, then I shall seek legal advice about the matter.'

'I'll – um – have to ask Mr Ludlam.'

'Aye, you do that. But I'll no' move from here until I've had what's due to me. And you can tell him that, too.'

After a hurried discussion Matthew authorised the payment of the wages, furious that someone he had dismissed would dare to demand things of him but wanting Hamilton out of the mill before his son returned.

When the money had been counted out of the cashbox, the clerk took out an envelope.

'A minute, if you please,' said Magnus, very haughtily. 'I'd be obliged if you'd fetch in another witness and get out the wages receipt book so that I can sign for this. And I'd like a copy receipt for myself as well. We don't want any confusion about this money, do we? There's already been enough confusion about my morals.'

When Reuben came back to the mill and discovered that Magnus had been dismissed out of hand, he went storming into his father's office where the two men had another furious argument. Reuben seriously considered walking out of the mill there and then, returning home and packing all his belongings. He could go to his grandmother's because he was pretty sure she would support him and give him a bed till he could decide what to do. He knew he was her favourite, for she was a lively old lady and had sighed over her son's increasing intransigence and resemblance to his father several times recently.

However, after some thought he decided he was better off staying where he was at least until the matter of Francis Rawley was resolved. If he needed help, there were several strong fellows in the workshop and Jim Marshall to hand.

'You're wrong to dismiss Hamilton,' he told his father, 'and you'll regret it.' Then he walked out of the office before he said too much.

His father's sarcastic tone followed him out. 'Why don't you get back to your own work? I'm not paying you to race round town interfering in other people's business.'

Reuben had to contain his frustration until later in the afternoon. When he met Bernard they agreed that it was a bit late to do anything until the next day, but both were determined to help Francis.

Cathie and Josie were walking along Market Street when they saw a tall figure in the distance. Cathie caught hold of her sister's hand. 'There's Magnus. Come and meet him.'

But when they ran across the street, she stopped in

dismay as he covered the last few yards that separated them. She had never seen Magnus look like this, so furiously angry. 'What's wrong?'

'I'll come into your hotel and tell you. It's no' something to be spoken of in the street.'

'My mother wants to meet you, anyway.'

'Aye, well, this may change her mind.' Then he realised how harshly he was speaking and looked down at her. 'Eh, lass, I'm sorry if I sound so curt.' For a moment they looked at one another, his expression softening and hers warm with affection. Then he realised she was not alone. 'And would this be your little sister, then?'

'Yes. Josie, this is Magnus.'

He offered his hand. 'Pleased to meet you, Josie. I'm sorry we couldna have met on a happier day.'

In silence they walked back to the hotel, where Cathie left him in the hall and hurried up to her mother's room.

'We met Magnus in town. Something else must have happened because he's absolutely furious. He wants to tell us about it in private.'

'We must go and find a sitting room downstairs.' Liza stood up and led the way down. When she was introduced to Magnus, she could not help thinking what a fine upright fellow he was and approved heartily of the fondness he and Cathie betrayed for one another in every glance, every gesture.

Just as she was about to ask a maid where they could talk in private, Dermott came running down the stairs whistling.

He stopped and looked at the group, noting Magnus's tight-lipped expression. 'What's happened now?'

'We're about to find out when we can find somewhere private to talk,' Liza told him.

'Come up to our sitting room.'

She hesitated, but he was looking at her in such a roguish, challenging way that she put up her chin defiantly and followed him. She would not spurn help, even from him.

When they were all settled, Magnus explained what had happened. 'I don't think Mr Reuben knows about this and I wish to assure you now, Mrs Caine, that nothing untoward has ever happened between your daughter and myself.' He paused to subdue another surge of anger. 'I was going to ask you for her hand in marriage today, but until I find other employment that's not possible. I think Mr Reuben will give me a reference so I should be able to get employment, but I canna be sure of it.'

'The Ludlams and Stephensons allus did stick together,' Dermott said cheerfully. 'And if this Mr Reuben won't write you a reference, I will.'

Magnus looked at him in puzzlement. 'But you don't know anything about me.'

'No one will know that. All they'll care about is that I'm a man of substance. We'll address it care of my wife's aunt, who's as respectable as they get.' He went to slap Magnus on the back. 'If you're smart, though, you'll work for yourself from now on. A clever fellow can earn a hell of a lot more that way.' He grinned. 'Even if he insists on absolute honesty.'

Cathie stood up and went to thread her arm through Magnus's. 'I don't care whether you have a job or not. It makes no difference to our engagement.'

'Well, I care. I care very much.'

Liza looked from one to the other. 'There is plenty of employment in Australia, Mr Hamilton. A hard-working man can make a decent life for himself and his family out there. And I'm sure my husband would help you.'

'I thank you for saying that but I don't want to leave England. Do you, love?'

Cathie's throat tightened and she looked at her mother, pleading for her understanding. 'No. I can't go back.'

Magnus turned back to her mother. 'I'll find something, Mrs Caine, don't worry.' He looked at her uncle. 'And you may be right, sir, about working for myself. I have had a bellyful of old fools who interfere in things they don't understand.'

'So,' said Dermott, 'now that's all settled, we'd better plan how to rescue Francis.'

Cathie forgave him a lot for that speech. 'Yes. That's the most important thing at the moment.'

'Mr Lorrimer and Mr Reuben went out to the Manor this morning but were denied entry,' Magnus said, for Reuben had come and told him what had happened before leaving for the foundry. 'It sounds as if the old man has brought some of the outdoor staff in to make sure no one gets near Francis.'

'Even grooms and gardeners have to sleep,' said Dermott, smiling a hungry tiger's smile.

'But we can't take the law into our own hands,' Liza protested. 'Cathie's already in trouble with the police. That matter still has to be settled.'

'Then we'll keep her out of it,' said Dermott.

'We certainly will,' Magnus agreed.

'Just you try!' she snapped. 'I know the inside of the house. You don't.'

'Jim knows it, too,' said Magnus. 'He'll show us the way.' He went to take her hands and gaze earnestly into her eyes. 'Stay out of this, love. Please. I don't want you getting hurt.'

'He's right, lass,' Dermott agreed. 'This is men's business.'

Christina, who had been listening on the other side of the door leading into the bedroom while she finished dressing, swept in just then with a rustle of silk shirts and a waft of perfume, demanding and getting everyone's attention.

Cathie was spared the necessity either of refusing point-blank or telling a lie. She hadn't changed her mind. She intended to help rescue her brother before it was too late, and no one, not even Magnus, was going to stop her.

CHAPTER TWENTY-THREE

September

———◆———

Late that afternoon Dermott left the hotel, telling Christina he was off for a stroll but actually intending to call on Bob Marshall and enlist his help. 'Fancy a bit of fun out at Rawley Manor tonight, lad?' he said as he walked into the shop.

'If you mean breaking in to rescue that lad, no, I bloody don't. It's all right for rich folk like you. If things go wrong, you can find yourself a lawyer and get away with it, but chaps like me are allus left holding the baby.'

Teddy peered out of the little workshop. 'What's up?' He blinked at Dermott and edged into the room, smiling. 'Eh, if it's not Dermott Docherty. You look just like your da! Poor old Con. He didn't make old bones, did he? How are you going, lad? Put on a bit o' weight, haven't you? Must be eating well.'

'Aye, I've done all right for mysen.'

Teddy had a sly expression on his face. 'We must drink to that sometime — when Bob gives me a copper or two. Mean, he is. Sits on the money like he's hatched it hissen. You got sons, Dermott? Well, don't let 'em take over when they grow up or you'll never be able to call your soul your own.'

Bob rolled his eyes, but said nothing. They'd had this argument too many times before.

Pulling five bob out of his pocket, Dermott pressed the coins into Teddy's hand. 'You go and buy yourself a drink on me, old fellow. I'll join you another time. I've got a bit of business with your Bob tonight.'

As Teddy thanked him profusely, Sal walked out of the scullery. 'You can buy a glass or two for your wife for once, Teddy Marshall, 'stead of spending it all on your useless friends.'

The pair were out of the house within a couple of minutes, already arguing about her demand for him to give her half the money.

'That'll keep them out of the road.' Dermott studied Bob, eyes narrowed. 'How about I slip you a bit of money to help us? Will that make you change your mind?'

'How much?'

'A pound.'

'Might be interested. Paid in advance. An' you'll have to promise to pay for a lawyer, too, if owt goes wrong.'

'It's a bargain.' Dermott shook hands then passed over some more money. 'Right then, you send someone to fetch your brothers an' I'll be back in a few minutes.'

'They'll want payin', too, mind.'

Dermott knew very well that Jim would help break into the Manor for nothing, but he enjoyed showing off his money and these small amounts meant nothing to him, so he nodded and went on to his next piece of business. 'Where does that Magnus Hamilton chap live? Whalley

Street? Right, I know where that is. I'll go and fetch him.'

'He'll not get mixed up in summat like this.'

'Care to bet on that?'

'No, I bloody don't.' Bob was going to nip home and give his money into his wife's safekeeping before he went anywhere. He and Min didn't intend to wind up like his father when they were old, not if hard work and frugality would prevent it.

Cathie could not settle. Josie was sitting with their mother. Funny how her little sister liked looking after sick people too, and it was lovely to see her looking so well.

Her mother was looking a lot better today and they'd had a lovely long talk together, so now it was time to do something about Francis. The more she thought about it, the more determined Cathie became to go and see him. If she went to the kitchen door at the Manor, she reckoned she might be able to slip into the house without anyone noticing or even get one of the maids to let her in. It was a pity Cook was no longer there. She'd have been the best ally of all.

Even if Francis was still too ill to leave, Cathie felt she would feel better just to know that he was recovering — and so would her mother, who had spoken so wistfully of him as a baby and asked innumerable questions about what he was like now. She didn't want to worry her mother, who was still not herself, so decided to slip out before anyone could stop her. She smiled, remembering how Magnus had said he'd tie her up, if necessary, to prevent her running into danger, and her uncle had agreed with him. Men never admitted that women could do things too.

She put on her darkest clothes and was just about to creep out of her room when Josie came in.

'Are you going out, Cathie?'

'Shhh!'

Josie lowered her voice only marginally. 'Can I come, too? Mum's fallen asleep and there's nothing to do here. I'm not at all tired.'

'Not this time, love.' Cathie glanced out of the window, hoping the rain would hold off. It was getting dark and the gas lamps were shining on the occasional puddle and showing the huddled shapes of people making their way home.

'Where are you going?'

Cathie hesitated, then looked at Josie very seriously. 'If I tell you, you must promise not to let anyone else know.'

The child nodded, eyes wide in her thin, freckled face.

'I'm going out to the Manor. I'm sure I can slip in by the servants' entrance without anyone noticing me. I have to see Francis and make sure he's all right.'

Josie's mouth fell open. 'Ooh, Cathie, they said you hadn't to. They said it was too dangerous.'

'I'll be very careful, I promise you.' She moved towards the door. 'I trust you to keep quiet about this, mind.' She didn't wait, but slipped out and went quickly downstairs.

Josie went to sit on the bed, kicking her heels against the side of it. She was bored. Had nothing to do. It wasn't fair. And they *had* told Cathie to stay away from the Manor. Tears welled in her eyes. What if something bad happened to her sister? She should tell her mother, only she'd promised not to.

The tears overflowed. She didn't like this. She didn't know why, but it didn't *feel* safe. Cathie always rushed into things and told people she'd be all right, but that wasn't true. Look what had happened to her sister in Liverpool. What if Cathie hadn't eventually remembered who she was? They might never have seen her again.

What if someone at the Manor killed their Cathie tonight? Josie whimpered and bit her hand to prevent herself from crying out.

Cathie made her way out towards the Manor, walking briskly to warm herself up. She slipped through the grounds as quietly as she could, her breath clouding the air in front of her, for there was a real nip in the air tonight. Avoiding the stables, where the head groom kept a particularly nasty dog, she stopped near the rear of the big house. The windows of the kitchen and servants' quarters were lit up so she crept forward till she could see inside.

The two maids were cooking dinner, both looking unhappy, and a man was sitting in a chair watching them. Surely that was one of the gardeners?

She fidgeted around, willing him to go away so that she could speak to the maids. It seemed a long time until he did and then, just as she was moving forward to make herself known, the butler came in, looking upset, so she stepped hastily back into the shadows. Gower was an old man, almost as old as his master, and his feet always hurt him. He sat down looking exhausted and said something to the maids, one of whom tossed her shoulder at him as if irritated by his remark.

A bell rang and Gower heaved himself to his feet and left.

Cathie didn't waste time but hurried across and tried the latch. The door wasn't locked so she simply walked in. As one of the maids looked up and saw her, she let out a screech. The other gaped for a moment, then as footsteps came towards the kitchen, gestured frantically towards the pantry.

Sighing with relief that Hilda had not given her away, Cathie slipped inside the pantry and stood very quietly, listening.

'What were you screeching about?' a man's voice asked.

'I nicked my finger,' Hilda said, sticking her forefinger into her mouth and sucking it as proof.

'Stupid bitch. You take care with your cooking. You burnt the meat last night.'

'I'm not employed as a cook.'

'You are now.'

As the footsteps went away again Hilda opened the pantry door. 'Eh, it's dangerous for you to come back here, Caitlin lass. The master can't speak your name without he curses you. What do you want?'

'To see Francis. Is he all right?'

'We aren't allowed near him any more. One of the men takes his food up and sees to him — well, they're *supposed* to see to him, but that lot spend more time lolling around than they do working.' And she was beginning to suspect that the grooms were taking things from the house, things the master might not notice — not in his present state — but which the maids who dusted every day had definitely missed. She and Ethel hadn't said anything. Well, they were afraid to, if truth be known. She'd never thought much of the outdoor staff, but they hadn't troubled her when they stayed outside. Now, things were changing by the hour and she didn't like it one bit.

'When's the best time to go upstairs?' Cathie asked.

'Eh, you'll never!'

'I have to see Francis.'

'When they're eating their meal, I suppose – but you'll need the key.' Hilda jerked her head in the direction of the butler's pantry. 'You could get it now while Gower's with the master. There's allus a spare key or two, and *he* won't notice if one's missing. Number six, top row, it is.'

'Thanks, Hilda.' Cathie hesitated. 'Look, if anything goes wrong tonight, you should fetch Mr Lorrimer. He'll help me.'

'You ought to get out while you can,' Ethel said sourly. 'If things don't get no better I'm leaving, even if I don't get my quarter's wages. One of them grooms tried to shove his hand down my dress this morning and I'm not having *that*! The cheek of it!'

Hilda shook her head. 'You hide in the broom cupboard for now, Cathie. I'll come and tap twice on the door when it's safe. But I shan't admit I've seen you, mind.'

'Thanks.' She went along to the butler's pantry, her nerves on edge, trying to make no sound as she walked. She took the key to Francis's room, then went and hid in the broom cupboard where time seemed to pass very slowly. She jumped at every noise of someone passing and was relieved when there were two knocks on the door.

✤

Francis had been left on his own for most of the day. He made sure he got up and walked around the bed several times, even though he still felt weak and dizzy. When they brought him food he ate as much as he could, determined to build up his strength. But it would take a few days, he knew, before he was fit enough to escape, so he tried to look weak and helpless when anyone was with him.

His uncle was acting so irrationally and looking at him with such hatred that Francis had begun to fear for his life.

The key turned in the lock and the door opened. When he saw Cathie walk in he thought for a moment he was feverish again and seeing things. Then he realised she was not an illusion, but was there in the flesh.

She flew across the room to hug him. 'You look a bit better,' she said, holding him at arm's length to study his face.

'I am. But I'm still so damnably weak. Oh, Cathie, what are you doing here? Has my uncle let you come back?'

'No. I sneaked into the house. I had to see you to make sure you were all right. I need to think first where I can hide, in case they come back.'

He stared frantically round the room. 'Under the bed is the only place. There isn't room in the wardrobe.'

She lifted the edge of the counterpane and bent to look under the bed, nodding, then locked the door again. Sitting next to him, she put her arm round his shoulders, which seemed all bone and no flesh. 'Francis, what is your uncle up to now?'

'He says he's going to make a man of me without the help of any women, and I'm to start on Monday by learning to ride properly.' He gave a bitter laugh and looked down at himself. 'As if I'll be well enough to go riding by then.'

She shivered. She could imagine the scene when Francis failed to do as ordered. 'Keep your voice low, love.'

'He won't let the maids near me any more,' Francis whispered, 'and when he comes, he rants on and on about you and your mother. Cathie, it's too dangerous for you here. Get out while you can. *Please!* He's lost his mind and – and I think he might really harm you.'

Even as he spoke, they heard someone approaching.

Cathie wriggled quickly under the bed while Francis lay down, trying to look as if he had just woken up. The door crashed back on its hinges and his uncle walked in.

Alexander Stephenson peered round the room. 'They shouldn't have left you on your own, boy. Won't have that.' He came right up to the bed to stare at Francis. 'All *her* fault you're such a weakling. Nicholas should have known better than to marry her, but then *he* was a great disappointment to us all as well.' He stretched out one bony hand and shook Francis's shoulder. 'Look at me when I'm talking to you. No manners, the young haven't.' He let go and walked out again.

Cathie poked her head out from under the bed, but Francis made a sign at her to get back and stayed where he was. He hadn't heard his uncle walk away. This happened sometimes. Sure enough, the door was flung open a minute later and Alexander rushed in again to stare round the room and then at his nephew. After a moment or two he walked out just as suddenly without a word of explanation.

Only when he had heard his uncle shuffle off along the corridor did Francis whisper, 'I think it's safe to come out now.'

'He looks dreadful,' Cathie said, shocked at how much her former employer had degenerated even in a few days. 'His face is all slack on one side and he's not walking properly. We have to get you away from here and let someone know about him. I'm going to stay till later and then we'll creep out together.'

'I don't think I have the strength.'

'You must!' She hesitated, then added, 'Our mother's arrived in Pendleworth and is longing to see you.'

He gaped at her as if he couldn't believe what he was hearing.

She went on gently to cover his confusion, 'She's been ill with the influenza, so she's not herself. Josie's with her. They're at the Railway Hotel.'

'Does she — want to see me?'

'Very much. It was one of the reasons she came to England.' When tears filled his eyes, she patted his hand and sat staring down at her lap, giving him time to recover.

He gave a shamefaced laugh. 'I'm not normally so prone to tears.' He smeared the moisture from his cheeks with the back of his hand. 'So *stupid!*'

She gave him another hug. 'We'll soon build you up again once we get you out of here. I'll stuff you full of food till you burst out of your clothes. Now, you try to get some rest and we'll wait for everyone to settle for the night.'

Dermott was enjoying himself. He'd had enough of sitting on his arse playing the rich man and relished the idea of a bit of action. Christina might spend half the day fancying herself up, but he felt like a stuffed fish in some of the clothes she insisted on him wearing. He was a man, not a tailor's dummy.

Magnus stood beside Dermott as they waited for Pat to arrive at the clogger's shop. He was not enjoying himself, had never in his life before planned to break the law and had only come along because if someone didn't rescue Francis, he was quite sure Cathie would try to do so herself. His expression softened for a moment at the thought of her then the worries came tumbling back. He hadn't even a job now. How could he marry without a way of supporting his wife?

The shop door clanged and Pat came tramping in, smelling of fresh air and beaming at them like a schoolboy offered a treat. 'Eh, the streets are quiet. I reckon we're the only ones awake now.'

Dermott took charge. 'Right, then. We need to plan this properly.'

'We can get in through the back after they're all asleep,' Jim said at once, not intending to kow-tow to Magnus Bloody Hamilton tonight.

Magnus looked across at him. 'I don't like breaking into someone's house.'

'Can you think of owt better?' Jim demanded. 'They're not going to open the door and *invite* us in, are they?'

Dermott pressed his point home. 'If we don't do something – an' quickly – our Cathie will. That lass is as wilful as they come. You've got yourself a right handful there, lad.'

Jim let out a snort of amusement at the thought of being brother-in-law to Magnus as well as step-brother to Francis Rawley. He was going up in the world an' would have folk kissing his arse at this rate. He just hoped he could find a way to get himself some money to match his new position.

'Right then, we might as well go,' Dermott decided, moving towards the door.

Magnus followed him out, grim-faced.

The three brothers looked at one another.

'Buggered if I know what to think about that one being involved,' Jim said.

'I like Magnus,' said Pat, who had been mainly silent but who was determined to earn his pound. Why, it'd pay off all their debts and still leave a bit in his Tess's purse.

The five men made their way through the quiet streets.

'I'm glad that rain's held off,' Jim said. 'I fair hate water dripping down my neck.'

'Shut your trap!' Dermott growled.

'Ah, there's no one to hear us here. An' I still think we should have took a cab.' Jim caught Dermott's eye, muttered something to his brother and shut up.

Dermott found himself walking next to Magnus, with Jim and Bob behind him and Pat trailing behind on his own. Funny bugger, the Scot, he thought, glancing sideways, but he and Cathie seemed happy with one another. He shivered. Eh, he'd forgotten how cold it always felt in this damp climate.

When they got to the edge of the town Jim took over, leading them on to the Rawley estate by a roundabout route that avoided the gatekeeper's cottage and, more importantly, his dog.

There were lights showing in the Manor and they could hear the noise from a distance.

'What the hell's going on?' Dermott muttered.

When they got round the back they saw a group of men sitting in the brightly lit servants' quarters, drinking, laughing and smoking pipes. There were several empty wine bottles on the table.

Through another window they could see two weary-looking maids clearing up the kitchen.

'They're not usually up this late,' Jim worried.

One of the men ambled into the kitchen and said something at which the older maid picked up a rolling pin and threatened him with it.

Dermott grinned, then the amusement faded. 'Looks like we'll have to wait a bit,' he whispered to Jim, who was standing next to him.

'Aye. Look at that lot sitting lording it inside. They normally stay in the stables.'

He led them into the vegetable garden where there were benches to sit on and they sat in silence, shoulders hunched against the cold, every one of them tense and on edge.

When Liza woke she felt better than she had for a long time and lay smiling across at the dying fire. She had found one of her missing children and would soon see the other. Poor Francis! If only she could take him home with her. Not till she started to get up did she look at the clock, surprised to see that it was nearly morning. When she heard a sound from the next room, she tapped on the connecting door and went in.

Josie, usually so cheerful, was lying weeping on the bed, still dressed, and there was no sign of Cathie. Liza rushed across to cuddle her. 'What's wrong, love?'

'It's Cathie. She's gone to rescue Francis. She went hours ago and she's not come back. I promised not to tell, but I'm so worried about her.' Josie pressed one hand to her heart. 'I'm worried *here*, Mum!' She sobbed even harder.

'Tell me exactly what she said.' Liza sat on the bed to listen to the whole tale, then stood up, her expression determined. 'I'm going to ask your Uncle Dermott to go after her.'

The corridor was quiet with a gas wall lamp burning low at one end. A light was still showing under Dermott's door, so Liza knocked.

Christina opened it. 'It's about time . . . Oh, it's you.'

'Can I speak to Dermott?'

'He went out.' She glanced back at the clock. 'He said he'd be late, but I didn't think he'd be gone this long.'

Liza moved into the room, not wanting to disturb the people nearby. 'Where on earth did he go at this time of night?'

Christina hunched one shoulder. 'He didn't tell *me*. I'm only his wife. Men are all alike. Think they know everything. Why? What's wrong?'

'I think Cathie may be in danger.' Liza thought things over quickly then asked, 'Do you know where Magnus Hamilton lives?'

'Heavens, no! Why should I?'

'They keep a night porter on duty. I'll see if he knows.' Liza made her way downstairs and asked the porter, but he had never heard of Magnus Hamilton. 'Find me a cab, then!' she ordered.

'At this hour? They'll all be at home asleep. Surely it can wait until morning, ma'am?'

'No, it can't. Send someone to wake a cab driver up, if you please. This is an emergency.'

She went back to her room to put on her outdoor things, worried sick. Her daughter should have been back hours ago. Something must be wrong. And of course Josie insisted on going with her. She would insist her younger daughter stay in the cab, though.

It was time to confront Alexander Stephenson.

About eleven o'clock, Cathie went to see what was happening in the rest of the house. She'd expected it to be fairly quiet, but it wasn't. Most of the noise was coming from the kitchen. It sounded like drunken men, which puzzled her. She tiptoed upstairs to the maids' rooms, but their bedroom was empty so she took the risk of going near Mr Stephenson's, but all was quiet there, too, with no sign of a light. Was he in bed or not?

She returned to Francis's room, taking the utmost care to move silently and to listen before she turned any corners. She found him leaning back against the pillows, fully dressed but looking exhausted, and her heart was wrung with pity.

'Is it time to leave now?' he asked, jerking upright. 'What's happening?'

'There are men in the servants' hall and they sound to be drinking heavily. I can't think where Hilda and

Ethel are. They're not in their rooms. And your uncle's bedroom was dark, so he's either asleep or still sitting in the library.'

'He doesn't seem to sleep much lately and wanders round at all hours of the day and night,' Francis worried. 'What if we bump into him?'

'We're stronger than he is. We'll push him out of the way and run for it,' she said cheerfully. But she doubted Francis could run anywhere, so they'd just have to take the utmost care how they moved around the house.

Suddenly there was the sound of someone walking along the corridor.

Cathie dived for the bed and wriggled under it, banging her head on the chamber pot. She heard Francis getting under the covers.

The door opened and the head groom spoke, sounding slurred and full of scorn. 'So there you are, all tucked up safe and sound, Master Francis. The master were worried you might have flown away so he sent me up to check.' He belched loudly and sniggered. 'That old fool doesn't know what time of day it is any more, but why should we care about him? We're having a fine old party down there. Don't you wish you could join us?'

'All I wish is to sleep.'

A loud burp, then, 'Ah, you're a milksop, you are. 'Tain't right you owning all this. He's right, you don't deserve it.' He went out, laughing derisively.

Cathie slid out from under the bed. 'Now's our chance. He won't come to check on you for a while.' Her voice grew gentler. 'You don't have to do anything but walk very quietly. Once we're out of the house, I'm going to take you to Mr Lorrimer's. That's not far.' She'd carry him if she had to, or push him in a wheelbarrow. She'd find a way to get him out of this dreadful place.

CHAPTER TWENTY-FOUR

September

Cathie and Francis tiptoed along the corridor and down the main stairs, because they would have to go out of the front door to avoid the revellers at the rear. However, Gower usually left the key in the lock, so she thought it'd be all right. If he hadn't done so tonight, she would go to the butler's pantry for it.

She was worried by how wobbly Francis felt as he leaned on her arm and how bloodless his face looked, but knew his only hope was to get away from here so didn't suggest going back.

When they reached the landing, she gestured to a small sofa and he sagged down on to it while she went to check the stairs and hall. They were empty and quiet. Pray they stayed so!

When she returned, Francis had his eyes closed. 'Come on, love,' Cathie said softly.

He nodded and forced a smile that was hardly more than a softening of the strained expression on his face, then let her help him to his feet.

They got down the stairs without mishap and she put one finger on her lips. He nodded and they stood still to listen. There was the faint sound of someone moving about in the library, presumably his uncle, but they could not let that stop them.

'Not far now,' she murmured in his ear.

When they got to the front door, the key was there and she closed her eyes for a moment, thankful for this small mercy, before turning it. The click of the lock sounded loud in the quiet hall and they both froze for a moment. But no one came.

Cathie turned the big brass handle gently and started to pull the door open.

From the back of the hall a voice screeched, 'What are you doing?'

She turned to see her worst fears realised.

Alexander Stephenson rushed towards them from the library, brandishing a walking stick and yelling for help at the top of his voice.

'The whore of Babylon's returned! Don't let her escape! Horace, where are you? "Vengeance is mine, saith the Lord." Now she'll pay the price of her sins.' He tried to hit her.

Francis stepped in front of her, but Cathie pushed him aside and as the stick came down towards her head, dodged quickly. She grasped it in both hands, tugging and bringing a further torrent of abuse from Alexander as they struggled for possession.

Francis wanted desperately to help her, but his legs were shaking so much he could only cling to a small table.

Cathie managed to wrest the stick from the old man but he rushed across the hall and grasped the bell pull, continuing to abuse her verbally. She turned to draw Francis across to the door, but even as she flung it open, men poured out from the rear of the hall.

Horace roared, 'Stop her!' and with yells the men rushed towards them.

Alexander cackled gleefully. 'Now we've got her. Kill the whore! Kill her!'

Cathie pushed Francis outside, whispering, 'Hide!' and turned to bar the way, brandishing the walking stick. For a few moments she fought them off while Francis staggered down the steps, but it was no use. Though she got in a few blows, eventually numbers prevailed. One man tore the stick from her hands and another leaped upon her, pushing her to the ground. Still she fought fiercely, using her nails and feet as weapons. But there were too many of them.

Outside at the rear of the house Jim watched as the men in the brightly lit servants' hall suddenly stopped talking and turned their heads. Then Horace shoved his chair backwards so roughly it fell over and he yelled something. As he led the way out, he was followed by the rest of the men.

Before the watchers had time to do anything, the two maids crept after the men, then came running back and rushed out of the back door, clearly fleeing.

'Catch 'em! Find out what's happening,' Dermott ordered.

Jim stepped forward, arms outstretched to stop the two women, but at the sight of him, Hilda only shrieked and tried to go round him, so Magnus caught her while Jim stopped Ethel.

'Stop that bloody screaming, you two! No one's going

to hurt you,' Dermott shouted when the hysterical women would not listen.

'It's all right, Hilda,' Jim said soothingly. 'These are friends of mine. We've come to rescue Francis.'

'What's happening in there?' Dermott demanded.

'They've caught Caitlin and Master Francis. There'll be murder done if you don't rescue them,' Hilda exclaimed.

'Caitlin's here?' Magnus asked in dismay.

'She came earlier, said she was here to rescue that poor lad.' Hilda cast a panic-filled look over her shoulder. 'We didn't hear anything, so we thought they must be biding their time, but the master suddenly started shouting for help and we saw them catch her, so me and Ethel decided to go over to Mr Lorrimer's for help, like Jim suggested.'

'I were going anyway, soon as I could slip out,' Ethel said indignantly. 'I reckon that lot were planning on having their way with us. They wouldn't let us go to bed, kept sniggering at one another and grabbing us when we were clearing up. It's not safe for a decent woman to work here any more and you wouldn't get me back, not if you paid me a hundred pounds, you wouldn't.'

'Good idea to go and fetch Lorrimer.' Dermott stepped back and waved them on. 'You tell him what's happening here and we'll see what we can do to save them two. Tell Lorrimer it's urgent, say we need a legal adviser.'

The two women ran off into the darkness.

Jim and Magnus were already running towards the house and the others followed.

The kitchen was still unoccupied, the outer door swinging open. Jim led the way towards the front of the house, looked back to check that the others were with him, then put one finger to his lips and opened the door to the main entrance hall. At first no one noticed them and they heard Cathie's voice, raised in anger.

'Can't you see he's run mad?' she begged. 'If we don't get help for Francis, that old man will kill him! Do you want to be involved in murder?'

'Kill her now!' Stephenson urged. 'She's a whore, like her mother.'

With a growl of anger, Magnus tried to push Dermott out of the way, but the other man held him back and hissed, 'Listen a minute. Let's find out what they're up to.'

Horace ignored his master and swaggered over to Cathie, who was held securely by two of his men. He raised her chin with his forefinger and laughed. 'We've got help for Francis now you're here, haven't we?' He eyed her in a suggestive way as he added, 'And you'll have other uses, too.'

'I'll be missed,' she threatened. 'They know where I am and they'll come looking for me.'

He snorted in amusement. 'Well, if they come, I'm sure you'll tell them you're working happily here again – for Francis's sake.'

As the implications of this sank in, she stared at him in shock.

Francis staggered across to her side. 'You'll not touch her. This is my house and—'

With a contemptuous laugh, Horace shoved him aside, sending him reeling into a statue that tottered on its plinth then crashed to the ground.

Cathie tried to get away from the men holding her, kicking and struggling, but they just laughed. Despair filled her. She had made things far worse by coming here tonight.

Then she heard a noise and turned to see Magnus stride forward from the rear of the hall, followed by her uncle and the three Marshall brothers. After staring for a moment in disbelief, she realised she was not seeing things and let out a sob of relief.

Magnus made straight for the two men holding his beloved and although they let go of her to face him, he punched one of them on the jaw so swiftly the man was knocked sideways before he could do anything. Once he fell, he did not move. The other one grabbed a bronze statuette from a side table and threatened Magnus with it. Before he could strike, Cathie grabbed the statuette from behind, allowing Magnus to get to him as well. Still holding it before her, she stepped hastily out of the way, pulling Francis with her. After a very short exchange of blows, the second man joined his companion on the floor, to lie dazed and groaning, not even trying to get up again.

In the centre of the hall the others were fighting, Dermott disposing of his opponent with ease and turning with a laugh to help Jim, who was fighting off two men.

As they made sure of their victory, a voice rang out from the door of the library. *'Stand still or I fire!'*

They all turned to see Stephenson standing there with a pistol in each hand. His eyes were glittering with malice and his hands were quite steady.

'If you don't get out of my house this minute, I shall be forced to shoot you. *Her* first!' He aimed one of the guns in Cathie's direction and said in a conversational tone, 'And believe me, I should be delighted to do that.'

Francis immediately stepped in front of his half-sister. 'Then you'll have to shoot me first, Uncle. Kill the last of the Rawleys. Are you prepared to do that?'

There was a moment's silence before Stephenson said, still in that chill controlled voice, 'Get out of the way or suffer the consequences.'

Francis did not move. As Cathie stirred behind him, he pushed her back.

Pat, who was slightly behind the others, seized the moment to hurl his cudgel at Stephenson. As it caught him on the shoulder one of the pistols went off and Dermott cursed loudly. The other pistol clattered to the ground. So fiercely did the old man fight, however, that it took all three Marshall brothers to subdue him and tie him to a chair.

Horace and three other men stayed where they were, standing at one side of the hall, nursing their injuries and scowling.

Magnus helped Francis to a chair then turned to Cathie, who flung herself into his arms.

Into this scene walked Bernard Lorrimer, to stand gaping near the front door at the sight of the destruction in the entrance hall and the two men lying on the ground.

Stephenson was quiet now, but he glared across the hall from the chair to which they'd tied him. 'You've come just in time to rescue me from these intruders. They were going to rob me.'

Bernard's eldest son hovered by the door, primed with instructions to run and fetch the police if it was too dangerous to intervene. He looked as shocked as his father by what he was seeing.

'What's happened?' demanded Bernard, looking at Magnus and ignoring Stephenson.

'These men have broken into my house,' Stephenson shouted. 'I want the police fetching at once. *At once!*'

'Someone shut the old fool up,' Dermott said, wincing.

Cathie realised that her uncle was holding his arm and blood was dripping from it on to the floor. She hurried across to look at it. 'You've been shot.'

'Aye. And the bugger wasn't even aiming at me,' he said.

'Jim, go and fetch a tea towel from the kitchen!' she ordered and, as he hurried off to do her bidding, began to ease Dermott's coat off.

Magnus explained to Bernard Lorrimer exactly what they were doing here, with interruptions from Stephenson who kept yelling, 'It's lies, all lies!'

Bernard thought quickly, knowing there was trouble ahead. 'I think we'd better go to my house and leave Mr Stephenson here in the care of his remaining servants.'

Magnus frowned. 'Is that wise? He'll only lie about what's happened here tonight.'

Bernard lowered his voice. 'He'll lie anyway, but we have the two maids and I'd rather take Francis to safety. I think I'll have enough credibility with the police for them to listen to me.' Even as he spoke, there was the sound of a carriage driving up to the house.

'Who the hell is that?' demanded Dermott, trying to twist out of Cathie's hands.

'My coachman, I hope,' Bernard said. 'I told him to follow me.'

'It's ours!' his son called from the doorway.

'Good, then this needn't take long. Francis and Mr

Docherty had better ride in the carriage. Cathie, you go with them. The rest of us can walk back to my house.'

Within minutes the hall was clear of everyone but the outdoor servants, the grooms and Stephenson, still tied to the chair.

Horace approached him and began to undo the knots in the curtain cord. 'Shall we get you to bed, Mr Stephenson?'

Stephenson batted his hand away. 'No, we shall *not*! Send for Matthew Ludlam. *At once*. As a magistrate, he has the authority to demand the return of my nephew.' He spoke more sensibly than he had for a day or two. 'Well? What are you waiting for?'

Only when Horace had left and the other men retreated to the kitchen to nurse their wounds did Stephenson start to mutter again, then, catching sight of himself in the mirror, he made his way up to his bedroom and rang for his man to set his clothing to rights.

'Not getting away from me,' he said several times as his valet helped him change. But his head felt strange and it was hard to stand up, so he sat down abruptly and forced himself to breathe slowly and carefully till the tingling sensation in his arm had gone.

The valet noticed, when his master resumed dressing, that he was moving awkwardly, but did not dare comment.

As soon as Bernard Lorrimer got home, he sent his coachman to fetch Sergeant Horly. The two cooks currently residing under his roof, helped by the maids from the Manor, got everyone hot drinks. While Cathie tended her uncle's arm, which the bullet had only grazed though it bled a lot, Edith Lorrimer persuaded Francis to lie down on the sofa.

The parlour was full of men with bruises, but there was an air of great relief and even jubilation about them all

Bernard, less sanguine that the affair was over, questioned everyone about the part they had played that night and asked Francis a lot of questions about his treatment in recent weeks, the answers to which horrified everyone.

Jim was able to confirm what he said in a gruff voice, trying and failing to hide his sympathy for the lad.

When the carriage was heard on the drive, Bernard went out to greet Sergeant Horly who had dressed hastily and brought the constable on night duty with him, realising from the coachman's garbled tale that there was big trouble among the 'nobs' of his small kingdom.

'Let me explain the situation first,' Bernard said smoothly, 'then you can question the others. A cup of tea, perhaps, as we speak?'

What Alfred Horly heard made his blood run cold. He definitely did not relish being caught in the midst of such a quarrel. 'I think you'd better send for the Chief Constable,' he said gruffly. 'I'll start questioning everyone, but it's all too much for me, sir, it really is.'

So the coachman was sent out again, and one by one the people involved went in to see the sergeant in Bernard's study, while the constable stood duty in the parlour to make sure the ones who had not yet been questioned did not collude about their stories.

When the coachman returned he was alone. 'The Chief Constable's been called out to the Manor,' he announced.

The sergeant was not the only one to experience a sinking feeling on hearing that.

Some time later they heard a horse approaching the house. Bernard looked out of the window. 'It's one of the grooms from the Manor.'

'What the hell's happening?' Dermott growled. His arm was now throbbing and he was angry that he had so tamely allowed this lawyer fellow to take over. They should have locked up Stephenson and sent for a doctor to certify him insane.

The message was for Sergeant Horly, who was requested to attend the Chief Constable at the Manor.

'I'm coming with you,' Bernard said.

'Better not, sir.'

On the way to the Manor on the spare horse the groom had brought, the sergeant overtook a cab also making for the house. Since he could make out a woman's silhouette inside it, he reined in and bent to speak to the occupant. 'Excuse me, ma'am, but there's trouble at the Manor. You should leave your visit until another time.'

'My daughter Cathie's there, probably at the centre of the trouble,' Liza said. 'She may need me.'

'Ah. Well, Miss Ludlam has moved to Mr Lorrimer's house now, so perhaps you should go there instead.'

'Thank you.'

He gave instructions to the cab driver and carried on, not looking forward to the scene he was sure would greet him at the Manor.

When Cathie saw who was getting out of yet another cab, she let out an exclamation of surprise. 'It's my mother. Mr Lorrimer, she hasn't seen Francis since he was a baby. Is there somewhere private they could meet?'

He led her and Francis into his wife's little sitting room and then went out to bring his visitor in.

Francis gripped Cathie's arm. 'I'm afraid.'

'Don't be.'

Liza paused in the doorway, glancing quickly at Cathie with a half-smile of greeting, then looking at her son, her eyes devouring him. Behind her Bernard closed the door quietly.

'Francis?' Liza asked in a voice husky with emotion.

He stared at her for a moment, this small woman with a mass of dark hair only lightly streaked with grey. He had had no idea what she looked like, only Cathie's description, and she was much younger than he had expected. He hesitated, then saw the love in her face and said, 'Mother,' the word more like a sob. As he walked towards her, tears ran down his cheeks.

Liza was sobbing aloud, so was he, and Cathie went over to put her arms round both of them and hug them wordlessly.

After a few minutes, Liza pulled back. 'Look at us all! And you hardly steady on your feet, Francis love.' As she and Cathie helped him across to the sofa, she murmured, 'What has that wicked old man done to you?'

Cathie would have liked to let them chat, but she was worried about the sergeant being summoned to the Manor.

'Mum, I think we're still in trouble. Mr Stephenson is mad, but he has lucid moments and if he persuades the Chief Constable that we are in the wrong, they might take Francis back to that place again.'

He gulped, 'I can't face it. They'll kill me this time.'

Liza straightened up, thinking furiously. 'Then we must act quickly to get you away.'

'How?' Cathie demanded. 'They've left a constable on duty here. And anyway, where can we go?'

'I know one person who would help us, I'm sure,' Liza said thoughtfully. 'We should get Francis away now, before they do anything else.'

'But what if the constable won't let him go?'

'We won't ask his permission.'

Francis looked from one to the other and smiled. 'You're very alike, you know.'

They both looked at him in surprise, then assessingly at each other.

'No, we're not,' said Cathie.

'Not in appearance, but in nature. Are you always so impulsive, Mother?'

Liza smiled reluctantly. 'It has been known. Now, how are we to arrange this?'

Cathie pursed her lips, then said, 'Magnus and Uncle Dermott.'

'You trust my brother?'

'Yes.'

A few minutes later, Cathie went back into the parlour. 'Time to change your bandages, Uncle Dermott.' Before he could stand up, she went to put her arm on his shoulder and squeeze it warningly. 'Magnus, will you help my uncle up the stairs, please? He's lost a lot of blood and I don't want him fainting on us.'

Dermott stared at her, then lowered his eyes and said in a feebler voice than usual, 'It is hurting again. I think you've got these bandages too tight.'

Magnus stood up without a word, his face expressionless. What was his lassie up to now? He'd not let her run into more danger and was relieved that she was at least not acting on her own, but turning to him.

The constable looked from one to the other. 'You're not to leave the house.'

'No, no. I'm just taking my uncle upstairs. He should probably lie down for a while,' Cathie said soothingly. 'Will that be all right, Constable? I want to give my mother and my half-brother some time alone together. She hasn't seen him since he was a baby.'

'As long as no one leaves the house,' the constable repeated doggedly.

Three hours later, the sergeant returned, accompanied by two more constables. He had not been able to persuade the Chief Constable that Mr Stephenson might be lying because somehow the old fellow had managed to appear near-normal. What he now had to do in the line of duty stuck in his throat.

'I have orders to take Francis Rawley back to his uncle,' he said to Bernard.

'You can't mean that? Isn't there going to be some sort of hearing first?'

'Mr Stephenson has agreed to drop all charges if the

476

'lad is returned,' Sergeant Horly said woodenly.

'Then it's a good thing the lad is no longer here.'

In the parlour Jim grinned at the constable, who was listening to this with a horrified expression on his face. 'Don't worry, lad. You couldn't be expected to keep watch on everyone, could you? And Francis getting away has probably prevented that old lunatic from murdering him.'

While the sergeant and his men searched the house from attic to cellars, braving sarcastic comments from the two cooks and what seemed to them like a whole regiment of uppity housemaids in the kitchen, Bernard Lorrimer sat in the parlour, arms folded.

'I shall have to ask you to come down to the station, sir, and to bring these gentlemen with you,' Sergeant Horly informed him at last, stiff with dignity.

'Certainly. What time would suit you?'

'Now.'

'Are we not to be allowed breakfast first?'

The sergeant hesitated.

'If I might suggest,' Edith Lorrimer put in, 'after such a night, we could all do with a good breakfast, the sergeant and his men included. It won't take long to serve up a quick meal.'

Sergeant Horly hesitated and was lost.

As he ploughed his way through a plate piled high with delicious ham and perfectly cooked eggs, he said not a word. When Bernard would have spoken to him, one of his men cleared his throat and shook his head warningly.

The food worked its usual magic. As the meal ended, the sergeant looked at his host. 'A word with you in private, sir, if you please.'

In the study he asked bluntly, 'What's going on?'

Bernard raised one eyebrow. 'Just between you and me?' Receiving a nod, he went over Alexander Stephenson's unreasonable hatred of Francis's mother and how the lad had been kept from her for all these years. 'Do you have sons, Sergeant?'

'Four, sir. And fine lads they are, too.' Horly could not hide his pride.

'Then you will understand what an unhappy life poor Francis has led. And you've already heard from Jim Marshall about how he was beaten and starved.'

'The Chief Constable won't believe me, sir. I tried to tell him, truly I did, but he thinks the sun shines out of old Stephenson's arse, begging your pardon for my language. He – er – is a bit inclined to kow-tow to the gentry, the Chief Constable is.'

After a short silence, Bernard said, 'I would be obliged if you'd allow me to send a message to Mr Reuben Ludlam and to change my clothes before we leave.'

As well be hanged for a sheep as a lamb, the sergeant reflected. 'If you're quick, sir.'

CHAPTER TWENTY-FIVE

September

———◆———

Reuben Ludlam received a message that his friend Bernard. Lorrimer was at the police station and needed his help urgently on a matter they had discussed before. Just as he was preparing to leave the house, a maid turned up to say that his grandmother would like to see him at once and he was not to delay an instant as it was a matter of life and death.

'Tell my grandmother I have another matter to deal with and shall be with her in an hour or two, Ruth,' he told the elderly maid, who had been with her mistress for over thirty years.

'Begging your pardon, Mr Reuben, but your grand-mother said not to let you go anywhere else *no matter who sends for you* till you've seen her. Please, sir.'

He frowned, trying to understand what this could mean. 'Can you not tell me why?'

'She said not to.'

'Then I'm afraid she'll have to wait. There's someone else who—'

Ruth clutched his arm, looked round as if afraid of being overheard and whispered, 'Mr Reuben, she's got Francis

Rawley there and the police are looking for him and I'm *that worried* she'll get herself into trouble. You know what she's been like since the old master died.'

She was wringing her hands and there were tears in her eyes, but it was the mention of Francis's name that did it. 'Very well. I'll send for the carriage and—'

'I have a cab waiting outside, Mr Reuben.'

Sophia Ludlam was waiting for her grandson in the parlour of her little house, eyes sparkling with mischief and belying her seventy years, stiff limbs and crown of silver hair.

'What are you up to now, Grandmother?' he asked, bending to kiss her wrinkled cheek and inhaling the scent of lavender that always hung around her.

'I'm seeing that justice is done.' For a moment she looked sad. 'At last I have a chance to make up for another of Saul's unkindnesses. The children he fathered are all grown up now and either married or in good employment. But this matter – well, it's been haunting me for years.'

'So what is it we need to do for Francis?' he asked gently. 'You are talking about him, aren't you?'

Sophia clicked her tongue in exasperation. 'I told Ruth not to mention the details until I'd checked that you would help me.'

'I'm glad she did. There are other people involved, and in trouble too, I think.'

'Tell me.' She listened intently.

Matthew Ludlam sat in the library of Rawley Manor, thinking how much Stephenson had aged lately and how rambling his speech was at times. But that was just the result of old age and some sort of minor seizure, nothing more sinister. Reuben was quite wrong about that. And since Stephenson was the legally appointed guardian of young Francis, no one had the right to try to take the boy away from him, and so Matthew would order as local magistrate.

There was a knock on the door and Gower came in. He bowed to his master. 'Excuse me, sir, but there's an urgent message for Mr Ludlam.'

Stephenson waved one hand and Gower handed over an envelope. 'The messenger said he'd been told to wait for a reply, sir.'

Matthew read the note impatiently, then gasped and read it again.

'Is something wrong?' Stephenson asked, fingers drumming on his chair arm.

'My mother wishes to see us both at her house at two o'clock this afternoon. She regrets her inability to come here, but she has difficulty walking these days.'

'I haven't got time to pay visits. Got to get the boy back.'

'It's about the boy that my mother wishes to see us.'

'What? Is he with her? If so, I'll send my men over at once to fetch him and—'

Matthew looked at the clock on the mantelpiece. 'It's only two hours to wait until the time she specifies. I think we should humour her in this.'

Stephenson glowered at him, then shut his mouth.

Matthew stood up. 'I'll send a carriage for you later, if you like.'

'I have my own carriage and Horace is perfectly capable of driving me there.'

When Matthew had left, he rang the bell and summoned his head groom, who was the only one who understood how he felt. They would take another couple of men in the carriage with them, strong ones, who could subdue the boy if necessary. They weren't coming back without his nephew.

'See how you like that!' he said aloud and began to pace up and down the library, talking of what he was going to do and why.

Horace left him to it. Funny how the old man could seem quite reasonable when he wanted to, then start rambling like this. However, Horace intended to ensure that the lad stood no chance of escaping again. He was looking forward to continuing this new and very enjoyable life, from which he intended to emerge with plenty of money after the old fool died.

After Francis had rested at Mrs Ludlam's house, he and his mother spent an hour chatting quietly of this and that while he picked at a tray of food and she persuaded him to eat 'just a little more, love'.

When he fell asleep suddenly Liza sat beside him, feasting her eyes on him, alternately marvelling at how much he resembled her second husband Nick Rawley and feeling bitterly angry about all the years she'd been kept away from her second son. She knew Cathie would understand her need to be with Francis and not resent it, and besides, Cathie had Magnus now, such a fine, reliable young man.

But, oh, Alexander Stephenson had a lot to answer for! And Liza did not intend to let him get his hands on her boy again. If Sophia Ludlam could not help her, then Liza would find someone who could and steal her son away, if necessary.

At half-past one she woke Francis gently and helped him to dress as smartly as possible in his newly laundered clothes. Afterwards she smoothed the collar of his shirt and reached up to pat his cheek, a motherly gesture that brought tears to his eyes.

'No one ever did such things for me before,' he said in a choked voice.

'Well, I'm going to drive you mad fussing over you from now on. But this is not the time to give way to our feelings,' she ordered, though she too felt like weeping. 'And besides, every minute we can spend together is so precious, my darling, that we mustn't waste time on regrets. Sadly I can't stay here for more than a few weeks. I have a home and husband in Australia.'

'I wish I could go there with you.'

'So do I. I'd love you to meet your brothers.' She brushed away a tear and scolded him gently. 'Look what you're doing to me.'

'Would your husband let me live with you, do you think?'

She smiled. 'Oh, yes. Benedict is a kind, generous man. If you were able to come, he'd welcome you with open arms and treat you as a son. Now let's go down and get you settled before they arrive, love.'

She'd called him 'love', Francis thought as they went

slowly down the stairs. She said it easily and tenderly, and every single time she used that simple word it made him want to weep.

Downstairs they found Cathie and Magnus waiting for them, though a sulky Josie had been relegated to the kitchen to help prepare some refreshments. Magnus had been home and changed into his Sunday best, a dark, slightly old-fashioned suit which seemed to make the burnished red-gold of his hair shine even more brightly in the small room. He and Cathie were gazing at one another in a fond, besotted way. Liza nudged Francis and winked at him as they watched this.

A cab came clopping along the lane and they all stopped talking to listen. Impatient as ever, Cathie slipped across to the window to check who it was. 'Only Uncle Dermott.'

Liza felt amazed that she could wait so comfortably for the brother who had once terrified her. She'd have said age had mellowed him, but she doubted it ever would, for he was still a rogue. You only had to look at his eyes to realise that. But he had never had the viciousness of Niall, so perhaps having money had softened him. He was talking now of bearding Christina's aunt in her den and making sure she named her niece as her heir. The poor woman would probably be putty in his hands, because he could be charming when he wanted, but Liza would never forgive him for burning them out — and she was quite sure he'd done that, whether he admitted it or not — even though she found it useful to form a temporary alliance with him.

Dermott entered the house with his arm in a sling and Christina beside him, magnificent in rustling fuchsia taffeta silk and an elaborately draped bustle. He introduced his wife to his hostess and nodded to everyone else.

'I think we'll need the chairs from the dining room,' Sophia said. 'Magnus, dear, could you fetch them in for us, please? I'm expecting quite a few people this afternoon.' She was already treating Magnus like a favourite nephew.

'I'll help you,' said Cathie at once, bouncing up.

Francis watched her with a half-smile. 'Isn't she *splendid*?' he said to his mother in a low voice. 'I've never seen a girl with so much life in her.'

'Yes.' But the thought was bitter-sweet to Liza. Cathie was far too full of life ever to settle down to the quiet of the bush. Well, it was clear to her now that her elder daughter's future lay here in Lancashire. That would always make her sad, but you could not hold your children prisoner.

Bernard Lorrimer was the next to arrive, bringing with him the three Marshall brothers, faces shiny with washing and hair carefully parted and slicked down. At first glance they looked like their father and that upset Liza, bringing back unhappy memories. Then she looked more closely and saw the difference in their expressions, the way they looked you straight in the eyes and stood close together for support in the face of all these rich people. They had a look of Cathie, too. No, they were definitely not like Teddy Marshall, who had once raped her so brutally.

Reuben Ludlam arrived next, accompanied by his father, both of them very stiff with one another.

And then came another man who was a stranger to most of the people there but whom Sophia greeted with a, 'Peter dear, I'm so grateful you could join us.'

The elderly gentleman smiled at her in a besotted way

that made Matthew glare at him, then modify the glare as Peter Corton, a fellow magistrate, turned and offered his hand with a warm smile.

Finally, the Chief Constable turned up with Sergeant Horly beside him, quiet and very alert.

When they were all seated, Sophia cleared her throat. 'If you will all bear with me for a few more moments, we have one more person still to come — Mr Stephenson — and given the antipathy he feels towards Liza, I feel she should leave us to deal with him.'

There was a chorus of murmurs of agreement.

'Liza, dear,' Sophia went on, 'I wonder if you would oblige me by waiting in the dining room, as we discussed earlier?'

Francis stared down at his hands and could not prevent them from trembling. His mother took one of them in hers and squeezed it, whispering, 'Courage, love!' before standing up. He nodded, but he could not help thinking that if they took him back to the Manor, he might die of terror — even before he died of further ill-treatment.

As Liza left, Cathie took her place on the sofa beside Francis, and Magnus went to stand protectively behind them.

An awkward silence fell and when it was broken by the sound of a carriage drawing up in the lane, Sergeant Horly was not the only one to let out a sigh of relief.

Alexander Stephenson was shown in by Ruth. He made a tight little bow to Sophia and said, 'Ma'am,' then saw his nephew and said, 'Aaah! I see you have caught him.'

Cathie bristled with indignation, but held her tongue. Sophia had assured them that she knew just how to deal with Mr Stephenson and they had to trust her judgement now, because he still had the law on his side. But Cathie didn't intend to let anyone take Francis back to that place, law or no law. They'd have to tear him out of her arms literally – and so she'd told Magnus and her kind hostess. She took hold of her brother's hand and felt it quiver in hers.

'Please be seated, Mr Stephenson,' Sophia said quietly. 'We have a few matters to discuss.'

'I think not, ma'am. All I have come for is my nephew whose guardian I am. I wish to keep him out of the hands of his half-sister, a woman of dubious morals and—'

'I'll no' stand silent if you start insulting my Caitlin,' Magnus announced, stepping forward and glowering at the old man, who lifted his nose and stared back with a sneering expression on his face.

'Please, Mr Stephenson,' Sophia said. 'Let us do this graciously.'

'I'll stay for a few minutes. That's all I can spare.' He took the chair she offered and sat on the edge of it, resting his hands on his walking stick and glaring at his nephew.

'There are a few things we wish to tell these two magistrates as we try to resolve this unhappy situation,' Sophia began. 'Gentlemen, Mr Stephenson may be the legal guardian of this lad, but he has abused the trust placed in him. Jim, will you please tell these gentlemen how Francis was treated?'

When Alexander tried to get to his feet, Magnus stood up and put his hands on the old man's shoulders to press him down.

The Chief Constable said quietly, 'Please listen to

this, sir. After all, if you're in the right, what have you to fear?'

'Of course I'm in the right. It's *she* who is in the wrong.' He cast a murderous glance in Cathie's direction.

Jim related how Francis had been beaten severely and starved for a long time until not only his health but indeed his life was threatened.

Matthew Ludlam, who had not heard the details before, listened with a look of distaste on his face, but when Jim stopped speaking, said coldly, 'Mr Stephenson is still the legal guardian, however. And since Francis has no other close relatives, we have no alternative but to . . .'

'But he does have other relatives,' Sophia said. 'He has a mother who has been prevented from seeing him since he was a baby, but who has paid for yearly reports on how he was growing and has written to me regularly all these years, so desperate was she for news of him. He most certainly does have other relatives.'

'That might be a better solution, you know,' Peter Corton proposed to Matthew. 'Sending him to join his mother for a few years.'

Alexander Stephenson started sputtering with rage.

'I cannot agree with that,' Matthew said. 'The woman is of common stock and not fit to raise a gentleman's son. She lived with us for a time, till it was discovered that she had foisted her bastard children on my brother Josiah. M'father told me all about it and I think . . .'

Sophia interrupted him. 'Your father didn't tell you the full truth, Matthew. Josiah was always aware that the children were not his but loved his adopted daughter so much that he gave his life to save hers. I've tried not to blacken your father's name to you, but Saul was a wicked man and I believe Mr Stephenson is cut from the same cloth.'

This time Sergeant Horly risked his superior's wrath by helping Magnus to hold Stephenson back.

'The two of them caused a great deal of unhappiness, not only to me,' Sophia went on, her voice faltering for a moment, 'but to Liza. And surely you can see that this poor maltreated boy needs a mother's care?'

Matthew's voice was cold. 'Not such a mother, I'm afraid.'

'You cannot judge that without meeting her.' Sophia sighed and raised her voice. 'Liza, I think you should join us now.' She had hoped to avoid this confrontation, but her son was a stubborn and bigoted man who saw everyone outside his class as inferior. Thank goodness her grandson did not take after him.

As the folding door opened, everyone turned round to watch Liza come into the room. She looked composed but pale as she paused for a moment to look round.

Stephenson shouted, 'This is a trick! That woman is not worthy to raise a Rawley. She is a whore and she—'

'Please, Mr Stephenson,' Peter Corton said. 'This abuse can do no good. If you would sit down again, we could discuss the boy's situation quietly, sir, then—'

'Discuss it? I'll discuss nothing.' Stephenson took a quick step sideways, dodging Sergeant Horly. He darted across the room and struck Liza across the side of the head with his stick, yelling, 'You'll never have him, you low-bred gutter bitch!'

She pushed him away but he raised the stick again.

Francis was on his feet, shouting, 'I'll not go back to him. I'd rather die!'

Just as Magnus and the sergeant reached Stephenson, he stiffened and let the stick fall. When he opened his mouth only a gurgling noise came out and he staggered sideways.

Liza stepped back, holding one hand to her stinging cheek.

'Don't let him hurt her!' Francis called.

But Alexander Stephenson was beyond hurting anyone. He crumpled slowly to the ground, where he lay twitching.

Sophia's voice cut through the noise: 'Another seizure. Someone loosen his clothing.'

Francis pushed past Magnus, ignoring his uncle and rushing to put his arm protectively round his mother. 'Are you all right? Did he hurt you?' He raised one hand to the weal across her cheek, nearly weeping. 'He did.'

She summoned up a smile. 'It's nothing, love.'

'Come over to the sofa,' he said urgently, putting his arm round her. 'Let Cathie look at your cheek.'

'Aye, you go and sit down, our Liza,' Dermott bellowed. 'That old sod's not going to hurt anyone else. He doesn't look to me like he'll be fit to look after himself from now on, let alone your lad.'

Francis sat down beside his mother, his arm still round her shoulders, feeling shaky but relieved. The sight of that red mark filled him with rage and horror that anyone could strike a woman like that.

Jim knelt by Stephenson while Cathie was still looking at her mother. He loosened the old man's collar and tie and slipped a cushion under his head. 'He's unconscious,' he told her as she joined him, 'but still breathing.'

Sophia hobbled across to join them. 'I doubt there's much anyone can do to help him. I think Mr Stephenson should be taken home and looked after carefully. I'm sure the doctor will confirm that his mind is disturbed as well as his body.' She looked across at her son. 'What now?'

'Well,' Matthew said grudgingly, 'this does change matters. Even if Mr Stephenson recovers, I doubt he'll be in a fit state to act as guardian to anyone.'

'And seizures can twist the mind as well as the body,' Sophia said sombrely. 'My own husband had to be restrained in his final weeks after such a seizure, as you will remember, Matthew.'

He nodded. He remembered only too well his father's final days. It had been a trying time for them all.

Silence fell as the old man was carried out. Once he had left a weight seemed to lift from the group and they began to talk again.

With Francis and Cathie on either side of her Liza struggled to pull herself together. Her cheek and head were still hurting for it had been a violent blow. She could feel no sense of triumph at what had happened to her attacker, though, because it was sad to see anyone brought to that state.

Sophia cleared her throat. 'I think we should settle this matter now, and I wish to state, for both magistrates' benefit,' she fixed her son with a stern gaze, 'that Mrs Caine lived with us for several months when the children were small, and I never found her anything but a caring and competent mother. She is in no way immoral and never has been. Does not Francis deserve a mother's care now? He clearly needs nursing back to health and he has had a very lonely and unhappy childhood with that wicked old man.'

'That's all very well,' Matthew said peevishly, annoyed at the turn events had taken, 'but she lives in Australia and his home is here.'

Francis spoke up suddenly, with a bitter edge to his voice. 'Rawley Manor is no home to me, sir. I have nothing but unhappy memories of that place. What I want, if you don't mind, Mother, is to come and live with you in Australia until I turn twenty-one, at least.'

Liza's smile was so radiant that it brought tears to Sophia's eyes and even Matthew Ludlam could not doubt the woman's love for her son.

'Francis, darling, I can think of nothing I'd like better than to take you home with me,' Liza said. 'Nothing in the whole world.'

'I have no objections to that,' Peter Corton declared, frowning at his pompous fellow magistrate, 'and if you wish to bring an application for custody of your son before me, Mrs Caine, I'll make a ruling to that effect.'

'The case is in *my* jurisdiction,' Matthew snapped, bristling. 'It's all very well to talk of sending the lad off to Australia – and I'm not denying that a sea voyage might do him a world of good, for I am shocked at how ill he looks – but who's to look after the Manor while he's away, not to mention overseeing the care of Mr Stephenson if he survives?'

'I don't care if that place falls into ruins,' Francis muttered. 'And I never want to see my uncle again.'

When Liza poked him with her elbow and shook her head slightly, he said nothing more.

'Why not let his prospective brother-in-law look after

the Manor?' Sophia asked. 'Magnus seems a very sensible and capable young man to me, and Reuben has always spoken well of him.'

Matthew scowled at the man he had dismissed only two days before. 'I don't think——'

'Good idea,' said Reuben. 'I cannot too highly recommend Magnus Hamilton. He's worked at the mill for over ten years and has risen to a position of responsibility there. Indeed, I have it in mind to go into partnership with him myself on another venture, so impressed am I by his capabilities.'

His father glared at him.

Cathie smiled to see her beloved flushing under this unstinted praise.

Bernard winked at Magnus from across the room.

'There is also the question of what to do with Mr Stephenson,' Matthew went on. 'He must be properly cared for, as befits his station.'

'I could do that, sir,' said Jim, seeing an opportunity. 'I don't want to go back to work in the mill. I like living in the fresh air. There are cottages on the estate. I dare say one could be found for my family – and perhaps for our Pat, too, because one man can't stay awake twenty-four hours a day and the old bug— er, fellow, hardly sleeps a wink these days. Me an' my brother will look after him right and proper.'

'Jim has taken excellent care of Francis,' Bernard Lorrimer put in.

'We can consider that, I suppose.' Matthew Ludlam pulled a sour face, but with his mother beaming and nodding at him, felt he could do no other than agree. 'But everything must be made comfortable for Mr Stephenson, as befits his station. And Francis must be raised properly and given an allowance of his own, as well as money being made available so that he can return to England when he reaches his majority – or sooner if he is unhappy in the Antipodes. Still, Patenby can see to all that, I suppose.'

'I'd rather Mr Lorrimer handled my affairs from now on,' said Francis. 'I trust him and I've never liked Mr Patenby.'

'Now, lad, you can't just . . .' Matthew began.

'I asked Patenby several times to help me,' Francis said, 'told him how bad things were with my uncle. But he refused to do anything.'

'I don't like the man, either,' Sophia agreed. Knowing how her son liked to be the one in charge when it came to details, and hoping this would assuage his wounded pride a little, she coaxed Matthew into supervising the handing over of all Rawley Estate business to Mr Lorrimer's practice.

'You will accept this responsibility and look after the Manor while Francis is away, Mr Hamilton, will you not?' she begged afterwards.

Magnus looked at her dubiously. 'I would enjoy trying, but I feel bound to admit that I have no experience of running an estate, ma'am.'

'You're used to handling men and organising work, though, and my grandson speaks very highly of you. We could perhaps give it a trial? What do you think, Matthew dear? Would that not be best for all concerned?'

He seized on that. 'Yes, a trial would be the best thing.' He cast a disapproving look at Magnus. 'I could ask our bailiff to work with Hamilton, and if he did not prove suitable . . .'

Magnus swallowed hard and looked at Cathie, his love for her showing clearly in his expression. 'Is that what you want, my love?'

'I'd like it very much.'

'You *are* getting married, I presume,' Matthew asked, with another of his disapproving looks.

Magnus gave him a glowing smile. 'Indeed we are, sir.'

'And the young woman will be staying with her mother until then?'

'Naturally! And I will repeat what I said before, sir. Nothing immoral has ever happened between the young lady and myself. I love her too much.'

Those words made Liza beam at him and then exchange smiles with her son.

Seeing that Francis was looking extremely weary, Sophia suggested he go and lie down for a while, and Matthew waved a hand at Liza. 'Yes, take him to lie down. He'll require careful nursing, mind.'

She managed to hold her tongue till they were out of the door, then laughed up at her tall, too-thin son and said, 'Let's get you tucked into bed, then, my lad. Magistrate's orders.'

She noticed Josie peering out of a door at the back of the hall. 'Come and help your new brother, darling,' she called and swept them both upstairs, giving Francis his first experience of how his mother could spread joy around her like a warm golden blanket.

*

When everyone had left, Magnus and Cathie walked back into town discussing their future.

'How soon can we be married, my little love?' he asked fondly.

'Only you could call me "little"! And we can be married as soon as you like. It takes three weeks to call the banns, doesn't it? Mum will be wanting to get back to Australia, but she'll stay for a few more weeks and by then Francis will be in a better condition to travel.'

'You're sure about staying here?' Magnus asked anxiously. 'You'll miss your family.'

'Very sure about staying. It's not just you' — she waved an arm around — 'but everything. I love it here in England. It's a sort of — don't laugh at me — but Lancashire is my inheritance, somehow.'

'You said once that your mother joked that you were her legacy from Lancashire.'

'Yes.' Cathie's expression grew sadder. 'It's going to hurt, though.'

'Losing your family?'

She nodded, looking up at him through tear-drenched eyes. 'I've heard people talk about it before in Australia, how they never stop missing the people and places they've left behind, even though they're happy with their new lives. I know Dad still misses the farm he grew up on, only his brother took that over, so there was no place for him here. I don't think Mum misses things as much as he does, though. And she has such a happy nature, she'd make herself at home anywhere. I just wish it didn't take so long to get there, so that I could go and visit them sometimes.'

'Maybe one day we'll manage a visit.'

'Maybe. But we're going to be busy for a while. Francis once told me the Manor was an unhappy place and said the tenants had been cowed and bullied. I'd like to make it feel happy again. And,' she blushed as she spoke, but said it nonetheless, 'I'm also hoping we have lots of children.'

'So am I.' They stopped walking to smile at one another and steal another kiss.

They went first to his house in Whalley Street, both reluctant to join the others. There they found two letters lying on the mat from the second post.

He picked them up, wondering who could have written to him, then gasped as he saw the handwriting.

Cathie, who had been moving towards the kitchen to make a cup of tea, turned round quickly. 'Is something wrong?'

He ripped open one of the envelopes and moved into the kitchen to read it in the light.

She stared in shock as tears began to roll down his cheeks. 'Magnus darling, what is it?' She went to put her arm round his waist. 'Tell me.'

He smiled at her through his tears and hugged her close with his left arm. 'This is from our Hamish. He wrote from Cape Town to prove that he won't forget to write to me. He's enjoying the voyage. Oh, Caitlin, lassie, he really did write to me.'

She knew how much that meant to him. 'You must let Mairi know at once. And maybe one day you'll hear from your other brothers.'

'Mebbe.' But even to know that one brother was not lost to him helped.

He dropped Hamish's letter on the table and began to

open the other. 'This one's from Mairi.' After a quick perusal, he beamed at her. 'She's expecting a child.'

'Oh, that's wonderful news! I'm going to be an aunt!' Cathie pulled his face down and kissed him very gently. 'And you're going to make the best uncle in the whole world. Now,' she forced herself to be brisk, 'you go and change out of your best things and I'll make us a cup of tea.'

A little later, refreshed by some quiet moments together, they set off for the hotel.

Liza saw them coming from her window. The two were arm in arm. Cathie was gesticulating energetically with her free hand as she talked and Magnus, head bent a little, was listening with a tender smile.

Liza had no doubt their future would be a happy one, whatever life brought. She liked Magnus and she had never seen Cathie looking as happy as she was now. After their wedding, she, Francis and Josie would have to start the long journey back. In the meantime she was determined to enjoy every moment with her two lost children, whose futures seemed set for happiness.

She blinked away a tear and turned to Josie. 'Do you want to be bridesmaid?'

Josie beamed at her and nodded.

Liza turned to Francis. 'And since Benedict can't be with us, you'll have to give Cathie away.'

He exchanged delighted glances with Josie, then said, 'I'd love to.'

'Right. We'll have to set matters in train quickly. Oh, my loves, it's going to be such fun!'

EPILOGUE

January 1877

As the ship docked in Albany, in the south of Western Australia, Liza stared at the crowd gathered to welcome them. Her heart lifted as she picked out Benedict, with Harry sitting on his shoulders. So he had got her letter in time to come and meet them! She waved furiously and saw the moment when his face lit up and he waved back.

'There's Dad!' squealed Josie, jigging up and down.

Francis stood silently beside them, nervous now. How would Liza's husband feel about him?

It was a while before they were able to leave the ship, but then Liza went rushing across to throw herself into Benedict's arms, careless of her dignity, and he swung her round and round, laughing with her, heedless whether anyone stared at them or not.

Harry rolled his eyes in embarrassment at his parents' antics and looked at Josie resentfully. 'You've grown. You're taller than me now. Seth wanted to come but he and Lucas have to look after the farm. They send their love.'

'This is Francis,' she said, aware of how nervous he was.

Harry looked up at him. 'You're our lost brother, aren't you?'

Francis nodded, unable to think of anything to say.

Harry studied him, lips pursed. 'You're very tall. Dad says I'll be tall when I grow up.' Then his mother swooped down on him to hug him in spite of his wriggles and protests.

Benedict went to swing Josie round and kiss her soundly, then turned towards the young man.

'It's very kind of you to let me come and visit, sir,' Francis began nervously.

'Eh, I've always got room for my Liza's son,' Benedict said. He took the hand Francis offered and used it to pull the lad into his arms and give him a proper hug, upset by how frail Francis looked. 'We'll have to feed you up. We'll get Dinny to make up some of her potions. She'll know what to do.'

Francis had not dared hope for a greeting so warm. 'You don't mind? My coming, I mean?'

'Eh, of course not, lad. There's always plenty of love to spare in our house.' Benedict grinned. 'And any road, I'll be setting you to work. We can always do with another pair of hands around the farm. Don't think you're going to live an idle life here.'

'I'll enjoy that.' Francis felt the last of his worries begin to fade.

They set off the next day in the big cart, travelling slowly. Benedict told them the amazing news that Ilse had married Matthieu Correntin and described the wedding. Liza shared with him her amusement at the way Dermott had brought his wife's posh Aunt Nora to Cathie's wedding, and how he already had her wrapped round his little finger.

'You've forgiven him, then?' Benedict said, scowling.

'Sort of. He did help us rescue Francis after all. That makes up for quite a lot.'

'Hmm.'

Because Francis was still not strong and because Benedict was enjoying this rest from his hard labours of the last few months, they did not hurry, taking their time to introduce Francis to the Australian countryside and the custom of offering generous hospitality to travellers when there were no towns or inns to stay at.

By the time they arrived at Lizabrook, Francis was looking tanned from the long sunny days and had found how much he loved the heat of the Australian summer.

Benedict stopped the cart at the spot he had planned and gestured towards the water. 'There, love, it's a proper lake now. Me and Matthieu hired some men and got it done.'

The water was rippling in the sun and beyond it stood their new home, already beginning to weather in the fierce heat of summer. Liza flung her arms round him. 'Oh, it looks wonderful, Benedict.'

'I sold one of your brooches and it gave me enough money to do all this. We didn't realise how valuable those jewels were, love. I'm going to finish the house next, if you'll agree to sell another piece of jewellery.'

'I've never cared about such things, only about you and my family.' Then she turned to beam at the three children in the rear of the cart. 'And my children of course — *all* my children!'

Benedict clicked his tongue and the big horses started

moving forward again. People were coming out of the two houses near the lake, waving and calling excitedly to one another.

As if she sensed his uncertainty, Liza reached behind her to take Francis's hand and Josie took his other one.

'It'll be all right,' Liza said softly.

Francis looked from his mother to his little sister and his heart swelled with love. He had never felt so happy in his whole life. Home, he thought wonderingly. I've got a real home and family now.